A PEOPLE BETRAYED

BY THE SAME AUTHOR

The Coming of the Spanish Civil War
The Triumph of Democracy in Spain
The Politics of Revenge
Franco: A Biography
¡Comrades! Portraits from the Spanish Civil War
Doves of War: Four Women of Spain
Juan Carlos: Steering Spain from Dictatorship to Democracy
The Spanish Civil War: Reaction, Revolution and Revenge
We Saw Spain Die: Foreign Correspondents in the Spanish Civil War
The Spanish Holocaust: Inquisition and Extermination in
Twentieth-Century Spain
The Last Stalinist
The Last Days of the Spanish Republic

A PEOPLE BETRAYED

A History of Corruption, Political Incompetence and Social Division in Modern Spain

Paul Preston

LIVERIGHT PUBLISHING CORPORATION

A Division of W. W. Norton & Company

Independent Publishers Since 1923

New York   London

Copyright © 2020 by Paul Preston
First American Edition 2020

First published in Great Britain in 2020 by William Collins, an imprint of
HarperCollins Publishers Ltd.

First published in book form (in Spanish translation) as Un pueblo traicionado:
España de 1876 a nuestros días: Corrupción, incompetencia política y división social;
Copyright © 2019 by Paul Preston; Copyright © 2019 by Penguin Random House
Grupo Editorial, S. A. U.; Translation copyright © 2019 by Jordi Ainaud

All rights reserved
Printed in the United States of America

For information about permission to reproduce selections from this book, write to
Permissions, Liveright Publishing Corporation, a division of W. W. Norton &
Company, Inc., 500 Fifth Avenue, New York, NY 10110

For information about special discounts for bulk purchases, please contact
W. W. Norton Special Sales at specialsales@wwnorton.com or 800-233-4830

Manufacturing by LSC Communications, Harrisonburg, VA
Production manager: Anna Oler

Library of Congress Cataloging-in-Publication Data

Names: Preston, Paul, 1946– author.
Title: A people betrayed : a history of corruption, political incompetence and social
    division in modern Spain / Paul Preston.
Other titles: History of corruption, political incompetence and social division in
    modern Spain
Description: First American edition. | New York : Liveright Publishing Corporation,
    A Division of W. W. Norton & Company, 2020. | Includes bibliographical
    references and index.
Identifiers: LCCN 2020012133 | ISBN 9780871408686 (hardcover) | ISBN
    9780871408709 (epub)
Subjects: LCSH: Political corruption—Spain—History. | Spain—Politics and
    government—20th century. | Spain—History—20th century.
Classification: LCC JN8386 .P74 2020 | DDC 946/.074—dc23
LC record available at https://lccn.loc.gov/2020012133

Liveright Publishing Corporation
500 Fifth Avenue, New York, N.Y. 10110
www.wwnorton.com

W. W. Norton & Company Ltd.
15 Carlisle Street, London W1D 3BS

1 2 3 4 5 6 7 8 9 0

For María Jesús González
and
Linda Palfreeman

Contents

Preface

The philosopher José Ortega y Gasset wrote in 1921: 'Starting with the monarchy and moving on to the Church, no national authority has thought of anything but itself. When has the heart, after all foreign, of a Spanish monarch or of the Spanish Church ever beat for ends that were deeply Spanish? As far as is known, never. They have done the exact opposite. They have ensured that their ends have been adopted as if they were in the national interest.'[1] In similar vein, the poet Antonio Machado, during the Spanish Civil War, wrote to a Russian friend, the novelist, David Vigodsky: 'The best thing in Spain is the people. That is why the selfless and heroic defence of Madrid, which has astounded the world, moves me but it does not surprise me. It has always been like that. In difficult times, the señoritos – our Boyars – invoke the fatherland and then they sell it; the people do not even mention it but they buy it back with their blood and they save it. In Spain, it is impossible to be a decent person and not love the people. For us, love of the people is a basic duty of gratitude.'[2]

Similar views were expressed in the nineteenth century by the English romantic travellers. The most celebrated, Richard Ford, author in 1845 of *A Handbook for Travellers in Spain* and one year later of *Gatherings in Spain*, portrayed ordinary Spaniards as generous and noble while referring constantly to bad government and misgovernment: 'The real permanent and standing cause of Spain's thinly peopled state, want of cultivation, and abomination of desolation, is BAD GOVERNMENT, civil and religious.' He claimed that, at all levels of government, there were despots always open to bribes.[3] Gerald Brenan agreed to a certain extent: 'Spain has been seen as the land of paradox where a people of great independence of character allowed themselves to be governed by corrupt and arbitrary rulers.' However, commenting on the extent to which such criticisms derived from an idealized image of Britain at the time when Ford was writing, Brenan remarked: 'He has much to say of Spanish mismanagement and poverty, yet who would not have preferred to be a Spanish workman in those days to an English miner or mill-hand or agricultural labourer?'[4]

The present volume is another work written by a British historian who loves Spain and one who has spent the last fifty years studying the country's history. As might be deduced from its title, this book echoes the spirit of Richard Ford and of many Spanish commentators such as Lucas Mallada, Ricardo Macías Picavea, Joaquín Costa, Manuel Azaña and José Ortega y Gasset. While drawing on the perceptions of Ford, it does not adopt his simplistic comparisons of a benighted Spain with an idealized Britain. Equally, while deriving great insight from the critical analysis of the regenerationists, it does not share the view of Costa that the problem called for an authoritarian solution – the 'iron surgeon'. This book makes no attempt to suggest that Spain is unique in terms of corruption or governmental incompetence. There are other European nations for which, at various historical moments, similar interpretations might be valid. For instance, while writing the book, I have lived, on a daily basis for the last three years, under the shadow of the Brexit process in Britain. It has been a painful experience to have to witness the combination of lies, governmental ineptitude and corruption that have bitterly divided the nation and threatened to provoke the break-up of the United Kingdom.

There are many possible approaches to the rich and tragic history of Spain. This book spans the period from the restoration of the Borbón monarchy in 1874 with Alfonso XII, to the early days of the reign of his great-great-grandson Felipe VI in 2014. It aims to provide a comprehensive and reliable history of Spain with a dramatic emphasis on the way the country's progress has been impeded by corruption and political incompetence. It demonstrates how these two features have resulted in a breakdown of social cohesion that has frequently been met with, and exacerbated by, the use of violence by the authorities. All three themes consistently emerge in the tensions between Madrid and Catalonia. Throughout the Restoration period, and most spectacularly during the Primo de Rivera dictatorship, institutional corruption and startling political incompetence were the norm. Popular disgust with this opened the way to the country's first democracy, the Second Republic.

From the inception of the Republic in 1931 until its demise in 1939, corruption was less toxic, not least because the newly installed political elite was inspired by many of the propositions of the regenerationists. That is not to say corruption did not exist. A recurring character in the book, the multi-millionaire Juan March, who was behind some of the most spectacular corruption during the Primo de Rivera period, was equally active during the Republic, as indeed he would be in the first decades of the Franco dictatorship. This was also true of Alejandro Lerroux, an important politician who was on March's payroll. A lifetime of shameless corruption reached its peak when, as Prime Minister in 1935, Lerroux brazenly sponsored a system of fixed roulette wheels, an outrageous operation that gave rise to the word *estraperlo* which has become a synonym for economic malfeasance.

The victory of General Franco saw the establishment of a regime of terror and pillage which allowed him and his elite supporters to plunder with impunity, enriching themselves while giving free rein to the political ineptitude that prolonged Spain's economic backwardness well into the 1950s. Ironically, throughout his life, Franco would express a fierce contempt for the political class that he held responsible for the loss of empire in 1898. In 1941, on the fifth anniversary of the outbreak of the civil war, he declared in a speech to the top brass of the Falange: 'when we started out in life … we saw our childhood dominated by the contemptible incompetence of those men who abandoned half of the fatherland's territory to foreigners'.[5] In fact, some of his own fatuous errors would far outdo those of the predecessors he mocked. That he would not scruple to put his determination to stay in power above national interests can be seen in his relationships with the Third Reich and later with the United States. His scatterbrained get-rich-quick schemes, ranging from alchemy and synthetic water-based gasoline to the disaster of his autarkic policies, contributed to Spain's backwardness until he was persuaded in 1959 to let others supervise the economy.

In denouncing politicians in 1941, Franco was far from alone. With brief intervals when optimism flowered, between 1931 and 1936 and the first decade of the rule of King Juan Carlos, the attitude of Spaniards towards their country's political class has often been one of disdain bordering on despair. Belief in the incompetence and venality of politicians has been an underlying constant of Spanish life since the

Napoleonic invasion if not before. Franco used rhetoric about corrupt politicians to justify a dictatorship under which corruption flourished unchecked and was indeed exploited ruthlessly by the Caudillo himself, both for his own enrichment and to manipulate his followers.

The humiliation of 1898 was just the final confirmation of a truth that had been coming for nearly a century. Spain's internal economic problems could no longer be alleviated by imperial plunder. A backward agrarian economy, an uneven and feeble industrial sector, the heavy hand of the Catholic Church, parasitical armed forces and growing regional divisions were endemic burdens. They were perpetuated, as was perceived by the far-sighted polymath Joaquín Costa, by a corrupt and incompetent political system which blocked social and economic progress and kept the Spanish people in the servitude, ignorance and misery which lay behind the contemporary slur that 'Africa begins at the Pyrenees'. However, the solution proposed by Costa, the iron surgeon, showed little confidence in the people and in democracy.

Other equally damaging, and inextricably linked, features of Spanish politics and society have endured since the late nineteenth century. The unspoken assumption that political and social problems could more naturally be solved by violence than by debate was firmly entrenched in a country in which for hundreds of years civil strife was no rarity. In modern times, certain forms of social violence have been a consequence of corruption and government incompetence. Electoral corruption excluded the masses from organized politics and challenged them with a choice between apathetic acceptance and violent revolution. The war of 1936–9 was the fourth such conflict since the 1830s.

Between 1814 and 1981, Spain witnessed more than twenty-five *pronunciamientos*, or military coups.[6] That crude statistic provides a graphic indication of the divorce between soldiers and civilians. In the first third of the nineteenth century, those *pronunciamientos* were liberal in their political intent, but thereafter a tradition of mutual misunderstanding and mistrust between the army and civil society developed to a point at which soldiers considered themselves more Spanish than civilians. Accordingly, a factor generating hatred within Spanish society was the repression by the army of deep-rooted social conflicts that had arisen in the wake of imperial decline and military defeat. Military resentment of politicians in general and of the left and the labour movement in particular was the other side of the same coin.

The role of violence in Spain was consolidated by the way in which the armed forces dealt with post-imperial trauma. A resentful officer corps, which blamed the humiliation of 1898 on the politicians who had provided inadequate support, came to consider itself the ultimate arbiter in politics. Determined to lose no more battles, it became obsessed not with the defence of Spain from external enemies but with the defence of national unity and the existing social order against the internal enemies of the regions and of the left. At one level, this was not surprising. After the Cuban disaster, the army was inefficient, overburdened by bureaucracy and ill equipped. An absurdly high proportion of the total military budget was absorbed by salaries, administration and running costs which left very little for training or equipment.

Spain's rulers had tried to shake off the immediate post-war shame with a disastrous new imperial endeavour in Morocco. Woefully unprepared, this African adventure stimulated massive popular opposition to conscription, thereby intensifying the mutual hatred of the military and the left. While working-class conscripts became militant pacifists in response to the appalling conditions in North Africa, there emerged within the military an elite corps of tough professional officers, the Africanistas, of whom Franco became the iconic example. They came to believe that they were a beleaguered band of heroic warriors alone concerned with the fate of the *patria*. This inevitably exacerbated their sense of apartness from a society which they felt had betrayed them. The Africanistas came to dominate the officer corps, particularly in the late 1920s when Franco was Director of the Military Academy. They would be at the heart of the coup of 1936 and then used against Spanish civilians the same terror tactics that they had perfected in Morocco.

They would be a favoured element of Franco's kleptocratic elite. The survival of their 'values' through and beyond the dictatorship would guarantee the determination of sectors of the armed forces to derail the new democracy established in the late 1970s. Fortunately, popular distrust of the armed forces came to an end with the democratization of the army after the military reforms carried out during the first Socialist government. Generational change within the officer corps and the entry of Spain into NATO have seen a dramatic reversal of popular perception of the armed forces and the Civil Guard, which are now among the most highly rated institutions in Spain. Popular perception of Spain's problems puts the political class second only behind unemployment.[7]

Equally damaging to Spain's attempts to attain modernity was the dead hand of the Catholic Church. In the civil wars of both the nineteenth and twentieth centuries, the Catholic Church took sides against the threat of liberalism and modernization. Besieged by violent popular anti-clericalism and impoverished by the disentailment of its lands in the 1830s and 1850s, the Church allied itself with the powerful. Already by the 1880s the Church, in its educational provision for the middle and upper classes, had become the legitimizing agent of the socio-economic and political system. The history of the Catholic Church in Spain in the twentieth century parallels that of the country itself. Almost every major political upheaval of a turbulent period – with the possible exception of the revolutionary crisis of 1917–23 – had its religious backcloth and a crucial, and often reactionary, role for the Church hierarchy.

What follows interleaves these themes of military and ecclesiastical influence, popular contempt for the political class, bitter social conflict, economic backwardness and conflict between centralist nationalism and regional independence movements. It also places these processes in an international context. The breakdown of the Second Republic and the coming of the civil war are incomprehensible without consideration of the influence of international developments, particularly fascism and communism, on domestic developments. The course of the Spanish Civil War will be analysed with particular attention to the interplay between domestic and international factors in determining its outcome. In many respects, the Spanish conflict can be seen as either a rehearsal for the Second World War or as the location of its first battles. Spanish neutrality in the Second World War played a key role in the outcome of the conflict in Europe. The process whereby the Franco dictatorship shook off international ostracism to become the valued ally of the Western powers will be fully considered.

The book shows how Spain went from utter despair in 1898 on a roller coaster that culminated in the present state of almost comparable pessimism. The civil war was the most dramatic of a series of uneven struggles between the forces of reform and reaction which had punctuated Spanish history from 1808 to the present day. There is a curious pattern in Spain's modern and contemporary history, arising from a frequent *desfase*, or lack of synchronization, between the social reality and the political power structure ruling over it. Lengthy periods during which reactionary elements have used political and military power to hold back social progress were followed by outbursts of revolutionary fervour. In the 1850s, in the 1870s, between 1910 and 1912, between 1917 and 1923 and above all during the Second Republic, efforts were made to bring Spanish politics into line with the country's social reality. This inevitably involved attempts to redistribute wealth, especially on the land, which in turn provoked reactionary efforts to stop the clock and reimpose the traditional order of social and economic power. Thus were progressive movements crushed by General O'Donnell in 1856, by General Pavia in 1874, by General Primo de Rivera in 1923 and by General Franco between 1936 and 1939. It took the horrors of the civil war and the nearly four decades of dictatorship that followed to break the pattern. The moderation shared by the progressive right and a chastened left underlay a bloodless transition to democracy.

The pattern of conflict between the political establishment and sociological development – progressive forces pushing for change until driven back by violence and the imposition of dictatorship – changed in 1977. Nevertheless, the new democratic establishment was tainted by the old ways. As asserted by Baltasar Garzón, one of the judges who has worked to eliminate corruption: 'In Spain, no one has ever been afraid to be corrupt. Given that its existence was taken for granted, corruption is not something that has bothered the average citizen. This indifference has ensured that its roots have grown deep and solid and sustain a structure of interests that is very difficult to bring down.' In the view of Garzón, the justice system has contributed to this situation: 'Judgments that are laid down after long years of delay, laughable sentences, incomprehensible dismissals or shelving of cases, unacceptable collusions and connivance ...'[8]

Throughout the entire period covered by this book, corruption and political incompetence have had a corrosive effect on political coexistence and social cohesion. Spain's transition to democracy has been widely admired. Nevertheless, the scale of uninterrupted corruption and periodic ineptitude demonstrated by the political class at various levels of society since 1982 has been remarkable. Politicians of both right and left have been unable or unwilling to deal with corruption and the pernicious clash between Spanish centralist nationalism and regional desires for independence. Only during brief periods in the early 1930s and in the first years of the transition to democracy was there a degree of public respect for politicians. However, widespread contempt and resentment have intensified anew during the economic crisis of recent years. The boom of the 1990s fostered corruption and witnessed political incompetence on an unprecedented scale. From the late 1980s to the present day, endemic corruption and renewed nationalist ferment has brought disillusionment with the political class almost full circle. While not at the unrepeatable low point of 1898, politicians are nevertheless rated by the Spanish population far lower than could have been imagined when the transition to democracy was being hailed as a model for other countries.

A PEOPLE BETRAYED

LA ARAÑA

Como es tan hermosa - la pobre España - cuanto mas la desnudan - está mas guapa. Los que la miran gozan la compadecen-los mas la envidian

A satirical cartoon published in the magazine *La Araña* in August 1885. 'Poor Spain. How beautiful she is. The more they strip her, the more beautiful she is.' Among the watching European leaders are Otto von Bismarck and King Umberto of Italy. Among those ripping the flag from her body are the architects of electoral corruption, Francisco Romero Robledo, Antonio Cánovas del Castillo and Práxedes Mateo Sagasta.

1

Spanish Stereotypes? Passion, Violence and Corruption

Spain has often been seen through the myths of national character. One of the most persistent has been that of corruption and dishonesty, which owed much to the numerous translations into other European languages of the first and hugely popular picaresque novels, the anonymous *Lazarillo de Tormes* (1554) and Francisco de Quevedo's *El buscón* (*o Historia de la vida del Buscón, llamado don Pablos; ejemplo de vagamundos y espejo de tacaños*) (written 1604, published 1626). During the eighteenth and nineteenth centuries, Spain was a frequent, and conveniently exotic, setting for operas by foreigners. Among the most extreme examples of operas based on myths of national character, especially Spanish, are almost certainly Mozart's *Don Giovanni*, Verdi's *Il trovatore* and *La forza del destino* and Bizet's *Carmen*. Artists wishing to portray violent passions drew upon a view of Spain, its history and its people as the embodiment of fanaticism, cruelty and uncontrolled emotion. This image went back to the Reformation, when a series of religiously inspired pamphlets had denounced the activities of the Spanish Inquisition, the Tribunal of the Holy Office and the terrors of the auto-da-fé. Religious hatreds aside, the European perception of Spain was confirmed by the experience of an empire in the Americas, Italy and Flanders built on greed and maintained by blood. The Peninsular Wars, or the wars of national independence, and the subsequent nineteenth-century series of civil wars did nothing to undermine stereotypes which survived into the twentieth century in the literature spawned by the Spanish Civil War.

Collectively, this view of Spain constituted what the Spaniards themselves came to call 'the black legend', the most extreme examples of which were collected in the celebrated work by the historian Julián Juderías, *La leyenda negra*. Combating the notion of universal laziness and violence, Juderías railed against 'the legend of the inquisitorial, ignorant, fanatical Spain, under the yoke of the clergy, lazy, incapable of figuring among civilized nations today as well as in the past, always ready for violent repressions; enemy of progress and innovations.[1] What Juderías had in mind were definitions of Spain such as that by Sir John Perrot, Elizabeth I's Lord Deputy of Ireland (1584–6), who observed: 'This semi-Morisco nation ... is sprung from the filth and slime of Africa, the base Ottomans and the rejected Jews.'[2] The stereotypes which caused greatest outrage to Spaniards, however, were fundamentally the product of the romantic era. From 1820 to 1850, British and French travellers were drawn to Spain by what they saw as the picturesque savagery of both its landscapes and its inhabitants. Rugged mountains infested by brigands, their paths travelled by convoys of well-armed smugglers, the bloody rituals of the bullfight, the ruins of Moorish palaces and castles, and erotic encounters (probably imagined) with languid olive-skinned beauties became the clichés of romantic literature about Spain. The stereotypes would be maintained even in the 1920s when bar owners in the sleazy Raval district of Barcelona exploited the reputation of the 'Barrio Chino' for the benefit of foreign tourists. They would stage 'spontaneous' incidents in which 'gypsies', apparently inflamed with jealousy by the sight of their women (the waitresses) flirting with the tourists, waved knives, the incidents being settled with rounds of expensive drinks.[3]

Bizet's *Carmen* remains perhaps the most famous 'Spanish' opera, largely because of its deployment of most of these Spanish stereotypes. *Carmen* presents the archetypes of the passionate Andalusian woman, the knife-wielding murderer and the bullfighter set in a context of smugglers, bandits, sex and violence. The notion that the Spaniards were sex-crazed underlay the fact that syphilis was known in France as *le mal espagnol*. The German writer August Fischer also wrote of the frantic, indeed fanatical, sexuality of Andalusian women – a view shared by Lord Byron, who visited Andalusia in 1809. The French diplomat Jean-François Bourgoing, in his *Nouveau voyage en Espagne* (1788; expanded in 1803 into the three-volume *Tableau de l'Espagne moderne*), complained about the open sensuality of flamenco dancing and excoriated the vice-ridden daily life of gypsies.[4] Rather more wistfully, Giacomo Casanova, the Venetian sexual athlete, praised the fandango thus: 'Everything is represented, from the sigh of desire to the final ecstasy; it is a very history of love. I could not conceive a woman refusing her partner anything after this dance, for it seemed made to stir up the senses.'[5]

It was Washington Irving's *Tales of the Alhambra* (1832) that really put Spain on the map for romantics. A decade later, he was outdone by Théophile Gautier whose *Un Voyage en Espagne* (1843) described the dusky, flashing-eyed Andalusian beauties who warmed his blood with their flamenco dancing and the blood-chilling gypsy knife fighters and their fancy cutlery.[6] English writers like George Borrow (*The Bible in Spain*, 1843) and Richard Ford (*Handbook for Spain*, 1845, and *Gatherings in Spain*, 1846) portrayed Spaniards' alleged obsession with honour, their religious fanaticism, their extremes of love and hate, and the proliferation of lawless cut-throats. This was intensified even more by Alexandre Dumas. Massively famous as a result of the success of *The Three Musketeers* and *The Count of Monte Cristo*, Dumas had been invited by the Duc de Montpensier to attend his wedding on 10 October 1846 to the Infanta Luisa Fernanda, daughter of King Fernando VII. Dumas spent two months in Spain on the basis of which he wrote his massive four-volume *De Paris à Cadix*. Here he described his disgust at Spanish food and at what he saw as the licentiousness and depravity of gypsy dancers in Granada. Yet, in Seville, he was delighted by the voluptuousness of professional flamenco dancers and rejoiced in the flirtations between young army officers and the pretty girls who worked in the great Fábrica de Tabaco.[7] Prosper Mérimée's novella *Carmen* (1845) concentrated all the romantic clichés about Seville in one personage. A cigarette factory worker, Carmen was also a flamenco dancer, lover of a bullfighter, accomplice of smugglers and bandits, voluptuous, independent, untamed – just the thing to titillate the Parisian bourgeois who seemed to view Spain as a kind of human zoo.[8] Mérimée's patronizingly anthropological attitude to his characters was popularized even further by Bizet's opera.

A context of readily familiar assumptions about Spain had long since been established by Marie-Catherine Le Jumel de Barneville, Baronne d'Aulnoy. Her *Mémoire de la cour d'Espagne* (1690), published in English as *Memories of the Court of Spain written by an ingenious French lady*, was a prurient account of the allegedly syphilis-ridden royal court in Madrid. Uninhibited by the fact that she had almost certainly never visited Spain at all, this armchair fantasist then quickly produced her immensely influential *Rélation du voyage d'Espagne*, which was first published in 1691 and was regularly reprinted in several languages well into the nineteenth century. Despite claiming to relate 'nothing but what I have seen', Madame d'Aulnoy described a country full of exotic animals including monkeys and parrots. Her cast of invented characters was based on other travel books, diplomatic memoirs and the plays of Calderón and other Spanish dramatists. Her wild exaggerations presented corrupt officials, aristocratic men ever ready to kill or die for questions of honour and promiscuous women invariably in the throes of passion.[9] Nevertheless, the caricatures created by Madame d'Aulnoy, including the notion that virtually the entire population was afflicted with venereal disease, allowed Bizet to present the insolent and primeval sexuality of Carmen as somehow typically Spanish.[10]

In Britain, the image of an exotic, semi-oriental Spain of crumbling cathedrals and mosques, castles and bridges, inhabited by colourful, passionate and sensual people, drew on the exquisite paintings and drawings of David Roberts and John Frederick Lewis in the 1830s and of Charles Clifford in the 1850s. Many of their most characteristic works became immensely popular through collections of best-selling lithographs. Their views of Spain were confirmed by many Spanish painters of the romantic era, particularly Genaro Pérez de Villaamil, whose work was exhibited and published in Paris.[11] Nothing symbolized the Spain of the romantic era more than Andalusian beauties and bandit-infested sierras. Foreign travellers returned home to dine out on stories of the risks they claimed that they had undergone.[12] Virtually all travellers to Spain, whatever their nationality and whatever they thought of the sex, the bandits, the bulls and the Inquisition, complained about the rutted tracks which passed for roads. They often declared confidently that Spain would never be penetrated by railways.[13] In fact, it was the introduction of railways from the late 1850s onwards that dramatically changed the stereotypes. As Spain enjoyed an extremely uneven industrial revolution, foreign investment increased. Thereafter, observers and travellers were concerned less with romantic stereotypes than with political instability, corruption and social violence.

In fact, the fundamentals of Spanish society had little to do with the steamy erotic stereotypes beloved of foreign travellers. The reality was altogether more mundane, its central characteristics the linked factors of social inequality and violence and political incompetence and corruption. In 1883, the Tribunal Supremo entitled part of its annual report on criminality 'On the Violent Customs of the Spanish People'.[14] It was symptomatic of Spain's dysfunctional society that, between 1814 and 1981, there were more than fifty *pronunciamientos*, or military coups. That crude statistic provides a graphic indication not just of the divorce between soldiers and civilians but of the extent to which the Spanish state did not adequately serve its citizens. A tradition of mutual misunderstanding and mistrust between the army and civil society developed to a point at which soldiers considered themselves more Spanish than civilians. The year 1833 saw the outbreak of the first of four civil wars with the battlefield hostilities of the last coming to a close in 1939. In fact, to some extent, the civil war of 1936–9 is the war that never ended. Indeed, in some respects, Spain still suffers today from some of the divisions of 1936.

The early 1830s experienced both the loss of the bulk of the once great Spanish empire and the beginning of dynastic conflict. The death in 1833 of Fernando VII, succeeded as queen by his infant daughter, Isabel, and the attempt by his brother Carlos to seize power provided the spark that ignited what came to be called the first Carlist War, which raged until 1840. Carlos sought support among deeply reactionary landowners and extreme ultramontane Catholics and was opposed by modernizing liberals led symbolically at least by Isabel's mother, the Queen-Regent María Cristina. Carlist forces were commanded, even more symbolically, by the Vírgen de los Dolores, a commitment to theocracy that guaranteed the support of the Church hierarchy. A second, rather more sporadic, Carlist war was fought from 1846 to 1849 and a third from 1872 to 1876. The active role of the Catholic Church in these Carlist Wars, with some lower clergy even taking up arms, contributed to the subsequent popular perception of priests as deeply reactionary.[15] In the 1860s, there had been fewer than 50,000 secular priests, monks and nuns in Spain. In the period between the monarchical Restoration of 1874 and the end of the century, the numbers would increase to more than 88,000. When the Primo de Rivera dictatorship fell in 1930, the clergy had swelled to over 135,000.[16] In the view of the anarchists, the Catholic Church commercialized religion but did not practise morality. They saw it as a corrupt and rapacious institution which exploited the people and also blocked social progress.

Thus, even though black, reactionary Spain was startled by the French revolution and was shaken out of its lethargy by the Napoleonic invasion of 1808, many of the European stereotypes of Spain lamented by Juderías, certainly those based on the violence of its political life, were confirmed rather than shattered by the cycle of nineteenth-century civil wars. The notion that deep social and political problems could be resolved by violence was to afflict Spain well into the twentieth century. The Franco regime which followed the civil war was a regime built on terror, plunder and corruption. None of these elements was the invention of Franco. Indeed, it is the central thesis of this book that the violence, corruption and incompetence of the political class have betrayed the population at least since 1833 and almost certainly before. There are many possible historical reasons to do with religion and empire but perhaps the most potent and enduring has been the lack of a state apparatus popularly accepted as legitimate. After a state of near civil war between the death of Franco in 1975 and the military coup of 1981, it looked as if Spain was witnessing the creation of a legitimate state. The prosperity of the late twentieth century masked the extent to which the new polity was as mired in corruption and incompetence as its predecessors. An especially vibrant economic boom fuelled by the cheap credit facilitated by Spain joining the euro drew a veil over rampant corruption that reached as far as the royal family. The recession that followed saw the veil torn away, the political establishment lose legitimacy and problems such as regional nationalism divide the country in, rhetorically at least, violent terms.

In the nineteenth century, the Spanish state was weak in the face of geographic obstacles, poor communications and historical and linguistic traditions utterly opposed to a centralized state. Unlike, say, France or Italy after 1871, Spanish governments failed to create an all-embracing patriotism and sense of nationhood. In other countries, this task was largely assumed by the armed forces. However, in Spain, the army was an engine of division, above all because of the appalling conditions faced by conscripts in overseas wars. By the early twentieth century, army officers were ripe for persuasion by extreme conservatives that it was their right and duty to interfere in politics in order to 'save Spain'. Unfortunately, that ostensibly noble objective actually meant the defence of the interests and privileges of relatively small segments of society. The armed forces were thus not the servants of the nation defending it from external enemies but the defenders of narrow social interests against their internal enemies, the working class and the regional nationalists. In the hundred years before 1930, it was possible to discern the gradual and immensely complex division of the country into two broadly antagonistic social blocs. Accordingly, popular hostility to the armed forces grew as deep-rooted social conflicts, at a time of imperial decline and military defeat, were repressed by the army. A further layer of the dialectic between violence and popular discontent was the way in which regional nationalism was crushed in the name of a patriotic centralism. Military resentments of politicians in general and of the left and the labour movement in particular were the other side of the same coin.

Ironically, it was in 1833 that the biggest step towards creating a state had been taken. This was the adoption of a highly centralized French territorial model with fifty broadly uniform provinces under the control of a civil governor appointed by Madrid. This systematized the distribution of patronage and therefore fostered corruption. Although the idea of Spain had long existed, the country seemed to be a flimsy collection of virtually independent provinces and regions whose languages and dialects were often mutually unintelligible. The 1833 definition of regions and provinces has subsequently been modified but, broadly speaking, it still holds good and can be recognized in the current system of so-called autonomies into which Spain is now divided. Similarly, further measures taken in the 1840s saw the beginnings of something resembling a central state with a crude and divisive taxation system and the creation of local and national police forces. However, with the exception of the Civil Guard, it was an inadequately implemented process. Taxation did not finance the state because wealth was not taxed, whereas consumption was. Ancient forms of politics, social influence and patronage, *caciquismo* or clientelism, took precedence over any kind of modern political machinery, poisoning what falteringly developed as electoral politics and leaving the state underfinanced and weak, other than in its coercive capacity.

After the process known as the disentailment or *desamortización*, Spain ceased to be a feudal society in legal and economic terms. However, it remained so in social and political terms. Traditional rural elites retained their power long after the Restoration of the monarchy in 1874 and the attempt to create a modern state by Antonio Cánovas del Castillo in his Constitution of 1876. That state worked only in so far as it was in the interests of the local bosses or *caciques* (a South American Indian word meaning 'chief') to allow it to do so. It was only with the growth of industry in the Basque Country, Asturias, Catalonia and Madrid that a different and more modern politics became even a remote possibility.

Then, the vested interests of the landed *caciques* ensured that their superior power was exerted over the reforming bourgeoisie which, itself under pressure from the first signs of working-class discontent, scurried to make an alliance in which it was the junior partner. Loss of empire would lead to a weakening of the alliance but it would always be consolidated when the industrial bourgeoisie needed the protection of the repressive machinery that was the state's principal asset. Pressure for political change and social development was simply dismissed as subversion.[17]

Richard Ford wrote in the 1840s: 'I once beheld a cloaked Spaniard pacing mournfully in the burial ground of Seville. When the public trench was opened, he drew from beneath the folds the dead body of his child, cast it in and disappeared. Thus, half the world lives without knowing how the other half dies.'[18] In a land in which oppressive poverty coexisted with an equally parasitical government and Church, the law was not respected and smugglers and bandits were the objects of hero worship. When Ford enquired of Spaniards where brigands hid, he was frequently told that 'it was not on the road that they were most likely to be found, but in the confessional boxes, the lawyers' offices, and still more in the *bureaux* of government'. Of the Civil Guard, Ford wrote that they were nothing but rogues 'used to keep down the expression of indignant public opinion, and, instead of catching thieves, upholding those first-rate criminals, foreign and domestic, who are now robbing poor Spain of her gold and liberties'.[19]

Founded by two royal decrees of 28 March and 13 May 1844, the Civil Guard was intended to be a disciplined nationwide police force, staffed by men seconded from the army. The corps was organized by the Inspector General of the Army, the Duke of Ahumada.[20] Between 1844 and the 1860s, the Civil Guard established itself as a dour and brutal army of occupation protecting the great estates and mines against the resentment of their workers. It became part of the army in 1878. Banditry was gradually eliminated, but the Civil Guard's ominous ubiquity forced the peasants to direct their rebelliousness against it and therefore against the state. 'Every Civil Guard became a recruiting officer for anarchism, and, as the anarchists increased their membership, the Civil Guard also grew.'[21] In fact, from the last quarter of the nineteenth century until the death of General Franco, many Civil Guards were actually recruited from the sons of men who had served in the corps.

The sense that the Civil Guard was a hostile institution imposed from outside was intensified by the fact that social interaction was forbidden between the rank and file and the inhabitants of the area where they served. Needless to say, this prohibition did not extend to the officers, who usually maintained cordial relations with the local clergy and those who owned the land, the mines and the factories. In small towns and villages, Civil Guards and their families lived in fortified barracks known as the *casa-cuartel*. In Asturias, the *casa-cuartel* was often paid for by the mining companies. In many places, it was common for the local *fuerzas vivas* (notables) and employers' organizations to subsidize the *casa-cuartel* with gifts of food, wine and, sometimes, furniture. Such gifts were publicized in the local press as well as in the official publications of the Civil Guard, which intensified the sense that the corps was a force at the service of the wealthy.[22] This perception was reinforced by the fact that a Civil Guard could not serve in the area where he or his wife had been born. In a country of fierce localism (*patriotismo chico*), where any stranger could be seen not just as an outsider but virtually as a foreigner, this increased the hostility towards the Civil Guard. In Asturian mining villages, for instance, the hatred of the Civil Guard was intense both for political reasons and also because they were often from Galicia. Guards were not permitted to move about unarmed or alone and so were usually in pairs (*la pareja*). Thus 'their relations with the working classes were of open hostility and suspicion. Living as they did among their enemies, they became unusually ready to shoot.'[23]

The Civil Guard responded to any social upheaval with aggression. In particular, signs of anarchist ideology were perceived as an especially pernicious and barbaric foreign doctrine. Anarchists were seen as 'harmful beasts', worse than common criminals because of their utopian ambitions for society. So the destructive influence of 'those who have ideas' had to be eliminated. Anarchists were the enemies of society and especially of the Civil Guards.[24]

Ford believed that bad government and poor communications were the principal cause of poverty and economic backwardness.

It has, indeed, required the utmost ingenuity and bad government of man to neutralise the prodigality of advantages which Providence has lavished on this highly favoured land, and which, while under the dominion of the Romans and Moors, resembled an Eden, a garden of plenty and delight, when in the words of an old author, there was nothing idle, nothing barren in Spain – 'nihil otiosum, nihil sterile in Hispania'. A sad change has come over this fair vision, and now the bulk of the Peninsula offers a picture of neglect and desolation, moral and physical, which it is painful to contemplate.

He added, 'Spain is a land which never yet has been able to construct or support even a sufficient number of common roads or canals for her poor and passive commerce and circulation.'[25]

For Ford, the essence of bad government in Spain was corruption. 'Public poverty', he wrote,

is the curse of the land, and all *empleados* or persons in office excuse themselves on dire necessity ... Some allowance, therefore, may be made for the rapacity which, with very few exceptions, prevails; the regular salaries, always inadequate, are generally in arrear, and the public servants, poor devils, swear that they are forced to pay themselves by conniving at defrauding the government; this few scruple to do, as all know it to be an unjust one, and that it can afford it; indeed, as all are offenders alike, the guilt of the offence is scarcely admitted. Where robbing and jobbing are the universal order of the day, one rascal keeps another in countenance ... A man who does not feather his nest when in place, is not thought honest, but a fool; *es preciso, que cada uno coma de su oficio*. It is necessary, nay, a *duty*, as in the East, that all should live by their office; and as office is short and insecure, no time or means is neglected in making up a purse ...

He offers an example:

We remember calling on a Spaniard who held the highest office in a chief city of Andalucia. As we came into his cabinet a cloaked personage was going out; the great man's table was covered with gold ounces, which he was shovelling complacently into a drawer, gloating on the glorious haul ... This gentleman, during the *Sistema*, or Riego constitution, had, with other 1oyalists, been turned out of office; and, having been put to the greatest hardships, was losing no time in taking prudent and laudable precautions to avert all similar calamity for the future. His practices were perfectly well known in the town, where people simply observed, '*Está atesorando*, he is laying up treasures,' – as every one of them would most certainly have done, had they been in his fortunate position ... *Donde no hay abundancia, no hay observancia.* The empty sack cannot stand upright, nor was ever a sack made in Spain into which gain and honour could be stowed away together; *honra y provecho, no caben en un saco o techo*; here virtue itself succumbs to poverty, induced by more than half a century of misgovernment, let alone the ruin caused by Buonaparte's invasion, to which domestic troubles and civil wars have been added.[26]

For all that Spanish intellectuals resented the belittling of their country by foreign writers, there were those who did it themselves, albeit in a different way. There was a substantial literature that lamented Spain's loss of empire, uninterrupted military failures, deep-rooted political instability and economic backwardness.[27] In November 1930, the intellectual Manuel Azaña, a future prime minister and president of the Second Republic, echoed Richard Ford's judgement. He described the political system as functioning with two mechanisms, despotic authoritarianism and corruption. The great practitioner of the first was the reactionary General Ramón María Narváez, who was seven times Prime Minister between 1844 and 1868. He was notorious for remarking on his deathbed: 'I have no enemies. I have shot them all.' The wizard of electoral falsification was Luis José Sartorius, who, in the 1840s and 1850s, according to Azaña, 'elevated political corruption into a system and became a master in the art of fabricating parliamentary majorities'. During their collaboration, in Azaña's view, 'the most illustrious elements of Spanish society applied themselves to squeezing profit out of politics'.[28]

The civil war of 1936–9 represented the most determined effort by reactionary elements in Spanish politics to crush any reforming project which might threaten their privileged position. The enduring dominance of reactionary forces reflected the continued power of the old landed oligarchy and the parallel weakness of the progressive bourgeoisie. The painfully slow and uneven development of industrial capitalism in Spain accounted for the existence of a numerically small and politically feeble commercial and manufacturing class. Spain did not experience a classic bourgeois revolution in which the structures of the *ancien régime* were broken. The power of the monarchy, the landed nobility and the Church remained more or less intact well into the twentieth century. Unlike Britain and France, nineteenth-century Spain did not see the establishment of an incipiently democratic polity with the flexibility to absorb new forces and to adjust to major social change. The legal basis for capitalism was established albeit without there being a political revolution and with the survival of elements of feudalism. Accordingly, with the obvious difference that its industrial capitalism was extremely feeble, Spain followed the political pattern established by Prussia.

Within this authoritarian model, until the 1950s capitalism in Spain was predominantly agrarian except for Asturias, Catalonia and the Basque Country in the north. Spanish agriculture is immensely variegated in terms of climate, crops and land-holding systems. There have long existed areas of commercially successful small and medium-sized farming operations, especially in the lush, wet hills and valleys of those northern regions which also experienced industrialization. However, throughout the nineteenth century and for the first half of the twentieth, the most politically influential sectors were, broadly speaking, the large landowners. In the main, the *latifundios*, the great estates, are concentrated in the arid central and southern regions of New Castile, Extremadura and Andalusia, although there are also substantial *latifundios* to be found scattered throughout parts of Old Castile and particularly in Salamanca. The political monopoly of the landed oligarchy saw occasional tentative challenges by the emasculated industrial and mercantile classes. However, reliant on the repressive power of the oligarchy, their efforts met with little success. Until well into the 1950s, the urban haute bourgeoisie was obliged to play the role of junior partner in a working coalition with the great *latifundistas*. Despite sporadic industrialization and a steady growth in the national importance of the political representatives of the northern industrialists, power remained squarely in the hands of the landowners.

In Spain, industrialization and political modernization did not go hand in hand. In the first half of the nineteenth century, the progressive impulses, both political and economic, of the Spanish bourgeoisie were diverted. The *desamortización* (disentailment) saw the expropriation of great swathes of Church and municipal lands and the lifting of mortmain, feudal restrictions on land transactions. The process had begun piecemeal in the late eighteenth century but was speeded up in 1836 by the Liberal Prime Minister Juan de Dios Álvarez Mendizábal. He had changed his name from Álvarez Méndez to hide the fact that he came from a Jewish family that sold second-hand clothes in Cadiz. He was a self-made businessman who had acquired a reputation as a financial genius as a result of having made a fortune in London. He saw the expropriation, and sale, of the lands of religious orders as a way of resolving royal financial problems created by the Carlist Wars of the 1830s. Mendizábal believed that he was thereby laying the basis for the future prosperity of Spain by creating a self-sustaining smallholding peasantry, 'a copious family of property owners'.[29] However, in the interests of the crown, the confiscated properties were sold at auction in large blocks, which meant that they were far beyond the means of even existing smallholders. Moreover, the fact that the lots were sold well below their market price, and often on credit which could be obtained only by the wealthy, ensured that one of the consequences was the consolidation of great estates. The other was that the privatization of property brought into cultivation land that had previously been idle or poorly cultivated. However, this was not enough to meet the needs of a steadily growing population, especially in the south.[30]

In 1841, General Baldomero Espartero extended the expropriations to all Church properties. Huge tracts of entailed ecclesiastical and common lands were liberated to pay for the Liberal war effort. This process was intensified after 1855 by the Ley Pascual Madoz which opened the way to the acquisition of common lands by private individuals, often simply by a combination of legal subterfuge and strong-arm tactics. The landed aristocracy benefited because their lands were taken out of mortmain but not expropriated. Thus they could buy and sell land and rationalize their holdings. By 1875, three-quarters of land that forty years previously had belonged to the Church or municipalities was in private hands. This not only diminished any impetus towards industrialization but, by helping to expand the great estates, also created intense social hatreds in the south. The newly released land was bought up by the more efficient among existing landlords, and also by lawyers and members of the commercial and mercantile bourgeoisie who were attracted by its cheapness and social prestige. The *latifundio* system was consolidated and, unlike their inefficient predecessors, the new landlords were keen for a return on their investment and saw land as a productive asset to be exploited for maximum profit. Having said that, neither the old nor the new landowners were prepared to invest in new techniques. The judgement on the 'general dilapidation' made by Richard Ford in the 1840s would still be valid ninety years later: 'The landed proprietor of the Peninsula is little better than a weed of the soil; he has never observed, nor scarcely permitted others to observe, the vast capabilities which might and ought to be called into action.'[31] One obvious consequence was an increase in thefts of domestic animals and assaults on bakeries and other shops. That is not to say that all crimes of violence were responses to social deprivation. Many others were sexual and honour crimes.[32]

The capital of the merchants of the great seaports and of Madrid bankers was diverted away from industry and into land purchases both for speculative purposes and also because of the social prestige that came with it.[33] Investment in land and widespread intermarriage between the urban bourgeoisie and the landed oligarchy weakened their commitment to reform. The weakness of the Spanish bourgeoisie as a potentially revolutionary class was exposed during the period from 1868 to 1873, which culminated in the chaos of the First Republic. Population growth in the middle of the century had increased pressure on the land. Unskilled labourers from country districts flocked to the towns and swelled the mob of unemployed who survived on the edges of society. This was especially the case in Barcelona, in large part because of the collapse of the wine industry as a result of the phylloxera crisis after 1880. Its population more than doubled between 1860, when it constituted an eighth of the Catalan total, and 1900, by which time it had swelled to more than a quarter. The living standards of the urban lower-middle class of teachers, officials and shopkeepers were almost as wretched as those of the unskilled labourers. One of the most explosive areas was the Catalan textile industry where the horrors of nascent capitalism – long hours, child labour, overcrowding in insanitary living conditions and starvation wages – produced acute social tensions and, soon, anarchist terrorism. When cotton supplies were choked off by the American Civil War in the 1860s, the consequent rise in unemployment was exacerbated by a depression in railway construction that saw the urban working class pushed to desperation. Until well into the twentieth century, Madrid governments, representing as they did agrarian interests, had little or no understanding of the problems of a growing and militant industrial proletariat in Catalonia. Consequently, the social problem was dealt with entirely as a public order issue. Of the eighty-six years between 1814 and 1900, for sixty of them Catalonia was under a state of exception, which effectively meant military rule. Moreover, a quarter of the nation's military strength was stationed in Catalonia, a region containing approximately 10 per cent of the Spanish population. This was directed as much at rural Carlism as at urban anarchism.[34]

In 1868, growing working-class discontent linked with middle-class and military resentment of the clerical and ultra-conservative leanings of the monarchy as well as financial and sexual scandals involving Queen Isabel II. In September 1868, a number of *pronunciamientos* culminating in one by General Juan Prim coincided with urban riots. This led to the overthrow and exile of the Queen. The two forces driving the so-called glorious revolution were ultimately inimical. The liberal middle classes and army officers had aimed to amend the constitutional structure of the country. Now, they were alarmed to find that they had awakened a mass revolutionary movement for social change and opened the way to the six years of instability known as the *sexenio revolucionario*. To add to the instability, between 1868 and 1878 Spain's richest surviving colony, Cuba, was riven by a rebellion against the metropolis. In November 1870, Prim finally offered the throne to Amadeo of Savoy, a son of Victor Emmanuel II of Italy. Amadeo had neither the political nor even the linguistic skills to cope with the problems that he faced. On 30 December, the very day of the new King's arrival in Spain, Prim was assassinated. From the beginning, Amadeo faced opposition from republicans, from supporters of Isabel II's thirteen-year-old son Alfonso and from the Carlists. In 1872, there began the third Carlist War. A successful rebellion across the Basque Country and Catalonia saw the establishment of a kind of Carlist state, disorganized and based on religiously inspired banditry.

In the Catalan countryside, the majority of small landowners and farmers were Carlist, not just because of the movement's clericalism but also because of its commitment to local freedoms and ultimately devolution. Thus in Catalonia, and also in the Basque Country, the Church's links to the Carlists fed into support for independence movements in both regions. From the middle of the nineteenth century, there had been a revival of Catalanist sentiment, of Catalan literature and of the language whose official use had been banned since the eighteenth century. This was intensified by the federalist movement from 1868 to the collapse of the First Republic. Nowhere was federalism as strong as in Catalonia. Another factor was almost certainly resentment of the lack of Catalan influence on the central government. Between 1833 and 1901, there were

902 men in ministerial office. Only twenty-four of them, 2.6 per cent of the total, were Catalan. In consequence, Catalanism was to be found not just in the rural areas but also in Barcelona, where it found enthusiastic adherents among the wealthy upper-middle classes. A loose federation of middle- and upper-class Catalanist groups formed the Unió Catalanista in 1892. Its programme, known as the Bases de Manresa, called for the restoration of an autonomous government, a separate tax system, the protection of Catalan industry and the institution of Catalan as an official language. With the exception of a brief period from 1906 to 1909, from 1868 until the Primo de Rivera dictatorship in the 1920s Catalan nationalism would be a largely conservative movement.[35]

Faced with civil war, a colonial revolt and a deeply divided political establishment, Amadeo abdicated in despair on 11 February 1873. With the establishment divided, elections in May saw a republican victory and the proclamation of the First Republic on 1 June. Under the presidency of the Catalan Federalist Francesc Pi y Margall, a decentralized structure was adopted and Spain was divided into eleven autonomous cantons. A series of bold reforms were proposed, including the abolition of conscription, the separation of Church and state, the provision of free compulsory education for all, the eight-hour day, the regulation of female and child labour, the expropriation of uncultivated estates and the establishment of peasant collectives. The combination of rapidly established cantons, land seizures, a violent revolutionary general strike in Alcoy, the Carlist rebellion, the Cuban unrest, an outburst of anti-clericalism and the alarm provoked by the planned reforms ensured that Pi y Margall's federal regime was perceived as an intolerable threat to the established order. The republican government was overthrown by the artillery General Manuel Pavia y Rodríguez de Alburquerque, who crushed the Cantonalist movement and established a more conservative government under General Francisco Serrano. Although the Carlists were on the verge of defeat, Serrano was unable to consolidate a conservative republic. On 29 December 1874, in Sagunto, the dynamic young Brigadier General Arsenio Martínez Campos proclaimed as King of Spain the now seventeen-year-old Prince Alfonso. One of the least scurrilous rumours concerning the sex life of his mother Queen Isabel II was that Alfonso's father had been Enrique Puigmoltó, a Valencian captain of the Engineers. Subsequent to his mother going into exile, Alfonso was educated, successively, in Paris, in Vienna and at Sandhurst.[36]

On 26 June 1878, Alfonso XII's wife María de las Mercedes de Orleans died of typhus two days after her eighteenth birthday. He was devastated and his consequent plunge into drink and sexual adventures did little for his own precarious health. Indeed, his wife's death was merely one of a series of misfortunes. Efforts to quell rebellion in Cuba would eventually lead to the loss of 200,000 lives and an unsustainable drain on state resources. In August 1878, there was a minor republican uprising in Navalmoral de la Mata in Cáceres. It was easily suppressed, but the fact that it had happened at all hinted at underlying problems. On 15 October that same year, Alfonso XII was the target of an unsuccessful assassination attempt by Joan Oliva i Moncasí, an anarchist cooper from Labra in the province of Tarragona. Oliva fired twice with a double-barrelled pistol but missed. He was executed by *garrote vil* on 4 January 1879. Fourteen months later, on 30 December, there was a second assassination attempt. The King had remarried only a month before, on 29 November. He was returning from a walk in the Retiro with his new wife, Queen María Cristina de Habsburgo-Lorena, when a twenty-year-old pastry chef from Galicia, Francisco Otero González, shot at them. Although he also missed, on 14 April 1880 Otero was similarly executed by *garrote vil*.[37]

For now, Arsenio Martínez Campos was achieving some success against the Cuban insurgents. By dint of a combination of energetic counter-guerrilla tactics, bribery and conciliatory negotiations, he had achieved the Peace of Zanjón. As Governor General, he urged thorough-going reform of education and the economy and especially of the Cuban tax burden and of Spanish tariffs on sugar, tobacco and coffee imports from the island. Cánovas was seriously alarmed because the proposed measures constituted a major threat to the Spanish economy. His solution was to invite Martínez Campos in June 1879 to form a government which he intended to control from the shadows. Cánovas's electoral fixer, Francisco Romero Robledo, had friends among the Cuban plantation owners who were bitterly opposed to Martínez Campos's proposed reforms and did everything possible to undermine the new Prime Minister. Deeply frustrated, Martínez Campos resigned a mere six months later on 7 December and was replaced by Cánovas. In the course of 1880 and 1881, only a few of Martínez Campos's reforms were implemented, which guaranteed that the Cuban War would be reignited. On 7 February 1881, Alfonso XII exercised his royal prerogative by withdrawing confidence from Cánovas and effectively making Práxedes Mateo Sagasta Prime Minister by giving him a decree to dissolve the Cortes and call new elections.[38] Little changed with the fall of Cánovas. Spain's domestic economic problems ensured that Martínez Campos, who had become Sagasta's Minister of War, remained unable to implement his proposed reforms. In addition to the plantation owners, wheat growers feared the loss of Cuban markets to North American producers. Catalan industrialists and the footwear manufacturers of Valencia and Alicante also relied on protected Cuban markets.

In many respects, the chaotic period 1873–4 was to Spain what 1848–9 had been elsewhere in Europe. Having plucked up the courage to challenge the old order and establish a short-lived Republic, the liberal bourgeoisie was frightened out of its reforming ambitions by the spectre of proletarian disorder. When the army restored the monarchy in the person of Alfonso XII, the middle classes abandoned their reformist ideals in return for social peace. The subsequent relation of forces between the landed oligarchy, the urban bourgeoisie and the remainder of the population was perfectly represented by the so-called Restoration political system created in 1876. Indeed, it would differ little in composition from what had gone before except that parties would alternate in power peacefully rather than by a combination of insurrections and military coups. A provisional government was established under the conservative Antonio Cánovas del Castillo, who quickly set about drafting a new Constitution. After sixty years of civil wars, disastrous rule by generals and political corruption, he was convinced that what was necessary was a period of tranquillity in which industries might develop.

Cultured and widely read, Cánovas believed that the prosperity enjoyed by the dominant power of the day, Great Britain, was the result of the stability provided by its two-party system. His admiration of the British parliamentary system allegedly extended to learning by heart some of the speeches of Gladstone and Disraeli. In a bid to emulate British success, he had set out to copy, outwardly at least, what he believed to be its secret. He was determined both to exclude the army from political power and to run no risks of a radical electorate undermining his plan to consolidate the recently restored monarchy. Thus an apparent working model of the British system was elaborated whereby the Conservative Party under Cánovas and the Liberal Party under Sagasta would take turns in power. The tool necessary for this to function without interference by the electorate was electoral falsification.[39] The system came to be known as the *turno pacífico*, that is to say the peaceful alternation in power of the two monarchist or 'dynastic' parties. Thus the *turno*, in the words of the liberal reformer Gumersindo de Azcárate, far from replicating the British system was merely 'a ridiculous parody in which everything is a farce and a lie'.[40] Salvador de Madariaga wrote that Cánovas 'relied on force and fiction' and described him as 'personally honest and honourable' but 'the greatest corrupter of political life which modern Spain has known'.[41]

The micro-managing of elections ensured that, for the next half-century, power would remain in the hands of the same families that had held it before 1876. Entire dynasties, fathers, sons and sons-in-law, brothers and brothers-in-law would monopolize parliamentary seats. Such would be the case of the family of Álvaro de Figueroa, the Conde de Romanones, in Guadalajara with tentacles in Baeza and Úbeda in Jaén, Castuera in Badajoz and Cartagena in Murcia. An equally striking example was the family of Eugenio Montero Ríos, the main *cacique* of the four provinces of Galicia, who was Minister of Development from 1885 to 1886, Minister of Justice between December 1892 and July 1893 and eventually Prime Minister in 1905. From his base in Lourizán in Pontevedra, he used his influence to promote the political careers of his sons and sons-in-law. Sagasta was equally watchful of the parliamentary welfare of his sons-in-law. Francisco Silvela y de Le Vielleuze, Cánovas's eventual successor at the head of the Conservative Party, was the all-powerful *cacique* of Ávila. Although he criticized the electoral falsification of the *turno pacífico*, he placed members of his family in some of the most important government positions. Juan de la Cierva y Peñafiel, the omnipotent *cacique* of Murcia, similarly promoted his family. Indeed, it was not uncommon for parliamentary seats, senior government administrative posts and sometimes even government ministries to be virtually bequeathed from father to son.[42]

The two political parties did not have strongly defined ideologies or policies but were rather groups of notables representing the interests of two sections of the landed oligarchy. The Conservatives looked mainly to the concerns of the wine and olive growers of the south while the Liberals protected the interests of the wheat growers of the centre. The differences between them were minimal. They were known as the 'dynastic' parties because they were both committed to the monarchy and were not divided on issues regarding the social order or the sanctity of property. As their name suggested, the Liberals were less authoritarian and, unlike the firmly Catholic Conservatives, inclined to be rather more critical of the Church. The main differences were to do with trade. The Conservatives favoured the free trade required by their constituency of export fruit growers and wine producers while the Liberals represented the needs of the inefficient wheat growers who wanted protection from the great international producers of Canada, Argentina and Australia. To give an example of the problem – in Barcelona in 1884, some 60 per cent of all wheat consumed came from Castile, yet two years later it was a mere 10 per cent. The various components of the northern industrial bourgeoisie were barely represented within the system but, for the moment, were content, as Cánovas had hoped, to devote their activities to economic expansion in an atmosphere of stability. Until, in the early twentieth century, they began to organize their own parties, the Catalan textile manufacturers tended to support the Liberals because of their shared interest in restrictive tariffs, in their case to protect the Spanish market against cheaper British and Indian competition. In contrast, the Basques, exporters of iron ore, tended to support the Conservative free traders. Nevertheless, because of its lack of representation, the Catalan industrial bourgeoisie was forced to act as little more than a pressure group. Thus, despite having interests in common with the agrarian protectionists, they could be attacked by Liberals and Conservatives alike as the mouthpieces of Catalan nationalism.[43]

It was virtually impossible for any political aspirations to find legal expression unless they were in the interests of the two great oligarchical parties. Liberal and Conservative governments followed one another with soporific regularity. Rafael Shaw, an English journalist who lived in Barcelona, wrote in 1910:

Ministerial changes in Spain are the outcome of a tacit arrangement made some thirty years ago between Antonio Cánovas del Castillo and Práxedes Mateo Sagasta, the then leaders of the two main parties, the Liberals and the Conservatives, and continued by their successors, that each side should have its fair share of the loaves and fishes. After one party had been in office three or four years it was agreed by common consent that the time had come for the other side to have a turn. Thus, as Major Martín Hume says: 'Dishonest Governments are faced in sham battle by dishonest Oppositions, and parliamentary institutions, instead of being a public check upon abuses, are simply a mask behind which a large number of politicians may carry on their nefarious trade with impunity.'

Shaw explained the impotence of the electorate to change this system as the consequence of 'the tentacles of the octopus of corruption which holds the whole country in its grip. The simple fact is that the great mass of the people have no voice at all in the election of their representatives. Nominally voting is free: actually it is not.'[44]

In theory, governments were in power for five years but in practice would resign because of defeat on a particular vote, hostile public opinion, the loss of party support for the Prime Minister or some intractable social or economic problem on the horizon. The King, in theory, as the mouthpiece of public opinion or, in reality, on the basis of his prejudices or caprice, had the power to change governments because he could force an administration to resign. He could then decide to whom to grant a royal decree of dissolution of the Cortes. The rather frivolous Alfonso XIII would abuse this power.[45] The newly chosen Prime Minister, often but not always the leader of the other party, would form a government. Then, he and his Minister of the Interior would spend the next few months arranging an electoral victory that both justified his party's presence in power and gave the outgoing party a decent presence in the Cortes. When the petitions of both parties had been examined, lists of candidates would be drawn up that would ensure a substantial majority for the new Prime Minister. This process was known as the *encasillado*, each candidate who was selected to win a seat placed in the pigeonhole (*casilla*). The agreement of both parties was forthcoming. Sometimes results were faked in the Ministry of the Interior but more often they were fixed at the local level. The task of ensuring the election of the selected candidates fell to the provincial governor of each province. He would then negotiate with the local town bosses or *caciques*. They would deliver the vote for the government's candidates in return for government patronage. The candidates chosen in Madrid, who were then 'parachuted' into the constituency, were known as *cuneros*. On average about half of successful candidates were *cuneros*, that is to say with no links to the area that they would represent. Nevertheless, sometimes the local oligarchs would accept a *cunero* willingly because his political influence boded well for the area.[46]

The two parties thus lived within a non-aggression pact which made a mockery of the apparently democratic system because the formation of governments had nothing to do with the will of the electorate. Only after governments had been appointed by the King were elections held. The results were then carefully arranged by the party in power and produced, on average, 65 per cent majorities. Such apparently humiliating defeats for one side were rendered acceptable by the certainty of an equally spectacular victory next time. Between them the two dynastic parties held 98 per cent of parliamentary seats in 1884 and 83 per cent in 1901. The republicans and the Carlists had relatively little representation. The relatively even alternation was illustrated by the fact that, between 1879 and 1901, of all the deputies 'elected' 1,748 were Conservatives and 1,761 were Liberals.[47] Electoral falsification ensured that the narrow interests represented by the system were never seriously threatened. The system rested on the social power of local town bosses or *caciques*. In the northern smallholding areas, the *cacique* could be a moneylender, one of the bigger landlords, a lawyer or even a priest, who held mortgages on the small farms. The threat of foreclosure could secure votes. In the areas of the great *latifundio* estates, New Castile, Extremadura or Andalusia, the *cacique* was usually the landowner or his agent, the man who decided who worked and therefore whose family did not starve. The *cacique* thus could acquire the votes of individuals by many means, ranging from the intimidation that came from ruthless control of the local labour market to the granting of favours and bribes.

Control of the local administrative and judicial apparatus enabled the *cacique* to provide favourable judgements in land disputes, jobs, reduction of tax bills or exemptions from military service for someone within the clientelist network. Each change of government would see a massive changeover of jobs from the most humble doormen and roadsweepers to civil governors, judges and senior civil servants, all of whom were expected to vote as instructed.[48] After the elections of 1875 had been arranged by Cánovas's Minister of the Interior, Francisco Romero Robledo, Sir Austen Henry Layard, the British Ambassador to Spain from 1869 to 1877, reported to the Foreign Office that virtually every salaried placeholder had been replaced by a supporter of Alfonso XII.[49] There was no permanent civil service or judiciary owing its service to the nation. The system itself fostered corruption by ensuring that public service was for private benefit. Thus the tradition which endures to this day was established whereby few of those who become mayors (*alcaldes*) leave the town hall poorer than when they entered.

General Eduardo López de Ochoa wrote in 1930 that the majority of judges and magistrates owed their places to political intrigues and passed sentences in the interests of their patrons. The same applied right down to secretaries and court clerks. It was said of the great *cacique* Juan de la Cierva that no leaf fell in the province of Murcia without his permission. López de Ochoa claimed that La Cierva had several judges of the Supreme Court in his pocket and could always count on judgments favourable to himself or his friends. López Ochoa quoted a law professor who had stated that 'larceny and robbery existed in Spain only in regard to amounts lower than one hundred thousand pesetas. Above that figure, they were called financial affairs.' In any issue, civil or criminal, that went through the courts, a sum had to be put aside to grease the wheels of 'justice'.[50]

Similar accusations to those made about Juan de la Cierva were made regarding numerous other powerful *caciques* who also controlled entire provinces: Álvaro de Figueroa y Torres, the Conde de Romanones in Guadalajara; the wheat baron Germán Gamazo in Valladolid; Juan Poveda and Antonio Torres Orduña in Alicante; Carlos O'Donnell, Duque de Tetuán, in Castellón; Pedro Rodríguez de la Borbolla in Seville; Manuel Burgos y Mazo in Huelva; Gabino Bugallal in Orense or Augusto González Besada in Lugo.[51] With the tax collector, the *alcalde* and the judge at his command, the *cacique* was able to take over parcels of common lands, let his cattle graze on his neighbours' lands, divert water away from the land of his enemies and towards his own or that of his friends and have works done on his property at the expense of the municipality. A landowning lawyer from Almería commented: 'Four pickpockets in top hats and four thugs usually make up the top brass of a party.' In a similar vein, the one-time Minister of Justice Pedro José Moreno Rodríguez claimed that 'those that the Civil Guard used to pursue now work as bodyguards for the authorities'. It was a symptom of how openly the system worked that despite the press publishing the most corrosive accounts of *caciquismo*, the outrage of public opinion changed nothing. The general view was that the lower orders of the *caciquismo* system, the *alcaldes* and secretaries, had often spent time in prison and, if they had not, their liberty had been maintained through the influence of the *caciques* that controlled the local judiciary.[52]

At a provincial level, the *cacique* was a highly privileged middleman between the government and the local vote. The incoming Minister of the Interior chose the provincial civil governors and he squared the *caciques*.[53] The influence that permitted the *cacique* to supply the required votes to the government depended in part on the distribution of patronage that was provided by the public purse. This might take the form of the rerouting of a road or railway or the building of a bridge that would extend his influence over a town or even an entire province. The loyalty of the *cacique*'s clientele also depended on the protection of family and friends from the law, from taxation or from conscription. It has been calculated that the more than a third of the correspondence written by the principal politicians of the Restoration period consisted of requests for votes or letters of recommendation for those whose votes were required. Moreover, the bulk of such correspondence was written just before or just after elections. It is said that the homes of Sagasta and Cánovas in Madrid were besieged on a daily basis by aspirants for government jobs or favours such as public works in their district. So frequently were roads built for the convenience of local *caciques* that they came to be known as parliamentary highways.[54]

On occasion, over-zealous local officials would produce majorities comprising more than 100 per cent of the electorate. It was not unknown for results to be published before the elections took place. As the century wore on, after the introduction of universal male suffrage, casual falsification became ever more difficult and, if the requisite number of votes could not be mustered, the *caciques* sometimes registered the dead in the local cemetery as voters. In Madrid in 1896, fictitious voters, known as Lázaros, used the names of deceased electors. More frequently, they sent gangs of paid voters from village to village to vote for the government party. In 1879, Romero Robledo used the technique of 'flying squads' – 200 Aragonese raced around Madrid from polling station to polling station using their votes. It was said that one man had voted forty-two times. The alteration of the electoral list or the addition or subtraction of votes was known as *pucherazo* or *tupinada*, the packing of the pot. Sometimes, announcements were placed in the local press announcing, falsely, that a rival had withdrawn his candidacy. More common was to change the timing of elections so that hostile voters would not arrive in time or having thugs present to intimidate rival voters. At other times, the voting urns were placed where voters would not want to go, in a fever hospital, a pigsty or on a high roof. In 1891, in one voting station in Murcia, the supervisor obliged voters to pass their voting slips through a window so that he could change them at his convenience. Advantage could also be taken of some who simply did not bother to vote. If the vote was not going as planned, there were thugs on hand to raid the polling station and seize the voting urns. Sometimes, those likely to vote for the unofficial candidate would be thrown in jail or else threatened with investigation of their tax status. Most common of all was simply the falsification of the count.[55]

The USS *Maine*, blown up in Havana harbour, the excuse for the Spanish-American war of 1898.

2

Violence, Corruption and the
Slide to Disaster

The consequence of the *turno* system was that politics became an exclusive minuet danced by a small privileged minority. As well as the *caciques* who were committed to one or other of the parties, the Conservative La Cierva or the Liberal Gamazo, there were amenable *caciques* who would work for both parties. This is illustrated by the oft-related story of the *cacique* of Motril in the province of Granada. When the coach with the election results arrived from the provincial capital, they were brought to him in the local rich men's club or Casino. Leafing through them, he declared to the expectant hangers-on: 'We the Liberals were convinced that we would win these elections. However, the will of God has decreed otherwise.' A lengthy pause. 'It appears that we the Conservatives have won the elections.' Excluded from organized politics, the hungry masses could choose only between apathy and violence. Their apathy allowed the local authorities to fabricate the results without too much opposition. Violent resistance guaranteed arrest, torture and perhaps execution. From 1876, the electorate consisted of men over the age of twenty-five who could afford to register to vote, by paying a 25 peseta tax on property or a 50 peseta tax on their economic activities. For the elections of 1879, 1881, 1884 and 1886, the electorate numbered approximately 850,000. The introduction of universal male suffrage in 1890 extended the electorate to just under four million for the elections of 1891, 1893, 1896, 1898, 1899, 1901 and 1903. By increasing the threat of the electorate using its votes in its own interests, the reform also intensified the use of electoral corruption in the interests of property.[1]

However, the electoral list had little to do with those whose votes were actually registered. Control of the local judiciary facilitated the removal of enemies and the addition of friends. In 1879, around 40 per cent of those who voted in Barcelona were government functionaries whose jobs depended on how they voted. In 1881, in Valencia, 75 per cent of those that voted had no right to do so. In 1884, Romero Robledo managed to reduce the potential electorate in Madrid from 33,205 to 12,250. That *alcaldes* were government nominees ensured that they would be willing electoral agents. Those who refused could simply be removed or forced to resign by threatening them with exorbitant fines for invented or trivial offences such as failure to respond to letters or to introduce the metric system.[2]

This all worked best in poor rural areas, particularly in Galicia and Andalusia, because the votes of a poverty-stricken and largely illiterate electorate could be falsified easily. Accordingly, the official turnout in rural areas was recorded as an utterly implausible 80 per cent. The cities, where it was so much more difficult for the techniques of *caciquismo* to be applied, recorded much lower electoral participation. As the century wore on, votes in the cities were increasingly the only ones that could be accepted as genuine. Thus, to neutralize them, the ministers of the interior of the dynastic parties had no compunction about resorting to gerrymandering, flagrantly changing electoral boundaries to swamp towns with the falsified votes of surrounding rural areas. This was possible while the Cortes was small and constituencies large. Even then, backward Galicia was over-represented in the Cortes while industrial Catalonia was dramatically under-represented. Between 1876 and 1887, there were only 210 deputies in the Cortes. After 1891, there were 348. By the turn of the century, urbanization saw an increasing influx of deputies from non-dynastic parties and even republicans.[3]

The quest for government jobs went on unabated. The queues of place-seekers outside his house obliged Sagasta on occasion to sleep in an hotel. Within two weeks of coming to power, he had replaced all the under-secretaries of all the ministries, virtually all the directors general in the ministries of the Navy, of Overseas Territories, of Finance and of Development, seven in the Ministry of the Interior and four in the Ministry of War, forty-seven civil governors, the Chief Justice of the Supreme Court and three of the eight captains general of the military regions. Sagasta's election fixer, Venancio González, emulated Romero Robledo and arranged a substantial Liberal majority in the late-summer elections of 1881. The immediate consequence was that, at provincial and municipal level, the number of sacked bureaucrats was legion.[4]

Under Cánovas, gambling casinos were illegal but were allowed to function when the appropriate bribes were paid. In Madrid, for instance, each casino paid 35,000 pesetas to the Civil Governor of Madrid, the Marqués de Heredia Spínola. Theoretically, the money was for charitable purposes, but there was no auditing. Heredia's successor, the Conde de Xiquena, tried to close the casinos, only for the owners to mount a bombing campaign in June 1881 which severely injured a number of children. It was later alleged by Xiquena that Romero Robledo had been one of the beneficiaries of the bribes paid by the gambling bosses. The accusation had to be abandoned when Cánovas threatened to bring the Cortes to its knees by leading a walkout of the Conservative Party.[5]

While the Liberals failed to introduce significant reform, working-class opposition to the system was growing. The Federación de Trabajadores de la Región Española (FTRE), the Spanish section of the *International Workingmen's Association* or 'First International', began to organize openly. It soon had 57,000 members, concentrated mainly in Andalusia and Catalonia, but was split over the relative efficacy of strikes and terrorism. The nucleus of the Socialist movement, the Asociación del Arte de Imprimir, was gaining ground through a successful strike by typesetters in 1882.[6] In January 1884, Alfonso XII had brought back Cánovas. His Minister of the Interior, Romero Robledo, presided over notoriously corrupt elections on 27 April that year and secured a Conservative majority of 295 seats against 90. Cánovas's government faced numerous problems – military subversion, the ongoing concerns about the alleged anarchist secret society called the Mano Negra, a cholera epidemic, unrest in Cuba and the fact that the King was facing a progressively more debilitating battle with virulent tuberculosis. In fact, Alfonso did not look after himself, failing even to wear warm clothing on hunting trips in bad weather.

Armed with such a big majority, the new cabinet's instinctive response to most problems was reactionary. Cánovas himself was seen as intolerably arrogant. The Cuban situation was worsened by the new Minister of Overseas Territories, Manuel Aguirre de Tejada, refusing to contemplate the abolition of slavery. This was not unconnected with the interests of Romero Robledo, who was the son-in-law of the fabulously rich sugar magnate Julián de Zulueta y Amondo. Known as 'the prince of the slavers', the Basque Zulueta had huge plantations and three sugar mills in Cuba and others in Álava.[7] That connection explains why

Romero Robledo would later, in November 1891, seek to be named Minister for Overseas Territories. Shortly after the 1884 elections, a minor republican uprising at Santa Coloma de Farners near Girona was easily suppressed. However, when courts martial failed to hand out death sentences for the two leaders, a major and a captain, the government went ahead and had them shot despite widespread protests, including from the King. On 20 November 1884, a minor student demonstration in favour of a professor who had been excommunicated for making a speech in favour of the theories of Charles Darwin was repressed with some violence by the Civil Guard. On Christmas Eve, a series of earthquakes in Andalusia left thousands homeless, many of whom died from cold and others from the cholera epidemic. A visit to the affected areas left the King disgusted with what he had seen of government neglect. He also ignored the Prime Minister's advice and visited areas affected by cholera.

Alfonso XII complained to the German envoy that Cánovas 'knows everything, decides everything and interferes in everything, even in military matters of which he knows nothing and that he gives no consideration to the King's views and wishes'. He believed that Cánovas was using funds that were needed to modernize the army's weaponry in order to fortify harbours because there were more opportunities for graft in construction. On 25 November 1885, Alfonso died, aged just twenty-seven. Apparently, Cánovas had been made aware of the seriousness of the King's condition by his doctor, who had told him that a warmer climate would probably prolong Alfonso's life. However, he had sworn the doctor to secrecy lest news of the King's weakness inflame the republican movement.[8] His wife María Cristina became Queen Regent and some months later gave birth to a child, the future Alfonso XIII. To ensure that the system established by Cánovas would endure, the two party leaders met at the Palace of the Pardo and signed a pact that consolidated the so-called *turno*.

In the south, land hunger was creating an increasingly desperate desire for change, the more so as Andalusian labourers came under the influence of anarchism. This was partly the consequence of the fact that, in November 1868, Giuseppe Fanelli, an Italian disciple of the Russian anarchist Mikhail Bakunin, had been sent to Spain by the First International. His oratory found fertile ground and soon inspired his own evangelists to take anarchism to village after village. Part of the message was that alcoholism, the frequenting of prostitutes and gambling were degrading. Alongside the advocacy of austerity, Fanelli also argued that justice and equality should be seized by direct action. This struck a chord among the starving day labourers or *braceros* and gave a new sense of hope and purpose to hitherto sporadic rural uprisings. Fanelli's eager converts took part in outbreaks of violence, crop burnings and strikes. However, poorly organized, these revolutionary outbursts were easily crushed and alternated with periods of apathy.[9]

Commenting in 1910 on why revolution was slow in developing, Rafael Shaw wrote:

> The patient submission of the labourer to conditions which he believes to be unalterable is partly the result of three hundred years of corrupt government, during which he has been steadily squeezed to provide money for the wars, luxuries, and amusements of the governing classes; partly of the terror of the Inquisition and the tradition of silence that it has left behind it; partly of Oriental fatalism; but is certainly not due to the animal indifference and stupidity to which his 'betters' attribute it. The peasant refrains from open complaint, not because he is contented and has nothing to complain of, but because long experience has taught him the uselessness and the danger of protest. He may offend his employer and lose his place, or, still worse, he may offend the Church and the Jesuits, in which case he will be a marked man, and can never hope to get permanent employment again.

Another reason for the lack of protest against the ease with which corruption dominated the political system was that, at the turn of the century, around 75 per cent of the population was illiterate. Thousands of villages had no school at all. Even in Madrid and Barcelona, there were fewer than half of the schools required by law. Where there were schools, attendance was not imposed and schoolteachers were poorly paid and often not paid at all. Rudimentary literacy skills were taught in the army.[10] At first, hunger and injustice had found their champions in the banditry for which the south was notorious, but the day labourers had not been long in finding a more sophisticated form of rebellion.[11] When they came, the inevitable outbreaks of protest by the unrepresented majority were repressed violently by the forces of order, the Civil Guard and, at moments of greater tension, the army.

The owners of the great estates, unwilling to engage in artificial fertilization or expensive irrigation projects, preferred instead to build their profits on the exploitation of the great armies of landless day labourers, the *braceros* and *jornaleros*.[12] The *latifundios* were usually administered by bailiffs, who took every advantage of a mass of surplus labour. When seasonal work was available, the *braceros* and *jornaleros* were obliged to work long hours, often from sun-up to sun-down. Work was often available only far from home which meant having to sleep in insanitary huts provided by the landowners. The labourers endured harsh working conditions on starvation wages and lengthy periods of unemployment. When the more easy-going clerics and nobles of an earlier age sold up and the common lands were enclosed, most of the social palliatives which had alleviated rural misery were curtailed. The encroachment on the lands of religious orders or the sleepier aristocrats saw the collection of windfall crops or firewood, the occasional hunting of rabbits or birds, the watering of domestic animals, which had hitherto kept the poverty-stricken south from upheaval, come to an end. Paternalism was replaced by repression. Thus was intensified the process of the proletarianization of a great army of landless labourers. The powder keg of resentment was kept in check by the institutionalized violence of the Civil Guard and armed thugs hired by the bailiffs.

Other devices were used, such as conspiracies fabricated or wildly exaggerated in order to justify the repression of the principal working-class organization, the FTRE. Its weekly journal, the *Revista Social*, was subject to censorship and occasional confiscation. In the last week of September 1882, the FTRE's second congress was celebrated in Seville. A total of 209 sections and nearly 50,000 members were represented, mainly from Andalusia (30,000) and from Catalonia (13,000). The FTRE was portrayed by the authorities as a band of bloodthirsty revolutionaries. In fact, the organization's immediate objective was the eight-hour day and its long-term ambition the collectivization of agriculture and industry. However, this relative moderation was undermined by the fact that members of the FTRE were being discriminated against by landowners and industrialists. In numerous towns, the *alcaldes* banned public meetings and the Civil Guard treated private ones as subversive. Accordingly, a breakaway group, Los Desheredados, advocated secret revolutionary action and the use of terrorism.[13]

A drought in the summer of 1881 led to crop failures across Andalusia but especially in the provinces of Cadiz and Seville. The consequent hunger the following winter saw landless labourers and their families begging in the streets of the towns. There were dramatic increases in the number of deaths from malnutrition and related illnesses such as measles, particularly among children. There were violent attacks on property, crop burning and sheep rustling, thefts from bakeries and other food shops and cases of banditry.[14] There were some towns where the authorities vainly tried to raise funds to ameliorate the predicament of the starving labourers and isolated incidents of charitable donations for the poor. In some cases, municipal resources were used to finance road mending or irrigation projects to give work to the unemployed. More often, however, labourers were simply advised to seek work in other provinces. By the autumn of 1882, social tension had intensified notably. A wave of strikes was met by heavy-handed repression at the hands of a substantially reinforced Civil Guard. In Jerez, there were demonstrations by labourers demanding work which soon degenerated into food riots. In December 1892, four murders were registered in the area.[15] The panic-stricken authorities seized the opportunity to claim that the killers in Jerez and the perpetrators of numerous other unconnected crimes, brawls and robberies belonged to the Mano Negra (Black Hand), a name referring to the dirty hands of manual labourers. The Mano Negra was said to be conspiring to avenge the crimes committed against the working class by the landowners. Allegedly, it aimed to wage war on the southern rich by means of murder, kidnappings and robbery. Furthermore, it was claimed that this secret organization had over 70,000 members. In this context, many workers were imprisoned on the basis of denunciations by a landlord, a magistrate or a Civil Guard, without any need for proof.

In the words of James Joll, the Mano Negra 'may never have existed outside the imagination of the police, who were always ready to attribute isolated, unconnected acts of violence to a single master organization'. Nevertheless, it is certainly the case that in 1880 some member organizations of the FTRE had agreed to carry out reprisals against the owners. By the spring of 1883, as a result of indiscriminate arrests of members of workers' societies and readers of (legal) anarchist newspapers, 5,000 prisoners were being held in Cadiz and Jerez. Little or no distinction was made between union activity and crime as confessions of membership of the Mano Negra were extracted by torture. The FTRE denied the existence of the Mano Negra and accused the government of concocting a supposed revolutionary organization out of unconnected criminal elements. In fact, it seems that, while there may possibly have existed since the late 1870s a small criminal mafia called the Mano Negra, the link between it and the transparent and moderate FTRE was an invention to justify the repression of the rural labourers' movement. Indeed, documents produced at the trial of its supposed members in the summer of 1883 revealed that the decisive 'proof' of the existence of Mano Negra just happened to have been provided by the commander of the Jerez garrison of the Civil Guard who had conveniently stumbled across a copy of this secret society's written constitution under a rock in the countryside. Many were sentenced to life imprisonment, which meant confinement in filthy dungeons, and seven were publicly executed by garrotte in June 1884.[16] The repression decimated the membership of the FTRE to the extent that, at a congress held in Valencia in September and October 1888, it was dissolved.[17]

The Spanish Socialist Party, the Partido Socialista Obrero Español (PSOE), was founded in 1879 but constituted little challenge to the anarchist movement. Its trade union strength was largely in the printers' union in Madrid, the Asociación General del Arte de Imprimir, and the textile union in Barcelona known as the Tres Clases de Vapor. The party's founder, Pablo Iglesias, admitted that, in the 1880s, the PSOE had only around 200 members. Rigidly Marxist, the PSOE leadership both refused alliances with bourgeois republicans and rejected the violent revolutionism of the anarchists. It thus remained isolated. It was not until 1886 that its newspaper El Socialista was published and only in 1888 that its trade union, the Unión General de Trabajadores (UGT), was established in Barcelona. So poor was its development that, in 1899, its headquarters were moved to Madrid. The key to the strategy adopted by Pablo Iglesias was to achieve political power by electoral means which rendered questionable the refusal to make alliances with the liberal republicans. For Pablo Iglesias, the purpose of strikes was not revolutionary but reformist, the improvement of working conditions, and thus insufficiently combative to attract workers in the miserable conditions of late nineteenth-century industrial Spain. By the end of the decade, the UGT was acquiring substantial support in the mining districts of the Basque Country and Asturias.[18]

Throughout the 1880s, and indeed beyond, the much larger anarchist movement was divided on tactics and strategy. Broadly speaking, on the one hand, there were the so-called collectivists who favoured the building of economic power through legal trade union activity that could eventually implement the social revolution. On the other, there were the so-called communists, who rejected this reformism as consolidating the capitalist system. In its stead, they advocated revolutionary violence. To replace its collectivist ideology, relative moderation and reliance on legal methods, there was emerging a more individualistic anarchism committed to 'propaganda by the deed' carried out by fragmented clandestine cells or 'affinity groups' such as those advocated by Los Desheredados.[19]

Strikes and demonstrations started to give way to acts of terrorism. As anarchism took ever deeper root in the small workshops of the highly fragmented Catalan textile industry, there was a wave of bomb outrages that provoked savage and indiscriminate reprisals from the forces of order. Between June 1884 and May 1890, there were twenty-five bomb incidents in Barcelona. The most frequent incidents came as a result of labour disputes and targeted factories, the homes of the managers or the owners, the offices of the industrialists' association, the Foment del Treball Nacional, and police stations. There were three fatalities and many injured. From 1890 to 1900, there would be another fifty-nine incidents which caused a further thirty-five deaths. The worst years in terms of violence would be those between 1893 and 1896. The intensification of social violence was not simply a result of the ideology of anarchist revolutionaries. Their ideas spread in the fertile soil of a Catalonia experiencing a profound process of social and economic transformation. Rural workers were being attracted to Barcelona and other cities by the growth of industries, especially in textiles. The recent arrivals, relying on insecure work, were forced to live in appalling shanty towns of unhygienic hovels without basic sanitation or adequate nutrition, resulting in high levels of infant, and indeed adult, mortality. Moreover, there was no schooling available for their children. Radicalization, similar to that taking place in France and Russia, was facilitated by the recent invention of dynamite which was available for purchase without restriction in Barcelona. It was not uncommon in the taverns of the poorer parts of Barcelona to encounter men passing the hat for 'a few pence for dynamite'.[20]

The social conflicts deriving from the painfully slow but inexorable progress of industrialization matched those arising in the southern countryside from the brutal social injustices intrinsic to the *latifundio* economy. The rural proletariat existed on the most meagre subsistence diet. There was rarely more than one meal per day, and it was usually poor-quality bread and gazpacho, a soup made from tomatoes, onions, cucumber, peppers and garlic. Such a diet never contained more than secondary sources of protein, since meat, fish and eggs were beyond the means of the day labourer. A common cold could be disastrous.[21] The 1890s were a period of economic depression which exacerbated the grievances of the lower classes, both in the urban slums and in rural areas.

The misery of the southern peasantry was the motive force behind direct action. The indiscriminate repression unleashed in the midst of the Mano Negra panic fostered the belief that any direct action up to and including individual terrorism was licit against the tyranny of the state. In a context of poor harvests with the consequent price inflation and mass unemployment, there were increasing levels of social violence in the form of sporadic estate occupations, thefts of livestock and grain and attacks on owners and estate managers. In late 1891, a building worker from Madrid, Félix Grávalo 'El Madrileño', preached anarchist ideas in the villages surrounding Jerez. Among his disciples grew the naive idea of seizing Jerez in order to create an anarchist stronghold as the first step to taking control of the entire province of Cadiz. On the night of 8 January 1892, more than 500 *braceros* from Arcos de la Frontera, Ubrique, Trebujena, Sanlúcar de Barrameda, El Puerto de Santa María and other towns in Cadiz and Lebrija in Seville, gathered on the outskirts of the city. Armed only with sickles, scythes, pitchforks and sticks but driven by hunger, they invaded the city centre. In part, they were intending to free dozens of workers recently imprisoned after the Mano Negra trials. Their battle cry was 'Brothers, we are coming for you!' However, parallel uprisings in several other towns of the province of Cadiz suggested Grávalo's wider revolutionary purpose. The *braceros* briefly held Jerez, although their belief that the local military garrison would join them was entirely misplaced. Their triumph was short-lived and the police swiftly regained control. Two innocent passers-by, a commercial traveller and an office worker, had been killed by elements of the mob in an outburst of class hatred. Because they were well dressed and wore gloves, they had been assumed to be 'oppressors'.[22] Fear of the spectre of revolution provoked by the Jerez events ensured that the consequent repression would be severe and extend right across western Andalusia. In subsequent military trials, despite lack of concrete evidence, other than the testimony of Grávalo obtained under duress, four labourers were condemned to life imprisonment. Four more were sentenced to death and executed by garrotte in the market place of Jerez.[23]

One of the consequences of the repression was the creation of an anarchist martyr in the form of the saintly Fermín Salvochea. He was accused of being the brains behind the entire event in Jerez despite already being in prison. In 1873 he had been Alcalde of Cadiz and had long been a target of the authorities who were frightened by his immense popularity. In April 1891, they had shut down his newspaper *La revolución social* and, after the May Day celebrations, arrested him. While in jail, he had been visited by the organizers of the Jerez invasion whom he had tried to dissuade from what he saw as a suicidal project. It was claimed that he was behind the assault on Jerez via 'El Madrileño' who was deemed to be his puppet. Several prisoners were taken out and tortured so that they would declare that Salvochea had offered the support of the anarchists of Cadiz for the Jerez operation. He was sentenced to twelve years' hard labour but was amnestied in 1899 after serving for eight years.[24]

The knowledge that confessions had been obtained by torture intensified the spread of anarchism in other parts of Spain. In particular, in Barcelona there were numerous acts of solidarity with the Andalusian labourers which in turn provoked state violence in the form of indiscriminate arrests, torture and executions in the Catalan capital. Initially, anarchist efforts to emulate the terrorist campaigns taking place in France and Russia were notable for their incompetence.[25] On 24 September 1893, as a direct response to the repression in Jerez, there was a failed attempt on the life of the Captain General of Barcelona, Arsenio Martínez Campos, who, it will be recalled, had led the military coup that had restored the monarchy in December 1874. He was noted for his open hostility to the workers' movement. The bomb attack during a parade in honour of the patroness of the city, the Virgin of Mercy (La Mare de Déu de la Mercè) was the beginning of three of the bloodiest years of terrorism in Barcelona. One Civil Guard and several horses were killed and sixteen people badly injured. Although Martínez Campos was thrown from his horse and had shrapnel in his leg, he was otherwise unharmed. The would-be assassin, a thirty-one-year-old printer and father of three, Paulí Pallàs, a member of an affinity group, made no attempt to escape and was arrested on the spot.

It is an indication of the inefficiency of the police that Pallàs was the first author of a bomb outrage to be caught. He was arrested and tried five days later. He declared that his only regret was not to have succeeded in killing 'that reactionary representative of the abuse of power'. He was sentenced to death on 30 September 1893 and executed by firing squad on 6 October. A huge crowd gathered and some of those present were heard to shout, 'Long live dynamite!' and 'Long live anarchy!' Pallàs's execution was the beginning of a major repression. In subsequent years, the police persecuted his wife, who had known nothing of his plans. In the immediate aftermath of the assassination attempt, sixty anarchists were arrested and six innocent men were executed on 21 May 1894, on the grounds of a non-existent complicity with Pallàs in the attack on General Martínez Campos. Two of them had been in prison at the time and one of those, Manuel Ars i Solanellas, would be avenged years later by his son Ramón in the assassination of the Prime Minister Eduardo Dato. Over the next two years, more than 20,000 men and women were imprisoned, many to be tortured. The blind lashing out by the police confirmed the working-class view that the state had declared war on them. At the same time, Pallàs was regarded in anarchist circles as a martyr. His last words were allegedly 'Vengeance will be terrible!' and calls for his death to be avenged began to be heard in anarchist circles. The bloodiest possible revenge would soon be carried out in the temple of the Catalan bourgeoisie, the Gran Teatre del Liceu.[26]

Terrorism was facilitated by the fact that, until 1895, the poorly paid and inadequately led police in Barcelona lacked a photographic archive and even a basic filing system. Its consequent incompetence was compensated for by its brutality. Despised by the working class, it was known as the 'muddle' or the 'stink'. It was not until September 1896, after one of the most extreme terrorist attacks, in the Carrer dels Canvis Nous, that the Conservative government of Cánovas del Castillo responded to the protests of prominent citizens and created a specialist unit or brigade for the investigation of political and social crimes. Given the inefficiency of the police, the government relied increasingly on the army. The high command considered that the only valid response to the threat of anarchist terrorism was blanket repression. Indiscriminate brutality hit those elements of the anarchist movement that condemned violence. The anarchists were already virulently anti-militaristic for both theoretical reasons and in response to the appalling experience of conscripts and their families who paid the cost of unjust colonial wars. As one anarchist newspaper declared: 'If the bourgeois want war, all they have to do is enlist and go to Cuba.' Repression exacerbated anarchist hostility to the army.[27]

Within one month of the execution of Paulí Pallàs, one of the most dramatic outrages took place on 7 November 1893, at the Gran Liceu de Barcelona, the opera house frequented by the wealthy bourgeoisie. Since there had been various warnings of an anarchist attack, to attend the opera in evening dress was an act of provocative irresponsibility. Before a packed house of 3,600 people, a performance of Rossini's *Guillaume Tell* opened the season. At the moment in Act 2 when William Tell swears he will free his country from oppression, the anarchist Santiago Salvador i Franch hurled two Orsini bombs from the fifth-floor balcony into the high-priced stall seats. Fortunately, only one exploded but, even so, twenty people died including a fourteen-year-old girl and nine women and a further thirty-five were injured by shrapnel, shards of glass and flying splinters from smashed seats. It was estimated at the time that had both bombs gone off, the death toll would have been massive.[28]

The subsequent repression was carried out implacably by the fifty-eight-year-old General Valeriano Weyler, who was appointed Captain General of Catalonia on 5 December 1893.[29] After more than 400 virtually indiscriminate arrests, six innocent men were put on trial. They were condemned to death after confessions of complicity in the attack on Martínez Campos had been secured by torture. Those death sentences were meant as a warning to the anarchists of the serious determination of the authorities to clamp down on terrorism. Santiago Salvador was not captured until 1 January 1894. A petty criminal of violent tendencies, he had previously been arrested for robbery and fighting. His family background was murky. In 1878, when he was thirteen, he had tried to murder his father, a notoriously violent man who was subsequently shot by the Civil Guard in 1891. In early 1893, Salvador had been badly beaten by the police in Valencia after which he is alleged to have said: 'every blow that I received would cost tears of blood'. He denied that his action was meant as revenge for the execution of Pallàs. Yet, at another time, he claimed that 'The death of Pallàs had a terrible effect on me and to avenge him, as a tribute to his memory, I decided to do something that would scare those who had derived pleasure from his death and thought that they no longer had anything to fear. I wanted to disabuse them and also enjoy myself.'

Salvador told a journalist that, after the explosion, he had remained in the street outside the Liceu to rejoice in the panic of the bourgeoisie. He had hoped to go to the funeral of the victims on 9 November to throw more bombs into the crowd of mourners, but his alarmed comrades refused to supply him with the necessary explosives. He and two others were not tried until 11 July 1894. While in prison, he faked reconciliation with the Catholic Church as a device to secure a more comfortable existence. In his well-appointed cell, he was surrounded by devotional books, holy pictures and crucifixes. He dropped the pretence when his sentence was confirmed and claimed that he had merely been playing one last joke on the bourgeoisie. When on 21 November, before a large crowd, he was executed by garrote vil, he died shouting, 'Long live anarchy and social revolution' and 'Down with religion'. Despite having murdered numerous innocents and then fled, he was hailed as a hero by some elements of the anarchist press, although severely condemned by others. Like Pallàs before him, Salvador seemed oblivious to the fact that, in addition to causing so many innocent deaths, his actions brought down a fierce repression on the anarchist movement, many of whose members were opposed to terrorism.[30]

The Liceu bombing came in the midst of a series of catastrophes which, taken together, did nothing to consolidate public confidence in the political establishment. In October 1893, small-scale conflict had broken out in Morocco. The military governor of the garrison town of Melilla, General Juan García Margallo, had initiated fortification works on land considered sacred by local Berber tribesmen. When the tomb of a Rifian saint was desecrated, 6,000 Rifeño tribesmen armed with Remington rifles attacked Melilla on 3 October. They were driven back by artillery fire which destroyed a mosque and so escalated the initial conflict into a jihad which necessitated considerable Spanish reinforcements. Then a strategic error by Garcia Margallo occasioned numerous Spanish losses in an action in which he himself was killed. It was rumoured that he had been shot with a revolver by a young lieutenant, Miguel Primo de Rivera, who in 1923 would establish a dictatorship.

Primo was allegedly indignant that the rifles with which the Moors were armed had been sold to them by the General. No proof was ever found, but the rumour exposed the entirely justified belief that the military administration was corrupt. Incidentally, Primo de Rivera was awarded Spain's highest military decoration, the Cruz Laureada de San Fernando, and promoted to captain. The campaign was ended only by a massive show of force that Spain could ill afford.[31]

Four days before the Liceu atrocity, there had taken place the greatest civilian disaster in nineteenth-century Spain. On 3 November 1893, the cargo ship *Cabo Machichaco* carrying dynamite caught fire in the harbour of Santander. While crew members from nearby ships and local firemen tried to extinguish the fire, a vast crowd gathered to watch. When the ship blew up, the explosion threw up a huge column of thousands of tons of water which hurled many people into the sea. The shock wave destroyed many buildings in the town and fragments of iron and body parts were blown immense distances. Five hundred and ninety people died and a further 525 were seriously injured, nearly 2 per cent of the population of the city. Among the dead were the principal military and civilian authorities including the Civil Governor whose baton of office was found several kilometres away.

In the wake of the Liceu attack, there were many demands for suppression of the anarchist movement. On 9 November, the government initiated a suspension of constitutional guarantees in the province of Barcelona which remained in force until 31 December the following year. For a brief period, vigilante groups patrolled the streets of bourgeois neighbourhoods. In July 1894, the law was strengthened to make the placing of bombs in public places or causing loss of life punishable by life imprisonment or death. It also widened the penalties against those suspected of conspiracy to commit terrorist acts. The exceptional measures did not just limit the rights of those of anarchist ideas but were also used to justify the arrests of republican workers, teachers from lay schools and other freethinkers. General Weyler's ruthless application of these measures provided Barcelona with nearly two years of tranquillity in large part because the horror provoked by the attack on the Liceu silenced any criticism of police methods.[32]

Posted to Cuba, Valeriano Weyler was succeeded in Barcelona in January 1896 by the somewhat more moderate General Eulogi Despujol i Dusay. Nevertheless, mass arrests followed a further terrorist outrage on 7 June that year. A bomb exploded in the midst of the Corpus Christi procession moving towards the beautiful Gothic church of Santa Maria del Mar in the Born district of Barcelona. This spectacular annual ceremony was a local tradition that was an excuse for dressing up and it always attracted large crowds. Unusually for a religious ceremony, the monstrance with the host and the ecclesiastical dignitaries did not lead the procession but came after the principal banner. This was always carried by the Captain General with its ribbons held by the Civil Governor and the Alcalde. As the banner was entering the basilica, an explosion was heard at the rear of the procession. The bomb exploded in the Carrer dels Canvis Nous as the crowd was kneeling before the monstrance. Because, a few moments earlier, it had started to rain, the bishop and the other clerical dignitaries had hastened into the church. The bomb killed twelve people including a six-year-old girl and an eleven-year-old boy and seriously injured a further fifty-four people. Since the bishop and other dignitaries were unhurt and all the victims were working-class citizens, there were suspicions that the perpetrator was a police agent provocateur. Another theory was that the culprit, ignorant of the particular arrangements of this procession, had assumed that the military and civil authorities would have been walking behind the monstrance. Whatever the doubts, the atrocity united public opinion in general and the bourgeois press of Barcelona and Madrid, Liberal and Conservative. The entire city of Barcelona declared mourning, the street lights dimmed.[33]

There were widespread demands for harsh reprisals against the anarchists who were assumed to be the culprits. The almost unanimous calls for revenge were the prelude to a brutal repression which would take place over the next months. Despite international condemnation, there was a hardening of the legal measures open to the Spanish authorities with the introduction that September of the law for the repression of anarchism. A new police squad was created which imitated the techniques of the Russian Okhrana, using bribery, informers, undercover operatives and agents provocateurs commanded by a Civil Guard, Lieutenant Narciso Portas Ascanio.[34] The Captain General placed the investigation in the hands of a military judge, Lieutenant Colonel Enrique Marzo Díaz-Valdivieso, who had presided over the trial after the attack on Martínez Campos that had led to the execution of six anarchists. The torture of prisoners was carried out under the supervision of

Lieutenant Portas. Admitting that they had no clues, the authorities proceeded to arrest more than 500 anarchists, republicans and freethinkers. Among them were the widows of previously executed anarchists such as Paulí Pallàs, writers, women who took food to those already imprisoned and even the staff of cafés frequented by leftists. Policemen were paid a bonus for every arrest, so local prisons were bursting at the seams. Workers' centres were closed down en masse. The majority of the anarchist and other leftist prisoners were held and interrogated in the bleak fortress of Montjuïc, the Spanish Bastille, which loured over Barcelona. The fact that among them were prominent anarchist intellectuals such as Anselmo Lorenzo, Federico Urales, Fernando Tarrida del Mármol and Teresa Claramunt and lawyers such as Pere Coromines ensured that articulate accounts of the abominable treatment of prisoners reached the outside world.[35]

One of the most effective of those drawing attention to the scandal was Alejandro Lerroux. Born in 1864 in Cordoba, he had started his adult life as a deserter from the army after squandering his Military Academy fees in a casino. As a fluent if rather lightweight journalist, he had acquired a spurious fame in 1893 by dint of an inadvertent victory in a duel with a newspaper editor. Elevated to the editorship of the then scandalmongering and left-wing *El País*, Lerroux acquired a popular following as a result of his exposés of the tortures in the Montjuïc prison. He achieved further celebrity with a series of revelations of military repression and government scandals. In March 1899, he launched a new weekly, *El Progreso*, in which he renewed the denunciation of what had happened in Montjuïc.[36]

It is probable that the explosion in the Carrer del Canvis Nous was the work of a French anarchist called either Jean or François Girault, who subsequently escaped to Buenos Aires after hiding in London.[37] The alleged principal culprit, also a Frenchman, Tomàs Ascheri, a police informer, was arrested two days after the bombing. His denunciations led to the arrest of two Catalan anarchists, Josep Molas and Antoni Nogués. After being subjected to intense tortures, they named others. Horrendous cruelties endured by those subsequently arrested included the crushing of bones, the tearing out of fingernails and toenails, the application of red-hot irons to flesh and the cutting out of tongues. Under these torments, one prisoner – Luis Mas – was driven insane, five died and another twenty-eight confessed to having placed the bomb. On the grounds that one of the victims had been a soldier, the accused were tried by court martial between 11 and 15 December 1896. The prosecutor demanded the death sentence for twenty-eight men. In the event, on the basis of the confessions extracted by torture, lengthy prison sentences were imposed on sixty-six and eight were condemned to death. Three death sentences and forty-six prison sentences were commuted by the Supreme Military Court. Among 194 men sentenced to banishment were numerous famous prisoners who then played a part in drawing international attention to the inquisitorial behaviour of the Spanish authorities. Finally, despite the doubts raised about confessions extorted by torture, five were executed. Before a large crowd, Ascheri as the alleged bomber and Molas, Nogués, Mas and Joan Alsina, the alleged bomb maker, as accomplices, were shot by firing squad at dawn on 4 May 1897 in the fortress moat. The four supposed accomplices died proclaiming their innocence. The prisoners condemned to hard labour suffered inhuman conditions in Spain's African colonies.[38]

International press exposures of the tortures brought immense discredit on Spain at the same time as the repression of independence movements in Cuba and the Philippines. In particular, the campaign in France likened the Spanish repression to that in Tsarist Russia. In Britain, a Spanish Atrocities Committee organized mass demonstrations. The exiled prisoners participated in mass meetings and provoked indignation when they showed their wounds and recounted the horrors of Montjuïc. Such campaigns stimulated support for the Cuban and Philippine rebels. However, the repression succeeded in putting an end to terrorism in Barcelona for some years at least. Some of the more violent militants had fled. Intellectuals like Tarrida and Anselmo Lorenzo advocated non-violent action. One of the last violent initiatives of this period took place in September 1897. The journalist Ramon Sempau shot and wounded Narciso Portas and his second-in-command, Joan Teixidó, in a public urinal in the Plaça de Catalunya. However, although Sempau was initially sentenced to death two days later by a military court, his case was passed to a civilian court – an indication of the impact on public opinion of the revelations about the Montjuïc atrocities. The following October, to widespread public approbation, he was found to have acted in self-defence. Portas became the target of public loathing. Cafés emptied when he entered them and he was the object of another failed assassination attempt in Madrid. He was obliged to go everywhere with several bodyguards. Alejandro Lerroux, at the height of his popu-larity in Barcelona, called him an 'executioner and a hitman', comparing him to Nero and Caligula. Portas challenged Lerroux to a duel. He refused on the grounds that a gentleman could have nothing to do with a torturer. Finally, Portas bumped into him in the Calle de Alcalá in Madrid. They went at each other with their walking sticks but neither could be said to have won the day.[39]

The Montjuïc trial and the preceding repression opened a new phase in the history of the anarchist movement. A direct consequence of the Montjuïc affair was the revenge assassination, on 8 August 1897, of the then Prime Minister, Antonio Cánovas del Castillo, by a twenty-six-year-old Italian anarchist journalist, Michele Angiolillo. It had been widely rumoured that the tortures had been carried out on the direct orders of Cánovas. This was suggested during demonstrations held in Paris and London in protest against the mistreatment of the prisoners. Angiolillo had attended a huge rally in Trafalgar Square at which some of the victims showed the burns and scars that they carried from Montjuïc. After meeting them, he travelled to Spain. He went to Santa Águeda near Mondragón in the Basque Country where Cánovas was taking the waters. He shot him three times. When Cánovas's wife Joaquina de la Osma shrieked 'assassin' at him, he bowed courteously and said: 'I respect you because you are an honourable lady but I have done my duty and I am calm. I have avenged my brothers from Montjuïc.' In fact, the savage violence inflicted on the anarchists was successful in curtailing individual terrorism and inclining the movement towards the use of the general strike.[40] Cánovas was replaced by the now seventy-two-year-old Sagasta, who immediately put an end to the strategy of total war in Cuba. In this sense, the assassination may have boosted the liberation movements in Cuba, the Philippines and Puerto Rico.

According to Joaquín Romero Maura,

the most significant factor of the Montjuich repression lies perhaps else-where. For the excesses committed by the police did not occur simply because the men in charge of the investigation happened to be heartless and brutal. The Spanish Administration was top-heavy, cumbersome, undisciplined and often corrupt. Scrupulous civil servants had only their conscience to restrain them from abuses. The legislation regarding civil service responsibilities was confused and rarely applied, and no efficient control mechanisms existed. Under these circumstances, with the police force as badly paid as most other lower grade civil servants, its recruitment totally haphazard and providing no security of tenure, scrupulousness could hardly be expected. But the conditions which in other branches of the civil service gave rise to bribery and tiresome delays, resulted in the police harassing individuals and making unwarranted arrests; arbitrariness was accentuated by a lack of self-assurance bred of inefficiency.[41]

The proliferation of social violence within Spain was matched and indeed intensified by the deterioration of the situation in what remained of the empire. The Cuban rebellion had resurfaced in 1895 and, despite the despatch of large numbers of troops, remained an immense drain on Spanish resources. Swift-moving and flexible guerrilla forces, known as the *mambises*, were more than a match for the Spanish garrisons. They were supported by consignments of arms, ammunition and other supplies from sympathizers in Florida. By the beginning of 1896, they had virtually won the war. The appointment of the ruthless General Weyler was Madrid's response. To deprive the *mambises* of the logistical support of the peasantry, Weyler adopted the policy of *reconcentración*. Large numbers of peasants were forcibly moved to concentration camps where, without adequate food, sanitation and medical care, around 160,000 died, nearly 10 per cent of the island's population. Weyler's brutal strategy intensified hatred of the colonial power and increased American support for the rebels. In October 1897, thanks to international censure and Sagasta's desire for conciliation with the rebels, Weyler was obliged to resign. However, it was too late for his departure to make a difference.[42]

In 1897, the Philippines were also in revolt with their defence an additional drain on Spanish resources. To make matters worse, on 15 February 1898 the battlecruiser USS *Maine* blew up in Havana harbour, killing 266 American sailors. The explosion may well have been accidental or possibly the work of Cuban anarchist provocateurs hoping to see the blame placed on Spain. This was certainly the consequence and it pushed American popular opinion further in favour of the Cuban rebels. Outrage in the United States at Weyler's measures together with their impact on American trade with Cuba forced President William McKinley to reiterate a demand first made in 1848 that Spain abandon Cuba, albeit by selling the island to the US. In Spain, a wide spectrum of jingoistic sentiment, excluding only the conscripts who had to go and fight, was in favour of war.[43]

On 25 April, President McKinley, egged on by Theodore Roosevelt, declared war on Spain. Spain's troops in Cuba, the Philippines and Puerto Rico numbered more than the entire United States army, nearly a quarter of a million to 28,000. However, they were scattered across many garrisons. In Cuba, the more efficient American forces, in alliance with powerful local guerrilla movements, quickly targeted key strategic objectives. Armed with rapid-fire Gatling guns, they seized the advantage over the demoralized Spanish conscripts. Moreover, the Americans had dramatically shorter supply lines and were favoured by British command of the seas. In naval terms, the difference was not just of superior resources but rather that the US strategy of heavily armoured battleships with long-range firepower had exposed the weaknesses of the Spanish option of swift cruisers with lighter guns. On the morning of 1 May 1898, at the Cavite naval station in the Bay of Manila, Commodore Dewey annihilated the Spanish Pacific fleet. On 3 July, the Spanish Atlantic fleet was also wiped out just outside the bay of Santiago de Cuba. The war had lasted less than three months. It was the end of Spanish naval power and prestige. The subsequent peace treaty in December 1898 saw Spain lose all its colonies apart from Morocco.[44]

Despite the reality that a vastly more numerous Spanish army had been defeated, there grew the myth cherished by General Franco that Spanish heroism had held out against overwhelming odds and been 'cheated' by technological superiority. Contemporary imagery about the greasy capitalist pig trampling on the dying Spanish lion contrasted with the American view that moral superiority and technical know-how had overcome a decadent enemy. Franco's perception would continue to reverberate through his career. He was five and a half when the great defeat at the hands of the United States occurred. Although, at such an age, he cannot have been aware of the significance of what was happening, he saw the coffins and the wounded being landed in the small naval garrison town of El Ferrol where he lived. Thereafter, the disaster had an ongoing effect that influenced him profoundly. Many of his schoolmates wore mourning, having been orphaned or lost relatives. Mutilated men were seen around the town for many years. Living in a military family, he heard the indignant conversations that his father had with colleagues from the naval base in which the defeat was blamed on dark forces such as freemasonry. An essentially middle-class intellectual movement, free-masonry was vilified by the Catholic Church for its anti-clericalism and by army officers because of its foreign links. Subsequently, when Franco became a cadet in the Military Academy, he encountered an atmosphere which had festered since 1898. Just as in Ferrol, in Toledo defeat was attributed to the machinations of American and British freemasonry and to the treachery of Spanish politicians who had sent naval and military forces into battle with inadequate resources.[45]

The aftermath of defeat saw private grief and public chagrin at the destruction of the illusion of Spanish great-power status. Newspaper editorials, intellectuals and politicians raked over the so-called 'dying nations' speech made on 4 May 1898 by the British Prime Minister Lord Salisbury to the Conservative Party's Primrose League at the Royal Albert Hall. Salisbury had stated that 'the living nations will gradually encroach on the territory of the dying'. His words were taken as an accurate prophecy of the future of Spain.

While the agonized inquest went on, the economic ruin that had been expected to follow the loss of empire failed to materialize. There was a minor economic boom as the return to peace brought lower inflation, less public debt and a higher level of capital investment. The drop in the value of the peseta occasioned by defeat stimulated an export boom to other European countries. Some products, such as footwear, olive oil and garlic, were still in demand in Cuba and Puerto Rico. Moreover, there were unexpectedly good harvests in both 1898 and 1899 which increased rural demand for industrial goods, as did the return of 200,000 colonial troops flush with wage arrears to spend on new clothes. Most important-ly, there was a massive repatriation of capital from Spanish America. The return of colonial settlers brought both investment and entrepre-neurial expertise to the areas, such as Galicia, from which they origi-nated. Nonetheless, although the consequences of 1898 were less dramatic than might have been feared, they were still deeply damaging for the Atlantic ports and the Catalan textile industry. Already ineffi-cient, built on a proliferation of small family firms with out-of-date machinery, Catalan textiles had survived on protection from foreign competition and a guaranteed overseas market. Both advantages disap-peared with the loss of Cuba.[46]

Moreover, the few favourable circumstances that followed the disaster were short-lived. The troops had soon spent their back pay. With subsequent harvests poor, domestic demand slumped. By the autumn of 1900, more than thirty factories in Catalonia had been closed and, in others, workers were being laid off. Industrial militancy was on the increase. Accordingly, the loss of Cuba fostered resentment of Madrid and accelerated the development of Catalan nationalism. Government measures to balance the budget and pay off the war debt provoked a taxpayers' strike, the so-called *tancament de caixes*, shop closures and riots. It also fostered the growth of the independence party, the Lliga Regionalista. Eventually, Catalan industry would find new markets, especially in Argentina, and would also diversify into automobiles, electricity and chemicals. However, there remained the problem that the army was assuaging its guilt by concentrating its anger on Catalonia. Since the middle of the eighteenth century, the Spanish army had known nothing but defeat at the hands of foreign enemies, its only successes being chalked up in domestic civil wars. It was hardly surprising that, when the last significant remnants of empire were lost, the army would cling to a determination that the final battle that would not be lost was the defence of national integrity. Ironically, the defeat which thus fed the flames of Spanish nationalism also breathed life into its greatest enemy.[47]

The reaction to this monumental humiliation, known thereafter as the 'Disaster of 1898', was a national examination of conscience. Regenerationism, as it was known, was an introspective analysis of what was wrong with Spain carried out by intellectuals and politicians in meetings, articles, books and private correspondence. The 'generation of 1898' grappled with the so-called *problema nacional*. The turmoil of the civil wars of the nineteenth century, the revolution of 1868, the chaos of the First Republic in 1873 and the loss of Cuba in 1898 had stimulated an endless poking through the national entrails. The progressive republican intellectual Ricardo Macías Picavea denounced the apparently legitimate institutions and democratic parliament of Restoration Spain as merely 'the wallpaper with pictures of a parliamentary system which hid the wall of brick and plaster, the *caciquismo* that was the harsh reality of our government'.[48] The towering figure of the regenerationist movement was the visionary Aragonese polymath, lawyer and agronomist Joaquín Costa Martínez. It was he who responded to the defeat with the war cry 'Schools, larders and double padlocks on the tomb of El Cid' – that is to say, no more military adventures. In 1902, at the age of fifty-six, he presented to the great intellectual club the Ateneo de Madrid his report 'Oligarchy and *caciquismo* as the present form of government in Spain'. He denounced *caciquismo* and the oligarchy, the political system and the political class as the principal problems of Spain. He compared the *cacique* to a cancer or tumour, an unnatural excrescence on the body of the nation. Accordingly, the political class had putrefied and blighted Spain through *caciquismo* and its corrupt practices, obstructing the forces of progress and thus keeping the nation in servitude, ignorance and misery. The solution had to be the iron surgeon who would sweep away *caciquismo* to facilitate democratic reform: 'That surgical policy, I repeat, has to be the personal burden of an iron surgeon, who knows well that anatomy of the Spanish people and feels for it an infinite compassion ... For Spain to be a parliamentary nation tomorrow, she must renounce it today.'[49] In fact, Costa insisted that his surgical solution was compatible with parliament and did not imply dictatorship.[50] Ultimately, regenerationism was open to exploitation by both the right and the left since among its advocates were both those who sought to sweep away by democratic reform the degenerate political system based on the power of local bosses or *caciques* and those who planned simply to destroy *caciquismo* by the authoritarian solution of 'an iron surgeon', to put an end to representative politics and restore the values that were thought to have made Spain great – unity, Catholicism and hierarchy.

The philosopher José Ortega y Gasset reflected on Cánovas and the system that he invented: 'the Restoration, gentlemen, was a panorama of phantasms and Cánovas the great impresario of phantasmagoria ... above and beyond being a great orator and a great thinker, Cánovas, gentlemen, was a great corruptor, as we might say, a professor of corruption. He corrupted even the incorruptible.'[51]

A demonstration in Barcelona in protest against the repression that followed the *Semana Tragica* or Tragic Week.

3

Revolution and War: From the Disaster of 1898 to the Tragic Week of 1909

With the humiliatingly swift defeat in an eight-month war against the United States, the effort to crush the rebels in Cuba and the Philippines came to a disastrous end. The shattering of the illusion of Spanish great-power status brought private grief and public chagrin to what had been a bellicose population. Lord Salisbury's 'dying nations' speech was echoed in newspaper editorials and on political platforms. As Sebastian Balfour puts it, 'the crisis occurred at the highest point in the age of empire, when the possession of colonies was seen as the bench-mark of a nation's fitness to survive'.[1] Yet the constitutional monarchy – which had gone into the war convinced that its own survival was at stake – did not suffer the fate of Napoleon III in 1870 or of Kaiser Wilhelm II in 1918. This was a reflection of the fact that the principal arbiters of politics – the military – were busy licking their wounds and administering the complex process of demobilization. The rest of Spanish society was excluded from a corrupt political system which offered workers and the rural dispossessed only the stark choice of violent resistance or apathy.

The fallout from the disaster of 1898 eventually hit several parts of the Spanish economy especially in Catalonia, for whose products Cuba had been a protected market. The sectors most dependent on colonial trade were badly hit, although a diversification of export targets and technological change eventually eased the difficulties. Uprooted Spanish entrepreneurs came back home with business know-how and substantial capital. Nonetheless, Catalan industrialists were driven to campaign for political change and modernization to increase domestic consumption. Moreover, the disaster of 1898 intensified the pre-existing alienation of the Catalan middle classes from the Spanish state. Already a cauldron of social tension as anarchist labourers migrated from the estates of Andalusia, Murcia and the Catalan hinterland, Barcelona was the scene of strikes and terrorist atrocities by both anarchists and government agents provocateurs. Although the Spanish economy remained predominantly agrarian, in the early years of the century a modern capitalist economy was developing around the textile and chemical industries of Cataluña, the iron and steel foundries of the Basque Country and the mines of Asturias.[2] Asturian coal was of lower quality and more expensive than that from British mines. Neither Catalan textiles nor Basque metallurgy could compete with British or German products in the international market, and their growth was stifled by the poverty of the Spanish domestic market. Nonetheless, even the hesitant growth of these industries led to the emergence of a militant industrial proletariat. Industrial development also fostered the beginnings of nationalist movements in Catalonia and the Basque Country born of resentment that Basque and Catalan industrialists paid a very high proportion of Spain's tax revenue but had little or no say in a government dominated by the agrarian oligarchy.

The notoriously corrupt elections of 19 May 1901 saw the machinery of *caciquismo* move from the exchange of favours for votes to outright purchase of them or the use of violence to force voting in one direction or another or simply to prevent voting altogether. Nevertheless, the Catalanist party, the Lliga Regionalista, won its first electoral victory. It had been established only three weeks earlier by uniting the most conservative elements of Catalan nationalism with the express intention of working 'by all legitimate means for the autonomy of the Catalan people within the Spanish State'. Its leader was the shrewd banker Francisco Cambó, the President of the industrialists' association, the Fomento Nacional. Between 1901 and 1905, the Lliga and the republicans destroyed the *turno* system in Barcelona. In the elections of 1901, all four Lliga candidates and both republicans won their seats. Henceforth, elections would be fought on left–right lines, between the various left-wing republican groups and the conservative and Catalanist Lliga.[3]

Elsewhere, the corrupt system of the Restoration survived, with the increase in electoral competition being met by an intensification of corrupt practices. At the turn of the century, the accounts of the March Hermanos Company of Mallorca revealed substantial payments made in cash, cigars and even cakes (*ensaimadas*) to secure votes in elections and to bribe frontier guards (carabineros), to turn a blind eye to tobacco smuggling.[4] In 1905, electors were abducted off the streets in Alicante.

In Guadalajara and other provinces, in 1905 and in most elections of the period, the Conde de Romanones used his immense fortune to establish an arsenal of favours and threats that his agents could use to gain votes.[5] The choice between the purchase of votes and the exercise of violence depended in part on the financial resources of the political group in question. Wealthy industrialists and mine owners in the Basque Country frequently resorted to purchase while the wheat growers of Old Castile were more often to be found using compulsion of one kind or another, especially the threat to foreclose mortgages or not to buy the wheat of the small producers. In order for any of this to happen, candidates had first to be authorized by the Ministry of the Interior. There, the *encasillado* (the list of candidates selected to win a seat) was drawn up according to the political needs of the day and the recommendations of influential figures.[6] Thus electoral fraud signified that there would be wild swings of votes from one election to the next, especially in rural areas. In some poor regions, such as Andalusia or Galicia, the government of the day was able to maintain control of the elections. In Andalusia, between 1899 and 1923, some 49 per cent of Cortes seats went to members of the Liberal Party and 44 per cent to members of the Conservative Party. Only 7 per cent of seats were 'won' by members of opposition parties and, even then, only because the Ministry of the Interior had included them in the *encasillado*.[7]

The impact of 1898 among intellectuals of the right and the left saw unmitigated criticism of the deficiencies of the political system. One response came from the austere Conservative Antonio Maura, who tried to reform Spanish politics between 1900 and 1910 by means of the so-called 'revolution from above'. Born in Palma de Mallorca in 1853, Maura had arrived in Madrid in 1868 to study law, barely able to speak Spanish. By the time he came to political prominence his eloquence in the language was legendary. He had long been committed to reform of Restoration politics, initially, as the brother-in-law of Germán Gamazo, in the Liberal Party. A rigidly austere Catholic, he would punish himself by renouncing smoking on any day on which an examination of his conscience revealed a sin.[8] His scathing oratorical skills could crush opponents and rendered him a divisive figure. In fact, his arrogant and authoritarian manner belied his relatively liberal ideology. Nevertheless, his desire for reform of the political system was inhibited by a fear of the masses.[9]

Maura would be Prime Minister five times, the first from December 1903 to December 1904; the longest (with a brief one-month interruption in March 1907) from January 1907 to October 1909 and finally for three short periods during the death agony of the Restoration system: March to November 1918, April to July 1919 and August 1921 to March 1922. His successes, and even more his failures, illustrate the problems of the Restoration system. If he was the great white hope of the system in his first governments, by 1918 he would be called upon, in the words of his friend César Silio, to be 'the fireman of the monarchy'.[10] After the death of Gamazo, he had taken the remnants of his faction into Francisco Silvela's Conservative Party in 1902. He had gradually come to believe that Silvela was more open to ideas of national regenerationism than the Liberals. In 1899, Silvela had underlined 'the need for a real revolution carried out from above with a determination to change profoundly our political, administrative and social way of being'. In July 1901, Maura declared in the Cortes that there had to be a revolution imposed by the government in order to forestall a more catastrophic revolution from below.[11]

In April 1903, as Minister of the Interior in Silvela's cabinet, Maura supervised 'clean' elections for the first time in the history of the Restoration. He undermined the networks of clientelism by appointing provincial civil governors without links to the local *caciques*. He also curtailed bribes to the press and refrained from using the *encasillado*, the imposition of governmental candidates on constituencies. His lifelong contempt for the press was reciprocated, which would always be a serious handicap. Since his speeches were often distorted, he declared that 'the diary of parliamentary proceedings is my newspaper'. Although, thanks to the entrenched power of the *caciques*, the Conservatives achieved a healthy majority, with government intervention limited, in the 1903 elections, thirty-four republican candidates were returned in Barcelona, Madrid and Valencia. The Queen Regent was furious, convinced that Maura had endangered the monarchy with what she regarded as self-indulgent moralism. Still having enormous influence over her recently enthroned son, she mobilized him against Silvela. The young King told Silvela that he must either oblige Maura to use the full arsenal of electoral chicanery or sack him. He refused. In fact, suffering ill health, he was more than ready to resign and, ironically, his departure saw Maura become leader of the Conservative Party.[12] This tension with the Royal Palace and Maura's austere manner explain why he was the only minister whom Alfonso XIII did not address with the informal *tú* form, but rather with the more respectful *usted* and 'Don Antonio'. This accounts for the underlying contradiction whereby, in the words of Maura's protégé Ángel Ossorio y Gallardo, 'the King would regard him with profound respect and uncontrollable antipathy'.[13]

From the beginnings of their relationship, the young Alfonso XIII resented Maura's attempts to make him act with the dignity becoming his role. The eighteen-year-old King was becoming obsessed with fast French cars. In early September 1904, several ministers expressed in cabinet their concern that Alfonso was risking his life with such powerful vehicles. Maura had declared: 'We have only him and, if anything happens to him, no one else.' The King bore a grudge. When Maura's Minister of War tried to name a new chief of the General Staff, Alfonso insisted on his own candidate, General Camilo García de Polavieja. Opposing the view of the entire cabinet, he refused to back down and forced the resignation of Maura's government. That his behaviour resembled an infantile tantrum was revealed when Alfonso took Maura's successor, the seventy-one-year-old General Marcelo de Azcárraga Palmero, to watch him driving a car over blazing logs and then told him to make sure that he told Maura what he had seen. General Azcárraga's government lasted little more than a month.[14]

After this brief hiatus, Maura returned to power following the election of 21 April 1907, managed by the Minister of the Interior, the thuggish Juan de la Cierva. It was one of the most corrupt in Spanish history. Maura disliked La Cierva's open espousal of electoral corruption yet came to rely on him. The relationship would consistently undermine his own career. Although the anarchists eschewed establishment politics, the Socialists and Republicans were slowly becoming ever more effective in mobilizing working-class votes in order to secure representation in the Cortes. Alejandro Lerroux's Radical Republican Party had also had some success in this regard in Catalonia in the elections of 1901 and 1903.[15] In consequence, La Cierva's 'skills' came to seem indispensable.

Elections aside, in the two decades before the First World War the principal challenges to the system came from a burgeoning anarcho-syndicalism and the more slowly growing Socialist movement. The Partido Socialista Obrero Español (PSOE), the Socialist Party founded in 1879, and its trade union organization, the Unión General de

Trabajadores (UGT), saw their ranks swelled by the working-class aristocracy of printers and craftsmen from the building and metal trades in Madrid, the steel and shipyard workers in Bilbao, and the coalminers of Asturias. Given the ideological differences between anarchism and socialism, there was never much likelihood of overall unity within the organized workers' movement. The possibility was definitively eliminated by the decision, in 1899, of the party's rigid leader Pablo Iglesias to move the headquarters of the UGT from the industrial capital, Barcelona, to the administrative capital, Madrid. To a large extent, this cut off the Socialist option for many Catalan workers. Moreover, the PSOE was further hobbled by its reliance on a rigid and simplistic French Marxism, mediated through the dead hand of Pablo Iglesias. He rendered the party isolationist, committed to the view that the Socialists should work legally for workers' interests, convinced of the inevitability of revolution, without, of course, preparing for it.[16]

The differences between the Socialists and the anarcho-syndicalists were illustrated by the general strike that paralysed Barcelona in mid-February 1902. In May 1901, the government had responded to a strike of tram workers by declaring martial law. So many workers were arrested that there was no room in the city prison and many were detained in the hold of the battlecruiser *Pelayo*.[17] This was followed in December by a strike of metalworkers in favour of a reduction of the working day from ten to nine hours. The metalworkers had faced fierce obstacles. They had no strike funds, and widespread unemployment made it easy for the factory owners to recruit blacklegs. Nevertheless, 10,000 workers managed to stay out for the next eight weeks. Then on 17 February 1902, the anarchist unions declared a general strike in solidarity with the metallurgical unions. Within a few days, it involved around 80,000 of Barcelona's workforce of 144,000. The city was without public transport, newspapers, shops, banks and cafés for a week. The response of the authorities was brutal. Martial law was declared within a week. Strike leaders were arrested and pickets broken up with cavalry charges. At least twelve workers were killed and several dozen injured. The strikers were defeated and returned to work on 24 February. The organized workers' movement in Catalonia was dramatically weakened. Trade unions were suppressed and the anarchist movement forced underground. The Socialist leadership had urged its militants to stand aside for fear of such consequences. Pablo Iglesias later denounced the anarchists for their irresponsibility and the party newspaper *El Socialista* accused the anarchists of being 'auxiliaries of the bourgeoisie'. Although it was a failure, the 1902 strike ultimately strengthened the anarchists and consolidated their hostility towards the Socialist movement.[18]

The long-standing monopoly of political power by the landed oligarchy was thus gradually being undermined by industrial modernization, but it would not be surrendered easily. Industrialization brought with it challenges from powerful industrialists and the organized working-class movement. The system was also opposed by an increasingly influential group of middle-class republicans. As well as distinguished individuals like Joaquín Costa, the philosopher Miguel de Unamuno and the novelist Vicente Blasco Ibáñez, there were dynamic new political groupings. In Asturias, the moderate liberal Melquiades Álvarez worked for a democratization of the monarchical system, in 1912 creating the Reformist Party. Álvarez's project for modernization attracted many young intellectuals who would later find prominence in the Second Republic. The most notable among them was the intensely learned man of letters Manuel Azaña, who would eventually become Prime Minister and later President of the Second Republic.

Some elements within the PSOE, notably the young Asturian journalist Indalecio Prieto, recognized that the non-violent triumph of socialism required the prior establishment of liberal democracy. The rise of republicanism inclined them to fight for an electoral alliance with middle-class Republicans. Anti-clericalism, anti-militarism and opposition to the Moroccan adventure was bringing the two closer together. Prieto's experiences in Bilbao had shown that, alone, the Socialists had little chance of electoral success while, with the Republicans, it was possible. His advocacy of a Republican–Socialist electoral combination in 1909 opened up the long-term prospect of building socialism legally from parliament. However, it also brought him into conflict with local leaders such as Facundo Perezagua, who advocated an exclusively syndicalist strategy of confrontational strike action. After a long and bitter struggle within the Federación Provincial Socialista de Vizcaya, Prieto eventually defeated Perezagua, and thereafter Bilbao became a stronghold of Republican–Socialist collaboration. That was enough to earn Prieto the lifelong hostility of the UGT Vice-President, Francisco Largo Caballero, who shared Perezagua's distrust of bourgeois Republicans. Republican–Socialist collaboration would be the basis of eventual PSOE success. Indeed, Pablo Iglesias himself was elected to parliament in 1910. Nevertheless, the unrelenting animosity of Largo Caballero would bedevil Prieto's existence and eventually, in the 1930s, have devastating consequences for Spain.[19]

Another Republican movement that seemed to be threatening the system was the brainchild of the outrageous rogue and virtuoso carpet-bagger Alejandro Lerroux. After his success on the back of the Montjuïc tortures, his popularity was consolidated by his exposure of a series of provocations by a Civil Guard named Captain Morales. In 1903, Morales fabricated a supposed anarchist conspiracy to set off bombs in Tarragona. Having then 'discovered' a cache of bombs and thus 'foiled' the plot, he had numerous workers arrested who, after being tortured, confessed their involvement. Lerroux played a leading part in exposing the farce and securing the release of the prisoners and the arrest, trial and imprisonment of Morales.[20] His skills as a rabble-rousing demagogue propelled him to the leadership of a mass Republican movement in the slums of Barcelona and his ability as an organizer built a formidable electoral machine. He was receiving money from the central government, a common practice in a period when politicians paid for news to be inserted in or excluded from newspapers. This gave rise to the widespread belief that he had been sent to Barcelona by Segismundo Moret, the Minister of the Interior in Mateo Sagasta's government, in order to deploy his rabble-rousing skills to divide the anarcho-syndicalist masses and undermine the rise of Catalan nationalism.

Probably no government slush fund could have achieved what he did. His links to anti-monarchical terrorist conspiracies would also have made him far from suitable as an agent of Madrid. He had been called to Barcelona to be a republican parliamentary candidate in the 1901 general elections. To become 'Emperor of the Paralelo', the Barcelona district where misery, criminality and prostitution held sway, required more genuine appeal than anything that could be conjured up in Madrid ministries. His sincere concern for the injustice suffered by the working class did not need bribery. His popularity would be built on the Radicals' provision of urban services, including libraries and *ateneos* (debating clubs) and, less salubriously, the near-pornographic techniques of his anti-clerical demagogy. Lerroux shared the profound anti-clericalism of immigrant labourers for whom the Church was the defender of the brutally unjust rural social order from which they had fled. It was only later that his venality saw anti-Catalanism and pro-militarism coming to the fore in his oratorical repertoire.[21]

The rural and urban proletariats believed that the Church was the ally and legitimizer of economic oppression. A factor that fed the notion was a deeply held conviction that priests systematically betrayed the secret of the confessional in the interests of the rich. It was believed that domestic servants were sent to confession so that the mistress might learn from the priest what the maid had been doing wrong and that crimes committed by the illegitimate children of clergymen were immune from prosecution. The religious orders were seen as parasites. Commenting on the 'silent defiance' of workmen, Rafael Shaw wrote: 'For years past I have noticed that no member of the working classes salutes a priest or friar in the streets.' Another factor in popular hostility was the fact that monasteries and convents undercut small tradespeople engaged in baking, laundry or needlework. Enmity was not one-sided. Through its press and pulpits, the Catholic Church carried out virulent and incendiary campaigns against lay education.[22]

There were two attempts on the life of the Prime Minister Antonio Maura in 1904, in Barcelona on 12 April and in Alicante two weeks later. Hoping to drive a wedge between Catalan Conservatives and the Republicans and anarchists, Maura had decided that it was time for King Alfonso XIII to visit Catalonia. For fear of terrorism, María Cristina had not been to Barcelona since 1888 and, since his coronation in May 1902, nor had her son. It was an adventurous gamble. On 4 April 1904, Lerroux wrote an article in *La Publicidad*, urging 'the poor, the paralysed and the beggars' to line the route of the King's procession in their shabbiest rags: 'Let them approach, let them see him at close range and observe how the monster of history has the face of a child and questioning eyes.' Tramps and the disabled in rags thronged the centre of the city. The King made some pro-Catalan gestures, such as asking for the members of the landowners' association, the Instituto Catalán de San Isidro, to address him in the language. Maura's gamble paid off. Alfonso received a degree of public acclaim and the visit seemed to have passed off without major incident. However, on 12 April, as the royal party was leaving the Cathedral after a Te Deum, a nineteen-year-old anarchist stonemason, Joaquim Miquel Artal, jumped on the running board of Maura's carriage, shouting 'Long live anarchy!' He leaned in and stabbed and slightly wounded Maura with a kitchen knife. He seems to have been acting, alone although he was carrying a copy of the newspaper with Lerroux's article. He was given a seventeen-year sentence and died in prison in Ceuta in November 1909, allegedly as a result of a savage beating. Maura was not harmed in the second attack in Alicante two weeks later and the unknown assailants were never caught. The attacks and his survival massively consolidated Maura's prestige.[23]

After the success of the Barcelona trip, Maura now decided that the image of Alfonso XIII could be improved even more by international visits. For Spanish revolutionaries, especially Lerroux, this constituted a threat to their efforts to present the Spanish monarchy as authoritarian and priest-ridden. It was also seen as an opportunity to kill the King and hasten the advent of a republic. By 1903, Lerroux, whose rhetoric was as radical as that of the anarchists, had managed to unite most republican groups into the Unión Republicana. Spanish revolutionaries exiled in Paris, led by the exiled republican Nicolás Estévanez, who had very briefly been Minister for the Army in the government of Pi y Margall, created a similar group, known as the Junta de Acción y Unión Republicana. Since early 1904, they had been publishing virulent pamphlets denouncing the monarchy as responsible for the tortures of Montjuïc and calling for Artal's example to be followed. One of the authors was an anarchist medical student, Pedro Vallina, a protégé of Fermín Salvochea. He had suffered some months in prison, having been framed by the police for involvement in an alleged conspiracy to assassinate Alfonso XIII during his coronation in May 1902. To avoid further police attention, Vallina had fled to France in October that year with a letter of introduction from Salvochea to Nicolás Estévanez. There, he had acquired some skill in bomb making.

Now, in response to news that Alfonso XIII was to make a state visit to France, the group began to plan his assassination. The mastermind and financier of the conspiracy was the fiercely anti-clerical educationalist Francesc Ferrer i Guàrdia, the wealthy director of the rationalist Escuela Moderna and of a number of lay schools in Barcelona. Ostensibly bookish and respectable, Ferrer was using his fortune to sponsor major acts of terrorism. There were close links between the Paris and Barcelona groups of anarchists and radical republicans. Indeed, Vallina had visited Barcelona in February 1905 where he had persuaded Lerroux that the death of the unmarried and childless King would expose divisions in the army and facilitate a republican coup. To this end, Ferrer had paid for

Vallina to set up a laboratory that could manufacture crude Orsini bombs in Barcelona. Lerroux and Estévanez made plans with sympathizers within the army. Lerroux also sent his friend Ricardo Fuente, the one-time editor of *El País*, to Paris, apparently to cover the royal visit but really so that he could telegraph him with the news of the outcome of the attempted regicide. The bombs to be used in Paris were prepared by Vallina. The bomb thrower was to be Mateo Morral Roca, the austere and highly educated son of a wealthy Catalan textile industrialist. Morral was a close collaborator of Ferrer, working as librarian and in the publishing section of the Escuela Moderna. He was also a devoted admirer of Estévanez whose pamphlet *Pensamientos revolucionarios* he had published and which Ferrer had paid for. On 25 May, the French police arrested Vallina and several other conspirators. Nevertheless, on the night of 31 May 1905, as Alfonso XIII and President Émile Loubet returned from the opera, Morral threw two bombs at the cavalcade as it passed down the Rue de Rohan. Only one exploded, injuring seventeen people, but the King and the President were unharmed.[24]

Morral escaped, but the planned coup in Spain came to nothing. The anarchists arrested alongside Vallina included an Italian, Carlo Malato, an Englishman, Bernard Harvey, and a Frenchman, Eugène Caussanel. Although Harvey was a teacher of English, his knowledge of chemistry had helped Vallina and Morral make the bombs. They were held for six months before eventually being put on trial in October 1906. Malato was a senior freemason and had influential political friends in the French establishment. A major campaign was mounted linking the trial to the scandal over the Montjuïc tortures and arguing that the assassination attempt had been a provocation prepared by the Spanish police in order to discredit the republicans in Spain. Among those who made eloquent speeches for the defence, as well as Lerroux and Estévanez, were the French Socialists Jean Jaurès and Aristide Briand. Despite overwhelming evidence of their involvement in the assassination plot, Vallina and the three others would be found innocent.[25]

The first years of the twentieth century thus saw an explosive cocktail of intransigence on the part of landowners, industrialists and the military and subversion from a disparate array of anarchists, Lerroux's Radicals, moderate republicans and regional nationalists. It was a period in which rapid albeit sporadic industrialization and increasing labour organization coincided with a resurgence of terrorism and post-imperial trauma in the armed forces. Disappointed by defeat in Cuba and subsequent budgetary restrictions, a resentful army turned inwards, determined to lose no more battles. Wounded pride turned into a neurotic sensitivity to perceived slurs on military honour. In the immediate aftermath of the disaster, General Camilo García de Polavieja, the Minister of War in Francisco Silvela's Conservative administration, blamed defeat on political incompetence and floated the idea of a military dictatorship.

The army's inflated sense of its importance in domestic politics was exaggerated by Alfonso XIII who saw himself as a soldier-king. He had been educated as an officer cadet and, like his admired cousin Kaiser Wilhelm II, he delighted in dressing up in uniform, presiding over parades and granting audiences to favoured officers. He encouraged senior generals to discuss problems with him directly rather than through the official channel of the Ministry of War. He exceeded his constitutional powers by interfering in military appointments, promotions and decorations, favouring his pet officers to a degree that smacked of corruption. According to one minister, the future President of the Second Republic Niceto Alcalá-Zamora, he behaved as if he was the Minister of War, in which capacity he frequently indulged petty personal caprices. He even charged the expenses of the deposed Austro-Hungarian monarchy to the Ministry's budget. By his identification with the army and his insistence on his personal prerogatives, the King impeded the modernization of the Restoration system. In a series of clashes between civilian and military power, he undermined the authority of various governments and encouraged military insubordination.[26]

The officer corps became obsessed with the defence of national unity and the existing social order and thus was increasingly hostile both to the left and to the regional nationalists. There were clashes with both Basque and Catalan nationalists. The military attitude to Catalanism was especially aggressive and bordering on racist. Catalans were denounced as cowardly traitors and misers. The anti-Semitic right frequently described Catalans as the Jews of Spain and this was reflected in the military press. A newspaper that claimed to represent army officers, *La Correspondencia Militar*, demanded that Catalan and Basque nationalists be forced from the country. 'Let them wander the world, without a fatherland, like the cursed race of the Jews. Let this be an eternal punishment.'[27] Since Cuba had been regarded as simply an overseas part of the *patria*, its loss was perceived as a diminution of the nation. Thousands of officers had served in Cuba and the Philippines and many had been killed or wounded in defence of Spanish hegemony. Traumatized by their loss, colonial officers saw the rising Catalan and Basque nationalist movements as threats comparable to the Cuban independence movement and thus an intolerable challenge. There was another practical consideration – military ambitions to rebuild the armed forces and regenerate Spain would be fatally undermined if Catalonia's wealth and its tax revenue were lost. Even if Catalan autonomy could be held off, Catalanists were regarded as anti-militarists keen to reduce the army budget and the size of the inflated officer corps.[28]

Denounced as 'separatists', the Barcelona bourgeoisie responded by mocking as unsophisticated hobbledehoys the officers stationed in Catalonia. Right-wing and centralist, army officers were easily needled by the anti-militarist views of Catalanist politicians and the sarcastic jibes of their press. ¡Cu-cut!, the Lliga Regionalista's weekly satirical journal, often published derisive cartoons portraying army and navy officers as pompous buffoons. In November 1905, the Lliga celebrated its victory in Barcelona's municipal elections by hosting a victory dinner for 2,500 guests. The report of the event in ¡Cu-cut! was illustrated with a cartoon in which a soldier asks a civilian what was being celebrated. 'The Victory Banquet', replies the civilian, to which the soldier comments 'Ah, they must be civilians then,' a clear reference to the 1898 colonial defeat and to the fact that the army had known no triumphs for nearly a century. In revenge, on the night of 25 November, 300 armed officers in uniform assaulted both the printing presses and offices of ¡Cu-cut! and the offices of Lliga's daily newspaper La Veu de Catalunya. Forty-six people were seriously injured.[29] This was merely the most violent of many attacks on newspapers and magazines that had criticized the army, such as those in Madrid in 1895 on El Globo and El Resumen, in Játiva in 1900 on El Progreso and in 1901 on El Correo de Guipúzcoa.[30]

The reaction to the ¡Cu-Cut! incident of both the high command and the King himself was to celebrate the Barcelona garrison's indiscipline. Not only were the culprits not punished but they were sent messages of congratulation by units all over Spain and the Moroccan colony. The Captain General of Barcelona, Manuel Delgado Zulueta, made a speech to a group of officers, congratulating them as if the attack on the press had been a heroic act of war. When parliamentary deputies debated what action to take, there were threats that the garrison of Madrid would assault the Cortes. Under the banner headline 'The Army in Defence of the Fatherland', *La Correspondencia Militar* demanded that 'Catalan deputies and senators be immediately expelled from the Parliament' on the grounds that there could be no room in the Spanish Cortes for those who represented ideas opposed to national unity.[31] The most damaging intervention was probably that of Alfonso XIII. He encouraged military sedition and diminished the credibility of the government in several ways. As 'the first soldier of the nation', he sent 'an affectionate greeting' and expressed his approval of what he called 'the legitimate aspirations of the Army'. He was pushing the government of Eugenio Montero Ríos to suspend constitutional guarantees in the province of Barcelona. The military press described the army as 'the sublime and august incarnation of the Fatherland'. According to Romanones, when the cabinet met in emergency session under the chairmanship of the King, 'his face revealed that his mind was far from the room where the cabinet had met and much nearer to the meetings being held in the officers' mess'. In these meetings, increasing numbers of officers were calling for legal prohibition of insults aimed at the armed forces. In fact, such safeguards existed through the civilian courts, but what the officers were now demanding was that perceived offences against the honour of the army, of the monarchy or of the *patria* should come under the jurisdiction of military tribunals.

Delegations of middle-rank officers came to put pressure on the Minister of War. Montero Ríos was determined to maintain civilian jurisdiction over the armed forces. Romanones commented later: 'Poor civilian power! We had nothing to defend it with!' Unprepared to sanction the proposed Law of Jurisdictions, Montero Ríos resigned. His successor, Segismundo Moret, was chosen by Alfonso XIII and given the specific task of introducing the required legislation. Moret's Liberal coalition government was essentially the puppet of the army. General Agustín Luque, who, as Captain General of Andalusia, had sent one of the most extreme messages in praise of the Barcelona garrison for the attacks on the Catalanist press, was appointed Minister of War. In the event, the Law of Jurisdictions was not as sweeping as had been desired by the military hotheads but it still constituted a dangerous step in the process whereby the officer corps came to consider itself to be the ultimate arbiter in politics. It also had consequences within Catalonia which were hardly what the government had hoped for.[32]

Support for the military came from an unexpected quarter. On his return from Paris where he had gone to make a statement on behalf of Vallina, Lerroux published a virulent article headed 'El alma en los labios' (Speaking from the heart). He attacked Catalan separatism as 'an overflowing sewer that had infected the city'. He praised army officers for avenging the fatherland declaring: 'if I had been a soldier, I would have gone to burn down *La Veu*, *¡Cu-Cut!*, the offices of the Lliga and the Bishop's Palace at the very least'. He called on the republicans of Barcelona not to ally with what he called 'the vile scum' of the regionalists. He later tried to row back but it was too late. He had made a serious mistake. The revelation of his pro-militaristic and centralist abhorrence of Catalanism exposed the fraudulence of his radicalism and ended any real chances that he had of middle-class support.[33]

The Spanish army was not prepared to be simply the defender of a despised constitutional regime. The officer corps wanted to rebuild its reputation with a new imperial endeavour in Morocco. This was made feasible by British desires for a Spanish buffer against French expansionism on the southern shores of the Straits of Gibraltar. The consequences could hardly have been worse for Spain's political stability. The bloodshed occasioned by the new adventure stimulated massive popular hostility against conscription and thereby intensified military contempt for the working class. Moreover, military failures could be attributed to a woeful lack of preparation, for which in turn officers blamed the political class.

The instability of Spanish politics did not diminish. The anarchist plan to assassinate the King and trigger a republican coup was not abandoned after the failure of May 1905 but revived one year later. This time the plot, in which Ferrer, Lerroux, Estévanez and Morral were again involved, was to kill him on the day of his wedding in Madrid, on 31 May 1906, to the English Princess Victoria Eugenie of Battenberg. On the grounds that Estévanez was going to Cuba and unlikely to return to Europe, Lerroux had successfully requested the Civil Governor of Catalonia, the Duque de Bivona, to grant him permission to enter Spain in mid-May and sail to Havana from Barcelona. The 68-year-old Estévanez was thus able to meet the other three conspirators and discuss the assassination and a subsequent seizure of the fortress of Montjuïc as the first step to a nation-wide insurrection. It has been suggested that Estévanez brought the bomb that Morral was to use to kill the royal couple.[34]

There was little or no security presence along the procession route from the Church of Los Jerónimos (San Jerónimo el Real), just behind the Prado, to the Royal Palace. As the parade passed down the Calle Mayor, Morral threw the bomb, hidden in a bouquet of flowers, at the royal carriage. The explosion killed twenty-three people and seriously wounded 108 more, but the royal couple were unhurt. Morral escaped. Later, near the village of Torrejón de Ardoz, he shot an estate guard who confronted him, and he then committed suicide. On the day of the royal wedding, Ferrer had presided over a meeting of anarchists to whom he had given money to buy arms for the hoped-for uprising. In Barcelona, he and Lerroux sat at separate tables in the same café in the Plaça de Catalunya waiting for the news that they fondly believed would be the trigger for a republican uprising. They waited in vain. Ferrer was arrested on 4 June and his property placed under embargo. The authorities had only circumstantial evidence of his involvement in the two assassination attempts. Nevertheless, his numerous influential monarchist and ecclesiastical enemies were convinced that he was responsible and they ensured that he remained in prison for a year under threat of the death sentence. Eventually, the Spanish government surrendered in the face of a huge international campaign in favour of Ferrer. Lerroux played a key role through *El Progreso*, which he had converted into a daily newspaper. After a four-day trial from 3 to 7 June 1907, Ferrer would be found innocent.[35]

That the attack on the royal couple had been possible reflected the reality that the Spanish police were hardly more efficient than they had been at the time of the reforms introduced after the bomb attack in the Carrer dels Canvis Nous in September 1896. They lacked technical expertise and modern equipment and were generally undermanned. Moreover, they were underfunded and wages were so low that recruits tended to be uneducated.[36] In 1903, La Cierva, recently named Civil Governor of Madrid, wrote in his memoirs, 'The police force in those days was a foul and dangerous outfit of officers appointed and sacked at the whim of the Governor and the Minister. They had no tenure or any kind of guarantee, although no particular qualifications were required to join. With annual wages of 1,250, 1,500 or 2,000 pesetas, it was easy to imagine what those officers would do in constant contact with every vice and every corruption.'[37] The chief of the Barcelona police, Antoni Tressols, nicknamed Vinagret, was virtually illiterate, corrupt and hated for his use of torture and for falsifying evidence against anarchists. Tressols had initially been employed as a rubbish collector before getting a job as a police informer. As he rose within the police force, he made a fortune by blackmailing criminals. A bomb was placed in his house on 18 October 1903 although it is possible that the culprit was not one of his victims but a rival officer who wanted his job. Tressol's wife died of nervous shock as a result of the explosion.[38]

Barcelona remained the centre of terrorist activity. This was considered locally to be partly the consequence of the totally ineffective police service. The Catalan nationalist Enric Prat de la Riba wrote in December 1906: 'The Spanish Police, like all the organs of the Spanish State, is powerless to function in areas of a high density of population. It is a primitive outfit, a useless fossil. To try to deal with the modern evil that Catalonia suffers – that is to say, anarchism – is like fighting with flint-head spears and stone axes against multitudes armed with Mausers and Krups. We cannot rely on the police because the State is incapable of organizing it any better.' Prat's complaint was merely one voice within an ever louder chorus of demands for the police to be restructured.[39]

It has been estimated that, in the streets of Barcelona, between April 1904 and the fall of the Maura government in October 1909 at least sixty-six bombs were placed, which either exploded or were found before they could do so. Eleven people were killed and a further seventy-one seriously injured. In February 1906, the Conservative Civil Governor of Barcelona, the Duque de Bivona (Tristán Álvarez de Toledo y Gutiérrez de la Concha), was approached by a twenty-five-year-old Catalan anarchist named Joan Rull i Queraltó who offered his services as a paid informer. Rull had recently been released from prison where he had been awaiting trial on suspicion of planting a bomb. Originally placed in a public urinal on the Ramblas on 4 September 1904, it had been taken by a policeman to the Palace of Justice where it exploded. The incident coincided with the return, the day before, of Alejandro Lerroux from a propaganda tour in Galicia, thus stimulating rumours that he was somehow involved. After fifteen months in prison awaiting trial, in December 1905 Rull was acquitted despite substantial evidence against him. The prosecution case had been badly drafted, a number of anarchist comrades had sworn that he was with them on the day that the bomb went off and, in addition, the jury had been intimidated. Despite being in prison at the time, Rull was also accused of responsibility for bombs that went off in November 1904 and May 1905.[40]

The subsequent career of Rull vividly illustrates the relationship between administrative corruption, political incompetence and social violence in Spain. In March 1908, awaiting trial for other subsequent crimes, Rull claimed that the years in prison had changed him, pushing him to conclude that anarchist terrorists were 'hyenas thirsting for human blood'. Accordingly, he said, he had decided to devote his life to pursuing them. The truth was somewhat different. An acquaintance, Antoni Andrés i Roig, alias 'Navarro', had suggested to him that he could make money as an informer. 'Navarro' introduced him to the wealthy Catalan industrialist Eusebi Güell. Güell reluctantly provided the pair with a letter of introduction to the Duque de Bivona. Wearing a suit bought with money provided by Tressols, Rull, accompanied by 'Navarro', went to see Bivona. They told him that they knew who was responsible for the most recent bombs and would be able to predict the time and place of their next atrocity and thus allow the authorities to catch them red-handed. Bivona handed over a substantial sum of money and, until he ceased to be Civil Governor on 28 June 1906, continued to pay Rull. During that time, only one bomb went off in Barcelona; placed on a tram, it harmed nobody. The lack of incidents could not be attributed to anything that Rull might have done – other, perhaps, than refraining from planting bombs himself. Since no actual perpetrators had been apprehended, Bivona was soon complaining about the lack of results. However, he was replaced before he could put pressure on Rull, and his successor Francisco Manzano Alfaro continued to pay Rull for some months.[41]

It was a period of growing tension in Catalonia. Six weeks before Rull's initiative, the veteran republican Nicolás Salmerón, in response to the passing of the Law of Jurisdictions, had created Solidaritat Catalana, a coalition of Catalanist parties uniting the Lliga Regionalista, the Carlists, the republican federalists, other Catalan nationalists and part of Unión Republicana. Given Lerroux's virulent anti-Catalanism, his followers left Unión Republicana and formed the Radical Party. On 20 May 1906, a crowd of around 200,000 people gathered in Barcelona to welcome home the Catalan deputies who had voted against the Law of Jurisdictions in the Cortes. Given its internal right–left contradictions, Solidaritat Catalana would last for barely four years. Nevertheless, its creation marked the beginning of effective Catalan nationalism. In the elections of November 1905, only seven Catalanist deputies had been elected, whereas in those of April 1907 they won forty-one of the possible forty-four seats. They had campaigned for both regional autonomy and national regeneration through honest elections. Lerroux lost his seat, which intensified his hostility to Solidaritat Catalana. Thereafter, the question of Catalan separatism became a much greater preoccupation of Madrid governments. Moreover, the Lliga's leader, Francesc Cambó, was starting to be seen as a major player in Spanish politics.[42]

Those April 1907 elections were called by the now 54-year-old Antonio Maura after the collapse of General Azcárraga's short-lived government. A formidable orator noted for his unflinching personal integrity, Maura had initially come to power in January with the ambition of sweeping away the corrupt electoral system of the Restoration and fostering widespread electoral participation. He planned to end political corruption by means of three laws: a law of municipal justice, an electoral law and a law of local administration. In order to have any chance of getting his projects approved, he needed a parliamentary majority. Given the challenges of the Catalans, the Socialists and the Republicans, that made him a hostage of the great electoral fixer, Juan de la Cierva, a master in the use of the methods that Maura was trying to eliminate. Thereafter, despite unflinching adulation of his boss, La Cierva would be an albatross around Maura's neck.[43] The first of Maura's projects aimed to separate executive and judicial power and remove one of the most powerful weapons in the *cacique*'s armoury – the capacity to exert pressure on and even blackmail rival candidates via the ability to appoint judges and magistrates who would then pass sentences in the interests of their patrons. To the outrage of *caciques* who henceforth would have to resort to bribery, Maura declared 'the orgy is over'. In the event, the law never got beyond his well-intentioned proposal.[44]

The electoral law was over-complicated (it had 409 clauses) and riddled with loopholes. Article 29, for instance, permitted the direct election of unopposed candidates, a gift to powerful caciques. In 1910, Article 29 permitted 119 seats in the Cortes, more than a quarter of the total, to be 'elected' without opposition; in 1923, the same procedure permitted the 'election' of 146 deputies. At a local level, there simply did not exist the machinery to ensure that the law was implemented. Maura's Liberal opponent, José Canalejas, pointed out that, in a country where, on average, over 40 per cent of the electorate was illiterate, rising to 70 per cent in the rural south, it was necessary first to educate the masses. The levels of illiteracy substantiated Costa's accusation that *caciquismo* kept the bulk of the population in ignorant servitude. Maura would face the same problem that had confronted Cánovas when he first elaborated the system in 1876 – what to do if the masses voted for left-wing options. Moreover, like others before him, he was more concerned to control working-class discontent than to open the system to participation by the lower classes.[45] The projected law of local administration which aimed to give municipalities independence from central government was weighed down in the Cortes with amendments and was never passed.[46]

Maura was a firm monarchist and Spanish patriot. Although born in Mallorca, he was hostile to Catalan nationalism. He was confident that he could exploit the divisions within Solidaritat Catalana. His commitment to political reform and determination to put an end to terrorism appealed to the industrialists of the Lliga. He thus established a close understanding with Cambó. Since his draconian law-and-order proposals were opposed by the Republicans within Solidaritat Catalana, they hastened the break-up of the coalition. In fact, the irony of Maura's ambitious plans to eliminate electoral fraud was that they damaged the interests of both the Liberal and Conservative Parties and boosted the challenges coming from the Lliga, the Radicals and the Socialists. Moreover, La Cierva's introduction of a fierce anti-terrorist law was abandoned after it provoked massive hostility and, along with opposition to the Moroccan war, inspired an anti-Maura campaign with the popular slogan 'Maura No'.[47]

The social conservatism of the dominant elements of Solidaritat Catalana permitted Lerroux to spin his anti-Catalanism into a cynical bid for working-class support. In line with his declaration of support for the army officers who had attacked the Catalanist media in November, Lerroux had been at war with Solidaritat Catalan since its creation. His followers stoned their meetings and smashed the presses of Catalanist publications. On 18 April 1907, the car taking Nicolás Salmerón and Cambó to an electoral meeting of Solidaritat Catalana was ambushed. Salmerón was unharmed but Cambó was shot and badly wounded. It was widely believed that Lerroux or his supporters were behind the attack. Although nothing was ever proved, it is likely that the revulsion against Lerroux's supporters contributed to the electoral victory of Solidaritat.[48]

Lerroux was in an ambiguous position. The constituency to which he hoped to appeal was the increasingly militant working class and the recently arrived immigrant population which, like himself, was anti-Catalan. However, as a fervent supporter of the army which was the principal instrument of the repression of the working class, he was vulnerable to losing followers to the anarchists. In a desperate bid to clinch left-wing support, on 1 September 1906, in the Unión Republicana newspaper *La Rebeldía*, Lerroux published his notorious article '¡Rebeldes!, ¡rebeldes¡' which contained an appeal that was to bestow greater notoriety on him:

> Young barbarians of today, enter and sack the decadent and miserable civilization of this unhappy country; destroy its temples, finish off its gods, lift the veil of the novice nuns and raise them up to the status of mothers to make the species more virile. Break into the property registries and make bonfires of its papers that fire might purify the odious social organization. Enter the homes of the humble and raise legions of proletarians so that the world might tremble before its awakened judges.[49]

It is difficult to know what impact this semi-pornographic appeal had, particularly on illiterate immigrant workers. Henceforth, Lerroux would go to considerable trouble to distance himself, usually physically, from incidents that might have been blamed on his rabble-rousing.

While the three-way struggle between Solidaritat Catalana, Madrid and Lerroux rumbled on, terrorism remained an issue in Barcelona. In the winter of 1906, since no arrests had been made as a result of information from Rull, Francisco Manzano told him that he would pay only on results. Rull was furious and, unsurprisingly, bombs started to be planted not only by Rull but also by his gang, which included members of his family. His main accomplice was his mother, Maria Queraltó. Between Christmas Eve 1906 and late January 1907, six bombs went off, killing one person and injuring eleven.[50] When Antonio Maura's Conservative government came to power in January 1907, his tough new Minister of the Interior, Juan de la Cierva, dismissed Manzano and replaced him with the brilliant young lawyer Ángel Ossorio y Gallardo. Both La Cierva and Ossorio were determined to resolve the terrorist problem. However, they faced two main problems. In the first place, the judiciary was reluctant to give harsh sentences as a result of international campaigns in favour of the accused which were often backed up by threats of violent retaliation. Efforts were made to put pressure on the judges and a more authoritarian anti-anarchist law, known as the Ley Maura, was prepared. However, this produced a welter of opposition and undermined the prestige of Maura's government. Thus the issue of the laxity of the judiciary remained unresolved.[51] The other problem was the inefficiency and corruption of the police.

On 31 January, the day after his arrival in Barcelona, Ossorio wrote to La Cierva that the police force that had awaited him 'is mainly comprised, not of villains, but of poor devils who haven't a clue what they are supposed to do. If blind justice were to be carried out, the whole lot should be sacked ... Strong measures should be taken soon.' Despite removing the most incompetent officers and generally raising standards, Ossorio faced internal obstruction from the old guard led by Tressols. Moreover, the daunting task of reforming a corrupt and shambolic police force also involved clearing the ground of networks of informers and parallel organizations.[52]

Rull offered his services to the new Civil Governor who, desperate for any means to put an end to terrorism, accepted. At this point, the bombs stopped. Rull had assembled a sizeable band of what he claimed were investigators and informers. In reality, it was a gang of hangers-on and potential bombers. He became over-confident in what was essentially blackmail, demanding more and more money for their pay and for travel and maintenance expenses. In early April 1907, Ossorio, tired of the lack of results and beginning to suspect that Rull was behind the bombs, offered only half the amount demanded. Rull responded that he had to pay in order 'to avoid something really big'. In fulfilment of the threat, two bombs went off on 8 April. In early July, to the delight of many anarchists in Barcelona, Ossorio issued orders for the police to arrest Rull, his brother Hermenegildo, his mother and father and other members of his gang. They were accused of responsibility for the eight incidents in December 1906 and January and April 1907 and for the accompanying blackmail. In fact, during that period, there were other terrorist acts. Accordingly, in addition to the belief that Rull's gang and other anarchists were responsible, contradictory suspicions circulated.

In a letter to La Cierva, Ossorio listed his suspects:

The anarchists themselves, so as to ruin, without running any risks, a powerful bourgeois society. The *lerrouxistas*, as a weapon against the Catalan nationalists. The separatists, as a means of wrecking the authority of the State (some distinguished and serious-minded members of the Unión catalanista have long maintained that Catalan national identity cannot be revived until after the present Catalan well-being is destroyed). Renegade anarchists, in order to harm their comrades. Greedy men, like Morales and Rull, for their own convenience. Some of these have been behind the bombs; perhaps several have been; perhaps all. But the hands that held them, the professionals of crime, the experts on explosions, we should seek nowhere but among the anarchist rabble … If these mercenaries did not exist, their paymasters would not find it so easy to hire them.[53]

Tressols and the Lerrouxistas claimed that the separatists were to blame but no proof has ever been found.[54] There were many Catalanists who believed that the Madrid government was paying agents provocateurs in order to justify repression against Solidaritat Catalana. Lerroux mounted a press campaign blaming Rull for the shooting of Cambó in April 1907. It is more likely that the majority of the incidents were the work of the anarchists and possibly the police. There were no further incidents until December, after which two people were killed and a further seven injured. After a trial lasting twelve months, Rull was condemned to death and his principal cronies to long prison sentences. This 'trafficker in terrorism', in the striking phrase of Antoni Dalmau, was executed by *garrote vil* on 8 August 1908. There was an explosion in the port of Barcelona on that day. Nine more bombs went off before the Semana Trágica of July 1909 (see Chapter 4), and a further seventeen in the three months leading up to the fall of the government of Maura on 22 October as a result of the repression that followed the events of July.[55] This suggested that Rull was executed both for his own crimes and for those of others unknown.[56]

From May 1907 there had been six months' respite; then the bombs began to go off again in December. Leading Catalan politicians had long since doubted the capacity of the police to protect their interests. In April 1907, the President of the Diputación Provincial de Barcelona, the prominent architect Josep Puig i Cadafalch, went to London, accompanied by the British Consul in Barcelona. He hired the head of the Scotland Yard

CID, Charles Arrow, who took early retirement and signed a three-year contract to set up a secret parallel police force. Known as the Oficina de Investigación Criminal (OIC), it occupied lavishly appointed offices in the city. Arrow and his assistants were promised, but never received, huge salaries. Arrow was compared to Sherlock Holmes, but he was hampered from the first by his inability to speak either Catalan or Spanish. His outfit was undermined by rivalry among his backers and his local staff, and by opposition from the anarchists, republicans and Lerroux's Radicals, as well as from Tressols, who laughed at the modern methods imported from London. According to the moderate anarchist Joan Peiró, Arrow was inhibited by discovering that some of the activities of the bombers were sponsored by members of the Catalan upper classes who wanted to foment hostility against the central government. Nevertheless, the creation of the OIC strengthened Ossorio's determination to reform the police force. In a letter to Maura in March 1908, he described the city's police services as 'until recently a real dung heap'. He increased pay, improved training and, to the chagrin of Tressols, tried to eradicate the use of torture. Arrow was dismissed in August 1909.[57]

In mid-1907, a variety of Socialists led by Antoni Fabra i Rivas and anarchist groups led by Anselmo Lorenzo and Tomás Herreros united to form an apolitical trade union known as Solidaridad Obrera. This was succeeded in September 1911 by the Confederación Nacional del Trabajo (CNT). It was initially an umbrella organization that gathered together the whole spectrum of anarchism together with Socialists and Republicans. In the minority, the latter were soon repelled by anarchists' view that strikes and industrial sabotage were the best weapons against bourgeois society. In consequence, the CNT was soon an exclusively anarcho-syndicalist organization.[58] Before long it would be Spain's largest union.

Juan de la Cierva, the *cacique* from
Murcia who fixed elections for
Antonio Maura.

4

Revolution and War: From the Tragic Week of 1909 to the Crisis of 1917–1918

The relatively brief honeymoon of Solidaritat Catalana came to an end in May 1909 when its essentially contradictory composition saw it divide and suffer defeat at the hands of Lerroux in local elections. The organization's fate was sealed by the events that took place in Barcelona two months later in July. The popular violence and the church burnings seen during that critical week hardened the conservative instincts of the Lliga which in turn generated working-class support for Lerroux. The origins of the Semana Trágica lay in the working-class pacifism that had been deepened by the disaster of 1898. This rendered it even more difficult for Spain to follow the example of France, Britain, Germany and Italy in using imperialist adventures to divert attention from domestic social conflict. Few poor families had not suffered one or more of their menfolk being killed or disabled during the long years of colonial war in the Philippines and Cuba. The survivors had brought back gruesome accounts of their experiences which had provoked widespread hostility to the governing classes held responsible for the disasters. The belief that conscripts were merely the cannon fodder of political corruption was based on knowledge of how the army had been poorly fed, inadequately armed and badly led. Nevertheless, many army officers were eager for an enterprise that could compensate for the colonial humiliation of 1898. Spain's consequent Moroccan entanglement was widely seen as being driven by the King and the owners of the iron mines, including, it was rumoured, the Jesuits.[1]

In the first week of July 1909, Rif tribesmen attacked the railway link from Melilla that was being built to facilitate commerce with what were wrongly believed to be important mineral deposits. The Minister of War in Maura's government, General Arsenio Linares, under pressure from army officers close to Alfonso XIII, from the King himself and from investors in the mines, reluctantly sent an expeditionary force and claimed that this was merely 'a policing operation' with no intention of it being extended into a military aggression. The Cortes was closed to prevent awkward questions being asked. From 11 July, large numbers of reservists, mainly married men with children, were called up and embarked from Barcelona with no provision being made for the upkeep of their families. For the rich, it was possible to buy exemption via a procedure known as cash redemption for 1,500 pesetas, the equivalent of a year's wages for a workman. It was a deeply unpopular privilege among those who could not afford to pay. The Socialist Party launched the slogan 'Everyone or No One' and there were waves of protest in the anarchist and republican press.[2] In fact, the scale of evasion of military service can be deduced from the fact that before 1895 and after 1898 the device brought into the exchequer between 9 and 12 million pesetas annually. During the three years of the Cuban War, it brought in 40 million pesetas per year.[3]

With no time for adequate preparation of the expedition, the reservists were being sent to a probable death. They had no wish to die to further the interests of what they considered to be a corrupt oligarchy or to satisfy the desire of the army to erase the memory of 1898. In Barcelona, on Sunday 18 July 1909, as the conscripts were marched towards the port, a pacifist demonstration pressured the Maura government into announcing that no further embarkations would take place. Nevertheless, a republican press campaign instigated by Lerroux's Radicals and the Catalan nationalists led by Antonio Rovira i Virgili kept anti-war sentiment at boiling point. The Radicals' youth wing, the Jóvenes Bárbaros (young barbarians), were noisily militant in nightly demonstrations that the police could not control. Within two days, similar disturbances took place in Madrid and in other cities with railway stations from which conscripts were being transported to Barcelona. Meanwhile, a broad spectrum of Catalan politicians sent a telegram to Maura demanding that he put a stop to the war, and the Socialist Party planned a general strike. Maura refused point blank and tension was heightened by news that ten of the reservists who had taken part in the Sunday demonstration had been court-martialled and might be executed. The Socialist plans were seconded by the anarcho-syndicalists. The Civil Governor Ángel Ossorio y Gallardo refused to deploy the hated Civil Guard, a stance which brought him into conflict with Maura's brutal Minister of the Interior, Juan de la Cierva, who believed that what was being planned was all-out revolution that must be crushed.[4]

On that same Sunday, Rif tribesmen intensified their resistance against the Spanish expeditionary force. Ill equipped and virtually untrained, the Spanish conscripts were subjected to constant harassment by an infinitely more skilful force. Over the course of the next week, anti-war sentiment spread within a population convinced that corrupt politicians were responsible for the deficient weaponry of the troops. The Spanish commander in Morocco, General José Marina Vega, success-fully requested more reinforcements, but his troops were defeated on Tuesday, 27 July at the battle of Barranco del Lobo.[5] On the previous day, a general strike had broken out in Barcelona and lasted until 1 August, seven days that came to be known as the tragic week (the Semana Trágica). Having decided to treat it as an insurrection, La Cierva instructed the Captain General of the region to declare martial law. In response, workers dug up thousands of paving stones and set up barri-cades. What had started as anti-conscription protests escalated into anti-clerical disturbances and church burnings. The maintenance of order was initially rendered difficult because many troops were frater-nizing with the strikers. Twenty-one churches and thirty convents were set alight, but assaults on clergy were rare. It was noteworthy that public buildings, banks and the mansions of the rich were left untouched. By Thursday, 29 July, the tide had turned with the arrival of additional troops and Civil Guards. As working-class districts were bombarded by artillery, the movement was put down by what Rafael Shaw called 'the terrorism exercised by the priest-ridden Government of Señor Maura'. In the course of the week, 104 men and six women were killed and around 300 treated for injuries. Five soldiers and two Civil Guards lost their lives. Three monks were killed during the rioting, one of them asphyxiated as he hid in the monastery cellar, although most of the violence was directed not at individual clerics but at the symbols of ecclesiastical power. Inflamed by Lerroux's lurid propaganda, the rioters burst into convents convinced that they would liberate nuns from torture and sexual servitude. Elsewhere in most Catalan towns, the strike went on and, in some, the Republic was declared.[6]

The Semana Trágica had serious consequences for Spanish politics. The officer corps of the army, determined to mask its feeble performance at Barranco del Lobo, became an ever more aggressive colonial lobby. The high command of the African Army successfully pushed for an expansion of military operations in Morocco, the costs of which quickly escalated, not just in financial terms. As both Liberal and Conservative governments had to turn to the army to suppress proletarian discontent, much of which was related to the human costs of the Moroccan adventure, the officer corps became increasingly intolerant of any civilian supervision.[7] Moreover, the events of July and August were followed by a fierce repression which moulded future working-class strategies. In Barcelona, the thoughtful Ángel Ossorio y Gallardo was replaced as Civil Governor by the hard-line Evaristo Crespo Azorín, who imposed martial law, banned most left-wing organizations and was particularly harsh on Solidaridad Obrera and the Radicals. Around 3,000 prisoners were taken and 1,725 cases were subsequently brought to trial by court martial. Seventeen men were sentenced to death, of whom five were actually executed. They included Francesc Ferrer and a charcoal burner whose crime was to have danced in the street with the desiccated corpse of a nun.

Ferrer's lay schools, like Spain's few Protestant schools, were subjected to furious and ceaseless abuse by the Catholic press. Ferrer himself was found guilty of masterminding the events in Barcelona despite there being only the flimsiest of evidence. Nevertheless, he had been involved in the planning and funding of both failed attempts on the life of Alfonso XIII. For the government and the military high command, the repression was deemed necessary because the disturbances combined elements of anti-militarism, anti-clericalism and Catalan separatism. In this sense, during the Semana Trágica the hostility between the military and the labour movement prefigured the violent hostilities of the civil war. Ironically, the Semana Trágica also saw the Catalan bourgeoisie scurry back to the protection of the Madrid government.

The execution of Ferrer on 13 October 1909 unleashed massive protest demonstrations across Spain and in several European capitals. The campaign with the slogan 'Maura No' was strengthened by the bullying policies of La Cierva. When the Liberal leader Segismundo Moret protested in the Cortes about the repression and called for Maura's resignation, La Cierva aggressively suggested that Moret's opposition to his methods was responsible for events such as the assassination attempts against the King. His tone was widely condemned, but Maura congratulated him on his speech. Although Maura had a substantial parliamentary majority, on 21 October Alfonso XIII seized the opportunity to get rid of Maura by precipitately accepting what the devastated Prime Minister had intended as merely a symbolic offer of resignation.[8] The King therefore ensured that the Conservative Party would henceforth be in the hands of elements opposed to substantial reform.[9] Alfonso then offered the government to Moret, who, unable to unite the faction-ridden Liberal Party, was replaced in February 1910 by José Canalejas, leader of the left wing of the Liberals and a politician genuinely concerned with social justice. There was an assassination attempt on Maura in Barcelona in the summer of 1911.[10]

In October 1908, to avoid imprisonment for his involvement in the assassination attempt on Alfonso XIII, Lerroux had gone to Argentina, where he remained until August 1909. Greeted by cheering crowds, he had returned a changed man. While in Argentina, he had received considerable gifts, including shares in meat-export companies and amusement parks as well as cash. In consequence, he began to invest in service companies that were then granted lucrative contracts by town councils controlled by the Radicals. The corruption of party members with positions in local administration helped Lerroux both to become a very rich man and to finance his party. And as he accumulated possessions, cars, jewellery and an estate in San Rafael, his rhetoric became ever more conservative. He was also involved in corrupt activities in the cement and building-supplies trade.[11]

The first elections called by Canalejas, on 8 May 1910, saw for the first time the election to the Cortes of a Socialist deputy. It has been suggested that Canalejas was, in his heart of hearts, a republican whose acceptance of the monarchy was purely pragmatic.[12] Certainly, he came to power determined to implement a regenerationist programme in the hope of weaning the working class away from anarchism and socialism. He was prepared to countenance state arbitration in wage settlements, to legislate on working conditions and even to contemplate the expropriation of the great *latifundio* estates on grounds of social utility. He introduced several important reforms including universal military service which put an end to the divisive practice whereby the rich could buy their way out. He also replaced the unjust tax on the consumption of food, drink and fuel known as the *impuesto de consumos* with taxes on the wealthy.

However, despite his reforming ambitions, he was beset by growing opposition. There was continued anti-war agitation and, in August 1911, some members of the crew of the warship *Numancia* mutinied and threatened to bombard Malaga in support of a republican coup. The intensification of left-wing and trade union agitation brought out Canalejas's instincts as a man of order. He used the army to repress strikes, most notably a nationwide general strike in September 1911 after which he suspended the CNT. There was a conviction within the anarchist movement that he was in collusion with Lerroux to destroy Solidaridad Obrera and subsequently the CNT. Indeed, he was the object of a hate campaign by both the left and the extreme right. Canalejas was shot dead by an anarchist in front of the Librería San Martín in Madrid's Puerta del Sol on 12 November 1912.[13]

Maura informed Alfonso XIII that he would not work with the Liberals because they were moving too close to republicanism. That decision together with the death of Canalejas left the two dynastic parties in chaos and marked the end of any serious attempt to reform the Restoration system. In 1913, when a government led by the Conde de Romanones fell, Alfonso XIII ignored the fact that Maura was leader of the Conservative Party and opened discussions with the lacklustre lawyer Eduardo Dato who, in contrast, was prepared to work with the Liberals. In protest at what they regarded as disrespect for their leader, Maura's more dynamic followers formed a group called Los Jóvenes Mauristas. Rather like the broader regenerationist movement, Maurismo would divide into two incompatible wings. On the one hand, led by Ossiorio y Gallardo, were those who shared their leader's desire to carry out political reform by putting an end to *caciquismo*. On the other hand, the majority, led by Antonio Goicoechea, would eventually develop into a key right-wing anti-republican group.[14]

The Liberal Party also divided into two major factions led respectively by Manuel García Prieto, the Marqués de Alhucemas, and Álvaro de Figueroa, the Conde de Romanones, the canny *cacique* of Guadalajara, an expert more in the exploitation than in the reform of the system. Nevertheless, in 1915, Romanones did bring the dynamic Santiago Alba into his government as Minister of the Interior. Alba was determined to reduce the size of the bureaucracy and the army in order to finance investment in both agriculture and industry. This seduced the Reformist Republicans of Melquíades Álvarez away from their alliance with the Socialists.

The CNT was becoming more radical as, gradually, the Socialists and Republicans became more moderate. In the course of the bitter industrial conflicts during the First World War, it became an exclusively anarcho-syndicalist movement. It mushroomed from its initial 15,000 members to over 700,000 by 1919, a reflection of the country's burgeoning industrial base. The number of workers engaged in non-agricultural activities had quadrupled from 244,000 in 1887 to 995,000 in 1900.[15] The leaders of the new organization rejected both individual violence and parliamentary politics, opting instead for what was called revolutionary syndicalism. This involved a central contradiction which would bedevil the organization until the Spanish Civil War. As recruits flooded in, the CNT had to act as a conventional trade union defending the interests of its members within the existing order while at the same time advocating direct action to overthrow that order. The involvement of its members in violent acts of industrial sabotage and revolutionary strikes meant the new organization would frequently be declared illegal.

Surprisingly, however, when the next challenge to the Restoration system came, it was not mounted by the rural anarchists or the urban working class but by the industrial bourgeoisie. Nevertheless, once the crisis started, proletarian ambitions came into play in such a way as to ensure that the basic hostilities within Spanish politics became more acute than ever. The social problems faced by the Restoration system, with political power concentrated in the hands of those who also enjoyed the monopoly of economic power, had been intensifying for decades. They were pushed to breaking point by the coming of the First World War. Given Spain's near bankruptcy and the parlous state of its armed forces, the Conservative government led by the wealthy lawyer Eduardo Dato had little choice but immediately to declare strict neutrality. Nevertheless, in a letter to Maura explaining his decision, Dato revealed his sympathies for the Austro-German Central Powers.[16] Political passions were aroused by an ongoing acrimonious debate about whether Spain should intervene and, if so, on which side. The army, most Conservatives, the Mauristas and the Carlists admired what they saw as Prussian discipline and efficiency and so supported the Central Powers. The Liberals, Lerroux's Radicals, the left and most intellectuals equated Germany with barbarism and so supported the Western Allies, whose cause they associated with civilization. The fiercely pro-Allied Romanones inspired a controversial article entitled 'Fatal Neutralities', although he quickly accepted that there was no alternative to neutrality. Heated polemics in the press (much of it owned or lavishly subsidized by Germans) and in mass meetings intensified the ever growing divisions within the Liberal and Conservative parties. Despite the lack of options, the political system would be torn apart by the economic consequences of the war, by the massive social upheaval that came in its wake and by the reverberations of the Russian revolution.[17] Within the polemics about Spain's possible participation in the conflict could be discerned the personal interests of some politicians. Needless to say, where there was corruption, Alejandro Lerroux could usually be found. His enthusiastic espousal of Spanish military intervention on the Allied side saw him attacked by pro-German gangs. While probably sincere, his stance was not unconnected with the exports by his companies, particularly of meat, to the French Republic.[18]

As a non-belligerent, Spain was in the economically privileged position of being able to supply both the Anglo-French Entente and the Central Powers with agricultural and industrial products. Manufacturers benefited from import substitution in the domestic market and from the possibility of filling the gaps left in their own export markets by the belligerent powers. Coalmines in Asturias, iron-ore mines and the shipping industry in the Basque Country, the Catalan textile and chemical industries, the Valencian and Mallorcan leather industries all experienced a frenetic boom which stimulated a dramatic take-off for the Spanish economy. The profits of Basque shipping lines increased from 4.43 million pesetas in 1913 to 52.69 million in 1915. In Bilbao, investment in new companies went up from 14.5 million pesetas in 1913 to 427.5 million by the end of the war.[19]

The boom had attracted rural labour to mines and factories in towns where the worst conditions of early capitalism prevailed, especially in Asturias and the Basque Country. The increase in the numbers of industrial workers would soon constitute a daunting challenge to the Restoration system. Between 1910 and 1918, the numbers of miners would rise from 90,000 to 133,000, of metallurgical workers from 61,000 to 200,000 and of textile workers from 125,000 to 213,000. At the same time, massive exports created domestic shortages, galloping inflation and plummeting living standards. Per capita consumption of basic foodstuffs, such as wheat, rice, chickpeas and potatoes, fell dramatically as prices rocketed during the war years. The Catalan bourgeoisie did not plough back profits into modernizing their factories. Rather, they frittered them away on building spectacular residences, buying luxury cars and frequenting the casinos, cabarets and brothels that sprang up. Working-class militancy was provoked by popular resentment of such conspicuous consumption together with the reluctance of the newly enriched bourgeoisie to concede wage increases.[20] As a result, in December 1915, the Dato government collapsed and the King called upon Romanones to replace him. Despite promises of clean elections, the contest of 9 April 1916 was rigged and saw Romanones gain a substantial majority. The new parliament was known as 'the Cortes of the relatives' since all the principal Conservative and Liberal leaders had managed to secure the election of family members. In fact, it was well known that party leaders maintained their position by nepotism, patronage and turning a blind eye to the plundering of state resources. The Socialist press revealed that the same political grandees sat on the boards of the country's most prosperous companies, citing this as proof that Spain was controlled by a small privileged elite.

Government ministers were actively involved in corruption. During the war, the Minister of Finance, Santiago Alba, made substantial sums of money from his alliance with the Mallorcan robber baron Juan March, who was making colossal profits from exporting food to both belligerents, as well as from his key business, tobacco smuggling. In this, March exploited the widespread nicotine addiction of Spaniards. Nearly three-quarters of a century earlier, Richard Ford had noted that 'a cigar is a *sine qua non* in every Spaniard's mouth, for otherwise he would resemble a house without a chimney, a steamer without a funnel'.[21] So successful was March's smuggling operation that government revenue from tobacco duty was plummeting to such an extent that it was decided to grant him the official monopoly for a fee.[22] Alba's reputation for venality was such that when he was appointed minister, some journalists said to March, 'Now you will have the doors of the Ministry wide open.' He smiled and replied smugly, 'I won't be the one visiting him. He will come to see me when I decide that the time is ripe.'[23]

The 'extreme friendship' that March demonstrated towards the young Liberal politician was expressed in many ways. On one occasion, March organized a banquet in Palma de Mallorca for him and presented Alba's wife with a bouquet of flowers in which were concealed ten 1,000-peseta notes. A striking example of how Alba expressed his gratitude for the friendship arose out of the introduction in 1915 of the Subsistence Law, the purpose of which was to bring under control the massive and highly profitable export of necessary foodstuffs to belligerent powers. Alba secured for March several exceptional export licences which allowed the Mallorcan plutocrat legally to bypass the restrictions imposed by the law. In 1916, the government prohibited the export of rice from Valencia. March's agents in the Valencian region began to stockpile huge quantities of rice and applied for an extraordinary licence on the grounds there was a surplus beyond the market's capacity to absorb. Without requiring any proof or instituting any inspection, Alba secured for March the necessary licence to allow him to sell the rice in Europe at inflated prices, having previously bought it at extremely low prices. Alba and the Conde de Romanones endeared themselves further to March by failing to make any serious effort to challenge his massive tobacco-smuggling activities. Alba's political ambitions received substantial financial support from March, especially in Mallorca. In return, Alba arranged for March to have a parliamentary seat in 1923. A number of extremely senior and influential government officials were alleged to be in March's pocket. It is hardly surprising that Alejandro Lerroux was also on the payroll of March, who contributed substantially to his electoral expenses as well.[24]

Romanones was no more successful than Dato in dealing with the social problems provoked by the world war. In 1916, a total of 2,415,304 working days were lost in strikes, more than six times as many as in the previous years, and there were also a number of dramatic bread riots.[25] Strikes secured some wage rises but these were not sufficient to keep up with the inflation of food prices. From 1913 to 1917, prices increased by 50 per cent, profits by 88 per cent and wages by only 10 per cent. Under pressure from the rank and file, the twelfth congress of the Socialist UGT on 12–13 May decided to call on the anarcho-syndicalist CNT to undertake joint action to resolve the social problems. The agreement was enshrined in the Pact of Zaragoza, signed on 17 July 1916, which coincided with a successful strike of Socialist railway workers in favour of recognition of their union. After more revolutionary proposals from the CNT had been rejected, the success of a one-day UGT strike in December 1916 encouraged hopes that a joint general strike might lead to free elections and then reform. The economic crisis thus brought about a remarkable alliance of the reformist UGT and the revolutionary CNT. Nevertheless, there was friction between the essential caution of the UGT and the militant élan of the CNT.[26] The survival of the alliance was facilitated by the fact that the CNT at the time was led by the thoughtful duo of the watch-mender Ángel Pestaña and the house painter Salvador Seguí. Known as El Noi del Sucre (the Sugar Boy) because of his sweet tooth, the affable Seguí was always elegant in public, usually wearing a hat and a starched collar and sporting a silk handkerchief in his breast pocket. The gruff Pestaña was more outspoken than his more subtle friend. Although later regarded as moderates, by 1917, believing that the monarchy was about to fall and that revolution was imminent, both countenanced violence to further those aims.[27]

As a result of the boom, the balance of power within the economic elite was beginning to shift. Although agrarian interests remained pre-eminent, industrialists were no longer prepared to tolerate their subordinate political position. Their dissatisfaction came to a head in June when Romanones's Minister of Finance, Santiago Alba, proposed paying for radical economic reforms by means of a tax on the notoriously spectacular war profits of northern industry without a corresponding measure to deal with the profits made by the agrarians. Accordingly, the measure was denounced by Basque, Catalan and Asturian industrialists as a tyrannical attempt to punish the productive classes. In fact, the outrage expressed on their behalf by Cambó and the Basque industrialist Ramón de la Sota was largely to do with the challenge to their profits. Largely at the hands of Cambó, Alba's initiative was blocked in December in the Cortes and thereby the possibility of alleviating the desperate situation of a substantial part of the population was frustrated.[28] Nonetheless, Alba's initiative so underlined the arrogance of the landed elite that it would precipitate a bid by the industrial bourgeoisie to implement political modernization. In the meantime, Romanones was coming under increasing pressure from the left for his inability to resolve the economic crisis and from the right for his pro-Allied stance. With Spanish shipping under attack from German submarines, he had proposed breaking off relations with the Central Powers. In response, the Germanophile Alfonso XIII forced him to resign and invited García Prieto to form a government.

In 1917, the working class, the military and the industrial bourgeoisie would all mount challenges to the existing order. Seemingly linked by their temporal coincidence, their aims were, however, starkly contradictory. The opposition to the Restoration system of Basque and Catalan industrialists had already seen the emergence of powerful regionalist movements backed by industrialists – the Partido Nacionalista Vasco

(PNV) and the Lliga Regionalista. The equivalent in Asturias was the Reformist Party led by Melquíades Álvarez. While there was a revolutionary air to these groups' opposition to the economic inertia and political incompetence of the rural oligarchy, they also pursued reactionary and oppressive policies against their own workforces. The leader of the Lliga, the shrewd financier Cambó, emerged as spokesman for the northern industrialists and bankers. He was convinced that drastic action was necessary to prevent the Restoration system being engulfed by a revolutionary cataclysm. His vision of a controlled revolution from above was based on the idea of an autonomous Catalonia as the dynamo of a new Spain.[29] Ironically, the reforming zeal of industrialists enriched by the war saw them ally briefly with the proletariat that was being impoverished by it. While industrialists and workers with significantly different agendas were agitating for change, middle-rank army officers were protesting at low wages, antiquated promotion structures and political corruption. A deceptive and short-lived alliance between all three was forged in part because of a misunderstanding on the part of the first two regarding the political stance of the army.

By 1916, already exiguous military salaries were being hit by wartime inflation, even more so than those of industrial workers who could secure some wage increases by means of strike action. Junior and middle-rank officers in Spain had to take on civilian jobs to maintain their families. This in turn fed a division within the army between those who had volunteered to serve in Morocco, the so-called Africanistas, and those who had remained in the Peninsula, the *peninsulares*. For the Africanistas, the risks were enormous but the prizes, in terms of adventure and rapid promotion, high. Brutalized by the horrors of the Moroccan tribal wars, the Africanistas had acquired a sense of being a heroic band of warriors alone in their concern for the fate of the *patria*. They felt contempt for professional politicians, for the pacifist left-wing masses, for Catalanists and, to a certain extent, for their peninsular comrades for whom the mainland signified a less well-paid but more comfortable, sedentary existence with promotion only by strict seniority. Inevitably, there was resentment among the *peninsulares* for the Africanistas who enjoyed the higher pay that came with quick promotion for battlefield merit.[30] They responded by creating the Juntas Militares de Defensa, a form of trade union, both to protect their rigid seniority system and to seek better pay as an escape from what they called 'the drip-feed of misery'. In the words of Cambó, 'the Juntas Militares de Defensa appeared, like frogs and mosquitoes in stagnant pools'.[31]

The Juntas' complaints were couched in the fashionable language of regenerationism, although the entire movement would turn out to be merely a significant step towards military dictatorship. In late May 1917, García Prieto ordered the dissolution of the Juntas Militares de Defensa and the arrest of the leaders. On 1 June, the Juntas threatened to launch a coup d'état if their comrades were not released and their movement not recognized as a legal military trade union. On 9 June, García Prieto was forced from power. The King, endlessly meddling, had toyed with the idea of a coalition government built around Santiago Alba and Francesc Cambó, despite the pair's mutual loathing. However, he replaced García Prieto with Dato, whose Conservative government recognized the Juntas.[32] Mouthing empty regenerationist clichés, they were acclaimed as the figureheads of a great national reform movement when, in fact, they were merely consolidating the army's belief that it was the ultimate arbiter of political life. For a brief, illusory moment, workers, capitalists and the military seemed to be united in the name of cleansing Spanish politics of the corruption of *caciquismo*. In the unlikely event of that three-pronged movement being successful in establishing a political system capable of permitting social adjustment, the civil war might perhaps have been avoided. In fact, the events of the crisis of 1917 simply gave slightly more power to the industrial and banking bourgeoisie without undermining the dominance of the entrenched landed oligarchy.[33]

The lengthy denouement of the crisis began when Dato suspended the Cortes. Cambó was also using a regenerationist rhetoric, claiming that a progressive Catalan capitalism could modernize backward agrarian Spain. His project guaranteed the hostility of Santiago Alba. To push it forward, and in response to Dato's closure of the Cortes, Cambó organized an alternative Assembly of Catalan deputies which met on 5 July 1917 in the Ajuntament de Barcelona and called for the reopening of the Cortes. They announced that if the government did not agree, a wider Assembly, with reforming parliamentarians from all over Spain, would meet in Barcelona as a kind of shadow Cortes. Dato declared the first Assembly seditious. Cambó went ahead with the threat and arranged the meeting of the Assembly for 19 July. Ossorio y Gallardo believed that it could carry out Maura's revolution from above. Cambó was anxious to secure the support of Maura himself to prevent the Assembly being smeared as a separatist and revolutionary initiative. Because it was illegal under the Constitution, Maura had refused to cooperate with the Assembly, denouncing it in a letter to his son as 'grotesque' and its members as 'a professional flea-market'.

Had Maura agreed, it would have brought the Juntas aboard and the momentum of the reform movement might have overthrown the monarchy. However, Maura had already denounced the Juntas as 'a monstrous freak of vintage depravity'. Despite maintaining a correspondence with Cambó, the leader of the Juntas, Colonel Benito Márquez, and his comrades were not prepared to collaborate with the Assembly movement because of its Catalanist emphasis and were certainly not ready to countenance any kind of revolutionary strike. Their hope was to see a government presided over by Antonio Maura, but, to the disappointment of his followers, he was not prepared to come out of retirement. In a letter to Ossorio, Maura referred to Cambó's plan as 'the subversive way' and went on to say: 'but I'm not one of those who have the vocation for such exploits'. Dato took an authoritarian approach. Much of the Catalan press was banned and he obliged the Madrid press to portray the Assembly as a Catalan separatist initiative. Extra reinforcements of the army and the Civil Guard were sent to Barcelona and a battlecruiser docked in the port. Nevertheless, projected as the progressive parliament that Spain would have if clean elections were possible, the Assembly met in the Palau del Parc de la Ciudadela. It called for an end to the dominance of the corrupt centralist oligarchy. Dato ordered the Assembly dissolved. The members were symbolically arrested by the Civil Governor placing his hand on their shoulders and immediately releasing them. They left the building to the cheers of a large crowd.[34]

Despite the apparent coincidence of their reforming rhetoric, the ultimate interests of workers, industrialists and army officers were contradictory and Dato skilfully exploited their differences. Despite the popular support for the Assembly movement, there were already significant differences between it and the Juntas. The UGT and the CNT had been preparing for a revolutionary strike, under the impression that they would enjoy the support of both the Lliga and the Juntas. This was highly unlikely since the fears provoked during the Semana Trágica had been reawakened by the February revolution in Russia. It was even more improbable that army officers would view a revolutionary strike with any sympathy. In any case, UGT–CNT collaboration was difficult. While the anarchists nurtured unrealistically extreme ambitions such as the dissolution of the armed forces and the nationalization of the land, the maximum aim of the Socialists was a provisional government capable of ending political corruption and dealing with inflation and food shortages. Nevertheless, in March 1917, a CNT delegation of Pestaña, Seguí and Ángel Lacort had gone to Madrid for meetings with the UGT. While there, they took part in a public meeting at which they and UGT representatives launched a manifesto that vehemently denounced the failure of the government to respond to the demands made during the UGT's one-day strike in December 1916. It was meant and was taken as a declaration of war on Dato, who duly had them arrested, but a public outcry forced their early release.[35]

The intransigence of the government pushed both the CNT and the UGT towards more militant positions, although the Socialists remained the more cautious of the two. Their unease derived from the fact that, from August 1916, extremist action groups on the fringes of the CNT had occasionally resorted to assassination attempts on recalcitrant employers, foremen and strike breakers. The more moderate elements, represented by Pestaña and Seguí, may have disapproved but were unable to disavow these activities. Pestaña wrote: 'tied by our love of the organization, not only did we not denounce such outrages but, if necessary, we would go out into the street to defend the organization when it was attacked'. The CNT's sporadic terror was met by a much more organized counter-terror lavishly funded by the industrialists. Over the next seven years, numerous murders were carried out by gangs led by the corrupt ex-police chief Manuel Bravo Portillo and a German agent, Friedrich Stallmann, who went by the name Baron de Koenig. The arrogant Bravo Portillo was tall and swarthy, sported a large curly moustache and tried to pass himself off as an aristocrat. He had made a fortune working for the Germans during the war. He had subsequently been dismissed and imprisoned, albeit for only six months, when it was discovered that he had revealed the sailing times of Allied ships from Barcelona, thereby permitting German submarines to torpedo them. The Bravo Portillo and Koenig gang also carried out attacks on industrialists who were exporting to France.[36]

By the time of their return to Barcelona after the meetings in Madrid, Pestaña and Seguí found their followers feverishly planning an armed uprising. Pestaña wrote later, 'The unions' cashboxes were emptied, down to the last cent to buy pistols and make bombs.' The Russian revolutionary Victor Serge wrote of those days:

> At the Café Espagnol, on the Paralelo, that crowded thoroughfare with its blazing lights of evening, near the horrible *barrio chino* whose mouldering alleys were full of half-naked girls lurking in doorways that gaped into hell-holes, it was here that I met militants arming for the approaching battle. They spoke enthusiastically of those who would fall in that fight, they dealt out Browning revolvers, and baited, as we all did, the anxious spies at the neighbouring table. In a revolutionary side-street, with a *Guardia Civil* barracks on one side and poor tenements on the other, I found Barcelona's hero of the hour, the quickening spirit, the uncrowned leader, the fearless man of politics who distrusted politicians: Salvador Seguí …

In long conversations, Seguí and Serge discussed what the latter called the 'dubious alliance' between the workers and the Catalan bourgeoisie. Seguí was aware that the CNT was being used by Cambó: 'we are useful in their game of political blackmail'. Nevertheless, he was optimistic: 'Without us, they can do nothing: we have the streets, the shock-troops, the brave hearts among the people. We know this, but we need them. They stand for money, trade, possible legality (at the beginning, anyway), the Press, public opinion, etc.'[37]

In contrast, the Socialists had initially planned only to support the Assembly movement for the establishment of a provisional government under Melquíades Álvarez with the participation of Lerroux, Pablo Iglesias and Largo Caballero. It would call elections for a Constituent Cortes to decide on the future form of the state. Such aims were compatible with those of Cambó. The discrepancies between the Socialists' limited ambitions and those of the CNT led to increasing tension.[38] When the CNT was about to hold an assembly on 20 June to decide on the immediate declaration of a revolutionary general strike, Largo Caballero hastened to Barcelona to try to restrain the anarchists. Used to working openly in Madrid, he was shocked to have to meet clandestinely at Vallvidrera in the hills outside the city. He was even more taken aback when confronted by a crowd of pistol-toting militants, who declared their readiness to use them to fight off the police or the Civil Guard. They accused the Socialists of being in cahoots with bourgeois politicians and demanded the immediate declaration of the strike.

In the event, Largo Caballero managed to persuade the assembly that the strike should not be declared before adequate preparations had been made. Only the intervention of the moderates Salvador Seguí and Ángel Pestaña saved the alliance.[39] On the day that the Assembly was about to meet in Barcelona, the Socialist leader Pablo Iglesias, himself en route to the meeting in the Parc de la Ciudadela, met Pestaña, Seguí and two other CNT leaders, Francesc Miranda and Enric Valero. They explained that the CNT was anxious to launch a general strike in support of the Assembly. To their barely concealed annoyance, Iglesias listened to them 'with contemptuous indifference'. Expressing surprise at how advanced their plans were, and clearly fearful of exacerbating military hostility, he tried to talk them out of strike action. When they argued that the time was ripe, he replied patronizingly: 'You, the manual workers see things like that but we, the intellectuals, see them differently.' They left him, utterly disillusioned, not to say disgusted, with the Socialist stance.[40]

Moreover, the CNT rank and file was suspicious of the Assembly movement, seeing it as an instrument of the bourgeoisie. In particular, there was considerable suspicion of Cambó, who was regarded as representing hated employers. Accordingly, the CNT was holding back, waiting to see if the Assembly would call for the overthrow of the monarchy. The Socialists, too, planned action only if the Assembly was repressed.[41] However, in Valencia, the left-wing republicans Marcelino Domingo and Félix Azzati convinced railway workers that the Assembly was the signal for the general strike. There were also agents provocateurs of the government present, stirring up militancy. The subsequent strike was not supported nationally by the UGT and was put down by the authorities at the cost of two dead and several wounded. The railway company took severe reprisals, dismissing hundreds of workers.[42]

Remembering their success the previous summer, the UGT's railway union threatened a nationwide strike in support of their demand for the sacked workers to be reinstated. The issue could have been settled easily, but Dato's government seized the opportunity to drive a wedge between the forces ranged against the establishment. Dato put pressure on the owners of the railway company to refuse to negotiate. Daniel Anguiano, Secretary General of the railway workers' union, was forced to fulfil the threat and he declared a strike on 10 August. Dato calculated that the intransigence of the railway owners would force the UGT to raise the stakes with a general strike in solidarity with the railway workers. His hope was that this would split off the Juntas and the Lliga from the reform movement. Accordingly, blindly confident of the backing of the Juntas and the Assembly, the UGT leadership optimistically decided three days later to support the railway workers with a nationwide strike. The instinctive politics of the military saw army officers – both *peninsulares* and Africanistas – happy to defend the established order.[43]

The manifesto for the strike that broke out on 10 August 1917 could hardly have been more moderate. Drafted by the PSOE Vice-President, the professor of logic Julián Besteiro, it echoed the demands of the Assembly and instructed the strikers to refrain from violence of any kind. Nevertheless, the government presented the strikers as bloodthirsty revolutionaries. With the UGT forced to act precipitately in support of the railway workers, the strike was poorly prepared, did not extend to the peasantry and was met with savage military repression. In Barcelona, the stoppage was total and artillery was used against the anarchists, who suffered thirty-seven dead. It lasted longest in Asturias where it was supported by Melquíades Álvarez who had been chosen to head the provisional government. It was easily crushed in Asturias and the Basque Country, two of the Socialists' major strongholds – the third being Madrid. Bilbao was occupied by troops who, on the orders of General José Souza, unleashed indiscriminate attacks on the population. In Asturias, the Military Governor General Ricardo Burguete y Lana declared martial law on 13 August. He accused the strike organizers of being the paid agents of foreign powers. Announcing that he would hunt down the strikers 'like wild beasts', he sent columns of regular troops and Civil Guards into the mining valleys where they unleashed an orgy of rape, looting, beatings and torture. With eighty dead, 152 wounded and 2,000 arrested, the failure of the strike was guaranteed.[44]

Manuel Llaneza, the moderate leader of the Asturian mineworkers' union, wrote of the 'odio africano' during an action in which one of Burguete's columns was under the command of the young Major Francisco Franco. The implication was that the Africanistas treated the proletariat in exactly the way they treated the colonial population in Morocco. In Madrid, Jóvenes Mauristas acted as auxiliary police and workers armed only with stones were fired on by soldiers with machine guns. Dato's ploy had secured a short-term success but at the cost of intensifying the hatred between the military and the proletariat and the hostility to his cabinet of both. In this way he inflicted fatal damage on both his government and the system.[45]

In contravention of his status as a parliamentary deputy, Marcelino Domingo was arrested and mistreated by Civil Guards, who were ready to execute him.[46] The UGT's four-man national strike committee, consisting of Besteiro, the UGT Vice-President, Francisco Largo Caballero, Andrés Saborit, leader of the printers' union and editor of the PSOE newspaper *El Socialista*, and Daniel Anguiano, the railway workers' leader, was arrested in a flat in Madrid. Having failed to take adequate security measures, they were blithely having dinner. To discredit them, the Minister of the Interior, José Sánchez Guerra, mendaciously announced that they were hiding – one in a wardrobe, another under a bed, and two others inside large flowerpots – and that vast amounts of Spanish and foreign currency were found in their belongings. Very nearly subjected to summary execution, from their insanitary cells they could hear the gallows being built. All four were tried by court martial. The Juntas demanded that they receive the death penalty, although they were finally sentenced to life imprisonment. In the event, they spent only some months in jail. Dato's failure to stand up to the Juntas severely damaged his reputation, just as their participation in the repression killed off the popularity that they had gained in previous months. After a nationwide amnesty campaign, the four members of the strike committee were freed when they were elected to the Cortes in the general elections of 24 February 1918 – Besteiro for Madrid, Saborit for Oviedo, Anguiano for Valencia and Largo Caballero for Barcelona. The entire experience was to have a damaging effect on the subsequent trajectory of all four. In general, the Socialist leadership, particularly the UGT bureaucracy, was traumatized, seeing the movement's role in 1917 as senseless adventurism.[47] The defeat of the strike put an end, for some time, to the possibility of reform from below. Nevertheless, it had demonstrated that the challenge of mass politics was something that the dynastic parties could resist only by recourse to the army. In the words of Francisco Romero, 'the army had stopped the revolution but who was going to stop the army?'[48]

Realizing that their role in the repression had fatally damaged their public image as a progressive element, the Juntas implausibly denied responsibility for the brutality meted out to civilians. They issued a statement, claiming that they had been put in an impossible position by the government.[49] On 26 October, despite Dato's efforts to ingratiate himself with the Juntas, they sent the King a note denouncing the incapacity of the present system and urging him to form a new national government. In fact, a wide spectrum of public opinion concurred that the *turno* system had to be replaced.[50] Despite defeating the strike, Dato had not resolved any of the social problems facing him prior to August. Alfonso XIII sacked him and shortly afterwards said to him, 'Teddy, I've been a scoundrel with you.' Despite his humiliation, Dato tried to protect the King, telling reporters that his resignation had not been precipitated by the Juntas' ultimatum. Romanones declared that the entire episode constituted the end of the *turno*. Cambó wrote in the press: 'I firmly believe that this is not the fall of a government but rather the defeat, the collapse of the system of revolving parties.'[51] It certainly marked the end of the credibility of Alfonso XIII as a moderating force and confirmed that the real power in the land was the army.

In the midst of the subsequent crisis which saw Spain without a government for eight days, the Assembly met in the Ateneo de Madrid, on 30 October, to demand a new constitution. In the middle of its deliberations, Cambó was invited to an audience with the King. The members of the Assembly believed that their movement had triumphed but Cambó was actually being bought off. To the consternation of the Assembly's more liberal and left-wing members, Cambó withdrew from the movement when the King offered the Lliga participation in a new coalition government. Negotiations over its composition were complicated by the Juntas' demand that they be represented, as Minister of War, by La Cierva, who was opposed by the left and the Assembly. Eventually, in return for the inclusion of two Catalan ministers, Joan Ventosa in Finance and Felip Rodés in Education, Cambó dropped the idea of a Constituent Cortes and on 1 November accepted the formation of a national coalition under García Prieto. To his furious critics in the Assembly, Cambó claimed, implausibly, that he was going to be able to reform the system from within, ensuring that Catalonia would be the Prussia of a regenerated Spain. However, already disliked by many for his brusque and imperious manner, he was widely regarded as having betrayed the forces committed to reform. What he had done was to ally the Lliga with the agrarian oligarchy and the army and had therefore put an end to any kind of legal reform of the system. He was convinced that, after the next elections, the Lliga would have between seventy and eighty deputies and he would be made Prime Minister. In the meantime, he boasted to colleagues that he could control García Prieto through Ventosa. However, the Prime Minister ran rings around the inexperienced Ventosa and Rodés. It was not long before Cambó came to believe that he had been deceived and to regret bitterly that he had not joined the government himself.[52]

In fact, the coalition had no agreed objectives and each of its components pursued their own agendas. Moreover, it would be opposed by every section of the left. According to Romanones, the legacy of the mistakes made by Dato rendered it an impossible enterprise.[53] The Juntas' representative, La Cierva, did everything possible to thwart the reforming intentions of the two Catalan ministers. The elections held on 24 February 1918 were among the most corrupt and venal of the entire Restoration period and demonstrated that the oligarchy's capacity to fix results was anything but neutralized. There were urban areas where the elections were relatively clean but the power of rural *caciquismo* remained solid. Thus Cambó's Lliga, although victorious in Catalonia, was a long way from gaining the number of seats necessary to permit him to implement a thoroughgoing reform. No party had an overall majority. Dato's Conservatives secured the most seats, but the combined Liberal groups under Romananones and García Prieto had more. Nevertheless, the results produced a deadlock, with the Cortes split into a number of factions. Moreover, a so-called Alianza de Izquierdas, a group led by Melquíadez Álvarez of the Reformist Party (9 deputies) and various Republican parties (20) and the Socialists (6) and the Lliga Regionalista (21) constituted a significant challenge to the establishment.

To the outrage of other members of the government and of Antonio Maura, La Cierva introduced by royal decree across-the-board pay rises for officers and promoted the ringleaders of the Juntas. Without consulting the Cortes, in a starving country he was massively inflating the military budget and undermining civilian sovereignty over the armed forces. His concern was to clinch military support for the monarchy. Constantly touring barracks, at the same time as he praised the patriotism of the Juntas, he banned the Non-Commissioned Officers' Junta and eliminated the regenerationist elements led by Benito Márquez. When Márquez protested that the Minister's pandering to the Juntas would eventually lead to the alienation of the army from the political system, La Cierva managed to get him expelled from the army. In February 1918, there began a strike of postal and telegraph workers. With characteristic heavy-handedness, La Cierva responded by militarizing those services and thereby rendering the strikers mutineers. Since the army lacked the expertise to run them, the consequence was total chaos in national communications. There was also public outrage that La Cierva had given in to the army but used force against civilians. La Cierva resigned and brought the government down. There were widespread rumours that he was planning to establish a dictatorship with a group of colonels. He later denied this.[54]

Alfonso XIII threatened to abdicate if a proper national government was not formed. The serious danger of a dictatorship under La Cierva was averted only when, on 21 March 1918, Maura was persuaded, in large part by Cambó, to preside over a broad national coalition government containing the principal party leaders. Dato, resentful because of the return of Maura, became Foreign Minister, García Prieto Minister of the Interior, Romanones Minister of Justice, Cambó Minister of Public Works and Santiago Alba Minister of Education. The public reaction was ecstatic, as if Spain had been saved and a new era inaugurated. Maura on the other hand was bitterly pessimistic. He wrote to his son: 'They kept me tied up there for nearly ten years which could have been the most profitable of my life, stopping me from doing anything useful, and now they want me to preside over all of them. Let's see how long this nonsense lasts.'[55]

Cambó defended his participation in the government in the Cortes on 17 April by claiming that it was necessary to avert anarchy.[56] Alarmed by the sight of revolutionary workers in the streets, the industrialists dropped their own demands for political reform and, lured by Maura's promises of economic modernization, permitted their leaders to support his administration. Yet again the industrial bourgeoisie had abandoned its political aspirations and allied with the landed oligarchy out of a fear of revolution. The coalition symbolized the slightly improved position of industrialists in a reactionary alliance still dominated by the landed interest.

In the event, despite apparently being a team of all the talents and making a highly promising and conciliatory start, the coalition was short-lived. With La Cierva absent, the strike of the communications workers was swiftly resolved. His military reform bill was revised and amnesty was granted for the events of August 1917. Nevertheless, there was considerable distrust within the government, especially between Dato and Maura and, most damagingly, between Alba and Cambó, who was trying both to further Catalan autonomy and to revitalize the Spanish economy. A crisis was provoked by the intensification of German attacks on Spanish shipping. The government issued an ultimatum to Berlin, but internal divisions were exacerbated by the Germanophile King's refusal to permit further action. In addition, the growing hostility between Alba and Cambó saw Maura's government collapse on 6 November 1918, five days before the armistice that brought the Great War to an end. Replaced by Romanones, an embittered Maura seemed to have reached the conclusion that the only solution was a military dictatorship. In fact, the fall of the second national government put an end to any remaining chance of effective reform of the system from above.[57]

Alfonso XIII with the coalition government formed by Antonio Maura on 21 March 1918 in response to his threat to abdicate.

5

A System in Disarray: Disorder and Repression, 1918–1921

The coming of peace in November 1918 brought an intensification of Spain's political crisis. The huge profits made in mines, steel production and textiles had not, in the main, been invested in new technology. Indeed, widespread publicity given to spending by the nouveaux riches on luxury items, at a time of food shortages, had intensified working-class resentment of what was seen as a parasitic plutocracy. The return to peacetime production of British, French and American industry plunged the Spanish economy into crisis.[1] Thus, while military brutality had permitted the discredited political system to survive the crisis of 1917, mass hunger and unemployment after the end of the war would intensify the pressure on the establishment. Already in 1918, there were strikes, bread riots and looting of shops. Nevertheless, the repression of the August 1917 strike had damaged the relationship between the Socialists and the anarchists and also divided both movements internally. The PSOE, too traumatized by the events of August 1917 to pursue further revolutionary action with the CNT, sought, instead, an electoral strategy in collaboration with the Republicans. This provoked a reaction from more militant elements that would eventually secede to form the Communist Party. While the Socialist leaders were worried by the success of the Bolsheviks in Russia, hard-line anarchists were thrilled. Oblivious to the authoritarian elements of Leninism, they believed that the events in Russia heralded the coming of a worldwide anarchist utopia. However, the more thoughtful syndicalists like Ángel Pestaña and Salvador Seguí would have been prepared to countenance joint strike action with the UGT.[2]

In the immediate aftermath of 1917, while UGT membership stagnated, the CNT grew substantially. One reason for this was the greater militancy of the anarcho-syndicalists. This had hitherto been rendered ineffective because the Catalan working class was dispersed into myriad small federations across individual trades and neighbourhoods. In 1917, there were 475 federations in Barcelona alone. The difficulty of arranging collective action played into the hands of the employers. The situation changed when the congress of the Catalan CNT, the Confederació Regional del Treball, held at Sants from 28 June to 1 July 1918, adopted a much more effective strategy. This was the creation of the so-called Sindicatos Únicos (united unions), in order to gather all the workers in each industry into a single body. It was further decided that all the Sindicatos Únicos in a given area would be grouped together in a local federation. Moreover, to prevent the growth of bureaucracy, union dues were abolished and paid administrative posts reduced to a bare minimum. With the help of some violent coercion of reluctant workers, the 475 small, weak unions in Barcelona were reduced to thirteen powerful ones. Henceforth, there would be fewer but much longer strikes, many of them initially successful. The Sindicato Único provided a channel for the resentments of the thousands of immigrant labourers who had arrived during the war years and were crammed into unhygienic tenements and paid starvation wages. The new union structure effectively imposed the militancy of the majority of these unskilled workers on the labour aristocracy and ensured that trade disputes quickly escalated. The brainchild of Seguí and Pestaña, the Sindicatos Únicos were adopted by the CNT nationally. By the end of 1918, the CNT had 70,000 members in Catalonia and 114,000 nationally. Within a year, this had swelled to 800,000.[3]

However, helped by the divisions within the working class and reinforced by the collaboration of the Lliga, the *turno* system was not quite dead yet. After the fall of the second national government, Alfonso XIII appointed a Liberal government under Manuel García Prieto, the Marqués de Alhucemas. It would be merely the first of ten brief administrations between November 1918 and September 1923, some of which would last for only a matter of weeks. La Cierva's presence was divisive but necessary to keep the army in check, albeit at a high price. By accepting the Juntas as an army trade union, La Cierva was effectively tolerating indiscipline and demands which were a step towards military dictatorship. Riddled with factionalism, incapable of agreeing on a common agenda, one government after another failed to resolve ever-intensifying problems.[4]

The cracks in the Restoration system were worsened by the machinations of the King. Concerned by the fall of other European monarchies
and fearing that his own downfall might be precipitated by the outbreak
of revolution in Barcelona, on 15 November Alfonso XIII tried to secure
the loyalty of Cambó. He told him that he saw Catalan autonomy as the
only certain way to divert the revolutionary threat. Cambó made the
mistake of falling for what was simply a cynical ploy and went ahead
with a project for autonomy. Although received sympathetically by
Romanones, who had formed a new government on 10 December 1918,
it was rejected violently in the Cortes by both the Liberals and Maura.
Niceto Alcalá-Zamora scored a direct hit when he pointed out the
contradiction between Cambó's two ambitions, autonomy for Catalonia
and hegemony of the Spanish state. He said: 'the problem with Cambó is
that he wants to be at the same time the Bolívar of Catalonia and the
Bismarck of Spain' – a phrase later accepted as true by Cambó himself.
The defeat of his aspirations for Catalonia deeply embittered Cambó and
led to the Catalan deputies withdrawing from the Cortes for six weeks.
Cambó himself was moved to break with Alfonso XIII. On 16 December,
he made a speech in Barcelona under the title 'Monarquia? República?
Catalunya!' in which he declared that the Lliga, while not expecting a
republic to bring about autonomy, would not abandon campaigning for
autonomy out of any concern that it might bring about the fall of the
monarchy.[5]

In 1919, the Liberal senator Amós Salvador, without naming him,
compared Alfonso XIII to a naughty child: 'Dealing with kings is like
dealing with children. One is inclined to let them do whatever they want
despite being convinced that there is no better way to do them the most
damage.'[6] In his memoirs, the Conservative Manuel Burgos y Mazo
wrote: 'After 1919, I promised myself that I would not serve again as a
minister for a disloyal King who could never be trusted by any one of his
advisers.'[7] Cambó had a similar perception, believing that the King was
behind the creation of the virulently anti-Catalan Unión Monárquica
Nacional, a group that would eventually play a key role in the conspiracy
to overthrow the Second Republic. Essentially, Alfonso XIII's meddling
would contribute to the definitive break between conservative
Catalanism and the monarchy.[8]

Despite these fissures and the aspirations of the coalition governments, at the end of the First World War Spain was still broadly divided

into two mutually hostile social groups, with landowners and industrialists on one side and workers and landless labourers on the other. Only one numerous social group was not definitively aligned within this broad cleavage – the smallholding peasantry. Significantly, in the course of the second decade of the century, the Catholic farmers of Old Castile were mobilized in defence of big landholding interests. As left-wing ideologies captured the urban working classes, the more far-sighted landowners realized that efforts had to be made to prevent the poison spreading to the countryside. Counter-revolutionary agrarian syndicates sponsored by landlords had begun to appear from 1906. The process was systematized by Ángel Herrera, the *éminence grise* of political Catholicism in Spain, and founder in 1909 of the Asociación Católica Nacional de Propagandistas (ACNP), a group of dynamic, high-flying Catholics in the professions. From 1912, Herrera and the Palencian landowner Antonio Monedero Martín set out to divert the smallholders away from socialism and anarchism by the implementation of the Christian-social encyclicals of Pope Leo XIII. In the next five years, through the efforts of the determined activists of the ACNP, a series of Catholic Agrarian Federations appeared in León, Salamanca and Castile and tried to prevent impoverished farmers turning to the left by offering them credit facilities, agronomic expertise, warehousing and machinery. Access to such assistance was made explicitly dependent on adherence to a militantly conservative Catholicism. Taken to its logical extremes, the rhetoric of the federations implied a challenge to the economic interests of big landowners. Only in the more prosperous north was it possible to maintain an uneasy balance between the mitigation of poverty and defence of the socio-economic status quo. By 1917, the various local federations were united as the Confederación Nacional Católico-Agraria (CNCA), but their implantation was intermittent outside the provinces of León and Old Castile. This was understandable since, in the south, the only palliative that landowners could offer the *braceros*, possession of the land, involved an unacceptable transfer of wealth.[9] The credibility, in the eyes of hungry labourers, of rich landowners arriving in limousines to establish a 'union', was necessarily minimal.[10]

The CNCA would almost certainly have remained confined to the smallholding areas of central and northern Spain had it not been for the massive upsurge in the revolutionary militancy of the rural proletariat of the south after 1917. Social tensions had been intensifying since the *desamortización*. Both the more ruthless exploitation of church and aristocratic lands by their new owners and the enclosure of the common lands had put an end to many practices that had eased rural hardship. The economic model of southern *latifundismo* was the exploitation of the labour of the landless rural proletariat.[11] For the majority, work was available only at harvest time and involved long hours of backbreaking labour often from sun-up to sun-down on starvation wages. The situation was dramatically worsened during the First World War. While landowners were enriched by the massive export of agricultural produce, the day labourers were impoverished by the inability of wages to keep pace with rocketing food prices.[12]

The consequence was a wave of strikes, land occupations and bread riots across Andalusia, especially in Cordoba, Jaén, Malaga and Seville, between 1918 and 1920. The period was termed the 'three Bolshevik years' by the great chronicler of the events, Juan Díaz del Moral, the liberal notary from Bujalance in Cordoba. The initial objectives were wage increases and better working conditions, although, inspired by the Russian revolution, some militant leaders saw the possibility of 'a red dawn'.[13] Even though the intentions of the majority of the strikers were considerably more reformist than revolutionary, the peasant agitations were seen by the big landowners as equivalent to the Russian revolution. Fear of insurrection provoked cursory interest in the CNCA from some *latifundistas*. That was hardly surprising since, as an acute observer of the revolutionary agitation of the spring of 1919, the distinguished agronomist Pascual Carrión, noted, 'we cannot forget the extension and intensity of the workers' movement; the strike in Cordoba, among others, was truly general and impressive, managing to frighten the landowners to such a degree that they were ready to hand over their estates'.[14]

From early 1919 until late 1920, the CNCA had received financial support each month from Alfonso XIII himself. As the class conflict intensified, however, he switched his support to the more aggressive landowners' organization, the Liga de Terratenientes Andaluces. There was a vain hope that this organization would collect money to combat 'the red wave', but during the *trienio bolchevista* it resorted to more violent measures. Throughout Andalusia, the sons of landowners formed cavalry units to support the Civil Guard in clashes with the workers.[15] In Andalusia, as in Catalonia, the King had little interest in promoting social cohesion, just like the majority of the *latifundistas*, whose

intransigent response to the strikes intensified the social resentments of
the rural south. The consequences of the *trienio bolchevista* would be
masked by the imposition of a military dictatorship between 1923 and
1930. Nevertheless, the conflicts of 1919–21 ended the previous uneasy
modus vivendi of the agrarian south. The repression intensified the
hatred of the *braceros* for the big landowners and their estate managers.
What remained of those elements of paternalism that mitigated the daily
brutality of the *braceros'* lives came to an abrupt end.

The CNCA began an extensive propaganda campaign in Andalusia in
January 1919, denouncing the blind egoism of the landowners, who were
'Catholics who boasted about their charity but then paid lower wages
and exacted higher rents than they would ever dare admit to their
confessor'. Teams of CNCA representatives toured the southern provinces and were egged on by the ACNP newspaper, *El Correo de Andalucía*,
which declared: 'Anarchy is spreading amongst those below and is being
fomented by the apathy of those above. We live in serious times; either
Andalusia will be saved now if she follows you or will die for ever in the
clutches of hatred and revolution … If the landowners of Andalusia
follow you, they will be saved; if they repudiate you, they will be drowned
in their own blood.' In the first months of the year, the CNCA campaign
was extremely successful with the owners, but the orators sent to workers' centres were booed off the stage. In their panic, a few *latifundistas*
put up money and made available small plots of wasteland for settlement
by suitably deferential labourers. However, the majority of landowners
were not prepared to make substantial concessions and preferred to
paralyse strikers with the unrestrained violence of their estate guards
(*guardas jurados*) backed by the Civil Guard. In some towns such as
Puente Genil, the local bourgeoisie created a well-armed militia to assist
the Civil Guard in clashes with strikers, a pre-echo of what would happen
in many Andalusian towns in the summer and autumn of 1936. Some
landowners abandoned their estates and fled to Madrid, while those who
stayed bought stocks of weaponry for themselves and their retainers. The
CNCA continued to preach the gospel of class collaboration, but its real
position was starkly exposed as conflict grew more acute.[16]

On 18 April 1919, Antonio Monedero Martín was made Director
General of Agriculture and his appointment was greeted by *El Socialista*
with the headline 'Scabs in power'. There was little proletarian faith in the
CNCA's declared ambition of creating a class of smallholding peasants.

Monedero soon confirmed the Socialist view that he was the puppet of the landowners when he called for the closure of working-class organizations and for the deportation or imprisonment of strike leaders. In mid-April, the government of Antonio Maura intensified the repression by suspending constitutional guarantees, declaring martial law in Cordoba and sending in cavalry units to reinforce the Civil Guard. The Africanista General Manuel de la Barrera was put in command of the 20,000 troops sent against the landless labourers. He declared that 'the Andalusian problem will not be solved without a cruel and energetic persecution of the propagandists who organise the masses'.[17] There were more than 2,000 arrests. The leaders of all unions, except Antonio Monedero's Catholic unions, were detained. Republican and Socialist leaders who had had nothing to do with the strike were deported from the province specifically to disrupt their campaigns for the April 1919 elections. With the area under virtual military occupation and the owners free to intimidate strikers, the revolutionary movement was gradually brought under control.[18] However, the repression of 1919–20 and the dictatorship of Primo de Rivera between 1923 and 1930 did nothing but douse an agitation which continued to smoulder until the Second Republic revived the spectre of land reform.

Indeed, Pascual Carrión noted that the landowners' instinctive intransigence and ready resort to repressive violence during the *trienio bolchevista* ensured that peasant rebellion was unlikely to end soon:

Nobody who knows the history of those movements could possibly think that, after that period, the *caciques* and the landowners would not recover their previous domination. The weight of the government repression, the deportations and reprisals carried out by a well-known general [Manuel de la Barrera] sent by the government in May 1919 to Andalusia, put an end to the proletarian movement. Instead of channelling that movement, it was crushed with cruelty as so often before and, for that reason, it is not surprising that hatred of the *latifundistas* was fomented among the humble classes and that now [in 1932] there is a resurgence of agitation and revolts with greater violence than ever.[19]

While the Spanish countryside seethed with conflict, the failures of the two national governments in 1918 were exacerbated by the social crisis in industrial cities that followed the end of the First World War. The

Basque iron and steel industry was hit by the dumping of the wartime surpluses accumulated in Britain and the United States. The shipping industry, which relied on transporting ore to Britain, was hit by the post-war slump in the British steel industry. During the war, Asturian mines and the Catalan textile industry had expanded but profits had not been ploughed back into achieving greater efficiency. Everywhere in industry and agriculture, the end of the war saw wages reduced and workers laid off.[20] Working-class militancy increased and was met by military intervention. The Spanish state faced similar challenges to those confronting the defeated belligerent nations of Europe. In Madrid, there were strikes and food riots during which trams were set alight. According to significantly understated official figures, the number of strikes mushroomed from 71,440 in 1917 to 244,684 in 1920, while the number of working days lost in those strikes increased from 1.75 million to 7.25 million.[21] Already terrified by the Russian revolution and the collapse of the German and Austro-Hungarian monarchies, the Spanish ruling classes were further alarmed by the foundation in Moscow of the Communist International (Comintern) in March 1919. Although defeat in 1917 had traumatized the Socialist leadership, it had not marked the end of the assault on the system. Between late 1918 and the beginning of 1921, industrial workers in northern Spain followed the example of the anarchist day labourers of the south. Industrialists responded to economic recession by limiting production, cutting wages and laying off large numbers of workers. This inevitably provoked greater worker militancy, to which industrialists in Catalonia and landowners in the south reacted by turning to the army.

In Catalonia in 1919, determined to crush the CNT, intransigent industrialists were backed by the hard-line Captain General of the IV Región Militar, Lieutenant General Joaquín Milans del Bosch y Carrió. He in turn enjoyed the support of the Juntas Militares de Defensa. Conflict intensified after a strike broke out on 8 February at the Anglo-Canadian-owned Barcelona Traction, Light and Power Company or Riegos y Fuerzas del Ebro, known as La Canadiense. It began in protest at the arbitrary dismissal of eight administrative staff for trying to unionize. It mushroomed as successively the sacked men's department, then the entire factory and finally, in a show of power by the Sindicato Único of Gas, Water and Electricity, all the power workers in Catalonia went on strike. By 21 February, three-quarters of Catalan industry had been forced to close down for lack of power. Trams were stalled in the streets, and cafés and theatres had to close. Milans del Bosch, himself an upper-class Catalan with connections to the industrialists, called for a declaration of martial law. The government of Romanones hesitantly agreed on 1 March. Workers were conscripted, a measure that exposed strikers to the threat of four years' imprisonment for mutiny. Despite the arrest of 3,000 workers, the strike did not fold. Romanones appointed a distinguished criminal lawyer, Gerardo Doval, as chief of police. He also named a conciliatory Civil Governor, Carlos Montañés, and sent the Under-Secretary of the cabinet office, José Morote, to negotiate with the strikers. Helped by the moderation of Seguí, these mediation initiatives led to the Canadiense agreeing in mid-March to rehire the workers and raise wages. At a mass meeting of nearly 30,000 initially hostile workers on 19 March, Seguí's oratory secured agreement for a return to work conditional on the release of prisoners. However, it was to be only a brief truce. Within five days, the city was again paralysed.[22]

Interestingly, in 1919, Lerroux had been placed on the payroll of the Canadiense (in addition to his many other income streams), in the hope that his rabble-rousing skills might help break the strike by undermining working-class solidarity. The company continued to pay him a monthly stipend for at least a further decade and half. In 1934, when he was Prime Minister, he was asked by the London offices of the Canadiense to try to reduce the company's fiscal obligations. It is not known what action he took.[23] Although the strike in the spring of 1919 had not been violent, the employers, shaken by the CNT's ability to shut down Barcelona, were determined to destroy the union. Moreover, Milans and the Juntas were infuriated by the readiness of Romanones to work for a peaceful solution. Even before the Canadiense strike, confident of the support of the army, the industrialists were becoming more militant. In February 1919, the recently formed Unión Monárquica Nacional had called for action against both strikers and Catalanists. Fearful of losing its conservative support, the Lliga-dominated employers' organization, the Foment Nacional del Treball, toned down its Catalanist aspirations and threw its support behind the coalition of the army and industrialists determined to destroy the Catalan section of the CNT, the Confederación Regional de Trabajo (CRT). The principal function of the industrialists' organization, the Federació Patronal de Catalunya, under its belligerent president Félix Graupera, was simply to combat the Sindicatos Únicos. To this end, it emulated the structure and tactics of the Sindicatos Únicos. Against the general strike would be deployed the general lock-out. The Catalan Federation belonged to the nationwide Confederación Patronal Española presided over by the equally militant Francisco Junoy. In Barcelona, as in Bilbao, Madrid and Valencia, the most hard-line members of the Confederación Patronal Española were owners of small and medium businesses in the metallurgical, building and woodworking industries who were badly hit by the post-war economic crisis and the rise in labour militancy.[24]

With the enthusiastic support of industrialists and businessmen, Milans del Bosch was already going onto a war footing against the CNT. On 22 March, he authorized a citizens' militia, the Somatén. Originally created in medieval times to repel Muslim raids, its name refers to the bells rung to summon the militia, *so emetent*, literally 'emitting sound' – that is, sounding the alarm. In fact, the revival of the Somatén had been long in preparation as a Guardia Cívica. However, now that it was armed by Milans del Bosch, this 8,000-strong auxiliary military force seriously worried Romanones, but he did not subject the Somatén to civilian authority. On 25 March, Milans decreed that anyone not a member of the Somatén caught carrying arms would be considered guilty of military rebellion.[25] The Somatén ran public transport and patrolled the streets, arresting and mistreating strikers and obliging shops and cafés to remain open. Milans also approved the use of a parallel police force financed by the Federació Patronal de Catalunya and led by the recently released Manuel Bravo Portillo. This gang of well-paid gunmen and cut-throats recruited in the underworld carried out assaults on trade union leaders that ranged from beatings to murder. To facilitate these activities, military funds financed the compilation of a huge card index of prominent CNTistas, the so-called Fichero Lasarte, compiled by a Civil Guard, Captain Julio de Lasarte Persino, who had worked with Baron de Koenig. With the encouragement of the recently appointed Military Governor, General Severiano Martínez Anido, Lasarte's often fabricated information was used to facilitate arrests and occasionally murders.[26]

Neither Milans del Bosch nor the Federació Patronal was interested in conciliation. When Milans refused to release prisoners, undermining the agreement for the return to work, the CNT was provoked into declaring a disastrous general strike on 24 March. With the loud support of the Barcelona garrison, martial law was reimposed, CNT offices were shut down and hundreds of union leaders, including Pestaña, arrested. The assault on the CNT was led by Martínez Anido, a brutal Africanista and a favourite of Alfonso XIII, who had been appointed Military Governor in February. The moderate syndicalists and the Romanones appointees, Montañés and Doval, were outflanked by the military. Milans was furious when Doval called on him to break up Bravo Portillo's gang. He sent the intimidating Martínez Anido and Colonel Julio Aldir of the Civil Guard to threaten Montañés and Doval that they would be imprisoned if they did not leave Barcelona immediately. With the strike effectively broken, it took the oratory of Seguí to persuade another mass meeting that a return to work was the only way to avoid further disaster. Unsurprisingly, the principal military newspaper denied, in rather vague language, that the Barcelona garrison had had anything to do with the expulsion of Montañés and Doval.[27]

The treatment of Montañés and Doval demonstrated the impotence of civilian rule. It provoked the fall of Romanones' cabinet and opened up a major political crisis in which a key role was played by Alfonso XIII.[28] Romanones asked the King to dismiss Milans, but Alfonso refused to accept the General's token resignation. In the light of the King's unreserved support for Milans, Romanones had no choice but to resign.[29] Alfonso's identification with the most reactionary elements of the army and the Church would consistently undermine any government attempts at conciliatory social policy. Indeed, the King was flirting ever more keenly with the idea of a military dictatorship. He chose to replace Romanones with a reluctant Maura on 15 April. It would be a temporary solution since Maura no longer represented the dominant sector of the Conservative Party, which was now led by Eduardo Dato. The shift in power within the party derived from disquiet at the methods of Juan de la Cierva and his links with the Juntas de Defensa. Dato and others inclined to a policy of negotiation with the moderate trade unionists. Suffering ill health, Dato had favoured a government under his ally, the moderate Conservative Joaquín Sánchez de Toca. However, the King granted Maura the dissolution decree. Despite his reputation as an opponent of electoral corruption, to secure success in the elections of 1 June 1919 Maura opted to exploit the worst kind of *caciquismo*. It was to no avail. Opposed by much of his own Conservative Party, he failed to win an overall majority. Moreover, his reputation was shattered and he resigned on 20 July.[30]

Under Maura and persisting after his fall, despite the defeat of the CNT's 'general strike', the dirty war against the organization continued in Catalonia. At the behest of Milans del Bosch, the Bravo Portillo gang maintained its offensive against trade unionists, eliminating moderates in order to disrupt industrial negotiations. Among those murdered had been Pau Sabater ('El Tero'), a distinguished leader of the textile Sindicato Único, whose bullet-riddled body was found on 20 July. Inevitably, there was a desire for reprisals. Moreover, the scale of the repression undermined the credibility of the moderate trade unionists among their own affiliates. And, as the economic repression bit harder and more workers were laid off, there were more men ready to take a small salary to become gunmen.[31] When Bravo Portillo was assassinated on 5 September, his gang would be taken over by the sinister Prussian Friedrich Stallman who, it will be recalled, went by the fake title of Baron de Koenig. He was described by the conservative politician Francisco Bastos Ansart as 'a prince of rogues'. Koenig was subsidized by the French secret service as well as by the bosses who paid him to murder trade union leaders. In turn, he also blackmailed the industrialists with a protection racket and was finally expelled from Spain in May 1920.[32]

To the delight of industrialists and landowners, in the twelve weeks that Maura was in government, aided by Antonio Goicoechea, his hard-line Minister of the Interior, he had responded with brutal force to social tension in Catalonia and the south. Constitutional guarantees were suspended and union leaders were imprisoned. As has been seen, he had sent General de la Barrera to Andalusia to smash the rebellion of the agricultural labourers. When Dato once more suggested as Maura's successor the moderate Joaquín Sánchez de Toca, Alfonso XIII resisted, pushing for Maura, even threatening to appoint the relatively left-wing Melquíades Álvarez. Eventually, Dato was able to secure the appointment he wanted. An enlightened team consisting of Sánchez de Toca, his Minister of the Interior, the devout social Catholic Manuel Burgos y Mazo, and a new Civil Governor of Barcelona, Julio Amado, adopted a conciliatory line towards the unions. According to Burgos y Mazo, there were 43,000 syndicalists in prison. Believing that repression could only encourage the extremist wing of the CNT, the government was inclined to recognize the unions as the legitimate representatives of the workers in dialogue with the industrialists. To this end, prisoners were released, martial law lifted and the eight-hour day introduced. The intelligent application of conciliation resolved strikes in Valencia and Malaga and saw a significant reduction in the number of assassinations in Barcelona. In return, Seguí, Manuel Buenacasa and other moderate syndicalists issued a manifesto declaring that if the CNT was legalized, strikes would be peaceful. They denounced state violence as the cause of left-wing terrorism.[33]

This coincided with a devastating speech in the Cortes by the thirty-nine-year-old republican deputy for Sabadell, Francesc Layret. The bearded Layret was severely disabled as a result of contracting polio at the age of two and needed iron leg braces and two sticks to walk.[34] A close friend of Seguí, Layret was a brilliant lawyer and frequently defended syndicalists in court. In his speech on 7 August 1919, Layret denounced the dictatorial role in Barcelona of Milans and the Juntas de Defensa. He revealed the threats made by Martínez Anido and Colonel Aldir to Gerardo Doval and Carlos Montañés and explained how the expulsion of both had precipitated the fall of Romanones. He went on to accuse Romanones of cowardice for resigning rather than sacking Milans del Bosch. Layret may have thereby signed his own death warrant. At the time, the response of Burgos y Mazo, far from attacking Layret, was to confirm his own conciliatory approach.[35]

The efforts of Sánchez de Toca, Burgos y Mazo and the Civil Governor of Barcelona, Julio Amado, to reach agreement with the unions were not at all what was wanted by La Cierva, the alarmed industrialists or the army. At the second congress of the Confederación Patronal Española, held in Barcelona in the last week of October 1919, it was decided to institute a lock-out of industrial workers (public services and the food sector were excluded) in order to starve the workers into leaving the CNT or provoke them into a reaction that would justify military intervention. The lock-out lasted until January 1920, left over 200,000 men out of work and intensified class hatred.[36] The credibility of the moderates in the CNT was undermined and workers increasingly placed their faith in the so-called *grupos de afinidad*, tightly knit action groups. Led by hard-liners such as Buenaventura Durruti, Juan García Oliver, Francisco Ascaso and Ricardo Sanz, groups such as 'Los Solidarios' and 'Nosotros' would eventually coalesce into the Federación Anarquista Ibérica.[37] At the same time as extremism flourished on the left, the provocations of the industrialists were matched by the activities of the Juntas. When a number of captains taking a course at the staff college (Escuela

Superior de Guerra) refused to join the Juntas de Defensa, they were subjected to an honour court and eventually expelled from the college, with the support of the Minister of War.[38]

This led to the fall of Sánchez de Toca's government on 9 December 1919. He was replaced by another Conservative follower of Maura, Manuel Allendesalazar, who was close to La Cierva. He appointed as Civil Governor of Barcelona the dour Francisco Maestre Laborde-Bois, Conde de Salvatierra, who had earned a reputation as a brutal Civil Governor of Seville. The outgoing Civil Governor, Julio Amado, bumped into Seguí and other CNT moderates who were returning from a congress in Madrid. 'Be very careful,' he warned them, 'those gentlemen want blood and I wasn't willing to spill it.'[39] With the industrialists' lock-out still in force, Salvatierra's repressive policies saw an intensification of street violence. Debilitated by the lock-out and the months without pay, their families and they themselves hungry, unable to pay their rent, the anarcho-syndicalists were weary. This situation discredited the moderate union leaders and ensured the rise of the action groups. The most determined of their leaders was Ramon Archs i Serra, Secretary of the metal-workers' union. On 4 January 1920, there was a failed assassination attempt on Salvador Seguí. On the following day, the President of the Federació Patronal, Félix Graupera, was wounded. The Conde de Salvatierra had over a hundred union leaders arrested and closed a large number of workers' centres and the syndicalists' newspaper *Solidaridad Obrera*. On 23 January, Salvatierra decreed the closing of all CRT–CNT unions. Without consulting the government, Milans del Bosch backed him by establishing martial law. He then demanded that the Somatén be given full military authority. A reluctant Allendesalazar agreed under pressure from garrisons from all over Spain as well as from the Somatén.[40]

In February, the publication of correspondence revealing his nefarious activities in previous years saw the dismissal of Milans del Bosch. There were rumours that he was preparing a coup, but he had insufficient ambition. Significantly, he was 'rewarded' by the King with the highly prestigious post of head of the royal household. He was replaced briefly as Captain General of Catalonia by the eighty-two-year-old hard-liner General Valeriano Weyler.[41]

Eduardo Dato took power on 5 May 1920 and Koenig was expelled from Spain. After the repressive interval of Allendesalazar, Dato returned to the moderate policies of Sánchez de Toca. He appointed the moderate

Francisco Bergamín as Minister of the Interior and the equally reasonable Federico Carlos Bas as Civil Governor of Barcelona. Bas noted that the majority of assassination attempts were directed against workers. In consequence, he was convinced that it was the vindictive approach of the Federació Patronal that kept terrorism alive. He began to release prisoners and lifted press censorship. The industrialists' opposition ensured that he was in post for barely six months. Thus Dato's moderation was to little or no avail. On 4 August, the Conde de Salvatierra, the ex-Civil Governor of Barcelona, was murdered in Valencia while returning from the port in a horse-drawn carriage.[42] Dato was forced to replace Bergamín with the hard-line Conde Gabino Bugallal. Tension was rising in Barcelona where a major strike in the metallurgical industries broke out in mid-October. Just as Seguí was bringing the strike to an end, virtually on the employers' terms, on 31 October, Jaume Pujol, the President of the federation of the employers in the electricity sector, was murdered.

Bas, who was negotiating with Seguí, was visited by the Military Governor, General Severiano Martínez Anido. In an intemperate confrontation, Martínez Anido declared that all social violence in Barcelona was the work of anarchists in the pay of Russia. He presented Bas with a list of seventy-eight anarchists, including Seguí and Pestaña, whom he demanded be shot immediately. Bas responded, 'I am neither an executioner nor a despot,' and presented his resignation to Bugallal. On 8 November 1920, Bas was replaced as Civil Governor by Martínez Anido, who was told by Dato: 'act as you see fit; the Government will put no obstacles in your way'. When Seguí learned of the appointment, he declared, 'they are going to massacre us'. Echoing the words of his predecessor Julio Amado, Bas asserted on leaving Barcelona, 'They are throwing me out because I am not prepared to be a murdering governor.'[43]

The entire operation to get rid of Bas had been choreographed by a group of businessmen and army officers including Martínez Anido himself, the chief of police, Colonel Miguel Arlegui Bayonés of the Civil Guard, and Captain Lasarte. Now Civil Governor, Martínez Anido was incensed by a revealing article by Andreu Nin, an up-and-coming figure in the CNT, who had written: 'Now we have a murderer as governor; the bosses can be pleased.'[44]

Despite the brief triumph of the Canadiense strike, already by the beginning of 1920 things were going badly for CNT. In addition to the various offensives being undertaken by the industrialists, the post-war economy was contracting. Wildcat strikes were hardly the best tactic to prevent lay-offs and wage-cuts. The employers' lock-out had left 200,000 men without work. Matters were made even worse by the promotion of the vicious Martínez Anido to Civil Governor of Barcelona. Now in overall charge of public order and in a position to wage war on the CNT, Martínez Anido, assisted by Miguel Arlegui, instituted a regime of terror. The tall Arlegui, beneath whose aquiline nose grew a small moustache, was even more sadistic than Martínez Anido. He enjoyed torturing prisoners. The upper and middle classes of Barcelona were ecstatic about the pair's appointment. On the basis of Lasarte's card index, sixty-four trade unionists and liberals, including Pestaña, Seguí and his friend the journalist Lluís Companys, were identified and arrested. Thirty-six were sent to the prison of La Mola in Mahon, Menorca. Martínez Anido had the gall to suggest that it was for their safety. In Barcelona, prisons were overflowing with a further 1,000 less prominent militants and many had to be confined on ships in the port. There was an increase in street shootings that could not be blamed on the anarchists since most of the likely suspects were in prison. Hundreds of CNT members were deported to distant Spanish provinces, forced to make the long journeys in chains, shod only in rope sandals. They were then left without sustenance to survive as best they could but obliged to report every day to the local Civil Guard post. Two hundred militants fled Barcelona and joined the Spanish Foreign Legion to fight in Morocco. Gunmen from the recently created scab organization the Sindicatos Libres were trained in military barracks.[45]

Shortly after midnight on 12 September 1920, a bomb exploded in a packed workmen's music hall, the Cabaret Pompeya in the Paralelo, killing six workers and seriously injuring eighteen more, including many moderates who opposed violence. The CNT, believing that the bomb was the work of assassins in the pay of the employers' association, declared its readiness to help in bringing the culprits to justice. Nevertheless, the police began to round up members of the Sindicato Único. Nearly 150,000 workers attended the funeral of those killed. It was eventually revealed that the perpetrator was Inocencio Feced Calvo, a diminutive and sickly ex-anarchist from Teruel who had tuberculosis. During the lock-out, in desperate need of money to buy medicine, he had agreed to become an informer. Thereafter, he had been blackmailed into becoming an agent provocateur by the threat of being exposed to his comrades.[46]

Arlegui implemented the so-called *ley de fugas* (the shooting in the back of prisoners forced to run but, allegedly, 'trying to escape'). This tactic enjoyed considerable approval within the army high command. General Miguel Primo de Rivera, at the time Captain General of Valencia, wrote to Eduardo Dato on 21 January 1921: 'Social disturbers should be rounded up, then, on their way to prison, a few bullets and the problem is solved. There is no other way to deal with this matter since ordinary justice and legislation are ineffective ...'[47] The principal targets of the gunmen seemed to be the more moderate elements of the CRT. On 17 November, for instance, José Canela, a close friend of Seguí, was assassinated. In the three weeks after Martínez Anido took over, there were twenty-two deaths on both sides. On 30 November, the republican parliamentary deputy Francesc Layret was murdered on his way to request the release of Companys. A huge multitude followed the funeral cortège of Layret.[48] It was Feced who later revealed that the assassination had been organized by Martínez Anido and Arlegui in conjunction with the leaders of the Sindicatos Libres, Ramón Sales Amenós and Juan Laguía Lliteras. The three gunmen were paid by the industrialist Maties Muntadas, who had previously financed the activities of Bravo Portillo.[49] Muntadas was not the only source of finance for Martínez Anido's murky activities. Luis Silvela, who held several ministerial posts under Alfonso XIII, including a brief stint as Minister of the Interior in late 1918, alleged that bribes from the owners of illegal gambling dens were used by Martínez Anido to pay *pistoleros*.[50]

The Basque novelist Pío Baroja composed a savage portrait of Martínez Anido: 'General don Severiano, short, stunted, red-faced, with the gloomy air of the true executioner, presented a disturbing image: he had a large head, his hair close cropped, short arms, square hands. Clumsy of speech, with misty eyes, he augured nothing good. He was the bulldog of the monarchy.' Pío Baroja alleged that Martínez Anido, 'a satyr like an orangutan', sexually abused the wives, daughters and sisters of prisoners who came to plead for their release. Once he had had his pleasure, he was as likely to order the execution as the release of the prisoners. It was also suggested that he was corrupt and used his power for 'dirty dealings'.[51]

As for Arlegui, Baroja was even more scathing, describing him as 'uncouth, clumsy, conceited: the typical Civil Guard sergeant raised up to an important post. He was a braggart always boasting about male virility. Deep down he was a cowardly chicken. Don Severiano is rather more interesting. Arlegui was gloomy, jumpy, neurotic, with stomach, heart and nerve problems.' On 19 January 1921, an action group led by Ramon Archs and Pere Vandellós shot Antonio Espejo, one of Arlegui's men who had been a member of the Bravo Portillo and Koenig gangs. Arlegui ordered reprisals. He then went to the mortuary where Espejo's body lay surrounded by a dozen or more of the anarchists shot on his orders. Hysterical, Arlegui addressed the corpse: 'Espejo, you cannot complain about me. There they are; they are the flowers with which I decorate your body.' His evil temper was perhaps linked to the pain from his stomach ulcers which caused him frequently to vomit blood.[52]

One of the most effective weapons at the disposal of Martínez Anido was the scab union, the Sindicatos Libres. With the CNT effectively paralysed by the repression orchestrated by the Civil Governor, many workers joined the Sindicatos Libres which, for seven years, would be the second largest union in Catalonia despite its poor labour record.[53] The Libres were secretly financed by a group of industrial magnates led by one of the richest men in Spain, Claudio López Bru, Marqués de Comillas. Previously, helped by advice from the Papal Nuncio, Comillas had also financed Catholic mineworkers' unions in Asturias and railway workers' unions in Valladolid, both of which had acted as strike breakers in 1917. He had also sponsored the so-called Uniones Profesionales which consisted largely of his employees, mainly shop assistants, never went on strike and were controlled by non-worker, often clerical, elements. Just as they were withering away, there was a revival of Carlism in Barcelona in reaction to the populist anti-clerical demagoguery of Lerroux's Radicals. Founded in October 1919, the Sindicatos Libres played the role of a scab union of paid thugs acting as terrorist strike breakers for both the Civil Governor and the patronal organizations. Martínez Anido called on the Libres to shoot ten anarchists for every one of their own killed.[54] In the course of 1921, casualties among the bosses were four murdered and nine wounded and, among the workers, sixty-nine murdered and fifty-nine wounded. CNT action groups responded in kind. As the more moderate elements were murdered or imprisoned, the action groups, made up of young militants, became more influential within the CNT. Martínez Anido could legitimately boast that he had destroyed the terrorist wing of the CNT, but the consequences would live on. He had ensured the division of the anarchist movement into the more moderate trade unionists and the insurrection-ary or terrorist groups which would later do so much damage to the Second Republic.[55]

In contrast to the CNT, as a result of the severity of the repression, over the next fifteen years the Socialist movement cautiously avoided risking conflict with the state apparatus. The defeat of the 1917 strike reinforced the Socialists' gradualist, reformist strategy. Indeed, whereas the anarchists greeted the Russian revolution with enthusiasm, the Socialists saw it as dangerously inopportune. The infirm Pablo Iglesias was more concerned with the probability that the Bolsheviks would seek a separate peace with Germany and thus undermine the Allied chances of victory. Shortly after the October revolution, *El Socialista* declared: 'The news we are getting from Russia fills us with distress. We sincerely believe, and we have always said so, that the mission of that great country is to put all her strength into the enterprise of crushing German imperi-alism.' No favourable comment on the Bolshevik revolution appeared until March 1918. This reflected a division within the movement between those for whom the defeat in 1917 meant that reformism should be accentuated and those who believed that the movement should prepare better for the next revolutionary attempt.[56]

Between 1919 and 1921, the PSOE was enmeshed in a civil war over its relationship with the Bolsheviks. The Secretary General of UGT since October 1918, Francisco Largo Caballero, was more concerned with the immediate material welfare of the trade union organization than with possible future revolutionary goals. He was determined never again to risk existing legislative gains and the movement's buildings and assets in a direct confrontation with the state.[57] Both Besteiro and Saborit also became progressively less radical. In different ways, all three perceived the futility of Spain's weak Socialist movement undertaking a frontal assault on the state. In the wake of the Russian revolution, continuing inflation and the rising unemployment of the post-1918 depression fostered a revolutionary group within the Socialist movement, particu-larly in Asturias and the Basque Country. Anguiano and others saw the events in Russia and the failure of the 1917 strike as evidence that reformism was pointless. In consequence, between 1918 and 1921 the Socialist movement was to be divided by a bitter three-year debate on the PSOE's relationship with the Comintern. The pro-Bolshevik tendency was defeated in a series of three party congresses held in December

1919, June 1920 and April 1921. In a closely fought struggle, the PSOE leadership won by relying on the votes of the strong UGT bureaucracy of paid permanent officials. Anguiano and the pro-Russian elements left to form the Spanish Communist Party.[58] Numerically, this was not a serious loss, but it accentuated the Socialists' ideological weakness at a time of grave economic and social crisis. The party's fundamental moderation was strengthened and, under a cautious and pragmatic leadership, there was a plunge in morale which lasted for nearly ten years. The Communists' influence was immediately felt in a series of strikes in the Asturian coalmines and the Basque iron and steel industry. In the aftermath of the defeat of 1917, the 1921 split left the Socialist leadership without a clear sense of direction and, in many respects, remote from the burning issues of the day. The syndical battles which raged elsewhere attracted less Socialist attention than the parliamentary campaign against the Moroccan war and eventually the King's involvement therein. In contrast, the essential moderate reformism of the Socialist movement was consolidated.[59]

Nevertheless, in the summer of 1920 the UGT was inclined to seek unity with the CNT. In the event, the negotiations did not prosper because the CNT leadership regarded the Socialists' parliamentary strategy as 'collaboration with the capitalist regime'. However, in early September, a provisional pact was signed in order to respond to the repression. Its manifesto stated:

> the government has met every demand of the bourgeoisie and has bent over backwards before the threats made by its organizations. They have suspended constitutional guarantees in order to close unions and dissolve important workers' groups; they have pursued savagely and, against all justice and in opposition to the law, have kept thousands of men in prison for the crime of having united to defend their right to life. They have agreed to close down our newspapers in those areas where protest against such arbitrary measures could endanger the bastard interests of the political clique that is under the thumb of the employers. They have decreed the shameful measure of deeming the collection of union dues to be the crime of fraud ... The government has legalized the arming of the bourgeoisie and has given it privileges which are the equivalent of a licence to commit murder.

The pact came to nothing when the Socialists refused to back CNT calls for a general strike in protest at the repression being carried out in Barcelona by Martínez Anido. This caused bitter resentment within the CNT towards Largo Caballero.[60]

The most extreme case of reprisal for the murderous policies of Martínez Anido took place on 8 March 1921 when the Prime Minister Eduardo Dato was assassinated in the Plaza de la Independencia in Madrid by three Catalan anarchists. He was the third Prime Minister to be murdered in the Restoration period. However, unlike those of Cánovas and Canalejas, his death was not the work of an isolated individual. There had been considerable debate within the anarchist movement about the need to respond to the repression with 'the big one'. The original intention had been to kill Conde Bugallal but it was too difficult. The murder was carried out by three militants. A fourth member of their group, who was never identified, dropped out. The car in which Dato was travelling was riddled with bullets from a motorcycle and sidecar ridden by Ramon Casanellas. The notion that a motorbike and sidecar would be the best way to catch Dato unawares came from Casanellas. The gunmen were Pedro Matheu in the sidecar and Luis Nicolau riding pillion.[61]

This act of revenge for the activities of Martínez Anido and Arlegui was planned by Ramon Archs who, at the behest of Casanellas, also secured the motorbike and sidecar. Archs had previously suffered several arrests and severe beatings by the police. He had an additional motive. When he was only seven years old, his father, Manuel Ars i Solanellas, was one of those executed, in May 1898, in Montjuïc, as a consequence of the failed assassination attempt on the Captain General of Barcelona, Arsenio Martínez Campos, in September 1893 by Paulí Pallàs. Ramon Archs, as Secretary of the CNT metalworkers' union in Barcelona and head of the CNT self-defence groups, had become an active militant in the war against the bosses, the police and the Sindicatos Libres. Ironically, he had come into contact with leaders of the Sindicatos Libres because his mother worked as a cook in the home of Martínez Anido. In late May 1921, Archs and Pere Vandellós were captured. Both were tortured before being shot. Some days later, the disfigured body of Archs was found dumped in the street, riddled with bullets, savagely stabbed and his genitals cut off. It was claimed that Miguel Arlegui boasted of having amused himself sticking a dagger into Archs's testicles. Of the three known perpetrators, Matheu was arrested on 13 March and Nicolau was detained in Berlin some months later. Both escaped the death penalty as a result of the deal brokered by the German authorities in return for the extradition of Nicolau. Ramon Casanellas, the speed-merchant who had insisted that a motorbike with sidecar be used, subsequently fled to the USSR and joined the Red Army, where he became an airman. He returned to Spain in 1931 to organize the Catalan Communist Party and in 1933 he died in a motorbike accident en route to a Partido Comunista de España (PCE) Congress in Madrid.[62]

Significantly, it was only during the period from late 1920 to October 1922, when Martínez Anido was Civil Governor, that the Sindicatos Libres took off as a meaningful trade union organization. This was possible after he had smashed the CNT with brutal violence. Martínez Anido authorized mass arrests, the torture of prisoners and Arlegui's use of the *ley de fugas*. He put the Sindicatos Libres under his protection. Their ranks provided many hitmen, Seguí and Layret being among their victims.[63] After the prohibition of the CNT and the arrest of many militants and the deportation to the south of others, many anarcho-syndicalists, bereft of an organization, began to seep into the Sindicatos Libres. By October 1921, there were 100,000 members of the Sindicatos Libres and, by the following July, 175,000. Only then did they begin to organize real strikes. However, the Libres never seriously challenged the CNT as defenders of working-class interests. That was hardly surprising given their central role in Martínez Anido's terror campaign. One of its leaders described them as the Governor's 'shock troops', 'ready to risk all' to prevent him leaving Barcelona. In the words of the well-informed journalist Francisco Madrid, 'they had at their right hand the personal power of General Martínez Anido'.[64]

Their pistol-toting leaders used a rhetoric of violence. The head of the Libres, the Catalan Carlist Ramón Sales Amenós, was short, fat and well known in the brothels of the *barrio chino*. Despite his unprepossessing appearance, he was an effectively aggressive orator. His deputy, the fanatical ex-Jesuit Juan Laguía Lliteras, was eventually expelled from the Sindicatos Libres in 1925 because of his uncontrollable aggression which had seen him, three years earlier, physically assault Indalecio Prieto in the Cortes. Like Sales, Laguía was a close crony of Martínez Anido. Moreover, the General was honorary President of one of the most numerous of the Libres' component unions, the cooks and waiters. With his approval, individual union gunmen were protected by the police, who often handed over CNT *pistoleros* to the Libres for quick disposal.[65] The 'pacification' masterminded by Martínez Anido was working. So many CNT militants were in prison that the union could barely function. Key leaders were being targeted and assassinated. However, the boasts of Martínez Anido that he could do as he liked without supervision from the government were causing increasing disquiet in Madrid. He was rightly suspected of collusion in the murder of Layret and had refused to do anything to prevent the mistreatment in custody of Vandellós. The influence of the Libres peaked in the summer of 1922 when Martínez Anido was eventually dismissed after being involved in a Libre plot to murder the CNT leader Ángel Pestaña and to mount a fake assassination attempt against himself. With the CNT legalized and the new Civil Governor cracking down on Libre gunmen, the masses left the Libres and the fighting started again.[66]

The ongoing unrest in Barcelona underlined the extent to which the Restoration political system was no longer an adequate mechanism for defending the economic interests of the ruling classes. In the background, the King, increasingly sympathetic to the hints of military right-wingers, was making ever more hostile comments about the constitutional system. On a visit to Cordoba in May 1921, he dined in the Casino de la Amistad with a group of local *latifundistas*. In his speech, he revealed his impatience with a parliamentary system in which his task was limited to signing projected laws that never reached the statute book:

the King is not an absolute monarch and all that he can do is put his signature to projects so that they can go to parliament but he can do nothing to get them approved. I am very happy not to have responsibilities. If I cannot have the responsibilities that were long ago taken from the crown and given to parliament, then I prefer to offer my life to the country. But it is very hard to stand idly by while what is in everyone's interest cannot progress because of the plotting and pettiness of politics. My government presents a project, it is opposed and the government falls. Its members then become the opposition to their own project. How could they want to help those who killed them! ... Some will say that I am exceeding my constitutional duties but I have been a constitutional King for nineteen years and I have risked my life too many times for anyone to

catch me out in a constitutional fault ... I think that the provinces should
start a movement of support for your King and the beneficial projects so
that Parliament will remember that it is subject to the orders of the people
... Then the King's signature will be an executive order and a guarantee
that projects beneficial for Spain will go forward.

To cover up this faux pas, Juan de la Cierva, who was with him, rapidly
scribbled an anodyne version of the speech and persuaded the accompanying press corps to use his text. However, the local press in Cordoba
reproduced Alfonso's actual words. In his memoirs, La Cierva excused
what the King had said by claiming that he had just got carried away by
the enthusiasm of his audience. Of course, the King was right – the
parliamentary system was utterly inefficient – but his words were totally
inappropriate for a constitutional monarch. He was widely applauded on
the right and thus encouraged the drift to dictatorship.[67]

Severiano Martinez Anido, the brutal
civil governor of Barcelona.

6

From Colonial Disaster to Dictatorship, 1921–1923

Already weakened by disorder in Barcelona, the credibility of the establishment was rocked by the overwhelming defeat of Spanish forces by Moroccan tribesmen at Annual in June 1921. Hostilities had broken out in 1919 after a lengthy period of inaction occasionally interrupted by skirmishes. Peace had been maintained largely by a culture of bribing tribal chieftains which fostered venality and complacence among the Spanish officer corps. While there was no fighting, there was gambling, recourse to prostitutes and dubious moneymaking schemes. These ranged from selling equipment to the tribesmen, via charging the government for the wages of fictitious native mercenaries, to conspiring with local tradesmen to cheat on materials used for road-building projects.[1] When systematic local resistance by the indigenous population began, the Spanish occupying forces were as poorly armed and trained as they had been in 1909. The most threatening rebellion was led by El Raisuni, the charismatic bandit chief of the Beni-Aros kabila (tribe) and leader of the Berbers of the north-western area of Jibala.[2]

The colonial occupiers were vulnerable because they held some important towns but little of their hinterland. The towns were linked by chains of wooden blockhouses, garrisoned by platoons of twenty-one men who lived in appallingly isolated conditions and whose morale was undermined by the uncertainty of the arrival of water, food and firewood every few days. The senseless loss of life saw popular hostility in Spain intensify and Madrid ever more reluctant to sink resources into a colonial war. The government had no stomach for anything beyond action in the immediate area around the two coastal enclaves of Ceuta and Melilla. This led to a deep division between politicians opting for a defensive policy of guarding the towns and the Africanist officer corps anxious to see the full-scale occupation of the Rif. Things improved in late 1919 when a new High Commissioner, General Dámaso Berenguer, began a long-term policy of slow occupation, fanning out from Ceuta. Part of his strategy was a commitment to pacifying the colony by means of negotiation with the tribes.[3]

One of his policy's greatest triumphs was the occupation, on 14 October 1920, of El Raisuni's headquarters, the picturesque mountain town of Xauen, the 'Sacred City'. However, the basic problem of controlling the marauding tribes between Xauen and Tetuán in the north and El Araich (Larache) to the west involved a ruinously expensive policing operation. Among those officers who thought that the answer was rapid full-scale occupation was Berenguer's friend the hotheaded Commander-in-Chief, General Manuel Fernández Silvestre. He was a favourite of Alfonso XIII, who encouraged his foolhardy temerity.[4] While Berenguer concentrated on squeezing El Raisuni's territory in the west, the impetuous Silvestre engaged in a more ambitious, indeed reckless, campaign in early 1921, moving swiftly westward from Melilla to occupy Monte Arruit (Al Aaroui) 40 kilometres to the south. This advance into inaccessible and hostile territory brought him into conflict with Abd el-Krim, the aggressive leader of the Beni-Urriaguel kabila of the Rif, who had begun to unify the other Berber tribes of that mountain region. In the third week of July 1921, Abd el-Krim inflicted a massive defeat on Silvestre's forces near Melilla.[5]

Beginning at the village of Annual, position after position fell in a domino effect over a period of three weeks, which saw the Spanish occupation rolled back as far as Melilla itself. As the Spanish troops fled, enthusiastic tribesmen joined the revolt. Garrison after garrison was slaughtered. The deficiencies of the poorly fed and equipped Spanish forces were brutally exposed.[6] Those deficiencies are all the more shocking given that in 1921 the military budget absorbed more than 35 per cent of the total budget of the state. The inefficiency of national politics was matched by the military inefficiency reflected in the excessive, indeed macrocephalic, size of the officer corps in relation both to the numbers of rank-and-file troops and to Spain's realistic military needs and capacity. There were more generals and fewer artillery pieces per 1,000 men than in the armies of Rumania, Montenegro or Portugal. There was an officer for every four rank-and-file soldiers. Accordingly, 70 per cent of the total military budget was absorbed by officers' salaries, ensuring that equipment was not modernized.[7]

Spain's long war in Morocco was of benefit only to those who had business interests in the protectorate, not least Alfonso XIII. The corollary of that was the undermining of social support for the monarchy. Hostility to the African adventure intensified popular hostility not only to the army but to all the institutions of the Restoration system.[8] The local tribes had been provoked by the brutality of the occupiers and now there were horrific revenge massacres at outposts near Melilla, Dar Drius, Monte Arruit and Nador. Within a few weeks, more than 9,000 Spanish soldiers had died and huge quantities of war materiel were lost. Silvestre was thought to have committed suicide. The tribesmen were on the outskirts of a panic-stricken Melilla. However, too preoccupied with looting, they failed to capture it, unaware that the town was virtually undefended.[9] Over the next two years, the territory was clawed back but the question was now starkly posed – withdrawal or occupation?

The murder of Dato had seen the return to power, on 13 March, of Manuel Allendesalazar, at the head of a hard-line coalition determined to put an end to the anarchist threat. However, within three months the disaster of Annual, blamed on the incompetence of his cabinet, particularly of the Minister of War, the Vizconde de Eza, exacerbated the crisis of the Restoration system. While near civil war raged in the streets of Barcelona, a deeply damaging national controversy began over the issue of responsibility for Annual. The Africanistas blamed the government for failing to commit enough funds for an efficient war. The left blamed the King and the army high command for its incompetence.[10] In desperation, Alfonso XIII turned again to Maura. Maura had long since abandoned his grand ambition of reforming the Restoration system and was deeply reluctant to return to active politics. He did so only because he felt that the monarchy was under threat and so reconciled himself to being the fireman of the system. He faced considerable difficulty in forming a government not least because of the mutual hostility of the followers of Dato and of La Cierva. Even greater was the mutual antipathy between the fiercely anti-Catalanist La Cierva and Cambó. In consequence, Maura's oddly assorted cabinet, including La Cierva as Minister of War and Cambó as Minister of Finance, was not settled until 14 August.[11]

In fact, the defeat in an already deeply unpopular colonial war had unleashed a wave of public hostility against both the King and the dynastic parties. It was popularly believed that Alfonso XIII had specifically encouraged Silvestre in his disastrous advance. The Moroccan situation saw successive governments faced with considerable economic demands.[12] In addition, the defeat intensified the divisions between the Junteros and the Africanistas. The consequent instability would conclude only with the establishment of a military dictatorship in September 1923.[13]

Maura was confronted by a daunting range of pre-existing problems: working-class discontent and subversion, particularly in Barcelona, the Catalan question and the profound economic difficulties following the end of the world war, all exacerbated by the Moroccan disaster. The cost of the military adventure had to be met and the responsibilities for it confronted. Maura wrote to his son on 26 August 1921: 'We shall see how long the wedding cake lasts. It will last as long as we don't squander with our mistakes the overwhelming weight of opinion currently running in our favour and divert it towards those who would be delighted to see the government have a spectacular failure.' Until October 1921, he governed with the Cortes closed. Nevertheless, over the following months, he achieved considerable practical success. In military terms, the territory lost in July 1921 was soon reconquered. As Minister of Finance, Cambó had reformed the banking system.[14] Moreover, the wave of left-wing opposition had been calmed by one of the Vizconde de Eza's last and most efficacious acts. Eza's principal concern had been to prove that he was not to be blamed for the debacle and, on 4 August 1921, he had appointed the sixty-four-year-old General Juan Picasso González to head an inquiry into the responsibilities for Annual. The much decorated General was uncle to the artist Pablo Picasso.[15]

There was generalized support for the massive revenge campaign that saw the recovery of the territory lost after Annual. The sight of masses of corpses of hideously tortured Spanish soldiers triggered vengeance of untrammelled savagery. The brutalization of the officer corps would be visited on the Spanish left during the civil war.[16] There was disagreement over Cambó's ambitious economic reform plans, although the central preoccupation was the reconquest of the Moroccan colony. Cambó clashed constantly with La Cierva who, with the encouragement of the King, pursued policies of ingratiation with the army as well as supporting the Unión Monárquica Nacional. Such was the tension between La Cierva and Cambó and indeed between La Cierva and other ministers that the government fell in the second week of March 1922.[17] In the hope of preventing Maura from resigning, Alfonso XIII had proposed, via Cambó, that the two should form a new government and rule by decree. Maura refused on grounds of age, saying 'It's already too late for me.'[18] Maura was replaced by José Sánchez Guerra. Sánchez Guerra's government lived in dread of the impending Picasso report on the responsibility for the Moroccan disaster. The Socialist Indalecio Prieto had travelled to North Africa on 24 August 1921 and toured the area indefatigably for seven weeks interviewing survivors, accompanying the troops, witnessing the most gruesome sights. His series of twenty-eight vividly written articles about conditions after Annual, published in *El Liberal* between 30 August and 18 October, constituted the first reliable account of the magnitude of the disaster. Written with objectivity and some sympathy for the military on the ground, the articles were widely reproduced by other newspapers. Prieto also made resounding speeches in the Cortes that, together with the articles, had a massive impact.[19]

When the Cortes debate began as a result of the official inquiry led by General Picasso, there were broadly three approaches. The government of Sánchez Guerra wanted to limit responsibilities to the military high command in Morocco. The first casualty within the high command was General Berenguer, who resigned as High Commissioner on 10 July 1922 and was replaced by General Ricardo Burguete.[20] The Liberals wanted to widen the issue to include the Allendesalazar government in power at the time of Annual. Prieto and the Socialists, however, wanted to go further and implicate the King.[21] Prieto took the lead with several powerful speeches in the Cortes, the first of which was delivered eight days after his return from Morocco. The Picasso report exposed the incompetence and corruption within the high command in relation to the disappearance of funds and the sale of food supplies to hotels and restaurants and of weaponry to the enemy. The issue went further in that the financial interests of the Spanish oligarchy in terms of mining, electricity and railways as well as shipping were protected by the army without any particular benefit to the nation. The military high command were involved in corrupt relations with the economic interests that they protected.[22] This was hardly new. For years, corruption had been denounced by the left-wing press, particularly in *La Lucha*, the newspaper of the Partit Republicà Català, which had been founded in 1917 by Marcelino Domingo, Lluís Companys and Francesc Layret.[23] Nevertheless, for the Picasso report to bring the matter to national prominence and in a way that demanded action constituted a bombshell.

In Melilla, large-scale funding for roads, for barracks and for equipment disappeared into the pockets of the colonels and generals. There were cases where money requisitioned for the bribery of non-existent Berber chieftains had been pocketed. These devices, together with large-scale selling of weaponry by senior officers, saw the accumulation of considerable fortunes. In the same way as underpaid government officials depended on bribes, lower-rank officers traded in army supplies of soap, building materials, food and arms and ammunition. It was discovered that, in just one ordnance depot, 77 million pesetas had been spent without any plausible account appearing on the books. Officers and their wives bartered guns and ammunition for fresh vegetables in the market places of the protectorate. Rank-and-file soldiers were often the victims in terms of poor-quality food and equipment. Indeed, they were often forced to go barefoot. Even more scandalous was the appalling state of military hospitals where the lack of pharmaceuticals was notorious. The military monopoly on all aspects of the colonial administration meant that contracts for garrison construction were often given to relatives of officers. Private individuals who wished to build houses were obliged to employ military engineers, who charged exorbitant fees for their work. While the corruption of the politicians could occasionally be reported in the press, the Law of Jurisdictions made it dangerous to comment on military misdeeds.[24]

Prieto's devastating oratory had a huge national impact. Speaking of the 'putrefaction' of Melilla, he highlighted government incompetence, military corruption and the atrocities committed against the Moroccan population by officers of the African Army, especially the frequency with which women were raped. He declared: 'Melilla is a brothel and a den of thieves.' He accused La Cierva – who had put obstacles in the way of Prieto's tour of Morocco – of so favouring the Juntas as to undermine military efficiency. He condemned the government for not issuing figures for the number of dead, which he put at 8,000. When seeking to allocate responsibility, he blamed the King for encouraging Silvestre and denounced 'this wretched reign'. He ended with the damning words: 'Those fields of colonial dominion are now fields of death; eight thousand corpses are gathered on the steps of the throne to demand justice.'[25] Eventually, Picasso's report would put the casualties at more than 13,000.

An indication of the scale of the corruption can be seen in the considerable fortune that Santiago Alba made in 1921 while he was Foreign Minister, with the help of Juan March, from the sale of weaponry to the Moroccan rebels. The arms were transported from Dutch and Portuguese ports and from Gibraltar. At the time, the Compañía Transmediterránea, of which March was one of the major shareholders, had the monopoly of troop and materiel transport for the North African coast for the duration of the war.[26] Military corruption was not confined to the Moroccan colony. Niceto Alcalá-Zamora, who was Liberal Minister of War in 1923, discovered that the quartermasters' corps (Intendencia) was involved in a massive swindle involving invented purchases of flour.[27]

Despite being preoccupied with establishing responsibility for Annual, Sánchez Guerra had embarked on a conciliatory social policy. To the fury of the Catalan industrialists, and even more so of Martínez Anido, he restored constitutional guarantees and opened the way to the legalization of the CNT. In fact, this coincided with a move to greater moderation within the CNT. A delegation was sent to Martínez Anido to request the reopening of workers' centres and the legalization of trade unions. He responded violently: 'I shit on Sánchez Guerra's order to restore constitutional guarantees. Here in Barcelona and its province, I'm in charge, not him. Get out of my sight immediately if you don't want a hard time.' With so many senior figures either dead or imprisoned, the leadership was in flux and Martínez Anido's response strengthened the more radical elements. Among the new figures there was intense enthusiasm for the Russian revolution and consequently a bitter conflict over the relationship of the CNT to the Comintern.[28]

The Secretary General of the CNT Evelio Boal López had been arrested in March 1921 and subsequently murdered by the police in a demonstration of the *ley de fugas*. Boal had been replaced by a young journalist, Andreu Nin. His sympathy for the Comintern was matched by that of Joaquín Maurín, who become leader of the CRT Federation in Lleida in April 1921. Nin was born in 1892 in El Vendrell in the province of Tarragona where he had been a pupil of the cellist Pau Casals. Maurín was born in 1896 in the tiny village of Bonansa in the province of Huesca. It had been decided in April 1921 to send a small CNT delegation to the inaugural congress of the Red International of Labour Unions (Krasnyi Internatsional Profsoyuzov, or Profintern) that took place in Moscow in July 1921. The visit confirmed Nin and Maurín in their view that the CNT should join the Comintern. Nin remained in Russia and eventually became a close collaborator of Trotsky. Maurín returned to Catalonia and replaced Nin as Secretary General of the CRT but faced a wave of hostility to the idea of adherence to the Comintern. However, he was arrested in February 1922.[29] The resurgence of the more moderate elements was confirmed at the Congress of Zaragoza on 11–12 June 1922. Ángel Pestaña had visited the Soviet Union in 1920 and returned deeply disillusioned. He had been arrested immediately on arrival in Spain and was therefore unable to put his views to the organization. Now, he and Seguí argued successfully against joining the Profintern. They both felt that it was important to reunite the anarchist movement and to seek legality. They were even ready to cooperate with liberal political groups. The moderate syndicalist Joan Peiró replaced Maurín.[30]

Both Martínez Anido and the employers' organizations, 'the Patronal', were dismayed by the re-emergence of the CNT, which they blamed for the more liberal policies of Sánchez Guerra. However, the triumph of the trade union wing of the CNT was, thanks to the Civil Governor's intransigence, paralleled by a resurgence of *pistolerismo* by the action groups. Needless to say, the Libres were not slow to retaliate. From March to October 1922, the Libres carried out eight assassinations and the anarchists five. Martínez Anido was engaging in a deliberate provocation to build up opposition to Sánchez Guerra. Criticism of the Libres in the Cortes by Indalecio Prieto saw the group's deputy leader, Juan Laguía Lliteras, travel to Madrid and, on 16 May, physically attack the Socialist deputy. On 7 August, Martínez Anido made a token offer of resignation which, under threats from Primo de Rivera and demonstrations of support from industrialists' organizations, Sánchez Guerra was obliged to refuse.[31]

Some weeks later, the Civil Governor was outraged to learn that Pestaña was going to make a speech in Manresa. On 25 August, Pestaña was waylaid by a gang of gunmen including Laguía Lliteras. The operation was ordered by Martínez Anido and financed by Muntadas. Pestaña was badly wounded, with one of the bullets puncturing a lung. He was laid up for two months during which time Arlegui had the Libres send another squad to surround the hospital with a view to finishing him off. In local brothels, they boasted about their intentions. The left and liberal press reported the case and Prieto delivered protests in the Cortes. Sánchez Guerra, more to prevent a scandal than to save Pestaña's life, instructed the Minister of the Interior, Vicente Piniés, to send Civil Guards to guard the hospital. He also ordered Martínez Anido to report daily on Pestaña's health. Nothing was done to arrest the Libre hit squad.[32]

There were several unsuccessful efforts by anarchist action groups to kill Martínez Anido. The most elaborate was actually a trap set up by the police. In the hope of justifying a massacre of anarchist militants, Arlegui commissioned the agent provocateur Inocencio Feced and Pere Mártir Homs, a labour lawyer on his payroll, to mount a fake assassination attempt on Martínez Anido. According to Ricardo Sanz, it was Homs who had organized the murder of Layret. In coordination with elements in police headquarters, including Captain Lasarte, Homs was the link to the paid assassins of the Libres. Now, Feced and a police agent called Florentino Pellejero infiltrated an anarchist group from Valencia led by José Claramonte and convinced them that it would be easy to kill Martínez Anido. Feced provided dummy bombs filled with sawdust which the others believed were to be thrown at the Civil Governor's car as he returned from the theatre.

As the group lay in ambush, Pellejero opened fire on them and shot Claramonte, who managed to shoot him in return. Another of the anarchists, Amalio Cerdeño, was captured and shot by the police, using the *ley de fugas*. However, he did not die immediately. He and other anarchists detained earlier in the proceedings were interrogated by a judge who quickly saw what Arlegui had planned. He informed the senior prosecutor, Diego Medina. In the early hours of the morning, Medina telephoned Sánchez Guerra, gave him details of what had happened and revealed that Arlegui and Martínez Anido had already planned to kill around 200 anarchists as a reprisal for the 'assassination attempt'. The Prime Minister seized on the excuse for getting rid of both. He telephoned Martínez Anido and informed him that, in view of these lamentable events, he was dismissing Arlegui. Justifying the attempt on the life of Pestaña, the Civil Governor commented: 'As long as the putrefaction that for many years has been hanging over Barcelona is not cleared away, expelling the scum that comes from all over, nothing useful can be done.' Unused to anyone challenging him and utterly furious, Martínez Anido had already declared that, if Arlegui were dismissed, he would resign. To his consternation, Sánchez Guerra replied that he reluctantly accepted his resignation.[33]

The Catalan financial and industrial elites were outraged and the conservative press in Barcelona declared that Sánchez Guerra's action had left the city defenceless. One week later, on 31 October, the Barcelona haute bourgeoisie gathered at the Ritz to give Martínez Anido a spectacular send-off.[34] However, the effect of his removal was somewhat diminished by Sánchez Guerra's appointment of Miguel Primo de Rivera as Captain General on 14 March 1922. Fiercely hostile to the CNT, Primo was furious that his close friends Martínez Anido and Arlegui had been dismissed. A delegation of employers' organizations had visited Primo on 27 October and had been reassured by his statement that he shared their distress at the loss of two 'most worthy officers'. The tension was increased when the government recognized the workers' right to free association. The new Civil Governor, General Julio Ardanaz, authorized the opening of workers' centres and the activities of Catalan trade unions.[35]

Feeling vulnerable, industrialists were heartened by the triumph of fascism in Italy. *El Eco Patronal*, the journal of the leaders of the Madrid building industry, declared that fascism was an example to be followed in Spain. Mussolini was praised as 'a modest man' and proudly declared to be 'one of our own' because he had been a building labourer. He was praised for 'restoring normality' to Italian political life, a euphemism for the crushing of left. The Somatén was compared with the Fascist Party and the editorial asked if it was not possible to find a Spanish Mussolini. The Duce was enviously seen as the model for the iron surgeon that Spain needed. Such enthusiasm naturally provoked fears on the left. The Confederación Patronal Española even launched an unsuccessful newspaper called *La Camisa Negra* (The Black Shirt) with editorial support from the extreme right-wing Maurista Manuel Delgado Barreto. The hard-line President of the Catalan federation, Félix Graupera, called for businessmen across Spain to emulate their Italian equivalents. It was hardly surprising that the patronal press approved of the violence used by the Fascists to crush the working-class movement in Italy, an operation it referred to as a 'necessary and inevitable evil'.[36]

Cambó, however, stressing its anti-democratic character, saw Italian fascism as merely chronologically parallel to events in Spain but not suitable for emulation.[37] The Conde de Romanones was aware of efforts to create a fascist party out of the Sindicatos Libres. The commander of the Barcelona garrison, Bartolomé de Roselló, held a meeting of officers in the Casino Militar in the spring of 1923 'to discuss the creation of a fascist party whose basis would be the Sindicato Libre, to which end the secretary is already in Italy'. The Secretary of the Libres, the notorious Juan Laguía Lliteras, had indeed gone to Rome. He held talks with the Fascists which came to naught. Discussions with the Partito Popolare were more fruitful. Important right-wing civilians were present at the meeting in the Casino Militar. The pro-fascist officers from the Barcelona garrison formed a group known as La Traza (the Project) with links to other garrisons. Emulating Mussolini's Black Shirts, they wore a blue shirt as their uniform. Their aim to become a nationwide organization failed totally. That there was never to be a full-scale Spanish equivalent of Italian fascism until the civil war was largely the consequence of Spanish neutrality in the Great War and the lack of thousands of post-war ex-combatants.[38]

The concerns of the Catalan elite about the departure of Martínez Anido were exacerbated by the continuing instability of the political system, over which hung the issue of responsibility for the disaster of Annual. The two principal parties were divided internally and the cabinet of Sánchez Guerra could not muster a parliamentary majority to get approval for the budget. Prieto had kept the issue at boiling point in the Cortes on 4 May 1922 with his stark analysis of the army's failure.[39] However, his most devastating intervention came after Sánchez Guerra, who had also assumed the portfolio of Minister of War, had responded to the widespread demand for action by agreeing, on 19 July, that General Picasso's findings could be discussed in the Cortes after a special parliamentary commission had analysed it. Prieto thanked him for this act of respect for the Cortes. Romanones, in contrast, was appalled. He was planning his own comeback with a grand coalition of the four main Liberal factions – his own more conservative grouping, the moderate centrist 'liberal-democrats' under García Prieto, the followers of the progressive, albeit personally corrupt, Santiago Alba and the Reformists under Melquíades Álvarez. Accordingly, he was aghast that Sánchez Guerra should have made this concession and thereby exposed García Prieto and other ministers to accusations of complicity in the disaster.[40]

The final Picasso report was presented to the Cortes on 15 November but not fully discussed until one week later.[41] Prieto, who was a member of the special commission, made a passionate speech to the Cortes over two days, on 21 and 22 November. He found reason to blame every government since 1909 but reserved his most pungent criticisms for that of Allendesalazar. He also criticized the three most senior generals at the time of Annual, Berenguer, Navarro, who was the captive of Abd el-Krim, and Fernández Silvestre, who was dead. The President of the Cortes was scandalized when Prieto quoted Silvestre as saying that he was going to Morocco to capture Alhucemas (the key to the Rif) 'because the King had authorized it and urged him to do so'. He ended with a sarcastic reference to the King's pleasure-seeking in Paris and on fashionable French beaches.[42]

Romanones was not alone in questioning the political wisdom of the Prime Minister. The King told Romanones that it was reckless folly to allow the Picasso report to be discussed by the Cortes.[43] Desperate for more stable government, he revealed further doubts about Sánchez Guerra when he implicitly compared him to Maura. He remarked to Maura's friend César Silio: 'We used to be in the Ritz Hotel and now we've ended up in the Posada del Peine.' (The Posada del Peine was a traditional and very modest inn in old Madrid.)[44] The King's solution was to turn to Cambó. Cambó was one of the few prominent politicians who seemed to be exempt from corruption, electoral or otherwise. On 30 November, Alfonso XIII offered him the post of Prime Minister, suggesting that he could rule with or without parliament. The King cited the exhaustion of Maura, the scale of government problems and Cambó's brilliant performances in the Ministries of Public Works and Finance. However, his offer of total power was conditional on Cambó's renunciation of Catalanism and taking up residence in Madrid. It was not much of an offer. Even if Cambó did give up his aspirations for Catalonia, the opposition of the dynastic parties was guaranteed and, if he renounced Catalanism, the Lliga would be finished.

Deeply offended by Alfonso's assumption that he would betray his principles in return for power, something that he perceived as a repetition of the King's duplicitous attempt to seduce him in November 1918, he took his revenge.[45] The opportunity arose later that evening. Cambó went as usual to the Cortes where a debate was taking place on the Picasso report. He heard Maura declare that, once responsibility had been established, the Cortes should take the case to the Senate which would act as a court of justice. At that moment, Cambó saw, as he wrote later, 'the opportunity to return the blow given me by the King that morning'. He knew that the King was desperate to avoid investigation into the question of responsibility for the disaster of Annual. Accordingly, later that evening and on the next day, 1 December, Cambó delivered measured speeches in which he accepted that there should be an examination of the possible responsibility of the Allendesalazar government which had been in power at the time, but hinted darkly that the blame lay elsewhere: 'As long as the Senate does not exonerate that Government under whose mandate the catastrophe took place or does not establish that the responsibility lies very specifically elsewhere, I believe that the Senate, if it wishes to do its duty, has to make a judgement in some direction and that it would be a disaster for the country and its prestige if it did not do so'. In the corridor afterwards, Romanones asked him what had happened between him and the King. Cambó, already wondering if he had gone too far, declined to respond.[46]

While his indignation was perfectly understandable, it is arguable that, in rejecting the King's offer, Cambó sealed the fate of the Restoration system.[47] Three of Sánchez Guerra's ministers, and the President of the Cortes, all of whom had served in the Allendesalazar government, felt obliged to resign. In part because of this and Cambó's intervention, the debate on the Picasso report grew more heated when it was renewed on 5 December. Having also been a member of Allendesalazar's cabinet, Juan de la Cierva furiously attacked Cambó, accusing him of corruptly using his position as Minister of Finance to support the Banco de Barcelona. There were physical confrontations as deputies jostled one another. Sánchez Guerra's cabinet resigned on 7 December.[48] It was the tenth government to fall since Antonio Maura's third, in November 1918. It was replaced by García Prieto's fifth cabinet, the bloc on which he had been working with Romanones and Alba. The strong man of the coalition was Santiago Alba, who was again Foreign Minister. It consisted of representatives of the various Liberal factions and the Reformist, José Manuel Pedregal, as Minister of Finance. Romanones became Minister of Justice and President of the Senate. Melquíades Álvarez was to be President of the Cortes. The cabinet was well received, the presence of the Reformists seen as likely to promote a tentative step towards democratization and a serious effort to pursue responsibility for Annual. However, most of the participants were far more interested in the spoils of office than in actually resolving the great problems of the day. As Romanones put it: 'We parcelled out the ministries like children divvying up treats at a picnic.' Accordingly, such was the scale of those problems – Morocco and the army, anarchism and social ferment, unemployment and soaring living costs and Catalan separatism – that the grand coalition was doomed to last only nine months.[49]

Morocco was probably the single most difficult issue. In an effort to limit the drain on resources and the simmering public discontent about casualties, Burguete had been ordered to attempt to pacify the rebels by bribery rather than by military action. On 22 September 1922, he had a deal with the now obese and burned-out El Raisuni whereby, in return for keeping the Berber tribes of the Jibala under control, he was given autonomy and a large sum of money. Since he was already under siege in his new headquarters at Tazarut, his power might have been squashed definitively had the Spaniards concentrated their forces against him. The policy of withdrawing troops from the territory of a man on the verge of defeat merely ensured his enrichment and the inflation of his reputation and power.

Burguete's objective in the accommodation in the west was to secure more freedom in his efforts to crush the altogether more dangerous Abd el-Krim in the east. After first pursuing negotiations with him for the ransom of the 375 prisoners of war held since Annual, Burguete moved on to the offensive in August.[50] He intended to dig in along a line to the south of Annual, using as his forward base Tizzi Azza, a fortified position extremely difficult to supply with food, water and ammunition. However, a pre-emptive attack by Abd el-Krim on a supply column at nearby Tifaruin was driven off only at the cost of numerous casualties. The Rif tribes then struck on a major scale at the beginning of November 1922. Safely ensconced in the slopes above the town, they fired down on the garrison causing 2,000 casualties and obliging the Spaniards to dig in for the winter.[51]

In the meantime, Cambó's break with Alfonso XIII ensured the continuation of unstable government and it also drew a line under his own political career. In June 1923, disgusted both with Alfonso XIII and with the sterility and intrigues of political life, Cambó would finally resign his seat in the Cortes, announcing that he was retiring from active politics. Perceptive observers predicted correctly that his departure would open the way to a radicalization of Catalanism. Indeed, the moderate regionalism of the Lliga was already being pushed aside by the more radical nationalists of Acció Catalana, the group that had broken away a year before and was starting to enjoy success in provincial elections. Acció Catalana was a belated reaction to what was seen as Cambó's betrayal of the Assembly movement in 1917.[52] Ironically, the man who had championed efforts to clean up Spanish politics would henceforth concentrate on augmenting his already substantial wealth as President of CHADE-CADE, the principal electrical company of Latin America.[53]

A somewhat more liberal line was adopted by the government of García Prieto, but it hardly constituted the daring step towards democratization suggested by Raymond Carr when he wrote of its eventual overthrow by the military coup of Primo de Rivera: 'Not for the first nor for the last time, a general claimed that he was killing off a diseased body when he was, in fact, strangling a new birth.' If anything, the riposte of Javier Tusell seems more plausible: 'The Captain General of Catalonia did not strangle a new-born but simply buried a corpse; the political system died of terminal cancer not of a heart attack.'[54] In fact, the limits of García Prieto's reforming ambition were revealed when he announced that his government would not undertake any constitutional revisions. The timidity of the cabinet was exposed further when clerical onslaught, backed by the King, obliged Romanones to withdraw a decree preventing the sale abroad of art treasures, most of which belonged to the Church.

Worse was to follow when the hierarchy made it clear that it would not tolerate any attempt to amend Article 11 of the Constitution, which denied freedom of public worship to other religions. When Romanones gave way, the Minister of Finance, José Manuel Pedregal, resigned in protest, but his party chief, Melquíades Álvarez, did not, thereby underlining that for him, as for his Liberal colleagues, power meant more than principle.[55] The clearest evidence of that came when the government finally got around to holding elections in April 1923. All the arts of electoral manipulation were put into practice in one of the most undemocratic elections of the entire Restoration period which recorded the highest ever number of deputies returned unopposed under Article 29. The various Liberal factions within the government engaged in the most unseemly rivalries over the *encasillado*. Among many corrupt arrangements, Santiago Alba managed to secure a seat for his benefactor, Juan March, who dispensed enormous sums of money. As so often before, the winner was the old fox Romanones. In fact, he and García Prieto each managed to secure seats in the Cortes for nine of their close relatives. In ironic contrast, the Socialists managed to win seven seats.[56] Cipriano de Rivas Cherif gives a vivid account of the scale of corruption in Puente del Arzobisbo in Toledo, the town where he was campaigning on behalf of his friend Manuel Azaña. In his contest against the local *cacique*, Azaña was financed by a Bilbao shipbuilder. Votes were bought on both sides but, when it came down to election day, the local officials, in the pocket of the *cacique*, simply falsified the votes. The *cacique* set out thereafter to ruin the local republicans who had supported Azaña.[57] The government was effectively following the unofficial law adumbrated in a diary entry by Natalio Rivas: 'a clean ballot means the straight road to political oblivion'.[58]

The coalition made vain efforts to deal with the great problems of the day. Santiago Alba hoped to resolve the Moroccan issue by replacing military rule over the protectorate with a civilian administration. This required a prior resolution of the colonial conflict, which in turn involved a choice between withdrawal and a massive campaign of conquest. Since neither was feasible, Alba became the object of virulent right-wing and military hostility. In late January and throughout February 1923, there had been intensifying discontent that Alba had managed, with the help of the Basque financier Horacio Echevarrieta, to secure the release of the prisoners held by Abd el-Krim. The idea that huge sums had been handed over was seen as an affront to military dignity because it implied that the army was incapable of rescuing its own men. The King did not bother to greet the prisoners when they reached Malaga, choosing instead to go hunting on the estate of the Duke of Tarifa in Huelva. This was unsurprising since he missed few opportunities for pleasure, particularly in the casino at Deauville. It was rumoured that, when he had heard of the scale of the ransom, he commented contemptuously: 'poultry is getting very dear'. Nevertheless, he did nothing to diminish the desire of many officers for revenge attacks on the Moroccan popula-tion.[59] In contrast, on 1 February, General Miguel Primo de Rivera wrote a letter of congratulation to Santiago Alba: 'Although, as you rightly say, it is neither a triumph nor an occasion for rejoicing, it is certainly worthy of congratulations for having relieved us of the nightmare of there being Spanish prisoners and the fear of them dying. There was no hope of freeing them by any better means than the one used. God willing, this will be the last episode of this reckless African adventure to hurt and humiliate us.'[60]

Alba and the Spanish High Commissioner, Luis Silvela, were trying to negotiate peace through the mediation of Dris-ben-Saíd, a pro-Spanish friend of Abd el-Krim. To the outrage of most of the high command, Dris-ben-Saíd had been authorized to offer substantial public works in the Rif. Alba's determination to bring about the peaceful resolution of the Moroccan problem brought him into conflict with the Minister of War, Alcalá-Zamora, who resigned on 25 May. On that day, there were fierce attacks by Abd el-Krim on Spanish positions. The new Minister of War, General Luis Aizpuru, responded by appointing Martínez Anido as commander of Melilla on 7 June. A few days later, Dris-ben-Saíd was shot in mysterious circumstances. Given Martínez Anido's track record in Barcelona, it was widely believed that he was behind the murder in order to put an end to the peace negotiations. He produced wildly ambitious plans for an amphibious expedition to seize Alhucemas which appalled Alba and provoked protests on the left. An influential article by Pablo Iglesias denounced this 'mad adventure' and referred to the entire Moroccan project as 'a huge tomb for Spanish youth'. After a detailed study by the General Staff which calculated that the operation would involve unacceptably high casualties, the cabinet turned down Martínez Anido's plans. Furious, he resigned on 10 August. He was regarded as a hero by the bulk of an officer corps that deeply resented what they saw as unwarranted civilian control over military policy. Right-wing disgust generated by Martínez Anido's departure soon deepened. Casualties were mounting as fighting intensified. Outraged supporters of the Africanistas spread alarmist rumours that another Annual could happen because of Alba's cost-cutting pacifist policies.[61]

On 23 August, in an echo of the Semana Trágica, in the port of Malaga a detachment of conscripts embarking for Melilla mutinied. Women chanted, 'Don't go to Morocco. They are taking you to the slaughterhouse', civilians were jostled and army officers assaulted. Some of the recruits were merely drunk, others were Catalan and Basque nationalists making political protests. Discipline was finally restored by the Civil Guard. This incident was planned to coincide with the outbreak of a Communist-organized general strike in Bilbao. An NCO in the Engineering Corps, José Ardoz, was killed and the crime was attributed to a Galician, Corporal José Sánchez Barroso. He was quickly tried by summary court martial and sentenced to death. In a context of wide-spread public revulsion against the Moroccan enterprise, there was an outcry against the death sentence. On 28 August, Sánchez Barroso was given a royal pardon, at the request of the cabinet. The officer corps was outraged by the Malaga incidents, by the subsequent public rejection of its cause in Morocco and by what it saw as the slight involved in the pardon. For the top brass, it was further evidence of the weakness of the Liberal government.[62]

As tensions festered in Morocco, the situation had grown more poisonous in Barcelona. Before the elections, in an effort to deal with the social problem, García Prieto had replaced General Ardanaz as Civil Governor of Barcelona with Salvador Raventós Clivilles, a Catalan deputy of his own Liberal Party. This, together with the introduction of arbitration committees in labour disputes, had permitted the more moderate elements of the CNT to continue rebuilding the trade unions under Salvador Seguí. After a clandestine meeting with Juan Laguía Lliteras, Seguí presided over a tacit truce with the Sindicatos Libres, who were inclined to be more conciliatory now that they no longer had Martínez Anido to protect them. The revival of the CNT infuriated the employers who, in the absence of Martínez Anido, could turn to the Captain General, his friend, Miguel Primo de Rivera. Moreover, they were further consoled by appointment of the hard-line Colonel Heraclio Hernández Malillos as chief of the Barcelona police and his choice of Captain Julio de Lasarte to be his deputy.[63] The hostility to the CNT of Primo and the bulk of the military high command was clinched when Seguí announced his readiness to collaborate with the Socialists in a campaign to push for Spanish withdrawal from Morocco. In any case, the brief truce between the CNT and the Libres ended in March 1923. The revival of the CNT under Pestaña, Peiró and Seguí had seen the return to the fold of many workers who had taken refuge in the Libres during the Martínez Anido persecution. Hard-liners among the Libres were ready to go to war again to undermine the growth of the CNT as a legitimate union.[64] Accordingly, their targets were the moderate anarcho-syndicalists. The renewal of violence began with the shooting on 24 February of Amadeu Campí, a leader of the Libres' textile finishing union. Although the CNT was accused, it is more likely that Campí was shot by Ramon Sales, with whom he had fallen out. Two other renegade members of the Libres were also shot.[65]

On 10 March, Seguí and his friend Francesc Comes were gunned down by a group of Libres, among whom was Inocencio Feced. The assassins' escape was covered by policemen led by Captain Lasarte. The action was organized by Pere Mártir Homs, who had previously set up the murder of Layret and the fake assault on Martínez Anido. Again, the operation was financed by the industrialist Maties Muntadas. Martínez Anido commented: 'I'm not really surprised. Those who play with fire sooner or later get burned.' It was later revealed by Feced that the Employer's Federation had financed the shooting. Certainly, Muntadas and other important members of the Patronal hoped for a military coup and believed that the murder of Seguí would provoke CNT retaliation that, in turn, would consolidate support for an army takeover. The death of Seguí was just one, albeit the most important, of a cycle of assassinations of both CNT and Libres militants. Over the following ten weeks, sixteen CNT militants and ten members of the Sindicatos Libres were shot dead and there were others wounded.[66] To avoid mass demonstrations, Salvador Raventós, the Civil Governor, arranged for Seguí's body to taken from the hospital and buried clandestinely. This provoked strikes in Barcelona, Gijón and Zaragoza with fighting between the police and action groups. When Comes was buried on 18 March, nearly 200,000 people followed the coffin.[67]

The murder of Seguí was a devastating blow to the CNT, which was left rudderless without the one man capable of bridging the gap between the trade unionists and the action groups.[68] In the aftermath of his death, a vain effort was made by Pestaña and the CNT Secretary General Joan Peiró to stop bloodshed. Significantly, the anarchists targeted by the Libres were those who had tried to put an end to the violence. Then Peiró himself was the target of two attacks. Others wanted revenge for the deaths of Seguí and Comes. Pestaña and Peiró reluctantly acquiesced, as much as anything in the desperate hope of counter-terrorism putting a stop to the Libres' onslaught. An action committee was set up to choose important targets, one of whom would be Martínez Anido. The actual dirty work was entrusted to a specialist unit. Its origins went back to 1920 when Manuel Buenacasa and Buenaventura Durruti were involved in a group called Los Justicieros which had unsuccessfully tried to kill the King in the Basque Country. They fled in early 1921 to Zaragoza, where they were joined by Francisco Ascaso. In September 1922, the group had moved to Barcelona and linked up with Juan García Oliver.

With Ricardo Sanz and Aurelio Fernández, they formed Los Solidarios in late 1922. They were all young. Durruti and Fernández were mechanics by trade, Ascaso a waiter and Sanz a textile worker. In May 1923, they tried in vain to catch Martínez Anido, first in San Sebastián and later in A Coruña.[69]

On 17 May 1923, in León, they killed Faustino González Regueral, one-time Civil Governor of Bilbao. On 4 June, Francisco Ascaso and Rafael Torres Escartín shot dead the Traditionalist Cardinal of Zaragoza, José Soldevila Romero. Deeply unpopular, Archbishop Soldevila was fiercely reactionary. He was believed in anarchist circles to finance gunmen from the Sindicatos Libres and to have plotted, with Martínez Anido and Arlegui, the murder of Seguí. He was alleged to have acquired a fortune from the ownership of brothels, gambling dens and a construction business. His corruption was said to permit him to live in spectacular luxury while being ministered to by a number of young nuns. He was shot while making his daily visit to a convent where it was rumoured that he had a sexual relationship with a nun to whom he left a fortune.[70] The assassination sent waves of horror across middle- and upper-class Spain.

Conscious of how this played into the hands of the industrialists and army officers who wanted a coup, Pestaña and Peiró disbanded the committee and vainly ordered the Solidarios to follow suit. However, the Solidarios were looking to create a revolutionary group – the Federación Anarquista Ibérica (FAI) – and embarked on a series of daring robberies to finance it. To make matters worse for the moderates, there was a major escalation of strikes as workers tried to recoup their living standards after years of the CNT being illegal.[71] After disputes in the construction industry, the biggest strike since La Canadiense, in this case of port workers, broke out in early May. Precisely to provoke a major confrontation, the employers responded with a lock-out of the dock workers. The Sindicato Único took the bait by calling a general strike of transport workers including rubbish collectors. As rubbish piled up in the streets and food distribution ground to a halt, middle-class opinion inclined towards authoritarian solutions. Primo de Rivera was seen by the upper and middle classes as the saviour lacking since the departure of Martínez Anido. He wanted to declare martial law and authorize the use of the Somatén. The efforts of the Civil Governor, Salvador Raventós, to resolve the strike were mocked as intolerable weakness. He resigned and was replaced by a Liberal deputy in the Cortes, Francisco Barber.[72]

The new Civil Governor quickly outraged the employers by continuing his predecessor's efforts to settle the strike by negotiation. They went over his head and appealed for help to Primo de Rivera. It was a reprise of what had happened during the Canadiense strike. As Milans del Bosch had done then, Primo expressed his sympathy with their views. On 8 June, the funeral of Josep Franquesa, a murdered member of both the Sindicatos Libres and the Somatén, was attended by 5,000 members of the two organizations. Barber was threatened and jostled and had to be rescued by Primo. Alarmed by Primo's support for the more extreme ambitions of the Catalan industrialists, and hoping to dismiss him, García Prieto summoned both him and Barber to Madrid. The King refused to sign the relevant decree replacing Primo. Already a broken man, Barber resigned after only three weeks in the post and, traumatized by his experience, died two months later. Primo used the time that he spent in Madrid to muster support for a military coup. He met a group of four generals, known as the Cuadrilátero (Quadrilateral), José Cavalcanti, Antonio Dabán, Leopoldo Saro and Federico Berenguer, brother of Dámaso, together with the Military Governor of Madrid, the Duque de Tetuán. Their concerns were that Morocco should not be abandoned and that the disorder in Barcelona should be resolved. All five were convinced royalists. Indeed, the King once told Alcalá-Zamora that neither Dabán nor Saro would move a muscle unless he ordered them to do so. Since the Cuadrilátero group was in regular contact with the King, he was fully apprised of Primo's machinations and hesitated to give his approval because of doubts about Primo's competence. Primo confessed his plans to Romanones, although he claimed that he would do nothing in the short term.[73]

Indeed, throughout 1923, Alfonso XIII received considerable encouragement for his inclination to lead a military coup. Indeed, at some unspecified point that year, he told Joaquim Salvatella, the Minister of Education and Fine Arts in the García Prieto government, that the only solution that he could see to the problems of the country was a government of colonels. There were deafening rumours that the man to lead a coup would be the 66-year-old General Francisco Aguilera y Egea, who had briefly been Minister of War under García Prieto in the spring of 1917. He enjoyed considerable support right across the army. As

President of the Supreme War Council, Aguilera had accepted that the colonial high command should take responsibility for the disaster, but he was not prepared to see the civilian politicians get away scot free. In early July 1923, he had written an insulting letter to the Conservative ex-Prime Minister Joaquín Sánchez de Toca, accusing him of trying to ensure that the political establishment would not face equal censure. He refused to apologize and challenged Sánchez de Toca to a duel. At this point, Sánchez Guerra and Romanones tried to mediate. As tempers rose, Aguilera and Sánchez Guerra jostled and the General came off worse. The ensuing scandal put an end to his possible candidacy as the future dictator.[74] In any case, Aguilera had already made it clear to Primo de Rivera that he thought the idea of a coup was madness.[75]

In August, Alfonso XIII discussed the idea of a coup with various people, including Gabriel Maura, who informed his father. Antonio Maura knew that the King, obsessed with Bolshevism and worried about the Picasso report, continued to toy with the idea of a dictatorship. He sent a note to the King with a devastating analysis: 'All my conclusions derive from my long-standing and ever firmer conviction that the current parties, without exception, have shown themselves incapable of governing, although this collective ineptitude is not the result of the personal failings of their leaders.' Maura stated that nothing was to be expected of yet another coalition government since the problem was to be found in the nature of the corrupt Restoration system. However, he believed that it would be suicide for the monarchy if the King took over the functions of government and assumed its day-to-day responsibilities. Accordingly, he believed that the answer lay in the army: 'It would be less harmful for those that have imposed their will in critical situations to assume the full responsibility of government themselves.'[76] This missive was interpreted by the King as Maura's permission for him to let the army take over. He did not, however, respond to Maura's prediction of disaster for the monarchy if he interfered in the subsequent dictatorship.

In the wake of his resignation, Barber was replaced by the immensely wealthy, trombone-playing, fifty-six-year-old Liberal from Galicia, Manuel Portela Valladares, a one-time member of the Foment de Treball Nacional. He immediately carried out a major crackdown on the CNT. He put troops on the streets by day and authorized the Somatén to patrol at night. The consequence was that Peiró lost control to García Oliver and the action groups, a development which worsened the sense that the social war was out of control and intensified middle-class desire for military intervention.[77]

Primo left Madrid convinced that his plotting had been discovered. He confided to a friend that he was amazed not to have been arrested during the journey back nor to have found news of his dismissal awaiting him.[78] When Primo reached Barcelona on 23 June, there was a huge demonstration at the railway station to greet him. It had a considerable impact on his vanity. In private meetings, Primo was being urged by the major industrialists to become the longed-for iron surgeon. Even before he had gone to Madrid, the employers had sent an open letter to him setting out their demands for the defeat of the strike and the subsequent return to draconian work conditions. His response, on 28 June, was to have CNT headquarters searched and eighteen leaders arrested. This exceeded his jurisdiction but he argued that it was a military necessity since the CNT was about to launch a revolutionary uprising. Portela Valladares did not object. In the face of such action, on 12 July the CNT called off a strike that had involved around 140,000 workers and left twenty-two dead.[79]

The success of Primo's tough action in ending the strike convinced the Catalan elite that more of the same was necessary to crush the CNT. Meanwhile, the action groups continued the social war with a series of bank robberies, the most spectacular of which was an assault on the Bank of Spain in Gijón on 1 September.[80] A cabinet reshuffle two days later was widely regarded as evidence of the weakness of the government.[81] Then, tension was ratcheted up by the events on 11 September, the Catalan national day, when groups of Catalan, Basque and Galician nationalists gathered in Barcelona and demonstrated in favour of home rule in all three regions. Anti-Spanish slogans were shouted, including some in favour of the Rif rebels, and there were clashes with the police. As was to be expected, the officers of the Barcelona garrison were outraged. As Captain General of the Catalan military region, Primo de Rivera overreacted and responded with a declaration of martial law.[82]

Primo de Rivera had made little secret of his wider plans. Apparently, he had visited the King's summer residence in San Sebastián to discuss the prospect with him. Afterwards, at a dinner in Cordoba, Alfonso XIII had confided in his hosts that Primo was preparing a movement that would resolve the problems of the day.[83] Primo returned to Madrid on 7 September and met the generals of the Cuadrilátero to make the final arrangements for a coup one week later. This secured the support of senior Africanistas. He had a vague commitment from General José Sanjurjo, the Military Governor of Zaragoza. Immediately on his return from Madrid on 23 June, he had courted the support of the Junteros. Primo admitted to General Eduardo López Ochoa, a freemason and republican, that he used different arguments with different interlocutors. He told López Ochoa that, in order to resolve the problems of Morocco, *pistolerismo* and Catalan nationalism, the coup would impose a competent civilian government with military backing, and that the army would remain in power only briefly. López Ochoa claimed later to have learned that Primo had made a deal with senior Catalanists, offering autonomy and a favourable customs regime in return for their support. He told another senior officer of the Barcelona garrison, General Mercader, a friend of the King, that the plan was to save the monarchy, while assuring López Ochoa that 'afterwards things would go very differently'.[84] This seems to be confirmed by a claim by Portela Valladares that, shortly after his arrival in Barcelona, Primo de Rivera confided in him his plans for a coup. Allegedly, Portela responded that his scheme would meet an insuperable obstacle in the King to which Primo replied: 'the day he gets in my way is the day I put him over the border'.[85] During this second sojourn in Madrid, he wrote letters to the generals in command of Ceuta (Enrique Marzo y Balaguer) and Melilla (Manuel Montero Navarro) to secure their support. These letters expressed his commitment to continued operations against Abd el-Krim.[86]

In the early hours of the morning of 13 September 1923, Primo's coup d'état was launched. He had long since ingratiated himself with the Catalan elite. It was alleged at the time that he had held secret meetings with Junoy, the architect Josep Puig i Cadafalch, President of the Catalan assembly of local councillors, the Mancomunitat, and other Catalan business leaders at the Font-Romeu health spa on the French side of the border. There, apparently, he agreed, in return for their support, to promote their ambitions in terms of greater autonomy, protectionist policies and public order.[87] In what must be presumed to be a cynical pantomime, he had made efforts to speak Catalan at public events and gave every sign of admiring Catalan culture, especially the national dance, the *sardana*. When he coincided with Cambó, he would always ask, 'How are you, my dear Chief?' He regularly dined with the leading industrial barons of the most conservative elements of the Lliga, such as Félix Graupera of the Federació Patronal, Domingo Sert of the Foment de Treball Nacional, the Marqués de Comillas and Ferran Fabra y Puig (Marqués de Alella).[88] In that sense, Primo's coup was more about meeting Catalan determination to see the CNT crushed than silencing the Picasso report on the responsibility for Annual, although that certainly clinched the support of both the Africanista generals and Alfonso XIII. The role of the King was crucial, not because he played an active role but rather because he irresponsibly stood and watched. When the crunch came, the response of the government was feeble largely because of a conviction that the overall political situation required desperate measures. Thus, despite knowing what Primo and the Cuadrilátero were up to, nothing was done to stop him returning to Barcelona. In fact, far from sure of success, he was fearful, as he had been in June, that he would be arrested on the way back. According to López Ochoa, Catalanist supporters had a car ready to spirit him across the French border if things went badly.[89]

Meanwhile, the carefree monarch was trying out a new sports car on the road between San Sebastián and Biarritz. On 12 September, Santiago Alba, the minister deputed to accompany Alfonso on his summer holiday learned of the imminence of the coup. Knowing how much military hatred was directed at his person, Alba resigned. Moreover, Martínez Anido, a key collaborator in the plot, was in San Sebastián with orders to arrest Alba as soon as the coup had succeeded, subject him to a summary court martial and shoot him. Warned of this and fearing for his life, Alba crossed the international bridge into France.[90] In Madrid, the government dithered. García Prieto was in favour of arresting Primo, but the Minister of War, General Luis Aizpuru, was reluctant to believe that he was involved in a plot. By the time of their inconsequential conversation, Primo de Rivera had already issued orders for the establishment of martial law in Barcelona, for the occupation of all major public buildings and for street patrols by the Somatén. At the same time, he published a manifesto to the nation in which he described himself as the long-awaited iron surgeon who would clear away the incompetence and corruption of the venal professional politicians as the first step to national regeneration. To do so, he would perform radical surgery on the sick body politic. Among the problems to be solved, he listed subversion, social violence, public disorder and separatism but was non-committal about his plans for Morocco, declaring only that he aimed to find a 'prompt, worthy and honourable' resolution.[91]

Without popular support, the government could do little to stand in the way of the army. Even less was it likely to stand against Alfonso XIII, who may not have been actively involved in the coup but certainly knew about it and was not displeased to see it prosper. He had long been indiscreet about his impatience with the inefficiency of various governments and their weakness in the face of revolutionary threats. He believed that he represented the national will better than any corruptly elected government. There had been his rash speech in May 1921 in Cordoba. In February and March 1923, rumours that he was thinking in terms of a dictatorship were fed by the right-wing daily *La Acción*, whose director, Manuel Delgado Barreto, was a prominent figure on the extreme right. Now there was the immediate advantage of preventing parliamentary discussion of the Picasso report.[92] It was therefore no surprise that, on 14 September, a beaming Alfonso XIII, wearing army uniform, arrived in Madrid and announced his support for the military rebels. He refused to dismiss the rebellious generals and thereby obliged his civilian government to resign. He then summoned Primo de Rivera to Madrid and named him head of a Military Directory with executive and legislative powers. García Prieto seemed more relieved than anything, commenting to journalists, 'I have a new saint to whom I can pray: St Miguel Primo de Rivera, because he has freed me from the nightmare of government.'[93] Around 4,000 well-dressed Catalans headed by the Mayor of Barcelona, the Marqués de Alella, the President of the Mancomunitat, Puig i Cadafalch, and the most prominent industrialists, were at the station on the evening of 14 September to bid farewell to Primo on his journey to Madrid to take power.[94] The significance of what had just happened has been frequently expressed in medical metaphors for the obvious reason that Primo himself adopted the classic regenerationist image of the iron surgeon. For Raymond Carr and Shlomo Ben-Ami, Primo butchered the mewling democracy of García Prieto's cabinet, while for Javier Tusell and José Luis García Navarro, he simply buried a corpse. Both views rather let Alfonso XIII off the hook. After all, without his intervention, the coup could easily have been stopped. By indulging his penchant for military government, the King left himself with no alternative when the military too ran out of ideas. More subtle altogether is the brilliant conclusion of

Francisco Romero: 'In fact, the "iron surgeon" had just switched off the life support system of the comatose patient. Having thought to do so himself, the chief consultant, King Alfonso XIII, was not troubled to sign the death certificate.'[95]

Miguel Primo de Rivera and Alfonso XIII,
together with the generals of the recently
formed Military Directory.

7

The Primo de Rivera Dictatorship: The Years of Success, 1923–1926

The manifesto published by Primo de Rivera on 12 September consisted of a diatribe against the nepotism and corruption of the political system of the constitutional monarchy. Primo invited the population to denounce any 'perversion of the course of justice, bribery or immorality' and promised 'to punish implacably those who had thereby offended, corrupted or dishonoured Spain'.[1] This laudable ambition seemed at odds with the fact that his own meteoric military career had benefited immensely from the patronage of his uncle, Fernando Primo de Rivera, and that he had tried unsuccessfully to achieve a parliamentary seat in Cadiz not by election but by getting a place in the *encasillado*. Ángel Ossorio described the manifesto as 'a hotchpotch of boorish, coarse clichés and idiotic vulgarity' and mocked its whitewashing of the responsibilities of the military for the condition of Spain. The choleric philosopher Miguel de Unamuno called it 'pornographic'. Honourable politicians were outraged; others, such as Juan de la Cierva, simply assumed that the criticisms were directed at others.[2]

It was typical of the frivolity of Alfonso XIII that he failed to realize that, as the King who had chosen the politicians of the old system, some of the mud splashed on him. Gabriel Maura wrote: 'it is very possible that neither he [Primo] nor the King perceived at the time, as most ordinary Spaniards did not notice until much later, that among the institutions overthrown by the new regime was to be found the monarchy'.[3] Thus Alfonso XIII blithely made the crucial individual decision not to support the constitutional government and to offer power instead to Primo. He delayed his return to Madrid, despite the pleas of the government, claiming that he was held up by bad weather. In fact, he was visiting Burgos, Valladolid and Zaragoza to take the pulse of the garrisons there. Advised by General Sanjurjo to keep these visits secret, he then returned to San Sebastián to begin his journey to Madrid.[4]

That the government of García Prieto had hardly been the harbinger of real democracy was revealed by how little opposition there was to the coup. Indeed, it was greeted without drama. In the towns, in cafés and around newspaper kiosks, the reaction ranged from indifference to enthusiasm.[5] There was rejoicing aplenty from the upper classes, many senior generals and, above all, the King. The Supreme War Council had been due to meet on 15 September and hear the case against the officers accused of responsibility for Annual. On 20 September, the special parliamentary commission charged with examining the Picasso report was also due to meet to finalize its conclusions that would then be debated on 1 October in the Cortes. Unsurprisingly, the King, after spending an anxious summer, was delighted by a coup that put an end to the judicial process. As one of Primo's fellow conspirators, General Cavalcanti, said: 'You will understand, Miguel, that I haven't made a revolution just to be found guilty.'

Indeed, one of Primo's first actions would be an attempt to seize the report and the supporting documentation. However, the commission's President, Bernardo Mateo Sagasta, anticipating this, had removed the material from the archive of the Cortes and hidden it.[6] On 27 June 1924, the Supreme War Council found General Berenguer guilty of responsibility for the collapse of the Melilla command and sentenced him to expulsion from the army. However, a wide-ranging amnesty one week later would annul the sentence and effectively draw a line under further investigation of the disaster of Annual. Primo airily dismissed the catastrophe as the consequence of 'the adversity that occasionally occurs in the best armies'. The amnesty included political offences.[7]

The nature of the new regime was in fact revealed when, on Primo's first day in Madrid, Alfonso XIII signed a decree establishing a Military Directory. Under the presidency of Primo, it consisted of a general from each of the eight military regions and an admiral, Antonio Magaz, who would serve as official Vice-President of the Directory. On the same day, martial law was imposed and would not be lifted until 16 March 1925. The press was subjected to rigid censorship. The Cortes was shut down and constitutional guarantees suspended. Ministries would continue to exist but be headed by under-secretaries, with Primo himself as a kind of super-minister with overall responsibility for all departments.

However, on 22 September, his crony Severiano Martínez Anido was named 'subsecretario de Gobernación', effectively Minister of the Interior and rather more his effective deputy than the merely symbolic Admiral Magaz. Martínez Anido's erstwhile deputy, the disgraced chief of police in Barcelona, General Miguel Arlegui, was restored to prominence as Director General of Public Order; his deputy was the sinister Captain Julio de Lasarte Persino, who specialized in fabricating 'information'.[8]

The three principal problems facing the new regime were the class war in Barcelona, the corrupt political system and the difficulties in the Moroccan Protectorate, although Primo's rhetoric focused on his proclaimed campaign against corruption. However, the group of largely inexperienced cronies assembled by Primo would have difficulty in resolving the latter issue given the extent of their own enjoyment of the spoils of office. In the caustic phrase of Eduardo Ortega y Gasset, elder brother of the philosopher José: 'There was too much fun to be had with arbitrary rule to leave any space in such mediocre minds for more serious work.'[9]

The inability of previous constitutional governments to resolve these problems explains the relief that greeted Primo de Rivera's coup. The first group to express support for the new regime was motivated by enthusiasm for its anticipated role in suppressing social disorder and by the prospect of an end to *caciquismo*. The Fomento Nacional del Treball was quick to inform Primo of 'its unshakeable commitment to the programme of government and regeneration of our motherland outlined in the manifesto with indisputable competence and authority'.[10] The other organizations of Catalan industrialists and landowners were not far behind. In a series of secret meetings with the top brass of the Lliga Regionalista and the Foment, Primo had made explicit promises that, once in power, he would expand Catalan autonomy in return for their support for his coup.[11] The President of the Mancomunitat, Josep Puig i Cadafalch, sent an optimistic note to Primo declaring: 'If the conflict is between an illegal act and corruption, we choose the former.' This was hardly surprising. Primo had made numerous earlier pro-Catalan and federalist statements. On this basis, Puig i Cadafalch was convinced that Primo could be relied upon to promote the importance of Catalonia within Spain. Accordingly, he went on to promise optimistically, 'we will collaborate with the generous project now begun'.[12]

Francesc Cambó, however, was much more cautious. Despite suggesting that the coup was 'the only sweetness tasted in many bitter years', he
advised his followers not to commit themselves to the Directory. Indeed,
he maintained that he had always believed that a dictatorship would be
a disaster for the country.[13] Shrewd as ever, he clearly saw that Primo's
pro-Catalanism was never more than at best superficial and at worst a
device to secure support for his plans. He could never have sold Catalan
autonomy to the rest of the army. His move against all regional nationalisms – seen specifically by Gabriel Maura as 'the anti-Catalan crusade'
– began on 18 September with a decree ordering that only the Spanish
flag could be flown on public buildings and that, at public events and in
schools, only Castilian Spanish could be used. In the Basque Country,
the Partido Nacionalista Vasco and its cultural clubs, the *batzokis*, were
banned. In Catalonia, the militant nationalist parties, Estat Català and
Acció Catalana, were dissolved. The *sardana* and the singing of the unofficial anthem 'Els Segadors' were banned and the Catalan half of bilin-
gual street signs removed. Primo declared that of the crimes of
syndicalism, communism and separatism, the latter was the worst. He
replaced Puig i Cadafalch as President of the Mancomunitat with the
centralist Alfonso Sala of the Unión Monárquica Nacional (UMN).
However, as his own Spanish nationalism intensified, against the advice
of his Director General of Local Administration, José Calvo Sotelo, he
abolished the Mancomunitat in the summer of 1924. From exile, Cambó
became a bitter critic of the government. More importantly for the
future, outrage at what was perceived as the betrayal by the Lliga saw the
leadership of the Catalanist cause pass to the left-wing groups.[14]

In fact, the swift jettisoning of the promises of Catalan autonomy and
the pre-eminence of Martínez Anido and Arlegui suggested that the
most important of the tasks assumed by Primo was the counter-
revolutionary one. Inevitably, the fortunes of the Libres were revived by
the return to prominence of the two. Membership was up to 111,252 by
1925 and to 197,853 by 1929, mainly in provincial Catalonia and
Valencia. This suggests that, with the CNT banned, those of the rank and
file who were not ideologically doctrinaire anarchists sought refuge in
any organization that could protect their wages. However, the political
preferences of Catalan workers would be seen clearly enough when, after
the fall of Primo de Rivera in 1930, support for the Libres evaporated
once again and there was a boom in CNT membership. In April 1931,

when the left Republican Esquerra came to power in Catalonia with CNT votes, the Libres were finished.[15]

The delight of the Catalan bourgeoisie was fed by the decree of 18 September which, as a step towards the militarization of society, established the Somatén in every town in Spain. Conservative citizens were invited to join these armed militias under army supervision and act as an auxiliary force to the police and army in order to put an end to the disorder of the years of *pistolerismo*.[16] As an armed militia, the Somatén was meant to be part of the regime's repressive machinery. Although the dictatorship cannot under any circumstances be seen as bloody, in many respects, including the leeway given to the Somatén, it would constantly abuse the rule of law. A decree of 14 October 1926 authorized the government to suspend any sentence that it adjudged to be 'prejudicial' to the interests of the administration. Members of the Somatén often committed acts of violence. In some cases, membership of the Somatén was used to cover up acts of poaching; in others, murder. On one occasion, a *somatenista*, in resisting eviction for failure to pay his rent, killed the house owner. When brought to trial, he asked: 'So, why did they give me this rifle?' If crimes committed by *somatenistas* came to trial, they were pardoned by the regime's decree of 16 May 1927, a decree denounced by the distinguished criminologist Quintiliano Saldaña as a 'juridical monster'.[17] Outside Catalonia, the Somatén was not the success anticipated by Primo. Many people joined only to avoid having to pay for a hunting licence. At the time of their creation on a nationwide basis, the Somatén had 21,868 members. This rose to a peak of 100,425 in 1925 and then declined rapidly until, by 1928, it was reduced to 22,492. Moreover, their main function was to provide numbers in official parades and ceremonies.[18]

One politician who could have no doubt of the manifesto's targets was Santiago Alba, since the manifesto announced that proceedings were in train against this 'depraved and cynical minister'. Primo and Alba, as advocates of the abandonment of the Moroccan colony, had previously had cordial relations, but now Primo made a cheap and unfounded accusation that, in going into exile, Alba had stolen a government car. He even blamed Alba for the military coup, telling a journalist from *El Imparcial*: 'the activity of this politician was the trigger for this movement. We have conclusive proof of his crimes which will be the basis of the prosecution.'[19]

These dark references hinted at Alba's murky relationship with Juan March. In an interview given three days after the coup, Primo repeated his accusation that Alba had provided a motive for his movement: 'Señor Alba has signed commercial contracts with capitalist elements for his personal benefit ... Señor Alba is mixed up in contraband.' The smuggling activities of Juan March were well known, but Primo and his fellow generals had no hard evidence against Alba. His house was searched by the police and his bank accounts frozen. An investigating magistrate was sent to Valladolid on a fishing expedition. His job was to implicate Alba in alleged corrupt dealings connected with a proposed railway from Valladolid to Toro that was paid for but not built. He found no evidence that Alba was involved. The Tribunal Supremo eventually dismissed the forty-one charges and also reprimanded the magistrate for making them up. However, the regime censorship prevented publication of its judgment.[20]

Given their previously warm relationship, the malice of Primo's persecution of Alba requires explanation. Alba was loathed by the military and by Catalan industrialists. During the First World War, as Minister of Finance he had infuriated the northern industrialists with proposals for a tax on their spectacular war profits without a corresponding measure to deal with the profits of his allies the agrarians. Alba's attempts to reduce the military budget, both in Morocco and in the Peninsula, were reviled within the army. More specifically, the Africanistas had never forgiven him for permitting the payments made to Abd el-Krim for the release of the prisoners taken after Annual. According to Francisco Franco, when the Foreign Legion attacked a Moroccan position, they advanced chanting 'Long live Spain! Death to Alba!' Thus an attack on Alba was part of Primo's strategy of consolidating support among his important early supporters.[21] There was also an element of personal resentment in that Primo unjustly blamed Alba for his failure to secure a seat in the Cortes. He believed, wrongly, that Alba had refused to persuade one of his political allies, the Liberal *cacique* of Cadiz, Primo's principal opponent in the province, to drop his opposition to Primo's candidacy.[22] Unsurprisingly, in exile, Alba would offer to finance the anarchists and others committed to the overthrow of the regime.[23]

One of the first initiatives in Primo's declared war on corruption and contraband was the beginning of an investigation into the massive tobacco smuggling that significantly diminished the revenue of the government monopoly, the Compañía Arrendataria de Tabacos. Inevitably, it focused on Juan March. An investigating magistrate was given material from various government departments relating to the issue and more than 400 house searches were carried out in Mallorca. It was alleged in the press that Juan March, like his puppet Alejandro Lerroux and Alba, had fled into exile and that he had a million pounds sterling (34 million pesetas) awaiting him in foreign banks. Frontier police had been given orders to arrest him. They were unable to do so because he had remained in Madrid. In fact, already, on 19 or 20 October, March had audaciously requested an interview with Primo. Whatever was said in that first of many meetings, March somehow persuaded Primo that his tobacco business benefited the state and that the regime would gain more from collaboration than from conflict with him.

Despite evidence that he was continuing with his smuggling activities, it soon became clear that the dictatorship no longer considered him one of its targets. March's shipping concern, the Compañía Trasmediterránea, began to receive significant government subsidies, his company Petróleos Porto Pi benefited from a change in the import duty on fuel and, in 1927, he was eventually granted the state tobacco monopoly for Morocco. Regarding the latter decision, Primo had had to overcome the misgivings of some ministers, most notably José Calvo Sotelo. In return for these favours, and at the explicit request of Primo himself, March supplied the tobacco needs of Spanish forces in Morocco, helped finance pro-regime newspapers such as *La Correspondencia Militar* and *La Nación*, bought land in Tangier for the Spanish state and paid for the building of a Catholic church there.

Juan March's corrupt activities during the dictatorship and before would be investigated by the Responsibilities Commission set up by the Cortes in 1931. A heated debate in the Cortes was provoked on 8 May 1934 when a lengthy speech by a member of the Commission, the Socialist Teodomiro Menéndez, detailed the long history of the corruption carried out by Juan March, from 1911 onwards, in securing the tobacco monopoly. Menéndez demonstrated that the investigations of the Responsibilities Commission had exposed how money provided by March, at the request of Primo, to bail out *La Correspondencia Militar* coincided exactly with the renewal of contracts for the tobacco monopoly. He also recounted how March had paid off huge debts accumulated by Queen Victoria Eugenia with various jewellers in Paris.

In the corridors of the Cortes afterwards, journalists overheard Cambó congratulate Menéndez for his speech while also pointing out that he was not the first politician to try to put a stop to March's corruption. Cambó then told the journalists that, when he was Minister of Finance, he had discovered that, to facilitate his smuggling operation, March had put numerous officers of the Carabineros on his payroll. Accordingly, to stop the practice, Cambó had threatened the senior commanders with disbanding the corps. He also discovered that, when March's vessels were captured by the navy, the cases against him were dismissed by naval courts and his ships returned to him. Cambó therefore introduced a law bringing smuggling offences into civilian juridiction. On receiving howls of complaint about this from the admirals who feared losing March's bribes, Cambó sent a message to them declaring that, if they didn't desist, he would reveal what they had been doing. Cambó also put a special watch on March, as a result of which ex-prime ministers and ex-ministers stopped visiting his house. He ended with an explosive declaration: 'The whole business of March is the most scandalous that the world has seen, because, for eleven years, he had one-time prime ministers and ministers at his service and effectively ran Spain. He could bring down governments whenever he liked and his influence even reached parliament.'[24]

Since securing Tangier for Spain was one of Primo's greatest ambitions, he expressed his delight at March's action by hosting a dinner in his honour. On the following day, he visited the Royal Palace for an audience with the King and, as he left, told the assembled courtiers: 'A great patriot has put his money at the service of the fatherland. You should all follow his example.' The loathing for Primo of Alfonso XIII's aristocratic intimates was thereby intensified. Also, at the behest of the Dictator, March had not only paid off the Queen's jewellery debts but, more importantly, had financed both the Instituto del Cáncer of which she was honorary president and the building of a tuberculosis sanatorium in Mallorca (which, as late as 1936, remained unfinished). In return, March would be the beneficiary in 1924 of Primo's interference in the judicial system and also of the Dictator's frequent public acknowledgement.[25]

Unamuno swiftly perceived that the rhetoric about the dictatorship, being merely a short-term project to clean up politics, was a cover for the principal objective of crushing revolution. He declared that the promises, couched in regenerationist language, of 'uprooting *caciquismo* and re-establishing authority' were just 'the theatrical scenery aimed at attracting the deluded idiots who have nightmares about communism and trades unions.'[26] If anything, the task was much easier than it might have seemed. There was little opposition from any of the working-class forces. Neither union organization had any interest in fighting to defend the corrupt constitutional system. The CNT was already a broken reed.[27]

The Socialists were concerned primarily with safeguarding their union structures. Their initial response to the news of the coup was cautious. Given the social agitation of the previous years, intense popular hostility to the Moroccan enterprise and the furore over responsibility for Annual, a military intervention was eminently foreseeable. Nevertheless, the Socialists neither predicted the coup nor showed great concern when it came, even though the new regime soon began to persecute other workers' organizations. While the King was still wending his leisurely way from San Sebastián to Madrid and rumours were circulating that Santiago Alba had been arrested, the front page of *El Socialista* carried a joint note of the PSOE and UGT executives declaring that 'no tie of solidarity or political sympathy links us to the governing class' and expressing 'the harshest reproaches for the way our politicians broke the promises made on the road to power'. Referring to Primo's claim that he would be putting an end to corruption and favouritism, the Socialist leadership was suspicious: 'With what authority can such claims be made by those who got to the top thanks to political favours influenced in their turn by royal suggestions?' The note ended ordering workers to take no initiatives without instructions from the executive committees of both the Socialist Party and the union. Primo's immediate appointment of Martínez Anido as his effective Minister of the Interior was another factor that counselled caution.

A second Socialist note instructed workers to abstain from initiatives likely 'to throw the proletariat into sterile movements that would justify precisely the repression longed for by reactionary forces'.[28] The Socialists speedily rejected an invitation from the CNT and the Communist Party to join them in a general strike. Indeed, the Socialist leadership not only did not try to impede the establishment of the regime but was also soon collaborating with it. This reflected the extent to which the leadership had emerged from the trauma of 1917 convinced of the need to stick to a legalist strategy, never again to risk the existence of the unions in direct clashes with the state, and to safeguard at all costs the achievements of existing social legislation.[29]

The Socialists' reluctance to oppose Primo's coup derived from the belief that, although the political struggle was suspended, daily trade union activity had to go on. Francisco Largo Caballero and the trade union bureaucracy believed that their first task was to use any means possible to protect the material interests of their members. Soon collaboration with the dictatorship would go from pragmatic realism to an opportunistic desire to steal an advantage over the anarcho-syndicalists. Ever since the breakdown of the pact with the CNT in December 1920, Largo Caballero had been determined to attract the rank and file of the CNT to the UGT.[30] He saw only advantage when the CNT and the Communist Party were banned and hundreds of their militants imprisoned.

Officially, the Dictator was not hostile to the working class, just to its radical elements. However, under the watch of Martínez Anido, anarchist prisoners suffered appalling mistreatment. They were subjected to savage beatings, kept in unhygienic conditions and fed virtually starvation rations.[31] Primo had paternalistic plans for the improvement of workers' living standards and himself suggested the possibility of collaboration with the Socialist movement whose initial passivity made him confident of a sympathetic response.

Primo's approach had come in a manifesto addressed to the workers on 29 September 1923. Inviting workers to feel proud of being Spaniards and urging them to be good, his text was clearly directed at the Socialists. On the one hand favouring social legislation, so dear to the reformists of the UGT, it then called upon the workers 'to distance themselves from the organizations which, seeming to offer benefits, only lead them along paths of ruin'. This dismissal of the CNT and the PCE was a scarcely veiled offer to the UGT that it could become the exclusive working-class organization and, in return for collaborating with the regime, eliminate its anarchist and Communist rivals. The Socialists' immediate response was to ask for more details of the new regime's proposed social legislation.[32]

The president of both the PSOE and the UGT, Pablo Iglesias, was soon gleefully predicting the downfall of the CNT, implying that the workers in its ranks had found themselves there either by mistake or because they were forced. Two days after publication of his manifesto, Primo personally made an offer to Manuel Llaneza, secretary general of the Asturian Miners' Union (Sindicato de los Obreros Mineros de Asturias – SOMA), inviting him to join a committee to examine the problems of the mining industry. Thinking that the SOMA would thereby be able to defend its achievements in terms of wages and hours, on the following day Llaneza persuaded an already favourably predisposed meeting of the joint national executives of the PSOE and UGT to support collaboration. There were three votes against this resolution, including those of Indalecio Prieto and Fernando de los Ríos, a distinguished law professor at the University of Granada. At the end of 1923, De los Ríos and Prieto wrote to the Vice-President of both the PSOE and the UGT, Julián Besteiro, to protest against collaboration, but on 9 January 1924 the National Committee of the PSOE ratified the collaborationist line.[33]

The integration of the Socialist leadership into the new regime would be thoroughgoing, and the UGT would be given representation on several state committees.[34] The Socialists' clubs, the Casas del Pueblo, remained open and most UGT sections were allowed to continue functioning, in contrast to total clampdown on the activities of the CNT and PCE. Nevertheless, in March 1924, workers' demonstrations were prohibited, prior to the planned May Day celebrations. In return for the workers' docility, the UGT was offered, and accepted, the prize of a seat on the Council of State and chose Largo Caballero as its representative. Within the UGT itself this had no unfavourable repercussions – Largo was the Secretary General. Prieto and De los Ríos both denounced Largo's opportunism, warning that it would be exploited by the Dictator for its propaganda value. They were right. On 25 April 1926, speaking in Alcalá de Henares, Primo quoted Largo's presence on the Council of State as a reason for not re-establishing democracy: 'Why do we need to elect anyone?' he asked rhetorically. After citing various consultative entities, he declared: 'we have the Council of State, organized so democratically that Largo Caballero is a member so that, in the name of the workers, he can honestly point out anything that is not well governed. Why then should we resuscitate that contraption called a parliament that countries that still suffer it are wondering how to get rid of?'[35]

On 10 December 1923, a plenum of the PSOE national committee ratified Largo's acceptance by fourteen votes to five. Prieto resigned and De los Ríos called unsuccessfully for a referendum among the rank and file. These divisions within the party would have repercussions right up to the civil war as a result of the personal enmities generated. Faced by rumours of schism within the party, Prieto declared publicly that the tactical discrepancies had not affected the cordiality and unity among the party's leaders. Nevertheless, it is clear that, both at the time and for many years thereafter, Largo Caballero harboured tremendous personal rancour against Prieto.[36]

The collaboration was consolidated despite evidence from Asturias that it did little to protect the workers' interests. Notwithstanding Primo's promises to Llaneza, the miners' union received no help from the regime in response to aggressive moves by mine owners to reduce wages and to meet the resulting strike action by sacking 350 workers. The UGT refused to join movements of resistance to the dictatorship. Pablo Iglesias claimed that, despite censorship and limits on meetings and strikes, both the UGT and the PSOE were growing under the dictatorship. The year 1926 was to see the most substantial cooperation yet by the UGT. Largo Caballero, speaking at the Madrid Casa del Pueblo, roundly condemned industrial sabotage, go-slows and strikes as likely to provoke lock-outs. He declared that opposition to the regime could prove disastrous for the working-class organization. Besteiro would not authorize any move against the regime unless it involved no risk for the Socialists.[37]

With the working class neutralized, until the mid-1920s the main opposition to the regime would come from liberal intellectuals like Unamuno, the wealthy novelist Vicente Blasco Ibáñez and the republican journalists Carlos Esplá and Eduardo Ortega y Gasset, all of whom, despite an amnesty of July 1924, chose to remain in exile. They used to meet in the Café Rotonde in Paris, once the haunt of Lenin and now frequented by a range of the Dictator's opponents from Santiago Alba and Generals Dámaso Berenguer and José Millán Astray to Marcelino Domingo, Joaquín Maurín and Andreu Nin. Backed financially by Blasco Ibáñez, from December 1924 to November 1925 Esplá, Unamuno and Ortega produced the overtly republican satirical broadsheet *España con honra*, with a print run of 50,000 copies that were widely distributed and read inside Spain. An even greater impact was achieved by the spectacular sales of Blasco Ibáñez's book *Alphonse XIII démasqué*, which was published in Paris and soon afterwards in several other languages.

Smuggled into Spain in enormous numbers, it severely damaged the King's image through its accusations of his direct responsibility for the disaster of Annual and of his facilitation of the dictatorship to prevent the Cortes debating the Picasso report. Alfonso was mocked for his frivolity and for his authoritarian ambitions, on account of which Blasco nicknamed him Fernando Seven and a Half, a feeble replica of his great-grandfather, the irresponsible absolutist Fernando VII. Equally damaging was Blasco's quotation of his dismissive comment about ransomed prisoners being over-priced poultry. The book had a considerable effect in France thanks to its assertions about Alfonso XIII's support for the German cause in the First World War. With information provided by Santiago Alba, Blasco Ibáñez claimed that the King had actively arranged for U-boats to refuel in Spanish ports and to be supplied with information about the movements of British, French, Italian and American shipping. Accounts of his pleasure-loving activities – polo, yachting, gambling, especially in the casino at Deauville, race-horses, women – were contrasted with his constant cries of poverty. Spending more than he received from a generous government allowance, he was involved in corrupt business deals which frequently saw him lending his name to dubious enterprises.[38] The accusations of Blasco Ibáñez were not unique. Alfonso was alleged to have been bribed by a swindler, Isidro Pedraza de la Pascua, to get government funding for the extravagant railway-building schemes of the Sociedad Española de Industrias y Tracción.[39]

In January 1925, the Spanish Embassy in Paris instituted legal proceedings against Blasco Ibáñez for offences against Alfonso XIII. The Ambassador, José María Quiñones de León, is alleged to have remarked to friends: 'The worst thing is that everything that Blasco says is true.'[40] After a widely publicized debate in the French parliament, the overall tone of which was broadly in favour of Blasco Ibáñez, the proceedings were stopped. This simply increased demand for the book and brought ridicule upon the dictatorship. Primo's concern about *España con honra* was revealed in December 1925 when the regime launched a legal action for lèse-majesté against Blasco Ibáñez, Ortega and Unamuno. By then, Unamuno had moved to Hendaye where, from April 1927, he would be involved with Ortega in the production of the journal *Hojas Libres*. The critical newssheets and pamphlets published in Paris were distributed widely in Spain by both the CNT and masonic networks. The Dictator made feeble attempts to denounce them in his *notas oficiosas* (official notes), not unlike Donald Trump's tweets, that were issued to the population on most days. He often composed them in the early hours, after his drunken return from a night of carousing. His attacks on *Hojas Libres* simply increased demand. When it first appeared, an ill-advised *nota oficiosa* denouncing its articles in detail provided priceless publicity. Primo's subsequent critiques ensured that the journal's accusations were devoured by readers in Spain.[41] Similar international ridicule was provoked by the Dictator's threat in September 1926 to pull Spain out of the League of Nations unless his country was made a permanent member of the Council.[42]

There were few who had lamented the promised demise of the *cacique* system. Primo de Rivera was greeted as if he was the iron surgeon of regenerationist dreams. He was only too keen to present himself in this light. Having assured a group of journalists that the Military Directory would be merely a 'constitutional parenthesis' lasting only three months, he declared: 'we are carrying out a surgical operation … But we are not doctors and, when the patient is convalescent, in the period that I have just mentioned, we will take him to a sanatorium where he can get stronger and be completely cured.'[43] The assertion that the Military Directory would be short-lived and make way for the election of a Constituent Cortes was soon undermined by the reality that the promised changes could not be achieved in three months.

The scale of the proposed war on *caciquismo* was underlined by a decree of 30 September which dissolved the *ayuntamiento* (local council) in every small town and village of Spain. Generals were appointed as civil governors in every province. Most would remain in post even after the Military Directory was replaced by a Civilian Directory in 1925. Elections for new *alcaldes* (mayors) and councils would be supervised by nearly 500 army officers sent as government delegates to the main towns in each province. Martínez Anido's instructions to the delegates required that the new councils consist of 'persons of high social prestige, of proven reliability and, if possible, with professional qualifications, or at least the highest taxpayers' – in other words, the people who had benefited most from the previous corrupt arrangements. This ensured that the same *caciques* remained in control of each town, as long as they were not known enemies of the Directory. Delegates were encouraged to investigate cases of *caciquismo* seriously, especially if the *cacique* was perceived to be a critic of the government. Those delegates who investigated friends of the government usually ended up being transferred. Notorious examples of *caciques* who escaped investigation were Leopoldo Saro in Jaén and Juan de la Cierva in Murcia, who nevertheless claimed in his memoirs that he had been persecuted. In contrast, there were serious investigations of the fiefs of the regime's critics – Niceto Alcalá-Zamora and José Sánchez Guerra in Cordoba, Santiago Alba in Valladolid, Romanones in Guadalajara and Manuel Burgos y Mazo in Huelva. The Directory arrogated to itself the right to name the *alcaldes* in cities of more than 100,000 inhabitants. In Madrid, Primo named Alberto Alcocer Rivocaba shortly after he had been dismissed from his post in the Development Ministry for absenteeism.[44]

The officers sent as government delegates were, in theory, anti-*caciquismo* commandos, given the monumental task of rooting out corruption and supervising local administration and elections. Typical of Primo's simplistic optimism about their regenerationist mission, they were enjoined to teach village children patriotism and personal hygiene, to persuade villagers to undertake gymnastics and keep bees and hens. An invitation for citizens to air their complaints about local officials and their abuses led to waves of arrests and trials on the basis of denunciations rather than evidence. Often the complaints merely reflected ongoing quarrels between rival *caciques*. According to the Socialist Antonio Ramos Oliveira, there were now two *caciques* in every town instead of one, and this was just the old politics dressed in military uniform. Those arrested were not the big provincial *caciques* but their agents or small-town *caciques*. The exposure of corruption saw large sums of money being returned to municipal treasuries. In the event, imprisonments were brief and trials led to little more than small fines. The crusade petered out because the number of complaints virtually paralysed local administration and many delegates were sacked because the *caciques* whose corruption they denounced were simply too powerful.[45]

Many municipal governments under inspection were accused of various irregularities. During the investigative process there were at least three suicides of municipal employees and still more examples of officials fleeing to Latin America or of archives burned before they could be consulted. The dearth of prosecutions of important *caciques* was inevitable given that the delegates tended to rely on prominent citizens, the commanders of the Civil Guard, the parish priests, judges, doctors and the local gentry with whom they socialized. This often meant that the delegates inadvertently did the dirty work of one group of *caciques* against another. The most virulent accusation of abuses often came from those who aspired to the posts of the accused. There were also cases of delegates who enriched themselves, having used their power to create their own *cacique* system. Primo himself was not above using the new system. He ensured that, in his own province of Cadiz, his state-sponsored or 'single' party, the Unión Patriótica (UP), would be dominated by friends and family: his cousin the right-wing poet José María Pemán, the Conde de los Andes and the *caciques* of Cadiz, Admiral Ramón de Carranza, the Marqués de Villapesadilla, and his son Ramón de Carranza, Marqués de Soto Hermoso.[46] Against such alliances, the new government delegates had little chance of eradicating corruption. In fact, in most places, the delegates had to choose between one faction of *caciques* and their rivals. The regime's blanket censorship deprived the losing *caciques* of the possibility of publicizing the abuses committed against them.[47]

Other measures taken by the regime ostensibly aimed at eradicating *caciquismo* also consolidated the system and permitted the survival of corruption. The Junta Inspectora de Personal Judicial was created to examine cases unresolved after five years. The scale of its task guaranteed that little would be done. Those who had believed Primo's initial promises of cleaning up the legal system placed greater hopes in the creation of the Junta Organizadora del Poder Judicial, which was to assess all appointments and promotions from President of the Tribunal Supremo down. However, what appeared to be a measure to give independence to the judiciary had the opposite effect. In all cases of a clash between the wishes of the Dictator and the law, the judiciary was overruled. The most notorious cases were those of his friend the drug-dealer 'La Caoba' (see below) in February 1924, an attempt to prosecute Juan March in April of the same year and a major fraud in the bank Crédito de la Unión Minera in 1925, all of which came to nothing because of official interference. When the Civilian Directory was created in December 1925, the powers of the Junta passed to the Ministry of Justice.

Another decree, in February 1924, on conflicts of interest of judges and magistrates, seemed to undermine the power of the *caciques* to control the judicial system at a local level. It strengthened existing government powers for judicial personnel to be transferred away from the area in which they worked. In practice, it merely made it easier for the government to interfere in the operation of justice to its own benefit or that of favoured *caciques*. The real thrust of these measures could be seen in the instruction sent by Martínez Anido on 5 January 1925 to *delegados gubernativos* to send secret reports on local judges who were lax in implementing government policy and in the report of the delegate from Loja in Granada who wrote, 'the principal and most important enemy of the Directory is the power of THE JUDICIARY. It is the greatest adversary to our work.'[48]

The principal problems facing the Directory could never have been solved in three months, all the more so given what Gabriel Maura called 'the encyclopaedic incompetence' of the regime.[49] In any case, the King was not interested in a short-term solution. This was revealed, on 12 November 1923, by his annoyance when the presidents of the Cortes and the Senate, the Conde de Romanones and Melquíades Álvarez, naively gave him a document reminding him of the constitutional requirement for the reopening of the two houses within three months of their closure. He received them, casually leaning on the doorframe. Without inviting them in, he coldly dismissed them. He passed the document to the Dictator, who published a sarcastic note: 'We have not overthrown an entire political system which was leading us to ruin and was loathed by all simply in order to return to the purchasing of votes, the falsification of electoral lists and the violence of recent, and indeed of all, elections that we can remember.'[50]

The process of consolidation of the new regime was confirmed shortly afterwards, when Primo and the King visited Italy during the last week of November 1923. Alfonso XIII introduced Primo to Vittorio Emmanuel as 'My Mussolini' and Primo came away dazzled by the Duce. He declared, 'Your importance is not just Italian but worldwide. You are the apostle of the campaign against dissolution and anarchy that was beginning in Europe.' In his audience with Pius XI, Alfonso XIII's militant rhetorical Catholicism, including an offer to lead crusades, shocked the Pontiff. His praise of Mussolini led to the French press calling him 'the black-shirted King'.[51]

It came as no surprise when, on 22 December 1923, there appeared a decree extending the state of exception constituted by the dictatorship. A note penned by Primo claimed that this was a response to unanimous popular demand.[52] Romanones and Melquíades Álvarez were not the only people to make an issue of the survival of the dictatorship beyond the promised three months. A few days later, Unamuno wrote to the editor of *Le Quotidien*, the Paris newspaper that published his frequent attacks on the regime:

> A pleasure-seeking general, of below average intelligence, eaten up with egoistic ambitions, issued a manifesto that constituted a supreme ignominy for the country. In it, he appealed to the dominant passion and envy of the inquisitorial mob. The same passion that produced in our fourteenth century the terrible Inquisition. As happened then, it invited denunciations. And thus was inaugurated a period of persecution of the intelligentsia. Since then, the private life of the Spaniards who love freedom, justice and humanity is hell.[53]

Unamuno's articles were to be a thorn in the Dictator's side. What initially infuriated Primo was the exposé by Unamuno and Rodrigo Soriano, the President of the Madrid Ateneo, of the relationship between the Dictator and La Caoba (Mahogany) – a nickname referring to her dark skin – an Andalusian cabaret artist who was alleged to be a prostitute and drug addict. When she was arrested for dealing in morphine and cocaine, Primo directed Prendes Pardo, the judge who had ordered the arrest, to release her. When he refused, he was expelled from the judiciary and Buenaventura Muñoz, the President of the Tribunal Supremo, who supported him, was forced to take early retirement.[54] In February 1924, for publicizing the case, Unamuno and Soriano were arrested and sent into exile on the barren and rocky Canary island of Fuerteventura and the Ateneo de Madrid was closed down. Primo had nursed ill feelings towards Soriano ever since he had insulted him in the Cortes in March 1906. Primo had reacted by challenging him to a duel with swords in which both were slightly wounded.[55]

The Directory dismissed Unamuno from his posts as Vice-Rector and Professor of Greek at the University of Salamanca, in both cases without consulting the university authorities. Although motivated by the case of La Caoba, the decision was formally justified by reference to a private letter in which Unamuno had denounced the monarchy as 'rotten'. Primo declared that he would happily repeat what he had done in her case because he was proud to say that he had always been kind and benevolent to women.[56] Two members of the board of the Ateneo, the prominent intellectual Gregorio Marañón and the poet Luis de Tapia, visited Martínez Anido to protest. Spitting with rage, he told them that Primo

was too kind-hearted and had prevented him employing his usual methods: 'I would cut off several heads of "intellectuals" so that they stop
being a nuisance. If I could carry out my programme, Unamuno would
not reach Fuerteventura alive. I don't give a shit about "intellectuals".' The
contempt was mutual. In a letter to a friend on 29 December 1925,
Unamuno wrote that there could be no return to 'liberty and normality
without a trial and punishment of the mutineers of 13 September, above
all of M. Anido, the epileptic pig whose crimes and theft of public funds
demand redress'.[57]

Unamuno's sojourn in Fuerteventura was brief. His escape, in June,
was organized by a coalition of freemasons, the editor of Le Quotidien
and the Ligue des Droits de l'Homme.[58] In Paris, his articles for Le
Quotidien infuriated Primo, who took the ill-advised step of asking the
French Prime Minister Édouard Herriot to silence Unamuno. When
Herriot made it clear that he could not intervene, Primo took the even
more impolitic step of writing directly to Le Quotidien. His letter started
with a declaration of his respect for the opinions of others and went on
to deny various allegations made by Unamuno, including references to
corruption within the African Army. It was printed on the newspaper's
front page together with Unamuno's reply, which mockingly pointed
out that Primo respected his opinion so much that he had exiled him
and deprived of his university chair before going on to repeat his
original allegations. Whereas Unamuno's exile enhanced his reputation,
Soriano's spiky personality saw him isolated on the fringes of the
opposition.[59]

Primo's peevish intolerance of criticism was further demonstrated by
the arrest of Ángel Ossorio y Gallardo on 11 September 1924 because he
had declared, in a private letter to Antonio Maura, that 'immorality and
barbarity abound everywhere in the most shameful way. You will have
seen that without any competition the young son of the Dictator has
been given a job as lawyer to the telephone company with a salary of
twenty or twenty-five thousand pesetas and similar things are happening
all over the place.' The 21-year-old José Antonio had only just finished
his law studies and was trying to make his way in the legal profession.
The incident revealed that the government intercepted the correspondence of Maura and many other political figures. It caused a scandal in the
legal profession that would do enduring damage to the regime. Primo's
own naive response, asserting that his son had a doctorate, was trilingual

in English, French and Spanish and had always got top marks at university, caused much merriment. While Osorio was in jail, the queues of journalists and politicians lining up to express solidarity with him impelled the King to advise the Vice-President, the Marqués de Magaz, to have him released. Nine days later, just as Ossorio was released on bail, Rafael Sánchez Guerra, the son of the ex-Prime Minister, was arrested on account of an article published in Cuba. The assault on prestigious intellectuals and their writings from exile fostered the growth of the republican movement.[60]

Primo himself had already revealed the police's illegal interception of private correspondence when he engaged in a polemic with Antonio Maura in August 1924. A group of Mauristas, headed by César Silio, had written to the grand old man requesting his opinion on the dictatorship and the Unión Patriótica. Although clandestinely circulated, Maura's reply had been opened by the police. In it, he expressed his abomination of the dictatorship and criticized its financial irregularities and arbitrary response to critics. He also suggested that those of his followers who had joined the Unión Patriótica, thinking it to be an instrument of regeneration, were mistaken. On 7 August, the Directory considered imprisoning Maura, but Primo decided instead to publish his letter along with what he thought would be a devastating commentary of his own. His feeble denial of Maura's criticisms gave them massive publicity.[61]

The fact that the regime had little serious interest in the eradication of corruption, particularly that of the Dictator's friends and collaborators, was underlined by the abortive attempt to prosecute Juan March for involvement in the murder of a rival. In April 1924, a judge, Francisco Serra, issued orders for the arrest of March in connection with the killing, in Valencia in September 1916, of Rafael, the son of José Garau, March's partner in the tobacco-contraband business. It was widely believed that March was involved because Rafael Garau had had an affair with March's wife, Eleonor Servera. There was also talk that the younger Garau was trying to undercut March's business with Gibraltar. At the time of the murder, the police had made little effort to apprehend the assassin. March had visited the examining magistrate to see if he had any evidence against him, which he did not. Nevertheless, the magistrate was shortly afterwards transferred to another province as a result, it was said, of the intervention of March's friends in government, which could only really mean Alba. Investigative journalists who were following the case were threatened and told to drop it. There the case lay until 23 December 1923 when, in a letter to Primo, Rafael Garau's brother Francisco revived the accusations against March. The Dictator felt obliged to pass the case to the Tribunal Supremo, and the incorruptible Francisco Serra was appointed to investigate the case. However, March was tipped off and fled to Paris disguised as a priest. While there, he arranged to finance Alba's rather luxurious exile in Le Claridge hotel on the Champs-Élysées. Francisco Serra was threatened by emissaries of March and also offered a large bribe. Serra was dismissed and the judge appointed to replace him in July shelved the case. March was able to return to Spain.[62]

The most serious attempt at rooting out local corruption was the work of the Director General of Local Administration, José Calvo Sotelo. As a disciple and ex-secretary of Antonio Maura, he believed that, to rid the country of *caciquismo*, it was necessary to introduce a reform of municipal administration. He claimed that Maura had told him that it was his 'sacred duty' to accept the job. He assembled a team of talented collaborators. Among them were would-be Christian Democrats from the Asociación Nacional Católica de Propagandistas (ANCP) inspired by Ángel Herrera, the editor of the Catholic newspaper *El Debate*. The ANCP was an elite Jesuit-influenced organization of about 500 prominent and talented Catholic rightists with a presence in the press, the judiciary and the professions.[63] The most prominent was Herrera's close collaborator José María Gil Robles, who would later come to prominence as leader of the legalist right during the Second Republic. The Estatuto Municipal of 1924 and the Estatuto Provincial of 1925 owed a lot to previous attempts at reform by Maura in 1907 and Canalejas in 1911. The laudable ambition of democratizing local life by allowing two-thirds of town councils to be elected was thwarted by a combination of the Dictator's determination to control all aspects of local existence through the continued presence of the *delegados gubernativos* and the residual power of the *caciques*.[64]

Behind the regime's anti-corruption rhetoric, there was considerable profit to be made and not just at a local level. In 1924, Primo created the Consejo de Economía Nacional, an organization that did more to protect the existing interests of both industry and the big landowners than to promote development. Its ruling council consisted of a number of pressure groups representing staunchly protectionist Catalan and Basque industrialists and the agrarian elite. Similarly, the Consejo Regulador de

Producción Industrial, created in 1926, imposed state control over any new industrial enterprise, effectively protecting existing corporations against new competition. Both tended to the creation of monopolies and, with them, corruption. The easy-handed concession of monopolies saw fortunes made by Primo's allies. José Juan Dómine, Juan March's partner in the Compañía Trasmediterránea shipping company, paid for special trains to bring crowds to Madrid to take part in pro-regime demonstrations. Unsurprisingly, the Trasmediterránea received substantial government subsidies. Companies involved in the dictatorship's ambitious railway-building programme were also the recipients of excessive subsidies.[65]

An astonishing case of the government's lax attitude to irregular and corrupt activities concerned the American art dealer Arthur Byne, who was the agent for the spectacularly rich and acquisitive William Randolph Hearst. Byne arranged the purchase and export to the United States of several historical buildings including the Monasterio de Santa María la Real de Sacramenia from Segovia. This was done stone by stone, at eye-watering expense. Though contrary to legislation passed by Eduardo Callejo de la Cuesta, the Minister of Education and Fine Arts, it was nevertheless permitted. Byne boasted to Hearst's architect, Julia Morgan, that violation of the law was facilitated by his lavish bribes to officials at the Ministry, allegedly including the Minister himself. Official acquiescence in Byne's activities would be underlined in 1927 when Byne was decorated, somewhat bizarrely, with the Cruz de Mérito Militar for his services to Hispanic Culture.[66]

The experience of Arthur Byne underlined how ministers, senior military figures and elements of the Dictator's single party, the Unión Patriótica, did not hesitate to use their position, and the lack of a vocal opposition, to obtain sinecures, take bribes or win lucrative government contracts.[67] According to Calvo Sotelo, in the Unión Patriótica 'there were crafty, hypocritical, professional frauds who had taken part for their personal benefit, despite their mental reservations'.[68]

Needless to say, the corruption facilitated by the Unión Patriótica was small beer by comparison with that made possible by the links between big business and the government. Rafael Benjumea y Burín, the Conde de Guadalhorce, for instance, combined being Minister of Development with his position on the board of directors of the hydro-electric company Canalización y Fuerzas del Guadalquivir which, in 1925, received government funds to pay half its expenses. Guadalhorce's brother Carlos profited from his investment in the company that built the highways from Oviedo to Gijón, from Madrid to Valencia and from Madrid to Irún.[69] A similarly favourable tax regime was accorded to another hydro-electric company, the Sociedad Saltos del Alberche, which Guadalhorce set up to build a dam on the Río Alberche, west of Madrid. On its board of directors was to be found the Minister of War, Juan O'Donnell, Duque de Tetuán, who entered government debt-ridden and died a rich man in 1928.[70] Three other civilian ministers had profitable links with banks, industrialists and landowners: José Calvo Sotelo (Finance) with the Banco de Cataluña and the Banco Central of whose board of directors he became President as soon as he left the government; José Yanguas Messia (Foreign Affairs) with the mine owners and the Conde de los Andes (Economy) with landowners. The Dictator's close friend José Sanjurjo was president of the company given the monopoly of civilian air transport in Spain, Concesionaria de Líneas Aéreas Subvencionadas SA (CLASSA), whose profits were boosted by government subsidies. Roberto Martínez Baldrich, the son of Martínez Anido, was given the national monopoly of rat extermination and disinfection works, an ironic parallel with his father's commitment to the extermination of reds.[71]

Martínez Anido was alleged to have accumulated a fortune during his time as Civil Governor of Barcelona. He once again used government funds for his own benefit. He needed to silence Pere Martir Homs, one of his key henchmen in the organization of assassinations during those days. Homs had incriminating information about him. Accordingly, he was established rent-free in a flat within the Ministry of the Interior and also paid a fat salary for a sinecure in the Telefónica.[72]

Some of the most byzantine ramifications of the Dictator's obsession with forming state monopolies were to be found in the creation of those concerning telephones and petroleum. The International Telephone and Telegraph Corporation of New York was given the monopoly in Spain's telephone services in August 1924. Granted generous subsidies and freedom from paying tax, ITT and its Spanish partners, all of whom had links to Primo, the Banco Urquijo, the Banco Hispano-American and the Catalan financiers the Marqués de Comillas and the Conde de Guell, made vast profits out of the arrangement.[73] Once Calvo Sotelo had been convinced by the idea for a petroleum monopoly, he put its implementation into the hands of his faithful collaborator the lawyer Andrés Amado, who worked with José Juan Dómine and Primo's private secretary, Lieutenant Colonel José Ibáñez García. It meant going into battle with Royal Dutch Shell and Standard Oil. Needless to say, his initiative enjoyed the enthusiastic support of Juan March's Porto Pi. Despite threats from the chairman of Shell, the Dutch-born Sir Henri Deterding, the assets and installations of the foreign giants were nationalized to create the Compañía Arrendataria del Monopolio del Petróleo SA (CAMPSA). There was generous compensation for the commercial entities that it replaced, some of which, it was alleged, went into the pockets of Primo's principal collaborators. CAMPSA came to be known popularly as the Consorcio de Amigos de Martínez Anido y Primo SA. Nevertheless, the operation was a success in the short term with the subsequent state revenue of CAMPSA more than doubling that previously raised by customs duties.[74]

In the long term, it was a disaster because the loans raised from foreign banks, particularly Rothschild, to pay compensation for the nationalizations, became an onerous burden on the state as a result of the collapse of the peseta in 1929. A loan of £1,100 million taken when the the pound was valued at 29.23 pesetas was due for repayment on 24 December 1930, by which time the exchange rate had risen to 46.25 pesetas to the pound. The scheme cost the state an additional 21.4 million pesetas. The combination of corruption and incompetence was best illustrated by the establishment of delegations of CAMPSA in every province with well-paid posts for military and civilian friends and relatives of the ministers of the dictatorship. Given that CAMPSA was a monopoly, there was little or no work for them to do. All this was exposed in the Cortes in May 1934 by Prieto and the Radical Minister of Finance, Manuel Marraco.[75]

One of Martínez Anido's closest friends was made an inspector of the monopoly in one province and the father-in-law of his son, Roberto Martínez Baldrich, given the position in another. Sanjurjo's son was made inspector for Zaragoza. Primo secured León for himself. Lieutenant Colonel Ibáñez García and another of his adjutants, Lieutenant Colonel Alfonso Elola Espín, were made national inspectors with fat salaries in addition to their military pay.[76] Martínez Anido's adjutant, Roberto Bahamonde, was given the newly created post of Director General of Supply. This opened up massive possibilities for corruption since government suppliers had to pay a bribe to secure contracts. Many similar profitable posts were invented for military comrades of the Dictator. Significantly, none went to artillery officers. When civilian courts looked into certain cases of corruption, efforts were made to transfer them to military tribunals.[77]

The regime's corruption was common knowledge. One of the most ill-advised, not to say comical, of the Dictator's *notas oficiosas* was put out on 5 July 1929. In response to a campaign being carried by *Hojas Libres* to expose Juan March's various dealings, a furious March complained to the Dictator and asked him issue orders to the frontier police to stop copies getting into Spain. To his dismay, Primo replied: 'Don't worry! I'll sort this out with a *nota oficiosa*.' March was horrified to read in the press the next day the promised note saying 'whatever the origins of this gentleman's enormous fortune, the fact is that he has put it at the disposal of the Directory for any and all of its patriotic objectives'. The consequence was that massive publicity was given to *Hojas Libres'* campaign against March and to Primo's flexible financial morality.[78]

There were many cases of fraud going unpunished thanks to the intervention of the government. One of several notorious examples was that of the Bilbao bank, the Crédito de la Unión Minera. As a result of administrative incompetence, irresponsible speculation and risky investments, the bank collapsed in 1925 with debts of 92 million pesetas. Several senior bank officials had used deposits for their own ends. In consequence, large numbers of people were ruined. A judge, Pedro Navarro, was appointed to investigate the bank's President, Juan Núñez, and several directors who had made fortunes out of the affair. Among those arrested were the Conde de Abásolo, the Marqués de Aldama and the Conde de los Gaitanes, all friends of Alfonso XIII. The Conde de Floridablanca, the son-in-law of Aldama, appealed to the King, who immediately summoned the chief prosecutor of the Tribunal Supremo, the endlessly obsequious Galo Ponte y Escartín, and ordered him to arrange the release of Abásolo, Aldama and Gaitanes. Ponte went to Bilbao, ordered Navarro to free them, destroyed the dossiers of evidence against them and punished Navarro by having him transferred. Heavy fines that had been levied on the accused were annulled by the Tribunal Supremo. It was alleged that the King received 1,500,000 pesetas for his part in the affair.[79]

As time went by, corrupt abuse of government positions would become more commonplace, not to say frenzied, especially once it became clear that the regime's days were numbered. Notorious examples ranged from the fortune spent on apartments in the Navy Ministry to a national subscription organized by the regime to reward the Dictator for the 'sacrifices' he had made for Spain. Companies and banks were informed officially that their, ostensibly voluntary, contribution would be fixed according to their turnover.[80] On 9 March 1929, Primo issued one of his most naive and hypocritical *notas oficiosas* explaining that the purpose of the national subscription was to present him with 'a house that would be a decorous location for my necessary repose after the hard struggle of recent years and also a solution to the needs of my family'. Over 4 million pesetas had been 'donated'.

Primo's declared reason for drawing attention to this was his proclaimed embarrassment that the heavy-handed enthusiasm of the scheme's organizers had led to accusations that contributions were obligatory. Accordingly, he invited anyone who felt that they had been pressured into contributing to reclaim their money. Those afraid to do so were assured that some of the money would go towards providing offices for the Unión Patriótica and the regional Somatén near his new house and some to the poor. He justified the subscription and his acceptance of the proceeds on the grounds that:

> above all, although I would be happy to die as poorly off as I have lived and live to this day, I went ahead with the scheme because, firstly, I believe in all conscience that my services to the country more than justify this beautiful homage; secondly, because I believe that it will be an example and a stimulus to those who come after me; thirdly, because I think that it is legitimate to ensure that my children do not have to move from apartment to apartment laden down with family heirlooms, as I have had to do, moving home in Madrid a dozen times; and fourthly, because I don't want the Unión Patriótica and the Somatén to have to make do with rented premises.

The idea that the Marqués de Estela, Andalusian landowner and senior general, had to permit this subscription lest he and his family be left in penury provoked not inconsiderable amusement.[81] At the end of September, it was announced that some of the money raised by the popular subscription had purchased for him a house in Jerez.[82] Four months later, he would again expose his naivety in relation to the benefits of his position. He responded to criticism in *Hojas Libres* of a junket to the United States his and Martínez Anido's sons had enjoyed as 'representatives' of the recently created Patronato de Turismo. He praised these young men for their sacrifice in making the trip.[83]

Primo's background as Captain General of Barcelona and intimate of the Catalan textile barons, as well as being the scion of a large landowning family in Jerez, made him the ideal praetorian defender of the interests of industrialists and landowners. On the other hand, it hardly prepared him for some of the problems that he faced. Nevertheless, at first he was immensely popular. Affable and approachable, he was a gargantuan eater, an inveterate gambler, a heavy drinker who loved binges and would frequently go on massive benders. His daughter claimed, implausibly, that he had never touched a drop of alcohol in his life.[84] A widower since his wife, Casilda Sáenz de Heredia, had died in June 1909, he was not averse to paying for the favours of women. On one occasion, he was hurt in a brawl provoked when he pressed unwanted attention on a hostess in a nightclub.[85] In another pre-echo of Donald Trump, he boasted of his success as a lothario, writing the following passage which he insisted was inserted in a semi-official biography:

> He has been a great lover. Among his loves there have been women of high and low origins. Of the first, apart from his wife, little is known since he is discreet in this regard ... Of the others, when he was widowed he had an affair, with a really feisty and attractive *madrileña* who flaunted her allure and wit as a waitress in a well-known Madrid bar. They say that he falls in love easily and has loved a lot, but they also say that he prefers flirting to fidelity.

According to his friend Jacinto Capella, he allegedly said that loss of virility limited his amorous activities.[86]

Primo's cousin José María Pemán described the Dictator's life as 'a frenzy of patriotism and an absence of books'. Salvador de Madariaga defined Primo as a café politician, 'spontaneous, intuitive, uninformed, impatient of delay, imaginative, intensely patriotic, apt to take simple views of things'.[87] Typical was his declared intention to put an end to the practice of functionaries brushing off problems with the mantra 'Come back tomorrow'. Two days after the establishment of the Military Directory, he issued a decree ordering government departments to post a list of all unresolved matters from the previous five years together with a reasoned justification of the delay. Inevitably, the problem of finding efficient and educated functionaries to deal with these issues was never solved. Moreover, Primo spent excessive time touring the country milking his popularity, particularly enjoying the admiration of the women who came to see him, and making patriotic speeches. He also found time to write his virtually daily notes to the press.[88]

Primo's accessibility was as notorious as his verbosity. José Calvo Sotelo commented that 'the doors of his office were never closed to anybody' and that he saw 'the clock as a useless bit of junk'. While Calvo Sotelo thought him eloquent, Unamuno regarded him as 'the royal goose' and 'simply a parrot'.[89] Primo considered himself to be a graduate of 'the university of life'. He was made an honorary Doctor of Law by the University of Salamanca in October 1926, allegedly as a result of the government repaying a substantial sum owed to the university. In his acceptance speech, he declared: 'Forgive me the immodesty, I have a doctorate in the science of life, and from it I have derived the lessons that prepared me for the exercise of government.'[90] Some of his apparently common-sense solutions to problems had wide appeal. For instance, in 1927, Calvo Sotelo convinced him that he had conjured up a fiscal surplus by dint of making the huge deficits disappear, which he did by producing one ordinary and one 'extraordinary' budget in which was parked the uncontrolled expenditure on public works and the preparation of the great exhibitions in Seville and Barcelona. Primo celebrated by devoting part of the 'surplus' to redeeming mattresses and clothes pawned by the needy. He also arranged for a subsidy for numerous families and created a 'disaster fund' to which the poor could apply. On another occasion, he decided to impose fines on hotels that overcharged.[91]

Two important contributions to the Dictator's honeymoon period were the general revulsion caused by the chaos of the previous six years and the fact that his arrival coincided with the first signs of economic recovery after the post-war crisis. The social peace imposed by Martínez Anido via the repression of the CNT and the PCE, together with Socialist collaboration with the regime, would endure until 1928. Rising wages, better social services and a drop in unemployment, thanks in part to

Primo's ambitious programmes of public works including a drive for cheap housing, saw working-class militancy neutralized by prosperity. The first years of the dictatorship coincided with a general international upturn and experienced significant development of the construction, chemical, steel and electricity-generating industries. The regime implemented many of the demands of the regenerationist thinkers in terms of massive irrigation schemes and a significant modernizing of transport and communications infrastructure. In 1928, damning accusations were made that huge sums of money had been accumulated by friends of the King and of Primo in deals relating to major irrigation projects. It was alleged that the published price paid by the state for the Canal de Henares in Guadalajara and the Canal del Esla in León was wildly inflated relative to the real price, with the difference going into their pockets.[92] The communications improvements were based on the building of sea and air ports as well as a network of roads and railways, all of which would bear fruit only thirty years later. The Ibero-American Exhibition in Seville and the International Expo in Barcelona were both successful and prestigious, albeit very costly.[93]

Nevertheless, there was little financial control over the various development schemes. Corruption was rife and gigantic profits were made by recently formed companies. Subsequently, there were allegations that the King had received bribes to help these companies get favourable contracts and that the Dictator himself derived financial benefit from the distribution of government contracts. When the Marqués de Cortina exposed some of these scandals in a specialized economic weekly, the journal was closed down and Cortina himself was arrested and exiled to the Canary Islands. References to corrupt dealings were silenced by the censorship. Articles exposing them in exiled publications were avidly devoured by those who could get access to smuggled copies.[94]

José María Pemán commented that Primo suffered from a need for public adulation, what he called 'a hunger for crowds'.[95] Primo's relatively short-lived popularity also owed much to government machinery. Blanket censorship, plus the organization of mass demonstrations of support, allowed him to proclaim that he was universally loved by all true Spaniards and that 'public opinion is on my side', even after 1926 when discontent was growing. The orchestration of cheering crowds at the parades and demonstrations of the Somatén and the Unión Patriótica could be considered part of the hidden corruption of the regime. They constituted a huge cost for the relevant municipal, provincial or national authorities.[96] There was thus a two-way process whereby the efforts to influence public opinion fed back into the Dictator's conviction that he was adored by all right-thinking Spaniards. A key part of the operation was the compulsory purchase of sixty regional newspapers and the creation by Martínez Anido of the daily *La Nación* under the editorship of the pro-fascist Manuel Delgado Barreto, an operation partially funded by Juan March. Nevertheless, *La Nación* never achieved a print run of more than 50,000 copies, many of which were either unsold or given away in the branch offices of the Unión Patriótica. The party's official bi-monthly magazine *Unión Patriótica* never sold more than 15,000 copies.[97] Despite these weak sales, Delgado Bareto's brother, Leoncio, with the approval of Martínez Anido, made money for the paper by blackmailing local authorities with the threat of inserting highly critical articles about their town or province.[98]

The entire press was turned into a vehicle for regime propaganda. The diverse editorial function of the independent press was replaced by the egoistical ramblings of Primo's *notas oficiosas*. His self-aggrandizement occasioned much mockery. For example, in one note he claimed that Alfonso XIII had asked him where he had learned to govern, to which he had allegedly replied, 'In the casino in Jerez' (the local landowners' club) – and the seemingly spell-bound King exclaimed, 'Ah, yes, it's true, you have lived the life of the people.' In another, he wrote: 'As I approached, the women separated into two lines so that they could see the saviour of the Fatherland.' His belief that women adored him was a constant refrain. In January 1926, at a banquet in his honour, one of the dignitaries present begged him not to give up power. A surprised Primo replied: 'Why would I? When I go out, women lift up their children so that they can know me and see the saviour of the Fatherland. On Sundays, when I go out for a walk alone in my Spanish cape, the people clap and cheer, and happy young seductive seamstresses tug on my cape to see if I really am General Primo de Rivera.' He even complained in his *notas oficiosas* that the press did not give adequate coverage to the scale of the admiration and affection showered on him by women.[99] All Spanish newspapers were obliged to insert the notes free of charge and they were placed in foreign newspapers despite the exorbitant cost.[100]

Primo banned criticism of the Italian Fascist regime in the Spanish press. While enjoying being compared with Mussolini, he had no interest in emulating the Fascist regime's ostensibly anti-capitalist order. Primo's conservative authoritarianism was built on the notion that the army was the embodiment of the nation and thus would impose a strong state to combat the threats of anarchism and Bolshevik communism and rise above the inefficiencies and corruption of the parliamentary system. The nearest to the Italian Fascist Party would be his single party, the Unión Patriótica. Based on several Uniones Patrióticas in several provinces of Castile, created by followers of Ángel Herrera, what passed for its ideology drew on the social Catholic ideas of the Confederación Nacional Católico-Agraria and the Asociación Nacional Católica de Propagandistas. Herrera was a fervent supporter of the new regime and anxious to see the creation of a mass organization to underpin it. However, much of its rhetoric was extreme. Primo's friend José María Pemán declared: 'the time has come for Spanish society to choose between Jesus and Barrabas'. For Pemán, the nation was bitterly divided between an anti-Spain embracing everything that was heterodox and foreign and an authentic Spain of traditional religious and monarchical values.[101]

Announced in April 1924 and organized over the next eighteen months, the aim of the Unión Patriótica was to consolidate Primo's achievements after the eventual transfer of military to civilian rule. In the event, it became less a party than an organization of the upper and middle classes who wished to manifest their support of the regime and so derive the corresponding benefits. Membership, reasonably priced at one peseta per year, became an unofficial requirement for access to government preferment. Its organization was the task of the government delegates. Their job was easiest where the CNCA was strongest, in the provinces of Old Castile and León, and where *caciques* dominated, in Andalusia and Extremadura. Almost half the total membership came from Cáceres and Huelva. The delegates often ended up having to favour one faction of *caciques* or their rivals. The Unión Patriótica was weakest in areas where *caciquismo* did not flourish. In Barcelona, for instance, with less than 4 per cent of the total membership, many members went to UP headquarters to read the press or to play cards.[102]

The efforts of Romanones and others to force a return to constitutional normality severely irritated the King. In April 1925, Alfonso rashly declared, in an interview for the newspaper *Paris-Midi*: 'The Constitution! What an empty word when compared with the security and calm that have just been restored to the people! ... if Parliament were opened again, we would soon see how the old parties, who led the country to ruin, would start their old disputes again and begin their inane chattering at the exact point at which they were interrupted by General Primo.' He told Romanones's sons that he was 'determined to make the present situation permanent'. He failed to realize that he was pushing many Liberals and Conservatives from passivity to active opposition.[103]

In any case, in the early months of the regime, threats to Primo's position were more likely to come from the army than from the workers. Africanista officers, and indeed many others, had been anything but enthusiastic about the coup. It was reported to the Dictator that, on hearing news of it, General Queipo de Llano had exclaimed, 'They've put Miguel Primo in power! He'll lead us into anarchy!' Once firm friends, this would be the beginning of a subsequent enmity inflamed because the ever irascible Queipo failed to abide by Primo's requirements for total submission.[104] Africanistas were fully aware of, and appalled by, Primo's widely publicized belief that Spain should abandon the Moroccan protectorate. They regarded it as an insult to the memory of their comrades who had died in an epic of patriotic sacrifice.[105] Typical in this regard was the rising star of the Foreign Legion, Lieutenant Colonel Francisco Franco Bahamonde. A favourite of the King, in January 1923 he had been named a *gentilhombre de cámara* (gentleman of the chamber), one of an elite group of military courtiers. This meant that, when on Monday, 22 October 1923 he got married to María del Carmen Polo in Oviedo, Alfonso XIII was his best man *in absentia*. By tradition, on marrying, a senior officer was required to 'kiss the hands' of the King, which he did in late October.

In later years, Franco himself asserted that, at their meeting, the King had quizzed him about how the army in Africa felt about the recent coup and the military situation in Morocco. Franco claimed to have told him that the army mistrusted Primo because of his belief in the need to abandon Morocco. When the King said that there was no solution to the Moroccan problem, Franco allegedly countered that the 'rebels' could be defeated and the Spanish protectorate secured. He explained that, so far, Spanish operations had been piecemeal, pushing back the tribal rebels from one small piece of ground after another, attempting to hold them and to retake them when they were recaptured. Primo de Rivera had been dismissed as Military Governor of Cadiz in 1917 for expressing an identical opinion. In the Senate on 25 November 1921, he had scornfully denounced the war as just a series of skirmishes, stating: 'I believe that, from a strategic point of view, the presence of a single Spanish soldier on the other side of the Straits is damaging for Spain.' For declaring that the only value of the Moroccan protectorate was as something to be exchanged for Gibraltar, he was dismissed as Captain General of the Madrid military region in 1919.[106] Now, in his conversation with the King, Franco advocated, not Primo's abandonism, but the same idea that had provoked Martínez Anido's resignation in August, that instead of tolerating an endless drain on men and materials, Spain should make an all-out attack on the headquarters of Abd el-Krim. The most direct route was by sea to the Bay of Alhucemas. Alfonso XIII allegedly responded by arranging for Franco to dine with the recently installed Dictator and tell him of his plan.[107]

If the meeting took place at all, Franco's typically Africanista views would have come as no surprise to Primo. Franco himself had already published a diary containing his opinion that all could be resolved at Alhucemas, 'the heart of anti-Spanish rebellion, the road to Fez'.[108] Although Franco later presented the idea for the Alhucemas landing as his own brainchild, plans for a landing there had been prepared by the General Staff long before Franco's conversation with the King.[109] Franco could not have told the Dictator anything that he did not already know. Primo was deeply concerned by the economic drain constituted by the colonial war but not so foolhardy as to think that he could go against the views of the Africanistas. Accordingly, Primo instructed the Ambassador in London, the Marqués de Merry del Val, to propose that the British government exchange Gibraltar for Ceuta. Had the plan been accepted, it might have made it possible for Primo to present withdrawal from Morocco as a triumph. However, for obvious strategic reasons, London had no interest in abandoning the uniquely defensible rock.[110] Moreover, by the spring of 1924 Abd el-Krim's power had grown enormously. Presenting himself as the leader of a wide Berber nationalist movement, he proposed establishing an independent socialist republic. In March, he made another attack on Tizzi Azza. Numerous tribes accepted his leadership and, under his self-bestowed title of 'Emir of the Rif', in June he formally requested membership of the League of Nations.[111]

Abd el-Krim's confidence reflected the tenuousness of Spain's foothold in Morocco. In the course of the Spanish offensives after Annual, the area around Melilla had been recaptured but, that aside, secure Spanish territory consisted only of the towns of Ceuta, Tetuán, Larache and Xauen. The High Commissioner, General Luis Aizpuru Mondéjar, had proposed a major advance from Melilla. Primo de Rivera had responded that that was impossible since Spain simply could not afford to maintain 115,000 troops in Morocco. He was convinced that full-scale pacification of the protectorate was beyond Spain's capacity and to cling to it, on the basis of strings of waterless, indefensible blockhouses, was ludicrous. He believed that 90,000 men were sufficient to repel Abd el-Krim's advance. In a speech in Zaragoza, he announced the immediate withdrawal of 25,000. The number of conscripts for 1924 was reduced by 20 per cent and there was early release for over 50,000 recruits.[112] Many garrisons were seriously disturbed by rumours that they were about to receive orders to withdraw. There was talk that, in the event of a retreat from Xauen, many officers, including Franco, would apply for transfers to the mainland. Aware of this, in July 1924 Primo de Rivera decided to inspect the situation on the ground personally despite fears in the local high command that he would be received with hostility. It was later alleged that some officers, including Franco, had plotted to take Primo hostage if he argued for the abandonment of the protectorate.[113]

During Primo's tour of the protectorate, there was a notorious incident in Ben-Tieb on 19 July 1924, which became the basis of another myth about Franco. This was the dinner at which, allegedly, Franco had arranged for Primo to be served a menu based entirely on eggs.[114] *Huevos* (eggs) being the Spanish slang for testicles, the message was clear: the visitor lacked *huevos* and the Legion had plenty to spare. In 1972, Franco denied that such a menu had been served but it was widely believed at the time. He certainly made a vehement speech arguing that Spanish Morocco should not be abandoned. Rather courageously, in the hostile context, Primo calmly reprimanded Franco for his insubordination and went on to explain firmly the logic behind plans for a total withdrawal. He argued that the conquest of Alhucemas was not worth the inevitable casualties and asked: 'Do you think that you enjoy the monopoly of patriotism?' This provoked hissing and heckling. Sanjurjo, who accompanied the Dictator, later told José Calvo Sotelo that, fearing that things could get out of hand, he had kept his hand on the butt of his pistol throughout the speeches. Primo's speech was greeted with total silence. The principal eyewitness, the journalist Emilio Herrero, said that he saw one *legionaro* draw his pistol with the intention of using it. Herrero was later arrested in Madrid for having published his account of the Ben-Tieb incident.[115] In his later recollections, Franco told his official biographer Ricardo de la Cierva that Primo had made light of the incident, inviting him to his quarters to argue for two hours on the need for a landing in Alhucemas. That is highly unlikely. Indeed, there were other officers who thought that Franco should have been court-martialled.[116]

Primo's abandonist position was not one of simple retreat and effective surrender to Abd el-Krim. He was also pursuing a complicated strategy of trying to play off El Raisuni and Abd el-Krim against one another. If this strategy failed, which it did, Spanish forces would be withdrawn behind a new defensive line. Efforts would be made to prevent munitions and food reaching the enemy while simultaneously pursuing a scorched-earth tactic of bombing Rif villages and surrounding farms with incendiaries, phosgene, chlorine and mustard gas and arming aircraft-mounted machine guns with toxic gas cartridges. In his Zaragoza speech, he declared: 'In the next operations, the air force will actively impose severe punishment on the Moors in order to make them recognize our sovereignty. We must remain active but with as few men as possible.'[117]

Despite the insubordinate behaviour of Franco and other officers of the Legion, Primo remained commited to abandoning Morocco not least because abandonism was immensely popular among the civilian population. It was his intention to reduce troop numbers to approximately 50,000 men by the end of September 1924.[118] However, Spanish attempts to deal with the terminally ill El Raisuni had consolidated support for Abd el-Krim, to whom peace overtures had not borne fruit. Already before his reconnaissance in Morocco, Primo had agreed to withdraw Spanish forces to a new line of defence and rely more on the bombing campaign. The consolidation of Spanish-held territory involved abandoning positions near Melilla in the east and a much bigger operation in the west. Relief operations had to be mounted for the various posts being besieged near the coast and near Tetuán, of which the most important was the holy city of Xauen.[119]

The idea of leaving the positions lost after Annual, and later retaken at enormous cost in casualties, outraged the Africanistas, but they had to recognize that something had to be done to relieve the siege of Xauen. It took a column led by General Castro Girona over a week to fight the

65 kilometres from Tetuán to Xauen. They arrived on 2 October. Over the next four weeks, units from remote positions gathered there until, by the beginning of November, there were 10,000 men in Xauen, many of them wounded, most exhausted. An evacuation was imperative. Primo assumed complete responsibility, naming himself High Commissioner on 16 October. He returned to Morocco and set up his General Staff in Tetuán. The evacuation of the Spanish, Jewish and pro-Spanish Arab inhabitants of Xauen was a daunting task. Women, children, the old and the sick, were packed onto trucks. The long and vulnerable column set off on 15 November. Moving slowly at night, their rear was covered by the Legion under Franco. Constantly harassed by raiding tribesmen, and severely slowed down by rainstorms that turned the tracks to deep mud, the evacuees took four weeks to reach Tetuán. The joureny cost nearly 2,000 dead plus 5,800 wounded but prevented Xauen becoming a second Annual.[120]

What changed Primo's policy was not the Africanistas' insubordination but rather a grave mistake made by Abd el-Krim on 13 April 1925. After entering Xauen, he had captured El Raisuni in January that year. Brimming with confidence, in pursuit of his ambition of creating a socialist republic, he invaded French Morocco and was initially successful. His forces came within 30 kilometres of Fez. Marshal Hubert Lyautey, Commander-in-Chief of French Forces in Morocco, called for an alliance with Spain against the Rif rebels. The subsequent Franco-Spanish Conference in Madrid from 17 June to 25 July 1925 established peace terms to be offered to Abd el-Krim and, if he refused them, an agreement between the two countries for joint military operations against him. Both parties feared that Abd el-Krim might establish an independent Riffian state. Believing that Moscow was behind a broad Muslim uprising against Christian Europe, Primo finally decided to implement the long-dormant plans for the invasion of Alhucemas.[121] He wrote to Sanjurjo while the conference was taking place, 'I fear that Abd el-Krim is being encouraged to form an independent state.'[122]

Talks on collaboration against Abd el-Krim were held between Primo and Marshal Philippe Pétain, the Inspector General of the French army, who replaced the seriously ill Lyautey. On 8 September 1925, an invasion from the south by a force of 160,000 French colonial troops coincided with the landing of 75,000 Spanish soldiers at Alhucemas before a successful push on Abd el-Krim's headquarters at Axdir. The Spanish contingent, under the overall command of General Sanjurjo, was transported in ships of Juan March's Compañía Transmediterránea. Franco was in command of the first party of troops to go ashore and had responsibility for establishing a bridgehead. In fact, the entire operation was characterized by Sanjurjo's poor organization and inadequate planning. Nevertheless, Axdir was captured on 2 October and Abd el-Krim's house looted. By the end of November, the rebels were in full retreat, although the Rif leader was still free and in control of much territory. Primo returned to Madrid, naming Sanjurjo as High Commissioner. There began a process of so-called pacification which signified fierce repression. On 26 May 1926, Abd el-Krim surrendered to the French authorities.[123]

In 1926, the Rif was given limited independence in agricultural, economic and administrative matters while still under Spanish military control. The Moroccan problem was resolved and, with it, the crippling drain on Spain's finances. It would later be seen as Primo's greatest achievement and, at the time, opened the way to the conversion of the Military Directory into a civilian one.[124] Having said that, it would be wrong to give him all the credit as did, among others, José Calvo Sotelo: 'This heroic feat was the personal, completely personal work of Primo de Rivera and of no one else. Everyone opposed the plan.'[125] Gabriel Maura wrote that 'this triumph of Spain would certainly not have been achieved without the personal intervention of the Marqués de Estella'. In fact, the Spanish forces enjoyed a strong element of luck since the landing took place on a different day, at a different time, on a different beach and with different tactics than had been laid down in the plans of the General Staff.[126]

It is certainly true that the idea of an Alhucemas landing prior to an invasion of the mountains of Beni Urriaguel had long been regarded as the only way of controlling the Rif and that Primo de Rivera provided the necessary initiative to make it happen. Certainly, he took the credit, writing to the Duque de Tetuán that the King had congratulated him for the decision to go ahead with the landing and apologized for opposing it.[127] For his triumph, he received numerous honours, of which the most notable was the awarding of the Gran Cruz Laureada de San Fernando, Spain's highest military honour, which came with an hereditary annual pension of 10,000 pesetas. He was also named *hijo adoptivo* (adoptive son) of Madrid, Barcelona and several other cities. The Ayuntamiento of

Jerez commissioned a statue of him and the government required town councils to make 'spontaneous' donations towards the cost. It was even proposed that the King make him Príncipe del Rif.[128] Had he resigned in 1926, when the economy was still buoyant, he would have been remembered as a great statesman and national hero. Unfortunately, his success had consolidated his conviction that he was a providential figure capable of resolving all Spain's problems.

José Calvo Sotelo, Primo's Minister of Finance who would be assassinated in 1936 just before the outbreak of Civil War.

8

The Primo de Rivera Dictatorship: The Years of Failure, 1926–1931

Ironically, the apparent apogee of Primo's popularity coincided with the emergence of opposition. The banning of CNT union activities and Martínez Anido's ruthless tactics in pursuing and arresting anarchist activists provoked a return to insurrectionary tactics. In 1927, the hard-line Federación Anarquista Ibérica was created. Ángel Pestaña's opposition to the move foreshadowed the divisions of the anarchist movement in the 1930s.[1] A crackdown on the anarchist extremists had followed the murder, on 7 May 1924, of Rogelio Pérez Cicario, the newly appointed executioner of the Barcelona High Court. Pérez Cicario was virtually unknown and his bodyguards were untouched during the assault. The assassination thus had the hallmarks of a Martínez Anido operation. It was almost certainly the work of police agents provocateurs seeking to justify the closure of union offices and the arrest of dozens of anarchists, both of which took place later the same day.[2]

The rather ineffective resistance to the dictatorship involved not only the anarchists but also various exiled republican groups loosely led by Marcelino Domingo, and the recently emerged Catalanist opposition. An extremely disparate Revolutionary Committee was established in Paris and secured promises of finance from Santiago Alba.[3] The hopes of the Lliga Regionalista and the Foment de Treball Nacional that their support for Primo's coup would obtain financial autonomy for Catalonia had been betrayed, but that had not diminished their need for the repressive arts of Martínez Anido. In consequence, the anti-Catalan measures of the regime saw the nationalist banner pass to more radical groups such as Acció Catalana and Estat Català, now in clandestinity. The leader of the latter was an ex-military engineer, Colonel Francesc Macià. A practising Catholic and by nature conservative, Macià had become a fervent nationalist in reaction to perceived betrayals by Madrid. In the course of his evolution, he had become a friend of Ángel Pestaña and Seguí, whose murder had contributed to his radicalization.[4]

The work of the new revolutionary committee was undermined by two precipitate actions carried out by the anarchist hard-liners, among whom Durruti and Juan García Oliver were prominent. The first was an ill-fated attack on the Atarazanas barracks in Barcelona that led to numerous arrests, including that of Ángel Pestaña. Two anarchists were tried by summary court martial and executed three days later.[5] The other action, equally precipitate, took the form of two incursions across the frontier. After receiving information, fabricated by police agents provocateurs, that a mass revolutionary uprising was imminent, several small groups of anarchists crossed the French frontier near Vera de Bidasoa in Navarre. One of the groups clashed with the Civil Guard and the frontier guards (Carabineros). In the subsequent shoot-out, three civilians and two Civil Guards were killed. The planned parallel operation into Girona was dismantled by the French police before it really got started.[6] Of those arrested at Vera de Bidasoa, four were tried by a court martial on 14 November. For lack of evidence, they were found not guilty of the deaths of the Civil Guards. The head of the Civil Guard, General Ricardo Burguete, was infuriated by the verdict. He persuaded the Captain General of the Burgos military region to imprison the officers who had acted as judges and to remove the prosecutor of the military judicial corps, Carlos Blanco Pérez. A fresh trial was ordered with the Captain General demanding the death sentence for three of the accused and six years' imprisonment for the fourth. The three were found guilty and sentenced to death. Two were garrotted and the third, Pablo Martín, committed suicide by diving head first from a high balcony on to the patio of the prison.[7] Both the infiltration of anarchist groups in France and the involvement of the sinister Captain Julio de Lasarte pointed to police manipulation of the affair. After his death on 29 January 1924, Arlegui had been replaced as Director General of Security by General Pedro Bazán Esteban, another crony of Martínez Anido. He had maintained Arlegui's team, including, as head of the secret police, the Brigada de Investigación Social, Santiago Martín Báguenas, and Luis Fenoll Malvasía as his deputy.[8]

The judicially questionable execution of the three men found guilty of the deaths at Vera de Bidasoa indicates that the regime, while hardly bloodthirsty on the scale attained by Franco, used the code of military justice to facilitate ready recourse to the death penalty. Death sentences were passed and implemented on those responsible for the robbery, near Aranjuez, of the Madrid–Andalusia express, on the night of 11 April 1924, during which a railway employee and one of the thieves was shot dead by the others. Since Martínez Anido was determined to present this case of common criminality as part of a Communist plot, it was necessary for the case to be tried by court martial. Galo Ponte, the prosecutor of the Tribunal Supremo, obligingly transferred the case to the military. Three death sentences, at least one of which was of doubtful validity, were passed. Similar outcomes followed armed robberies of casinos in Badalona in May 1924 and in Zaragoza in July 1927. Those responsible were sentenced to death by a court martial.[9]

On 3 December 1925, buoyed up by the popularity bestowed by the victory at Alhucemas, Primo took a further step in the institutionalization of his hitherto provisional regime. With the enthusiastic approval of Alfonso XIII, he instituted a Civilian Directory. Committing the future of the monarchy to Primo, the King expressed his confidence in the Directory and gave Primo power to form and preside over a government.[10] Primo chose the cabinet of ministers himself, remaining as before the all-powerful super-minister. Martínez Anido was named deputy Prime Minister and Minister of the Interior. An immediate problem was that some civilian functionaries revealed themselves as less docile than the military personnel they replaced. Considerable embarrassment was caused when the regime's anti-corruption rhetoric was taken seriously by the Under-Secretary of the Ministry of Labour, Juan Flórez Posada. He was dismissed, after barely six weeks in office, for writing critical reports about dubious financial initiatives involving senior regime figures, including the King.[11]

The most powerful civilian ministers were the engineer Rafael Benjumea y Burín, the Conde Guadalhorce, at Development, José Calvo Sotelo, at Finance, and the Catalan Eduardo Aunós, one-time Lliga Regionalista deputy for Lleida, as Minister of Labour, Commerce and Industry. Aunós, one-time private secretary to Cambó, was described by Amadeu Hurtado as 'that fat and dozy young man'.[12] Primo's control over the judiciary was clinched by the appointment of the notoriously incompetent and corrupt Galo Ponte. In 1923, then a magistrate in Seville, Ponte had sent Primo an enthusiastic telegram congratulating him on the success of his coup. As a reward for his sycophancy, Ponte was made the prosecutor of the Tribunal Supremo. For his services to the regime, including elaborating the legal device whereby the robbery on the Andalusia express could be tried by court martial and his role in the Crédito de la Unión Minera case, he was rewarded again by being made Minister of Justice in the Civilian Directory.[13]

Galo Ponte's principal task as minister was to curb the remaining independence of the judiciary. A decree of 16 May 1926 granted the government the power to impose sentences with no other limiting factor than 'the good of the country'. Moreover, all legal obstacles to this measure were suspended and there was to be no appeal other than directly to the Council of Ministers. A further decree of 14 June 1926 established the so-called Consejo Judicial with the power to revise any judicial decision and to dismiss any judge whose actions displeased the government. A further decree of 14 October 1926 gave the government power to overturn decisions of the Tribunal Supremo and removed all possibility of judicial appeal against decisions of the government. In response to growing opposition to the regime, any possibility of judicial restraint of the executive was stripped away. Another decree of 22 December 1928 gave the government the power to remove, transfer or forcibly retire any judge, magistrate or prosecutor. This power was extended by a further decree of 3 February 1929 which permitted the government to transfer, suspend or dismiss any functionary who expressed hostility to the regime or hindered its policies in any way.[14]

Galo Ponte's various illegal actions resulted in his arrest in the early days of the Second Republic. The future Prime Minister and later President of the Republic Manuel Azaña had served as a minor functionary in Ponte's ministry. He wrote in his diary on 2 September 1931 that he felt sorry for him, since he had lost his job and the Republic had deprived Primo's ministers of redundancy compensation. Now the lawyers who had suffered his arrogance were making sure that he could not get work: 'he is penniless and none of the old hitmen and collaborators who used to do his dirty work will help him. He has to eat prison rations.' When Ponte was put on trial, he was defended by the Dictator's son, José Antonio.[15]

In early 1926, Primo began to talk of being tired and wanting the King to appoint a successor as head of the Civilian Directory. He broached the subject with Juan de la Cierva and the Conde de Guadalhorce.[16] Nothing came of these overtures and, by the summer of 1926, he was toying with a faux-parliamentary solution to legitimize his regime. This was to be a corporative, non-elected National Assembly that 'will in no way share sovereignty with the King or the government which will continue to run the Dictatorship in the mild form that it has done to date'. In September 1926, on the anniversary of the original coup, a plebiscite was held on whether there was popular support for the scheme. There were no controls to avoid falsification. Blank papers were distributed at poll stations manned by members of the Unión Patriótica and the Somatén. Despite the lack of legal supervision and the massive scale of pro-regime propaganda mounted through the controlled press and the Unión Patriótica, only a 57 per cent majority of eligible voters was secured. The Assembly would be a consultative body only, made up of hand-picked members from the army, the Church, the Civil Service, the universities, the Socialist trade unions and employers' organizations. Interestingly, only fourteen of the 159 politicians who had been ministers between 1902 and 1923 would be chosen as members. Primo offered six Socialists seats and all six rejected his offer.[17]

Sánchez Guerra told Alfonso XIII that the proposed National Assembly was an 'illegitimate and factious act' that signified long-term commitment to dictatorial rule. He warned the King that approval of the scheme would undermine support for the monarchy. The censorship prevented the publication of his arguments, but Primo gave them currency by publishing his own reply. However, the owner of the influential monarchist daily *ABC*, Torcuato Luca de Tena, refused to publish Primo's note without it being accompanied by Sánchez Guerra's manifesto. When the King approved the scheme for the Assembly, Sánchez Guerra went into exile. His house in Paris became the centre of conservative opposition to the regime. Over the next two years, he found that he could count on the support not only of Romanones and other ex-ministers who wanted the restoration of the 1876 Constitution but also of the republicans who wanted a Constituent Cortes to decide Spain's future, and of a wide range of army officers, as well as of some anarchists like Pestaña. Other leftists, like Maurín, regarded him as essentially reactionary.[18]

The 1924 Vera de Bidasoa episode had been just the first of several cross-border incursions by resistance groups based in France. Somewhat more serious, particularly in the long term, was the growing involvement of the Catalanist opposition led by Colonel Macià. One of the first actions of Estat Català had been a plot by young militants of two sections of the party, La Bandera Negra (Black Flag) and Els Escamots (The Squads). They allegedly planned to assassinate Alfonso XIII, in June 1925, as he returned to Madrid after a visit to Barcelona. The royal train was to be blown up as it passed through a tunnel in the Costers del Garraf, near Sitges. They were betrayed by an informer, arrested, kept incommunicado for several months and tortured. They were tried, illegally, by court martial and four of them were sentenced to life imprisonment on the basis of confessions that they claimed had been obtained by violence.[19]

A second incursion at Vera de Bidasoa was set up by General Bazán Esteban and Luis Fenoll, who had replaced Martín Báguenas as head of the secret police, the BIS. They fabricated an incident on the French frontier that was to be blamed on Blasco Ibáñez, Unamuno and Ortega and justify a request to Paris for their extradition. That this was a constant objective of the regime would be revealed in December 1927. On returning to Spain after visiting Unamuno in Hendaye, his wife Concha was arrested in Irún and briefly imprisoned in San Sebastián for the crime of possessing four copies of *Hojas Libres*. She was released after twenty-four hours but her passport was confiscated to prevent her visiting her husband and to force him to return to Spain.[20]

In *Hojas Libres*, Unamuno and Ortega y Gasset demonstrated that 'the second Vera incident' had been a set-up by the police. They argued that, on 8 October 1925, a team from the secret police led by Fenoll had bought fifty pistols in Hendaye. These pistols were then 'discovered' allegedly in the possession of some anarchists crossing the frontier. The commander of the Carabinero station in Vera, Captain Juan Cueto, in letters published in the Cuban daily *Diario de la Marina* and in a later interview in *Hojas Libres*, demonstrated that the entire affair was a police provocation mounted by Fenoll. At the time, Cueto had reported his findings to his superiors, in punishment for which he had been first transferred to Asturias. When he continued to denounce Fenoll, he was arrested and court-martialled. General Bazán was awarded the Gran Cruz de Mérito Militar by Primo, and Fenoll was also decorated for his part in 'discovering' the plot.[21]

Evidence that opposition was widening was provided by the failed military coup on 24 June 1926. It was known as the Sanjuanada because that day was the feast of the birth of San Juan Bautista. The 89-year-old

General Valeriano Weyler turned against Primo because of his blatant interference in the promotion system. He had long since despised Primo as a 'palace toady and a loud-mouthed bully' and was outraged to be removed as chairman of the committee overseeing the promotion of generals and colonels, the Junta de Clasificación.[22] Primo had shamelessly bypassed the committee, issuing instructions directly to the Under-Secretary of War, the Duque de Tetuán, to promote his allies and punish his critics, most notably General Eduardo López Ochoa. Primo also took every opportunity to try to humiliate Weyler. In a letter to the Captain General of Madrid, Adolfo Vallespinosa, he referred to Weyler as 'envious', 'doddery' and 'a sheep in wolf's clothing'. General Francisco Aguilera y Egea had also resigned as President of the Supreme War Council because of Primo's arbitrary interference.[23]

Together with Romanones and Melquíades, the two veteran generals planned a coup to restore the 1876 Constitution. It was a scheme with little chance of popular support. Their plot had only tenuous links to the various republican groups that, in February 1926, had formed the Alianza Republicana. The group included the Catalans under Marcelino Domingo, Alejandro Lerroux's Radicals, together with Unamuno, Ortega y Gasset and Gregorio Marañón. Alianza Republicana was sympathetic to the generals' plot but not actively involved. In the event, the Sanjuanada was hatched with little security and there were big differences between the aspirations of those involved, who ranged from Generals Queipo de Llano and López Ochoa, via Romanones and Blasco Ibáñez, to Juan-Simeón Vidarte of the Juventud Socialista and Lerroux (who was suspected of being on Primo's payroll and was almost certainly on that of Juan March). It was easily dismantled by the authorities.[24]

Primo himself mocked the coup attempt as the work of 'a few people, blinded by passion, ambition or spite'. He derided what he called 'the grotesque mosaic of conspirators', claiming that they were nostalgic for the period before his regime: 'they enjoyed terrorism, separatism, immorality, the lack of monetary credit, international contempt, chaos in Morocco and the ruin and abandonment of agrarian and industrial production'. He shrewdly refrained from making martyrs, limiting the punishment of those found guilty to crippling fines, which in the case of the notoriously miserly Romanones was the colossal sum of 500,000 pesetas.[25]

Not long afterwards, in November 1926, Colonel Macià organized with the anarchists and some exiled Italian anti-Fascists a raid across the frontier from headquarters established at Prats de Molló. As with the Vera de Bidasoa incursion, the hope was to provoke a rising in Spain. The preparations were well known to the police in both Paris and Madrid. The poorly equipped invaders, disguised as hikers, were easily forestalled by the French police on the frontier and at Perpignan and the few who managed to cross the border were detained by the Spanish police. Nevertheless, the publicity made it something of a propaganda coup for Macià. He and about ninety others were deported to Belgium.[26]

The regime was not shaken by the Sanjuanada, but it reflected the reality that, in addition to a broad spectrum of liberal and left-wing opposition, some sections of the army were turning against the regime. It was in this area that Primo made one of his most damaging errors. As a one-time *abandonista*, he was aware that the army was unsustainably expensive in large part because of its inflated officer corps. The regime spent almost as much on a huge programme of military modernization as on public works, although the increase in the number of mechanized units was immensely disappointing.[27] Related efforts to streamline the officer corps severely undermined the regime. Primo's clumsy efforts to resolve divisions between the corps that favoured battlefield promotions and those that opposed them, the question which had given birth to the Juntas de Defensa in 1917, had disastrous effects.

Divisions between the Africanistas and the necessarily more educated artillerymen and engineers arose from the fact that it was much easier for an infantry or cavalry officer fighting Rif tribesmen to gain promotion by merit than for an engineer or an artilleryman. The artillery corps had sworn in 1901 to accept no promotions other than on grounds of strict seniority and to seek instead other rewards or decorations. With decrees of 21 October 1925 and 30 January 1926, Primo gave himself the freedom to promote brave or capable officers even when it meant flouting the traditions of the artillery. This was perceived as opening the way to corruption. Primo, whose own meteoric rise owed much to his uncle's influence, now used the promotions system, as he did the judicial system, to favour his supporters and punish his critics. Existing tension was increased when, on 9 June 1926, he issued a decree imposing merit promotions on the artillery. Those who had accepted medals instead of promotions were now deemed retrospectively to have been promoted. Hostility within the mainland officer corps to a range of tactless encroachments on military sensibilities by the Dictator was fostering the links between officers and the opposition that had emerged in the Sanjuanada.[28]

In August, in reaction to the imposition of merit promotions, there was a near mutiny by artillery officers. With the King's support, Primo responded by declaring martial law and suspending all artillery officers without pay. In Pamplona, shots were fired by infantrymen sent to put an end to one such 'strike' of artillerymen. The officers concerned were handcuffed and arrested by Civil Guards. The repression was conducted by Martínez Anido, whose devotion to the task saw Primo call him 'a nun with spurs'. For refusing to hand over the Artillery Academy of Segovia, its Director was condemned to death, a sentence later commuted to life imprisonment.[29] A small role in the conflict was played by General Queipo de Llano. He had been removed from his position as Military Governor of Cordoba for repeating at a dinner a joke that was going around Seville to the effect that the Unión Patriótica did not have an office in the city but did have a club in the Plaza de San Fernando, a reference to the sign 'U.P.' (Urinario Público) over the square's splendid public urinals. As a result, he was refused promotion to major general and, on 31 March 1928, relegated to the reserve list on the grounds that he was 'rather undisciplined, rebellious and inclined to disobey orders'. He indignantly refused Primo's offers of lucrative civilian posts. Moreover, because the King had promised not to sign the order consigning him to the reserve, Queipo joined the republican movement and set up home in Madrid where he actively encouraged the opposition of the artillery to the regime.[30]

Unwilling to unleash military action against the regime, the artillery officers eventually gave in on 6 September. However, Primo's victory had been won at the cost of dividing the army and of severely undermining its loyalty to the King. The clash lay behind the inclination of many officers from the artillery, the engineers and the medical corps to move in the direction of the republican movement. Thus, by January 1930, important elements of the army would stand aside and permit Primo's downfall. The damage to Alfonso XIII's standing with the officer corps was such that even the Africanistas would not be prepared to fight to prevent the coming of the Second Republic in April 1931.[31]

It took a year after its creation before the National Assembly began to function. This was partly in response to the opposition reflected in the Sanjuanada, the Prats de Molló plot and the conflict with the artillery. Moreover, Primo was preoccupied by the refusal of many of those invited to join a meaningless institution. The Socialists rejected the invitation in 1927 because they were not allowed to choose their delegates. They did so again in 1929 because of growing evidence that collaboration with the regime was having a deleterious effect on the UGT's membership rolls. In November 1926, Eduardo Aunós had set up the National Corporative Organization. On the basis of a study tour that he had made in Fascist Italy, and incorporating much existing social legislation, its long-term aim was to eliminate the class struggle.[32] Its most practical manifestation was the creation of arbitration committees, *comités paritarios*. The UGT decided to participate, on the grounds that there were immediate material benefits to be obtained. If the best wages and working conditions were negotiated through the committees, with the workers' representation exclusively in the hands of the UGT, then non-Socialist workers would flock to its ranks. They were wrong about the impact on union membership. Nevertheless, employers, especially in Catalonia, resented the boost given to organized labour.[33]

Somewhat bizarrely, the Dictator's image was undermined by the publicity given, in early 1928, to his proposed marriage with an aristocratic volunteer nurse called Mercedes 'Nini' Castellanos. The popular press was full of the romance between the portly fifty-eight-year-old widower and the forty-year-old stepdaughter of the Conde de San Felix. Barely a day went by in April and May without sycophantic references to her in the press. They were seen together at society events and she accompanied him on official journeys. She became a popular figure and several town councils, including those of Murcia, Oviedo and Almagro, obsequiously named her honorary mayoress. The wedding was due to take place in September, but on 9 June, without explanation, it was announced that the marriage would not take place. The brusqueness of the announcement and the jilting of 'Nini' was yet another motive for popular ridicule and aristocratic disdain for Primo.[34]

All this time, opposition was growing. Student unrest had long been brewing because of the regime's persecution of notable professors and intellectuals. At the end of April 1926, for defending six students who had protested against the appointment of a priest to Unamuno's chair of

Greek at the University of Salamanca, the Socialist law professor Luis Jiménez de Asúa had been arrested and exiled for three months to the tiny Chafarinas islands near Melilla. The students were imprisoned for two weeks. When the student leader, Antoni Maria Sbert, had been arrested on 20 May 1925, the Dictator told him, 'a student is a soldier who has no right to represent other students or to complain to the government other than via his superiors'. Sbert was arrested again March 1929.[35]

In April 1929, the student union, the Federación Universitaria de Estudiantes, protested against the government's decision to permit Catholic private universities to confer degrees. Since university degrees were essential certificates for government jobs, this constituted a challenge to the bulk of lay students. The immediate response was a wave of strikes, assemblies and demonstrations. By early April 1928, the dispute had spread to all universities except Zaragoza. Primo responded contemptuously, ordering the military occupation of some universities and imprisoning the most militant students. The universities of Madrid, Barcelona and Oviedo were suspended. Student opposition provided mass support for the existing resistance of the exiled intellectuals. Unamuno became a hero to student rebels, publishing open letters in characteristically intemperate language lambasting the Dictator as 'the miserable bandit, a vile, rapacious cheat, a coward and a felon who tyrannizes Spain'. Primo talked of reducing the number of universities because Spain had too many lawyers and doctors. He remarked that professors were notorious absentees and students naturally lazy.[36]

The seriousness of the threat constituted by the various groups opposing the regime was becoming ever clearer. Partly because of international factors and partly because of the huge budget deficit, the value of the peseta was falling. Juan March, concerned by this and hedging his bets as always, was not only financing the exile of Alba and Lerroux, but now also supporting the activities of Sánchez Guerra. In conjunction with a wide spectrum from the conservatives, via Alianza Republicana and the Catalanists of Macià and Lluís Companys, to the CNT and army officers, there were plans for a *pronunciamiento* to be led by Alberto Castro Girona, the Captain General of Valencia. The political figurehead was to be Sánchez Guerra. It was impossible to maintain secrecy because so many groups were involved, each with different objectives and levels of commitment. The secret police were following many suspects and, on 11

September 1928, Martínez Anido had ordered the arrests of over 4,000 republicans and army officers.[37]

On the evening of 19 January 1929, Sánchez Guerra landed in Valencia to put himself at the head of eighteen artillery garrisons. In fact, only the rising in Ciudad Real was successful. To the alarm of Primo, there was no resistance from the Somatén or the Unión Patriótica. He told Calvo Sotelo of his disillusion on discovering that the Unión Patriótica would not fight to defend the regime.[38] The plot failed because the Captain General of Valencia, Castro Girona, on whose support the plotters had relied, doubting its success changed his mind at the last minute. Rather than flee, Sánchez Guerra surrendered himself to Castro Girona, who had effectively betrayed him. An embarrassed Castro Girona offered to let him escape, but he refused. Primo's *nota oficiosa*, allegedly drafted when he was drunk, called the movement 'comical', claiming that it had failed because the government knew about it beforehand, that it was disorganized, that those involved were 'riff-raff' and that the people of Valencia had been much more interested in the finals of the Miss Spain beauty contest, which was won by Miss Valencia, Pepita Samper. Outraged that the conspiracy had been justified on the grounds that his regime was illegitimate, he responded with a list of his own achievements: 'No government has done more than the Dictatorship in terms of the religious traditions of the country, of elevating women, of protecting the less fortunate'; he also boasted about what he had done for widows, orphans and the old.

To put pressure on the government, Sánchez Guerra consistently declared that his aim was rebellion and described his activities in the exact words of the criminal code which defined sedition and required the death penalty. He was kept imprisoned on a warship until October 1929, but eventually he had to be tried. A court martial, with six generals as judges, found him not guilty on the implicit grounds that rebellion against an illegal government could not be condemned. Around thirty officers involved in the plot in Ciudad Real were sentenced to imprisonment. They were cheered as the train carrying them passed through each station between Madrid and Pamplona, where they were to be held. There, a large demonstration greeted them. The verdict on Sánchez Guerra was a challenge to the regime and made it clear that the highest reaches of the army had lost faith in Primo. The conspiracy in itself had suggested that the monarchy was facing a very major crisis because so many significant figures of the old politics – Melquíades Álvarez, Sánchez Guerra, Santiago Alba, Manuel Burgos y Mazo, even Romanones – had been prepared to work with the republicans.[39]

At the beginning of March, pointing out that the three major opposition groups were in concert, Romanones unsuccessfully urged Alfonso XIII to return to the 1876 Constitution. The situation was nearing crisis point. Although his relationship with the Dictator was deteriorating, the King was prepared to shelve his misgivings, hoping that Primo's plans for constitutional reform might offer a way out.[40] Primo was talking ever more frequently about his readiness to leave government. He felt disillusioned and isolated, leaking support across the social spectrum as the economic situation deteriorated. The UGT was turning against him, particularly because it was losing agricultural members. Nothing had come of Primo's suggestions of a scheme to provide credit for labourers. Aunós's half-hearted attempts to establish rural *comités paritarios* were fiercely opposed by the landowners of the south and by the CNCA.[41] Sixty-five rural sections of the UGT, with 15,000 members, were closed down by 1928. Before the dictatorship, the UGT had had over 65,000 members; by December 1929 that was down to 30,000. The UGT's virtual monopoly within the state industrial arbitration machinery had not produced the expected effect on membership. One of the UGT's strongest sections, the Asturian miners, had suffered appreciable losses during the dictatorship. This was persuading Largo Caballero to move towards Prieto's position of alliance with the republican opposition to the regime.[42]

Right-wing hostility to the *comités paritarios* was intensified by the collapse of the peseta. The world slump had seen emigrant remittances diminish, exports plummet and prices rocket. Inevitably, falling living standards affected all classes of society, but especially the working class. However, where it had the most immediate impact on the regime was within the officer corps of the armed forces, which was now the last remaining, but tottering, pillar of the dictatorship. Officers, in the words of Gabriel Maura, 'were roused by the ever more aggressive mutterings of their fellows and their civilian relatives who were unanimous in blaming them, either for bringing about the Dictatorship or for not overthrowing it'.[43]

Throughout the autumn of 1929, Primo vainly tried to shore up his regime by granting additional powers to Sanjurjo, now head of the Civil

Guard, and by reorganizing the National Assembly and the Unión Patriótica. No previous Prime Minister accepted nomination. The Colegio de Abogados elected as its members well-known figures of the opposition. The University of Valladolid chose Unamuno.[44] On 3 December, the members of the Directory met for dinner at Madrid's Lhardy restaurant to celebrate their fourth anniversary. Primo talked about resigning and passing the presidency of the Directory to the Conde de Guadalhorce.[45] With crisis in the air, at a cabinet meeting on 30 December he made unworkable suggestions for a transition based on corporative elections to provide some of the deputies in a reformed National Assembly, with the remainder appointed by the government. On the next day, the proposals were put before the King, who now realized that the survival of the monarchy required the removal of Primo. Without an obvious replacement, he shrank from dismissing Primo and told him that he needed time to mull over the proposals. Nevertheless, in the words of Calvo Sotelo, 'on that day, the death sentence of the Dictatorship was signed'.[46]

Alfonso was ever more responsive to courtiers who despised the Dictator for his crude manners, his innumerable snubs of the aristocracy, his links with Juan March and his shoddy treatment of Mercedes Castellanos.[47] On the day after his meeting with the King, in a rambling article entitled 'Hablemos claro' (Let's speak plainly), Primo accepted that the succession was now urgent. Acknowledging that he had lost the support of major sectors of society, he still managed to attribute selfish motives to them all: the aristocracy because of lost privileges, the leaders of the old parties because they were tied to what he called the 'contrivance' of the 1876 Constitution, functionaries because, although paid better, they were expected to turn up to work, bankers because they had to pay taxes, industrialists because he recognized workers' rights. He claimed that, despite accusations to the contrary, neither he nor any of his collaborators had enriched themselves, bizarrely insisting that, although free to do what he liked with the 4 million pesetas received from the national subscription, he had not invested the money outside or inside Spain.[48]

Throughout January 1930, the crisis intensified. When Primo refused to lift sanctions against students and professors, there was another strike. The Rector of the University of Madrid closed the university in order to prevent the entry of the Civil Guard. A team from the security services led by Luis Fenoll was in the south investigating a coup being planned by General Manuel Goded, the Military Governor of Cadiz. Goded had support right across the armed forces, the constitutionalist opposition and the republicans. The plans enjoyed the sympathy of Goded's superior, the Captain General of the second military region, Carlos María de Borbón Dos Sicilias, who urged the King, his brother-in-law, to remove Primo. Rather than risk precipitating the plot by taking active measures against it, Primo opted instead for a *nota oficiosa* dismissing it as a 'trivial incident'.[49]

Most damaging to the regime was the collapse of the peseta. Foolishly regarding the exchange rate with the pound sterling as a measure of national prestige, Primo encouraged Calvo Sotelo to use Spain's gold and currency reserves to buy pesetas on the international market. After this intervention allowed speculators to make fortunes, the peseta eventually had to be devalued, dropping from 29.50 to the pound in July 1928 to 38 in January 1930. Cambó blamed this on the regime's inflationary policies and the ineptitude of Calvo Sotelo. He pointed out the absurdity both of his 'extraordinary' budget and of the defence of the peseta when it would have been more sensible to sell pesetas and build up reserves of sterling and US dollars.[50]

On 3 December 1929, the day of the dinner at Lhardy, the government had decided to issue government bonds of 350 million gold pesetas in a vain effort shore up the peseta. The bonds were not covered despite, on 21 December, Primo congratulating himself on the success of the operation. Three days later, he admitted that, driven by patriotism, even when it became obvious that the intelligent strategy would have been to sell pesetas and buy pounds and dollars, he and Calvo Sotelo behaved 'like the gambler on a losing streak, who goes for broke to try to recoup his losses'.[51] On 9 January, he issued a pathetic *nota oficiosa* in which he stated that there were three reasons for the fall of the peseta – economic ones, political ones and imponderable ones. In any case, he declared, the collapse merely hit the rich. He told journalists that there was no explanation for the fall of the peseta. Confirming Cambó's accusation of his incompetence, Calvo Sotelo produced an equally weak explanation, attributing the collapse to a temporary case of 'stock-market madness'. That provoked widespread mockery, with *La Vanguardia* expressing the hope that the Minister might receive some divine illumination.[52] On 20 January, Calvo Sotelo resigned, citing exhaustion, and was replaced by the Conde de los Andes. Still believing in the magic of his 'extraordinary' budget, Calvo Sotelo claimed that the treasury enjoyed a surplus. Similarly, he continued to assert that the crisis of the peseta was the consequence of an international hurricane that would soon pass. The ministerial crisis brought the end of the regime ever nearer.[53]

Primo was exhausted and suffering from diabetes linked to his alcoholism. On 26 January 1930, after a sleepless night, he confessed to journalists his worries about student unrest and the peseta. He claimed that the bulk of the population still supported him. Since this could not be proved and since he had been brought to power 'by military proclamation', he proposed now to ask the ten captains general and other senior commanders in the army, navy and Civil Guard if he still had their support. It was indicative of his attitude to Alfonso XIII that he did not consult him first, since only the King had the right to dismiss the Dictator. An indignant Alfonso summoned Primo to the palace. Reeling from a furious dressing-down, Primo claimed that he was not usurping royal prerogative but merely trying to undermine the coup being plotted by Goded. It hardly mattered since the non-committal replies of the senior military figures, over the course of 27 January, made it clear that they were keen to distance themselves from the regime. Even close friends such as Emilio Barrera, the Captain General of Catalonia, Severiano Martínez Anido and Sanjurjo stated that their loyalty was to the King. Yet, still convinced that public opinion was on his side, Primo did not resign. Accordingly, Alfonso sent the new Finance Minister, Primo's friend the Conde de los Andes, to convince him. Deeply saddened, he resigned on the following day.[54]

The tone of Primo's meeting with Alfonso XIII can be deduced from his final, and tragicomic, *nota oficiosa*. He apologized lest he might have alarmed the nation, explaining that 'In the early hours of Saturday, giving free rein to my pencil, I wrote at top speed the pages of the *nota oficiosa* published on Sunday. I didn't check with anyone else, not even with myself, not rereading them. With the cyclist about to take them to the Press Office, without losing a minute, as if the very salvation of the nation depended on it, I fainted.' He went on to thank the military top brass for their 'patriotic' replies and, without revealing the contents thereof, went on to say that they, together with his health crisis, had 'the inevitable and immediate consequence of my retirement from the government'. The rest of his Directory resigned with him. Primo gave the

King a list of suggestions for the next government. As President, he recommended one of Generals Emilio Barrera, Martínez Anido or Dámaso Berenguer. Alfonso asked Berenguer to form a cabinet. After some soul-searching, he accepted. Throughout the crisis, there were pro-republican demonstrations in front of the Royal Palace and in other parts of Madrid.[55]

Despite resigning, Primo seems not to have realized that he had failed. He remained in Madrid and on 31 January held a meeting of his ex-ministers. In the course of it, he was telephoned with the news that a bitter critic, Santiago del Valle, had been named as chief prosecutor of the Tribunal Supremo. Revealing that he was fully aware that he had committed serious irregularities while in power, he said: 'I'm sure he's going to press charges against us.' There was talk in the press of investigations into the responsibilities of his regime. He began to mutter about a new coup. On 13 February, he went to Barcelona, where Emilio Barrera convinced him that it was too early to be thinking of a comeback and advised him to go to Paris. Seriously ill, he died there four weeks later, on 16 March.[56]

The republican demonstrations emphasized the scale of the crisis faced by the King, who had handed the rather more honest and cultured Berenguer a poisoned chalice. Since Primo's own ideas for the future based on the National Assembly and the Unión Patriótica had been shown to be non-starters, there remained only three possible options – a more repressive dictatorship, a gradual return to the pre-1923 constitutional system or free elections with the risk of a republic. With a divided army, the first was impossible and the third anathema. Only the second was acceptable. The exiled opposition had not overthrown the dictatorship but it had fostered contempt for it and support for republicanism. The mishandling of conflict with the artillery and engineers had undermined military support for the monarchy and prompted some important military figures to join the republican ranks. The crisis of the peseta had dissipated the backing of the banking and industrial elites. The dwindling efficacy of the *comités paritarios*, enough nonetheless to irritate both industrial and landowning elites, had seen the support of the Socialist movement disappear.

The old dynastic parties had withered away, their networks of *caciquismo* broken. Their leaders could not forgive the King's cavalier abandonment of the Constitution of 1876. During the dictatorship, he had either spurned them or ignored them. Another bulwark of the monarchy, the Lliga Regionalista, had been debilitated by the anti-Catalan policies of the regime. In mid-March 1931, the principal left Catalanist groups, Acció Catalana and Estat Català, would unite in Esquerra Republicana de Catalunya under Francesc Macià and Lluís Companys. The bulk of the membership of the Reformist Party of Melquíades Álvarez soon joined republican groups. Most members of the Unión Patriótica simply drifted away, with the more committed joining either the CNCA and the ACNP or the Unión Monárquica Nacional. Without party organization, neither would have much influence in 1930.[57]

For the more right-wing Mauristas, like Calvo Sotelo, having thrown themselves wholeheartedly into the service of the Dictator, there could be no going back. They joined the UMN, believing that the only solution to the challenges faced by the right was a military monarchy. They would form the general staff of the extreme right during the Second Republic and provide much of the ideological content of the Franco regime. The paucity of UMN support in 1930 was revealed when Calvo Sotelo, Guadalhorce and José Antonio Primo de Rivera undertook a propaganda tour of Galicia in the late summer. There were numerous violent incidents of which the worst was in Lugo where stones were hurled at them. The police intervened and wounded five protesters, which provoked strikes across Galicia. In Valladolid, students attacked a meeting of the Partido Nacionalista Español founded by Dr José María Albiñana. The extremist Albiñana had left the UMN because he considered it too lukewarm in pursuing the central task of annihilating the covert enemies of Spain.[58]

Without the shield of the dictatorship, it was with scant hope of success that Alfonso XIII began his fight for the throne. Primo had failed to use the economic breathing space of the years 1923 to 1927 to construct a lasting political replacement for the decrepit constitutional monarchy. Widespread opposition to his arbitrary rule had developed into a burgeoning republican movement. The various republican groups that had united in 1926 into a loose coalition, the Alianza Republicana, had developed well-organized local, regional and provincial networks. Ironically, the modernization overseen by the regime had led to a doubling of student numbers and so the universities were at the heart of resistance.

Berenguer's first difficulty was to assemble a cabinet. Cambó, recovering from throat cancer, declined the invitation to become Minister of

Finance. So few were the willing candidates that there was a brief possibility that the King's dentist, Florestán Aguilar, might be appointed Minister of Education.[59] Berenguer started in an open spirit, taking in good part a stunt perpetrated by Manuel Fontdevila Cruixent, editor of the republican newspaper *Heraldo de Madrid*. Pretending to be calling from the Prime Minister's office, he telephoned the Madrid fire brigade and ordered the removal of the huge National Assembly plaque from the façade of the Cortes. He had a photographer present when they did the job on the next morning. Berenguer cancelled sanctions against university professors, army officers and students. Exiles returned. Numerous provincial and municipal authorities overthrown by the dictatorship were restored. Berenguer's published programme promised the re-establishment of the 1876 Constitution and elections. Early elections might have saved the monarchy, but his cautious hesitations for fear of failure stimulated the growth of republican sentiment.[60]

Unfortunately, the economic downturn occasioned by the world depression was inadvertently accelerated by the new Minister of Finance, Manuel de Argüelles. As a fierce critic of Calvo Sotelo's inflationary policies, he imposed rigid budgetary austerity with an immediate ban on new public works. The consequences were catastrophic. Construction on all new railway lines was stopped and all orders for new locomotives were cancelled, to the severe detriment of the entire metallurgical industry. The reduction of activity in this and other sectors quickly inflamed working-class militancy. Moreover, the termination of the work on the Barcelona and Seville exhibitions, coinciding with the return of immigrants, had already created a dangerous situation, particularly in the construction industry. In Barcelona, there were already clashes between the CNT and the Sindicatos Libres.[61]

The monarchy quickly seemed to be under siege. In San Sebastián on 20 February, Miguel Maura, the second son of Antonio Maura, announced his conversion to republicanism. A few days earlier, he had informed the King of his decision. A complacent Alfonso XIII mocked him: 'You're crazy! As long as I am alive, the monarchy is in no danger. Après moi, le déluge.' Maura's speech was overshadowed by that of Sánchez Guerra, on 27 February, in the Teatro de la Zarzuela in Madrid. He was greeted as a hero. Although he did not declare himself republican, he said that he had lost confidence in Alfonso XIII and argued for elections to a Constituent Cortes. His statement that the King had 'ridiculed, humiliated and trampled on' the Constitution was loudly cheered, as was his declaration that 'I am not republican but I recognize Spain's right to be so, if it wishes.' The event was followed by a huge pro-republican demonstration in the surrounding streets. The new Director General of Security, General Emilio Mola, regarded the speech and the public response as 'the death sentence of the monarchy'.[62]

Even more damaging was a speech in Valencia, on 13 April, by the one-time Minister of War and *cacique* of Priego in Cordoba, Niceto Alcalá-Zamora. With his characteristically flowery oratory, he denounced the corruption of the dictatorship and called for free elections and the establishment of a republic. His conversion owed much to the damage done to his personal interests by the dictatorship. It was the first of several speeches across Spain that had a major impact. The next in line was Ángel Ossorio y Gallardo who, on 4 May, in Zaragoza, defined himself as 'a monarchist without a king', called for the abdication of Alfonso XIII and demanded honest elections.[63] These conservative converts shared an instinctive desire to ensure that the inevitable collapse of the monarchy would not facilitate social revolution. When Alcalá-Zamora spoke at the Madrid Ateneo on 30 May, an alarmed *ABC* commented: 'he has undertaken the gigantic task of burying the Spanish monarchy with words. He has travelled many kilometres across Spain, sowing salt and curses to dry out the roots of monarchism. Wherever his devastating words pass, the shoots of monarchism wither and die.'[64]

Despite poor health, Berenguer worked hard to appease the various groups victimized by the dictatorship, but he was unable to halt the rising tide of republicanism. On 14 July, Alcalá-Zamora and Miguel Maura created the Derecha Liberal Republicana (Liberal Republican Right), underlining the gloomy prophecies of *ABC*. With the new republican parties still in embryo, the PSOE was the only fully organized political party. The UGT was also in a strong position, since the CNT and Communists needed time to recover from Martínez Anido's persecution. Nevertheless, a joint UGT–PSOE manifesto condemned Berenguer's regime as illegitimate but gave no hint of active opposition, merely calling for the re-establishment of political liberties. On the day Berenguer assumed power, he received a report from the Director General of Security, General Bazán, describing the Socialists' role under the dictatorship as 'frankly governmental' and still a guarantee of the political order in contrast to the far more dangerous CNT and FAI.[65]

Bazán's successor, General Mola, had made his name in counter-espionage during the Moroccan campaigns and saw his main task as the repression of political subversion. Francisco Franco's brother Ramón, a celebrated aviator, believed that Mola would treat the Spanish population in the same way as he had treated the tribesmen of the Rif.[66] To this end, Mola kept on most of the secret police inherited from Bazán. The renamed División de Investigación Social was still headed by Santiago Martín Báguenas, with Luis Fenoll as his deputy. Mola was confident, mistakenly, that the revival of the Lliga Regionalista and the authorization of the Catalan language and the flag would neutralize the Catalan opposition. He believed that the UGT trade union bureaucracy could be relied on to prevent militant action, and even help combat anarchist and Communist agitation. He was sure that many senior officials of the UGT, who had well-paid jobs in the *comités paritarios* and other state organizations, had a vested interest in making the wage-arbitration machinery work.[67]

As the inchoate republican forces coalesced into political parties, the first off the mark was Lerroux's Radical Party. Wealth and age had seen the one-time fiery demagogue recycle himself as the voice of moderate opposition to the crown. Acción Republicana under the intellectual Manuel Azaña challenged both Lerroux's tepid opposition and the 'monarchy without a king' line of the recent conservative converts. Francesc Macià returned illegally from exile in September as a hero, only to be exiled again a few days later, which actually boosted support for Estat Català. Other significant regional republican groups emerging were Santiago Casares Quiroga's Organización Republican Gallega Autónoma and the Unión Republicana Autonomista de Valencia, formed by followers of the late Blasco Ibáñez under the leadership of his son Sigfrido. As early as mid-February, led by Marcelino Domingo's fiercely anti-clerical Partido Republicano Radical-Socialista, a wide range of left-ist, centrist and conservative republicans swelled Alianza Republicana. When joined by Casares Quiroga's ORGA in May, only the Socialists and the Catalans remained outside the coalition.[68]

Not only was Prieto the most inspirational figure of the nascent republican movement, he also had a unique network of civilian and military contacts. As the republican forces mounted pressure on the Socialists to add their weight to the movement against the monarchy, he was their greatest ally. His brilliant speech 'El momento político' on 25 April in the

Madrid Ateneo had an enormous impact. It linked his earlier campaign to expose responsibility for Annual with an exposure of the corruption of Primo and his collaborators, corruption in which the King himself was involved. Prieto made scathing criticisms of their venality, particularly in relation to the railway scandal and the telephone and petrol monopolies. Denouncing the payments made to Primo's ministers and their relatives and in-laws, he delighted the audience by mentioning the rat-extermination monopoly granted to Martínez Anido's son which, he declared, 'let several political and military rats get fat instead of dying'. Inevitably, press reports were heavily censored. To the chagrin of both Besteiro's group and Largo Caballero, Prieto advocated a revolutionary movement against the monarchy with the participation of the Socialist masses.[69]

Tensions ran high when Unamuno arrived in Madrid on 1 May. Huge crowds greeted him and then assembled for his speeches at the Ateneo and in the Cine Europeo. The intervention of the police provoked serious student demonstrations. This led to the closing of the Universities of Madrid, Valencia, Zaragoza, Salamanca, Valladolid and Granada.[70] Over the summer, Largo Caballero began to move towards Prieto's position on Socialist collaboration with the republicans. The intensifying economic crisis, particularly in the mining and agricultural sectors, was destabilizing the UGT rank and file. The CNT had been legalized on 30 April and recovered its old strength with astonishing speed. Mola and the police were seriously concerned about the possibility of a renewal of anarchist conflict with the Sindicatos Libres. Mola interviewed both Ángel Pestaña and Ramón Salas of the Libres and made it clear that he would not tolerate any renewal of *pistolerismo* by either side. He also strengthened the units of secret police investigating the activities of both the PCE and the CNT, as well as extending his network of informers.[71] By June, CNT-inspired strikes were breaking out in Catalonia, the Levante, Aragon and Andalusia. The Communists did not attain the same influence, but they had substantial militant support in the Basque Country and in Seville. Nineteen-thirty saw, in comparison with 1929, four times as many strikes, involving five times as many strikers, with the loss of ten times as many working days. A disastrous olive harvest in Andalusia was caused by heavy spring storms followed by a severe summer drought that seriously damaged the cereal crop. The resulting unemployment ranged from 12 per cent in Cadiz to 50 per cent in Jaén and Seville. In a context of constant strikes, feeling was growing that only a republic could solve Spain's economic and social problems through fundamental agrarian reform.[72]

For fear of losing members to the more aggressive CNT, above all in the south, the UGT embarked on general strikes in Seville, Granada and Malaga. By September, Galicia, Asturias and the Basque Country were also becoming active, with economic aims being overtaken by demands for a change of regime.[73] Largo was alarmed that his efforts to restrain militancy were contributing to the gains in membership being recorded by the CNT and, to a lesser extent, by the Communist Party. He was also aware that the Asturian Socialist Federation was following Prieto's lead in making local alliances with republicans.[74] He was annoyed to learn that, in a personal capacity, Prieto had attended the meeting in San Sebastián, on 17 August, at which a wide range of republican leaders, including the Catalans, signed the Pact of San Sebastián. This would be the basis of the republican revolutionary committee and the future provisional government. The Catalan delegates demanded total autonomy for Catalonia. After tense debate, it was agreed that the Republic would bring a draft autonomy statute to the future Constituent Cortes.[75]

A few days after the meeting, Azaña and Prieto coincided with Juan March in the famed Nicolasa restaurant in San Sebastián. Prieto joked, 'You could part with two million pesetas to ingratiate yourself with the revolution and make sure it doesn't go after you.' In the company, as so often, of a beautiful young blonde, March just smirked. At various points in 1930, Maura and Lerroux offered to mortgage their properties to March if he would finance the republican movement. When approached by Lerroux, he replied, 'I cannot and must not become the banker of the revolution.' March refused because, as Azaña later reflected, he did not believe that it would succeed. However, he kept in touch with the senior republicans to get information on their plans and resources in order to inform the government.[76]

With great reluctance, Largo Caballero moved towards Prieto's position on collaboration with the republicans. He wrote later: 'I have never believed that the bourgeois Republic could be the cure for all the evils of the capitalist regime but I considered it an historical necessity.'[77] He was pushed nearer by the weight of public opinion as manifested in a series of huge pro-republican meetings. On 28 September, 20,000 people came from all over Spain to hear speeches at the Madrid bullring by Azaña,

Maura, Alcalá-Zamora, Lerroux, Marcelino Domingo and other republican leaders, all of whom insisted on the need for unity. Similar meetings were held all over Spain, the largest being one that attracted 25,000
people in Valencia, on 20 October. Thus, on 16 and 18 October, meetings
of the executive committees of the PSOE and the UGT accepted the
revolutionary committee's offer of two PSOE ministries in a future
republican government in return for the Socialists calling a general strike
in support of a coup d'état. The moderate anarcho-syndicalists led by
Pestaña were also inclining towards supporting the great republican
coalition.[78]

The republican leaders had no faith in Berenguer's promise of eventual elections, not least because of the constitutional monarchy's track
record of electoral corruption. They were convinced that a coup d'état
was the only way forward. This required cooperation from army officers,
which was easily secured in the aftermath of Primo's conflict with the
artillery and the engineers, his interference in promotion procedures
and his enmity towards key individuals such as López Ochoa and Queipo
de Llano. A military revolutionary committee was created under the
chairmanship of Queipo who, along with Ramón Franco, elaborated
detailed plans for the seizure of key communication centres and military
barracks. Followed by Mola's agents, Ramón Franco was travelling
around Spain liaising with other conspirators, trying to persuade his
anarchist friends to join the movement, attempting to buy arms and
organizing the making of bombs.[79]

In October, the composition of a provisional government was
announced. By way of reassurance that, despite its name, the revolutionary committee did not intend social revolution, the two major posts
went to conservative Catholics, Alcalá-Zamora as Prime Minister and
Maura as Minister of the Interior. A suggestion that Lerroux be given the
Ministry of Justice was dismissed after Maura remarked that it would
lead to his corrupt friends auctioning judgments in the Puerta del Sol.[80]
Meeting either at the Ateneo or in Maura's house, the committee agreed,
in late October, to prepare a military coup backed by a UGT general
strike. After various delays, it was scheduled for 15 December. The
committee was encouraged by the steady increase in the number of
strikes. Mola admitted later that the republican movement was backed
by workers, students, government functionaries, army officers, businessmen, industrialists, doctors, lawyers and other professionals and even

some priests. Nevertheless, his network of secret agents kept him well informed of the preparations for a rising.[81]

A major blow was delivered to the government on 13 November. A massive demonstration of over 150,000 people accompanied the funeral cortège of four building workers killed when a building collapsed in Calle Alonso Cano in Madrid. Security forces opened fire, killing two and wounding forty-nine people. The response was a nationwide forty-eight-hour general strike by the UGT which rocked the government.[82] This was compounded on 15 November in the form of a devastating article by José Ortega y Gasset. Under the title 'El error Berenguer', he declared that, after seven years of abnormality, the project of restoring normality was doomed.[83]

The key to the republican plot in Madrid was the Cuatro Vientos military airfield. Its prospects of success were diminished, however, by an uprising by the garrison of the tiny Pyrenean mountain town of Jaca in the north of the province of Huesca. On 12 December, Captains Fermín Galán, Ángel García Hernández and Salvador Sediles jumped the gun three days before the agreed date for the nationwide action. They declared the Republic and then set off to start a rising in the garrisons of Huesca, Zaragoza and Lérida. A promised CNT strike in Zaragoza did not take place. Galán's cold, wet and hungry column was stopped at Cillas, 3 kilometres from Huesca, by troops of the Captain General of the Aragonese military region, General Fernández de Heredia. The Jaca revolt was put down.[84] Galán and Garcia Hernández, as the two ringleaders, were tried by summary courts martial, on 13 December, and sentenced to death. Under pressure from the King, Berenguer made the disastrous mistake of approving the sentence and they were shot on the next day. In the view of Manuel Burgos y Mazo, the executions converted what could have been a disaster for republican hopes into a monument to martyrs.[85]

Nevertheless, the defeat of the Jaca rebels was a debilitating reverse for the plotters, provoking the withdrawal of numerous officers, particularly from the artillery. Although the planned rebellion went ahead on 15 December, it was with justified pessimism. Rebel aviators captured the air base at Cuatro Vientos, but they were isolated once the expected general strike had failed to materialize. In an effort to seize the initiative, Ramón Franco set off to bomb the Royal Palace. Watched by Alfonso XIII from a balcony as he flew over the palace, Ramón abandoned the raid after seeing children playing in the gardens and returned to Cuatro Vientos. Other flyers dropped leaflets proclaiming the general strike. After the initial success at the airfield, the next step was to neutralize the nearby army garrison of Campamento, but Queipo delayed and lost all possibility of surprise, with the result that the aerodrome was retaken. The entire affair ended in a fiasco, albeit one that was later to see the protagonists hailed as heroes. The main plotters fled first to Portugal and then on to Paris.[86]

The way the Besteirista leadership of the UGT dragged their feet had effectively sabotaged the strike. On 10 December, Andrés Saborit refused point-blank to have the revolutionary manifesto for the day of the strike printed at the Socialist printing works.[87] Then, on the morning of 14 December, Largo Caballero gave the final instructions for the strike in Madrid to Besteiro's follower, Manuel Muiño, the President of the Socialist Casa del Pueblo. Muiño did not pass them on and even confided in Mola that the UGT would not join in the strike on the following day. Years later, Besteiro would admit that he was responsible for the December 1930 failure.[88] None of the powerful unions controlled by the Besteirista syndical bureaucracy stopped work in Madrid. Elsewhere, the UGT was prominent in stoppages throughout Asturias and the Basque Country and even in Barcelona, where the CNT had hesitated to call the strike because of the news from Madrid.[89]

The government arrested some members of the revolutionary committee – Maura, Alcalá-Zamora, Largo Caballero, Fernando de los Ríos, Álvaro de Albornoz and Casares Quiroga. Prieto managed to escape arrest in Bilbao and got across the Bay of Biscay to France. He lived on a shoestring in Paris where, by dint of a voluminous correspondence and frequent meetings with delegations from Spain, he continued to be the dynamic force that kept the Republican–Socialist coalition together. Suspiciously, no arrest warrant had been issued for Lerroux.[90]

Public outrage over the deaths of Galán and García Hernández mortally wounded the monarchy. In contrast, many senior military figures, including Francisco Franco, believed the executions to be legitimate, especially after the death of the military governor of Huesca, General Manuel de las Heras, who had been wounded in the clash between his forces and the Jaca rebels.[91] Berenguer resigned on 14 February when the senior Liberals Romanones and García Prieto withdrew their support from the government, partly in response to public outrage over the executions and partly because of concern that the planned elections would be rigged in favour of the Conservatives. Sánchez Guerra tried to form a government and even visited the imprisoned republican leaders in a predictably unsuccessful effort to secure their collaboration.[92]

On 17 February, the Captain General of the Navy, Admiral Juan Bautista Aznar, formed a cabinet with the top brass of the old monarchist parties, from Romanones as Foreign Minister to La Cierva as Minister for Development, with Berenguer as Minister for the Army and Gabriel Maura as Minister of Labour.[93] Gabriel described the unworldly Aznar as 'politically from the moon and geographically from Cartagena' and wrote later: 'I had always predicted that my political career would end in the funeral cortège of the Crown.' His more liberal brother, Miguel, described the members of Aznar's cabinet as 'the gravediggers of the Monarchy'.[94]

Between 13 and 16 March 1931, there took place in Jaca the trial of Captain Salvador Sediles and seventy-one other officers and men who had been involved in the December rebellion. Admiral Aznar declared that he would ask the King for clemency whatever the verdicts. Nevertheless, the publication of the sentences – death for Captain Sediles, four life terms and other lesser sentences – provoked a vigorous public campaign in favour of clemency. The universities across Spain were in a ferment of constant agitation. In the run-up to the municipal elections called, on 6 March, for 12 April, there was no more potent subject than that of the executions of Galán and García Hernández. Accordingly, all the sentences were commuted on 18 March.[95] On 20 March, the trials began of the civilian signatories of the revolutionary manifesto. The cheering crowds that lined the route taking the prisoners from the Cárcel Modelo to the Palacio de Justicia in the Plaza de las Salesas converted their passage into a triumphal republican procession. The lawyers put the monarchy on trial, arguing that rebellion against an illegitimate regime was no crime. The President of the court, General Ricardo Burguete, a friend of Maura's lawyer, Ossorio y Gallardo, and an enemy of Berenguer, allowed them free rein. The accused were absolved and carried out of the court on the shoulders of enthusiastic workers and students.[96]

The government was principally occupied with the preparation of the municipal elections, scheduled for 12 April, although neither Admiral

Aznar nor his Minister of the Interior, the Marqués de Hoyos, invested much energy in the issue. As Marqués de Zornoza, Marqués de Vinent and Vizconde de Manzanera, the patrician Hoyos was entirely distanced from the world of daily politics. It was left to Romanones to toil desperately to secure a united monarchist candidacy. However, uniting Conservatives, Liberals, the Unión Patriótica, the Unión Monárquica and groups like Albiñana's ultra-right-wing Legionarios de España was a thankless task. The representatives of the old parties squabbled over how many seats each should have.[97] In every respect, the Republican–Socialist coalition was more united and more efficient in the way its campaign was run. The positive case for the monarchy could not match the negative charge-sheet mustered by the republicans based on the Semana Trágica, Annual and the dictatorship. Monarchist scare stories about the republicans being the puppets of Jewish Bolsheviks bent on abolishing property and imposing the common ownership of women were neutralized by the presence in the Republican–Socialist coalition of Catholic conservatives like Miguel Maura and Alcalá-Zamora.[98]

The over-confidence of the King and his supporters was remarkable. Many members of the aristocracy simply did not bother to vote. The 12th of April being a sun-drenched Sunday, most wealthy Madrileños had headed for the sierra.[99] The results saw the Republican–Socialist coalition sweep the board in forty-five of the provincial capitals, with monarchists winning only in the rural areas where the social domination of the *caciques* remained intact. In the towns, however, it was effectively a plebiscite against the monarchy. To the utter consternation of Romanones and La Cierva, their fiefs in Guadalajara and Murcia fell to the coalition. Pedro Rico, the portly republican candidate for major, was cheered as the hero of the hour when he appeared at the Madrid bull-ring.[100] In Barcelona, a wide coalition of the Catalan left, led by Macià and Companys, enjoyed an overwhelming triumph. The Lliga Regionalista was eclipsed and crowds chanted 'Visca Macià!' (Long live Macià) and 'Mori Cambó!' (Death to Cambó).[101] Sanjurjo informed members of the cabinet that he could not guarantee the loyalty of the Civil Guard in the event of mass demonstrations against the monarchy.

In any case, at a cabinet meeting on 13 April Berenguer declared his opposition to the use of military force. He had sent a telegram to the captains general of the eight military regions instructing them to keep calm and maintain the discipline of the men under their command as 'the guarantee that the destinies of the Fatherland may follow without damaging disorders the logical course that the supreme national will imposes on them'. With republican demonstrations on the streets and with city after city declaring the Republic, there was growing agreement in the cabinet that the King should go into brief exile. Alfonso XIII himself seemed oblivious to the gravity of his situation until the very last moment but eventually conceded that he must withdraw from Spain. On hearing of the decision, Sanjurjo visited Miguel Maura and simply said, 'At your orders, Minister.' It was the end for the monarchy. The King did not abdicate but departed optimistic that his followers would soon be able to engineer a situation in which he would be begged to return. The Second Republic was established on 14 April.[102]

In later years the Primo de Rivera dictatorship was to be regarded as a golden age by the Spanish middle classes and became a central myth of the reactionary right. Eduardo Aunós referred to 13 September 1923 as 'the wedding day of Primo with immortality'. Ironically, in 1942, Franco would hail a period of relentless corruption as 'the happy years of the glorious General Primo de Rivera, years of good government, six exemplary years of Moroccan victories, of peace and of progress'.[103]

A poster published in Valencia in 1831 to
commemorate the Second Republic.

9

The Second Republic: Reform and Frustration, 1931–1933

The Second Republic was established on 14 April 1931 amid outbursts of popular rejoicing in the main towns. Crowds chanted insults directed against the King for his alleged corruption. The novelist Ramón de Valle Inclán wrote: 'the King is not being thrown out for breaking the constitution but as a thief'.[1] Outrage at the abuses of the monarchy and the dictatorship had fed into exaggerated expectations of what the new regime could deliver.[2] In fact, in a context of world depression, the Republic faced massive problems. Emigrants were flooding back into rural Spain, as were the unskilled construction workers laid off as the dictatorship's public works extravaganza ended. This intensified the need for reform in terms of social welfare and landownership, but the Republic would have little economic capacity to initiate change because of both the financial burden left by Primo and the suspicion of the international banking community.

The new Minister of War, Manuel Azaña, declared proudly in the Cortes that the monarchy had been overthrown without a single window being broken.[3] The euphoric crowds in town squares were oblivious to the hostile climate into which the Republic had been born. On the far right, devotees of the dictatorship in both the Unión Monárquica led by the Conde de Guadalhorce and the Carlist Comunión Tradicionalista were already plotting to destroy the Republic. The somewhat more moderate groups inspired by Ángel Herrera would use all means 'within legality', to regain everything that has been lost'.[4] Herrera was described by Miguel Maura as 'a bird of ill omen'. Moderate conservatives hoped that a symbolic sacrifice, the substitution of the disgraced Alfonso XIII by a president, would be sufficient to pacify the masses that were demanding reforms.[5] As their expectations were thwarted, they would turn to right-wing parties. Moreover, collaboration with the dictatorship by Largo Caballero and the UGT trade union bureaucracy had generated CNT anti-Socialist hostility on a scale that would deeply damage the Republic. The anarchist attitude to the Republic was summed up in the headline 'All governments are detestable and it is our mission to destroy them.'[6]

The greatest immediate tensions were generated in southern Spain. The misery of the southern landless labourers had been intensified by the disastrous floods that had destroyed the year's olive harvest, leaving them with less work and the landowners determined to recoup their losses by slashing wages. The system whereby the authorities tried to mop up surplus labour with public works could not cope with the scale of unemployment. Landowners fiercely resisted the device of *alojamiento*, the 'placing' of workers on an estate. Disorder soon followed. Bakeries were assaulted in villages in the province of Cadiz and shops were looted in Jaén. Around 1,800 workers occupied Antequera, in Malaga, from 5 to 20 November 1930, until they were expelled by Civil Guards and regular army infantry and cavalry units sent from Morocco.[7] The sporadic social war in the south dramatically diminished the Republic's ability to establish a regime of coexistence.

In April 1931, few Spaniards believed that the country's problems could be solved only by violence. Perceived as a threat by the most privileged members of society, the Republic raised inordinate hopes among the most humble. Ultimately, the new regime would be destroyed for trying and failing to implement reform. Within weeks of its establishment, both the erstwhile supporters of Primo and a significant minority of anarchists were working to undermine it. In their separate ways, they ensured that, within five years and three months, large sections of the population would come to believe that war was inevitable.

The creation of a new regime did not alter the balance of social and economic power. The wealth and influence of landowners, industrialists and bankers were not diminished on 14 April. Political power, in contrast, had fallen into the hands of a broadly moderate coalition of the most reformist section of the organized working class, the Socialists, and a disparate collection of middle-class republican parties. Their apparent strength concealed a fatal weakness. United during the later years of the dictatorship by the immediate goal of removing the monarchy, the coalition's members had different agendas. To its right, the conservatives, led by a landowner and one-time Liberal Minister of War under the monarchy, Niceto Alcalá-Zamora, and Miguel Maura, had already fulfilled their principal ambition, the departure of Alfonso XIII.[8] Only marginally to their left was the Radical Party of Alejandro Lerroux. No longer the firebrand of yore, now a crony of Juan March and congenitally corrupt, Lerroux spouted anti-revolutionary rhetoric and was deeply distrusted by the other members of the provisional government. Not all the Radicals were as venal as their leader and his henchman Emiliano Iglesias, but many were in politics to derive profit from access to the levers of power.[9] To the left of the coalition, the Socialists and the Alianza Republicana, including the rather Jacobin Radical-Socialists, had ambitious reforming objectives ranging from the destruction of the reactionary influence of the Church and the army, via meeting the autonomy demands of Basque and Catalan regionalists, to agrarian reform and more equitable industrial relations. However, republicans like Manuel Azaña and Marcelino Domingo saw the political objectives as a greater priority than the social changes pursued by the Socialists.

Given that both economic power (ownership of the banks, industry and the land) and social power (control of the press and the radio and of the largely private education system) remained unchanged, the coalition's reforming ambitions constituted a dauntingly tall order. For the first time, relatively free elections had allowed the oligarchy to be threatened, but its defences were strong and varied. While the army and Civil Guard remained determined to repel attacks on property, religion and national unity, the Catholic Church retained immense influence over the hearts and minds of a large proportion of the population. The combined strength of these forces would frustrate reform at the cost of the radicalization of the left, to which their response would be the military coup of 1936.

One of the legacies of the struggle against the monarchy was the call for the punishment of the beneficiaries of the old regime. In July 1930, an informal 'responsibilities commission' had been formed in the Madrid Ateneo in the hope of bringing Alfonso XIII and the collaborators of the dictatorship to justice. Six members of the provisional government – Azaña, Fernando de los Rios, Prieto, Marcelino Domingo, Maura and Alcalá-Zamora – had belonged to the Commission and Eduardo Ortega y Gasset, the scourge of the dictatorship's corruption, was now Civil Governor of Madrid. Allocating responsibility was a symbolic cause but also a poisoned chalice, splitting the republican coalition and creating enemies. On 8 May 1931, the findings of the Commission were handed to the new Attorney General, Ángel Galarza. He ordered the seizure of the King's properties and the arrests of Galo Ponte and Generals Berenguer and Mola for their part in the executions of Galán and García Hernández. The King was accused of administrative immorality. Nevertheless, before the Commission could prevent him, he had taken a fortune of 85 million pesetas out of Spain. Like him, other possible targets, including Calvo Sotelo and Martínez Anido, had fled into exile.[10]

The work of the Commission in the early months of the regime helped keep popular republican fervour at boiling point, but it exacted a high price in the long term. Few individuals were successfully prosecuted and, although the Commission was independent of the government, its work created an image of a vindictive Republic. On 2 September, Azaña was furious that there had been numerous arrests of aged generals – motivated, he thought, by the desire for sensational headlines. Azaña commented that the friends of Galo Ponte had all abandoned him and now boasted of being republicans: 'In the glory-holes of the administration, the most abject individuals take refuge.' The arrested generals were quickly presented as victims by the right-wing press. Azaña wrote, 'No one remembers most of these men. Now we have created a collective symbol for the counterrevolution and given it leaders.'[11]

With Largo Caballero as Minister of Labour, landless labourers began to flood into the Socialist land workers' union, the Federación Nacional de Trabajadores de la Tierra (FNTT). By late 1932, they made up nearly 40 per cent of the UGT's membership. Once a union of skilled craftsmen, the UGT was becoming the political representative of the unsophisticated *braceros* who were in the front line of the southern class war.[12] While many landowners funded organizations committed to the defence of the old order by violence, others sought more pragmatic, legal solutions. For some, this meant a renewed interest in the CNCA and its political offshoots, first Acción Popular, and later in 1933 the Confederación Española de Derechas Autónomas. Others, more liberal, or perhaps more cynical, threw in their lot with conservative Republican parties, especially the Radicals. There were thus two transmission belts of rural antagonisms into Madrid politics: on the one hand, the aspirations of landless labourers passed from the FNTT to the PSOE and, on the other, those of the big landowners passed via various local organizations to Acción Popular and the Agrarian Minority.

In 1931, there was far less change than was either expected by the rejoicing crowds in the streets or feared by the upper classes. Along with the two key positions in the provisional government assumed by Alcalá-Zamora and Maura, the Minister of the Economy was the liberal Catalan Lluis Nicolau d'Olwer. Lerroux was made Minister of Foreign Affairs because it gave him the fewest opportunities for embezzlement. When members of the revolutionary committee had been in jail in December 1930, he had organized a subscription on their behalf and the proceeds had disappeared. According to Largo Caballero, Alcalá-Zamora despised Lerroux. It will be recalled that, in October 1930, Maura had opposed Lerroux becoming Minister of Justice in the provisional government on the grounds that it would lead to his corrupt friends auctioning judgments in the Puerta del Sol.[13] As Foreign Minister, Lerroux would be a disaster. At the League of Nations at Geneva, he would cut a ridiculous figure. His limited French prevented his following the proceedings or understanding the speeches written for him by Salvador de Madariaga.[14] Lerroux's deputy, the altogether more honest Diego Martínez Barrio, became Minister of Communications. The remainder of the cabinet consisted of four left Republicans and three reformist Socialists, unanimous in their desire to build a republic for all Spaniards. However, Azaña would soon be lamenting that the two Radical-Socialists, Álvaro de Albornoz in Development and Marcelino Domingo in Education, could not control the extremists in their party, nicknamed the 'wild boars' (*jabalíes*) by José Ortega y Gasset.[15]

The Socialist leadership hoped that political power would permit the improvement of the living conditions of the southern *braceros*, the Asturian miners and other sections of the industrial working class. They realized that the overthrow of capitalism was a distant dream. What they initially failed to perceive was that the great landlords and mine owners would regard any attempt at reform as a revolutionary challenge. However, trapped between the impatient mass demand for reform and the dogged hostility to change of the rich, the Socialists approached the Republic in a spirit of self-sacrifice and optimism. In Madrid on 14 April, militants of the Federación de Juventudes Socialistas prevented the burning of General Mola's house and formed a human barrier around the Royal Palace to protect Alfonso XIII's family.[16] As Minister of Finance, Indalecio Prieto ensured that the royal family was given time and facilities to have its belongings properly packed for shipping from the palace. Moreover, in a gesture to the wealthy classes, he announced that he would meet all the financial obligations of the dictatorship.[17] According to Miguel Maura, in the first months Prieto was the driving force in the Republican–Socialist cabinet. However, as the obstacles to progress mounted, frustration soon set in within the Socialist movement.

Rightist hostility to the Republic was quickly revealed. Prieto announced at the first cabinet meeting that the peseta was being undermined by a large-scale flight of capital. He spent substantial sums in a vain effort to maintain the value of the currency but flinched from the stabilization measures used by Berenguer's minister, Manuel de Argüelles, for fear of undermining economic activity. Although the peseta fell by 22 per cent against the US dollar, this favoured exports and diminished some of the effects on Spain of the world crisis. His determination to eradicate corruption earned him the hostility of the business community. He frequently threatened and insulted bankers, regularly calling them 'thieves'.[18] On several occasions, he made accusations against Juan March. On 6 November, a furious March replied to accusations made by Galarza. Azaña likened him to a cornered animal. It was perhaps the day on which March declared war on the Republic. A week later, on 13 November, when March was mentioned in the Cortes, Prieto shouted from the government benches: 'They should have hanged him in the Puerta del Sol. And I would have happily swung from his feet.' This brusque departure from their once cordial relations reflected what Prieto could now see as the impact on public finances of March's activities.[19]

From the first, the Unión Monárquica Nacional was preparing resistance against the Republic. Money was collected from aristocrats, landowners, bankers and industrialists to publicize authoritarian ideas, to finance conspiratorial activities and to buy arms. The Republic's commitment to improving the living conditions of the poorest members of society required a major redistribution of wealth. At a time of world depression, wage increases and the cost of better working conditions could not simply be absorbed by higher profits. In a contracting economy, they were revolutionary challenges to the economic order.

The threat to the *latifundio* system came in the form of a series of decrees passed from late April to early July, by the Socialist Ministers of Labour, Francisco Largo Caballero, and of Justice, Fernando de los Ríos. De los Ríos rectified the imbalance in rural leases which favoured landlords. Eviction was made almost impossible and rent rises blocked as long as prices were falling. Largo Caballero's measures were more dramatic. The so-called Decree of Municipal Boundaries prevented the hiring of outside labour in a municipality while any local workers remained unemployed. It struck at the landowners' most potent weapon, the power to break strikes and keep down wages by the import of cheap blackleg labour. In early May, he did what Primo de Rivera had tried and failed to do – he introduced arbitration committees (the *comités paritarios* were now called *jurados mixtos*) for rural wages and working conditions. One of the rights now to be protected was the newly introduced eight-hour day. Previously, the *braceros* had been expected to work from sun-up to sun-down, but now the owners would have to either pay overtime or else employ more men to do the same work. Finally, a decree of obligatory cultivation prevented the owners sabotaging these measures by leaving their land fallow. None of these decrees was applied ruthlessly. Nothing was done about the owners who ignored them. Indeed, armed estate guards assaulted trade union officials who complained. Moreover, preparations for a law of agrarian reform alarmed the landowners who protested loudly that agriculture was being ruined.[20]

The implementation of the reforming decrees would depend on the efficacy and commitment of the civil governor of each province. The Republican government faced great difficulty in finding competent functionaries. The men recommended as potential provincial governors to Miguel Maura by his fellow ministers were often comically inadequate – one he rejected was a shoeshine boy (*limpiabotas*) who had lent money to Marcelino Domingo in harder times. Another confessed that he wanted to be Governor of Segovia so that he could help his friend open a café in the Plaza de la Catedral. In his memoirs, Maura wrote: 'Governors! After thirty years, just thinking about them still gives me gooseflesh.' Few governors would be capable of standing up to the landowners who openly flouted legislation. In their weakness, they often ended up more loyal to local elites than to central government.[21]

There were two rightist responses to the reforming challenge, known as 'accidentalist' and 'catastrophist'. Inspired by Ángel Herrera, the editor of *El Debate*, the most modern right-wing daily in Spain, the 'accidentalists' adopted a legalist tactic based on the notion that forms of regime, republican or monarchical, were 'accidental' and not fundamental. What really mattered, and could be controlled legally, was the social content of a regime. The 'accidentalists' were members of the Asociación Católica Nacional de Propagandistas, most of whom had belonged to Primo de Rivera's Unión Patriótica. They had influence in the press, the judiciary and the professions. From this pool of talent, an organization called Acción Popular was fashioned by the clever lawyer José María Gil Robles. He was described by Miguel Maura as 'a round-faced young man who looked like a carved chickpea, in an ill-fitting suit, but highly pretentious, almost pedantic, with the air of a demagogue'. The rank and file consisted of Catholic smallholders from the provincial groups of the Confederación Nacional Católico-Agraria. Its few elected deputies used every possible device to block reform in the Cortes. Extensive and skilful propaganda campaigns persuaded the Catholic smallholding farmers of northern and central Spain that the Republic's agrarian reforms damaged their interests every bit as much as those of the big landowners. The Republic was presented as a godless, rabble-rousing instrument of Soviet communism poised to steal their lands and dragoon their wives and daughters into an orgy of obligatory free love. With their votes, by 1933 the legalist right would be able to wrest political power back from the left.[22]

The three principal 'catastrophist' groups aimed simply to destroy the Republic by means of a military uprising. The oldest was the Traditionalist Communion of the Carlists, anti-modern advocates of a theocracy to be ruled by warrior priests. Antiquated though its ideas were, it had substantial support among the farmers of Navarre and among some Andalusian landowners. The Carlists had a fanatical militia called the Requeté which, between 1934 and 1936, was training in Mussolini's Italy. The best-financed and most influential of the 'catastrophists' were the Alfonsine monarchists. With their journal *Acción Española* and their political party Renovación Española, they were the general staff and the paymasters of the extreme right. Both the rising of 1936 and the structure and ideology of the Francoist state owed an enormous amount to them.

Finally, several efforts were made to create a Spanish fascism by the deranged surrealist Ernesto Giménez Caballero, by the eccentric Dr José María Albiñana, by the would-be Nazi and translator of *Mein Kampf* Onésimo Redondo Ortega and by the post-office functionary and Germanophile Ramiro Ledesma Ramos.[23] Albiñana's Partido Nacionalista Español, and his blue-shirted, roman-saluting Legionarios de España, despite a fascist and anti-Semitic rhetoric, eventually fused with the monarchists.[24] Ledesma Ramos's La Conquista del Estado, created in February 1931, was the first overtly fascist group.[25] Three months later, Onésimo Redondo, a functionary of the sugarbeet growers' association, founded a fascist group in Valladolid under the name La Junta Castellana de Actuación Hispánica. In October 1931, these two diminutive organizations fused into Las Juntas de Ofensiva Nacional-Sindicalista (JONS), a tiny, penurious outfit whose greatest asset was their symbol, the yoke and the arrows.[26] Inspired by Hitler, they eventually merged, early in 1934, with José Antonio Primo de Rivera's Falange Española as Falange Española y de las JONS. Subsidized both by the Alfonsine monarchists and by Mussolini, the rank-and-file Falangists supplied the cannon fodder of the 'catastrophist' option, attacking the left and provoking the street fights which permitted other groups to denounce the 'disorder' of the Republic.[27]

Among the Republic's enemies, two of the most powerful were the Church and the army. Both were to be easily drawn into the anti-Republican right, in part because of errors made by the Republic's politicians but also because of the actions of the Church's own hard-liner fundamentalists or *integristas*. They were committed to the necessity of a 'Confessional State' that forcibly, by civil war if necessary, would impose the practice of the Catholic religion and prohibit all others. Prominent among them were the Cardinal Primate of All Spain, the Archbishop of Toledo, Pedro Segura, and the Bishop of Tarazona in the province of Zaragoza, Isidro Gomá. They formed a semi-clandestine group within the Church, whose members communicated with one another in code, as was revealed when left-wingers found the secret archives of Isidro Gomá in the Archbishop's palace at Toledo in July 1936.[28]

On 1 May, a major scandal was provoked by the pastoral issued by the ambitious and irascible Archbishop Segura, one of whose obsessions was the prohibition of any dancing involving physical contact between the partners. His pugnacity in matters theological led the monarchist intellectual José María Pemán to call him 'a bullfighter in doctrinal and pastoral issues'.[29] Segura's pastoral letter, addressed to the bishops and the faithful of Spain, called for the mass mobilization of all in a crusade of prayers to unite 'seriously and effectively to ensure the election to the Constituent Cortes of candidates who guarantee to defend the rights of the Church and the social order'. In the context of popular enthusiasm for the Republic, his praise of the monarchy and its links to the Church was irresponsibly provocative. The equally belligerent Bishop of Barcelona, Manuel Irurita, declared that the Church needed swords and artillery.[30]

The government petitioned the Vatican for Segura's removal but, before a response was received, fearing reprisals he fled to Rome. However, on 11 June, he returned to organize clandestine meetings of priests. Miguel Maura, without consulting the rest of the cabinet, ordered his expulsion. Newspaper photographs of the Cardinal Primate of Spain being escorted by police and Civil Guards from a monastery in Guadalajara were immediately produced as evidence that the Republican government consisted of 'freemasons, atheists and judaizers' committed to persecution of the Church. One week later, Maura also expelled the Bishop of Vitoria, Mateo Múgica, a Basque-speaker and militant nationalist, when he refused to cancel a mass demonstration of Carlists and Basque nationalists in Bilbao that was likely to provoke street violence.[31]

The clashes with Segura and Múgica had hardened the Republican view that the Church was the bulwark of black reaction. On Sunday, 10 May, young monarchists of the Círculo Monárquico Independiente had provoked a disturbance in Madrid's Calle Alcalá by playing the Marcha Real from the window of their headquarters and then chanting 'Long live the King!' and 'Death to the Republic!' Having tried unsuccessfully to attack the building, a crowd instead marched on the offices of the monarchist daily ABC. Maura wanted to employ the Civil Guard but was restrained by Azaña and Prieto. On the following two days, churches and convents were burned in Madrid, Malaga, Seville, Cadiz and Alicante. Again, Maura's cabinet colleagues prevented him mobilizing the Civil Guard. Azaña proclaimed that 'all the convents in Madrid are not worth the life of one Republican'. Order was finally and easily re-established by a declaration of martial law. The fires were set by young hotheads from the Ateneo and the anarchist movement, in the belief that the Church was the spider at the heart of the web of reactionary politics in Spain. Both the Republican press at the time and Maura later claimed that right-wing agents provocateurs were involved. Witnesses claimed that members of the Círculo Monárquico Independiente had paid young men to buy petrol and burn religious buildings. On 22 May, full religious liberty was declared. The monarchist daily ABC and the

Catholic *El Debate* howled abuse and were briefly closed down by the government.[32]

Several issues were to cause friction between the Republic and the armed forces but none more than the new regime's readiness to concede regional autonomy. The vote in the elections of 12 April had seen a victory for Colonel Macià's Esquerra Republicana de Catalunya (Republican Left of Catalonia), for which many CNT militants had voted.[33] On 14 April, Lluís Companys had proclaimed the Republic. Shortly afterwards, Macià declared an independent Catalan republic and was proclaimed its President. In previous, and indeed later, times, such situations led to bloody confrontation. Now, a pacific resolution was achieved by a deputation of three ministers from Madrid, Fernando de los Ríos and two Catalans, Marcelino Domingo (Education) and Lluís Nicolau d'Olwer (Economy). Their suggestion that the Catalan administration be given the symbolic title of the old medieval government, the Generalitat, and the promise of a rapid statute of autonomy persuaded Macià to make what he described as 'the greatest sacrifice of my life'. A team from the Generalitat began to draft a Statute of Autonomy.[34]

Inevitably, this aroused the suspicions of the fiercely centralist army. Moreover, Azaña, as Minister of War, wished to reduce the army to a size commensurate with the nation's economic capacity, to increase its efficiency and to eradicate the threat of militarism from Spanish politics. Azaña was influenced by those sections of the army which had opposed the dictatorship, mainly artillerymen and airmen. Infuriated Africanistas began to mutter that Azaña was in thrall to a group of officers denounced on the right as the 'black cabinet'.[35] His necessary and generous reform saw 8,000 surplus officers offered voluntary retirement on full pay. However, military sensibilities were inflamed when Azaña's decree of 3 June 1931, on the so-called *revisión de ascensos* (review of promotions), reopened some of the 'merit' promotions given during the Moroccan wars. Many right-wing generals, including Francisco Franco, faced the prospect of being reduced to the rank of colonel. The commission carrying out the revision took more than eighteen months to report, causing unnecessary anxiety for the nearly 1,000 officers affected, of whom only half had their cases examined. On 30 June, Azaña closed the General Military Academy in Zaragoza both for budgetary reasons and because it was a hotbed of reactionary militarism. This guaranteed Azaña the eternal enmity of its Director, Franco.[36]

Many officers regarded Azaña's reforms as a savage attack on their own interests because they abolished military jurisdiction over civilians deemed to have insulted the army. Those that were retired, having refused to take the oath of loyalty to the Republic, were left with the leisure to plot against the regime. This was encouraged by the conservative newspapers read by most Army officers, *ABC*, *La Época* and *La Correspondencia Militar*, which presented the Republic as responsible for the breakdown of law and order, disrespect for the army and anticlericalism. In particular, a campaign was mounted alleging that Azaña's intention was to *triturar el Ejército* (crush the army). Azaña never made any such remark. In fact, far from depriving the army of funds and equipment, having made a lifetime study of civil–military relations he merely ensured that funding would be used more efficaciously. He wanted to give Spain a non-political army while right-wingers wanted an army that would defend their social and economic interests. Accordingly, he was portrayed by rightist propaganda as a corrupt monster, determined to destroy both the army and the Church.[37] From the very first days of the Republic, right-wing extremists disseminated the theory that the new regime was the plaything of a sinister foreign alliance, a Jewish–masonic–Bolshevik conspiracy, a filthy concubinage that had to be exterminated.[38]

The success of such propaganda lay in the future. The general election of 28 June 1931 was won by the Socialists in coalition with the various Republican groups. This considerable triumph was achieved because the right was poorly organized and many Catholics and conservatives did not vote at all or else voted for Lerroux's Radical Party. Although part of the coalition, the Radical Party was already on the road to becoming anti-Socialist. Before the elections, *El Debate* had declared that the right placed its hopes in Lerroux and would support him until its own forces were organized. With an unashamedly conservative campaign, the Radicals had gained ninety-four seats and become the second largest party in the Constituent Cortes. Nevertheless, Martínez Barrio told Azaña that no more than forty or fifty of these deputies were actually republicans and the remainder were 'as monarchist as the followers of Gil Robles or even more so'.[39] Understandably, Lerroux denounced the 'utopia' of agrarian reform. In August 1931, he would openly admit that the Radical Party was now fundamentally conservative and opened its arms to ex-monarchists. In many parts of the south, to the horror of the rightist press, many monarchists decided that they could best defend their interests from within a republican party and so had joined the Radicals.[40]

In preparation for the June elections, to the chagrin of the right, Maura annulled the notorious Article 29 of the 1907 electoral law by which unopposed candidates were directly elected, a gift to powerful *caciques*. The electoral regulations were drafted to ensure strong government majorities and avoid the political fragmentation that had undermined the Weimar Republic. In each province, 80 per cent of the seats went to the candidate list with most votes over 40 per cent of those cast. The other 20 per cent block of seats went to the list that was second past the post. Inevitably, the system required the formation of coalitions. The elections for the 470-seat Constituent Cortes registered a major victory for the parties of the provisional government. There is still doubt over the exact numbers but, broadly speaking, the Socialists won 116 seats, the left Republicans (that is to say Marcelino Domingo's Radical-Socialists with 56 and Azaña's Acción Republicana with 26) won 82 and the Catalan and Galician regionalists 57 seats. In the centre, the Radicals won 94, Alcalá-Zamora's Derecha Liberal Republicana 22 and the group of intellectuals known as Al Servicio de la República 13. The disunited groups of the right gained only 48 seats. The biggest group consisted of Acción Popular and the twenty-four Castilian deputies known in the Cortes as the Agrarian Minority. Future government changes would oscillate dramatically since the electoral system saw small fluctuations in the number of votes cast producing massive swings in the number of parliamentary seats won. The polarization brought about by the pendulum effect of a big left-wing victory in the 1931 elections followed by an equally dramatic rightist triumph in 1933 was partly the consequence of the Radicals changing sides.[41]

The 1931 Cortes faced appalling difficulties. For the Republic to survive, it had to increase wages and cut unemployment and do so in the context of the world depression. With agricultural prices falling, landowners had let land fall out of cultivation. The landless labourers, who lived near starvation at the best of times, were in a state of revolutionary tension. Industrial and building workers were similarly hit. To make matters worse, the wealthy classes were hoarding or exporting their capital. This posed a terrible dilemma for the Republican government. If the labour demands for expropriation of the great estates and factory takeovers were met, the army would probably intervene to destroy the Republic. If revolutionary disturbances were put down in order to appease the upper classes, the government would find the workers arrayed against it. In trying to tread the middle course, the Republican–Socialist coalition ended up enraging both sides.

This was demonstrated within a week of the Cortes' first session. The anarchists' brief honeymoon with the Republic had already ended when CNT–FAI demonstrations on 1 May were repressed violently. Then a general strike called by the anarchists, on 18 July, led to thousands of CNT telephone workers leaving work, mainly in Seville and Barcelona. The government was anxious to prove its ability to maintain order. Determined to dominate the CNT, Largo Caballero declared the strike illegal. In Seville, when the CNT attempted to convert the strike into an insurrection, Maura imposed martial law and sent in the army. The Civil Governor permitted local rightist volunteers to form a 'Guardia Cívica' which then murdered several leftists, including four anarchists shot in cold blood in the Parque de María Luisa on 24 July. Maura also authorized the artillery shelling of an anarchist meeting place, the Casa Cornelio. These incidents severely discredited the Republic. The revolutionary strike frightened the wealthy, while the violence of the repression – thirty killed and 200 wounded – confirmed anarchist hostility to the Republic.[42]

The CNT was increasingly falling under the domination of the extremist Federación Anarquista Ibérica, founded in 1927. Some FAI leaders saw strikes as revolutionary instruments and thus were determined to gain control of the CNT. They were not the only anarchist radicals that hoped to submerge the CNT in revolutionary fantasies and denounced pragmatic trade unionists led by Ángel Pestaña as counter-revolutionaries. Some strikes were called, not to gain improvements in wages or working conditions, but as weapons against the state. The inevitable split began at the extraordinary CNT Congress in June 1931. In answer to the FAI victory, Ángel Pestaña, Joan Peiró and twenty-eight others issued, in August, the manifesto of the Treintistas. Their pressure for the creation of a trade union movement saw some of the reformist elements of the CNT leave, and others were expelled. The bulk of the anarcho-syndicalist movement was left in the hands of those who aspired only to make revolution and to pursue a bitter rivalry with the UGT in revenge for its collaboration with Primo de Rivera. Mass unemployment created a potentially explosive situation, and the Republican response to social disorder was similar to that of the monarchy. In October 1931, the Law for the Defence of the Republic was passed with the enthusiastic backing of Largo Caballero. It was followed in August 1933 by the even more draconian law against vagrancy (Law of Vagrants and Malefactors). Inevitably, such legislation favoured the FAI's hard line. Thereafter, and until the CNT was uneasily reunited in 1936, the FAI pursued a policy of insurrectionary strikes which invariably failed because of poor coordination and fierce repression, but enabled the rightist press to identify the Republic with violence and upheaval.[43]

In the autumn of 1931, however, before the waves of anarchist agitation were fully under way, the Cortes was occupied with the elaboration of the new Constitution. A committee, under the Socialist law professor Luis Jiménez de Asúa, met, on 28 July, with less than a month to draft a text, and some of its unsubtle wording gave rise to three months of acrimonious debate. Presenting the project on 27 August, Jiménez de Asúa described it as a democratic, liberal document with great social content. Article 1 read: 'Spain is a republic of workers of all classes.' Article 44 stated that all the wealth of the country must be subordinate to the economic interests of the nation and that all property could be expropriated, with compensation, for reasons of social utility. The text approved on 9 December was democratic, laic, reforming and liberal on matters of regional autonomy. Inevitably, it appalled the most powerful interests in Spain – landowners, industrialists, Churchmen and army officers.[44]

The right-wing opposition to the Constitution crystallized around Articles 44 and 26. The latter concerned the cutting off of state financial support for the clergy and religious orders; the dissolution of those orders, such as the Jesuits, bound by foreign oaths of allegiance; and the limitation of the Church's right to wealth. The Republican–Socialist coalition believed that the creation of a modern Spain needed the Church's stranglehold on many aspects of society to be broken. That reasonable perception failed to acknowledge the sensibilities of Spain's millions of Catholics. Religion was not attacked as such, but Article 26's attack on the Church's privileged position was perceived on the right as a vicious onslaught on traditional values. The debate on Article 26, coming in the wake of Azaña's military reforms, intensified existing polarization.

Indeed, the passing of the Constitution dramatically identified the new regime with the Jacobinism of a Cortes majority that was hardly representative of the entire country. The Catholic middle classes were gratuitously offended by the incendiary speeches of the Radical-Socialist 'wild boars', men like Juan Botella Asensi, José Antonio Balbontín, Eduardo Ortega y Gasset and Ramón Franco. One of them, Joaquín Pérez Madrigal (later a fervent Francoist), called for the imprisonment of the entire clergy. Azaña was alarmed by 'a party full of unruly and impetuous types'. Alcalá-Zamora later wrote that the greatest damage was done to the Republic by the 'unequalled dementia' of this 'short-lived and disastrous party'.[45]

Maura and Alcalá-Zamora, in despair, saw the constitutional draft as a declaration of religious war. The perceived ferocity of its anti-clericalism would soon break up the Republican–Socialist governing coalition and accelerate the drawing together of the hitherto divided right.[46] During the debate of 13 October, later described by Alcalá-Zamora as the saddest night of his life, the defence of the religious clauses of the Constitution fell to Azaña. In his speech, he remarked that 'Spain has ceased to be Catholic'.[47] This provocative comment was taken by the right and many clergy as the satanic war cry of a vengeful lay inquisitor. In fact, Azaña's attitude to the Church was more reasonable and – to the annoyance of the Radical-Socialists – his speech persuaded the left-wing majority not to push for the complete dissolution of the religious orders. The cordial relations of Manuel Azaña with liberal Churchmen such as Cardinal Vidal i Barraquer belied the cries that the Church was being mercilessly persecuted. Nevertheless, even Vidal expressed alarm at the sectarian nature of the Constitution's religious clauses.[48]

Azaña's notorious remark was inopportune but reflected the sociological reality that religiosity was in decline. The Church's legitimation of the injustices of the *latifundio* system occasionally incited landless labourers to hurl stones at missionary priests. Despite the military triumphs of the Reconquista against Islam, Andalusia and Extremadura had never been fully conquered for the Church. In Azuaga in Badajoz, a town of 18,000 people, only ten men and 200 women attended Sunday Mass. It was reported that 80 per cent of the population of Extremadura did not know the words of the 'Hail Mary' or the 'Our Father'.[49] In the autumn of 1932, Cardinal Eustaquio Ilundáin, Archbishop of Seville, compiled a report for the Pope on religious practice in his archdiocese, based on information from parish priests. It was reported from Lepe in Huelva that 80 per cent of the townspeople did not attend Sunday Mass or fulfil their Easter duties of confession and communion and from Palos de la Frontera that no men attended Mass. When Ilundáin instructed parish priests to create committees of adult, male, practising Catholics of good moral character to raise money to support the clergy, nearly all of them replied that no such persons existed. Alienation from the Church was even higher in the working-class districts of industrial towns and cities.[50]

Azaña's speech effectively saved the Constitution, but a cabinet crisis was precipitated because the senior Catholics in the government, Alcalá-Zamora and Maura, resigned. Azaña's performance, and the prolonged applause with which it was greeted, made him the obvious person to become Prime Minister. He had the support of both the Socialists and the left Republicans. Lerroux's known corruption ensured that he would not be chosen but he was outraged, writing later, 'the Republic needed at the head of its government a republican with history, experience and authority, all of which I had and more than anyone'. Azaña reluctantly accepted the post but had inadvertently clinched the enmity not only of Lerroux but also of Alcalá-Zamora, who was elected President of the Republic on 10 December. Alcalá-Zamora never forgave Azaña for what had happened on 13 October. Moreover, his overwhelming self-importance would lead to him being known in political circles as 'Alfonso XIV' and 'the paperback Alfonso'. In the government formed on 17 December, there was no place for the Radicals, who went into opposition. Azaña was obliged to rely more upon the Socialists and the Radical-Socialist hotheads. This in turn made it more difficult for him to avoid provoking the enmity of the right.[51]

The breach between Lerroux and the rest of the Republican–Socialist coalition was confirmed by the Responsibilities Commission's investigation into corruption. One of its principal targets was Juan March. By the end of April, Maura had ordered his arrest and, on 10 May, Galarza had charged him with contraband offences and bribery in connection with the tobacco monopoly awarded him by Calvo Sotelo in 1927. To avoid prosecution, March had secured parliamentary immunity by deploying his considerable wealth to secure a seat in the June Cortes elections as an independent deputy for the Balearic Islands. Galarza and other members of the Commission, Jerónimo Bugeda and Eduardo Ortega y Gasset, were told repeatedly by emissaries of March that they would be killed if they did not abandon the case. Nevertheless, the tobacco monopoly was annulled. In the Cortes on 5 November, accused by Galarza, now Director General of Security, a nervous March inadvertently revealed his inside knowledge of the secret proceedings of the Commission. The Radical deputy for Las Palmas, Rafael Guerra del Río, was informing March of the investigation's progress. Moreover, Joan Simó Bofarull, Radical deputy for Tarragona, the chairman of the subcommittee investigating March, had been offered 25,000 pesetas to obstruct the process. The intermediary was March's lawyer in Barcelona, Emiliano Iglesias, probably the most venal of Lerroux's cronies. To bribe Simó, March had given 200,000 pesetas to Iglesias who planned to pocket the difference.[52]

The entire affair clinched the determination of the Socialists not to collaborate in a cabinet with Lerroux. The parliamentary immunity of March and Calvo Sotelo was revoked only until 8 June 1932, since there was insufficient evidence to justify a permanent ban. Calvo Sotelo, who was in exile in France, was fiercely defended by Gil Robles. Held in the Cárcel Modelo while awaiting trial, and later in the provincial prison of Alcalá de Henares, March enjoyed conditions akin to those of a first-class hotel. He had a suite of rooms and a chef on his payroll and received 'conjugal visits' from ladies of the night. He distributed largesse both to the officials and to fellow prisoners. The latter included members of the FAI. It was said that he aimed to use them in an assassination attempt on Azaña. One of March's employees was later secretary to Joaquín Ascaso of the FAI. The Republic had acquired a fabulously wealthy enemy. As Jaume Carner said in the Cortes on 14 June: 'Either the Republic controls him or he will control the Republic.' From 1933 onwards, March used his financial control of several influential Madrid newspapers – *Informaciones, La Libertad, El Sol, La Voz* and *Luz* – to wage war on Azaña's government. Along with absurd accusations against Besteiro and De los Ríos were allegations that Azaña and Prieto had accumulated enormous fortunes.[53] In fact, the Responsibilities Commission had run out of steam by the autumn. The only other harsh sentence to result from its work – of two parallel terms of twelve years' imprisonment and the loss of all political and pension rights – was passed against Martínez Anido. He was in any case in exile but he would exact implacable revenge during the civil war as Franco's head of security and public order.[54]

The alienation of the Radicals and March isolated the Republican–Socialist coalition at a difficult moment. The Constitution's legalization of divorce and dissolution of some religious orders infuriated the Catholic establishment and the right-wing press attributed the measures to evil Jewish–masonic machinations. During the late-night debate on 13 October 1931, Gil Robles had declared to the Republican–Socialist majority: 'Today, in opposition to the Constitution, Catholic Spain takes its stand. You will bear responsibility for the spiritual war that is going to be unleashed in Spain.' Five days later, in the bullring at Ledesma (Salamanca), he called for a crusade against the Republic, claiming that 'while anarchic forces, gun in hand, spread panic in government circles, the government tramples on defenceless beings like poor nuns'.[55] Substantial popular support for right-wing hostility to the Republic was secured during the subsequent campaign to revise the Constitution. Opposition to the religious clauses was equalled in bitterness by that to the clauses concerning regional autonomy for Catalonia and agrarian reform.

In addition, agrarian violence was a constant problem facing Azaña's cabinet. Fed by the crippling poverty of rural labourers, it was kept at boiling point by the anarchists. The CNT and the FNTT were calling for expropriation of estates and the creation of collectives. The middle-class Republicans respected property and were not prepared to go that far. Largo Caballero had lowered social tensions somewhat with the four decrees that he had introduced in the spring. However, the limits of such piecemeal reform were starkly exposed in December 1931 when the Badajoz section of the FNTT called a general strike. It was in the main a peaceful one. In the remote village of Castilblanco, however, there was bloodshed. The FNTT members there had already spent the winter without work. On 31 December, while they were holding a peaceful demonstration, the Civil Guard started to break up the crowd. After a scuffle, a Civil Guard opened fire, killing one man and wounding two others. The hungry villagers, in a frenzy of fear, anger and panic, fell upon the four guards and beat them to death.[56]

General Sanjurjo, now Director General of the Civil Guard, compared the local workers to the Moorish tribesmen whom he had fought in Morocco – 'In a corner of the province of Badajoz, Rif tribesmen have a base' – and claimed mendaciously that the corpses of the Civil Guards had been savagely mutilated. This identification of rural labourers with the rebels of the Rif indicated that, for the Africanistas, the Spanish proletariat was 'the enemy'. Perhaps inflamed by Sanjurjo's words, his men wreaked a bloody revenge that killed eighteen people. Three days after Castilblanco, the Civil Guard killed two workers and wounded three more in Zalamea de la Serena (Badajoz). Two days later, a striker was shot dead and another wounded in Calzada de Calatrava and one striker was shot in Puertollano (both villages in Ciudad Real), while two strikers were killed and eleven wounded in Épila (Zaragoza), and two strikers killed and ten wounded in Jeresa (Valencia). On 5 January 1932, there took place the most shocking of these actions, when twenty-eight Civil Guards opened fire on a peaceful demonstration at Arnedo, a small town in the northern Castilian province of Logroño. Several workers had been sacked from the local shoe factory, at the end of 1931, for belonging to the UGT. At the ensuing public protest, the Civil Guard shot dead a worker, four women and the two-year-old son of one of them, a twenty-six-year-old pregnant mother. Bullet wounds were suffered by a further fifty townspeople, including many women, children and babes-in-arms. Over subsequent days, five more people died of their wounds and many had to have limbs amputated, among them a five-year-old boy and a widow with six children.[57]

Then, in early 1932, an anarchist strike was put down with considerable severity, especially in Alto Llobregat in Catalonia. There were arrests and deportations that left anarchist and Socialist workers losing faith in the Republic, without diminishing the right-wing conviction that the Republic meant only chaos and violence. In the *latifundio* areas of Salamanca, Extremadura and Andalusia, unionized labour was locked out either by land being left uncultivated or by simply being refused work and told to *comed República* (literally 'eat the Republic', meaning 'let the Republic feed you').[58] Right-wing press networks spouted virulent prophecies of the doom that would result from reform. There was no machinery with which to enforce the new decrees in the remote villages of the south. The social power consequent on being the exclusive providers of work remained with the owners. The Civil Guard was skilfully cultivated by, and remained loyal to, the rural upper classes. Socialist deputies from the south regularly complained in the Cortes that the provincial civil governors did nothing to implement legislation or to prevent the Civil Guard defending the landowners' interests. In Jaén, the gathering of acorns, normally pig food, of firewood or of windfall olives and the watering of beasts were denounced as 'collective kleptomania'. Peasants caught doing such things were savagely beaten by the Civil Guard or armed estate guards.[59]

Throughout 1932, the FNTT worked hard to contain the growing desperation of its southern rank and file. The law of obligatory cultivation was ignored and no labour was hired to do the tasks essential for the spring planting. *Braceros* were refused work if they belonged to the FNTT. Nonetheless, the union adhered to a moderate line, and appealed to grassroots militants to refrain from extremism and not to expect too much from the statute of agrarian reform which was staggering through the Cortes. Throughout 1933, Acción Popular and the Agrarian Minority – with Gil Robles at the helm – obstructed reform. In the debates on the draft law on rural leases, 250 amendments were tabled as part of a planned technical obstruction. The frustration thereby created so discouraged attendance at the Cortes that, when the time came to vote, a quorum could never be obtained.[60] In any case, the statute promised little because its cautious provisions had been drawn up for the Ministry of Agriculture by conservative agronomists and property lawyers. After a painfully slow progress through the Cortes between July and September, it set up an Institute of Agrarian Reform to supervise the break-up of estates over 22.5 hectares. Therefore, it did nothing for the smallholders of the north. Nor did it do anything for the labourers of the south, given the loopholes and exceptions in the reform law's provisions. Nevertheless, the hostility of right-wing landowners towards the Republic was undiminished.[61]

Another source of fierce opposition to the Republic was the statute of Catalan autonomy, which was regarded by the army and the conservative classes as an attack on national unity. In the Cortes, a determined Azaña had to deal with the filibustering of around forty right-wing deputies and thirty Radicals who tabled 200 amendments. A boycott of Catalan products was mounted in the Castilian provinces. In fact, the statute of Catalan autonomy was not maximalist. Nevertheless, ministers were loath to allow the Generalitat, and particularly Colonel Macià, real autonomy since they regarded the Esquerra as an opportunistic coalition, reliant on the votes of the CNT rank and file. Nevertheless, the right portrayed Azaña as determined to destroy Spanish unity.[62]

However, religion was the most potent weapon in the right-wing armoury and it was reinforced by Republican and Socialist anti-clericalism. Given the Church's historic links with the most reactionary elements in Spanish society and its legitimation of social injustice, popular anti-clericalism was widespread. However, gratuitous distress was caused to ordinary Catholics by measures directed not against the institutional Church but against the shared rituals that were so important in much of provincial life. Some left-wing mayors (*alcaldes*) imposed a tax on Catholic burials or prohibited funeral processions. The removal of crucifixes and religious statues from schools and public hospitals along with the prohibition on the ringing of church bells inclined ordinary Catholics to view the Republic as their enemy. Municipal authorities were forbidden to make financial contributions to the Church or its festivals and some towns and villages provocatively banned religious processions. In Seville, fear of attack led to more than forty of the traditional fraternities (*cofradías*) withdrawing from the Holy Week procession. Despite the efforts of the Republican authorities to protect the processions, the issue was used to create the impression of religious persecution. Members of the *cofradías* who were militants of Acción Popular and of the Carlist Comunión Tradicionalista began to use the phrase 'Seville the martyr'. All this reinforced the myth that the Republic was the puppet of the Jewish–masonic–Bolshevik conspiracy.[63]

It was thus but a short step to claims that the Republic must be destroyed and its supporters exterminated. Army officers enraged by both the military reforms and the autonomy statute were joined by monarchist plotters in persuading General Sanjurjo that the country was on the verge of anarchy and ready to rise at his bidding. In the wake of Castilblanco and Arnedo, Sanjurjo had been relieved of the command of the Civil Guard in January 1932 and made Director General of the Carabineros (frontier guards).[64] His attempted coup took place on 10 August 1932. Although enjoying financial support from Juan March and encouragement from Lerroux, and from Mussolini, it was badly planned and was easily defeated both in Seville, by a general strike of CNT, UGT and Communist workers, and in Madrid where the government, warned in advance, quickly rounded up the conspirators. In a sense, this attack by one of the heroes of the old regime benefited the government by generating a wave of pro-Republic fervour. The Radicals abandoned their obstruction of the agrarian reform bill and the Catalan autonomy statute which both passed successfully through the Cortes in September. Nevertheless, among those involved in the coup attempt were the same rightists responsible for the 1931 shootings in the Parque de María Luisa. They would soon be at liberty and well in time to repeat their exploits in 1936.[65]

The government's prestige was at its height, yet the situation was less favourable than it seemed. Much of the right-wing press, including *Acción Española*, was temporarily banned, but there were no executions. In cabinet, Azaña successfully argued for clemency, and Sanjurjo and others were imprisoned but amnestied in April 1934.[66] In his prison cell, Sanjurjo received frequent visits from right-wing admirers. He wrote to *Acción Española* to say how much it had 'comforted his spirit'.[67] The feeble punishments emboldened the conspirators to plan for a more successful future venture. They had learned valuable lessons. Within one month of Sanjurjo's failure, members of Acción Española and Captain Jorge Vigón of the General Staff created a committee to begin preparations for a coup. With the encouragement of the exiled Alfonso XIII, a small fortune was collected from rightist sympathizers to buy arms and to finance the political destabilization for which agents provocateurs from the CNT–FAI were hired. Juan March contributed 2 million pesetas. This committee had an intelligence network run by Santiago Martín Báguenas, who had been head of the secret police under General Mola. They tried to get Martínez Anido involved but he declined, preferring to enjoy his gilded retirement in Nice, financed by the spoils of his corrupt activities in the 1920s.[68] The key objective of the committee was the creation of subversive cells within the army, a task entrusted to Lieutenant Colonel Valentín Galarza Morante of the General Staff. Galarza became the link between the monarchist conspirators and the clandestine association of army officers, the Unión Militar Española (UME), created at the end of 1933 by the retired Colonel Emilio Rodríguez Tarduchy, a close friend of Sanjurjo and an early member of the Falange. Tarduchy was soon succeeded by Captain Bartolomé Barba Hernández of the General Staff, an Africanista friend of Franco.[69]

Sanjurjo's failure contrasted with Gil Robles's success in stalling reform by parliamentary obstruction. The coup's defeat showed that the 'catastrophist' tactic damaged the material interests of the right and that frontal attacks could only strengthen the Republic. An assembly of Acción Popular was called on 22 October to resolve the tensions between legalists and catastrophists within the organization. Despite denials by

El Debate, Gil Robles knew about the preparations for the coup and there is no reason to suspect that he would have been displeased had it been successful.[70] After heated debate, the assembly agreed that violent rebellion against the Republic had been counter-productive and voted for the legalist tactic. In consequence, preparations were begun to create a federal Catholic party at another assembly to be held in early 1933. The conspiratorial right created their own party, Renovación Española.[71] There was no acrimony about the split and the members of both groups continued to mix socially, to attend each other's meetings, to read each other's press and even to belong to both organizations.

While the right was reorganizing, the government coalition was crumbling, a process accelerated by the insurrectionism of the CNT. The rightist press did not make subtle distinctions between the CNT, the UGT and the FNTT, portraying them all as 'communists'. Despite the CNT's hostility towards the Republic, its strikes and uprisings were blamed on the Republican–Socialist coalition which was working hard to control them. The extreme right in the countryside made sweeping condemnations of disorder, most dramatically in the wake of a nation-wide revolutionary strike called by the CNT for 8 January 1933 and of its bloody repercussions in the village of Casas Viejas in the province of Cadiz. In the lock-out conditions of 1932, four out of five workers in Casas Viejas were unemployed for most of the year, dependent on charity, occasional roadmending and scouring the countryside for wild asparagus and rabbits. Their desperation, inflamed by an increase in bread prices, ensured a ready response to the CNT call for revolution. The villagers' hesitant declaration of libertarian communism led to a savage repression in which twenty-four people died.[72]

The right-wing press initially applauded the Civil Guard's repression of the strike.[73] But when it became apparent that there was political capital to be made, crocodile tears were shed for the victims. Barba Hernández of the UME fuelled the subsequent smear campaign with a mendacious claim that Azaña had personally ordered the massacre. The right-wing newspapers and Juan March's press network howled that the Republic was as barbaric, unjust and corrupt as its monarchist predecessors. Lerroux, ever anxious for power, had moved further to the right and began a policy of obstruction in the Cortes. The government was virtually paralysed by acerbic Cortes debates. Although the Socialists stood loyally by Azaña, Casas Viejas undermined the coalition. Azaña was so embittered by the behaviour of the Radicals and the *jabaliés* that he contemplated abandoning politics.[74]

Casas Viejas underlined the cost to the Socialist movement of participation in the government. The defence of the bourgeois Republic against the anarchists was sacrificing Socialist credibility with their own rural supporters. The anarchists, meanwhile, stepped up the tempo of their revolutionary activities. The latent violence at local level was the basis of ever increasing hostility between the PSOE and Gil Robles's new party, the Confederación Española de Derechas Autónomas (CEDA). Inspired by Ángel Herrera, it was based on Acción Popular, the Agrarians and about forty other rightist groups. At the founding congress in Madrid, at the end of February 1933, Gil Robles compared his anti-revolutionary objectives with those of Hitler in Germany. On the same day, at another meeting in Madrid, he spoke approvingly of fascism as a cure for the evils of Spain.[75] Unsurprisingly, the Socialists believed that the CEDA aimed to establish fascism in Spain, a charge only casually denied by Gil Robles. Inevitably, this accelerated the radicalization of the followers of Largo Caballero.[76]

Gil Robles's speeches were peppered with double-edged pronouncements that fuelled the Socialists' sensitivity to the danger of fascism. Weimar was persistently cited as an example by the right and as a warning by the left. The Catholic press applauded the Nazi destruction of the German Socialist and Communist movements. Nazism was admired for its emphasis on authority, the fatherland and hierarchy – all three oft-repeated slogans of CEDA propaganda. *El Debate* pointed out alarmingly that Hitler had attained power legally. A constant refrain of the paper was that Spain needed an organization like those that had crushed the German and Italian left, hinting that the CEDA could fulfil that role.[77]

Alongside the Casas Viejas campaign, the implementation of Article 26 of the Constitution via a Law of Congregations infuriated the Church hierarchy and intensified conservative opposition to the government. Conscious of growing opposition and personally unhappy about the Law of Congregations, Alcalá-Zamora was keen to remove Azaña. Their relations were increasingly tense. Azaña commented, 'he can't stomach me'.[78] The President's manoeuvres to replace him with Lerroux led the journalist César Jalón to conclude that he was 'a pocket Machiavelli'. An opportunity arose in early June when Azaña proposed a reshuffle to replace his terminally ill Finance Minister, Jaume Carner. There was talk of a broad government coalition under Prieto, but both Lerroux and Largo Caballero refused to participate in the same cabinet. Largo Caballero's antipathy to Prieto thus deprived the PSOE of a significant opportunity: both to avoid immediate elections and to have a role in determining when and how they were eventually called. Accordingly, Azaña was obliged, on 6 June, to cobble together a slightly different Republican–Socialist cabinet which soldiered on through the summer but faced mounting difficulties.[79]

As reform was ever more successfully blocked by the right, Largo Caballero's followers in the Federación de Juventudes Socialistas (FJS) were demanding that the PSOE end its collaboration with the Republicans. Addressing them on 23 July in Madrid, Largo Caballero declared that the Socialists should seek to govern alone.[80] On 6 August, at the FJS summer school at Torrelodones near Madrid, Prieto defended Socialist collaboration in government with the Republicans. He criticized hopes of instant social transformations as 'infantile optimism'. Stressing the immense power of a resurgent right, he argued that an exclusively Socialist government was not a realistic aspiration. This speech was not what Prieto's youthful listeners wanted to hear and *El Socialista* refused to publish it.[81]

At the beginning of September, elections were held for the Tribunal of Constitutional Guarantees, which would adjudicate on the constitutional validity of laws and on conflicts between the autonomous regions and the central state. Among other conservatives, Calvo Sotelo was elected, as was Juan March, a success that reflected his lavish spending in the Balearic Islands rather than any juridical expertise. However, the outstanding charges against him of bribery and treason kept him in prison.[82] To the alarm of the Socialists, on 12 September Alcalá-Zamora used the results of the Tribunal elections to justify asking Lerroux to form a government. To avoid certain parliamentary defeat, Lerroux governed with the Cortes closed. On 19 September, the PSOE executive voted to break its undertakings with the left Republicans, a decision passionately defended by Largo Caballero in speeches in Madrid.[83] When the Cortes reopened on 2 October, Prieto dutifully undertook the painful task of announcing the end of the Republican–Socialist coalition to which he had dedicated much of his life. Lerroux lost a vote of confidence and Alcalá-Zamora called on Martínez Barrio to form a government to preside over new elections.[84]

In the elections called for 19 November, in contrast to 1931 the left went to the polls in disarray while the right was able to mount a united campaign. Gil Robles had just returned from the Nuremberg rally strongly influenced by what he had seen. Determined on victory at any price, the CEDA election committee decided on a single counter-revolutionary front. Thus the CEDA went into the elections in some areas in coalition with 'catastrophist' groups such as Renovación Española and the Carlists or, in others, with the corrupt Radicals. The French Catholic philosopher Georges Bernanos later wrote sarcastically that Gil Robles and Ángel Herrera, having been offered by Lerroux the gangrenous remnants of the Radical Party, 'always welcome the prodigal son as long as he brings the fatted cow'.[85]

The Socialists were embittered by the ease with which, throughout the summer, Largo Caballero's social legislation had been virtually abandoned. Rank-and-file faith in the Republic was diminished.[86] The radical elements simultaneously blamed the left Republicans for the limitations of reform while confidently, and mistakenly, assuming that all the votes cast in June 1931 for the Republican–Socialist coalition would stay with the PSOE. The Radical Party was now on the right and the bitterness generated by much Republican legislation would ensure much anarchist abstention. Prieto's defence of the coalition was dismissed out of hand and so the irresponsible decision to go it alone was taken. It would be a fatal strategic error.[87] With an electoral law that favoured coalitions and Gil Robles's tactical alliances with a range of bedfellows, twice as many Socialist votes as rightist ones would be needed to elect a deputy. One of the few glimmers of common sense in the PSOE's preparations was Prieto's inclusion of both Azaña and Marcelino Domingo in the Socialist electoral list for Vizcaya.[88]

The CEDA's election fund was enormous, based on generous donations from the well-to-do, especially from Juan March. The climax of the CEDA's campaign came in a belligerent speech given in Madrid by Gil Robles: 'It is necessary now to defeat socialism inexorably. We must found a new state, purge the fatherland of judaizing freemasons ... What does it matter if we have to shed blood! ... When the time comes, either parliament submits or we will eliminate it.'[89]

Just as the campaign was beginning, on 3 November, March escaped from prison. He later told an official of the British Embassy that, on 2 November, in the presence of a warder, he had said to a visiting friend:

'I am escaping tomorrow morning at six, I will telegraph you from Gibraltar.' When the alarmed friend looked at the warder, March reassured him, saying: 'I have bought the gentleman and the guards at the gate.' He was accompanied by two bodyguards provided by the FAI. His flight was treated by both the rightist and anarchist press as an heroic act by a persecuted (and generous) man.[90] Initially, March sought refuge in Gibraltar, before taking up residence in a luxury hotel in Paris. His wealth would see him elected and he was soon able to return to Spain with parliamentary immunity, having gained a seat for Mallorca by dint of the disbursement of large sums.[91]

The PSOE could not match the well-funded right-wing campaign. Gil Robles dominated the right-wing campaign as Largo Caballero dominated that of the Socialists. The latter delighted his supporters with calls for the dictatorship of the proletariat to carry out the economic disarmament of the bourgeoisie. His radicalism antagonized middle-class voters and helped justify the right's dire warnings.[92] The results brought bitter disappointment to the Socialists. After local deals between the CEDA and the Radicals had enabled them to exploit the electoral law, the two parties finished with 115 and 104 deputies respectively. With the connivance of the Radicals, the right had regained control of the apparatus of the state. It was determined to use it to dismantle the reforms of the previous two years. However, expectations had been raised during that time which could only ensure burning popular fury when the right put back the clock to 1930.

In the two years following the November elections, known subsequently as the 'two black years' (bienio negro), the existing conflicts in Spanish politics were dramatically intensified. Power had passed to a right wing determined to avenge the perceived injuries and indignities suffered at the hands of the Constituent Cortes. Bitter polarization was inevitable. Industrial workers and landless labourers had already been driven to desperation by the ease with which the reforms of 1931–3 had been bypassed. The decrees introduced by Largo Caballero had been ruthlessly blocked by landowners in the south, despite evidence that the jurados mixtos had prevented 80 per cent of potential strikes.[93] The complete demolition of those reforms could only provoke violence. At the end of 1933, as many as 619,000 men, 12 per cent of Spain's workforce, were unemployed and in the south the figures were nearer 20 per cent. The UGT's success in negotiating wage increases through the jura-

dos mixtos had provoked a violent reaction among employers. The response of the Federación Patronal Madrileña was particularly fierce. In Madrid, unemployment was averaging 30 per cent and in the construction industry would soon reach 40 per cent. Employers celebrated electoral victory by cutting wages and sacking workers while landowners evicted tenants and raised rents. As landowners ignored social legislation entirely and took reprisals for the discomforts of the previous two years, unemployment rose even further. By April 1934 it had reached 703,000.[94]

Socialist outrage knew no bounds. As well as the tactical error in not allying with the Republicans, there were other crucial contributions to their defeat. The loss of forty seats may have owed something to anarchist abstention which could be linked to March's subsidies to the anarchist press, particularly *La Tierra*, whose Director, Salvador Cánovas Cervantes, was reckoned to be open to bribery. The one-time leading CNT militant and subsequently founder of the Marxist POUM Joaquín Maurín wrote of March's influence on the anarchist press, 'The CNT made several mindless uprisings when there was a Republican–Socialist government. In the reactionary Lerroux–Gil Robles period, they refrained from doing so.'[95]

Of course, CNT abstention was not exclusively the work of Juan March. It was also driven by outrage at the Republican repression. In the words of the influential Dr Isaac Puente: 'Whoever wins, whether Right or Left, will be our enemy, our jailer, our executioner. It will be whoever is served by the truncheons of the Assault Guard, the bullying of the police, the rifles of the Civil Guard, and the mentality of prison guards. The proletariat will have exactly what it already has: the shadow of the jailer, spies, hunger, bruises and welts.' The Assault Guard was a Republican corps intended to be more progressive in its outlook than the Civil Guard. Denouncing all candidates as equally miserable cynics and right-wing, the CNT press called for workers not to vote.[96] March was not the only sponsor of abstention. In Cadiz, supporters of José Antonio Primo de Rivera paid for the local anarchist abstention campaign.[97] The introduction of female suffrage in Article 36 of the Constitution had seen the reactionary influence of the clergy impel the majority of Catholic women to vote for the right. Nevertheless, the Socialist rank and file were convinced that the elections had been fraudulent. In the south, they had good reason to believe that they had been swindled out of seats by the *caciques'* power over the starving *braceros*. In rural areas of high unemployment, it had been easy to get votes with promises of jobs or threats of dismissal. The deputy for Badajoz, Margarita Nelken, saw local *caciques* buy votes from starving peasants with chorizo and bread while upper-class women, escorted by machine-gun-toting Civil Guards, bought votes in brothels and at the voting stations. Armed thugs employed by the *caciques* prevented Socialist campaigners speaking at some meetings and were a louring presence next to the glass voting urns on election day.[98]

The PSOE's 1.5 million votes had won it 58 seats in the Cortes, while the Radicals' 800,000 votes had been rewarded with 104 seats. According to calculations made by the PSOE, the united parties of the right had together obtained 3,345,504 votes and 212 seats at 15,780 votes per seat, while the disunited left had received 3,375,432 votes and only 99 seats at 34,095 votes per seat. In some areas of the south – Badajoz, Cordoba and Malaga, for example – the margin of right-wing victory was small enough for electoral malpractice to have made all the difference. In Badajoz, the difference in votes meant the difference between winning three or eleven seats and the Radical representation rose from two to ten.[99] Azaña later denounced the 'miserable corruption' and 'frightening immorality' of the right's campaign.[100]

The question of Juan March's contribution to the right's electoral war chest was raised during an acrimonious debate in the Cortes on 8 May 1935. In a lengthy speech, Teodomiro Menéndez, reporting on the work of the Responsibilities Commission, recounted the acts of corruption perpetrated by March since 1911. He related that murky record to the efforts made by the right to secure the financial backing of March: 'It has been simply a course of action against the interests of Spain and in the interests of a private individual whom you have now enthroned in this chamber, this Juan March who has contributed with his money to the recent elections ... The Sultan of Spain is Juan March and you are his subjects.'[101]

Demonstration in the Madrid bull-ring during the Popular Front election
campaign in February 1936 in support of the 30,000 Austrians imprisoned after
the October 1934 uprising.

10

The Black Years and the Coming of War, 1933–1936

The bitterness aroused in the Socialist rank and file by the cynical union of Radicals and the CEDA was soon compounded by the untrammelled offensive of the employers. Popular outrage was all the greater because of the restraint and self-sacrifice that had characterized Socialist policy between 1931 and 1933. Several politicians, ranging from Azaña to Botella Asensi, now in the Radical Party, called for new elections. Most frantic was the response of Largo Caballero. Sensitive to the social distress being experienced by the UGT's rank and file, he played a dangerous game, adopting an apparently revolutionary rhetoric which was merely an empty threat intended to scare the right into limiting its belligerency and to persuade Alcalá-Zamora to call new elections. No real plans for a rising were made. When the President did not succumb to this vacuous pressure, the Socialists were faced with the choice of stepping up their threats or losing credibility with their own militants. The resulting situation could be of benefit only to the CEDA.[1]

Although not prepared to call new elections, Alcalá-Zamora did not invite Gil Robles to form a government despite the fact that the CEDA was the biggest party in the Cortes. He feared his ambition to establish an authoritarian, corporative state. In any case, Gil Robles's victory was much more precarious than it appeared. Even if invited by the President to form a government, he could not have done so. All the rightist elements in the Cortes did not make up an absolute majority. Besides, a cabinet containing the declared enemies of the Republic could only excite the fervour of the left, including a substantial section of the Radical Party. With leftist divisions healed, any such rightist government would be defeated. Then there would either be a coalition of left and centre Republicans or new elections. It was inconceivable that the Socialists would make the same tactical error twice. Anxious, therefore, not to have to risk his fragile victory in further elections, Gil Robles sought another solution. Lacking the force to seize power by violence, he turned to the idea of a government controlled by CEDA votes. Thus Lerroux, as leader of the second largest party, became Prime Minister with the Radicals as the CEDA's puppets. *El Debate* explained: 'First support Lerroux; then collaborate with Lerroux; and later replace Lerroux'.[2]

Gil Robles made it brutally clear to Lerroux what he expected in return for CEDA votes. There was little about his requirements that might calm social tensions. In a speech in the Cortes on 19 December, claiming that the election results had revealed a national revulsion against the policies of the first *bienio*, he called for an amnesty for those imprisoned for Sanjurjo's coup, for a revision of the religious legislation of the Constituent Cortes and for the repeal of the measures that had most alleviated the distress of the landless peasantry – municipal boundaries, obligatory cultivation, the eight-hour day and mixed juries – and a reduction of the area of land subject to expropriation under the agrarian reform bill. In return for the harsh social policies desired by the CEDA's wealthy backers, the Radicals would be allowed to enjoy the spoils of office. The Radical election campaign had been about moderating, not destroying, the reforming achievements of the first *bienio*. CEDA demands challenged the liberal beliefs of many Radicals, including Martínez Barrio. However, at the age of sixty-nine, Lerroux was not about to reject his last chance of power.[3]

The Socialists were appalled. During the election campaign, Largo Caballero had declared that, in the Radical Party, there were those who 'if they have not been in jail, deserve to have been'. He was referring both to Lerroux's long history of financial corruption and to his collusion in Sanjurjo's 1932 coup.[4] Miguel Maura was of like mind, writing later of the inexhaustible supply of anecdotes and incidents involving the immorality of Lerroux's friends and relations. In the summer of 1933, anticipating that he would soon be in power, Lerroux had offered Maura a ministry. Maura refused, telling him that he could never take part in any government of his, 'not exactly because of you but because of the undesirables that surround you who will end up bringing you down'. Lerroux responded blithely that he always looked after his friends, calling it 'the price of fame'. He brushed off their activities as 'peccadilloes'. Shortly afterwards, Lerroux's secretary asked Maura if he would like to make a fortune out of a deal in the Ministry of the Interior. Maura returned and reported this to Lerroux who simply responded: 'These lads! I'm going to tweak his ears.'[5]

Maura was not the only conservative politician worried by Lerroux's easy-going approach to financial probity in public life. It was a concern shared by Alcalá-Zamora, Gil Robles and Joaquín Chapaprieta, the independent conservative republican deputy for Alicante. It was well known that Lerroux had always hankered after a life of luxury. Once in government, Lerroux bombarded other ministers with requests for official positions for his relatives and cronies. Alcalá-Zamora lamented that his criteria for such appointments were the candidates' need for money and their personal likeability. This provoked real alarm in the President when it was a question of senior positions in banks.[6]

Azaña later recalled with bitter amusement that, shortly after entering government, Lerroux's deputies set up an office to distribute state favours, monopolies, government procurement orders, licences and so on. Azaña called it 'the maternity ward for jobs', comparing the scale of corruption with the worst days of Romero Robledo: 'They wanted more than the political posts that always change with changes of government. With enormous skill and patience, commensurate with their greed, they divided among themselves government and other official and semi-official positions both inside Spain and elsewhere. There was not a single ministry, monopoly, delegation, administrative office, consortium, confederation, authorized dealership, private company carrying out government business, institution etc., etc., into which they did not get their claws.'[7] Similarly, Félix Gordón Ordás, who joined Diego Martínez Barrio in creating Unión Republicana in September 1934, declared in Bilbao, at the end of May 1935, that 'the majority of the governments led by Lerroux, and especially the present one, are virtual cartels for fabulous business deals'.[8]

Throughout 1935, evidence of Radical corruption would mount. *El Socialista* alleged that three Radical deputies – Fernando Rey Mora, Basilio Álvarez, and Emiliano Iglesias – each demanded 30,000 pesetas from a Sr Serrano Pérez to ensure that his son was appointed secretary to the Court of Constitutional Guarantees. There were many allegations of embezzlement of municipal funds by Radical town councillors and of rake-offs being taken by senior Radicals, including Lerroux's adopted son, Aurelio, in return for permitting illegal casinos to function. Among others implicated were Lerroux's cronies Emiliano Iglesias, Juan Pich y

Pon and Manuel Marraco. Other accusations related to public contracts given to businesses owned by Lerroux himself. Ironically, Lerroux complained to the monarchist Pedro Sainz Rodríguez that his own staff were dishonest and had even stolen his shirts.[9]

The Socialists believed that the Radicals had betrayed the basic ideals of the Republic by undertaking to protect the agrarian oligarchy's material interests in return for a licence to indulge in corruption.[10] Although on nothing like the same scale, it is certainly the case that, during the first *bienio*, there were examples of Socialists and left Republicans accumulating official positions. In February 1933, a right-wing lawyer with suspicious links to the CNT, Joaquín del Moral, published a diatribe against the Republican–Socialist coalition alleging infractions of the 1931 Constitution and the enjoyment of the spoils of power (*enchufismo*). Hailed by the extreme right, it became a runaway best-seller. More virulent calumnies were published by Dr Albiñana of the Partido Nacionalista.[11] The *enchufismo* of which the Republicans were accused was small beer by comparison with that indulged in during the dictatorship by the same monarchists who applauded Del Moral.[12]

Despite the threatening stance of Largo Caballero, the first violent working-class protest came from the anarchists. With irresponsible naïvety, a futile uprising was called for 8 December 1933. However, the government had been forewarned and quickly declared a state of emergency. Leaders of the CNT and the FAI were arrested, press censorship was imposed and unions were closed down. In traditionally anarchist areas, Aragon, the Rioja, Catalonia, the Levante, parts of Andalusia and Galicia, there were sporadic strikes, some trains were blown up and Civil Guard posts were assaulted. The movement was quickly over in Barcelona, Madrid and Valencia. In the Aragonese capital, Zaragoza, however, the rising did get off the ground. Workers erected barricades, attacked public buildings and engaged in street fighting. The government sent in the army, which took four days, with the aid of tanks, to crush the insurrection.[13]

Violent incidents involving the CNT diverted attention from the intensifying social problems in the south. This was the result not only of the landowners slashing wages and refusing work to union members but also of significant rises in the price of basic necessities. The Radical government had removed price control on bread and costs had risen by 25 per cent to 70. Demonstrations of starving women, children and old people calling for bread became a frequent sight. The increase in unemployment, sharp reductions in wages and the consequent hunger was reflected in the incidence of anaemia and tuberculosis among the children of the region. When the landless labourers protested or tried to collect windfall crops, they were beaten by the Civil Guard. Rising hunger in the south was reflected in the growing militancy of the FNTT. Its moderate president, Lucio Martínez Gil, was replaced by one of the radical young followers of Largo Caballero, Ricardo Zabalza Elorga. At the end of 1933, Largo Caballero reacted to the rising tide of militancy by intensifying his threats, although his rhetoric was not matched by any serious revolutionary intentions.[14]

With a pliant Radical government in power, the success of Acción Popular's 'accidentalist' tactics was clear. Nevertheless, for the 'catastrophists', even a strong rightist government was inadequate. Franco's friend Joaquín Arrarás claimed that the life-and-death struggle of 'the forces of order and the fatherland against the forces of anarchy and the anti-fatherland' required the outright crushing of the revolution. Calvo Sotelo lamented the lack of a strong state able to 'discipline' the working class.[15] Accordingly, the extreme right prepared, on three loosely linked fronts, for a final violent showdown: military conspiracy, Carlist militias and fascist street fighters. The weakness of the JONS had finally led, in mid-February 1934, to its fusion with José Antonio Primo de Rivera's Falange Española.[16] Two months before its own launch on Sunday, 29 October 1933, Falange Española had accepted funding from the monarchists of Renovación Española. The so-called Pacto de El Escorial tied the Falange to the military conspiracy against the Republic.[17] With its rhetoric of 'lead and blood' and celebration of 'the music of pistols and the barbaric drumbeat of lead', the monarchists saw the Falange as the perfect instrument of political destabilization. That its leader was a landowning aristocrat, a cosmopolitan socialite and, of course, political heir of his father calmed any anxiety that the Falange might get out of control in the way of its German and Italian equivalents. The Falange would provoke street brawls and thereby help to generate the lawlessness which, exaggerated by the right-wing press, would 'justify' the military rising.[18]

In a separate initiative, a joint delegation of Alfonsine and Carlist monarchists went to Rome on 31 March in search of financial help and weaponry. The delegation included Antonio Goicoechea, head of Renovación Española, General Emilio Barrera, of the Unión Militar

Española, and Antonio Lizarza Iribarren, the recruiter for the Carlist Requeté (armed militia). Barrera began by saying that he was moved by the honour of speaking to Mussolini and 'thanked him for the help given by Italy for the coup of 10 August, a failure but rich in lessons'. Mussolini offered financial assistance to the tune of 1.5 million pesetas and 20,000 rifles, 20,000 hand grenades and 200 machine guns which were delivered via Tripoli and Portugal. Arrangements were also made for several hundred Requetés to be trained by the Italian army as instructors.[19] Under its newly elected leader, Manuel Fal Conde, the Carlist Comunión Tradicionalista was creating a full-scale citizen army. Trained by the Africanista Colonel José Enrique Varela, a well-armed force of 30,000 'red berets' would be at the disposal of the military conspirators in the spring of 1936.[20]

The monarchists' immediate objective was an amnesty for the collaborators of the dictatorship and those involved in Sanjurjo's coup. Eventually secured on 24 April 1934, this saw the return of their most dynamic leader, José Calvo Sotelo, who replaced the ineffectual dandy Goicoechea. Seeing the Falange as the possible party of the future, Calvo Sotelo tried to join and make it his own. José Antonio Primo de Rivera, who despised him, refused, saying that he could never be a potential caudillo because 'he couldn't ride a horse'.[21] The word 'caudillo' which was adopted by Franco as the Spanish equivalent of Duce and Führer originally meant 'bandit chieftain'. Soon, the monarchist press, in addition to abusing Gil Robles's weakness, would talk of the 'installation' of a new authoritarian monarchy rather than of the restoration of Alfonso XIII. This meant the conquest of the state in order to build a new authoritarian regime.[22]

Deeply sensitive to such developments, the Socialists were determined to avoid the fate of the German and Austrian left. As 1934 progressed there were growing numbers of street battles. Events within the orthodox political arena did little to cool tempers. An important group within the Radical Party, led by Martínez Barrio, was unhappy about Lerroux's drift to the right and his appointment of the aggressively conservative Agrarian deputy for Zamora, José María Cid Ruiz Zorrilla, as Minister of Communications. When the Agrarians' leader, José Martínez de Velasco, had announced that the Agrarian Party would accept the Republic, something Gil Robles consistently failed to do, eight of his thirty-one deputies joined the CEDA in protest. In an interview in the monarchist magazine *Blanco y Negro* in February, Martínez Barrio declared that a wide coalition of the centre-right would be preferable to a minority Radical government hobbled by its commitments. However, this would require unequivocal acceptance of the Republic by the CEDA and the Agrarians. In the Cortes, Gil Robles insinuated that his party had already made too many sacrifices and threatened obliquely that any attempt to put legal obstacles in the way of his programme would provoke violence.[23]

As he demanded harsher repression of such 'criminality' as the theft of acorns and olives by hungry day labourers, the Socialists saw that the Radical government, to maintain CEDA support, was dismantling more of the progressive measures introduced since 1931. Gil Robles was steadily eliminating the moderate members of the cabinet. In speeches on 19 and 26 February, he had threatened to bring down the government unless critics of the CEDA were silenced. Concerns were intensified further when *El Debate* stated that the repression, in February, of the Austrian Socialist movement by Engelbert Dollfuss was a lesson to be followed.[24] On 1 March, Gil Robles withdrew his support from the government, secured what he called 'the defeat of the extremist sector of the Radical Party' and demanded a cabinet more closely corresponding to the forces in the Cortes. Martínez Barrio and two other moderate Radical ministers, Antonio de Lara y Zarate (Finance) and José Pareja Yébenes (Education), were forced to resign.[25]

To the delight of Gil Robles, the reactionary and volatile Rafael Salazar Alonso, who had close personal ties to the landowning oligarchy in Extremadura, became Minister of the Interior. Salazar immediately outlined his plans for his 'anti-revolutionary coordination' of the entire apparatus of public order – the Civil Guard, the police and the Assault Guard.[26] Gil Robles declared that, as long as the Minister of the Interior defended the social order like this, the government could count on CEDA support. The CEDA press was calling for anti-strike legislation similar to that of Fascist Italy, Nazi Germany, Portugal and Austria. Although Lerroux refrained from illegalizing all strikes, he delighted the right by announcing that strikes with political implications would be ruthlessly suppressed. For the CEDA and Salazar Alonso, all strikes were deemed to be political. He provoked a number of strikes throughout the spring and summer of 1934 which enabled him to pick off the most powerful unions one by one, beginning with the printers in March. The government extended its repressive armoury by increasing the numbers of the Civil Guard and the Assault Guard and by re-establishing the death penalty.[27]

Nevertheless, this was not enough for the CEDA. Pressure was piled on Lerroux for a law to reinstate state support for the clergy and then to move forward with the amnesty bill, something for which he was keen given his links with Sanjurjo. The amnesty text was drafted by Gil Robles, Antonio Goicoechea, José Martínez de Velasco and the Carlist leader, the Conde de Rodezno. The Socialists and left Republicans, fearing the return to the army of officers determined to overthrow the regime, vainly opposed it. Alcalá-Zamora withheld his consent over the weekend of 20–23 April before finally signing.

While he hesitated, Gil Robles applied pressure. On 22 April 1934, the CEDA youth organization, the Juventud de Acción Popular (JAP), announced that 50,000 militants would attend a rally at Philip II's monastery of El Escorial, a provocatively anti-Republican gesture. Seduced by Mussolini's examples, it was hoped to precipitate a 'March on Madrid' to seize power. A concerned Alcalá-Zamora asked Salazar Alonso, 'will they be flying their flags? And will they do their stiff-arm salutes?' The Socialists, fearing a Nazi-style rally, tried to stop it by means of a general strike in Madrid and efforts to disrupt transport. In the event, only 20,000 people gathered, some of them smallholders paid for the day by their landlords. Ramón Serrano Súñer, CEDA deputy for Zaragoza and later architect of Franco's National-Syndicalist state, fulminated against 'degenerate democracy'. Luciano de la Calzada, CEDA deputy for Valladolid, listed those with no right to call themselves Spaniards: 'Jews, heretics, protestants, comuneros, moriscos [Moorish converts to Christianity], Encyclopaedists, afrancesados [admirers of the French revolution], freemasons, Krausists, liberals and Marxists'. Gil Robles's own speech was greeted with chants of '¡Jefe! ¡Jefe! ¡Jefe!' – the Spanish equivalent of Duce.[28]

After his disagreement with Alcalá-Zamora over the amnesty, Lerroux, following protocol, made a token offer of his own resignation. To his surprise, Alcalá-Zamora accepted and offered the premiership to the Minister of Labour, the obscure and ineffectual Ricardo Samper.[29] Lerroux gave Samper permission to form a government, fearing that, if he did not, the President would dissolve the Cortes and call new elections. Gil Robles saw an opportunity to exploit the situation. His fellow deputy from Salamanca, Cándido Casanueva, suggested that CEDA, monarchist and Radical deputies unite to pass a vote of confidence in Lerroux and thereby provoke Alcalá-Zamora's resignation. The manoeuvre would then be completed by the elevation of Lerroux to the presidency of the Republic. The idea was for Lerroux then to invite Gil Robles to form a government. Confident that he would soon be Prime Minister again, Lerroux was too wily to fall for the manoeuvre.[30]

Alcalá-Zamora had precipitated far more than just a cabinet reshuffle. His opposition to the amnesty was perfectly justifiable but it was a mistake to remove Lerroux. He had never trusted him and probably saw him as a potential rival for the presidency. This emotional decision triggered a series of unforeseen consequences that contributed to the polarization of the Republic. He made an enemy of Lerroux and provoked a crisis within the Radical Party. Twenty deputies led by Martínez Barrio left the party in May, leaving the rump even more dependent on CEDA whims.[31]

Lerroux's support for the amnesty bill had exposed his links with the conspirators of 1932. Now, the Samper government, with a belligerent Minister of the Interior, could hardly be more to the liking of Gil Robles. A decree of 4 May annulled the post-Sanjurjada expropriations and another on 23 May repealed the Law of Municipal Boundaries.[32] It was increasingly difficult for the Socialist leaders to hold back their followers. Largo Caballero tended to pander to the revolutionary impatience of the masses, although his rhetoric consisted of little beyond Marxist platitudes. No concrete reference to the contemporary political scene was ever made in Largo's speeches and no timetable for the future revolution was ever given. Nevertheless, the radicalization of the Socialist movement, particularly from its youth movement, the Federación de Juventudes Socialistas (FJS), and its Madrid organization, the Agrupación Socialista Madrileña, intensified throughout 1934. Efforts by Besteiro to slow down the process of bolshevization earned him the hostility of the radical youth. Out of party loyalty, Prieto reluctantly went along with the revolutionary tactic.[33]

Trouble had been building since March. Rural labourers were suffering immense hardship through increased aggression from employers. The repeal of the Law of Municipal Boundaries, coming just before the harvest, permitted landlords to bring in cheap Portuguese and Galician migrant workers to undercut local wages. The defences of the rural proletariat were falling rapidly before the right-wing onslaught. The last vestige of protection that landless labourers had for their jobs and wages came from Socialist mayors who tried to oblige local landowners to observe social legislation or used municipal funds for public works to provide some employment. Salazar Alonso systematically removed them, using flimsy pretexts such as 'administrative irregularities' – which often meant debts inherited from their monarchist predecessors – or a failure 'to inspire confidence in matters of public order' – which usually meant Socialists.[34]

In Badajoz, starving labourers were begging in the streets of the towns. Rickets and tuberculosis were common. Workers who refused to rip up their union cards were denied work. The owners' boycott of unionized labour and the notorious 'Comed República' campaign were designed to reassert pre-1931 forms of social control. The FNTT leadership reacted with moderation, sending a series of reasoned appeals to the Ministers of Labour, Agriculture and the Interior for the implementation of the law regarding obligatory cultivation, work agreements, strict job rotation and labour exchanges.[35]

When nothing was done, a meeting of the FNTT National Committee, on 11 and 12 May, decided to combat the patronal offensive with strike action, to begin on 5 June. Older heads within the UGT were opposed to what they saw as a rash initiative that might squander worker militancy. The harvest was ready at different times in each area, so the selection of a single date for the strike posed problems of coordination. Moreover, a general strike, as opposed to staggered ones limited to large estates, would cause hardship to leaseholders and sharecroppers who needed to hire one or two workers. Largo Caballero pointed out that a nationwide peasant strike would be denounced as revolutionary and risked a terrible repression. Thus, there would be no solidarity strikes by industrial workers. The FNTT was under extreme pressure from a hungry rank and file pushed beyond endurance by the constant provocation of *caciques* and Civil Guard. The executive informed the UGT that to ignore their members' demand for action would be to abandon them to hunger wages and lock-out. As the FNTT newspaper declared, 'All of Spain is becoming Casas Viejas.' The strike declaration was made in strict accordance with the law, ten days' notice being given, in the hope that the mere threat of a strike would be sufficient to oblige the government to do something to respond to mass hunger.[36]

Unsurprisingly, Salazar Alonso seized his chance to strike a blow at the largest section of the UGT. In meetings with the head of the Civil Guard and the Director General of Security, he had already made specific plans for the repression of such a strike. Accordingly, just as Zabalza's hopes of compromise negotiations between the FNTT and the Ministers of Agriculture and Labour were coming to fruition, Salazar Alonso criminalized the strikers by declaring the harvest a national public service and the strike a 'revolutionary conflict'. Liberal and left-wing individuals in the country districts were arrested wholesale, including four Socialist deputies in flagrant violation of Articles 55 and 56 of the Constitution. Several thousand peasants were loaded at gunpoint onto lorries, transported hundreds of kilometres from their homes and dumped without food or money to make their own way back. Workers' centres were closed down and many elected town councils were replaced by government nominees. Although most of the labourers arrested were soon released, emergency courts sentenced prominent workers' leaders to four or more years of imprisonment. The workers' societies in each village, the Casas del Pueblo, were closed and the FNTT was effectively crippled until 1936. In an uneven battle, the FNTT had suffered a terrible defeat. Salazar Alonso had effectively put the clock back in the Spanish countryside to the 1920s.[37]

The actions of Salazar Alonso could only intensify the conviction on the left that Samper's cabinet was merely Gil Robles's Trojan Horse. The Radical–CEDA determination to undermine the Republic's most loyal support became clear when the government clashed successively with the Catalans and the Basques. The sympathy shown by the Constituent Cortes to autonomist aspirations was now replaced by right-wing centralist bias, particularly in the case of Catalonia. In April, the Generalitat had passed an agrarian reform, the Llei de Contractes de Conreu, an enlightened measure to protect tenants from eviction by landowners and give them the right to buy land they had worked for eighteen years. On 8 June, to the delight of the landowners of the Lliga Regionalista, the predominantly right-wing Tribunal of Constitutional Guarantees overruled the law. Presenting the text unchanged to the Corts Catalanes on 12 June, the President of the Generalitat, Lluís Companys, described the Tribunal's decision as yet another centralist attempt to reduce the region's autonomy.[38] The consequent political tension was skilfully manipulated by Gil Robles in such a way as to provoke the left. In a tense debate in the Cortes, he called for the sternest application of the law against the Generalitat for flying the 'flag of rebellion'. As Samper vacillated, Gil Robles's support for the government began to waver. Throughout the crisis *El Debate* called for the government to make the Catalans submit. Meanwhile, the government began to infringe the Basques' tax privileges and, to silence protest, cancelled municipal elections on 12 August and imprisoned hundreds of Basque town councillors. Such high-handed centralism confirmed leftist fears of the accelerating drift to the right.[39]

The politics of reprisal were beginning to generate an atmosphere, if not of imminent civil war, certainly of worsening violence. The left saw fascism in every action of the right; the right smelt revolution in every left-wing move. Violent speeches were made in the Cortes and, at one point, guns flourished. In the streets, there were shots exchanged between Socialist and Falangist youths. Juan Antonio Ansaldo, a wealthy monarchist playboy and aviator, had joined the Falange in the spring to organize terrorist squads known as the Falange of Blood. A plan to blow up the Madrid Casa del Pueblo was thwarted when the police discovered a large cache of arms and explosives. The actions of the Falangist hit squads provoked reprisals by the extremists of the FJS.[40]

The attacks on regional autonomy and Gil Robles's increasingly threatening rhetoric were part of a build-up of pressure on Alcalá-Zamora to invite the CEDA to join a coalition government. Already in mid-August, Gil Robles told Samper that the cabinet was no longer to the CEDA's liking and could not depend on its parliamentary support. On 5 September he warned both Samper and Salazar Alonso that, at a JAP rally to be held four days later, he would publicly announce his discontent with the government's approach to public order. The rally, on 9 September, was held at Covadonga in Asturias, the starting point for the Reconquista. This warlike symbol echoed Sanjurjo's comparison of the rural proletariat with Moroccan tribesmen and foreshadowed the Francoist use of a violent crusade rhetoric. Gil Robles spoke passionately of the need to annihilate the 'separatist rebellion' of the Catalans and the Basque nationalists. Revelling in the adulation of the assembled ranks of the JAP, the supreme 'Jefe' worked himself up to a frenzy of patriotic rhetoric calling for nationalism to be exalted 'with ecstasy, with paroxysms, with anything; I prefer a nation of lunatics to a nation of wretches'. Behind this apparently spontaneous vehemence lay a cold-blooded determination to inflame the left to prevent the CEDA coming to power.[41]

Both he and Salazar Alonso were confident that the left could not succeed. The young Socialists' preparations for revolution had consisted largely of Sunday picnics in Madrid's Casa del Campo during which military drills without weapons were practised. The police easily located the few revolvers and rifles that had been acquired in expensive encounters with unscrupulous arms dealers. Thanks to informers in the PSOE or to the arms dealers themselves, when the police subsequently raided the houses of militants or Casas del Pueblo, they knew exactly where guns were concealed behind partitions or under floorboards. The most notorious arms purchase was carried out by Prieto. Arms – initially ordered by exiled enemies of the Portuguese dictatorship who could then not pay for them – were shipped to Asturias on the steamer *Turquesa*. In a bizarre incident, the shipment fell largely into the hands of the police, although Prieto escaped. Only in Asturias was the working class armed – with dynamite from the mines and small arms pilfered from local factories.[42]

Salazar Alonso, like Gil Robles, was confident that the entry of the CEDA into the government would trigger a Socialist reaction that would, in turn, justify a pre-emptive blow against the left. At a cabinet meeting on 11 September, he proposed that the CEDA join the government precisely in order to provoke a revolutionary strike in anticipation of which martial law would be declared. Both Samper and other ministers were horrified by such irresponsible cynicism. Six weeks earlier, Salazar Alonso had written to his lover, the wife of a *latifundista* from Extremadura, boasting that his aim was to provoke an action by the left so as to smash it: 'People believe in me, they turn to my puny figure and they see the man of providence who can save them.' In the evening of 11 September, he wrote to her again recounting what he had tried to do at the cabinet meeting. In his published account of his role, he declared: 'The problem was simply to start the counter-revolutionary offensive to put an end to the evil.' Salazar Alonso was determined both to smash the immediate revolutionary bid and to ensure that the left did not raise its head again.[43]

Gil Robles later admitted that he shared Salazar Alonso's provocative intentions. They both knew that the Socialists would react violently to what they would see as an attempt to establish a Dollfuss-type regime and were confident that the chances of revolutionary success were remote. Speaking in the Acción Popular offices in December, he recalled complacently:

> I was sure that our arrival in the government would immediately provoke a revolutionary movement ... and when I considered the blood that was going to be shed, I asked myself this question: 'I can give Spain three months of apparent tranquillity if I do not enter the government. If we enter, will the revolution break out? Better let that happen before it is well prepared, before it can defeat us.' This is what Acción Popular did: precipitated the movement, confronted it and implacably smashed the revolution from within the government.[44]

On 26 September, Gil Robles opened the crisis by announcing that he could no longer support a minority government. Republicans – from Martínez Barrio, via Azaña, to Largo Caballero – expected Alcalá-Zamora to resolve the situation by calling elections, and the Socialists began to step up their revolutionary rhetoric in the hope of convincing him of the dangers of bringing the CEDA into government.[45] The conviction that they would not have to unleash the threatened revolution is the only plausible explanation for the Socialists' lack of preparation for any action. As Minister of the Interior, Salazar Alonso knew this only too well but continued to claim that the revolution was about to break out.[46]

On 1 October, in the Cortes, Gil Robles threateningly demanded CEDA participation in the government: 'we are conscious of our strength both here and elsewhere'. Samper was forced to resign and Alcalá-Zamora invited Lerroux to form a government. The Radical leader hesitated, fearing that, in coalition with Gil Robles, it would be harder to exploit the financial benefits of public office, and uneasy about his party being pushed further to the right. Alcalá-Zamora wanted to limit CEDA participation to one ministry but Gil Robles insisted on three in the knowledge that this would provoke the left. Accordingly, Lerroux's cabinet, announced late at night on 3 October, included three CEDA ministers.[47]

The three CEDA choices were Rafael Aizpún (Justice), Manuel Giménez Fernández (Agriculture) and José Oriol y Anguera de Sojo (Labour). Aizpún, CEDA deputy for Pamplona and a Carlist sympathizer, was anything but a convinced republican. Giménez Fernández, as deputy for Badajoz, was inevitably assumed to be as faithful a representative of the aggressive landlords of that province as Salazar Alonso and likely, as Minister of Agriculture, to intensify the awful repression that had followed the harvest strike. Such suppositions were wrong, since he was a moderate Christian Democrat. The most alarming choice in the eyes of the left was Anguera de Sojo. An integrist Catholic, whose mother was being considered by the Vatican for canonization, he was the lawyer for the Benedictine Monastery of Montserrat. He had been the public prosecutor responsible for a hundred confiscations and numerous fines suffered by *El Socialista*. Moreover, as a Catalan rightist, he was a bitter enemy of Companys's Esquerra Republicana de Catalunya. As a hardline Civil Governor of Barcelona in 1931, his uncompromising strike-breaking policies had accelerated the CNT move to insurrectionism. The Esquerra had pleaded with Alcalá-Zamora for Anguera's exclusion. When Gil Robles rejected the intercession, the President retaliated by insisting that Salazar Alonso be dropped as Minister of the Interior. Lerroux compensated him for his bitter disappointment by appointing him Mayor of Madrid.[48]

The left saw the new cabinet as the first step towards the imposition of fascism. Leading Republicans denounced the move and even the conservative Miguel Maura broke off relations with the President. Azaña's Izquierda Republicana declared that 'the monstrous action of surrendering the Government of the Republic to its enemies is treachery'.[49] The Socialists were paralysed with doubt.[50] Their threats of revolution had failed to persuade Alcalá-Zamora to call new elections. Now the UGT gave twenty-four hours' notice of a pacific general strike which simply allowed the police time to arrest working-class leaders and suspect army officers. The leadership rejected anarchist and Trotskyist offers of revolutionary collaboration. In most parts of Spain, the strike was a failure largely because of the prompt action of the government in declaring martial law and bringing in the army to run essential services. The Socialist leaders who managed to avoid arrest either went into hiding, as did Largo Caballero, or went into exile, as did Prieto. Their followers were left standing on street corners awaiting instructions and within a week the strike had petered out. The talk of a seizure of power by revolutionary militias was revealed as empty bluster.[51]

Elsewhere, events were more dramatic. In Asturias, a fierce conflict with the Civil Guard from 5 to 6 October saw the miners seize control of the coalfields and capture Oviedo.[52] In Barcelona, in an attempt to outflank extreme Catalan nationalists, Companys proclaimed an independent state of Catalonia 'within the Federal Republic of Spain' in protest against what was perceived as the betrayal of the Republic. The CNT stood aside since it regarded the Esquerra as a purely bourgeois affair. In fact, the rebellion of the Generalitat was doomed when Companys refused to arm the workers.[53]

A cabinet meeting was held on 6 October to evaluate how best to react to events in Catalonia and Asturias. The Minister of War, Diego Hidalgo, with the enthusiastic backing of the three CEDA ministers, proposed sending General Franco to take over operations in Asturias. However, the views of Alcalá-Zamora, Lerroux and his more liberal cabinet colleagues prevailed and General Eduardo López Ochoa was sent instead.[54] In the event, it made no difference because Diego Hidalgo then effectively put Franco in overall charge of the repression by appointing him as an unofficial Chief of the General Staff. The Minister, marginalizing his own staff, slavishly signed the orders drafted by Franco who thus enjoyed an intoxicating taste of unprecedented politico-military power.[55] The declaration of martial law effectively transferred to the Ministry of War the responsibility for law and order normally under the jurisdiction of the Ministry of the Interior. Diego Hidalgo's total reliance on Franco effectively gave him control of the functions of both ministries. The excessively harsh manner in which Franco directed the repression from Madrid gave a stamp to the events in Asturias that they might not have had if Hidalgo had left matters to the permanent staff of his ministry.[56]

Bloodshed was avoided in Catalonia by the moderation of both Companys and General Domingo Batet, the commander of the Catalan military region. General Batet showed great restraint in restoring the authority of the central government. He ordered his men to be 'deaf, dumb and blind' in the face of provocation. By so doing, he incurred the wrath of Franco, who had sent warships to bombard the city and troops of the Foreign Legion. Batet refused to use the Foreign Legion and thereby kept casualties to a minimum. In avoiding the exemplary violence that Franco regarded as essential, Batet was paving the way to his own execution during the civil war.[57]

The right was delighted when Franco responded to the rebellious miners in Asturias as if he were dealing with the recalcitrant tribes of

Morocco. Uninhibited by the humanitarian considerations which made other officers hesitate, he mobilized the hardened mercenaries of the Army of Africa against the miners. The miners organized a revolutionary commune with transport, communications, hospital facilities and food distribution, but had few weapons beyond dynamite. They were reduced to submission by heavy artillery attacks and bombing raids. The Foreign Legion, commanded by Franco's crony Colonel Juan Yagüe Blanco, then committed appalling atrocities. Women were raped and prisoners tortured. When the principal cities, Gijón and Oviedo, fell, the army carried out summary executions of leftists.[58] López Ochoa subsequently lamented that he had been unable to prevent the atrocities. At the time, Yagüe complained to both Franco and Gil Robles about López Ochoa's humane treatment of the miners. Franco commented casually to a journalist, 'This war is a frontier war and its fronts are socialism, communism and any force that attacks civilization in order to replace it with barbarism.'[59] On 17 October, Juan March gave 100,000 pesetas to a subscription to reward the armed forces for their part in the Asturian repression.[60]

The events in Asturias demonstrated that the left could implement change only by legal means and convinced the right that the best way to prevent change lay with the instruments of violence provided by the armed forces. While the Socialists recovered their faith in democracy, the right moved close to a military coup. The October revolution had terrified the middle and upper classes for which they exacted a revenge that obliged the left to accept the need to reunite in order to win power electorally. The Socialist movement was, in fact, badly scarred by the events of October 1934. The repression unleashed in its aftermath was truly brutal. Around 30,000 workers were imprisoned. Virtually the entire UGT executive was in jail. The Socialist press was silenced. The Catalan autonomy statute was suspended and Companys was sentenced to thirty years' imprisonment. Azaña was arrested on the absurd grounds that he had prepared the Catalan revolution. The feeble basis of the accusation was that he had gone to Barcelona at the end of September to attend the funeral of Jaume Carner. In fact, while there, he had tried to persuade members of the Generalitat not to respond to provocation from Madrid with an insurrection. In contravention of his parliamentary immunity, he was arrested in Barcelona on 8 October and imprisoned on a ship in the harbour until the end of December. Vilified by the right-wing press, he became a symbol for all those in Spain who were suffering from the repressive politics of the Radical–CEDA coalition. His eventual release saw a massive outpouring of support.[61]

Nothing was done in the fifteen months after October to reconcile the hostilities aroused on the right by the revolution and on left by its repression. Gil Robles pressed for the harshest punishments. At a cabinet meeting on 12 October, Lerroux proposed pardoning the officers involved in the rebellion of the Generalitat. Alcalá-Zamora refused to confirm their death sentences, just as he had done with those implicated in the Sanjurjada of 1932. He was subjected to intense pressure from the three CEDA ministers but, to their consternation, he met their threats of resignation with what Giménez Fernández called 'astounding equanimity'. On 18 October, faced with his own threat of resignation, the cabinet agreed to the pardon. Furious, Gil Robles toyed with sponsoring a military coup but was told by Generals Manuel Goded and Joaquín Fanjul that they were not confident of defeating the left.[62]

When the Cortes reopened on 5 November, Gil Robles called for an investigation into responsibility for the events of October. This opened the way to an assault by the monarchists on the previous government for alleged negligence. Goicoechea called for the chamber to announce its 'moral incompatibility' with the left, a prelude to the outlawing of the Socialist Party. On the next day, Calvo Sotelo attacked both Samper and Diego Hidalgo. As the attacks intensified, the intervention of Gil Robles led to the resignations of both on 15 November. Gil Robles continued to demand the 'calm, inflexible but not cruel implementation of the law' and some exemplary bloodshed. These demands, together with a call for the dissolution of unions implicated in the rising, were defeated by the Radicals.[63]

The strategy of eliminating 'liberal' elements and restructuring the cabinet along lines more acceptable to the CEDA soon took a further step forward. Gil Robles selected as his next target the Minister of Public Instruction, Filiberto Villalobos, whose liberalism he regarded as sectarian. On 21 December, Villalobos was forced to resign after questioning the CEDA's loyalty to the Republic. Gil Robles declared that 'it was the second reshuffle that I was obliged to provoke'.[64]

Gil Robles's much vaunted, and utterly insincere, aims of defeating revolution by a programme of social reform were blocked – with his connivance – by right-wing intransigence. The new Minister of

Agriculture, Manuel Giménez Fernández, one of the few sincere social Catholics within the CEDA, horrified the right when it was reported in the press that he had told his staff that 'the disturbances against the state did not start on the rebels' side of the street but on ours, because the state itself has created many enemies by consistently neglecting its duties to all citizens'. He put forward a series of mildly reformist measures between November 1934 and March 1935. Without tackling the key problem of land distribution, they aimed to mitigate some of its worst abuses. This provoked an onslaught of embittered opposition from the monarchists and from within the CEDA, especially from Gil Robles's fellow deputies from Salamanca. Responding to pressure from landowners' organizations, they blocked progressive features such as the proposal to give long-term tenants the right to buy the land they farmed. Giménez Fernández was subjected to what he termed 'poisonous' personal abuse in the Cortes, called 'a Marxist in disguise' and even denounced as a Leninist in the landowners' clubs of Seville. Gil Robles, when he next provoked a cabinet crisis at the end of March 1935, replaced Giménez Fernández with a pliable Radical, Juan José Benayas.[65]

The next crisis came in March after twenty death sentences had been passed by military courts on Socialists implicated in the October rising, including two prominent followers of Prieto, Teodomiro Menéndez and Ramón González Peña. Lerroux and Alcalá-Zamora favoured clemency. When the CEDA failed to secure death penalties, an enraged Gil Robles ordered the resignation of his three ministers.[66] The ease with which he was able to move crablike towards taking power was facilitated by Lerroux's lack of interest in day-to-day government and his infrequent appearances in the Cortes. Gil Robles kept Lerroux on a short leash by regular insinuations about the Radicals' abuse of public funds.[67]

During tortuous negotiations throughout April, a cabinet made up of friends of Lerroux and Alcalá-Zamora governed with the Cortes closed. At one point, attempting to recruit a young economist, Lerroux revealed his attitude to public office: 'I'm offering not to make you a minister but something much better, an ex-minister,' referring to the lavish lifetime pensions enjoyed by ministers irrespective of how long they had been in office. This attitude partly explains the vertiginous turnover of ministers in Radical cabinets.[68] Alcalá-Zamora hoped for a broad coalition cabinet including more Republican elements, but Gil Robles was immovable. He wanted to be Prime Minister and have six ministries. Eventually, fearing that the President might call new elections which, in the wake of the repression, would see a surge of support for the left, he ceded a little. Lerroux's new government, finally announced on 6 May, contained five Cedistas, including Gil Robles himself as Minister of War, but only three Radicals.[69] It heralded a period of open reaction.

Landlords halved wages and order was brutally restored in the countryside. Gil Robles was determined to strengthen the repressive power of the government. Seeing the army as a bulwark against the social aspirations of the masses, he had been disturbed by its difficulties in Asturias and by the generals' inability to support him with a coup in October 1934. Accordingly, he purged the army of loyal Republican officers and promoted known opponents of the regime. Against opposition from Alcalá-Zamora, who remarked that 'young generals aspire to be fascist caudillos', Franco was made Chief of the General Staff; Manuel Goded was made Inspector General, and Joaquín Fanjul Under-Secretary of War. Aware of his own ignorance in military affairs, Gil Robles left Franco to run the ministry. Azaña's military reforms were overturned. Much was done to facilitate the later rebel war effort, especially the building of fortifications overlooking Madrid and manoeuvres in Asturias against a projected working-class enemy. To the delight of Sanjurjo, Franco secretly brought General Mola, head of military forces in Morocco, to Madrid to prepare for the use of the colonial army on the mainland in the event of further left-wing unrest. Franco encouraged the conspiratorial activities of one of his deputies in the General Staff, Valentín Galarza.[70]

The CEDA turned a blind eye to Radical financial misdeeds and was far from free of corruption itself. A close friend of Cándido Casanueva was Diego Martín Veloz, a wealthy gambler who had bought up land and buildings in Salamanca. Investing in gambling and prostitution, he became the key figure in the brothels and gambling dens of Salamanca, Valladolid, Zamora and Palencia. One of the richest men in Salamanca, he owned a large part of the provincial capital and came to be known as 'The boss of Salamanca'. When the government began to close down his casinos, he built a political base, buying the newspaper *La Voz de Castilla* and creating the Farmers and Cattle Breeders League, a party with widespread support throughout the province. Casanueva was his political factotum and his link to Gil Robles. It was believed that Martín Veloz bought votes for Casanueva, just as it was believed that Casanueva bought votes for Gil Robles. In the spring of 1936, Martín Veloz and Casanueva worked with the local military in the preparation of the uprising.[71]

In the summer of 1935, Casanueva was involved in another shady operation. Gil Robles was anxious to increase military striking power by means of a huge rearmament programme. It was intended to purchase the bulk of requirements in Germany, starting with machine guns, armoured cars and vehicles for the rapid transportation of artillery. In the negotiations with the Reich Federation of Industry, the CEDA liaison was Eduardo de Laiglesia, acting under instructions from Casanueva. His task was to use the transaction to generate electoral funds for the CEDA by the overcharging of the Ministry of War. The deal was going ahead until the German firms became concerned about Laiglesia's extravagant demands for commission. It is not clear whether he was seeking personal profit on top of Casanova's requirements. Before alternative arrangements could be made, the government fell and new elections were on the horizon.[72]

In any case, the machinations of Casanueva and Laiglesia were overshadowed by the revelation of a series of scandals involving what Gordón Ordás called 'Lerroux and his gang of thieves'. The twin scandals known as Estraperlo and Nombela which broke in October 1935 brought about the ruin of Lerroux. Even before, Alcalá-Zamora had been alarmed to discover that Lerroux was planning to pocket the proceeds of a national subscription created after the events of the October 1934 risings. When the President protested, Lerroux replied that he would personally accept only those donations from members of his own party. Other monies already subscribed by banks, businesses and their employees would be used for an unspecified 'particular purpose' that the President suspected meant the enrichment of Lerroux.[73]

All this was small beer by comparison with what happened in mid-September. There was a crisis, for once not engineered by Gil Robles, whose outcome undermined his plans to use the Radicals to leapfrog his way to power without risking elections. Two resignations by ministers of the Agrarian Party coincided with the imminent implementation of a scheme, devised by the Minister of Finance, Joaquín Chapaprieta, to slash government expenditure by reducing the number of ministries. Knowing that the Estraperlo scandal was about to explode, Alcalá-Zamora resolved the crisis by inviting Chapaprieta to form a government. Lerroux was demoted to the Foreign Ministry. Chapaprieta's austerity plan saw the cabinet reduced in size from thirteen to nine, with CEDA participation down to three. However, by doubling porfolios, the CEDA still controlled what had previously been five ministries. Moreover, Chapaprieta was happy for Gil Robles to drive policy.[74]

The word 'Estraperlo', which henceforth came to be used in Spanish as a synonym for corruption, derived from a racket involving three individuals, Daniel Strauss, Joachim Perlowitz and Frieda Lowann. They had invented an electric roulette wheel that could be manipulated by the casino owners. In fact, roulette was legally prohibited in Spain but Strauss and Perlowitz had managed to get their machines installed in two casinos, in Formentor (Mallorca) and San Sebastián, through cash payments and expensive gifts including gold watches for Lerroux, Salazar Alonso (when Minister of the Interior) and other key members of the Radical Party through the liaison of Lerroux's adopted son, Aurelio, and Juan Pich y Pon. The scandal burst when Salazar Alonso and other bribe takers reneged and measures were taken to remove the devices. Strauss, claiming that the operation had cost him a fortune, responded by exposing the entire chain of corruption. He gave an incriminating dossier to Alcalá-Zamora, who passed on the information to Chapaprieta and the leaders of the other parties. Lerroux was forced to resign and Salazar Alonso removed as Alcalde of Madrid. However, the party immediately became involved in another scandal, occasioned by efforts to make payments from public funds to a friend of Lerroux, Antonio Tayá, owner of a shipping company. Tayá's contract to link the colonies of Equatorial Guinea and Fernando Poo had been cancelled in 1929 for alleged failure to provide the service offered, an accusation he disputed. Lerroux, keen to see Tayá compensated, but anxious to avoid parliamentary scrutiny of the operation, proposed that he be paid directly from 'the colonial treasure'. However, Antonio Nombela, the Inspector General of Colonies, refused to authorize what he deemed to be misuse of the fund. As a result, Nombela was sacked in July 1935. When he was refused redress, Nombela had taken his case to Chapaprieta who already had ample reason to suspect Lerroux's financial probity. He was aware of Lerroux's efforts to secure substantial commission for himself through a shady deal involving the tobacco monopoly.[75]

By the time that all this reached its climax, Chapaprieta, deeply frustrated because the CEDA was blocking his proposed tax reforms, resigned on 9 December.[76] Gil Robles was convinced that power was virtually in his grasp and refused to collaborate in any cabinet other than one led by himself. Alcalá-Zamora had no faith in the CEDA leader's democratic convictions. After all, only some weeks previously, Gil Robles's followers of the JAP had starkly revealed that the legalist tactic was merely a device to reach power: 'with the weapons of suffrage and democracy, Spain must prepare itself to bury once and for all the rotting corpse of liberalism. The JAP does not believe in universal suffrage nor in parliamentarism, nor in democracy.'[77]

Alcalá-Zamora's suspicions of Gil Robles were such that, throughout the subsequent political crisis, he had the Ministry of War surrounded by Civil Guards and the principal garrisons and airports placed under special vigilance. Gil Robles was outraged and so, as he later confessed to the Portuguese journalist Armando Boaventura, he and his close friend Cándido Casanueva had investigated the possibilities of staging a coup d'état. Again, the generals consulted, Fanjul, Goded, Varela and Franco, felt that, in the light of the strength of working-class resistance during the Asturian events, the army was not yet ready.[78] Gil Robles had overplayed his hand. On 11 December, the President told him that he was not going to invite him to form a government. When Alcalá-Zamora stated that the present Cortes was incapable of sustaining stable governments, Gil Robles could hardly reply that the instability, artificially created by himself to facilitate his road to power, would stop if he were made Prime Minister. To his fury, Alcalá-Zamora invited his friend Manuel Portela Valladares to form a government based on a wide Republican coalition and then to hold elections.

Alcalá-Zamora's distrust of Gil Robles was such that he was prepared to put his own career in jeopardy. Constitutionally, he had the right to call extraordinary elections only twice and he had already done so once in November 1933. To use up his second 'chance' was the only way to stop Gil Robles. Since Portela was seen as a wizard of electoral management, Alcalá hoped that elections would see a new party of the centre, heavily influenced by himself, emerge as arbiter of the Cortes. This could be done only at the expense of the CEDA and Gil Robles was determined to prevent it. He effectively brought down the cabinet on 30 December by declaring that the CEDA would make no electoral alliances with any groups supporting Portela, all of whom were aware that to go to the polls in opposition to the CEDA would be electoral suicide. A new cabinet of

Portela's friends was installed without parliamentary support and with no ambition beyond organizing the next elections. To this end, Portela changed large numbers of civil governors.[79]

In response to the intransigence of the two years of Radical–CEDA collaboration, the left had grown in strength, unity and belligerence. In jail, political prisoners had absorbed revolutionary literature. Outside, the economic misery of large numbers of peasants and workers, the savage persecution of the October rebels and the attacks on Manuel Azaña combined to cement solidarity among all sections of the left. Azaña, after his release from jail, and Prieto, from his Belgian exile, campaigned to ensure that the disunity behind the 1933 electoral defeat would not be repeated. Azaña worked hard to reunite the various tiny Republican parties, while Prieto concentrated on countering the revolutionary extremism of the Socialist left under Largo Caballero. Three gigantic mass meetings in Valencia on 26 May in Bilbao on 14 July and in Madrid on 20 October saw hundreds of thousands of people applaud Azaña's appeals for an electoral coalition. The enthusiasm for left-wing unity shown by those who came from all over Spain to attend these *discursos en campo abierto* (open-air speeches) helped convince Largo Caballero to abandon his opposition to what eventually became the Popular Front.

Another pressure on Largo's stance as the conscience of the working class was awareness that the key figures of the anarchist movement were also in favour of the Popular Front because it promised to release political prisoners.[80] At the same time, the Communists, prompted by Moscow's desire for alliance with the democracies, and anxious not to be excluded, also used their influence with Largo in favour of the Popular Front. They knew that, in order to give it the more proletarian flavour that he wanted, Largo Caballero would insist on their presence. In this way, the Communists found a place in an electoral front which, contrary to rightist propaganda, was not, in Spain, a Comintern creation but the revival of the broad 1931 Republican–Socialist coalition. The left and centre left closed ranks with a programme of amnesty for prisoners, of social and educational reform and trade union freedom. They were thus able to take advantage of the electoral regulations so disastrously ignored in 1933.[81]

Elections were announced for February. Gil Robles could not manufacture a corresponding right-wing coalition. The leader of the Partido

Nacionalista Vasco, José María Aguirre, would not collaborate with the CEDA because Gil Robles opposed a Basque statute of autonomy. Accordingly, the Basque nationalists neither joined the Frente Popular nor allied with the CEDA.[82] The 'catastrophist' monarchists demanded excessive representation in joint candidacies. Gil Robles refused because he realized that, in the event of victory, a sizeable Renovación Española group would be able to do to the CEDA what he had done to the Radicals. Moreover, to accept their hard-line programme would preclude alliance in many areas with the Republican right and in others with the Carlists or the Falange. Therefore, the right went into the election campaign with a kaleidoscope of local alliances. In areas of left-wing strength, like Badajoz, Jaén, Cordoba and Asturias, the CEDA allied with any group not part of the Popular Front. In the areas of strongest reactionary sentiment, Salamanca, Navarre and most of Castile, Gil Robles saw that links with groups not of extreme rightist character would lose votes. In Badajoz, Giménez Fernández was dropped as a candidate because the local right regarded his social Catholicism as dangerous leftism. In Salamanca, the alliance was with Carlists and Agrarians only; in Asturias, with the local Liberal Democrats of Melquíades Álvarez; in Pontevedra, with the Radicals; in Navarre, with the Carlists; in the Balearic Islands, with the all-powerful Juan March. In the great Republican strongholds of Catalonia, a highly implausible coalition of the CEDA, the Radicals, the Carlists and the Lliga united in a 'law and order' front.[83]

Unsurprisingly, the election campaign was fought in a frenetic atmosphere. Already, in late October, Gil Robles had requested a complete range of Nazi anti-Marxist propaganda pamphlets and posters, to be used as a model for CEDA publicity material. In practical terms, the right enjoyed an enormous advantage over the left. Juan March contributed huge sums to rightist electoral funds which dramatically exceeded the exiguous funds of the left.[84] Ten thousand posters and 50 million leaflets were printed for the CEDA. Distributed to small villages by fleets of trucks and dropped on remote farms from aircraft, they presented the elections in terms of a life-or-death struggle between good and evil, survival and destruction. Looting and the common ownership of women were predicted as the result of a left-wing victory. The Popular Front based its campaign on the threat of fascism and the need for an amnesty for the prisoners of October.[85] Key anarchist leaders, including Durruti, campaigned against the traditional abstention policy and for a vote against fascism.[86]

In the course of the campaign, forty-six people were killed in clashes either between rival groups or with the forces of order or were murdered by gunmen, and a further forty were badly hurt. More than half the eighty-six victims were militants of either the PSOE or the PCE. In fact, the incidence of violence was not significantly higher than in the 1933 elections, which have been considered exemplary by some commentators. On the day of the elections, 16 February, thanks to preventive measures taken by the government, voting was not disrupted by violence.[87] A narrow overall victory for the Popular Front in terms of votes, because of the system favouring coalitions, was translated into a massive triumph in terms of power in the Cortes. The Popular Front won in all the largest cities – Madrid, Barcelona, Bilbao, Valencia, Zaragoza and Murcia and in all the principal towns of Extremadura, Asturias, Andalusia (except Granada), Catalonia, the Canary Islands and the coastal towns of Galicia. Even in several very conservative provinces such as Valladolid, León, Ciudad Real and Albacete, the Popular Front won. Out of a total of 473 seats, the Popular Front gained 259. A second round on 4 March to decide places without a decisive result added another 8. Subsequent elections in forty-one disputed seats added a further 19, bringing the total to 286.[88]

The parties of the right increased their vote by more than three-quarters of a million votes, largely as a result of the disintegration of the Radical Party and the transfer of most of its votes to the CEDA or to Republican parties of the centre. Lerroux lost his seat and there were only five Radical deputies in the Cortes.[89] Despite the expenditure of vast sums by the right, the left increased its vote by 1 million votes. In terms of the amounts spent on propaganda, a vote for the right cost more than five times one for the left. Moreover, all the traditional devices of electoral chicanery had been used on behalf of the right, which had far greater resources to exert social pressure on the poor.[90] In 1939, a committee established by the victorious Franco regime would claim that the military coup was a response to fraudulent elections.[91]

The legitimacy of the elections and the final result were confirmed in 1971 by a thoroughgoing investigation carried out by a team led by Javier Tusell. Their conclusions have held sway for nearly five decades until challenged recently by a study that has provoked a fierce polemic, *1936*.

Fraude y violencia by Manuel Álvarez Tardío and Roberto Villa García. Like the 1939 Francoist commission, the title and conclusions of the book suggest that the Popular Front came to power by dint of fraud and violence, although its detailed research does not sustain that thesis. The authors' extensive local research has discovered manipulation of results in some constituencies during the second round of elections when the left was back in power. However, they do not examine in the same detail the manipulation of the vote by the right during the first round – chicanery admitted by Gil Robles himself. He wrote in his memoirs of his 'infinite' repugnance at taking advantage of Portela's mechanisms of corruption, 'But how else could we prevent our defeat in constituencies with high numbers of voters?'[92] The authors have not significantly altered Tusell's broad voting figures and they concede that the additional seats gained by manipulations after 19 February did not change the fact that the Popular Front won.[93]

Because the election results represented an unequivocal statement of the popular desire for a strong Republican–Socialist government, they were taken by many on the right as proving the futility of legalism. The brutality of rightist policies during the previous two years ensured that the left would be unlikely to repeat Largo Caballero's errors of 1933 and that anarchist abstention would be less. Precisely because the left had gone into the elections united, it took an average of just over 19,150 votes to get a Popular Front deputy elected, whereas it took 23,700 to get a right-winger into the Cortes, a reverse of the case in 1933 and sufficient to convince the 'catastrophists' that their time had come. The CEDA's youth sections and many of the movement's wealthy backers were also convinced of the necessity of securing by violence what was unobtainable by persuasion. Henceforth, the right would be more concerned with destroying the Republic than with taking it over. Military plotting began in earnest.

Gil Robles himself accepted that the legalist tactic had now outlived its usefulness. In the early hours of the morning on 17 February, he woke Portela. Claiming to speak for all the forces of the right, Gil Robles told him that the Popular Front successes meant anarchy and asked him to declare martial law. Portela demurred but did agree to declare a state of alert (the stage prior to martial law) and to discuss with Alcalá-Zamora the imposition of martial law. At the same time, via his secretary, Gil Robles urged Franco, still Chief of the General Staff, to plead with Portela not to resign and to deploy the army. Franco then took a series of initiatives. He instructed Valentín Galarza to alert key UME officers in provincial garrisons to be ready for action. Franco also tried unsuccessfully to persuade the Director General of the Civil Guard, Sebastián Pozas, to commit his men to a coup. He also asked the Minister of War, General Nicolás Molero, to declare martial law. Molero refused but agreed to urge Portela to convene a cabinet meeting to discuss the declaration of martial law.

Franco's next move was to convince Portela to order Pozas to mobilize the Civil Guard against the populace but could not see him until 7 p.m. on the 18th. Before then, at midday, the cabinet met, under the chairmanship of Alcalá-Zamora, and declared the state of alert for eight days. It also approved, and the President signed, a draft decree of martial law to be kept in reserve and used only when Portela judged it necessary. Meanwhile, General Goded tried to bring out the troops of the Montaña barracks in Madrid, but the officers there and in other garrisons refused to rebel without a guarantee that the Civil Guard would cooperate. Franco, informed by Molero of the blank decree, used its existence to justify ordering local commanders to declare martial law. Without authority, he was arrogantly assuming the de facto powers of both Minister of War and Minister of the Interior that he had exercised during the Asturian crisis. Despite the illegality of his position, on his orders martial law was declared in Zaragoza, Valencia, Oviedo and Alicante and was about to be declared in Huesca, Cordoba and Granada. Meanwhile, Gil Robles waited at CEDA headquarters for news of the expected coup, in order to take power. However, most Civil Guard commanders checked with Pozas and were told that there had been no declaration of martial law. When Franco saw Portela later in the evening, he urged him to implement the blank decree while mendaciously claiming that he personally was not involved in any conspiracy.

With rumours abounding of an imminent coup, Pozas, backed up by General Miguel Núñez de Prado, the Inspector General of the Army, had already reassured Portela earlier on the 18th that the Civil Guard would oppose any coup attempt. Pozas surrounded all suspect garrisons with Civil Guard detachments. Just before midnight on the 18th, José Calvo Sotelo and the militant Carlist Joaquín Bau visited Portela and urged him to authorize Franco, the officers of the Madrid military garrison and the Civil Guard to impose order. When he refused, a last despairing effort was made by Gil Robles, who secretly met Portela on the outskirts of Madrid at 8.30 the next morning.[94] The efforts of Gil Robles, Calvo Sotelo and Franco did not divert Portela and the rest of his panic-stricken cabinet from their determination to resign and probably pushed them to do so sooner. At 10.30 a.m., they agreed to hand over power to Azaña immediately, instead of waiting for the opening of the Cortes. With a Popular Front electoral victory seeming assured, Alcalá-Zamora asked Azaña to form a government. Since Portela failed to inform Azaña of Franco's disloyalty, his mutinous activities went unpunished and he was left free to play a crucial role in the military coup five months later.[95]

Having failed to engineer a coup, Gil Robles did nothing to stem the flow of CEDA members to more extremist organizations. He was fully apprised of the development of military conspiracy. Key liaison between the military and civilian elements was provided by Cedistas. On 8 March, a crucial meeting of Generals Mola, Franco, Orgaz, Villegas, Fanjul and Varela was held in the home of José Delgado, a prominent stockbroker who had been an unsuccessful CEDA candidate in the February elections.[96] Made aware of that meeting, either through his old Moroccan contacts with the Africanista generals or perhaps through Francisco Herrera and Gil Robles, Juan March would provide invaluable encouragement and financial support.[97] Throughout the spring of 1936, Gil Robles worked hard, in parliament and the press, to generate the atmosphere which made a military rising appear to the middle classes as the only alternative to catastrophe.[98]

Popular Front victory saw an almost instant return to the rural lockout of 1933 and renewed aggression from industrialists and landowners, who also switched their financial support to the conspiratorial right. The rural and industrial working classes were equally militant, determined to secure some redress for the anti-union repression of the last two years. Helpless in the midst of the conflict stood the government. Indeed, the central factor in the spring of 1936 was the fatal debility of the Popular Front cabinet. This was the consequence not only of right-wing hostility but also of Largo Caballero's opposition to Socialist ministerial participation. Prieto knew that the situation demanded Socialist collaboration in government, but Largo Caballero, fearful of a rank-and-file drift to the CNT, blocked the formation of a strong Republican–Socialist coalition. He had supported the electoral coalition only to secure political amnesty for the victims of the post-October repression. Believing that only an exclusively Socialist cabinet could transform society, he insisted that the Republicans govern alone to implement the Popular Front electoral programme. The Socialists would replace them once they reached their bourgeois limitations. If this provoked a fascist uprising, he naively believed that it would be easily defeated by a proletarian revolution.[99]

Largo Caballero's empty revolutionary rhetoric intensified the fears of a middle class already terrified by both rightist propaganda and increasing disorder on the streets. In the southern countryside, where rightist persecution had gone furthest, the tables were being turned. Azaña wrote of his 'black despair' at assaults on prisons, church burnings and attacks on right-wingers. Demonstrations in favour of amnesty for those imprisoned after the rural strikes of 1934 saw the clubs of the rich (*casinos*) and local offices of Acción Popular ransacked. In the *ayuntamientos* imposed in 1934 by Salazar Alonso, returning Socialists and Republicans replaced the nominees of the *caciques*. To the outrage of the landowners, they re-established *jurados mixtos* and levied local taxes to provide work for the unemployed. Some prohibited religious festivals. Legal once more, the FNTT encouraged the occupations of estates that were on illegally enclosed common lands. There were cases of demonstrators burning deeds to property in municipal land registries.[100]

The task facing Azaña was enormous. In the first half of March, a campaign of armed attacks on prominent left-wing and liberal politicians began in order to provoke reprisals. The terrorism of action squads manned by Falangists and financed by the monarchists was facilitated by the fact that, in the previous two years, over 270,000 gun licences had been issued to rightists. The most successful operation of this kind was carried out in Granada on 9–10 March. Falangist gunmen fired on a group of workers and their families, wounding many women and children. In response, the local unions called a general strike in the course of which offices of the Falange and Acción Popular were set on fire, those of the ACNP newspaper, *Ideal*, destroyed, and two churches burned. In Granada and elsewhere, incidents were often caused by strangers who disappeared as quickly as they had appeared and many 'anarchists' and 'Communists' were later revealed to have been Falangists in disguise. On 12 March, Falangists tried to kill Socialist law professor Luis Jiménez Asúa, and, four days later, Largo Caballero's house was fired upon by a rightist terror squad.[101] Meanwhile, the right was printing leaflets, supposedly emanating from the UGT, containing detailed plans for revolution and blacklists of the left's enemies.[102]

The debates held by the committee for examining electoral validity, the Comisión de Actas, were used by the CEDA at the time and the Franco regime thereafter as part of the effort to convince right-wing opinion that democratic coexistence was impossible. The Comisión added around 37 to the Frente Popular majority, but many were the result of the correction of real electoral abuse during the campaign and the actual election process.[103] The committee, although often partisan, sometimes benefited the right. In Santander and Albacete, for instance, allegations of intimidation of Republican voters were ignored for lack of notarized witness statements and the rightist victory was confirmed. Other decisions went in favour of the right in the provinces of Ciudad Real, Toledo and Avila, for similar reasons. In Zaragoza province, evidence of intimidation aside, the results for seventy-eight villages were simply made up by the Civil Governor. Nevertheless, the rightist victory was approved because of a lack of documentary proofs. The results in the Balearic Islands, the fief of Juan March, were not even questioned.[104]

The CEDA contrived to obscure its own involvement in electoral malpractice, claiming that it was being persecuted. Gil Robles and Cándido Casanueva in Salamanca, Calvo Sotelo in Orense and Goicoechea in Cuenca were all in danger of losing their seats. If the most flagrantly dishonest elections of all, those of Granada, were invalidated, the CEDA stood to lose five deputies. In a bid to prevent this, Giménez Fernández, the CEDA representative on the Comisión, led a temporary withdrawal of the CEDA deputies from the Cortes and *ABC* claimed that the right had been expelled.[105]

Azaña's cabinet was barely equal to the problems it faced. The likeable Minister of the Interior, Amós Salvador, was unable to stop the spiral of provocation and reprisal. On 15 April, Azaña presented his programme to the Cortes. He was subjected to a concerted attack first by Calvo Sotelo and then by Gil Robles. Calvo Sotelo declared that any government reliant on PSOE votes was only a step away from Russian dominance. Gil Robles stated that government impotence was making solutions of force inevitable. In apocalyptic terms that wildly exaggerated the threat of anarchy and completely ignored the rightist part in political violence, he issued a threat: 'Half the nation will not resign itself to die. If it cannot defend itself by one path, it will defend itself by another.' He claimed that civil war was being fomented by the revolutionary elements of the Popular Front and declared belligerently, 'When civil war breaks out in Spain, let it be known that the weapons have been loaded by the negligence of a government unable to fulfil its duty towards groups which have stayed within the strictest legality ... It is better to know how to die in the street than to be trampled on as a coward.'[106]

The wealthy conservatives who had previously financed Gil Robles as the most effective defender of their interests were now switching funds to the Falange and the Sindicatos Libres of Ramón Sales, who had close relations with Calvo Sotelo. At the beginning of March, *ABC* opened a subscription for a newly formed Federación Española de Trabajadores, the brainchild of Sales. By the end of April the fund had reached 350,000 pesetas, donated by aristocrats, landowners, industrialists and many anonymous 'fascists' and Falangists. The money was never used for union purposes and, since many individuals arrested for acts of violence turned out to be members of the Sindicatos Libres, there was little doubt that this fund was financing professional gunmen.[107]

The denunciations of violence by Gil Robles and Calvo Sotelo were utterly cynical. Since parliamentary debates received full uncensored press coverage, they listed every possible incident of crime and disorder, irrespective of whether it was politically motivated, to demonstrate that the Republic was being engulfed by left-wing violence while conveniently failing to mention the role of Falangist terror squads. In Madrid, the American Ambassador Claude Bowers was regaled by rightists with spine-chilling tales of uncontrolled mobs butchering monarchists and feeding their bodies to pigs.[108] There was indisputably disorder during the spring of 1936 but it is impossible to apportion responsibility with the certainty of the recriminations made by both sides at the time. However, having won the elections, no element of the Popular Front had any need to provoke violence in order to take power. The creation of an atmosphere of turmoil and disorder could, on the other hand, justify the resort to force to establish a dictatorship of the right.

Recent research has shown that the left suffered more from the violence. In fact, only two groups stood to benefit from the lawlessness – the extreme left and the 'catastrophist' right. The Communist Party had no plan to seize power in the midst of a total breakdown of law and order. Its policy was aimed both at broadening support among the middle classes as part of the Popular Front tactic imposed by Moscow and at gradually taking over the Socialist movement through unification with the Federación de Juventudes Socialistas, the UGT and eventually the PSOE left. The Socialist dailies *El Socialista* and *Claridad* constantly warned their readers to ignore rightist provocation. Some anarchists were readier to use random violence, but it was not part of their overall strategy.[109] However, the rhetorically belligerent parliamentary replies to Calvo Sotelo made by Casares Quiroga, first as Minister of the Interior and later as Prime Minister, sustained the right-wing argument that the Popular Front government was so partisan that it had to be brought down by violence if necessary.[110]

As long as Azaña remained Prime Minister, the government maintained a degree of authority. However, this soon changed disastrously. In order to put together a strong government team, Azaña and Prieto plotted to remove Alcalá-Zamora from the presidency. He was constantly meddling in the work of the government and had little liking for Azaña. He was loathed by the left for inviting the CEDA into government in October 1934 and the right despised him for failing to make Gil Robles Prime Minister at the end of 1935. In the Cortes on 7 April, Azaña and Prieto combined to have him impeached on the grounds that he had exceeded his constitutional powers by dissolving the Cortes. His removal seemed to open up the prospect of overcoming Largo Caballero's hostility to Socialist participation in government. Between them, Prieto and Azaña had the skill and the popularity to stabilize the tense situation of the spring of 1936. With the former as Prime Minister and the latter as President, it might have been possible to maintain reform on a scale that might diminish left-wing militancy while dealing determinedly with right-wing conspiracy and terrorism.[111]

Their optimism was misplaced. The first part of their plan worked but not the second. Azaña was elevated to the presidency on 10 May and immediately offered the government to Prieto, who had detailed plans for social reforms and for a crackdown on the extreme right. However, he needed the backing of Largo Caballero, who was president of the UGT, of the powerful Agrupación Socialista Madrileña and also of the parliamentary party which he ruled with a rod of iron. Prieto faced his fellow parliamentary deputies twice, on 11 and 12 May. When he had backed Azaña for the presidency, he knew that Largo Caballero and his followers would oppose his forming a government. He could have created a cabinet with the Republicans and about a third of the Socialist deputies, but he could not bring himself to split the party to which he had devoted his life. Moreover, Prieto later claimed ruefully that Azaña had preferred the eventual nominee, his more malleable friend Santiago Casares Quiroga.[112] The consequences could not have been worse. A shrewd and strong Prime Minister was lost and, on assuming the presidency, Azaña increasingly withdrew from everyday politics. He took enormous delight in his ceremonial functions, in the restoration of monuments and palaces and in being a patron of the arts.[113]

Natural disaster was intensifying the social misery of the south. After drought in 1935, 1936 had begun with heavy rainstorms that decimated olive, wheat and barley production. With unemployment rocketing, the FNTT was urging its members to take at its word the Popular Front's proclaimed commitment to rapid reform. In Salamanca and Toledo, in Cordoba and Jaén, there were invasions of estates by peasants who stole olives or cut down trees. The most substantial land seizures took place in Badajoz. On 29 May, in Yeste in the province of Albacete, seventeen peasants were killed, and many others wounded, by the Civil Guard. They had attempted to chop wood on once common land that had been taken from the village by legal subterfuge in the nineteenth century. What most alarmed the landlords was the assertiveness of once servile labourers who were now determined not to be cheated out of reform as they had been between 1931 and 1933. Many landowners withdrew to Seville or Madrid, or even to Biarritz or Paris, where they enthusiastically joined, financed or merely awaited news of ultra-rightist plots against the Republic.[114]

Gil Robles's role in the preparation of the coup was considerable. As he later boasted, he made an incalculable contribution to the creation of mass right-wing militancy: 'I cooperated with advice, with moral stimulus, with secret orders for collaboration, and even with economic assistance, taken in appreciable quantities from the party's electoral funds.' This assistance, which he later tried to deny, consisted of 500,000 pesetas given to General Mola. His efforts to block, and later to dismantle, reform had done much to undermine Socialist faith in the possibilities of bourgeois democracy but, now that his day had passed, his efforts were concentrated on facilitating the military conspiracy. Nothing more starkly demonstrated the change in atmosphere than the rise of the Falange. Cashing in on middle-class disillusionment with the CEDA's legalism, the Falange expanded rapidly, its numbers swelled by the bulk of the JAP.[115]

The Falangist terror squads worked hard to accelerate the spiral of mindless violence which rendered impossible rational discussion. With young activists of right and left clashing on the streets and the UME plotting to overthrow the regime, there was acute need for the decisive government that Casares Quiroga, suffering from tuberculosis, was hardly able to provide. While Prieto counselled caution, Largo Caballero did exactly the reverse. Intoxicated by Communist flattery – *Pravda* called him 'the Spanish Lenin' – he toured Spain, prophesying the triumph of the coming revolution to crowds of cheering workers. His loyal followers were determined to oust Prieto from the PSOE and turn it into an instrument of revolution.[116] Largo Caballero's dearest ambition was to bring the whole of the workers' movement under Socialist control. However, he made the naive error of permitting the fusion of the Socialist and Communist youth movements. The Communists happily agreed that the new organization should carry a name which gave the impression of a Socialist takeover – Juventudes Socialistas Unificadas (JSU). The JSU quickly fell totally under the dominance of the more dynamic Communists. This meant the eventual loss of 40,000 young Socialists of the FJS to the PCE. Santiago Carrillo, the FJS leader, had long since drawn close to Moscow. Indeed, he had already started attending meetings of the Central Committee of the Communist Party.[117]

Always a pragmatist concerned to further the interests of his UGT members, Largo Caballero tended to 'lead from behind', going along with the rank and file out of a determination not to be out of step. For all his rhetoric, the only real weapon at the left's disposal in early 1936, the revolutionary general strike, was never used. When proposals for revolution were made in April by Joaquín Maurín, one of the leaders of the quasi-Trotskyist Partido Obrero de Unificación Marxista (POUM), he was scorned as a dangerous utopian by Largo Caballero's supporters. The Caballeristas' regular statements about the death agony of capitalism and the inevitable triumph of socialism were regarded by Prieto as insanely provocative. The May Day marches, the clenched-fist salutes, the revolutionary rhetoric and the violent attacks on Prieto all contributed to middle-class alarm. On 31 May, Prieto and other PSOE moderates were greeted with a hail of bullets, stones and bottles from members of the Caballerista youth at a meeting in Écija in Seville.[118]

Even if Largo Caballero's threats of revolution were vacuous, they pushed conservative voters to approve of the violent rightist strategies that promised to rescue them from their apparently impending doom. While the political and personal divisions between Largo and Prieto effectively paralysed the strongest party of the Popular Front, Casares Quiroga seemed unaware of the need to use the apparatus of the state to defend the Republic. Under constant attack in the Cortes from an angry right wing, harassed by the destruction of public order by the Falange and the anarchists and undermined by the lack of Socialist support, Casares nonetheless seemed oblivious to the gravity of the situation. He shrugged off Prieto's warnings about military plotters with the offensive comment 'I will not tolerate your menopausal outbursts.' He told Largo Caballero to ignore the scare stories of bored and embittered officers.[119]

The government could do little to prevent politics degenerating into open conflict. There were ever closer links between the conspirators of the UME and the Falange, the Carlists, the JAP and sections of the CEDA. Ángel Herrera's brother Francisco allowed his home to be used by the plotters. A shield was provided by Gil Robles, who admitted later that his performances in the Cortes were coordinated with the conspirators: 'My task was to tire the left in parliament.'[120] In response to Largo Caballero's empty prophecies of revolution, Calvo Sotelo talked chillingly of violent counter-revolution and provided the army with a theory of political action against the twin threats of 'communism' and 'separatism', which he presented as consubstantial with the Republic. His speeches provoked scuffles in the Cortes. On the day that Casares Quiroga presented his new government, Calvo Sotelo called the Socialist deputy for Santander, Bruno Alonso, 'a nonentity, a pigmy'. The irate Socialist offered to fight him in the street and cried, 'The honourable member is a braggart.'[121] In his last major speech on 16 June, Calvo Sotelo declared himself a fascist and made an unmistakable overture to the army, saying, 'the soldier who, faced with his destiny, is not prepared to rise for Spain and against anarchy, is out of his mind'.[122]

Many senior officers, witnessing the disorder attributed to the Popular Front, much of it orchestrated by their rightist allies, were only too happy to intervene in politics. In the wake of the meeting of 8 March, the military uprising of 17–18 July 1936 was more carefully planned than any previous coup. The lesson of the Sanjurjada of 10 August 1932 had been well learned. General Mola, the 'Director' of the plot, had prepared a coordinated seizure of garrisons of all of Spain's fifty provinces and a swift annihilation of the organized working class. The first of his secret instructions, issued in April 1936, recognized the importance of terror: 'It will be realized that extreme violence will be required for the swift reduction of the enemy which is strong and well organized. Of course, all leaders of political parties, societies and trade unions not linked to our movement will be imprisoned and exemplary punishment imposed on them in order to strangle any rebellion or strikes.'[123] In his first speech at the beginning of the war, he declared: 'It is necessary to spread terror. We have to create the impression of mastery, eliminating without scruples or hesitation all those who do not think as we do.'[124]

To impede the preparation of a coup, on 21 February Franco had been sacked as Chief of Staff and sent to the Canary Islands as military commander, Goded was removed as Inspector General and transferred to the Balearic Islands as military commander and Mola was posted away from command of the Army of Africa to be Military Governor of the Navarrese capital, Pamplona. This last transfer was short-sighted. Pamplona was the headquarters of the Carlist movement and its militia, the Requetés. Consequently, Mola found himself in an excellent place from which to organize plans for the mainland insurrection. The obvious figurehead was the veteran of African wars and earlier coups, Sanjurjo. However, the crucial impetus for the conspiracy came from junior officers, many of whom had trained under Franco when he was director of the Military Academy in Zaragoza.[125]

The conspiracy was facilitated by the government's complacency in the face of repeated warnings. The Director General of Security, José Alonso Mallol, worked tirelessly to combat Falangist terrorism and to monitor the activities of hostile officers. In May, he gave Azaña and Casares Quiroga a list of more than 500 conspirators whom he believed should be arrested immediately. Fearful of the possible reactions, Azaña and Casares failed to act. Mallol pointed the finger at Mola but nothing was done. Shortly after Casares was appointed Prime Minister, he dismissed information from the Navarrese Communist Jesús Monzón about the Carlist accumulation of weaponry. He similarly ignored regular reports on conspiratorial activity in military units collected by Communist Party members and forwarded to him by Enrique Líster.[126] His military aide, the air force Major Ignacio Hidalgo de Cisneros, informed him that a group of anti-Republican pilots were collecting machine guns and bombs. When they reported this to Azaña, the President interrupted Hidalgo, saying brusquely that it was dangerous to make such accusations. On their way back to Madrid, Casares said, 'After what you've just seen, you'll understand how difficult it is for me to take action against suspects.'

On 12 June, in response to deafening (and accurate) rumours that Colonel Juan Yagüe, commander of the Foreign Legion in Ceuta, was organizing the military conspiracy in Morocco, Casares summoned him to the Ministry of War. Hidalgo de Cisneros urged him to replace Yagüe with a trustworthy officer. Offered a transfer to desirable posts either on the Spanish mainland or as a military attaché abroad, Yagüe replied that he would burn his uniform rather than leave the Legion. After a long meeting, Casares emerged, declaring to Hidalgo, 'Yagüe is a gentleman, a perfect officer, and I am sure that he would never betray the Republic. He has given me his word of honour and his promise as an officer that he will always loyally serve the Republic and men like Yagüe stand by their word.' By permitting Yagüe to return to Morocco, Casares committed a major political blunder.[127]

Three days later, Casares compounded this error. On 15 June, at the Monastery of Irache, near Estella in Navarre, Mola held a secret meeting with the commanders of the garrisons of Pamplona, Logroño, Vitoria and San Sebastián. On discovering this, the Mayor of Estella informed the Civil Governor of Navarre, who posted units of Civil Guards around the monastery. When he telephoned Casares Quiroga for further instructions, the Prime Minister indignantly ordered their removal, saying, 'General Mola is a loyal republican who, therefore, deserves the respect of the authorities.' Fearful of the possible reactions, Azaña and Casares failed to act on the list of conspirators compiled by Mallol.[128]

Just over a week went by before yet another mistake seems to have been made. A curious warning was later claimed to have come from the pen of General Franco. Some weeks after the military coup, the Francoist press published the text of a letter allegedly sent to Casares Quiroga on 23 June. Of labyrinthine ambiguity, the text both suggested that the army would be loyal if treated properly and insinuated that it was hostile to the Republic. The clear implication was that, if only Casares would put Franco in charge, the plots could be dismantled. In later years, his apologists presented the letter as either a skilful effort to put Casares off the scent or a last magnanimous peace-making gesture. There is no evidence that the letter was ever received. If it was, Casares took no more notice of Franco than he had of other warnings and failed to seize the opportunity to neutralize Franco, either by buying him off or by having him arrested.[129] Similarly, Casares blocked a plan by officers of the Unión Militar Republicana Antifascista (UMRA) to kidnap senior military plotters in Morocco. UMRA leaders denounced the activities of Goded, Mola, Fanjul, Varela, Franco, Yagüe and others, but Casares assured them that there was no possibility of a rising.[130]

The monarchist conspirators had already taken giant steps towards a successful coup. Contacts with Mussolini's government regarding the agreement made in 1934 had been assiduously maintained by Goicoechea. In mid-June, he wrote a report on behalf of Renovación Española and the Falange to Ernesto Carpi, a mutual friend of Don Juan de Borbón and of the prominent Fascist Italo Balbo. Carpi was the monarchists' liaison with the Fascist regime. The report confirmed that plans for a coup were well advanced and requesting 1 million pesetas to be used to guarantee hesitant plotters financial support for their families in the event of failure. A week earlier, the Italian military attaché in Tangiers had informed Rome that the coup in Morocco was imminent. On 1 July, Pedro Sainz Rodríguez signed contracts with Mussolini's government for the purchase of a large quantity of armament, including forty aircraft, bombs, artillery shells and machine guns. Payment was to come from Juan March. These preparations demonstrate that the conspirators anticipated a harder task than a simple *pronunciamiento*.[131]

Franco's position was extremely ambiguous, but Mola and the other conspirators were loath to proceed without him. He had enormous influence in the officer corps, as a result of his time as Director of the Military Academy in Zaragoza and as Chief of the General Staff under Gil Robles. In particular, he was revered in the Moroccan Army. The coup had no chance of succeeding without the colonial army and Franco was the obvious man to lead it. Moreover, his role in crushing the rising in Asturias in 1934 had made him a hero among the more conservative sections of the middle and upper classes. Neverthless, Sanjurjo, still bitter about Franco's failure to join him in 1932, commented suspiciously, 'Franco will do nothing that commits him; he will always be in the shadows because he is sneaky.'[132] Mola and Sanjurjo were exasperated by the risks of having to plan around a doubtful element, but they rightly sensed that his commitment would clinch the involvement of many others.

When Franco finally decided to join in, he was given a vitally important but still second-rank role. The head of state once the coup had triumphed was intended to be Sanjurjo. Mola, as technical mastermind of the plot, was then expected to play a decisive role in the politics of the victorious regime. Then came a number of generals each of whom was assigned a region, among them Franco with Morocco. Greater subsequent importance was expected for Joaquín Fanjul, who was in charge of the rising in Madrid, and Manuel Goded, who was given Barcelona. However, that situation changed with astonishing rapidity and, in the eyes of some observers, with sinister symmetry.

The logistics of Franco's part in the coup were organized even before his participation was finally confirmed. Gil Robles's friend Francisco Herrera arranged for Juan March to cover the cost of chartering an aircraft to take Franco from the Canaries to Morocco, where he was to assume command of the African Army.[133] The arrangements were made in London in early July by the Spanish aeronautical expert Juan de la Cierva and Luis Bolín, the correspondent of the monarchist daily *ABC* who had established links with Franco in Morocco in the 1920s. Bolín hired a de Havilland Dragon Rapide in Croydon and arranged for a set of apparently holidaying passengers to mask the aeroplane's real purpose. The Foreign Office was apprised of the enterprise and there remains a suspicion that the British Secret Intelligence Service was aware of what was happening. Leaving Croydon on 11 July, the plane arrived four days later at the airport of Gando near Las Palmas on the island of Gran Canaria.[134]

In the meantime, however, dramatic events had been taking place on the Spanish mainland. On the afternoon of 12 July, Falangist gunmen had shot and killed Lieutenant José del Castillo of the Republican Assault Guard. Castillo was number two on a blacklist of pro-Republican officers compiled by the UME. The first man on the list, Captain Carlos Faraudo, the officer who helped train the Socialist militias, had already been murdered on 7 May by a joint UME–Falangist squad. Now enraged comrades of Castillo responded with a massive and irresponsible reprisal. In the early hours of 13 July, they set out to avenge his death by seizing a prominent right-wing politician. Failing to find Gil Robles, who was holidaying in Biarritz, they kidnapped and shot and killed Calvo Sotelo. The huge political scandal that followed the discovery of the body played neatly into the hands of the military plotters. On the evening of the 13th, Indalecio Prieto led a delegation of Socialists and Communists to demand that Casares Quiroga distribute arms to the workers before the military rose. The Prime Minister refused, but there was now virtually open war.[135]

There were madcap schemes on the part of the lunatic fringe of the extreme right. Eugenio Vegas Latapié (later to be tutor to the future King Juan Carlos), with other members of Renovación Española and young army officers, toyed both with the assassination of Azaña and with a suicide attack on the Cortes with poison gas. Neither scheme came to fruition, the first because the plotters could not get hold of a machine gun and the second because they could not get gas canisters.[136] Calvo Sotelo's murder provided stark justification for the argument that only military intervention could save Spain from anarchy. It clinched the commitment of many ditherers, including Franco, and masked the extent to which the coup had been long in the making. It also deprived the conspirators of an important leader. As a prestigious figure with wide international connections, Calvo Sotelo might have been the senior civilian leader after the coup. Now his death removed an important political rival to Franco.

In the short term, the murder gave a new urgency to the conspiracy. Franco had acute immediate problems which took precedence over any long-term ambitions. With the rising scheduled to start on 18 July, he needed to leave for Morocco on the 17th at the latest. As military commander of the Canary Islands, his headquarters were in Santa Cruz de Tenerife but the Dragon Rapide from Croydon had landed on Gran Canaria, perhaps because of the low cloud which afflicts Tenerife or because of fears that Franco was being watched. There was no certainty that Franco would be able to get to Gran Canaria since, to leave his post, he needed the authorization of the Ministry of War. His request for permission to make an inspection tour of Gran Canaria was refused. That he reached the aircraft at all was thus the result of either an amazing coincidence or foul play.

On the morning of 16 July, General Amado Balmes, military commander in Gran Canaria, and an excellent marksman, was shot in the stomach, allegedly while trying out various pistols in a shooting range. Francoist historiography presented the incident as a tragic, but fortunately timed, accident. To counter suspicions that Balmes had been removed by the military plotters, Franco's official biographer claimed that Balmes was himself an important figure in the plot. In fact, Balmes was a loyal officer who had withstood intense pressure to join the rising and so put his life in mortal danger. Recent research has demonstrated that he was murdered. Franco was thus 'obliged' to preside over his funeral, the perfect excuse to travel to Las Palmas on 17 July.[137] Coordinated risings were planned to take place all over Spain on the following morning. However, fear that the conspirators in Morocco were about to be arrested saw the action brought forward there to the early evening of 17 July. The garrisons rose in Melilla, Tetuán and Ceuta. In the early morning of 18 July, Franco and General Luis Orgaz took over Las Palmas.

The anarchist journalist Salvador Cánovas Cervantes claimed that a group of journalists stopped Casares Quiroga in the corridors of the Cortes and told him that there was about to be a military uprising, to which he allegedly replied, 'Let them rise. I, in contrast, am going to bed.' When news reached Madrid of the rising in Morocco, Azaña asked Casares what Franco was doing, to which he replied complacently, 'He's in storage in the Canary Islands.' Casares telephoned his friend the distinguished physiologist Professor Juan Negrín and told him, 'This coup is guaranteed to fail. The Government is master of the situation. It will all be over soon.'[138] The Spanish Civil War had begun and already the government was at a major disadvantage.

'The Last Pirate of the Mediterranean', the
fabulously rich Juan March who helped
finance Franco's war effort.

11

Civil War: Hatred, Incompetence and Profit, 1936–1939

The rising took place on the evening of 17 July 1936 in Spain's Moroccan colony and in the Peninsula itself on the next morning. The plotters were confident that it would all be over in a few days. Had they faced only the Republican government, their predictions might have come true. The coup was successful in the Catholic smallholding areas which voted for the CEDA – the provincial capitals of rural León and Old Castile, cathedral market towns like Ávila, Burgos, Salamanca and Valladolid. However, in the left-wing strongholds of industrial Spain and the great estates of the south, the uprising was defeated by the spontaneous action of the working-class organizations. Yet, ominously, in towns like Cadiz, Cordoba, Granada and Seville, left-wing resistance was swiftly and savagely crushed.

For the military rebels, a programme of terror and extermination was central to their planning and preparations. To combat the numerical superiority of the urban and rural working classes, they believed that the immediate imposition of a reign of terror was crucial. With the use of forces brutalized in the colonial wars in Africa, backed up by local landowners, this process was supervised in the south by General Gonzalo Queipo de Llano. In the deeply conservative regions of Navarra, Galicia, Old Castile and León, where the military coup was almost immediately successful and left-wing resistance minimal, General Mola's application of terror was disproportionately severe.[1]

Wherever the rising was successful, there began a bloody repression of Republicans, from the revolutionary left of anarchists, Communists and Trotskyists to moderate Socialists and centre-left Republicans. All those who were perceived as challenging the pre-1931 social, economic and political order were potential victims. Hence the targeting of women. Murder, torture and rape would be generalized punishments for the gender liberation embraced by many liberal and left-wing women during the Republican period. Thousands were subjected to extreme sexual abuse, the humiliation of head shaving and being forced to ingest castor oil to make them soil themselves in public. Those who came out of prison alive suffered deep lifelong physical and psychological problems.[2] Mola's belief in the value of terror was revealed in a speech to an assembly of the *alcaldes* (mayors) of the province in Pamplona: 'It is necessary to spread terror. We have to create the impression of mastery, eliminating without scruples or hesitation all those who do not think as we do.'[3] At the end of July, on being told that the French press had reported that Prieto had proposed a negotiated settlement to avoid more bloodshed, Mola barked, 'Negotiate? Never! This war has to end with the extermination of Spain's enemies.'[4] The ruthlessness of the rebel repression reflected the strength derived from the imposition of military discipline. This contrasted with the divisions of the Popular Front government that derived from Largo Caballero's refusal to permit the Socialist Party to participate in a cabinet under Prieto.

The moderate liberal cabinet of Santiago Casares Quiroga was utterly indecisive. Despite the flood of disturbing news, he failed to see the seriousness of the situation. At 6.00 p.m. on 18 July, he rejected Largo Caballero's call to arm the workers, a measure that might have prevented the success of the rising in many areas. By 9.00 p.m., Casares had resigned and Azaña consulted the moderate Republican Diego Martínez Barrio, the conservative Republican Felipe Sánchez Román and Largo Caballero and Prieto about a new cabinet. Largo Caballero stubbornly blocked Prieto's call for Socialist participation while Sánchez Román, as a sop to the rebels, suggested the prohibition of strikes and a total crackdown on left-wing militias. The outcome was a cabinet of the centre under Martínez Barrio. When he telephoned Mola at 2 a.m. on 19 July, he rejected out of hand the new Prime Minister's proposals for compromise.[5]

In any case, the idea of negotiation was unacceptable to the left-wing masses. Within hours, Martínez Barrio had been replaced by the Minister for the Navy, the chemistry professor José Giral, a friend of Azaña. Giral courageously took the crucial decision to arm the workers.[6] Without it, the coup being led in Madrid by General Joaquín Fanjul at the Montaña barracks could not have been defeated.[7] The same was even truer of the defeat of General Goded in Barcelona after anarchist workers had seized a weapons depot, which also rendered the Generalitat of Lluís Companys virtually powerless.[8] With power in the streets held by the workers, Giral's cabinet was hardly distinguishable from that of Casares Quiroga. Given Largo Caballero's veto, and also with an eye on the hostile international context, there were no ministers from the working-class parties. Yet, to Largo Caballero's irritation, from 20 July to 4 September Prieto would be the virtual Prime Minister in the shadows while apparently merely adviser to Giral's cabinet. From an office in the Navy Ministry, he worked unceasingly to impose order and direction on the government shambles.[9]

Within days, the country was split into two war zones. The rebels controlled one-third of Spain in a northern block of Galicia, León, Old Castile, Aragon and part of Extremadura and an Andalusian triangle from Huelva to Seville to Cordoba. They had the great wheat-growing areas, but the main industrial centres remained in Republican hands. In its favour, Giral's cabinet controlled the nation's gold and currency reserves and most of Spain's industrial capacity. However, the revolution that the military rebels claimed to be forestalling was itself precipitated by the coup. In every city not conquered by the insurgents, the coup provoked the collapse of the state apparatus and saw power assumed by the workers who had helped defeat the rising. It would take several months before the middle-class Republican left, the moderate Socialists and the Communist Party could combine to play down the revolution and restore power to the bourgeois Republic. In the meantime, the collapse of the machinery of the state inevitably facilitated popular violence of all kinds against those seen as rebel supporters. 'Revolutionary' tribunals, autonomous police forces and detention centres, known as *checas*, were set up by political parties, trade unions or militia groups. In the absence of most of the structures of law and order, there was also an element of sheer criminality. Resentment of years of social injustice, the opening of the prisons and the release of thousands of common criminals all combined to produce a situation which would soon diminish the international prestige of the Republic.[10]

The rebels, having expected near instant success, were shocked by the scale of Republican resistance. The columns sent by Mola against Madrid were halted by workers' militias at the Sierra to the north. What they lacked in training they made up in an enthusiasm that could not be matched by the conscripts of the rebel army. In the navy, left-wing sailors had mutinied against their right-wing officers.[11] There would, however, be several major differences between the two sides that would eventually decide the conflict – the African Army, the geographical division of the officer corps within Spain and the roles of the great powers. At first, the rebels' strongest card, the ferocious colonial army under Franco, was blockaded in Morocco by Republican warships. However, the situation was reversed by an unprecedented airlift and a blockade-breaking 'victory convoy' of fishing boats carrying troops.[12] The news that the bloodthirsty Foreign Legion and mercenary Regulares Indígenas (Native Regulars) had landed on the mainland spread fear throughout the Republican zone.[13]

Only four of the Republic's eighteen most senior generals joined the coup. However, eighteen out of thirty-two brigadier generals, the bulk of the General Staff, more than 80 per cent of colonels and below, forty-four of the most important garrisons and half the forces of public order sided with the rebels. The Army of Africa was among the 150,000 armed and trained men at the disposal of the conspirators. In contrast, the Republic was dependent on untrained volunteer militias. They were often ineffective even when led by loyal Republican officers, whom they did not trust and, on occasion, murdered. About half the 600,000 rifles in Spain at the beginning of the war were in the Republican zone but, especially in anarchist-controlled areas, they were often used not at the battlefront but in revolutionary and repressive activities in the rearguard. The discrepancy in naval forces was equally dramatic. The Republic had a short-lived numerical advantage in aircraft. However, its aged machines were swiftly overtaken by the modern German and Italian models soon at the disposal of the rebels. The pre-existing military structures enjoyed by the rebels together with ample numbers of professional officers facilitated the creation of new units from volunteers and conscripts, something impossible for the Republic for several months.[14]

Although he was only one of the conspirators, Franco had ambitions far beyond immediate victory. Within days of reaching Morocco, he set up both diplomatic and press offices. The international press was soon receiving communiqués that referred to him as supreme commander of the 'Nationalist' forces. The rebels adopted the term 'Nationalist' to imply that they were fighting a foreign enemy. Franco quickly persuaded the local representatives of Nazi Germany and Fascist Italy that he was the man to back. On 25 July, he told the Italian military attaché, Major

Giuseppe Luccardi, that five of Spain's eight military regions, the Balearic Islands, the Canary Islands and all of Spanish Morocco were 'in his possession'. By the end of July, Junkers 52 and Savoia-Marchetti 81 transport aircraft were undertaking the first major military airlift in history across the Straits of Gibraltar to Seville.[15] Fifteen thousand men crossed in ten days and a coup d'état going wrong became a long and bloody civil war. Within days, Franco's troops would be advancing northwards to Madrid under the command of the ruthless Colonel Juan Yagüe. Heading out of Seville, the African Army took village after village, leaving a horrific trail of slaughter in its wake.[16]

This initial, and crucial, aid from Fascist Italy and Nazi Germany was soon followed by a regular stream of modern technological assistance. State-of-the-art equipment arrived from Germany and Italy, complete with technicians and spare parts. After 1 November 1936 when, in a speech in the Piazza del Duomo in Milan, Mussolini gave the name Axis to the growing collaboration between the fascist powers, aid deliveries to Franco increased even further. In contrast, the Republic was shunned by the democracies and, until Soviet aid arrived, had to make do with what could be bought from commercial, and often dishonest, arms dealers. The politicians responsible for weapons procurement often innocently bought over-priced and obsolete equipment. To make matters worse, they had to work with banks whose directors were sympathetic to the military rebels.[17] The dominance in Republican Spain enjoyed by the unions and their militias undermined Giral's efforts to secure aid from the Western democracies.

Financial support was easier for Franco. He issued a threatening appeal to bankers and businessmen: 'CAPITALIST! The National Movement, Saviour of Spain, allows you to continue enjoying your income. If you dither for a moment in lending your moral and material help with generosity and disinterestedness, you will be not only a bad patriot but a wretch unworthy of a place in the strong Spain that is beginning to be reborn. Your gold and jewels must immediately swell the National Treasury of the Burgos Government.' Those who were remiss were denounced as Jews.[18]

One capitalist unstinting in his generosity was Juan March, from whom financial support was urgently sought by Franco. His telegraphed request was published in the Republican press with comments like 'the swine March was the financier of the subversive movement ... Juan

March was the banker of the rebellion.[19] Such well-founded accusations impelled Franco to leap to the defence of both March and himself: 'Those like Juan March who have lent their support to our movement have not done so to gain any advantage, which at no point have they been promised. They did it to reach a better Spain, and they have given their mite for a more just Spain.' Needless to say, March would derive reward in many ways over the next years.[20] In a speech in Lugo on 21 August 1942, Franco revealed more than he intended about his notion of 'a more just Spain' when he declared that 'Our Crusade is the only struggle in which the rich who took part in the war emerged richer.'[21]

March had gone into exile in Paris even before the results of the February elections, fearing that a Popular Front victory would see him subjected to renewed persecution. Given his hostility to the Republic, he was delighted to learn of the 8 March meeting of conspiratorial generals but was alarmed to hear of their fears about the risks, particularly in the case of Mola. He sent him a message: 'You mustn't worry about your Family. If anything happens to you, Juan March will look after their needs. Moreover, he guarantees you, up front, one million pesetas.' This permitted Mola to settle his wife and four children in Biarritz and Franco some days later to send his wife and daughter on the German ship *Waldi* to Le Havre. March's intermediary with Mola was the retired Colonel Tomás Peire and, with Franco, the diplomat José Antonio Sangróniz. March had secured seats for Peire as a Radical deputy in the Cortes, in 1931 for Huesca and in 1933 for Ceuta.[22]

In mid-June, Goicoechea had recognized the importance of March's financial guarantees, writing to his principal Italian contact, the secret agent Ernesto Carpi, about many hesitant officers. He acknowledged what had already been done: 'A special financial effort to win them over was made to guarantee them against the economic risks that might be faced by their families. Although not motivated by money, they won't act unless their future livelihood is guaranteed in the event of failure.' He requested a further 1 million pesetas to be distributed among other doubters.[23] Throughout the spring of 1936, March made financial guarantees to overcome the hesitations of several key generals and keep them in the conspiracy. In March, for the purchase of arms, he also provided Franco and Mola with a credit of £500,000 through the Kleinwort Bank. This was increased to £800,000 in August and to £942,000 in December. In Biarritz during the spring of 1936, arms purchases were on the agenda of Mola's frequent meetings with March who, typically, imposed harsh repayment and interest conditions.[24] He also paid more than £20,000 for the Dragon Rapide that took Franco from the Canary Islands to Morocco.[25] March's lavish contribution to the preparation of the coup totally discredits subsequent Francoist claims that it was carried out on a shoestring.[26] March later boasted to an official of the British Embassy about his contribution to Franco's victory, claiming that he was 'mainly responsible for persuading wavering financiers and grandees to risk their money on General Franco, and in many cases it was the knowledge that March was prepared to triple their stakes (rather than General Franco's military situation) which gave them the necessary confidence'.[27]

Once the rising had begun, March transferred funds from the Kleinwort Bank in London to pay the Italian government for the twelve Savoia-Marchetti aircraft that were to transport Franco's troops from Morocco to the mainland. According to the official historian of the bank, he deposited 'staggering amounts of bullion in the Bank of Italy to finance Italian involvement in the war'. On 3 September, he deposited 49.5 metric tons (one metric ton was worth over £37,000,000 in 2019 prices) and a further 72 metric tons six days later.[28] It has been suggested that to guarantee aircraft deliveries to Franco, March bought a majority of the shares in the Savoia-Marchetti Company. He was almost certainly the main financier of the rising in the early months of the war. At considerable profit to himself, he used his sources of foreign currency to act as purchaser of equipment for the rebels. It has been calculated that March advanced approximately 8–10 per cent of the cost of Franco's war effort.[29] Despite Franco's protestations, this was more than a mite (óbolo) and was not given disinterestedly. When March called in the debt, it was alleged that Franco had authorized the sale of the fabulous treasures of the Cathedral of Zaragoza. Moreover, as a result of his financial help to the rebels his fortune had more than doubled by the end of the war. This was not unconnected with the fact that the huge donations to the rebel cause made by Spanish aristocrats in cash, shares and jewellery were held in March's Kleinwort account.[30] Gil Robles, who later became one of March's principal legal representatives, was the rebels' agent in Lisbon. His activities, together with those of Franco's brother Nicolás in an unofficial embassy, were financed by March. Indeed, in the opinion of Diego Hidalgo, who had been Minister of War when Franco was military commander of the Balearic Islands, Franco was actually the puppet of

March, with whom he had frequent contact at that time. Certainly, as a marine engineer, Nicolás had worked for March's shipping interests as long ago as 1914.[31]

It was fighter aircraft and other military equipment sent from Italy at March's expense that secured Mallorca for the rebels. In fact, Mussolini also had a crucial interest in an island that was the key to maritime traffic in the Mediterranean. The coup in Mallorca had been initially successful, although it was not so in the other Balearic Islands. A Republican attack led by Captain Alberto Bayo began on 5 August and successfully captured the smaller islands. Bayo's attack on Mallorca went well at first. Much of the propaganda that accompanied it was directed against March: 'We just want to free the island from the clutches of the bandit March.' However, thanks to the disorganization of the invading forces, particularly the anarchist contingent, and with Italian aircraft and other equipment paid for by March, the rebels had recaptured the island by the beginning of September. Thereafter, Mallorca was a key military base for rebel bombing attacks on the Catalan and Valencian coasts and for the Francoist navy to block deliveries of food and weapons to Republican ports.[32] For the next four months, a terrible repression was mounted by the head of the small Italian invasion force, the deranged Fascist Arconovaldo Bonacorsi, known as Conte Rossi.[33]

March's crony Alejandro Lerroux played no part in the civil war. His contacts with the military conspirators had ensured that he was given prior warning of the rising. He left his home in San Rafael on the evening of 17 July en route for Portugal. While there, much of his fortune in Spanish banks was confiscated by the Republic, but he seems to have lived well in exile thanks to funds not discovered and to help from Juan March. Throughout the war, he wrote sycophantic letters to Franco in the vain hope of being allowed to return to Spain. After the war, while still trying to get permission to return, he wrote memoirs in which he justified the military coup.[34]

The financial aid given to the rebels by Francesc Cambó was almost as important as that provided by Juan March. He heard of the rising while on an Adriatic cruise on his 100-ton yacht *Catalònia* and was alleged to have responded, 'Those with money should give it and those of military age should fight.' He placed his considerable fortune at the disposal of the rebels. It was used to establish an immensely influential pro-rebel propaganda operation in Paris. Through his collaborator José

Bertrán y Musitu, he financed a rebel espionage service, the Servicio de Información de la Frontera Noroeste España.[35] He became a key element in persuading moderate international opinion of the righteousness of the rebel cause.[36] Cambó would later express private regret that economic interest had obliged him to support Franco's 'politics of petulance and illiteracy'. He felt little but contempt for Franco, whom he compared to General Primo de Rivera 'but with much less talent'. As the war progressed, his concerns grew that, if victorious, the rebels would pursue anti-Catalan policies. Nevertheless, he put his economic interests ahead of his Catalanism.[37]

To a large extent, the reaction of foreign powers would dictate the course of the civil war. The policies of four of the five major international protagonists, Britain, France, Germany and Italy, were substantially influenced by hostility to the fifth, the Soviet Union. Suspicion of the Soviet Union had been a major determinant of the international diplomacy of the Western powers since the revolution of October 1917, and the Spanish conflict was to be the most recent battle in a European civil war.[38]

There was a prevailing belief in London, fanned by the fiercely right-wing Ambassador to Madrid, Sir Henry Chilton, and by the militantly anti-Republican Consul in Barcelona, Norman King, that the Popular Front triumph in February had signified the beginning of a pre-revolutionary crisis. In despatch after despatch, Chilton asserted that the Popular Front cabinet was the puppet of extreme-left Socialists and Communists. On 26 March, less than three weeks after the meeting of the conspirators, he had written: 'If the military coup d'état, which it is generally believed is being planned, does not succeed, things will be pretty awful.'[39] These despatches fell on fertile ground. On 20 July, Maurice Hankey, the deeply conservative Cabinet Secretary, prepared a memorandum for the British government on the League of Nations which concluded: 'in the present state of Europe, with France and Spain menaced by Bolshevism, it is not inconceivable that before long it might pay us to throw in our lot with Germany and Italy, and the greater our detachment from European entanglements the better'.[40] This prepared the way for British policy towards the Spanish crisis to be one of non-intervention. This institutionalized hypocrisy was in response to a suggestion by the French. On 19 July, Giral had sent a telegram to the Prime Minister of the Front Populaire government in Paris, Léon Blum:

'Surprised by dangerous military coup. Beg you to help us immediately with arms and aeroplanes. Fraternally yours, Giral'. Blum's initial reaction was to help the legitimate Frente Popular government. To do so favoured French strategic interests since the security of both the Pyrenean frontier and the North African colonies depended on a friendly or neutral regime in Spain. If the military rebels won, there would be a danger of a right-wing Spain establishing close links with France's enemies, Fascist Italy and Nazi Germany. On 22 July, a more specific formal request was received from Giral for twenty bombers, fifty light machine guns, eight artillery pieces, 1,000 rifles, 250,000 machine-gun bullets, 4 million cartridges and 20,000 bombs.[41]

The British government was informed about Giral's request and Blum's response by Charles Corbin, the French Ambassador in London. Blum was in London on 25 July to discuss a British–French–Belgian response to the German occupation of the Rhineland. While there, the Prime Minister Stanley Baldwin and his Foreign Secretary, Anthony Eden, left Blum in no doubt about their concerns. According to Blum himself, in the vestibule of Claridge's hotel, Eden, whom he trusted implicitly, asked him if he planned to send arms to Madrid. When Blum confirmed that this was his intention, Eden said: 'It's your business; I ask only one thing of you, I beg of you, be careful.'[42]

Blum's inevitable preoccupation was intensified by dramatic events at home. The Spanish Military Attaché, Lieutenant Colonel Antonio Barroso, a rebel sympathizer, had leaked to the French right-wing press Blum's positive response to Giral. This provoked a vicious press campaign against both Blum and the Spanish Republic. After a cabinet meeting on 25 July, overshadowed by concerns of civil violence between left and right being provoked by events in Spain, a communiqué was issued to the effect that France would not deliver war materiel to Spain. It was the beginning of a process over the next two weeks that led to a complete reversal of Blum's commitment to helping the Spanish Republic. By 1 August, the French government had decided to propose the feeble compromise of a non-intervention agreement and by 8 August had opted for a complete arms embargo.[43]

There can be little doubt that there were strong, and decisive, hints that, in the event of war, France would be left without crucial British support.[44] It was hoped in London that, if non-intervention could be imposed, the Spanish war would peter out for lack of arms and ammunition. On 15 August, London and Paris exchanged diplomatic notes agreeing to non-intervention in Spain. It was announced that a strict embargo on the delivery of weapons and munitions to Spain would begin as soon as the governments of Germany, Italy, the Soviet Union and Portugal agreed.[45]

Like the French, the British government was committed at all costs to diminishing the risks of a European conflagration. Moreover, where the Spanish war was concerned, Conservative decision makers in London tended to let their class prejudices prevail over the strategic interests of Great Britain. The journalist Henry Buckley was told by a British diplomat that 'the essential thing to remember in the case of Spain is that it is a civil conflict and that it is very necessary that we stand by our class'.[46] Mussolini and his Foreign Minister Count Galeazzo Ciano were confident that Britain approved of their actions. On 28 July 1936, Ciano told the French Ambassador that 'because Portugal had declared its sympathy with the insurgents and as the Portuguese hardly ever came out in the open on any matter without first being assured of British support, owing to the long-standing Anglo-Portuguese alliance, Great Britain was in favour of the rebels'.[47] Even as the first Italian aircraft were on their way to Morocco, the Italian Chargé in London, Leonardo Vitetti, reported that widespread sympathy for the Spanish rebels and for Italian Fascism was to be found within the highest reaches of the Conservative Party.[48]

Franco never ever admitted in public that 'perfidious Albion' had made an enormous contribution to his eventual success. However, within the hastily created rebel administration, the Junta de Defensa Nacional, British sympathy was confidently assumed to be assured on the basis of London's toleration of the support being given to the rebels by Portugal.[49] In early August, Juan de la Cierva, the Spanish inventor of the autogyro (the precursor of the helicopter), who had helped arrange Franco's flight from the Canary Islands to Morocco, told Vitetti that he had bought all the aircraft available on the free market in Britain for General Mola and that 'the British authorities had given him every facility even though they knew only too well that the aircraft were destined for the Spanish rebels'.[50]

The British were inclined by their considerable commercial interests in Spain to be hostile to the Republic. The business community believed that the anarchists and other Spanish revolutionaries were liable to seize and collectivize British holdings.[51] Equally, members of the British government and the diplomatic corps, for reasons of class and education, sympathized with the anti-revolutionary aims of the Nationalists as they did with those of Hitler and Mussolini. Moreover, it was commonplace for Spanish aristocrats and the scions of the main sherry-exporting families to be educated at English Catholic public schools like Beaumont, Downside, Ampleforth and Stonyhurst. This nexus of upper-class contacts and friendship intensified the underlying hostility of British Conservatives to the Spanish Republic.[52] Ostensibly intended to neutralize and localize the Spanish war, non-intervention hobbled the Spanish Republic far more than it did the military rebels. The manner in which the financial authorities turned a blind eye to the operations of British banks in favour of the rebels underlines the point.[53]

In this increasingly favourable international context, the rebels conducted two campaigns which dramatically improved their situation. Franco's African forces advanced rapidly using the techniques of terror honed during the Moroccan wars. They were opposed by untrained labourers, armed only with shotguns, ancient blunderbusses, knives and hatchets. The shock units of the Spanish colonial army took villages and towns in the provinces of Seville and Badajoz. They were equipped with artillery and enjoyed total air superiority provided by Savoia-Marchetti 81 flown by Italian air force pilots and Junkers Ju 52 flown by Luftwaffe pilots. By 10 August, they had captured Mérida and united the two halves of Nationalist Spain. Yagüe's troops then turned back to capture Badajoz, the capital of Extremadura, near the Portuguese border. It was not a strategic necessity since Badajoz was isolated and could have been picked off at the rebels' leisure. After heavy artillery and bombing attacks, the walls were breached, and a savage repression began during which nearly 2,000 people, including many innocent civilians, were shot. Rivulets of blood ran down the streets and piles of corpses provided scenes of what the Portuguese journalist Mário Neves called 'desolation and dread'. Franco was sending a message to the citizens of Madrid about what they could expect if they did not surrender before the arrival of the African columns.[54]

Meanwhile, in early August, Mola began a campaign to cut off the Basque Country from the French border. Irún and Fuenterrabía were shelled from the sea and attacked daily by German and Italian bombers. They dropped rebel pamphlets threatening to repeat what had been done in Badajoz. Irún's poorly armed and untrained militia defenders fought bravely but were overwhelmed on 3 September. Thousands of panic-stricken refugees fled across the international bridge from Irún over the River Bidasoa to France. The Basque Country, Santander and Asturias were now isolated from France as well as from the rest of Republican Spain. Rebel forces occupied San Sebastián on Sunday, 13 September 1936.[55]

The rebels consolidated their position throughout August and September as General José Enrique Varela connected up Seville, Cordoba, Granada and Cadiz. For the Republicans, there were only retreats and two frustrating operations which were a drain on resources. For more than two months from 21 July, the rebel garrison of Toledo that had taken refuge in the Alcázar fortress was unsuccessfully besieged by Republican militiamen who wasted time, energy and ammunition trying to capture this strategically unimportant target.[56] Similarly, on 23 July, enthusiastic anarchist militia columns had set out from Barcelona to recapture Zaragoza. Like Seville, the Aragonese capital was a CNT stronghold and had also fallen quickly to the rebels. It thus became a point of honour for the CNT to retake Zaragoza. They got within striking distance and then halted because of insufficient weaponry. Along the way, they engaged in deeply divisive attempts forcibly to collectivize smallholdings.[57]

By late August, Franco's African columns were rapidly moving north-eastwards to Talavera de la Reina. Giral, aware of the inadequacies of a government lacking the support of the CNT and the UGT, urged a change to a more broadly based government. Survival required a cabinet representative of the working-class forces that had defended the Republic against the coup. That meant involving Largo Caballero, but he, despite international hostility to the Republic, had no sympathy for Prieto's view that the need to placate the Western powers and also to consolidate popular support required a cabinet backed by both the working-class parties and the bourgeois Republicans. On 26 August, interviewed by the Soviet journalist Mikhail Koltsov, Prieto spoke frankly about his rival: 'He is a fool who tries to pass himself off as clever. He is a cold bureaucrat who plays the role of a wild fanatic, he creates havoc and is a meddler who pretends to be a methodical bureaucrat. He is a man capable of ruining everything and everyone ... And, despite all that, he is, today at least, the only man, or rather, the only name that can appropriately head a new government.'[58]

Largo Caballero refused to join the government merely as Minister of War, demanding also to be Prime Minister. The thought of making him Prime Minister horrified Azaña, who remarked to his brother-in-law, Cipriano Rivas Cherif, 'He is not the Spanish Lenin; he will sink and the Republic will go down with him.'[59] When his appointment seemed inevitable, Koltsov wrote of general concerns that 'his rudeness, his unsociability and his impatience will make it impossible for anyone to collaborate with him'. Prieto's friend the renowned physiologist Dr Juan Negrín commented on the appointment: 'I cannot imagine a more ludicrous mistake from both a national and an international perspective. Is the idea to lose the war? Is it meant to be a challenge to Europe?'[60]

For Azaña, Prieto, the Spanish Communists and Stalin, the realistic option was a purely Republican–Socialist coalition but, regarding himself as the hero of the entire working class and confident that he could unite it, Largo Caballero made the inclusion of two Communists a condition of accepting the post. He also insisted on the participation of three other Socialists and there was some hope that Prieto could be Minister of Defence. However, Largo Caballero wanted the ministry for himself and so, in the government announced on 4 September, the three Socialists were Prieto as Navy and Air Minister, the brilliant Negrín as Minister of Finance and Anastasio de Gracia as Minister of Industry.[61] Although popular among workers, Largo Caballero lacked the energy, determination and vision to direct a successful war effort. Indeed, his incompetence would be deeply damaging to the Republic. Assembling a cabinet was not easy given the conflicting agendas of the various left-wing forces, but he did not consult even with party colleagues over the distribution of portfolios.[62] On taking over the Ministry of War, his first order was for the table piled with telephones, maps and plans used by his predecessor, General Juan Hernández Saravia, to be removed. The General Staff was not permitted to disturb him without an appointment, which prevented the rapid and flexible resolution of problems. His telephone number was a closely guarded secret. Largo kept an extremely rigid timetable. He was at his desk at 8 a.m. He took only a short lunch break and, at 8 p.m., he withdrew to bed, leaving strict orders that he was never to be disturbed except in the event of the gravest emergency.[63]

Fighting not only Franco and his armies but also the military and economic might of Hitler and Mussolini, and snubbed by France and

Britain, Giral turned to Moscow. The initial reaction of the Soviet Union was one of deep embarrassment. The Kremlin did not want events in Spain to undermine its delicately laid plans for an alliance with France. However, by mid-August, the flow of help to the rebels from Hitler and Mussolini threatened an even greater disaster if the Spanish Republic fell. That would severely alter the European balance of power, leaving France with three hostile fascist states on its borders.[64] Stalin also wished to ensure that Soviet aid would be paid for. In fact, by late September, Negrín had decided to send Spain's gold reserves to Russia because of the hostile machinations of the international banking system, the insecurity of the gold reserves within Spain and the fact that the Soviet Union was the only major power likely to help the Republic. This led to the Kremlin launching what was called 'Operation X'.[65] Distance and organizational chaos meant that it was late September before any equipment left for Spain. The first shipment of ancient rifles and machine guns arrived on 4 October. Then Stalin took the decision to send modern aircraft and tanks – which had to be paid for at inflated prices.[66]

While the Republic floundered in search of foreign assistance and its disorganized militias fell back on the capital, the rebels tightened up their command structure. On 21 September, at an airfield near Salamanca, the leading rebel generals met to choose a commander-in-chief both for obvious military reasons and to facilitate ongoing negoti- ations for aid from Hitler and Mussolini. Franco had let both monarchists, through General Alfredo Kindelán, and Falangists, via Colonel Juan de Yagüe, think that he would further their aims. Kindelán organized the meeting on 21 September. With the exception of the head of the Burgos Junta, Miguel Cabanellas, all agreed that a commander-in-chief was needed to replace Sanjurjo who had died in a plane crash in Portugal on 20 July. At the Salamanca meeting, Franco was chosen as single commander despite reluctance on the part of some of his fellow generals.[67]

On the same day, his African columns had reached Maqueda, where the road from the south divided to go north to Madrid or east to Toledo. The columns could either press on towards Madrid, or turn to Toledo, to relieve the besieged garrison. He opted to send them to Toledo, a deci- sion that revealed that a swift military victory was not his first priority. He lost an unrepeatable chance to attack Madrid before its defences were ready. However, the relief of the Alcázar on 26 September clinched his own power with an emotional victory and a great media coup. A blood-bath ensued.[68] The liberation was restaged on the following day for news-reel cameras. After cinema audiences across the world saw him touring the rubble of the Alcázar, Franco became the internationally recognized symbol of the rebel war effort. At a second meeting of generals on 28 September, with considerable chicanery by General Kindelán and Franco's brother Nicolás, it was agreed that Franco be given the rank of Generalísimo with the function of 'Head of the Government of the Spanish State as long as the war lasts'. However, with characteristic duplicity, Franco had the official text altered and, henceforth, simply arrogated to himself the full powers of head of state.[69]

On 7 October the Army of Africa resumed its march on Madrid. Wracked with indecision, Largo Caballero had made no plans for the defence of the capital other than the militarization of the militias.[70] In an effort to rally the population, on 4 November, he added two anarcho-syndicalist ministers to his cabinet. However, Franco's delay had permit-ted the morale of the defenders to be boosted by the arrival, in early November, of aircraft and tanks from the Soviet Union, together with the columns of volunteers known as the International Brigades. Volunteers from the democracies were motivated by anxiety about what defeat for the Spanish Republic might mean for the rest of the world. For Italian, German and Austrian refugees from Fascism and Nazism, Spain was the first real chance to fight back and eventually to go home. The early volunteers arrived in Spain in October and were trained at Albacete. Some were out of work, others were intellectuals, a few adventurers, but all had come to fight fascism.[71]

They reached a Madrid gripped by terror, inundated with refugees and beset by major supply problems. Refugees from the south brought horrific tales of the atrocities carried out by the African columns that were now at the city's outskirts.[72] On 6 November, Largo Caballero, expecting the capital to fall, ordered the evacuation of the government to Valencia, a prudent decision that irrevocably damaged his prestige. The city was left in the hands of a semi-autonomous government, the Communist-dominated Junta de Defensa de Madrid, under the formal presidency of General José Miaja.[73] It was in this context that anarchists and Communists collaborated in the elimination of right-wing prison-ers, especially army officers who had pledged to join their rebel comrades. The greatest single atrocity in the Republican zone was the murder of

2,500 prisoners at the village of Paracuellos de Jarama, on the outskirts of the capital, carried out by anarchists and Communists in collaboration.[74] The unkempt Miaja rallied the population while his brilliant Chief of Staff, Colonel Vicente Rojo, organized the city's forces. The first units of the International Brigades reached Madrid on 8 November. Some had fought in the First World War or else had some experience of military service. Sprinkled among the Spanish defenders at the rate of one to four, the brigaders both boosted their morale and trained them in basic military know-how. Franco's African columns were successfully resisted and, by late November, he had to acknowledge his failure. The besieged capital would hold out for another two and a half years.

However, riven by internal dissensions, and still without a conventional army, the Republic could not capitalize on victory at Madrid. Constant bombing raids exacerbated the refugee problem. On 4 December alone, German aircraft unloaded 36 tons of bombs. Many were left homeless and others suffered acute hunger, queueing for hours for tiny rations of beans, rice and bread, often in vain.[75] In contrast, Franco's forces were soon strengthened by nearly 50,000 Italian 'volunteers' shipped to Spain between mid-December 1936 and mid-February 1937. This Corpo di Truppe Volontarie (CTV) consisted of Fascist militiamen, hastily recruited workers and some regular troops.[76] Franco now made a series of attempts to encircle the capital. At the battles of Boadilla (December 1936), Jarama (February 1937) and Guadalajara (March 1937), his forces were beaten back albeit at enormous cost to the Republic. The defence of Madrid had meant the neglect of other Republican fronts, particularly in the case of Malaga. Defended only by poorly armed militiamen, it fell to the CTV in early February. That Mussolini could claim the triumph caused Franco intense chagrin.[77] The loss of Malaga destroyed the myth of Largo Caballero as an effective war leader. He had slept through the final hours of the city. His incompetence was exposed and the Communists were now determined to remove him.[78]

Franco saw no easy victories near Madrid. At the Jarama, the Nationalist front had advanced a few kilometres, but failed to make the key strategic gain of cutting the road to Valencia. In heavy rain and piercing wind, with poor communications, the rebels lost 20,000 and the Republicans 25,000 including some of the best British and American members of the Brigades. The British contingent was almost wiped out in one afternoon.[79] In March, Franco made further efforts to encircle Madrid by attacking near Guadalajara, 60 kilometres north-east of Madrid. He was torn between his need for Italian aid and concern that an unstoppable Italian attack directed from Rome would see him humiliated by having to accept victories benevolently bestowed by Mussolini. The Duce wanted a spectacular triumph; Franco proceeded as if the Italians were just a diversion for his beleaguered troops in the Jarama. Accordingly, he failed to provide the support expected by the Italians for what they perceived as a major joint operation. Caught in heavy snow and sleet, the reluctant Italian volunteers were inadequately prepared and clothed, many dressed in colonial uniforms. Stranded on muddy improvised airfields, their aircraft made perfect targets for the Republican fighters flying from permanent runways. The consequence was the defeat of the CTV.[80]

The rebel failure at Guadalajara imposed on Franco a momentous strategic volte-face. Evidence that the Republic was concentrating its best troops in the centre of Spain and neglecting other fronts led him reluctantly to abandon his obsession with Madrid and to destroy the Republic by instalments elsewhere. By late March, priority was being shifted to operations in the north aimed at the seizure of the armaments factories and coal, iron and steel reserves of the Basque provinces.[81] In March, Mola led 40,000 troops in an assault on the Basque Country. This was accompanied by a largely fictitious naval blockade aimed at starving the population of Bilbao, a violation of the freedom of international waters. It was countenanced by the British Conservative government which pressured British merchant ships not to take supplies to Bilbao, citing the largely non-existent blockade to justify what was effectively support for Franco. Its hypocrisy was exposed by the *Times* journalist George Steer and Labour and Liberal MPs.[82]

Even after Guadalajara, the rebels still held the initiative since each reverse for Franco saw his Axis allies increase their support. Nevertheless, anxious to speed up his war effort, they advocated the use of terror bombing. In a rehearsal for the Blitzkrieg in Poland and France, Guernica was annihilated on 26 April 1937. That the operation was designed to cause the greatest possible number of civilian victims may be deduced from the choice of projectiles – a combination of explosive bombs and light incendiaries. The first targets were the municipal water tanks and the fire station, to prevent the fires being put out. Terrified citizens who fled to the surrounding fields were herded back into the town by the machine-gun strafing of Heinkel He 51 fighters that circled the town in what the German commander, Wolfram von Richthofen, called 'the ring of fire'. The effect on Basque morale undermined the defence of the capital, Bilbao, which fell on 19 June.[83]

Victory in the Basque Country was accompanied by a political triumph for Franco that both eliminated divisions among his supporters and created a mass political movement. This process was masterminded by his brother Nicolás and his brother-in-law, Ramón Serrano Súñer. They cunningly plotted the unification of the two largest organizations within the rebel coalition – the Falange and the Carlist Traditional Communion. First, they exploited a bitter power struggle between the two principal groups within the Falange, the more radical fascists led by the proletarian Manuel Hedilla and the so-called 'legitimists' of relatives and friends of José Antonio Primo de Rivera led by Agustín Aznar. They orchestrated a clash in Salamanca in mid-April which gave Franco the excuse to arrest the Aznar faction. On 18 April, Hedilla was made National Chief of the Falange. However, on the next day, a decree of unification – drafted without consultation with either Hedilla or the Carlists – announced the creation of a united Falange Española Tradicionalista y de las Juntas de Ofensiva Nacional Sindicalista. When Hedilla protested, he was arrested on 25 April, tried and given a death sentence, commuted to four years' imprisonment. Thereafter, the Movimiento (Movement), as the new single party was known, had little or no political autonomy and became a corrupt machine for the distribution of patronage.[84] Franco similarly had few competitors within the army. Sanjurjo had been killed at the outset, Goded and Fanjul executed by the Republicans in August 1936. The only potential rival was Mola and he was killed in an air crash on 3 June 1937.

While Franco eliminated internal dissent, the Republic, in addition to the hostile international environment, faced massive internal problems. The collapse of the bourgeois state in the first days of the war had seen the rapid emergence of revolutionary organs of parallel power – the committees and militias linked to left-wing unions and parties. A collectivization of agriculture and industry took place. Exhilarating to participants and foreign observers like George Orwell, the great collectivist experiments begun in the autumn of 1936 did little to create a war machine. Opposing beliefs about whether to prioritize war or revolution saw an undeclared internal mini-civil war simmering until the defeat of the revolutionary elements in May 1937.[85] Liberal Republicans and moderate Socialists believed that a conventional state apparatus, with central control of the economy and of mass mobilization, was essential for an efficacious war effort. The Communists and the Russian advisers agreed and they hoped that halting the revolutionary activities of Trotskyists and anarchists would reassure the bourgeois democracies being courted by the Soviet Union.[86]

However, there was a problem in the person of the Prime Minister. The British correspondent Philip Jordan defined Largo Caballero as 'that shabby myth whose vanity did so much to dissipate the early strength of Republican Spain.'[87] From February 1937, the Communists were seeking ways to remove him but were aware that the anarchists were determined to keep the 'Spanish Lenin' in power.[88] Ironically, he had been the figure-head behind whom the process began of pacifying the revolutionary elements. On 1 February 1937, in a speech to the Cortes, he exposed the limits of his own revolutionary bluster, declaring, 'there have been enough experiments'. He had clawed back for the central state the revolutionary advances of the summer of 1936, nationalized collectivized industries and militarized the militias.[89] Nevertheless, he now faced an alliance of Republicans, moderate Socialists and Communists determined to curtail even further the proletarian revolution.

Defeat at Malaga had convinced the Communists and their Russian advisers that there had been not just incompetence but also sabotage and treachery. This put the spotlight on the local 'Trotskyists', the Partido Obrero de Unificación Marxista, led by Trotsky's erstwhile, but now estranged, secretary Andreu Nin. Events came to a head in May 1937 in Barcelona where political conflict was intensified by economic and social distress. The arrival of 350,000 refugees had led inevitably to shortages and inflation which provoked bread riots. The Generalitat and the Catalan Communist Party, the Partit Socialista Unificat de Catalunya (PSUC), were already on a collision course with the CNT and the POUM over control of war industries, rural and industrial collectives, the autonomy of anarchist militias, and public order. Determined to put an end to anarchist excesses, Companys had already re-established conventional police forces in October.[90]

On 3 May, the crisis exploded in Barcelona when a Generalitat raid to seize the central telephone exchange from the CNT detonated an outbreak of street fighting – a small-scale civil war within the civil war. Barricades went up in the city centre. The CNT, the POUM and the revolutionary anarchist group, the Friends of Durruti, confronted the forces of the Generalitat and the PSUC over several days. Far from being planned by the Communists, reports from Barcelona to Moscow show that the events shocked them. Nevertheless, the Communists and moderate Socialists seized the chance to break the power of the CNT and limit that of the Generalitat. The CNT was confronted with the dilemma that to win in Barcelona meant combating the Generalitat and defeating both the central Republican government and the Francoists. The Generalitat's Ministry of Defence was held by Francisco Isgleas Piarnau of the CNT and his deputy, Juan Manuel Molina. They confidently instructed CNT militia units not to return to Barcelona from Aragon since they controlled the principal garrisons in Barcelona and also had anti-aircraft and coastal artillery batteries trained on the Generalitat building. Nevertheless, faced with the enormity of what was involved, the CNT leadership reluctantly ordered their militants to lay down their arms. The government in Valencia provided the decisive police reinforcements on 7 May which determined the outcome. All this was happening as the Basque Country was falling to Franco.[91]

The entire cabinet, Republicans, Socialist and Communist ministers, and President Azaña, were by now exasperated by Largo Caballero's ineptitude. Giral told Azaña that, when he and other ministers asked Largo Caballero about the progress of the war effort, he would reply, 'You will find out by reading the papers.'[92] At a fractious cabinet meeting on 13 May, the PCE ministers Jesús Hernández and Vicente Uribe demanded stronger measures in public order, the dissolution of the POUM and the arrest of its leaders. Largo Caballero, determined to remove the Communists, refused and, as he had hoped, the two Communist ministers resigned. However, Prieto and Negrín announced that they could not remain in the government without them. Largo was forced to resign.[93] Stalin had been willing to see Largo Caballero remain as Prime Minister but not as Minister of War. His Socialist colleagues also wanted to see him replaced as Minister of War by Prieto.[94] The premiership was offered to Dr Juan Negrín after Prieto refused, preferring to take overall charge of the war effort in a new Ministry of National Defence combining the Ministries of War and of Navy and Air. Two weeks later, Azaña noted his satisfaction with Negrín's energy and decisiveness: 'Now when

I speak with the Prime Minister, I no longer feel that I am talking to a dead man.'[95]

Thereafter, Largo Caballero devoted his efforts to undermining the Republican government. After the war, the PSOE General Secretary, Ramón Lamoneda, wrote: 'the obstinate old rogue Caballero, a master of stubbornness, a back-street shyster who set new standards of dishonesty, managed to palm on to others the blame for the disasters he imposed on the party between 1933 and 1937. He thereby went into exile free of responsibility for the wartime period, jumping on the anti-Negrín band-wagon of the enemies of the Republic as if Spain had been an earthly paradise while he was in government.' Lamoneda concluded that Caballero's behaviour after his loss of power was aimed at preparing a comfortable exile for himself and his followers – projecting anti-communism 'to go into exile bleached of all traces of red, reneging on his recent Russophilia – Oh, the Spanish Lenin – and making themselves agreeable to the police, to the bourgeoisie and to the reactionary governments'.[96]

In the wake of the May 1937 crisis, there were arrests of CNT and, even more so, of POUM militants. Andreu Nin and the other POUM leaders had far exceeded the CNT in the militancy of their revolutionary pronouncements. However, the POUM was merely suspended pending an investigation into its possible criminal activity and officially dissolved only after the trial in October 1938.[97] The Russian security services made the elimination of Nin a major objective. The NKVD chief in Spain, Aleksandr Orlov, orchestrated an elaborate plot to frame Nin as a German agent. Nin was arrested and, held in the custody of Orlov in Alcalá de Henares, assassinated there by NKVD agents, in late July 1937, after a charade aiming to demonstrate that he had been liberated by the Gestapo.[98]

While recognizing that Prieto was absolutely the man to run the war effort, Azaña was concerned that his volatility would make him a poor choice as Prime Minister. He preferred Negrín, 'still young, intelligent, cultivated, he knows what the problems are and understands them; and can prioritize and see issues in context'.[99] The scale of what Negrín had undertaken was soon revealed. Barely two weeks later, Bilbao fell and he had to deal with the reaction of Prieto. Prieto was inconsolable, stating, 'I have judged myself so severely for my own responsibility that, not only did I send the prime minister a letter of resignation, but I also contemplated suicide.'[100] Negrín managed to persuade him to remain at the Ministry of National Defence. Faced with the growing advantages enjoyed by Franco, Negrín put his faith in the brilliant strategist Colonel Vicente Rojo, who tried to halt the rebels' inexorable progress by a series of diversionary offensives. At Brunete, in arid scrubland west of Madrid, on 6 July, 50,000 troops smashed through enemy lines, but Franco had enough reinforcements to plug the gap and considerable air superiority. For ten days, in one of the bloodiest encounters of the war, the Republicans were pounded by air and artillery attacks. At enormous cost in men and equipment, the Brunete offensive delayed only slightly the eventual collapse of the north. In a battle involving 90,000 men, nearly 40,000 were killed or wounded. Brunete itself was razed to the ground.[101] As would happen in subsequent battles, Franco was able to bring up reinforcements with a fleet of trucks, supplied on credit by the Ford Motor Company. The pro-Nazi President of the Texaco oil company, Thorkild Rieber, supplied rebel fuel needs also on credit. The risks were guaranteed by March, who also purchased fuel for the rebels from other sources.[102]

The arrival of Negrín as Prime Minister curtailed some, albeit not all, of the chaos, inefficiency and corruption characteristic of the Largo Caballero government. Negrín's cabinet contained nine ministers as against Largo's eighteen. José Giral, on taking over the Foreign Ministry, discovered that there were hardly any archives. He was horrified to discover that 600 diplomatic passports had been issued in the first five months of 1937 and that the diplomatic bag was used for personal business including contraband. Even more alarming was his discovery of the huge profits being made by foreign embassies in return for certificates of naturalization, passports and refuge for Francoist supporters. Negrín told Azaña about the persistence of the corrupt habits associated with the Radical Party, noting that Diego Martínez Barrio, President of the Cortes, was using his influence to get lucrative government jobs for fellow members of Unión Republicana. Azaña was not surprised since all political groups, even the CNT–FAI, were doing the same.[103]

Azaña feared that the armed forces were so riddled with fifth columnists that the plans of Rojo were frequently known in advance by the Francoist General Staff.[104] This was not always the case. In August 1937, Rojo made a bold pincer movement against Zaragoza. At the small town of Belchite, as at Brunete, the Republicans gained an initial advantage, but lacked the force for the killer blow. Thereafter, the rebel army, amply supplied with Italian troops and equipment, captured Santander on 26 August and took 45,000 prisoners.[105] Asturias was quickly mopped up during September and October. Northern industry was now at the service of the rebels. This gave them a decisive advantage to add to their already considerable superiority in men, tanks and aeroplanes. Prieto again offered his resignation but it was refused by Negrín. That the military balance was tipping increasingly towards Franco could be deduced from the transfer of the Republican government from Valencia to Barcelona in early November 1937. This was justified as facilitating the mobilization of the resources of Catalonia for the war effort, but there was an element of defeatism in the government's removal to a place nearer the French frontier prior to the anticipated rebel push against Valencia.[106]

In December 1937, Rojo launched a pre-emptive attack against Teruel, in the hope of diverting Franco's latest assault on Madrid. In bitter cold, his plan initially worked. Surprise was achieved and the rebels, caught unawares, found their aeroplanes grounded by the weather. For the first time, Republican forces captured an enemy-held provincial capital, Teruel falling on 8 January 1938. It would have made strategic sense for Franco to abandon Teruel and press ahead with his plans to cut off Madrid. The capture of Madrid would have hastened the end of the war cheaply since Rojo had thrown everything into the Teruel offensive. However, Franco could not permit the enemy such successes. In April 1937, he had told the Italian Ambassador that his aim was 'the necessarily slow task of redemption and pacification'. This meant crushing the Republican army completely, a project which, along with the repression in the captured areas, was intended to lay the foundations for an enduring dictatorship. It was a strategic vision that appalled his Axis allies and many of his own generals.[107] Although at heavy cost to his own forces, Franco could not resist the opportunity to destroy a large body of the Republic's best units. Accordingly, the Republican triumph was short-lived and Rojo's forces were dislodged after six weeks of heavy battering by artillery and bombers. After another costly defence of a small advance, the Republicans had to retreat on 21 February 1938, when Teruel was about to be encircled. The casualties on both sides had been enormous. In trying to hold a gain of little strategic importance, the Republic suffered disastrous losses in men and equipment.[108]

The Republicans were exhausted, short of guns and ammunition and demoralized after Teruel. The successive breakdowns of Rojo's three offensives at Brunete, Belchite and Teruel demonstrated that the sheer material superiority enjoyed by Franco's forces would always prevail over the courage of the loyalist troops. Each time, the Republicans were unable to follow up their initial advantage. By early 1938, Franco had a 20 per cent advantage in terms of men and an overwhelming one in terms of aircraft, artillery and other equipment.[109] His exploitation of that superiority in regaining Teruel made it the turning point of the war. He seized the initiative with a huge offensive through Aragon and Castellón towards the sea. A hundred thousand troops, 200 tanks and nearly 1,000 German and Italian aircraft began a rapid advance on 7 March. By early April, the rebels had reached Lerida and then moved down the Ebro valley cutting off Catalonia from the rest of the Republic. By 15 April, they had captured 6,400 square kilometres of territory and reached the Mediterranean. Franco's forces had lost around 350 dead and 1,200 wounded. The Republican dead numbered nearly 5,000 and over 5,500 men fell prisoner.[110] The brutal repression inflicted by Franco's forces as they invaded first Lleida then Tarragona revealed a savage anti-Catalanism. An appalled Cambó commented prophetically that this would embitter future relations between Catalonia and Spain.[111]

In parallel with the Republic's military reverses, the home front saw intensifying food shortages exacerbated by floods of refugees.[112] Morale was eroded on the Mediterranean coast by ever more frequent and intense bombing raids. Barcelona was hit badly in December 1937 and March 1938. Civilian areas, crammed with refugees, were targeted.[113] With the Republic's exiguous foreign currency and gold reserves devoted to arms procurement, food imports were limited. In contrast, the rebels controlled the wheat- and cattle-producing areas of western Andalusia, Extremadura and Castile. The Republic's agricultural land was dwindling. Moreover, the armed forces desperately scavenged eggs, poultry, fruit and vegetables during the frantic retreat through Aragon to Catalonia in the spring of 1938. With rations limited to 150 grams of rice, beans or lentils, despite aid efforts from the Quakers, deaths from malnutrition among children and the elderly quadrupled between 1936 and 1938.[114]

After his triumph in Aragon, always more interested in the total destruction of the Republican forces than in rapid victory, Franco ignored the opportunity to turn against a poorly defended Barcelona.[115] Instead, in July, he launched a major attack on Valencia. Dogged Republican defence made progress slow and exhausting but, by 23 July 1938, the city was under direct threat, with the Nationalists only 40 kilometres away.[116] Vicente Rojo responded with a spectacular diversion in the form of a great push across the River Ebro to restore contact with Catalonia. The army that Rojo was able to put into the field included recent conscripts as old as thirty-five and as young as sixteen who received only five days' training. This had a negative impact on the Catalan economy and society. War weariness, already generated by hunger and the billeting of troops, was intensified by conscription's drain on the labour force.

In the hardest-fought battle of the war, 80,000 men crossed the river and broke through the Francoist lines, although at great cost to the International Brigades. By 1 August, they had reached Gandesa. However, Franco's fleet of trucks enabled reinforcements to be rushed in. His massive air and artillery superiority saw the Republicans subjected to three months of fierce bombardment in sweltering heat. By mid-November, at horrendous cost in casualties, the Francoists had pushed the Republicans out of the territory captured in July. Approximately 6,100 Francoists and 7,150 Republicans were killed and, in roughly similar proportions, about 110,000 were wounded. They left behind them many dead and much precious materiel.[117]

More than the losses on the battlefield, the greatest defeat was Munich. Part of the logic behind the Ebro offensive had been to keep the war going until the Western democracies woke up to the danger from the Axis. The outbreak of a general European war would, Negrín hoped, see the Republic aligned with France, Britain and Russia against Germany and Italy. His hopes were dashed when the Republic was virtually sentenced to death by the British reaction to the Czechoslovakian crisis. British foreign policy had long since been orientated in favour of a Francoist victory. Rather than risk war with Hitler, Chamberlain surrendered Czechoslovakia at the Munich Agreement of 29 September 1938. This made Stalin rethink his strategy on Spain. The Republic now stared defeat in the face. Franco's logistical superiority in terms of air cover, artillery and troop numbers was greater than ever. Confident that, after Munich, the Republic would not find salvation in a European war, Franco gathered over 30,000 fresh troops. He granted extensive mining concessions to the Third Reich in return for substantial deliveries of equipment.[118] The Ebro was a strategic disaster for the Republic since it used up vast quantities of equipment and opened the way to the rebel conquest of Catalonia. Barcelona fell on 26 January 1939 and 450,000 Republicans trudged into exile.[119]

Around 30 per cent of territory in central and south-eastern Spain remained to the Republic. Negrín still nurtured hopes of hanging on until a European war started. However, in Madrid, on 5 March, the commander of the Republican Army of the Centre, Colonel Segismundo Casado, revolted against the Republican government. He claimed in his highly mendacious memoirs that he did so to stop more senseless slaughter but, as his close links with the Francoist fifth column have revealed, his principal aim was to secure his own future. He exploited the resentments of both the supporters of Largo Caballero and the anarchists against Negrín and the Communists. He also convinced many army officers that he could secure their pensions in a Francoist future. His action received wide support because it tapped into mass hunger and demoralization. The coup derived a veneer of legitimacy from the participation of the distinguished Socialist philosophy professor Julián Besteiro. Himself in contact with the fifth column, he naively believed that the post-war repression would be minimal. The coup sparked off a six-day civil war within the Republican zone and rendered pointless the bloodshed and the sacrifices of the previous three years. Negrín was forced into exile and Casado defeated pro-Communist forces. His promises of Franco's benevolence came to naught and his Junta de Defensa Nacional failed to arrange the evacuation of the tens of thousands under threat from the Francoists. He thereby guaranteed a major humanitarian disaster.[120]

Franco's forces entered an eerily silent Madrid on 27 March. Their victory was institutionalized as the Franco dictatorship. The repression of the defeated enmeshed Franco's coalition of supporters in what has been called 'the covenant of blood', uniting them in fear of retribution should the Republicans ever return. For many Spaniards, the war was not over. Until the early 1950s, Franco's armed forces were engaged in operations against armed groups vainly attempting to reverse the result of the war. It is remarkable that there was any opposition at all other than the purely passive. The Spanish left had been militarily defeated and its most dynamic and representative cadres had been decimated during three years of bloodshed. Around 450,000 Republicans went into exile, where those who did not have the luck to reach Latin America were quickly swept up by the whirlwind of world war. Those left behind quickly realized that Francoist policy towards the defeated would be every bit as brutal as the wartime purges of captured territory. Moreover, the anti-Francoist forces were hindered by internal divisions. Pre-existing conflicts within the left were multiplied by bitter mutual recriminations about responsibility for defeat. The history of the anti-Francoist opposition in the 1940s was the story of continual and debilitating fragmentation.

Francisco Franco, as Generalísimo and his wife, Carmen Polo.

12

World War: Survival, Hypocrisy and Profit, 1939–1945

Armed struggle against the dictatorship, from 1939 to 1944, came from the so-called *huídos* or fugitives, Republicans who took to the hills rather than surrender. The repression, hunger, families destroyed by death and exile and, above all, the intense weariness left by the titanic struggles of the previous three years ensured that there would be no popular uprising. The *huídos* never constituted a threat to the regime. Their primary goal was survival.[1] Things would change in 1944 when the exiles who had played a key role in the French resistance turned their gaze to Spain as defeat for the Germans approached.

Until then, Franco's concerns for his future related to rivals within his own coalition. He would demonstrate masterly skill in manipulating the 'families', involving them in corruption, fomenting their mutual suspicions to leave them reliant on the supreme arbiter. The ability to estimate almost instantly the weakness and/or the price of a man enabled him to secure loyalty with the promise of a ministry, an embassy, a military promotion, a job in a state enterprise, a decoration, an import licence or just a box of cigars. His choice of ministers was less to do with their potential competence than with his moves on the political chessboard. Francesc Cambó attributed the basis of his success to 'His agile left hand. He toys with men – especially his generals – with consummate skill.'[2]

Basking in constant adulation, Franco now saw himself as the imperial heir to Charles V and Philip II, as the natural partner of Hitler and Mussolini, able to build a new colonial empire in North Africa. He established absolute power with the Law of the Head of State on 8 August 1939 which gave him 'the supreme power to issue laws of a general nature' and to issue specific decrees and laws without discussing them first with the cabinet 'when reasons of urgency so advise.'[3] It was power of a kind previously enjoyed only by the kings of medieval Spain. His perception of himself as heir to the great warrior kings of a glorious imperial past was enshrined in the ceremonial and choreography of his regime. However, even before the civil war was over, on 9 February, a law (not published in the official gazette as it was legally supposed to be) was introduced that created a special fund ostensibly to stimulate exports. It effectively gave the Minister of Industry and Commerce the power to distribute those 'bonuses, compensations and returns' to counteract the negative impact on exports produced by a series of mysterious factors. These were blamed on the destruction caused by the enemy but were really the consequence of internal inflation and a hugely overvalued peseta. Since all import and export operations were subject to ministerial authorization, the opportunities for profit to those who granted the authorizations were massive.[4]

The regime's central pillar until well after the Second World War would be repression. Over a million Spaniards spent time in prison or in labour camps while tens of thousands were executed. As was revealed both by Franco's deliberately slow war effort and in explicit interviews, he was making an investment in terror. With battlefield hostilities over, the war against the Republic would continue in military courts, in prisons and concentration camps, in labour battalions and, with the help of the Gestapo, in the pursuit, and subsequent execution, of prominent exiles such as Lluís Companys and Julián Zugazagoitia. The immediate tasks were the classification and punishment of those trapped in the eastern seaports and the purging of the recently conquered provinces. Hundreds of thousands of prisoners were confined in overcrowded, unhygienic camps and improvised prisons where untold numbers died of malnutrition, disease, torture and beatings. Imprisoned women also endured horrendous sexual abuse and the theft of their children. The long-term institutionalization of Franco's victory required the perfection of the machinery of state terror to protect and oversee the original investment. For that reason, the martial law declared in July 1936 was not rescinded until 1948.[5]

With hundreds of thousands of workers either in exile or in prisons or concentration camps, Spain faced a major labour shortage. The regime's answer was the ruthless exploitation of prisoners, a measure justified by the regime's pseudo-religious rhetoric of the need for the defeated to seek redemption through sacrifice. The device whereby sentences were reduced in return for work facilitated the capital accumulation behind the economic boom of the 1960s. Prisoners were rented out to private companies. The forced – effectively slave – labour of penal columns used in mines, railway building and the reconstruction of the so-called 'devastated regions' made immense fortunes for construction giants, such as Banús Hermanos, San Román, Huarte, Agromán and Dragados y Construcciones, railway companies such as Norte, MZA and Renfe, mining concerns such as Carbones Asturianos, Minera Estaño Silleda, Duro Felguera, Minería Industrial Pirenaica and Minas de Sillada and metallurgical and shipbuilding enterprises such as Babcock & Wilcox, Astilleros de Cádiz and La Maquinista Terrestre. Many prisoners died working in excessively dangerous conditions in coal and mercury mines.[6]

The gigantic irrigation scheme, the Canal de Riegos del Bajo Guadalquivir, was carried out by prisoners who were kept in appalling conditions. It greatly increased the productivity of the large estates of the region and the profits of the landowners who had hitherto made little effort to resolve the problem of constant drought.[7] The destruction of trade unions permitted starvation wages which in turn allowed banks, industry and the landholding classes to record spectacular increases in profits. An extreme example of the corrupt exploitation of Republican prisoners was Franco's personal caprice, the gigantic basilica and towering cross of the mausoleum of the Valle de los Caídos, a monument to his victory which revealed his megalomaniac concept of his own place in history. Twenty thousand prisoners were employed, on minimal wages, in its construction. Many died from malnutrition and others were killed or badly injured in accidents.[8]

The repressive judicial system was based on the administrative machinery and the pseudo-legal framework developed throughout the war. The bizarre central premise of the subsequent trials was described by Ramón Serrano Súñer as 'back-to-front justice.'[9] It deemed those who had legitimately opposed the coup of 1936 to be guilty of military rebellion, and thus subject to court martial and the death sentence. The sophistry went further in that all left-wing or trade union activities from the beginning of October 1934 were regarded as 'support for military rebellion' on the grounds that they had contributed to the alleged disorder which necessitated the military coup which was, of course, the only rebellion.[10] This fiction was the basis of the thousands of subsequent summary courts martial. The accused were usually denied the possibility of defending themselves. The military would choose the judge, the prosecutor and the defence 'lawyer', this latter always being an officer junior to the judge and prosecutor. Groups of prisoners, unknown to one another and accused of notably different offences, would be tried together. The 'case' against them usually consisted of accusations read out without evidence. They were not permitted to call witnesses or present any evidence of their own. In 'emergency summary trials', the charges were not even read out. In no cases were appeals permitted.[11]

The repression was not confined to terror. The dictatorship was also a regime of pillage. Hundreds of thousands of people lost their livelihoods as public positions became the monopoly of, often unqualified, regime supporters. Property was confiscated on a colossal scale through the juridical monstrosity of the Law of Political Responsibilities, announced in Burgos on 9 February 1939. It ensured the punishment of any Republican who had either opposed the military rebellion or, through the 'crime' of 'serious passivity', not supported it. The punishments involved heavy fines and/or the confiscation of property ranging from businesses and houses, via bank savings and shareholdings, to household furniture, crockery and cutlery. Through systematic extortion, the law did not just punish the defeated but also made them pay for the war that had been inflicted upon them. It was applied retroactively and criminalized activities, from membership of a political party to government service, that were perfectly legal when they were carried out. Fines imposed on dead or exiled Republicans were collected by the confiscation of their families' goods.[12]

Systematic persecution would continue in virtually every aspect of daily life well into the 1950s. Republicans would suffer grinding poverty, with families deprived of their menfolk, women forced into prostitution, workers obliged to take starvation wages and a rationing system which intensified social division. The impact on the defeated has to be seen in a context of the economic consequences of the war. The destruction of infrastructure and the scale of wartime casualties and exile constituted an incalculable cost. Afflicted by droughts and harvest failure, the Second World War years in Spain were characterized not only by intense hunger, especially for the defeated, but also by generalized corruption. Social and economic privation were an additional mechanism of humiliation for the defeated.[13]

Agricultural production fell to pre-1914 standards as a consequence of the loss of machinery and animal power, hostile climatic conditions and also the dismemberment of the labour force. During the years of the Second World War, urgently needed agricultural products were exported to pay Franco's debt to Hitler. Believing himself to be an economist of genius, Franco rashly adopted fascist-style policies of autarky without taking into account the reality that Spain did not possess the necessary technological and industrial base.[14] His first peacetime government was announced on 9 August 1939. Franco's lifelong friend, and wartime Minister of Industry and Commerce, Juan Antonio Suanzes was replaced by the even more incompetent Luis Alarcón de la Lastra, an aristocratic landowner who had been an artillery commander during the civil war. To the alarm of José Larraz, the able new Finance Minister, days before Alarcón entered the ministry he was seen swotting up on basic economics. Alarcón, who obeyed Franco in everything, was to be one of his most incompetent ministers and lasted for only fourteen months.[15]

When Franco explained to Larraz his commitment to autarky and his conviction that Spain would soon be a major military power, the new Minister was shocked. Franco told him at interminable length that he refused to seek foreign credits and that a massive modernization of the army, navy and air force could be paid for by simply printing money. Larraz was appalled by the Caudillo's combination of ignorance and prejudice. He was even more alarmed by inconsequential cabinet meetings in which Franco declared his plans and the only discussion was of issues like the price of rope sandals. His attempts to impose an austere and realistic economic policy clashed with Franco's wild fantasies.[16] For instance, on 1 September 1939, Franco announced the construction of nearly 200 naval vessels, including four battleships, fifty-four destroyers and fifty submarines. He frequently informed Larraz that money printed for public works did not cause inflation. Among other schemes never carried out, and likened by Larraz to the ideas of Jules Verne, were a tunnel under the Straits of Gibraltar, a canal from the Bay of Biscay to the Mediterranean and a massive house-building project.[17] The stunned Minister regarded the Caudillo's conviction of his own economic omniscience as laughable. Realizing that there was no point arguing with him, Larraz devoted himself to some basic reform of the tax system and to unifying the monetary systems of the two wartime zones, a process that saw the savings of the defeated Republicans effectively pillaged. All banknotes issued in the Republican zone during the war were made valueless and an abusive discount was applied to bank accounts. Larraz was replaced in May 1941.[18]

In October 1939, Franco announced a simplistic ten-year plan for Spain's future prosperity based on misplaced optimism in the country's capacity to substitute imports, increase exports, rely on its own raw materials and do so without foreign investment, despite negligible fuel sources. For ideological reasons and on the advice of Suanzes, with whom he shared his flawed comprehension of economics, Franco turned his back on the economic growth that neutrality had brought to Spain during the First World War. He believed that he could convert Spain into a great military power by a combination of autarky and public works schemes financed simply by printing money. His disastrous decision to maintain the peseta at a dramatically overvalued rate undermined exports. A lack of foreign currency limited imports and provoked acute shortages.[19]

These egregious errors were compounded by Franco's touchingly naive faith in magical wheezes. In the late 1930s, he had been persuaded that he could create international pre-eminence with unlimited gold reserves provided by an alchemist, a mysterious Hindu named Savarpoldi Hammaralt who may have been a British agent. To facilitate Hammaralt's work, Franco put the science laboratories of the University of Salamanca at his disposal. This may have been behind his rash declaration in his end-of-year message in 1939 that Spain possessed gigantic gold reserves, which it certainly did not.[20] Equally astonishing was his belief in the imaginary synthetic gasoline offered to him by an Austrian petty thief and confidence trickster, Albert von Filek. Franco was sure that Filek's unbounded admiration for him was why he rejected spectacular international offers for his invention in order to give it to the Caudillo. Enthusiasts for the idea included Alarcón de la Lastra, Franco's wife Carmen and his brother-in-law, Felipe Polo. It has been alleged that the Franco family stood to make a significant profit from the project. Eventually, after substantial government funds had been invested in the project, doubts were expressed by Larraz and the Falangist businessman Demetrio Carceller and proper tests were carried out, with the result that the deception was exposed and Filek imprisoned.[21]

The consequences of autarky for the bulk of the population were exacerbated by the incapacity of the state to redistribute wealth or even remedy the systematic fraud of the tax system.[22] The principal instrument of autarky was the Instituto Nacional de Industria under the direction of Suanzes. On 25 September 1941, Suanzes told Franco that he could easily industrialize Spain, and he informed representatives of German industry that his intention was 'to eliminate the influence of British capital'. His interventionist policies, particularly in terms of import control, would have disastrous effects.[23]

Shortages necessitated rationing which led to black-marketeering and corruption on a spectacular scale. The suffering which the Spanish people had to undergo throughout the years of hunger in the 1940s, in large part as a result of Franco's economic delusions, is incalculable. The defeated lived on the verge of starvation.[24] In contrast, those who financed his war effort were generously recompensed. Prominent supporters were rewarded with contracts to supply ministries with goods or services or for public works. Others benefited from the granting of public positions, often to untrained and incompetent individuals who were incapable of replacing those who were either dead, in exile, in prison or starving. The greatest institutionalized corruption was the use of the state apparatus for private benefit. Major beneficiaries were those with contacts in the ministries and those who simply bribed ministers. The gatekeepers of access to Franco were his brother Nicolás, his sister Pilar and his brother-in-law Felipe Polo, from all of whom could be purchased letters of introduction to ministers.[25]

Those who could secure import licences for scarce products, such as, needless to say, Juan March, made spectacular profits. An example was the Segarra footwear company which, holding the monopoly of supplies to the armed forces, was able to import leather that contributed to its civilian production. One of the regime's more austere generals, Rafael Latorre Roja, commented on Nicolás Franco:

apart from the good luck of getting the magnificent Lisbon embassy, where he enjoys himself to excess and like a heathen, he is the chairman, deputy chairman or a director of innumerable companies created with the support and under the protection of the regime. What enormities and immoralities could be told about this! Who was Nicolás Franco in industry and finance and what was his economic position in 1936? Just one example: a factory in Valladolid, of whose board of directors he was chairman, was going from bad to worse until one fine day it was decreed that the foreign products that it needed to import would be protected from customs duties.[26]

There was corruption everywhere. The espionage services of the Falange reported to Franco that a subscription in support of the División Azul was being skimmed by Miguel Primo de Rivera, the Civil Governor of Madrid, to finance his extravagant lifestyle.[27] When the idealistic Falangist poet Dionisio Ridruejo was received by Franco after being invalided out of the División Azul at the end of April 1942, he reported that, among his comrades, there was much criticism of the corruption in Spain. Franco replied complacently that in other times victors were rewarded with titles of nobility and lands. Since that was now difficult, instead he kept his supporters happy by turning a blind eye to venality. On 7 July, Ridruejo wrote to Franco repeating his criticisms and stating that those who dominated the regime were inept, reactionary and hypocritical mediocrities. He resigned all his posts because of what he described as the 'tragic trick' being played on Spain by the regime. Ridruejo's reward for his frankness was eight months' confinement in the remote town of Ronda.[28]

Franco ignored both the corruption of his supporters and the suffering of the poor consequent on autarky. Malnutrition accounted for the return of diseases long thought eradicated. Both British and German diplomats and Franco's own security service commented with horror on the sight of starving people scavenging from dustbins and fetid rubbish piles.[29] The Minister of War, General José Varela, received letters from senior colleagues complaining about the scandalous inadequacy of rations for soldiers.[30] For the poor, use of the black market, the so-called estraperlo, was an inadequate strategy of survival. Even if not deliberately conceived as such, the black market was an additional instrument of repression. Corrupt local authorities did little to restrain those making the greatest profits while imposing draconian punishment on the small-scale operators. For the wealthy, it guaranteed decent food and luxuries and, for many agricultural producers, it meant huge profits.[31]

The black market facilitated the appearance of an entirely new class of corrupt businessmen. Thanks to their proximity to the regime, it was possible for them to accumulate fortunes. One of the most notorious was Julio Muñoz Ramonet. Because of his family's close links with General

Luis Orgaz, Muñoz Ramonet and his brother received permits for the distribution of cotton. Their speculation with these permits allowed them to ruin around twenty textile factories that they then bought at knock-down prices and relaunched. They had functionaries and judges on their payroll and built up a business empire that included the Hotel Ritz in Barcelona as well as chains of department stores and insurance companies in Spain and banks in Switzerland and the Dominican Republic.[32]

Franco felt no magnanimity towards the vanquished Republicans and saw the repression as a long-term undertaking. In fact, his policies in this regard were of a piece with his identification with the anti-Semitism of the Third Reich. In Madrid on 19 May 1939, at his spectacular victory celebrations, he declared the need to remain alert against 'the Jewish spirit that permitted the alliance of big capital with Marxism' and which 'cannot be extirpated in just one day'.[33] This reflected the explicitly racist rules for entry into Spain introduced eight days earlier by the Ministry of Foreign Affairs. Spaniards and foreigners were required to obtain visas which were refused to anyone who had not supported the Francoist cause. Refusal was automatic for those who 'had a markedly Jewish character, freemasons, and Jews other than those who were proven friends of Franco's Spain'. It was not specified how 'a markedly Jewish character' was to be identified by the consuls to whom application was made.[34] In September 1939, Franco compared atrocities against the clergy by 'the red hordes' with the 'limitless cruelty of an accursed race'. In his New Year's Eve broadcast, he gave thanks in virulently anti-Semitic terms for the expulsion of the Jews in 1492 by Isabel la Católica. On 29 May 1942, he boastfully compared himself to Isabel and praised her for achieving 'racial unity' and laying the foundations of 'a totalitarian and racist policy'.[35]

One of Franco's central beliefs was the 'Jewish–masonic–Bolshevik conspiracy'. He was convinced that Judaism was the ally of both American capitalism and Russian communism.[36] Although the biggest enemy of the three for Franco was always freemasonry, regime media projected a fierce anti-Semitism. The Francoist establishment was aware of the treatment of Jews in Nazi-occupied Europe. Even if the full horrors were not known until 1944, the language used, such as 'filthy and diseased' and 'there are no greater parasites than individuals of Jewish origin', and the repetition of terms like 'the destruction', 'the end' and 'the dissolution' of Judaism leave little doubt regarding the regime's anti-Semitism.[37]

On 5 May 1941, in response to the dangers allegedly posed by Jews resident in Spain, the Director General of Security, the pro-Nazi José Finat Escrivá de Romaní, Conde de Mayalde, ordered the creation of an archive of their names. 'Circular no. 11' was sent to all civil governors, requesting individual reports on 'the Israelites, Spanish and foreign, resident in the province', indicating their political views, their income, their potential danger and any information on them held by the police. The document specified that special attention be paid to Sephardic Jews born in Spain because their assimilation of Spanish habits and culture gave them greater possibilities of 'hiding their origins' and thus facilitating their 'worrying intrigues'.[38] In fact, on 24 June 1940, the Francoist Spanish authorities had blocked the transit from France of several thousand Jewish refugees in possession of Portuguese visas. Moreover, there had been arrests of Jews since late 1940. It is likely that the 'archive' was being prepared to facilitate the deportation of Jews in the event of Spanish entry into the war on the side of the Axis. Allegedly, when Mayalde arrived in Berlin as Ambassador in June 1941, he gave the list to Himmler.[39] There had been a close collaboration between the Francoist police and the Gestapo since 1937.[40] At the behest of Franco himself, his headquarters created the Judaeo-Masonic Section of the military intelligence service which used the lists of supposed Jews and freemasons compiled by Father Juan Tusquets.[41]

Despite the demonstrable anti-Semitism of the Dictator and his regime, a myth was carefully constructed to claim that Franco's regime had saved many Jews from extermination.[42] The myth was further undermined by the dictatorship's policy of providing refuge for many hundreds of Nazi war criminals and thousands of members of the Vichy French militia. By the device of granting them Spanish nationality, it was possible to deny that they had been given asylum. Spaniards previously employed by the Gestapo were incorporated into Franco's security services.[43] Franco himself worked shamelessly at reinventing the past. He would present this outrageous untruth to the North American journalist Merwin K. Hart in San Sebastián on 18 August 1947: 'Having been asked to receive thousands of Jewish children, Spain offered model accommodation, guaranteeing them religious freedom supervised by those doctors of their faith that wished to accompany them. Although, to the grave detriment of those unfortunate creatures, international intrigues prevented this, Spain's noble and tolerant position was clearly demonstrated.'[44]

Franco's anxiety to wipe away the stigma of anti-Semitism was further underlined in the autumn of 1949 with the publication, in French, English and Spanish, of a lengthy pamphlet, *España y los Judíos*. It was a reply to the statement made at the General Assembly of the United Nations by the Ambassador of Israel, Abba Eban, that Franco's dictatorship had been 'an active and sympathetic ally of the regime' that was responsible for the extermination of the Jews and 'had welcomed, accepted, congratulated and upheld the prospect of Nazi supremacy in Europe and the world'.[45] The pamphlet responded with the claim that Franco had saved thousands of Jews from France, French Morocco, Hungary, Bulgaria, Rumania and Greece – in contrast, it alleged, to the indifference of Great Britain.[46] In the immediate aftermath of the collapse of the Third Reich, these myths were a crucial element in the domestic operation mounted to prove the Caudillo's divinely inspired perspicacity and consequent indispensability. Internationally, that propaganda helped keep him in power, providing a flimsy justification for the Western powers, anxious to incorporate Franco into the anti-Communist front of the Cold War, to forget about his innumerable hostile acts of word and deed during the war. Spanish neutrality was indeed crucial to the eventual outcome of the Second World War but it was not the heroic achievement of Franco but rather the consequence of Allied fuel and food diplomacy.[47]

Franco's denunciations of Jewish greed coincided with the accumulation, between 1937 and 1940, of a personal fortune of 34 million pesetas of the period (388 million euros of 2010). The beginning of what would eventually be a considerable property portfolio came in November 1937. José María de Palacio y Abarzuza, Conde de las Almenas, in gratitude for Franco's 'magnificent reconquest of Spain', bequeathed him an estate in the Sierra de Guadarrama near Torrelodones, known as Canto del Pico. Its 820,000 square metres were dominated by a large mansion called the Casa del Viento, which contained many valuable works of art. Almenas died in 1940. The estate was sold by the Franco family in 1988 for 320 million pesetas.[48]

While that gift awaited the death of the Conde, on 5 December 1938 Franco took time off from the war to visit his native La Coruña to take possession of a 'gift' that derived from a combination of corruption and servile adulation. Julio Muñoz Aguilar, Civil Governor of the province, and Pedro Barrié de la Maza, a local businessman, had organized a 'popular' subscription ostensibly to enable the people of the province to express their gratitude for their salvation at the hands of Franco. The proceeds were used for the purchase and extensive renovation of a splendid country house, known as the Pazo de Meirás, which had belonged to the Galician novelist Emilia Pardo Bazán. The house lay in grounds of 110,000 square metres. The renovation was supervised by Carmen Polo who, during the process, was the recipient of many gifts. Some contributions to the scheme were voluntary. However, many people were coerced into contributing and, in the case of public employees, their 'donations' were simply deducted from their salaries. Others contributed for fear of being denounced as disloyal. Muñoz Aguilar was rewarded with the lucrative posts of Head of Franco's Household and administrator of the Patrimonio Nacional of the properties and art treasures of the royal family. Barrié de la Maza was later ennobled by Franco. In May 1939, Franco's propagandist, Víctor Ruiz Albeniz, 'El Tebib Arrumi', wrote an article praising Franco's austerity and claiming that his only wealth was his army salary of 1,500 pesetas monthly. The Pazo estate, subsidized by the provincial administration and the central government, was converted into a profitable agricultural business and sumptuous summer residence, theoretically for the head of state.[49] In 1941, Franco had fraudulently had the property put in his own name, which permitted its subsequent exploitation by his family.[50]

An important source of Franco's disposable wealth was his appropriation of subscriptions ostensibly organized to meet the cost of the rebel war effort. Contribution to these initiatives was usually obligatory. The proceeds were generally kept secret which facilitated the transfer of funds to one of his bank accounts under the name 'National Subscription at the Disposal of General Don Francisco Franco Bahamonde'. This account name was later changed to 'Gifts at the Disposal of the Head of State'. After the civil war, with some of this money, Franco bought a large estate known as Valdefuentes near Móstoles on the outskirts of Madrid. It consisted of 10 million square metres and cost 2.5 million pesetas. By 1953, he would have invested nearly 8 million pesetas in extensive improvements, machinery and buildings. These would see the property producing a healthy annual income. One-third of the property would be eventually be sold by the Franco family for 10 million euros.

These properties were the tip of a colossal iceberg. There were gifts of many kinds ranging from gold medallions to luxury automobiles, including two Hispano Suizas, a Chrysler, a Mercedes, a Cadillac, a Packard and a Lincoln. Franco received from Hitler a Daimler-Benz four-wheel-drive vehicle valued in 2015 prices at nearly 400,000 euros. In 1940, the Compañía Telefónica Nacional de España began to make a monthly payment to Franco of 10,000 pesetas which would have been worth around 100,000 euros in 2010. Franco also obtained over 7.5 million pesetas from the sale of coffee through the black market. The largest part derived from a gift to the Spanish people made in 1939 by the Brazilian dictator Getúlio Vargas of 600 tons of coffee which Franco sold to the Comisaría de Abastecimientos of the Ministry of Industry. The equivalent in modern terms is difficult to calculate but was not less than 400 million euros.[51] The various properties would continue to grow in value and they would generate considerable income after 1945. Similarly, Franco's accumulated cash was invested in stocks and shares. The fortune left on his death would be worth more than 1 billion euros in 2010 values.[52]

Franco was not the only general to be spectacularly enriched during the civil war. In Seville, Queipo de Llano's reign of terror was accompanied by systematic impoverishment of the population of Western Andalusia. He created what Rúben Serém has called the 'Kleptocratic State', 'the economic equivalent of the military scorched earth policy adopted by the Army of Africa', with Seville the testing ground for the rest of rebel Spain.[53] Donations of gold and silver by the better-off were usually voluntary. However, sheer intimidation saw local workers' societies handing over their funds. Numerous more formal devices were invented to facilitate economic plunder. Obligatory fund-raising, effectively organized extortion, had the dual function of financing the war effort and punishing Republicans. 'Subscriptions' were announced for various causes – allegedly to buy aircraft, to support the army, to buy the battlecruiser *España*. With no sense of irony, Queipo praised the patriotic spirit of workers who handed over their wages for the subscriptions. Refusal to cooperate was regarded as subversion punishable with fines for the rich and imprisonment or execution for the poor.[54]

Queipo was one of the greatest beneficiaries of the system. In August 1937, a subscription was launched, apparently at his own initiative, in order to pay him homage in the form of a substantial gift. In his broadcasts, he constantly declared that he had no need of tributes. However, on 16 August, referring to 'the subscription being made as a tribute to my person', he let slip the phrase 'because of my own felicitous initiative'. Within four months, the contributions, including those by the poor, reached the astonishing sum of 2 million pesetas. This permitted the purchase of a magnificent estate called Gambogaz, in Camas on the outskirts of Triana. To mask his personal gain, he used the remaining money to buy land for war wounded and the poor. He also claimed, in his broadcast of 24 December 1937, that Gambogaz was to be used 'for social purposes, to help and improve the lot of agricultural workers and implement agrarian reform'. In fact, it was his personal retreat where, particularly in retirement, he would pursue an interest in horse and cattle breeding.[55]

The personal enrichment of Franco and his supporters was guaranteed. His hopes of national profit lay with the Axis. In fact, even before the outbreak of war, in August 1939, Franco, entirely on his own initiative, had made preparations for an attack on Gibraltar. A year later, he negotiated with Portugal a free hand for the attack and in a letter of 22 September 1940 boasted to Hitler of his preparations.[56] Barely two months after the German invasion of Poland, he proposed to the Chief of the General Staff and the three Army, Navy and Air Force Ministers an ambitious rearmament plan, the mobilization of 2 million men and preparations to close the Straits of Gibraltar to undermine the maritime trade of the two countries seen as Spain's principal enemies, Britain and France.[57] Franco nearly took Spain into war on the Axis side in the summer of 1940 and on several subsequent occasions. Although the most feasible moment had passed by late 1940, Franco experienced his 'Axis temptation' most intensely after the German invasion of Russia in the summer of 1941. In the final analysis, however, his ambitions in foreign policy were restrained by two overriding considerations, his own domestic survival and Spain's limited economic and military capacity for war. Franco's inability to participate in what he fervently hoped would be an Axis victory was recast by his propaganda apparatus into the myth that, by dint of astute caution, he hoodwinked Hitler and bravely kept Spain out of the Second World War.[58]

Inevitably, in 1940, the strategic importance of Spain made Franco the object of courtship by both sides, the Germans to bring him into the war and the British to keep him out. The British used the carrot and stick made available by the naval dominance that enabled them to control Spanish supplies of food and fuel. The Germans on the other hand took it for granted that Franco would do what they wanted without any special wooing. That attitude owed much to Franco's frequently and fulsomely expressed enthusiasm for the Axis cause. It led to the ruthless German recovery of civil war debts through exports of Spanish foodstuffs and minerals to the Reich. In 1941, for instance, the entire Spanish production of olive oil was sent to Germany.[59] The Franco regime also smuggled narcotics from Argentina to Nazi Germany. It has been alleged that, in 1940, during the negotiations for a trade agreement with Argentina, a warrant was issued in Buenos Aires for the arrest of the head of the Spanish delegation, Eduardo Aunós, for illegally exporting 5 kilos of cocaine.[60]

In the war's final days, Franco still nurtured secret hopes of Hitler's wonder weapons turning the tide in favour of the Third Reich, believing that Nazi scientists had harnessed the power of cosmic rays.[61] When Berlin fell, the regime's tightly controlled press printed tributes to the inspirational presence of Hitler in the city's defence and *Informaciones* declared that Hitler had preferred to sacrifice himself for Europe rather than unleash his secret weapons. Allied victory was presented as the triumph of materialism over heroism.[62]

Franco's alleged services to Spain and the Allies as the man who heroically held back the Nazi hordes were to be a central theme of his propaganda until his death. The myth bore little relationship to the reality. On 10 June 1940, confident of an early German victory, he sent his Chief of the General Staff, General Juan Vigón, to Berlin with an effusive letter of congratulation for Hitler.[63] In fact, Hitler kept Spain at arm's length.[64] Expecting an imminent British surrender, he had no intention of paying a high price for services for which he believed he had no need. Franco knew that an economically prostrate Spain could not sustain a long war effort but, if France and Britain might be annihilated by a new German world order, he hoped to enter the war at the last minute to gain a ticket for the distribution of the booty.

Franco repeated the offer of Spanish entry into the war in the autumn of 1940. Needing only passage through Spain for an attack on Gibraltar, Hitler was unwilling to meet the crippling costs of turning Spain into an effective ally by reconstructing its economy and armed forces. Nor could he satisfy Franco's ambitions for large chunks of the French empire without undermining relations with Vichy France and Italy. Without offering anything, Germany enjoyed ample Spanish benevolence. The controlled Spanish press was enthusiastically committed to the Axis cause. The German war effort in the Atlantic was boosted by the refuelling and provisioning of destroyers and submarines in Spanish ports. German reconnaissance aircraft flew with Spanish markings. There were navigation stations at the service of the Luftwaffe at Lugo in the north-west and Seville in the south-west. The export of valuable raw materials to the Third Reich, although diminished by the spring of 1944, continued until 1945. The Spanish merchant fleet was used to carry supplies to German forces in North Africa and the Spanish navy escorted German convoys in the Mediterranean. German military intelligence was allowed to establish substantial operations on Spanish soil for espionage and sabotage activities against Gibraltar.[65] Similarly, Italian bombers making long-range attacks on Gibraltar were granted refuelling facilities in Spain to permit their return to Italy.[66]

The unexpected obstinacy of British resistance and the defeat of the Luftwaffe in the Battle of Britain led Hitler to abandon his invasion plan, Operation Sea Lion. Instead, the Germans hoped for victory by intensifying U-boat warfare and seizing the nerve centres of the British empire, Gibraltar and Suez. The need to capture Gibraltar made Spain's entry into the war superficially more attractive.[67] However, analysis of the costs and benefits diminished enthusiasm for a Spanish declaration of war. Spanish belligerency might offer control of the Straits but it might provoke possible English counter-seizures of the Canary Islands, Tangier and the Balearic Islands and perhaps even an extension of the Gibraltar zone or English landings in Portugal or Morocco. To sustain a Spanish war effort would mean an intolerable drain on Axis supplies of food and fuel. The German high command reported that the Spanish army could sustain only a few days of hostilities.[68] German officials began the process of quantifying Spain's essential civilian and military needs. The figures presented by Madrid for civilian needs alone, in terms of fuel, wheat and a wide range of raw materials, were enormous but realistic, that is to say not an invention to frighten off the Germans.[69] By the winter of 1940, continued British resistance and the deterioration of Spain's economy left Franco ever more vulnerable to Anglo-American pressures and blandishments.[70]

The precariousness of the Spanish position was made starkly clear to Ramón Serrano Súñer, Franco's brother-in-law and Minister of the Interior, in Berlin in mid-September 1940. The German Foreign Minister Joachim von Ribbentrop informed him that, in return for German supplies of military equipment, Spain must meet its civil war debts to Germany through deliveries of raw materials. He demanded French and English mining properties in Spain and Spanish Morocco as well as military bases. Spain would be integrated into a German-dominated European economy, with a subordinate role, limited to agriculture, the production of raw materials and industries 'indigenous to Spain'. Spain's colonial ambitions were brusquely dismissed by Ribbentrop, who demanded one of the Canary Islands for a German base and further bases in Spanish Morocco.[71] Despite being informed by Serrano Súñer that, in Hitler's new order, Spain would be a mere satellite, Franco did not waver in his determination to ensure Spanish participation in the division of the spoils. Far from astutely holding the Germans at bay, he remained anxious to convince them that he was an ally to be trusted.[72] The letters that he sent to Serrano during his stay in Berlin reveal that Franco not only believed blindly in the victory of the Axis but that he was fully determined to join in the war at its side. His tone was of wide-eyed adulation of Hitler.[73] Franco's warlike ambition was restrained by growing opposition to entry into the war within his own high command in response to continued British resistance. The General Staff reported that the navy had no fuel, there was neither a functioning air force nor effective mechanized units, and after the civil war widespread hunger meant that the population could not sustain more sacrifices. Moreover, tensions were brewing between monarchists and Falangists. Nevertheless, Franco was more confident than the Germans themselves that their victory in the world war was near.[74]

On 28 September 1940, Hitler told Ciano in Berlin that Spanish intervention 'would cost more than it is worth'. Hitler had to balance the conflicting demands of Franco, Pétain and Mussolini.[75] Meanwhile, Spain's intensifying food shortage forced Franco to make overtures to the British and Americans. On 7 October, he sent a telegram to Roosevelt saying that Spain would stay neutral if the USA would send wheat.[76] However, within a week, Franco's commitment to the Third Reich was underlined by his dismissal of his two most pro-Allied ministers. The Anglophile Colonel Juan Beigbeder was replaced as Foreign Minister by

Serrano Súñer and Luis Alarcón de la Lastra, a man as economically illiterate as his master, as Minister of Industry and Commerce by the wily Demetrio Carceller. Alarcón's rapid departure had been hastened by Carceller's exposure of the Filek swindle.[77] Spanish promises to join the Axis were reiterated, albeit not converted into binding contractual commitments at the historic meeting between Hitler and Franco at Hendaye on 23 October 1940. Hitler had not come to demand that Franco go to war immediately. Rather, concerned that Mussolini was about to get involved in a costly Balkan war by attacking Greece, he was engaged on a reconnaissance mission, meeting Pierre Laval on 22 October at Montoire-sur-le-Loir near Tours, en route to seeing Franco and then Pétain on 24 October again at Montoire on his way back. Hitler was starting to think that it was better to leave the French to defend their own colonies rather than satisfy Franco.[78] The German high command was convinced that the Spanish economy was on the verge of collapse and that Spain's domestic situation was so rotten as to make the country useless as an ally.[79]

   That one meeting of the two dictators was to be the central plank in the construction of the myth of Franco courageously securing Spanish neutrality by resisting Hitler's threats. In the words of his hagiographers, 'the skill of one man held back what all the armies of Europe, including the French, had been unable to do'.[80] In reality, Hitler exerted little pressure for Spanish belligerence and it was Franco who pushed to be part of a future Axis world order. He failed because Hitler believed that Vichy offered the better deal. Hitler was unmoved by Franco's irritating recital of his requirements and his boast that Spain could take Gibraltar alone.[81] After being in Franco's company for nearly nine hours, Hitler told Mussolini later that 'Rather than go through that again, I would prefer to have three or four teeth taken out'.[82] Serrano Súñer suggested years later that Franco's African ambitions were such that, if Hitler had offered him French Morocco, he would have entered the war.[83] The Hendaye meeting thus decided little. A protocol was signed, committing Spain to join the Axis cause at a date to be decided only after military preparations were complete. Serrano Súñer repeated three times to the American Ambassador on 31 October 1940 that 'there had been no pressure, not even an insinuation on the part of either Hitler or Mussolini that Spain should enter the war'.[84]

   There was no question of hostile German action against Spain. Hitler's central obsession was the destruction of the Soviet Union. Planning for the attack on Russia from the summer of 1940, the Wehrmacht had little spare capacity for an assault on Spain. Already receiving valuable cooperation from Franco, Hitler had no need to contemplate one.[85] Thereafter, in the entire course of the Second World War, Spain came no nearer than it had in 1940 to joining the Axis. The Caudillo's sympathies continued to lie with Germany and Italy. If Hitler had met the asking price, Franco would almost certainly have joined him. However, his own survival was always Franco's paramount ambition and the tensions between the army and the Falange over whether or not to go to war imposed caution. The most obvious example of his circumspection and its link to domestic issues was his non-interference during Allied preparation for the invasion of French North Africa in November 1942, Operation Torch.

Franco still manifested pro-Axis fervour but the economic crisis inside Spain was deepening dramatically and there were signs that Axis triumphs were slowing down. Hitler, shaken by the British naval victory over the Italians at Taranto in November 1940, was keener on an attack on Gibraltar.[86] However, as Hitler's planners quickly discovered, Franco had not exaggerated about the feeble condition of the Spanish economy. The different rail gauges on either side of the Franco-Spanish border and the general disrepair of Spanish track and rolling stock were notorious. Moreover, a disastrous harvest meant that Spain needed even more grain than specified in its earlier requests to the Germans. With famine conditions in many parts of the country, Franco had no choice but to seek to buy food in the United States and that necessarily involved postponing a declaration of war. The best that he could do for Hitler was to allow German tankers to be stationed in remote bays on the northern coast for the refuelling of Kriegsmarine destroyers. Spain's colossal food shortage obliged Franco to admit that Spain could enter the war only when England was about to collapse.[87]

Despite having to pull back at the crucial moment, Franco still declared vehemently to German Ambassador Eberhard von Stohrer, on 20 January 1941, that his faith in Hitler's victory was undiminished and that 'it was not a question at all of whether Spain would enter the war; that had been decided at Hendaye. It was merely a question of when.'[88] On 5 February 1941, Hitler wrote to Mussolini asking him to try to persuade Franco to change his mind and permit a German assault on Gibraltar.[89] With the economic situation in Spain deteriorating daily, there was little possibility of that happening. German consuls were reporting that there was no bread at all in parts of the country and there were cases of highway robbery and banditry. The Director of the Economic Policy Department in Berlin regarded Spain's consequent requests for economic support as utterly unrealizable.[90]

Franco's meeting with Mussolini took place on 12 and 13 February at Bordighera.[91] Shortly before, Franco had received news of the annihilation of Marshal Graziani's army by the British at Benghazi. The Italian rout in Cyrenaica by a much smaller British force and the British naval bombardment of Genoa on 8 February had a significant impact on opinion within the Francoist establishment.[92] At Bordighera, Franco boasted to Mussolini that he could easily capture Gibraltar but admitted, 'Spain wishes to enter the war; her fear is to enter too late.' The Duce asked Franco if he would declare war if given sufficient supplies and binding promises about his colonial ambitions. The Caudillo replied that, even if all the supplies requested were delivered, which was impossible, given Hitler's other commitments, Spain's military unpreparedness and famine conditions would still mean several months before it could join in the war.[93] The Duce informed Hitler that it was pointless to try to persuade Franco to join the Axis war effort in the short term just as the German Department of Economic Planning was reporting that Spanish demands could not be met without endangering the Reich's military capacity. Ribbentrop instructed Stohrer to take no further steps to secure Spanish belligerence.[94]

There was no question of Hitler forcing the issue since he had already committed his military machine to rescuing Italy from its disastrous involvement in the Balkans.[95] Nevertheless, a change in his approach to Franco could be perceived at the end of February in firmer German insistence on the repayment of Spain's civil war debts, which were agreed at 372 million Reichsmarks.[96] In marked contrast, in order to isolate Serrano Súñer, on 7 April, the British government granted Spain credits of £2.5 million.[97] Pressure on Franco intensified when a small-scale, but crucially important, power struggle broke out in late April after Vigón informed him that, if Serrano Súñer's power were not curtailed, the military ministers would resign en bloc.[98]

The outcome of the crisis would be one of the first fruits of a British plan, instituted ten months earlier, to bribe important elements in the Spanish high command. Inevitably, where bribery was concerned, Juan March was not far away. With his unerring capacity to end up on the winning side, March believed that Britain would be the eventual victor and had decided to put his financial weight behind London. At the heart of the scheme was Captain Alan Hillgarth, Naval Attaché at the British Embassy in Madrid from 1939 to the autumn of 1943, and effective head of British intelligence in Spain. Hillgarth learned much about Juan March during his time as consul in Mallorca and regarded him as 'a scoundrel of the deepest dye'.[99] The British Ambassador, Sir Samuel Hoare, shortly after his arrival in Madrid, had received from Hillgarth a devastatingly frank analysis of the defeatism of the staff of the Embassy and the defects of its security arrangements. Hoare wrote to Churchill to say how greatly this had impressed him.[100]

Hillgarth's acquaintance with March, his prior friendship with Churchill and the respect of Hoare made it possible to mount the bribery operation to bolster the opposition of key generals both to Serrano Súñer and to Spanish entry into the war. A total of $14 million was eventually distributed, through Antonio Aranda, to Generals José Varela, Luis Orgaz, Alfredo Kindelán and Carlos Asensio, Colonel Valentín Galarza and Franco's brother Nicolás.[101] The idea of corrupting Spanish generals probably originated with March, so familiar with the power of bribery, rather than with Hillgarth.[102] March's financial guarantees to the military conspirators in the spring of 1936 had demonstrated their readiness to accept his money. Hoare enthusiastically adopted the idea of dispersing a sum so colossal that Sir Antony Eden would later refer to its beneficiaries as a 'corrupt gang of generals', 'a wretched lot'. The first payments were organized in June 1940, although the recipients believed that the money came, not from the British government, but from March: Nicolás Franco $2 million, Aranda $2 million, Varela $2 million, Galarza $1 million, Kindelán $500,000.[103] The total amount spent by London on this has been calculated as being, in contemporary terms, the equivalent of somewhere between £270 million and £899 million.[104]

A problem arose between September 1941 and February 1942, because the money had to come from a bank in New York. The American entry into the war saw an embargo placed on dollar accounts held in the USA and elsewhere by non-American residents. Ironically, this included one of the illegal accounts held by Franco in contravention of his own Law of Currency Offences. This account contained some of the monies donated to the rebel cause. The issue of the blocked funds was eventually resolved in an immensely complex process involving March, Hoare, Hillgarth, Churchill, Halifax, Eden and others.[105]

When Vigón made his threat about Serrano Súñer, the generals in question were already hostile to Spanish entry into the war on the Axis side.[106] Kindelán and Varela had been collecting information on the limited capabilities of the Spanish army. The growing weight of alarmist reports, only partly inspired by the bribes, led Serrano Súñer to suspect 'some hidden influence'.[107] Since replacing Beigbeder as Foreign Minister, on 17 October 1940, Serrano Súñer maintained control of his previous Ministry of the Interior through its Under-Secretary, José Lorente Sanz. He also dominated the Falange. Inevitably, Franco began to suspect that his brother-in-law was growing too powerful. He was alerted by Serrano's call for the Falange to assume greater power and his efforts to get his protégés into the government. Faced with mounting anti-Serrano Súñer criticism from his high command, on 5 May 1941 Franco made Galarza Minister of the Interior, replacing him as Under-Secretary to the Presidency with the thirty-six-year-old Captain Luis Carrero Blanco of the Naval General Staff.[108] Hugh Dalton, the Minister of Economic Warfare in London, commented: 'In Spain, the Cavalry of St George have been charging, hence some of the recent changes; hence also Attaché H's concern for J.M.'s tinplate' (where 'H' was Hillgarth and 'J.M.' Juan March).[109]

When Valentín Galarza replaced his key men, Lorente Sanz, the Director General of Security (the Conde de Mayalde) and the Falangists in charge of Press and Propaganda, Serrano Súñer resigned as Foreign Minister. The hostility between the military and the Falange reached boiling point with clashes between the police and Falangists. This badly weakened Serrano Súñer's standing in Franco's eyes.[110] After an intervention by Stohrer, control of the press was restored to Serrano Súñer, who withdrew his resignation.[111] The crisis was finally resolved by cabinet changes on 19 May that seemed to suggest his victory but would eventually undermine his position. Fearing that the removal of Serrano Súñer would leave him as the prisoner of the monarchist generals, Franco appointed two additional Falangist ministers, Miguel Primo de Rivera as Minister of Agriculture and José Luis de Arrese as Minister-Secretary of the Falange. The pro-Nazi José Antonio Girón was already Minister of Labour. However, Franco guaranteed the loyalty of the three with promises of preferment.[112] The May 1941 crisis was the beginning of Serrano's downfall. Moreover, during the crisis, Franco had learned how cheaply the Falange could be bought.[113]

However, German victories in the spring of 1941 in North Africa, Yugoslavia and Greece rekindled Franco's pro-Axis fervour and strengthened Serrano Súñer's position. Hoare wrote to Eden on 31 May that, in the wake of the crisis, Serrano was 'determined to obtain complete control of the Government and to drive the country into war before the end of the summer. One of our best sources reports that in order to achieve these two objectives he is plotting with the Germans to eliminate Franco.'[114] Nevertheless, after the British evacuation of Crete in the last week of May, Franco believed that Suez would soon be in Axis hands.[115] On 8 June, Hoare wrote to Eden: 'Generals, including Vigón, are now convinced that Suner's [sic] policy is endangering Spain's neutrality and that he must be eliminated. Ways and means are being seriously considered, bearing in mind danger of doing nothing on the one hand and on the other hand that of provoking Germany.'[116] Franco's belief in Axis victory was dangerously inflamed by the Nazi invasion of the Soviet Union on 22 June 1941. This countered the reverses suffered in the May crisis by Serrano who informed Stohrer that he and Franco wished to send volunteer units of Falangists to fight in Russia.[117]

The controlled press rejoiced and the British Embassy was stormed by Falangists on 24 June, an assault facilitated by a truckload of stones thoughtfully provided by the authorities. Three days later, Spain moved from non-belligerency to what Serrano Súñer called 'moral belligerency' and preparations began to send the Blue Division of nearly 50,000 Falangist volunteers to fight alongside the German invaders. In addition, an agreement was made on 21 August 1941 between the Deutsche Arbeitsfront and the Falangist Syndicates for 100,000 Spanish workers to be sent to Germany. Theoretically 'volunteers', but more often levies chosen by the Falange to fit Germany's industrial needs, between 15,000 and 20,000 were eventually sent.[118] The Blue Division was intended to show enough commitment to the Axis cause to earn a share in the future division of the spoils. For the same reason, Franco gave full support to German anti-Allied espionage and sabotage activities on Spanish soil.[119]

On 9 July, Hoare reported to Eden on a conversation between David Eccles, the representative of the Ministry of Economic Warfare in the Iberian Peninsula, and Demetrio Carceller and his chief adviser. Both told Eccles 'that Suñer [sic] was so intolerable that he ought to be liquidated, and by this horrible expression they obviously meant killed'. Hoare continued: 'from an almost equally important source I have further information that the Generals are contemplating liquidating Suñer in the next week or two and, with a view to avoiding German retaliation following the liquidation, by an immediate signing of the Triple Pact with the Axis'. His source was almost certainly Aranda or Kindelán. Hoare had sent a message to the generals that this would be suicidal.[120] In fact, Carceller had admitted to Eccles that the assassination of Serrano would be dangerous in terms of the likely reactions both of the Germans and of Franco himself.

Carceller's comments reflected his desire to maintain commercial links with the Anglo-Saxon bloc at a time when the pro-Axis policy of Franco and Serrano Súñer was threatening crucial wheat and fuel deliveries that needed the approval of London and Washington. This was confirmed some weeks later when Carceller spoke to Willard Beaulac, the Economic Counsellor at the US Embassy. Without mentioning any homicidal projects, Carceller told him that Serrano 'was an evil man with unbounded ambition' who should be replaced.[121] In September, Carceller told Emil Karl Josef Wiehl, the Director of Economic Policy in the German Foreign Ministry, that the immediate survival of the Franco regime required a rapprochement with the Anglo-American bloc.[122] In each of the three conversations, Carceller expressed enthusiasm for the country of his interlocutor.

Franco, in contrast, continued to assert that the Allies had lost the war. On the fifth anniversary of the outbreak of the Spanish Civil War, 17 July 1941, he addressed the National Council of the Falange and applauded Hitler's Russian venture at 'this moment when the German armies lead the battle for which Europe and Christianity have for so many years longed, and in which the blood of our youth is to mingle with that of our comrades of the Axis'. He added, 'I do not harbour any doubt about the result of the war. The die is cast and the first battle was won here in Spain. The war is lost for the Allies.' He spoke of his contempt for 'plutocratic democracies', of his conviction that Germany had already won the war and that American intervention would be a 'criminal madness' leading only to useless prolongation of the conflict and catastrophe for the USA.[123]

The frequent attacks of Franco's controlled press on Britain and the USA and praise for German triumphs saw imports of essential goods begin to dry up as Spain found it harder to get American export licences and British navicerts (the safe-conducts for the passage of neutral shipping through the blockade).[124] Shortages of coal, copper, tin, rubber and textile fibres presaged an imminent breakdown of Spanish industry. Since the requested supplies from Germany did not materialize, by 6 October 1941 Franco was forced to admit to the US Ambassador Alexander Weddell that, given Spain's shortages of wheat, cotton and gasoline, he wanted to see an improvement of economic relations with the USA.[125]

Franco's initial delight at the Japanese attack on Pearl Harbor on 7 December 1941 was cut short when the USA entered the war. Moreover, the second flowering of his pro-Axis enthusiasm would soon wither along with the fortunes of the German armies in Russia. Nevertheless, it took him some time to accept that American involvement meant that Germany now faced a long and titanic struggle. The precise moment when he postponed Spanish entry into the war indefinitely is difficult to locate for the simple reason that it was never definitive. On 13 February 1942, he could still tell the Portuguese Premier, António de Oliveira Salazar, in Seville that an Allied victory was impossible and that he would send a million Spanish troops to defend Germany from the Bolsheviks.[126] On the next day, apparently unconcerned by the catastrophic German situation in Russia, he told a group of high-ranking army officers of his 'absolute certainty' that the Reich would survive and publicly repeated what he had told Salazar, that 'if the road to Berlin were open, then it would not merely be one Division of Spanish volunteers but one million Spaniards who would be offered to help'.[127]

Neutrality, far from being the result of brilliant statecraft or foresight, was the fruit of the good fortune that Germany would not or could not pay the price demanded for entry into the war. The internal political situation in Spain also played its part. Military hostility to Serrano Súñer was reaching boiling point.[128] Moreover, after Franco's initial enthusiasm for the Japanese assault on the United States, economic and political realism had prevailed. Less anti-American material was appearing in the press. The Caudillo's key political talent was his ability to balance the internal forces of the regime coalition. Serrano had long since been the target of fierce complaints from senior military figures, especially the beneficiaries of the Cavalry of St George. However, the balance tipped against him when Franco was irked by rumours that he, Serrano, was the real ruler of Spain. Started by an innocent question from Franco's daughter Carmen, the rumours were carefully fomented by Serrano's rivals, Arrese and Carrero Blanco. Even more sensitive to these insinuations was Franco's wife Carmen, furious because Madrid high society was buzzing with gossip about Serrano's affair with Consuela (Sonsoles) de Icaza y León, the wife of Lieutenant Colonel Francisco Díez de Rivera, the Marqués de Llanzol.

The crisis was triggered by an incident at the Santuario de la Virgen de Begoña in Bilbao in mid-August when a Falangist attempt on the life of Varela seriously wounded seventy-two bystanders. This was exploited by the Ministers of War and the Interior, Varela and Galarza. Franco reacted to their scheme to limit the power of the Falange by dismissing them, a blow to the British bribery scheme centred largely on both. However, the cabinet secretary, Luis Carrero Blanco, whispered in Franco's ear that the crisis should have 'winners and losers' since the sacking of the two ministers might be interpreted as proof of Serrano Súñer's pre-eminence. On 3 September 1942, Serrano was replaced as Foreign Minister by General Francisco Jordana. This did not mean that Franco had adopted a pro-Allied position. Neither the Germans nor the Italians were upset, seeing Serrano Súñer as 'too difficult'.[129] Franco wrote to Mussolini on 18 September 1942 and asserted that the decision was motivated by domestic politics and 'did not in the least affect our position in foreign affairs'.[130]

In the autumn of 1942, when clear evidence of Allied preparations for Operation Torch raised doubts about eventual Axis triumph, Franco reacted, not with prophetic awareness of the ultimate outcome, but rather with understandable caution.[131] This probably reflected the influence of those generals who were receiving colossal bribes from London precisely for that purpose. (Kindelán, for example, received 4 million pesetas, the equivalent of more than 34 million euros in 2017. Orgaz may have received four times as much.)[132] The massing of force on his borders was hardly the best moment to cross swords with the Allies, particularly in the wake of Rommel's defeat in Egypt. On 8 November 1942, when Anglo-American forces landed in the French Moroccan and Algerian territories coveted by Franco, he instructed his Ambassador in London to seek rapprochement with the Western Allies. That did not mean that he had lost belief in ultimate Axis victory; it was, rather, a typically cynical attempt to exploit German difficulties.

Franco's strategy was now to demand that Berlin provide military aid to permit him to resist the Allies. Four days after the landings, his Foreign Ministry drafted a document calling on Germany for weaponry without conditions, without payment and without supervising officers or technicians. On 4 December, the Spanish Ambassador discussed this with Hitler and, on the 29th, Jordana told the Führer's emissary Admiral Canaris that, if Germany would not provide armaments, Spain would seek them elsewhere. Franco was trying to exploit Axis difficulties exactly as he was exaggerating German threats in order to squeeze benefits from the Allies.[133] Franco told the newly arrived German Ambassador, Hans Adolf von Moltke, in late January 1943 that Germany was his friend; Britain, America and the 'Bolsheviks' his enemies. He swore that he would 'support Germany in the struggle imposed upon her by destiny'. However, the weapons did not arrive.[134] Moreover, in the wake of Torch and the removal of Serrano Súñer, the work of the Cavalry of St George was rendered easier. In the absence of Varela and Galarza, it was facilitated by Franco's brother Nicolás.[135]

In early 1943, it was obvious that the international context had changed dramatically. Torch had shifted the strategic balance, but until the fall of Mussolini in the summer Franco remained convinced that the Allies could not win and that their successes in Africa were of marginal importance. However, in the wake of German defeat at Stalingrad in February, he sent a delegation under General Carlos Martínez Campos to Berlin in March with a list of armaments requirements. That Germany could not spare such materiel was masked by a ten-day tour of the Nazi war industries during which Martínez Campos was seduced by tales about the new wonder weapons with which the Third Reich would easily win the war. On his return to Spain, he convinced a bedazzled Caudillo that the German war machine remained invincible.[136] Inspired by Martínez Campos's report, Franco expressed renewed enthusiasm for the Axis cause just as the Allies were preparing the invasion of Sicily in the summer of 1943. In an effort to help the Third Reich, he played an inadvertently damaging role in ensuring the spectacular success of the British deception plan codenamed Operation Mincemeat to mask the preparations. The operation involved placing in Spanish waters near Huelva the corpse of a fictional Major Martin (later known as 'The Man Who Never Was'), carrying documents seemingly showing that the Allied assault would be in the Western Mediterranean. Franco personally authorized that these documents with their misinformation be given to Captain Wilhelm Leissner, the counter-espionage specialist in the German Embassy, for onward transmission to Berlin.[137]

In January 1943, José María Doussinague, Jordana's deputy, had instructed Spanish diplomats to make no commitment to saving Jews and to avoid allowing Sephardic Jews to be identified as Spanish. However, the Jews were told to register their wealth which 'in some sense, is part of the nation's patrimony'. Some weeks later, the German Embassy in Madrid informed Franco's government that the Third Reich was going to suspend the 'special treatment' granted to Spanish Jews who, from the end of March, would have to leave German occupied territories or expect the same treatment as non-Spanish Jews. Doussinague advised Jordana that this posed a serious dilemma. If Spain allowed Sephardic Jews to be subjected to German measures, it ran the risk, especially in America, of being accused of complicity in murder. Doussinague's note revealed that he was fully aware of German atrocities against the Jews and did not find them objectionable. He wrote, 'the solution of bringing these Jews to Spain is not acceptable because their race, their money, their Anglophilia and their freemasonry would make them agents of all kinds of intrigue'.

Doussinague proposed, instead, only to allow them passage through Spain to any other country that gave them an entry visa. Two months later, with evident reluctance, he extended this suggestion. Jews would be permitted to remain in Spain until they had negotiated such visas, since not to allow this would damage Spain's international image. At a cabinet meeting, it was decided that 'they could enter Spain only with a cast-iron written guarantee that it was simply for transit and for very few days'. The Minister of the Interior, Blas Pérez, demanded assurance that the strictest control would be applied to Jews in transit. The entire process was subject to lengthy bureaucratic delays. Only twenty-five Jews were allowed in at a time, and only after they had departed would another twenty-five be admitted. While in Spain, Jews had to be cared for by international refugee agencies. Franco was concerned about his image in the international press and so grudgingly accepted suggestions from his brother Nicolás and Jordana that relations with the World Jewish Congress must be improved. There was no humanitarian dimension to Franco's Jewish policy. He accepted Jordana's advice because he feared that defeat for the Third Reich would see the world run by the

Jewish–Bolshevik–masonic conspiracy.[138] There were Jews saved, not by Franco, but by the courageous individual action of the Spanish consuls in Athens, Sebastián Romero Radigales, and in Budapest, Ángel Sanz Briz.[139]

In early May, during a tour of Andalusia, Franco made speeches on the theme of his neutrality and desire for peace.[140] The Allied invasion of Sicily and the subsequent fall of Mussolini in July had convinced senior generals of the need for urgent consideration of the future. On 15 September, eight of them, including the main recipients of British bribes, Kindelán, Varela and Orgaz, presented a timid letter to Franco request-ing that he consider a monarchical restoration. Gil Robles believed that their timidity derived from their reluctance to be separated from the benefits of 'the Francoist racket'. Equally concerned by the situation and aware of monarchist machinations, Franco announced the withdrawal of the Blue Division, although volunteers were to be permitted to stay on in German units. On 1 October 1943, in a speech to the Falange, Franco now described Spain's position as one of 'vigilant neutrality'. That did nothing to prevent incidents such as Falangist attacks on the British Vice-Consulate in Zaragoza and the American Consulate in Valencia.[141] Nor did it inhibit Spanish exports of vital wolfram to the Third Reich.

The corruption of ministers was widely known, with Carceller and Girón being the most notorious. It is alleged that Carceller created a company to which, as minister, he granted 2,000 import licences for cars and trucks. Acquiring the necessary currency at the rate of 11 pesetas per US dollar, for each $5,000 purchased he was able to buy a truck that was then sold in Spain for 1 million pesetas. Juan March, of all people, complained to Gil Robles, on 10 January 1944, about 'new and tremen-dous cases of undeniable administrative immorality'. Two months later, March told Gil Robles that corruption was increasing 'on such a scale that British and American diplomats are informing their governments that certain ministers are pilfering the national patrimony'.[142] In early April, March told the British Press Attaché Tom Burns that the enmity of Girón and Carceller had led to Galarza being ordered to confiscate March's passport and put him under house arrest. Galarza had warned March in time for him to leave Spain. March had written to Franco deny-ing the allegations against him and offering to disprove them, but only at a cabinet meeting, at which he would be obliged to demonstrate the corruption of three ministers and it would then be up to the cabinet to

decide who went to prison, him or the ministers. The letter went un-
answered, but police surveillance of March was lifted and he kept his
passport. March went into detail with Burns about the scale of corruption in Franco's government.[143] This raises the issue of how Franco could
have failed to know about the British bribery operation. The amounts
received were colossal; his brother Nicolás was involved and, in any case,
Franco had all his generals under surveillance. Aranda, a notorious
gossip, for instance, was known by Franco to be in touch with both the
British and the Germans and with the anti-regime opposition. His
frequent claims that an anti-Franco coup was imminent led British
diplomats to regard him as 'a weathercock', 'unreliable and illogical'.[144]
Nevertheless, a monarchist conspiracy involving Aranda and Gil Robles
in Lisbon benefited from Juan March's contribution to their activities of
a million Swiss francs.[145]

   The sinuous and corrupt Orgaz was a member of the monarchist
'opposition' but unreliable probably because, from early September 1943,
Franco had on his desk a report on Orgaz's involvement in corrupt business deals in North Africa.[146] In 1944, he learned that Orgaz was
complaining about Varela's preoccupation with his wealth and investments.[147] Varela's wealth was clearly not just based on that of his wife,
Casilda Ampuero. Accordingly, Franco had to be aware of the accumulation of riches among his generals. He certainly knew that some were
taking German bribes. Several senior officers received substantial
commissions for appearing fraudulently as directors of German-held
mining operations in order to make them seem to be Spanish-owned.[148]
In fact, Franco was not only aware of corruption but also used that
knowledge to control members of his coalition. He had no interest in
preventing corruption in itself, preferring rather to use his knowledge
thereof as leverage over those involved. Indeed, he often repaid those
who informed him of corruption not by taking action against the guilty
but by letting them know who had informed on them.[149]

   In the army, many officers with business interests used their soldiers,
as well as Republican prisoners of war, as cheap, or cost-free, labour.
Others used military vehicles for private purposes. There were frequent
cases of smuggling by senior officers. General Joaquín Ríos Capapé, one
of Franco's friends, owned a bar in Madrid's Gran Vía. He used Spanish
air force planes to bring in spirits, coffee and tobacco from the Tangier
free port. His wife sold petrol coupons in the bar. Other generals

imported contraband from the Canary Islands. The military budget was used for private purposes such as the sumptuous coming-out party of the daughter of General Carlos Asensio when he was Minister of War. The cost of spectacular gifts from the captains general was met by an obligatory contribution from the entire officer corps. Senior officers doubled and tripled their salaries with well-paid posts in the civil administration or on the boards of private companies. The luxurious lifestyle of some captains general such as Rafael García Valiño shocked their more austere comrades.[150] At a lower level, junior officers used conscripts as domestic servants, handymen, babysitters and the like. Franco was aware of this and was happy to let it be known that he knew. On only two occasions did he use that knowledge to have a senior officer expelled from the army. One was General Francisco Borbón y de la Torre, who was accused of illegally trafficking in foodstuffs. The other was the prominent Africanista General Heli Rolando de Tella y Cantos. Despite his highly distinguished record, Tella was stripped of all military honours for 'administrative irregularities' committed through the use of military vehicles and personnel in connection with his flour factory and the rebuilding of his country mansion while he was Military Governor of Lugo. Since Franco rarely considered corruption a serious crime, subsequent assaults and an assassination attempt convinced Tella that he had been persecuted because of his pro-monarchist activities.[151]

A fertile area for corruption was the mining and export of wolfram, a crucial ingredient in the manufacture of high-quality steel for armaments. American policy had been to try to limit Franco's exports to Germany by pre-emptive purchase of Spanish wolfram. On 3 December 1943, Franco told Moltke's successor, Hans Heinrich Dieckhoff, that his own survival depended on an Axis victory and that an Allied triumph 'would mean his own annihilation'. He declared that 'a neutral Spain furnishing Germany with wolfram and other products is at this moment of greater value to Germany than a Spain which would be drawn into the war'.[152] Allied restrictions on the export of wolfram opened up opportunities for corruption. Carceller allegedly made a lot of money in return for permitting illicit exports to the Reich, although it was only part of his enrichment as minister.[153] March told Tom Burns, 'wolfram has been a comparatively small element, and almost every import and export of Spain has paid its due to Sr. Carceller's pocket. It is sufficient to recall that Sr. Carceller was a man without great fortune up to the time of becoming a minister, thenceforward – when he was ostensibly not engaged in business for private gain – he made his fortune.' Burns commented: 'It is true that J.M. criticises Sr. Carceller much as a bank-robber might a pickpocket, but the criticism is none the less expert for that.'[154]

By early 1944, with North Africa secure and Italy out of the war, Washington was furious about Germany's continued import of Spanish wolfram paid for with gold looted from prisoners in extermination camps.[155] There was uproar in the United States when Franco sent congratulations to José P. Laurel on his installation by the Japanese as puppet Governor of the Philippines. On 27 January 1944, Hoare visited Franco to complain that Madrid was providing new facilities for German wolfram purchase, that, despite the formal withdrawal of the Blue Division, the Falange was continuing to recruit for the small Spanish Legion still in Russia with a unit of the Spanish air force and that German agents were still conducting anti-Allied espionage and sabotage with the help of Spanish military personnel.[156]

In response to Franco's brinkmanship over wolfram, the Americans precipitately curtailed petroleum exports to Spain.[157] Franco was forced to restrict monthly deliveries of wolfram to a near token amount. On 2 May 1944, Franco signed an agreement to close down the German Consulate in Tangier, to withdraw Spanish units from Russia and to expel German spies and saboteurs from Spain. Throughout the rest of 1944, Hoare protested almost daily at Franco's failure to expel the German agents. German observation posts and radio interception stations were maintained in Spain until the end of the war.[158] Many ex-members of the Blue Division volunteered for the Wehrmacht and the Waffen SS and took part in the defence of Berlin and of the Chancellery.[159]

Franco also ignored an opportunity to diminish the hostility felt towards him in Allied circles. The death of Jordana in August 1944 and the need to appoint a new foreign minister made possible a clean break with the pro-Axis past. Instead, Franco replaced Jordana with José Félix Lequerica, the fiercely pro-Nazi Ambassador to Vichy. Nevertheless, a half-hearted diplomatic initiative was begun to convince the Allies that Franco had never meant them any harm and that his Axis links had been aimed at the Soviet Union. On 18 October, he proposed a future Anglo-Spanish anti-Bolshevik alliance to destroy communism. He dismissed his own pro-Axis activities as a series of small incidents. He made the astonishing claim that the only obstacle to better Anglo-Spanish relations in previous years had been British interference in Spain's internal affairs.[160]

Ironically, on the following day, 19 October, approximately 5,000 Spanish Republican guerrilla fighters began to enter Spain through the Pyrenees with the principal attack focused on the snow-bound Val d'Aran. The invasion was over-optimistic and played into the hands of Franco's huge land forces. Over the next three weeks, the invaders chalked up a few successes, some units getting more than a hundred kilometres into the interior, others defeating units of the Spanish army and capturing large numbers of prisoners. However, 40,000 Moroccan troops led by experienced Francoist generals, José Monasterio, Juan Yagüe, Rafael García Valiño and José Moscardó, overcame the relatively small invading army. There was never any real hope of triggering an anti-Franco uprising. The regime's iron control of the press ensured that the *guerrillero* invasion took place amid a deafening silence.[161]

His praetorian guard aside, what saved Franco from his own ambitions was not immense skill or vision but rather a fortuitous combination of the skill of Anglo-American carrot-and-stick economic diplomacy and Hitler's commitment of enormous German resources to Italian rescue operations and his obsession with attacking Russia. As the Under-Secretary at the Ministry of Foreign Affairs, Juan Peche, commented: 'we did not enter the war as a result of Franco resisting German pressure, but because Hitler did not want us to or because it was not even part of his plans'.[162]

It was hardly surprising, as the German Ambassador Eberhard von Stohrer remarked to General Krappe in October 1941, that the Führer should conclude that Spain was more useful to Germany under the mask of neutrality as its only outlet from the British blockade. This was confirmed by Hitler himself on 10 February 1945 when he told his private secretary, Martin Bormann,

> Spain was burning to follow Italy's example and become a member of the victor's Club. Franco, of course, had very exaggerated ideas on the value of Spanish intervention. Nevertheless, I believe that, in spite of the systematic sabotage perpetrated by his Jesuit brother-in-law, he would have agreed to make common cause with us on quite reasonable conditions – the promise of a little bit of France as a sop to his pride and a

substantial slice of Algeria as a real, material asset. But as Spain had really nothing tangible to contribute, I came to the conclusion that her direct intervention was not desirable. It is true that it would have allowed us to occupy Gibraltar. On the other hand, Spain's entry into the war would certainly have added many kilometres to the Atlantic coast-line which we would have had to defend – from San Sebastian to Cadiz ... By ensuring that the Iberian Peninsula remained neutral, Spain has already rendered us the one service in this conflict which she had in her power to render. Having Italy on our backs is a sufficient burden in all conscience; and whatever may be the qualities of the Spanish soldier, Spain herself, in her state of poverty and unpreparedness, would have been a heavy liability rather than an asset.[163]

Franco addresses crowd from the balcony
of the Royal Palace of Madrid.

13

The Franco Regime: Corruption and Terror, 1945–1953

As the Second World War was reaching its final days, the regime's controlled media began to proclaim 'Franco's Victory'.[1] Selling that story to the Spanish population, however, was an easier proposition than peddling it to the victorious Allies. At home, Franco's propaganda machine promoted the absurd notion that Spain was the object of a ruthless international siege.[2] British diplomats were fully aware that Franco had supplied the last German garrisons in southern France with food and ammunition from Spanish ports on the Bay of Biscay. They knew too that, despite international publicity being given to the horrors of German extermination camps, Nazi officials were being given certificates of Spanish nationality and Franco's press was praising Hitler's heroism during the struggle for Berlin. The regime formally broke off diplomatic relations with the Third Reich only on 8 May, VE Day. Only then were the swastikas removed from the German Embassy building.[3]

Behind the effort that Franco and his propaganda machine put into rewriting his role in the Second World War, there was an element of fear. Accordingly, the most outrageous lies were propagated about his activities during the world war. For the rest of his life, he maintained the fiction of his commitment to Spanish neutrality, telling his doctor, Ramón Soriano, 'I never considered entering the war.' He told his friend Max Borrell that, at the October 1940 meeting at Hendaye, he had enjoyed making Hitler nervous. In fact, there exist many photos and newsreels that show that it was Franco who was the nervous one in the presence of the great man.[4]

The defeat of the Third Reich ended Franco's ambitions of building a new empire. However, always the supreme pragmatist, his commitment to the survival of his regime was not conditioned by any long-term ideological vision. Feeling no obligation to die in the ruins of the bunker, he brazened out the hostility of the Allies with a level of cunning that makes it unwise to understate his extraordinary political instincts. He lost no opportunity to remind the Spanish people of what their service had cost him. Footage of his public appearances always opened the daily state-controlled cinema newsreels of the Noticiario Español and its later manifestation, the NO-DO (Noticiarios y Documentales – News and Documentaries). They insistently projected the image of the tireless and vigilant Caudillo: 'the Chief of State, victorious Caudillo of our war and our peace, reconstruction and labour, devotes himself to the task of ruling over and governing our people'.[5]

From 1945 to 1950, Franco convinced himself that he and Spain were under deadly siege. With opposition re-emerging and hoping for backing from the Allies, many of the Caudillo's followers wavered during what has been called 'the black night of Francoism'.[6] Franco's strategy with regard to the great powers was to rewrite his role in the Second World War and with regard to the Spanish population rewrite what was happening outside the country. After nearly ten years of daily adulation, he was incapable of perceiving a difference between his personal political needs and those of Spain. He dismissed foreign criticism of himself as the fruit of a masonic conspiracy against Spain. Throughout the Cold War, he used the press shamelessly as an instrument to guarantee his own survival. It was repeated almost daily that the man who had diligently courted Hitler had personally saved Spain from the world war. The international ostracism provoked by his Axis links was presented as a perverse international siege motivated by the envy of the democracies for what he had done for Spain.

Although a guerrilla war was being fought against his regime and despite the fact that starvation afflicted large swathes of the population, he congratulated himself on 'the order, the peace and the joy which makes Spain one of the few countries still able to smile in this tormented Europe'.[7] He believed that popular distress had no objective cause but was simply generated by Communist agitators and sinister freemasons. This distance from reality gave Franco total confidence in himself. A stranger to self-criticism, his conviction that he was always right gave him the flexibility to adapt ceaselessly to changes in national and international circumstances.

In domestic policy, he worked to consolidate the loyalty of the triple pillars of the regime, the Church, the army and the Falange.

Simultaneously, his foreign policy emphasized the Catholic and monarchical elements of a regime that was presented as uniquely Spanish. While he projected this image, he took the precaution of surrounding himself with a praetorian guard of Axis stalwarts. Monarchist generals were kept away from senior posts while Falangist militants were given commissions as junior officers. He also created the Guardia de Franco, a paramilitary formation of Falangist zealots.[8] He described the Falange as 'a bulwark against subversion', a safety valve that 'gets the blame for the government's errors'. It was also the machine for mobilizing the crowds that greeted him on his tours around Spain.[9]

Franco had the gift of being convinced by his own lies. He was soon presenting his regime as essentially a kind of constitutional monarchy. A pseudo-constitution was announced on 17 July 1945 in the form of the Fuero de los Españoles (Spaniards' Charter of Rights) whose superficial guarantee of civil liberties did not permit opposition to the 'fundamental principles of the State' or allow political parties or trades unions. Franco declared that his regime would eventually be succeeded by a traditional monarchy. On the following day, he removed the more obviously Axis-tainted ministers from his cabinet and appointed conservative Christian Democrats, such as Alberto Martín-Artajo as Foreign Minister, to give credibility to his new image as an authoritarian Catholic. The appointment of Juan Antonio Suanzes, as Minister of Commerce and Industry, presaged poor economic performance. The key appointment was Martín-Artajo, who was assured by Franco that he could facilitate a transition to the promised monarchy. He was unaware that Franco was simultaneously reassuring Falangists that nothing would change. In fact, he would keep control over foreign policy merely using Artajo as the acceptable face of his regime for the international community.[10]

To neutralize the monarchists in his coalition and present a more acceptable face to the Western powers, Franco planned to introduce a law to make Spain a kingdom. However, he had no intention of bringing back a royal family that he regarded as tainted by constitutionalism as well as being an impediment to his own power.[11] He was confident that his own survival would be assured by the inevitable break-up of the Allies' wartime alliance with the Soviet Union leaving Spain as a potentially valuable asset for the West.[12] Much patience would be needed. At the founding conference of the United Nations, held in San Francisco between 25 April and 26 June 1945, Mexico successfully proposed the exclusion of any country whose regime had been installed with the help of the states that had fought against the United Nations. The proposal could apply only to Franco's Spain.[13] The Caudillo responded with a shameless denial. Interviewed by the United Press, he said: 'when Germany seemed to be winning the war, some members of the Falange tried to identify Spain with Germany and Italy, but I immediately dismissed all persons so inclined. I never had the slightest intention of taking Spain into the war.'[14] The Mexican resolution was adopted by the three great powers at the Potsdam conference when, on 2 August, Spain was excluded from the United Nations because of the origins, nature, record and Axis links of the Franco regime.[15]

Franco replied brazenly, on 5 August, that Spain did not beg to join any international organization and would accept only a position commensurate with its historical importance, size of population and services to peace and culture. He praised Spanish wartime neutrality as an 'outstanding record of nobility'.[16] In frequent declarations, he portrayed Spain as a unified oasis of peace in a troubled world in which Communist hordes were ceaselessly on the prowl.[17] Martín-Artajo shared his belief that Spain's geostrategic position rendered it invaluable to the Western powers. 'Spain', he said, 'has only to sit waiting at her door to see the funeral procession of the enemies which she defeated in 1939.'[18]

In August, Franco's ever more influential assistant Luis Carrero Blanco presented a sycophantic report on the regime's survival. It praised Franco's achievements and echoed his prejudices. The monarchists were dismissed as a few ambitious egoists. The critical attitudes of London and Washington were dismissed as resentment that 'Spain is now independent, politically free, vigorous and on the way up'. Carrero Blanco was confident that Britain and the United States would never risk opening the door to communism in Spain by supporting the exiled Republicans. He advised Franco that 'the only formula possible for us is order, unity and hang on for dear life. Good police action to foresee subversion; energetic repression if it materializes, without fear of foreign criticism, since it is better to punish harshly once and for all than leave the evil uncorrected.' Franco regarded any foreign pressure for democratic change as 'the masonic offensive'. He told a cabinet meeting on 8 September that there were 15 million freemasons in England who all voted Labour.[19] Nevertheless, with typical duplicity, he bought time by letting Martín-Artajo assure foreign diplomats that he would hand over to the heir to the throne, Don Juan de Borbón 'within the next two years'.[20]

Carrero Blanco's memorandum had proposed an entirely reasonable strategy. Churchill and later Ernest Bevin, the Foreign Secretary in Clement Attlee's government, had made it clear that Britain would never intervene in Spain. Despite intense public hostility to Franco, the French President General de Gaulle sent a secret message to Franco to the effect that he would resist pressure and maintain diplomatic relations with him.[21] Without external opposition, Franco was able to concentrate on his domestic position. In late 1945 and early 1946, he made key speeches to the army top brass calling for defence of the unity of the *patria*, which effectively meant in defence of his position.[22] At the same time, he rejected suggestions that he should limit his reliance on the Falange.[23] The Día del Caudillo on 1 October 1945, the ninth anniversary of his exaltation to supreme power, saw ceremonies all over Spain involving the Church, the armed forces and contingents of Falangists orchestrated to project an image of popular and institutional support for Franco.[24]

To disband the Falange would barely diminish popular hostility towards Franco in the Western democracies while maintaining it provided constant adulation from the hundreds of thousands of hangers-on who lived off the Movimiento's sprawling bureaucracy, a gigantic apparatus staffed by those who had nowhere else to go and whose survival depended on loyalty to the Caudillo. At a week-long cabinet meeting from 3 to 11 October, Franco ruled out any reform beyond cosmetic changes such as banning the fascist salute. Talking of 'wearing a democratic suit as an insurance policy', he ordered a propaganda emphasis on the Fuero de los Españoles and a law to establish the eventual succession. When Artajo suggested a partial amnesty for political prisoners, Franco replied, 'We do not wipe the slate clean.'[25] He made a linked threat that efforts to remove him would mean another civil war.[26] To get rid of Franco depended on the army and he consistently consolidated its support by hints that, if he disappeared, 'the days of fat living' would end.[27]

Against the left, he applied implacable repression. Imprisonment, executions, torture and exile had already taken a savage toll on the Republican opposition. Hunger and the difficulty of getting work without safe-conducts for travel and certificates of political reliability further diminished the capacity for resistance. The impact of autarky, corruption and incompetence could be seen in food prices. In 1936, a kilo of beef cost 2 pesetas 40 cents, a kilo of potatoes 30 cents and a litre of olive oil 1 peseta 70 cents. By 1945, if these items were actually available, a kilo of beef cost between 35 and 40 pesetas, a kilo of potatoes 5 pesetas and a litre of olive oil 68 pesetas 70 cents. In the case of cooking oil, olive oil had been exported throughout the Second World War and, in its stead, low-quality soya oil had been imported which had caused several cases of food poisoning.[28]

Between 1945 and 1951, the war against left-wing *guerrilleros* was pursued ruthlessly. In the budget for 1946, while only 6 per cent of public spending was dedicated to education, the instruments of repression, the police, the Civil Guard and the army, received 45 per cent.[29] In the war against the *guerrilleros*, a scorched-earth policy saw the Civil Guard raze entire villages to the ground. Eventual peasant rejection of the *guerrilleros* was accelerated by the actions of special Civil Guard units of agents provocateurs. Disguised as *guerrilleros*, they would enter a village seeking food and shelter. When sympathizers came forward, they were arrested or executed. Sometimes, the fake *guerrilleros* would attack villages, raping and plundering. By the late 1940s, the real *guerrilleros* could no longer count on peasant sympathy and had to steal simply to survive.[30]

The economy continued to languish but criticism of Franco's policies was dismissed as 'typical of credulous simpletons in economics'.[31] Publication in the United States of German documents revealing Franco's commitment to the Axis was brushed off as evidence of a Communist–masonic conspiracy dedicated to destroying Spain. In a bizarre speech in September 1945, Franco declared that, despite defeating the 'satanic machinations' of perverted freemasons, Spain was coming under attack from 'the masonic super-State' which controlled the world's press and radio stations as well as many key politicians in the Western democracies. Franco carried this message to the people on punishing tours around the country at which his speeches were hailed by crowds mobilized by the Falange.[32]

Despite presenting his regime to the outside world as monarchist, Franco was infuriated when the royal heir refused to come to Spain unless it was to assume the throne. In early February 1946, Don Juan took up residence in Estoril near Lisbon. As many as 458 of the most important figures of the Spanish establishment, including twenty ex-ministers, the presidents of the country's five biggest banks, many aristocrats and prominent university professors, signed a collective letter to Don Juan expressing their wish to see the restoration of the monarchy, 'incarnated by Your Majesty'.[33] Franco was livid, telling a cabinet meeting on 15 February, 'This is a declaration of war. They must be crushed like worms.' He planned to imprison all the signatories without trial, desisting only when senior ministers explained the damaging international repercussions of doing so. Instead, he punished them by withdrawing their passports, subjecting them to exhaustive tax inspections or dismissing them from their posts. Seeing Kindelán as the ringleader, he exiled him to the Canary Islands.[34]

Franco's treatment of the monarchists was mild in comparison with the fate of the left. On 21 February, one of the leaders of the guerrilla movement and a hero of the French resistance, Cristino García, was executed along with nine others, after the most cursory of trials.[35] Franco rejected pleas for clemency from the French government to reinforce the message projected during his tour of Falangist rallies. A few days later, thirty-seven members of the PSOE were given heavy prison sentences for trying to reorganize the party.[36]

The French government was furious and wanted to put the Spanish question on the agenda of the United Nations Security Council. Determined to do nothing that might encourage civil war in Spain, the British and American governments persuaded the French to accept an anodyne compromise. On 4 March, a Tripartite Declaration of the United States, Great Britain and France announced that 'As long as General Franco continues in control of Spain, the Spanish people cannot anticipate full and cordial association with those nations of the world which have, by common effort, brought defeat to German Nazism and Italian Fascism, which aided the present Spanish regime in its rise to power.' It went on to state that 'There is no intention of interfering in the internal affairs of Spain. The Spanish people themselves must in the long run work out their own destiny.' The pious hope that, without risking civil war, 'leading patriotic and liberal-minded Spaniards may soon find the means to bring about a peaceful withdrawal by Franco, the abolition of the Falange and the establishment of an interim or caretaker Government' illustrated the limits of the Western powers' hostility to the Caudillo revealed by the Potsdam Declaration.[37] Nevertheless, in cabinet Franco fumed that Russia was behind the Tripartite Declaration and

France its 'Quisling'. He referred to the leaders of the democracies as 'those bandits'.[38]

Franco perceived that the Anglo-American policy of non-intervention was based on a determination to prevent the Iberian Peninsula falling under Soviet influence.[39] On the day after the Tripartite Declaration, Churchill's celebrated 'Iron Curtain' speech at Fulton, Missouri, convinced him that it was only a matter of time before the West recognized his value. Two days later, at the Army Museum, Franco reminded his supporters that the best defence against the return of a vengeful left was to unite around him. He spoke of shared 'sacrifices and discomfort, of austerity and long vigils, of service and sentry duty. But in such service, you can occasionally rest. I cannot; I am the sentry who is never relieved, the one who receives the unwelcome telegrams and dictates the solutions; the one who is watchful while others sleep.' From self-glorification, he passed to self-pity, lamenting the costs of his selfless dedication: 'I, as Chief of State, see my private life and my hobbies severely limited; my entire life is work and meditation.'[40]

On 1 April, the annual civil war victory parade was turned into a massive demonstration of support for Franco.[41] On 6 April, the Falangist Minister of Labour, José Antonio Girón de Velasco, and a delegation of civil war ex-combatants gave a delighted Franco fifty albums containing 300,000 signed affirmations of grateful loyalty.[42] In mid-April, the Russian and Polish delegations at the United Nations jointly proposed the suspension of diplomatic relations with Spain, on the grounds that an ally of the Axis was a danger to world peace. It was countered by the British and American representatives who proposed merely that the accusations be investigated by a subcommittee.[43] On 14 May, Franco replied in the Cortes. Speaking for over two hours, he denied coming to power with Axis assistance and claimed that Spain was being attacked because it had suppressed freemasonry and defeated communism. He praised himself for his generosity in 1940 towards a defeated France and claimed that Spain had saved Britain from defeat.[44]

In its report of 31 May, the subcommittee confirmed the Axis-assisted origins and fascist nature of the Franco regime, its pro-Axis conduct during the Second World War, its continuing support for Nazi war criminals and the execution, imprisonment and repression of its political opponents. However, since Franco had not threatened international peace, it was unable to recommend that the Security Council interfere in

Spain. Nonetheless, concluding that Franco's Spain represented 'a potential threat to international peace and security', the subcommittee recommended that the United Nations call on its members to break off relations with Spain.[45] Franco, through Artajo, responded with an indignant protest that this constituted an intolerable interference in Spain's internal affairs. In fact, nothing came of the subcommittee's report beyond a feeble agreement that the Spanish question should be subject to constant vigilance by the Security Council.[46]

Meanwhile, Franco's propaganda apparatus was working frantically to persuade Spaniards that they were the victims of an international siege to which was attributed responsibility for the country's appalling economic situation. In fact, the real culprit was the policy of autarky, which permitted Spanish manufacturers to import crucial raw materials and machinery only with government licences. This fostered both corruption and incompetence.[47] For Spain to share in the benefits of international post-war economic reconstruction, Franco would have had to accept political reform. This he categorically refused to do. The 'siege' was a convenient excuse for almost every failing of the regime.[48]

Ever more complacent, Franco told Artajo that 'the world squabbles and leaves us in peace'.[49] The flow of adulation was unabated. On the tenth annual Día del Caudillo, on 1 October, in elaborate celebrations in Burgos, after a Te Deum in the Cathedral Franco received a shield of gold and platinum encrusted with rubies, diamonds and emeralds, the gift of the authorities of the fifty Spanish provinces.[50] He dismissed as a Soviet-inspired plot United Nations calls, in late 1946, for him to give way to a provisional representative government.[51] An extensive propaganda campaign to give the impression of total national unity was organized by the Falangist ministers Girón and Fernández Cuesta.[52] A throng of Falangists and ex-combatants gathered in the Plaza de Oriente, on 9 December 1946, waving banners with slogans attacking Russia, the French and foreigners in general. Franco addressed the crowd as if Spain were still in the midst of the civil war, virulently attacking communism and the democracies. He invited his supporters 'to unite the force of our righteousness to the fortress of our unity' and ended with the boast that 'the proof of Spain's resurgence is that the rest of the world dangles from our feet'. Chants of '¡Franco! ¡Franco! ¡Franco!' could be heard for an hour after his speech.[53]

The final agreed resolution on Spain, adopted at the General Assembly on 12 December 1946, excluded Spain from the United Nations and called on all members to withdraw their ambassadors.[54] Four days later, at a ceremony in Zaragoza to celebrate Spanish resistance against the Napoleonic invasion, Franco declared that his superior system placed Spain ten years ahead of other nations in moral standing and social evolution. He also authorized a new coinage to be minted on which would appear his head and the words 'Caudillo by the grace of God'.[55] Despite the pretence that Spain was facing international aggression, the United Nations had effectively endorsed the Anglo-American policy of non-intervention. There would be no economic or military sanctions. Most countries withdrew their ambassadors but continued to run their embassies as normal under a chargé d'affaires. Franco, however, was delighted to be able to use the toothless international hostility to create the myth that he was the heroic captain of a besieged garrison.[56] Within two days of the United Nations resolution, he began a series of occasional articles in *Arriba*. Published over the next five years under the pseudonym Jakim Boor (the two pillars of the masonic temple), they revealed his enduring hostility to 'the Jews of the world, the army of speculators'.[57] The UN Secretary General, the Norwegian Trygve Lie, and the President of the General Assembly, the Belgian Paul-Henri Spaak, were reviled as freemasons and lackeys of Moscow. The articles argued that freemasonry, which for Franco was consubstantial with liberal democracy, was conspiring with communism to destroy Spain.[58] Franco's obsession with freemasonry was fed by a network of spies. Although the information that they supplied was extremely dubious, he treated it with total credulity.[59]

Despite his contempt for the Western democracies, Franco was working with Carrero Blanco on schemes to make his regime acceptable in the international arena. This involved institutionalizing the regime as a monarchy with Franco remaining as head of state and regent for life. Changing the name of the regime to 'kingdom' would not alter its substance. On 22 March 1947, Carrero Blanco suggested that Franco name his own royal successor.[60]

Around this time, after a visit to Spain, Juan March commented to Gil Robles that all he saw was 'cowardice, egoism and corruption'.[61] Franco himself acknowledged this in early January 1947. Leading a delegation of older generals, the venerable Andrés Saliquet expressed concern about the United Nations' decision. Franco replied cruelly: 'There's nothing to worry about. Anyway, isn't your soap factory doing well?' He thereby demonstrated his awareness of how networks of corruption sustained his cause. Many generals enjoyed directorships in companies happy to pay for their influence in the quest for rare raw materials or electrical power. He then told the generals that the growing antagonism between Russia and America guaranteed that he would soon be courted by Washington.[62] He had diplomatic reports on his desk confirming that British Conservatives and important elements in the Pentagon saw him as a bulwark against Soviet advances.[63]

The tide was indeed turning for Franco. On 12 March 1947, in response to British inability to sustain military aid to Greece and Turkey, the Truman doctrine of support for 'free peoples to work out their own destinies in their own way' was announced.[64] As the international context became more favourable, Franco continued to clothe his regime with the trappings of acceptability. A draft of the Law of Succession was announced in early April. Spain was declared to be a Catholic kingdom whose head of state was Franco. The Axis dalliance was simply brushed under the carpet while the small print showed that nothing had changed in the dictatorship. Franco would govern until prevented by death or incapacity and would have the right to name his own royal successor. Ideally, the scheme required the acquiescence of Don Juan de Borbón. However, on 7 April, an outraged Don Juan issued the 'Estoril Manifesto' denouncing the succession law as illegal since neither the heir to the throne nor the people had been consulted. Franco, Artajo and Carrero agreed that Don Juan had thereby eliminated himself as a suitable successor to the Caudillo. Don Juan's manifesto saw Franco's press denounce him as the tool of international freemasonry and communism.[65] Both London and Washington were totally sceptical of Franco's scheme but, in the Cold War context, had no stomach to do anything about it.[66]

In response to the plummeting living conditions of the working class, and despite heavy police repression, industrial unrest finally erupted at the beginning of May 1947. A series of strikes broke out across the country, mainly in the Basque Country and also in Catalonia, in Madrid and in the shipyards of El Ferrol.[67] The regime responded with characteristic brutality. Bilbao was flooded with units of the Foreign Legion, the Civil Guard and an additional 2,500 armed police. Employers were ordered to sack strikers, and those who did not were imprisoned.[68] Rather than seeing the strike wave as the popular action against the regime called for by the UN condemnation of December 1946, London and Washington chose to interpret it as Communist-inspired mischief.[69]

In June 1947, General George C. Marshall, the US Secretary of State, announced the European Recovery Programme, from which Spain was excluded. The Spanish government responded by distributing in Washington pamphlets claiming that, without Spain, the Marshall Plan was doomed to failure.[70] Ironically, the Marshall Plan, even with Spain excluded, favoured Franco's survival. By preventing its Eastern European dependants from accepting US aid, Moscow hastened the division of Europe into two blocs and thereby increased Spain's strategic value to the West.

In the meantime, food from Argentina was crucial in sustaining the regime until US attitudes changed. Juan Domingo Perón had disobeyed the UN resolution and, in January 1947, sent a new ambassador whose arrival was greeted by orchestrated demonstrations and euphoric press coverage.[71] Even more spectacular propaganda was generated when the glamorous María Eva Duarte de Perón (Evita) visited Spain in the summer. Vast crowds were mobilized by the Falange whenever Evita was seen in public with Franco.[72] The visit coincided with the referendum to ratify the Law of Succession being organized by Blas Pérez, the Minister of the Interior.[73] Calls for a 'yes' vote in the referendum appeared opposite coverage of Evita's tour. The Franco–Perón Protocol was signed, guaranteeing further credit and wheat deliveries until 1951.[74]

Blanket propaganda for the referendum claimed that a 'no' vote meant abandoning Catholic Spain to international Marxism.[75] The full power of the Church was activated and officials insisted that ration cards would not be valid unless presented and stamped at the polling booths. According to the debatable official figures, in the referendum held on Monday 6 July, 15,219,565 Spaniards voted, 89 per cent of those eligible. Of these, 14,145,163 or 93 per cent voted 'yes'; 4.7 per cent (722,656) voted 'no' and there were 2.3 per cent (351,746) blank or spoiled ballot papers. Even accounting for abstention in the big cities, the propaganda barrage, the intimidation and falsification, the results showed that Franco now enjoyed considerable popular support.[76] Although hardly convinced by the democratic validity of the referendum, by mid-July 1947 British and American policymakers were beginning to accept that Franco would be around for some time to come.[77] They reluctantly acknowledged his value in the Cold War. In October that year, the US State Department opted for a rapid normalization of economic and political relations with Spain.[78]

The Spanish question was discussed at the General Assembly, held at the temporary UN headquarters in Lake Success on the edge of New York City. Despite evidence that Franco's Law of Succession was a sham, that thousands of his opponents were kept in inhuman prison conditions and that he continued to grant asylum to large numbers of Nazi war criminals, proposals for full-scale economic sanctions did not succeed. Many ambassadors were already drifting back to Madrid in contravention of the 1946 UN Resolution and, in January 1948, State Department officials were discussing possibly sending an American ambassador to Madrid. Franco had survived the worst, and the Communist takeover in Czechoslovakia in February 1948 and the Berlin blockade from June 1948 to May 1949 would do the rest.[79] Franco felt able to devote ever more time to his pleasures. Fishing in Asturias occupied his Easter holidays and deep-sea fishing in the Atlantic on his yacht *Azor* took up much of the summer. He always found time too for hunting trips that hosted much of the regime's corrupt dealing.[80]

Although the US Congress approved Spain's inclusion in the Marshall Plan on 30 March 1948, President Truman pointed out that only the members of the European Recovery Programme could decide. He was taking account of popular opinion in Britain and France and was also appalled at the lack of religious freedom in Franco's Spain.[81] Meanwhile, Franco arranged a meeting with Don Juan on the *Azor* in the Bay of Biscay, on 25 August.[82] They spoke alone for three hours, although Franco did most of the talking. Franco's aim was to ensure that Don Juan's ten-year-old son Juan Carlos would complete his education in Spain. He wanted the boy as a hostage both to justify his continued enjoyment of the role of regent and to control the eventual monarchical restoration.[83] Don Juan told an official of the American Embassy that prior to the meeting he was making no progress in his relations with Franco and that now he had got 'his foot in the door', although he was aware that any agreement on Juan Carlos would be manipulated by Franco to imply that he had abdicated.[84]

The benefits of the meeting were all on Franco's side. He had undermined a rapprochement between monarchists and Socialists.[85] He leaked news that Juan Carlos would be educated in Spain, and Don Juan was forced to agree to send his son to Spain, where he arrived on 9 November. A group of teachers professing firm pro-Francoist loyalty was assembled. When Juan Carlos visited Franco at his official residence, the El Pardo palace on the outskirts of Madrid, the controlled media gave the impression that the monarchy was subordinate to the Dictator.[86] In the context of worsening international tension, this apparent 'normalization' of Spanish politics was greeted eagerly by the Western powers. Don Juan soon realized that he had been duped, but it was too late. Franco had squeezed every drop of benefit out of the apparent closeness between them.[87]

To consolidate his position with Washington, in March 1948 Franco sent José Félix de Lequerica to Washington with the specious title of 'Inspector of Embassies and Legations' and copious amounts of cash to build up political, military, religious and financial support for the regime. Lequerica cultivated an enthusiastically pro-Franco lobby of influential Catholics, anti-Communists, military planners, anti-Truman Republicans and businessmen with interests in Spain.[88] He successfully arranged the visit to El Pardo on 30 September of a US military mission.[89] Since it occurred during the annual Día del Caudillo celebrations, the media presented the visit as an American endorsement of Franco's rule.[90] The worst was over. Don Juan was tamed. Senior American military men were beating a path to his door. On 4 October in Paris, General Marshall told the British and French Foreign Ministers, Ernest Bevin and Dr Robert Schuman, that recognizing Franco presented no problem for the United States. It was too early for public opinion in Britain and France to go that far, but Spanish entry into the United Nations would soon be on the agenda.[91]

Anxious to clinch relations with the United States, Franco unsuccessfully proposed a bilateral economic arrangement with the USA, even including the possibility of military bases in Spain and in the Canary and Balearic Islands.[92] Given that the Labour Party was in power in Britain, Franco concentrated his diplomatic efforts on the United States and the Vatican. The piously Catholic Joaquín Ruiz-Giménez was despatched as Ambassador to the Holy See at the end of November 1948 with the task of securing a Concordat which Franco wanted as a public seal of divine approval for his regime.

So powerful was Franco's apparatus of repression that he gave little thought to the left. In working-class districts of major towns, people in rags could be seen hunting for scraps, and the streets were thronged with beggars. Most major cities had shanty towns on their outskirts where people lived in appallingly primitive conditions. Just outside Barcelona and Malaga, some lived in huts made of cardboard or corrugated iron and others in caves. State medical and welfare services were virtually non-existent. The situation worsened with massive internal migration after 1945 and the uncontrolled growth of industrial cities. In the absence of urban planning, the need to accommodate the recently arrived population saw huge fortunes made in the construction industry through the creation of shoddy, overcrowded speculative neighbourhoods. They usually lacked basic services, clinics, schools, public transport, functioning lifts and safety facilities and were nicknamed vertical shanty towns. The possibilities for corruption were almost unlimited as public officials needed to be bribed to ensure the necessary reclassification or rezoning as well as to provide the permits for basic building materials such as cement, steel and wood which were rationed until 1959.[93] Hardship, malnutrition, epidemics and the growth of prostitution and the black market were consequences of his regime's policies, but the plight of the victims did not bother Franco.[94] Despite speeches claiming that he had bestowed prosperity on his people, when there was speculation about Spain joining the soon-to-be-launched NATO he indicated that the price for military cooperation should involve some relief of the country's economic plight.[95]

Spain's economic situation was so desperate that the Minister of Industry and Commerce, Juan Antonio Suanzes, predicted that, without American financial aid, total collapse could be anticipated within six months. Persistent drought was causing severe electricity restrictions which hit industrial production. Predictions of the wheat harvest were consistently being scaled down. The bread ration was reduced to 150 grams per day after Perón had refused to send more wheat without fulfilment of Spanish commitments to Argentina.[96] However, Franco's boundless optimism in such parlous conditions was boosted by the success of the Spanish lobby. On 8 February 1949, it was announced that two New York banks had loaned the Spanish government $25 million.[97] In early April 1949, NATO was created without Spain but with Salazar's Portugal as a member. That reflected the strategic value of the Azores, the hostility towards Franco of public opinion in most European countries and the fact that Salazar had handled his wartime neutrality with infinitely greater subtlety than Franco.[98] Nevertheless, there were hopeful signs for Franco. When the UN General Assembly met in New York in early May that year to discuss the continued ostracism of Spain, Britain, France and the USA abstained from voting on a Latin American proposal to restore full diplomatic relations. After bitter arguments on 11 and 16 May, the Latin American resolution came within four votes of reaching the required two-thirds majority.[99] Two days later, Franco gave a speech to the Cortes both justifying his past and claiming a prime place in the international community. He boasted that his regime was a world leader whose social achievements distinguished it from both liberal capitalism and Marxist materialism. The speech contained an account of his imaginary economic achievements. He also insinuated that the only obstacle to his desired understanding with the USA was the malice of Britain and France.[100]

At this time, the Spanish government was involved in a dubious operation with Juan March, who came out of it massively enriched.[101] It involved the Barcelona Traction, Light and Power Co. (BTLP), the principal electricity-generating company in Catalonia. Registered in Canada, hence its nickname La Canadiense, its major shareholder was a Belgian company, SOFINA, which also owned the Compañía Hispano-American de Electricidad (CHADE), the biggest electricity-generating company in Latin America. Although CHADE was not active in Spain, its profits in Latin America were paid into its headquarters in Spain and enjoyed very favourable tax privileges from Franco. March had been buying up shares in BTLP since the end of the Second World War through a company in Tangiers. In April 1947, his emissaries informed its chairman, the American Daniel Heineman, that, if the CHADE did not sell the BTLP to him, the Spanish government would attack CHADE. In preparation for this operation, March had abandoned his advocacy of the cause of Don Juan in order to repair his relations with El Pardo.

His first target was Blas Pérez, who received permission from Franco to see him. March's pretext was to talk about public health in Mallorca since Blas Pérez was also Minister of Health. He left the interview declaring: 'He is the most intelligent Minister that Franco has. I'm in love with him.' What incentives were discussed is not known, but criticisms of CHADE soon began to be voiced both in cabinet and in the Cortes by Pérez and Suanzes, with whom March had close links. March told Heineman that he could stop the attacks in return for a controlling interest in Barcelona Traction. When Heineman refused, in July 1947 Suanzes implemented restrictive fiscal measures against CHADE. It has been alleged that March gave a block of shares to the Spanish government. Certainly, Blas Pérez later became a board member of March's Transmediterránea shipping company.

Barcelona Traction was a profitable company. Its assets were about £10 million (about $500 million in 2010). However, for the convenience of some of its foreign investors, BTLP had issued some bonds in sterling on which the interest was payable in pounds. Suanzes's commitment to autarky had seen currency restrictions imposed by the Instituto Español de Moneda Extranjera which made it impossible for BTLP to acquire the necessary sterling to pay the interest. The company's assets would be sufficient to pay the arrears of interest whenever the restrictions were relaxed. However, agents secretly acting for March bought up the bonds, taking advantage of the fact that, as the debt in back interest increased, the share price dropped. When he had enough (21 per cent), March called for the payment of interest. In February 1948, his agents brought a case in a court in Reus, claiming that the BTLP was in default and demanding immediate relief. The judge, who had allegedly been bribed, agreed and awarded ownership of all Barcelona Traction's assets to the complainants (effectively to March). The company's foreign owners appealed, but got no relief from Spanish courts. They were supported by the governments of Belgium, Canada and the USA, but their initiatives were skilfully blocked by March's lawyers.

By June 1951, March had most of the shares and pushed for the company to be sold. The conditions of the auction were that the buyer had to pay all the interest owed, most of which was owed to March. In his actions, March had the support of Blas Pérez, Suanzes and Franco, who all believed that this was an opportunity for the company to be nationalized. When Suanzes was replaced by Manuel Arburúa in July 1951, March got him on board. The only bidder able to meet the conditions of the auction was Fuerzas Eléctricas de Cataluña SA, which belonged to March. For 10 million pesetas, he acquired a company that was valued at a minimum of 1,500 million and possibly 6,000 million. The initial reaction of Franco was to call it 'a daring triumph of nationalism'. It has been suggested that Franco's support was his payment for March's support during the civil war. Suanzes was furious when the company was not nationalized and all the profit went to March. Larraz regarded it as 'the swindle of the century'.[102] The Belgian government appealed to the International Court of Justice in The Hague in 1958, to no avail. Serrano Súñer who acted as one of the lawyers for the Belgian government called it 'the most fabulous stunt ever perpetrated in the history of commercial law'.[103]

Although the BTLP profit went to March, things were going well for Franco on other fronts. When Don Juan suggested preventing his son's return to Spain after the 1949 summer holidays, Franco countered with a threat to pass a law specifically excluding Don Juan from the throne. He capitulated.[104] News of the Soviet explosion of an atom bomb in August intensified pressure within the United States for a rapprochement with Spain to secure air and naval bases.[105] A powerful advocate of an alliance with Franco was Admiral Forrest Sherman, who was convinced of Spain's geostrategic importance to the USA. As Commander-in-Chief of the US Sixth Fleet, he visited many Spanish ports. His son-in-law was Assistant Naval Attaché in Madrid in 1947. When Sherman and his wife visited their daughter in the Spanish capital, Franco ensured that they were pampered by the authorities.[106] Other key figures in the US defence establishment were keen to secure bases in Spain. Lequerica's Washington lobby could count on the support of several influential political and military figures and, thanks to funds authorized by Franco, increasing numbers of senators and congressmen paraded through Madrid at Spain's expense.[107]

Mao Zedong's establishment of the Chinese People's Republic in early October 1949 further benefited Franco. To Western policymakers, it seemed as if another huge area of the world had fallen into the Soviet orbit, although Mao was not the stooge of Moscow. In this context an operation to show the Western Allies the value of the Iberian Peninsula was mounted from 22 to 27 October 1949. Franco visited Portugal on board the battlecruiser *Miguel de Cervantes* at the head of a flotilla of eleven warships. At the mouth of the Tagus, he was met by four Portuguese destroyers and escorted to Lisbon. There followed a fly-past of Hurricanes and Spitfires and a parade of 15,000 Portuguese soldiers. The 27th of October was declared a public holiday in Spain and, to greet Franco's return, the streets of Madrid were lined by crowds of Falangists and peasants bussed in from the Castilian provinces.[108]

Meanwhile, Spain's food crisis was worsening. Shortly after Christmas 1949, Varela told Franco of his concern about both administrative corruption and the desperate wheat shortage. The Caudillo replied complacently that he could easily get the foreign credits to buy food but was not prepared to pay the price of the necessary political changes. He preferred to wait, certain that 'the world needs Spain more than Spain needs the world'. Varela suggested that he limit the regime's corruption by granting more freedom to the press and the Cortes. Franco objected that the negative consequences would be worse. Corruption was a central instrument of his power. The interview ended with Franco telling Varela: 'I will not give Spain any freedom in the next ten years. Then, I will open my hand a little.'[109]

Franco's confidence reflected his awareness of pressure in both the British and American governments for a more favourable policy towards Spain.[110] Admitting that the 1946 resolution had failed, on 18 January 1950 Truman's Secretary of State, Dean Acheson, stated in a widely reproduced letter that the United States would be prepared to vote for a UN resolution permitting member nations to send ambassadors to Madrid and admitting Spain to international technical agencies. Acheson indicated that fuller integration into Western European institutions, including presumably NATO, would require political liberalization in Spain.[111] The writing was on the wall. When Acheson's letter was published in Spain, it was taken as proof that the United States recognized that the Caudillo had been right all along. The call for liberalization was denounced as an impertinent interference in Spain's internal affairs.[112] Franco knew that the regime's worst difficulties were over. Moreover, despite critical declarations about his Axis links, Western European governments wanted access to Spain's agricultural products.[113]

Behind the media smokescreen of Franco's dedication to his country, the appalling living standards of the working class coexisted with the fat living and corruption of the elite. Some of the more austere generals protested. However, as Franco's remarks to Saliquet indicated, austerity in the higher echelons was the exception, particularly within the Caudillo's own family. In a speech made in March 1950, General Juan Yagüe, Captain General of the VI Military Region (Burgos), complained bitterly about the 'ignorant and the uneducated, with no more qualification than their ability to buy consciences, who enrich themselves rapidly and proudly boast of their shamelessness; others get important jobs and no one knows what black hand elevates them and keeps them there'.[114]

Franco considered himself to be a man of exemplary austerity. Certainly, he did not womanize, did not smoke, drank wine in moderation at meal times and did not gamble beyond a small-scale flutter on the national lottery or when playing cards with friends – and later on the pools. However, the entire resources, antiques and artworks, palaces and estates of the one-time royal patrimony were at the exclusive disposal of his family, a privilege of which he took full advantage, particularly for hunting. The expense of his hunting and fishing expeditions was enormous. Deep-sea fishing required the year-round maintenance of the yacht *Azor* and the provision of naval escorts when he chased tuna and whales far into the Atlantic. Both hunting and freshwater fishing involved moving large retinues around Spain. Moreover, there were the hidden costs of the neglect of government business, since not only Franco but also several of his ministers would be involved in these jaunts. There was also the effort that went into ensuring that his trips were successful by dint of baiting large areas of the sea and of feeding deer and other game at strategic points on hunting reserves.

The corruption of the Franco family increased on a significant scale with the marriage of his daughter 'Nenuca' (Carmen), on 10 April 1950, to a minor society playboy from Jaén, Dr Cristóbal Martínez-Bordiú. That he was soon to inherit the title of Marqués de Villaverde endeared him to the snobbish Carmen Polo.[115] The preparations and the accumulation of presents were such that the press was ordered to say nothing for fear of provoking unwelcome contrasts with the famine and poverty that afflicted much of the country.[116] Those wishing to ingratiate themselves with Doña Carmen took advice from her inseparable companion, Pura, the Marquesa de Huétor, on the most appropriate presents. The wedding was on a level of extravagance that would have taxed any European royal family. Guards of honour, military bands and hundreds of guests including the cabinet, the diplomatic corps and a glittering array of aristocrats, took part in what became a major state occasion. Reports of the ceremony, which took place in the chapel at El Pardo, failed to mention the gifts. Editorial comments praising the austerity of the occasion were, however, laughably at odds with the coverage, on other pages, of the banquet offered at El Pardo for 800 people.

Popular attention was caught by the beautiful jewellery worn by the bride and by the bridegroom's elaborate uniform as a Knight of the Holy Sepulchre, complete with sword and crested helmet. The Caudillo, dressed in the ornate dress uniform of a captain general of the armed forces, gave away his daughter.[117] Nenuca's marriage would change Franco's life. Between 1951 and 1964, she would give him seven grandchildren on whom he would lavish an indulgent affection hitherto absent from his life. Martínez-Bordiú exchanged the old motorbike on which he had visited his fiancée for a series of Chrysler and Packard convertibles and was soon known by Madrid wags as the Marqués de Vayavida (What a life). He took full advantage of his link to the Dictator's family to foster his business interests. General Latorre Roca commented: 'the light-fingered and pompous Marqués de Villaverde far exceeds Nicolás in many regards, but principally as an exceptional commercial traveller as the representative of several foreign companies who provided goods to Spanish government departments'. Together with Pura's husband, the Marqués de Huétor de Santillán, the head of Franco's household, Martínez-Bordiú made a fortune from various sources, particularly the acquisition of the exclusive licence for importing Vespa motor scooters from Italy, at a time when Spain had little foreign currency for imports. The machines were in a standard green and, in Madrid, his nickname changed to the Marqués de Vespaverde. Madrid wits quipped that VESPA stood for Villaverde Entra Sin Pagar Aduana (Villaverde enters without paying customs duties).[118]

A Villaverde clan emerged, of which the financial brains was Martínez-Bordiú's uncle and godfather José María Sanchiz Sancho. Sanchiz's father, José Martínez Ortega, the Conde de Argillo, had worked for the Third Reich during the Second World War and helped hide Nazi funds from the Allies afterwards.[119] Sanchiz was soon handling Franco's finances. He made a fortune for the Villaverde clan with speculation in property and import–export licences and his success saw him acquire considerable banking interests. Sanchiz helped Franco buy, and then acted as administrator of, a substantial estate at Valdefuentes, near Móstoles on the Extremadura road out of Madrid. Eventually, the numerous members of the Villaverde clan came to displace the families of Franco's brother Nicolás and sister Pilar at the Pardo.[120] A senior Falangist who kept records of bribery and corruption within the Francoist elite described Sanchiz as 'an adventurer with the soul of a jackal' for whom 'politics cannot be regarded as selfless service for the common good but rather as cunning dealing on a dirty counter whose greasy profits have to be seen immediately in one's own bank account.

He besmirches everything he touches and leaves a slimy trail wherever he goes.'[121] The Villaverde clan were probably the most successful of the many people who exploited their personal connections with Franco. The Caudillo's opinion of Sanchiz is not known although, despite the lucrative dealings that he had undertaken for him, he never released him from the obligation to address him as *Excelencia* and to use the formal *usted* mode of address. Franco had no interest in investigating corruption given his own involvement and the extent to which it kept the elite loyal to him.

Overall, it has been calculated that Franco received gifts worth 4,000 million pesetas (approximately £4 million/$7.5 million) during his rule. That calculation probably does not include the value of the hundreds of commemorative gold medals given to Franco by towns and organizations all over Spain which Doña Carmen had melted down into ingots.[122] In addition to the estate at Valdefuentes, the Franco family accumulated a further fifteen properties. In 1945, Doña Carmen bought an entire apartment building in Madrid. In August 1962, she acquired the magnificent Palacio de Cornide in La Coruña. The complex, and dubious, machinations for this latter purchase involved a rigged auction facilitated by Pedro Barrié de la Maza and the city's Mayor.[123]

It was only after the connection with the Villaverdes had been sealed that Doña Carmen gave free rein to her passion for antiques and jewellery. In this, she was urged on by Pura Huétor, who assured her that everyone in Spain with a high standard of living owed everything to the Caudillo.[124] The meanness and acquisitiveness of La Señora became legendary. It has been claimed that the jewellers of Madrid and Barcelona set up unofficial insurance syndicates to indemnify themselves against her visits. In La Coruña and Oviedo, jewellers and antique-dealers often shut up shop when they heard that she would be visiting. The shopkeepers that received her visits were told to send the bill to the Casa Civil of El Pardo and those that dared do so were duly paid. What is noteworthy, given the much-vaunted probity and austerity of the Franco family, is that these bills – for items destined for Carmen's private collection – were met from state funds.[125] Members of the El Pardo court, led by Pura, were the advance guard that arranged with antique dealers which pieces should be given to La Señora. Pura and her husband's second-in-command at the Casa Civil, General Fernando Fuertes de Villavicencio, also gave advice to ambitious sycophants on the kind of gift that would be acceptable. Unwanted gifts were exchanged for more desirable ones.[126] The Huétors exploited their connections with Doña Carmen to profit from their apparent closeness to Franco. José Antonio Girón, a man not fastidious in ethical matters, complained to Franco's cousin, Francisco Franco Salgado-Araujo, 'Pacón', about Pura Huétor's business dealings. Pacón told him resignedly that Doña Carmen was amused by it and considered it of no importance. Franco's sister Pilar, herself not averse to murky dealings, claimed to be shocked by Doña Carmen's links with Pura Huétor.[127]

Pilar always presented herself as a poverty-stricken widow who never took advantage of being the Dictator's sister. In fact, her relationship with her brother secured her positions on the boards of several companies that flourished precisely because it was assumed that Franco himself had an interest in them. Despite having only a small widow's pension in 1941 when her husband died, by the 1950s Pilar was a very rich woman. She had a residence in a fashionable Madrid neighbourhood that cost 12 million pesetas. She had managed to buy apartments for each of her ten children, was able to rent out another two, owned an estate in Puentedeume, near A Coruña and had substantial stock-market holdings. Her most profitable enterprise was carried out in 1957. An 81-year-old swindler, Manuel Bruguera Muñoz, falsified maps and deeds allowing him to sell an area of land in Madrid that already had owners. This was a fraud similar to those in which confidence tricksters sold the Eiffel Tower or the Statue of Liberty.

For 100,000 pesetas, Pilar Franco purchased for herself and her friend María Queipo de Llano, the niece of General Gonzalo Queipo de Llano, the land in an area due for major development (the prolongation of O'Donnell and Sainz de Baranda across Dr Esquerdo). The law practice of José María Gil Robles was retained to defend the interests of the real owners. According to Jaime Sánchez-Blanco, the lawyer who took on the case, Pilar then used her political influence to derive the greatest possible profit from the fraudulent operation. First of all, the Ayuntamiento of Madrid and the property registry were mobilized to get the land inscribed as actually belonging to her. When investigations were initiated, Franco's lifelong friend Camilo Alonso Vega was Minister of the Interior and the documents establishing the rightful ownership mysteriously disappeared from the Tribunal Supremo. Shortly after Bruguera died, the crime of falsification was declared to have fallen under the statute of limitations. The land was subjected to compulsory purchase orders when the expected urban development commenced in 1964. At that point, the Ministers of both Public Works and Finance ensured that Pilar got substantial compensation of 3 million pesetas for one part of the land and 15 millions for another. In July 1973, she received a further 134 million pesetas in compensation, the figure having been inflated when the assessors were told that the land 'belonged' to Pilar Franco.[128]

It was one of the most spectacular cases of fortunes being made through dubious reclassifications of land use, another being the wealth accumulated by the Falangist José Antonio Girón. Appointed Minister of Labour in May 1941, he remained in post for sixteen years. Within the regime, he was accused of misuse of public funds in his programme of creating *universidades laborales* (technical colleges), which saw friends make money from generous building contracts. José Solís accused him of being worse than the Sicilian mafia. Prior to leaving the ministry, he prepared his post-political career carefully. He had bought a house in Fuengirola in the province of Malaga from where he devoted himself to property deals. This was facilitated by Hans Hoffmann, a German with whom he had established close links during the Second World War. Hoffmann had worked as an interpreter for the División Azul and was then attached to the Third Reich's Embassy in Spain. Hoffmann used his connection with Girón to get information about the Spanish government that he then reported to Berlin. After 1945, he was a prominent member of the Nazi exiled community in Spain and became the key link between Konrad Adenauer and the Franco government. For this, he was rewarded by being made German Consul first in Algeciras and then in Malaga.

Throughout the 1960s, Hoffmann was the intermediary in purchasing numerous plots of land in the name of Girón's wife, María Josefa Larrucea Samaniego. Girón established himself in Fuengirola in 1949 after his friend, the Alcalde and head of the local Falange, Salvador Sáenz de Tejada Moreno, browbeat some peasants into selling a farm known as the Finca Santa Amalia to Hoffmann's wife for 15,000 pesetas. One year later, the land was sold to Girón's wife for the same amount. Girón then proceeded to build a sumptuous house on part of the land that encroached on the archaeological protection zone of the Arab castle of Fuengirola (Sohail). Hoffmann and Girón systematically began to buy up chalets, apartments, shops and plots of land.[129] The land rocketed in value after Girón used his political influence to have its legal status altered from agricultural use to permit construction. He was also helped by his friendship with another Falangist Alcalde, Clemente Díaz Ruiz. His holdings grew in value even more after he was named President in 1964 of the newly created Cooperativa de Promotores de la Costa del Sol. This body brought to the area major developers, bankers and hoteliers, such as Banús, Marsans, Meliá and the banker Ignacio Coca Gascón, who had close links to the Franco family.[130] This was the beginning of the process whereby large tracts of Spain's coastline became a wall of concrete.[131]

Domestic corruption had no impact on the readiness of both the United States military establishment and the British Conservative Party to incorporate Franco into the Western defensive orbit. However, both the Labour Party and President Truman continued to regard the Franco regime as a repugnant police state.[132] The Caudillo indignantly attributed British and American hostility to masonic plots, a view encouraged by despatches from Lequerica.[133] However, Western hostility to Franco was about to be swept aside. News of the Soviet acquisition of the atomic bomb, the triumph of Mao Zedong and several espionage scandals had already fed American fears that the United States was under threat from communism.[134] Fearing a Soviet takeover of Europe, the Joint Chiefs of Staff pressed for alliance with Spain as 'the last foothold in continental Europe' from which to launch a fightback. At first, Truman regarded this as politically unrealistic, but his doubts were forgotten when, on 24 June 1950, North Korean troops invaded South Korea, which had been under United States control since 1945.[135]

Wild speculation about the scale of Soviet imperialist intentions saw the Truman administration move from a strategy of containment to a more aggressive response. If, as many supposed, there was going to be a third world war, there would be no question of action against Franco.[136] On 26 September 1950, with American troops committed in Korea and the United Nations reconsidering diplomatic relations with Spain, Franco offered to send 500,000 troops to fight in Korea.[137] On 4 November, the General Assembly of the United Nations voted to authorize the return of ambassadors to Madrid and to admit Spain to the UN Food and Agriculture Organization. Britain and France abstained while the United States voted in favour. Franco acclaimed the decision as full-scale international endorsement of his policies.[138]

Determined to squeeze every possible advantage from the changed situation, Franco claimed that Spain was owed compensation for the post-war economic hardship which he blamed on the international ostracism.[139] That was nonsense. Economic difficulties were largely the consequence of his refusal to allow the political reform that would have brought international aid. Instead, he had persisted with crippling policies of autarky and high exchange rates. In the event, economic help came because Washington accepted that Franco's army needed rearming. In mid-November 1950, the Truman administration authorized a $62.5 million loan to Spain and secretly agreed to appoint an ambassador to Madrid.[140] At the end of the month, 200,000 Chinese troops pushed the United Nations troops back into South Korea. Spain's formal incorporation into the anti-Soviet bloc began when the appointment of Stanton Griffis as American Ambassador was made public on 27 December.[141]

The decision was hailed in Spain as proof that Franco had heroically overcome the international siege. In his end-of-year message on 31 December, he congratulated himself for the great social and economic advances achieved in the face of an international conspiracy to keep Spain weak. He claimed that no regime in Spanish history had created more wealth than his. By presenting toothless international opprobrium as a ruthless siege, bent on unleashing the horrors of civil war, he had consolidated popular support considerably. He had tamed the monarchist opposition, crushed the guerrilla resistance and seen the Church and the army become more Francoist in their loyalties. A fearsome apparatus of repression remained in place. His confidence was shown when he named Lequerica as Ambassador to Washington and settled the grudge he had borne since Truman rejected Lequerica as envoy in 1945.[142] The exchange of ambassadors was the beginning of a process which would see Spain admitted to UNESCO in November 1952; sign a Concordat with the Vatican in August 1953; sign the Pact of Madrid with the United States in September 1953 and be admitted to the United Nations in December 1955.

Aware that European political hostility made membership of NATO unlikely, Franco concentrated on securing a bilateral relationship with the United States.[143] In February 1951, interviewed by the Hearst press chain, he boasted that Spain was the only European country to have eliminated communism, claimed that he admired the USA's greatness and called for direct collaboration with North America outside NATO.[144] Less because of his propaganda and more because of geo-politics, the USA was seeking future cooperation with the Spanish military and the establishment of American air and naval bases on Spanish territory. Given Spain's combination of military weakness and strategic import- ance, and given the political objections to its inclusion in NATO, the British Chiefs of Staff agreed that the only solution was a separate US– Spanish bilateral agreement.[145]

In contrast to Franco's boasts about his foreign and domestic achievements, the repression and disastrous economic policies were reflected in food shortages, inflation and growing labour militancy. Per capita meat consumption in Spain in 1950 was only half what it had been in 1926 and bread consumption only half what it had been in 1936. Since 1939, prices had risen more than twice as fast as working-class wages. Moreover, inadequate rations meant that working-class families had to buy food on the black market where prices were more than double the official rate.[146] Inefficient agriculture left Spain dependent on food imports at a time of dwindling foreign currency reserves. The prices of raw materials were rocketing in the context of the Korean War. Energy shortages were leaving factories idle and workers laid off. For Franco, the consequent labour unrest was a law-and-order issue generated by Communist agitators. Nevertheless, worsening living conditions impelled him to make an astonishing admission in a speech to the National Congress of Workers on 11 March 1951. Contrary to his outrageous claims of bringing unprecedented prosperity, he declared: 'We must wipe from Spaniards' minds the puerile mistake that Spain is a rich country.'[147]

Inevitably, plummeting working-class living standards saw social tensions in Barcelona finally boil over. Franco's cabinet had permitted the hated Civil Governor of Barcelona, the Falangist Eduardo Baeza Alegría, to increase fares on Barcelona's decrepit trams by 40 per cent, twice the rate in Madrid. By late February, there was a boycott of public transport and trams were stoned.[148] By 12 March, the city was paralysed with more than 300,000 workers on strike involving Communists, some Falangists, activists of HOAC (the Hermandad Obrera de Acción Católica – the Workers Fraternity of Catholic Action) and members of the middle class. When a number of cars and buses were overturned, Baeza Alegría requested troops and Franco overreacted by sending three

destroyers and a minesweeper to Barcelona. Marines marched through
the streets. Fortunately, the Captain General of Barcelona, the monarchist General Juan Bautista Sánchez, refused to use the army to repress
disorder provoked by Baeza's irresponsibility. He prevented bloodshed
by calmly confining the garrison to barracks. In fact, within two or three
days, fearing for their jobs, most workers were drifting back to work.
Nevertheless, there were nearly a thousand arrests.[149]

Baeza was dismissed on 17 March. When the first choice to replace
him, the Conde de Mayalde, asked if he could release supplies of bread
and olive oil, the Minister of the Interior, Blas Pérez, told him to forget
conciliation and use the Civil Guard. A shocked Mayalde withdrew and
Baeza was replaced by the hard-line General Felipe Acedo Colunga.[150]
The tram stoppage saw solidarity strikes by students in Granada and
Madrid. The textile industry in Manresa was still closed when, on 23
April, 250,000 men began a forty-eight-hour strike in the shipyards,
steelworks and mines of the Basque Country. Again, Falangists and
members of HOAC joined in alongside leftists and Basque nationalists.
The regime denounced the strike as the work of foreign agitators. The
employers, unprepared to lose skilled labour, ignored the regime's orders
to sack strikers. Despite police brutality and the imprisonment of strike
leaders in a concentration camp near Vitoria, industrial action continued for several weeks. In late May, there was another transport strike in
Madrid.

At a cabinet meeting on 5 April, Franco blamed the economic situation on Spain's foreign enemies and dismissed the labour discontent as
mutiny.[151] In May, he called the strikes 'criminal' and claimed that false
news about them was broadcast by the BBC on masonic orders. A press
campaign denounced the strikes as the work of French and British freemasons.[152] In the Cold War atmosphere, his response was applauded in
America as evidence of his fierce anti-communism. Moreover, his
repressive labour legislation, fostering as it did high profit margins, made
Spain attractive to foreign investors. Meanwhile Franco was discussing
with Stanton Griffis whether Spain might join NATO. When Griffis told
him that a bilateral pact with the USA would be difficult, Franco agreed
to join a wider defence effort and give the USA air, land and naval
bases.[153]

Aware of the growing closeness between Franco and Washington,
Don Juan wrote to Franco on 10 July to suggest that the recent strikes,

the economic situation and government corruption meant that he should negotiate a transition to the monarchy. Franco replied two months later claiming that his regime was free of corruption and that the economic situation was entirely favourable.[154]

By late June 1951, General Eisenhower, NATO Commander-in-Chief, the Pentagon and the Joint Chiefs of Staff agreed that a US military mission could be sent to Spain to negotiate a bilateral pact. Military necessity outweighed the misgivings of the British, French and other European members of NATO.[155] Truman told Admiral Sherman, now the Chief of Naval Operations, 'I don't like Franco and I never will but I won't let my personal feelings override the convictions of you military men.'[156] By mid-July, Sherman and his staff were in Spain discussing the leasing of air and naval bases. Franco claimed that, since US bases in Spain would provoke a Soviet attack, Spanish forces needed to be brought to a level that would enable them to resist the Russians. This would not be cheap since they had no radar and were short of aircraft, heavy tanks, anti-aircraft and anti-tank equipment. He also told Sherman that military collaboration would not be possible because Spain did not have sufficient stocks of fuel, wheat and other commodities to allow it to go to war. Sherman promised that the US General Staff and the Department of Defense would seek credits from Congress. Despite his haggling, Franco was desperate to clinch the deal and, when Sherman asked when the military mission could start work, he replied: 'Immediately.' Within a month, high-powered American military and economic study groups were in Spain.[157]

Two days after the Sherman interview, Franco remodelled his cabinet. Other than appointing the deeply Catholic Joaquín Ruiz-Giménez as Minister of Education, his growing confidence saw him reassert the Falangist tone of the regime. The Ministry of War went to General Agustín Muñoz Grandes, the commander of the Blue Division who had been awarded the Iron Cross by Hitler. He would be responsible for negotiating the military agreement with the Americans. A newly created Ministry of Information would sell that agreement to the nation. The Minister was Gabriel Arias Salgado, who had run the controlled press in the interests of the Third Reich during the Second World War. Franco was making Falangists accomplices in the surrender of sovereignty to the United States to diminish any possible nationalist backlash. Carrero Blanco was promoted to ministerial rank. With the Americans pressing for economic liberalization, Suanzes, the architect of autarky, remained as President of the Instituto Nacional de Industria (INI) but was replaced as Minister of Industry and Commerce by the quick-witted economist Manuel Arburúa at Commerce and by an artillery general, Joaquín Planell, at Industry.[158]

The new cabinet would tentatively start to open up the economy to external market forces. Unwilling to commit suicide with political reform, Franco was buying American support by sacrificing autarky. The rewards would be massive: in the short term, American friendship; in the long, economic growth.[159] However, the change signified an incipient distance between Franco and his regime. Soon highly trained technocrats rather than old military chums would be required to run an economy that was getting beyond his comprehension. The American teams sent to investigate Spain's economy and military preparedness were shocked by the appalling condition of both. Encouraged by Lequerica, Franco's expectation that American money would put everything right led him to stall negotiations.[160] On opening the Cortes on 17 May 1952, the Caudillo announced that the deal would bring economic and military aid without any diminution of sovereignty. He heaped praise on what he saw as his uniquely democratic system. His words made a cruel commentary on the brutal repression that was being imposed in the wake of the strikes of the previous year.[161]

After assuming the presidency on 20 January 1953, Eisenhower sent James C. Dunn as Ambassador to Madrid. He was an advocate of an agreement with Spain. Nevertheless, although Franco was dragging out negotiations in the hope of forcing better terms, in the face of American pressure he was forced, rather than lose the alliance, to drop his extreme demands and accept what was virtually an American text.[162] He was worried by the prospect of conceding bases to a foreign power and diminishing national sovereignty. Accordingly, he used news that the recently crowned Queen Elizabeth II would visit Gibraltar in 1954 as a smokescreen. British citizens in Spain were harassed. Franco gave a militantly anti-British interview to *Arriba* as a cheap and effective way of whipping up nationalist support by stressing the sinister intentions of imperialist Britain and diverting attention from the costs of the agreement with the USA.[163]

At the end of August 1953, the lengthy Concordat negotiations with the Vatican were successfully concluded. While less important than the regime claimed, the Concordat was a major step towards international recognition for Franco. In return, he gave the Church a pre-eminent voice in education and social morality as well as confirming Catholicism as the official state religion.[164] Franco got the Papal seal of legitimacy for his semi-monarchical rule, to justify both the coins on which were stamped 'Caudillo by the grace of God' and his assumption of royal status in entering and leaving churches under the canopy previously reserved for the kings of Spain. Nevertheless, his dealings with the Church would sometimes be conflictive. His assumption of the royal prerogative to choose bishops from a three-name list presented by the Nuncio would provoke clashes with the hierarchy, especially in areas of strong local nationalisms such as Catalonia and the Basque Country.[165]

The importance of the Concordat was overshadowed by the signing of the Defence Pact with the USA, on 26 September 1953. Many details remained to be resolved about the conditions governing American use of the bases in wartime and ultimate Spanish jurisdiction over them.[166] The ambiguities and grey areas in the final agreement favoured the Americans. Despite his protestations to the contrary, Franco had renounced a considerable tranche of national sovereignty. A future wartime emergency, with only minutes to get fighters airborne, would preclude further negotiations. This was acknowledged in secret, additional clauses to the treaty whereby, in the event of Soviet aggression, the United States was obliged only to 'communicate the information at its disposal and its intentions' to Madrid. If Spain were attacked by a non-Communist aggressor, the USA was not obliged to come to its aid. Indeed, large areas of Spain remained without adequate defence coverage. Franco had not accepted satellite status but he had revealed how high a price he was prepared to pay to keep himself in power.[167]

In the final stages of the haggling, he had told his negotiators, 'in the last resort, if you don't get what you want, sign anything they put in front of you. We need the agreement.'[168] When the agreements were made public, Franco forgot that desperation. Photomontages presented Franco as the equal partner of Eisenhower. The media claimed that the nations of the world were reeling with amazement at the Caudillo's triumph.[169] The mutual defence pact brought $226 million in military and technological assistance. General economic aid was limited to infrastructural projects with military use, the building of roads, ports and defence industries. Deliveries of military equipment consisted largely of weapons, aircraft and vehicles already used in the Second World War and/or Korea. In return, Franco permitted the establishment of American air bases at Torrejón near Madrid, Seville, Zaragoza and Morón de la Frontera and a small naval base at Rota in Cadiz, as well as a wide range of smaller air force installations and naval refuelling facilities in Spanish ports. American military personnel stationed in Spain were exempt from Spanish law and tax systems. The Caudillo had bargained away neutrality and sovereignty without distinguishing between the good of Spain and the good of Francisco Franco. In particular, the siting of bases next to major cities constituted an act of sheer irresponsibility.[170]

International ostracism was ended at the cost of a diminution of sovereignty and the danger of war in the atomic age. In return, Spain was integrated into the Western system, and the military high command were delighted. Economic aid came with requirements such as a realistic exchange rate for the peseta and balancing the budget, which implied changes in the very nature of the regime.[171] In fact, it would not be American pressure but the collapse of the Spanish economy which would oblige Franco to permit economic liberalization. He clung on to autarky for another six years, finally abandoning it both reluctantly and uncomprehendingly. Ironically, the agreements provided the economic stimulus that would expose the structural rigidities of Francoist autarky and were a step towards the economic and social development that would eventually render the Caudillo an irrelevance.

On 1 October 1953, Franco presented the bases agreement to the Cortes as the pinnacle of a selfless commitment, since 1936, to defend Western civilization. On that day, the Día del Caudillo, the Movimiento mounted a great rally in the Plaza de Oriente. Workers and peasants were bussed in from all over Spain, with a day's pay and a packed lunch. The sycophantic newspaper editor Luis de Galinsoga proclaimed him 'Caudillo of the West', the only truly great man of the twentieth century, a giant by the side of such dwarfs as Churchill and Roosevelt.[172] That Spain was now more vulnerable to Soviet aggression was not mentioned.[173] Even so, by becoming an ally, however subordinate, of the USA, Franco had made things easier for himself and opened the way to entry into the United Nations and full international recognition.

Lest subservience to Washington and the Vatican offend Falangist sensibilities, Franco arranged a huge public demonstration of his commitment to the Movimiento. On 29 October 1953, the twentieth anniversary of the foundation of Falange Española, Franco addressed 125,000 'Falangists' at the Real Madrid stadium at Chamartín. The correspondent of *Le Monde* estimated that 80 per cent of the crowd were peasants or unemployed agricultural labourers brought in from the provinces and paid a day's wage. Franco triumphantly presented the agreements as a second victory over communism.[174]

The Pact of Madrid reduced pressure on Franco by slowing the decline in living standards. It was also an excuse for a revival of anti-Communist propaganda to keep alive the spirit of the civil war. Moreover, the enormous investment in terror made between 1936 and 1945 was paying off in the political apathy of the bulk of the population. Franco's opponents had learned their lesson and torture, prisons and occasional executions served as a reminder for those who forgot. The Civil Guard, the armed police and the secret police did their gruesome work, tirelessly crushing efforts to rebuild parties and unions.

The heir to the Spanish throne, Don Juan de Borbón, in 1963 with his son Juan Carlos, the future King of Spain.

14

The Franco Regime: Corruption and Complacency, 1953–1969

In the wake of the treaties with Washington and the Vatican, Franco's confidence could be seen in his greater devotion to his hobbies – hunting, freshwater and deep-sea fishing with Max Borrell, golf, watching westerns in the private cinema in El Pardo, painting, and developing his large estate at Valdefuentes. Able to draw on the manpower and machinery of the Ministry of Agriculture, and producing wheat, potatoes and even tobacco, it became immensely profitable. When he was in residence at El Pardo, Franco would go to Valdefuentes most afternoons to take the air after a late lunch.[1] He had always left his ministers to get on with the technical side of their ministries, to enrich themselves or merely to be efficient or even incompetent, while he dictated the broad lines of policy, especially foreign policy. After 1953, he increasingly left the drudgery of day-to-day government to others. He continued to ignore corruption, whether committed by his political servants or by his extended family, as long as absolute loyalty was maintained.

1954 saw the completion of the crypt at the Valle de los Caídos. It had been an obsession, 'the other woman', ever since the inauguration of the works in 1940. More than any other legacy of his regime, it mirrored Franco's conception of himself as an historic figure on a par with Philip II. He had had it doubled in size from the original conception and the crypt was finished on 31 August. It had been a colossal undertaking, dug out from solid granite, 262 metres long and 41 high. Many of the great building companies of the Francoist boom got their start there: Banús, Agromán and, particularly, Huarte, awarded the contract to build the cross, which was not finished until September 1956. Weighing 181,620 metric tons, the cross was 150 metres high, with arms 46 metres long.[2]

The biggest problem facing Franco was the muted opposition of the monarchists who, to his discomfort, reminded him of his unfulfilled promise to restore the monarchy. In July 1954, under the influence of Gil Robles, Don Juan clashed with Franco over the education of Juan Carlos. Don Juan wanted his son to begin his university education at Louvain whereas Franco intended him to spend time in the Military Academy at Zaragoza followed by time at the naval and air academies and the social science and engineering faculties of Madrid University, and then to shadow Franco himself in government. Franco informed Don Juan that those who hoped to govern Spain should be educated in Spain, dismissively implying that Don Juan did not figure in his plans for any restoration and threatening that the monarchy might not be restored at all. Franco used the word 'installation' to emphasize that there would be no restoration of the legitimate Borbón line, only the imposition of a Francoist king who had to be chosen and trained to ensure the continuation of his regime. Alarmed by the prospect of breaking totally with Franco, Don Juan backed down.[3]

The Concordat and the Pact of Madrid made it harder to maintain the myth of a siege that Franco had exploited since 1945. His greatest skill, the manipulation of his supporters, was also a diminishing asset. He had handled the rivalry of the Falange and the monarchists in the army up to 1945 and of the Falange and the Catholic monarchists in the post-war period with preferment and jobs. Now, generations were coming to maturity who had not fought in the civil war and were blasé about the Caudillo's achievements as the 'saviour' of Spain. Younger men less bewitched by the aura of the Caudillo began openly to jockey for position. Alongside Falangists and Martín-Artajo's conservative Christian Democrats, there were supporters of Don Juan and prominent bankers, lawyers and professors of the increasingly powerful Catholic secular order, the Opus Dei, who had aspirations to liberalize the administration and modernize the economy.[4]

Many of Franco's supporters were beginning to think about the future and the Caudillo himself was concerned about those who supported Don Juan. In February 1954, he had received a visit from several generals, including Juan Bautista Sánchez, who pressed him to prepare for the monarchist succession after his death. He was alarmed when many upper- and middle-class Spaniards went to Estoril to celebrate the coming out of Don Juan's daughter, the Infanta María Pilar.[5] Although Franco's position was hardly under threat, the celebration of municipal elections in Madrid on 21 November 1954, the first since the civil war, suggested that things were changing. Despite the fact that the electorate was extremely limited, the four monarchist candidates were intimidated by Falangist thugs and by the police. To ensure that the four Movimiento candidates would win, Carrero Blanco, Blas Pérez, Gabriel Arias Salgado and the Minister Secretary of the Falange, Raimundo Fernández Cuesta, had agreed on detailed electoral falsification. Notwithstanding that the official results gave a substantial victory to the Falangist candidates, the monarchists claimed to have won over 60 per cent of the vote.[6] Blas Pérez told Franco that the results signified popular acclaim, something that was belied by bitter complaints from influential monarchists, including the Minister of Justice, the traditionalist Antonio Iturmendi. To make matters worse, the military intelligence services had discovered that the bulk of the Madrid garrison had voted for the monarchy. Franco privately accepted that Blas Pérez had lied and that, despite the official results still standing, the regime had lost the elections. To neutralize military monarchism, he arranged to meet Don Juan.[7]

His international position consolidated and his repressive apparatus ensuring his domestic security, Franco was now principally concerned to ensure that he be succeeded by a Falangist monarchy. However, the Falange was increasingly anachronistic while Don Juan's liberal-monarchist option seemed more in tune with the outside world. Moreover, the autarky associated with the Falange was intensifying Spain's economic problems. Franco arranged to meet Don Juan only to convince monarchists of his own sincerity. The limits of his good faith were revealed, on 2 December 1954, in a letter to Don Juan in which he reiterated that he would hand over only on his death or total incapacity and then only to a king committed to the unconditional maintenance of the dictatorship. Thus he insisted that Juan Carlos be educated in the principles of the Movimiento. The letter ended with Franco criticizing Don Juan for his supporters running against the Movimiento in the municipal elections.[8]

The meeting took place at Las Cabezas, the estate of Don Juan's representative in Spain, the Conde de Ruiseñada. Franco repeated what he had said in his letter and dismissed Don Juan's advisers as free-masons on the grounds that Don Juan called for freedom of the press, an independent judiciary, social justice, trade union freedom and polit-ical representation. His unmistakable message was that, if Don Juan did not allow Juan Carlos to be educated under Franco's tutelage, he would be renouncing the throne. Don Juan thus agreed that Juan Carlos be educated at the three service academies, at the university and at Franco's side. With the greatest reluctance, Franco agreed to a joint communiqué that implicitly recognized the hereditary rights to the throne of the Borbón dynasty.[9] The meeting had given the impression of progress but, in his end-of-year message on 31 December 1954, he made it clear that he had conceded nothing to Don Juan. Using the royal 'we', he emphasized that there would be no restoration of a constitutional monarchy and stressed his right to choose a successor who would guarantee the continuity of his regime. He denounced calls for reform as the work of bad Spaniards in the service of sinister foreign enemies. In a subsequent interview, he dispelled any hopes of an early transition to the monarchy.[10]

The Falange's functionaries were guaranteed well-paid jobs and sinecures and the continuation of the one-party state in return for accepting a monarchist succession.[11] Similarly, the monarchists had to accept that the monarchy would be restored only within the Movimiento. Don Juan was mortified when the press published a fabricated interview which gave the impression that he was committed to the Movimiento.[12] Political apathy generated by years of carefully applied state terror was being gradually translated into mass acceptance of the regime, or 'sociological Francoism'.[13] Franco could delegate ever more and spend more time hunting and fishing. His intimates began to notice a reluctance to give attention to day-to-day political developments.[14] There would still be crises to overcome but, those aside, he let politics be a smaller drain on his time. A large proportion of the time devoted to official business was ceremonial. He seemed uninterested in major state problems, of which the most acute was continuing inflation and economic stagnation.[15] By the end of 1954, he was spending Saturdays, Sundays and Mondays hunting in the season and, occasionally, entire weeks at a time. Hunting parties were organized around his presence and became the notorious epicentre of regime corruption. Ministers developed an interest in hunting because they could not afford to be absent from what was perceived as the Caudillo's charmed circle. Their consequent neglect of government business seemed not to bother him. While hunting, he was subjected to adulation and to malicious gossip about those who were not present, as well as to constant requests for favours. Businessmen sponsored costly hunting parties in order to get near to ministers.[16]

By the mid-1950s, Franco was spending less time on politics and more with his family and at his pleasures. However, despite his conviction that all problems were the work of satanic minorities radio-controlled from masonic lodges and left-wing internationals abroad, the municipal elections of November 1954 and the meeting at Las Cabezas had put the post-Franco succession firmly on the agenda. He had no inclination to give up power but was out of touch with the broader reality of social change and the aspirations of much of the Spanish population. His mantra of the good Spaniards who had won the civil war and the bad, anti-Francoist losers was being made irrelevant by generational change. Encouraged by Carrero Blanco and others, he believed in a Spain in which he was the beloved father of his people protecting them from freemasons and Communists.

Throughout the 1950s, the Moroccan independence movement had been growing in opposition to both France and Spain. On 7 April 1956, both European nations relinquished their Moroccan protectorates. Franco was bitterly distressed to have to sign the declaration of independence.[17] Along with the Moroccan crisis, domestic political problems arose which reminded him that permitting anything that replicated party politics was too risky. Ever since the meeting at Las Cabezas, he had been trying to ignore sporadic evidence of discontent within the Falange. There were elements impatient with the endless postponement of the great ambition of the Falange, its so-called *revolución pendiente*, and the relegation of the party to the status of Caudillo's claque. In February 1955, the extreme Falangist militia the Guardia de Franco chanted insulting slogans against Juan Carlos and allegedly called Franco a traitor for dallying with Don Juan.[18] This was unavoidable evidence of the erosion of the Movimiento's hitherto unquestioning loyalty.

Things were shifting behind the repressive façade of regime uniformity. Liberal initiatives in the universities by the Minister of Education, Joaquín Ruiz-Giménez, exacerbated tensions within the Movimiento. The rumblings of the mid-1950s were something different from earlier rivalries between military monarchists and senior Falangists. Spanish students, even left-wing and liberal ones, were almost exclusively from comfortable middle-class families and could not simply be subjected to the savage repression casually meted out to working-class strikers. However, Franco had neither the time nor the flexibility to learn about these new forces. Accordingly, he did not take seriously either the student unrest or the Falangist rejection of the slide into conservative monarchism. In El Escorial at the November 1955 commemoration of the anniversary of the death of the Falange's founder José Antonio Primo de Rivera, a voice from the ranks of the guard of honour shouted: 'We want no idiot kings.' Franco was not unduly bothered.[19] However, he seriously misread the student unrest, failing to see it as symptomatic of how the regime was out of step with Spanish society. His comforting assumption that any opposition was of Communist or masonic inspiration was no longer adequate.

Franco was gradually forced to confront evidence that a majority of students regarded the political and military authorities as incompetent and immoral.[20] He referred to the university tensions in his 1955 end-of-year broadcast. The pretence that unity was the essential response to a non-existent international siege was no longer plausible. Since he would not contemplate reform, instead of the usual résumé of his great achievements Franco devoted this annual message to the dangers of subversion. He implied that the success of his 'captaincy' had let Spaniards become complacent and easy prey to the foreigners who wanted to divide them. He referred to the libertinage of the airwaves.[21] Franco's negativity was applauded only by the most hard-line sections of the Falange. He agreed with the anti-liberal, anti-masonic, anti-Communist elements of their rhetoric, and he knew that any concession to the monarchists would weaken his own position, since their loyalties lay elsewhere. In contrast, the Falange depended on him for its very existence. The discontent was not limited to Falangist tantrums. There was also growing working-class discontent at appalling housing conditions and living standards.[22]

On 8 February, demonstrations in the University of Madrid by progressive students were broken up by violent bands of Falangists.[23] The extremist Guardia de Franco drew up blacklists of 'traitors' including Ruiz-Giménez. Outraged senior generals, among them the Minister for the Army, Muñoz Grandes, visited Franco to express their displeasure.[24] Sympathizing with the Falangists and convinced that the crisis was the work of Communist agitators, the Caudillo was inclined to do nothing.[25] However, when Muñoz Grandes told him that, if any of those on the blacklist were harmed, the army would take over Madrid, Franco allegedly promised to have the Falangist conspirators arrested.[26] Nevertheless, he was sufficiently unconcerned to set out immediately at the head of a large hunting party along with Muñoz Grandes, Arburúa and a group of aristocrats and businessmen.

Franco was furious with Ruiz-Giménez because he believed that his liberal tendencies had allowed left-wing elements to flourish in the universities and with Fernández Cuesta for allowing the emergence of anti-Franco tendencies within the Movimiento.[27] He was especially annoyed that the resurgence of hostility between the Falange and the military high command should interrupt his hunting. He replaced Fernández Cuesta with the fiercely ambitious Arrese and Ruiz-Giménez with Jesús Rubio García-Mina, a Falangist professor whose view on the recent disturbances was that 'students should study'.[28] The events of February 1956 confirmed that Franco was losing touch with the evolving political situation. He had underestimated the seriousness of the crisis only partly because he had been preoccupied by the Moroccan problem. His solution was a short-term one. He had little choice but to cling to the Falange since otherwise he would be putting his fate into the hands of those senior army officers who wanted a restoration of the monarchy.[29]

Hard-line Falangist discontent had been building up since the meeting at Las Cabezas. At the end of 1955, Franco was presented with a memorandum demanding the swift implementation of the Falangist revolution in the form of a more totalitarian one-party state structure.[30] He let his regime get more out of touch with international and domestic change by permitting Arrese, as Minister Secretary, to try to implement the memorandum's demands. In April, devastated by the loss of Morocco, Franco grasped at Arrese's scheme for the *refalangistización* of the regime as a way of revitalizing his rule.[31] Far from calming divisions, Arrese's plans caused intense polarization. Traditionalists, Juanista monarchists and Catholics saw them as a neo-Nazi scheme to block any future liberalization under a restored monarchy and so perpetuate the Falangist domination of the regime.

It was symptomatic of Franco's failing acuity that he was not suspicious of Arrese's ambition, perhaps seduced by a scheme presented in the most sycophantic wrapping. Since the decadence of liberal monarchy was one of Franco's favourite themes, Arrese convinced him that he was preparing crucial safeguards to prevent the risk of democratic reform under a weak king.[32] Throughout March, Arrese elaborated his plans while Franco was distracted with both the imminent decolonization of Spanish Morocco and growing economic and social discontent. The cost of living index had risen by 50 per cent over the previous twelve months. When the cabinet met on 3 March to discuss rising working-class militancy, Girón, the Falangist Minister of Labour, supported by Arrese, urged wage increases of 23 per cent. The Minister of Commerce, Manuel Arburúa, was overruled when he stressed the inflationary consequences of such a strategy.[33] The wage rises did not come in time to delay a series of strikes which began in the shoe-manufacturing industry in Pamplona, in April, and then spread through the Basque steel industry and into the Asturian coalfields.[34]

Franco's greatest skill was always to let each group of the Francoist coalition believe that he really backed them. It was remarkable that in 1956 he permitted Arrese to close off all options for the succession but the Falangist one. He wanted to enjoy the present and to guarantee the future of his regime. As he slid into comfortable routine, the various regime forces tried more actively to secure their own futures. This, paradoxically, confirmed Franco as the arbiter who held the system together. Franco himself, of course, was happy to go on being indispensable. Arrese's plans for a Falangist monopoly of the Francoist future provoked the monarchists into action. Ruiseñada prepared a plan for an early restoration of the monarchy with Franco becoming temporary regent and the day-to-day running of government assumed by General Bautista Sánchez. The involvement of the highly respected Bautista Sánchez helped secure the support of other monarchist generals against Arrese.[35]

Aware of these manoeuvres, Franco embarked on a propaganda tour of Andalusia. Egged on by Arrese, his speeches became ever more militantly Falangist. In Seville, on 24 April, he declared that his regime bore comparison with the best regimes ever known or even imaginable. Arrese ensured that the Caudillo would be greeted by crowds of delirious Falangists and then convinced him that this reflected mass enthusiasm for a stronger Falangist line. In Huelva, on 25 April, Franco delighted his audience with insulting references to the monarchists and to Juan Carlos. He declared that 'we take no notice of the clumsy plotting of several dozen political intriguers nor their kids', and threatened to 'unleash a flood of blue-shirts and red berets to crush them'. At a Falangist rally in Seville on 1 May, he passionately denounced the enemies of the Falangist revolution as the tools of masonic lodges and Communist internationals, working himself up to the declaration that 'the Falange can live without the monarchy but what could not survive is a monarchy without the Falange'.[36]

It is striking that Franco, who had maintained the political balance by shrouding his intentions in nebulous vagueness, should have gone so far. Enthused by Arrese's talk of a glorious Falangist future, he had made uncharacteristically explicit declarations that alarmed many monarchists who had been happy to accept the regime as long there was a possibility of their ambitions being fulfilled. Now, in addition, even greater disquiet was generated by Arrese arrogantly talking as if he could dictate the next cabinet changes.[37] Fernández Cuesta told the British Ambassador that Arrese's draft constitution would give the Falange a pre-eminence comparable to that of the Communist Party in Russia.[38] Even Carrero Blanco was concerned, as was the Minister of Justice, Antonio Iturmendi, who was following Arrese's efforts with hostility. He commissioned a report by the brilliant Catalan monarchist and professor of administrative law Laureano López Rodó of the Opus Dei.[39]

At first, Franco was supportive of Arrese's plans.[40] However, senior generals were disturbed by the 1 May speech. On 1 July, General Antonio Barroso, the new head of the Caudillo's Military Household, protested to him about the Arrese plan. He and two other generals broached the Ruiseñada plan to the Caudillo. He suggested that a Military Directory take over and hold a plebiscite on the issue of monarchy or republic, confident that there would be overwhelming support for the monarchy.[41] Now worried, Franco began to treat Arrese with notable coolness.[42] Nevertheless, a speech to the Consejo Nacional of the Falange on 17 July 1956, the twentieth anniversary of the military uprising, partly drafted by Arrese, was Falangist in tone. The Consejo Nacional was a symbolic body and had not met since 1945. Its revival was part of Arrese's plans as the watchdog of the ideological purity of Franco's successor.[43] The speech confirmed the central role of the Movimiento in the succession and calmed Falangist fears that a future king might use his powers to bring about a transition to democracy.[44] Martín-Artajo was alarmed by Franco's praise of Fascist Italy and Nazi Germany and his sneering reference to the post-war democratic systems 'imposed' on the defeated Axis powers by frightened and envious Western Allies. These anti-democratic remarks were omitted from the published version of the speech.[45]

General Barroso was also disturbed by the unrestrained ostentation of the Franco family, as were others in the generally austere high command. Since Nenuca's marriage to Martínez-Bordiú in 1950, Doña Carmen had plunged into high society and indulged her passion for jewellery and antiques. This had led to her acquiring the popular nickname Doña Collares (Doña Necklaces).[46] She even doctored her husband's past by restructuring and refurnishing the Franco family home in El Ferrol when it was converted into a museum. The house and its modest furnishings had reflected the income of a middling naval officer with four children. By stocking it with expensive period antiques and porcelain, she set out to create an upper-middle-class or semi-aristocratic past for her husband.[47]

On 29 September, a huge Falangist rally was held in Salamanca to celebrate Franco's elevation to the headship of state. Franco's speech had not mentioned the 'Fundamental Laws' being prepared by Arrese.[48] Uproar was provoked in the Francoist establishment when he circulated his final draft. Although it recognized Franco's absolute powers for life, it left his successor at the mercy of the Consejo Nacional and of the Secretary General of the Falange, a position which Arrese envisaged for himself. Monarchists, Catholics, archbishops and generals joined in opposing a text giving the Movimiento totalitarian control over all aspects of Spanish life.[49] There was outrage in the army at what seemed like an attempt to block the return of the monarchy. Three of the four Spanish cardinals sent Franco a letter denouncing Arrese's text for flouting Papal encyclicals with a draft constitution similar to those of Nazism, Fascism and Peronism.[50] In response to the various protests, Franco, despite his partiality to Arrese's schemes, obliged him to water them down.[51] It suggested that he was no longer the ultimate arbiter of regime politics.

Between the extremes of Ruiseñada's negotiated transition to Don Juan and a retreat into Arrese's fortress Falangism, there emerged the middle option favoured by Carrero Blanco. Ultimately adopted by Franco, it aimed to create the legislative framework for an authoritarian monarchy that would guarantee the survival of Francoism after his death. The job of producing a blueprint was entrusted to López Rodó.[52] As Secretary of the Presidencia (the office of the cabinet President), Carrero Blanco was Franco's political chief of staff and gradually assuming some of the tasks of a prime minister. López Rodó, in turn Carrero's chief of staff, was creating an administrative machine to confront the complex technical problems of a modern economy that were beyond Franco.

Meanwhile, Bautista Sánchez was building support for Ruiseñada's plan to marginalize Franco and place Don Juan upon the throne. Bizarrely suspecting the fervently Catholic Bautista Sánchez of being a freemason, Franco had him followed by the secret service.[53] Things came to a head in mid-January 1957, when a transport users' strike and anti-regime demonstrations by students broke out in Barcelona.[54] The Civil Governor, General Felipe Acedo Colunga, evacuated the university with some violence to prevent demonstrations in favour of the strikers. Franco was annoyed when Bautista Sánchez criticized Acedo Colunga's harsh methods.[55] He believed that Bautista Sánchez was fostering the strike as an excuse for a coup in favour of the monarchy.[56] He added two regiments of the Legion to manoeuvres being supervised by Bautista Sánchez and sent Muñoz Grandes to inform him that he was being dismissed as Captain General of Catalonia.[57] On the next day, 29 January, Bautista Sánchez was found dead. Despite rumours that he had been murdered, he probably died of a heart attack after his painful interview with Muñoz Grandes.[58]

The combination of the opposition provoked by Arrese, the Barcelona strike and serious economic problems forced Franco to reshuffle his cabinet. Despite supporting Girón against Arburúa, he was obliged to acknowledge that rocketing inflation was matched by a disastrous balance of payments. This was the consequence partly of the ineptitude of his ministers but also of his commitment to autarky and the central role of Suanzes's Instituto Nacional de Industria. The Minister of Public Works, General José María Fernández Ladreda, warned him in stark terms: 'the entire funds of the national budget over many years would not be enough to maintain this diabolical monstrosity'.[59] The INI's show-piece projects made demands on scarce resources of capital and materials. Franco's failure to attend to administrative detail allowed ministerial overspending which was resolved by printing money. Moreover, wage rises sanctioned by Girón had increased industrial and agricultural costs by more than 40 per cent.[60]

Franco hesitated to initiate a reshuffle, fearing that Arburúa was irre-placeable as Minister of Commerce. He was dazzled by the Minister's expertise in what he saw as the mysteries of international trade and finance.[61] Indeed, he admired Arburúa for starting his working life as liveried attendant or 'buttons' in a bank and ending up as a multi-millionaire. It was alleged that the basis of his fortune was his granting of import licences to friends and influential contacts. They could be resold for fabulous sums because there was an annual demand for 40,000 cars but only 6,000 licences. This gave rise to the catchphrase 'Gracias, Manolo'. At one point, the deputy minister's office acknowledged that there was no documentation for many import licences granted 'by a higher authority'.[62] Franco understood neither the damage caused by autarky nor Spain's need for sophisticated economic techniques. He reluctantly acquiesced in the idea of trade liberalization and Spain's integration into the Organization for European Economic Co-operation (OEEC) and the International Monetary Fund (IMF). However, by altering his cabinet accordingly, he relinquished further his own control over Spanish politics.

The cabinet reshuffle of February 1957 marked the beginning of Franco's transition from active dictator to symbolic figurehead. The details were worked out in collaboration with the ever more influential Carrero Blanco, whose grasp of economics was as rudimentary as that of his master. However, he could rely on the talented López Rodó.[63] The long-term implications of the cabinet changes that they recommended went beyond anything anticipated by Franco. They signified not just the political disarmament of the Falange but, within two years, the abandonment of Franco's economic policies and the embrace of modern capitalism. That would bring massive foreign investment, industrialization, population migration, urbanization and educational expansion. The social consequences were to turn Franco and the Falange into historical anachronisms. In the event, the Caudillo would take the credit for economic development, as he had for wartime neutrality and for surviving the Cold War.

Arrese was replaced as Minister Secretary by the sycophantic José Solís Ruiz, head of the Falangist syndicates.[64] Girón was replaced as Minister of Labour by the colourless Fermín Sanz Orrio. Arrese was kept on, as a sop to the Falange, in the innocuous post of Minister of Housing.[65] Martín-Artajo was replaced by Fernando María de Castiella, the one-time Falangist now reinvented as a Christian Democrat. The end of autarky was signalled by the inclusion of the 'technocrats' whose task would be to integrate Spain into the world economy. The new Minister of Finance, Mariano Navarro Rubio, was a Catholic lawyer and a director of the Opus Dei-controlled Banco Popular. Arburúa was replaced as Minister of Commerce by Alberto Ullastres Calvo, an economics professor and, like López Rodó, a member of Opus Dei whose vows of poverty distinguished him from his predecessor. There was speculation that the trio were a sinister bloc controlled by a Catholic freemasonry. Over the next few years, they would lay the basis for the regime's survival through its economic and political transformation. This fuelled resentment within the displaced Falange that they had hijacked the Caudillo and the Movimiento.[66]

The arrival of the technocrats was a pragmatic response to the realization that by 1957 the regime faced political and economic bankruptcy. Franco and Carrero Blanco needed new blood and fresh ideas. López Rodó was the nominee of Carrero Blanco. Navarro Rubio was the Caudillo's choice. Ullastres was recommended by both López Rodó and Navarro Rubio. Without being a monolithic unit, the three worked together as a team, despite occasional friction, to push for the administrative and economic modernization of the regime.[67] López Rodó did not become a minister yet his influence would be immense, hastening Franco's withdrawal from active politics. While more than a ceremonial head of state, the Caudillo would have less involvement in the daily machinery of government. The Decree Law of the Juridical Regime of the Administration of the State, drafted by López Rodó, reorganized the government. Ratified by the Cortes in mid-July 1957, it elevated Carrero Blanco's Presidencia to a ministry. With López Rodó as its technical secretary, it became a prime minister's office able to initiate, draft and programme legislation. An Office of Economic Coordination and Planning, headed by López Rodó, would provide technical services for the key economic ministries. Government became more administrative and less political. Franco's hunting and fishing passions meant that henceforth strategic policy would be much more likely to be made by Carrero Blanco and López Rodó.[68]

Initially, the technocrats laboured to resolve the economic problems inherited from their incompetent predecessors. Franco's acceptance of Girón's claim, in 1956, that strikes could be avoided by massive wage rises without any impact on prices had unleashed a major inflationary spiral. By the spring of 1957, pressure on living standards generated another strike wave. Franco saw industrial unrest as the work of Communist agitators and freemasons. He regarded talk of inadequate wages and hunger as foreign propaganda.[69] The technocrats knew that economic modernization needed the Caudillo to be marginalized.

Shortly after the cabinet changes, López Rodó told Ruiseñada, 'it is impossible to talk to Franco about politics because he thinks that they want to move him from his seat or prepare the way for his replacement. The trick is to make him accept an administrative plan to decentralize the economy. He doesn't see that as directed against him personally. He will give us a free hand and, then, once inside the administration, we will see how far we can go with our political objectives, which have to be masked as far as possible.'[70] López Rodó's plan was to create a secure structure of institutions and constitutional laws and then have Juan Carlos officially proclaimed royal successor in 1968, when he would reach thirty, the age at which the Law of Succession permitted him to assume the throne.[71]

The displaced Falangists suspected that economic liberalization masked a project of political transformation, especially after Ullastres devalued the peseta from five to the US dollar to the more realistic forty-two and announced the lifting of price controls. Franco seemed unconcerned by these economic changes or by López Rodó's drafting, on Carrero Blanco's instructions, of constitutional texts for the eventual installation of the monarchy.[72] As López Rodó explained to Don Juan in Lisbon on 17 September, the texts were meant to calm Franco's fears that, after his death, his successor might dismantle his life's work. Thus, in accordance with the Law of Succession, whoever was chosen would have to accept the basic principles of the Francoist state, which Don Juan was reluctant to do.[73]

In the spring of 1958, there was another wave of strikes in the Asturian mines and Catalonia. Franco again blamed them on foreign agitators and the laziness of the working class.[74] Increasingly, he left his ministers to get on with the work of government while he went hunting and fishing. His job was increasingly ceremonial. In the Cortes, on 17 May, in a speech written by López Rodó, he unveiled the first fruit of the constitution project, the 'Declaration of the Fundamental Principles of the Movimiento Nacional'. It declared that 'the political form of the Spanish State is the traditional, Catholic, social and representative monarchy' and thus decoupled the regime from Falangism.[75]

On 10 June 1958, with Spain's foreign exchange reserves dwindling, Navarro Rubio presented to the cabinet the report that outlined the harsh monetary stabilization programme which underlay Spain's subsequent economic development. Although unaware that this constituted a reversal of twenty years of Francoism, Franco was sufficiently alarmed by the political implications to insist that the report remain secret.[76] By the summer, however, his thoughts had turned again to fishing and hunting.[77] While he was at his pleasures, difficulties were brewing. In the late autumn, the new Pope John XXIII instituted a liberalization of the Catholic Church which would cause severe problems for Franco. Combined with increasing involvement of Spanish clerics in the worker-priest movement, it signalled an end to the Church's monolithic pro-Francoism. A more immediate problem was the collapse of the Spanish economy amid rocketing inflation and growing working-class discontent. Franco seemed unaware of the gravity of the situation.[78] He was more concerned that, on 29 January 1959, supporters of Don Juan launched an association known as Unión Española at a dinner in Madrid's Hotel Menfis. Inspired by a monarchist lawyer and industrialist, Joaquín Satrústegui, the speeches argued that the monarchy, to survive, could not be installed by a dictator but had to be restored with the popular support of a majority of Spaniards. Franco furiously fined Satrústegui 50,000 pesetas.[79] Unión Española was only one of several more or less Christian Democrat groups springing up alongside left-wing and regionalist opposition in the universities and the labour movement. Alarmed Falangists mounted a defence of hard-line Francoism through extremist organizations such the Vieja Guardia (Old Guard) and the Círculos José Antonio.[80]

Franco seemed happy to leave matters to his technocrats until the arrival of an International Monetary Fund mission, in early 1959, to investigate the problems of the Spanish economy. Both the delegation and Navarro Rubio saw the free convertibility of the peseta as a key step towards the necessary integration of the Spanish economy into the international system.[81] Franco opposed any further devaluation of the peseta and, on 18 February, refused Ullastres permission to accept an offer from the IMF to elaborate a stabilization plan for the Spanish economy because he distrusted foreigners. Only after Navarro Rubio had bombarded him with evidence of Spain's parlous financial state did Franco shrug his shoulders and authorize the opening of formal talks with the IMF.[82] He suspected that once economically dependent on international goodwill, he might be pushed into political reform or even resignation.[83] After the IMF links had been established, pressure for a further devaluation of the peseta from forty-two to the US dollar to sixty became irresistible. Franco's hostility was overcome when Ullastres revealed just how near Spain was to bankruptcy.[84]

The stabilization plan adopted on 6 March 1959, further devaluation of the peseta and a reduction in public spending all had acute social consequences. Many companies were forced to close and unemployment was rising. However, despite ministerial opposition as budgets were slashed, Franco backed the policy.[85] He accepted technical arguments because the issues were of a complexity way beyond his understanding.[86] At the same time, he permitted the monarchists in his cabinet to elaborate their own constitutional scheme for the succession. Carrero Blanco gave him the first draft on 7 March together with a sycophantic note urging the completion of the 'constitutional process lest the King inherit the Caudillo's powers and be able to change everything'. As if addressing a medieval king, Carrero wrote: 'We must ratify the lifetime character of the magistracy of Your Excellency who is Caudillo which is greater than King because you are founding a monarchy.'[87] Fearing to hasten his own departure, Franco did nothing with the constitutional draft for another eight years.

His conviction that nothing was really changing was boosted by the celebrations of the twentieth anniversary of the end of the civil war which included the inauguration of the Valle de los Caídos on 1 April. Franco's delight was out of tune with the mood of most Spaniards. The stabilization plan, drawn up under the supervision of the IMF and the Organization for European Economic Co-operation, aimed to cut domestic consumption by massive devaluation of the peseta, fierce credit restrictions and cuts in public spending. The devaluation was intended to boost exports, bring in hard currency to finance imports of capital goods and hasten economic modernization. The working class paid the social costs as wages were frozen, unemployment rose and there were shortages of basic consumer goods. By the late 1950s, there was a revival of clandestine trade union activity, orchestrated by Catholic groups as well as by the Communist Party and other left-wing organizations. Franco believed that Spain was under siege again from international Communism and freemasonry.[88]

On 21 December, a thrilled Franco hosted a brief visit by President Eisenhower. His declared admiration for the USA led his sister to comment, 'If only Hitler and Mussolini could have heard him.'[89] The efforts of Ullastres and Navarro Rubio started to bear fruit after 1960.

Franco, and his supporters, attributed to his genius and foresight an 'economic miracle' that was the result of liberal economics and integration into the international capitalist system, both of which had been excoriated by Franco since 1939. Moreover, both he and Carrero Blanco still hankered after a return to autarky.[90]

Spain's boom took place in a period of sustained international growth. That context allowed the export of excess labour, largely to Northern Europe. Migrant workers remitted their earnings back in foreign currency. Disposable income in the pockets of German, French and British workers saw a tourist boom that brought valuable foreign currency. Franco's contribution was inadvertent: the anti-communism that brought American aid in the mid-1950s and the repressive labour legislation that attracted foreign investors. Combined with the repression of strikes and good facilities for the repatriation of profits, Spain was an attractive target for foreign capital in the early 1960s. In giving the technocrats their head, Franco was furthering the process whereby he was being sidelined. He was happy to take credit for economic triumphs brought about by policies that he did not entirely understand.

Anxiety about the future was fuelled by gossip about the Caudillo's failing health as he neared seventy. News that a third meeting with Don Juan had been scheduled for late March 1960 stoked unfounded rumours that he planned to hand over power to him. In fact, Franco did not trust Don Juan because of his declared intention to be the King of all Spaniards, of both left and right. He had more faith in Juan Carlos, because of his education in Francoist Spain.[91] The encounter on 29 March was short and inconsequential. Franco made no mention of his intentions lest he lose monarchist support. He did, however, repeat his accusations that Don Juan was surrounded by freemasons.[92] They agreed on a joint statement that the talks had been cordial and that Juan Carlos's education in Spain did not prejudge the question of the succession. However, on returning to Madrid late in the evening of 29 March, Franco simply amended the text to make it seem that Don Juan had accepted the terms of the Law of Succession. Don Juan was understandably annoyed by Franco's underhand dealing.[93]

In fact, Franco was imperceptibly drifting from the centre of political life. In response to economic modernization, a society was emerging with concerns incomprehensible to someone locked into the mindset of the civil war and its aftermath. Moreover, partly as a result of his obsession with his hobbies and partly in response to the sheer complexity of government, he was increasingly leaving the detail of government to Carrero Blanco and the technocrats. Throughout the summer, conflict simmered between the technocrats and the Falangist ministers as the stabilization plan slashed the budgets of the Ministries of Labour, Education, Interior and the Movimiento and thus diminished the Falange's politically crucial power of social patronage. With Spaniards concerned about living standards and anxious to forget the civil war and the hunger of the 1940s, Franco's refrains about past triumphs made him seem irrelevant. The political elite still needed him as ultimate arbiter but less and less as day-to-day ruler. The technocrats were significantly strengthened by the relative success of the stabilization plan. The political and economic changes implicit in their policies provoked a sense of desperation within the Falange and some feeble expressions of discontent during official ceremonies.[94]

On 19 December 1960, Navarro Rubio announced the first Development Plan, which had been drafted in collaboration with the World Bank. Franco continued to long for autarky and believed that the World Bank advisory mission on the Development Plan was part of a plot by freemasons.[95] Obsessed with freemasonry and the civil war, still an admirer of Hitler and Mussolini, he was increasingly isolated from his ministers, many of whom were twenty to thirty years his junior. He believed that the American government was dominated by freemasons ready to open the door to communism and regarded the newly elected President, John F. Kennedy, as a dangerous liberal.[96] In February 1961, Carrero Blanco produced a report warning that any American pressure for political liberalization must be resisted.[97]

1961 saw the stabilization plan begin to bear fruit. It was also the twenty-fifth anniversary of the military rebellion of 1936. Franco's speeches were nostalgic and far removed from the domestic and international reality of the 1960s. He seemed unaware that his enemies were not those of 1936, but young factory workers ready to strike against long hours, low pay and hazardous conditions, students and liberal Basque and Catalan priests denouncing the repression of regionalism. With Kennedy determined to beat communism by aggressively projecting the benefits of capitalism, the Caudillo seemed a fossilized survivor. On 3 June, inaugurating the new Cortes, in a speech nearly two hours long,

Franco boasted about his achievements and denounced political parties.[98]

The year had been choreographed so as to emphasize that Franco would not be stepping down any time soon. On 1 October, he inaugurated a carefully orchestrated set of ceremonies to celebrate his election as Caudillo with a nostalgic and self-congratulatory speech in Burgos.[99] Meanwhile, López Rodó and Carrero Blanco pressed him to announce that the constitutional law drafted in 1957, the Organic Law of the State, would be submitted to the Cortes. However, Franco was not ready to choose a particular option for a succession that he assumed to be still far in the future.[100] That was underlined on 2 October, at a meeting of the Consejo Nacional of the Falange in his honour.[101] The Movimiento's abject subordination was emphasized when José Solís, the Minister Secretary, opened proceedings by addressing Franco simply as 'Señor', a form of address reserved for kings. In his own arrogantly boastful speech, Franco gave himself credit for the recent economic growth.[102]

Conflict between the Falange and the technocrats took the form of a competition 'to furnish Franco's head with ideas'.[103] In fact, the Movimiento had been thoroughly domesticated under Arrese, Fernández Cuesta and Solís. Bright, hard-working functionaries were emerging who were more concerned to get top jobs in the state apparatus than to implement the ideology of Falangism. Men like López Rodó and Navarro Rubio were defined by their membership of the Opus Dei but were more accurately seen as examples of what came to be called the 'bureaucracy of number ones', those who had won competitive examinations for the civil service or university chairs while still young. Similarly, other prominent regime administrators in the 1960s, such as Manuel Fraga and Torcuato Fernández Miranda, were usually described as Falangists. Yet they could all more properly be identified as meritocratic functionaries.[104]

The technically competent functionaries who came to the fore between 1957 and 1973 saw themselves as 'apolitical' in that their central concern was efficient administration rather than loyalty to a particular faction of the Movimiento. Their professional competence marginalized Franco from the ever more complex day-to-day running of government, yet paradoxically strengthened his position in two ways. First, he got credit for their economic achievements and second, having no political clientele, they owed their well-remunerated prominence entirely to him.

There were still factions but none had the clout of earlier times. The Caudillo's position as the keystone of the Francoist arch was impregnable. With the technocrats' policies working, no one Francoist faction would take the risk of destabilizing a situation from which all derived benefit. Each hoped for Franco's support against the others. With growing prosperity, Franco's own position seemed to be threatened only by his health. Nevertheless, the social turmoil unleashed by economic change boosted opposition in the factories, the universities and the regions.

Panic about Franco's mortality was provoked by a hunting accident at the end of 1961. His shotgun exploded, badly damaging his left hand.[105] Franco activated none of the mechanisms established in the Law of Succession. He merely telephoned Carrero Blanco and ordered him to inform only the military ministers and the General Staff of the army. He asked his friend Camilo Alonso Vega, the hard-line Minister of the Interior, to 'keep an eye on things'. Franco was justifiably confident that between them Alonso Vega, the Director General of Security Carlos Arias Navarro and the Director General of the Civil Guard could maintain public order. Rumours that he had been the target of an assassination attempt were unfounded. The explosion was attributed to his loading incorrect ammunition from his daughter's gun.[106] Nonetheless, the incident impelled many Francoists to turn their attention to the succession.[107] Their anxieties for the future would be intensified when large-scale strikes swept across Asturias and much of the industrial north in the spring of 1962.

Franco himself gave no public hint of preoccupation. The instruction to Alonso Vega presaged the appointment of a hard-line regent to guarantee that the eventual monarch would not stray from the authoritarian path. That watchdog role would be entrusted first to Muñoz Grandes and then to Carrero Blanco, although Franco would outlive them both. Despite Franco's close relationship with Carrero, who was committed to Juan Carlos, there was still doubt regarding his choice of a royal candidate. In the meantime, in January 1962, López Rodó was given the powerful position of head of the Commissariat for the Development Plan, a central planning body suggested by the World Bank advisers. López Rodó's elevation meant that the Falange had lost a key battle in the war for the post-Franco future. López Rodó believed that administrative and economic reform were better guarantees of the survival of the system than the resistance to change (*inmovilismo*) seen in Franco's reluctance to resolve the succession.[108]

At sixty-nine, Franco would now be distanced even further from the centre of gravity. Since neither he nor Carrero understood the full complexity of what López Rodó was doing, he had considerable autonomy as Comisario. Moreover, over the next few years, he came to dominate the cabinet subcommittee for economic affairs formally chaired by Franco. The committee was soon attended not just by the various ministers with responsibility for economic matters. As it became the real locus of power, issues other than economic ones were discussed and other ministers sought excuses to attend. Just as previously, as Secretary to the Presidencia, López Rodó had prepared and prioritized cabinet business, now he had a similar and even more powerful role, in initiating and coordinating economic policy. Franco became aware of the issues only when they came, pre-wrapped, to the subcommittee.[109] Since he had no reason to question the loyalty of Carrero Blanco's protégé, he was delighted to be relieved of irksome economic detail so that he could return to frequent hunting parties. In addition, he also spent many hours watching movies and sport on the many television sets placed around El Pardo. He began to do the pools every week and won twice.[110]

To maintain the momentum of economic reform initiated by the technocrats, Castiella and the economic ministers persuaded a reluctant Franco to allow a petition to join the European Economic Community. Believing the Community to be in the hands of freemasons, he feared that membership would see Spain blackmailed into political liberalization. In the event, the EEC agreed to negotiations for some form of economic agreement but insisted that major constitutional change would be necessary before any form of political link could be contemplated.[111] The Community's refusal to open political negotiations merely convinced Franco that Spain was still surrounded by hostile forces determined to bring him down. This belief was reinforced by the outbreak of strikes in the Asturian mines and the Basque steel industry in the spring of 1962. There was a massive and brutal deployment of the Civil Guard and armed police against both miners and their womenfolk. Nevertheless, the strikes spread to Catalonia and Madrid. They were stopped not by repression but by wage increases, a triumph for a new clandestine working-class movement.[112] In the economic revival which followed the harsh austerity of the stabilization plan from 1959 to 1961, the victory of the workers showed that state-owned enterprises and private sector industrialists were prepared to pay to avoid interrupting valuable production. Franco again attributed unrest to outside agitators and was perplexed by the support of many priests for the workers, particularly in the Basque Country. Privately and in public, he reverted to explanations in civil war terms of the 'enemy' and foreign Communist and masonic agitators.[113]

The regime's abortive overtures to the EEC and the 1962 strikes boosted sympathy in Europe for the anti-Franco opposition. To capitalize on this, from 5 to 8 June 1962, around eighty monarchists, Catholics and repentant Falangists from inside Spain met thirty-eight exiled Socialists and Basque and Catalan nationalists in Munich at the IV Congress of the European Movement. The meeting, covertly financed by the CIA's Congress for Cultural Freedom, issued a moderate and pacific final communiqué calling for evolution in Spain. A furious Franco saw only a conspiracy to undermine the regime by freemasons, Jews and Catholics. He insisted on the suspension of the flimsy constitutional guarantees of the Fuero de los Españoles.[114] Many of the Spanish delegates, including Dionisio Ridruejo and José María Gil Robles, were arrested and sent into exile for their part in what was denounced both in the state media and in Franco's speeches as the 'filthy Munich cohabitation'.[115] The myth of the regime's invulnerability had already been undermined by the Caudillo's shooting accident and the strike waves. Munich seemed to justify the Communists' claims that their policy of 'national reconciliation', adopted in 1956, was about to bear fruit in a wide front of anti-Franco forces. Moreover, there had been glimmers of conflict with the Catholic Church since the Second Vatican Council in 1959. The Pope's encyclical of 1961, *Mater et Magistra*, had alarmed the hard-liners in Franco's cabinet with its talk of just wages and humane conditions for industrial and agricultural labourers, redistributive taxes and trade union rights.[116]

Franco's reaction to Munich had been a serious error. He was informed by Castiella and the ambassadors in Paris, José María de Areilza, and in Washington, Antonio Garrigues, of the damage caused to their efforts to improve Spain's international position. Always alert to threats to his survival, he responded with a major cabinet reshuffle on 10 July.[117] The technocrats' economic line was consolidated with the appointment of the dynamic thirty-eight-year-old Gregorio López Bravo, as Minister of

Industry. Other more 'progressive' Opus Dei technocrats replaced Falangists: Manuel Lora Tamayo as Minister of Education and Jesús Romeo Gorría as Minister of Labour. Solís was kept on, both as a sop to the Falange and as a reward for the energy that he had displayed during the strikes. In his seventieth year, Franco needed familiar faces as well as the dynamic technocrats. Thus he kept on the 73-year-old Alonso Vega as Minister of the Interior, appointed the 64-year-old Admiral Nieto Antúnez as Minister for the Navy and named the 66-year-old hard-liner General Agustín Muñoz Grandes as Vice-President of the cabinet. The latter job was largely fulfilled by Carrero Blanco, who thus accumulated more power.[118] A key change was the promotion of the 40-year-old Manuel Fraga Iribarne to the Ministry of Information to remedy the misguided press reaction to Munich. Usually labelled a Falangist, the energetic and ambitious Fraga was a versatile and flexible apparatchik. Along with the economic changes being hastened by the technocrats, his partial liberalization of the press would make him, like them, one of the inadvertent gravediggers of the regime.[119]

To ensure his permanence in power, Franco pinned his hopes on a combination of brutal repression and more economic growth. Arrests and torture of leftist militants were still commonplace. A new strike wave in Asturias and Catalonia during August and September was countered by ferocious police measures. Under the development plans, GDP doubled in the course of the 1960s but it lagged behind that of Italy. Spain remained desperately poor. Moreover, industrialization created social problems as internal migration led to the growth of over-crowded housing estates of shoddily built tower blocks. Inevitably, the new working class living in these blocks responded to their social deprivation with greater militancy.[120] Along the way, huge fortunes were made for speculative builders in cahoots with public officials. In Barcelona, for instance, under the Alcalde Josep Maria Porcioles, the Ayuntamiento rezoned private and public property such as sports grounds and compulsorily purchased terrain. Then Porcioles's own notary's office would arrange the necessary building permits for the construction company belonging to Josep Maria Figueras, whose brother-in-law also happened to be the head of the urban services of the Ayuntamiento.[121] In Valencia, when the Civil Governor was the Falangist Adolfo Rincón de Arellano, the population grew by 1 million between 1960 and 1975, reaching 3 million inhabitants. The concomitant urban expansion saw much speculative building and fortunes made out of the traffic in permits and licences.[122]

Fraga loosened the censorship and managed the image of Franco and the regime more skilfully. In public, albeit not in private, Franco talked more of economic achievements than of freemasons and the enemies of the true Spain. Alongside the claim that the present growth had been planned all along, the mantra coined by Fraga and López Rodó was 'the Spanish miracle'.[123] The successes of the modernizers permitted Franco to spend ever more time on his leisure pursuits and leave daily administration to his ministers.[124] However, the new cabinet contained two groups with different plans for the future. The restoration of the monarchy was the goal of Carrero Blanco, the military conservatives and the technocrats who saw economic modernization as a prior condition in a context of political stability.[125] Castiella, Fraga, Solís and Nieto Antúnez were keener on political modernization. Fraga was anxious to open up the regime with a more liberal information policy and Solís was talking of a limited pluralism within the Movimiento with 'political associations'. The subsequent tension between Solís and Carrero Blanco was permitted by Franco, who intervened only rarely to make peace.[126] Convinced by the Vatican Council that the Curia was infiltrated by freemasons and Communists, and disgusted by Don Juan's determination to be King of all Spaniards, he had no stomach for reform. 'It is inconceivable', he said, 'that the victors of a war should cede power to the defeated'.[127]

The social dislocation that accompanied economic progress, fuelling strikes and unrest, was met with harsh repression. Yet Franco was convinced that his Spain was a paradise of individual freedom.[128] In fact, the barbaric nature of the regime in general and of Franco in particular was revealed by the trial and execution of the Communist Julián Grimau García in 1963.[129] It provoked a wave of demonstrations against Franco in the major cities of Europe and America. Unfortunately for the regime, the Grimau trial coincided with Pope John XXIII's great reforming encyclical *Pacem in Terris* advocating human rights such as freedom of association and expression and political participation. It confirmed Franco's belief that the Vatican was a nest of freemasons and Communists.[130] He ignored pleas for clemency by ecclesiastical dignitaries and political leaders including Nikita Khrushchev, Willy Brandt, Harold Wilson and Queen Elizabeth II. Despite the international repercussions, Franco was adamant that Grimau must die.[131] The resulting wave of international revulsion undermined efforts to improve the regime's image. In France, the popular outrage sabotaged General de Gaulle's plans to hasten a closer association of Spain with the European Economic Community.[132] Four months later, after a brief trial, two anarchists, Francisco Granados Gata and Joaquín Delgado Martínez, were garrotted for alleged implication in a bombing incident at Madrid police headquarters. The international clamour, although more muted than in the case of Grimau, was considerable.[133] Such political faux pas, along with economic change, were damaging the regime. Even the Falange was less reliable: its senior militants were geriatric and corrupt, its young men cynical and ambitious functionaries. The liberalization of the Church through the Vatican Council would have an impact. News that the liberal Cardinal Montini had been elected as Pope Paul VI reached Franco during a cabinet meeting on 21 June 1963. He exclaimed bitterly, 'A jug of cold water.'[134]

Under the slogan invented by Manuel Fraga, 'Twenty-Five Years of Peace', at immense cost massive celebrations of the anniversary of the end of the civil war would be mounted throughout 1964. An array of hagiographic books and articles set out to transform Franco, whose legitimacy had previously been based on war, into an icon of peace.[135] The year 1964 would have been an appropriate moment for him to announce his choice of successor, but he ignored the opportunity to do so. Confident that his technocrats could be left to provide increased prosperity and efficient administration, his main concern, beyond his hobbies, was to ensure the continuity of the regime after his death. Franco would take an inordinately long time to decide. That was partly a reflection of the difficulty of finding a candidate both committed to the perpetuation of Francoism and also acceptable to all the regime families. At the same time, he was reluctant to contemplate death or the abandonment of power. Nevertheless, that he could spend years musing on the topic was a measure of the extent to which his position was secure. Within five years, that situation was to change dramatically.

On 9 April 1964, he gave the Consejo Nacional his self-congratulatory interpretation of his rule, attributing economic development to his own foresight. He stressed his efforts to provide for the continuity of the regime after his disappearance but made no specific announcement about the future.[136] For the reformists in the cabinet who hoped that the 'peace' celebrations might encourage him to promulgate the Organic Law of the State and name his successor, it was a disappointment. Watching him read out the speech, Fraga was struck by how he had aged. A week later, in a private audience, the impression that Franco was fading fast was overwhelming.[137] On 30 April 1964, he was presented with a medal to commemorate the twenty-five years of peace. In his speech of thanks, he said that he looked forward to a similar ceremony in another twenty-five years' time.[138]

In April, the celebrations were marred by a resurgence of strikes in the Asturian mines in protest against a new labour law. A savage repression saw men dismissed and strikers arrested, many of whom would languish in prison until 1970. This led to cabinet clashes. The Minister of Labour, Romeo Gorría, accused the Minister of Industry, López Bravo, of being too ready to buy off strikers. Franco supported López Bravo, commenting that the Ministry of Labour and Falangist Syndical Organization were infiltrated by Communists. He told his cousin, Pacón, that many mineworkers 'obey hidden powers'. Alonso Vega wanted to intensify the repression, but Fraga, Castiella and the reformists managed to persuade Franco that more violence would be counter-productive.[139]

Franco's delight in the 1964 celebrations increased both his reluctance to plan for the future and his conviction that he was indispensable. During the summer, he cited the applause that greeted him on his public appearance as his principal argument when his ministers suggested change. Addicted to popular adulation, he showed ever less interest in reform.[140] Domestic popular acclaim made him more sensitive to foreign criticism. The rising tide of strikes, student demonstrations and agitation in the regions was widely reported by the press of Europe including some Catholic publications.[141] Franco assumed that subversion in Spain was the work of sinister foreign forces and was puzzled by the implicit criticisms of his rule emanating from the Vatican Council. His belief in his own divine purpose was unshaken, often confirmed by extravagant praise from some sections of the Spanish Church hierarchy.[142] He saw Vatican unease about the imprisonment, torture, exile and even execution of the regime's enemies, together with the growth of the Catholic workers' organization HOAC, as proof of Communist infiltration. The reformers of the regime were again disappointed at the opening of the Cortes on 8 July 1964 when Franco denounced liberal democracy as an exhausted system repudiated by the masses.[143] The siege mentality of both Franco and Carrero Blanco was at odds with the humanist and pluralist renewal of Catholicism being elaborated in Rome.[144] The evolving attitudes of many senior members of the hierarchy was matched by the radicalization of worker priests. They experienced at first hand the privations of migrant workers living in the slums of the great industrial cities. In the Basque Country and Catalonia, the close relationship between the clergy and the faithful was reflected in a growing ecclesiastical sympathy with regionalist aspirations.[145] In September, when the Vatican Council approved a resolution requesting nations to renounce their privileges of intervening in the nomination of bishops, Franco refused categorically to negotiate lest the Papal Nuncio name bishops in the interests of their regional communities rather than as servants of the state.

Despite his continuing passion for arduous hunting and fishing jaunts, Franco was showing signs of deteriorating health. He was developing Parkinson's disease.[146] In public, he spoke less frequently and more briefly as it became harder to conceal the symptoms of the disease – a rigid stance, an unsure walk and a vacant, open-mouthed facial expression. He brushed aside encouragement from all sides of the regime to proceed with the Organic Law, claiming that he was working on it.[147] The urgency was underlined by serious university disturbances in the spring of 1965 in Madrid and Barcelona. At the 5 March cabinet meeting, Carrero Blanco, supported by all the ministers, proposed that the Organic Law be drafted as soon as possible. Franco claimed that he was delayed by the difficulty of finding a solution that would please everyone.[148] On 1 April, Franco read to Carrero Blanco a near final draft of the Organic Law but weeks later had made no further progress.[149] In July, after endless doubts and hesitations, he reshuffled the cabinet. With greater priority being given to relations with the EEC, Ullastres became Ambassador to the Community and was replaced as Minister of Commerce by another Opus Deista, Faustino García Moncó. López Rodó remained as Comisario of the Development Plan and became Minister without Portfolio. Carrero's battle with Solís would henceforth be assumed directly by López Rodó.[150]

At the cabinet meeting of 13 August 1965, discussion began about Fraga's Press Law. Over subsequent months, the text was debated, with fierce opposition coming from Alonso Vega and other reactionary elements who tried to persuade Franco that it threatened the very foundations of the regime. Nevertheless, by February 1966, it was ready for submission to the Cortes for rubber-stamping.[151] An even more contentious issue was the possible nomination of Juan Carlos as Franco's successor. The Caudillo himself watched from the sidelines throughout 1966 as acrimonious conflicts developed between López Bravo and López Rodó on the one hand and Solís and Romeo Gorría on the other. The Falangists supported the questionable claim to the succession of Alfonso Borbón-Dampierre, son of Don Juan's brother, Jaime. Partly out of apathy and a reluctance to face another reshuffle and partly to spite Don Juan, Franco let the squabbles continue. He did nothing when the government's economic policy was attacked by Solís's Movimiento press.[152] Girón complained of the Caudillo's loosening grip as cabinet meetings became fewer and shorter.[153]

The future remained the most divisive issue. On 9 February 1966, López Rodó pressed Franco to resolve the succession to avoid chaos on his death. He agreed but then complained about having to choose between so many candidates, using it as an excuse to keep his options open.[154] He knew that, once he had named his successor, there would be a rush of opportunists eager to ingratiate themselves with the nominee, which could only diminish his own power. Moreover, he was concerned by secret police reports on Juan Carlos's contacts with progressive elements.[155] He would not proceed without the certainty that Juan Carlos would swear to be bound by the principles of the Movimiento. He told Fraga at the beginning of June that Don Juan was out of the question.[156] He was furious because Don Juan, despairing of ever being made successor, had established a secretariat, a virtual shadow cabinet, headed by José María de Areilza. Areilza was convinced, by the international storms over Munich and Grimau, and by an icy interview with Franco, that the regime was in a cul-de-sac.[157] The decline of Franco's health was unmistakable, although the evidence of senility alternated with long periods of fitness.[158] Nevertheless, with age and the succession on his mind, on 13 June he gave Carrero the final draft of the Organic Law of the State.[159] There would be no discussion of the complex law. It would be submitted first to the Cortes and then to the Spanish people without any public justification or explanation.[160]

When he presented the Organic Law of the State to the Cortes on 22 November 1966, in a haltingly weak voice Franco read a boastful speech about his lifetime achievements. The tone was valedictory but he proclaimed that he had no intention of retiring. He gradually descended into an unintelligible mumble. Without discussing its ten sections, sixty-six articles and many additional clauses, he just called on the *procuradores* (deputies) to give their assent, which they did by acclamation.[161] Three weeks later, he spoke to the nation on television and radio to seek a 'yes' vote in the forthcoming referendum on the Organic Law. In line with the official slogan '¡Franco sí!', he made the referendum a vote of confidence in himself personally. He stated that democracy was a fiction and foreign hostility was proof of international admiration of his regime. He asked for a 'yes' vote as a reward for all he had done for Spain.[162] The speech was the opening shot in a massive campaign mounted by Fraga with the full weight of the media. The streets and highways were plastered with gigantic placards of a beaming, benevolent patriarch. It was reiterated that to vote 'no' was to vote for Moscow. On 14 December, 88 per cent of the eligible electorate voted and fewer than 2 per cent of them voted 'no'. There had been no discussion of the virtually incomprehensible law. The opposition had been silenced. There were cases of multiple voting and even places where official efficiency ensured that more than 120 per cent of the electorate voted 'yes'. In others, voting slips were not counted and the desired result merely recorded. The greatest level of abstentions and 'no' votes was in the industrial towns.[163] The referendum was, despite the massive electoral fraud and the social pressures, a victory for Franco. Many had voted 'yes' in gratitude for the past and for growing prosperity, but many did so also in the hope of bringing nearer the transition from Franco's dictatorship to the monarchy.

By 1967, with the technical arrangements for the succession in place, there was little left for Franco to do except actually name his successor. Now seventy-four years old, he seemed at times barely a shadow of his former self. In newsreels, there was an ever more noticeable rigidity in movement and a lack of energy in his speeches. Even with the Organic Law in place, uncertainty about the succession saw many of the regime elite continue to behave as if he were still entirely in control. The machinery of government was in the hands of Carrero Blanco and López Rodó. The years of state terror banked between 1936 and 1944 had paid off handsomely in mass political apathy. The central issue was the post-Franco future and that gave rise to a process of jockeying for position in which he played a marginal role. That he was no longer the major player in the game of Spanish politics was reflected in the media's tendency to photograph him more often playing with his grandchildren, hunting or fishing. Smiling timidly, Franco was now the distant patriarch, the grandfather of his people.

The technocrats hoped that, within the terms of the new Organic Law, Franco would name Carrero Blanco President of the Council of Ministers. Finally, Franco made him Vice-President on 21 September 1967, effectively handing him the reins of government. Carrero had served him loyally since 1941 and their views were almost indistinguishable. However, his commitment to the cause of Juan Carlos generated alarm among the Falangists. They feared that, if Franco backed Juan Carlos, it would open the way to a liberal monarchy and the end of their privileges. They fought a war against the Opus in the mid-1960s through the Movimiento press network.[164] An insidious private struggle was carried on by a circle of right-wingers who gathered in El Pardo in an attempt to mobilize an increasingly decrepit Franco to the cause of *inmovilismo*. Consisting of Cristóbal Martínez-Bordiú, Doña Carmen and hard-line Falangists like Girón, they had links with military hard-liners who saw the army as the praetorian guard of the regime. By the late 1960s, the most prominent of the so-called 'blue' or Falangist generals, such as Alfonso Pérez Viñeta, Tomás García Rebull, Carlos Iniesta Cano and Ángel Campano López, were reaching key operational positions. In his last years, mainly because of his disease and the drugs taken to mitigate the symptoms, Franco became a passive shuttlecock between these groups. He was largely committed to the Carrero Blanco–López Rodó vision of the transition to an authoritarian monarchy. However, as he grew older, his instincts made him more prone to listen to the alarmist accounts of what was happening put his way by this clique.[165]

Just turned seventy-five, infuriated by university disturbances in early 1968, Franco was convinced that they were the work of foreign agitators and that radical priests were Communists in disguise. He was delighted by the violent repression of left-wing and liberal priests and university students imposed by General Pérez Viñeta, the Captain General of Barcelona.[166] There would be no reconciliation with his enemies. He was bewildered by the increasing liberalism of the Catholic Church and by the activities of bishops who condemned police repression.[167] As more priests became involved in support of the labour and regionalist opposition to the regime, in the summer of 1968 Franco authorized the creation of a prison for priests at Zamora which held over fifty priests.[168] As part of the Church moved leftwards, ultra-right-wing anti-clericalism emerged within the regime, in the Falange, among the Carlists and in the military. Several tiny neo-Nazi groups, including the Partido Español Nacional-Sindicalista, Blas Piñar's Fuerza Nueva (New Force), the Guerrilleros de Cristo Rey (the Warriors of Christ the King) and CEDADE (Círculo Español de Amigos de Europa), attacked with armed terror squads anything liberal or leftist from priests to workers.[169]

Franco gave little sign of concern that his cabinet was virtually paralysed by the hostility between the Falangists and the technocrats. In the second half of 1968, he ignored the calls of Carrero, Fraga and others that he renew the government.[170] Symptoms of his decreasing energy were impossible to ignore.[171] He delayed for another five years before responding to appeals from several ministers to name a president of the government.[172] At a meeting with the American Secretary of State, Dean Rusk, on 18 November 1968, to discuss the renewal of the bases agreement, a barely lucid Franco did no more than grunt monosyllables.[173] His end-of-year broadcast, on 30 December, was a lifeless condemnation of the unrest in the universities.[174] He showed every sign of aiming to remain in power, but he could now manage only fortnightly cabinet meetings. However, his hesitations about the succession were largely resolved by the autumn of 1968.[175] On 8 January 1969, interviewed by the official news agency EFE, Juan Carlos unreservedly accepted the idea of the installation of a Francoist monarchy. Franco was delighted and, on 15 January, more or less told Juan Carlos that he would be naming him as his successor before the end of the year.[176] However, the chances of a smooth succession were nearly scuppered by the reaction of Alonso Vega, Carrero Blanco, Nieto Antúnez and Solís to renewed university agitation. At a cabinet meeting on 24 January, they demanded a state of emergency, a tacit admission of helplessness before the growing clamour of workers, students and Basque activists. Apart from the absurdity of the regime dinosaurs trying to hold back the consequences of social change, López Rodó and the modernizers were concerned that this would see Franco delay again since Juan Carlos could not be named as successor while the state of emergency remained in force.[177] At the cabinet meeting of 21 March, after Fraga had claimed that it would damage the tourist trade, the state of emergency was lifted by a reluctant Franco, who always preferred public order to international goodwill. He still hesitated to name his successor.[178]

Other problems were emerging. In early May, Carrero told Franco about the growing threat of the Basque revolutionary separatist organization Euskadi ta Askatasuna (Basque Homeland and Liberty). Carrero pointed out that the extirpation of ETA required enormous delicacy if the operation were not to damage relations with the Basque Country and with the Church.[179] Not fully on top of events, Franco left the struggle against ETA to hard-line elements in the army, and Carrero's pessimistic predictions would come true.

At the end of May, Franco told Carrero Blanco that he would name Juan Carlos as his successor before the summer.[180] Then, pressed by the Falangists not to do so, he hesitated again, fearful, as he told Carrero Blanco, of deserting his loyal followers. With the technocrat ministers becoming impatient, he opted to make the announcement on 17 July. He failed to tell Juan Carlos, who was about to visit his father in Portugal, and informed him only on his return on 12 July. He thereby cunningly engineered a rupture between the two since Don Juan assumed that Juan Carlos had known and had betrayed him with his silence. Relations between them were strained for some time afterwards.[181] Juan Carlos was given the title of Príncipe de España, and not Príncipe de Asturias, the traditional title of the heir to the throne. Thus Franco severed both the continuity and the legitimacy of the Borbón line. The new monarchy would be his.[182] Speaking to the Cortes on 22 July, he took pride in the precision of the instruments created for the succession.[183] The Prince swore fidelity to the principles of the Movimiento, having first been assured by his adviser Torcuato Fernández Miranda that this oath would not prevent a future process of democratic reform. Franco trusted Juan Carlos sufficiently to give him a free hand.[184] It seems that the Prince, having learned from his mentor how to keep his cards close to his chest, planned all along to deceive him by working for the transition to democracy after his death.

Shortly after the nomination of Juan Carlos, Solís presented a Statute of Associations to the Consejo Nacional, in an attempt to establish the regime's 'limited pluralism' and head off more meaningful change. It permitted the creation, not of political parties, but of associations in which there could be a 'contrast of legitimate opinion'. There was no context in which associations could be subjected to a popular vote. They had to have a minimum membership of 25,000 and had to be authorized by the Consejo Nacional. Rejected by the democratic opposition, the idea was taken up only by Francoist factions. The most ultra-reactionary was Blas Piñar's extreme Falangist Fuerza Nueva. Franco did not object to a cosmetic veneer of liberalism for foreign consumption, but his obsessive hatred of political parties ensured that Solís's reform would remain meaningless.[185]

Franco's belief that, with the succession resolved, he could enjoy a trouble-free future was to be rudely shattered in the second half of 1969. ETA was a threatening black cloud. More immediately, in mid-August 1969, there erupted the political volcano known as the Matesa scandal. Matesa (Maquinaría Textil del Norte de España SA) was a textile-machinery manufacturer in Pamplona. Under its Director, Juan Vilá Reyes, Matesa had developed a shuttleless loom which it was exporting to Europe, Latin America and the USA. The apparent success of Vilá Reyes made him the toast of the technocrats. To qualify for export credits, he set up subsidiaries in Latin America which ordered large numbers of looms. Financial irregularities were discovered in late 1968, and it was alleged that the subsidiaries and their orders were a fraudulent device to qualify for the credits and that misappropriation of state funds in the region of 10 billion pesetas had been used to finance Opus Dei ventures abroad as well as to enrich Vilá Reyes. The ministers accused of complicity were Faustino García Moncó (Commerce), Juan José Espinosa San Martín (Finance) and Gregorio López Bravo (Industry), together with the Governor of the Bank of Spain, Mariano Navarro Rubio.[186] Franco was unconcerned, having been convinced by Vilá Reyes that the company was merely bending archaic regulations to boost much-needed exports.[187]

However, the company's problems intensified when the Movimiento press used the issue to unleash a violent campaign against the Opus with *Arriba* denouncing a national disaster.[188] Solís hoped to break the hegemony of the Opus Dei technocrats before the post-Franco future began under Juan Carlos, but his ploy backfired badly. Deeply puritanical, Franco and Carrero were already disturbed by Fraga's press liberalization and were now outraged by this blatant attempt to overturn the Opus Dei scenario for Juan Carlos's succession. It was thus easy for Carrero and López Rodó to turn the potentially damaging Matesa crisis to their advantage. Carrero's report for Franco contrasted the 'lamentable negligence' of the ministers involved with the damage to Spain's international credibility done by the media campaign. Franco did not regard the offences as serious and delighted in the absolute loyalty of the Opus ministers. Now heavily medicated for Parkinson's disease, he did not follow all the ramifications of the affair and was easily persuaded by Carrero's report that Solís's press network and Fraga's Ministry of Information were attempting to undermine the government. Espinosa San Martín and García Moncó resigned, but Franco did not doubt their honesty.[189]

Carrero Blanco was determined that Fraga and Solís would also have to go. He convinced Franco that Solís was trying to build an independent power base and that Fraga's Press Law permitted pornography and Communist propaganda.[190] Franco responded with a cabinet reshuffle on 29 October 1969 in which, for the first time, Carrero, with help from López Rodó, was instrumental in the choice of ministers. Franco's presidency was little more than nominal. The dynamic Gregorio López Bravo replaced Castiella as Foreign Minister. Fraga was replaced by the Opus Deista Alfredo Sanchez Bella, Solís by the sinuously intelligent Torcuato Fernández Miranda, a member of Opus Dei and a key adviser to Juan Carlos. The Opus controlled Education, Information, Foreign Affairs and the four economic ministries of Finance, Commerce, Industry and the Development Plan. Alonso Vega was replaced by a bureaucratic military lawyer, Tomás Garicano Goñi. This so-called monochrome government was united in support of Juan Carlos.[191]

The intra-regime squabbles over Matesa went far beyond the competition for the spoils of power. They also reflected growing concern about labour, student and regionalist unrest. Franco's supporters were beginning to break up into factions reflecting not the traditional divisions into Falangists, monarchists and Catholics but shifting groups seeking options for their survival after Franco's death. The technocrats believed that prosperity and efficient administration would permit a painless transition to a Francoist monarchy under Juan Carlos. Others believed that modernization had opened the floodgates to opposition and so advocated a return to hard-line Francoism. Blind to the incapacity of his dictatorship to cope with a dramatically different Spain, Franco assumed that this cabinet would be capable of resolving the serious problems already on the agenda. Soon, however, the inability of the new team to settle the ferment of Spanish society saw Franco and Carrero instinctively return to the siege mentality of the 1940s. Nevertheless, in his end-of-year message on 30 December 1969, the Caudillo confidently declared, in what was to become the nautical catchphrase of his twilight years, that 'all is lashed down and well lashed down'. It reflected his view that Juan Carlos would be obliged to maintain the regime. In other words, he believed that it was the Prince who was lashed down.[192]

Prince Juan Carlos of Spain and Princess Sophia of Greece in Athens, married by
the Greek Orthodox rite, May 1962.

15

The Twilight Years of a Corrupt Regime, 1969–1982

There had been no more dramatic indication of how things were changing for Franco than Pope Paul VI's appointment, in February 1969, of
Monsignor Vicente Enrique y Tarancón as Primate of Spain. Committed
to the liberalizing spirit of the Second Vatican Council, he was to be the
instrument whereby Rome distanced itself from the regime. At the same
time, intensifying opposition in the universities, factories and regions
reflected the limitations of the economic growth of the 1960s. The
Development Plans had been accompanied by inefficiency, corruption
and high social cost and had done nothing to redistribute wealth or to
diminish regional imbalances. Once the economic boost consequent
upon the opening up of Spain to world trade got under way, long-term
planning was replaced by short-term policies to control inflation and
balance of payments deficits. Accordingly, when the 1960s boom began
to slow down, the technocrats responded with austerity measures.
Inevitably, strikes increased in number. Growth had created a new working class whose militancy could be controlled only by continuously
improved living standards or heavier repression.

Even the defeated Falangists saw Carrero as the best guarantor of the
essence of Francoism, despite his links to the technocrats. They believed
that he would be able to prevent any reformist ambitions on the part of
Juan Carlos. Certainly, his monochrome cabinet was committed to a
post-Franco Francoism built on continued prosperity rather than political liberalization. Thus, before 1969 was out, Fernández Miranda was
obliged to scrap the Solís project of political associations, presumably for
fear that they might spawn real parties. In the event, Carrero's plans
would end with his own assassination in 1973 and massive economic
crisis. The combination of worldwide recession and the structural weaknesses of the Spanish economy would ensure that 1974 would see

one-time Francoists toying with political liberalization as a substitute for failed prosperity. The inability of the Carrero team to resolve the contradictions between the regime and a changing society saw a deterioration of labour relations throughout 1970. The year began with 20,000 miners on strike in Asturias and coal imports needed to keep the iron and steel industries going.

By the summer, there would be serious disputes in the shipyards, the Granada and Madrid construction industries and the Madrid metro. Some 3,800 metro workers were forced to return to work when the cabinet decreed their military mobilization, rendering them liable to court martial for mutiny. Such brutal responses were symptomatic of the regime's crisis of authority. During the Asturian strike, the Archbishop of Oviedo, Gabino Díaz Merchán, condemned government reprisals against the miners. On 21 July, the police fired on a demonstration by around 2,000 building workers in Granada, killing three and wounding several others. Granada Cathedral and some local churches gave strikers refuge from the police. While the Movimiento press accused the local clergy of provoking the strike, on 28 July the Archbishop of Granada, Benavent Escuín, condemned police violence against the workers.[1] Trials of priests for supporting worker or regionalist aspirations also drove wedges between Catholics and the Francoist state. The anxiety provoked in banking and industrial circles by the unrest was echoed within the political establishment. There was misgiving about the regime's ability to deal with so many problems, above all, in the Basque Country, where ETA's terrorist activities were destroying the regime's myth of invulnerability. Yet, as his health declined, Franco was oblivious to the fact that positions were being taken up for the aftermath of his demise.

Stoppages in the autumn were driven by rocketing prices. Increases in transport, heating, clothing and food costs left the average two-child family needing a monthly income of 12,000 pesetas in order to survive. The legal minimum wage was 120 pesetas per day and many workers received less. The most precarious situation was to be found among unskilled and casual labour. There were strikes across the country, of which the most bitter involved 20,000 workers in the Madrid construction industry. The siege mentality of the regime ensured a brutal response that persuaded many workers and middle-class professionals of the need for political change.

The Communist Party saw the strikes as evidence of popular backing for their strategy of a broad alliance of anti-regime forces, known as the Pact for Liberty. Throughout the 1960s, the party had extended its membership in the universities and the factories where its clandestine Comisiones Obreras (Workers' Commissions) were challenging the Falangist syndicates.[2] The growth of highly politicized student movements and powerful semi-clandestine unions reflected the vertiginous economic growth of the 1960s. The PCE became increasingly involved in the mass struggle against the regime. By 1970, Santiago Carrillo talked about the party emerging from the catacombs and collaborating with other liberal and leftist groups in student, worker and neighbourhood groups. PCE members became more involved in legal associations of housewives, consumers, residents, parents and teachers, while party lawyers were prominent in the defence of trade unionists on trial.[3]

The party called for a great national strike on 3 November to demand amnesty for political prisoners. Without an immediate economic motivation and given the scale of police repression, the popular response was uneven. The greatest impact was among Madrid and Barcelona metallurgical workers, shipyard workers in the Basque Country and El Ferrol and building workers in Seville. Nevertheless, even the exaggeratedly low official estimate acknowledged 25,000 strikers across the country. The public support given openly for the first time by many intellectuals, artists, students and housewives was evidence of the deepening solidarity of opposition forces.[4] In contrast, there were widening divisions within the Francoist establishment. As Franco drifted into senility and the economic situation deteriorated, the technocrats became edgy. Carrero was reverting to his hard-line instincts. In March, he had written an article comparing efforts to democratize Spain with trying to get a reformed alcoholic to take a drink.[5] The conflict over Matesa had eliminated reformist Falangism as an option, and even such an unrepentant Francoist as Manuel Fraga began to move to a more progressive position.

Between 1969 and 1975, anticipation of Franco's eventual demise saw divisions within different sectors of the regime. Bright young functionaries and politicians with directorships and consultancies in dynamic enterprises perceived the need for change. In contrast to these more far-sighted elements, others were ridden with a gnawing fear that the golden days of corruption and unpunished repression were coming to an end. Regime forces were divided between the so-called *aperturistas* led by Fraga, the grey technocrats known as *continuistas* and the intransigent ultras or *inmovilistas*. Older hard-line Falangists, Blas Piñar's Fuerza Nueva, officers of the police, the army and the Civil Guard and, crucially, Franco's family circle were united in a readiness to fight progress to the bitter end. Accordingly, they were known by the Hitlerian nickname of 'the bunker'. In opposition to the technocrats' advocacy of Juan Carlos, they championed Alfonso de Borbón-Dampierre, son of Don Juan's elder brother Jaime and soon to be fiancé of Franco's eldest grandchild, María del Carmen Martínez-Bordiú, a great favourite of Doña Carmen.[6]

At the end of September 1970, Richard Nixon landed in Madrid accompanied by Henry Kissinger, who found Franco's Spain 'as if suspended, waiting for a life to end so that it could rejoin European history'. Washington was still interested in Spain strategically and was anxious to see a moderate evolution after Franco's death. US policy was to maintain a working relationship with his regime while extending contacts within the moderate opposition. There was discreet American pressure to persuade him to hand over to Juan Carlos before incapacity deprived him of control of the transition. When Nixon and Kissinger met Franco for what were meant to be 'substantive talks', they were startled to see the seventy-eight-year-old Dictator dozing off even as the President began to talk. Soon the Caudillo and Kissinger were snoozing gently while Nixon talked to López Bravo.[7]

Symptomatic of Franco's declining judgement and Carrero's political insensitivity was the fact that hard-line *generales azules* convinced Franco to reply to ETA with a show trial of sixteen Basque prisoners, including two priests. The regime's judicial farces were usually held in camera. Because priests were among the accused, the Vatican had pressed for the trial to be held in public. The trials that began on 3 December at Burgos were among the longest ever mounted by the dictatorship. The stance of the military prosecutors focused world attention on the nationalist aspirations shared by all sixteen defendants and many other Basques. The regime inadvertently confirmed this by imposing a state of emergency in Guipúzcoa. In the courtroom, the defendants emphasized the brutality to which they had been subjected in jail. Effectively, the regime was itself put on trial by the ETA defendants and by the world's press. When the Basque hierarchy condemned the trial procedures and called for pardons for anyone sentenced to death, the Movimiento media reacted hysterically.[8]

After violent clashes between the police and protesters in Madrid, Barcelona, Bilbao, Oviedo, Seville and Pamplona, on 14 December four captains general visited Franco to demand more energetic government. Under pressure from the Minister of the Interior, General Garicano Goñi, and the three military ministers, Franco agreed to the suspension of constitutional guarantees.[9] It was the beginning of a counter-offensive by the regime hard-liners that deepened the cabinet divisions. The hard-liners could appeal to those elements of the regime who saw their privileges under threat. They blamed the Opus Dei as much as they did the 'reds' and 'separatists' of the opposition. On 16 and 17 December, there were enormous pro-Franco demonstrations in Burgos and Madrid. Government employees were given the day off to attend. Peasants were bussed into Madrid from rural Castile, given a day's pay and a packed lunch. This day of 'national affirmation' was organized by a group of senior Falangists, army officers and ex-ministers who had been supplanted by technocrats. In the Plaza de Oriente in Madrid, the crowds shouted for Franco. A bewildered Franco and his wife set out from El Pardo. She gave the fascist salute and he raised both hands to acknowledge the anti-Opus Dei chants of the crowd.[10] The trials ended with three of the ETA militants found guilty of two capital charges each and given two death sentences each. López Rodó and Carrero Blanco agreed that it would be politically disastrous for Franco to approve them. At the cabinet meeting on 30 December, López Bravo argued for commutation. Franco reluctantly made a magnanimous gesture and commuted them to terms of imprisonment.[11] His end-of-year message that day ended with the promise: 'You will be able to count on the strength and resolve of my spirit as long as God gives me life to continue ruling over the destiny of our Fatherland.'[12]

The regime's clumsy handling of the trials and the attitude of the Church boosted the opposition. More progressive Francoists were abandoning what they saw as a sinking ship. The reliance of both Franco and Carrero on the most reactionary *inmovilistas* boded ill in the short term for the modernizers but actually signified Franco's loosening grip as the regime's options were running out. Surrounded by the ultras in El Pardo, he was gradually losing control. By the early 1970s, the symptoms of Parkinson's disease – unsteady hands, rigid movements, vacant expression – were ever more unmistakable. In February 1971, General Vernon A. Walters, deputy Director of the CIA, was sent by Nixon to Madrid to ask Franco what would happen after his death. He replied that Juan Carlos would succeed him without any disorder and that 'the Army would never let things get out of hand'. Walters found Franco 'old and weak. His left hand trembled at times so violently that he would cover it with his other hand. At times he appeared far away and at others he came right to the point.'[13]

In January 1971, Juan Carlos and his wife Princess Sofía visited Washington. The Prince gave press interviews about the future, implying a commitment to change. On his return to Spain, Juan Carlos, expecting Franco to be furious, was surprised to find that he had assumed that the Prince had set out to deceive his audience.[14] In fact, trapped between the grey technocrats and the ultra-right of the bunker, Franco became more susceptible to pressure from the El Pardo clique and the hard-line Falangists, especially Girón. He and Carrero were resorting to the army to defend the regime. This was reflected in promotions for the *generales azules*. Tomás García Rebull was made Captain General of Madrid; Carlos Iniesta Cano, Director General of the Civil Guard; and Ángel Campano López, Military Governor of Madrid.[15]

The strengthening of the regime's defensive armoury did nothing to resolve the enormous social problems facing the government. Police brutality against workers was commonplace. During strikes in Seville, the police entered factories and arrested workers. A coalition of lawyers, professors, doctors, architects and workers presented the Cardinal-Archbishop of Seville with a detailed denunciation of police excesses. In Pamplona, a metalworkers' strike in January was met by police violence. On Holy Thursday, 8 April, a document outlining the torture of workers, signed by 200 priests, was read out in 80 per cent of the churches of Navarre. In Pamplona Cathedral, in the presence of local Francoist dignitaries, the auxiliary Bishop stated: 'I have seen with my own eyes, here in Pamplona, the tortures, the arbitrary interrogations and the unjustifiable and inexplicable arrests. Those who practise, order, tolerate or ignore them cut themselves off from the Church.'[16]

Despair at the regime's retreat into the habits of the 1940s saw even distinguished Francoists publicly express alarm at the lack of progress towards political evolution. In July, Ramón Serrano Súñer spoke in Burgos about the need for a gradual return to a party system. In

November, Juan Manuel Fanjul Sedeño, a prominent element of the Movimiento and a monarchist member of Opus Dei, claimed that the survival of the system required democratic reform. It was he who was inadvertently instrumental in coining the expression 'the bunker' when he declared six months later that 'the only thing that happens when you retreat to the cellars of the Chancellery is that you provoke the collapse of the Chancellery on top of you'. Manuel Cantarero de Castillo, one-time head of the Falange's youth front, would soon call for those in power to recognize the need for *apertura*.[17]

It was in vain. In response to the rising waves of opposition, Carrero introduced tougher measures, making more offences subject to military law. Fines, suspensions and closures of the more liberal press became ever more frequent.[18] On 1 October, the Ministry of the Interior used the structures of the Movimiento to organize a massive celebration of the thirty-fifth anniversary of Franco's elevation to power. The hope of the Falangists was for a reassertion of hard-line Francoism and its fulfilment would be reflected in Franco's declaration that 'the enemy has not disappeared and tries to divide us'. On the following day, a delighted *Arriba* would comment that 'the living and also the dead chanted and cheered with us'. For the technocrats, the intention was to put an end to the Matesa scandal. It was alleged that Vilá Reyes had threatened that, if he was not released from jail, he would reveal information damaging to the Opus Dei technocrats.[19]

Hundreds of trains and buses provided free transport to Madrid and thousands of soldiers attended in civilian clothes. The Movimiento claimed that a million people were present, although the Plaza de Oriente could barely hold a quarter of that number. Nevertheless, delighted by the chants and banners, Franco was moved to make a speech in which the old clichés were mixed with conviction that the future was secure. As intended, he announced a pardon for most of those on trial for the Matesa affair and thereby confirmed his attitude to corruption: 'If, for political reasons, I have had to pardon the ETA assassins, why can I not do the same with good collaborators who have simply made a mistake or been negligent?'[20]

On opening the Cortes on 19 November, he cited the demonstration as an endorsement of his years in power. He acknowledged Solís's plan for a 'contrast of opinions' in associations and fraternities within the Movimiento, but slammed the door on anything that might lead to political parties. Typically, he cited recent strikes in the state-owned SEAT car plant as proof of the ever-present international siege. He did not mention the brutality with which the strikers had been treated.[21]

The regime establishment was rattled by the accelerating liberalization of the Church under Cardinal Enrique y Tarancón. On 13 September, Tarancón inaugurated a joint assembly of bishops and priests which rejected the divisive civil war ideology of the dictatorship with the words: 'We recognize humbly that, when it was necessary, we were not able to be true ministers of reconciliation and we beg forgiveness.' In December 1971, the Vatican made Tarancón Archbishop of Madrid-Alcalá, thereby underlining that the diocese was the centre of Church power. He was replaced as Primate by the Archbishop of Barcelona, Marcelo González Martín, an appointment which saw the vacancy in Barcelona filled by the liberal Catalan Archbishop Narcís Jubany Arnau.[22] Under the direction of the Bishop of Huelva, Rafael González Moralejo, the Church's Pax et Justitia Commission denounced the regime's brutality. Franco reacted to Tarancón, Jubany and González Moralejo as if the Church had joined the enemy. In his end-of-year message on 31 December 1971, he insinuated that the regime would take action against the liberal positions adopted by liberal bishops. His threats had the effect of hardening the stance of the liberals. The Bishop of Malaga declared that the hierarchy would not be silenced.[23]

Working-class discontent continued to intensify in response to low wages, poor housing and inadequate educational facilities. The Communist Party invested immense effort in helping to resolve daily social problems through ostensibly non-political neighbourhood associations that would become an ever more powerful element of opposition. Strikes in Madrid, Barcelona and Asturias were met by police violence.[24] Many employers were disturbed as labour disputes were intensified by government intervention. In the more advanced industries, they were coming to see the regime's repressive mechanisms as an obstacle to workable labour relations. Many began to bypass the official syndical structures and negotiate directly with the Comisiones Obreras. Regime intransigence was boosting the Communist Party strategy of the Pact for Liberty, especially in Catalonia. Throughout 1971, representatives of all the principal Catalan opposition forces were uniting. On 7 November, about 300 delegates gathered secretly in Barcelona for the first Assemblea de Catalunya. Representing a broad political spectrum from the Communist Partit Socialista Unificat de Catalunya and the Comisiones Obreras, and liberal monarchists, Catholics, professional organizations and women's groups, the Assemblea adopted a programme for political amnesty and liberty that was supported by several prominent members of the Catalan industrial and banking bourgeoisie.[25] As the regime returned to the past, influential sectors of Spain's economic oligarchies were making arrangements for the future. The Assemblea was soon replicated elsewhere, especially in Madrid and Seville.

Carrero was acquiescing in ever greater violence against those perceived as enemies of the regime. Gelling around the magazine *Fuerza Nueva* and its editor, Carrero's friend Blas Piñar, several neo-fascist terrorist squads emerged under names like the Guerrilleros de Cristo Rey, the Partido Español Nacional-Socialista, the Comandos de Lucha Antimarxista and other seemingly spontaneous groups. The churches of progressive priests were invaded and clergy and congregations attacked. In the universities, liberals and leftists were terrorized. In working-class districts, union leaders were assaulted. Art galleries and bookshops were destroyed. These groups, made up of paid thugs, Falangist extremists and some off-duty policemen, acted with an impunity that suggested official connivance. In fact, they were organized by Carrero's intelligence service, the Servicio de Documentación de la Presidencia del Gobierno. Ostensibly independent, such a violent extreme right made the government seem to be of the centre. The Minister of the Interior, Garicano Goñi, even protested to Franco about the dangers posed by these extremists.[26]

Right-wing terrorism was one sign that society was changing beyond the capacity of institutionalized Francoism to control it. Another was the increase in police brutality against strikers and students. In mid-January 1972, more than fifty people were hurt in clashes at Madrid University.[27] In March, during a strike at the state-owned Bazan shipyards in El Ferrol, the police opened fire on a demonstration of 3,000 strikers, killing two and wounding another fifteen. This provoked solidarity strikes all over Galicia, in the Asturian mines, in Catalonia and in the Basque Country.[28] The regime's sense of its own vulnerability was generated by the bombings, robberies and attacks on industrialists and members of the security forces carried out by ETA activists. On 12 January 1973, in support of striking workers at the Torfinosa company in Pamplona, ETA kidnapped the owner, Felix Huarte. It was a clever propaganda ploy since there were well-signposted Huarte construction sites in most Spanish towns. Increasingly, the struggle against ETA was seen by the regime as a military matter to be entrusted less to the police and more to the army and Civil Guard. In response, ETA began making plans to kidnap Carrero Blanco.[29]

Meanwhile, throughout 1972 the stench of corruption at Franco's court grew stronger. The Caudillo's brother Nicolás had a vast network of business interests that had come his way because of their relationship. He was implicated in one of the greatest financial scandals of the dictatorship, the so-called *aceite de Redondela* affair. Four million kilos of olive oil, held as a state reserve stock in tanks belonging to a fat and edible-oil refining company, REACE (Refinerías del Noroeste de Aceites y Grasas SA), were found to be missing. Assuming that the stocks would not be called upon, the company had been speculating with the oil. Nicolás was a major shareholder in the company. In the course of the subsequent investigations, six people involved in denouncing the affair met violent deaths. A major cover-up was being mounted to silence the links between Nicolás and those accused of fraud.[30]

Franco's lack of concern about corruption was underlined by the fact that his long hours of work when not on hunting and fishing trips had given way to time spent in front of the television. He needed lengthy siestas. In cabinet meetings and audiences, he said virtually nothing, and often dozed off. When awake, his hands were seen to tremble uncontrollably. His sight was deteriorating, he suffered from fungal infections in the mouth and from related pains in the leg which limited his hunting trips. The annual 1 October reception was shortened because he was unable to stand for a long period. The medication for Parkinson's disease caused him to become increasingly indecisive.[31] In private, he was obsessed with 'traitors' or 'the ungrateful' which often meant the technocrats.[32] His family was becoming more hostile to the Carrero Blanco–López Rodó–Juan Carlos option. As Franco grew more infirm, his wife was egged on to assume a more dominant role by the wives of the *generales azules* and of hard-line Francoists like Girón that she entertained at weekly tea parties at El Pardo. She told Carrero vehemently that Garicano Goñi was weak and López Bravo disloyal. Within El Pardo, she and Cristobal Martínez-Bordiú openly criticized Carrero Blanco as weak and Juan Carlos as treacherous.[33]

On 4 December 1972, Franco reached his eightieth birthday. His response to Doña Carmen's fears was to watch more television.[34] His legs were swollen and the recording of his end-of-year speech had to be interrupted several times for him to rest. In this speech, he seemed decrepit, yet, in a near inaudible mumble, he repeated his prohibition of the Church daring to judge the activities of the regime. He assured the viewers that he would hang on indefinitely: 'Here you will find me, with the same resolve as always, looking out for the future of the Fatherland, for as long as God wants me to continue.'[35] Symptomatic of the extent to which anxiety about Franco's health was being compounded by worsening social and political tensions was Carrero's resort to ultra-rightist terror squads.[36] The hardening of repressive violence, both official and furtive, merely intensified divisions within the regime forces and strengthened the opposition.

As the repression of strikes provoked wider solidarity actions in industrial towns, there was growing Communist confidence that the Pact for Liberty, backed by a national general strike, could effect a transition from dictatorship to democracy. The hoped-for sequence of events was for the regime to be brought to its knees by the strike and then the forces of the Pact would form a provisional government and call constituent elections.[37] In contrast, the Partido Socialista Obrero Español had no specific project and was still engaged in rebuilding after years of impotence. At the PSOE's XII Congress-in-exile, held in Toulouse in mid-August 1972, an influential group of militants, led by Felipe González from Seville and Nicolas Redondo from Bilbao, had supplanted the aged exiled leadership. Like the Communists, their strategy, an echo of how the PSOE had come to power in 1931, rested on the working class playing the crucial role while the leadership sought alliances with other opposition forces.[38]

The political bankruptcy revealed by Carrero's inability to resolve social tensions, other than by a resort to violence, saw the moderate opposition swelled by defectors from the regime. Generally speaking, they sought a transition without the outright conflict implicit in the leftist strategies. Among academic theorists and politicians, the idea began to emerge that there were loopholes in the Francoist constitution that could be exploited to permit a real evolution.[39] In the forefront was Torcuato Fernández Miranda, who had been Juan Carlos's political science tutor and had become his close adviser. At the same time, Areilza,

Antonio Garrigues, who resigned as Ambassador to the Holy See, and other leading figures of the moderate opposition began to see Juan Carlos as the key to securing a 'legal' evolution to democracy. Once embraced by Juan Carlos, this project would be crucial in 1976.

In early April 1973, the shooting of a striker by police in San Adrian de Besos triggered solidarity strikes all over Catalonia.[40] During the May Day demonstration in Madrid, a secret police inspector, Juan Antonio Fernández Gutiérrez, was fatally stabbed by a member of the ultra-leftist Frente Revolucionario Antifascista y Patriota (FRAP), an organization later revealed to be riddled with police agents provocateurs. Two other secret policemen were also wounded. The incident provided the perfect excuse for reprisals by the hard-liners of the regime. There were mass arrests and leftists were tortured. The most significant events took place at the funeral of Fernández Gutiérrez, whose cortège was led by General Iniesta. There was a demonstration of police officers demanding more repressive measures while 3,000 Falangist war veterans screamed for vengeance. Their placards praised the neo-Nazi ultras and demanded firing squads for the 'red archbishops'. That a police mutiny in the presence of Carrero Blanco was tolerated was a clear indication that the tide was running in favour of the ultras. This was confirmed on 7 May, when Garicano Goñi resigned, frustrated by the lack of will for reform and alarmed at the growing influence of extreme rightists.[41]

The El Pardo clique finally convinced Franco that the cabinet had failed in the primordial task of maintaining public order. On 3 May, the Caudillo told a reluctant Carrero Blanco that he was going to be made President of the cabinet and that he should start planning its composition. His choices brought the technocrat's dominance to an end. To please Doña Carmen, López Rodó was exiled to the Ministry of Foreign Affairs with the task of putting a moderate veneer on an essentially reactionary cabinet. Further evidence of the influence of the El Pardo clique could be seen in the appointment of two hard-line Falangist followers of Girón, José Utrera Molina at Housing and Francisco Ruiz-Jarabo at Justice, and the belligerent Julio Rodríguez, the new Minister of Education. Surprisingly, as Vice-President and Minister Secretary General of the Movimiento, Carrero chose Torcuato Fernández Miranda. Franco accepted the list with only one change. Having been convinced by his wife and son-in-law that the government was too soft, Franco insisted on the appointment as Minister of the Interior of Don Camilo's one-time strong-arm Director General of Security, Carlos Arias Navarro. As Mayor of Madrid since 1963, Arias had become a personal favourite of Doña Carmen. During the Civil War, his ruthlessness as a prosecutor had earned him the nickname 'the butcher of Malaga'. Carrero was seventy and had neither popular nor military support. The composition of what Madrid wits called 'the funeral cabinet' dashed hopes of progressive change.[42]

If Franco had died first, it is unlikely that Carrero would have had the will, the authority or the ideas to be able to rule for long thereafter. By November 1973, his cabinet was adrift in a sea of industrial unrest in Catalonia, Asturias and the Basque Country, provoked by the austerity measures taken to stem inflation. With the first energy crisis brewing and Spain heavily dependent on imported energy, the technocrat strategy of buying off political discontent with rising prosperity was no more. Carrero Blanco's only response was intensified repression. This was to be symbolized by the 'Proceso 1.001', a show trial of ten members of the Comisiones Obreras, charged with illegal association to demonstrate the cabinet's determination to crush the underground unions. Just as it was beginning on 20 December, an ETA squad assassinated Carrero Blanco by detonating an explosive charge under his car as he returned from daily Mass. ETA calculated that his murder would destroy Franco's plans for the continuation of his regime and exacerbate its internal divisions.[43]

Franco seemed overwhelmed. Unable to eat, he took refuge in his study. He was more vulnerable now to the El Pardo clique than he had been six months earlier.[44] Fernández Miranda automatically became interim Prime Minister. However, preparations were made for the coming power struggle. In a gross abuse of his authority, the Director General of the Civil Guard, Carlos Iniesta, issued an order for his men to make unlimited use of firearms to repress demonstrators and subversives. Cooler heads prevailed. After taking advice from the Chief of the General Staff, Manuel Díez-Alegría, Fernández Miranda, Arias Navarro, the senior military minister, Admiral Gabriel Pita da Veiga, and the head of Carrero's private intelligence service, Lieutenant Colonel José Ignacio San Martín, combined to prevent a bloodbath. Iniesta was forced to rescind his telegram and was placed briefly under house arrest. Two ministers, Julio Rodriguez and José Utrera Molina, appeared at the office of the Madrid police chief, Colonel Federico Quintero Morente, and offered to join a revenge squad to find and kill the assassins. Blas Piñar was ordered to keep his followers under control.[45]

On the day after the assassination, tempers ran high: at a mass for Carrero, Archbishop Enrique y Tarancón was jostled and insulted by extreme right-wingers. Franco chaired a cabinet meeting at which he broke down in tears and stared at Carrero's empty chair. He quickly composed himself and opened the meeting at which the only business was the posthumous conferment on the murdered Prime Minister of the title Duque de Carrero Blanco. On the next day, 22 December, he attended another funeral mass at the Church of San Francisco el Grande, weeping and groaning quietly throughout. When the first shock had passed, Franco – left to make choices about the future – was subjected to pressure from the ultra clique and the final outcome was more of their making than of his. Regarding the succession to Carrero Blanco, Doña Carmen and Cristobal Martínez-Bordiú played a major part in blocking the promotion of Fernández Miranda, perceiving him as an accomplice to what they assumed would be liberalization under Juan Carlos.[46] Easily persuaded not to name Fernández Miranda, Franco was inclined to have the complex succession procedures manipulated to ensure the appointment of his old friend Admiral Pedro Nieto Antúnez. As a senior military Francoist, 'Pedrolo' seemed a safe choice. However, the regime 'ultras' and the El Pardo clique saw things differently. Since Pedrolo was only six years younger than Franco and five years older than Carrero Blanco, the problem of a replacement could arise again soon. The clique was also alarmed because Pedrolo planned to name the now openly – albeit temporarily – reformist Fraga as Vice-President.

Accordingly, Franco was pressured by Doña Carmen and Vicente Gil to change his mind in favour of the tough Arias Navarro because of his hard-line reputation in security matters.[47] In his six months as Minister of the Interior, public order policy had been inspired by his mentor General Alonso Vega. He had mounted major offensives against ETA, with nine militants shot, against the PCE, with several regional networks broken up, and against the Comisiones Obreras. On the other hand, he was the minister responsible for security failures before and after the assassination. No controls had been imposed at Barajas airport or on roads out of Madrid for five hours after the explosion. Suspicions were voiced about the ease with which the ETA commando had tunnelled under a street near the US Embassy and other well-guarded official buildings. Arias was partly redeemed by the fact that Carrero had ignored his warnings to change his rigidly regular daily route.[48]

In his end-of-year message on 30 December 1973, Franco briefly paid tribute to Carrero Blanco. Dismissing the assassination as the work of a tiny minority radio-controlled from abroad, he took pride in the functioning of the Francoist institutions during the crisis. Referring to his thirty-seven years in power, he offered to go on indefinitely: 'Spain can always rely on my dedication which will not be lacking, given that my entire life has been, is and will be devoted to the service of the Spaniards.' The words 'no hay mal que por bien no venga' (it's an ill wind that blows nobody any good) were inserted in his own handwriting in the typed text of the message. This was assumed in the inner circles of the regime to be an acknowledgement that Franco now saw the Carrero Blanco period as a mistake.[49] The appointments of Arias and his cabinet constituted Franco's last major political decisions. He would be largely a bystander to the transition to democracy that had now started. The process was triggered, not by Carrero's assassination, but because Francoism had been rendered obsolete by the economic reforms of the technocrats. Now the dwindling of his physical and mental powers coincided with a burgeoning opposition and a more critical international context.

Arias's government, announced on 3 January 1974, constituted a rickety bridge between hard-liners and progressives. The inclusion of three vice-presidents – the Ministers of the Interior, Finance and Labour – suggested that the main concerns would be the closely linked issues of public order, inflation and working-class unrest. Arias retained eight of Carrero's ministers in his new cabinet and added some hard-line Falangists. The liberal wing included Antonio Carro as Minister of the Presidencia and Pío Cabanillas as Minister of Information, both followers of Fraga, and Antonio Barrera de Irimo as Minister of Finance and Vice-President for economic matters. Barrera was a representative figure of the more dynamic sectors of Spanish capitalism and a devotee of Juan Carlos. The most reactionary elements were two fanatical Falangists: José Utrera Molina as Minister Secretary of the Movimiento and Francisco Ruiz-Jarabo as Minister of Justice. Their inclusion reflected the influence of Girón. Utrera's appointment was specifically intended to prevent any reform of the institutions of the Movimiento along the lines timidly broached by the previous Minister Secretary, Torcuato Fernández

Miranda. José García Hernández, the Minister of the Interior and Vice-President in charge of internal security, was, like Arias himself, a one-time assistant to Alonso Vega.[50] Arias's suggestion of Fraga as Foreign Minister was vetoed by Franco, who wanted López Rodó to continue. Since Arias was adamant that he did not want him, they compromised on the diplomat Pedro Cortina Mauri, another El Pardo favourite.[51]

Girón's influence in El Pardo ensured the appointment of Utrera Molina, who told Arias that he would not let the Movimiento be a herd of political sheep. His ceremonial induction into the post was attended by an array of bunker celebrities – the Falangists Arrese, Fernández Cuesta, Solís and Girón and *generales azules* like Iniesta Cano and García Rebull.[52] The El Pardo clique was pleased that Arias had not bothered to consult with Juan Carlos about the composition of his cabinet. However, Arias Navarro would not fulfil their expectations. The structural problems of the regime would oblige Arias to embrace more change than Carrero had ever done. He inherited disputes in the Asturian mines, the Basque steel industry and the Catalan textile sector as well as in Zaragoza, Valladolid and Alcoy.

They were the consequences of a combination of inflation about to exceed 25 per cent per annum and a wage freeze of 15 per cent. Rocketing crude oil prices hit Spain badly because of its lack of domestic energy reserves. Energy costs were passed on directly to consumers. In the first quarter of 1974, electricity prices rose by 15 per cent, petrol by 70 per cent, butane gas, the most widely used fuel for heating and cooking, by 60 per cent and transport costs by 33 per cent. There would be no early end to the strike wave. To make matters worse, two major sources of foreign currency, tourism and remittances from emigrant workers, would soon be dramatically diminished as the energy crisis hit Northern Europe.[53] Arias retained Carrero's Minister of Labour, the Falangist Licinio de la Fuente, as Vice-President for social affairs. Despite De la Fuente's reputation for social concern, Arias's cabinet would not permit him to exercise the flexibility so urgently needed on the labour front.[54]

The Minister of the Presidency, and effective head of the civil service, Antonio Carro Martínez, was linked to the Tácito pressure group as were many of the regime's most talented functionaries. Conservative Christian Democrats committed to peaceful reform of the system and linked to the Catholic pressure group, the Asociación Católica Nacional de

Propagandistas, their collective identity came from influential newspaper articles published from 1972 in the Catholic daily *Ya*. Signed 'Tácito', their articles advocated reform of the system from within. Their links to the banking and industrial world and to the ecclesiastical hierarchy ensured that Arias could not ignore them. When the leading Tácito, Alfonso Osorio García, offered Arias the backing of the group if he would commit to reform, he accepted. On Carro's recommendation, he appointed four members of the group as under-secretaries.[55]

Despite his authoritarian instincts, Arias was sufficiently vain to be concerned with his public face. Carro, Osorio and Pío Cabanillas persuaded him that, to survive, he and Francoism needed a change of image. Accordingly, on 12 February 1974, he broadcast a tepidly progressive programme. The text, drafted by Carro's office, later known as 'the spirit of 12 February', proposed wider political participation, albeit within the limits of the Francoist laws. Mayors and local officials were to be elected rather than appointed by the government. There was to be an increase from 17 to 35 per cent of those Cortes deputies not simply appointed but elected through a strictly limited suffrage. The vertical syndicates were promised greater bargaining power. Political associations, but not political parties, were promised. Ritual praise for Franco was followed by the statement that responsibility for political change could no longer be only his responsibility. Despite a vehemently expressed determination to stamp out 'subversion', it was the most liberal declaration ever made by a minister of Franco. But the opposition remained unimpressed.[56]

A more liberal approach to the press and publishers from Pío Cabanillas's Ministry of Information and the toleration shown the most moderate opposition groups seemed to give credence to Arias's speech. In practice, however, behind the promise of liberalization, Arias responded to social unrest with unflinching harshness. This reflected both his own instincts and the ease with which the bunker could mobilize Franco against reform by claiming that freemasons were pushing Spain into an abyss of pornography and disorder. After Arias, Franco's closest contact in the government was Utrera Molina. In January 1974, when Utrera outlined his plans for the ideological rearmament of the Movimiento, Franco was delighted. After Arias's speech, he asked Utrera to explain 'the spirit of 12 February'. Thoroughly alarmed by that explanation, Franco said: 'if the regime lets its doctrinal essence be attacked and its defenders fail to defend what is fundamental, we must suspect that some are contemplating a cowardly suicide'.[57]

With prices rocketing in the wake of the energy crisis, worker militancy intensified in early 1974. Unable to offer major change, Arias found that his position was becoming impossible. Paradoxically, Franco's first intervention was to restrain the Prime Minister's reactionary instincts. The ultra-right-wing newspaper *El Alcázar* had even urged violence against what it saw as the 'betrayal' of the regime by the liberal Church hierarchy. This was partly a reaction to the presence of many Basques among the offending clergy. The traditionally close links between the Basque clergy and their parishioners ensured that they were affected by the fall-out from the war between ETA and the regime. Arias was on the verge of expelling from Spain the Bishop of Bilbao, Monsignor Antonio Añoveros, for allowing the publication, on 24 February, of homilies quoting Pope John XXIII in defence of ethnic minorities. Añoveros was defended by both Tarancón and Pope Paul VI. Unwilling to risk the excommunication of his Prime Minister, Franco obliged Arias to back down.[58]

This was the exception. Already, in the first two months of 1974, the police had arrested over 150 militants of working-class organizations, ETA and leftist groups. Franco refused to commute the death sentences passed on the Catalan anarchist Salvador Puig Antich and the Pole Heinz Chez, both accused of killing members of the forces of order. Despite an international outcry recalling the Grimau and Burgos trials, with protests from the Vatican, the EEC and several heads of state, the executions were carried out, by *garrote vil*, on 2 March.[59] This led to the condemnation of the regime by the European Parliament. If that did not surprise the inhabitants of the bunker, more disturbing was the fall of the Portuguese dictatorship on 25 April, which greatly cheered the opposition in Spain. Three days later, on 28 April, the ultras' fear of the impact of the Portuguese events was reflected in a vehement attack by Girón in *Arriba* on Arias and the liberals in his cabinet. Franco let Utrera know that he was not displeased by this so-called *Gironazo*.[60]

As part of the same operation, the retired General García Rebull denounced political parties and politicians. This was the first salvo in a scheme intended to allow Iniesta to sidestep his imminent retirement as head of the Civil Guard and replace the liberal Manuel Díez-Alegría as Chief of the General Staff. The bunker feared that Díez-Alegría might do in Spain what had been done in Portugal by General António de Spínola. Indeed, ever since the Portuguese revolution, he was reported to have received hundreds of monocles in the post like those sported by Spínola. With Iniesta as CGS, General Ángel Campano would take over the Civil Guard and officers suspected of liberalism would be purged. The scheme enjoyed the support of the El Pardo clique, although the failing Caudillo was not told. When Arias was informed about the plot by the Minister for the Army, General Francisco Coloma Gallegos, he hastened to see Franco and threatened to resign. Deeply disturbed, Franco, who regarded seniority procedures as sacrosanct, backed Arias, forcing Iniesta to retire on schedule on 12 May.[61]

Arias tried vainly to find a middle way between the bunker and the opposition, newly resurgent after the Portuguese events. On the one hand, arrests of leftists increased. On the other, he presented a half-hearted project for political associations strictly limited to groups within the Movimiento.[62] Meanwhile, Franco seemed oblivious to what was going on. On 26 June, Fraga found him tired and distant.[63] He went into hospital on 9 July with phlebitis in his right leg. The treatment was complicated by the fact that medication to alleviate his Parkinson's disease was causing gastric ulcers which were worsened by the anti-coagulants to treat the blood clot of the phlebitis. As his condition worsened, on 19 July, Arias and the President of the Cortes persuaded Franco to implement Article 11 of the Organic Law of the State whereby Juan Carlos would take over as interim head of state. Doña Carmen and Villaverde were furious. Juan Carlos himself was unwilling to take over so shortly after the Antich execution and the Añoveros affair. He was concerned that he would be tarnished by association with an unpopular government which he had not chosen and whose President had never consulted him.[64] However, he had little choice if he was not to risk his succession.

It turned out to be a humiliating experience. Cristóbal Martínez-Bordiú, who had arrogated to himself the role of head of the family, was openly rude to Juan Carlos.[65] Franco was able to leave hospital on 30 July, albeit not to return to work. Vicente Gil urged him, for the sake of his health, to renounce power. A furious Martínez-Bordiú physically attacked Gil and then had him dismissed as Franco's physician. Distraught at the prospect of losing their privileges, the El Pardo clique convinced Franco that Juan Carlos was not to be trusted and pressed him to resume his powers, which he did on 2 September.[66] Their panic was justified. Franco's illness had boosted the morale of the opposition. This could be seen in the growth of democratic juntas and round-tables. The most successful was the Assemblea de Catalunya which, in addition to its substantial popular support, included bankers and industrialists among its leaders. News of Franco's illness had triggered the launch by Santiago Carrillo, in Paris on 30 July 1974, of the Junta Democrática. It consisted of the Comisiones Obreras, the minuscule Partido Socialista Popular of Enrique Tierno Galván, various regionalist groups, the Carlists and some prominent individual independents including the Opus Deista Rafael Calvo Serer.[67] The Junta's programme called for power to be assumed by a provisional government; a total political amnesty; the legalization of political parties and trade unions; freedom of speech and of the media; independence of the judiciary; regional autonomy; the separation of Church and state and free elections within eighteen months. Despite the absence of the Christian Democrats and the Partido Socialista Obrero Español, the Junta and its programme of a complete break with the regime (*ruptura democrática*) energized the opposition circles and intensified the bunker's sense of being under siege.[68]

The Socialists refused to join the Junta because of differences over strategy. After years of lethargy, the PSOE was undergoing a process of revitalization. The old leadership was sidelined at the party's XIII Congress-in-exile held at Suresnes, near Paris, in mid-October 1974. A dynamic alliance of Enrique Múgica and Nicolas Redondo from Bilbao and Felipe González and Alfonso Guerra from Seville took over the party leadership. They regarded as unrealistic the PCE plan to overthrow the Franco regime with a national general strike. The new Secretary General, Felipe González, believed, reluctantly, that it would be necessary to negotiate with regime reformists.[69]

The El Pardo clique's victory over Juan Carlos in securing Franco's return to power was soon followed by an assault on the most liberal minister in the cabinet, Pío Cabanillas. Franco was given a dossier of Spanish magazine pages containing advertisements for beachware and camping equipment featuring bikini-clad models skilfully interleaved with explicit photographs from Playboy, to give the impression that such material was published in Spain. He was easily convinced that Pío Cabanillas must go. He was especially outraged by evidence in the dossier that, as Fraga had done with Matesa, Pío Cabanillas was permitting the press to publicize the *aceite de Redondela* case which had finally come to trial. On 24 October, he ordered Arias to remove Cabanillas. In solidarity, Antonio Barrera de Irimo resigned. Arias proposed to strike a balance with the removal of Utrera and Francisco Ruiz-Jarabo. Franco refused categorically on the grounds that they were both 'very loyal'.[70]

It was a pyrrhic victory for the ultras since it merely accelerated the crumbling of the regime. As stock prices fell, influential sectors of the oligarchy were beginning to demand reform. Throughout 1974, there had been virtually open meetings of prominent industrialists and financiers with members of the moderate opposition. Among the most notable were those hosted by the lawyer Joaquín Garrigues Walker, Areilza's son-in-law and a key figure in the business world.[71] The crisis that saw the departure of Barrera and Cabanillas exposed the regime's bankruptcy. It confirmed that Arias was incapable of introducing real change and was followed by the resignations of the key functionaries belonging to the Tácito group led by Pío Cabanillas's Under-Secretary, Marcelino Oreja. Their published verdict on Arias's 12 February reform project pronounced it dead.[72]

The bunker reacted by mobilizing its forces in the form of a massive Confederación Nacional de Ex-Combatientes under the leadership of Girón. That Arias was losing control of events was demonstrated when the police, without his authorization, arrested the leaders of the moderate opposition at the end of November. They had been meeting in Madrid to discuss the creation of a rival front to the Junta Democrática. The incident caused another international scandal similar to that surrounding the Añoveros case. After a few days, they were released. But immense damage had been done to Arias Navarro's position.[73]

All this seemed to be passing Franco by. By late 1974, he was showing ever more marked signs of senility. His mouth gaped in a permanent yawn. Occasionally, he would tune into normality but the general impression was of impenetrable distraction.[74] Yet, for political reasons, he was pushed into a programme of activities that alarmed his doctors. His passion for hunting and fishing, combined with the determination of the El Pardo clique that he be seen to be active, led to him joining tiring expeditions in inclement weather. During the winter of 1974–5, he took part in several shooting parties in wet blustery weather, with temperatures often near or below zero. During the first such excursion

of 1975, at the beginning of January in the Sierra Morena, the need to
stand still for long periods, so as not to disturb the prey, provoked
nephritis (inflammation of the kidneys).⁷⁵ His health was deteriorating
rapidly, with the greatest distress caused by dental problems.⁷⁶ In his
end-of-year broadcast on 30 December 1974, he gave thanks for his
complete recuperation from his recent illness and boasted about how
well his institutions had functioned during his absence.⁷⁷ He seemed
unaware of the disintegration of the Francoist coalition.

The first skirmish of 1975 took place in February. Arias was infuriated
when the Movimiento press failed to commemorate the anniversary of
his 12 February speech and he ordered Utrera to sack Antonio Castro
Villacañas, director of the Movimiento's press and radio networks, and
Antonio Izquierdo, the editor of *Arriba*. Utrera refused and hastened to
inform Franco, only for a feeble and fearful Caudillo to tell him to obey
Arias so as to avoid trouble.⁷⁸ The medication for Parkinson's disease had
left him timorous. Utrera brought proof of Arias's plans to dissolve the
Movimiento and tapes of him criticizing Franco. When Utrera said
'Arias is a traitor,' Franco began to cry and sobbed: 'Yes, yes, Arias is a
traitor, but don't tell anyone. We must be careful.'⁷⁹ The ultra campaign
redoubled its intensity. The hard-liners in the cabinet blocked legislation
to introduce a limited right to strike. On 24 February, Licinio de la
Fuente, Minister of Labour since 1969, and a Francoist beyond suspicion
of liberal tendencies, resigned in frustration.⁸⁰

At last, Arias was impelled to fight back against the bunker. He told
Franco that he wanted to replace not only De la Fuente but also other
ministers. When Franco refused, Arias threatened to resign, alleging that
Utrera had fabricated evidence against him, and browbeat a weak old
man into agreeing to a ministerial reshuffle in which both Ruiz-Jarabo
and Utrera were removed. Fernando Herrero Tejedor, the chief prosecutor of the Supreme Court, arrived as the great new liberal promise as
Minister Secretary General of the Movimiento. A flexible opportunist,
with a good relationship with Franco, Herrero Tejedor was an Opus
Deista with irreproachable Movimiento credentials. He was widely
tipped to be Arias's eventual successor and the man to organize the transition to the monarchy. Herrero made contact within the tolerated
moderate opposition of the Christian Democrats and Ridruejo's Social
Democrats. He also set about the thankless task of giving credibility to
the empty project for political associations.⁸¹ When Franco read Fraga's

draft proposal for an association, he is said to have asked Nieto Antúnez what country Fraga had in mind.[82]

When Utrera went to El Pardo on 11 March to take his leave, an emotional Franco praised his loyalty. As the audience came to an end, he asked him never to change. Deeply moved, Utrera promised to remain on guard until his last breath. At that, Franco embraced him and wept copiously. Utrera stepped back, stood to attention and, with his arm raised in the fascist salute, barked out the Falangist greeting: 'Caudillo, a tus órdenes, ¡Arriba España!' Franco stood pathetically with his own trembling arm raised in response.[83] His decline was reflected in the fact that State Department policy was inclining away from the Caudillo and towards Juan Carlos. When the US President Gerald Ford arrived on 31 May for a two-day visit, he spent rather more time with the Prince than with Franco.[84]

On 23 June 1975, Herrero Tejedor died in a car crash. Franco was much affected by the news, which he took as a providential sign that the experiment with associations did not have divine approval.[85] The logical successor should have been Herrero's ambitious deputy, Adolfo Suárez, who had joined the Opus Dei and used his friendship with Herrero to establish links with key regime figures. General Alonso Vega made him Civil Governor of Segovia in 1968. As he neared the top, Suárez worked hard to attract the attention of Franco and to become friendly with Juan Carlos. The Prince recommended him to Carrero Blanco, who in 1969 made him Director General of Spanish Television, RTVE. He used this position to promote the image of Juan Carlos. He also ingratiated himself with ministers and senior generals by making television time available to them and by sending flowers to their wives. By February 1975, he had risen to the key position of Vice-Secretary of the Movimiento.[86]

Having seen divine intervention in the death of Herrero Tejedor, Franco was not inclined to promote Suárez. Instead, Franco insisted that the new Minister Secretary should be José Solís. He was reflecting the belief in the El Pardo clique that, to repel the opposition, he should surround himself with his reliable old guard. Martínez-Bordiú and Doña Carmen, in cahoots with Girón and Alejandro Rodríguez Valcárcel, the President of the Cortes, persuaded Franco to extend the life of the present Cortes by six months. They hoped thereby to gain the time necessary to push Arias out and secure the elevation of Solís, Rodríguez Valcárcel or even Girón, to the presidency.[87] However, others saw the future in

Suárez. The perceptive commentator Luis María Anson named him 'politician of the month' in the magazine *Blanco y Negro* on 2 July. At that stage, future reform meant working within the Francoist system along the lines envisaged by Torcuato Fernández Miranda. It was to be the sheer weight of working-class, regionalist and student pressure over the next eighteen months that would put full-scale democratic change onto the political agenda.[88]

Those who wanted to block even the most limited reform were ridden with anxiety about their own futures and needed Franco to stay alive.[89] The Caudillo was exhausted and anxious to rest, even talking of emulating Charles V and retiring to a monastery to die. Panic-stricken, his wife persuaded him not to abandon politics just as his equally worried son-in-law later kept him alive electronically.[90] In his final months, the bunker worked on his fears and prejudices, their efforts facilitated by his undying conviction of the sinister threat of freemasonry.[91] On 15 July, Franco told a delegation of the Hermandad Nacional de Alféreces Provisionales (National Fraternity of Provisional Lieutenants), a bunker stronghold, that they must defend to the death the civil war victory.[92]

In the summer of 1975, the sense of the regime crumbling rendered plans for associations irrelevant. Rightist terror squads stepped up attacks on left-wing lawyers and clergymen, on bookshops and workers. This was particularly so in Vizcaya and Guipúzcoa where a state of exception had been declared, provocatively, on 26 April, the anniversary of the bombing of Guernica. This was a response to the continuing success of ETA's terror campaign. However, the measure was counter-productive. It strengthened opposition unity and confirmed the determination of liberal elements in the Church to distance themselves from the regime.[93] The state of exception unleashed police terror against the two provinces. The homes and offices of suspects were vandalized. The Bilbao bullring had to be used to hold the large numbers of detainees. Torture and beatings were commonplace. The womenfolk of wanted men were seized as hostages and abused. Mass intimidation was intensified by the activities of the ultra-rightist terror squads. Using names such as Antiterrorismo ETA or the Batallon Vasco-Español, they machine-gunned and bombed the bars frequented by *abertzales* (as Basque militant nationalists were known), the offices of lawyers, publishing houses and the businesses of ETA sympathizers. Far from cowing the population, the right-wing terror campaign provoked a massive reaction in the Basque Country, backed by solidarity actions all over Spain.[94]

Rigid censorship saw many newspapers and magazines seized. The return to untrammelled repression could not hold back the surging waves of strikes. Liberal Francoist elements were alarmed at the savagery displayed by the bunker and its international impact. FEDISA, the political 'study society' founded by Fraga, Areilza and Cabanillas, issued a plea for progress towards democracy. The plea reflected the mood of increasing numbers of bankers and industrialists. The possibility of a bloodbath sent shares plummeting and they saw Spain's chances of entering the EEC dwindling.[95]

While Franco was on holiday in Galicia, rumours spread that, on his return, he would replace Arias with Solís. A cabinet meeting held at the Pazo de Meirás on 22 August introduced a harsh anti-terrorist law covering all aspects of opposition to the regime.[96] The first results were a series of trials that led to the final black episode in Franco's life. On 28 August, a court martial in Burgos sentenced to death two members of ETA and, on 19 September, another in Barcelona passed a third death penalty. In between, two more court martials on 11 and 17 September, held at an army base near Madrid, sentenced eight members of FRAP to death. In a worldwide wave of fierce protest, fifteen European governments recalled their ambassadors. There were demonstrations and attacks on Spanish Embassy buildings in most European countries. The President of Mexico, Luis Echevarría, called for the expulsion of Spain from the United Nations. Pope Paul VI and every Spanish bishop appealed for clemency. Don Juan sent an appeal through his son. Similar requests came from governments around the world. An indignant Franco ignored them all. At a cabinet meeting held on 26 September, presided over by an extremely infirm Caudillo, five death sentences were confirmed. At dawn on the following day, the condemned were shot. The international protests intensified, with the Pope among the most outspoken. The European Commission called for a suspension of trade with Spain. The Spanish Embassy in Lisbon was sacked.[97]

The prestige of the opposition mounted in inverse proportion to the disgust provoked by the regime's brutality. The creation of the Junta Democrática had been followed in June 1975 by the birth of the Plataforma de Convergencia Democrática, which united the PSOE with Dionisio Ridruejo's Unión Social-Demócrata Española, Joaquín Ruiz-Giménez's Izquierda Demócrata Cristiana and several regionalist groups, including the Partido Nacionalista Vasco. The Plataforma was more open to dialogue with the regime reformists than was the Junta Democrática, which was committed to the PCE strategy of strikes and mass demonstrations. However, the executions overcame the mutual suspicion of both fronts which began negotiations for their fusion. The support of Don Juan de Borbón for the Plataforma provoked panic among regime reformists.[98]

The end was nigh for Franco. Infirm and under the influence of the bunker, he was losing weight and having trouble sleeping. On 1 October, the thirty-ninth anniversary of his elevation to the headship of state, he appeared before a huge crowd at the Royal Palace, many bussed in by the Movimiento. In the previous days, state radio and television had been urging people to attend. Offices, factories and shops were officially closed to facilitate this. On this last public appearance, the now diminutive, hunched Caudillo croaked out the eternal paranoiac clichés. Spain's problem was, he declared 'a masonic left-wing conspiracy within the political class in concubinage with Communist-terrorist subversion in society'. He took his leave of the crowd weeping and with both hands raised.[99]

On the same day, four policemen were shot by a newly emerged allegedly Marxist-Leninist terrorist group, GRAPO (Grupos de Resistencia Antifascista Primero de Octubre). Over the next five years, GRAPO was to act as a dangerous agent provocateur with suspicious connections to elements of the police.[100] In the meantime, demonstrations, strikes and shootings punctuated Franco's rapidly deteriorating health. Assassinations carried out by FRAP and ETA were quickly followed by reprisals from ultra-rightist terrorists. Exposure to the stabbing autumn winds of Madrid at his Plaza de Oriente appearance on 1 October set off the escalation of medical crises which culminated in his death. On 14 October, he manifested acute symptoms of influenza. The following morning, Franco awoke with pains in his chest and shoulders: he had suffered a serious heart attack. Despite this, he continued to work, holding eleven formal audiences on Thursday the 16th.[101] Against the advice of his doctors, he insisted on chairing a cabinet meeting on the next day. His alarmed doctors insisted that he wear electrodes connected to a heart monitor. During the session, news came in that Moroccan nationalists were conducting a 'green march' on Spanish Sahara. The shock caused him to have a relapse.[102]

On 18 October, Franco got up and worked in his study for the last time, probably writing his last will and testament. On Sunday the 19th, he heard Mass and took communion. At 11 p.m. on the night of the 20th, he had another mild heart attack and over the next days his condition began to deteriorate badly. He had a third heart attack on 22 October and a fourth on the 24th. His dental problems flared up again and he began also to suffer abdominal distension as a result of stomach haemorrhage. On Saturday 25 October, he was given extreme unction. After a further internal haemorrhage, by 29 October he was receiving constant blood transfusions. Throughout this time, although the Caudillo was in acute pain, Martínez-Bordiú tried to prevent his real condition becoming public knowledge. By 30 October, there were signs of peritonitis. When he was told of the gravity of his condition, Franco ordered that Article 11 of the Organic Law of the State be implemented. This ended his regency and passed the headship of state to Juan Carlos. Martínez-Bordiú and Arias, now united in panic, vainly tried to get him to accept an interim position, but he refused. Within days, the Prince revealed in *Newsweek* his wish to be 'the symbol of national unity and reconciliation'. The more liberal press now promoted his image and talked of Franco in the past tense.[103]

Juan Carlos's residence, the Zarzuela Palace, became a place of pilgrimage for liberal Francoists. Arias's half-hearted solution to Francoism after Franco had shattered on the rocks of bunker intransigence. The executions in September had exposed the obsolescence of the regime and created a broader desire for change that linked the democratic opposition with wide areas of the economic oligarchy, the middle classes and the administration. Hopes were now centred on Juan Carlos. Throughout November, prices on the Madrid stock exchange rose. There were doubts on the left about the extent to which Juan Carlos would be in thrall to the Francoist establishment. However, in Franco's last weeks, his contacts with European emissaries and with liberals inside Spain suggested that he was likely to attempt to steer Spain towards democracy.[104]

By the night of 2–3 November, Franco was suffering agony from cardiac, dental and abdominal problems. The medication to alleviate one worsened another. His intestinal haemorrhages were intensifying. The twenty-four specialists now in attendance believed that he was beyond help. However, Martínez Bardiú pressured them into conducting an emergency operation in an improvised theatre in the guards' first-aid post at El Pardo. In the course of a three-hour procedure, they discovered that an ulcer had opened an artery. Franco survived but was now suffering uraemia (a morbid condition of the blood due to the retention of urinary matter normally eliminated by the kidneys).[105] Needing dialysis, he was taken in a military ambulance to a properly equipped hospital, the Ciudad Sanitaria La Paz. Three days later, with the uraemia intensifying, at 5.30 p.m. on 5 November another operation began; it lasted four and a half hours and saw two-thirds of his stomach removed.[106] Thereafter, he was kept alive by a formidable panoply of life-support machines, regaining consciousness occasionally to murmur 'How hard it is to die.' Martínez-Bordiú was infuriated when Vicente Gil remarked that Franco should be allowed to die with dignity.[107] The hospital was besieged by journalists. Enormous sums were offered for photographs of the dying dictator. Gil's replacement as Franco's personal physician, Dr Vicente Pozuelo, indignantly rejected fabulous offers only to discover later that the Marqués de Villaverde had already made profitable use of his own camera.[108] On 15 November a further massive haemorrhage began. Franco's stomach was inflated as a result of the peritonitis. A third operation began in the early hours of the morning, after which Manuel Hidalgo Huerta's team remained deeply pessimistic.[109] The determination of the El Pardo entourage to keep Franco alive despite his intense suffering was linked to the fact that the term of office of Alejandro Rodríguez Valcárcel as President of the Consejo del Reino and of the Cortes was due to end on 26 November. If Franco could recover sufficiently to renew Rodríguez Valcárcel's mandate, the clique would have a key man in a position to ensure that Juan Carlos would choose a 'reliable' prime minister.[110]

Franco was alive but only just, barely conscious and entirely dependent on the complex life-support machinery. Finally, his daughter Nenuca insisted that he be allowed to die in peace. At 11.15 p.m. on 19 November, the various tubes connecting him to the machines were removed on the grudging instructions of Martínez-Bordiú. He probably died shortly afterwards. The official time of death was given as 5.25 a.m. on 20 November 1975; the official cause was announced as endotoxic shock brought about by acute bacterial peritonitis, renal failure, bronco-pneumonia, cardiac arrest, stomach ulcers, thrombophlebitis and Parkinson's disease.[111] He died a rich man with a fortune in the region of 400 million euros in 2015 terms.[112]

Any fears that Doña Carmen had of reprisals were unfounded. Within several days of his investiture as King, Juan Carlos granted her the title of La Señora de Meirás and her daughter that of Duquesa de Franco. La Señora had time to supervise the process that saw innumerable crates of jewellery, antiques, pictures and tapestries packed, loaded onto lorries, along with the Caudillo's papers, and either distributed around the various family properties in Spain or else spirited off to safe foreign havens. It is alleged that some of the priceless items properly belonged to the nation and that there was no vigilance by officials of the Patrimonio Nacional.[113] Despite the loss of Franco, the family remained immensely rich. Carmen's collection of jewellery was colossal. In her apartment, there was a room in which the walls were covered from floor to ceiling with forty columns of twenty narrow drawers. Some contained 'a disordered chaos of jewels: necklaces, tiaras, earrings, garlands, brooches, cameos'. Other drawers were full of gold and silver and individual stones, pearls, diamonds, rubies, emeralds and topazes. And the most valuable pieces were in bank vaults. These were gifts from Spaniards and foreigners presented in the hope of securing the goodwill of the Dictator. In the big house (Caserón) of the estate known as Canto del Pico left to the Franco family in 1937, there were tons of gifts given to the Caudillo and his wife.[114] Elsewhere, there were entire warehouses containing other gifts that had been sent to them. In addition to her accumulated wealth, Doña Carmen received lavish pensions from the state as widow of the head of state, of a captain general and of the holder of various medals. It has been estimated that the combined value of the pensions gave her an income double that of the Prime Minister (about 350,000 euros per year in 2019 terms).[115]

When Franco's death was announced, people danced in the streets of Basque towns. Although there was considerable apprehension in the air, Madrid and Barcelona were quietly drunk dry of champagne. No significant head of state, other than the Chilean dictator General Pinochet, attended Franco's funeral. In contrast, Juan Carlos's coronation would be attended by the French and West German presidents, the Duke of Edinburgh, the US Vice-President and the West German premier, Willy Brandt, who had fought in the International Brigades. Enormous goodwill, both inside and outside Spain, greeted the beginning of Juan Carlos's reign. Nevertheless, enormous obstacles lay in his path. The legacy of hatred in the Basque Country would bedevil Spanish politics for years to come. The bunker was entrenched in the army, the police and the Civil Guard. Over 100,000 Falangists were still authorized to carry guns. The problem was illustrated starkly on 22 November at the ceremony in the Cortes at which Juan Carlos was proclaimed King. As required, he swore fidelity to the Fundamental Laws and the Principios del Movimiento but, in a mildly progressive speech, he omitted references to the rebel victory in the civil war. It was received coldly by the *procuradores*. At his coronation, the bunker was outraged that Cardinal Enrique y Tarancón had called on him to be 'King of All Spaniards'.[116]

Progress without bloodshed depended on the skill of Juan Carlos, especially in relation to the armed forces, on the ministers that he chose and on the leaders of the opposition. His advisers had kept him informed of the desire of important sectors of Spanish capitalism to ditch the political mechanisms of Francoism. Married to a Greek princess, he was conscious of the consequences of her family's failure to go with the tide of popular democratic sentiment. On the other hand, he was equally aware of the strength and ill-will of the bunker. Moreover, anything that he did would have to be within the narrow limits of the Francoist Constitution to which he owed his accession. Accordingly, in the early days of his reign, he stepped cautiously. While popular pressure for reform intensified on the streets, he was engaged in complex negotiations behind closed doors. He managed to remove Rodríguez Valcárcel as President of the Cortes and get him replaced by his chosen candidate, his close adviser Torcuato Fernández Miranda. For his Prime Minister, he reluctantly kept on Arias, whom he regarded as obstinate and blinkered. He was only too aware that to replace both Rodríguez Valcárcel and Arias would be seen as a provocative challenge by the bunker.[117]

It has been suggested that Franco knew and approved of Juan Carlos's plans to democratize Spain. If so, it is strange that he did nothing to prepare his supporters for any such outcome. Indeed, on the contrary, he assured his ministers that his institutions would tie the future King to the principles of the Movimiento and 'the spirit of 18 July 1936'.[118] Arias accepted the premiership, stating patronizingly that he had been nominated by Franco and not by Juan Carlos. Along with the rounding up of leftists and the passing of an amnesty that released few political prisoners, this boosted the bunker's optimism that Juan Carlos would have to be faithful to his oaths and to his mentor. By nominating his own royal successor, and ignoring the legitimate heir to the throne, Franco seemed to have destroyed any political neutrality that Juan Carlos might have.[119] Taking a similar view, the clandestine left-wing press greeted the coronation with headlines that proclaimed: 'No to an imposed King!' and 'No to the Francoist King!'[120] The fact that Juan Carlos's first acts were aimed at consolidating his position within the army confirmed opposition suspicions. On 22 November, he sent a message to the armed forces, renewing his oath of fidelity to the flag and acknowledging their position as defenders of Franco's Fundamental Laws.[121]

Spanish President Adolfo Suarez and King Juan Carlos, two of the architects of
Spain's transition to democracy.

16

The Painful Creation of a Democracy, 1975–1982

The cabinet announced by Arias on 10 December 1975 contained enough Francoist hard-liners to please the bunker and worry the opposition. However, under pressure from the King, in turn advised by Fernández Miranda, Arias had included some notable reformists. Fraga as Minister of the Interior, Areilza as Foreign Minister and Antonio Garrigues as Minister of Justice, among others, had links with prominent Spanish companies and important multi-national corporations like United States Steel, IBM, Rank Xerox and General Electric.[1] At Juan Carlos's suggestion, Alfonso Osorio was appointed to the crucial Ministry of the Presidency, which gave him control over the cabinet agenda and responsibility for the national patrimony, the perfect cover for his frequent meetings with the King. However, the key to all of Juan Carlos's plans lay in the appointment of Fernández Miranda as President of the Cortes and of the Consejo del Reino. His knowledge of both Francoist constitutional law and of the entire regime elite would allow Juan Carlos to pursue reform without breaking his oaths. He ensured that he would have a mole in the cabinet by persuading Arias to give his protégé Adolfo Suárez the key post of Minister Secretary General of the Movimiento. Arias believed that Franco had wanted José Solís to remain in the post, but Fernández Miranda sidestepped the problem by suggesting that he give Solís the Ministry of Labour. Although ostensibly acceptable to the bunker, Suárez was not what he seemed. The same was true of the young Falangist Rodolfo Martín Villa as Minister for the official unions of the Movimiento.[2]

The challenge awaiting Juan Carlos and Fernández Miranda was underlined by Arias's thoroughly Francoist speech to the Consejo Nacional del Movimiento on 19 January 1976. He praised Franco's achievements and announced his determination to follow his example.

He assured his listeners that he nurtured 'neither murky desires of revisionism nor suicidal aims of stirring up our institutional system because of an itch for novelty or mad irresponsibility'. He went even further on 28 January when he presented his programme in a televised speech to the Cortes. The most that could be expected was that he might try to make enough of a democratic gesture to neutralize the left without provoking the bunker.[3]

A joint committee of senior cabinet ministers and members of the Consejo Nacional was established to examine possible institutional reform. At its first meeting, on 11 February 1976, Arias reaffirmed his determination to perpetuate Francoism and combat its enemies. He envisaged only minor cosmetic change.[4] The opposition was demanding full political amnesty, legalization of all political parties, free trade unions, the dismantling of the Movimiento and the Sindicatos, and free elections. The next six months would see a trial of strength between Arias's intransigence and the reformist ambitions of Fernández Miranda and the King. The balance would be tipped in favour of reform by mass militancy throughout Spain and violence in the Basque Country. Amnesty demonstrations and large-scale industrial strikes spread in early 1976, reaching a level in the Basque Country not seen elsewhere. The scale of popular militancy was a legacy of the violence of the forces of order during the state of exception of 1975. Equally, the Francoist instincts of both Arias and Fraga, as Minister of the Interior, were reflected in violent police charges against amnesty demonstrations and groups of strikers. Postmen, Madrid underground and national railway workers were militarized and the army used to run services.[5]

Behind the scenes, the liberals in the cabinet tried to reach out to the opposition and seek foreign support. Juan Carlos himself garnered considerable popularity on a tour of Catalonia.[6] However, reformist credibility was undermined by the authoritarianism of Arias and Fraga. The Madrid strikes were followed in February by 80,000-strong amnesty demonstrations on successive Sundays in Barcelona.[7] Militancy was even greater in the Basque Country. The pardon issued on coronation day had affected fewer than 10 per cent of the 750 Basque prisoners. Many Basques believed that ETA violence was a justifiable response to the institutional violence of Francoism. An intensive amnesty campaign of demonstrations was backed by labour disputes, sit-ins, hunger strikes and mass resignations by municipal officials. ETA remained active. In the first three months of 1976, several Civil Guards were killed taking down booby-trapped Basque flags (*ikurriñas*), a number of alleged informers were shot and an industrialist was kidnapped and murdered. This inevitably enraged both the bunker and Fraga, whose hostility to the Basques had been revealed in early March. A two-month strike in the town of Vitoria culminated on 3 March in a massive demonstration. A charge by riot police killed five and injured over seventy. In reply, a general strike was called throughout the Basque Country. The events of Vitoria destroyed any credibility that the government had had in the region. Fraga declared war on ETA on 8 April. The intensification of police activity, backed by the re-emergence of the ultra-rightist hit squads, reinforced popular support for ETA. While militancy elsewhere in Spain might diminish if democracy was established, any return to normality in Euskadi (the Basque Country) was a long-term problem.[8] The democratic fronts established in the rest of Spain, which were constantly widened to include moderates, never took root in the Basque Country.[9]

In the meantime, the Communist Party was having to accept that its hopes of a 'national democratic action' to overthrow the Francoist system were flimsy beyond Madrid and Barcelona. Santiago Carrillo saw that the *ruptura democrática* could come only from some process of negotiation between the reformists in the government and the more moderate elements of the opposition. Despite the numerical superiority and greater discipline of the PCE's rank and file, relative to the rest of the opposition, negotiations would favour the more obviously 'respectable' Socialists and Christian Democrats. To avoid the PCE being marginalized, Carrillo accepted the need for unity between the Junta Democrática and the Plataforma de Convergencia Democrática. This meant abandoning the *ruptura democrática*, in favour of the Plataforma's strategy of *ruptura pactada*. In late March, they united as Coordinación Democrática, popularly known as the Platajunta. Although its political diversity diminished the coalition's capacity for decisive action, its creation facilitated negotiation with the Francoist reformists and exposed divisions inside the cabinet.[10]

Arias was oblivious to these developments. More flexible ministers, like Areilza, Suárez and Osorio, were open to dialogue but Fraga flouted their advice. Unleashing his despotic instincts, he arrested the opposition leaders who met on 29 March to launch the Platajunta.[11] Discredited by the events in Vitoria, he began to curry favour with the hard-line Francoists, especially within the army. He told the Valencian Christian Democrat Emilio Attard that he planned to 'smash to pulp' the demonstrators at an amnesty rally in Valencia. His authoritarianism was further revealed at a dinner where he told Felipe González that the Socialists would not be legalized in eight years and the Communists never. 'Remember, I represent power and you are nothing.' The abandonment of reformism was a miscalculation that eliminated him as a possible successor to Arias.[12] In contrast, the crisis of Vitoria both united the left and boosted the career of Adolfo Suárez. As acting Minister of the Interior (Fraga being absent in Germany), he prevented a military intervention and subsequently, with the aid of Alfonso Osorio, convinced the King that his firm handling of events had avoided more bloodshed.[13]

Suárez was consolidating his position without provoking the suspicions of Arias or the bunker. They were convinced that he was a Falangist who intended only to use the apparatus of the Movimiento to create a veneer of democratic change. However, contacts with Fernández Miranda had convinced him that his future lay in a greater commitment to democracy. He was already establishing links with the 'tolerated opposition' of the Christian Democrats linked to Fernando Álvarez de Miranda. The group was close to the King, who began to see Suárez as someone who might be able to link disparate sectors of Francoist politics.[14] This view was confirmed when with great eloquence he presented Arias's Law of Political Associations to the Cortes. For the moment, he was hobbled by a lack of contacts on the left precisely at the moment when the Platajunta was opening up the opposition front to include centre and even right-of-centre groups while simultaneously isolating the government.[15]

Although wary of provoking the bunker, Juan Carlos was infuriated by both Arias' obstruction of reform and his arrogant assumption that he was irreplaceable. Arias made no secret of his contempt for the King. In the hope of provoking Arias's resignation, Juan Carlos gave an interview to *Newsweek* in which he described the Prime Minister as 'an unmitigated disaster' because he represented the interests of the bunker. On 9 June, after Suárez's speech, the Cortes passed the Law of Political Associations but refused to amend the penal code to permit the legalization of political parties as envisaged by the law. Juan Carlos knew that his own survival depended on a transition to democracy and that in turn required a politician capable of dealing with both the bunker and the opposition. Accordingly, on a highly successful trip to the USA in early June, he sought assurances of support from the White House. Having received them, on 1 July, Juan Carlos asked for Arias's resignation.[16] The King's delay in doing so led many observers to suspect that his commitment to democratization was flimsy. They underestimated the power of the bunker in general and of the armed forces in particular. The subsequent emergence of military subversion (*golpismo*) underlines the extent to which Juan Carlos had to operate with extreme caution where the army was concerned. His success in that regard was a crucial contribution to the coming of democracy. Similarly, the limited scale of Arias's reforms and the bunker's resistance to them discredited the ultra-right in the eyes of the remainder of the Francoist elite. The inadequacy of Arias's schemes persuaded many Francoist bureaucrats and businessmen to join the reformist camp. At the same time, Fraga's clumsy repression consolidated opposition unity. That unity, and the popular support behind it, provided the pressure that pushed the most flexible and reformist functionaries to think about the future. The opprobrium generated by the extreme right in the Arias period also inclined international opinion in favour of the democratic left.

The success of the democratic project would depend on the person chosen to succeed Arias. Both Areilza and Fraga assumed that it would be one of them, but Juan Carlos regarded them both as unsuitable, the one for his arrogance, the other for his authoritarian style. The rules required the King to choose from a three-man shortlist (*terna*) selected by the Consejo del Reino. Fernández Miranda skilfully arranged its key meeting on 3 July so as to ensure the inclusion of Adolfo Suárez alongside the Opus technocrat Gregorio López Bravo and Federico Silva Muñoz, the dourly conservative Christian Democrat. The Consejo presented the list in the confidence that the choice would be between the two senior candidates. To the bitter disappointment of both Areilza and Fraga, Suárez was appointed on 3 July.[17] He owed his elevation to his knowledge of the Movimiento, which would enable him, with guidance from Fernández Miranda, to use the system to initiate reform. In the short term, his Francoist credentials neutralized the bunker, although they alarmed the opposition. As Suárez later admitted, the consequent amnesty demonstrations in the second week of July convinced him of the urgency of speedy and thorough reform.[18]

The immediate difficulty was to assemble a cabinet after Areilza and Fraga had refused to take part. Suárez had to avoid the fatal step of forming a team of his own cronies from the Movimiento. Fernández Miranda and the King persuaded Alfonso Osorio to become Vice-President of the cabinet and Minister of the Presidency. Osorio then persuaded other Tácitos to accept posts. Suárez's eventual list of conservative Catholics with links to the more progressive sectors of Spanish capitalism, like Marcelino Oreja, at Foreign Affairs, and Landelino Lavilla, at Justice, would have more success in bringing reform than his critics had believed possible.[19] His programme, eloquently presented on television, recognized popular sovereignty, promised a referendum on political reform and elections before 30 June 1977. It won him considerable popular sympathy, but he had to manoeuvre between the opposition and a hostile bunker. Carrillo was living clandestinely in Spain and the Communist Party was in the forefront of mass pressure for change. There were ten times more strikes in 1976 than in 1975. Without provoking the army, Suárez's strategy was to introduce measures faster than the hard-liners could react. Nevertheless, he still had to get the opposition to accept that democratization could take place only within Francoist 'legality'.[20]

To take the initiative away from the left, Suárez had to make substantial concessions while splitting the united front of the opposition. The priority was to force back the Communists from setting the pace of opposition demands to a more defensive position of trying to prevent their own isolation. Suárez successfully devoted August to making contact with a wide range of opposition personalities, including Felipe González. The PSOE leader had already accepted that a constitution elaborated by a freely elected Cortes would in itself constitute a rupture but that it would require negotiation with the government. He was much impressed by Suárez's readiness to listen and readiness to contemplate the creation of a genuinely democratic regime.[21] Through third parties, Suárez secured assurances from Carrillo that he would not disrupt a pacific transition.

On 4 September, several liberal, Social Democrat and Christian Democrat groups gathered in Madrid to discuss with the Platajunta and other regional opposition fronts the elaboration of a united strategy. The opposition was recruiting ever more refugees from the establishment. The creation of a liaison committee was sufficient to oblige Suárez to accelerate his project of political reform.[22] This in turn provoked concern within the army. The reactionary General Fernando de Santiago y Díaz de Mendívil, as Vice-President and Minister of Defence, was a key link between the military and the civilian bunkers in their efforts to obstruct democratic reform. His influence was countered somewhat by the appointment of the liberal General Gutiérrez Mellado as Chief of the General Staff. On 8 September, Suárez sought support for his reform project from the military ministers, the nine captains general and the Chiefs of Staff of the three services. Because they were backed by Juan Carlos, Suárez's persuasively expounded plans were accepted with reluctance, albeit with a demand that the Communist Party be excluded from any future reform. Suárez assured them that the international loyalties enshrined in the PCE's statutes would prevent its legalization. He did not tell them that through his secret contacts with Carrillo he was working towards a change in those statutes and an eventual legalization of the Communist Party.[23]

Two days later, the cabinet approved the Law for Political Reform without any opposition from the four military ministers. However, within days, General Santiago opposed a draft project for trade union reform so vehemently that on 21 September Suárez obliged him to resign and replaced him with Gutiérrez Mellado. Osorio was concerned that this was a mistake given Santiago's immense influence among the right-wing opponents of reform. He was right. Henceforth, Suárez's relations with the military would deteriorate rapidly. The fierce reaction of both Santiago and General Iniesta Cano constituted a declaration of war against Gutiérrez Mellado. A cabinet meeting on 1 October decided to punish both Santiago and Iniesta by relegation to the reserve list. An appeal by Iniesta was upheld and the government's action was declared improper. The bunker was delighted and Suárez's cabinet had been made to look ridiculous and vindictive. Henceforth, Iniesta and Santiago would promote anti-democratic subversion, or *golpismo*, within the armed forces through articles in *El Alcázar*.[24] Nevertheless, Gutiérrez Mellado was able to begin the urgent task of promoting a new generation of officers loyal to the coming democratic regime.[25]

When the reform text was made public, opposition reactions were mixed. The fact that the promised elections would be presided over by the existing government raised fears of electoral corruption. The Communist Party denounced the text as an 'anti-democratic fraud'. Other groups were readier to be convinced, seeing evidence of reform in the functioning of the press and in the freedom enjoyed by the non-Communist left. The PSOE was allowed to prepare to hold its first congress in Spain since the civil war. Martín Villa, now Minister of the Interior, had prohibited all Communist public activities yet a blind eye was being turned to the PCE. Suárez insinuated to the Socialists and the left Christian Democrats that he would make even greater concessions provided that they did not provoke the army by insisting on the legalization of the PCE. He skilfully manoeuvred Felipe González into accepting that premature legalization was unrealistic.[26]

By dint of cunning and the skill of Fernández Miranda, Suárez managed to steer the reform project through the Francoist institutions. On 8 October, it was approved with minor amendments by the Consejo Nacional and, in mid-November, in the Cortes, in both cases by huge majorities. Some hard-liners were sent on an official junket to Panama, via the Carribean, and others were promised seats in the future Senate. Many *procuradores* naively assumed that they would be re-elected in the forthcoming elections. It was, in the later judgement of Suárez, a collective suicide by the '*procuradores del harakiri*'. Their voluntary suicide was only relative, however, since they maintained their well-paid jobs in industry, the banks and financial entities and frequently also in regional and provincial administrations.[27]

The opposition remained distrustful. At a meeting on 4 November in Las Palmas, a wide opposition front rejected Suárez's plans for a referendum on his political reform project. A call for abstention would be in vain. A strike wave did not disrupt the timetable for reform since the bulk of the population welcomed the changes introduced by Suárez. Although more than a million workers were involved, the general strike on 12 November did not become the great national action against the Suárez reform hoped for by the Communists. That was in large part because of the elaborate precautions taken by the Minister of the Interior. Martín Villa's counter-strategy saw arrests of workers' leaders in Madrid, Barcelona, Valencia, Bilbao and Seville which neutralized the nerve centres of the movement and so appreciably limited its impact.[28]

The relative failure of the strike contributed to Suárez's success three days later when he submitted his project to the Cortes. Many opposition groups now accepted that dealing with Suárez could lead to real reform.[29] The PSOE was inclined to moderation. This was revealed at the XXVII Congress of the PSOE held in Madrid at the beginning of December. The party leadership feared that, even if, in solidarity with the Communists, they refused to participate in the elections, people would go to the polls anyway and PSOE votes would go to rival groups. The presence of Europe's major Socialist leaders was used to endorse Felipe González's unequivocally moderate line. He made it clear that the PSOE would participate in the elections even if all parties had not been legalized beforehand.[30]

The wisdom of the Socialists' moderation was confirmed on 15 December when the referendum on political reform saw the project approved by 94 per cent of the vote. The abstention calls of the opposition were ignored by the left-wing rank and file. The result was a victory for Suárez but also for the mass pressure throughout 1976 that had pushed the government towards democratization.[31] He still faced two major problems in relation to his uneasy truce with the army: the legalization of the PCE and terrorism. The former would eventually be solved by his characteristic wheeling and dealing, albeit at the cost of toxic resentment in military circles. The latter, in contrast, was to prove intractable and, in the long run, was to be Suárez's undoing. Already immersed in the monumental task of steering a path to democracy, he had little understanding of ETA demands. He was unable to see their roots in Francoist excesses and atrocities. Unfortunately, he left the question of terrorism to Martín Villa, who had been Civil Governor of Barcelona in September 1975 when 'Txiki' Paredes was executed there. He was thus guaranteed intense hostility in Euskadi. To solve the problem would have required amnesty for all ETA prisoners and the legalization of the Basque flag, the *ikurriña*. Such conciliatory gestures were more than he or Martín Villa, let along the bunker, could countenance.[32]

In contrast, the legalization of the PCE was relatively uncomplicated. Aware that the rest of the opposition was unlikely to risk its own gains in order to help the Communists, Carrillo daringly set about clawing back some of the initiative from Suárez. Living clandestinely in Madrid, he decided to force the pace by holding a press conference with over seventy Spanish and foreign journalists on 10 December. It was a provocation that deeply embarrassed Martín Villa, but Carrillo's words to the assembled reporters were conciliatory. He stated that, provided the PCE was allowed to take part in the elections, the Communists would cooperate in the elaboration of a social contract to deal with the economic crisis, a significant offer given the Communist influence in the Comisiones Obreras. Martín Villa ordered Carrillo's arrest. He was detained for eight days but eventually Suárez had to release him, since a trial would have damaged his reforming credibility. By freeing Carrillo, Suárez was taking a substantial step towards legalizing the PCE.[33]

This could only infuriate the bunker, especially in the upper reaches of the armed forces where terrorist activity kept nerves on edge. After Suárez had made the first announcement of his reform project, GRAPO began a highly orchestrated effort to destabilize Spain along the lines practised by the extreme right in South America and Italy. It started with a bombing campaign then, on the eve of the referendum, escalated with the kidnapping of Antonio María de Oriol y Urquijo, President of the Consejo del Estado. Disappointed that it had not impeded a huge referendum vote in favour of change, the campaign was escalated further on 24 January 1977 with the kidnapping of General Emilio Villaescusa Quilis, President of the Consejo Superior de Justicia Militar. On the same day, right-wing terrorists murdered five people, four of whom were Communist labour lawyers, in an office in the Atocha district of Madrid. Carrillo did not take the bait and instead issued appeals for calm. At the funeral of the victims, the PCE organized a gigantic display of silent solidarity. Not only was Suárez deeply impressed by this demonstration of Communist strength and discipline, but popular hostility to the legalization of the party was diminished. In return for promises of action against the bunker's violence, an opposition delegation offered Suárez a joint statement denouncing terrorism and calling for national support for the government. Suárez's position was boosted by the implicit acknowledgement that he belonged to the democratic forces.[34]

Suárez was advancing towards the promised elections but that was merely a step towards his final goal. The purpose of the project was to guarantee the political and economic interests of that broad spectrum of the Francoist establishment which, unlike the bunker, had thrown in its lot with the monarchy. To that end, it would be necessary to create a centre-right party with good electoral prospects. The progressive ex-Francoists now in the democratic ranks were thus engaged in frantic preparation for the forthcoming elections.[35] Fraga opted to create a right-wing party in collaboration with six other ex-Francoist figures including Laureano López Rodó. The so-called magnificent seven hoped to appeal to the sector of society that had been moulded by nearly forty years of Francoist propaganda. Rigid control of the media and the education system had created what came to be called 'sociological Francoism'. With substantial backing from the banks, Fraga's party Alianza Popular was created rapidly in the second half of September 1976.[36]

An element of its financing came illegally from West Germany via Franz Josef Strauss's Christian-Social Union. Hans Hoffmann, Girón's factotum in Malaga, created the Hanns Seidel Stiftung through which money was funnelled to Alianza Popular.[37] In fact, like its successor, the Partido Popular, Fraga's party would be the object of frequent accusations of corruption. The PSOE also received German money, from the Stiftung Friedrich Ebert. In time, the quest for electoral funding would see other parties involved in corruption.[38]

The creation of Alianza Popular convinced Suárez that his own best chance of success lay with a centre party. He created the Unión de Centro Democrático by exploiting the desperate need of many small centre-right parties for alliances. His trump card was the government's control of Radio-Television Española and of local administrative machinery.[39] UCD was a fusion of five main groups, each in its turn composed of several others. The most substantial segment consisted of two groups of conservative Christian Democrats – the followers of Alfonso Osorio and Fernando Álvarez de Miranda, together with some Tácitos and the Partido Popular, including the Valencian lawyer Emilio Attard, along with Pío Cabanillas and Areilza. They united as Centro Democrático in mid-January 1977. On the left of UCD were the various Social Democrats led by Francisco Fernández Ordóñez and several liberal groups under Joaquín Garrigues. Both would eventually be instrumental in the fragmentation of the party but, that year, all were desperate to be part of an electorally viable party. Ideological, personal and moral considerations took a back seat to the ruthless quest for profitable alliances. The fifth and key group, known as Azules because of their Falangist past, were important Movimiento officials tempted to join by promises of places in the future regime.[40]

The formal agreement for the electoral coalition known as UCD was signed on 3 May 1977. Since the candidate lists had to be submitted by 9 May, frantic deals were made over the next five days. Suárez's control of the state electoral machinery gave him enormous power. He was able to eliminate Areilza. However, he had incurred commitments to many Azules in exchange for votes to get his reform project through the Cortes.

Inevitably, the UCD's candidate lists were filled by men who had been *procuradores* in Franco's Cortes, officials in provincial and municipal government, state industries or RTVE or top functionaries. Real power in UCD would lie with Suárez and these ex-Movimiento cronies and, to a lesser extent, the 'barons' of the component groups. Suárez's inner circle came to be known as *la empresa* (the firm).[41] In power, UCD's deputies were ambitious men committed to little except their own careers. Most had close relations with business, industry and especially the banks. UCD was thus the ideal instrument to ensure that in the transition from a dictatorial to a democratic regime, real government power would remain in the hands, if not of the same people as before, at least of sufficiently conservative individuals to guarantee the existing structure of economic and social power.[42]

As UCD was coalescing, other parties were being legalized. The problem was the PCE. The bunker and the army were fiercely opposed to its legalization but, without it, democracy would be incomplete. Suárez delayed it as long as he could, but on 27 February he met Carrillo. In return for legal status, Carrillo undertook to recognize the monarchy, adopt the red-yellow-red monarchist flag of Spain and offer his support for a future social contract. On 9 April, with most of the Madrid political and military elite out of town for the Easter weekend, Suárez, blithely confident of army acquiescence, announced the legalization of the PCE. It guaranteed him the unrelenting hatred of the bunker who saw it as a vile betrayal of Franco's civil war victory. The Minister for the Navy, Admiral Pita da Veiga, resigned. Despite Suárez's efforts, on 11 April, to justify to the high command what he had done, it was obvious that military opposition was considerable. As a safety precaution, key military units were kept short of petrol. The legalization of the PCE was a necessary part of the transition, but it was a gift for the ultras. Propaganda denouncing Suárez's 'treachery' was distributed in military barracks by a series of 'patriotic juntas', assumed to be the brainchild of extremists like Girón, Utrera Molina and Blas Piñar. Sectors of the army had reached the conclusion that an intervention in politics was needed. Daily incitements to military subversion appeared in the bunker press, *El Alcazar, El Imparcial* and *Fuerza Nueva*.[43]

Although the continued existence of ETA intensified the bunker's opposition to the democratic process, the election campaign proceeded in an atmosphere of popular fiesta. There were huge meetings mounted by the PSOE and the PCE. UCD's campaign centred on television, press and radio.[44] Eighteen million people voted, nearly 80 per cent of the total electorate, and 90 per cent of them voted clearly for change. The popular desire for change but not confrontation favoured Suárez and Felipe González. In contrast, Carrillo and Fraga awakened memories of the past. Despite ample finance, Alianza Popular's line-up of prominent Francoists did not help its cause, especially given the unrepentantly Francoist nostalgia of Arias Navarro and the vehemence of Fraga.[45] To generate fear of another civil war, the right-wing press exploited the presence in the PCE lists of wartime figures like Carrillo and Dolores Ibárruri. In contrast, the modern image of Felipe González and the prestige conferred by the support of European Socialist leaders made him a serious rival to Suárez.[46]

Suárez refused to take part in any debate with other party leaders, relying on the media and a large-scale, well-financed advertising campaign. The UCD propaganda machine worked hard to appeal to women, building on Suárez's film-star looks to create an image of the devoted family man and practising Catholic. As was to be expected, UCD won the elections, with 34.3 per cent of the vote; but the Socialists were not far behind with 28.5 per cent. The PCE came third with 9.3 per cent and Alianza Popular fourth with 8.4 per cent.[47] So 15 June 1977 saw the end of the Franco regime but not of Francoism. Forty years of brainwashing guaranteed that Francoist attitudes would survive for decades. The creation of a democratic polity, in such a context, was made possible by the skill of Adolfo Suárez and his advisers, by the determination of Juan Carlos but, especially, by the moderation displayed by González, Carrillo and the other leaders of an opposition that made immense sacrifices in the interests of the immediate goal of democracy.

Formal political democracy was a great achievement after thirty-eight years of dictatorship, but it was only a timid first step. Moreover, it did nothing to eradicate corrupt practices inherited from the Franco regime and before. The simple problem of presenting candidates for election at national and local level often meant that the ethics of new recruits were not adequately checked. Practices that were considered normal under Franco, such as the private use of official vehicles and lavish travel and entertainment expenses, were exploited on the basis of 'it's our turn now'. This was inevitable, particularly when it came to raising party funds, since electoral success was the main priority. Hopes of social and economic reform were quietly abandoned. There was no retribution for those who had enjoyed the fruits of civil war victory nor justice for their victims. Many Francoist cadres remained in positions of power by dint of a simple transfer from the Movimiento to UCD. Perhaps inevitably, in a context of rising inflation and unemployment, the next four years would see popular enthusiasm turn to disenchantment.[48]

On 15 June, the voters had opted overwhelmingly for moderation. In opinion polls, 80 per cent of Spaniards described themselves as belonging to the area between right and left of centre.[49] However, the problems that were to undermine democracy over the next four years – military subversion, terrorism and economic stagnation – could not be resolved merely by the existence of a moderate electorate. Inevitably, given its close links to the financial and industrial elite, the UCD had little interest in structural reform. The priority of the new cabinet was the maintenance of the unity of a fragmented party whose cadres were mainly concerned with securing highly paid official posts. Suárez's personal friends were well represented, especially his new Vice-President for Political Affairs, Fernando Abril Martorell, an agronomist whom he had met in Segovia when he was Civil Governor there.[50]

Suárez's ability to fulfil the expectations of the electorate was limited by the costs of keeping his disparate party together; by his lack of an overall parliamentary majority; by the need to elaborate a universally acceptable constitutional framework; by the demands of autonomous regions; and above all by the daily erosion of energy by the anti-democratic violence of the extreme right and left. Prior deals both within UCD and with other parties were always required before major Cortes votes. Natural inclination and the problems facing him accelerated Suárez's withdrawal into smoke-filled rooms. His secretive style of backstairs dealing and the way that a spiral of ETA terrorism and military subversion carried apprehension and fear into daily life were to convert the optimism of 1977 into the disenchantment of 1980.

Bitter tensions in the Basque Country engendered under Franco festered largely because of the behaviour of the unreformed forces of order. Elsewhere in Spain, people were ready to believe that, despite the Francoist background of many cabinet members, real change was under way. However, many Basques believed that fascist oppression continued to exist under another name. Habits of police violence died hard and, even outside Euskadi, there were several scandals in 1977. On 27 August, the Socialist deputy for Santander, Jaime Blanco, was beaten up by policemen at a political rally. In December, the police opened fire at a gathering of Andalusian nationalists in Malaga, killing one man and wounding six others. A few days later, a student was shot at the University of La Laguna in Tenerife. When Martín Villa supported the police and took no action against those responsible, Alfonso Guerra again denounced him in the Cortes as a Francoist. Martín Villa, with the police, and Gutiérrez Mellado, with the army, were confronted with the identical problems of having to rely on personnel trained in anti-democratic habits. Necessary reforms were shirked for fear of mutiny. Until 1979, Martín Villa was unable to introduce reform of the police.[51]

The legalization of the PCE intensified anti-democratic conspiracy in the higher echelons of the armed forces. It was fomented by the ultra press, and military barracks were flooded with pamphlets calling for military intervention. The intelligence services failed to pass on information about the plotters. Originally created to eradicate liberalism in the armed forces, military intelligence was hard-line Francoist in composition, objectives and methods. Accordingly, military enemies of the democratic regime could count on invaluable assistance. Elements of the varied military intelligence services were later involved in the Tejero coup attempt of 23 February 1981. The Suárez government tried to reform the intelligence services by creating the Centro Superior de Información de la Defensa (CESID). Inheriting the personnel of its various Francoist predecessors, the CESID formed a parallel power structure which did not share the loyalty to the King of the military hierarchy under Gutiérrez Mellado. Despite evidence that the CESID was spying on ministers and other politicians while failing to investigate military subversion, the government turned a blind eye.[52]

Anti-democratic ferment in the army was perceptible in the autumn of 1977. It fed off bitterness because of the PCE's legalization, the government's failure to quash Basque terrorism and rumours of an imminent purge of older officers which would deprive them of career and pension prospects. Already in mid-September, General Fernando de Santiago hosted a three-day meeting of senior generals in Játiva in the province of Valencia. They wanted the King to appoint a government of national salvation under Santiago. Despite official denials, widespread rumours about this attempt to carry out a bloodless coup d'état brought the threat of military intervention into the open.[53] Civilian support networks for subversion were being organized. Those organizing the propaganda campaigns of the 'patriotic juntas' were allegedly preparing their followers to take over the civil service, local government and communications in the event of a coup.[54] Fearful of precipitating military intervention, the government took no action against those involved in the Játiva meeting.

Instead, Gutiérrez Mellado tried to bring the military under control by means of strategic postings and promotions such as the removal of the extreme rightist Jaime Milans del Bosch from command of the Brunete Armoured Division. The División Acorazada (DAC) was the key to any coup attempt. Milans was made Captain General of the Third Military Region, centred on Valencia, which put him in a more powerful position. Gutiérrez Mellado's changes merely nourished military suspicion that the government was indecisive, meddlesome and vindictive. Evidence of weakness was provided when Lieutenant Colonel Antonio Tejero was punished only by being confined to barracks for one month despite nearly provoking a massacre in Malaga on 8 October. On Tejero's orders, a legally authorized rally in favour of a reduction in the voting age to eighteen was broken up by fully armed Civil Guards. His irresponsible brutality was making him a cult figure among ultras.[55]

Despite the festering problems of military subversion and Basque terrorism, Suárez made remarkable progress towards solving the potential problem of Catalonia. Through the mediation of the banker Manuel Ortínez, Suárez established a close relationship with the 77-year-old exiled President of the Generalitat de Catalunya, Josep Tarradellas, which facilitated a political coup. An awareness of a 'Catalan problem' was brought home to Suárez by the results of the 15 June elections in Catalonia. The UCD had been swamped by the so-called *partidos sucursalistas* (branch parties), the PSC and PSUC, the Catalan branches of the Socialist and Communist parties. Accordingly, in late June, Tarradellas was invited to Madrid and began arduous negotiations with Suárez. Juan Carlos played a key role in smoothing the path to agreement. In return for the re-establishment of the Generalitat, through an adaption of the 1932 Statute, Tarradellas pledged Catalan loyalty to the monarchy, acceptance of the unity of Spain and respect for the armed forces. The meeting was a theatrical gesture which diminished the electoral victory of the Catalan left-wing parties as well as reaffirming Suárez's penchant for government by private negotiation. The deal with Tarradellas was an immense popular success, but a high price would be paid in terms of military resentment. Tarradellas returned in triumph to Barcelona on 23 October.[56]

Progress with the Basques would be much slower because of the issue of amnesty for imprisoned Etarras (members of ETA). By the beginning of October, opposition pressure was building for an amnesty not just for Etarras but also for army officers who had fought for the Republic during the civil war and even for the ultra-right terrorists responsible for the Atocha massacre. Suárez met representatives of all parties on 8 and 9 October but warned them that he was hampered by what he called the *poderes fácticos*, that is to say, the powerful elements invigilating the democratic regime – the army, the banks and, to a lesser extent, the Church. This explained the exclusion from the amnesty passed in the Cortes on 14 October of both the Republican officers and those involved in the Unión Militar Democrática. Nevertheless, the amnesty, backed by a nearly unanimous vote, seemed to symbolize reconciliation. As the basis of the so-called pact of oblivion, it would be one of the pillars of the transition to democracy. The law effectively stated that acts of terrorism in opposition to the Franco dictatorship and crimes against human rights in its defence could not be subject to judicial proceedings. It rested on a tacit, collective agreement of the great majority of the Spanish people to renounce any settling of accounts with the Franco regime. Given the numerical discrepancy between the relatively few people involved in acts of violence against the regime and the many involved in its brutal imposition and subsequent defence, it constituted a major sacrifice made by the democratic forces in order to avoid further blood-shed. The law was also accompanied by the systematic destruction of the archives of the Franco regime's repressive apparatus.[57]

The spectre of military resentment hovered over negotiations about Basque autonomy. The Basque government-in-exile was a more substantial entity than the symbolic Generalitat represented by Tarradellas. Suárez would not contemplate an arrangement with the Basque President or Lendakari, Jesús María de Leizaola, like that concluded with Tarradellas. Instead, in complicated circumstances, the Minister for the Regions, the Andalusian Manuel Clavero Arévalo, negotiated with parliamentary representatives of the Partido Nacionalista Vasco and of the Basque branches of the PSOE and of UCD the creation of the Consejo General Vasco with which the government would negotiate autonomy issues. The hard-line separatists were therefore excluded and regarded the process with suspicion.[58] The most conflictive issue was the status of Navarre. For Basque nationalists, the province was part of Euskadi; for the army, the UCD and the right in general and the Navarrese right in particular, it was the cradle of Spanish nationalism. Moreover, neither the PSOE nor the PCE were in favour of including Navarre within the Basque Country. Accordingly, the Basque autonomy statute eventually implemented on 25 October 1979 was limited to the three indisputably Basque provinces of Vizcaya, Guipúzcoa and Álava. Albeit a step towards peace in Euskadi, it faced the undisguised hostility of both the army and the *abertzales*.[59]

For most army officers, any autonomy concessions were an assault on Spanish unity. For the *abertzales*, the UCD was rendering Basque autonomy innocuous by diluting it in a sea of autonomies. In fact, autonomy demands were emerging from the most unlikely parts of Spain as a reaction both to the corruption and inefficiency of local government under Franco and to the economic imbalances bequeathed by his regime. Clavero Arévalo tried to cater to local aspirations without provoking the military by creating a two-tier system. The three historic nationalities, Catalonia, Euskadi and Galicia, were permitted to elaborate an autonomy statute which had then to be submitted to local referendum. Thirteen other regions, some small like Cantabria, others large like Andalusia, were subjected to vaguer arrangements. Needless to say, it inflamed military disaffection with the democratic regime.

On other issues, however, the autumn and winter of 1977 saw cooperation and sacrifice among the main political parties. This was symbolized by the social contract signed in late October by thirty-one representatives of virtually all parties and known as the Moncloa Pact because the ceremony took place at the Prime Minister's official residence, the Palacio de la Moncloa. Suárez exploited Santiago Carrillo's acceptance that the country was economically too weak and the health of the newborn democracy too fragile to stand right–left polarization.[60] The Pact was essentially an austerity package, although it aimed to establish a common response to terrorism as well as to inflation, unemployment and the growing trade deficit.[61] With inflation at 29 per cent, the left accepted wage-rise ceilings of 20–22 per cent and various monetarist measures to restrict credit and public spending. In return, the government promised major structural reform, especially in agriculture and the tax system, reorganization of the police and the return of the buildings, newspapers and funds of the trade unions confiscated by the Francoists after the civil war. In fact, the government fulfilled few of its promises and the working class bore the brunt of the economic crisis. Over the next three years, inflation dropped to 15 per cent, although it was still nearly twice the OECD average, and unemployment soared from 7 per cent to nearly 13 per cent as monetarist policies provoked bankruptcies and plant closures.[62] In the wake of expectations that democracy would solve all Spain's ills, such harsh austerity brought the widespread disillusionment known as the *desencanto*.

The elaboration of a Constitution was a detailed juridical task that inevitably failed to capture the excitement of the end of Francoism and the election campaign. A truce between parties, the Pacto Constitucional, facilitated this momentous task. At the beginning of August 1977, the Constitutional Committee of the Cortes elected a drafting committee, or Ponencia. It consisted of seven parliamentary deputies, three from UCD and one each from the PSOE, Catalan conservative party, Convergencia i Unió, the PSUC and Alianza Popular. Working in a spirit of compromise, they had produced a draft text by mid-November. At the beginning of 1978, a more refined draft was submitted to the thirty-six members of the Constitutional Committee. Despite some friction over such issues as abortion, autonomies, private education and the death penalty, steady progress was maintained under the chairmanship of Emilio Attard.[63] Deliberations were completed on 20 June and the text was ratified by the Cortes and the Senate on 31 October 1978. It did not satisfy right-wing ultras and Basque nationalists at the time nor Catalan nationalists forty years later, but the text's moderation and guarantee of basic liberties ensured a broadly favourable popular reception.[64] The widespread belief in Euskadi that Martín Villa approved of the brutality of the police and Civil Guard fuelled support for ETA. On 11 January 1978, a policeman and two Etarras had been killed in a shoot-out in Pamplona. When asked for comment by journalists, Martín Villa unwisely remarked, '2–1 to us.'[65]

Suárez's run of success would come to an end in the course of 1978. A rise in street crime reflected spiralling unemployment and it was exploited by the ultra press to foment middle-class panic about a collapse of law and order. The ultra-right claimed that the criminals were leftists released from prison by amnesty measures. The left argued that the police were trying to undermine democracy by letting crime get out of hand. There was certainly a remarkable contrast between the brutal efficacy of the police under Franco and its apparent helplessness in the democratic regime.[66] The law-and-order issue was eroding the popular credibility of the Suárez government, although it would be ETA terrorism and the military response to it that would eventually destroy Suárez. In the shorter term, the steady rise in unemployment and the government's failure to implement the reforms promised by the Moncloa Pact saw the PSOE and liberal press conclude that UCD was the puppet of the right-wing employers' organization, the Confederación Española de Organizaciones Empresariales. Suárez's popularity ratings began to plummet.[67]

He was loathed by many army officers. The passage of time had not reconciled the armed forces to the democratic regime. Necessary efforts by Gutiérrez Mellado to promote liberal officers had obliged him to bypass the rigid system of promotion by strict seniority, which offended traditionalists who were not necessarily subversives. Large increases in military budgets, with salaries raised by 21 per cent, did little to foster military loyalty. The government was trapped between the hostility of senior officers to the process of regional devolution and Basque pressure for it to be accelerated. The eighty-five terrorist victims in 1978 tripled the tally of the previous two years. The military wing of ETA was primarily, if not exclusively, responsible. It remained determined to establish an independent Basque state including the four Spanish and three French Basque provinces. Its intensification of violence against policemen and soldiers provoked the brutality that maintained its support. ETA-Militar (ETA-M) and the extreme right created a counterpoint of repression and terror. The police and Civil Guard were partially out of government control in the second half of 1978. Martín Villa told the Cortes that he did not dare to try to purge the police and was later quoted to the effect that he could trust only twenty officers.[68]

His impotence before acts of brutality confirmed the widespread Basque perception of the Spanish forces of order as a rapacious foreign army of occupation and ETA's actions as legitimate self-defence. The government seemed to be paralysed in the face of almost weekly ETA assassinations of policemen or Civil Guards. Acts of indiscriminate terrorism began to diminish ETA's popular support, albeit not enough to help Suárez. The wave of killings led to various government attempts to negotiate a truce with ETA. They were in vain because ETA-M wanted to provoke the army into occupying Euskadi and thus, it was hoped, igniting a national revolutionary rising.[69] Military intervention was entirely possible whereas a popular revolutionary action was highly unlikely. Sympathy for ETA was maintained largely because of the activities of rightist terror squads and the police indiscipline. ETA-M seemed undeterred, imposing a 'revolutionary tax' on Basque businessmen and continuing to attack army officers throughout the autumn and winter of 1978. The ultra-rightist press drew comparisons with the situation prior to the military uprising of 1936 and denounced the new Constitution as a Communist-inspired assault on national unity. It was in the context of a descent into violence that the Cortes approved the Constitution on 31 October 1978, by 363 votes to 6, with 13 abstentions.[70]

Although the ongoing violence favoured the ultras' cause, Gutiérrez Mellado's policy of strategic promotions was gradually undermining their strength in the army. Some believed that they had to act before democracy was further consolidated by the constitutional referendum fixed for 6 December. A plan was made to kidnap Suárez and his cabinet on 17 November as the first step towards the imposition of a government of 'national salvation' to suspend parliament and step up the existing 'dirty war' against ETA. It was called Operación Galaxia, after the cafeteria where it had been hatched by Lieutenant Colonel Tejero of the Civil Guard and Captain Ricardo Sáenz de Ynestrillas of the police. The date was chosen because the King and many key officers were scheduled to be out of Madrid, and large numbers of ultras, many armed, were expected to arrive for the commemoration, on 20 November, of the anniversary of Franco's death. In the event, the plot was uncovered in time. Tejero and Sáenz de Ynestrillas were arrested, but nothing was done to prevent activities linked to the projected coup. Many officers and the intelligence services knew about the plot but did not report it, preferring to wait and see what would happen. Tejero's apparent impunity fed the belief that he and his ilk were immune from investigation. Moreover, out of fear, the entire political spectrum, including the government, increasingly deferred to the military hierarchy.[71]

Talk of military coups did not deter ETA-M from increasing attacks on policemen and Civil Guards. Accordingly, the referendum was held on 6 December in a spirit of trepidation. Nevertheless, despite national abstention levels of 32.3 per cent, the result was a clear popular ratification of the Constitution.[72] The abstentions were a symptom of the growing disenchantment with politics. The government was concerned by the results in Euskadi, with 51.1 per cent abstentions and 23.5 per cent negative votes of those who did vote. In many places to have voted at all risked denunciation of collaboration with the central government. Nevertheless, the 76.5 per cent of affirmative votes undermined ETA claims that Euskadi had rejected the Constitution.[73] It remained the case that the government needed rapidly to draft a satisfactory autonomy statute for Euskadi. To get parliamentary authority for such a course, Suárez called general elections for 1 March 1979. The campaign took place in an atmosphere of tension racked up by the activities of ultra-right *golpistas* and by ETA attacks on policemen, Civil Guards and army officers. Popular disillusionment was reflected in a high abstention rate. Nevertheless, the UCD won thanks to the support of the Church hierarchy and Suárez's skilful appeal to the fear vote by exploiting the PSOE's self-definition as a Marxist party.[74]

Suárez's attacks accelerated a process whereby the PSOE ditched Marxism, consolidated the leadership of Felipe González and acknowledged that the immediate priority had to be winning elections and not the establishment of socialism. Suárez's electoral triumph was followed by an inexorable decline. The UCD achieved poor results in the municipal elections of 3 April 1979 whereas the PSOE and the PCE gained control of twenty-seven provincial capitals, representing 10.5 million people. In contrast, the UCD won only twenty-three, representing just 2.5 million people. When Suárez presented his programme of government in the Cortes, his prestige was badly damaged by Felipe González's quotation of pro-Franco speeches he had made as Secretary General of the Movimiento.[75] Suárez's new cabinet had neither the drive nor the imagination to resolve the problems of regional autonomy, terrorism, unemployment and military subversion. An impression of incapacity was created by the departure of major figures like Rodolfo Martín Villa, exhausted after three years at the Ministry of the Interior. Moreover, Suárez was increasingly absent as a result of an acute dental problem. Terrorism, crime and military subversion filled the newspapers on most days. ETA-M was more committed to violence than ever and the ultras were more dominant in the army, and especially in the intelligence services and key units such as the DAC.[76]

Disenchantment with Suárez intensified as a result of his failure to solve the overwhelming political and economic problems that beset

Spain. His many difficulties were exacerbated by the UCD's lack of an overall majority in the Cortes, which was constantly endangered by its fragile unity. The ideological differences between the various component groups of 1977's cynical electoral coalition were beginning to come to the surface.[77] ETA attacks on senior military personnel and atrocities by agents provocateurs such as GRAPO were provoking increasingly vociferous calls for a coup. The response of the government was generally one of appeasement of the military ultras. The exceptions, which intensified the fury of the ultras, were the appointments of the liberal José Gabeiras Montero as Chief of the General Staff of the army and Guillermo Quintana Lacaci as Captain General of Madrid.[78] Negotiations for a Basque autonomy statute saw Suárez trapped between the aspirations of the *abertzales* and the hostility of the ultras. In the event, a text was agreed with the majority Partido Nacionalista Vasco and then approved by a Basque referendum on 25 October 1979.[79] Although this justified a hope for peace, ETA-M remained active and popular support for its actions was generated by the campaign of ultra-rightist terror squads, often involving off-duty policemen and Civil Guards.[80]

It was hardly surprising that the most senior right-wing generals, including Milans del Bosch and Jesús González del Yerro, Captain General of the Canary Islands, were openly denouncing the democratic regime as responsible for terrorism, insecurity, inflation, unemployment and pornography.[81] Planning had begun for a coup involving the key Madrid-based unit, the Brunete Armoured Division. The DAC was commanded by an ultra, General Luis Torres Rojas, who mounted manoeuvres to practise seizing the nerve centres of Madrid and controlling the main access roads.[82] Torres Rojas was involved in plans for the Brigada Paracaidista (Parachute Brigade) of Alcalá de Henares, known as the BRIPAC, to seize the Moncloa Palace with helicopter support while armoured vehicles of the DAC neutralized the capital. The plotters could not raise sufficient support for such a scheme and, on 24 January 1980, Torres was merely removed from command of the DAC and sent to be Military Governor of La Coruña.[83] The government thus continued to massage the military ego. The trial of the Galaxia conspirators in early May saw Tejero and the newly promoted Major Sáenz de Ynestrillas sentenced to only seven and six months' detention respectively. Taking into account time served while awaiting trial, this ensured their immediate release. A greater encouragement for plotters could hardly have been imagined.

Forced in on himself by his dental agonies, Suárez's popularity was being diminished by the attrition of terrorism, street crime, inflation and unemployment. Moreover, his inactivity and isolation were under relentless attack from the PSOE in the Cortes and the press.[84] In private, the Socialists were negotiating with the Social Democrat wing of UCD led by Fernández Ordóñez. The possibility of their departure was merely one symptom of the UCD's fragmenting unity. The four main groups within UCD – Christian Democrats, ex-Movimiento bureaucrats associated with Rodolfo Martín Villa, Social Democrats and Liberals under Joaquín Garrigues – were divided on a range of social, economic and religious issues. As Suárez's popularity declined, they wondered if they might not survive better without him. Fernández Ordóñez was reconsidering his future. The Christian Democrats, the most coherent UCD component group, wanted the party to be more openly conservative and confessional and opposed Suárez's projected divorce reform.[85] Internal divisions, government impotence and poorly planned campaigns contributed to a series of damaging electoral reverses for UCD in Andalusia, the Basque Country, Catalonia and Galicia.[86]

UCD's popular support was crumbling with nearly half its voters in 1979 declaring that they would not vote again for the party. Rising unemployment and energy restrictions added to the ongoing tensions of a system beset by fears of Basque terrorism and military subversion. The widespread sense of *desgobierno*, of not being governed at all, was exacerbated by Suárez's infrequent appearances in the Cortes, at press conferences and even at cabinet meetings. He retreated into the Moncloa Palace, screened from the real political world, and even from his own party colleagues, by an inner circle of advisers known as the *fontaneros* (plumbers).[87] By the spring of 1980, internal dissent in the party was impossible to conceal. The new cabinet announced on 2 May excluded Garrigues's Liberals and Fernández Ordóñez's Social Democrats. The Christian Democrats were now the dominant faction. UCD barely survived a PSOE censure motion in a televised Cortes debate between 28 and 30 May in which Felipe González shone as a viable presidential candidate.[88]

The 'barons' or faction leaders were plotting to replace Suárez. He headed off the threat temporarily by granting them more control of policy. However, internal divisions saw the loss of his greatest ally, Abril Martorell, who resigned in the summer.[89] By the autumn of 1980, Suárez found himself isolated from his cabinet, his party and the press, facing the outright hostility of Felipe González and unable to deal with rapidly rising unemployment. ETA-M's determination to see Navarre incorporated into Euskadi constituted a declaration of war on the army. Military subversion had been kept at boiling point throughout the spring and summer of 1980 by the attempts of both ETA-M and GRAPO to assassinate senior generals.[90]

In a last bid to regain control of his party, on 9 September, Suárez reshuffled his cabinet to create a 'government of the barons'. He secured the temporary loyalty of some of them. However, the appointment of Francisco Fernández Ordóñez as Minister of Justice with responsibility for Church–state relations, alienated the Christian Democrats because of his commitment to divorce reform. Moreover, the loss of Abril Martorell, previously his parliamentary shield, exposed Suárez to attacks in the Cortes. Without Abril as fireman, according to José Oneto, 'the fire soon reached the very gates of the palace'.[91] Meetings with González, on 1 October, with Carrillo, on 6 October, and with the Basque Lendakari, Carlos Garaicoetxea, on 12 October, led to hopes that Suárez was about to achieve a new Moncloa Pact.[92] However, the flames were being fanned by ETA attacks and military conspiracy. Suarez's rally had come too late.

The situation soon began to worsen inexorably. Conspiracy in the army was taking place almost openly. The right-wing press was speculating about the most suitable military candidates to form a government. On 17 October, twenty-six of the most prominent ultras in Spain met in Madrid to discuss finance and civilian support for a coup. There was talk about 'Operation De Gaulle', a veiled reference to the activities of General Alfonso Armada, the one-time head of the King's Military Household. Now Military Governor of Lérida, he was seeking support for a non-violent substitution of UCD by a government of national salvation under his own presidency. On 22 October, at a lunch in the home of the Socialist Alcalde of Lérida, Antoni Ciurana, Armada broached the idea with Enrique Múgica of the PSOE and Joan Raventós of the PSC. Felipe González was immediately informed and passed on the information to Suárez. On 17 November, insinuating that he was acting under instructions from the King, Armada spoke in similar terms to Milans del Bosch.[93]

Suárez was paralysed as Socialist hostility intensified. On 23 October, forty-eight children and three adults were killed in an accidental propane-gas explosion at the village school of Ortuella in Vizcaya and three Basque UCD members were assassinated by an ETA-M offshoot. Suárez responded with apparent indifference. He remained coldly in the Moncloa Palace, made no parliamentary statement about either the disaster or the terrorist attacks and neither visited the stricken village nor attended the funerals of his party colleagues.[94] Moreover, the murders were followed by more mindless violence in the Basque Country. On 31 October, ETA-Político-Militar (ETA-PM) murdered another UCD member and, on 3 November, ETA-M killed four Civil Guards and a Partido Nacionalista Vasco (PNV) member and wounded six other customers in a bar in Zarauz. Again, Suárez did not attend the funerals. In fact, the violence of the autumn of 1980 was finally provoking an anti-ETA reaction in the Basque Country itself. On 9 November, a silent all-party demonstration of 30,000 marched through San Sebastián, local PSOE, UCD and PNV leaders linking arms. Increasing numbers of businessmen were also refusing to pay the 'revolutionary tax' demanded by ETA. Awareness that ETA's assault on Spain's democratic regime had to be countered before it was too late led to the establishment of a Basque Peace Front involving the PSOE, the PCE, moderate Basque parties, UCD and the Carlists. However, this tentative beginning did little to diminish military dissent.[95]

The Turkish military coup of 12 September was greeted with envious enthusiasm by groups of officers. This led to press talk of the 'Turkish temptation' and the 'Ankara syndrome'.[96] It worried both Manuel Fraga and Felipe González, who informed the King of their readiness to join in a caretaker coalition government in circumstances of extreme gravity. They saw it as a sacrifice that might have to be made to forestall a full-scale coup.[97] Suárez was concerned by speculation about a broad coalition under Armada or his friend Alfonso Osorio who had already broached the idea of a strong all-party government with key members of the PSOE, with his fellow UCD Christian Democrats and even with Jaime Ballesteros of the PCE. Given both alarming rumours about a violent coup of the colonels and Suárez's incapacity to resolve the problems of ETA and unemployment, a coalition led by a general began to seem almost an attractive option.[98]

In this context, UCD was a cauldron of intrigue. Suárez was under attack from the Christian Democrats who were also in collusion with Fraga's Alianza Popular. On 12 January 1981, Landelino Lavilla, in a devastating and widely publicized newspaper interview, accused Suárez of accumulating and misusing arbitrary power. A showdown was expected at the second congress of UCD, scheduled to be held in Mallorca on 29 January.[99] Physically and psychologically exhausted after the travails of the previous four and a half years, over the weekend of 24–25 January 1981 Suárez decided to resign. He knew that seventeen senior generals had met on 23 January to discuss a military intervention in politics and that the King had been sufficiently alarmed to curtail a hunting trip. Victory at the congress could gain him only a brief respite. With his party crumbling, he had no stomach for a coalition government. Moreover, opinion poll figures gave him only 26 per cent of popular support as against 43 per cent for Felipe González. Concluding that there was no alternative, he planned to announce his resignation at the party congress.[100]

When an air controllers' strike saw the congress postponed, Suárez informed his cabinet, the party leadership and the King and then announced his departure in a television broadcast on 29 January. The ultra-right was jubilant. Juan Carlos was kept aware of the anti-democratic sentiment in the army by his one-time mentor Armada, among others. Nevertheless, like Suárez, the King was anxious to avoid military intervention against the democratic regime.[101] There were widespread rumours in Madrid about two possibilities – a softer option, the plan for a coalition government under Armada, and a hard-line Turkish-style coup of the colonels.[102] Suárez's ignominious decline, the deterioration of his image, his unease in parliament and his retreat behind a bodyguard of *fontaneros* should not obscure his achievements. Despite all the problems that he had inherited, between 1977 and 1980 he had contributed substantially to the creation of a constitutional democracy, the nurturing of parliamentary coexistence and the concession of regional autonomy. Whatever his shortcomings, Suárez's honourable place in the history of Spanish democracy was assured.

On the other hand, his departure could not stop the fragmentation of the UCD. Since the competing 'barons' neutralized one another, his successor was the cabinet Vice-President, Leopoldo Calvo Sotelo. His wide banking contacts and administrative competence made him a reasonable compromise candidate.[103] However, he still faced internal plotting and army readiness to intervene in politics. This was intensified when Juan Carlos and Queen Sofia made a conciliatory visit to the Basque Country from 3 to 5 February. The trip was seriously marred by desultory anti-Spanish demonstrations at Vitoria airport and in the Basque parliament, the Casa de Juntas in Guernica. The King handled with great dignity and aplomb disruptions to his speech by members of the *abertzale* party, Herri Batasuna. His response had an enormously favourable impact on Basque opinion. However, the insult to the supreme commander of the army inflamed the *golpistas*.[104]

Two kidnappings by ETA exacerbated the situation. That of the wealthy industrialist Luis Súñer was for the purpose of extortion. The other was of José María Ryan, the chief engineer at the Lemoniz nuclear power station. Denouncing the power station as a symbol of Spanish exploitation, ETA-M demanded that it be demolished. International appeals and mass demonstrations for Ryan's release were ignored and he was murdered on 6 February. Protests against ETA's actions saw a general strike and mass demonstrations in Euskadi.[105] As ETA-M seems to have hoped, Ryan's murder provoked ultra-rightist fury in the army. It was expressed in an inflammatory article by the retired General Fernando de Santiago y Díaz de Mendívil. Under the headline 'Situación Límite' (This Cannot Go On), he railed against the state's impotence in the face of the long list of ETA kidnappings and assassinations. He cited growing electoral abstention as evidence that the people had rejected the *contubernio politico* (the politics of intrigue) and wanted the army to save Spain.[106]

Since mid-December 1980, *El Alcázar* had been publishing virtually open appeals for a military coup under the byline of 'Almendros' (almonds), a hint that something was being plotted for the second half of February when the almond tree normally blossoms. As well as staff of the newspaper, the 'Almendros' collective included several well-known ultra officers including General Santiago and Colonel San Martín, now Chief of Staff at the DAC. The group was supported by influential civilian ultras, including Girón de Velasco and Juan García Carrés. They hoped for a coup more openly Francoist than either Armada's soft option or the 'Turkish' plans of the colonels. These hopes were pinned on Milans del Bosch.[107] Military conviction about government helplessness was not diminished by the UCD Congress which eventually took place in Palma de Mallorca on 6 February. Out of government, Suárez no longer had the resources of patronage, nor perhaps the will, to keep his loose coalition together. Deep division was evident. The Christian Democrats wanted to push UCD into a more confessional and reactionary direction against the more reformist views of the party apparatus. The fragility of party unity merely inflamed military suspicions of the government's impotence.[108]

Calvo Sotelo faced the Cortes for the formal investiture procedure on 20 February amid deafening rumours of a coup. The suspicious death in police custody of the Etarra Joseba Iñaki Arregui Izaguirre negated the anti-ETA sentiment provoked by Ryan's murder and set off vehement anti-Spanish demonstrations. It also deprived Calvo Sotelo of the votes of the PNV. He gained a simple majority of 169 votes to 158 against and 17 abstentions but not the overall majority of 176 votes necessary to confirm him as President.[109] He was now obliged to wait two days for a second vote for which only a simple majority was required. The voting had just begun on 23 February when, at 6.20 p.m., 320 Civil Guards under Colonel Tejero burst into the chamber and, claiming to be acting in the name of the King, held the entire political class hostage. Tejero telephoned the headquarters of Milans del Bosch and confirmed that the objective had been achieved. He announced to the chamber that a senior military personality would shortly arrive to take control.[110]

Shortly after Tejero reached the Cortes, Milans del Bosch declared a state of emergency in the Valencian region, put public service personnel under military command, imposed a 9.00 p.m. curfew and banned all political activities. Tanks took up positions alongside important public buildings. There were troop movements in various parts of Spain. In Madrid, for instance, the broadcasting studios at Prado del Rey were briefly taken over by a unit from the DAC. They insisted that the radio broadcast only military marches. The *éminence grise* behind all this was General Armada who, in his role as second-in-command of the General Staff, was ostensibly working to make Tejero release the Cortes deputies. In fact, Armada was playing a risky game, exploiting the fanatical Tejero to implement his own De Gaulle-style government of national salvation. To end the dangerous situation in the Cortes, he would make the 'patriotic sacrifice' of forming a government without ever seeming to have played any part in initiating the coup.

The coup would fail because the decisive action of the King and his close collaborators exposed the ambiguities and inadequate preparations of the plotters. The three main conspiracies simmering throughout 1980 had come together in a rashly precipitate manner. Milans and the DAC colonels planned a Turkish-style coup with a brutal purge of the left, a 'dirty war' against ETA and a return to rigid centralism. Their hopes of royal approval led to the link-up with Armada who wanted to use the threat of the colonels to blackmail the political class into supporting his plan for an all-party government of national salvation. The conviction of both Tejero and Milans that they would enjoy the King's approval can only have come from Armada.[111]

The coup was dismantled by a triumvirate of the King himself, the Secretary General of the royal household, General Sabino Fernández Campos, and the new Director General of Security, Francisco Laína García. They were backed by the Chief of the Army General Staff, General José Gabeiras Montero, the Captain General of Madrid, Guillermo Quintana Lacaci, the Inspector General of the Police, General José Sáenz de Santamaría and the Director General of the Civil Guard, General José Aramburu Topete. A provisional government consisting of the under-secretaries of each ministry was established under the direction of Laína in the Ministry of the Interior. Juan Carlos and his aides engaged in a battle by telephone to secure the loyalty of the captains general of the other military regions. Most were sympathetic to Milans, and only the King stood between Spanish democracy and its destruction. The task of the King's team in the Zarzuela was hindered by the complex game that Armada was playing.

It turned out that Armada was in fact the 'senior military personality' that Tejero had been waiting for. Armada entered the Cortes at 12.30 on the morning of the 24th and spoke to Tejero for about three-quarters of an hour. He wanted to propose his government of national salvation to the hijacked deputies who were then to put this 'constitutional solution' to the King. Tejero wanted a Pinochet-style junta to crush the left and revoke regional autonomies and so he angrily rejected the idea of a coalition government with Felipe González as Vice-President and a Communist, Jordi Solé Tura, as Minister of Labour – which suggests that he had not been privy to Armada's intentions. In any case, the coup began to falter when Juan Carlos appeared on television at 1.15 a.m. on 24 February and announced that the crown opposed any attempt to overthrow by force the democratically ratified Constitution. When the King informed Milans that he opposed the coup, that he would not abdicate nor leave Spain and that to succeed the rebels would have to shoot him, Milans withdrew his troops from the streets at 4 a.m.[112] Tired and frustrated, Tejero finally negotiated his surrender with Armada, who was himself arrested some days later.[113]

The events of 23 February have generated immense amounts of speculation and controversy. The biggest issue has concerned the role of Juan Carlos. There are many, including myself, who regard him as having put his prestige and personal safety on the line to save democracy.[114] Others have accused him of collusion in a coup being prepared by the CESID to frighten the political class into accepting a coalition government under the presidency of Armada. The King was certainly conscious of both the military discontent generated by the Basque issue and public disenchantment with the economic situation and the UCD's apparent inability to deal with the nation's problems. It is also probable that he had some inkling of what was being prepared by Armada and Milans and that his silence about it may have encouraged subversion. However, even if all that is true, it did not constitute active complicity. The objective of a coalition government led by Armada could easily have been achieved legally when Suárez resigned. After all, the proposed ministers in the cabinet list shown by Armada to Tejero in the Cortes had already expressed a willingness to serve. That being the case, it is difficult to see how a military coup, with all the negative consequences for Spain's international position, could have benefited Juan Carlos.[115]

The investiture of Calvo Sotelo was approved on the next day by 186 votes to 158. On 27 February, 3 million people demonstrated in favour of democracy in Madrid and other cities, albeit not in the Basque Country. The defeat of the so-called Tejerazo or 23-F did not resolve the democratic regime's difficulties but it did offer a second chance. When Juan Carlos received the main political leaders on the evening of 24 February, he pointed out it should not have been necessary for him to risk his prestige and safety. The emollient response to military subversion taken by Spain's political class in general and the UCD in particular had misfired. After the achievements of the period 1976–9, Suárez's various governments had been incapable of dealing with inflation, unemployment, terrorism and military subversion.

Calvo Sotelo's first cabinet distributed power evenly within UCD. However, wide, and ultimately fatal, divisions soon appeared, derived from the hostility of the Christian Democrats to Fernández Ordóñez's commitment to legalizing divorce. In the short term, the main priority had to be the elimination of *golpismo*, a task entrusted to the new Minister of Defence, Alberto Oliart Saussol. In the aftermath of the events of 23 February, the King had warned the leaders of the parliamentary groups that a harsh response would risk a military backlash. However, Oliart's approach was so conciliatory as to generate a suspicion that Armada had succeeded, in that the military authorities were now a kind of government in the shadows.[116]

In fact, the coup had some inadvertently positive outcomes. The Spanish people began to revalue their democratic institutions. Calvo Sotelo was more approachable than Suárez and appeared more frequently in parliament and before the press. He also consulted regularly with the leaders of the other parties and with senior generals. González, Fraga and Carrillo reciprocated and supported the government in the Cortes. ETA-PM announced an indefinite ceasefire. The revelation of the readiness of Tejero, Milans and others to resort to bloodshed together with the scale of Spain's massive economic problems terminated the euphoric expectations of 1977–9. Democracy was now seen as a deadly serious business. However, Calvo Sotelo's ability to take advantage of the new spirit of national cooperation was fatally undermined by the divisions in the UCD and the uninspiring nature of his policies: entry into NATO, reduction of public expenditure, more private investment, wage restraint, a revamped anti-terrorist campaign and a slowing down of progress towards regional autonomy. This was enshrined in the notorious Organic Law on the Harmonization of the Autonomy Process (Ley Orgánica de Armonización del Proceso Autonómico, or LOAPA) of 29 September 1981 which granted the military one of its principal aspirations.[117]

The government was pushing for entry into NATO in the hope that integration into the Western defence system would divert the armed forces from their obsession with domestic politics. The PSOE opposed entry and many officers who welcomed access to modern weaponry in NATO were unhappy with what they saw as UCD's humiliating readiness to join without adequate recognition of what Spain would bring to NATO.[118] However, the sense that democracy was under military surveillance was intensified when many of the minor participants in the 23-F were released throughout March and April. The more prominent conspirators were being kept in extremely comfortable conditions. The attempted coup was openly justified in *El Alcázar*.[119] Fear of military subversion was fuelled by the continuing terrorist activities of ETA-M and the provocations of GRAPO.[120]

Mass anxiety was kept at fever pitch by numerous incidents, including the seizure by armed men (rumoured to be Civil Guards) of the Banco Central in Barcelona. They demanded the release of Tejero and other participants in the 23-F coup. The bank was finally liberated by special forces.[121] Concerns were raised that only 32 of the nearly 300 officers involved in the coup were to be tried. Moreover, attempts were made to undermine faith in the King and the political class by means of claims about their alleged complicity in the coup. Then, on 21 June, two colonels were arrested for trying to organize another coup.[122] A further blow to the government was a scandal concerning public health. Since early May, forty-eight people, including several children, had died from a mysterious illness diagnosed as 'atypical pneumonia'. Over 8,000 more were in hospital suffering from appallingly painful symptoms. The cause of the epidemic was rapeseed oil which had been adulterated with industrial oil and various chemicals to make it smell like olive oil and then sold from street stalls. The Ministry of Agriculture had ignored warnings about the illegal cooking oil. Spain's limited consumer-protection laws and the lack of action by the Ministry of Health led to a wave of public hostility against the government.[123]

Alarming details emerged of the plot uncovered in June. A bombing campaign was meant to culminate in the bloody disruption of a huge Catalanist rally scheduled to take place in Barcelona on 23 June at the Nou Camp football stadium. Simultaneously, the King would be seized and forced to abdicate. A military junta would be established. Blacklists of democrats to be liquidated had been drawn up.[124] Calvo Sotelo's problems were mounting as UCD's post-Tejerazo unity began to fragment. As the Christian Democrats moved further towards an understanding with Fraga's Alianza Popular, Fernández Ordóñez's Social Democrats left UCD and joined the PSOE in November.[125] The decline of UCD was exposed at the regional elections in Galicia on 20 October when it suffered a massive loss of votes. The PSOE was surging ahead with Felipe González topping opinion polls as Spain's most popular leader.[126]

The PSOE's standing as a responsible opposition was enhanced by its exposure of the government's inept handling of the rapeseed-oil scandal in which the death toll had reached over 130. The PSOE's anti-NATO campaign also enhanced its popularity. Moreover, the PSOE was unchallenged to the left because Carrillo's Communist Party was embroiled in its own internal bloodletting.[127] Throughout November, UCD was playing out its death agony.[128] As the party crumbled, the Minister of Defence, Alberto Oliart, gave a lamentable display of sycophancy towards the military hard-liners. During preparations for the trial of those involved in the February coup, outbursts against the King went unpunished. Senior officers of questionable loyalty were promoted and Milans del Bosch was awarded a medal for 'sufferings for the Fatherland'. The signatories of the 'Almendros' articles issued a manifesto denouncing the Constitution. This was believed to be part of ongoing efforts to resuscitate the colonels' plot or else force the appointment of a coalition government, similar to that proposed by Armada, to be led by General González del Yerro.[129]

Renewed talk of *golpismo* coincided in early 1982 with a massive extortion campaign launched by ETA-M that generated a wave of outrage within the Basque Country. And all the while the UCD continued to crumble with ever more frequent desertions.[130] Ironically, constant military subversion and ETA terrorism were changing the popular mood. Confidence in the King and in Spain's democratic institutions was inadvertently consolidated by the *golpistas* during the trial that began on 19 February and dominated the media for the next three and a half months.[131] The defendants revealed themselves to be ill-mannered bullies whose arrogance and moral bankruptcy provoked public dismay. Despite the efforts of *El Alcázar* to present the proceedings as a trial of the entire army, many officers were disgusted by the efforts of the defendants to shift the blame for 23-F onto the King.[132] As a concession to military sensibilities, they were tried by court martial rather than by a civilian court. Although it had not been the intention, this forestalled any claim that the entire military estate was being tried by civil society. After the trial, anti-democratic declarations which previously had enjoyed silent approbation if not open admiration were now more likely to draw severe rebukes from the military authorities. The change in attitudes was also the fruit of the promotions policy initiated by General Gutiérrez Mellado.

Calvo Sotelo's position was deteriorating by the day. ETA-M's extortion campaign and the massive inconvenience caused by its destruction in mid-April of the Madrid telephone exchange augmented a sense of government incapacity. Opinion polls showed that the PSOE would easily win the next general elections. Elections to the Andalusian parliament on 23 May saw the PSOE win 52 per cent of the vote and sixty-six seats. Alianza Popular came second with seventeen seats and UCD trailed in third with only fifteen.[133] Torn apart by recriminations, the UCD was in its death throes. The banks were treating UCD with a growing coolness and pumping money into Alianza Popular which was enjoying a recruiting boom of 1,000 new members per week. Calvo Sotelo's position was not helped by the publication on 3 June of the relatively mild sentences on the 23-F plotters. Although Tejero and Milans del Bosch received the maximum possible thirty years, Armada was sentenced to only six. Twenty-two of the thirty-two defendants were condemned to three years or less which permitted them to return to the ranks after they had served their sentences. After a government appeal to the Supreme Court, the sentences would be substantially increased, most notably in the case of Armada. However, at the time, a stunned political class perceived the sentences as proof that nothing had changed.[134]

The lugubrious Calvo Sotelo seemed as isolated as Suárez had been in January 1981. During the summer of 1982, his popularity plummeted as that of both Fraga and González rocketed. By refraining from trying to force early elections and stressing that the PSOE's mission was to ensure the survival of the democratic regime, Felipe González built an image of moderation and strength, gaining in credibility. It was known that he was discussing a possible centre-left coalition with Suárez, who announced his own departure from UCD on 28 June. Calvo Sotelo announced, on 30 July, that he would not be the UCD's presidential candidate in the next elections.[135] In contrast, Felipe González gave the impression of being the future Prime Minister. The self-destruction of the UCD was being matched by that of the PCE. Internal feuding among the Communists had reached such a peak that Carrillo was able to hold on to power by the dangerous gesture of a short-lived resignation on 7 June.[136]

UCD's disarray reached its most dramatic point at the end of July when it began to break up into its component parts. The more conservative Christian Democrats formed the Partido Demócrata Popular and announced an electoral coalition with Fraga. Suárez formed a new party, Centro Democrático y Social, and announced that, after the poll, he would support a Socialist government.[137] A greatly diminished UCD went into elections for which opinion polls predicted a sweeping Socialist

victory, with Alianza Popular also doing well.[138] The PSOE's programme
was moderate, promising to create 800,000 new jobs through state
investment backed by agreement with private enterprise.[139] After the
self-destruction of the centre, the only substantial challenge to the PSOE
came from Fraga's Alianza Popular with a traditionalist conservative
programme of law and order, a free-market economy and defence of the
family and national unity.

On 3 October, news broke of a projected coup scheduled to take place
on the eve of the 28 October elections. Exposed by the military intelligence services, it was a carefully prepared version of the colonels' coup,
inspired by Milans del Bosch. The Zarzuela and Moncloa Palaces, the
headquarters of the Joint Chiefs of Staff, various ministries, key public
buildings, railway stations, airports, radio and television transmitters
and newspaper offices were to be seized and the political elite 'neutralized' in their homes. The King was to be deposed for having betrayed his
oath of loyalty to the Movimiento.[140] The elections took place under the
ongoing threat of military intervention, but the popular vote was a
massive rejection of the *golpistas* and their claim to be doing what was
best for Spain. The Socialists won 10,127,092 votes, 47.3 per cent of those
cast, and 202 seats. Alianza Popular came second with 5,548,335 votes,
25.9 per cent, and 107 deputies. UCD limped home behind the Catalan
Convergencia i Unió with 1,323,339 votes, 6.2 per cent, and 11 deputies.
Calvo Sotelo failed to gain a seat. Although Carrillo was elected, the PCE
dropped from nearly 11 per cent to 3.6 per cent and lost three-quarters
of its deputies.[141]

The decisiveness of the PSOE's victory demolished the pretence that
the army could interpret the national will better than elected politicians.
Nevertheless, the tasks awaiting Felipe González were enormous. The
linked problems of ETA terrorism and military subversion required skill
and authority. Enjoying good relations with moderate Basque forces, the
PSOE had perhaps a better chance of success against ETA than UCD had
ever had. The shrewd and tactful Narcís Serra, as Minister of Defence,
would inaugurate a programme of military modernization, redeploy-
ment and professionalization that would finally eliminate the Third
World *golpista* mentality from the armed forces. The restructuring of
Spanish industry, with its obsolete sectors, its high energy dependence,
its regional imbalances and its technological deficiencies, would require
vision and sacrifice. The same was true of agrarian reform. No one

expected short-term triumphs. However, the fact that the PSOE was prepared to confront tasks shirked by UCD ensured remarkable public tolerance for immediate measures like devaluation of the peseta, tax increases and fuel-price rises. The Socialists had been elected by a serious electorate which had undergone the agonies of terrorism and military conspiracy.

The road from 1969 had been rocky. Nevertheless, despite the hostile context bequeathed by Franco, a constitutional framework and the structures of regional autonomy had been created in a spirit of sacrifice and cooperation. Despite the daunting obstacles of military subversion and ultra-nationalist terrorism, the elections of 28 October 1982 saw the popular will prevail. The transition was over. The political class could now begin to face up to long-term social and economic problems as well as to divisions relating to the legacy of the civil war, the hostilities between Spanish and Catalan nationalism and the continuing scourge of corruption.

The celebration in the Cortes of the 40th anniversary of the Spanish constitution in 2018. Four surviving prime ministers in the front row (from right to left: Felipe González, José María Aznar, José Luis Rodríguez Zapatero and Mariano Rajoy).

17

The Grandeur and Misery of a Newborn Democracy, 1982–2004

A big change would come in terms of external support for Spanish democracy in June 1982 when Spain joined NATO. This held the key to eventual membership of the EEC and indeed to diverting the Spanish military from its obsession with domestic politics. Initially, the PSOE opposed NATO membership, but, once in office, Felipe González did not withdraw Spain from the Atlantic Alliance although he did halt the process of incorporation into the integrated military command. Throughout the year following the attempted coup, the King was the most determined advocate of military discipline just as he was an enthusiast for Spain's entry into the EEC.[1] The era of UCD appeasement of the military – during which the King, as he commented bitterly, had had to be called out regularly as a 'fireman' – came to an end with the elections of 28 October 1982. The Socialists won 47.3 per cent of the vote and 202 of the 350 seats in parliament, the largest majority ever gained by any party. In total, Felipe González would win four general elections, in 1982, 1986, 1989 and 1993, the first three of which were with overall majorities.

Despite the scale of the Socialist victory, Felipe González still faced enormous difficulties. It was only six years since his party had been legalized and three since dropping its Marxist label. His government inherited a state apparatus and an economy both in urgent need of reform. González had reached power by ditching aspirations for a Socialist transformation in favour of pragmatism or, as it has been called, 'coming to terms with reality'.[2] Both he and Alfonso Guerra believed that the survival of democracy required a readiness to introduce austerity policies and even to tolerate Francoist survivals. Thus there would be no judicial investigations into, or punishment of, the illegality of the 1936 military coup or the atrocities of the Francoist repression. The senior staff of the army and the security forces were still mainly Francoists. Accordingly, the Socialists' pragmatism led them to go along with the policies of their predecessors and acquiesce in state terrorism against ETA, a dirty war that would be one of the factors that would eventually bring them down. Nevertheless, the consolidation of democracy in Spain after the elections of 1982 would see a long list of achievements, especially in terms of the control of military subversion and economic reform.

Reform required vision and sacrifice. Unemployment was unacceptably high at 16 per cent and inflation at 14 per cent. The conservative policies of the Minister of Finance, Miguel Boyer, saw the peseta devalued by 8 per cent, monetary policy tightened and the trade unions obliged to limit wage demands. Most of Spain's heavy industry was uncompetitive, much of it belonging to Franco's massive autarkic state holding company, the Instituto Nacional de Industria. A process of industrial reconversion lifted the dead hand of INI through the privatization of some public companies and the closure of others. The equally conservative Minister of Industry, Carlos Solchaga, proceeded to dispose of loss-making divisions, including the car-maker SEAT, sold to Volkswagen. The dramatic process of deindustrialization included the closure of Altos Hornos, and various other steel-producing works in the Basque Country, in Cantabria, Asturias, Galicia and Valencia which led to the loss of half a million jobs with the attendant social costs. The ending of paternalistic practices inherited from the Francoist Movimiento to make the labour market more flexible led to an increase in unemployment within three years to 21.5 per cent and a fall in inflation to 8.8 per cent. When the Socialists left power in 1996, inflation was approaching 2 per cent but unemployment remained above 20 per cent.[3]

Nevertheless, over the first three years of Socialist government, exports rose and foreign investment increased. Growth rates between 1986 and 1990 hovered around 5 per cent, well in excess of the rates being recorded by other members of the European Economic Community. Carlos Solchaga, now Minister of Economy and Finance, boasted in 1988 that 'Spain is the country in Europe and perhaps in the world where the most money can be made in the shortest time.' He was inadvertently endorsing the ubiquity of rapid, and often corrupt, profit that went with speculation, later called 'sleaze culture'.[4] Economic success had been consolidated by Spain's incorporation into the EEC in January 1986. Since that success had been facilitated by membership of NATO, the issue of Socialist opposition to the Atlantic Alliance had to be resolved. In accordance with a pledge made in the 1982 election campaign, a referendum was held on 12 March 1986. Not without internal frictions, the PSOE campaigned for a 'yes' vote with the slogan 'NATO in Spain's interests'. On a turnout of 59.4 per cent, the vote to remain in NATO won by 53 per cent to 40.3 per cent. The highest share of 'no' votes, 67.6 per cent, was recorded in the Basque Country. Felipe González seized the opportunity to bring forward to 22 June the elections scheduled for late November. With 184 seats, eighteen fewer than in 1982, the PSOE still had a comfortable absolute majority.[5]

As well as increasing foreign trade and investment, EEC membership brought other benefits. The establishment of the EEC's cohesion fund in December 1992, designed to bring the economies of the poorer countries up to the EEC average, and the influx of structural funds saw a transformation of the Spain's transport infrastructure in terms of road networks, airports and the introduction of a high-velocity railway system. However, it also facilitated corrupt profiteering. Economic success was to go into decline from 1993 as austerity measures were applied. Moreover, Spain was bedevilled by a level of corruption that involved virtually every institution in the country from the monarchy, via all the principal political parties, the banks and employers' organizations, to the trade unions and local administrations. Under the Socialists, public spending almost doubled. In part, this was as a result of a 40 per cent increase in public sector employment. Around 70 per cent of party members and sympathizers were rewarded with some of the 500,000 jobs created between 1982 and 1994. This practice fed on, and consolidated, the belief that private benefit could be derived from public service.[6] Spending also grew between 1982 and 1996 as a result of successful efforts to improve on the Francoist state's exiguous welfare provision. This was particularly true in health care, pensions and education.[7]

Unfortunately, the successes of the Socialists would be undermined by two major problems – terrorism and corruption. The previous resort by UCD, and now the Socialists, to the unreformed security forces, particularly the Civil Guard, saw no let-up in ETA hostility to the central state. In response to ETA assassinations, UCD had permitted the use of right-wing death squads with links to the security services on both sides of the French–Basque frontier. Made up of French, Italian and Argentinian rightists as well as mercenary killers, they used a variety of names of which the most common was the Batallón Vasco Español. The Socialist Minister of the Interior, José Barrionuevo, and his Secretary of State for Security, Rafael Vera, retained officers from the Francoist secret police. Between October 1983 and July 1987, they used government slush funds to finance these groups now operating as the Grupos Antiterroristas de Liberación (GAL). The murders of twenty-seven ETA activists in the French Basque Country were aimed at forcing the French authorities to clamp down on ETA's safe havens in the area. On 4 December 1983, the GAL mistakenly kidnapped Segundo Marey, an innocent French citizen unconnected to ETA. The operation was eventually revealed to have had the complicity of Vera and Julián Sancristóbal, the Civil Governor of Vizcaya, and was run by a Francoist police superintendent, José Amedo Fouce. After dogged investigation by the examining magistrate, Baltasar Garzón, into the financing of the GAL and its activities, including the kidnapping of Marey, Barrionuevo, Vera, Sancristóbal and Amedo would all be imprisoned. The political scandal surrounding the GAL and government complicity strengthened anti-Madrid sentiment in the Basque Country and did immense damage to Felipe González. He always rebutted insinuations that he might have been 'Señor X', the person suspected, but not named, by Garzón as the authority that had sanctioned the GAL. His widely reported comment that 'the rule of law has also to be defended in the sewers' did nothing to stifle rumours.[8]

An early example of corruption arose when, to alleviate rural underemployment, benefits were increased and subsidies under the Plan de Empleo Rural (PER) were introduced. This encouraged fraud, of which a characteristic case was exposed in Pinos Puente, Granada. The Alcalde from 1987 to 1991, Juan Ferrándiz, allegedly opened an account in a local bank in which a deposit of 300 pesetas could purchase the certificate of having worked the sixty days needed to qualify for the 28,000 peseta unemployment benefit under the PER. Between 1988 and 1990, the Ayuntamiento certified that 200,000 days had been worked by 4,000 local residents at a cost to the Instituto Nacional de Empleo of 990 million pesetas. In June 1986, Ferrándiz was sentenced to eighteen months' imprisonment and fined 100,000 pesetas. There were other similar cases.[9]

In Andalusia, where the Socialists governed without interruption until 2018, there were many scandals, but all paled in comparison with the so-called ERE (Expediente de Regulación de Empleo) cases in which nearly 1 billion euros was swindled between 2000 and 2012 from a fund supposedly to assist those faced with redundancy or seeking early retirement. In one notorious example, the retirement sum due one man was calculated on the assumption that he had worked for the same company since the day he was born. Javier Guerrero, Director General of Labour and Social Security of the Junta de Andalucía was at the heart of the racket. His lavish grants included 1.3 million euros to his chauffeur and 430,000 euros to his mother-in-law. However, a further 266 individuals, including two ex-presidents, numerous senior politicians and administrators of the regional government, were accused of involvement in the embezzlement of the ERE funds.[10]

One of the biggest corruption scandals was exposed in 1985. It involved the Catalan financier Javier de la Rosa Martí, a man with a taste for yachts, private planes and luxury cars who belonged to a dynasty of swindlers. His father, Antonio, was in hiding in South America after it was discovered that, between 1975 and 1979, he had embezzled 1.2 billion pesetas through the fictitious purchase of non-existent land for the Consorcio de la Zona Franca of Barcelona, of which he was Secretary. This entity, with funding from the Ayuntamiento and the central government, was embarking on the construction of a major logistics and industrial centre midway between the Barcelona Free Port and the airport. The stolen money was spent on prostitutes and the purchase of a fleet of luxury cars. Javier de la Rosa's son would later be involved in the corrupt dealings of Jordi Pujol, who was President of the Generalitat de Catalunya from 1980 to 2003.[11]

In 1974, a meteoric rise though the financial world had seen Javier de la Rosa become the director of the Banca Garriga Nogués, the investment subsidiary of the Banco Español de Crédito (Banesto). His management of the bank was ruinous, particularly as a result of an investment in Quash-Tierras de Almería, a speculative agro-business. An investigation by Banesto of the Banca Garrigues Nogués in 1988 discovered that there was a black hole of 98,500 million pesetas, sixteen times bigger than the bank's nominal capital.[12] When the bank collapsed, an investigation by the recently installed head of Banesto, Mario Conde, was shelved, allegedly after De la Rosa produced a dossier containing evidence of Conde's own shady business dealings.[13] By that time, De la Rosa had moved on to become the representative in Spain of the Kuwait Investment Office (KIO), buying up a wide range of companies, some profitable in chemicals, fertilizer, paper, food production and real estate, others in crisis, which were then subjected to asset stripping. The resulting conglomerate run by De la Rosa was called Grupo Torras. After Saddam Hussein's invasion of Kuwait in August 1990, a total of 167,000 million pesetas were transferred from Torras to tax havens in Jersey, Gibraltar, the Cayman Islands, Switzerland and Panama. Some 70,000 millions of this money seem to have ended up in accounts belonging to De la Rosa. He later claimed to have given the money to political parties to foster the Kuwaiti cause. The KIO declared that it had invested $5 billion in Torras of which $950 million had been stolen and the rest lost by mismanagement. When the Torras group was declared bankrupt, after the collapse of the holding company Grand Tibidabo which, among other schemes, was behind the amusement park Port Aventura, many thousands of workers lost their jobs and 10,500 shareholders lost their savings. De la Rosa and some members of the Kuwaiti royal family were accused of fraud, the misuse of public funds and the bribery of politicians. In October 1994, De la Rosa was found guilty of fraud, falsification of documents and the theft of 1 billion pesetas from the company Grand Tibidabo. He was jailed but, in February 1995, he was released on bail of 1 billion pesetas.[14]

The stain of corruption would eventually reach the royal family but, in the early years of Socialist rule, the King's popularity would increase despite the continued hostility of ETA and several assassination attempts.[15] The process was helped by visits to the Basque Country and the marriage in Barcelona Cathedral of his daughter Cristina to the Basque handball star Iñaki Urdangarín Liebaert, on 4 October 1997. The wedding, together with the fact that Cristina lived in Barcelona and could speak Catalan, saw 200,000 people in the streets to cheer the couple and their parents.[16] The King's relations with Catalonia, while not without difficulty, were significantly easier than with the Basque Country and were helped by his enthusiastic support for Barcelona's candidacy for the Olympic Games of 1992.[17] Juan Carlos also collaborated fully with Narcís Serra in efforts to resolve the problem of military subversion. At the Pascua Militar celebrations on 6 January 1984, for instance, as supreme commander, he called on the armed forces to remain united and to collaborate 'without doubts or reservations' in the government's military reforms. The following year, he emphasized the advantages of modernization within NATO.[18] With great energy, and the full support of the King, Serra set about incorporating the military administration into the civilian administration of the state. This was facilitated by Spain's membership of NATO, which brought the armed forces into ever more regular contact with the officers of other democratic countries. Serra reduced overmanning in the army, particularly at the highest levels.[19]

In the long term, the military situation was destined to improve massively. Meanwhile, however, during Easter 1985, another reactionary coup, scheduled for 2 June, was deactivated by the main intelligence agency, the Centro Superior de Información de la Defensa (CESID). The plan was for a bomb to be detonated under the podium from which the King would preside at the Day of the Armed Forces celebrations in A Coruña. Had the plot gone ahead, Juan Carlos, Sofía and the Infantas, as well as Felipe González, Narcís Serra, the higher echelons of the armed forces and other invited guests would have been killed. The explosion would then have been attributed to ETA and this would have provided the excuse for the imposition of a military junta. It was the last serious plot against the King.[20]

After victory in 1986, the next elections were not due until July 1990. However, Felipe González brought them forward to October 1989 in response to growing disquiet on several fronts. The most surprising was the dissent between the Socialist government and the UGT. The economic growth of the period from 1985 to 1992 was achieved by the liberalization of the labour market through the closure of obsolete industries, sweeping redundancies with reduced compensation, decreased job security and a wage ceiling. The increase in the minimum pension contributions from ten to fifteen years, delays in the introduction of the forty-hour week and the spread of insecure temporary contracts of employment generated working-class discontent and confrontations between workers and the forces of order. The outright opposition to the government of the head of the UGT, Nicolás Redondo, led to the massive general strike of 14 December 1988 in which the UGT and Comisiones Obreras collaborated to bring out 8 million workers and paralyse the entire country.[21]

The election saw the PSOE win 175 seats, nine fewer than in 1986 and one short of an absolute majority. Felipe González was able to govern as if he had such a majority because the four deputies of Herri Batasuna refused to take up their seats. Alianza Popular had been restructured and renamed Partido Popular (PP) and was now under the leadership of the 43-year-old José María Aznar. Uncharismatic, a poor public speaker, this one-time tax inspector, a Francoist in his youth, was premier of the autonomous region of Castilla-León. The ex-intimate of Fraga and Secretary General of Alianza Popular, Jorge Verstrynge, claimed that he left the PP because Aznar 'increasingly droned on about his conversations with St Teresa of Ávila and ended up dismissing his adversaries as "Jewish dogs"'. Nevertheless, he admired Aznar as a serious and efficient administrator.[22]

The PP won 107 seats, two more than in 1986. The decline of the PSOE's support reflected the clash with the UGT, disquiet over increasing revelations about the GAL and disenchantment over corruption. The deterioration of the PSOE's position would have been worse had it not been for the electorate's reluctance to vote for the Partido Popular, a party perceived as Francoist.[23] Nevertheless, while economic improvements had been achieved at the cost of damaging effects on working-class living standards, huge fortunes were made by individuals such as Mario Conde and Javier de la Rosa in the get-rich-quick culture known as the *pelotazo*. Since this involved some high-profile Socialists, the *pelotazo* undermined the PSOE's popularity.

It would soon get worse as a series of spectacular corruption scandals came to the fore. The case of Juan Guerra, the brother of the deputy Prime Minister, Alfonso, was the first to hit the PSOE directly and was to be the starting pistol that set journalists off to investigate others. When the Socialists came to power, the previously unemployed Juan Guerra was given a modest salary as assistant to Alfonso and the use of his brother's office in the central government's delegation in Seville. The scandal broke in mid-1989 when Juan's deserted wife vengefully revealed to Manuel Fraga that her husband had become an important shareholder in several businesses and had acquired an estate, horses and expensive cars. By the end of the year, the press was full of revelations that he had acted as broker on behalf of companies and individuals seeking contracts, the rezoning of land and/or building licences within the region, the province or various town councils. He was accused of bribery, tax fraud, the peddling of political favours, embezzlement of public funds, money laundering and perverting the course of justice. Although initially deny-ing his brother's wrongdoing, Alfonso was eventually obliged to resign as deputy Prime Minister in January 1991, which marked the beginning of a division between the government and the PSOE. Juan Guerra was initially supported by his party on the grounds that, at least until 1994, he had not been found guilty in a court of law. As is still the case, the judiciary moved extremely slowly and was accused of political interference. Both the Socialist and subsequent Partido Popular governments were able to appoint party sympathizers to leading posts in the Constitutional Court, the Supreme Court and, especially, the General Council of the Judiciary, which has overall responsibility for Spain's legal system. Thus Juan Guerra's relatively easy passage through the courts was associated with the presence of Socialists within the judicial apparatus in the early 1990s. This led to relations between the PSOE and the Partido Popular becoming greatly embittered. However, both the appointment of sympathizers and the device of ensuring that those accused of corruption would not have to admit to political responsibility until criminal charges were resolved would similarly be used by the PP when it came to power.[24]

As well as cases of personal gain, a number of scandals were related to the financing of both the PSOE and the Partido Popular. At the end of May 1991, on the basis of information from a disgruntled ex-employee, *El Mundo* revealed that, between 1988 and 1991, illegal funds in the region of 1 billion pesetas had been channelled through three tiny interconnected front companies known as Filesa, Malesa and Time Export, the latter a company with hardly any staff, bought by Filesa for 400 pesetas. The vast profits from the sale of fictitious consultancy reports for large-scale public and private enterprises including major banks were used to pay for electoral campaign publicity in 1989. It was alleged that Guillermo Galeote, the man in charge of the party's finances, oversaw the operation. In one case, a seventeen-page report produced for a supermarket chain at a cost of $250,000 contained fourteen pages which were merely photocopies of local council planning documents. A six-year investigation followed which culminated in the imprisonment of several senior members of the PSOE.[25] Galeote was not among them but he was obliged to resign as head of the party's finance division 'to avoid damage to the party's image.' In a similar but smaller case, in 1992, it was claimed that, during the negotiation for the high-speed rail link between Madrid and Seville, there had been attempts to swell PSOE funds with commissions from companies bidding for contracts. Julián García Valverde, President of the national railway, RENFE, from 1985 to 1991, and now Minister of Health, was obliged to resign. In fact, he was subsequently absolved of responsibility.[26]

During the lengthy Filesa investigation, key pieces of evidence disappeared. Nevertheless, the detailed accounts had been published by the press. The case did less damage to the PSOE than it might have done because it was preceded by a similar case of illegal financing in the Partido Popular. In April 1990, an investigating magistrate ordered the arrest of several senior members of the Partido Popular including the national treasurer, Rosendo Naseiro, his predecessor, Ángel Sanchís, and a Valencia city councillor, Salvador Palop, who was head of the municipal purchasing committee. They were accused of using inside information provided by Palop to arrange for construction companies to be awarded public works contracts in return for substantial contributions to party funds in the form of anticipated commission on the deals. The racket had come to light as a result of telephone taps in a separate investigation into drug trafficking involving Palop's younger brother Rafael, which had inadvertently exposed this system of party financing in Valencia. However, the case was dismissed because the telephone taps were ruled inadmissible and subsequently destroyed. Although this meant that the PP individuals were not subjected to criminal charges, their political careers were ruined and Aznar's hopes of an early election victory were undermined because the contents of the tapes had long since been revealed in the press. It was never entirely clear how much of the proceeds of the scam actually went to the PP.[27] After a brief spell in prison, Naseiro deposited with a lawyer in Alicante a series of documents that demonstrated the existence of the Partido Popular's slush fund. Among these documents was a sworn statement that every decision that he had taken as treasurer had always been 'under the supervision, instructions and opinions of Don José María Aznar'. Then, from the fax machine in the lawyer's office, he sent copies to Aznar, threatening that they would be published if the party made him the scapegoat in the case.[28]

Among the most shocking revelations of the inadmissible tapes was a conversation, on 11 February 1990, between Palop and Eduardo Zaplana, soon to be President of the PP in Alicante, then progressively Alcalde of Benidorm in 1991, President of the Generalitat of Valencia in 1995 and Minister of Labour in 2002, in Aznar's second government. In a lengthy conversation in which they discussed illegal commissions on property sales, Zaplana admitted to Palop that he needed to get rich because he was spending all his money on his political career: 'I have to get rich. I must earn lots of money. I need lots of money to live. Just now I need to buy a car.'[29] In May 2018, in the so-called Operación Erial, Zaplana was arrested on charges of corruption while he was President of the Generalitat, between 1995 and 2002. This particularly involved rake-offs and fake invoices during the construction of the massive and ultimately failed theme park Terra Mítica. The charges included bribery, perversion of the course of justice, embezzlement of public funds, influence peddling, falsifying documents, money laundering, conspiracy and tax fraud and having money in foreign bank accounts in Andorra, Uruguay and Paraguay.[30]

The UGT was raising money through a cooperative, Promoción Social de Viviendas, ostensibly to build 22,000 cheap homes for union members. It was declared bankrupt in February 1994 after revelations of fraudulent accounting and speculation with the cooperative's funds in unrelated schemes. The UGT Secretary General, Nicolás Redondo, was forced to resign.[31] Such revelations about corruption together with a resurgence of interest in the GAL case gave the impression that the PSOE was rotten. Indeed, when the report on Filesa by the Finance Ministry was published in March 1993, Felipe González was jeered by students at the Universidad Autónoma de Madrid who shouted 'thief' and 'crook' (*chorizo*). The elections of 6 June 1993 were bitterly fought. To counter emerging scandals, the PSOE campaigned on its considerable achievements in power, most recently the Barcelona Olympics and the Universal Exhibition in Seville in 1992, the preparations for which had seen massive investment in the infrastructure of both cities. The Francoist origins of the Partido Popular were also stressed. To convince the electorate that action was being taken against corruption, Baltasar Garzón, the investigating magistrate in the GAL case, was included as an independent among the PSOE candidates. The result saw the PSOE win but lose its absolute majority with 159 seats and 38 per cent of the vote. The surge of PP support to nearly 35 per cent of the vote and 141 seats underlined its position as a serious contender for power.[32]

After the general elections of June 1993, the fourth Socialist government was weakened by the differences between the modernizers of Felipe González in the cabinet and the followers of Alfonso Guerra in the party. The party was also bedevilled by almost daily revelations of corruption involving *los beautiful*, a number of individuals notorious for flaunting their opulent lifestyles, several of whom were associated with the party. These included the former Finance Minister Miguel Boyer who was married to Isabel Preysler, the glamorous and extremely rich ex-wife of the singer Julio Iglesias. Another with links to the Socialist government was the buccaneering President of the Banco Español de Crédito (Banesto), Mario Conde, whose rapid and ruthless rise earned him the nickname of the Shark. In the wake of the Juan Guerra case, revelations in April and May 1994 saw the government undermined by more scandals that led to the resignations of several past or current ministers. The most damaging involved the heads of hitherto highly respected national institutions, Mariano Rubio, the Governor of the Bank of Spain, and Luis Roldán, the first civilian head of the Civil Guard. In the words of Joaquín Leguina, the President of the Comunidad de Madrid, 'the man in charge of the guards fled with the money and the man in charge of the money was in the custody of two guards'. At the ceremony to celebrate the 150th anniversary of the creation of the Civil Guard, González was booed and shouts of 'Chorizo!' were heard.[33]

Rubio served a brief prison sentence for tax fraud and for providing information that facilitated insider trading at Ibercorp investment bank. Also imprisoned was Ibercorp's President, Manuel de la Concha, the former President of the Madrid stock exchange. The beneficiaries of the scam included Miguel Boyer, Isabel Preysler and several leading figures in the world of finance. This led to the resignation of Carlos Solchaga, the government's parliamentary spokesman who, as Minister of Finance, had initially appointed Rubio. It also led to the resignation of Vicente Albero, the Minister of Agriculture, who admitted tax fraud related to his involvement in a racket set up by De la Concha.[34] Almost as sensational was the downfall of Mario Conde. After an emergency audit discovered a 3,000 million euro black hole in Banesto's accounts in December 1993, Mario Conde was arrested and sentenced to twenty years' imprisonment for fraud and embezzlement and ordered to repay 22.6 million euros to the swindled shareholders.[35]

Luis Roldán was a municipal politician from Zaragoza who, with falsified academic qualifications, had risen through the provincial administration and been appointed government delegate to Navarre. In this difficult job, he had endeared himself to the Civil Guard. In

November 1986, he was made Director of the Civil Guard with the mission of modernizing the institution.[36] One of his projects was the refurbishment of Civil Guard barracks. In November 1993, an investigation into his activities by journalists from *Diario 16* revealed that, over the course of seven years, he had accumulated a fortune of 400 million pesetas, a significant property portfolio in Spain and France and a Swiss bank account. The money had come from a variety of sources: kickbacks on the construction of Civil Guard buildings, money paid to non-existent informers, the funds of the Civil Guard's orphans' college, payments from businessmen for non-existent protection from ETA and arms sales in Angola. By early December, Roldán had been dismissed from his post and was under investigation. When he fled Spain in April 1994, the Minister of the Interior, Antoni Asunción, resigned.[37]

In an interview with *El Mundo* in Paris on 29 April, Roldán claimed that the use of slush funds to boost the salaries of senior figures in the Ministry of the Interior had been authorized by the security chief Rafael Vera who, so he said, was one of the principal beneficiaries. He alleged, without proof, that the two Ministers of the Interior before Asunción, José Barrionuevo and José Luis Corcuera, had also taken money from the same sources. Roldán was eventually captured in February 1995, allegedly in Laos but almost certainly in Paris, brought back to Spain and sentenced to thirty-one years in prison for bribery, falsification of documents, misuse of public funds, blackmail and tax fraud. Only around one-third of the stolen money was recovered.[38]

At this point the King's name began to be bandied about. The departure of Sabino Fernández Campo as head of the royal household in January 1993 had removed a barrier between the King and Mario Conde and other jet-set financiers who wanted to exploit royal favour.[39] Along with Mario Conde, another who had tried, without notable success, to get close to the King was Javier de la Rosa. When both Conde and De la Rosa fell foul of the authorities from late 1993 onwards, they seemed to believe, because of their business dealings with Juan Carlos's friend and unofficial ambassador Manuel Prado y Colón de Carvajal, that they could somehow expect royal protection from justice. Their hopes that the King would save them were frustrated. It has been alleged that, after he had been imprisoned for embezzlement, in mid-October 1994, an enraged De la Rosa tried to blackmail Prado y Colón de Carvajal over the missing KIO funds. He backed up his attempts with vague threats of damaging revelations about the King. In 1997, he claimed that he had donated some of the defrauded funds to the Catalan section of the Partido Popular.[40]

After the 1993 elections, hostility between the PSOE and the Partido Popular reached such a point that the next three years of Socialist government came to be known as 'the legislature of endless tension'. Internal unity within the PSOE was consolidated by the absence of Alfonso Guerra and the creation of a strong leadership team with Narcís Serra as Vice-President, Javier Solana as Foreign Minister and Pedro Solbes as Finance Minister. However, José María Aznar was inevitably able to use the resignations of Solchaga, Corcuera, Asunción and Albero to make damaging accusations against the government and demand early elections. His constant attacks bore fruit in the June 1994 European elections which saw the PSOE vote drop to 30.7 per cent from 39.6 per cent in 1989 while the PP vote rose from 21.4 per cent to 40.2 per cent. It was a significant shift in momentum to the PP and it began to look likely that Aznar would form the next government. At the PSOE's annual Jaime Vera Summer School some weeks later, Felipe González accepted that his party's poor results were a reflection of the corruption scandals. In particular, they were an indication of growing public concern about government involvement in the GAL case revealed by documents stolen by the recently dismissed deputy head of the CESID, Colonel Juan Alberto Perote.[41]

After Garzón's 1993 election to the Cortes, he had been made the Socialist drug tsar. However, he resigned in May in protest at the lack of government dynamism in the fight against corruption and returned to investigating the GAL and Roldán cases. He was disappointed not to have been made Minister of Justice in order to supervise the process.[42] The man who did get the job, Juan Alberto Belloch, created, in 1995, the Office for the Prosecution of Corruption and Organized Crime. As Garzón's investigations continued, leaks about the GAL case, in the newspapers *El Mundo* and *ABC*, perhaps did more to harm the government than any of the other scandals. That they coincided with the fraud case against Mario Conde led to suspicions that he was using his wealth to influence the press and blackmail the government. Conde was in contact with the embittered Colonel Perote. The material that he had taken from the CESID included not only classified documents but also tape recordings of telephone conversations with senior members of the government. The timing of press revelations from this material coincided with judicial actions against Conde and Perote and was deeply damaging to the PSOE. Significantly, the editor of *El Mundo*, Pedro J. Ramírez, was in communication with Aznar's future deputy, Francisco Álvarez Cascos. The disclosures provoked the resignations of the head of the CESID, General Emilio Alonso-Manglano, of the deputy Prime Minister, Narcís Serra, who was Minister of Defence when the phone taps were made, and of his successor in the Ministry, Julián García Vargas.[43]

The government also suffered as a result of a sharp economic downturn. The peseta had been devalued three times since June 1992 and unemployment had risen to 23 per cent. Thanks to the influx of funds from the European Union and various structural reforms implemented by Pedro Solbes, the worst of the recession was over by the end of 1994. However, defeats in regional elections in Galicia and in European elections, and a massive rise of the PP votes in many municipalities, indicated that Socialist hegemony was coming to an end. In early 1996, Felipe González was obliged to call elections for 3 March, although they were not due until July 1997. The catalyst came in the autumn of 1995 with the withdrawal, by his coalition partner, Jordi Pujol's Convergència i Unió (CiU), of support for the PSOE's budget proposals for the following year. The PSOE narrowly lost the election, with 37.6 per cent of the votes and 141 Cortes seats as against the PP's 38.8 per cent and 156 seats, which was still twenty short of an absolute majority. The PSOE's credibility had been seriously undermined by the involvement of party figures in the Ibercorp, Roldán and GAL cases and the widespread perception that the spectacular malfeasance of Mario Conde and Javier de la Rosa had been facilitated by government negligence.

A series of ETA outrages intended to force the PSOE to hasten Basque independence redounded in favour of the PP. In particular, the dour Aznar won a degree of personal popularity because of the coolness he displayed after he narrowly escaped an assassination attempt by ETA in April 1995. Nevertheless, despite predictions of a huge PP victory, the PSOE's defeat was by a far smaller margin than had been anticipated, a consequence of González having greater popularity and charisma than Aznar.[44] Felipe González unexpectedly resigned as Secretary General of the PSOE at the XXXIV Congress in June 1997. He was replaced by Joaquín Almunia, who inherited a divided party and had to cope with the renewed popular opprobrium towards the PSOE when the sentences in the Filesa, Roldán and GAL cases were made public.[45]

Without an absolute majority, José María Aznar had to seek support in the Cortes from Pujol's CiU with sixteen seats, the PNV with five and Coalición Canaria with four. This was the prelude to both the Basque Country and Catalonia securing more control over their own affairs. Over almost two months, Pujol's Economy Minister, Macià Alavedra, and Joaquim Molins, the leader of CiU in the Cortes, negotiated a deal with Mariano Rajoy and Rodrigo Rato. The so-called Pact of the Hotel Majestic was sealed by Aznar and Pujol at a dinner on 28 April. Similar negotiations took place between the PP and the PNV. The agreements eliminated the post of civil governor, brought an end to compulsory military service, doubled the percentage of tax revenue that Catalonia could keep (from 15 per cent to 30) and granted control over policing, transport infrastructure and ports.[46] Aznar's Vice-President and head of the cabinet office (Minister of the Presidency) was Francisco Álvarez Cascos and his second Vice-President and Minister of Economy and Finance and was Rato. Aznar's eventual successor, Rajoy, became Minister of Public Administration. The PP set about a programme of economic liberalization and deregulation. To facilitate relations with Pujol and to compensate for the weakness of the PP in Catalonia, the Catalan economist Josep Piqué was made Minister of Industry with the mission of privatizing sections of the public sector. The rancorous tone of relations with the PSOE established in the previous legislature was intensified. The entire civil service was swiftly purged of all personnel in any way linked to the PSOE. The first practical task undertaken was to complete the liquidation of the Instituto Nacional de Industria begun by Carlos Solchaga and Pedro Solbes. They had divided the component parts of INI into two sections. On the one hand, there were saleable assets such as Telefónica, the oil giant Repsol, the state electricity and gas corporations Endesa and Enagás and the state banking entity Argentaria. These were placed under the jurisdiction of Sociedad Estatal de Participaciones Industriales. Loss makers became part of the Agencia Industrial del Estado. In total, forty-three companies passed into the private sectors with the loss of around 60,000 jobs. The sales of state assets contributed, during this first PP government, to the economic growth, with inflation dropping below 2 per cent and unemployment dropping from 23 per cent to 15.[47]

Despite the Pacto del Majestic, there was considerable dissatisfaction in Catalonia, the Basque Country and Galicia over the clear desire of central government to limit the process of decentralization. In July 1998, representatives of CiU, the PNV and the Bloque Nacionalista Galego signed the Declaración de Barcelona in protest against the evident Spanish centralism of Aznar's government. The three wanted recognition of their status as 'nationalities' and not just regions, a distinction blurred by the official use of the term 'autonomous communities'. This did not mean that ultra-nationalist parties were in the ascendant in Catalonia. In the regional elections of October 1999, a surge in the vote for the PSC, led by the highly popular ex-Mayor of Barcelona, Pascal Maragall, had the paradoxical consequence of the CiU being able to remain in power only with the support of the Catalan PP.[48]

Aznar came to power with a pledge to provide 'clean government' and to find individuals to run state enterprises who were wealthy enough not to need to steal from them. His choices, often of personal friends, seemed to undermine the sincerity of his anti-corruption credentials. For instance, suspicion surrounded Piqué's links with Javier de la Rosa. Piqué had been President, from 1989 to 1992, of the refinery company Ertoil, a subsidiary of the oil company Ercros, which was part of the Grupo Torras-KIO. Questions were raised about his involvement in the labyrinthine operation to sell Ertoil, in 1991, behind which was the hand of De la Rosa. When the case was finally investigated a decade later, the judge shelved it for lack of evidence. Piqué held several ministries, finally leaving government in 2003 and going on to a prosperous future as president, director or adviser in twenty-five different state and private enterprises.[49]

One of Aznar's friends, Juan Villalonga, was made head of Telefónica. Villalonga converted Telefónica into a spectacular international telecommunications power by dint of expansion into Latin America and several deals with telecom companies in Britain and the USA. This saw a massive increase in its share price. However, in June 2000, an investigation by *El Mundo* claimed that Villalonga, along with the banking and construction magnate Alberto Cortina Alcocer, one of the more prominent of *los beautiful*, had made a fortune through insider trading in 1998. It was alleged that they used privileged stock options to buy shares prior to major expansions of Telefónica and so permit the later sale of shares whose value had risen steeply. On 24 July, the Stock Exchange

Commission, the Comisión Nacional del Mercado de Valores (CNMV), began its own investigation. The consequent rumours led to pressure from Aznar's government for Villalonga to resign as Chairman. The CNMV investigation was closed on 2 August after concluding that there was insufficient evidence of insider trading to justify opening a case.[50]

Villalonga was replaced as the President of the state tobacco monopoly, Tabacalera, by César Alierta, whose track record was not unlike that of his predecessor. In early 2002, another investigation by *El Mundo* revealed that Alierta and his wife had formed an investment company which, in 1997, they sold to their nephew Luis Javier Plácer. In late 1997, Tabacalera's share value was boosted with the acquisition of the American tobacco company Havatampa of Florida. With inside information about the impending purchase from his uncle, Plácer's company bought a large number of Tabacalera shares. When they were sold six months later, they realized a profit of 309 million pesetas. As a result of *El Mundo*'s allegations, the Office for the Prosecution of Corruption and Organized Crime began to investigate Alierta for influence peddling and insider trading. The case came before the Madrid provincial court, but was dropped in November 2005 because the statute of limitations had run out. However, the Supreme Court insisted that the case should go to trial. Further delays saw the case definitively dropped in July 2009. Alierta went on to a highly successful career with Telefónica.[51]

All that was in the future. On 10 March 1999, in response to the circulation of dossiers with accusations of corruption by members of the PP, Aznar declared to the Socialists in the Cortes: 'Unlike when you were in government, in Spain there is no big corruption problem.' On that day and again one week later, he had to resort to claiming that PSOE corruption had been worse and the current examples of PP corruption were simply 'errors'.[52] In fact, the scale of corruption that would be reached while the PP was in power would make Aznar's claims laughable. The bitterness between the parties was intensified in September 1999 when the PP was the only party in the Cortes to refuse to condemn the military uprising of 1936.[53]

During the first PP government, war was declared on ETA. The Minister of the Interior, Jaime Mayor Oreja, secured cooperation in France. Popular repugnance was provoked by ETA's kidnapping, in January 1996, of José Antonio Ortega Lara, a prison official and PP militant. Ortega was subsequently subjected to horrendous captivity in a tiny dungeon for 532 days. ETA unsuccessfully demanded that all the organization's prisoners be brought to prisons in the Basque Country. Ortega Lara was rescued on 1 July 1997. Just over a week later, ETA sought another victim and kidnapped Miguel Ángel Blanco, a PP councillor from Ermua, and made the same demand. When it was ignored by the government, Blanco was murdered in cold blood on 13 July. The murder prompted huge demonstrations and stimulated the so-called spirit of Ermua, a wave of popular revulsion which dramatically undermined support for ETA. Nevertheless, during the first PP government, 135 ETA prisoners were moved to prisons in the Basque Country and a further 207 of the 535 prisoners were released.[54]

Aznar called elections for 12 March 2000 to take advantage of the positive economic situation, the aura of corruption that still surrounded the PSOE and the fact that the corruption of major PP figures had still not hit the headlines. He won an absolute majority in the Cortes with 10.3 million votes and 183 seats, twenty-seven more than in 1996. The PSOE gained only 125, sixteen fewer than four years earlier. The Communist successor party Izquierda Unida also fell from twenty-one to eight.[55] Joaquín Almunia resigned as Secretary General of the PSOE and was succeeded by José Luis Rodríguez Zapatero. In September 2001, Vicente Martínez Pujalte, PP spokesman on the economy, declared that corruption was impossible while his party governed. It would not be long before accusations of bribery and corruption involved senior PP members including, by 2016, Martínez Pujalte.[56] Even before the elections, considerable media attention was being given to the so-called flax scandal.

The cultivation of flax, for the production of linseed oil and linen, was subsidized by the European Union to the tune of 120,000 euros per hectare. While Loyola de Palacio y del Valle-Lersundi was Minister of Agriculture, from 1996 to 1998, immense areas were sown with flax on land belonging to relatives of senior officials of the Ministry and to prominent figures including the Duquesa de Alba and Mario Conde. Planted on 200 hectares in 1994, flax cultivation rocketed to 30,000 hectares in 1998 despite being an unsuitable crop for the areas in question and taking over land previously used for wheat and other useful crops. Most of the flax grown, which could not be sold, was either left to rot in the fields or else burned. In April 1999, Nicolás López de Coca, the Director General of the entity responsible for negotiating subsidies with the European Union, the Fondo Español de Garantía Agraria (FEGA), resigned when it was revealed that members of his family were among the beneficiaries of the subsidies. In December 2000, the Fiscalía Anticorrupción began to look into possible criminal charges and informed the European Commission that there had been fraud in connection with EU subsidies to textile flax. The PP vehemently denied that there had been wrongdoing by Loyola de Palacio, who was by this time Vice-President of the European Commission. In April 2007, the Audiencia Nacional (National Court) judged that those who had taken advantage of the EU subsidies had done nothing illegal.[57]

Government-linked corruption was kept in the headlines by the cases of Gescartera in 2001 and BBVA in 2002. In June 2001, the CNMV discovered that the stockbroker firm Gescartera had defrauded clients, including several bishops, thirty religious orders and the police mutual fund, of sums later calculated at 88 million euros. The PP's deputy Finance Minister, Enrique Giménez-Reyna, resigned on 21 July. His sister Pilar was the company's Managing Director who was accused of embezzling funds. In September, Enrique Giménez-Reyna was investigated for having facilitated contacts between his sister and Pilar Valiente, head of the CNMV. This led to the resignation of Pilar Valiente on 21 September after she had been accused of passing confidential information to, and receiving gifts from, Gescartera. When the case finally came to trial in 2007, the court sentenced the company's owner, Antonio Camacho Friaza, to eleven years in prison and its President Pilar Giménez-Reyna to three.[58] In January 2002, it was revealed that Baltasar Garzón had begun a major investigation into secret accounts of the BBVA held in tax havens. Two directors of BBVA resigned in December 2001 and a further four in April 2002. They were all allegedly implicated in tax evasion and embezzlement of pension funds, and holding secret accounts in tax havens.[59]

Public scrutiny of Aznar's much vaunted austerity was provoked by the wedding of his daughter Ana to one of his advisers, Alejandro Agag. Celebrated in the monastery of El Escorial on 5 September 2002, the event was on a scale appropriate for a royal wedding. The 1,100 guests included the King and Queen and the prime ministers of the United Kingdom, Italy and Portugal, as well as a range of Spanish politicians and celebrities. There were twenty-five witnesses at the ceremony, one of whom was Francisco Correa, who was later at the heart of the notorious

Gürtel scandal. In 2009, Agag denied ever having any commercial deal-ings with Correa, but his name appeared in the secret books kept by one of Correa's key partners, his accountant José Luis Izquierdo López. Correa owned several successful travel and events companies and had already organized holidays for senior members of the PP, to whom he had been introduced by friends in the youth wing of the party, Nuevas Generaciones, of which Agag was the secretary. Questions were asked at the time about how Aznar, a one-time tax inspector, could afford the lavish reception, the cost of which was partly met by gifts from wine producers. Eleven years later, investigations into Gürtel revealed that 32,452 euros had been given by Correa to cover the sound and lighting expenses and that gifts for the couple had been charged to Gürtel accounts. Aznar always denied that public money was involved. However, in addition to the prodigious expense of the wedding reception, the substantial costs of transport, crowd control and parking for the guests were met by the municipality of El Escorial.[60]

In the background, smaller-scale corruption, particularly in relation to the construction industry and land sales, proliferated. One of the key and ultimately most damaging measures implemented by Aznar's first government was the deregulation of land use. Together with the arrival of cheap credit in the wake of Spain's entry into the euro, this change in the law would generate the building boom that was to be the engine of Spain's economic growth over the next ten years. The availability of easy money triggered a whole range of questionable practices including the fraudulent reclassification of land, the adjudication of service contracts with rake-offs for the political decision makers and the building of unnecessary infrastructure and iconic projects such as the Ciudad de las Artes y de las Ciencias in Valencia. The latter cost nearly 1.3 billion euros, more than four times over budget, and was described by Antonio Muñoz Molina as one of 'the most useless and most expensive structures in Europe'. At a local level, there emerged a confusion of public and private entities to which, without institutional control or vigilance, were outsourced activities from urban planning, rubbish collection, street cleaning, water and energy supply and public transport to the mounting of public events. One of the most adept operators in this context was Francisco Correa, who induced local officials to rig certain contracts in favour of companies that he controlled. The price of the contract would be inflated and the politicians paid off.[61] Often, membership of a political party would transport totally unqualified candidates to senior positions in provincial savings banks, and either their greed or that of their political masters would lead to the collapse of the bank and the loss of the savings of the small investors.[62]

Spain wasted between 80 and 90 billion euros on 'unnecessary, abandoned, under-used or poorly planned infrastructure' between 1995 and 2016, according to a recent investigation into the complex nexus of waste, inefficient use of public resources and corruption. The lack of regulation, transparency and accounting permitted contracts for unnecessary public works to be adjudicated at inflated prices to cartels in what has been called 'crony capitalism'. One-third of this amount (26.2 billion euros) went into unnecessary parts of the high-speed rail network, including railway stations on lines that were quickly closed because of lack of use or left unfinished. The airport of Castellón was opened in March 2011 without the appropriate licences for flights and inevitably faced enormous losses for several years. The 4-kilometre runway at Ciudad Real is the longest in Spain. Although the town has fewer than 74,000 inhabitants, the airport was planned for an anticipated 2.5 million passengers per year. Opened in October 2008, it ran up debts of 300 million euros and was closed four years later. It was sold in 2016 for one-twentieth of the original 1 billion euro cost.[63]

Suitcases full of money would be given by construction companies to municipal officials in return for reclassification of land use. Over the course of the PP's two periods in power, unemployment fell to 11.5 per cent as a result of the jobs created during the boom in the construction industry. The sweeping deregulation enshrined in the April 1998 Land Law dramatically increased the area available for development but not enough to prevent construction firms seeking more, often by corrupt means. This was reflected in the fact that the number of housing starts increased fourfold under the Partido Popular. By 2010, more than 150 *ayuntamientos* were under investigation by the tax authorities for fiscal fraud, money laundering and/or bribery of public officials. Most were to be found on the Mediterranean coast of Andalusia and Valencia.[64] The most common form of corruption in the building industry related to cases in which the owner of unprofitable agricultural land would bribe the relevant municipal or provincial officials to get it illegally reclassified as 'urbanizable' which massively increased its value. Officials also sold developers illegal building permits, allowing thousands of homes to be built illegally on agricultural land. The purchasers then faced the threat from other municipal officials that their houses would have to be demolished. In the case of Catral (Alicante), over 1,200 houses had been built after town hall officials had provided illegal permits to developers, some of whom were their relatives.[65] Many of the victims were foreigners who had been deceived by lawyers in the pay of the developers.[66] The Junta de Andalucía has acknowledged that there are approximately 250,000 illegal properties in the region, leaving the owners in a juridical limbo.[67]

Another typical example was what took place in Andratx in Mallorca. In November 2006, the Alcalde, Eugenio Hidalgo, Mallorca's Director General of Urban Affairs, Jaume Massot, the municipal official responsible for public works, Jaume Gibert, and the legal adviser to the Ayuntamiento, Ignacio Mir, were arrested. They were charged with taking bribes in return for providing certificates to allow construction on protected rustic land of a chalet for the Alcalde, a restaurant and eleven houses with swimming pools. Initially, the government of the Balearic Islands, headed by the notoriously corrupt Jaume Matas of the Partido Popular, had refused to act on denunciations of the offences.[68] Convicted on charges of falsification of documents, accepting bribes, crimes against the environment and knowingly flouting the laws concerning urban planning regulations, Hidalgo, Massot and Gibert were imprisoned and Mir fined.[69]

Aznar's Minister of the Environment from 2003 to 2007, Jaume Matas, and his wife, María Teresa Areal, were notable for their expenditure on sumptuous properties and luxury goods, including a 23,000 euro Rolex watch. As President of the Govern Balear, Matas was involved in several corrupt enterprises. The most notorious was the Palma Arena velodrome for which the original budget of 27 million euros was exceeded by 83 million. As well as his personal enrichment, this money was used to pay for the electoral expenses of the PP in 2007. It led to his trial for embezzlement of public funds, money laundering and perversion of the course of justice. Investigations into the Palma Arena case discovered a labyrinth of corruption involving Mata and many others, including the King's son-in-law, Iñaki Urdangarín.[70]

Another scandal that seriously implicated the PP was the so-called Brugal case. The name 'Brugal' was the acronym given by the police to the original case concerning corruption in the adjudication of lucrative contracts for rubbish collection in the province of Alicante, 'Basuras

Rurales Gestión Alicante. The investigation began in March 2006 and was soon extended to include the blackmail and bribery of public officials in connection not just with rubbish-collection contracts but also with the considerably more profitable area of the reclassification of agricultural land for construction. At the centre of 'Brugal' was Ángel Fenoll, the owner of several businesses in Orihuela, in both rubbish collection and land speculation. He was to be a key protagonist and also the informer whose revelations sparked off a massive thirteen-year investigation into corruption in Alicante. For many years, with a hidden camera in his office, he had been recording his business conversations with municipal and provincial authorities. The affair started in 2006 when a tendering competition for the rubbish-collection contract in Orihuela, between Fenoll's company and four other businesses including Urbaser, his fiercest rival, was not going his way. He believed that Urbaser would win because of bribes offered to the Alcalde, José Manuel Medina of the Partido Popular, and other councillors. Moreover, Fenoll was worried that Medina was about to reclassify a tract of agricultural land to enable the building of 3,000 houses. Illegality of this kind would not normally have bothered him but, in this case, the land in question abutted his own, where he kept both his rubbish dump and a large zoo of animals from Africa and Asia.

Accordingly, to put pressure on Medina, Fenoll supported Mónica Lorente as the mayoral candidate for the upcoming elections for the Orihuela town hall and also threatened to publish compromising tapes. He had mixed success in his war on Medina. Lorente was elected Alcaldesa (mayoress) in June 2007 but, some weeks earlier, Fenoll and five others, including his son, were arrested on charges of blackmail. After being released on bail, a deeply embittered Fenoll made dark insinuations that he could publish his recordings of meetings with businessmen and politicians from Alicante. To give credibility to his threats, as a sample of his armoury, he recalled his relationship with Luis Fernando Cartagena, who had been the PP Alcalde in Orihuela from 1986 to 1995 and also Minister of Public Works in the Generalitat of Valencia from 1995 to 1998, under the presidency of Eduardo Zaplana. In 1997, Cartagena had given Fenoll the rubbish-collection contract for the entire coast of the region in return for covering up a crime. Fenoll provided fake invoices to account for 49,000 euros stolen by Cartagena in 1993. The money had been donated to Orihuela for social projects by the

Carmelite nuns of the San Juan de Dios municipal old people's hospice. When the case was exposed in 1997, Cartagena needed the invoices to make it look as if the money had indeed been spent on social causes. Both had been tried for this fraud and Cartagena jailed and Fenoll fined. After receiving the huge contract from Cartagena, Fenoll had shown his gratitude by giving sinecures in his businesses to the relatives of top PP officials, such as Carmen Zaplana, sister of Eduardo, by financing a local radio station that supported the PP and on one occasion by paying for two busloads of PP militants to swing the vote at a meeting. Now Fenoll declared threateningly: 'I have lots more recordings. Let's hope that I don't have to use them. I will do so if my businesses are in danger.'

In February 2010, the case became more complicated when Fenoll and seventeen other businessmen and municipal officials were accused of massive tax fraud involving thousands of false invoices. Further investigations into the case saw nine people arrested in June, including José Joaquín Ripoll, the President of the provincial council of Alicante (Diputación Provincial) and leader of the Partido Popular in Alicante. The anti-corruption prosecutor accused Ripoll, the Alcaldesa of Alicante, Sonia Castedo, and her predecessor as Alcalde, Luis Díaz Alperi, of corrupt involvement related to the implementation of the new arrangements for land reclassification in the province, the Plan General de Ordenación Urbana. They were accused of demanding bribes, influence peddling and selling privileged information to Enrique Ortiz, a notoriously shady local construction magnate. Among his interests, Ortiz was the principal shareholder of Hércules Football Club. He was also accused of bribing Córdoba CF and other teams to lose against Hércules during the 2009–10 season, in order to ensure his team's promotion to the First Division. Sonia Castedo denied the charges, although she admitted having accepted a trip to the Balearic Islands on Ortiz's yacht. The anti-corruption prosecutor also accused directors of Bancaja and the ex-President and a director of the Caja Mediterráneo of involvement in the land-reclassification racket. In 2012, the investigation was extended to twenty-nine people including the past Alcalde and present Alcaldesa of Orihuela, José Manuel Medina and Mónica-Isabel Lorente. It was alleged that she had taken bribes to ensure that Fenoll got the contract for rubbish collection denied him by Medina. The complex ramifications of the case were such that the first trials did not start until March 2019 and the trials of some of the defendants, including Ripoll and Castedo, have been postponed still further.[71]

In the summer of 2008, a judicial investigation began into the finances of Carlos Fabra, the President of the Diputación of Castellón from 1995 to 2011, a major figure in the Partido Popular in the Valencian region and an ally of Zaplana. Fabra was an hereditary *cacique* – his father, his grandfather, his great-grandfather, two brothers of his great-grandfather and a great-great-uncle had been President before him. It was discovered that 15 million euros had been paid into more than a hundred bank accounts opened in his name. At least 6 million euros of this money had been paid in cash without documentary justification or any tax being paid. Overall, it was estimated that numerous cash payments of between 40,000 and 100,000 euros accounted for thirty times his income as declared to the tax authorities. In 1999, for instance, his declared income was 73,000 euros but he had hidden an additional 800,000 euros. He claimed to have won 2.2 million euros on the lottery in seven prizes between 2000 and 2004. This unlikely good fortune was the result of a money-laundering device whereby a winning ticket is bought at an inflated price which permits the collection of the prize money tax-free. When Fabra was first accused, Rajoy came to his aid, saying that he was an exemplary citizen. Fabra was notorious for arranging for the construction of the airport of Castellón, a useless vanity project which cost the province a fortune. On November 2013, after being found guilty of bribery, influence peddling and tax fraud, he was sentenced to four years in jail.[72]

Other parties as well as the PSOE and the PP were involved in corruption. The offences of CiU came to light after it lost support in Catalonia because of its close links to the PP. The main beneficiary among Catalanist forces was the Esquerra Republicana de Catalunya (ERC). In the November 2003 elections, the Socialist Pasqual Maragall defeated Pujol's successor, the suave economist Artur Mas, but did not win an absolute majority.[73] In December, Maragall became President of the Generalitat at the head of a coalition of the Catalan Socialist Party, the ERC and the Iniciativa per Catalunya Verds (itself a coalition of Communists and Greens). The so-called tripartite coalition held power from 2003 until 2010.[74]

Like the Partido Popular, Convergència i Unió had been financed illegally by means of commissions charged on government contracts. This hit the headlines as a result of a debate in the Catalan parliament, on 24 February 2005, about the collapse in the Carmel district of construction work on the new metro. In response to accusations of government negligence by the leader of CiU, Artur Mas, the Socialist President of the Generalitat, Paqual Maragall, stated: 'You have a problem and it's called 3%,' a reference to rumours about CiU collecting a 3 per cent commission when adjudicating public works contracts. When Mas threatened to end support for reform of the Catalan autonomy statute, Maragall was forced to withdraw the accusation. Subsequent judicial investigations into the case revealed that CiU had received commissions on contracts for public works awarded to construction companies. When a company was granted a contract, it would make a 'charitable donation', equivalent to 3 per cent of the contract, to the cultural foundation, the Fundació Orfeó Català-Palau de la Música. Part of this money was then transferred to the Fundació CatDem, the cultural foundation of Convergència i Unió. For instance, Ferrovial, via the Palau, paid commissions totalling 5.1 million euros on contracts such as the massive law-courts complex known as the Ciutat de la Justícia and the ambitious Line Nine of the Barcelona metro.[75]

In 2013, the long-running investigations into the illicit financing of CiU exposed personal corruption by Jordi Pujol. The scandal came to light when María Victoria Álvarez, the ex-lover of his eldest son, Jordi Pujol Ferrusola, revealed that the family held substantial bank accounts in the tax haven of Andorra. In response to ongoing media revelations, in July 2014 Jordi Pujol claimed that this referred to an inheritance received from his father and that he had simply been too busy to declare it to the tax authorities. However, María Victoria Álvarez asserted that the money derived from commissions received in return for the adjudication of public works. This caused a minor earthquake in Catalan politics. The scandal was linked in turn to the collapse of the Banca Catalana but more frequently to accusations that the Pujol clan had been collecting commissions from businessmen during the twenty-three years of his presidency of Catalonia. The Audiencia Nacional judge in charge of the case, José de la Mata, effectively vindicated Maragall when he identified more than a hundred companies that had been awarded contracts from the Generalitat and CiU-controlled town councils and had paid commissions amounting to 11.5 million euros to the Pujol family in return for the contracts.[76]

Another large Catalan case involved important figures of both CiU and the Partit Socialista de Catalunya (PSC). In 2009, Garzón began investigating the Caso Pretoria, a network of urban corruption involving three *ayuntamientos* in the province of Barcelona and several one-time senior government officials of CiU and the PSC. The racket, operating since 2002, concerned a number of conspiracies to manipulate public contracts and illegally reclassify land in municipalities to the north of Barcelona, mainly in Santa Coloma de Gramenet, but also in Badalona and Sant Andreu de Llavaneres. Between municipal and government officials, twenty people were under investigation in a complex network that manipulated, for substantial commissions, the adjudication of public contracts. It involved Lluís Prenafeta, one-time right-hand man of Jordi Pujol and his first cabinet secretary, and Macià Alavedra, who had served in Pujol's government for fifteen years as Minister of the Interior from 1982 to 1987, of Industry from 1987 to 1989 and of the Economy from 1989 to 1996. Both were accused of conspiracy, influence peddling and money laundering. Also arrested were the ex-Alcalde of Santa Coloma, a Socialist Bartomeu Muñoz, who was accused of conspiracy, demanding and receiving bribes, fraud and falsification of official documents. Under investigation too were the town councillor for urban affairs, Manuel Dobarco, and Pascual Vela, the Director of Urban Services who sought the deals with construction companies for which commissions were paid. The brains behind the affair was Luis García Saéz, 'Luigi', a one-time parliamentary deputy of the PSC, who, in addition to facing the same charges as those levelled against Muñoz, was accused of money laundering and influence peddling. Also under investigation were the heads of the companies that paid for contracts and relatives of the officials involved. The investigation against Pascual Vela was eventually lifted, but the rest of the case inched its way slowly through the justice system.[77]

The protagonists of the Gürtel political corruption case.

18

The Triumph of Corruption and Incompetence, 2004–2018

On Aznar's watch, major scandals that would not come to light for more than a decade began to fester. Aznar chose Luis Bárcenas as PP manager in 1989. Eduardo Zaplana was his protégé. He named Rodrigo Rato President of Bankia, the bank that would be at the heart of a massive corruption scandal in 2011.[1] All three would be involved in huge corruption cases. The first began in 2009 when, as part of the Gürtel investigation into PP finances, Garzón asked the Swiss authorities if Bárcenas had funds in banks in Geneva. To the alarm of the PP leadership, it emerged that he had a personal fortune there of 48.25 million euros. This had been acquired during the years that he had worked with Álvaro Lapuerta, the PP treasurer between 1993 and 2008 before Bárcenas succeeded him. The pair had used the parallel accounting system first exposed in the Naseiro scandal to funnel huge undeclared and illegal cash donations to the PP. Apart from the amounts Bárcenas kept for himself, this money was the basis for a slush fund used to pay various party expenses and to boost the salaries of senior officials. When Bárcenas was first under investigation, Rajoy claimed that this was a politically motivated attack on the PP. After the Swiss accounts had been revealed, he obliged Bárcenas to resign as PP treasurer and as a member of the Senate. To soften the blow, the party agreed to give him the title of adviser, with an annual salary of 255,600 euros, to meet his legal costs up to 200,000 euros and to continue to provide him with a car and secretary.[2]

The anti-corruption authorities stepped up their inquiries, which led, in 2012, to greater collaboration between the Spanish courts and the Swiss authorities. In consequence, the Partido Popular, already under pressure because of the brewing Bankia crisis involving Rodrigo Rato, decided not to support Bárcenas.[3] On 31 January 2013, *El País* published revelations from a series of handwritten pages from Bárcenas's parallel accounts relating to 1990–3 and 1996–2008. The incomings, mainly donations from construction companies but also including money from Francisco Correa's business empire, violated the law on party financing. The outgoings, equally illegal, took the form of supplements to the salaries of senior PP figures. The principal beneficiary was Mariano Rajoy, who figured thirty-five times in Bárcenas's accounts, receiving 322,231 euros over eleven years including three of the years that he served as minister in Aznar's cabinet. Between 1990 and 2008, other major beneficiaries were Álvarez Cascos, who allegedly received the equivalent of 321,391 euros, Rodrigo Rato with 216,711 euros and Jaime Mayor Oreja with 181,440 euros. José María Aznar received the more modest amount of 9,198 euros in 1990, when he was one of six vice-presidents of the PP and had overall responsibility for party finances. Later on the same day that the so-called *papeles secretos* were published, Bárcenas denied that such payments had been made. Four months later, he admitted to the editor of *El Mundo*, Pedro J. Ramírez, that the papers were genuine. He accepted that both he and his predecessor as party treasurer, Álvaro Lapuerta, had based the slush fund on cash received from businessmen. For the next five years, Rajoy would claim ignorance of the activities of Bárcenas, his family friend and party colleague. He did so despite proof of his collusion being published in *El Mundo* in the form of supportive text messages that he sent to Bárcenas and his wife Rosa, such as 'Be brave' and 'Be strong'.[4]

Gürtel is the biggest case to implicate senior officials of the PP. It is closely linked to the Bárcenas case. It came to public notice in early 2009, although trials of the accused did not start until October 2016 as a result of various efforts by the PP to challenge the judges. The police used the codeword 'Gürtel' (belt in German) as a reference to the principal suspect, Francisco Correa Sánchez, since *correa* is Spanish for belt. Correa's skill in pandering to the rich and powerful saw his influence grow to the point at which he got commissions to organize electoral events including spectacular rallies in bullrings. The investigation by Baltasar Garzón started after information had been given to the police by two whistle-blowers, both municipal officials in the Madrid region, José Luis Peñas from Majahonda and Ana Garrido Ramos from Boadilla del Monte. The consequent accusation against the PP Alcalde of Boadilla, Arturo González Panero, led to his resignation and exile. The police called for the arrest of his successor, Juan Siguero. The PP mayors of Majahonda, Boadilla, Pozuelo de Alarcón and Arganda del Rey and former members of the PP-run Madrid regional government were accused of receiving more than 4 million euros for illicitly adjudicating contracts and granting building permits.[5]

As with most such cases, the principal accusations were of bribery, money laundering and tax evasion. In this case, they applied to a network, overseen by Correa, of businessmen and PP politicians. They were involved in illegal activities regarding party funding and the rigging of tenders for public contracts in regions under PP control, mainly Valencia and Madrid, but also in Galicia.[6] Through Orange Market, an events-organizing business belonging to Correa, gifts and cash payments were made to PP politicians including payment for luxury suits for Francisco Camps, Ricardo Costa and other officials of the Valencian PP. Those payments and others were made, in cash with 500-euro notes, by the one-time organization secretary of the Galician PP, Pablo Crespo, the administrator of Orange Market and one of Correa's key partners. The tailor who exposed the racket regarding the gifts of suits lost his job.[7] It has been estimated that the activities of the network in terms of tax evasion and unnecessary or inflated contracts for building work and municipal services cost the public purse at least 120 million euros.[8] Correa's personal profit has been variously estimated at nearly 9 million euros.[9]

Cash flowed on such a scale that Correa – known to his friends as 'Don Vito' – was said to count substantial sums openly at dinner in the exclusive restaurant, Sorolla, that he used to frequent. He allegedly arranged sex parties for politicians and spent so much time at a nearby brothel called Pigmalion that he and his associates referred to it as 'the office'.[10] To manage his ever more complex empire, Correa assembled a team of advisers, of accountants who kept records of the bribes and gifts and of lawyers who created the companies within companies in Spain and elsewhere in order to hide money. Through Pablo Crespo, the initial network around Madrid was expanded to the Valencian PP.

The investigations began after José Camarasa Albertos, a Socialist deputy in the Valencian Cortes, voiced suspicions about irregular business deals by Orange Market. Run in Valencia by Correa's partner, Álvaro Pérez Alonso, known as El Bigotes (Moustaches), the firm organized propaganda meetings, conferences and congresses, as well as hiring publicity experts for the election campaigns of the PP in Valencian regional elections in 2007 and in the general elections of 2008. At his trial in 2018, El Bigotes claimed that when the company first began to work for José María Aznar 'We gave him a fresh, dynamic image; people thought that he had had plastic surgery; I got rid of his permanently evil look.' The investigation centred on Pablo Crespo and the ex-Secretary General of PP in Valencia, Ricardo Costa. The defence of the PP was that it was all a plot mounted by the PSOE.[11]

Correa was arrested along with several of his colleagues in February 2009. He was unable to afford the astronomical bail set at 15 million euros. He was in jail for three years while investigations continued and then the bail was reduced to 1 million.[12] In June 2009, investigations began into the activities of Luis Bárcenas. The process meandered along with numerous changes in the judicial personnel, including Garzón, who was dismissed from the judiciary for authorizing illegal wiretaps of conversations between the accused and their lawyers.

Finally, in January 2016, the trial began of thirty-seven of those involved. Correa testified that his relationship with the PP began in 1993 through links to Álvarez Cascos and Bárcenas. He confessed that he gave envelopes of money to the Alcalde of Pozuelo, Jesús Sepúlveda, to Luis Bárcenas and to other senior officials, as well as helping to finance electoral campaigns in Pozuelo, Majadahonda and Valencia. He also gave substantial gifts, including two luxury cars, to Sepúlveda and his wife, Ana Mato, a PP deputy and, from 2011 to 2014, Minister of Health. Correa said of PP headquarters at Génova 13: 'I used to spend all day in Génova. I spent more time there than in my office. It was my home.' He said that, at the suggestion of Bárcenas, he had acted as an intermediary between the PP and major companies, negotiating big public contracts in return for large commissions in cash. He kept part of the proceeds and gave the rest to Bárcenas.[13] One of the most important moments in the trial took place in June 2017 when Mariano Rajoy appeared. He was the first Prime Minister obliged to appear at a trial, albeit only as a witness. Despite the evidence of the Bárcenas papers, he denied receiving supplements to his salary and claimed to have no knowledge of the PP's involvement in the rackets admitted by Correa. He insisted that he merely set the party's political policy and played no part in its finances.[14] In January 2019, Bárcenas claimed that the police had seized documentation proving that Rajoy and other PP leaders had received money.[15]

On 17 May 2018, the High Court (Audiencia Nacional) found twenty-seven individuals, and the Partido Popular, guilty of fraud and money laundering. Correa got fifty-one years and eleven months; Crespo, thirty-seven years and six months; Bárcenas, thirty-three years and four months and a fine of 44 million euros; his wife Rosalía Iglesias Villar, fifteen years and one month; Guillermo Ortega (ex-Alcalde of Majadahonda), thirty-eight years and three months; José Luís Izquierdo López, seventeen years and seven months; Jesús Sepúlveda, fourteen years and four months; José Luis Peñas (one-time councillor in Majadahonda who informed on Gürtel), four years and nine months. Álvaro Pérez Alonso was found not guilty. The PP was fined over 245 million euros for its part in the Gürtel racket. Through its use of a parallel accounting system, in return for public contracts, commissions from commercial companies were used to fund the party and to enrich individual members. The judge stated that Rajoy's claim to know nothing of this illicit money was not 'sufficiently credible'. The damage to the reputation of the party was incalculable and saw it lose power to the PSOE within a month, after losing a no-confidence motion on 1 June.[16] During the debate on the motion of censure, Irene Montero of the anti-austerity party Podemos listed sixty major cases of corruption. In the trial regarding the illegal funding of the Valencian PP, the judgment was that 3.5 million euros had been used for electoral expenses for the PP, including mounting a smear campaign against the PSOE Secretary General José Luis Rodríguez Zapatero.[17]

In 2005, Operación Ballena Blanca, an extensive police investigation into money laundering by organized crime in drugs, prostitution, arms dealing and kidnapping, searched several lawyers' offices in Marbella. Among the cases that were exposed was that concerning the Alcalde of Manilva (Malaga), Pedro Tirado. On 13 October 2005, he was arrested along with his brother-in-law, Francisco Calle. When their houses were searched, Pedro Tirado was found to have 770,000 euros in plastic rubbish bags and Francisco Calle 20,000 euros. They were linked to Royal Marbella Estates, a company that was allegedly a mechanism for laundering drug money. In 2003, Tirado arranged for the rezoning for building of a piece of farmland of 1.3 million square metres, the Cortijo La Parrada, and dramatically increased the number of permitted houses. Royal Marbella Estates, which had bought the land for 12 million euros, then sold it to five developers for 160 million. Tirado was accused of bribery, perverting the course of justice, influence peddling and accepting gifts in return for making unjust decisions. He claimed that the money came from anonymous donations and he was eventually sentenced to a fine of 12,000 euros and Calle was acquitted for lack of proof.[18]

The principal discovery of Operación Ballena Blanca was the so-called Malaya case in the Ayuntamiento of Marbella which was notorious for corruption during the years it was controlled by the Grupo Independiente Liberal (GIL), the party created by the shady property magnate Jesús Gil, who was Alcalde from 1991 to 2002. In April of that year, he was banned for twenty-eight years from holding public office, forced to stand down as mayor and imprisoned for six months for a range of offences including influence peddling, falsifying documents, embezzlement of public funds and swindling funds from Atlético Madrid and from the Ayuntamiento of Marbella. He took 450 million pesetas (2.7 million euros) from the Ayuntamiento claiming that it was to pay for the town's name appearing on the club's shirts. The scam not only profited him financially but also boosted his electoral campaign to become Alcalde in 1991. Between 1991 and 1995, Gil and six accomplices swindled the Ayuntamiento of 35.2 million euros as expense payments to four nonexistent companies. One of the accomplices was Juan Antonio Roca, the head of urban planning in the Ayuntamiento of Marbella.[19]

Gil had died before investigations by the anti-corruption authorities began in November 2005. Under his protection, in the 1990s, Juan Antonio Roca, through bribery and blackmail, had created a network of businessmen, lawyers, policemen and even judges, using the contacts established by the German Consul in Malaga, Hans Hoffmann, and his son Juan. It will be recalled that Hans Hoffmann was the frontman for the land deals in nearby Fuengirola that enriched José Antonio Girón de Velasco.[20] During the property boom, Roca had masterminded infringements of urban planning regulations that enriched himself and several mayors and town councillors. Cash from businessmen was used by Roca to pay off councillors to ensure planning approvals and construction licences from which he and Gil profited. Investigations into their activities led to around one hundred corruption cases with names like Saqueo I, Saqueo II, Minutas, Belmonsa, Urquía and most importantly Malaya, which saw Roca imprisoned for eleven years. During the first of several trials, it was shown that Roca had acquired an illegal fortune of more than 1 billion euros.[21]

In March 2006, police raids on homes and offices in Marbella, Malaga, Madrid, Murcia, Cadiz and Huelva seized documents, enormous quantities of valuables and cash amounting to 2.4 billion euros. Numerous properties belonging to Roca, ranging from vast estates to hotels and apartment blocks, were searched. On his sprawling estate in Marbella, Finca La Caridad, in March 2006 were found boxes of jewellery, several luxury cars, 245 valuable paintings, including one by Miró hanging in a bathroom, a helicopter, a pavilion full of hunting trophies in the form of stuffed elephants, zebras, giraffes and leopards and a stable of more than a hundred thoroughbred horses. In Finca La Morisca in Jimena de la Frontera (Cadiz), there were a hundred fighting bulls and a valuable collection of historic bullfighting paraphernalia.[22] The search of the Madrid home of Marbella's ex-Councillor of Traffic, Victoriano Rodríguez, found between 300,000 and 400,000 euros presumably prepared for bribery since the money was in envelopes labelled with amounts and names. These discoveries led to the arrests of Roca, of Rodríguez, of the Alcaldesa of Marbella, Marisol Yagüe, and of her deputy Isabel García Marcos. The government took the unprecedented decision to dissolve the town council in April and created an emergency management committee until the elections of May 2007, which were won by the PP.[23]

A second phase of the operation took place on 27 June 2006 when 300 financial crimes agents raided premises in Malaga, Granada, Cordoba, Seville, Madrid and Pamplona. They arrested thirty people including thirteen one-time councillors of the Ayuntamiento de Marbella and construction magnates.[24] On 17 July, there were further arrests including Jesús Gil's successor as Alcalde, Julián Felipe Muñoz. Subsequently, Muñoz's lover, the singer Isabel Pantoja, was sentenced to two years in prison for money laundering. Other politicians and celebrities were involved and the notoriety of the case led to it being made into a TV miniseries.[25] On 14 November, a third phase of the investigation saw the arrest of eleven people, including Muñoz's ex-wife, Maite Zaldívar, who unwisely commented during a television appearance that 'bags and bags of money used to come into our house'.[26] In July 2007, ninety-five people were charged, of whom fifty-two were eventually found guilty in October 2013. Roca was sentenced to eleven years and given a 240 million euro fine, Yagüe six years and Muñoz two years.[27]

Aware of his own plummeting popularity since his decision one year earlier to join George Bush and Tony Blair and take Spain to war with Iraq, Aznar had decided not to stand in the elections scheduled for 14 March 2004. Despite the waves of corruption, he was confident of victory for the PP, seemingly convinced that his chosen candidate, Mariano Rajoy, would not face a punishment vote for the Iraq decision.[28] Moreover, three days before voting was due to start, nail bombs on four commuter trains entering Atocha station in Madrid killed 192 people and injured 1,800 more. The attack was the work of an Al Qaeda cell, in revenge for Spain's part in the war with Iraq. An Al Qaeda-affiliated website advocated attacks on Spain and claimed that they would secure the victory of the PSOE and the withdrawal of Spanish troops from Iraq. That claim was based on a statement in 2003 by the Socialist José Luis Rodríguez Zapatero that, if he won the next elections, he would withdraw Spain's forces from Iraq. Initially, the Prime Minister of the Basque government, Juan José Ibarretxe, blamed ETA, as did Aznar himself, who personally telephoned newspaper editors and assured them of ETA's guilt. Spanish ambassadors were instructed to stress the point. It was a reasonable deduction since ETA had previously targeted Madrid railway stations, albeit without success. However, forensic evidence soon accumulated that incriminated Al Qaeda. The discovery of an audiotape of recordings of the Quran and a van containing seven detonators led to the arrest of three Moroccans. The government held on to this new information and, when it was finally released, suspicions grew that this had been in order to boost the PP's electoral chances. The election results were a spectacular reversal of Aznar's expectations. The Socialists won with 164 seats, thirty-nine more than in 2000, sixteen more than Rajoy's PP whose 148 represented a loss of thirty-five.[29]

The damaging information not released by the government was that, on 13 March, a videocassette had been found near Madrid's main mosque showing an Al Qaeda spokesman claiming responsibility for the killings carried out as a response to Spain's role in Afghanistan and Iraq. At demonstrations at PP headquarters across Spain, protesters chanted 'Your wars, our dead'. An investigation set up by the PSOE, the so-called 11-M Commission, proved that the bombing was the work of Islamic terrorists and not ETA. It also showed that Aznar's government had indeed hidden the truth for electoral purposes. It also affirmed that the government had underestimated the Islamic terrorist threat to Spain.

When the report of the 11-M Commission came before the Cortes, its findings were approved by all parties except the PP. Indeed, two years later, senior figures of the PP were still refusing to accept that the atrocity had not been the work of ETA.[30]

Without an absolute majority, Zapatero had to seek the support of Izquierda Unida and Esquerra Republicana de Catalunya. That was one of several reasons inclining him to progressive policies. Another was the execution by the military rebels of his paternal grandfather, a captain in the Spanish army in 1936, because he refused to fight against the Republic. Zapatero's cabinet included as many women as men and his deputy was María Teresa Fernández de la Vega. An equality law was passed aiming to make political parties name women as at least 40 per cent of their candidates, and companies with more than 250 employees to give 40 per cent of the seats on their boards to women. A law against domestic violence aimed to protect and support victims and introduced heavy penalties for perpetrators. To the outrage of the right, homosexual marriage was legalized in 2005. Abortion laws were liberalized and fast-track divorce was introduced along with unprecedented welfare support for people unable to live independently because of illness, disability or age. These liberal measures provoked fierce opposition from the Catholic Church. The conservative Cardinal Archbishop of Madrid, Antonio Rouco Varela, accused Zapatero of turning Spain into Sodom and Gomorrah.[31]

One of the most controversial measures was the Law of Historical Memory. It was too little too late and was systematically blocked and sabotaged by the Partido Popular.[32] In the early years of the transition, fear of another civil war and a return to dictatorship had inhibited any inclination to investigate the crimes of the Francoists during the civil war and after. Despite the curtain of silence drawn over the past in the interests of a still fragile democracy, many historians continued to research into the civil war and the subsequent repression. Atrocities committed by leftists in the Republican zone had been fully investigated by the Franco regime and the victims commemorated. However, both the generation of Republicans that had experienced the war and their children still lived in fear. The fact that the police, the Civil Guard and the judiciary went unreformed for years was a significant factor. Even when the PSOE came to power in 1982, there had been no appetite to meet the latent demand for an investigation. It was considered too risky. Moreover, to untangle the subsequent fate of property plundered during and after the war and to annul the thousands of cases of people unjustly executed or imprisoned were problems riddled with too many legal complications.

The impetus to do something came from the grandchildren of the victims. In the hostile climate generated by Aznar's government, there gradually emerged a feeling that democracy was strong enough to sustain a debate about the recent past. Inspired after 2000 by the efforts of a young Navarrese sociologist, Emilio Silva-Barrera, to investigate the fate of his grandfather who had disappeared in León in the first months of the war, there has grown a mass movement in favour of what has come to be called 'the recovery of historical memory'. All over Spain there emerged branches of the Association for the Recovery of Historical Memory. They have received thousands of requests for help in locating the remains of relatives. Volunteers began to excavate common graves and to record the testimonies of survivors. Regional (not national) television companies produced disturbing documentaries about the repression. Zapatero's government declared 2006 the 'Year of Historical Memory'. In 2007, the Spanish parliament approved the so-called Law of Historical Memory. There were important regional initiatives, such as the creation by the Catalan Generalitat of the department known as Memorial Democràtic, the provision in Galicia of public funding for the research into 'historical memory' and the creation in Andalusia of the huge project 'Todos los Nombres' (All the Names). However, the hopes raised by the law were gradually dashed. Conservative town councils would not finance excavations. Moreover, the Spanish judiciary showed little readiness to investigate the disappearance of tens of thousands of people between 1936 and 1939.[33]

This historical memory movement generated discomfort, not just for the perpetrators or their relatives, but also among those who felt nostalgia for Franco and the wider sections of society that, over time, derived benefit from the dictatorship. A number of highly successful polemical works have pandered to this audience. Berating Spain's many serious researchers, a small group of authors and broadcasters heckle raucously from the sidelines in the manner of football hooligans. They claim that the sufferings of Republican victims are no more than an exaggeration of a sinister conspiracy of politically correct historians and add that their sufferings were, in any case, their own fault. There is negligible new research in these self-styled 'revisionist' works, which essentially recycle the basic theses of Francoist propaganda. In books and libellous *tertulias* (radio debates) they dismiss as liars and idiots the authors of the new critical historiography.[34] When the Partido Popular returned to power in 2011, the already inadequate funding for most of the activities made possible by the Law of Historical Memory came to an end. Accordingly, there is still no nationwide census of the dead or funding for DNA testing. In contrast, the PP government contributed to the upkeep of the graves of Falangist volunteers who fought with the Germans on the Eastern Front.[35]

Rodríguez Zapatero inherited a strong economy, in no small part owing to Spain's membership of the euro. Incorporation into the euro had required liberalization of the market and brought cheap credit, an inflow of EU funds and foreign investment. GDP growth was largely due to the construction boom which had created millions of jobs and fostered corruption. The period of easy money was inaugurated when membership of the euro led to interest rates falling from 14 per cent to nearer 3 per cent. German and French banks lent money to Spanish banks which permitted their customers to buy German and French consumer goods and a first or second home. During Zapatero's first term in office, the economy grew by around 3 per cent per year and unemployment fell from 11.5 per cent in March 2004 to 8 per cent in 2007. Per capita income overtook the EU average and passed that of Italy, but both public and private debt were out of control and the entire economy too dependent on the construction sector. The first signs of crisis emerged in mid-2007 when the Spanish economy was already slowing down. The bubble burst after the international financial crisis of 2008 saw GDP drop by 4.6 per cent by the end of 2009. There began a recession that would last until 2013. Economic growth dropped from 3.6 per cent in 2007 to below 1 per cent in 2008. The construction industry contracted by 35 per cent between 2007 and 2010. One million jobs were lost with the consequent knock-on effect on the rest of the economy. Unemployment soared to 25 per cent and youth unemployment to 55 per cent.[36]

In addition to the economic crisis, it was during Zapatero's first period in government that there were sown the seeds of a political crisis in Catalonia that would tear Spain apart. Catalonia holds 16 per cent of Spain's population but accounts for approximately 20 per cent of the economy. Inevitably, then, the reluctant and painfully slow transfer of powers from Madrid to Barcelona had generated dissatisfaction in

Catalonia. Pujol had long since pursued a policy of consolidating a sense of national identity based on language and culture. In 1990, he had commissioned a team of Catalan intellectuals to draft 'The Strategy for Catalanization'. It was a programme aimed at demonstrating to the population that Catalonia was hobbled culturally and economically by the discrimination of the Spanish state.[37] The development of an autonomous education system and Catalan-language radio and television fed support for independence as did the fact that many Catalans depended on jobs in the Generalitat.[38] There was a growing appetite for a resolution of the deficiencies, as perceived in Barcelona, of both the 1978 Spanish Constitution and the 1979 Catalan autonomy statute. In 2005–6 around 14 per cent of Catalans favoured full independence from Spain and another 34 per cent were in favour of independence within a federal Spain.[39] A revised text was drafted by Maragall's first tripartite coalition. Debated in, and approved by, the Catalan parliament, it was then submitted for approval to the Spanish Cortes. All parties except the Partido Popular agreed to consider the proposal. The majority PSOE was uneasy because the text defined Catalonia as a nation. Mariano Rajoy, however, was unambiguous. At a rally of nearly 50,000 PP members, in Madrid's Puerta del Sol, he declared in December 2005: 'There is only one nation, the Spanish one.'[40]

After difficult negotiations, the new Catalan statute was approved in the Spanish Cortes in June 2006. Despite the concessions made during the process, mainly on financial matters, the principal Catalan parties accepted the text approved in Madrid since it recognized that Catalonia was a nation. It was then endorsed by the Catalans in a referendum on 18 June. There were high levels of abstention, with fewer than half of eligible voters participating. Of those who did, 74 per cent voted in favour. The principal nationalist party, Esquerra Republicana de Catalunya, had campaigned for a 'no' vote on the grounds that the text did not go far enough. The PP argued that the results were an indication that independence was not a burning issue.[41] Even this watered-down Statute for Catalonia came in for bitter criticism from the right-wing press in much of Spain. The PP put 500,000 euros into a divisive campaign in favour of a boycott of Catalan products and, in some media, including the highly popular COPE, the radio station of the Episcopal Conference, there were expressions of hostility bordering on ethnic hatred.[42]

In late July 2006, on the point of becoming law, the statute was challenged on constitutional grounds by the PP and referred to the deeply conservative Constitutional Tribunal.[43] The consequent four-year delay fomented hard-line independence sentiment. The court's 881-page judgment, finally published on 28 June 2010, declared unconstitutional 14 of the statute's 233 articles including those that gave the Catalan language preferential status and granted Catalonia control over its tax revenue. Moreover, references to the 'indissoluble unity of the Spanish nation' were inserted. Ernest Benach, the President of the Catalan parliament, denounced the court's judgment as provoking a 'crisis of state' and argued that it 'breaks the pact between Catalonia and Spain and scorns the will of the Catalan people'. The consequent hardening of pro-independence sentiment was reflected in a massive protest demonstration in Barcelona on 10 July, with the slogan 'We are a nation. We decide'.[44]

The Tribunal's judgement coincided with the onset of austerity, imposed by the government in Madrid because of the financial crisis, rising unemployment and increasing disquiet about corruption. Support for Catalan independence within a federal Spain had dropped slightly to 31 per cent. Support for full independence increased significantly to 24.5 per cent and rose steadily thereafter.[45] In response to widespread disappointment with the Tribunal's truncation of the autonomy statute, Mas campaigned in the Catalan elections of 28 November 2010 on a pro-independence line, emphasizing the disproportionate Catalan contribution to the Spanish economy. The second tripartite government, led, since 2006, by José Montilla, was defeated. CiU gained sixty-two seats. Still six short of an absolute majority in the 135-seat Parlement, Mas governed with the support of independents.[46] Inheriting substantial debts from the tripartite government, with the support of the Catalan PP, Mas was forced to adopt harsh austerity policies. His deeply unpopular cuts saw unemployment deepening. This exacerbated the annoyance that, with only 16 per cent of the Spanish population, the contribution to the national coffers of 8 per cent of Catalan GDP constituted 21 per cent of the national tax revenue, yet Catalonia had received back only 8 per cent of state investment in infrastructure. In fact, a comparable inequality prevailed in Spain's richest region, Madrid.[47]

Zapatero's government had been slow to respond to the signs of the global economic crisis. Measures such as a substantial tax rebate for all taxpayers helped secure an election victory on 9 March 2008. The PSOE won 169 seats, five more than in 2004; the PP won 154, an increase of four. With no absolute majority, Zapatero would need circumstantial alliances, yet he emanated confidence. In New York, on 24 September 2008, nine days after the collapse of Lehman Brothers detonated the financial crisis, he spoke to a group of directors of multinational corporations and investment banks. On the basis of reports given him by the Governor of the Banco de España, Miguel Ángel Fernández Ordóñez, and his Minister of Economy and Finance, Pedro Solbes, he boasted that 'Spain has perhaps the most solid financial system in the international community. It has had a regulatory and supervisory framework internationally recognized for its quality and rigour.'[48] As the recession began to bite, tax revenues fell and the budget deficit rose to 11.1 per cent of GDP in 2009. On 11 May 2010, Barack Obama telephoned Zapatero, since Spain then held the presidency of the European Union, to urge him to undertake the necessary reforms to deal with the economic problems of Spain and the EU. Just as the Constitutional Tribunal was about to report on the Catalan statute, additional pressure from the European Union and the International Monetary Fund obliged Zapatero to adopt austerity policies to reduce the deficit. This led, in 2011, to a 5 per cent limit to wage increases on 2.8 million civil servants, an increase of VAT from 16 to 18 per cent, a reduction in redundancy payments and a freeze on the annual increase in pension payments.[49]

Zapatero did not immediately perceive that the Spanish banking system faced a monumental crisis. Numerous local banks were dramatically over-exposed in terms of loans on property development, often linked to corruption. When the recession hit, many developers and construction firms defaulted on their loans. This undermined the banking sector as a whole but was particularly disastrous for the forty-five provincial and regional savings banks (cajas), which made up nearly 50 per cent of Spain's banking system. Governed by boards of directors who were mainly political appointees and local businessmen, they had been vulnerable to the temptations of projects which seemed to promise easy profit and/or political prestige. The first to collapse, in March 2009, was Caja Castilla La Mancha as a result of its enormous loans to the construction sector and the financing of the unnecessary airport at Ciudad Real. In late June 2009, the government was obliged to take measures to reorganize and restore solvency to the most compromised small and medium-sized entities. To this end, it created a restructuring fund

(Fondo de Reestructuración Ordenada Bancaria – FROB). Next in line to be placed under administration were the Church-owned CajaSur, based in Cordoba, and the Valencia-based Caja de Ahorros del Mediterraneo (CAM), both of which had excessive exposure to toxic loans in property as well as some spectacularly overpaid and underqualified executives and board members who benefited from massive interest-free loans.[50]

The two major commercial banks, Santander and BBVA, survived the crisis, but the plight of the *cajas* was worsened by the Bank of Spain's inadequate vigilance. The actions of the FROB saw the number of *cajas* reduced from forty-five to eleven by 2012, largely through mergers overseen by the Bank of Spain. The CAM was sold to Banco Sabadell.[51] In December 2010, seven *cajas*, including Caja Madrid, merged into one large bank, the Banco Financiero de Ahorros, BFA-Bankia. The retail arm of the bank, Bankia, was launched on the stock exchange by its newly appointed President, Rodrigo Rato, Aznar's one-time Minister of the Economy and later chairman of the International Monetary Fund. Rato made great play of Bankia's apparent assets. The reality was that it was burdened with 31.8 billion euros of toxic debt which was deposited in BFA, the 'bad bank'. The intended solution to the crisis of the *cajas* initiated a colossal banking catastrophe. After it was announced in March 2012 that profits in 2011 were 305 million euros, within days it was revealed that the bank had suffered losses of 2.79 billion euros. The 347,338 small investors who bought shares in Bankia lost most of their savings when the share price dropped 80 per cent in 2011. The bank needed a state rescue totalling 23.5 billion euros, as a result of which, in May 2012, it was nationalized and the anti-corruption authorities opened an investigation into alleged mercantile fraud and false accounting committed by Rodrigo Rato and thirty-two other directors of the bank.[52]

In the meantime, public indignation about high unemployment, austerity and the collapse of the *cajas* merged with outrage about the inflated salaries that bank executives paid themselves and the perceived impunity of those implicated in corruption cases.[53] This had led, on 15 May 2011, to the beginning of a month-long occupation of Madrid's Puerta del Sol by more than a thousand mainly, but not only, young people disillusioned with politicians and bankers. This *movimiento de los indignados* was replicated by a camp of *indignados* in the Plaça de Catalunya in Barcelona and other such camps across Spain. It was supported by unemployed workers, older people hit by reductions in pension payments and dispossessed home owners. The latter were victims of Spain's draconian mortgage legislation by which failure to meet payments meant both the loss of the property and the obligation to pay the outstanding loan. The 15-M movement drew on a generalized disgust with the venality of the political class and inspired the 'Occupy Wall Street' movement.[54] It led to the emergence, under the leadership of the pugnacious Pablo Iglesias, of the left-wing party Podemos that was devoted to exposing the crimes of the political and business elite, which it referred to as 'the caste'. Disaffection with the political class and economic institutions did not bear fruit only on the left. It also fostered the Spanish nationalist party Ciudadanos that originally came to prominence in Catalonia in 2006 as a centrist anti-nationalist party under the leadership of Albert Rivera, a dynamic young lawyer.

In a context of economic decline and financial scandals, Zapatero called elections for 20 November 2011. He chose not to stand as candidate for the presidency and handed that task to Alfredo Pérez Rubalcaba. Mariano Rajoy argued powerfully that the economic situation required a dramatic change. The PSOE lost power spectacularly, with Pérez Rubalcaba gaining only 110 seats in the Cortes, fifty-nine down on 2008. Rajoy's PP gained 186. Under pressure from the European Commission, the European Central Bank and the International Monetary Fund, Rajoy continued the austerity policy already introduced by Zapatero. In fact, the banking crisis had been facilitated by the negligence of the Bank of Spain and the CNMV in failing to exercise proper vigilance. In July 2012, the Governor of the Bank of Spain, Luis Linde, appeared before the Cortes' economic committee, and acknowledged that there had been insufficient vigilance because 'there was a euphoria that led us not to see, or not to want to see, the accumulating risks'. Spain's external debt of 92 per cent of GDP was equivalent to those of Portugal, Ireland and Greece. Linde called for a restructuring of the banking system by which the institutions without the strength to guarantee their future would have to be merged or liquidated.[55]

The growth in support for Catalan independence began to accelerate when, after its landslide victory in the Spanish general election of November 2011, the Partido Popular exacerbated the brewing Catalan crisis through its combination of recentralization and austerity policies that obliged the Generalitat to cut spending on public services, especially

health and education. Unemployment was generating home reposses-
sions. Echoing the outrage of the nationwide 15 May movement
prompted by the effects of the recession and austerity, in March 2012 the
Assemblea Nacional de Catalonia (ANC) was created and channelled
these socio-economic grievances into pressure for a referendum on full
Catalan independence. The economic circumstances were feeding
pro-independence sentiment which rose to 34 per cent while federalist
support dropped to 28.7 per cent.[56] Mas was caught between trying to
maintain his deeply unpopular economic policies and retaining support
for CiU. His solution was the intensification of separatist rhetoric. On 11
September, the Catalan national day, the Diada, the ANC brought out
over a million people to demonstrate in favour of independence under
the slogan 'Catalònia nou estat d'Europa'. Mas was trying to negotiate a
fiscal pact with Madrid but, prior to a meeting scheduled for 20
September, Rajoy provocatively declared that, given Catalonia's debts
and 700,000 unemployed, this was no time for 'gibberish, muddles,
polemics and disputes'. This was seen in Barcelona as inflammatory since
the Generalitat believed that Catalonia needed to request a rescue package of 5 billion euros precisely because, since the 2010 judgment by the
Constitutional Tribunal, the region was being strangled by an unjust
financial settlement. When the meeting took place, Rajoy dismissed
outright any possible change in the fiscal relationship.[57]

Mas responded to Rajoy's refusal by aligning CiU more closely with
the pro-independence ERC and Iniciativa per Catalunya Verds. Popular
support for a federal solution had dropped to 25.5 per cent and that for
full independence had risen to 44 per cent.[58] On 27 September, Mas
joined ERC and ICV to pass a motion calling for a popular consultation
on independence for Catalonia and convoked early elections.[59] In the
campaign for the elections of 25 November 2012, indignation over
Rajoy's refusal to negotiate a fiscal pact in the context of PP corruption
was expressed by Mas's conservative deputy. Josep Antoni Duran i
Lleida, leader of the Christian Democrat Unió Democràtica de Catalunya
(UDC), declared, 'the Spanish state is a sewer'.[60] However, Mas's intensified pro-independence line lost him support among those in his party
who opposed separation from Spain. CiU's representation fell from
sixty-two to fifty while the ERC gained twenty-one seats (eleven more
than in 2010) and ICV thirteen (three more). The most militant separatist group, the Candidatura d'Unitat Popular or Popular Unity

Candidacy (CUP), kept its three seats. Overall, therefore, the combined vote of CiU, ERC, ICV and CUP had risen from eighty-five to eighty-seven. Mas was confirmed as President on 19 December, after signing a pact with the others that included a commitment to a public consultation on the future status of Catalonia.[61]

Despite warnings from the Constitutional Tribunal, throughout 2013 the nationalist parties went ahead with preparations for an independence referendum, to be held in November 2014. When the proposal to hold a referendum was put to the Spanish Cortes in April 2014, it was defeated by 299 votes to 47. The pro-independence parties in the Catalan parliament then elaborated a law permitting non-binding consultations. Rajoy reacted by putting the case to the Constitutional Tribunal, which prohibited the consultation. Mas responded with the device of declaring that it was a citizens' consultation to be managed by volunteers.[62] In the event, turnout on 9 November was only 37 per cent of the electorate, a reflection of the fact that many working-class Catalans were of Castilian-speaking immigrant origin. Ciudadanos had taken advantage of the weakness of the corruption-tainted PP by expressing vehement opposition to the referendum. Although the vote in favour of Catalan independence was 80.8 per cent, the low turnout hardly justified Mas's claim that it opened the way to a process of full independence.[63] Within days, the state prosecutor brought charges of civil disobedience, perversion of the course of justice and misuse of public funds against Mas, the Vice-President Joana Ortega and the Minister of Education, Irene Rigau.[64]

To build on the 9 November consultation, Mas called another snap election for 27 September 2015, claiming that it could become a plebiscite if pro-independence parties included independence in their manifestos.[65] On 30 March, CiU, ERC and representatives of pro-independence civic groups, Carme Forcadell of the ANC and Muriel Casals of Òmnium Cultural, agreed on a 'road map for the Catalan sovereignty process'. This included a unilateral declaration of independence within eighteen months if their coalition, running as Junts pel Sí (Together for Yes), won the elections. On the next day, Rajoy warned that no central government would permit any infringement of national integrity.[66] Since Duran i Lleida opposed any illegal separatist action in opposition to the Madrid government, in June 2015 Unió Democràtica withdrew its ministers from the Generalitat and CiU was dissolved. Convergència and UDC would run separately in the elections.[67] Nine days before the elections *El Mundo* revived the scandal of companies given public contracts allegedly being obliged to make a 'charitable donation' equivalent to 3 per cent of the contract to the Palau de la Música Catalana, from which money was then funnelled to the Fundació CatDem. Now, the newspaper falsely alleged that some of this money had gone into the private bank accounts of Artur Mas and his father, and of Jordi Pujol and his wife Marta Ferrusola.[68] It would subsequently be revealed that, since the 2012 Diada, the PP government, with the knowledge and encouragement of Rajoy, had been running covert and illegal police operations to investigate and smear Catalan politicians. One of the masterminds of the so-called Operación Cataluña was a sinister ex-policeman, José Manuel Villarejo.[69]

On 27 September, with 39 per cent of the vote and sixty-two seats, Junts pel Sí won a simple majority in the Parlement, far from the hoped-for sweeping plebiscite in favour of independence. The coalition of Podemos and ICV, known as Catalunya sí que es pot (Catalonia Can), which wanted reform of the autonomy statute, got 8.9 per cent of the vote and eleven seats. The Socialists who advocated a federalist solution got 12.7 per cent of the vote and sixteen seats. Totally opposing any move towards independence were the right-of-centre Ciudadanos with 17.9 per cent and twenty-five seats and the Catalan PP with 8.5 per cent and eleven seats. Mas believed that it would be possible to move ahead with the 'sovereignty process' in collaboration with the ultra-nationalist and fiercely anti-capitalist CUP which had achieved 8.2 per cent of the vote and ten seats. Those ten seats made the CUP the arbiter of Catalan politics, determined to exchange its parliamentary support only for a commitment to an early declaration of independence. In the Parlement, on 27 October, Junts pel Sí and the CUP called for the opening of the process to create an independent Catalan republic. Opposed by the PP, Ciudadanos and the Catalan Socialist Party, the proposal was passed on 9 November. Rajoy immediately took the independence proposal to the Constitutional Tribunal, which declared it unconstitutional.[70]

Whatever timetable Mas had for progress to independence, things would accelerate now that the Generalitat was being pushed by the CUP and the grassroots ANC and Òmnium Cultural. As one commentator put it, the process had neither steering wheel nor brakes. In revenge for his implementation of austerity, the CUP refused to support Mas for the presidency and demanded that Junts pel Sí come up with another candidate. Accordingly, Mas was replaced in January 2016 by the one-time Mayor of Girona, Carles Puigdemont.[71] At the congress of Convergència in July 2016, it was decided to change the party's name. This was a response to the damage inflicted by the 2014 revelations of the corruption scandal involving the fortune hidden by Pujol in various tax havens and also to the 2015 split with Unió Democràtica de Catalunya. After lengthy negotiations, Convergència became, in September 2016, the Partit Demòcrata Europeu Català (PDeCat).[72] In January 2017, about to be tried for holding the illegal referendum in 2014, Artur Mas resigned as President of PDeCat in order to devote his efforts to his defence.[73] He was found guilty of civil disobedience and perversion of the course of justice and sentenced to disqualification from public office for two years. He was also required to pay the costs to the public purse of holding the referendum.[74]

In the meantime, in the rest of Spain, public outrage about the Bankia scandal intensified when it was revealed in October 2014 that, between 2003 and 2012, the directors of Caja Madrid and Bankia had enjoyed the use of 'black' credit cards, which they used for personal expenses totalling 15.5 million euros. Although they already benefited from salaries and expense accounts linked to their professional undertakings, they had used the cards for travel, entertainment, clothes and cash withdrawals. The largest amounts had been spent by Rodrigo Rato (54,800 euros) and Miguel Blesa, the President of Caja Madrid (436,700 euros). In February 2017, sixty-five directors of both banks were sentenced to a total of 120 years in prison, with Blesa at the top of the list with six years, followed by Rato with four and a half. Blesa committed suicide in July 2017.[75]

The festering crisis in Catalonia did not create the alarm that it might have done because media attention was more concerned with the links between the head of state and corruption. The taboo that used to inhibit public criticisms of the crown no longer functioned after 2007. Indeed, the economic crisis and the reduction in welfare saw hostile questions about the royal budget being posed by members of the PNV and the ERC.[76] Disenchantment with the monarchy spread during the post-2010 economic crisis as part of the general resentment of corruption. On 8 May 2010, Juan Carlos underwent a lung operation which was at first thought to be for cancer. It was the beginning of a cycle of deteriorating health, including knee and hip replacements. The situation went downhill for the King in 2012, beginning with a fraud investigation into the financial affairs of his son-in-law, Iñaki Urdangarín. Matters worsened further after his fall during an elephant hunt in Botswana in April 2012. This provoked vehement criticism not least because it exposed his relationship with the German-Danish businesswoman Corinna Larsen, who had accompanied him on the fateful trip. He had met her in February 2004 when the then forty-year-old was still married to Prinz Casimir zu Sayn-Wittgenstein, whom she divorced shortly afterwards.[77] In the context of financial crisis, with unemployment higher than 25 per cent, his absence from Spain on a safari and his affair massively undermined his popularity.[78]

With pro-republican sentiment growing, the 'Urdangarín case' further impaired the credibility of the monarchy. The scandal was provoked by Urdangarín's role in the supposedly non-profit-making research consultancy known as the Instituto Nóos. In 2004, Urdangarín, who on his marriage to the Infanta Cristina had been made the Duque de Palma, became the administrator, and she a director, of the Instituto Nóos. Between 2004 and 2006, Urdangarín and his partner, Diego Torres, organized events for which they charged astronomical fees.[79] Their role was initially uncovered as part of the notorious Palma Arena corruption case involving the ex-President of the PP in the Balearic Islands, Jaume Matas. The investigation discovered that, thanks to Urdangarín's perceived royal influence and so without facing public competition, the Instituto Nóos had been awarded extravagant public funds in the Balearics and Valencia for fictitious or wildly overpriced services.[80]

Two conferences in 2005 and 2006 on tourism and sport organized for the tourism promotion entity, the Illes Balears Forum, each cost more than 1 million euros. The expenses charged included 80,000 euros for 'four lunches, three dinners and six coffee breaks' for the guests.[81] Similarly, in Valencia, the Generalitat and the Ayuntamiento were charged more than 3 million euros for the organization of three 'Valencia Summit' conferences on the advantages for cities in hosting sports events. The real cost per meeting was barely 100,000 euros.[82] According to the tax authorities, the Instituto Nóos and its linked companies invoiced at least 16 million euros to various public and private entities, with almost 40 per cent of its profits coming from public finances. Documents seized from Nóos revealed that huge quantities of money had been funnelled to fiscal paradises such as Belize.[83]

In 2005, Urdangarín and his wife bought a luxury residence in the exclusive Barcelona district of Pedralbes for 6 million euros, which aroused suspicions about public funds having been diverted through Nóos.[84] The royal household was sufficiently concerned about Urdangarín's probity to arrange a golden exile for his family, having him posted to Washington, as representative of Telefónica, in April 2009, on an annual salary of 1 million euros.[85] In June 2011, Urdangarín's partner, Diego Torres, was placed under investigation and, on 7 November, anti-corruption prosecutors searched the headquarters of the Instituto Nóos in Barcelona. Two days later, both Torres and Urdangarín were charged with falsifying documents, fraud and embezzlement of public funds. When Urdangarín refused to join in a united defence strategy, a furious Torres began, in April 2012, to publish compromising emails from Urdangarín.

Over the next months, these emails implied that the King had helped Urdangarín get contracts and revealed that Corinna zu Sayn-Wittgenstein had been involved in the 'Valencia Summit' events. In a celebrated interview with Ana Romero, Corinna denied any involvement in Nóos but admitted that the King had asked her to get Urdangarín a job in her world of international sports sponsorship. When the Infanta Cristina was put under investigation, the royal household decided that Urdangarín would have to be cast aside and left to organize his own defence. Cristina's defence was that she knew nothing and did what she did out of blind affection for her husband.[86] The scale of the King's consequent anxiety was noticeable in his 2011 Christmas speech. In response to the intensifying criticism from the left and from the Basque, Catalan and Galician nationalists, without mentioning Urdangarín, he spoke of corruption and stated that justice was the same for everyone.[87] On 29 December 2011, Urdangarín was formally charged with offences relating to the perversion of the course of justice, misuse of public funds, defrauding the public purse and tax evasion. In June 2018, he was sentenced to five years and ten months in jail.[88] The damage to the crown was immense. The King had had to authorize the charging of his daughter in the interests of the monarchy's survival.[89]

It increasingly seemed that the King had exhausted the enormous political capital that he had built up between 1975 and 1982. Republican sentiment was on the rise, especially among those under thirty-five.[90] Nevertheless, in the spring of 2012, it appeared that the robust, albeit belated, reaction to the Urdangarín situation was remedying matters. Ironically, on 14 April, the eighty-first anniversary of the establishment of the Second Republic, a crisis exploded with the news that the King needed surgery for a triple fracture of his femur and a right hip replacement as a result of the fall in Botswana.[91] His hunting jaunts had already provoked the indignation of pro-animal activists and of deputies of the PNV and ERC about the cost, given that the jaunts had coincided with cuts in the health and education budgets.[92]

In fact, the 750,000 euro cost of the hunting party in Botswana had been met by a Saudi Arabian friend. However, the beneficial impact of this news was swamped by the revelation that he had been accompanied by the by now 48-year-old divorcee who still used the title Serene Highness Princess Corinna zu Sayn-Wittgenstein. When they met, Corinna worked for Boss & Co., the London bespoke gunmakers, organizing luxury safaris for wealthy clients. In 2006, she opened her own consultancy company, Apollonia Associates, which arranged high-level sports sponsorship. The elephants and the German-Danish Princess had combined to burst the media dyke which had previously shielded the King's private life.[93] For years, rumours about difficulties in his marriage with Queen Sofía had steadily diminished the popularity of the monarchy. As he had grown closer to Corinna, his treatment of Sofía became more hostile, and he was allegedly heard to say: 'I can't stand her. I hate her.'[94] The twin scandals of the hunting party and the affair intensified criticisms. The President of the PNV, Iñigo Urkullu, declared that he was 'astonished and embarrassed' by the King's behaviour and denounced the Botswana hunting party as 'absolutely frivolous'. The UGT and Comisiones Obreras called the trip inopportune and demanded explanations.[95] On 30 May 2012, Izquierda Unida (IU), Esquerra Republicana de Catalunya (ERC) and the Bloque Nacional Gallega (BNG) united in the Cortes to call for an investigative commission to establish methods of parliamentary control and transparency over the public activities of the King and the royal family.[96] Along with criticism of the irresponsibility of the Botswana adventure and of Urdangarín, there was scurrilous gossip about Juan Carlos's deteriorating marital situation. The most unrestrained criticism related to his relationship with Corinna and the fact that she frequently accompanied him on foreign trips, sometimes assumed official functions and was even in possession of a diplomatic passport.[97]

While he was in hospital, the King and his advisers were greatly affected by the wave of public censure and he was advised to make a statement to the nation. Accordingly, when he left the clinic, there were TV cameras awaiting him. He spoke in terms never previously heard from the lips of any Spanish head of state, whether royal or republican: 'I am so sorry. I made a mistake and it will not happen again.' His remorse permitted the government, the PP, the PSOE and CiU to come out in his support. The first official mention of Corinna came when journalists were told that 'Juan Carlos will henceforth observe greater discretion regarding the personal friends who accompany him on his private trips and activities. However, the King will not give up these friends, including the close relationship that for some years he has maintained with the German businesswoman and safari organizer Princess Corinna zu Sayn-Wittgenstein who also accompanied the King on the hunt in Botswana.'[98] In September 2013, Corinna told an American journalist that she and Juan Carlos had been lovers but now 'We are close friends. Some people don't understand that things can happen at a certain point in time, and then they end, but the friendship doesn't end.'[99]

Along with his dwindling popularity, Juan Carlos's health was deteriorating. In November 2012, he needed a left hip replacement; in March 2013, he suffered a spinal disc hernia and six months later was to be hospitalized when his left hip prosthesis became infected. There was much public speculation about the need for him to abdicate, not just because of his health problems but also because the economic crisis was seen as proof of the incompetence and corruption of the political establishment of which he was the keystone. On 5 January 2014, his seventy-sixth birthday, El Mundo published a poll suggesting that 62 per cent of the population favoured his abdication. On the next day, overtired after a trip to London, he was barely able to complete his speech at the annual armed forces celebration. A day later, on 7 January, Cristina was charged. As one media disaster followed another, he began to weigh up abdication and benefited from the advice of Felipe González. There was concern that, if Spain, as is often said, was JuanCarlista rather than monarchist, his departure might mean the end of the monarchy.[100] An article in El País, by the prestigious historian Santos Juliá, had immense influence on both public opinion and the King himself.[101]

Convinced that there was little chance of recuperating the popularity which had to be the basis of the monarchy's survival, or simply too tired to try, he decided to make a clean break and give his son Felipe VI the best chance of remaining on the throne for a long time. He abdicated on

2 June 2014.[102] Subsequently, his image would be damaged further by the publication, in July 2018, of tape recordings made in 2015 of a conversation in London between Corinna, Juan Villalonga and the ubiquitous José Manuel Villarejo. The corrupt Villarejo had made a fortune from money laundering and blackmail in the course of dirty-tricks operations on behalf of private and public clients.[103] Claiming later that she was unaware that she was being recorded, Corinna said that Juan Carlos had asked her to marry him. She also made damaging allegations about his financial affairs. She claimed that he had encouraged Urdangarín's activities in the Instituto Nóos, held secret bank accounts in Switzerland, had put properties in her name in Monaco and had made a fortune in commissions on business deals in Saudi Arabia, not least via the help he gave to Spanish firms to get the contracts to build the high-speed rail link between Mecca and Medina.[104]

The consequent deterioration of the image of the monarchy was not the only problem bequeathed by Juan Carlos. If it was not obvious in 2014, it would be starkly clear by 2018 that Felipe VI had inherited a bitterly divided country with a broken political system, the results of corruption and political incompetence. Even before the final erosion of his father's position, outrage about widespread political corruption had finally begun to have a serious impact on public opinion. In 2015, the consequence could be seen in the rise of the leftist populist party Podemos. In the general elections on 20 December, the combined votes of the PSOE and the PP would slump to an all-time low of 51 per cent. The PP gained 123 of the 350 seats (down sixty-three) and the PSOE 90 (down twenty). Their joint dominance of the Cortes was undermined by Podemos with forty-two and the right-of-centre Ciudadanos with forty. The Cortes was gridlocked and, with no agreement on the formation of a new government, Rajoy remained as acting Prime Minister until equally inconclusive elections on 26 June 2016.[105] The PP won again but, with only 137 seats, it was still short of an absolute majority. The Socialists came second but had lost five seats. The anti-corruption coalition of Unidos Podemos, consisting of Podemos, Izquierda Unida and several small regionalist groups, had seventy-one seats.[106]

The weakness of the Madrid government, the legacy of corruption, would boost independence sentiment in Catalonia, with support for a fully independent state rising to 47 per cent by mid-2016.[107] Pushed by the CUP, in July 2016 Puigdemont's new nationalist coalition would try to take advantage of the central government's debility by pressing ahead with the referendum on Catalan independence that had already been banned by the Constitutional Tribunal. This would open the way to a calamitous process of confrontation between Madrid and Barcelona, the ramifications of which would bitterly divide not just Spain but also Catalonia. The culpable mishandling of the Catalan situation by both Rajoy and Puigdemont could only lead to disaster. Puigdemont's recklessness would allow Rajoy to bolster his own position by taking a strong anti-Catalan position instead of seeking to reach out to the majority of Catalans who were not committed to outright separatism.[108] Hoping to exploit the anti-Catalanism that had been nurtured in Spain over the previous decade, Rajoy gambled that a hard line would boost the PP's popularity in the rest of Spain. In doing so, he was ignoring the pattern in the last hundred years of Spain's history whereby Catalan separatism has fed off Madrid's centralist intransigence.[109]

The Catalan crisis came to a head with the referendum on 1 October, called in violation of the Spanish Constitution. It provoked the inevitable harsh reaction from Madrid with unfortunate efforts by the Spanish forces of order to prevent it taking place. Although less than half the electorate took part and there were no trustworthy controls, the result registered a majority for independence. The levels of uncertainty and tension saw King Felipe VI make a televised speech on 3 October in support of Spanish unity and of the Catalans not in favour of independence. After a declaration of an independent Catalan Republic on 27 October, the government activated Article 155 of the Constitution, imposed direct rule from Madrid and called regional elections. State prosecutors laid charges of sedition, rebellion and misuse of public funds. Puigdemont and four of his ministers fled abroad and other members of the Catalan cabinet were arrested and faced prosecution calls for thirty-year prison sentences.[110] The powers of the Generalitat were restored as a result of the Catalan elections of December 2017. After tortuous negotiations, the presidency of the Generalitat passed, in May 2018, to the militant separatist, Joaquim Torra, who rejected any compromise with Madrid and was totally committed to full independence.[111]

The PP clung on to power with support from Ciudadanos until May 2018 when the comment of the judge in the Gürtel case that Rajoy's testimony was not 'sufficiently credible' justified the bold strike by Pedro

Sánchez, on 1 June, of tabling a no-confidence motion. Rajoy's position had already been undermined by his poor handling of the Catalan crisis and opinion polls showed that support for the PP was plummeting. The PP lost the no-confidence vote. Gürtel had finally put an end to insouciance about corruption to the extent of seriously undermining trust in public institutions and the political class.[112] This led to the electoral success, for the first time since democracy was re-established, of the far right. In the general elections of 28 April 2019, the relatively new party Vox benefited from the PP's spectacular loss of seventy-one seats. Vox got 10.6 per cent of the vote and twenty-four deputies after campaigning on an extreme anti-Catalan, anti-immigration and anti-feminism line. The PSOE returned to power without an absolute majority in another deadlocked Cortes.[113]

Much had changed since 1982. Juan Carlos de Borbón was no longer a national hero. The Partido Popular had ceased to be the party which had alternated in power with the PSOE for nearly four decades. The PSOE was only precariously back in power. Both had been undone by a combination of corruption and arrogance. The lack of clear boundaries between the political elite and the judiciary – which had, of course, been most scandalously the case during the Franco years – had induced a sense of invulnerability and a sense that, after the institutionalized corruption of the Franco dictatorship, it was the turn of others to derive the profits of power. In that sense, the culture of greed was a reaction to the pillage enjoyed by the Francoist elite. After the transition, the prodigious economic growth under the PSOE, boosted by entry into the EEC, facilitated considerable inward investment. Vast sums were thus available to be used for speculation, which was further encouraged by financial deregulation measures consequent upon Spain's entry into the European Community. Corruption was also a response to the sheer expense of democratic politics in the age of television and mass media. Some of the most notorious early corruption scandals – such as the Filesa and Naseiro cases – were initially a response to the needs of political party electoral financing. Of course, once the money began to flow in, some of it was diverted into private pockets at every level of the political pyramid, from the throne down to the lowliest *ayuntamiento*. With glacial slowness, the judiciary is dealing with corruption. Whether anyone can resolve endemic political incompetence remains to be seen. Until it is, the social consequences of both will continue to divide Spanish politics.

Acknowledgements

This book draws on my work on Spain over the last fifty years. During that time, I have been fortunate to make some wonderful friendships and to have learned an enormous amount from many admired colleagues. Inevitably, the debts that I have incurred are numerous.

Over the many years during which I have been writing this book, I have received invaluable advice, comments and documentation from the following friends and colleagues: Fernando Arcas Cubero, Sebastian Balfour, Francisco Camas García, Julián Casanova, Luis Castro Berrojo, Ángela Cenarro, Javier Cervera Gil, Soledad Fox Maura, Eduardo González Calleja, José Luis de la Granja, Harold Heckle, Santos Juliá, Frances Lannon, Martin Minchom, Ricardo Miralles, Enrique Moradiellos, Francisco Moreno Gómez, Josep Palomero, Manuel Pérez Lorenzo, Alberto Reig Tapia, Michael Richards, Panxo Borja de Riquer, Josep Sánchez Cervelló, Ismael Saz, Angel Smith, Josep Maria Solé i Sabaté, Joan Maria Thomàs, Sandra Souto Kustrín, Enric Ucelay de Cal, Joan Villarroya i Font and Boris Volodarsky.

In particular, I would like to thank Carlos Barciela for help on matters relating to the economy; the late Gabriel Cardona for his insights into the Spanish military; William Chislett for his understanding of present-day Spain; Jaume Claret for material on military corruption; Antoni Dalmau for opening my eyes to *pistolerismo* and repression in Catalonia during the Restoration period; Carlos García Santa Cecilia for material on the exile during the Primo de Rivera dictatorship; Paul Heywood, for help in understanding the mechanics of corruption; Josep Massot i Muntaner for all things to do with Catalonia and the Balearic Islands, Hilari Raguer for endless advice on matters to do with the Catholic Church; Ricardo Robledo for his encyclopaedic knowledge of agrarian problems. In a category apart is Estanislao Sánchez Méndez

(Tani), whose uncanny mastery of obscure digital resources has been invaluable.

Over many decades, the interchange of ideas and opinions with Paco Espinosa Maestre, Helen Graham and Ángel Viñas has been constant and, for me, indispensable.

I am especially grateful to a number of friends who have read and commented on the manuscript of the book and saved me from many errors: Nicolás Belmonte, Chris Ealham, Lala Isla, Linda Palfreeman and Francisco Romero Salvadó. I am especially indebted to Peter James, whose hawk-eyed copy-editing always enhances my books.

I owe special thanks to my colleagues in the LSE's Cañada Blanch Centre, Susana Grau, Álvaro Cepero and Stephen Rainbird for their unstinting and good-humoured support. In the early stages of my research into the history of corruption in Spain, I was fortunate to be able to count on the collaboration of Jaume Muñoz Jofre.

The book is dedicated to María Jesús González Hernández and Linda Palfreeman, whose friendship and kindness over many years has done so much to keep me going.

Notes

Preface

1. José Ortega y Gasset, *España invertebrada*, 15th edn (Madrid: Revista de Occidente, 1967) pp. 68–9.
2. Antonio Machado, 'Carta a David Vigodsky, Valencia, 20 February 1937', *Hora de España*, No. IV, April 1937, pp. 5–10.
3. Richard Ford, *A Handbook for Travellers in Spain*, 3rd edn, 2 vols (London: John Murray, 1855) I, pp. 28, 74, 155, 162, 253, II, pp. 598, 660, 838; Richard Ford, *Gatherings from Spain* (London: John Murray, 1861) pp. 8–9, 46, 55, 332; Raymond Carr, 'Spain through true blue eyes', *Spectator*, 4 March 2004; Tom Burns Marañón, *Hispanomanía* (Barcelona: Plaza y Janés, 2000) pp. 130–3; María Jesús González, *Raymond Carr: The Curiosity of the Fox* (Brighton: Sussex Academic Press, 2013) pp. 133–8.
4. Gerald Brenan, 'Hispanophilia', *New York Review of Books*, 26 January 1967.
5. *La Vanguardia Española*, 18 July 1941.
6. *El País*, 24 February 1981.
7. http://www.cis.es/cis/export/sites/default/-Archivos/Indicadores/documentos_html/TresProblemas.html; http://sociometrica.es/category/valoracion-de-instituciones/.
8. Baltasar Garzón, *El fango. Cuarenta años de corrupción en España* (Barcelona: Debate, 2015) pp. 19, 25.

Chapter 1: Spanish Stereotypes? Passion, Violence and Corruption

1. Julián Juderías, *La leyenda negra y la verdad histórica. Contribución al estudio del concepto de España en Europa, de las causas de este concepto y de la tolerancia política y religiosa en los países civilizados* (Madrid: Tipografía de la Revista de Archivos, 1914). References here are to the greatly expanded fourth edition, Julián Juderías, *La leyenda negra. Estudios acerca del concepto de España en el extranjero*, 4th edn (Barcelona: Editorial Araluce, 1917) pp. 208, 333.
2. John Walter Stoye, *English Travellers Abroad 1604–1667* (New York: Octagon Books, 1968) p. 326.
3. Adolfo Bueso, *Recuerdos de un cenetista*, Vol. II: *De la Segunda República al final de la guerra civil* (Barcelona: Ariel, 1978) pp. 74–9.
4. David Mitchell, *Travellers in Spain* (London: Cassell, 1990) pp. 25, 36.
5. *The Memoirs of Jacques Casanova De Seingalt 1725–1798*, Vol. 6:

Spanish Passions, ch. 3. First English edn 1894, reprinted London: Elek Books, 1960. I have used the digital edition by Project Gutenberg at https://www.gutenberg.org/files/2981/2981-h/2981-h.htm. The quotation is from p. 3082. See also Fernando Royuela, 'Casanova o la pasión de amar', *El País – Babelia*, 12 April 2008.

6. Théophile Gautier, *A Romantic in Spain* (Oxford: Signal Books, 2001) pp. 157–8, 266–8; Mitchell, *Travellers*, pp. 62–4.

7. Alexandre Dumas, *From Paris to Cadiz* (London: Peter Owen, 1958) pp. 25, 37–8, 124–7, 198–9.

8. Prosper Mérimée, *Carmen and Other Stories* (Oxford: Oxford University Press, 1989) pp. 14–15.

9. Madame D'Aulnoy, *The Ingenious and Diverting Letters of the Lady ——: Travels into Spain* (London: Routledge, 1930) pp. 3, 47–8, 222–3, 289–91, 309, 326–33. The long introductory article by R. Foulché-Delbosc analyses her sources and concludes that she was never in Spain. See esp. pp. xxxii–xxxvii, lxi–lxvii.

10. *Ibid.*, pp. 294–5.

11. María Dolores Cabra Loredo, *España en la litografía romántica* (Madrid: Compañía Literaria, 1994) pp. 34–5, 40–1, 44–6, 51, 53–5, 58, 73–5, 79–81, 107; David Howarth, ed., *The Discovery of Spain: British Artists and Collectors – Goya to Picasso* (Edinburgh: National Galleries of Scotland, 2009) pp. 46–81.

12. Dumas, *From Paris to Cadiz*, pp. 42–3.

13. Germà Bel, *Infrastructure and the Political Economy of Nation Building in Spain, 1720–2010* (Brighton: Sussex Academic Press/Cañada Blanch, 2012) pp. 11–12, 17–18, 40–2.

14. 'Exposición que dirige al Gobierno de SM el Fiscal del Tribunal Supremo, 15 de septiembre de 1883' (Madrid: Ministerio de Justicia, 1883), pp. 17–18, quoted by Gutmaro Gómez Bravo: '"De las costumbres violentas de la sociedad española": visiones y enfoques para el siglo XIX y primer cuarto del siglo XX', *Bulletin of Spanish Studies*, 2017, p. 1.

15. Maria Thomas, *The Faith and the Fury: Popular Anticlerical Violence and Iconoclasm in Spain, 1931–1936* (Brighton: Sussex Academic Press/Cañada Blanch, 2012) pp. 71–2.

16. Ángel Herrerín López, *Anarquía, dinamita y revolución social. Violencia y represión en la España de entre siglos (1868–1909)* (Madrid: Los Libros de la Catarata, 2011) pp. 129–30; Nigel Townson, 'Anticlericalism and Secularization: A European Exception?', in Nigel Townson, ed., *Is Spain Different?: A Comparative Look at the 19th and 20th Centuries* (Eastbourne: Sussex Academic Press, 2015) p. 74.

17. Juan José Linz and Miguel Jérez, 'Los diputados en las Cortes de la Restauración y de la Segunda República', in *Obras Escogidas*, Vol. 6: *Partidos y elites políticas en España* (Madrid: Centro de Estudios Políticos y Constitucionales: 2013) p. 31; Juan José Linz, 'Continuidad y discontinuidad en la elite política española: de la Restauración al régimen autoritario', in *ibid.*, pp. 753–5.

18. Richard Ford, *Gatherings from Spain* (London: John Murray, 1846) p. 248 (Everyman edn, p. 269).

19. *Ibid.*, p. 188 (Everyman edn, p. 204).

20. Diego Garrido López, *La Guardia Civil y los orígenes del Estado centralista* (Barcelona: Crítica, 1982) pp. 46–59, 73–113, 168–84.

21. Gerald Brenan, *The Spanish Labyrinth* (Cambridge: Cambridge University Press, 1943) pp. 156–7.

22. Eduardo González Calleja, *La razón de la fuerza. Órden público, subversión y violencia política en la España de la Restauración (1875–1917)* (Madrid: Consejo Superior de Investigaciones Cientificas, 1998) pp. 43–5; Michael M. Seidman, *Workers against Work: Labor in Paris and Barcelona during the Popular Fronts* (Berkeley: University of California Press, 1991) p. 24.

23. Manuel Ballbé, *Orden público y militarismo en la España constitucional (1812–1983)* (Madrid: Alianza Editorial, 1983) pp. ii–iv, 141–54; Adrian Shubert, *The Road to Revolution in Spain: The Coal Miners of Asturias 1860–1934* (Urbana/Chicago: University of Illinois Press, 1987) pp. 72, 86; Julian A. Pitt-Rivers, *The People of the Sierra*, 2nd edn (Chicago: University of Chicago Press, 1971) pp. 130–1, 156.

24. Gerald Blaney, 'The Civil Guard and the Spanish Second Republic, 1931–1936', unpublished PhD thesis, London School of Economics, 2010, ch. 1.

25. Ford, *Gatherings from Spain*, pp. 2–8, 47–9 (Everyman edn, pp. 10–17, 58–60); Bel, *Infrastructure*, pp. 34–43.

26. Ford, *Gatherings from Spain*, pp. 280–2 (Everyman edn, pp. 303–6).

27. For example, Ángel Ganivet, *Idearium español* (Granada: Tip. Lit. Vda. e Hijos de Sabatel, 1897); Joaquín Costa, *Oligarquía y caciquismo como la forma actual de gobierno en España. Urgencia y modo de cambiarla* (Madrid: Establecimiento Tipográfico de Fortanet, 1901).

28. Manuel Azaña, 'Tres generaciones del Ateneo', 20 November 1930, *Obras completas*, 4 vols (Mexico City: Ediciones Oasis, 1966–8) II, pp. 619–37.

29. Francisco Martí Gilabert, *La desamortización española* (Madrid: Ediciones Rialp, 2003) p. 151.

30. Francisco Tomás y Valiente, *El Marco Politico de la Desamortización en España* (Barcelona: Ariel, 1972) pp. 44–91; Richard Herr, *An Historical Essay on Modern Spain* (Berkeley: University of California Press, 1974) pp. 68, 84–5; Gabriel Tortella, 'Agriculture: A Slow-moving Sector 1830–1935', in Nicolás Sánchez Albornoz, ed., *The Economic Modernization of Spain 1830–1930* (New York: New York University Press, 1987) pp. 44–8; Gabriel Tortella, *The Development of Modern Spain: An Economic History of the Nineteenth and Twentieth Centuries* (Cambridge, Mass.: Harvard University Press, 2000) pp. 53–61.

31. Herr, *An Historical Essay*, pp. 102–3; Tomás y Valiente, *El Marco Politico*, pp. 97–127; Ford, *Gatherings from Spain*, p. 268 (Everyman edn, p. 290).

32. Gómez Bravo, 'De las costumbres violentas', pp. 6–8, 12–13, 16–18.

33. Herr, *An Historical Essay*, pp. 93–4.

34. Albert Balcells, *Cataluña contemporánea I (Siglo XIX)*, 2nd edn (Madrid: Siglo XXI de España, 1979) pp. 85–6, 92; Albert Balcells, *Historia contemporánea de Cataluña* (Barcelona: Edhasa, 1983) pp. 93–7.

35. Edgar Allison Peers, *Catalonia Infelix* (London: Methuen, 1937) pp. 93–4, 136–42; Balcells, *Cataluña contemporánea I*, pp. 73–4, 89–100; Brenan, *The Spanish Labyrinth*, pp. 27–9.

36. Raymond Carr, *Spain 1808–1939* (Oxford: Oxford University Press, 1966) pp. 303–42; Brenan, *The Spanish Labyrinth*, pp. 147–54; Juan Avilés Farré, *La daga y la dinamita. Los anarquistas y el nacimiento del terrorismo* (Barcelona: Tusquets Editores, 2013) pp. 73–7.

37. Avilés Farré, *La daga y la dinamita*, pp. 89–90; Herrerín López, *Anarquía, dinamita y revolución social*, pp. 46–7; Josep Termes, *Anarquismo y Sindicalismo en España. La Primera Internacional (1864–1881)* (Barcelona: Ariel, 1972) pp. 240–1.

38. Earl R. Beck, *A Time of Triumph and of Sorrow: Spanish Politics during the Reign of Alfonso XII 1874–1885* (Carbondale: Southern Illinois University Press, 1979) pp. 101–25.

39. Brenan, *The Spanish Labyrinth*, pp. 2–5; Miguel Martorell, 'El parlamento en el orden constitucional de la Restauración', in Mercedes Cabrera, *Con luz y taquígrafos. El Parlamento en la Restauración (1913–1923)* (Madrid: Taurus, 1998) pp. 23–64; Linz, 'Continuidad y discontinuidad', p. 754.

40. Gumersindo de Azcárate, *La constitución inglesa y la política del continente* (Madrid: Imprenta de Manuel Minuesa de los Ríos, 1878) pp. 136–8; Joaquín Costa, *Oligarquía y caciquismo como la forma actual de gobierno en España. Urgencia y modo de cambiarla*, 2 vols (Madrid: Ediciones de la Revista de Trabajo, 1975) I, p. 81.

41. Salvador de Madariaga, *Spain: A Modern History* (London: Jonathan Cape, 1961) p. 69.

42. Javier Moreno Luzón, *Romanones. Caciquismo y política liberal* (Madrid: Alianza Editorial, 1998) pp. 31–3, 190–2.

43. Balcells, *Cataluña contemporánea I*, p. 84.

44. Rafael Shaw, *Spain from Within* (London: T. Fisher Unwin, 1910) pp. 228–33.

45. Linz and Jérez, 'Los diputados en las Cortes', pp. 15–18; Mercedes Cabrera, ed., *Con luz y taquígrafos. El Parlamento en la Restauración (1913–1923)* (Madrid: Taurus, 1998) pp. 33–6; Borja de Riquer, *Alfonso XIII y Cambó. La monarquía y el catalanismo político* (Barcelona: RBA, 2013) pp. 27–32.

46. José Varela Ortega, *Los amigos políticos. Partidos, elecciones y caciquismo en la Restauración (1875–1900)* (Madrid: Alianza, 1977) pp. 404–5; Salvador Forner and Mariano García, *Cuneros y caciques* (Alicante: Patronato Municipal del V Centenario de la Ciudad de Alicante, 1990) pp. 67–72; Ramón Villares and Javier Moreno Luzón, *Restauración y Dictadura* (Barcelona: Crítica-Marcial Pons, 2009) pp. 116–18.

47. Villares and Moreno Luzón, *Restauración y Dictadura*, pp. 96–102; María Gemma Rubí i Casals, *Els catalans i la política en temps del caciquisme. Manresa, 1875–1923* (Vic: Eumo Editorial, 2006) pp. 29–36.

48. Villares and Moreno Luzón, *Restauración y Dictadura*, pp. 110–11.

49. Varela Ortega, *Los amigos políticos*, pp. 121–2, 415; Costa, *Oligarquía y caciquismo*, I, pp. 25–7.

50. Juan de la Cierva y Peñafiel, *Notas de mi vida* (Madrid: Instituto Editorial Reus, 1955) pp. 22–3; Eduardo López de Ochoa, *De la Dictadura a la República* (Madrid: Zeus, 1930) pp. 63–5.

51. Carlos Dardé, Rogelio López Blanco, Javier Moreno Luzón and Alicia Yanini, 'Conclusiones', in José Varela Ortega, ed., *El poder de la influencia. Geografía del caciquismo en España (1875–1923)* (Madrid: Centro de Estudios Políticos y Constitucionales/Marcial Pons, 2001) pp. 563–5.

52. The classic definition of *caciquismo* was presented to the Ateneo de Madrid in 1902 by Joaquín Costa (Madrid: Ateneo, 1902). The edition used here is Joaquín Costa, *Oligarquía y caciquismo como la forma actual de gobierno en España. Urgencia y modo de cambiarla*, 2 vols (Madrid: Ediciones de la Revista de Trabajo, 1975) I, pp. 21–6.

53. *Ibid.*, pp. 35–40.

54. Carr, *Spain 1808–1939*, pp. 366–9; Moreno Luzón, *Romanones*, pp. 445–8; Villares and Moreno Luzón, *Restauración y Dictadura*, pp. 104–7, 118.

55. Varela Ortega, *Los amigos políticos*, pp. 411–16; Forner and García, *Cuneros y caciques*, pp. 135–9.

Chapter 2: Violence, Corruption and the Slide to Disaster

1. Juan José Linz and Miguel Jérez, 'Los diputados en las Cortes de la Restauración y de la Segunda República', in *Obras Escogidas*, Vol. 6: *Partidos y elites políticas en España* (Madrid: Centro de Estudios Políticos y Constitucionales: 2013) p. 9; María Gemma Rubí i Casals, *Els catalans i la política en temps del caciquisme.*

Manresa, 1875–1923 (Vic: Eumo Editorial, 2006) pp. 36–46; Raymond Carr, *Modern Spain 1875–1980* (Oxford: Oxford University Press, 1980) p. 12; Gemma Rubí and Josep Armengol, *Vots, electors i corrupción. Una reflexió sobre l'apatia a Catalunya (1869–1923)* (Barcelona: Publicacions de l'Abadia de Montserrat, 2012) pp. 145–52.

2. José Varela Ortega, *Los amigos políticos. Partidos, elecciones y caciquismo en la Restauración (1875–1900)* (Madrid: Alianza, 1977) pp. 406–11, 415.

3. Salvador Forner and Mariano García, *Cuneros y caciques* (Alicante: Patronato Municipal del V Centenario de la Ciudad de Alicante, 1990) p. 13; Carlos Dardé, Rogelio López Blanco, Javier Moreno Luzón and Alicia Yanini, 'Conclusiones', in José Varela Ortega, ed., *El poder de la influencia. Geografía del caciquismo en España (1875–1923)* (Madrid: Centro de Estudios Políticos y Constitucionales/Marcial Pons, 2001) p. 562; Carr, *Modern Spain*, pp. 10–15; Rubí i Casals, *Els catalans i la política*, p. 49; Varela Ortega, *Los amigos políticos*, pp. 404–3; Dardé et al., 'Conclusiones', in Varela Ortega, ed., *El poder de la influencia*, p. 562.

4. Earl R. Beck, *A Time of Triumph and of Sorrow: Spanish Politics during the Reign of Alfonso XII 1874–1885* (Carbondale: Southern Illinois University Press, 1979) pp. 126–32.

5. *Ibid.*, p. 133.

6. Manuel Tuñón de Lara, *El Movimiento obrero en la historia de España* (Madrid: Taurus, 1972) pp. 276–82; Ángel Herrerín López, *Anarquía, dinamita y revolución*

social. *Violencia y represión en la España de entre siglos (1868–1909)* (Madrid: Los Libros de la Catarata, 2011) pp. 53–64; Juan Avilés Farré, *La daga y la dinamita. Los anarquistas y el nacimiento del terrorismo* (Barcelona: Tusquets Editores, 2013) pp. 131–7.

7. Hugh Thomas, *Cuba or the Pursuit of Freedom* (London: Eyre & Spottiswoode, 1971) pp. 136–7, 155; Ramón Villares and Javier Moreno Luzón, *Restauración y Dictadura* (Barcelona: Crítica-Marcial Pons, 2009) p. 18.

8. Beck, *A Time of Triumph*, pp. 165, 170–2, 191–3.

9. Anselmo Lorenzo, *El proletariado militante* (Madrid: Alianza Editorial, 1974) pp. 38–44; José Álvarez Junco, *La ideología política del anarquismo español (1868–1910)* (Madrid: Siglo XXI de España, 1991) pp. 483–510.

10. Rafael Shaw, *Spain from Within* (London: T. Fisher Unwin, 1910), pp. 30–1, 263–82.

11. E. J. Hobsbawm, *Primitive Rebels: Studies in Archaic Forms of Social Movements in the 19th and 20th Centuries* (Manchester: Manchester University Press, 1959) pp. 74–92.

12. Pascual Carrión, *Los latifundios en España* (Madrid: Gráficas Reunidas, 1932) p. 45.

13. George R. Esenwein, *Anarchist Ideology and the Working Class Movement in Spain, 1868–1898* (Berkeley: University of California Press, 1989) pp. 86–92; Avilés Farré, *La daga y la dinamita*, pp. 132–7; Max Nettlau, *La Première Internationale en Espagne (1868–1888)* (Dordrecht: Reider, 1969) pp. 343–4.

14. Demetrio Castro Alfín, *Hambre en Andalucía. Antecedentes y circunstancias de la mano negra*

(Cordoba: Ayuntamiento de Córdoba, 1986) pp. 93–114; Avilés Farré, *La daga y la dinamita*, pp. 137–9.

15. Castro Alfín, *Hambre en Andalucía*, pp. 117–26, 141–6, 151–2.

16. There is some dispute as to whether the Mano Negra really existed and, if it did, its real status. In a celebrated essay published in 1919, Constancio Bernaldo de Quirós, *El espartaquismo agrario y otros ensayos sobre la estructura económica y social de Andalucía* (Madrid: Ediciones de la Revista de Trabajo, 1978) pp. 162–7, took the Mano Negra seriously, although the examples of its alleged crimes that he gave could easily have been the consequence of unrelated and unconnected disputes. Clara E. Lida, 'Agrarian Anarchism in Andalusia. Documents on the Mano Negra', *International Review of Social History*, Vol. 14, No. 3, December 1969, pp. 315–52, provides documentary evidence that the society existed while casting doubt on links with the FTRE and acknowledging that most of those arrested had nothing to do with the FTRE. See also Clara E. Lida, *Anarquismo y revolución en la España del XIX* (Madrid: Siglo XXI de España, 1972) pp. 247–60; Castro Alfín, *Hambre en Andalucía*, pp. 153–63; Eduardo González Calleja, *La razón de la fuerza. Órden público, subversión y violencia política en la España de la Restauración (1875–1917)* (Madrid; Consejo Superior de Investigaciones Cientificas, 1998) pp. 234–6, and Avilés Farré, *La daga y la dinamita*, pp. 139–66. The view that it was an invention of the authorities is also common. See, for example, James Joll, *The Anarchists,*

2nd edn (London: Methuen, 1979) pp. 110, 214; Tuñón de Lara, *El Movimiento obrero*, pp. 278–82; Diego Abad de Santillán, *Contribución a la historia del movimiento obrero* (Puebla, Mexico: Editorial Cajica, 1962) p. 321; Temma Kaplan, *Anarchists of Andalusia 1868–1903* (Princeton, NJ: Princeton University Press, 1977) pp. 126–34; Esenwein, *Anarchist Ideology*, pp. 85–97; María García Alonso, 'Historias de la mano negra', *Boletín de la Institución Libre de Enseñanza*, Nos 40–1, 2001, pp. 149–65.

17. Esenwein, *Anarchist Ideology*, pp. 93–6, 117–22.

18. *Ibid.*, p. 162; Paul Heywood, *Marxism and the Failure of Organised Socialism in Spain 1879–1936* (Cambridge: Cambridge University Press, 1990). Cf. Juan José Morato, *El Partido Socialista Obrero*, 2nd edn (Madrid: Editorial Ayuso, 1976); Juan José Morato, *La cuna de un gigante. Historia de la Asociación General del Arte de Imprimir*, facsimile of 1925 edn (Madrid: Ministerio de Trabajo y Seguridad Social, 1984); Juan José Morato, *Líderes del movimiento obrero español 1868–1921* (Madrid: Edicusa, 1972); Juan José Morato, *Pablo Iglesias Posse. Educador de muchedumbres*, 2nd edn (Barcelona: Ariel, 1968); Santos Juliá Díaz, *Los socialistas en la política española 1879–1982* (Madrid: Taurus, 1997).

19. Esenwein, *Anarchist Ideology*, pp. 98–116; Álvarez Junco, *La ideología política del anarquismo español*, pp. 341–74; González Calleja, *La razón de la fuerza*, pp. 236–46; Antoni Dalmau, *El procés de Montjuïc. Barcelona al*

final del segle xix (Barcelona: Ajuntament de Barcelona/Editorial Base, 2010) pp. 23–5; Avilés Farré, *La daga y la dinamita*, pp. 274–5.

20. Dalmau, *El procés de Montjuïc*, pp. 26–8, 38–50; Avilés Farré, *La daga y la dinamita*, pp. 274–80; Temma Kaplan, *Red City, Blue Period: Social Movements in Picasso's Barcelona* (Berkeley: University of California Press, 1992) pp. 28–35.

21. José Aguilar Villagrán, *El asalto campesino a Jérez de la Frontera en 1892* (Jerez: Centro de Estudios Históricos Jérezanos, 1984) pp. 9–11.

22. *Ibid.*, pp. 28–9, claims that more than 1,500 peasants were involved. Enrique Montáñez, 'El anarquismo en Andalucía. De la F.R.E. a la Mano Negra y el asalto campesino a Jérez', in Manuel González de Molina and Diego Caro Cancela, eds, *La utopía racional. Estudios sobre el movimiento obrero andaluz* (Granada: Editoria Universidad de Granada, 2001) pp. 53–79; Kaplan, *Anarchists of Andalusia*, pp. 170–5; Pascual Carrión, *Los latifundios en España* (Madrid: Gráficas Reunidas, 1932) pp. 27–8; Bernaldo de Quirós, *El espartaquismo agrario*, pp. 169–70.

23. Aguilar Villagrán, *El asalto campesino a Jérez*, pp. 79–104; Kaplan, *Anarchists of Andalusia*, pp. 175–85; Bernaldo de Quirós, *El espartaquismo agrario*, pp. 171–2; Gérard Brey, ed., *Seis estudios sobre el proletariado andaluz (1868–1939)* (Cordoba: Ayuntamiento de Córdoba, 1984) pp. 113–18; Avilés Farré, *La daga y la dinamita*, pp. 213–22.

24. Esenwein, *Anarchist Ideology*, pp. 176–83; Avilés Farré, *La daga y la dinamita*, pp. 222–6.

25. José Álvarez Junco, *El Emperador del Paralelo* (Madrid: Alianza, 1990) p. 147.

26. Rafael Núñez Florencio, *El terrorismo anarquista 1888–1909* (Madrid: Siglo XXI de España, 1983) pp. 31–3, 41–2, 48–50; Dalmau, *El procés de Montjuïc*, pp. 52–92, 203–13; Avilés Farré, *La daga y la dinamita*, pp. 280–3; Angel Smith, *Anarchism, Revolution and Reaction: Catalan Labour and the Crisis of the Spanish State, 1898–1923* (New York: Berghahn Books, 2007) pp. 107–8.

27. Dalmau, *El procés de Montjuïc*, pp. 28–36, 247; Álvarez Junco, *La ideología política*, pp. 255–65; Carlos Serrano, *El turno del pueblo. Crisis nacional, movimientos populares y populismo en España (1890–1910)* (Barcelona: Península, 2000) pp. 143–64.

28. Dalmau, *El procés de Montjuïc*, pp. 99–10, 115–21; Avilés Farré, *La daga y la dinamita*, pp. 283–7. Designed by the Italian Nationalist Felice Orsini, the bombs had first been used in his attempt to kill Napoleon III in 1858.

29. Gabriel Cardona and Juan Carlos Losada, *Weyler. Nuestro hombre en La Habana* (Barcelona: Planeta, 1997) p. 139.

30. Dalmau, *El procés de Montjuïc*, pp. 121–40, 148–84, 187–97, 216–20, 223–35; Avilés Farré, *La daga y la dinamita*, pp. 287–95; Esenwein *Anarchist Ideology*, pp. 186–8.

31. David S. Woolman, *Rebels in the Rif: Abd el Krim and the Rif Rebellion* (Stanford, Calif.: Stanford University Press, 1969) pp. 33–4; Stanley G. Payne, *Politics and the Military in Modern Spain* (Stanford, Calif.: Stanford University Press, 1967) pp. 62–3; Manuel

Leguineche, *Annual 1921. El desastre de España en el Rif* (Madrid: Alfaguara, 1996) pp. 166–8; Gerald Brenan, *The Spanish Labyrinth* (Cambridge: Cambridge University Press, 1943) p. 61; Manuel Ciges Aparicio, *España bajo la dinastía de los Borbones* (Madrid: M. Aguilar, 1932) p. 377.

32. Dalmau, *El procés de Montjuïc*, pp. 141–8, 185–7; Cardona and Losada, *Weyler*, pp. 146–51; Álvarez Junco, *El Emperador del Paralelo*, pp. 148–50; Avilés Farré, *La daga y la dinamita*, pp. 295–7.

33. Dalmau, *El procés de Montjuïc*, pp. 249–74; Amadeo Hurtado, *Quaranta anys d'advocat. Història del meu temps 1894–1936* (Barcelona: Edicions 62, 2011) pp. 25–43; Herrerín López, *Anarquía, dinamita y revolución social*, pp. 130–1; Avilés Farré, *La daga y la dinamita*, pp. 299–303; Esenwein, *Anarchist Ideology*, pp. 191–4; Joaquín Romero Maura, 'Terrorism in Barcelona and its Impact on Spanish Politics 1904–1909', *Past & Present*, No. 41, December 1968, pp. 130–83, esp. pp. 131–2.

34. González Calleja, *La razón de la fuerza*, pp. 281–3; Avilés Farré, *La daga y la dinamita*, pp. 318–24.

35. Esenwein, *Anarchist Ideology*, pp. 194–7; Dalmau, *El procés de Montjuïc*, pp. 364–81; Antoni Dalmau i Ribalta, *Per la causa dels humils. Una biografía de Tarrida del Mármol (1861–1915)* (Barcelona: Publicacions de l'Abadia de Montserrat, 2015) pp. 63–78.

36. Álvarez Junco, *El Emperador del Paralelo*, pp. 148–70; Dalmau, *El procés de Montjuïc*, pp. 456–8; Joan B. Culla i Clarà, *El republicanisme Lerrouxista a Catalunya (1901–*

1923) (Barcelona: Curial, 1986)
p. 16.

37. Romero Maura, 'Terrorism in
Barcelona', p. 131, n. 1; Dalmau, *El
procés de Montjuïc*, pp. 424–43;
Avilés Farré, *La daga y la dinamita*,
pp. 338–9; Herrerín López,
*Anarquía, dinamita y revolución
social*, pp. 147–52; Joan Peiró,
Escrits 1917–1939 (Barcelona:
Edicions 62, 1975) pp. 473–4.

38. Dalmau, *El procés de Montjuïc*,
pp. 275–84, 387–90, 432. Lists of
those arrested, *ibid.*, pp. 285–340;
on tortures and prison conditions,
pp. 341–60; on Marzo Díaz-
Valdivieso, pp. 364–8; on legal
consequences, pp. 382–6; on
Ascheri, pp. 391–9; on the trial and
executions, pp. 405–20; Hurtado,
Quaranta anys d'advocat, pp. 31–6;
Avilés Farré, *La daga y la dinamita*,
pp. 303–18.

39. Dalmau, *El procés de Montjuïc*,
pp. 373–9; Álvarez Junco, *El
Emperador del Paralelo*, p. 79; Joan
B. Culla, *El republicanisme
lerrouxista a Catalunya (1901–
1923)* (Barcelona: Curial, 1986)
p. 61; Alejandro Lerroux, *Mis
Memorias* (Madrid: Afrodisio
Aguado, 1963) pp. 390–4; González
Calleja, *La razón de la fuerza*,
pp. 290–2; Herrerín López,
*Anarquía, dinamita y revolución
social*, pp. 167–72.

40. González Calleja, *La razón de la
fuerza*, pp. 293–5; Esenwein,
Anarchist Ideology, pp. 197–9;
Avilés Farré, *La daga y la dinamita*,
pp. 324–6; Robert Hughes,
Barcelona (London: Harvill, 1992)
pp. 418–22; *The Times*, 5 May 1897;
Francesco Tamburini, 'Michele
Angiolillo, el anarquista que asesinó
a Cánovas del Castillo', *Historia 16*,
Madrid, 1997, pp. 28–39; Herrerín
López, *Anarquía, dinamita y*

revolución social, pp. 157–61.

41. Romero Maura, 'Terrorism in
Barcelona', pp. 130–83,
esp. pp. 131–3.

42. Cardona and Losada, *Weyler*,
pp. 173–237; Hugh Thomas, *Cuba
or the Pursuit of Freedom* (London:
Eyre & Spottiswoode, 1971)
pp. 331–53; Fernando J. Padilla
Angulo, '*Reconcentración* in Cuba
(1895–1898): An Uncomfortable
Past', in Fernando Puell de la Villa
and David García Hernán, eds, *War
and Population Displacement:
Lessons of History* (Brighton: Sussex
Academic Press, 2018) pp. 117–35.

43. Sebastian Balfour, *The End of the
Spanish Empire 1898–1923* (Oxford:
Clarendon Press, 1997) pp. 11–28;
Conde de Romanones, *Las
responsabilidades políticas del
antiguo régimen 1875–1923*
(Madrid: Renacimiento, 1924)
p. 33.

44. Balfour, *The End of the Spanish
Empire*, pp. 33–46.

45. Pilar Jaraiz Franco, *Historia de una
disidencia* (Barcelona: Planeta,
1981) p. 37; Luis Suárez Fernández,
Francisco Franco y su tiempo, 8 vols
(Madrid: Fundación Nacional
Francisco Franco, 1984) I, pp. 71–3;
George Hills, *Franco: The Man and
his Nation* (New York: Macmillan,
1967) p. 24.

46. Balfour, *The End of the Spanish
Empire*, pp. 50–5; R. J. Harrison,
'Catalan Business and the Loss of
Cuba, 1898–1914', *Economic
History Review*, 2nd Series, Vol.
XXVII, No. 3, August 1974,
pp. 431–5.

47. Balfour, *The End of the Spanish
Empire*, pp. 56–63; Harrison,
'Catalan Business and the Loss of
Cuba', pp. 435–41.

48. Ricardo Macías Picavea, *El
problema nacional. Hechos, causas,*

remedios (Madrid: Librería General de Victoriano Suárez, 1899) pp. 251–2.

49. Costa, *Oligarquía y caciquismo*, I, pp. 5–6, 12–21, 67–75, 152–3; Manuel Azaña, 'El cirujano de hierro, según Costa', *España*, No. 397, 24 November 1923.

50. Costa, *Oligarquía y caciquismo*, I, pp. 152–3.

51. José Ortega y Gasset, *Vieja y nueva política* (Madrid: Renacimiento, 1914), reproduced in *Obras completas*, Vol. I (Madrid: Revista de Occidente, 1950) pp. 281–2.

Chapter 3: Revolution and War: From the Disaster of 1898 to the Tragic Week of 1909

1. Sebastian Balfour, *The End of the Spanish Empire 1898–1923* (Oxford: Clarendon Press, 1997) pp. 49, 92–131.

2. Xavier Cuadrat, *Socialismo y anarquismo en Cataluña (1899–1911). Los orígenes de la C.N.T.* (Madrid: Ediciones de la Revista de Trabajo, 1976) pp. 51–74; Romero Maura, *La rosa de fuego*, pp. 87–93.

3. Balfour, *The End of the Spanish Empire*, pp. 145–8.

4. Pere Ferrer, *Juan March. El hombre más misterioso del mundo* (Barcelona: Ediciones B, 2008) pp. 26, 34. See also Frank Jellinek, *The Civil War in Spain* (London: Left Book Club, 1938) pp. 76–82.

5. Salvador Forner and Mariano García, *Cuneros y caciques* (Alicante: Patronato Municipal del V Centenario de la Ciudad de Alicante, 1990) p. 139; Javier Moreno Luzón, *Romanones. Caciquismo y política liberal* (Madrid: Alianza Editorial, 1998) pp. 139, 157–8, 349–51.

6. Juan José Linz and Miguel Jerez, 'Los diputados en las Cortes de la Restauración y de la Segunda República', in Linz, *Obras escogidas (6) Partidos y elites políticas en España* (Madrid: Centro de Estudios Políticos y Constitucionales, 2013) p. 16.

7. M. A. Peña Guerrero and M. Sierra, 'Andalucía', in José Varela Ortega, ed., *El poder de la influencia. Geografía del caciquismo en España (1875–1923)* (Madrid: Centro de Estudios Políticos y Constitucionales/Marcial Pons, 2001) p. 39.

8. María Jesús González Hernández, *El universo conservador de Antonio Maura. Biografía y proyecto de Estado* (Madrid: Biblioteca Nueva, 1997) pp. 7–28; Raymond Carr, *Modern Spain 1875–1980* (Oxford: Oxford University Press, 1980) pp. 72–3.

9. For perceptive summaries of Maura's character and career, see Francisco J. Romero Salvadó, 'Antonio Maura from Messiah to Fireman', in Alejandro Quiroga and Miguel Ángel del Arco, eds, *Right-Wing Spain in the Civil War Era: Soldiers of God and Apostles of the Fatherland* (London: Continuum, 2012) pp. 1–26, and María Jesús González, '"Neither God Nor Monster": Antonio Maura and the Failure of Conservative Reformism in Restoration Spain (1893–1923)', *European History Quarterly*, Vol. 32, No. 3, pp. 307–34.

10. María Jesús González Hernández, *Ciudadanía y acción. El conservadurismo maurista 1907–1923* (Madrid: Siglo XXI de España, 1990) p. 217.

11. Duque de Maura and Melchor Fernández Almagro, *Por qué cayó Alfonso XIII* (Madrid: Ediciones Ambos Mundos, 1948) pp. 40–2.

12. *Ibid.*, pp. 49-51; González Hernández, *El universo conservador*, pp. 47-57.
13. Ángel Ossorio y Gallardo, *Mis memorias* (Buenos Aires: Losada, 1946) p. 67.
14. Maura and Fernández Almagro, *Por qué cayó Alfonso XIII*, pp. 71-9; Joaquín Romero Maura, *'La rosa de fuego'. El obrerismo barcelonés de 1899 a 1909* (Barcelona: Grijalbo, 1975) pp. 382-3.
15. Carr, *Modern Spain*, pp. 73-5; Joaquín Romero Maura, 'Terrorism in Barcelona and its Impact on Spanish Politics 1904-1909', *Past & Present*, No. 41 (December, 1968), pp. 130-83.
16. Paul Heywood, *Marxism and the Failure of Organised Socialism in Spain 1879-1936* (Cambridge: Cambridge University Press, 1990) pp. 9-28.
17. Cuadrat, *Socialismo y anarquismo en Cataluña*, p. 74.
18. *Ibid.*, pp. 75-92; Romero Maura, *'La rosa de fuego'*, p. 207; Alfonso Colodrón, 'La huelga general de Barcelona de 1902', *Revista de Trabajo*, No. 33, 1971, pp. 99-109; *El Socialista*, 21 February 1902.
19. Juan Pablo Fusi, *Política obrera en el País Vasco* (Madrid: Ediciones Turner, 1975) pp. 333-58; Octavio Cabezas, *Indalecio Prieto, socialista y español* (Madrid: Algaba Ediciones, 2005) pp. 56-71.
20. Alejandro Lerroux, *Mis memorias* (Madrid: Afrodisio Aguado, 1963) pp. 390, 646-7
21. José Álvarez Junco, *El Emperador del Paralelo* (Madrid: Alianza, 1990) pp. 151-69, 315-98; Romero Maura, *'La rosa de fuego'*, pp. 111-27; Joan B. Culla Clarà, *El Republicanisme Lerrouxista a Catalunya (1901-1923)* (Barcelona: Curial, 1986) p. 16; Eduardo

González Calleja, *La razón de la fuerza. Órden público, subversión y violencia política en la España de la Restauración (1875-1917)* (Madrid: Consejo Superior de Investigaciones Cientificas, 1998) p. 401.
22. Rafael Shaw, *Spain from Within* (London: T. Fisher Unwin, 1910) pp. 73-86, 91-108; Romero Maura, *'La rosa de fuego'*, pp. 521-2, 190-5.
23. Lerroux, *Mis memorias*, pp. 452-9; Romero Maura, 'Terrorism in Barcelona', pp. 135-7; González Calleja, *La razón de la fuerza*, pp. 414-15; Ángel Herrerín López, *Anarquía, dinamita y revolución social. Violencia y represión en la España de entre siglos (1868-1909)* (Madrid: Los Libros de la Catarata, 2011) pp. 214-17; González Hernández, *El universo conservador*, pp. 75-6; Álvarez Junco, *El Emperador del Paralelo*, pp. 292-4.
24. Juan Avilés Farré, *Francisco Ferrer y Guardia. Pedagogo, anarquista y mártir* (Madrid: Marcial Pons, 2006) pp. 145-57, 170, 174, 188-91; Romero Maura, 'Terrorism in Barcelona', pp. 137-44; Lerroux, *Mis memorias*, pp. 449-51, 535; Dr Pedro Vallina, *Mis memorias* (Madrid/Seville: Libre Pensamiento/Centro Andaluz del Libro, 2000) pp. 65-79, 232, 267; Herrerín López, *Anarquía, dinamita y revolución social*, pp. 217-23; Álvarez Junco, *El Emperador del Paralelo*, pp. 295-8.
25. Avilés Farré, *Francisco Ferrer*, pp. 157-63; Herrerín López, *Anarquía, dinamita y revolución social*, pp. 223-4; Álvarez Junco, *El Emperador del Paralelo*, pp. 298-300.
26. Carolyn P. Boyd, 'El rey-soldado. Alfonso XIII y el ejército', in Javier

Moreno Luzón, ed., *Alfonso XIII. Un político en el trono* (Madrid: Marcial Pons, 2003) pp. 215-19, 222-6; María Jesús González Hernández, 'El rey de los conservadores', in Moreno Luzón, ed., *Alfonso XIII*, p. 124; Conde de Romanones, *Notas de una vida* (Madrid: Marcial Pons Ediciones, 1999) pp. 160-2; Niceto Alcalá-Zamora, *Memorias* (Barcelona: Planeta, 1977) pp. 74-8.

27. *La Correspondencia Militar*, 4 October 1905.

28. On military conceptions of honour, see Emilio Mola Vidal, *Obras completas* (Valladolid: Librería Santarén, 1940) pp. 991-5; Gabriel Cardona, *El poder militar en la España contemporánea hasta la guerra civil* (Madrid: Siglo XXI de España, 1983) pp. 41-3, 47-50; Balfour, *The End of the Spanish Empire*, pp. 175-8.

29. Claudi Ametlla, *Memòries polítiques 1890-1917* (Barcelona: Editorial Pòrtic, 1963) pp. 238-40; Amadeu Hurtado, *Quaranta anys d'advocat. Història del meu temps 1894-1936*, 2nd edn (Barcelona: Edicions 62, 2011) pp. 79-80; Joaquín Romero Maura, *The Spanish Army and Catalonia: The 'Cu-Cut! Incident' and the Law of Jurisdictions, 1905-1906* (London: Sage, 1976) pp. 5-7, 13, 18-21; Álvarez Junco, *El Emperador del Paralelo*, pp. 317-18; Balfour, *The End of the Spanish Empire*, pp. 178-81.

30. Juan Antonio Lacomba Avellán, *La crisis española de 1917* (Madrid: Editorial Ciencia Nueva, 1970) p. 105.

31. *La Correspondencia Militar*, 28 November 1905.

32. Romanones, *Notas de una vida*, pp. 208-11; Ametlla, *Memòries polítiques 1890-1917*, pp. 241-2;

Romero Maura, *The Spanish Army and Catalonia*, pp. 18-29; Cardona, *El poder militar*, pp. 50-2; Borja de Riquer, *Alfonso XIII y Cambó. La monarquía y el catalanismo político* (Barcelona: RBA, 2013) pp. 49-50.

33. In *La Publicidad*, 9 December 1905; Álvarez Junco, *El Emperador del Paralelo*, pp. 320-6, 356-7.

34. Avilés Farré, *Francisco Ferrer*, pp. 167-96; Lerroux, *Mis memorias*, pp. 459-67; Romero Maura, 'Terrorism in Barcelona', pp. 145-6; Herrerín López, *Anarquía, dinamita y revolución social*, pp. 220-7; Álvarez Junco, *El Emperador del Paralelo*, pp. 304-6.

35. Avilés Farré, *Francisco Ferrer*, pp. 170-96; Romanones, *Notas de una vida*, pp. 220-3; Álvarez Junco, *El Emperador del Paralelo*, pp. 306-7.

36. Richard Bach Jensen, *The Battle against Anarchist Terrorism: An International History, 1878-1934* (Cambridge: Cambridge University Press, 2014) pp. 315-24.

37. Juan de la Cierva y Peñafiel, *Notas de mi vida* (Madrid: Instituto Editorial Reus, 1955) pp. 56-8.

38. Romero Maura, 'Terrorism in Barcelona', pp. 135, 165, 172-3; González Calleja, *La razón de la fuerza*, pp. 279, 283-4, 351, 354-5, 393; Antoni Dalmau Ribalta, *El Cas Rull. Viure del terror a la ciutat de les bombes (1901-1908)* (Barcelona: Columna Edicions, 2008) p. 33. There is some confusion about the spelling of his name. Dalmau uses 'Tresols'; virtually all others use 'Tressols'.

39. González Calleja, *La razón de la fuerza*, pp. 390-2.

40. Romero Maura, 'Terrorism in Barcelona', pp. 149-52; González Calleja, *La razón de la fuerza*,

pp. 390, 398; Rafael Núñez
Florencio, *El terrorismo anarquista
1888-1909* (Madrid: Siglo XXI de
España, 1983) pp. 81-2; Dalmau
Ribalta, *El Cas Rull*, pp. 61-6, 81,
109-13, 118-52.
41. Dalmau Ribalta, *El Cas Rull*,
pp. 153-72; Núñez Florencio, *El
terrorismo anarquista*, pp. 207-9.
42. Ametlla, *Memòries polítiques 1890-
1917*, pp. 242-7; Hurtado,
Quaranta anys, pp. 102-8; Riquer,
Alfonso XIII y Cambó, pp. 50-3.
43. Romero Salvadó, 'Antonio Maura',
in Quiroga and Del Arco, ed.,
Right-Wing Spain, pp. 4-5;
González Hernández, *Ciudadanía y
acción*, pp. 24-5.
44. González Hernández, *El universo
conservador*, pp. 134-7, 143-5.
45. *Ibid.*, pp. 146-50.
46. *Ibid.*, pp. 153-9.
47. González Hernández, *Ciudadanía y
acción*, pp. 14-15.
48. Romero Maura, *'La rosa de fuego'*,
pp. 427-30; Ametlla, *Memòries
polítiques 1890-1917*, pp. 248-54;
Balfour, *The End of the Spanish
Empire*, pp. 155-7.
49. *La Rebeldía*, 1 September 1906;
Joan B. Culla y Clarà, 'Ni tan
jóvenes, ni tan bárbaros. Juventudes
en el republicanismo lerrouxista
barcelonés', *Ayer*, No. 59 (3), 2005;
Álvarez Junco, *El Emperador del
Paralelo*, pp. 324-8; Dalmau
Ribalta, *El Cas Rull*, pp. 186-7.
50. Romero Maura, 'Terrorism in
Barcelona', pp. 156-7; González
Calleja, *La razón de la fuerza*,
pp. 392-3, 397-9; Dalmau Ribalta,
El Cas Rull, pp. 177, 181-202,
211-33; Herrerín López, *Anarquía,
dinamita y revolución social*,
pp. 265-6.
51. Romero Maura, 'Terrorism in
Barcelona', pp. 176-82.
52. *Ibid.*, pp. 170-4.

53. Ossorio to La Cierva on 9 January
1908, *ibid.*, pp. 158-60.
54. Dalmau Ribalta, *El Cas Rull*,
pp. 332-5.
55. Herrerín López, *Anarquía,
dinamita y revolución social*,
pp. 267-72; Dalmau Ribalta, *El Cas
Rull*, pp. 236-7, 244-7, 255-60.
56. Dalmau Ribalta, *El Cas Rull*,
pp. 329-30.
57. *Ibid.*, pp. 234-44, 265-98, 307-25;
González Calleja, *La razón de la
fuerza*, pp. 399-417; Romero
Maura, 'Terrorism in Barcelona',
pp. 163-7, 171-3; Núñez Florencio,
El terrorismo anarquista, pp. 101-2;
Joan Peiró, *Escrits 1917-1939*
(Barcelona: Edicions 62, 1975)
pp. 473-4.
58. Cuadrat, *Socialismo y anarquismo
en Cataluña*, pp. 179-209.

Chapter 4: Revolution and War: From the Tragic Week of 1909 to the Crisis of 1917-1918

1. Rafael Shaw, *Spain from Within*
(London: T. Fisher Unwin, 1910)
pp. 18, 199-203.
2. María Jesús González Hernández,
*El universo conservador de Antonio
Maura. Biografía y proyecto de
Estado* (Madrid: Biblioteca Nueva,
1997) pp. 108-9, 309-13; Romero
Maura, *'La rosa de fuego'*, pp. 501-6;
María Rosa de Madariaga, *En el
Barranco del Lobo. Las guerras de
Marruecos* (Madrid: Alianza
Editorial, 2005) pp. 43-52, 60-4;
Sebastian Balfour, *Deadly Embrace:
Morocco and the Road to the
Spanish Civil War* (Oxford: Oxford
University Press, 2002) pp. 8-27.
3. Sebastian Balfour, *The End of the
Spanish Empire 1898-1923* (Oxford:
Clarendon Press, 1997) p. 93.
4. Juan de la Cierva y Peñafiel, *Notas
de mi vida* (Madrid: Instituto
Editorial Reus, 1955) pp. 136-42;

Joan Connelly Ullman, *The Tragic Week: A Study of Anti-Clericalism in Spain 1875–1912* (Cambridge, Mass.: Harvard University Press, 1968) pp. 132–6, 142–63; González Hernández, *El universo conservador*, pp. 320–2; José Álvarez Junco, *El Emperador del Paralelo* (Madrid: Alianza, 1990) pp. 375–8; Madariaga, *En el Barranco del Lobo*, pp. 62–6.

5. Madariaga, *En el Barranco del Lobo*, pp. 53–7.

6. Connelly Ullman, *The Tragic Week*, pp. 141–58, 167–282, 326–8; Álvarez Junco, *El Emperador del Paralelo*, pp. 379–83; Shaw, *Spain from Within*, p. 35; Romero Maura, 'La rosa de fuego', pp. 509–19.

7. Carolyn P. Boyd, *Praetorian Politics in Liberal Spain* (Chapel Hill: University of North Carolina Press, 1979) pp. 23–5.

8. La Cierva, *Notas*, pp. 146–52; Duque de Maura and Melchor Fernández Almagro, *Por qué cayó Alfonso XIII* (Madrid: Ediciones Ambos Mundos, 1948) pp. 145–59; Connelly Ullman, *The Tragic Week*, pp. 284–304; Joaquín Romero Maura, 'Terrorism in Barcelona and its Impact on Spanish Politics 1904–1909', *Past & Present*, No. 41, December 1968, pp. 130–83, esp. pp. 141–6; Shaw, *Spain from Within*, pp. 147–8, 190–1; Balfour, *The End of the Spanish Empire*, pp. 128–31, 160–2.

9. González Hernández, *El universo conservador*, pp. 174–5.

10. Alejandro Lerroux, *Mis memorias* (Madrid: Afrodisio Aguado Editores, 1963) pp. 467–9.

11. Álvarez Junco, *El Emperador del Paralelo*, pp. 419–22.

12. Morgan C. Hall, 'El Rey imaginado. La construcción política de la imagen de Alfonso XIII', in Javier

Moreno Luzón, ed., *Alfonso XIII. Un político en el trono* (Madrid: Marcial Pons, 2003) p. 65.

13. Conde de Romanones, *Notas de una vida* (Madrid: Marcial Pons Ediciones, 1999) pp. 286–8, 292–8; Raymond Carr, *Spain 1808–1939* (Oxford: Oxford University Press, 1966) pp. 492–5; Balfour, *The End of the Spanish Empire*, pp. 204–9; Xavier Cuadrat, *Socialismo y anarquismo en Cataluña (1899–1911). Los orígenes de la C.N.T.* (Madrid: Ediciones de la Revista de Trabajo, 1976), pp. 457–62, 535–85.

14. Ángel Ossorio y Gallardo, *Mis memorias* (Buenos Aires: Losada, 1946) pp. 102–4; Romanones, *Notas de una vida*, pp. 369–71; María Jesús González Hernández, *Ciudadanía y acción. El conservadurismo maurista 1907–1923* (Madrid: Siglo XXI de España, 1990) pp. 22–3, 44–67, 122.

15. Cuadrat, *Socialismo y anarquismo en Cataluña*, pp. 179–209, 462–92; Manuel Tuñón de Lara, *El movimiento obrero en la historia de España* (Madrid: Taurus, 1972) pp. 305–7.

16. Maura and Fernández Almagro, *Por qué cayó Alfonso XIII*, pp. 472–3.

17. Francisco J. Romero Salvadó, *Spain 1914–1918: Between War and Revolution* (London: Routledge/Cañada Blanch, 1999) pp. 6–19, 68–70.

18. Álvarez Junco, *El Emperador del Paralelo*, pp. 424–5; Octavio Ruiz Manjón, *El Partido Republicano Radical 1908–1936* (Madrid: Ediciones Giner, 1976) pp. 108–9.

19. Santiago Roldán, José Luis García Delgado and Juan Muñoz, *La formación de la sociedad capitalista en España, 1914–1920*, 2 vols (Madrid: Confederación Española

de Cajas de Ahorros, 1973) I, pp. 48–53, 70–4; Joseph Harrison, *An Economic History of Modern Spain* (Manchester: Manchester University Press, 1978) pp. 89–95; Joseph Harrison, 'Heavy Industry, the State and Economic Development in the Basque Region, 1876–1936', *Economic History Review*, 2nd Series, Vol. XXXVI, No. 4, November 1983, pp. 540–1; Romero Salvadó, *Spain 1914–1918*, pp. 22–6.

20. Juan Antonio Lacomba Avellán, *La crisis española de 1917* (Madrid: Editorial Ciencia Nueva, 1970) pp. 31–9; Pedro Gual Villalbí, *Memorias de un industrial de nuestro tiempo* (Barcelona: Sociedad General de Publicaciones, 1923) pp. 104–21; Ángel Pestaña, *Terrorismo en Barcelona (Memorias inéditas)* (Barcelona: Planeta, 1979) pp. 101–2.

21. Richard Ford, *Gatherings from Spain* (London: John Murray, 1846) p. 335 (Everyman edn, p. 362).

22. Jehanne Wake, *Kleinwort Benson: The History of Two Families in Banking* (New York: Oxford University Press, 1997) p. 251.

23. Pere Ferrer, *Juan March. El hombre más misterioso del mundo* (Barcelona: Ediciones B, 2008) p. 74.

24. *Ibid.*, pp. 75–7; Mercedes Cabrera, *Juan March (1880–1962)* (Madrid: Marcial Pons, 2011) pp. 60–2, 103, 108–11, 126; Bernardo Díaz Nosty, *La irresistible ascensión de Juan March* (Madrid: Sedmay Ediciones, 1977) pp. 31–4, 98–100, 115; Fabián Estapé, *Sin acuse de recibo* (Barcelona: Plaza y Janés, 2000) p. 58.

25. Roldán, García Delgado and Muñoz, *La formación de la sociedad capitalista*, I, pp. 127–43, 239–51.

26. Francisco Largo Caballero, *Mis recuerdos. Cartas a un amigo* (Mexico City: Editores Unidos, 1954) pp. 51–2; Andrés Saborit, *Julián Besteiro* (Buenos Aires: Losada, 1967) pp. 86–9; Angel Smith, *Anarchism, Revolution and Reaction: Catalan Labour and the Crisis of the Spanish State, 1898–1923* (New York: Berghahn Books, 2007) pp. 264–5; Lacomba Avellán, *La crisis española de 1917*, pp. 216–21; Romero Salvadó, *Spain 1914–1918*, pp. 30–40, 86; Benjamin Martin, *The Agony of Modernization: Labor and Industrialization in Spain* (Ithaca, NY: Cornell University Press, 1990) p. 179; Chris Ealham, 'An Impossible Unity: Revolution, Reform and Counter-Revolution and the Spanish Left, 1917–23', in Francisco J. Romero and Angel Smith, eds, *The Agony of Spanish Liberalism: From Revolution to Dictatorship* (London: Palgrave Macmillan, 2010) pp. 108–9.

27. On Seguí, see Antonio Soler, *Apóstoles y asesinos. Vida, fulgor y muerte del Noi del Sucre* (Barcelona: Galaxia Gutenberg, 2016) pp. 75, 112, 120 and *passim*; Martin, *The Agony of Modernization*, pp. 184–7.

28. Roldán, García Delgado and Muñoz, *La formación de la sociedad capitalista*, pp. 255–322, 459–77; Francesc Cambó, *Memòries (1876–1936)* (Barcelona: Editorial Alpha, 1981) pp. 236–7, 242–9; José Varela Ortega, *Partidos, elecciones y caciquismo en la Restauración (1875–1900)* (Madrid: Marcial Pons, 2001) p. 286.

29. Jesús Pabón, *Cambó*, 3 vols (Barcelona: Editorial Alpha, 1952–69) I, pp. 501–7; Lacomba Avellán, *La crisis española de 1917*, pp. 169–70.

30. For an Africanista critique of the Juntas, see Emilio Mola Vidal, *Obras completas* (Valladolid: Librería Santarén, 1940) pp. 997–1016; Stanley G. Payne, *Politics and the Military in Modern Spain* (Stanford, Calif.: Stanford University Press, 1967) pp. 125–45; Boyd, *Praetorian Politics*, pp. 51–60.

31. Pabón, *Cambó*, I, p. 491; Cambó, *Memòries*, pp. 259–60.

32. Boyd, *Praetorian Politics*, pp. 61–6; Borja de Riquer, *Alfonso XIII y Cambó. La monarquía y el catalanismo político* (Barcelona: RBA, 2013) pp. 81–3; Cambó, *Memòries*, pp. 231–2, 247–9.

33. Lacomba Avellán, *La crisis española de 1917*, pp. 150–60; Maura and Fernández Almagro, *Por qué cayó Alfonso XIII*, pp. 298–308; J. M. Capo, *Las Juntas Militares de Defensa* (La Habana: Los Rayos X, 1923) pp. 23–33.

34. Pabón, *Cambó*, I, pp. 512–19; Cambó, *Memòries*, pp. 261–5; Lacomba Avellán, *La crisis española de 1917*, pp. 172–87, 190–209; Maura and Fernández Almagro, *Por qué cayó Alfonso XIII*, pp. 298, 486–9, 494–7, 505; Boyd, *Praetorian Politics*, pp. 79–82; Romero Salvadó, *Spain 1914–1918*, pp. 45–54, 105–15.

35. Lacomba Avellán, *La crisis española de 1917*, pp. 226–9; Ángel Pestaña, *Lo que aprendí en la vida* (Madrid: M. Aguilar, 1933) pp. 57–8.

36. Pestaña, *Lo que aprendí*, pp. 79–80, 171–7; Ángel Pestaña, *Terrorismo en Barcelona (Memorias inéditas)* (Barcelona: Planeta, 1979) pp. 98–104; Gerald Brenan, *The Spanish Labyrinth* (Cambridge: Cambridge University Press, 1943) pp. 69, 72; Smith, *Anarchism*, pp. 250–3; Francisco J. Romero Salvadó, *The Foundations of Civil*

War: Revolution, Social Conflict and Reaction in Liberal Spain, 1916–1923 (London: Routledge, 2008) pp. 60–1; Capo, *Las Juntas Militares*, pp. 128–34; Pío Baroja, *El cabo de las tormentas* (Madrid: Caro Raggio, 1974) pp. 93–7.

37. Pestaña, *Lo que aprendí*, p. 59; Victor Serge, *Memoirs of a Revolutionary 1901–1941* (London: Oxford University Press, 1963) pp. 54–7.

38. Romero Salvadó, *Spain 1914–1918*, pp. 101–4.

39. Largo Caballero, *Mis recuerdos*, pp. 52–4; Pestaña, *Lo que aprendí*, pp. 59–61.

40. Pestaña, *Lo que aprendí*, pp. 62–3.

41. Smith, *Anarchism*, pp. 278–81.

42. Lacomba Avellán, *La crisis española de 1917*, pp. 229–33; Romero Salvadó, *Spain 1914–1918*, pp. 120–1; Juan-Simeón Vidarte, *No queríamos al Rey. Testimonio de un socialista español* (Barcelona: Grijalbo, 1977) pp. 73–4.

43. Lacomba Avellán, *La crisis española de 1917*, pp. 233–47; Largo Caballero, *Mis recuerdos*, pp. 54–7; Saborit, *Julián Besteiro*, pp. 89–102; Romero Salvadó, *Spain 1914–1918*, pp. 123–4; Gerald H. Meaker, *The Revolutionary Left in Spain, 1914–1923* (Stanford, Calif.: Stanford University Press, 1974) pp. 82–6. For the Socialists' strike manifesto, see Vidarte, *No queríamos al Rey*, pp. 74–6.

44. Smith, *Anarchism*, pp. 275–83; Boyd, *Praetorian Politics*, pp. 84–5, 286; Enrique Moradiellos, *El Sindicato de los Obreros Mineros Asturianos 1910–1930* (Oviedo: Universidad de Oviedo, 1986) pp. 58–9; Lacomba Avellán, *La crisis española de 1917*, pp. 247–72; Antonio Bar, *La C.N.T. en los años rojos (del sindicalismo*

revolucionario al anarcosindicalismo 1910–1926) (Madrid: Akal, 1981) pp. 417–27; Meaker, *The Revolutionary Left*, pp. 86–91.

45. Llaneza, letters from prison, published in *El Minero de la Hulla*, August and September 1917, reprinted in Manuel Llaneza, *Escritos y discursos* (Oviedo: Fundación José Barreiros, 1985) pp. 206–14; Romero Salvadó, *The Foundations*, pp. 91–5. On Franco's role, see Francisco Aguado Sánchez, *La revolución de octubre de 1934* (Madrid: Editorial San Martín, 1972) p. 193; Luis Galinsoga and Francisco Franco-Salgado, *Centinela de occidente (Semblanza biográfica de Francisco Franco)* (Barcelona: Editorial AHR, 1956) pp. 35–6; Brian Crozier, *Franco: A Biographical History* (London: Eyre & Spottiswoode, 1967) p. 50.

46. Capo, *Las Juntas Militares*, pp. 61–5; Claudi Ametlla, *Memòries polítiques 1890–1917* (Barcelona: Editorial Pòrtic, 1963), pp. 388–9.

47. Romero Salvadó, *The Foundations*, p. 91; Largo Caballero, *Mis recuerdos*, pp. 56–63; Vidarte, *No queríamos al Rey*, pp. 78–9, 99–102; Paul Heywood, *Marxism and the Failure of Organised Socialism in Spain 1879–1936* (Cambridge: Cambridge University Press, 1990) pp. 53–4; Romero Salvadó, *Spain 1914–1918*, pp. 137–40.

48. Romero Salvadó, *Spain 1914–1918*, p. 135; Martin, *The Agony of Modernization*, p. 195.

49. Maura and Fernández Almagro, *Por qué cayó Alfonso XIII*, pp. 307–8; Lacomba Avellán, *La crisis española de 1917*, pp. 272–4; Pabón, *Cambó*, I, pp. 546–9.

50. Maura and Fernández Almagro, *Por qué cayó Alfonso XIII*, p. 507; La Cierva, *Notas*, pp. 186–7; Lacomba

Avellán, *La crisis española de 1917*, pp. 296–301; Romero Salvadó, *Spain 1914–1918*, pp. 142–5.

51. María Jesús González Hernández, 'El rey de los conservadores', in Moreno Luzón, ed., *Alfonso XIII*, p. 144; Romanones, *Notas de una vida*, pp. 419–20; Lacomba Avellán, *La crisis española de 1917*, pp. 301–4.

52. Lacomba Avellán, *La crisis española de 1917*, pp. 315–20; Riquer, *Alfonso XIII y Cambó*, pp. 88–97; Romanones, *Notas de una vida*, pp. 420–2; Cambó, *Memòries*, pp. 269–71; Pabón, *Cambó*, I, pp. 563–82; Ametlla, *Memòries polítiques 1890–1917*, pp. 384–7; Romero Salvadó, *Spain 1914–1918*, pp. 149–55.

53. Romanones, *Notas de una vida*, p. 420.

54. Maura and Fernández Almagro, *Por qué cayó Alfonso XIII*, p. 320; Capo, *Las Juntas Militares*, pp. 88–9, 103–119; Lacomba Avellán, *La crisis española de 1917*, pp. 323–44; Boyd, *Praetorian Politics*, pp. 94–8; Payne, *Politics and the Military*, pp. 140–5; Romero Salvadó, *Spain 1914–1918*, pp. 157–63, 215–16; Romero Salvadó, *The Foundations*, pp. 106–10.

55. Romanones, *Notas de una vida*, pp. 427–30; Maura and Fernández Almagro, *Por qué cayó Alfonso XIII*, pp. 309–11; Riquer, *Alfonso XIII y Cambó*, pp. 99–102; Cambó, *Memòries*, pp. 272–5; La Cierva, *Notas*, pp. 187–207; Pabón, *Cambó*, I, pp. 595–609.

56. *Diario de las Sesiones de Cortes*, 17 April 1918, reproduced in Francesc Cambó, *Discursos parlamentarios (1907–1935)* (Barcelona: Editorial Alpha, 1991) pp. 485–8.

57. Cambó, *Memòries*, pp. 275–97; Maura and Fernández Almagro, *Por*

qué cayó Alfonso XIII, pp. 312–23; Romanones, *Notas de una vida*, pp. 422–4; Pabón, *Cambó*, I, pp. 640–78; Riquer, *Alfonso XIII y Cambó*, pp. 103–9, 136.

Chapter 5: A System in Disarray: Disorder and Repression, 1918–1921

1. Juan Antonio Lacomba Avellán, *La crisis española de 1917* (Madrid: Editorial Ciencia Nueva, 1970) pp. 47–50; José Peirats, *Los anarquistas en la crisis política española* (Buenos Aires: Editorial Alfa, 1964).

2. Gerald H. Meaker, *The Revolutionary Left in Spain, 1914–1923* (Stanford, Calif.: Stanford University Press, 1974) pp. 103–8; Angel Smith, *Anarchism, Revolution and Reaction: Catalan Labour and the Crisis of the Spanish State, 1898–1923* (New York: Berghahn Books, 2007) pp. 284–6.

3. Antonio Bar, *La C.N.T. en los años rojos (del sindicalismo revolucionario al anarcosindicalismo 1910–1926)* (Madrid: Akal, 1981) pp. 356–8, 367–80; Benjamin Martin, *The Agony of Modernization: Labor and Industrialization in Spain* (Ithaca: Cornell University Press, 1990) pp. 196–200; Smith, *Anarchism*, pp. 245–50; Alberto Balcells, *El sindicalismo en Barcelona 1916–1923* (Barcelona: Editorial Nova Terra, 1965) pp. 51–65; Joaquín Romero Maura, 'The Spanish Case', *Government and Opposition*, Vol. 5, No. 4, 1970, pp. 469–72.

4. Francesc Cambó, *Memòries (1876–1936)* (Barcelona: Editorial Alpha, 1981) pp. 275–97; Duque de Maura and Melchor Fernández Almagro, *Por qué cayó Alfonso XIII* (Madrid: Ediciones Ambos Mundos, 1948) pp. 312–20; Jesús Pabón, *Cambó*, 3

vols (Barcelona: Editorial Alpha, 1952–69) I, pp. 640–78; Borja de Riquer, *Alfonso XIII y Cambó. La monarquía y el catalanismo político* (Barcelona: RBA, 2013) pp. 103–9, 136.

5. Diario de las Sesiones de las Cortes, 10 December 1918; Maura and Fernández Almagro, *Por qué cayó Alfonso XIII*, pp. 323–4; Riquer, *Alfonso XIII y Cambó*, pp. 111–26; Cambó, *Memòries*, pp. 298–304; Pabón, *Cambó*, II: *Parte primera: 1918–1930*, pp. 15–20.

6. Javier Moreno Luzón, 'El Rey de los Liberales', in Javier Moreno Luzón, ed., *Alfonso XIII. Un político en el trono* (Madrid: Marcial Pons, 2003) p. 153.

7. María Jesús González Hernández, 'El rey de los conservadores', in Moreno Luzón, ed., *Alfonso XIII*, pp. 141, 146.

8. Riquer, *Alfonso XIII y Cambó*, pp. 128–36; Cambó, *Memòries*, p. 328.

9. Juan José Castillo, 'Notas sobre los orígenes y primeros años de la Confederación Nacional Católico Agraria', in José Luis García Delgado, ed., *La cuestión agraria en la España contemporánea* (Madrid: Siglo XXI de España, 1976) pp. 203–48; Josefina Cuesta, *Sindicalismo católico agrario en España (1917–1919)* (Madrid: Editorial Narcea, 1978) *passim*.

10. Juan José Castillo, *El sindicalismo amarillo en España* (Madrid: Edicusa, 1977) p. 41.

11. Pascual Carrión, *Los latifundios en España* (Madrid: Gráficas Reunidas, 1932) p. 45.

12. Francisco Cobo Romero, '"The Red Dawn" of the Andalusian Countryside: Peasant Protest during the "Bolshevik Triennium", 1918–20', in Francisco J. Romero

and Angel Smith, eds, *The Agony of Spanish Liberalism: From Revolution to Dictatorship* (London: Palgrave Macmillan, 2010) pp. 121–43.

13. Juan Diaz del Moral, *Historia de las agitaciones campesinas andaluzas*, 3rd edn (Madrid: Alianza Editorial, 1973) pp. 265–86; Ángeles González, 'La construcción de un mito. El trienio bolchevique en Andalucía', in Manuel González de Molina and Diego Caro Cancela, eds, *La utopía racional. Estudios sobre el movimiento obrero andaluz* (Granada: Editoria Universidad de Granada, 2001) pp. 175–219; Francisco Cobo Romero, *Conflicto rural y violencia política. El largo camino hacia la dictadura. JAÉN, 1917–1950* (Jaén: Publicaciones de la Universidad de Jaén, 1999) pp. 114–27; Sebastian Balfour, *The End of the Spanish Empire 1898–1923* (Oxford: Clarendon Press, 1997) pp. 223–4.

14. Pascual Carrión, *Los latifundios en España* (Madrid: Gráficas Reunidas, 1932) p. 415; Constancio Bernaldo de Quirós, *El espartaquismo agrario y otros ensayos sobre la estructura económica y social de Andalucía* (Madrid: Ediciones de la Revista de Trabajo, 1973) pp. 183–92.

15. González Hernández, 'El rey de los conservadores', in Moreno Luzón, *Alfonso XIII*, p. 146; María Jesús González Hernández, *El universo conservador de Antonio Maura. Biografía y proyecto de Estado* (Madrid: Biblioteca Nueva, 1997) p. 379; Juan José Castillo, *Propietarios muy pobres. Sobre la subordinación política del pequeño campesino* (Madrid: Instituto de Estudios Agrarias, 1979) pp. 140–2; Eduardo González Calleja, *El máuser y el sufragio. Orden público, subversión y violencia política en la*

crisis de la Restauración (1917–1931) (Madrid: Consejo Superior de Investigaciones Científicas, 1999) pp. 44–5; Francisco J. Romero Salvadó, *The Foundations of Civil War: Revolution, Social Conflict and Reaction in Liberal Spain, 1916–1923* (London: Routledge/Cañada Blanch, 2008) p. 199.

16. Castillo, *Propietarios muy pobres*, pp. 202–8.

17. *El Socialista*, 23 July 1919.

18. Diaz del Moral, *Las agitaciones*, pp. 361–76; Edward E. Malefakis, *Agrarian Reform and Peasant Revolution in Spain* (New Haven, Conn.: Yale University Press, 1970) pp. 147–52; Castillo, *Propietarios muy pobres*, pp. 209–20; Ricardo Robledo, 'El Trienio Bolchevique de Díaz del Moral y su visión conservadora del cambio social', in Francisco Acosta Ramírez, ed., *La aurora de rojos dedos. El Trienio Bolchevique desde el sur de España* (Granada: Comares y Diputación Provincial de Córdoba, forthcoming).

19. Carrión, *Los latifundios*, p. 415.

20. Joseph Harrison, 'Heavy Industry, the State and Economic Development in the Basque Region, 1876–1936', *Economic History Review*, 2nd Series, Vol. XXXVI, No. 4, November 1983, pp. 541–2; Adrian Shubert, *The Road to Revolution in Spain: The Coal Miners of Asturias 1860–1934* (Urbana: University of Illinois Press, 1987) pp. 48–51, 85–6, 114–28; Antonio L. Oliveros, *Asturias en el resurgimiento español (apuntes históricos y biográficos*, 2nd edn (Gijón: Silverio Cañada, 1989) pp. 113–77.

21. Martin, *The Agony of Modernization*, p. 206.

22. 'Historia de la huelga de "La Canadiense"'; 'El Sr Morote explica a los lectores de "El Sol" la historia de todo lo ocurrido'; 'Declaraciones del Sr. Doval', *El Sol*, 3, 20 March, 1 August 1919; Amadeu Hurtado, *Quaranta anys d'advocat. Història del meu temps 1894-1936*, 2nd edn (Barcelona: Edicions 62, 2011) pp. 341-2; Pere Foix, *Apòstols i mercaders. Seixanta anys de lluita social a Catalunya*, 2nd edn (Barcelona: Editorial Nova Terra, 1976) pp. 69-71; Balcells, *El sindicalismo*, pp. 73-84; Smith, *Anarchism*, pp. 290-6; Conde de Romanones, *Notas de una vida* (Madrid: Marcial Pons Ediciones, 1999) pp. 432-6; Javier Moreno Luzón, *Romanones. Caciquismo y política liberal* (Madrid: Alianza Editorial, 1998) pp. 367-9.

23. This was discovered in the company's archives in 1958 by the lawyer Fabián Estapé, who was writing a report for the International Tribunal of The Hague on a long-running case involving the Barcelona Traction, Light and Power Company. See Fabián Estapé, *Sin acuse de recibo* (Barcelona: Plaza y Janés, 2000) pp. 122-5.

24. Manuel Burgos y Mazo, *El verano de 1919 en Gobernación* (Cuenca: Imprenta de Emilio Pinos, 1921) pp. 500-35; Soledad Bengoechea and Fernando del Rey, 'En vísperas de un golpe de Estado. Radicalización del patronal e imagen del fascismo en España', in Javier Tusell, Julio Gil Pecharromán and Feliciano Montero, eds, *Estudios sobre la derecha española contemporánea* (Madrid: UNED, 1993) pp. 301-26, esp. p. 304; Romero Salvadó, *The Foundations*, pp. 194-5.

25. Eduardo González Calleja and Fernando del Rey Reguillo, *La defensa armada contra la revolución* (Madrid: Consejo Superior de Investigaciones Científicas, 1995) pp. 71-80, 91-6.

26. Pere Foix, *Los archivos del terrorismo blanco. El fichero Lasarte 1918-1936* (Madrid: Ediciones de la Piqueta, 1978) p. 54; Manuel Casal Gómez, *La Banda Negra. Orígen y actuación de los pistoleros en Barcelona (1919-1921)*, 2nd edn (Barcelona: Icaria Editorial, 1977) pp. 66-8, 153-5; González Calleja, *El máuser*, pp. 80-1, 146-7, 152-9, 165; José Peirats, *La CNT en la revolución española*, 2nd edn, 3 vols (Paris: Ediciones Ruedo Ibérico, 1971) I, p. 34.

27. Speech of Francesc Layret, *Diario de Sesiones de las Cortes*, 7 August 1919, pp. 841-2; Smith, *Anarchism*, pp. 297-9; 'Afirmaciones Terminantes', *La Correspondencia Militar*, 17 April 1919; 'Declaraciones del Sr. Doval', *El Sol*, 1 August 1919; 'Nota de Montañés', reprinted in Romanones, *Notas de una vida*, pp. 436-40; Casal Gómez, *La Banda Negra*, pp. 59-62.

28. Balcells, *El sindicalismo*, pp. 85-99; Hurtado, *Quaranta anys*, pp. 343-6; Smith, *Anarchism*, pp. 294-5.

29. Carolyn P. Boyd, 'El rey-soldado. Alfonso XIII y el ejército', in Moreno Luzón, ed., *Alfonso XIII*, pp. 232-3. See the ambiguous account of Romanones, *Notas de una vida*, p. 436.

30. Moreno Luzón, *Romanones*, pp. 370-1; Romero Salvadó, *The Foundations*, pp. 199-200; Moreno Luzón, 'El Rey de los Liberales', in Moreno Luzón, *Alfonso XIII*, pp. 178-9.

31. González Calleja, *El máuser*, pp. 118-22; Smith, *Anarchism*,

pp. 300–2; Angel Pestaña, *Lo que aprendí en la vida* (Madrid: M. Aguilar, 1933) pp. 76–8, 81–4, 165–7; Casal Gómez, *La Banda Negra*, pp. 68–77; Ángel Pestaña, *Terrorismo en Barcelona (Memorias inéditas)* (Barcelona: Planeta, 1979) pp. 105–12.

32. Casal Gómez, *La Banda Negra*, pp. 62–8, 153–5; Francisco Bastos Ansart, *Pistolerismo (Historia trágica)* (Madrid: Espasa Calpe, 1935) pp. 35–41; Pestaña, *Terrorismo en Barcelona*, pp. 94–6, 102–16; Manuel Buenacasa, *El movimiento obrero español 1886–1926* (Gijón: Ediciones Júcar, 1977) p. 55; Adolfo Bueso, *Recuerdos de un cenetista*, Vol. I: *De la Semana Trágica (1909) a la Segunda República (1931)* (Barcelona: Ariel, 1976) pp. 126–8; González Calleja, *El máuser*, pp. 146–7, 152–5; Pío Baroja, *El cabo de las tormentas* (Madrid: Caro Raggio, 1974) pp. 93–8.

33. Romero Salvadó, *The Foundations*, pp. 202–5; Salvador de Madariaga, *Spain: A Modern History* (London: Jonathan Cape, 1961) pp. 328–31; Smith, *Anarchism*, pp. 302–8.

34. Antonio Soler, *Apóstoles y asesinos. Vida, fulgor y muerte del Noi del Sucre* (Barcelona: Galaxia Gutenberg, 2016) pp. 27–8.

35. *Diario de Sesiones de las Cortes*, 7 August 1919; Romero Salvadó, *The Foundations*, p. 202; Burgos y Mazo, *El verano de 1919*, pp. 305–13.

36. Romero Salvadó, *The Foundations*, pp. 205–9; Smith, *Anarchism*, pp. 308–15.

37. Ricardo Sanz, *El sindicalismo y la política. Los 'Solidarios' y 'Nosotros'* (Toulouse: Imprimerie Dulaurier, 1966) pp. 51–6; Balcells, *El sindicalismo*, pp. 104–6; Juan García Oliver, *El eco de los pasos*

(Barcelona: Ruedo Ibérico, 1978) pp. 31–2; Angel Pestaña, *Lo que aprendí en la vida* (Madrid: M. Aguilar, 1933) p. 186; González Calleja, *El máuser*, pp. 226–36.

38. Madariaga, *Spain*, pp. 331–2.

39. Smith, *Anarchism*, p. 315.

40. *ABC*, 7, 8, 11, 13 January 1920; García Oliver, *El eco*, pp. 30–1; Meaker, *The Revolutionary Left*, pp. 314–19; Smith, *Anarchism*, pp. 315–17, 336–7; Romero Salvadó, *The Foundations*, p. 236.

41. Gabriel Cardona and Juan Carlos Losada, *Weyler. Nuestro hombre en La Habana* (Barcelona: Planeta, 1997) pp. 289–91; Balcells, *El sindicalismo*, pp. 135–6.

42. *ABC*, 5, 6 August; *El Globo*, 6 August 1920; Foix, *Apòstols*, pp. 39–40; Robert Kern, *Red Years/ Black Years: A Political History of Spanish Anarchism, 1911–1937* (Philadelphia: Institute for the Study of Human Issues, 1978) pp. 54–6.

43. Francisco Madrid, *Ocho meses y un día en el gobierno civil de Barcelona* (Barcelona: La Flecha, 1932) pp. 78–93 (for Bas's own account of his period in office) and pp. 93–102 (for Bas's clash with Martínez Anido); Romero Salvadó, *The Foundations*, pp. 222–5; Smith, *Anarchism*, pp. 329–30; Roberto Muñoz Bolaños, 'Severiano Martínez Anido (1862–1937) Militar y represor', *Anatomía de la Historia*, 2013, pp. 7–9.

44. González Calleja, *El máuser*, p. 168; Pelai Pagès i Blanch, *Andreu Nin. Una vida al servicio de la clase obrera* (Barcelona: Laertes, 2011) p. 101.

45. González Calleja, *El máuser*, pp. 182–3; Meaker, *The Revolutionary Left*, pp. 328–36; Albert Pérez Baró, *Els 'feliços' anys*

vint. Memòries d'un militant obrer 1918–1926 (Palma de Mallorca: Editorial Moll, 1974) pp. 88–106; Jacinto León-Ignacio, *Los años del pistolerismo* (Barcelona: Planeta, 1981) pp. 150–4.

46. Smith, *Anarchism*, pp. 329, 335; León-Ignacio, *Los años del pistolerismo*, pp. 102, 148, 167. On Feced, see Romero Salvadó, *The Foundations*, p. 261; Paco Ignacio Taibo II, *Que sean fuego las estrellas. Barcelona (1917–1923)* (Barcelona: Crítica, 2016) pp. 269–70.

47. Romero Salvadó, *The Foundations*, p. 231.

48. Bueso, *Recuerdos de un cenetista*, p. 139; Madrid, *Ocho meses*, pp. 107–10; Burgos y Mazo, *El verano de 1919*, pp. 553–65; Foix, *Apòstols*, pp. 76–7, 82–3; Romero Salvadó, *The Foundations*, pp. 225–32; Casal Gómez, *La Banda Negra*, pp. 143–9; Smith, *Anarchism*, pp. 331–3, 356; León-Ignacio, *Los años del pistolerismo*, pp. 156–61.

49. The confessions of Feced were reprinted in Peirats, *La CNT*, I, pp. 33–6.

50. Letter of Miguel de Unamuno to *Le Quotidien*, Paris, 29 December 1923, reproduced in Valentín del Arco López, 'Unamuno frente a Primo de Rivera. De Salamanca Al Exilio, 1923–1924', in Dolores Gómez Molleda, ed., *Actas del Congreso Internacional, Cincuentenario de Unamuno* (Salamanca: Ediciones de la Universidad de Salamanca, 1986) pp. 150–1.

51. Baroja, *El cabo*, pp. 75, 79, 103–6.

52. *Ibid.*, pp. 79–80, 104–10; Andreu Navarra Ordoño, 'Pistolas, carnavales y pronunciamientos: Baroja y las rebeliones sociales de los años veinte y treinta', *Sancho el*

Sabio, No. 36, 2013, pp. 47–60; Smith, *Anarchism*, pp. 334–7.

53. Pestaña, *Terrorismo en Barcelona*, pp. 159–63; Smith, *Anarchism*, pp. 337–9; Colin M. Winston, *Workers and the Right in Spain, 1900–1936* (Princeton, NJ: Princeton University Press, 1985) pp. 185–208.

54. Madrid, *Ocho meses*, p. 67; Winston, *Workers and the Right*, pp. 49–50, 108–36; Castillo, *El sindicalismo amarillo*, pp. 37–9, 89–90, 126–43. Regarding Comillas's business empire, see Castillo, *El sindicalismo amarillo*, pp. 253–73.

55. Balcells, *El sindicalismo*, p. 162; Smith, *Anarchism*, pp. 335, 337; Romero Salvadó, *The Foundations*, pp. 227–30.

56. 'Sería bien triste …' and 'Los revolucionarios rusos', *El Socialista*, 10 November 1917 and 1 March 1918; Meaker, *The Revolutionary Left*, pp. 108–9.

57. Julio Aróstegui, *Largo Caballero. El tesón y la quimera* (Barcelona: Debate, 2013) pp. 122–33.

58. *Ibid.*, pp. 148–59; Meaker, *The Revolutionary Left*, pp. 225–384; Heywood, *Marxism*, pp. 54–83; Manuel Tuñón de Lara, *El Movimiento obrero en la historia de España* (Madrid: Taurus, 1972) pp. 681–717.

59. Heywood, *Marxism*, pp. 54–84; Chris Ealham, 'An Impossible Unity: Revolution, Reform and Counter-Revolution and the Spanish Left, 1917–23', in Francisco J. Romero and Angel Smith, eds, *The Agony of Spanish Liberalism: From Revolution to Dictatorship* (London: Palgrave Macmillan, 2010) pp. 112–14.

60. Francisco Largo Caballero, *Presente y futuro de la Unión General de*

Trabajadores de España (Madrid:
Javier Morata, 1925) pp. 135–59,
176–84; Smith, *Anarchism*,
pp. 335–6; Buenacasa, *El
movimiento obrero*, pp. 74–80.
61. Antonio Sánchez, 'Anatomía de un
magnicidio. Pedro Mateu "Yo maté
a Dato"', *Interviu*, 11–17 November
1976, pp. 35–6; Bueso, *Recuerdos de
un cenetista*, pp. 139–45; Sanz, *El
sindicalismo y la política*, pp. 73–4;
León-Ignacio, *Los años del
pistolerismo*, pp. 180–95; Romero
Salvadó, *The Foundations*,
pp. 211–12; Smith, *Anarchism*,
p. 337.
62. Juan Ruiz, 'Manuel y Ramón Archs.
Dos militantes de acción', *Tierra y
Libertad*, No. 233, December 2007;
Antoni Dalmau i Ribalta, 'Manuel
Ars i Solanellas (1859–1894),
l'estampador afusellat injustament a
Montjuïc', *Revista d'Igualada*, No.
28, April 2008, pp. 16–41, on
Ramón, pp. 38–40; Abel Rebollo,
'Dos generaciones: Paulí Pallàs i
Latorre (1862–1893) y Ramón
Archs (1887–1921)', in Manel Aisa
et al., *La Barcelona rebelde. Guía de
una ciudad silenciada* (Barcelona:
Octaedro, 2004) pp. 277–8; García
Oliver, *El eco*, pp. 30–6, 625–6.
63. Meaker, *The Revolutionary Left*,
pp. 331–4, 338–9; Winston,
Workers and the Right, pp. 139–41.
64. Madrid, *Ocho meses*, pp. 108–9.
65. Ibid., pp. 118–19; Winston, *Workers
and the Right*, pp. 112–14, 132–3,
142–63.
66. Foix, *Apòstols*, pp. 43–4; Romero
Salvadó, *The Foundations*,
pp. 234–6.
67. *El Defensor de Córdoba*, 24 May
1921; *ABC*, 24 May 1921; Juan de la
Cierva y Peñafiel, *Notas de mi vida*
(Madrid: Instituto Editorial Reus,
1955) pp. 233–5; Madariaga, *Spain*,
pp. 337–9; González Hernández, *El

universo conservador*, p. 379; José
María García Escudero, '¿Rey
autoritario o rey constitucional?',
Historia y Vida, No. 56, 1972,
pp. 52–62; José Luis Gómez
Navarro, *El régimen de Primo de
Rivera* (Madrid: Cátedra, 1991)
pp. 115–16; Rafael Borràs Betriu, *El
Rey perjuro. Alfonso XIII y la caída
de la Monarquía* (Barcelona: Los
Libros de Abril, 1997) pp. 85–7;
Javier Tusell and Genoveva García
Queipo de Llano, *Alfonso XIII. El
Rey polémico* (Madrid: Taurus,
2001) pp. 379–84.

**Chapter 6: From Colonial Disaster to
Dictatorship, 1921–1923**
1. Francisco J. Romero Salvadó, *The
Foundations of Civil War:
Revolution, Social Conflict and
Reaction in Liberal Spain, 1916–
1923* (London: Routledge/Cañada
Blanch, 2008) pp. 237–41; Pablo La
Porte, *La atracción del imán. El
desastre de Annual y sus
repercusiones en la política europea
(1921–1923)* (Madrid: Biblioteca
Nueva, 2001) pp. 60–2; Arturo
Barea, *The Forging of a Rebel*
(London: Davis-Poynter, 1972)
pp. 244–8, 262–5; Arturo Barea, *La
forja de un rebelde* (Buenos Aires:
Losada, 1951) pp. 253–9, 276–81.
2. On El Raisuni, see David Woolman,
*Rebels in the Rif: Abd el Krim and
the Rif Rebellion* (Stanford, Calif.:
Stanford University Press, 1969)
pp. 46–51; María Rosa de
Madariaga, *En el Barranco del Lobo.
Las guerras de Marruecos* (Madrid:
Alianza Editorial, 2005) pp. 104–6,
119–25.
3. Gabriel Cardona, *El poder militar
en la España contemporánea hasta
la guerra civil* (Madrid: Siglo XXI
de España, 1983) pp. 70–1; Carolyn
P. Boyd, *Praetorian Politics in

Liberal Spain (Chapel Hill: University of North Carolina Press, 1979) pp. 160, 286.

4. Javier Tusell and Genoveva García Queipo de Llano, *Alfonso XIII. El Rey polémico* (Madrid: Taurus, 2001), pp. 391, 395–7.

5. For an eloquent account of the background to the defeat, see Romero Salvadó, *The Foundations*, pp. 242–7.

6. Madariaga, *En el Barranco del Lobo*, pp. 118–54; Woolman, *Rebels*, pp. 83–90; Juan Pando, *Historia secreta de Annual* (Madrid: Ediciones Temas de Hoy, 1999) pp. 101–69; Manuel Leguineche, *Annual 1921. El desastre de España en el Rif* (Madrid: Alfaguara, 1996) pp. 169–82, 212–21; La Porte, *La atracción del imán*, pp. 63–73.

7. Fernando Reinlein García-Miranda, 'Del siglo XIX a la guerra civil', in Colectivo Democracia, *Los Ejércitos … más allá del golpe* (Barcelona: Planeta, 1981) pp. 13–33; Pando, *Historia secreta*, pp. 78–9; C. Seco Serrano, *Militarismo y civilismo en la España contemporánea* (Madrid: Instituto de Estudios Econòmicos, 1984), p. 233.

8. Pablo La Porte, 'The Moroccan Quagmire and the Crisis of Spain's Liberal System, 1917–1923', in Francisco J. Romero and Angel Smith, eds, *The Agony of Spanish Liberalism: From Revolution to Dictatorship* (London: Palgrave Macmillan, 2010), pp. 246–7; Eduardo González Calleja, *La España de Primo de Rivera. La modernización autoritaria, 1923–1930* (Madrid: Alianza Editorial, 2005) p. 31; Alberto Bru Sánchez-Fortún, 'Padrino y patrón. Alfonso XIII y sus oficiales (1902–1923)', *Hispania Nova. Revista de Historia Contemporánea*, No. 6, 2006, p. 2.

9. Madariaga, *En el Barranco del Lobo*, pp. 155–63; Pando, *Historia secreta*, pp. 169–71; Woolman, *Rebels*, pp. 90–5; Sebastian Balfour, *Deadly Embrace: Morocco and the Road to the Spanish Civil War* (Oxford: Oxford University Press, 2002) pp. 71–5.

10. The most widely publicized accusations were those levelled by Vicente Blasco Ibáñez, *Alfonso XIII Unmasked* (London: Eveleigh, Nash & Grayson, 1925) pp. 78–83, and Eduardo Ortega y Gasset, *España encadenada. La verdad sobre la dictadura* (Paris: Juan Dura, 1925) pp. 39–43.

11. Duque de Maura and Melchor Fernández Almagro, *Por qué cayó Alfonso XIII* (Madrid: Ediciones Ambos Mundos, 1948) pp. 338–44; Fidel Gómez Ochoa, 'El gobierno de concentración en el pensamiento y la acción política de Antonio Maura (1918–1922)', *Revista de Estudios Políticos* (Nueva Epoca), No. 69. July–September 1990, pp. 244–9.

12. Juan de la Cierva y Peñafiel, *Notas de mi vida* (Madrid: Instituto Editorial Reus, 1955) pp. 239–40; Carlos Seco Serrano, *Alfonso XIII y la crisis de la restauración* (Barcelona: Ediciones Ariel, 1969) pp. 142–5.

13. La Porte, *La atracción del imán*, pp. 83–8; Boyd, *Praetorian Politics*, pp. 173, 189–94.

14. Maura and Fernández Almagro, *Por qué cayó Alfonso XIII*, pp. 347–51; Fidel Gómez Ochoa, 'La alianza Maura–Cambó de 1921: una experiencia de reformismo conservador durante el reinado de Alfonso XIII', *Revista de historia contemporánea*, No. 5, 1991, pp. 96–7; Gómez Ochoa, 'El gobierno de concentración',

pp. 249–51; La Cierva, *Notas*, pp. 242–58; María Jesús González Hernández, *Ciudadanía y acción. El conservadurismo maurista 1907–1923* (Madrid: Siglo XXI de España, 1990) pp. 113–18; Francisco J. Romero Salvadó, 'Antonio Maura from Messiah to Fireman', in Alejandro Quiroga and Miguel Ángel del Arco, eds, *Right-Wing Spain in the Civil War Era: Soldiers of God and Apostles of the Fatherland* (London: Continuum, 2012) pp. 16–17; Francesc Cambó, *Memòries (1876–1936)* (Barcelona: Editorial Alpha, 1981) pp. 337–50.

15. Pando, *Historia secreta*, pp. 268–72.

16. Indalecio Prieto, *Con el Rey o contra el Rey* (Mexico City: Ediciones Oasis, 1972) pp. 101–3; Balfour, *Deadly Embrace*, pp. 84–8; Pando, *Historia secreta*, pp. 272–97.

17. La Cierva, *Notas*, pp. 250–64; Cambó, *Memòries*, pp. 352–4.

18. Jesús Pabón, *Cambó, II: Parte primera 1918–1930* (Barcelona: Editorial Alpha, 1969) pp. 349–55; Cambó, *Memòries*, p. 353; Borja de Riquer, *Alfonso XIII y Cambó. La monarquía y el catalanismo político* (Barcelona: RBA, 2013) pp. 137–42.

19. The articles were reprinted in Prieto, *Con el Rey*, pp. 9–117.

20. Madariaga, *En el Barranco del Lobo*, pp. 316–17.

21. Javier Moreno Luzón, *Romanones. Caciquismo y política liberal* (Madrid: Alianza Editorial, 1998) p. 388.

22. Maria Teresa González Calbet, *La Dictadura de Primo de Rivera. El Directorio Militar* (Madrid: Ediciones El Arquero, 1987) pp. 185–6.

23. Antonio Soler, *Apóstoles y asesinos. Vida, fulgor y muerte del Noi del Sucre* (Barcelona: Galaxia Gutenberg, 2016) pp. 138–9.

24. Alfred Mendizábal, *Aux origines d'une tragédie: la politique espagnole de 1923 à 1936* (Paris: Desclée de Brouwer, n.d. [1937?]) pp. 69–70; Woolman, *Rebels*, pp. 97–100; Balfour, *Deadly Embrace*, pp. 215–17; Manuel Leguineche, *Annual 1921. El desastre de España en el Rif* (Madrid: Alfaguara, 1996) pp. 142–3; Gerald Brenan, *The Spanish Labyrinth* (Cambridge: Cambridge University Press, 1943) pp. 61–2.

25. *Diario de las Sesiones de Cortes*, 27 October 1921; Prieto, *Con el Rey*, pp. 121–58; Octavio Cabezas, *Indalecio Prieto, socialista y español* (Madrid: Algaba Ediciones, 2005) pp. 125–9.

26. Jaume Muñoz Jofre, *La España corrupta. Breve historia de la corrupción en España. De la Restauración a nuestros días (1875–2016)* (Granada: Comares, 2016) pp. 38–9; Pere Ferrer, *Juan March. El hombre más misterioso del mundo* (Barcelona: Ediciones B, 2008) pp. 177–8.

27. Nicolás Alcalá-Zamora, *Memorias* (Barcelona: Planeta, 1977) p. 83.

28. Joan Manent i Pesas, *Records d'un sindicalista llibertari català 1916–1943* (Paris: Edicions Catalanes, 1976) pp. 75–8; Manuel Buenacasa, *El movimiento obrero español 1886–1926. Historia y crítica* (Gijón: Ediciones Júcar, 1977) pp. 73–4, 81; Gerald H. Meaker, *The Revolutionary Left in Spain, 1914–1923* (Stanford, Calif.: Stanford University Press, 1974) pp. 390–2.

29. Pelai Pagès i Blanch, *Andreu Nin. Una vida al servicio de la clase obrera* (Barcelona: Laertes, 2011) pp. 98–111; Antoni Monreal, *El pensamiento político de Joaquín Maurín* (Barcelona: Ediciones Península, 1984) pp. 11–18;

Meaker, *The Revolutionary Left*, pp. 392–403, 417–26, 440–1; Andrew Charles Durgan, *B.O.C. 1930-1936. El Bloque Obrero y Campesino* (Barcelona: Editorial Laertes, 1996) pp. 21–5.

30. Pere Gabriel, 'Introducció', in Joan Peiró, *Escrits, 1917–1939* (Barcelona: Edicions 62, 19) pp. 13–14; Durgan, *B.O.C. 1930-1936*, pp. 25–8; Ángel Pestaña, *Lo que yo pienso. Setenta días en Rusia*, 2nd edn (Madrid: Doncel, 1976) *passim*; Juan García Oliver, *El eco de los pasos* (Barcelona: Ruedo Ibérico, 1978) pp. 66–9.

31. Manent, *Records*, pp. 76–8; Eduardo González Calleja, *El máuser y el sufragio. Orden público, subversión y violencia política en la crisis de la Restauración (1917–1931)* (Madrid: Consejo Superior de Investigaciones Científicas, 1999) pp. 211–12.

32. Pere Foix, *Apòstols i mercaders. Seixanta anys de lluita social a Catalunya*, 2nd edn (Barcelona: Editorial Nova Terra, 1976) pp. 188–9; José Peirats, *Los anarquistas en la crisis política española* (Buenos Aires: Editorial Alfa, 1964) p. 35; Manent, *Records*, pp. 78–9; Jacinto León-Ignacio, *Los años del pistolerismo* (Barcelona: Planeta, 1981) pp. 225–36.

33. 'La torva historia de Anido', *Hojas Libres*, Vol. 2, May 1927, pp. 85–6; Manent, *Records*, pp. 79–100; Amadeu Hurtado, *Quaranta anys d'advocat. Història del meu temps 1894–1936*, 2nd edn (Barcelona: Edicions 62, 2011) pp. 398–9; Ricardo Sanz, *El sindicalismo y la política. Los 'Solidarios' y 'Nosotros'* (Toulouse: Imprimerie Dulaurier, 1966), pp. 56–7, 71–2; Juan Oller Piñol, *Martínez Anido. Su vida y su obra* (Madrid: Librería Victoriano Suárez, 1943) pp. 151–7; Peirats,

Los anarquistas, pp. 36–9; González Calleja, *El máuser*, pp. 197, 212–17; León-Ignacio, *Los años del pistolerismo*, pp. 238–46.

34. *La Correspondencia Militar*, 27 October 1922.

35. Romero Salvadó, *The Foundations*, pp. 261–3, 369 nn. 18, 19 and 20; Angel Smith, *Anarchism, Revolution and Reaction: Catalan Labour and the Crisis of the Spanish State, 1898–1923* (New York: Berghahn Books, 2007) pp. 344–5; Buenacasa, *El movimiento obrero*, pp. 83–8.

36. *ABC*, 19 December 1922; Soledad Bengoechea and Fernando del Rey, 'En vísperas de un golpe de Estado. Radicalización del patronal e imagen del fascismo en España', in Javier Tusell, Julio Gil Pecharromán and Feliciano Montero, eds, *Estudios sobre la derecha española contemporánea* (Madrid: UNED, 1993) pp. 304–12.

37. Francesc Cambó, *En torn del feixisme italià* in *Llibres* (Barcelona: Editorial Alpha, 1984) pp. 211, 225–36.

38. Bengoechea and Del Rey, 'En vísperas de un golpe', pp. 317–24; Colin M. Winston, *Workers and the Right in Spain, 1900–1936* (Princeton, NJ: Princeton University Press, 1985) pp. 157–9; González Calbet, *La dictadura de Primo de Rivera*, pp. 130–1; Javier Tusell, *Radiografía de un golpe de Estado* (Madrid: Alianza, 1987) p. 52; Stanley G. Payne, 'Fascist Italy and Spain, 1922–45', *Mediterranean Historical Review*, Vol. 13, Nos 1–2, June–December 1998, p. 100.

39. *Diario de las Sesiones de Cortes*, 4 May 1922.

40. *Ibid.*, 19 July 1922; Conde de Romanones, *Notas de una vida* (Madrid: Marcial Pons Ediciones,

1999) pp. 464–6; Moreno Luzón, *Romanones*, pp. 387–90; Ramón Villares and Javier Moreno Luzón, *Restauración y Dictadura* (Barcelona: Crítica-Marcial Pons, 2009) pp. 491–2.

41. Diario de las Sesiones de Cortes, 15 November 1922.

42. *Ibid.*, 21, 22 November 1922; reprinted as Dictamen de la Minoría Socialista, *El desastre de Melilla. Dictamen formulado por Indalecio Prieto como miembro de la Comisión designada por el Congreso de los Diputados para entender en el expediente Picasso* (Madrid: Sucesores de Rivadeneyra, 1922), and in Prieto, *Con el Rey*, pp. 201–63.

43. Romanones, *Notas de una vida*, p. 465.

44. Pabón, *Cambó*, II: *Parte primera*, p. 405.

45. Cambó, *Memòries*, pp. 364–5; Pabón, *Cambó*, II: *Parte primera*, pp. 399–407; Riquer, *Alfonso XIII y Cambó*, pp. 143–50; Tusell and García Queipo de Llano, *Alfonso XIII*, pp. 364–5.

46. Cambó, *Memòries*, p. 364; Diario de las Sesiones de Cortes, 30 November, 1 December 1922; Francesc Cambó, *Discursos parlamentaris* (Barcelona: Editorial Alpha, 1991) pp. 783–8; Pabón, *Cambó*, II: *Parte primera*, pp. 407–16.

47. Cambó, *Memòries*, p. 365; Seco Serrano, *Alfonso XIII*, p. 148; Riquer, *Alfonso XIII y Cambó*, p. 151.

48. Diario de las Sesiones de Cortes, 5 December 1922; La Cierva, *Notas*, pp. 287–9; Cambó, *Memòries*, pp. 365–6; Pabón, *Cambó*, II: *Parte primera*, pp. 416–18.

49. Romanones, *Notas de una vida*, pp. 467–8; Francisco Hernández

Mir, *La Dictadura ante la Historia. Un crimen de lesa patria* (Madrid: Compañía Ibero-Americana de Publicaciones, 1930) pp. 14–20; Romero Salvadó, *The Foundations*, pp. 269–70; Moreno Luzón, *Romanones*, pp. 389–91.

50. See interviews with the prisoners and Abd el-Krim in Luis de Oteyza, *Abd-el-Krim y los prisioneros*, 3rd edn (A Coruña: Ediciones del Viento, 2018) pp. 45–57, 67–81.

51. Woolman, *Rebels*, pp. 106–8, 120; Madariaga, *En el Barranco del Lobo*, pp. 228–9, 317–19.

52. Pabón, *Cambó*, II: *Parte primera*, pp. 369–92; Hurtado, *Quaranta anys*, pp. 387–8.

53. Borja de Riquer, *Cambó en Argentina. Negocios y corrupción política* (Barcelona: Edhasa, 2016) pp. 56ff.; Alberto Balcells, *El sindicalismo en Barcelona 1916–1923* (Barcelona: Editorial Nova Terra, 1965) pp. 164–5.

54. Raymond Carr, *Spain 1808–1975* (Oxford: Clarendon Press, 1982) p. 523; Shlomo Ben-Ami, *Fascism from Above: The Dictatorship of Primo de Rivera in Spain 1923–1930* (Oxford: Oxford University Press, 1983) pp. 19–26; José Luis Gómez Navarro, *El régimen de Primo de Rivera* (Madrid: Cátedra, 1991) pp. 490–4; Tusell, *Radiografía*, p. 267.

55. Romero Salvadó, *The Foundations*, pp. 271–2; Romanones, *Notas de una vida*, pp. 468–73; Moreno Luzón, *Romanones*, pp. 390–4; Alcalá-Zamora, *Memorias*, p. 82.

56. Moreno Luzón, *Romanones*, pp. 393–6; Tusell, *Radiografía*, pp. 21–2; Mercedes Cabrera, *Juan March (1880–1962)* (Madrid: Marcial Pons, 2011) pp. 123–30.

57. Cipriano de Rivas Cherif, *Retrato de un desconocido. Vida de Manuel*

Azaña (Barcelona: Grijalbo, 1980) pp. 118–24.
58. Francisco J. Romero Salvadó, 'Building Alliances against the New? Monarchy and the Military in Industrializing Spain', in Helen Graham, ed., *Interrogating Francoism: History and Dictatorship in Twentieth-Century Spain* (London: Bloomsbury, 2016) p. 50.
59. *ABC*, 28, 29, 31 January, 2, 24 February 1923; Madariaga, *En el Barranco del Lobo*, pp. 230–1; Pando, *Historia secreta*, p. 338; Woolman, *Rebels*, pp. 112–13; Balfour, *Deadly Embrace*, p. 91. On the King's pleasure-seeking, see Javier Moreno Luzón, 'Fernando Siete y medio. Los escándolos de corrupción de Alfonso XIII', in Borja de Riquer, Joan Lluís Pérez Francesch, Gemma Rubí, Lluís Ferran Toledano and Oriol Luján, eds, *La corrupción política en la España contemporánea* (Madrid: Marcial Pons Historia, 2018) pp. 262–5.
60. Hernández Mir, *La Dictadura*, p. 21.
61. 'Como fue asesinado Dris-ben-Said', *Hojas Libres*, Vol. 5, August 1927, pp. 50–8; Ortega y Gasset, *España encadenada*, pp. 73–7; Madariaga, *En el Barranco del Lobo*, pp. 286–8; *ABC*, 25, 26, 27, 28, 30, 31 August 1923; Óscar Pérez Solís, *Memorias de mi amigo Óscar Perea* (Madrid: Renacimiento, n.d. [1930]) pp. 318–19.
62. Alcalá-Zamora, *Memorias*, pp. 71–2, 86–8; Madariaga, *En el Barranco del Lobo*, pp. 178–9, 324–32; Tusell, *Radiografía*, pp. 110–12; Boyd, *Praetorian Politics*, pp. 258–60; Romero Salvadó, *The Foundations*, pp. 273–7.

63. León-Ignacio, *Los años del pistolerismo*, p. 253; González Calleja, *El máuser*, p. 306.
64. Ángel Pestaña, *Terrorismo en Barcelona (Memorias inéditas)* (Barcelona: Planeta, 1979) pp. 148–52.
65. Smith, *Anarchism*, pp. 345–7; Soler, *Apóstles y asesinos*, pp. 400–8.
66. *ABC*, 13, 15 March 1923; Pestaña, *Terrorismo en Barcelona*, pp. 148–51; Manent, *Records*, pp. 264–74; Foix, *Apòstols*, pp. 111–18; González Calleja, *El máuser*, pp. 216–17; Soler, *Apóstoles y asesinos*, pp. 415–35; José Peirats, *La CNT en la revolución española*, 2nd edn, 3 vols (Paris: Ediciones Ruedo Ibérico, 1971) I, p. 34.
67. *ABC*, 13, 14, 20 March; *La Vanguardia*, 13, 14, 15, 16, 20 March 1923; Manent, *Records*, pp. 100–4; León-Ignacio, *Los años del pistolerismo*, pp. 265–70.
68. Adolfo Bueso, *Recuerdos de un cenetista*, Vol. I: *De la Semana Trágica (1909) a la Segunda República (1931)* (Barcelona: Ariel, 1976) pp. 175–6.
69. Sanz, *El sindicalismo y la política*, pp. 95–109; García Oliver, *El eco*, pp. 628–32; Abel Paz, *Durruti en la revolución española* (Madrid: Fundación Anselmo Lorenzo, 1996) pp. 92–3; Smith, *Anarchism*, pp. 343–4.
70. Jesús Cirac, 'El asesinato del Cardenal Soldevila por Francisco Ascaso y Rafael Torres Escartín. Noventa años después', *El Agitador*, 12 June 2013; Carlos Forcadell, 'El asesinato del Cardenal Soldevila', *Tiempo de Historia*, No. 47, October 1978, pp. 16–23; Paz, *Durruti*, pp. 47, 92–106; García Oliver, *El eco*, pp. 631–2; León-Ignacio, *Los años del pistolerismo*, pp. 284–9.

71. Smith, *Anarchism*, pp. 347–50;
León-Ignacio, *Los años del
pistolerismo*, pp. 287–8; Foix,
Apòstols, pp. 114–16; García Oliver,
El eco, pp. 119, 630–5; Paz, *Durruti*,
pp. 94–106; Sanz, *El sindicalismo y
la política*, pp. 103–18.

72. Hurtado, *Quaranta anys*,
pp. 419–20; Smith, *Anarchism*,
pp. 350–1.

73. Romanones, *Notas de una vida*,
pp. 473–4; González Calleja, *El
máuser*, pp. 260–1; Boyd,
Praetorian Politics, pp. 253–4;
Tusell, *Radiografía*, pp. 74–8.

74. Romanones, *Notas de una vida*,
pp. 473–6; Hurtado *Quaranta anys*,
pp. 418–19; Boyd, *Praetorian
Politics*, pp. 255–7; Francisco Alía
Miranda, *Duelo de sables. El
General Aguilera de ministro a
conspirador contra Primo de Rivera
(1917–1931)* (Madrid: Biblioteca
Nueva, 2006) pp. 127–45; Tusell,
Radiografía, pp. 74–5.

75. Pabón, *Cambó, II: Parte primera*,
p. 447.

76. Gabriel Maura, *Bosquejo histórico
de la Dictadura*, Vol. I (Madrid:
Tipografía de Archivos, 1930)
pp. 28–31.

77. González Calleja, *El máuser*, p. 224;
Tusell, *Radiografía*, pp. 80–1; Smith,
Anarchism, pp. 350–4; Manuel
Portela Valladares, *Memorias.
Dentro del drama español* (Madrid:
Alianza Editorial, 1988) pp. 100–3.
Regarding the trombone, see
Portela Valladares, *Memorias*,
p. 19.

78. Hernández Mir, *La Dictadura*,
pp. 40–1.

79. *La Vanguardia*, 23 June 1923;
Romero Salvadó, *The Foundations*,
pp. 287–8.

80. *ABC*, 8 September 1923; Paz,
Durruti, pp. 110–15.

81. *ABC*, 5 September 1923.

82. Romero Salvadó, *The Foundations*,
pp. 288–9; Alejandro Quiroga,
*Making Spaniards: Primo de Rivera
and the Nationalization of the
Masses, 1923–1930* (London:
Palgrave Macmillan, 2007)
pp. 32–3.

83. Stanley G. Payne, *Politics and the
Military in Modern Spain* (Stanford,
Calif.: Stanford University Press,
1967) pp. 195, 491 n. 17.

84. General E. López Ochoa, *De la
Dictadura a la República* (Madrid:
Editorial Zeus, 1930) pp. 22–7;
Hernández Mir, *La Dictadura*,
pp. 42–4; Gonzalo Queipo de
Llano, *El general Queipo de Llano
perseguido por la dictadura*
(Madrid: Javier Morato, 1930) p. 32;
Pabón, *Cambó, II: Parte primera*,
pp. 447–50; Tusell, *Radiografía*,
p. 154; Boyd, *Praetorian Politics*,
pp. 262–5; González Calbet, *La
Dictadura*, pp. 55–9; Romero
Salvadó, *The Foundations*,
pp. 288–9.

85. Portela Valladares, *Memorias*,
pp. 102–3.

86. Hernández Mir, *La Dictadura*,
pp. 44–6.

87. Ortega y Gasset, *España
encadenada*, pp. 328–30; Artur
Perucho i Badia, *Catalunya sota la
dictadura (Dades per a la Història)*,
2nd edn (Barcelona: Publicacions
de l'Abadia de Montserrat, 2018; 1st
edn 1930) pp. 53–7; Enrique Ucelay
Da Cal, 'Estat Català: The Strategies
of Separation and Revolution of
Catalan Radical Nationalism
(1919–1933)', PhD thesis, Columbia
University, 1979 (Ann Arbor,
Michigan: University Microfilms
International, 1979) p. 139.

88. Cambó, *Memòries*, p. 375; Maura,
Bosquejo, I, pp. 101–2; Pabón,
Cambó, II: Parte primera,
pp. 449–50; Francesc Cambó, *Per la*

concòrdia, in *Llibres* (Barcelona: Editorial Alpha, 1984) pp. 465–515 at p. 469; Ben-Ami, *Fascism from Above*, pp. 45–6.

89. López Ochoa, *De la Dictadura a la República*, pp. 30–2; Tusell, *Radiografía*, pp. 71–83, 94; González Calbet, *La Dictadura*, pp. 65–72.

90. Ortega y Gasset, *España encadenada*, pp. 81–90, 171–5; Francisco Villanueva, *La dictadura militar (Crónica documentada de la oposición y la represión bajo el directorio) (1923–1926)* (Madrid: Javier Morata Editor, 1931) pp. 75–6; Perucho, *Catalunya sota la dictadura*, pp. 57–9; Ángel Ossorio y Gallardo, *Mis memorias* (Buenos Aires: Losada, 1946) p. 130; Salvador de Madariaga, *Spain: A Modern History* (London: Jonathan Cape, 1961) pp. 339–40.

91. *ABC*, 14 September 1923; Tusell, *Radiografía*, pp. 151–7, 163–72; González Calbet, *La Dictadura*, pp. 77–80; Romero Salvadó, *The Foundations*, pp. 290–1.

92. Tusell and García Queipo de Llano, *Alfonso XIII*, pp. 411–12; Maura and Fernández Almagro, *Por qué cayó Alfonso XIII*, pp. 361–2; Gómez Navarro, *El régimen de Primo*, pp. 107–21; Tusell, *Radiografía*, pp. 127–33, 236–9, 268–9.

93. *ABC*, 15 September 1923; Tusell, *Radiografía*, pp. 230–1.

94. Fernando del Rey, 'El capitalismo catalán y Primo de Rivera: en torno a un golpe de Estado', *Hispania*, Año 1988, Vol. 48, No. 168, pp. 289–308.

95. Romero Salvadó, *The Foundations*, p. 294; Boyd, *Praetorian Politics*, pp. 236–7.

Chapter 7: The Primo de Rivera Dictatorship: The Years of Success, 1923–1926

1. *ABC*, 14 September 1923.

2. Ángel Ossorio y Gallardo, *Mis memorias* (Buenos Aires: Losada, 1946) pp. 131–2; Dionisio Pérez, *La Dictadura a través de sus notas oficiosas* (Madrid: CIAP, 1930) pp. 13–21; Juan de la Cierva y Peñafiel, *Notas de mi vida* (Madrid: Instituto Editorial Reus, 1955) pp. 295–6; Eduardo Ortega y Gasset, *España encadenada. La verdad sobre la dictadura* (Paris: Juan Dura, 1925) pp. 160–3.

3. Gabriel Maura, *Bosquejo histórico de la Dictadura*, Vol. I (Madrid: Tipografía de Archivos, 1930) pp. 45–7.

4. Ortega y Gasset, *España encadenada*, pp. 97–112; Shlomo Ben-Ami, *Fascism from Above: The Dictatorship of Primo de Rivera in Spain 1923–1930* (Oxford: Oxford University Press, 1983) pp. 63–5.

5. Francisco Villanueva, *La dictadura militar (Crónica documentada de la oposición y la represión bajo el directorio) (1923–1926)* (Madrid: Javier Morata Editor, 1931) pp. 29–32; Pedro Sainz Rodríguez, *Testimonio y recuerdos* (Barcelona: Planeta, 1978) pp. 82–3.

6. Ortega y Gasset, *España encadenada*, pp. 31, 35–46, 149; Salvador de Madariaga, *Spain: A Modern History* (London: Jonathan Cape, 1961) pp. 346–7; Juan Pando, *Historia secreta de Annual* (Madrid: Ediciones Temas de Hoy, 1999) pp. 312–13.

7. *ABC*, 28, 29 June, 5 July 1924; Maura, *Bosquejo*, I, pp. 138–40.

8. María Teresa González Calbet, *La Dictadura de Primo de Rivera. El Directorio Militar* (Madrid: Ediciones El Arquero, 1987)

pp. 117–21, 206–7; Ramiro Gómez Fernández, *La dictadura me honró encarcelándome* (Madrid: Javier Morata Editor, 1930) pp. 24–5.

9. Ortega y Gasset, *España encadenada*, p. 236.

10. Joaquín Maurín, *Los hombres de la Dictadura* (Madrid: Editorial Cenit, 1930) pp. 122–6.

11. Artur Perucho i Badia, *Catalunya sota la dictadura (Dades per a la Història)* (Barcelona: Publicacions de l'Abadia de Montserrat, 2018) pp. 52–6.

12. Ortega y Gasset, *España encadenada*, pp. 332–4; González Calbet, *La Dictadura*, pp. 81–4; Jesús Pabón, *Cambó, II: Parte primera 1918–1930* (Barcelona: Editorial Alpha, 1969) pp. 448–53, 469; Perucho, *Catalunya sota la dictadura*, pp. 82–3.

13. Francesc Cambó, *Memòries (1876–1936)* (Barcelona: Editorial Alpha, 1981) pp. 375–9.

14. Perucho, *Catalunya sota la dictadura*, pp. 131–51; Pabón, *Cambó, II: Parte primera 1918–1930*, pp. 459–61; Maura, *Bosquejo*, I, pp. 101–5; José Calvo Sotelo, *Mis servicios al Estado. Seis años de gestión: apuntes para la Historia* (Madrid: Imprenta Clásica Española, 1931) pp. 66–71; González Calbet, *La Dictadura*, pp. 171–82.

15. Colin M. Winston, *Workers and the Right in Spain, 1900–1936* (Princeton, NJ: Princeton University Press, 1985) pp. 284–90

16. *ABC*, 18 September; *El Socialista*, 15, 18 September 1923; Eduardo González Calleja and Fernando Rey Reguillo, *La defensa armada contra la revolución. Una historia de las Guardias Cívicas en la España del siglo XX* (Madrid: Consejo Superior de Investigaciones Científicas, 1995) pp. 177–200.

17. Q. Saldaña, *Al servicio de la justicia. La orgía áurea de la dictadura* (Madrid: Javier Morata, 1930) pp. 28–9, 34–9; Eduardo González Calleja, *El máuser y el sufragio. Orden público, subversión y violencia política en la crisis de la Restauración (1917–1931)* (Madrid: Consejo Superior de Investigaciones Científicas, 1999) pp. 166–9, 178–82.

18. See, for example, *ABC*, 21 January, 26 November 1925, 18 August 1927; *La Vanguardia*, 1 June 1926, 13 December 1927, 4 September 1928, 28 March 1929; González Calleja and Rey Reguillo, *La defensa armada*, pp. 200–1; González Calbet, *La Dictadura*, pp. 157–62; Ortega y Gasset, *España encadenada* p. 231; Rosa Martínez Segarra, *El Somatén Nacional en la Dictadura de Primo de Rivera* (Madrid: Editorial de la Universidad Complutense, 1984) pp. 263–77; Alejandro Quiroga, *Making Spaniards: Primo de Rivera and the Nationalization of the Masses, 1923–1930* (London: Palgrave Macmillan, 2007) pp. 146–64.

19. Villanueva, *La dictadura militar*, pp. 76–7.

20. Bernardo Díaz Nosty, *La irresistible ascensión de Juan March* (Madrid: Sedmay Ediciones, 1977) pp. 114–15; Rafael Salazar Alonso, *La justicia bajo la dictadura* (Madrid: CIAP, 1930) pp. 31–42; Ortega y Gasset, *España encadenada*, pp. 263–6; Villanueva, *La dictadura militar*, pp. 76–7.

21. Ben-Ami, *Fascism from Above*, pp. 56–7; Javier Tusell, *La crisis del caciquismo andaluz (1923–1931)* (Madrid: Cupsa Editorial, 1977) p. 18.

22. Pérez, *Notas oficiosas*, pp. 14–15; Ortega y Gasset, *España encadenada*, pp. 177–9.
23. González Calleja, *El máuser*, p. 319.
24. *Diario de Sesiones de las Cortes*, 8 May; *El Socialista*, 9, 11, 12 May; *El Progreso*, 11 May; *El Diario de la Marina* (Havana), 11 May 1934.
25. Díaz Nosty, *Juan March*, pp. 114–30, 142–9; Manuel Benavides, *El último pirata del mediterráneo* (Barcelona: Imprenta Industrial, 1936) pp. 231–6, 253–4, 296–8; Ramón Garriga, *Juan March y su tiempo* (Barcelona: Planeta, 1976) pp. 186–92, 200–4, 211–16; Pere Ferrer, *Juan March. El hombre más misterioso del mundo* (Barcelona: Ediciones B, 2008) pp. 202–9; Mercedes Cabrera, *Juan March (1880-1962)* (Madrid: Marcial Pons, 2011) pp. 134–7, 150–66, 170–85.
26. Julián Casanova and Carlos Gil Andrés, *Historia de España en el Siglo XX* (Barcelona: Ariel, 2009) p. 92; Valentín del Arco López, 'Unamuno frente a Primo de Rivera. De Salamanca Al Exilio, 1923-1924', in Dolores Gómez Molleda, ed., *Actas del Congreso Internacional, Cincuentenario de Unamuno* (Salamanca: Ediciones de la Universidad de Salamanca, 1986) pp. 129–79; Ortega y Gasset, *España encadenada*, pp. 235–7.
27. José Peirats, *La CNT en la revolución española*, 2nd edn, 3 vols (Paris: Ediciones Ruedo Ibérico, 1971) I, pp. 37.
28. *El Socialista*, 13, 14, 18, 27 September 1923; Antonio Ramos Oliveira, *Nosotros los marxistas. Lenin contra Marx*, 2nd edn (Madrid: Ediciones Júcar, 1979) pp. 145–7; Amaro del Rosal, *Historia de la UGT de España 1901-1939*, 2 vols (Barcelona:

Grijalbo, 1977) I, pp. 260–70; Julio Aróstegui, *Largo Caballero. El tesón y la quimera* (Barcelona: Debate, 2013) pp. 171–4; José Luis Martín Ramos, *Historia de la UGT*, Vol. II: *Entre la revolución y el reformismo, 1914-1931* (Madrid: Siglo XXI de España, 2008) pp. 143–6
29. *El Socialista*, 15 September 1923.
30. Francisco Largo Caballero, *Presente y futuro de la Unión General de Trabajadores* (Madrid: Javier Morata, 1925) pp. 42–3, 176–84; Enrique de Santiago, *La UGT ante la revolución* (Madrid: Tipografía Sáez Hermanos, 1932) pp. 24–5, 44; Manuel Cordero, *Los socialistas y la revolución* (Madrid: Imprenta Torrent, 1932) p. 64; *Convocatoria y orden del día para el XII congreso ordinario del PSOE* (Madrid: Gráfica Socialista, 1927) p. 91.
31. Juan García Oliver, *El eco de los pasos* (Barcelona: Ruedo Ibérico, 1978) pp. 77–9.
32. *El Socialista*, 29 September, 1 October; *ABC*, 29 September 1923.
33. *El Socialista*, 2 October, 1 November 1923; David Ruiz, *El movimiento obrero en Asturias* (Oviedo: Amigos de Asturias, 1968) pp. 188–9; Martín Ramos, *Historia de la UGT*, pp. 146–8; *Convocatoria*, p. 96.
34. Santiago, *UGT*, p. 39; Ramos Oliveira, *Nosotros los marxistas*, pp. 158–60; Manuel Tuñón de Lara, *El Movimiento obrero en la historia de España* (Madrid: Taurus, 1972) p. 776.
35. *ABC*, 27 April 1926; Manuel Tuñón de Lara, *La España del siglo XX*, 2nd edn (Paris: Librería Española, 1973) p. 151.
36. *Convocatoria*, p. 103; *El Socialista*, 11, 13 December 1923; Virgilio Zapatero, *Fernando de los Ríos. Los problemas del socialismo*

democrático (Madrid: Editorial Cuadernos para el Diálogo, 1974) p. 77; Largo Caballero, *Presente y futuro*, pp. 42–7; Francisco Largo Caballero, *Mis recuerdos. Cartas a un amigo* (Mexico City: Editores Unidos, 1954) pp. 90–2.

37. David Ruiz, *El Movimiento obrero en Asturias* (Oviedo: Amigos de Asturias, 1968) pp. 190–1; Cordero, *Socialistas*, p. 74; Ramos Oliveira, *Nosotros los marxistas*, pp. 151–3; *El Socialista*, 12 May 1925, 26 February 1926.

38. Vicente Blasco Ibáñez, *Alfonso XIII Unmasked* (London: Eveleigh, Nash & Grayson, 1925) pp. 24–8, 73–83, 40–50, 60–5.

39. 'La veritat sobre la SEITE o el negoci dels tres millons', in *Pasquin Rev. 000, 1, 3* (Leipzig, 1924), reproduced in Jordi Casassas Ymbert, *La dictadura de Primo de Rivera (1923–1930). Textos* (Barcelona: Editorial Anthropos, 1983) pp. 226–30.

40. Casassas Ymbert, *La dictadura*, p. 126.

41. *España con honra*, Nos 5, 6, 7, 8, 17, 24, 31 January, 7 February 1925; Francisco Madrid, *Los desterrados de la Dictadura* (Madrid: Editorial España, 1930) pp. 15–16, 28–34, 130–60; Eduardo Comín Colomer, *Unamuno, libelista. Sus campañas contra Alfonso XIII y la Dictadura* (Madrid: Vasallo de Mumbert, 1968) pp. 88–9; Valentín del Arco López, 'La prensa como fuente: *España con honra*. Un semanario contra la Dictadura de Primo de Rivera', *Studia Histórica. Historia Contemporánea*, Vol. 6, 1988, pp. 113–42.

42. Madrid, *Los desterrados*, pp. 170–6, 182–90; Yolanda Gamarra Chopo, 'La ilusión española de la Sociedad de Naciones', in Yolanda Gamarra

Chopo and Carlos R. Fernández Liesa, eds, *Los orígenes del Derecho internacional contemporáneo. Estudios conmemorativos del Centenario de la Primera Guerra Mundial* (Zaragoza: Institución Fernando el Católico, 2015) pp. 289–93.

43. *ABC*, 18 September 1923.

44. Tusell, *La crisis del caciquismo*, pp. 77–84; González Calbet, *La Dictadura*, pp. 152–7, 219–24, 235–6; La Cierva, *Notas*, pp. 295–7; Carmelo Lisón-Tolosana, *Belmonte de los Caballeros: A Sociological Study of a Spanish Town* (Oxford: Clarendon Press, 1966) pp. 216–17.

45. José Tomás Valverde, *Memorias de un alcalde* (Madrid: Talleres Gráficos Escelicer, 1961) pp. 51–4; Ortega y Gasset, *España encadenada*, pp. 224–9; Ramos Oliveira, *Nosotros los marxistas*, pp. 147–8; Tusell, *La crisis del caciquismo*, pp. 85–116; González Calbet, *La Dictadura*, pp. 128–9, 221–6; Casanova and Gil Andrés, *Historia*, pp. 90–2; James H. Rial, *Revolution from Above: The Primo de Rivera Dictatorship in Spain, 1923–1930* (Fairfax, Va.: George Mason University Press, 1986) pp. 80–3; González Calbet, *La Dictadura*, pp. 128–9, 221–6.

46. Ortega y Gasset, *España encadenada*, pp. 295–8; Gonzalo Álvarez Chillida, *José María Pemán. Pensamiento y trayectoria de un monárquico (1897–1941)* (Cadiz: Universidad de Cádiz Servicio de Publicaciones, 1996) pp. 22–9; Xavier Tusell Gómez, 'The Functioning of the Cacique System in Andalusia, 1890–1931', in Stanley G. Payne, ed., *Politics and Society in Twentieth-Century Spain* (New York: New Viewpoints, 1976) pp. 22–3.

47. Carlos Blanco, *La dictadura y los procesos militares* (Madrid: Javier Morata Editor, 1931) pp. 119–21.

48. José Pemartín, *Los valores históricos en la dictadura española*, 2nd edn (Madrid: Publicaciones de la Junta de Propaganda Patriótica y Ciudadana, 1929) pp. 405–18; Saldaña, *Al servicio de la justicia*, pp. 46–51; González Calbet, *La Dictadura*, pp. 228–37; General E. López Ochoa, *De la Dictadura a la República* (Madrid: Editorial Zeus, 1930) pp. 63–7.

49. Maura, *Bosquejo*, I, p. 110.

50. *ABC*, 14 November 1923; Maura, *Bosquejo*, I, pp. 78–81; Romanones, *Notas*, pp. 480–3; Moreno Luzón, *Romanones*, p. 402.

51. *ABC*, 20, 21, 23, 24, 25 November 1923; Maura, *Bosquejo*, I, pp. 86–92; Ben-Ami, *Fascism from Above*, pp. 131–2; González Calbet, *La Dictadura*, pp. 124–5; Javier Tusell and Genoveva García Queipo de Llano, *Alfonso XIII. El Rey polémico* (Madrid: Taurus, 2001) pp. 446–9.

52. *ABC*, 22 December 1923; Pérez, *Notas oficiosas*, p. 40.

53. Del Arco López, 'Unamuno frente a Primo de Rivera', pp. 150–1.

54. *ABC*, 6 February 1924; Salazar Alonso, *La justicia*, pp. 21–5; Maura, *Bosquejo*, I, pp. 112–15; Pérez, *Notas oficiosas*, pp. 42–8; Ortega y Gasset, *España encadenada*, pp. 269–70; López Ochoa, *De la Dictadura a la República*, pp. 68–9.

55. *ABC*, 23 September 2015; Primo to General Federico Madariaga, 2 April 1925, José Manuel and Luis de Armiñán Odriozola, eds, *Epistolario del Dictador. La figura del General Primo de Rivera, trazada por su propia mano* (Madrid: Javier Morata, 1930) pp. 87–8.

56. *ABC*, 21, 23, 27, 28 February, 22 March 1924; Villanueva, *La dictadura militar*, pp. 111–34; Salazar Alonso, *La justicia*, pp. 298–307; Comín Colomer, *Unamuno, libelista*, pp. 56–62.

57. Ortega y Gasset, *España encadenada*, pp. 251–8; Arco López, 'La prensa como fuente: España con honra', p. 120.

58. Comín Colomer, *Unamuno, libelista*, pp. 65–8.

59. Madrid, *Los desterrados*, pp. 42–51, 237–42.

60. *ABC*, 12, 20 September 1924; Blanco, *La dictadura*, pp. 113–30; Salazar Alonso, *La justicia*, pp. 27–30, 267–9; Ossorio, *Mis memorias*, pp. 138–41; Antonio Miguel López García, *Ángel Ossorio y Gallardo. Biografíá política de un conservador heterodoxo* (Madrid: Reus Editorial, 2017) pp. 166–7; Julio Gil Pecharromán, *José Antonio Primo de Rivera. Retrato de un visionario* (Madrid: Temas de Hoy, 1996) pp. 69–72; Pérez, *Notas oficiosas*, p. 60.

61. *ABC*, 8 August 1924; Maura, *Bosquejo*, I, pp. 149–55; Pérez, *Notas oficiosas*, p. 58; 'Policiaquismo', *Hojas Libres*, No. 5, 1 August 1927, pp. 84–6.

62. Ferrer, *Juan March*, pp. 32, 103–13, 164–5, 189–200; Díaz Nosty, *Juan March*, pp. 42–55, 135–41; Benavides, *El último pirata*, pp. 255–74; Madrid, *Los desterrados*, pp. 32–4; Cabrera, *Juan March*, pp. 62–75, 139–41, 144–50.

63. A. Sáez Alba (pseudonym of Alfonso Colodron), *La Otra 'cosa nostra'. La Asociación Católica Nacional de Propagandistas* (Paris: Ruedo Ibérico, 1974) pp. ix–xxii; José María García Escudero, *Conversaciones sobre Ángel Herrera*

(Madrid: Rialp/Biblioteca de Autores Cristianos, 1986) pp. 16–20; Juan Jose Castillo, 'Notas sobre los orígenes y primeros años de la Confederación Nacional Católico Agraria', in José Luis García Delgado, ed., *La cuestión agraria en la España contemporánea* (Madrid: Siglo XXI de España, 1976) pp. 203–48; Pedro Carlos González Cuevas, *Acción Española. Teología política y nacionalismo autoritario en España (1913-1936)* (Madrid: Editorial Tecnos, 1998) pp. 97–100.

64. Calvo Sotelo, *Mis servicios*, pp. 14–21; González Calbet, *La Dictadura*, pp. 238–46.

65. *España con Honra*, No. 9, 14 February 1925; 'Van saliendo los chanchullos', *Hojas Libres*, No. 6, 1 September 1927, pp. 84–7; Maura, *Bosquejo*, I, pp. 340–6; Calvo Sotelo, *Mis servicios*, pp. 256–60; José Luis García Delgado and Juan Carlos Jiménez, *Un siglo de España. La Economía* (Madrid: Marcial Pons, 1999) pp. 62–72; Ben-Ami, *Fascism from Above*, pp. 243–5.

66. *ABC*, 9 June 1927; David Mitchell, *Travellers in Spain* (London: Cassell, 1990) p. 127; Josefa Paredes, 'El americano que expolio España', *El Mundo*, 4 December 2005.

67. 'Algunas sinecuras de los renovadores', *Hojas Libres*, No. 7, 1 October 1927, pp. 75–8.

68. Calvo Sotelo, *Mis servicios*, p. 332.

69. 'Relación de chanchullos de la Dictadura (continuación)', *Hojas Libres*, No. 8, 1 November 1927, pp. 7–10.

70. 'La Inmoralidad de la Dictadura', *Hojas Libres*, No. 15, June 1927, pp. 65–70; Maura, *Bosquejo*, I, p. 345; López Ochoa, *De la*

Dictadura a la República, p. 161; Ben-Ami, *Fascism from Above*, pp. 245–6.

71. José Luis Gómez Navarro, *El régimen de Primo de Rivera* (Madrid: Ediciones Cátedra, 1991) p. 170; Jaume Muñoz Jofre, *La España corrupta. Breve historia de la corrupción (de la Restauración a nuestros días, 1976-2016)* (Granada: Comares, 2016) p. 47.

72. 'La torva historia de Anido', *Hojas Libres*, No. 2, 1 May 1927, pp. 81–6.

73. Saldaña, *Al servicio de la justicia*, pp. 169–76.

74. Calvo Sotelo, *Mis servicios*, pp. 194–203; 'Grandes negocios. El monopolio petrolífero', *Hojas Libres*, No. 4, 1 July 1927, pp. 74–6; 'Primo y sus amigos. Estafa de más de dos millones de pesetas', *Hojas Libres*, No. 9, December 1927, pp. 24–5; Ben-Ami, *Fascism from Above*, pp. 248–50; Ramón Tamames, *Ni Mussolini ni Franco. La dictadura de Primo de Rivera y su tiempo* (Barcelona: Planeta, 2008) pp. 329–31.

75. *Diario de Sesiones de las Cortes*, 18, 22, 23 May 1934.

76. 'La Dictadura de Monipodio', *Hojas Libres*, No. 9, December 1927, pp. 45–8; Artur Perucho i Badia, *Catalunya sota la dictadura* (Barcelona: Publicacions de l'Abadia de Montserrat, 2018) pp. 308–10.

77. 'Primo y sus amigos', *Hojas Libres*, No. 9, December 1927, pp. 24–9.

78. Miguel de Unamuno, 'Democracia y cleptocracia', *Hojas Libres*, No. 19, 1 January 1929; Gabriel Maura, *Al servicio de la historia. Bosquejo histórico de la Dictadura*, Vol. II (Madrid: Javier Morata Editor, 1930) pp. 71–2; Perucho, *Catalunya*

sota la dictadura, note by Josep Palomero, pp. 308–9; Pérez, *Notas oficiosas*, pp. 272–3.

79. 'Van saliendo los chanchullos', *Hojas Libres*, No. 6, 1 September 1927, pp. 82–4; Salazar Alonso, *La justicia*, pp. 177–84; López Ochoa, *De la Dictadura a la República*, pp. 69–70; Pedro María Velarde and Fermín Allende Portillo, 'Un año selectivo para la banca en Bilbao', in Pablo Martín Aceña and Montserrat Gárate Ojanguren, eds, *Economía y empresa en el norte de España (Una aproximación histórica)* (Bilbao: Universidad del País Vasco, 1994) pp. 171–4.

80. 'La Inmoralidad de la Dictadura', *Hojas Libres*, No. 15, June 1927, pp. 70–1; 'El homenaje bochornoso al Dictador', *Hojas Libres*, No. 11, February 1928, pp. 74–81; 'La casa del homenaje y el Código Penal', *Hojas Libres*, No. 12, March 1928, pp. 65–6.

81. Francisco Hernández Mir, *La Dictadura ante la Historia. Un crimen de lesa patria* (Madrid: Compañía Ibero-Americana de Publicaciones, 1930) pp. 245–58; *ABC*, 9 March 1929.

82. *ABC*, 29 September 1929.

83. Pérez, *Notas oficiosas*, pp. 270–2; 'Los últimos chanchullos', *Hojas Libres*, No. 12, March 1928, p. 62.

84. Pilar Primo de Rivera, *Recuerdos de una vida* (Madrid: Ediciones Dyrsa, 1983) p. 29.

85. Miguel de Unamuno, 'Psicología de tafetán', *Hojas Libres*, No. 2, 1 May 1927, pp. 1–9.

86. Jacinto Capella, *La verdad de Primo de Rivera. Intimidades y anécdotas del Dictador* (Madrid: Imprenta Hijos de Tomás Minuesa/Librería San Martín, 1933) pp. 16–17, 27–30, 101–2; Andrés Révesz, *Frente al Dictador* (Madrid:

Biblioteca Internacional, n.d. [1926]) p. 44.

87. José María Pemán, *Mis almuerzos con gente importante* (Barcelona: Dopesa, 1970) pp. 17–18; Madariaga, *Spain*, pp. 342–5; Gerald Brenan, *The Spanish Labyrinth*, 2nd edn (Cambridge: Cambridge University Press, 1950) pp. 78–80.

88. Ortega y Gasset, *España encadenada*, p. 236; González Calbet, *La Dictadura*, pp. 120–1.

89. Calvo Sotelo, *Mis servicios*, pp. 236–7; Antonio Cordón, *Trayectoria (Recuerdos de un artillero)* (Seville: Espuela de Plata, 2008) p. 249; Tusell and García Queipo de Llano, *Alfonso XIII*, p. 452; Brenan, *The Spanish Labyrinth*, pp. 79–80.

90. *ABC*, 1, 2, 3 October 1926; 'Vanidad Triangular', *Hojas Libres*, No. 1, April 1927, p. 71; Gabriele Ranzato, *El eclipse de la democracia. La guerra civil española y sus orígines, 1931–1939* (Madrid: Siglo XXI de España, 2006) p. 103.

91. Saldaña, *Al servicio de la justicia*, pp. 109–11; Calvo Sotelo, *Mis servicios*, pp. 244 (pawnshops), 391 (double budget); Pérez, *Notas oficiosas*, pp. 267–8.

92. 'Los últimos chanchullos', *Hojas Libres*, No. 12, March 1928, pp. 59–61.

93. Tuñón de Lara, *La España del siglo XX*, pp. 135–51; Paul Preston, *The Coming of the Spanish Civil War: Reform, Reaction and Revolution in the Second Spanish Republic*, 2nd edn (London: Routledge, 1994) pp. 12–19; Germà Bel, *Infrastructure and the Political Economy of Nation Building in Spain, 1720–2010* (Brighton: Sussex Academic Press, 2012) pp. 70–1, 78, 118.

94. Ortega y Gasset, *España encadenada*, pp. 237–45, 298–303; Saldaña, *Al servicio de la justicia*, pp. 179–255; Perez, *Notas oficiosas*, pp. 41–2.

95. Pemán, *Mis almuerzos*, p. 41.

96. Hernández Mir, *La Dictadura*, pp. 237–9.

97. *Ibid.*, pp. 237–8; Alejandro Quiroga, 'Cirujano de Hierro. La construcción carismática del general Primo de Rivera', *Revista Ayer*, No. 91, Vol. 3, 2013, pp. 154, 159, 163; Cabrera, *Juan March*, pp. 156–7.

98. 'La gira de "La Nación"', *Hojas Libres*, No. 5, 1 August 1927, pp. 86–9.

99. *ABC*, 24 June 1924; Saldaña, *Al servicio de la justicia*, p. 96; Pérez, *Notas oficiosas*, pp. 75–6, 258.

100. Pérez, *Notas oficiosas*, pp. 17–18, 316–18; Saldaña, *Al servicio de la justicia*, pp. 93–8; Brenan, *The Spanish Labyrinth*, p. 79; Quiroga, *Making Spaniards*, p. 34.

101. José María Pemán, *El hecho y la idea de la Unión Patriótica* (Madrid: Imprenta Artística Sáez Hermanos, 1929) pp. 28–9, 105, 308–9.

102. Quiroga, *Making Spaniards*, pp. 165–71; González Calbet, *La Dictadura*, pp. 130–41; Gómez Navarro, *El régimen de Primo*, pp. 230–4.

103. González Calleja, *El máuser*, pp. 274–5; Moreno Luzón, *Romanones*, pp. 406–8.

104. Hernández Mir, *La Dictadura*, p. 97; Primo to General Madariaga, 2 April 1925, Armiñán, *Epistolario*, pp. 89–94.

105. Francisco Franco Salgado-Araujo, *Mi vida junto a Franco* (Barcelona: Planeta, 1977) p. 66; Emilio Mola Vidal, *Obras completas* (Valladolid: Librería Santarén, 1940) pp. 1024–5; Ignacio Hidalgo de Cisneros,

Cambio de rumbo (Memorias), 2 vols (Bucharest: Colección Ebro, 1964) I, pp. 108–9; Arturo Barea, *The Forging of a Rebel* (London: Davis-Poynter, 1972) pp. 449, 459–61.

106. Francisco Hernández Mir, *La Dictadura en Marruecos. Al margen de una farsa* (Madrid: Javier Morata, 1930) p. 145; Pabón, *Cambó*, II: *Parte primera*, pp. 261, 309; Duque de Maura and Melchor Fernández Almagro, *Por qué cayó Alfonso XIII* (Madrid: Ediciones Ambos Mundos, 1948) p. 356; Javier Tusell, *Radiografía de un golpe de Estado. El ascenso al Poder del General Primo de Rivera* (Madrid: Alianza Editorial, 1987) pp. 35–6.

107. Francisco Franco Salgado-Araujo, *Mis conversaciones privadas con Franco* (Barcelona: Planeta, 1976) pp. 62–3, 377–8; George Hills, *Franco: The Man and his Nation* (New York: Macmillan, 1967) pp. 133–5.

108. Comandante Franco, *Diario de una bandera* (Madrid: Editorial Pueyo, 1922) p. 278.

109. Franco's role was exaggerated by his hagiographers, Joaquín Arrarás, *Franco* (Burgos: Imprenta Aldecoa, 1938) pp. 113–14; Brian Crozier, *Franco: A Biographical History* (London: Eyre & Spottiswoode, 1967) p. 83. Cf. David S. Woolman, *Rebels in the Rif: Abd el Krim and the Rif Rebellion* (Stanford, Calif.: Stanford University Press, 1969) p. 187.

110. Primo to Merry del Val, 7 June 1925, Armiñán, *Epistolario*, pp. 151–9; Susana Sueiro Seoane, *España en el Mediterráneo. Primo de Rivera y la 'cuestión marroquí' 1923–1930* (Madrid, UNED, 1992) pp. 134–5.

111. Hernández Mir, *La Dictadura en Marruecos*, pp. 144–6; Luis Suárez Fernández, *Francisco Franco y su tiempo*, 8 vols (Madrid: Fundación Nacional Francisco Franco, 1984) I, p. 171.

112. González Calbet, *La Dictadura*, p. 194; Hernández Mir, *La Dictadura en Marruecos*, p. 149; Shannon E. Fleming and Ann K. Fleming, 'Primo de Rivera and Spain's Moroccan Problem, 1923–27', *Journal of Contemporary History*, Vol. 12, No. 1, January 1977, p. 87.

113. Gómez Fernández, *La dictadura me honró*, pp. 115–16; Gonzalo Queipo de Llano, *El general Queipo de Llano perseguido por la dictadura* (Madrid: Javier Morato, 1930) p. 105; González Calbet, *La Dictadura*, pp. 195–6; Ricardo de la Cierva, *Francisco Franco. Biografía histórica*, 6 vols (Barcelona: Planeta, 1982) I, pp. 225–6, 236–7.

114. Ortega y Gasset, *España encadenada*, pp. 311–14; La Cierva, *Francisco Franco*, I, pp. 232–5; Barea, *Forja*, pp. 472–3; Stanley G. Payne, *Politics and the Military in Modern Spain* (Stanford, Calif.: Stanford University Press, 1967) p. 211.

115. Calvo Sotelo, *Mis servicios*, pp. 238–9; Gómez Fernández, *La dictadura me honró*, pp. 116–21, 128–9.

116. Cordón, *Trayectoria*, pp. 249–51; Arrarás, *Franco*, pp. 100–1; Luis de Galinsoga and Francisco Franco Salgado, *Centinela de occidente (Semblanza biográfica de Francisco Franco)* (Barcelona: AHR, 1956) pp. 88–91; General Francisco Javier Mariñas, *General Varela (de soldado a general)* (Barcelona: AHR, 1956) pp. 35–6; Franco Salgado-Araujo, *Mis*

conversaciones, pp. 137–8; La Cierva, *Franco*, I, pp. 235, 238–40.

117. Cordón, *Trayectoria*, pp. 251–5; Hernández Mir, *La Dictadura en Marruecos*, p. 149; Fleming, 'Primo de Rivera', pp. 87–8; Sebastian Balfour, *Deadly Embrace. Morocco and the Road to the Spanish Civil War* (Oxford: Oxford University Press, 2002) pp. 94–6. For devastating accounts of the development and consequences of the Spanish chemical war, see Balfour, *Deadly Embrace*, pp. 131–56, and María Rosa de Madariaga, *En el Barranco del Lobo. Las guerras de Marruecos* (Madrid: Alianza, 2005) pp. 351–4; Hidalgo de Cisneros, *Cambio de rumbo*, I, pp. 132–5.

118. Fleming, 'Primo de Rivera', pp. 88–9.

119. Hernández Mir, *La Dictadura ante la Historia*, pp. 172–9; Informe del general Primo de Rivera, November 1924, Armiñán, *Epistolario*, pp. 39–47; Balfour, *Deadly Embrace*, pp. 96–103.

120. Suárez Fernández, *Franco*, I, pp. 175–80; Galinsoga and Franco Salgado, *Centinela*, pp. 93–100; Payne, *Politics and the Military*, pp. 214–17; Fleming, 'Primo de Rivera', pp. 89–90; González Calbet, *La Dictadura*, p. 197; Balfour, *Deadly Embrace*, pp. 103–4. General José Millán Astray, *Franco, el Caudillo* (Salamanca: M. Quero y Simón Editor, 1939) p. 14, claimed, absurdly, that the entire operation had been masterminded by Franco.

121. Primo to Magaz, 21 June, to Jordana, 23 June 1925, Armiñán, *Epistolario*, pp. 227–38; Fleming, 'Primo de Rivera', pp. 90–1; González Calbet, *La Dictadura*, pp. 198–200; Balfour, *Deadly Embrace*, pp. 104–8.

122. Primo to Sanjurjo, 4 June 1925, Armiñán, *Epistolario*, pp. 123-6.
123. Madariaga, *En el Barranco del Lobo*, pp. 346-50; Balfour, *Deadly Embrace*, pp. 109-20; Cabrera, *Juan March*, pp. 170-1.
124. On the massive costs of the Moroccan war, see Calvo Sotelo, *Mis servicios*, pp. 416-17; Villanueva, *La dictadura militar*, pp. 203-4; Pemartín, *Los valores históricos*, Gráficos Nos 19 and 22, between pp. 176-7; González Calbet, *La Dictadura*, pp. 201-3.
125. Calvo Sotelo, *Mis servicios*, pp. 233-4.
126. Maura, *Bosquejo*, I, pp. 231-3; Balfour, *Deadly Embrace*, pp. 110-11; Francisco Franco, diary entry for 8 September 1925, 'Diario de Alhucemas', *Revista de Historia Militar*, No. 40, 1976, p. 229; Woolman, *Rebels*, pp. 191-3.
127. Woolman, *Rebels*, p. 187. For Primo's views on the landing, see his letters from Tetuán, to Magaz, 1, 10, 12 September, to Duque de Tetuán, 11 September, to Sanjurjo, 15 September 1925, Armiñán, *Epistolario*, pp. 257-304. The comment on the King is on p. 77.
128. *ABC*, 13 October 1925; Armiñán, *Epistolario*, pp. 327-30; 'Vanidad Triangular', *Hojas Libres*, No. 1, April 1927, pp. 68-70.

Chapter 8: The Primo de Rivera Dictatorship: The Years of Failure, 1926-1931

1. Antonio Elorza, 'El anarcosindicalismo español bajo la dictadura (1923-1930). La génesis de la Federación Anarquista Ibérica', *Revista de Trabajo*, Nos 39-40, 1972, pp. 123-477; Eduardo González Calleja, *El máuser y el sufragio. Orden público, subversión y violencia política en la crisis de la*

Restauración (1917-1931) (Madrid: Consejo Superior de Investigaciones Científicas, 1999) pp. 321-44.
2. Ricardo Sanz, *El sindicalismo y la política. Los 'Solidarios' y 'Nosotros'* (Toulouse: Imprimerie Dulaurier, 1966) pp. 150-2; Adolfo Bueso, *Recuerdos de un cenetista*, Vol. I: *De la Semana Trágica (1909) a la Segunda República (1931)* (Barcelona: Ariel, 1976) p. 203.
3. González Calleja, *El máuser*, pp. 306-14.
4. Francisco Madrid, *Los desterrados de la Dictadura* (Madrid: Editorial España, 1930) pp. 193-200; Enrique Ucelay Da Cal, 'Estat Català: The Strategies of Separation and Revolution of Catalan Radical Nationalism (1919-1933)', PhD thesis, Columbia University, 1979 (Ann Arbor, Michigan: University Microfilms International, 1979) pp. 74-91, 95-103, 130-8; Edgar Allison Peers, *Catalonia Infelix* (London: Methuen, 1937) pp. 168, 175; Enric Jardí, *Francesc Macià. El camí de la llibertat (1905-1931)* (Barcelona: Aymà Editora, 1977) pp. 76-123.
5. Sanz, *El sindicalismo y la política*, pp. 140-2; Madrid, *Los desterrados*, pp. 245-50; González Calleja, *El máuser*, p. 315.
6. José Peirats, *La CNT en la revolución española*, 2nd edn, 3 vols (Paris: Ediciones Ruedo Ibérico, 1971) I, pp. 37-42; Juan García Oliver, *El eco de los pasos* (Barcelona: Ruedo Ibérico, 1978) pp. 99, 111, 115-16; Pío Baroja, *La selva oscura. La familia de Errotacho* (Madrid: Espasa Calpe, 1932) pp. 111-80; González Calleja, *El máuser*, pp. 315-20.
7. Baroja, *La selva oscura*, pp. 201-2, 244-8, 269-82; Ramiro Gómez

Fernández, *La dictadura me honró encarcelándome* (Madrid: Javier Morata Editor, 1930) pp. 24–9; Ernest Hemingway, *Death in the Afternoon* (London: Jonathan Cape, 1966) p. 258. The ramifications of the affair are lucidly analysed by Miriam B. Mandel, *Hemingway's 'Death in the Afternoon': The Complete Annotations* (Lanham, Md: Scarecrow Press, 2002) pp. 113–21.

8. *ABC*, 30 January 1924; González Calleja, *El máuser*, pp. 221 n. 370, 286–7; José Luis Vila-San-Juan, *La vida cotidiana en España durante la dictadura de Primo de Rivera* (Madrid: Argos Vergara, 1984) pp. 263–6; Manuel Tuñón de Lara, *La España del siglo XX*, 2nd edn (Paris: Librería Española, 1973) pp. 157–8.

9. *ABC*, 13, 15 May 1924; Carlos Blanco, *La dictadura y los procesos militares* (Madrid: Javier Morata Editor, 1931) pp. 73–112, 209; Rafael Salazar Alonso, *La justicia bajo la dictadura* (Madrid: CIAP, 1930) p. 86; Francisco Villanueva, *La dictadura militar (Crónica documentada de la oposición y la represión bajo el directorio) (1923–1926)* (Madrid: Javier Morata Editor, 1931) pp. 164–73; María Teresa González Calbet, *La Dictadura de Primo de Rivera. El Directorio Militar* (Madrid: Ediciones El Arquero, 1987) pp. 208–10.

10. *ABC*, 3 December 1925.

11. González Calbet, *La Dictadura*, p. 127. On the King's investments, see Guillermo Cortázar, *Alfonso XIII. Hombre de negocios* (Madrid: Alianza Editorial, 1986).

12. On Aunós, see Amadeu Hurtado, *Quaranta anys d'advocat. Història del meu temps 1894–1936*, 2nd edn

(Barcelona: Edicions 62, 2011) p. 488; Pedro Carlos González Cuevas, *Acción Española. Teología política y nacionalismo autoritario en España (1913–1936)* (Madrid: Editorial Tecnos, 1998) pp. 102–5. On Calvo Sotelo, Aurelio Joaniquet, *Calvo Sotelo. Una vida fecunda, un ideario política, una doctrina económica* (Madrid: Espasa Calpe, 1939) pp. 44–91; Eduardo Aunós, *Calvo Sotelo y la política de su tiempo* (Madrid: Ediciones Españolas, 1941) pp. 33–55; Alfonso Bullón de Mendoza, *José Calvo Sotelo* (Barcelona: Ariel, 2004).

13. 'Figuras del régimen – Don Galo Ponte', *Hojas Libres*, Nos 13 and 14, May 1928, pp. 63–4; Q. Saldaña, *Al servicio de la justicia. La orgía áurea de la dictadura* (Madrid: Javier Morata, 1930) pp. 21–2; Salazar Alonso, *La justicia*, pp. 84–7.

14. José Luis Gómez Navarro, *El régimen de Primo de Rivera* (Madrid: Cátedra, 1991) pp. 153–7.

15. Manuel Azaña, *Obras completas*, 4 vols (Mexico City: Ediciones Oasis, 1966–8) IV, p. 116; 'Informe en la defensa de don Galo Ponte', in José Antonio Primo de Rivera, *Obras*, 4th edn (Madrid: Sección Feminina de FET y de las JONS, 1966) pp. 15–36.

16. Juan de la Cierva y Peñafiel, *Notas de mi vida* (Madrid: Instituto Editorial Reus, 1955) pp. 298–300, 305–6.

17. Dionisio Pérez, *La Dictadura a través de sus notas oficiosas* (Madrid: CIAP, 1930) pp. 123–6; Juan José Linz, 'Continuidad y discontinuidad en la elite política española: de la Restauración al régimen autoritario', in *Obras Escogidas: Partidos y elites políticas en España*, 7 vols (Madrid: Centro

de Estudios Políticos y Constitucionales, 2008–13) VI, p. 765; Javier Tusell, *La crisis del caciquismo andaluz (1923–1931)* (Madrid: Cupsa Editorial, 1977) pp. 156–64.

18. José Sánchez Guerra, *Al servicio de España. Un manifiesto y un discurso* (Madrid: Javier Morato, 1930) pp. 11–38; Gabriel Maura, *Al servicio de la historia. Bosquejo histórico de la Dictadura*, Vol. II (Madrid: Javier Morata Editor, 1930) pp. 15–26; Pérez, *Notas oficiosas*, pp. 143–9; Gómez Navarro, *El régimen de Primo*, pp. 265–8; González Calleja, *El máuser*, pp. 471–80; 'Una entrevista con el Conde de Romanones', *Hojas Libres*, No. 7, 1 October 1927, pp. 30–8; Joaquín Maurín, *Los hombres de la Dictadura* (Madrid: Editorial Cenit, 1930) pp. 51–4, 60–6.

19. Blanco, *La dictadura y los procesos*, pp. 131–7; Joan Crexell i Playà, *El complot de Garraf* (Barcelona: Publicacions de l'Abadia de Montserrat, 1988) pp. 51–74, 92–8; Artur Perucho i Badia, *Catalunya sota la dictadura (Dades per a la Història)*, 2nd edn (Barcelona: Publicacions de l'Abadia de Montserrat, 2018; 1st edn 1930) pp. 289–90.

20. Miguel de Unamuno, 'A mis hermanos de España, presos en ella', *Hojas Libres*, No. 10, January 1928, pp. 1–10.

21. 'Los sucesos de Vera', *Hojas Libres*, No. 1, April 1927, pp. 16–26; 'Un interviú con el Capitán Cueto', *Hojas Libres*, No. 3, June 1927; Blanco, *La dictadura y los procesos*, pp. 20–72, 207; Eduardo Ortega y Gasset, *España encadenada. La verdad sobre la dictadura* (Paris: Juan Dura, 1925) pp. 274–81;

Perucho, *Catalunya sota la dictadura*, pp. 284–8; Salvador de Madariaga, *Spain: A Modern History* (London: Jonathan Cape, 1961) pp. 356–7; Villanueva, *La dictadura militar*, pp. 174–80; Vicente Marco Miranda, *Las conspiraciones contra la Dictadura*, 2nd edn (Madrid: Tebas, 1975) pp. 35–8; González Calleja, *El máuser*, pp. 288–9; Aurelio Gutiérrez, 'Juan Cueto, Bera sucesos octubre 1925', http://bidasoaikerketazentroa.blogspot.co.uk/2013/11/juan-cueto-bera-sucesos-octubre-1925.html.

22. Gabriel Cardona and Juan Carlos Losada, *Weyler. Nuestro hombre en La Habana* (Barcelona: Planeta, 1997) pp. 297–301.

23. Primo to Duque de Tetuán, 2, 23 April, 8 October, to Jordana, 5 June, to Magaz, 6 October, to Vallespinosa, 8 October 1925, José Manuel and Luis de Armiñán Odriozola, eds, *Epistolario del Dictador. La figura del General Primo de Rivera, trazada por su propia mano* (Madrid: Javier Morata, 1930) pp. 77–83, 131–7, 241–5, 309–11, 319–23, 327–30; General E. López Ochoa, *De la Dictadura a la República* (Madrid: Editorial Zeus, 1930) pp. 78–105; Gómez Fernández, *La dictadura me honró*, pp. 167–73.

24. Marco Miranda, *Las conspiraciones*, pp. 53–63; Gómez Fernández, *La dictadura me honró*, pp. 174–5, 189–92; Cardona and Losada, *Weyler*, pp. 302–5; Eduardo González Calleja, *La España de Primo de Rivera. La modernización autoritaria 1923–1930* (Madrid: Alianza Editorial, 2005) pp. 365–7; González Calleja, *El máuser*, pp. 451–66; Shlomo Ben-Ami, *Fascism from Above: The*

Dictatorship of Primo de Rivera in Spain 1923–1930 (Oxford: Oxford University Press, 1983) pp. 360–1; Gabriel Cardona, *El poder militar en la España contemporánea hasta la guerra civil* (Madrid: Siglo XXI de España, 1983) pp. 86–91.

25. *ABC*, 26 June 1926; Maura, *Bosquejo*, I, pp. 317–22; Gómez Fernández, *La dictadura me honró*, pp. 27–47; Pérez, *Notas oficiosas*, pp. 86–7; Javier Moreno Luzón, *Romanones. Caciquismo y política liberal* (Madrid: Alianza Editorial, 1998) pp. 405–11; Conde de Romanones, *Notas de una vida* (Madrid: Marcial Pons Ediciones, 1999) pp. 487–8; José María Pemán, *Mis almuerzos con gente importante* (Barcelona: Dopesa, 1970) pp. 46–9.

26. Blanco, *La dictadura y los procesos*, pp. 73–95, 207; Madrid, *Los desterrados*, pp. 225–33; Jardí, *Francesc Macià*, pp. 136–54; Ucelay Da Cal, 'Estat Català', pp. 268–77; Peers, *Catalonia Infelix*, pp. 184–5; González Calleja, *El máuser*, pp. 388–402.

27. Michael Alpert, *La reforma militar de Azaña (1931–1933)* (Madrid: Siglo XXI de España, 1982) pp. 106–9, 120; Ben-Ami, *Fascism from Above*, pp. 356–8.

28. López Ochoa, *De la Dictadura a la República*, pp. 106–24; Hernández Mir, *La Dictadura ante la Historia*, pp. 259–72; Marco Miranda, *Las conspiraciones*, pp. 75–7.

29. López Ochoa, *De la Dictadura a la República*, pp. 118–24; Maura, *Bosquejo*, I, pp. 325–37, 360–77; González Calleja, *El máuser*, pp. 466–70.

30. Gonzalo Queipo de Llano, *El general Queipo de Llano perseguido por la dictadura* (Madrid: Javier Morato, 1930) pp. 214–29; Antonio Olmedo Delgado and General José

Cuesta Monereo, *General Queipo de Llano (Aventura y audacia)* (Barcelona: AHR, 1958) p. 71.

31. Ben-Ami, *Fascism from Above*, pp. 361–4; Duque de Maura and Melchor Fernández Almagro, *Por qué cayó Alfonso XIII* (Madrid: Ediciones Ambos Mundos, 1948), pp. 368, 395.

32. Eduardo Aunós, *La política social de la Dictadura* (Madrid: Real Academia de Ciencias Morales y Políticas, 1944) pp. 46–63.

33. Maurín, *Los hombres*, pp. 188–91; *Boletín de la Unión General de Trabajadores de España*, August, September 1929; *El Socialista*, 1 September 1929; Juan Andrade, *La burocracia reformista en el movimiento obrero* (Madrid: Ediciones Gleba, 1935) pp. 208–9; Sanz, *El sindicalismo y la política*, p. 149; Ben-Ami, *Fascism from Above*, pp. 330–4.

34. Interview with Mercedes Castellanos, *Estampa*, 24 April 1924; *ABC*, 24, 28, 29 April, 1, 2, 8, 15, 22, 23, 27, 29, 30 May, 1, 9 June 1924; Ramón Garriga, *Juan March y su tiempo* (Barcelona: Planeta, 1976) pp. 236–8.

35. Luis Jiménez de Asúa, *Notas de un confinado* (Madrid: Compañía Ibero-Americana de Publicaciones, 1930) pp. 33–59; Gómez Fernández, *La dictadura me honró*, pp. 134–40, 200–22; Eduardo Comín Colomer, *Unamuno, libelista. Sus campañas contra Alfonso XIII y la Dictadura* (Madrid: Vasallo de Mumbert, 1968) pp. 74–9.

36. 'La reforma universitaria', *Hojas Libres*, No. 15, June 1926, pp. 89–95; Pérez, *Notas oficiosas*, pp. 239–49; Saldaña, *Al servicio de la justicia*, pp. 119–40; Comín Colomer, *Unamuno, libelista*, pp. 79–83;

Ben-Ami, *Fascism from Above*, pp. 351–4.

37. Maura, *Bosquejo*, II, pp. 168–70; López Ochoa, *De la Dictadura a la República*, pp. 136–42; González Calleja, *El máuser*, pp. 476–81, 494; Mercedes Cabrera, *Juan March (1880–1962)* (Madrid: Marcial Pons, 2011) pp. 184–6.

38. Joaquín Arrarás, *Historia de la Cruzada española*, 8 vols, 36 tomos (Madrid: Ediciones Españolas, 1939–43) I, tomo 2, p. 177.

39. *ABC*, 30 January, 3 February 1929; Rafael Sánchez Guerra, *El movimiento revolucionario de Valencia (Relato de un procesado)*, 3rd edn (Madrid: CIAP, 1930) pp. 63–72, 89–97, 107–11, 127–33; Madariaga, *Spain*, pp. 358–60; Blanco, *La dictadura y los procesos*, pp. 163–9; Maura, *Bosquejo*, II, pp. 206–20, 294–7, 329–30; Pérez, *Notas oficiosas*, pp. 226–33; López Ochoa, *De la Dictadura a la República*, pp. 143–68; González Calleja, *El máuser*, pp. 482–93.

40. *ABC*, 5, 27 November, 17 December 1929; Maura, *Bosquejo*, II, pp. 78–86; Pérez, *Notas oficiosas*, pp. 253, 274–5, 293–300; José Calvo Sotelo, *Mis servicios al Estado. Seis años de gestión: apuntes para la Historia* (Madrid: Imprenta Clásica Española, 1931) p. 338.

41. Juan José Castillo, *Propietarios muy pobres: sobre la subordinación política del pequeño campesino* (Madrid: Instituto de Estudios Agrarias, 1979) pp. 337–59; Eduardo Aunós, *Itinerario histórico de la España contemporánea* (Barcelona: Bosch, 1940) pp. 377–9; Eduardo Aunós, *España en crisis (1874–1936)* (Buenos Aires: Librería del Colegio, 1942) pp. 289–93.

42. Enrique de Santiago, *La UGT ante la revolución* (Madrid: Tipografía Sáez Hermanos, 1932) p. 45; Gabriel Morón, *El Partido Socialista ante la realidad política española* (Madrid: Editorial Cénit, 1929) pp. 124–35; Maurín, *Los hombres*, pp. 188–9.

43. Maura, *Bosquejo*, II, p. 309.

44. Dámaso Berenguer, *De la Dictadura a la República* (Madrid: Editorial Plus Ultra, 1946) pp. 9–10; Ben-Ami, *Fascism from Above*, pp. 365–71, 378–82.

45. *ABC*, 4, 10 December 1929; Calvo Sotelo, *Mis servicios*, pp. 338–41; Ben-Ami, *Fascism from Above*, pp. 380–4.

46. Maura, *Bosquejo*, II, pp. 324–8; Calvo Sotelo, *Mis servicios*, pp. 341–52.

47. Ortega y Gasset, *España encadenada*, pp. 246–7; Aunós, *España en crisis*, pp. 310–13; Julián Cortés Cavanillas, *La caída de Alfonso XIII. Causas y episodios de una revolución*, 7th edn (Madrid: Librería de San Martín, 1933) pp. 58–9, 62.

48. *ABC*, 1 January 1930.

49. Maura, *Bosquejo*, II, pp. 331–2; Pérez, *Notas oficiosas*, pp. 305–7; González Calleja, *El máuser*, pp. 494–7; Aunós, *España en crisis*, pp. 313–14.

50. Francesc Cambó, *La valoració de la pesseta* (Barcelona: Llibreria Catalonia, 1929), page references to the edition in *Llibres* (Barcelona: Editorial Alpha, 1984) pp. 302–6, 318–21.

51. *ABC*, 4, 21, 24 December 1929; Pérez, *Notas oficiosas*, pp. 301–4; Calvo Sotelo, *Mis servicios*, p. 214; Maura, *Bosquejo*, II, pp. 274–6; Ben-Ami, *Fascism from Above*, pp. 342–3.

52. *La Vanguardia*, 8, 10 January; *ABC*, 9 January 1930; Pérez, *Notas oficiosas*, pp. 314–16.

53. *ABC*, 21, 22 January 1930; Calvo Sotelo, *Mis servicios*, pp. 354–8; Maura, *Bosquejo*, II, pp. 310–12; Cabrera, *Juan March*, pp. 185–6.

54. *ABC*, 26 January 1930; Maura, *Bosquejo*, II, pp. 334–6; Maura and Fernández Almagro, *Por qué cayó Alfonso XIII*, pp. 369–70; Pérez, *Notas oficiosas*, pp. 320–31; Francisco Villanueva, *¿Qué ha pasado aquí?* (Madrid: Javier Morata Editor, 1930) pp. 173–9; Berenguer, *De la Dictadura*, pp. 17–18; Ana de Sagrera, *Miguel Primo de Rivera. El hombre, el soldado y el político* (Jerez de la Frontera: Ayuntamiento de Jerez de la Frontera, 1974) p. 348; Ángel Ossorio y Gallardo, *Mis memorias* (Buenos Aires: Losada, 1946) p. 154.

55. *ABC*, 29, 30 January 1930; Pérez, *Notas oficiosas*, pp. 324–31; Villanueva, *¿Qué ha pasado aquí?*, pp. 185–6; Berenguer, *De la Dictadura*, pp. 20–34.

56. Eduardo Aunós, *Primo de Rivera. Soldado y gobernante* (Madrid: Editorial Alhambra, 1944) pp. 219–25; Calvo Sotelo, *Mis servicios*, pp. 370–3.

57. Miguel Maura, *Así cayó Alfonso XIII* (Mexico City: Imprenta Mañez, 1962) pp. 44–5; Berenguer, *De la Dictadura*, pp. 112–13; Gómez Navarro, *El régimen de Primo*, pp. 520–9.

58. *ABC*, 9 September 1930; Emilio Mola Vidal, *Obras completas* (Valladolid: Librería Santarén, 1940) pp. 396–7; Julio Gil Pecharromán, *José Antonio Primo de Rivera. Retrato de un visionario* (Madrid: Temas de Hoy, 1996) pp. 109–13; Alfonso Bullón de Mendoza, *José Calvo Sotelo* (Barcelona: Ariel, 2004) pp. 261–2; Julio Gil Pecharromán, 'Sobre

España inmortal, sólo Dios'. José María Albiñana y el Partido Nacionalista Español (1930–1937) (Madrid: Universidad Nacional de Educación a Distancia, 2000) pp. 77–94.

59. Berenguer, *De la Dictadura*, pp. 44–9, 58–63; Ossorio, *Mis memorias*, p. 155.

60. *ABC*, 7 February 1930; Hurtado, *Quaranta anys*, pp. 531–2; Berenguer, *De la Dictadura*, pp. 68–75, 81–93; López Ochoa, *De la Dictadura a la República*, pp. 219–22.

61. Calvo Sotelo, *Mis servicios*, pp. 361–70, 375–461; Berenguer, *De la Dictadura*, pp. 70–1; Ricardo Robledo, 'Mercado de trabajo, guerra social y "complot" anarquista en el campo sevillano. Las bombas de mayo (1932)', *Historia Social*, No. 92, 2018, pp. 23–45.

62. Maura, *Así cayó*, pp. 50–7; Sánchez Guerra, *Al servicio*, pp. 53–92; Berenguer, *De la Dictadura*, pp. 98–104; Mola, *Obras*, pp. 254–6; Hurtado, *Quaranta anys*, pp. 535–6.

63. *El Sol*, 13, 15, 29, 30 April, 1, 6, 25, 29, 30, 31 May 1930; Niceto Alcalá-Zamora, *Discursos* (Madrid: Editorial Tecnos, 1979) pp. 474–96; Niceto Alcalá-Zamora, *Memorias* (Barcelona: Planeta, 1977) pp. 127–32; Ossorio, *Mis memorias*, pp. 165–6.

64. *ABC*, 1 June 1930; Shlomo Ben-Ami, *The Origins of the Second Republic in Spain* (Oxford: Oxford University Press, 1978) pp. 56–7.

65. Berenguer, *De la Dictadura*, pp. 49–54; Carlos Sambricio, *Memorias inéditas de Secundino Zuazo, 1919–1940. Madrid y sus anhelos urbanísticos* (San Sebastián: Nerea Editorial, 2003) pp. 181–2.

66. Comandante Franco [Ramón], *Madrid bajo las bombas* (Madrid: Zeus S.A. Editorial, 1931) p. 102.

67. Mola, *Obras*, pp. 240–51, 259–60, 276–7, 352–5; González Calleja, *El máuser*, pp. 509–11. On the official posts held by Socialists, see Andrade, *La burocracia reformista*, pp. 242–8.

68. Ben-Ami, *The Origins*, pp. 49–51, 54–6, 59–63, 73–6; Octavio Ruiz Manjón, *El Partido Republicano Radical 1908–1936* (Madrid: Ediciones Giner, 1976) pp. 139–47; Nigel Townson, *The Crisis of Democracy in Spain: Centrist Politics under the Second Republic 1931–1936* (Brighton: Sussex Academic Press, 2000) pp. 12–14; Manuel Azaña, *Obras completas*, 4 vols (Mexico City: Ediciones Oasis, 1966–8) II, pp. 7–17, III, pp. 573–6.

69. *El Sol*, 26, 27, 29 April 1930; Indalecio Prieto, *Con el Rey o contra el Rey* (Mexico City: Ediciones Oasis, 1972) pp. 289–306; Berenguer, *De la Dictadura*, p. 126; Maura, *Así cayó*, pp. 57–9; Gabriel Mario de Coca, *Anti-Caballero. Crítica marxista de la bolchevización del Partido Socialista* (Madrid: Ediciones Engels, 1936) p. 18.

70. *El Sol*, 2, 3, 4, 6 May 1930; Mola, *Obras*, pp. 329–33.

71. Mola, *Obras*, pp. 282–9, 308–9, 314–25.

72. Constancio Bernaldo de Quirós, 'Informe acerca del paro de los jornaleros del campo de Andalucía durante el otoño de 1930', in Ministerio de Trabajo y Previsión Social, *La Crisis andaluza de 1930–1* (Madrid: Ministerio de Trabajo, 1931) pp. 8–35; Manuel Cordero, *Los socialistas y la revolución* (Madrid: Imprenta Torrent, 1932) pp. 93–4.

73. Cordero, *Socialistas*, p. 88; Mola, *Obras*, pp. 353–4, 373, 394, 399, 404, 421, 437–46.

74. Manuel Tuñón de Lara, *El Movimiento obrero en la historia de España* (Madrid: Taurus, 1972) p. 790; David Ruiz, *El movimiento obrero en Asturias* (Oviedo: Amigos de Asturias, 1968) pp. 214–17.

75. *El Sol*, 19 August 1930; Maura, *Así cayó*, pp. 70–2; Mola, *Obras*, pp. 382–3, 394; Alejandro Lerroux, *La Pequeña historia. Apuntes para la Historia grande vividos y redactados por el autor* (Buenos Aires: Editorial Cimera, 1945) pp. 54–6; Ben-Ami, *The Origins*, pp. 76–84. On the disparate nature of the committee, see Joaquín Pérez Madrigal, *Pérez (Vida y trabajos de uno)* (Madrid: Instituto Editorial Reus, 1955) pp. 68–79.

76. Azaña, diary entry for 3 April 1923, *Obras*, IV, p. 367; Lerroux, *La Pequeña historia*, pp. 63–4; Bernardo Díaz Nosty, *La irresistible ascensión de Juan March* (Madrid: Sedmay Ediciones, 1977) pp. 164–70.

77. Coca, *Anti-Caballero*, pp. 20–3; Francisco Largo Caballero, *Mis recuerdos. Cartas a un amigo* (Mexico City: Editores Unidos, 1954) p. 109; Ben-Ami, *The Origins*, pp. 76–84.

78. *El Sol*, 27, 30 September, 21 October 1930; Ben-Ami, *The Origins*, pp. 84–6; Aróstegui, *Largo Caballero*, pp. 215–22; José Peirats, *Los anarquistas en la crisis política española* (Buenos Aires: Editorial Alfa, 1964) pp. 53–65.

79. Mola, *Obras*, pp. 349, 394–5, 408–12, 435; Franco, *Madrid bajo las bombas*, pp. 87, 104–14; Ramón Garriga, *Ramón Franco, el hermano maldito* (Barcelona: Planeta, 1978) pp. 173–8, 182–9; Carmen Díaz, *Mi*

vida con Ramón Franco (Barcelona: Planeta, 1981) pp. 94–153; Gonzalo Queipo de Llano, *El movimiento reivindicativo de Cuatro Vientos* (Madrid: Tipografía Yagües, 1933) pp. 54–5, 63–4.
80. Maura, *Así cayó*, pp. 81–5, 92–3; Indalecio Prieto, *Convulsiones de España. Pequeños detalles de grandes sucesos*, 3 vols (Mexico City: Oasis, 1967–9) II, pp. 323–5.
81. Maura, *Así cayó*, pp. 102–4; Mola, *Obras*, pp. 417–21, 429–35, 471–82.
82. Mola, *Obras*, pp. 437–49; Berenguer, *De la Dictadura*, pp. 212–15; González Calleja, *El máuser*, pp. 555–8.
83. *El Sol*, 15 November 1930; Berenguer, *De la Dictadura*, pp. 126–8; Hurtado, *Quaranta anys*, pp. 554–6; Ossorio, *Mis memorias*, pp. 157–9.
84. José María Azpíroz Pascual and Fernando Elboj Broto, *La sublevación de Jaca* (Zaragoza: Guara Editorial, 1984) pp. 33–40, 81–7; Graco Marsá, *La sublevación de Jaca. Relato de un rebelde*, 2nd edn (Madrid: Zeus S.A. Editorial, 1931) pp. 57–81, 159–89; Maura, *Así cayó*, pp. 109–12; Mola, *Obras*, pp. 471–5; Berenguer, *De la Dictadura*, pp. 237–46; Franco Salgado-Araujo, *Mi vida*, p. 92; Manuel Tuñón de Lara, 'La sublevación de Jaca', *Historia 16*, No. 1, 1976, pp. 57–64; Ben-Ami, *The Origins*, pp. 94–6.
85. Ossorio, *Mis memorias*, pp. 161–3; Henry Buckley, *Life and Death of the Spanish Republic* (London: Hamish Hamilton, 1940) pp. 29–30; Azpíroz and Elboj, *La sublevación*, pp. 109–17; Julio Alvarez del Vayo, *The Last Optimist* (London: Putnam, 1950) pp. 197–8; Manuel de Burgos y Mazo, *De la República*

a ...? (Madrid: Javier Morata, 1931) pp. 83–4.
86. Franco, *Madrid bajo las bombas*, pp. 164–75; Garriga, *Ramón Franco*, pp. 202–4; Queipo de Llano, *El movimiento reivindicativo*, pp. 91–113, 121–8; Ignacio Hidalgo de Cisneros, *Cambio de rumbo (Memorias)*, 2 vols (Bucharest: Colección Ebro, 1964) I, pp. 214–24; Maura, *Así cayó*, pp. 112–13.
87. *El Socialista*, 8–13 October 1932; Alvarez del Vayo, *The Last Optimist*, p. 198.
88. Mola, *Obras*, pp. 447, 543; Largo Caballero, *Mis recuerdos*, pp. 111–13; Andrés Saborit, *Julián Besteiro* (Buenos Aires: Losada, 1967) pp. 195–8; *Diario de sesiones de las Cortes*, 11 April 1934.
89. Peirats, *Los anarquistas*, pp. 67–8; Mola, *Obras*, pp. 544–5, 557–65; Berenguer, *De la Dictadura*, pp. 253–4; Rafael Sánchez Guerra, *Proceso de un cambio de régimen (Historia y murmuración)* (Madrid: CIAP, 1932) pp. 42–4, 49–57, 61–87.
90. Maura, *Así cayó*, pp. 105–9; Buckley, *Life and Death*, p. 168; Indalecio Prieto, *De mi vida. Recuerdos, estampas, siluetas, sombras ...* 2 vols (Mexico City: Ediciones Oasis, 1968) I, pp. 101–5.
91. Azpíroz and Elboj, *La sublevación*, p. 66; *ABC*, 14, 15 February 1931.
92. Maura, *Así cayó*, pp. 119–25; Sánchez Guerra, *Proceso*, pp. 141–6; Joaquín Chapaprieta Torregrosa, *La paz fue posible. Memorias de un político* (Barcelona: Ariel, 1971) pp. 146–8; Burgos y Mazo, *De la República*, pp. 85–95.
93. *ABC*, 17, 18, 19 February 1931; Berenguer, *De la Dictadura*, pp. 320–33; Marqués de Hoyos, *Mi testimonio* (Madrid: Afrodisio

Aguardo, 1962) pp. 47-51;
Ben-Ami, *The Origins*, pp. 202-5.
94. Maura, *Así cayó*, pp. 126-7; Maura
and Fernández Almagro, *Por qué
cayó Alfonso XIII*, pp. 382-5.
95. *ABC*, 14, 17, 19 March 1931;
Azpíroz and Elboj, *La sublevación*,
pp. 144-9; Mola, *Obras*, pp. 735-8;
Maura, *Así cayó*, pp. 131-2; Hoyos,
Mi testimonio, pp. 73-4.
96. *ABC*, 21, 22, 25 March 1931;
Maura, *Así cayó*, pp. 132-8; Mola,
Obras, pp. 739-50; Berenguer, *De la
Dictadura*, pp. 345-8; Hoyos, *Mi
testimonio*, pp. 77-100.
97. *ABC*, 7, 8, 10, 20, 21, 24, 25 March
1931; Hoyos, *Mi testimonio*,
pp. 107-10; La Cierva, *Notas*,
pp. 359-60; Ben-Ami, *The Origins*,
pp. 218-27.
98. *ABC*, 8, 10, 12 April; *El Debate*, 8, 9,
10 April 1931; Ben-Ami, *The
Origins*, pp. 228-37.
99. Ramón de Alderete, ... *y estos
borbones nos quieren gobernar*
(Paris: Edición del Autor, 1974)
p. 31; Mola, *Obras*, pp. 825-31,
836-43, 850-1.
100. Maura, *Así cayó*, pp. 146-50; Conde
de Romanones, *Y sucedió así.
Aportación para la Historia*
(Madrid: Espasa Calpe, 1947)
pp. 23-38; La Cierva, *Notas*,
pp. 361-2; Conde de Romanones,
*Las últimas horas de una
monarquía. La República en España*
(Madrid: Javier Morata Editor,
1931) pp. 91-3.
101. Hurtado, *Quaranta anys*, pp. 576-7;
Peers, *Catalonia Infelix*, pp. 190-2;
Arnau González i Vilalta, *Lluís
Companys. Un home de govern*
(Barcelona: Editorial Base, 2009)
pp. 145-6.
102. Berenguer, *De la Dictadura*,
pp. 355-8, 361-71; Hoyos, *Mi
testimonio*, pp. 126-43; Maura, *Así
cayó*, pp. 165-9; Ben-Ami, *The

Origins, pp. 238-52; Rafael Borràs
Betriu, *Cambio de régimen. Caída
de la Monarquía y proclamación de
la República* (Barcelona: Flor de
Viento Ediciones, 2001) p. 233.
103. Eduardo Aunós, *Calvo Sotelo y la
política de su tiempo* (Madrid:
Ediciones Españolas, 1941)
pp. 46-7; Francisco Franco
Bahamonde, *Palabras del Caudillo
19 abril 1937-7 diciembre 1942*
(Madrid: Ediciones de la Vice-
Secretaría de Educación Popular,
1943) p. 214.

**Chapter 9: The Second Republic:
Reform and Frustration, 1931-1933**

1. Javier Moreno Luzón, 'Fernando
Siete y medio. Los escándolos de
corrupción de Alfonso XIII', in
Borja de Riquer, Joan Lluís Pérez
Francesch, Gemma Rubí, Lluís
Ferran Toledano y Oriol Luján, eds,
*La corrupción política en la España
contemporánea* (Madrid: Marcial
Pons Historia, 2018) pp. 259-60.
2. Rafael Cruz, *Una revolución
elegante. España 1931* (Madrid:
Alianza, 2014) pp. 74-101.
3. Azaña speech, 19 November 1931,
Manuel Azaña, *Obras completas*, 4
vols (Mexico City: Ediciones Oasis,
1966-8) III, pp. 81-3.
4. Shlomo Ben-Ami, *The Origins of
the Second Republic in Spain*
(Oxford: Oxford University Press,
1978) pp. 169-74, 183-6; Martin
Blinkhorn, 'Right-wing Utopianism
and Harsh Reality: Carlism, the
Republic and the Crusade' and Paul
Preston, 'Alfonsist Monarchism and
the Coming of the Spanish Civil
War', both in Martin Blinkhorn, ed.,
*Spain in Conflict 1931-1939:
Democracy and its Enemies*
(London, Sage Publications, 1986)
pp. 160-3, 183-90; Julio Gil
Pecharromán, *Conservadores*

subversivos. La derecha autoritaria alfonsina (1913–1936) (Madrid: Eudema, 1994) pp. 69–86; Miguel Platón, *Alfonso XIII. De Primo de Rivera a Franco. La tentación autoritaria de la Monarquía* (Barcelona: Plaza y Janés, 1998) pp. 271–4.

5. Diego Martínez Barrio, *Memorias* (Barcelona: Planeta, 1983) p. 77; Miguel Maura, *Asi cayó Alfonso XIII. De una dictadura a otra*, 2nd edn by Joaquín Romero Maura (Madrid: Marcial Pons Historia, 2007) p. 404.

6. *Tierra y Libertad*, 15 September 1933.

7. Constancio Bernaldo de Quiros, 'Informe acerca del paro de los jornaleros del campo de Andalucía durante el otoño de 1931', reprinted in his *El espartaquismo agrario y otros ensayos sobre la estructura económica y social de Andalucía* (Madrid: Ediciones de la Revista de Trabajo, 1973) pp. 99–126; *El Socialista*, 14, 29 January, 18 March 1931; Jacques Maurice, *La reforma agraria en España en el siglo XX* (Madrid: Siglo XXI de España, 1975) pp. 22–4.

8. Niceto Alcalá-Zamora, *Memorias* (Barcelona: Planeta, 1977) pp. 170–4, 203–4; Joaquín Romero Maura, 'Introducción', in Maura, *De una dictadura a otra*, pp. 109–11.

9. Nigel Townson, *The Crisis of Democracy in Spain: Centrist Politics under the Second Republic 1931–1936* (Brighton: Sussex Academic Press, 2000) pp. 13–16.

10. Carolyn P. Boyd, 'Responsibilities and the Second Spanish Republic 1931–6', *European History Quarterly*, Vol. 14 (1984), pp. 151–82; Moreno Luzón, 'Fernando Siete y medio', pp. 260–1, 272–4; Ángel Ossorio y Gallardo,

Mis memorias (Buenos Aires: Losada, 1946) pp. 185–8.

11. *El Debate*, 3 September; *ABC*, 5 September 1931; Alcalá-Zamora, *Memorias*, pp. 178–9; Azaña, diary entries for 2 and 11 September 1931, *Obras*, IV, pp. 115–16, 124; Boyd, 'Responsibilities', p. 164.

12. *El Obrero de la Tierra*, 10, 17 September 1932; *Boletín de la UGT*, November 1931. The PSOE also grew dramatically in the south. See Actas de la Comisión Ejecutiva del PSOE, Fundacion Pablo Iglesias (henceforth FPI, Actas), AH-20-1, 26 May, 4, 10 September 1931, 14, 28, January, 11 February 1932.

13. Francisco Largo Caballero, *Mis recuerdos. Cartas a un amigo* (Mexico City: Editores Unidos, 1954) p. 121; Alcalá-Zamora, *Memorias*, pp. 141–4; Miguel Maura, *Así cayó Alfonso XIII* (Mexico City: Imprenta Mañez, 1962) pp. 84–5.

14. Azaña, diary entry for 9 October 1931, *Obras*, IV, p. 163.

15. Azaña, diary entry for 28 August 1931, *Obras*, IV, p. 107; Joaquín Pérez Madrigal, *Pérez (Vida y trabajos de uno)* (Madrid: Instituto Editorial Reus, 1955) pp. 84–102, 108–16.

16. *Renovación*, 20 April, 10 May 1931; Largo Caballero, *Mis recuerdos*, p. 117; Juan-Simeón Vidarte, *Las Cortes Constituyentes de 1931–1933* (Barcelona: Grijalbo, 1976) p. 22.

17. Maura, *Así cayó*, pp. 209–10, 216–22; Jordi Palafox, *Atraso económico y democracia. La segunda República y la economía española, 1892–1936* (Barcelona: Crítica, 1991) p. 180.

18. Santos Juliá Díaz, *Historia del socialismo español (1931–1939)* (Barcelona: Conjunto Editorial, 1989) pp. 43–4; Palafox, *Atraso*

económico, pp. 155, 192–3, 209; Maura, *Así cayó*, p. 201; Azaña, diary entry for 9 January, 11 May 1932, *Obras*, IV, pp. 302, 382.

19. Azaña, diary entries for 6 and 13 November 1931, *Obras*, IV, pp. 216–17, 227.

20. Edward E. Malefakis, *Agrarian Reform and Peasant Revolution in Spain* (New Haven, Conn.: Yale University Press, 1970) pp. 166–71; *BUGT*, May and June 1931; Alejandro López López, *El boicot de las derechas a las reformas de la Segunda República. La minoría agraria, el rechazo constitucional y la cuestión de la tierra* (Madrid: Instituto de Estudios Agrarios, 1984) pp. 245–62.

21. Maura, *Asi cayó*, pp. 264–72.

22. *El Debate*, 21 April, 9, 30 May, 17 June 1931; José Monge Bernal, *Acción Popular (Estudios de biología política)* (Madrid: Imprenta Saez Hermanos, 1936) pp. 114–15, 122, 126–9; Manuel Álvarez Tardío, *José María Gil-Robles: Leader of the Catholic Right during the Spanish Second Republic* (Brighton: Sussex Academic Press, 2018) pp. 30–49; Maura, *De una dictadura a otra*, pp. 404, 423–5.

23. Ismael Saz Campos, *Mussolini contra la II República. Hostilidad, conspiraciones, intervención (1931–1936)* (Valencia: Edicions Alfons el Magnànim, 1986) pp. 97–101; Enrique Selva Roca de Togores, 'Giménez Caballero en los orígenes ideológicos del fascismo español', *Estudis d'Història Contemporània del País Valencià*, No. 9, 1991, pp. 183–213.

24. José María Albiñana, *Después de la dictadura. Los cuervos sobre la tumba*, 2nd edn (Madrid: CIAP, 1930) pp. 252–9; Julio Gil Pecharromán, 'Sobre España

inmortal, sólo Díos'. José María Albiñana y el Partido Nacionalista Español (1930–1937) (Madrid: Universidad Nacional de Educación a Distancia, 2000) pp. 133–7.

25. Ramiro Ledesma Ramos, *¿Fascismo en España?*, 2nd edn (Barcelona: Ariel, 1968) pp. 77–81; Ferran Gallego, *Ramiro Ledesma Ramos* (Madrid: Editorial Síntesis, 2005) pp. 64–92; Tomás Borrás, *Ramiro Ledesma Ramos* (Madrid: Editora Nacional, 1971) pp. 216, 248–50; Herbert Rutledge Southworth, 'The Falange: An Analysis of Spain's Fascist Heritage', in Paul Preston, ed., *Spain in Crisis: The Evolution and Decline of the Franco Regime* (Hassocks: Harvester Press, 1976) p. 6.

26. *Onésimo Redondo Caudillo de Castilla* (Valladolid: Ediciones Libertad, 1937) pp. 18–37; Ledesma Ramos, *¿Fascismo?*, p. 99; Gallego, *Ramiro Ledesma Ramos*, pp. 94–115.

27. Raffaele Guariglia, *Ambasciata in Spagna e primi passi in diplomazia 1932–1934* (Naples: Edizioni Scientifiche Italiane, 1972) pp. 304–5; Saz, *Mussolini contra la segunda República*, pp. 111–12, 140–5; Pedro Sainz Rodríguez, *Testimonio y recuerdos* (Barcelona: Planeta, 1978) pp. 220–2; José María Gil Robles, *No fue posible la paz* (Barcelona: Ariel, 1968) pp. 442–3.

28. Hilari Raguer, *La pólvora y el incienso. La Iglesia y la guerra civil española* (Barcelona: Ediciones Península, 2001) pp. 43–5; Arxiu Vidal i Barraquer, *Esglesia i Estat durant la Segona República espanyola 1931/1936*, 4 volumes in 8 parts (Monestir de Montserrat: Publicacions de l'Abadia de Montserrat, 1971–90) I, 1st part, p. 24.

29. José María Pemán, *Mis almuerzos con gente importante* (Barcelona: Dopesa, 1970) p. 143.

30. Santiago Martínez Sánchez, *Los papeles perdidos del cardenal Segura, 1880–1957* (Pamplona: Ediciones Universidad de Navarra, 2004) pp. 238–47; Hilari Raguer, "'España ha dejado de ser católica'. La Iglesia y el "alzamiento'", in Francisco Sánchez Pérez, ed., *Los mitos del 18 de julio* (Barcelona: Crítica, 2013) pp. 244–7.

31. Maura, *Así cayó*, pp. 293–307; Juan de Iturralde (pseudonym of Juan José Usabiaga Irazustabarrena), *La guerra de Franco. Los vascos y la Iglesia*, 2 vols (San Sebastián: Publicaciones 'Clero Vasco', 1978) I, pp. 201–3; Raguer, *La pólvora*, pp. 48–51.

32. Maura, *Así cayó*, pp. 240–64; Azaña, diary entry for 10 January, *Obras*, IV, pp. 302–5; Henry Buckley, *Life and Death of the Spanish Republic* (London: Hamish Hamilton, 1940) pp. 64–6; interview with Miguel Maura in Gabriel Jackson, *Historian's Quest* (New York: Alfred A. Knopf, 1969) pp. 114–15; evidence of witness no. 30 in the Basque Clergy's compilation *El Pueblo vasco frente a la cruzada franquista* (Toulouse: Editorial Egi-Indarra, 1966) pp. 23–4; Ossorio, *Mis memorias*, pp. 183–5; Pérez Madrigal, *Pérez*, pp. 102–7.

33. John Brademas, *Anarcosindicalismo y revolución en España 1930–1937* (Barcelona: Ariel, 1974) p. 57; Joan Peiró, *Escrits 1917–1939* (Barcelona: Edicions 62, 1975) pp. 303–6.

34. *ABC*, 15 April; *La Vanguardia*, 15 April 1931; Enric Jardí, *Francesc Macià. President de Catalunya* (Barcelona: Publicacions de l'Abadia de Montserrat, 1981)

pp. 15–91; Amadeu Hurtado, *Quaranta anys d'advocat. Història del meu temps 1894–1936*, 2nd edn (Barcelona: Edicions 62, 2011) pp. 592–9; Carles Pi Sunyer, *La República y la guerra. Memorias de un político catalán* (Mexico City: Ediciones Oasis, 1975) pp. 30–4.

35. Ramón Salas Larrazábal, *Historia del Ejército popular de la República*, 4 vols (Madrid, 1973) I, pp. 7, 14, 19–23; Felipe Díaz Sandino, *De la conspiración a la revolución 1929–1937* (Madrid: Libertarias, 1990) pp. 78–82; Santos Juliá Díaz, *Vida y tiempo de Manuel Azaña 1880–1940* (Madrid: Taurus, 2008) pp. 279–84.

36. Mola, *Obras*, pp. 1056–8; Michael Alpert, *La reforma militar de Azaña (1931–1933)* (Madrid: Siglo XXI de España, 1982) pp. 133–50, 216–28; Mariano Aguilar Olivencia, *El Ejército español durante la segunda República* (Madrid: Econorte, 1986) pp. 65–83.

37. *La Correspondencia Militar*, 18 June, 17, 31 July 1931; Mola, *Obras*, pp. 1045–65; Eduardo Espín, *Azaña en el poder. El partido de Acción Republicana* (Madrid: Centro de Investigaciones Sociológicas, 1980) pp. 323–34; Alpert, *La reforma militar*, pp. 293–7; Maura, *Así cayó*, p. 227.

38. Juan Tusquets, *Orígenes de la revolución española* (Barcelona: Editorial Vilamala, 1932) pp. 30–44, 137–42; Martin Blinkhorn, *Carlism and Crisis in Spain 1931–1939* (Cambridge: Cambridge University Press, 1975) pp. 46, 179; Gonzalo Álvarez Chillida, *El antisemitismo en España. La imagen del judío (1812–2002)* (Madrid: Marcial Pons, 2002) pp. 181, 334–8.

39. Azaña, diary entry for 7 August 1937, *Obras*, IV, p. 717.

40. *El Debate*, 23, 24, 26, 30 June, 25 August; *ABC*, 12, 24, 28 June 1931; *El Socialista*, 26, 28 November, 1 December 1933; *El Pueblo Católico*, 4 May 1933; Joaquín Chapaprieta Torregrosa, *La paz fue posible. Memorias de un político* (Barcelona: Ariel, 1971) pp. 149–58; Octavio Ruiz Manjón, *El Partido Republicano Radical 1908–1936* (Madrid: Ediciones Giner, 1976) pp. 186–91, 205–6; Azaña, diary entry for 2 October 1931, *Obras*, IV, p. 161; Townson, *Crisis of Democracy*, pp. 54–7; Fernando del Rey, *Paisanos en lucha. Exclusión política y violencia en la Segunda República española* (Madrid: Biblioteca Nueva, 2008) pp. 107–11.

41. Maura, *De una dictadura a otra*, pp. 393–4, 399–407; Julio Gil Pecharromán, *Historia de la Segunda República Española 1931–1936* (Madrid: Biblioteca Nueva, 2002) pp. 55–8; Javier Tusell, Octavio Ruiz-Manjón and Genoveva García Queipo de Llano, 'Las Constituyentes de 1931: una elecciones de transición', *Revista de Derecho Político* (Madrid: UNED, 1981–2) Vol. 12, pp. 189–236 and Vol. 13, pp. 137–95, 237–70.

42. José Manuel Macarro Vera, *La utopía revolucionaria. Sevilla en la segunda República* (Seville: Monte de Piedad y Caja de Ahorros de Sevilla, 1985) pp. 147–60; Eduardo de Guzmán, *Sevilla la trágica. Ocho días que estremecieron a España* (Madrid: Ediciones Minuesa, 1931) pp. 16–21, 32–48; Francisco Espinosa Maestre, *La justicia de Queipo. (Violencia selectiva y terror fascista en la II División en 1936) Sevilla, Huelva, Cádiz, Córdoba, Málaga y Badajoz*, 2nd edn (Barcelona: Crítica, 2005) pp. 19–21; Maura, *De una dictadura*

a otra, pp. 365–72, 417–21; Manuel Ballbé, *Orden público y militarismo en la España constitucional 1812–1983* (Madrid: Alianza Editorial, 1983) pp. 322–3.

43. Julián Casanova, *De la calle al frente. El anarcosindicalismo en España (1931–1939)* (Barcelona: Crítica, 1997) pp. 20–31; Chris Ealham, *Class, Culture and Conflict in Barcelona 1898–1937* (London: Routledge Cañada Blanch, 2004) pp. 90–101, 131–2; Ballbé, *Orden público*, pp. 317–23; José Peirats, *La CNT en la revolución española*, 2nd edn, 3 vols (Paris: Ediciones Ruedo Ibérico, 1971) I, pp. 51–73; Eulàlia Vega, *El Trentisme a Catalunya. Divergències ideològiques en la CNT (1930–1933)* (Barcelona: Curial Edicions Catalanes, 1980) pp. 132–48; Eulàlia Vega, *Anarquistas y sindicalistas durante la segunda República. La CNT y los Sindicatos de Oposición en el País Valenciano* (Valencia: Edicions Alfons el Magnànim, 1987) pp. 145–67; Joaquín Romero Maura, *La romana del diablo. Ensayos sobre la violencia política en España (1900–1950)* (Madrid: Marcial Pons, 2000) pp. 201–3; Richard Purkiss, *Democracy, Trade Unions and Political Violence in Spain: The Valencian Anarchist Movement, 1918–1936* (Brighton: Sussex Academic Press, 2010) pp. 139–40.

44. Luis Jiménez de Asúa, *Anécdotas de las Constituyentes* (Buenos Aires: PHAC, 1942) pp. 21–45; Niceto Alcalá-Zamora, *Los defectos de la constitución de 1931 y tres años de experiencia constitucional*, 2nd edn (Madrid: Editorial Civitas, 1981) pp. 42–8.

45. Azaña, diary entry for 28 August 1931, *Obras*, IV, p. 107; Alcalá-

Zamora, *Memorias*, p. 175; Martínez Barrio, *Memorias*, pp. 70-1; Fernando Vázquez Ocaña, *Pasión y muerte de la segunda República española* (Paris: Editorial Norte, 1940) p. 41; Gabriel Morón, *El fracaso de una revolución* (Madrid: Gráfica Socialista, 1935) pp. 121-5.

46. Maura, *De una dictadura a otra*, pp. 433-5.

47. Azaña, speech in Cortes, 13 October 1931 in defence of Article 26 of the Constitution, *Obras*, III, pp. 49-58; Alcalá-Zamora, *Memorias*, pp. 190-4; Raguer, "'España ha dejado de ser católica'", pp. 239-41; Martínez Barrio, *Memorias*, pp. 70-7.

48. Cardinal Vidal i Barraquer to Pacelli, 16 October, to Azaña, 24 and 25 November 1931, Arxiu Vidal i Barraquer, *Esglesia i Estat*, II, 1st part, pp. 159-63, 2nd part, pp. 391-7; Víctor Manuel Arbeloa, *La semana trágica de la Iglesia en España (1931)* (Barcelona: Galba Edicions, 1976) pp. 257-67.

49. William J. Callahan, 'Was Spain Catholic?', *Revista Canadiense de Estudios Hispánicos*, Vol. 8, No. 2, 1984, pp. 167-71.

50. Juan Ordóñez Márquez, *La apostasía de las masas y la persecución religiosa en la provincia de Huelva 1931-6* (Madrid: Instituto Enrique Flórez, 1968) pp. 26-31, 90, 101, 148-9, 161-2, 172; Frances Lannon, *Privilege, Persecution, and Prophecy: The Catholic Church in Spain 1875-1975* (Oxford: Clarendon Press, 1987) pp. 9-19; William J. Callahan, *The Catholic Church in Spain 1875-1998* (Washington, DC: The Catholic University of America Press, 2000) pp. 240-50, 289-90.

51. Azaña, diary entry for 14 October 1931, *Obras*, IV, pp. 183-6; Maura, *De una dictadura a otra*, pp. 437-43; Vidarte, *Las Cortes Constituyentes*, pp. 284-9; César Jalón, *Memorias políticas. Periodista, ministro, presidiario* (Madrid: Guadarrama, 1973) p. 76; Alejandro Lerroux, *La pequeña historia. Apuntes para la Historia grande vividos y redactados por el autor* (Buenos Aires: Editorial Cimera, 1945) pp. 118-21; Martínez Barrio, *Memorias*, pp. 77-81, 90-1; Townson, *Crisis of Democracy*, pp. 77-82.

52. Boyd, 'Responsibilities', pp. 169-72; *Diario de sesiones de las Cortes Constituyentes* (henceforth *DSCC*), 5, 6, 10 November 1931; Azaña, diary entries for 5, 6, 7 and 13 November 1931, *Obras*, IV, pp. 215-223; Ramón Garriga, *Juan March y su tiempo* (Barcelona: Planeta, 1976) pp. 298-313; Bernardo Díaz Nosty, *La irresistible ascensión de Juan March* (Madrid: Sedmay Ediciones, 1977) pp. 183-210; Pere Ferrer, *Juan March. El hombre más misterioso del mundo* (Barcelona: Ediciones B, 2008) pp. 241-62; Townson, *Crisis of Democracy*, pp. 83-6; Mercedes Cabrera, *Juan March (1880-1962)* (Madrid: Marcial Pons, 2011) pp. 206-13.

53. Manuel Benavides, *El último pirata del mediterráneo* (Barcelona: Imprenta Industrial, 1936) pp. 358-60; Azaña, diary entries for 30 April, 3 May 1933, 19 July 1937, *Diarios, 1932-1933. 'Los cuadernos robados'* (Barcelona: Grijalbo-Mondadori, 1997) pp. 251-2, 261, *Obras*, IV, p. 685; *DSCC*, 8, 14 June 1931; Morón, *El fracaso*, pp. 118-21; Garriga, *Juan March*, pp. 321-31; Ferrer, *Juan March*,

pp. 268-77; Cabrera, *Juan March*, pp. 217-32, 243-4; Díaz Nosty, *La irresistible ascensión*, pp. 210-16, 223-50.

54. Paul Preston, *The Spanish Holocaust: Inquisition and Extermination in Twentieth-Century Spain* (London: HarperCollins, 2012) pp. 440, 486, 490-2.

55. *DSCC*, 13 October 1931; *El Debate*, 20, 23 October 1931; Maura, *De una dictadura a otra*, pp. 435-7; Mary Vincent, *Catholicism in the Second Spanish Republic: Religion and Politics in Salamanca 1930-1936* (Oxford: Clarendon Press, 1996) pp. 180-1.

56. Manuel Albar, 'Sobre unos sucesos. El verdadero culpable', *El Socialista*, 2 January 1932; Vidarte, *Las Cortes Constituyentes*, pp. 290-309. The judicial proceedings were published as Luis Jiménez Asúa, Juan-Simeón Vidarte, Antonio Rodríguez Sastre and Anselmo Trejo, *Castilblanco* (Madrid: Editorial España, 1933).

57. *El Socialista*, 6 January; *La Rioja*, 6, 8, 9, 10, 12 January; *El Debate*, 6 January 1932; Carlos Gil Andrés, *La República en la Plaza. Los sucesos de Arnedo de 1932* (Logroño: Instituto de Estudios Riojanos, 2003) pp. 24-33, 43-9; Malefakis, *Agrarian Reform*, pp. 310-11.

58. López López, *El boicot de las derechas*, p. 254; Ricardo Robledo and Luis Enrique Espinosa, '"¡El campo en pie!". Política y reforma agraria', in Ricardo Robledo, ed., *Esta salvaje pesadilla. Salamanca en la guerra civil española* (Barcelona: Crítica, 2007) pp. 23-5.

59. *La Mañana* (Jaén), 1 October 1932, 21, 27 January, 3, 18 February, 5 April 1933, 16 January 1934; *El Adelanto* (Salamanca), 19 October 1932; *Región* (Cáceres), 24 February

1933; *El Obrero de la Tierra*, 14 January, 4 March 1933, 6, 13, 20 January, 17 February 1934; *El Socialista*, 21 January, 20 April, 1 July 1933. See also Paul Preston, *The Coming of the Spanish Civil War: Reform, Reaction and Revolution in the Second Spanish Republic 1931-1936*, 2nd edn (London, Routledge, 1994) pp. 101-2, 111, 134-5, 140, 148-9, 184-5.

60. Malefakis, *Agrarian Reform*, pp. 268-73; José María Gil Robles, *Discursos parlamentarios* (Madrid: Taurus, 1971) pp. 263-7.

61. *El Obrero de la Tierra*, 19 November 1932, 14, 28 January, 4 March 1933; *Boletín del Instituto de Reforma Agraria*, March 1933; *Región* (Cáceres), 24 February 1933; *El Pueblo Católico*, 14 March 1933; *ABC*, 26 January, 26 March 1933; *La Mañana*, 21, 27 January, 3, 18 February, 5 April 1933; *El Socialista*, 21 January, 20 April, 1 July 1933.

62. Jardí, *Francesc Macià*, pp. 213-306; Hurtado, *Quaranta anys*, pp. 685-702.

63. Leandro Álvarez Rey, *La derecha en la II República. Sevilla, 1931-1936* (Seville: Universidad de Sevilla, 1993) pp. 203-6, 215-35; Vincent, *Catholicism*, pp. 185-6; Lannon, *Privilege, Persecution*, pp. 15, 181-9.

64. Azaña, diary entry for 8 January 1932, *Obras*, IV, pp. 299-301.

65. Espinosa Maestre, *La justicia de Queipo*, pp. 33, 77-9; Álvarez Rey, *La derecha*, pp. 252-60; Martínez Barrio, *Memorias*, pp. 138-48; Emilio Estéban Infantes, *La sublevación del general Sanjurjo* (Madrid: Imprenta de J. Sánchez Ocaña, 1933) pp. 24-37; Eduardo González Calleja, *Contrarrevolucionarios. Radicalización violenta de las*

derechas durante la Segunda República, 1931-1936 (Madrid: Alianza Editorial, 2011) pp. 82-102; Townson, *Crisis of Democracy*, pp. 136-45; Cabrera, *Juan March*, pp. 235-7.

66. Julio Alvarez del Vayo, *The Last Optimist* (London: Putnam, 1950) p. 228; Manuel Azaña, diary entries for 24-28 August 1932, *Diarios, 1932-1933*, pp. 41-51; Joaquín del Moral, *Lo del '10 de agosto' y la justicia* (Madrid: CIAP, 1933) pp. 99-108; Maura, *De una dictadura a otra*, pp. 457-63.

67. Letter from Sanjurjo, 12 December 1933, *Acción Española*, No. 43, December 1933, p. 629; Pedro Carlos González Cuevas, *Acción Española. Teología política y nacionalismo autoritario en España (1913-1936)* (Madrid: Editorial Tecnos, 1998) p. 172.

68. Juan Antonio Ansaldo, *¿Para qué ...? (de Alfonso XIII a Juan III)* (Buenos Aires: Editorial Vasca Ekin, 1951) pp. 47-51; Eugenio Vegas Latapié, *Memorias políticas. El suicidio de la monarquía y la segunda República* (Barcelona: Planeta, 1983) pp. 150-2, 156-8; Azaña, diary entries for 29 August 1932 and 5 March 1933, *Diarios, 1932-1933*, pp. 53, 206; González Cuevas, *Acción Española*, pp. 173-6.

69. Antonio Cacho Zabalza, *La Unión Militar Española* (Alicante: Egasa, 1940) pp. 13-19, 30; Julio Busquets and Juan Carlos Losada, *Ruido de sables. Las conspiraciones militares en la España del siglo XX* (Barcelona: Crítica, 2003) pp. 50-60; Gabriel Cardona, *El poder militar en la España contemporánea hasta la guerra civil* (Madrid: Siglo XXI de España, 1983) pp. 193-5; Stanley G. Payne,

Politics and the Military in Modern Spain (Stanford, Calif.: Stanford University Press, 1967) pp. 293-4.

70. Gil Robles, *No fue posible*, pp. 82-91; *El Debate*, 8 October 1933.

71. *El Debate*, 21, 23, 25 October 1932; José R. Montero, *La CEDA. El catolicismo social y político en la II República*, 2 vols (Madrid: Revista de Trabajo, 1977) I, pp. 259-71.

72. Ramón Sender, *Viaje a la aldea del crimen* (Madrid: Pueyo, 1934) pp. 33-42, 70-130; Eduardo de Guzmán, *La tragedia de Casas Viejas, 1933. Quince crónicas de guerra, 1936* (Madrid: Ediciones Vosa, 2007) pp. 15-48; Gérald Brey and Jacques Maurice, *Historia y leyenda de Casas Viejas* (Bilbao: Editorial Zero/ZYX, 1976) pp. 65-75; Jerome R. Mintz, *The Anarchists of Casas Viejas* (Chicago: University of Chicago Press, 1982) pp. 189-225.

73. *El Debate*, 15 January 1932.

74. *DSCC*, 3, 23, 24 February, 2, 3, 16 March 1933; *El Debate*, 24 February 1933; Azaña, diary entry for 13 January, 23 February 1933, *Diarios, 1932-1933*, pp. 136, 186; Maura, *De una dictadura a otra*, pp. 483-8; Townson, *Crisis of Democracy*, pp. 153-7; Cabrera, *Juan March*, pp. 247-9.

75. *El Debate*, 1, 2, 3, 5, 7, 8 March; *CEDA*, 1 May 1933; Gil Robles, *No fue posible*, pp. 86, 90; Montero, *La CEDA*, I, pp. 271-303.

76. *El Socialista*, 31 January, 5, 10, 11 February, 10 March, 2, 21 April, 1, 4, 6 May 1933.

77. *El Debate*, 28 June, 16, 25 July, 4, 17, 25 August 1933; *El Socialista*, 21 July, 7 September 1933.

78. Azaña, diary entries for 31 May, 1, 2 June 1933, *Diarios, 1932-1933*, pp. 316-17, 323-7.

79. Azaña, diary entries for 5, 10, 11 June 1933, *Diarios, 1932–1933*, pp. 328–9, 345–55; Martínez Barrio, *Memorias*, pp. 176–84; Jalón, *Memorias*, pp. 69–77; Morón, *El fracaso*, pp. 232–40; Vázquez Ocaña, *Pasión y muerte*, pp. 41–2; Santos Juliá Díaz, *Manuel Azaña. Una biografía política* (Madrid: Alianza Editorial, 1990) pp. 262–70; Townson, *Crisis of Democracy*, pp. 162–5.

80. *El Socialista*, 25 June 1933; Julio Aróstegui, *Largo Caballero. El tesón y la quimera* (Barcelona: Debate, 2013) pp. 314–17.

81. Indalecio Prieto, *Discursos fundamentales* (Madrid: Ediciones Turner, 1975) pp. 160–80; Indalecio Prieto, *Cartas a un escultor. Pequeños detalles de grandes sucesos* (Buenos Aires: Editorial Losada, 1961) pp. 83–8.

82. Cabrera, *Juan March*, pp. 251–4; Díaz Nosty, *La irresistible ascensión*, pp. 256–8; Ferrer, *Juan March*, pp. 311–16.

83. *El Socialista*, 20, 24 September, 3 October 1933; Francisco Largo Caballero, *Discursos a los trabajadores* (Madrid: Gráfica Socialista, 1934) pp. 69–85; Aróstegui, *Largo Caballero*, pp. 317–23.

84. Lerroux, *La pequeña historia*, pp. 172–84; Alcalá-Zamora, *Memorias*, pp. 244–6; Townson, *Crisis of Democracy*, pp. 180–3; Juliá Díaz, *Historia del socialismo*, pp. 196–8.

85. Georges Bernanos, *Les grands cimitières sous la lune* (Paris: Plon, 1938) p. 93.

86. *El Debate*, 15, 17, 22, 23, 29 August, 2, 15, 19 September; *El Socialista*, 13 August; 3, 8 October; *El Obrero de la Tierra*, 12, 20 August, 9, 16, 23 September 1933;

Malefakis, *Agrarian Reform*, pp. 268–73.

87. Juliá Díaz, *Historia del socialismo*, pp. 197–8.

88. Juan Simeón Vidarte, *El bienio negro y la insurrección de Asturias* (Barcelona: Grijalbo, 1978) p. 21; FPI, Actas, AH-20-1, 24, 25, 27, 31 October, 22, 29 November 1933 (Archivo Histórico de la Fundación Pablo Iglesias, Madrid).

89. *El Debate*, 3 November 1933; Díaz Nosty, *La irresistible ascensión*, pp. 271–2; Cabrera, *Juan March*, pp. 265–6.

90. T. F. Burns, Memorandum for Hoare, 11 April 1944, Templewood Papers, Cambridge University Library, XIII/6/28; *Tierra y Libertad*, 10 November 1933; Benavides, *El último pirata*, pp. 56–7; Díaz Nosty, *La irresistible ascensión*, pp. 258–60.

91. *El Socialista*, 5 November, 10 December 1933; Díaz Nosty, *La irresistible ascensión*, pp. 260–75; Cabrera, *Juan March*, pp. 257–64; Ferrer, *Juan March*, pp. 322–36; David Jato, *Gibraltar decidió la guerra* (Barcelona: Acervo, 1971) pp. 198–200.

92. *El Debate*, 12, 17, 18, 24 October, 7, 17, 18 November; *El Socialista*, 7, 14, 15 November 1933; Aróstegui, *Largo Caballero*, pp. 327–33; Santiago Carrillo, *Juez y parte. 15 retratos españoles* (Barcelona: Plaza y Janés, 1996) pp. 44–5.

93. *El Obrero de la Tierra*, 30 January, 5, 13, 20 February, 5, 12, 26 March, 8 October 1932, 8 October 1933; *La Mañana*, 1, 2, 6, 7, 16 April, 11 May, 24 June, 18 November 1932, 27 January, 18 February 1933; Vázquez Ocaña, *Pasión y muerte*, p. 44; Manuel Pérez Yruela, *La conflictividad campesina en la provincia de Córdoba 1931–1936*

(Madrid: Servicio de Publicaciones
Agrarias, 1979) pp. 111–18, 155–70;
Francisco Moreno Gómez, *La
República y la guerra civil en
Córdoba I* (Córdoba: Ayuntamiento
de Córdoba, 1982) pp. 117–19,
131–4, 147–53, 163–74, 199–213;
Mario López Martínez, *Órden
público y luchas agrarias en
Andalucía* (Madrid: Ediciones
Libertarias/Ayuntamiento de
Córdoba, 1995) pp. 273–308.

94. *Boletín del Ministerio de Trabajo*,
January 1935; Santos Juliá Díaz,
*Madrid, 1931-1934. De la fiesta
popular a la lucha de clases*
(Madrid: Siglo XXI de España,
1984) pp. 295–306, 452–3;
Malefakis, *Agrarian Reform*, p. 288;
Francisco Cobo Romero,
*Labradores, campesinos y jornaleros.
Protesta social y diferenciación
interna del campesinado jiennense
en los orígenes de la Guerra Civil
(1931-1936)* (Cordoba:
Publicaciones del Ayuntamiento de
Córdoba, 1992) pp. 400–5.

95. Andrew Durgan, 'The 1933
Elections in Spain', unpublished
MA dissertation, Queen Mary
College, University of London,
1981, p. 40; Díaz Nosty, *La
irresistible ascensión*, pp. 276–7. On
Cánovas Cervantes's alleged
venality, see Guillermo Cabanellas,
*La guerra de los mil días.
Nacimiento, vida y muerte de la II
República española*, 2 vols (Buenos
Aires: Grijalbo, 1973) I, p. 239.

96. 'Ante la agudización del mito
electoral, abstención a toda costa',
CNT, 24 October, 'Ahora toca
hablar a los abstenidos', 6
November; '¡Trabajadores, no
votar!', *Tierra y Libertad*, 10
November 1933.

97. Francisco Bravo Martínez, *José
Antonio. El hombre, el jefe, el*

camarada (Madrid: Ediciones
Españolas, 1939) pp. 31–2.

98. Nelken, 'Con el fango hasta la boca',
El Socialista, 30 November 1933;
Margarita Nelken, *Por qué hicimos
la revolución* (Barcelona/París/New
York: Ediciones Sociales
Internacionales, 1936) pp. 69–71.

99. Appendix to Largo Caballero,
Discursos, pp. 163–6. With a
different emphasis, the PSOE's
conclusions are broadly confirmed
by Roberto Villa García, *La
República en las urnas. El despertar
de la democracia en España*
(Madrid: Marcial Pons, 2011)
pp. 336–52, 533–64. See also Juan-
Simeón Vidarte, *El bienio negro y la
insurrección de Asturias* (Barcelona:
Grijalbo, 1978) pp. 32–6; Townson,
Crisis of Democracy, pp. 192–5.

100. Azaña, speech in Barcelona, 7
January 1934, *Obras*, II, p. 904.

101. *Diario de sesiones de las Cortes*, 8
May 1935; *El Progreso*, 11 May
1934; *El Diario de la Marina*
(Havana), 11 May 1934.

**Chapter 10: The Black Years and the
Coming of War, 1933–1936**

1. Diego Martínez Barrio, *Memorias*
(Barcelona: Planeta, 1983)
pp. 211–12; Niceto Alcalá-Zamora,
Memorias (Barcelona: Planeta,
1977) p. 260.

2. *El Debate*, 15 November 1934.

3. *Diario de sesiones de las Cortes*
[henceforth *DSC*], *Congreso de los
Diputados, comenzaron el 8 de
diciembre de 1933*, 19 December 33;
Nigel Townson, *The Crisis of
Democracy in Spain: Centrist
Politics under the Second Republic
1931-1936* (Brighton: Sussex
Academic Press, 2000) pp. 184–8,
196–8, 201–4.

4. *El Socialista*, 16 November 1933;
Francisco Largo Caballero, *Discursos*

a los trabajadores (Madrid: Gráfica Socialista, 1934) pp. 54-9;

5. Miguel Maura, *Así cayó Alfonso XIII* (Mexico City: Imprenta Mañez, 1962) pp. 88-93.

6. Alcalá-Zamora, *Memorias*, p. 310; Joaquín Chapaprieta, *La paz fue posible* (Barcelona: Ariel, 1971) pp. 243-5; José María Gil Robles, *No fue posible la paz* (Barcelona: Ariel, 1968) pp. 163-4.

7. Azaña, diary entry for 28 June 1937, Manuel Azaña, *Obras completas*, 4 vols (Mexico City: Ediciones Oasis, 1966-8) IV, pp. 635-6.

8. *La Libertad*, 29 May 1935.

9. Rafael Salazar Alonso, *Bajo el signo de la revolución* (Madrid: San Martín, 1935) p. 265; Pedro Sainz Rodríguez, *Testimonio y recuerdos* (Barcelona: Planeta, 1978) p. 157; Townson, *Crisis of Democracy*, pp. 208-11.

10. *El Socialista*, 17, 19, 23 January 1934.

11. *ABC*, 10 February 1933; Joaquín del Moral, *Oligarquía y 'enchufismo'* (Madrid: Imp. Galo Sáez, 1933) pp. 72-81; Doctor Albiñana, *Prisionero de la República* (Madrid: Imprenta El Financiero, 1932) pp. 215-24; Doctor Albiñana, *Confinado en las Hurdes (una víctima de la Inquisición republicana)* (Madrid: Imprenta El Financiero, 1933) pp. 193-7, 231-2, 362-3; Gabriel Morón, *El fracaso de una revolución* (Madrid: Gráfica Socialista, 1935) pp. 106-7; Townson, *Crisis of Democracy*, pp. 205-10; Raymond Carr, *Spain 1808-1939* (Oxford: Oxford University Press, 1966) pp. 625-6, describes the allegations as 'contemptible'.

12. See speech by Prieto, *DSC*, 18 May 1934.

13. Enrique Montañés, *Anarcosindicalismo y cambio político. Zaragoza, 1930-1936* (Zaragoza: Institución Fernando el Católico, 1989) pp. 98-100; José María Azpíroz Pascual, *Poder político y conflictividad social en Huesca durante la II República* (Huesca: Ayuntamiento de Huesca, 1993) pp. 161-9; Enrique Pradas Martínez, ed., *8 de diciembre de 1933. Insurrección anarquista en La Rioja* (Logroño: Cuadernos Riojanos, 1983) *passim*; Salvador Forner Muñoz, *Industrialización y movimiento obrero. Alicante 1923-1936)* (Valencia: Edicions Alfons el Magnànim, 1982) pp. 354-7; Manuel Pérez Yruela, *La conflictividad campesina en la provincia de Córdoba 1931-1936* (Madrid: Servicio de Publicaciones Agrarias, 1979) pp. 169-71; Francisco Moreno Gómez, *La República y la guerra civil en Córdoba I* (Córdoba: Ayuntamiento de Córdoba, 1982) pp. 244-8; José Manuel Macarro Vera, *La utopía revolucionaria. Sevilla en la segunda República* (Seville: Monte de Piedad y Caja de Ahorros de Sevilla, 1985) p. 368.

14. See speech by Margarita Nelken, *DSC*, 25 January 1934.

15. Joaquín Arrarás, 'Actualidad española', *Acción Española*, No. 42, 1 December 1933, pp. 574-5; José Calvo Sotelo, 'Principios informadores de un programa de Gobierno', *Acción Española*, No. 43, 1 December 1933, pp. 664-7.

16. Anon. (Javier Martínez de Bedoya), *Onésimo Redondo Caudillo de Castilla* (Valladolid: Ediciones Libertad, 1937) pp. 85-90.

17. The only reliable contemporary report of this agreement is Guariglia to MAE, 1 September

1933, in Raffaele Guariglia, *Ambasciata in Spagna e primi passi in diplomazia 1932-1934* (Naples: Edizioni Scientifiche Italiani, 1972) pp. 304–5; Ismael Saz Campos, *Mussolini contra la II República. Hostilidad, conspiraciones, intervención (1931-1936)* (Valencia: Edicions Alfons el Magnànim, 1986), pp. 111–12; Sainz Rodríguez, *Testimonio*, pp. 220–2, 375–6; Gil Robles, *No fue posible*, pp. 442–3; Juan Antonio Ansaldo, *¿Para qué ...? (de Alfonso XIII a Juan III)* (Buenos Aires: Editorial Vasca Ekin, 1951) p. 89.

18. Emmet John Hughes, *Report from Spain* (London: Latimer House, 1947) pp. 34–5; Herbert Rutledge Southworth, *Antifalange. Estudio crítico de 'Falange en la guerra de España' de Maximiano García Venero* (Paris: Ediciones Ruedo Ibérico, 1967) pp. 26–9; Felipe Ximénez de Sandoval, *'José Antonio' (Biografía apasionada)* (Barcelona: Editorial Juventud, 1941) pp. 204–5, 210–12, 299, 316–17, 330, 358, 437–40; Francisco Bravo Martínez, *Historia de Falange Española de las JONS*, 2nd edn (Madrid: Editora Nacional, 1943) pp. 213–14; Sainz Rodríguez, *Testimonio*, p. 220.

19. Colloquio del Capo del Governo con i rappresentanti della destra spagnola, 31 March 1934, *I Documenti Diplomatici Italiani, 7ª serie, vol. XV (18 marzo–27 settembre 1934)* (Rome: Istituto Poligrafico e Zecca dello Stato/ Libreria dello Stato, 1990) pp. 64–8; Antonio Lizarza Iribarren, *Memorias de la conspiración*, 4th edn (Pamplona: Editorial Gómez, 1969) pp. 34–41; *How Mussolini Provoked the Spanish Civil War: Documentary Evidence* (London:

United Editorial, 1938) pp. 5–10; Eduardo González Calleja, *Contrarrevolucionarios. Radicalización violenta de las derechas durante la Segunda República, 1931-1936* (Madrid: Alianza Editorial, 2011) pp. 184–7; José Ángel Sánchez Asiaín, *La financiación de la guerra civil española. Una aproximación histórica* (Barcelona: Crítica, 2012) pp. 77–89; Ángel Viñas, *¿Quién quiso la guerra civil? Historia de una conspiración* (Barcelona: Crítica, 2019) pp. 85–95.

20. Javier Ugarte Telleria, *La nueva Covadonga insurgente. Orígenes sociales y culturales de la sublevación de 1936 en Navarra y el País Vasco* (Madrid: Editorial Biblioteca Nueva, 1998) pp. 74–8, 266–71; Eduardo González Calleja, 'La violencia y sus discursos. Los límites de la "fascistización" de la derecha española durante el régimen de la Segunda República', *Ayer*, No. 71, 2008 (3), pp. 98–102; Jordi Canal, *Banderas blancas, boinas rojas. Una historia política del carlismo, 1876-1939* (Madrid: Marcial Pons, 2006) pp. 44–6; Martin Blinkhorn, *Carlism and Crisis in Spain 1931-1939* (Cambridge: Cambridge University Press, 1975) pp. 116–18, 131–40.

21. Julio Gil Pecharromán, *Conservadores subversivos. La derecha autoritaria alfonsina (1913-1936)* (Madrid: Eudema, 1994) pp. 178–83; González Cuevas, *Acción Española*, pp. 230–53; Ximénez de Sandoval, *'José Antonio'*, pp. 420–7; Eugenio Vegas Latapié, *Memorias políticas. El suicidio de la monarquía y la segunda República* (Barcelona: Planeta, 1983) pp. 217–18; Ansaldo, *¿Para qué ...?*, pp. 63–5.

22. Joaquín Arrarás, 'Actualidad española', *Acción Española*, 16 June 1934, No. 55, p. 74.

23. *DSC*, 7 February 1934; Alejandro Lerroux, *La pequeña historia. Apuntes para la Historia grande vividos y redactados por el autor* (Buenos Aires: Editorial Cimera, 1945) pp. 216-21, 232-6; Martínez Barrio, *Memorias*, p. 217.

24. *El Debate*, 7, 14-17, 20, 22, 28 February 1934; *El Socialista*, 13, 18, 20 February, 4, 7 March 1934.

25. Gil Robles, *No fue posible*, p. 118; *El Debate*, 20, 28 February, 2 March 1934; Lerroux, *La pequeña historia*, pp. 216-38; Martínez Barrio, *Memorias*, pp. 216-17.

26. Salazar Alonso, *Bajo el signo*, pp. 33-5.

27. *El Debate*, 2, 8, 10, 11, 22, 27 March 1934; *El Socialista*, 29 March 1934; *DSC*, 8 March 1934.

28. *El Debate*, 22, 24 April 1934; *El Socialista*, 22, 24 April 1934; José Monge Bernal, *Acción Popular (Estudios de biología política)* (Madrid: Imprenta Saez Hermanos, 1936) pp. 258-60; Salazar Alonso, *Bajo el signo*, pp. 75-8; Henry Buckley, *Life and Death of the Spanish Republic* (London: Hamish Hamilton, 1940) pp. 126-7; Sid Lowe, *Catholicism, War and the Foundation of Francoism: The Juventud de Acción Popular in Spain, 1931-1939* (Brighton: Sussex Academic Press, 2010) pp. 15-19.

29. Gil Robles, *No fue posible*, pp. 119-22; Salazar Alonso, *Bajo el signo*, pp. 85-93; Lerroux, *La pequeña historia*, pp. 247-59; *DSC*, 20 April; *El Debate*, 12, 21 April; *El Socialista*, 12 April 1934.

30. Lerroux, *La pequeña historia*, pp. 260-2; Octavio Ruiz Manjón, *El Partido Republicano Radical 1908-*

1936 (Madrid: Ediciones Giner, 1976) pp. 424-32.

31. Martínez Barrio, *Memorias*, pp. 223-8.

32. *DSC*, 17, 23 May 1934.

33. Gabriel Mario de Coca, *Anti-Caballero. Una crítica marxista de la bolchevización del Partido Socialista Obrero Español* (Madrid: Ediciones Engels, 1936) pp. 137-42; *Renovación*, 10, 17 February, 8 March 1934; *El Sol*, 20, 21 April 1934.

34. *El Debate*, 26 May 1934; *El Socialista*, 24, 25 May 1934; Salazar Alonso, *Bajo el signo*, pp. 121-9; Francisco Cobo Romero, *Labradores, campesinos y jornaleros. Protesta social y diferenciación interna del campesinado jiennense en los orígenes de la Guerra Civil (1931-1936)* (Cordoba: Publicaciones del Ayuntamiento de Córdoba, 1992) pp. 17-20; Mario López Martínez, *Órden público y luchas agrarias en Andalucía* (Madrid: Ediciones Libertarias/Ayuntamiento de Córdoba, 1995) pp. 330-45.

35. *El Obrero de la Tierra*, 24 February, 3, 24, 31 March, 14, 21 April 1934.

36. *El Obrero de la Tierra*, 19, 26 May 1934.

37. *DSC*, 30 May 1934; Juan-Simeón Vidarte, *El bienio negro y la insurrección de Asturias* (Barcelona: Grijalbo, 1978) pp. 151-9; Paul Preston, *The Coming of the Spanish Civil War: Reform, Reaction and Revolution in the Second Spanish Republic*, 2nd edn (London: Routledge, 1994) pp. 147-53.

38. Frederic Escofet, *Al servei de Catalunya i de la República*, 2 vols (Paris: Edicions Catalanes, 1973) I, pp. 199-205; Edgar Allison Peers, *Catalonia Infelix* (London: Methuen, 1937) pp. 222-8; Manuel

Azaña, *Mi rebelión en Barcelona* (Madrid: Espasa-Calpe, 1935) pp. 28–38.

39. *DSC*, 25 June, 4 July; *El Debate*, 13, 19 June, 8 July 1934; Azaña, *Obras*, II, pp. 902, 977–98; Gil Robles, *No fue posible*, pp. 124–6; *El Socialista*, 2 May, 9, 13, 17 June, 3 July 1934; José Luis de la Granja Sainz, *El oasis vasco. El nacimiento de Euskadi en la República y la guerra civil* (Madrid: Tecnos, 2007) pp. 116–17; Santiago de Pablo, Ludger Mees and José A. Rodríguez Ranz, *El péndulo patriótico. Historia del Partido Nacionalista Vasco I 1895–1936* (Barcelona: Crítica, 1999) pp. 258–60.

40. Ansaldo, *¿Para qué ...?*, pp. 71–3; Ramiro Ledesma Ramos, *¿Fascismo en España?*, 2nd edn (Barcelona: Ariel, 1968) pp.161–4; Miguel Ramos González, *La violencia en Falange Española* (Oviedo: Ediciones Tarfe, 1993) pp. 75–6; David Jato, *La rebelión de los estudiantes (Apuntes para una Historia del alegre S.E.U.)* (Madrid: CIES, 1953) p. 109.

41. *El Debate*, 11 September; *CEDA*, 15 September; *El Socialista*, 11, 20 September 1934; Gil Robles, *No fue posible*, pp. 127–30; Manuel Grossi, *La insurrección de Asturias (Quince días de revolución socialista)* (Barcelona: Gráficos Alfa, 1935) pp. 17–18.

42. Francisco Largo Caballero, *Escritos de la República* (Madrid: Fundación Pablo Iglesias, 1985) pp. 143–9; Amaro del Rosal, *1934: el movimiento revolucionario de octubre* (Madrid: Akal, 1983) pp. 233–49; Bernardo Díaz Nosty, *La Comuna asturiana. Revolución de octubre de 1934* (Bilbao: ZYX, 1974) pp. 105–7; Indalecio Prieto, 'La noche del Turquesa', in

Convulsiones de España. Pequeños detalles de grandes sucesos, 3 vols (Mexico City: Ediciones Oasis, 1967–9) I, pp. 109–11; Grossi, *La insurrección*, p. 23; Salazar Alonso, *Bajo el signo*, pp. 226–51; Manuel Benavides, *La revolución fue así (octubre rojo y negro) reportaje* (Barcelona: Imprenta Industrial, 1935) pp. 9–20.

43. *El Sol*, 12 September 1934; Salazar Alonso, *Bajo el signo*, pp. 316–20; Salazar to Amparo, 30 July, 11 September 1934, reprinted in José García Pradas, 'La conversión ejemplar de un "pobre hombre" que llegó a Ministro de la República', *CNT*, 17 January 1937.

44. *CEDA*, nos 36–7, December 1934.

45. *El Socialista*, 25, 27, 30 September 1934.

46. Salazar Alonso, *Bajo el signo*, pp. 324–5.

47. *El Debate*, 26, 27, 28 September; *DSC*, 1 October 1934; Gil Robles, *No fue posible*, pp. 134–9; Alcalá-Zamora, *Memorias*, pp. 285–6; Townson, *Crisis of Democracy*, pp. 265–9.

48. Vidarte, *El bienio negro*, p. 233; Coca, *Anti-Caballero*, p. 107; Lerroux, *La pequeña historia*, p. 302. On Anguera, see Francisco Madrid, *Ocho meses y un día en el gobierno civil de Barcelona* (Barcelona: La Flecha, 1932) pp. 185–98; Ramon Corts Blay, Joan Galtés Pujol and Albert Manent Segimon, eds, *Diccionari d´història eclesiàstica de Catalunya*, 3 vols (Barcelona: Generalitat de Catalunya/Claret, 1998–2001) III, p. 459; Salazar Alonso, *Bajo el signo*, pp. 324–6.

49. *El Sol*, 3 October 1934; Antonio Ramos Oliveira, *La revolución española de octubre* (Madrid: Editorial España, 1935) pp. 55–61;

Martínez Barrio, *Memorias*, pp. 251–3.
50. *El Socialista*, 3, 4 October 1934.
51. Grandizo Munis, *Jalones de derrota, promesa de victoria* (Mexico City: Editorial Lucha Obrera, 1948) pp. 130–40; Joaquín Maurín, *Hacia la segunda revolución. El fracaso de la República y la insurrección de octubre* (Barcelona: Gráficos Alfa, 1935) pp. 147–67; testimony of Madrid CNT Secretary, Miguel González Inestal, to the author; Enrique Castro Delgado, *Hombres Made in Moscú* (Barcelona: Luis de Caralt, 1965) pp. 176–83; Andrés Nin, *Los problemas de la revolución española* (Paris: Ruedo Ibérico, 1971) pp. 156–7; Santos Juliá Díaz, 'Fracaso de una insurrección y derrota de una huelga: los hechos de octubre en Madrid', *Estudios de Historia Social*, No. 31, October–December 1984.
52. Díaz Nosty, *La Comuna asturiana*, pp. 169–99; Adrian Shubert, 'The Epic Failure: The Asturian Revolution of October 1934', in Paul Preston, ed., *Revolution and War in Spain 1931–1939* (London: Methuen, 1984) pp. 128–31.
53. Escofet, *Al servei*, I, pp. 109–17; J. Costa i Deu and Modest Sabaté, *La nit del 6 d'octubre a Barcelona. Reportatge* (Barcelona: Tipografía Emporium, 1935) pp. 43–55; Enrique de Ángulo, *Diez horas de Estat català (Reportage)* (Valencia: Librería Fenollera, 1934) pp. 41–5.
54. General López Ochoa, *Campaña militar de Asturias en octubre de 1934 (narración táctico-episódica)* (Madrid: Ediciones Yunque, 1936) pp. 26–30; Gil Robles, *No fue posible*, pp. 140–1; Vidarte, *El bienio negro*, pp. 358–9; César Jalón, *Memorias políticas. Periodista.*

Ministro. Presidiario. (Madrid: Guadarrama, 1973) pp. 128–31; Coronel Francisco Aguado Sánchez, *La revolución de octubre de 1934* (Madrid: Editorial San Martín, 1972) pp. 188–93.
55. Diego Hidalgo, *¿Por qué fui lanzado del Ministerio de la Guerra? Diez meses de actuación ministerial* (Madrid, 1934) pp. 77–81; Concha Muñoz Tinoco, *Diego Hidalgo, un notario republicano* (Badajoz: Diputación Provincial, 1986) pp. 93–5; Elsa López, José Álvarez Junco, Manuel Espadas Burgos and Concha Muñoz Tinoco, *Diego Hidalgo. Memoria de un tiempo difícil* (Madrid: Alianza Editorial, 1986) pp. 171–5; Alcalá-Zamora, *Memorias*, p. 296; Vidarte, *El bienio negro*, pp. 290–1.
56. Alcalá-Zamora, *Memorias*, p. 296; Vidarte, *El bienio negro*, pp. 290–1; Ballbé, *Orden público*, pp. 371–2; Paul Preston, *Franco. Caudillo de España*, 3rd edn (Barcelona: Debate, 2015) pp. 132–5.
57. Enric Ucelay-Da Cal, *La Catalunya populista. Imatge, cultura i política en la etapa republicana (1931–1939)* (Barcelona: Edicions de La Magrana, 1982) pp. 208–20; Maurín, *Segunda revolución*, pp. 123–44; Escofet, *Al servei*, I, pp. 109–44; Josep Dencàs, *El 6 d'octubre des del Palau de Governació* (Barcelona: Edicions Mediterrània, 1935) pp. 70–89; Hilari Raguer, *El general Batet. Franco contra Batet. Crónica de una venganza* (Barcelona: Ediciones Península, 1996) pp. 135–86.
58. Díaz Nosty, *La Comuna asturiana*, pp. 355–69. Among the most convincing witness accounts of the atrocities committed by the African Army in Asturias are those collected at the time by two

relatively conservative individuals, Vicente Marco Miranda, a Republican prosecutor, and Félix Gordón Ordás of Martínez Barrio's Unión Republicana. They are reproduced in Margarita Nelken, *Por qué hicimos la revolución* (Barcelona/París/New York: Ediciones Sociales Internacionales, 1936) pp. 172–255. See also Narcis Molins i Fábrega, *UHP. La insurrección proletaria de Asturias,* 2nd edn (Gijón: Ediciones Júcar, 1977) pp. 169–74, 184–7, 196–219; Leah Manning, *What I Saw in Spain* (London: Gollancz, 1935) pp. 167–221; Fernando Solano Palacio, *La revolución de octubre. Quince días de comunismo libertario en Asturias* (Barcelona: Ediciones El Luchador, 1936) pp. 176–82.

59. López Ochoa in Vidarte, *El bienio negro,* pp. 358–62; Franco in Claude Martin, *Franco, soldado y estadista* (Madrid: Fermín Uriarte, 1965) pp. 129–30; Francisco Franco Bahamonde, 'Apuntes' personales sobre la República y la guerra civil (Madrid: Fundación Nacional Francisco Franco, 1987); Juan José Calleja, *Yagüe, un corazón al rojo* (Barcelona: Editorial Juventud, 1963) pp. 63–7.

60. *La Vanguardia,* 18 October 1934.

61. *DSC,* 5 November 1934; Manuel Azaña, *Mi rebelión en Barcelona* (Madrid: Espasa-Calpe, 1935) pp. 133–64; Cipriano de Rivas-Cherif, *Retrato de un desconocido. Vida de Manuel Azaña* (Barcelona: Grijalbo, 1980) pp. 294–9; A. C. Márquez Tornero, *Testimonio de mi tiempo (Memorias de un español republicano)* (Madrid: Editorial Orígenes, 1979) pp. 115–16; Townson, *Crisis of Democracy,* pp. 278–9. Lerroux's mendacious account, *La pequeña historia,* pp. 318–20.

62. *El Debate,* 24 October 1934; Gil Robles, *No fue posible,* pp. 146–8; Jalón, *Memorias,* pp. 141–9; Lerroux, *La pequeña historia,* pp. 333–40; Alcalá-Zamora, *Memorias,* pp. 292–4; Javier Tusell and José Calvo, *Giménez Fernández. Precursor de la democracia española* (Seville: Mondadori/Diputación de Sevilla, 1990) pp. 60–1.

63. *El Debate,* 16, 17 November 1934; *DSC,* 5, 6, 15 November 1934; Gil Robles, *No fue posible,* pp. 149–53; Hidalgo, *¿Por qué fui lanzado?,* pp. 19–36; Alfonso Bullón de Mendoza, *José Calvo Sotelo* (Barcelona: Ariel, 2004) pp. 462–4.

64. *DSC,* 21 December; *El Debate,* 28 December 1934; Gil Robles, *No fue posible,* pp. 157–8; Santos Juliá, 'Gil Robles contra Villalobos: la cuestión educativa (1934)', in Ricardo Robledo, ed., *Esta salvaje pesadilla. Salamanca en la guerra civil española* (Barcelona: Crítica, 2007) pp. 53–69; Antonio Rodríguez de las Heras, *Filiberto Villalobos, su obra social y política 1900-1936* (Salamanca: Centro de Estudios Salmantinos, 1985) pp. 218–20, 233–4, 257–65.

65. *El Debate,* 24 November, 1, 5, 7, 20, 21 December 1934, 2, 6 February, 1, 19 March 1935; *DSC,* 5, 11, 12, 13 December 1934, 23 January, 27 February, 14 March 1935; Gil Robles, *No fue posible,* pp. 172–88; Edward E. Malefakis, *Agrarian Reform and Peasant Revolution in Spain* (New Haven, Conn.: Yale University Press, 1970) pp. 347–55; Tusell and Calvo, *Giménez Fernández,* pp. 57–60, 70–106, 110; Leandro Álvarez Rey, *La derecha en la II República. Sevilla, 1931-1936*

(Seville: Universidad de Sevilla, 1993) p. 420.

66. *El Debate*, 10 February, 19, 27, 30 March 1935; Lerroux, *La pequeña historia*, pp. 369–75; Gil Robles, *No fue posible*, pp. 212–17; Alcalá-Zamora, *Memorias*, pp. 301–4.

67. *El Debate*, 20 October, 8 November 1934; 5, 26 February, 19, 24, 26, 27 March 1935; Townson, *Crisis of Democracy*, pp. 282–3, 287.

68. Buckley, *Life and Death*, pp. 186–7; Townson, *Crisis of Democracy*, p. 290.

69. *El Debate*, 2, 3, 21, 23, 28, 30 April, 4, 7 May 1935; Gil Robles, *No fue posible*, pp. 218–31; Lerroux, *La pequeña historia*, pp. 387–91.

70. Gil Robles, *No fue posible*, pp. 234–62; Franco, *Apuntes personales*, pp. 13–15; José María Iribarren, *Mola, datos para una biografía y para la historia del alzamiento nacional* (Zaragoza: Librería General, 1938) p. 44; González Calleja, *Contrarrevolucionarios*, pp. 290–6; Ricardo de la Cierva, *Francisco Franco. Un siglo de España*, 2 vols (Madrid: Editora Nacional, 1973) pp. 392–8; *ABC*, 31 July 1936.

71. On Martín Veloz, see Javier Infante, 'Sables y naipes: Diego Martín Veloz (1875–1938). De cómo un matón de casino se convirtió en caudillo rural', in Robledo, ed., *Esta salvaje pesadilla*, pp. 264–79, 425, 428; José Venegas, *Andanzas y recuerdos de España* (Montevideo: Feria del Libro, 1948) pp. 74–85; Indalecio Prieto, *De mi vida. Recuerdos, estampas, siluetas, sombras ...* 2 vols (Mexico City: Ediciones Oasis, 1965) I, pp. 183–92.

72. Reports of Reich Federation of Industry and of Wilhelmstrasse, 24 September, 4 October, 4 December 1935, *Documents on German Foreign Policy*, Series C, vol. IV (London: HMSO, 1964) pp. 641–50, 698–9, 880–6.

73. Félix Gordón Ordás, *Mi política fuera de España*, 5 vols (Mexico City: Autor, 1965–72) II, p. 131; Alcalá-Zamora, *Memorias*, pp. 310–11.

74. *El Debate*, 20, 24–26 September 1935; Lerroux, *La pequeña historia*, pp. 411–40; Chapaprieta, *La paz fue posible*, pp. 207–30, 246–8; Gil Robles, *No fue posible*, pp. 286–91; Jalón, *Memorias*, pp. 219–28.

75. *DSC*, 28 October; *El Debate*, 23, 27, 29, 30 October 1935; Gil Robles, *No fue posible*, pp. 304–12; Primo de Rivera, *Obras*, pp. 665–8; Lerroux, *La pequeña historia*, pp. 446–55; Chapaprieta, *La paz fue posible*, pp. 243–80; Jalón, *Memorias*, pp. 228–32; Townson, *Crisis of Democracy*, pp. 315–29, 332–7.

76. Chapaprieta, *La paz fue posible*, pp. 292–309; Gil Robles, *No fue posible*, pp. 341–58.

77. *JAP*, 12 October 1935; *El Debate*, 10 November 1935; González Calleja, *Contrarrevolucionarios*, pp. 285–9; Lowe, *Catholicism*, pp. 78–80.

78. Armando Boaventura, *Madrid-Moscovo – Da Ditadura a República e a Guerra Civil de Espanha* (Lisbon: Parceria António Maria Pereira, 1937) pp. 191–2; Ansaldo, *¿Para qué ...?*, pp. 110–11; Tusell and Calvo, *Giménez Fernández*, pp. 148, 153–9; Chapaprieta, *La paz fue posible*, pp. 315–30; Alcalá-Zamora, *Memorias*, pp. 340–5; Joaquín Arrarás, *Historia de la Cruzada española*, 8 vols, 36 tomos (Madrid: Ediciones Españolas, 1939–43) II, tomo 8, p. 277; Gil Robles, *No fue posible*, pp. 145–8.

79. *El Debate*, 10–15, 17, 18, 28 December 1935; Gil Robles, *No fue posible*, pp. 358–403; Chapaprieta,

La paz fue posible, pp. 324–32, 343–77; Manuel Portela Valladares, *Memorias. Dentro del drama español* (Madrid: Alianza Editorial, 1988) pp. 152–60; José Luis Martín Ramos, *El Frente Popular. Victoria y derrota de la democracia en España* (Barcelona: Pasado y Presente, 2015) pp. 141–4.

80. Chris Ealham, *Class, Culture and Conflict in Barcelona 1898–1937* (London: Routledge Cañada Blanch, 2004) pp. 167–8.

81. On the roles of Azaña and Prieto, see Paul Preston, *¡Comrades! Portraits from the Spanish Civil War* (London: HarperCollins, 1999) pp. 217–20, 256–8. For more detail, see Santos Juliá, *La izquierda del PSOE (1935–1936)* (Madrid: Siglo XXI de España, 1977) pp. 53–111; Vidarte, *Bienio negro*, pp. 387–514; Manuel Azaña, *Discursos en campo abierto* (Madrid: Espasa-Calpe, 1936) pp. 103–242; Azaña, *Obras*, III, pp. 229–93; Márquez Tornero, *Testimonio*, pp. 118–21; Buckley, *Life and Death*, pp. 182–5; Azaña to Prieto, 7 August 1935, Azaña, *Obras*, III, pp. 603–4.

82. José Luis de la Granja Sainz and Luis Sala González, *Vidas cruzadas. Prieto y Aguirre. Los padres fundadores de Euskadi en la República y la guerra civil* (Madrid: Biblioteca Nueva, 2017) p. 43; De la Granja, *El Oasis*, pp. 72–3.

83. Gil Robles, *No fue posible*, pp. 404–30; Javier Tusell, *Las elecciones del Frente Popular*, 2 vols (Madrid: Edicusa, 1971) I, pp. 42–133; *El Socialista*, 11, 18 January 1936; Tusell and Calvo, *Giménez Fernández*, pp. 162–5; Blinkhorn, *Carlism*, p. 204.

84. Díaz Nosty, *La irresistible ascensión*, pp. 290–5; Gil Robles, *No fue posible*, p. 472.

85. *El Socialista*, 18, 19, 30 January, 9, 13 February; *El Debate*, 3, 10, 11, 15, 17 January, 2, 7, 9, 11, 14, 16 February; *JAP*, 21, 28 December 1935, 4 January, 14 February; *ABC*, 7 February; *Ideal*, 3, 14, 15, 28, 29 January, 11, 12, 14, 16 February; *El Defensor*, 14, 19, 22, 23, 24, 28 January, 1, 11, 6, 15–20 February, 5–7 March; *Ideal*, 3, 14, 15, 28, 29 January, 11, 12, 14, 16 February 1936; Gil Robles, *No fue posible*, pp. 464–73; Tusell, *Las elecciones*, I, pp. 150, 211–19, 229–47, 273–85, II, pp. 123–91, Appendix 7, pp. 371–401; Díaz Nosty, *La irresistible ascensión*, pp. 290–1.

86. Chris Ealham, *Living Anarchism: José Peirats and the Spanish Anarcho-Syndicalist Movement* (Oakland, Calif.: AK Press, 2016) pp. 82–3.

87. Manuel Álvarez Tardío and Roberto Villa García, *1936. Fraude y violencia en las elecciones del Frente Popular* (Barcelona: Espasa, 2017) pp. 254–73, 279–84, 353–61.

88. Eduardo González Calleja, Francisco Cobo Romero, Ana Martínez Rus and Francisco Sánchez Pérez, *La Segunda República Española* (Barcelona: Pasado y Presente, 2015) pp. 832–6; Martín Ramos, *El Frente Popular*, pp. 144–6.

89. Townson, *Crisis of Democracy*, pp. 339–43; Ruiz Manjón, *El Partido Republicano Radical*, pp. 556–77; Jalón, *Memorias*, pp. 236–42; Martín Ramos, *El Frente Popular*, pp. 144–50.

90. *El Debate*, 3 January; *El Socialista*, 30 January 1936; Claude G. Bowers, *My Mission to Spain* (London: Gollancz, 1954) pp. 182–7; Buckley, *Life and Death*, pp. 190–1; Constancia de la Mora, *In Place of Splendour* (New York: Harcourt, Brace, 1939) p. 207.

91. Ministerio de la Gobernación, *Dictamen de la Comisión sobre ilegitimidad de poderes actuantes en 18 de julio de 1936* (Barcelona: Editora Nacional, 1939) pp. 31–45.

92. Gil Robles, *No fue posible*, pp. 431–5.

93. Álvarez Tardío and Villa García, *1936. Fraude y violencia*, pp. 380–1, 408–9, 419, 423, 491–8, 515–16; Enrique Moradiellos, 'Las elecciones generales de febrero de 1936: una reconsideración historiográfica', *Revista de Libros*, 13 September 2017, pp. 1–38; Santos Juliá, 'Las cuentas galanas de 1936', *El País* (Babelia), 1 April 2017, p. 8; Stanley G. Payne, '1936. Fraude y violencia', *ABC*, 7 May 2017.

94. *El Sol*, 19 February; *El Socialista*, 19 February 1936; Gil Robles, *No fue posible*, pp. 492–8, 500–2; Azaña, diary entry, 19 February 1936, *Obras*, IV, pp. 563–4; Portela, *Memorias*, pp. 175–90; Franco, *Apuntes personales*, pp. 25–30; Ricardo de la Cierva, *Historia de la guerra civil española* (Madrid: Editorial San Martín, 1969) I, pp. 639–42; Arrarás, *Cruzada*, II, tomo 9, pp. 440–3; Juan-Simeón Vidarte, *Todos fuimos culpables. Testimonio de un socialista español* (Mexico City: Fondo de Cultura Económica, 1973) pp. 40–2, 47–9; Servicio Histórico Militar, *Historia de la guerra de liberación* (Madrid: Editorial San Martín, 1945) I, p. 421; Manuel Goded, *Un 'faccioso' cien por cien* (Zaragoza: Heraldo, 1938) pp. 26–7; Martínez Barrio, *Memorias*, pp. 303–7; Servicio Histórico Militar, *Historia de la guerra de liberación* (Madrid: Editorial San Martín, 1945) I, p. 421.

95. Cipriano de Rivas Cherif, *Retrato de un desconocido. Vida de Manuel*

Azaña (Barcelona: Grijalbo, 1980) pp. 320–2.

96. Gil Robles, *No fue posible*, pp. 719–20; Arrarás, *Cruzada*, II, tomo 9, p. 467; Franco, *Apuntes personales*, pp. 33–4; Iribarren, *Mola*, pp. 45–6; José María Iribarren, *Con el general Mola. Escenas y aspectos inéditos de la guerra civil* (Zaragoza: Librería General, 1937) pp. 14–15; Felipe Bertrán Güell, *Preparación y desarrollo del alzamiento nacional* (Valladolid, 1939) pp. 116–17.

97. Gil Robles and March were in touch during the Republic and in later years had a business relationship, Gil Robles, *No fue posible*, pp. 772, 780, 789–90, 794, 798. On March's direct contacts with the generals, see Gustau Nerín, *La guerra que vino de África* (Barcelona: Crítica, 2005) pp. 132–3.

98. Lowe, *Catholicism*, pp. 139–47.

99. Louis Fischer, *Men and Politics: An Autobiography* (London: Jonathan Cape, 1941) p. 309.

100. Azaña to Rivas Cherif, 17 March 1936, in Rivas Cherif, *Retrato*, pp. 665–6; Moreno Gómez, *La República*, pp. 352–68; Pérez Yruela, *La conflictividad*, pp. 205–7; Cobo Romero, *Labradores*, pp. 445–53; Malefakis, *Agrarian Reform*, pp. 364–9.

101. *El Socialista*, 7, 8, 15 March 1936; speech by Rodolfo Llopis, *DSC*, 15 April; *El Debate*, 18, 19 March 1936; Gil Robles, *No fue posible*, pp. 575–6; Vidarte, *Todos fuimos culpables*, p. 53; Lowe, *Catholicism*, pp. 111–24; González Calleja, *Contrarrevolucionarios*, pp. 307–29.

102. *El Socialista*, 22 March; *Claridad*, 6 April, 30 May 1936.

103. Ministerio de la Gobernación, *Dictamen*, pp. 33–46, 128–9; Richard, A. H. Robinson, *The*

Origins of Franco's Spain: The Right, the Republic and Revolution, 1931–1936 (Newton Abbot: David & Charles, 1970) pp. 255–7; Stanley G. Payne, *Spain's First Democracy: The Second Republic, 1931–1936* (Madison, Wis.: Wisconsin University Press, 1993) pp. 296–301; Tusell, *Las elecciones*, II, pp. 190–1; Alcalá-Zamora, *Memorias*, pp. 350–3; Gil Robles, *No fue posible*, pp. 541–7; Álvarez Tardío and Villa García, *1936. Fraude y violencia*, pp. 383–409, 454–73, 491–8.

104. *DSC*, 20, 24, 31 March, 1, 2 April; *El Debate*, 28, 29, 31 March 1936; Vidarte, *Todos fuimos culpables*, p. 71; José Venegas, *Las elecciones del Frente Popular* (Buenos Aires: PHAC, 1942) pp. 47–8; Gil Robles, *No fue posible*, pp. 548–9; Prieto, prologue to Luis Romero Solano, *Vísperas de la guerra de España* (Mexico City: El Libro Perfecto, n.d. [1947]) pp. 6–7.

105. *DSC*, 31 March; *ABC*, 1 April 1936; Tusell and Calvo, *Giménez Fernández*, pp. 184–7.

106. *DSC*, 15 April 1936; Bullón de Mendoza, *Calvo Sotelo*, pp. 598–603.

107. *ABC*, 4, 5, 11 March, 2, 19, 29 April 1936; Colin M. Winston, *Workers and the Right in Spain 1900–1936* (Princeton, NJ: Princeton University Press, 1985) pp. 306–22; Ansaldo, *¿Para qué ...?*, pp. 76–8; Buckley, *Life and Death*, p. 129; De la Mora, *In Place of Splendour*, pp. 214–15; Stanley G. Payne, *Falange: A History of Spanish Fascism* (Stanford, Calif.: Stanford University Press, 1961) pp. 98–105; Stanley G. Payne, *Fascism in Spain 1923–1977* (Madison, Wis.: Wisconsin University Press, 1993) pp. 185–201.

108. Bowers, *My Mission*, pp. 200–10, 224–5.

109. For analyses of political violence during the spring of 1936, see Eduardo González Calleja, *Cifras cruentas. Las víctimas mortales de la violencia sociopolítica en la Segunda República española (1931–1936)* (Granada: Editorial Comares, 2015) pp. 285–93; Rafael Cruz, *En el nombre del pueblo. República, rebelión y guerra en la España de 1936* (Madrid: Siglo XXI de España, 2006) pp. 164–70.

110. Bullón de Mendoza, *Calvo Sotelo*, pp. 612–25, 634–42.

111. Alcalá-Zamora, *Memorias*, pp. 359–71.

112. Vidarte, *Todos fuimos culpables*, pp. 115–18; Indalecio Prieto, *Cartas a un escultor. Pequeños detalles de grandes sucesos* (Buenos Aires: Editorial Losada, 1961) pp. 44–5.

113. Manuel Azaña, *Apuntes de memoria inéditos y cartas 1938–1939–1940* (Valencia: Pre-Textos, 1990) pp. 17–18.

114. *El Obrero de la Tierra*, 18 April 1, 16, 23, 30 May, 13, 20, 27 June; *Claridad*, 6, 9, 18 June; *DSC*, 5 June 1936; Manuel Requena Gallego, *Los sucesos de Yeste (mayo 1936)* (Albacete: Instituto de Estudios Albacetenses, 1983) pp. 83–100; Manuel Ortiz Heras, *Violencia política en la II República y el primer franquismo. Albacete, 1936–1950* (Madrid: Siglo XXI de España, 1996) pp. 58–63.

115. Gil Robles, *No fue posible*, pp. 719, 728–30, 789, 798; Gil Robles to Mola, 29 December 1936 and 1 January 1937, in Francisco Franco Salgado-Araujo, *Mi vida con Franco* (Barcelona: Planeta, 1977) pp. 202–3; Sánchez Asiaín, *La financiación*, pp. 1143–7.

116. *El Socialista*, 26 March; *Claridad*, 9, 10, 11, 12, 16, 18, 19, 22 April; 11 May, 1, 6, 9, 18 June, 1, 2, 13 July 1936.

117. Paul Preston, *The Last Stalinist: Santiago Carrillo 1915-2012* (London: William Collins, 2014) pp. 58-66.

118. *Claridad*, 20 May, 1 June 1936; Prieto, *Convulsiones*, III, pp. 159-60; Vidarte, *Todos fuimos culpables*, pp. 199-200, 859-61; Helen Graham, *Socialism and War: The Spanish Socialist Party in Power and Crisis, 1936-1939* (Cambridge: Cambridge University Press, 1991) pp. 28-40; José María Varela Rendueles, *Rebelión en Sevilla. Memorias de un Gobernador rebelde* (Seville: Ayuntamiento de Sevilla, 1982) pp. 51-6.

119. Vidarte, *Todos fuimos culpables*, pp. 93-5, 99-100, 146-7, 190-2; Prieto, *Convulsiones*, III, pp. 143-4; Francisco Largo Caballero, *Escritos de la República* (Madrid: Fundación Pablo Iglesias, 1985) pp. 304-6; Prieto, *Cartas a un escultor*, p. 57.

120. Payne, *Falange*, pp. 104-5; Blinkhorn, *Carlism*, pp. 234-5; Rafael Valls, *La Derecha Regional Valenciana 1930-1936* (Valencia: Edicions Alfons el Magnànim, 1992) pp. 227-34; Lowe, *Catholicism*, pp. 131-40; Ugarte, *La nueva Covadonga insurgente*, p. 67; Vincent, *Catholicism*, pp. 242-3; Vicent Comes Iglesia, *En el filo de la navaja. Biografía política de Luis Lucia Lucia* (Madrid: Biblioteca Nueva, 2002) pp. 350-61.

121. *DSC*, 19 May, 16 June; *ABC*, 20 May, 17 June 1936.

122. *DSC*, 16 June; *ABC*, 17 June 1936.

123. Fernando Puell de la Villa, 'La trama militar de la conspiración', in Francisco Sánchez Pérez, ed., *Los mitos del 18 de julio* (Barcelona:

Crítica, 2013) pp. 71-7. For all Mola's instructions, see *ibid.*, pp. 341-67.

124. Juan de Iturralde, *La guerra de Franco, los vascos y la Iglesia*, 2 vols (San Sebastián: Publicaciones del Clero Vasco, 1978) I, p. 433.

125. B. Félix Maíz, *Alzamiento en España*, 2nd edn (Pamplona: Editorial Gómez, 1952) pp. 53-6, 61-3, 67.

126. Pedro Luis Angosto, *José Alonso Mallol. El hombre que pudo evitar la guerra* (Alicante: Instituto de Cultura Juan Gil-Albert, 2010) pp. 199, 212-14; Dolores Ibárruri, *El único camino* (Madrid: Editorial Castalia, 1992) p. 349; Enrique Líster, *Nuestra guerra* (Paris: Colección Ebro, 1966) pp. 30-1.

127. Ignacio Hidalgo de Cisneros, *Cambio de rumbo*, 2 vols (Bucharest: Colección Ebro, 1964-70) II, pp. 131-5; Juan José Calleja, *Yagüe, un corazón al rojo* (Barcelona: Editorial Juventud, 1963) pp. 75-6.

128. Mariano Ansó, *Yo fui ministro de Negrín* (Barcelona: Planeta, 1976) pp. 122-3; Carlos Fernández Santander, *Casares Quiroga, una pasión republicana* (Sada-A Coruña: Ediciós do Castro, 2000) pp. 235-40.

129. *Gaceta de Tenerife*, 26 August; *The Times*, 7 September 1936.

130. Joaquín Gil Honduvilla, 'La sublevación de julio de 1936: Proceso militar al general Romerales 2004', *Historia Actual Online*, No. 4, Spring 2004, pp. 107-8. For contrasting accounts of the role of Romerales, see Julio Busquets and Juan Carlos Losada, *Ruido de sables. Las conspiraciones militares en la España del siglo XX* (Barcelona: Crítica, 2003) pp. 63-8.

131. Saz Campos, *Mussolini contra la II República*, pp. 166–74; Morten Heiberg, *Emperadores del Mediterráneo. Franco, Mussolini y la guerra civil española* (Barcelona: Crítica, 2004) p. 51; Morten Heiberg and Manuel Ros Agudo, *La trama oculta de la guerra civil. Los servicios secretos de Franco 1936–1945* (Barcelona: Crítica, 2006) pp. 30–8; Sainz Rodríguez, *Testimonio*, pp. 232–3; Ángel Viñas, 'La connivencia fascista con la sublevación y otros éxitos de la trama civil', in Sánchez Pérez, ed., *Los mitos*, pp. 90–106. The contracts are reproduced in Sánchez Pérez, ed., *Los mitos*, pp. 169–81.

132. Vegas Latapié, *Memorias*, p. 184; Sainz Rodríguez, *Testimonio*, p. 247; Ansaldo, *¿Para qué …?*, p. 121.

133. Gil Robles, *No fue posible*, p. 780; José Ignacio Luca de Tena, *Mis amigos muertos* (Barcelona: Planeta, 1971) p. 164; Torcuato Luca de Tena, *Papeles para la pequeña y la gran historia. Memorias de mi padre y mías* (Barcelona: Planeta, 1991) pp. 207–8.

134. Interviews with Bebb and Pollard, *Guardian*, 7 July 1966; Douglas Jerrold, *Georgian Adventure* (London: Right Book Club, 1937) pp. 367–73; Antonio González Betes, *Franco y el Dragón Rapide* (Madrid: Ediciones Rialp, 1987) pp. 96–121; Peter Day, *Franco's Friends: How British Intelligence Helped Bring Franco to Power in Spain* (London: Biteback, 2011) pp. 15–26, 70–88; Graham D. Macklin, 'Major Hugh Pollard, MI6, and the Spanish Civil War', *Historical Journal*, Vol. 49, Issue 1 (2006) pp. 277–80. The definitive forensic analysis of the evidence is by Ángel Viñas, *La conspiración del General Franco y otras revelaciones acerca de una guerra civil desfigurada*, 2nd edn (Barcelona: Crítica, 2012) pp. 30–74. On Bolín in Africa, Nerín, *La guerra*, p. 136.

135. Julián Zugazagoitia, *Guerra y vicisitudes de los españoles*, 2 vols (Paris: Librería Española, 1968) I, pp. 28–32; Prieto, *Convulsiones*, I, pp. 157–63; Vidarte, *Todos fuimos culpables*, pp. 213–17; Ian Gibson, *La noche en que mataron a Calvo Sotelo* (Barcelona: Argos Vergara, 1982) pp. 15–22.

136. Vegas Latapié, *Memorias*, pp. 310–15.

137. Ángel Viñas, Miguel Ull Laita and Cecilio Yusta, *El primer asesinato de Franco. La muerte del general Balmes y el inicio de la sublevación* (Barcelona: Crítica, 2018) pp. 110–24, 175ff.

138. Gil Robles, *No fue posible*, p. 743; *Solidaridad Obrera*, 24 February 1937; S. Cánovas Cervantes, *Apuntes históricos de Solidaridad Obrera* (Barcelona: Ediciones CNT, 1937) p. 447.

Chapter 11: Civil War: Hatred, Incompetence and Profit, 1936–1939

1. On the repression behind the lines, see Paul Preston, *The Spanish Holocaust: Inquisition and Extermination in Twentieth-Century Spain* (London: HarperCollins, 2012).

2. *Ibid.*, pp. 137, 139, 156, 169, 187, 212, 310, 315, 321, 326; Pura Sánchez, *Individuas de dudosa moral. La represión de las mujeres en Andalucía (1936–1958)* (Barcelona: Crítica, 2009) pp. 215–31.

3. Juan de Iturralde, *La guerra de Franco, los vascos y la Iglesia*, 2 vols (San Sebastián: Publicaciones del Clero Vasco, 1978) I, p. 433.

4. José María Iribarren, *Con el general Mola. Escenas y aspectos inéditos de*

la guerra civil (Zaragoza: Librería General, 1937) p. 169.

5. *Ibid.*, pp. 64-6; Diego Martínez Barrio, *Memorias* (Barcelona: Planeta, 1983) pp. 358-64; Carlos Blanco Escolá, *General Mola. El ególatra que provocó la guerra civil* (Madrid: La Esfera de los Libros, 2002) pp. 284-6.

6. Julian Zugazagoitia, *Guerra y vicisitudes de los españoles*, 2nd edn, 2 vols (Paris: Librería Española, 1968) I, p. 65; Helen Graham, *The Spanish Republic at War 1936-1939* (Cambridge: Cambridge University Press, 2002) pp. 82-3; Indalecio Prieto, *Convulsiones de España. Pequeños detalles de grandes sucesos*, 3 vols (Mexico City: Ediciones Oasis, 1967-9) p. 149; Manuel Azaña, *Obras completas*, 4 vols (Mexico City: Ediciones Oasis, 1966-8) pp. 487-9.

7. Maximiano García Venero, *El general Fanjul. Madrid en el alzamiento nacional* (Madrid: Ediciones Cid, 1967) pp. 338-44; Luis Enrique Délano, *Cuatro meses de guerra civil en Madrid* (Santiago de Chile: Editorial Panorama, 1937) pp. 12-13; Joaquín Arrarás, *Historia de la Cruzada española*, 8 vols, 36 tomos (Madrid: Ediciones Españolas, 1939-43) IV, tomo 17, pp. 403-9, 434-68; José Martín Blázquez, *I Helped to Build an Army: Civil War Memoirs of a Spanish Staff Officer* (London: Secker & Warburg, 1939) pp. 111-17; Zugazagoitia, *Guerra y vicisitudes*, I, pp. 69-71; Luis Romero, *Tres días de julio (18, 19 y 20 de 1936)*, 2nd edn (Barcelona: Ariel, 1968) pp. 414-16, 432-5, 457-62, 469-91, 543-58.

8. Frederic Escofet, *Al servei de Catalunya i la República*, 2 vols (Paris: Edicions Catalanes, 1973)

II, pp. 205-435; Manuel Goded, *Un 'faccioso' cien por cien* (Zaragoza: Librería General, 1939) pp. 44-59.

9. Mijail Koltsov, *Diario de la guerra de España* (Paris: Ruedo Ibérico, 1963) p. 55; Juan-Simeón Vidarte, *Todos fuimos culpables* (Mexico City: Fondo de Cultura Económica, 1973) p. 476.

10. For more detail on the consequences of the coup in the Republican zone, see Preston, *The Spanish Holocaust*, chs 7 and 8.

11. Michael Alpert, *La guerra civil española en el mar* (Madrid: Siglo XXI de España, 1987) pp. 40-55; Daniel Sueiro, *La flota es roja. Papel clave del radiotelegrafista Benjamín Balboa en julio de 1936* (Barcelona: Editorial Argos Vergara, 1983) *passim*; Manuel D. Benavides, *La escuadra la mandan los cabos*, 2nd edn (Mexico City: Ediciones Roca, 1976) pp. 123-58.

12. Arrarás, *Cruzada*, III, tomo 10, pp. 118-19; Francisco Franco Salgado-Araujo, *Mi vida junto a Franco* (Barcelona: Planeta, 1977) pp. 181-2; José Manuel Martínez Bande, *La campaña de Andalucía*, 2nd edn (Madrid: Editorial San Martín, 1986) pp. 55-8; Alfredo Kindelán Duany, *La verdad de mis relaciones con Franco*, 2nd edn (Barcelona: Planeta, 1981) pp. 176-7.

13. María Rosa de Madariaga, *Los moros que trajo Franco* (Madrid: Alianza Editorial, 2015) pp. 187-98; Francisco Sánchez Ruano, *Islam y Guerra Civil Española. Moros con Franco y con la República* (Madrid: La Esfera de los Libros, 2004) pp. 149-50; Gustau Nerín, *La guerra que vino de África* (Barcelona: Crítica, 2005) pp. 169-91, 237-42; Sebastian

Balfour, *Deadly Embrace: Morocco and the Road to the Spanish Civil War* (Oxford: Oxford University Press, 2002) pp. 285-94; Ali Al Tuma, *Guns, Culture and Moors: Racial Perceptions, Cultural Impact and the Moroccan Participation in the Spanish Civil War* (London: Routledge, 2018) pp. 110-16.

14. Gabriel Cardona, 'Factores militares esenciales de la guerra civil española', in Enrique Fuentes Quintana and Francisco Comín Comín, eds, *Economía y economistas españoles en la guerra civil*, 2 vols (Barcelona: Real Academia de Ciencias Morales y Política & Círculo de Lectores, 2008) pp. 279-99.

15. Paul Preston, *Franco: A Biography* (London: HarperCollins, 1993) pp. 153-63; Ángel Viñas, *Franco, Hitler y el estallido de la guerra civil. Antecedentes y consecuencias* (Madrid: Alianza Editorial, 2001) pp. 335-402; Paul Preston, 'Mussolini's Spanish Adventure: From Limited Risk to War', in Paul Preston and Ann Mackenzie, eds, *The Republic Besieged: Civil War in Spain 1936-1939* (Edinburgh: Edinburgh University Press, 1996) pp. 21-51.

16. The fullest account is by Francisco Espinosa Maestre, *La columna de la muerte. El avance del ejército franquista de Sevilla a Badajoz*, 2nd edn (Barcelona: Crítica, 2017).

17. Zugazagoitia, *Guerra y vicisitudes*, I, pp. 102-3; Gerald Howson, *Arms for Spain: The Untold Story of the Spanish Civil War*, 2nd edn (New York: St Martin's Press, 1999) pp. 75-80; Ángel Viñas, *El escudo de la República. El oro de España, la apuesta soviética y los hechos de mayo de 1937* (Barcelona: Crítica, 2007) pp. 89-121.

18. Rafael Abella, *La vida cotidiana durante la guerra civil*, Vol. I: *La España Nacional* (Barcelona: Planeta, 1978) pp. 51-4.

19. *El Socialista*, 25 July 1936; Mercedes Cabrera, *Juan March (1880-1962)* (Madrid: Marcial Pons, 2011) pp. 277-8, 295-307.

20. Bernardo Díaz Nosty, *La irresistible ascensión de Juan March* (Madrid: Sedmay Ediciones, 1977) p. 303.

21. Francisco Franco Bahamonde, *Palabras del Caudillo 19 abril 1937-7 diciembre 1942* (Madrid: Ediciones de la Vice-Secretaría de Educación Popular, 1943) pp. 231-5.

22. Arturo Dixon, *Señor Monopolio. La asombrosa vida de Juan March* (Barcelona: Planeta, 1985) p. 134; Luis Romero, *Tres días de julio (18, 19 y 20 de 1936)*, 2nd edn (Barcelona: Ariel, 1968) p. 20; Franco Salgado-Araujo, *Mi vida*, p. 150; Pilar Franco Bahamonde, *Nosotros los Franco* (Barcelona: Planeta, 1980) pp. 98-100; Díaz Nosty, *La irresistible ascensión*, pp. 303-7; Ramón Garriga, *Juan March y su tiempo* (Barcelona: Planeta, 1976) pp. 373-6. On March and Sangróniz, see Ramón Garriga, *La Señora de El Pardo* (Barcelona: Planeta, 1979) pp. 90, 120; José Antonio Vaca de Osma, *La larga guerra de Francisco Franco* (Madrid, Ediciones RIALP, 1991) pp. 117-20. On Peire, see Ricardo de la Cierva, *Historia de la guerra civil española*, Vol. I (Madrid: Editorial San Martín, 1969) p. 748.

23. Ismael Saz Campos, *Mussolini contra la II República. Hostilidad, conspiraciones, intervención (1931-1936)* (Valencia: Edicions Alfons el Magnànim, 1986) pp. 166-74.

24. Jehanne Wake, *Kleinwort Benson: The History of Two Families in Banking* (New York: Oxford

University Press, 1997) pp. 250-4; José Ángel Sánchez Asiaín, *La financiación de la guerra civil española. Una aproximación histórica* (Barcelona: Crítica, 2012) pp. 119-20, 180-5, 199-204.

25. José Ignacio Luca de Tena, *Mis amigos muertos* (Barcelona: Planeta, 1971) pp. 83, 162-4; Torcuato Luca de Tena, *Papeles para la pequeña y la gran historia. Memorias de mi padre y mías* (Barcelona: Planeta, 1991) pp. 200, 207, 210; Cabrera, *Juan March*, pp. 293-4; Asiaín, *La financiación*, pp. 186-90; Ángel Viñas, 'La connivencia fascista con la sublevación y otros éxitos de la trama civil', in Francisco Sánchez Pérez, ed., *Los mitos del 18 de julio* (Barcelona: Crítica, 2013) pp. 114-18; Wake, *Kleinwort Benson*, pp. 252-3.

26. Francisco Franco Bahamonde, *'Apuntes' personales sobre la República y la guerra civil* (Madrid: Fundación Francisco Franco, 1987) p. 35; 'La historia del Alzamiento Nacional contada por su Jefe de Estado Mayor', *Falange*, 15 March 1939.

27. T. F. Burns, Memorandum for Hoare, 11 April 1944, Templewood Papers, Cambridge University Library, XIII/6/28, p. 2.

28. Wake, *Kleinwort Benson*, p. 252.

29. On the negotiation and payment for the Italian aircraft, see Paul Preston, 'Mussolini's Spanish Adventure: From Limited Risk to War', in Preston and Mackenzie, eds, *The Republic Besieged*, pp. 33-5; José Gutiérrez Ravé, *Antonio Goicoechea* (Madrid: Celebridades, 1965) pp. 34-6; Díaz Nosty, *La irresistible ascensión*, pp. 307-18, 325-34; Ángel Viñas, *Las armas y el oro. Palancas de la guerra civil, mitos del Franquismo*

(Barcelona: Pasado y Presente, 2013) pp. 360-4; Cabrera, *Juan March*, pp. 276-87; Sánchez Asiaín, *La financiación*, pp. 168-9, 177-85, 190-3 199-205, 222-5; Garriga, *Juan March*, pp. 379-82.

30. Wake, *Kleinwort Benson*, pp. 253-4; Mariano Sánchez Soler, *Ricos por la guerra civil de España* (Madrid: Editorial Raíces, 2007) pp. 41-4; Viñas, *Las armas*, pp. 368-70.

31. Cabrera, *Juan March*, pp. 278-9, 287-8, 302-4; Sánchez Soler, *Ricos*, pp. 85-9; Ramón Garriga, *Nicolás Franco, el hermano brujo* (Barcelona: Planeta, 1980) pp. 19-20.

32. Tomeu Ferrer, *Vint dies de guerra* (Palma de Mallorca: Edicions Documenta Balear, 2005) pp. 216-18; Alberto Bayo, *Mi desembarco en Mallorca (de la guerra civil española)* (Palma de Mallorca: Miquel Font Editor, 1987) pp. 85-150; Josep Massot i Muntaner, *El desembarcament de Bayo a Mallorca, Agost-Setembre de 1936* (Barcelona: Publicacions de l'Abadia de Montserrat, 1987) pp. 60, 92, 110, 138-40, 252, 268; José Manuel Martínez Bande, *La invasión de Aragón y el desembarco en Mallorca*, 2nd edn (Madrid: Editorial San Martín, 1989) pp. 143-211; Sánchez Asiaín, *La financiación*, pp. 206-22.

33. Bayo, *Mi desembarco*, pp. 134-5; Josep Massot i Muntaner, *Arconovaldo Bonacorsi. El 'Conde Rossi'. Mallorca, agost-desembre 1936. Màlaga, gener-febrer 1937* (Barcelona: Publicacions de l'Abadia de Montserrat, 2017) pp. 127-70; Josep Massot i Muntaner, *Guerra civil i repressió a Mallorca* (Barcelona: Publicacions de l'Abadia de Montserrat, 1997) pp. 59-126.

34. Alejandro Lerroux, *Mis memorias* (Madrid: Afrodisio Aguado, 1963) pp. 637–9; Lerroux to Franco, 18 July 1937, 25 February 1938, 29 March 1939, reprinted in Franco Salgado-Araujo, *Mi vida*, pp. 373, 375, 381–2; Alejandro Lerroux, *La Pequeña historia. Apuntes para la Historia grande vividos y redactados por el autor* (Buenos Aires: Editorial Cimera, 1945) pp. 588–91.

35. Sánchez Asiaín, *La financiación*, pp. 138–49; Borja de Riquer i Permanyer, *L'últim Cambó (1936–1947). La dreta catalanista davant la guerra civil i el franquisme* (Barcelona: Eumo Editorial, 1996) pp. 52–65, 99–102, 178–89; Morten Heiberg and Manuel Ros Agudo, *La trama oculta de la guerra civil. Los servicios secretos de Franco 1936–1945* (Barcelona: Crítica, 2006) pp. 17, 59–60, 100–3, 258–9. The account by José Bertrán y Musitu, *Experiencias de los Servicios de Información del Nordeste de España (S.I.F.N.E.) durante la guerra* (Madrid: Espasa Calpe, 1940) does not mention Cambó.

36. See for example Francesc Cambó, 'Democracy and Spanish Conflict' and 'Spain under Shadow of Anarchist Rule', *Daily Telegraph*, 28, 29 December 1936.

37. Francesc Cambó, diary entries for 13 July 1937, 23, 24 March 1938, *Meditacions: dietari (1936–1940)* (Barcelona: Editorial Alpha, 1982) pp. 147, 303–4.

38. Paul Preston, 'The Great Civil War: European Politics, 1914–1945', in Tim Blanning, ed., *The Oxford History of Modern Europe* (Oxford: Oxford University Press, 2000) pp. 153–84.

39. Chilton to Eden, 10 January (TNA FO 371/20520, W344/62/41), 21 February 1936 (FO 371/20520,

W1639/62/41), 3 March (FO 371/20520, W2014/62/41), 24 March (FO 371/20520, W2868/62/41), 26 March (FO 371/20520, W2888/62/41), 7 April (FO 371/20521, W3224/62/41), 18 April (FO 371/20521, W3449/62/41), 2 May (FO 371/20521, W3947/62/41), Ogilvie-Forbes to Eden, 3 March (FO 371/20520, W2015/62/41), 17 June 1936 (FO 371/20522, W5670/62/41); Enrique Moradiellos, *La perfidia de Albión. El Gobierno británico y la guerra civil española* (Madrid: Siglo XXI de España, 1996) pp. 64–87; Douglas Little, *Malevolent Neutrality: The United States, Great Britain, and the Origins of the Spanish Civil War* (Ithaca, NY: Cornell University Press, 1985) pp. 184–220.

40. Sir M. Hankey, 'The Future of the League of Nations', Cabinet minutes, 20 July 1936, TNA CAB 63–51.

41. Jean Lacouture, *Léon Blum* (New York: Holmes & Meier, 1982) pp. 305–6; Hugh Thomas, *The Spanish Civil War*, 3rd edn (London: Hamish Hamilton, 1977) pp. 337, 343–4; Julian Jackson, *The Popular Front in France: Defending Democracy, 1934–1938* (Cambridge: Cambridge University Press, 1988) p. 202.

42. David Carlton, 'Eden, Blum and the Origins of Non-Intervention', *Journal of Contemporary History*, Vol. VI, No. 3, 1971, pp. 41–5; Anthony Eden, *Facing the Dictators* (London: Cassell, 1962) p. 405; Joel Colton, *Léon Blum: Humanist in Politics* (New York: Alfred A. Knopf, 1966) p. 241.

43. David Wingeate Pike, *La Galia dividida. Los franceses y la Guerra Civil española* (A Coruña:

Ediciones del Viento, 2016)
pp. 54–7; *The Times*, 26 July 1936;
Carlton, 'Eden, Blum', pp. 47–52;
John E. Dreifort, *Yvon Delbos at the
Quai d'Orsay: French Foreign Policy
during the Popular Front* (Lawrence,
Kan.: University Press of Kansas,
1973) pp. 44–9; Moradiellos, *La
perfidia*, pp. 64–87; Eden, *Facing
the Dictators*, pp. 401–3.

44. Lacouture, *Léon Blum*, pp. 311–12;
Dreifort, *Yvon Delbos*, pp. 50–1.

45. Moradiellos, *La perfidia*, pp. 71–2.

46. Zara Steiner, *The Triumph of the
Dark: European International
History 1933–1939* (Oxford: Oxford
University Press, 2011) pp. 202–3;
Henry Buckley, *Life and Death of
the Spanish Republic* (London:
Hamish Hamilton, 1940) p. 321.

47. Ingram to Eden, 28 July 1936,
*Documents on British Foreign
Policy*, 2nd Series, Vol. XVII
(London: HMSO, 1979) pp. 31–2;
Nino D'Aroma, *Un popolo alla
prova. Dieci anni di guerra (1935–
1945)*, 4 vols (Palermo: Editore
Cusimano, 1967) I, pp. 282–3.

48. Vitetti to Ciano, 29 July, 3 August,
Ciano to Vitetti, 30 July 1936, *I
Documenti Diplomatici Italiani, 8ª
serie, vol. IV (10 maggio–31 agosto
1936)* (Rome: Istituto Poligrafico e
Zecca dello Stato/Libreria dello
Stato, 1993) pp. 711–13, 719–20,
736–7; Saz Campos, *Mussolini
contra la II República*, pp. 204–5;
Enrique Moradiellos, *Neutralidad
benévola. El Gobierno británico y la
insurrección militar española de
1936* (Oviedo: Pentalfa Ediciones,
1990) pp. 172–3.

49. Enrique Moradiellos, 'El mundo
ante el avispero español.
Intervención y no intervención
extranjera en la guerra civil', in
Santos Juliá, ed., *Historia de España
Menéndez Pidal Tomo XL*.

República y guerra civil (Madrid:
Espasa Calpe, 2004) p. 253; Archivo
del Ministerio de Asuntos
Exteriores, legajo R-981, Expediente
5 (AMAE: R-981, E-5); José
Antonio Durango, 'La política
exterior del general Franco, 1938–
1940', unpublished doctoral thesis,
Universidad de Zaragoza, 1992,
pp. 1–5; Francisco Serrat Bonastre,
*Salamanca, 1936. Memorias del
primer 'ministro' de Asuntos
Exteriores de Franco* (Barcelona:
Crítica, 2014) pp. 162–3.

50. Vitetti to Ciano, 7 August 1937, *I
Documenti Diplomatici Italiani, 8ª
serie, vol. IV*, p. 774.

51. Moradiellos, *Neutralidad benévola*,
pp. 95–103; Steiner, *The Triumph*,
p. 201.

52. Paul Preston, 'The Answer lies in
the Sewers: Captain Aguilera and
the Mentality of the Francoist
Officer Corps', *Science & Society*,
Vol. 68, No. 3, Fall 2004, p. 289;
Peter Day, *Franco's Friends: How
British Intelligence Helped Bring
Franco to Power in Spain* (London:
Biteback, 2011) pp. 10–14.

53. Jean-François Berdah, *La
democracia asesinada. La República
española y las grandes potencias,
1931–1939* (Barcelona: Crítica,
2002) pp. 247–74; Viñas, *Las armas*,
pp. 254–5.

54. Espinosa Maestre, *La columna de la
muerte*, pp. 8–95, 205–34; Preston,
The Spanish Holocaust, pp. 304–24;
Mário Neves, *La matanza de
Badajoz* (Badajoz: Editora Regional
de Extremadura, 1986) pp. 43–53;
Herbert Rutledge Southworth, *El
mito de la cruzada de Franco* (Paris:
Éditions Ruedo Ibérico, 1963)
pp. 217–31.

55. *The Times*, 29, 31 August, 1, 2, 4, 5
September 1936; José Manuel
Martínez Bande, *Nueve meses de*

guerra en el norte (Madrid: Editorial San Martín, 1980) pp. 64–86.

56. José María Ruiz Alonso, *La guerra civil en la provincia de Toledo. Utopía, conflicto y poder en el sur del Tajo (1936–1939)*, 2 vols (Ciudad Real: Almud, Ediciones de Castilla-La Mancha, 2004) I, pp. 166–85; Rafael Casas de la Vega, *El Alcázar* (Madrid: G. del Toro, 1976) pp. 38–77; Antonio Vilanova Fuentes, *La defensa del Alcázar de Toledo (epopeya o mito)* (Mexico City: Editores Mexicanos Unidos, 1963) pp. 107–92; Gregorio Gallego, *Madrid, corazón que se desangra* (Madrid: G. del Toro, 1976) pp. 154–8.

57. José Peirats, *La CNT en la revolución española*, 2nd edn, 3 vols (Paris: Ediciones Ruedo Ibérico, 1971) I, pp. 157–62; Preston, *The Spanish Holocaust*, pp. 242–51; Josep Termes, *Misèria contra pobresa. Els fets de la Fatarella del gener de 1937. Un exemple de la resistència pagesa contra la col·lectivització agrària durant la guerra civil* (Catarroja, Valencia: Editorial Afers, 2005) pp. 53–74, 81–107.

58. Koltsov, *Diario*, p. 55; Franz Borkenau, *The Spanish Cockpit* (London: Faber & Faber, 1937) pp. 130–2.

59. Cipriano de Rivas Cherif, *Retrato de un desconocido. Vida de Manuel Azaña* (Barcelona: Grijalbo, 1980) p. 351.

60. Dolores Ibárruri et al., *Guerra y revolución en España 1936–39*, 4 vols (Moscow: Editorial Progreso, 1966–77) II, pp. 46–8; Koltsov, *Diario*, p. 65; Zugazagoitia, *Guerra y vicisitudes*, I, pp. 144–5.

61. Ángel Viñas, *La soledad de la República. El abandono de las

democracias y el viraje hacia la Unión Soviética* (Barcelona: Crítica, 2006) pp. 198, 206–9; Vidarte, *Todos fuimos culpables*, pp. 478–85; Enrique Moradiellos, *Negrín. Una biografía de la figura más difamada de la España del siglo XX* (Barcelona: Ediciones Península, 2015) pp. 194–200.

62. Julio Álvarez del Vayo, *Freedom's Battle* (London: Heinemann, 1940) pp. 202–3.

63. Martín Blázquez, *I Helped to Build an Army*, p. 190; Antonio Cordón, *Trayectoria (Recuerdos de un artillero)* (Paris: Colección Ebro, 1971) p. 258.

64. Yuri Rybalkin, *Stalin y España. La ayuda militar soviética a la República* (Madrid: Marcial Pons Historia, 2007) pp. 40–56.

65. The standard work on the gold remains Ángel Viñas, *El oro español en la guerra civil* (Madrid: Instituto de Estudios Fiscales, 1976). For a broader, updated study, see his *La soledad de la República*, pp. 197–398. See also Boris Volodarsky, *Stalin's Agent: The Life and Death of Alexander Orlov* (Oxford: Oxford University Press, 2015) pp. 156–67; Moradiellos, *Negrín*, pp. 200–13.

66. Howson, *Arms for Spain*, pp. 128–45, 278–84; Viñas, *La soledad de la República*, pp. 345–58.

67. Preston, *Franco*, pp. 173–9; Garriga, *Nicolás Franco*, pp. 97–104; Guillermo Cabanellas, *La guerra de los mil días*, 2 vols (Buenos Aires: Grijalbo, 1973) pp. 196, 305–6; José María Iribarren, *Mola, datos para una biografía y para la historia del alzamiento nacional* (Zaragoza: Librería General, 1938) pp. 232–3.

68. H. R. Knickerbocker, *The Siege of Alcazar: A War-Log of the Spanish Revolution* (London: Hutchinson,

n.d. [1937]) pp. 172–3; Webb Miller, *I Found No Peace* (London: The Book Club, 1937) pp. 329–30, 335–7; Herbert L. Matthews, *The Yoke and the Arrows: A Report on Spain* (London: Heinemann, 1958) p. 176; Alberto Risco SJ, *La epopeya del Alcázar de Toledo*, 2nd edn (Burgos: Editorial Española, 1937) pp. 216–18, 225–6.

69. Preston, *Franco*, pp. 179–86; Ramón Garriga, *La España de Franco. Las relaciones con Hitler*, 2nd edn (Puebla, Mexico: Cajica, 1970) p. 73; Charles Foltz, Jr, *The Masquerade in Spain* (Boston: Houghton Mifflin, 1948) p. 178; Jean Créac'h, *Le coeur et l'épée: chroniques espagnoles* (Paris: Librairie Plon, 1958) p. 182; Ramón Serrano Suñer, *Entre el silencio y la propaganda, la Historia como fue. Memorias* (Barcelona: Planeta, 1977) pp. 163–4.

70. Julio Aróstegui and Jesús A. Martínez, *La Junta de Defensa de Madrid* (Madrid: Comunidad de Madrid, 1984) pp. 26–45; Gallego, *Madrid*, pp. 164–5.

71. The literature on the International Brigades is enormous. The main study of the entire operation remains Andreu Castells, *Las Brigadas Internacionales de la guerra de España* (Barcelona: Ariel, 1974). The best national studies are Rémi Skoutelsky, *L'Espoir guidait leurs pas. Les volontaires français dans les Brigades internationales, 1936–1939* (Paris: Bernard Grasset, 1998); Peter N. Carroll, *The Odyssey of the Abraham Lincoln Brigade: Americans in the Spanish Civil War* (Stanford, Calif.: Stanford University Press, 1994); Richard Baxell, *Unlikely Warriors: The British in the Spanish Civil War and the Struggle against Fascism*

(London: Aurum Press, 2012); Franco Giannantoni and Fabio Minazzi, eds, *Il coraggio della memoria e la guerra civile spagnola, 1936–1939. Studi, documenti inediti e testimonianze* (Milano: Edizioni Arterigere/Amici del Liceo Scientifico di Varese, 2000).

72. Koltsov, *Diario*, pp. 182, 200.

73. Santiago Carrillo, *Memorias* (Barcelona: Planeta, 1993) p. 189; Aróstegui and Martínez, *La Junta de Defensa de Madrid*, pp. 54–61; Antonio López Fernández, *Defensa de Madrid. Relato histórico* (Mexico City: Editorial A. P. Márquez, 1945) pp. 82–4.

74. Preston, *The Spanish Holocaust*, pp. 341–75; Julius Ruiz, *'Paracuellos': The Elimination of the 'Fifth Column' in Republican Madrid during the Spanish Civil War* (Brighton: Sussex Academic Press, 2017) *passim*.

75. Koltsov, *Diario*, p. 275; Virginia Cowles, *Looking for Trouble* (London: Hamish Hamilton, 1941) p. 18; Josep Maria Solé i Sabaté and Joan Villarroya i Font, *España en llamas. La guerra civil desde el aire* (Madrid: Ediciones Temas de Hoy, 2003) pp. 45–60; Anthony Beevor, *The Battle for Spain: The Spanish Civil War (1936–1939)* (London: Weidenfeld & Nicolson, 2006) pp. 182–4.

76. Paul Preston, 'Italy and Spain in Civil War and World War, 1936–1943', in Sebastian Balfour and Paul Preston, eds, *Spain and the Great Powers* (London: Routledge, 1999) pp. 160–76.

77. Preston, *Franco*, pp. 205–19; Emilio Faldella, *Venti mesi di guerra in Spagna* (Florence: Le Monnier, 1939) pp. 230–51; Alberto Rovighi and Filippo Stefani, *La partecipazione italiana alla guerra*

civile Spagnola, 2 vols, each in two parts Testi & Allegati (Rome: Ufficio Storico dello Stato Maggiore dell'Esercito, 1992-3) I, Testo, pp. 185-216.

78. Zugazagoitia, *Guerra y vicisitudes*, I, pp. 236-43.

79. José Manuel Martínez Bande, *La lucha en torno a Madrid* (Madrid: Editorial San Martín, 1968) pp. 71-111; Jesús González de Miguel, *La batalla del Jarama. Febrero de 1937, testimonios desde un frente de la guerra civil* (Madrid: La Esfera de los Libros, 2009) pp. 37-48 and, on the casualties, 707-17; Luis Diez, *La batalla del Jarama* (Madrid: Oberón, 2005) pp. 27-58, 241-4; Beevor, *The Battle*, pp. 189-96, 208-15.

80. Faldella, *Venti mesi di guerra*, pp. 252-75; Rovighi and Stefani, *La partecipazione italiana*, I, Testo, pp. 238-317; Olao Conforti, *Guadalajara. La prima sconfitta del fascismo* (Milan: Mursia, 1967) pp. 51ff.; Preston, *Franco*, pp. 229-36; Martínez Bande, *La lucha en torno a Madrid*, pp. 117-70; Preston, *Franco*, pp. 221-33; Leonardo Pompeo D'Alessandro, *Guadalajara 1937. I voluntari italiani fascisti e antifascisti nella guerra di Spagna* (Roma: Carocci Editore, 2017) pp. 143-72.

81. Alfredo Kindelán Duany, *Mis cuadernos de guerra*, 2nd edn (Barcelona: Planeta, 1982) pp. 120-3; General Jorge Vigón, *General Mola (el conspirador)* (Barcelona: AHR, 1957) pp. 303-4.

82. Paul Preston, 'Britain and the Basque Campaign of 1937: The Government, the Royal Navy, the Labour Party and the Press', *European History Quarterly*, Vol. 48, No. 3, 2018, pp. 490-515; James Cable, *The Royal Navy and the Siege of Bilbao* (Cambridge: Cambridge University Press, 1979) pp. 35-6, 46-53, 66-76, 88-98.

83. Xabier Irujo, *El Guernica de Richthofen. Un ensayo de bombardeo de terror* (Guernica-Lumo: Guernicako Bakearen Museoa Fundazioa, 2012) pp. 14, 59-60, 73-4, 257-301; Paul Preston, *The Destruction of Guernica*, e-book 2nd edn (London: William Collins, 2017) pp. 11-22, 31-6; Herbert Rutledge Southworth, *Guernica! Guernica!: A Study of Journalism, Propaganda and History* (Berkeley: University of California Press, 1977) pp. 239-325, 368-84.

84. Preston, *Franco*, pp. 248-71; Martin Blinkhorn, *Carlism and Crisis in Spain (1931-1939)* (Cambridge: Cambridge University Press, 1975) pp. 279-93; Sheelagh Ellwood, *Prietas las filas. Historia de Falange Española, 1933-1983* (Barcelona: Crítica, 1984) pp. 90-110; Ramón Serrano Súñer, *Entre el silencio y la propaganda, la Historia como fue. Memorias* (Barcelona: Planeta, 1977) pp. 169-87, 165; Maximiano García Venero, *Falange en la guerra de España. La Unificación y Hedilla* (Paris: Ruedo Ibérico, 1967) pp. 338-427; Herbert Rutledge Southworth, *Antifalange. Estudio crítico de 'Falange en la guerra de España' de Maximiano García Venero* (Paris: Ruedo Ibérico, 1967) pp. 179-218.

85. For a compelling statement of the revolutionary positions, see, from the anarchist perspective, Vernon Richards, *Lessons of the Spanish Revolution* (London: Freedom Press, 1972) and from the POUM, Grandizo Munis, *Jalones de derrota, promesa de victoria [España 1930-*

1939] (Mexico City: Editorial Lucha Obrera, 1948) pp. 237–319.

86. Helen Graham, "'Against the State": A Genealogy of the Barcelona May Days (1937)', *European History Quarterly*, Vol. 29, No. 4, 1999, pp. 485–542; Paul Preston, 'Lights and Shadows in George Orwell's *Homage to Catalonia*', *Bulletin of Spanish Studies*, 2018 DOI: 10.1080/14753820.2018.1388550.

87. Philip Jordan, *There Is No Return* (London: Cresset Press, 1938) p. 18.

88. Franz Borkenau, *The Spanish Cockpit* (London: Faber & Faber, 1937) pp. 195–6.

89. Munis, *Jalones*, p. 296; Helen Graham, 'The Spanish Popular Front and the Civil War', in Helen Graham and Paul Preston, eds, *The Popular Front in Europe* (London: Macmillan, 1987) pp. 122–5.

90. Josep Maria Bricall, *Política Económica de la Generalitat (1936–1939). Evolución i formes de la producción industrial* (Barcelona: Edicions 62, 1978) pp. 33–40, 44–50, 138–55; Graham, *The Spanish Republic*, pp. 254–61; Rafael Abella, *La vida cotidiana durante la guerra civil*, Vol. II: *La España Republicana* (Barcelona: Planeta, 1976) pp. 192–6.

91. Graham, *The Spanish Republic*, pp. 261–76; Manuel Cruells, *Mayo sangriento. Barcelona 1937* (Barcelona: Editorial Juventud, 1970) pp. 50–91; Agustín Guillamón, *Barricadas en Barcelona. La CNT de la victoria de julio de 1936 a la necesaria derrota de mayo de 1937* (Barcelona: Ediciones Espartaco Internacional, 2007) pp. 148–70; Juan García Oliver, *El eco de los pasos* (Barcelona: Ruedo Ibérico, 1978) pp. 420–31; Adolfo Bueso, *Recuerdos de un cenetista*, Vol. II:

De la Segunda República al final de la guerra civil (Barcelona: Ariel, 1978) pp. 229–446; Burnett Bolloten, *The Spanish Civil War: Revolution and Counterrevolution* (Hemel Hempstead: Harvester Wheatsheaf, 1991) pp. 414–61, 899; Zugazagoitia, *Guerra y vicisitudes*, I, pp. 268, 270–2; Peirats, *La CNT*, II, pp. 138–43. On the artillery, Diego Abad de Santillán, *Por que perdimos la guerra. Una contribución a la historia de la tragedia española*, 2nd edn (Madrid: G. del Toro, 1975) pp. 164–9.

92. Azaña, *Obras*, IV, pp. 591–2.

93. *Ibid.*, pp. 592–8; Viñas, *El escudo de la República*, pp. 549–62; Ibárruri et al., *Guerra y revolución en España 1936–39*, III, pp. 79–84; Francisco Largo Caballero, *Mis recuerdos. Cartas a un amigo* (Mexico City: Editores Unidos, 1954) pp. 217–22; Julio Aróstegui, *Largo Caballero. El tesón y la quimera* (Barcelona: Debate, 2013) pp. 580–606; Graham, *The Spanish Republic*, pp. 299–305.

94. Georgi Dimitrov, *The Diary of Georgi Dimitrov* (New Haven: Yale University Press, 2003) pp. 58, 60; Fernando Hernández Sánchez, *Guerra o revolución. El Partido Comunista de España en la guerra civil* (Barcelona: Crítica, 2010) pp. 191–206.

95. Azaña, *Obras*, IV, p. 603.

96. Ramón Lamoneda, 'El secreto del anticomunismo' ms, Archivo de la Fundación Pablo Iglesias, ARLF-166-40, pp. 1–4.

97. Bueso, *Recuerdos*, II, pp. 244–51; García Oliver, *El eco*, pp. 431–5; Josep Coll and Josep Pané, *Josep Rovira. Una vida al servei de Catalunya i del socialismo* (Barcelona: Ariel, 1978) pp. 173–5; Zugazagoitia, *Guerra y vicisitudes*, I,

p. 272; Antonio Elorza and Marta Bizcarrondo, *Queridos Camaradas. La Internacional Comunista y España, 1919–1939* (Barcelona: Planeta, 1999) pp. 362–73.

98. Volodarsky, *Stalin's Agent*, pp. 280–9; John Costello and Oleg Tsarev, *Deadly Illusions* (New York: Crown Publishers, 1993) pp. 288–92, 470; Preston, *The Spanish Holocaust*, pp. 407–15; Javier Cervera Gil, *Madrid en guerra. La ciudad clandestina 1936–1939*, 2nd edn (Madrid: Alianza Editorial, 2006) pp. 304–10; Zugazagoitia, *Guerra y vicisitudes*, I, pp. 291–4; Vidarte, *Todos fuimos culpables*, pp. 727–9; Pelai Pagès i Blanch, 'El asesinato de Andreu Nin. Más datos para la polémica', in *Ebre 38. Revista Internacional de la Guerra Civil 1936–1939*, No. 4, 2010, pp. 57–76.

99. Azaña, *Obras*, IV, p. 603.

100. Zugazagoitia, *Guerra y vicisitudes*, II, p. 14.

101. Enrique Líster, *Nuestra guerra* (Paris: Colección Ebro, 1966) pp. 132–48; Rafael Casas de la Vega, *Brunete* (Madrid: Fermín Uriarte, 1967) *passim*; José Manuel Martínez Bande, *La ofensiva sobre Segovia y la batalla de Brunete* (Madrid: Editorial San Martín, 1972) pp. 101–233; Beevor, *The Battle*, pp. 276–86; Severiano Montero Barrado, *La batalla de Brunete* (Madrid: Editorial Raíces, 2010) pp. 42–208; Juan Barceló, *Brunete. El nacimiento del Ejército Popular* (A Coruña: Ediciones del Viento, 2018) pp. 97–293.

102. Sánchez Asiaín, *La financiación*, pp. 194–6; Díaz Nosty, *La irresistible ascensión*, pp. 318–21; Pere Ferrer, *Juan March. El hombre más misterioso del mundo* (Barcelona: Ediciones B, 2008)

pp. 361–2; Dixon, *Señor Monopolio*, p. 144.

103. Azaña, diary entry for 28 June 1937, *Obras*, IV, pp. 635–6.

104. *Ibid.*, p. 636.

105. José Manuel Martínez Bande, *El final del frente norte* (Madrid: Editorial San Martín, 1972) pp. 39–105.

106. Martínez Bande, *El final del frente norte*, pp. 107–97; Zugazagoitia, *Guerra y vicisitudes*, II, p. 44.

107. Roberto Cantalupo, *Fu la Spagna. Ambasciata presso Franco. Febbraio–Aprile 1937* (Milan: Mondadori, 1948) pp. 230–3; Gabriel Cardona, *Historia militar de una guerra civil. Estrategias y tácticas de la guerra de España* (Barcelona: Flor del Viento, 2006) p. 198.

108. General Vicente Rojo, *España heróica. Diez bocetos de la guerra española*, 3rd edn (Barcelona: Ariel, 1975) pp. 117–25; Beevor, *The Battle*, pp. 316–22; José Manuel Martínez Bande, *La batalla de Teruel*, 2nd edn (Madrid: Editorial San Martín, 1990) pp. 52–64; Vicente Aupí, *El General Invierno y la Batalla de Teruel* (Teruel: Dobleuve Comunicación, 2015) pp. 93–122; Milagro and Fernando Lloréns Casani, *Héroes o traidores. Teruel, la verdad se abre camino* (Linares: Ediciones Lloréns, 2005) pp. 127ff.

109. *Documents on German Foreign Policy* (henceforth *DGFP*), Series D, vol. III (London: HMSO, 1951) pp. 554–7; Gerald Howson, *Aircraft of the Spanish Civil War 1936–1939* (London: Putnam, 1990) pp. 20–8.

110. José Manuel Martínez Bande, *La llegada al mar* (Madrid: Editorial San Martín, 1975) pp. 25–179.

111. Preston, *The Spanish Holocaust*, pp. 458–61; Cambó, diary entries

for 1, 6 April, 24 December 1938, 1 January 1939, *Meditacions*, pp. 308–9, 311, 454–5, 461.

112. Joan Serralonga i Urquidi, *Refugiats i desplaçats dins la Catalunya en guerra 1936–1939* (Barcelona: Editorial Base, 2004) pp. 29–69, 163–212.

113. Solé i Sabaté and Villarroya i Font, *España en llamas*, pp. 139–97; Joan Villarroya i Font, *Els bombardeigs de Barcelona durant la guerra civil (1936–1939)*, 2nd edn (Barcelona: Publicacions de L'Abadia de Montserrat, 1999) pp. 211–80; Pedro Payá López, 'Guerra total y propaganda', in Roque Moreno Fonseret, ed., *La aviación fascista y el bombardeo del 25 de mayo de Alicante* (Alicante: Publicaciones Universitat d'Alacant, 2018) pp.107–28; Gaspar Díez Pomares, '25 de mayo de 1938: el trágico bombardeo del Alicante en la documentación italiana', *Historia Actual Online*, Vol. 46, No. 2, 2018, pp. 123–36.

114. Graham, *The Spanish Republic*, pp. 351–4; Gabriel Jackson, *The Spanish Republic and the Civil War* (Princeton, NJ: Princeton University Press, 1965) pp. 446–50; Julián Casanova, *Anarquismo y revolución en la sociedad rural aragonesa 1936–1938* (Madrid: Siglo XXI de España, 1985) pp. 110–13. On the Quakers, see Farah Mendlesohn, *Quaker Relief Work in the Spanish Civil War* (Lewiston, NY: Edwin Mellen Press, 2002) *passim*.

115. Cardona, *Historia militar*, pp. 229–37.

116. José Manuel Martínez Bande, *La ofensiva sobre Valencia* (Madrid: Editorial San Martín, 1977) pp. 11–41.

117. José Manuel Martínez Bande, *La*

batalla del Ebro, 2nd edn (Madrid: Editorial San Martín, 1988) pp. 103–269; Beevor, *The Battle*, pp. 349–59; Jorge Martínez Reverte, *La Batalla del Ebro* (Barcelona: Crítica, 2003) *passim*.

118. *DGFP*, D, III, pp. 760–1, 767–8, 775–9, 782–8, 802.

119. José Manuel Martínez Bande, *La campaña de Cataluña* (Madrid: Editorial San Martín, 1979) pp. 41–53; 189–214; General Vicente Rojo, *¡Alerta los pueblos! estudio político-militar del período final de la guerra española*, 2nd edn (Barcelona: Ariel, 1974) pp. 79–154; Paul Preston, *L'anti-catalanisme dels rebels militars. De la batalla de l'Ebre a l'ocupació total del país* (Tarragona: Universitat Rovira i Virgili, 2013) pp. 9–23; Helen Graham, 'Casado's Ghosts: Demythologising the End of the Spanish Republic', *Bulletin of Spanish Studies*, Vol. 89, Nos 7–8, 2012, pp. 255–78; Ángel Viñas, 'Playing with History and Hiding Treason: Colonel Casado's Untrustworthy Memoirs and the End of the Spanish Civil War', *Bulletin of Spanish Studies*, Vol. 91, Nos 1–2, 2014, pp. 295–323.

120. On the Casado coup and its consequences, see Paul Preston, *The Last Days of the Spanish Republic: The Final Betrayal* (London: William Collins, 2016); Ángel Bahamonde Magro and Javier Cervera Gil, *Así terminó la Guerra de España* (Madrid: Marcial Pons, 1999); Ángel Bahamonde Magro, *Madrid 1939. La conjura del coronel Casado* (Madrid: Ediciones Cátedra, 2014); Graham, 'Casado's Ghosts: Demythologizing the End of the Spanish Republic', pp. 255–78; Viñas, 'Playing with History and Hiding Treason', pp. 295–323.

Chapter 12: World War: Survival, Hypocrisy and Profit, 1939–1945

1. Francisco Moreno Gómez, *La resistencia armada contra Franco. Tragedia del maquis y la guerrilla* (Barcelona: Crítica, 2001) pp. 31–238; Julio Aróstegui and Jorge Marco, eds, *El último frente. La resistencia armada antifranquista en España 1939–1952* (Madrid: Los Libros de la Catarata, 2008) *passim*.

2. Francesc Cambó, diary entry for 8 May 1944, *Meditacions. Dietari (1941–1946)* (Barcelona: Editorial Alpha, 1982) p. 1449.

3. *Boletín Oficial del Estado*, 9 August; *Arriba*, 9 August; *Ya*, 9 August 1939; Enrique Moradiellos, *Franco. Anatomía de un dictador* (Madrid: Turner, 2018) pp. 174–6.

4. Ángel Viñas, Julio Viñuela, Fernando Eguidazu, Carlos Fernández Pulgar and Senen Florensa, *Política comercial exterior en España (1931–1975)*, 2 vols (Madrid: Banco Exterior de España, 1979) I, pp. 210–11, 258–67.

5. Paul Preston, *The Spanish Holocaust: Inquisition and Extermination in Twentieth-Century Spain* (London: HarperCollins, 2012) ch. 13. On the treatment of women, see Fernando Hernández Holgado, *Mujeres encárceladas. La prisión de Ventas: de la República al franquismo, 1931–1941* (Madrid: Marcial Pons, 2003) pp. 113–82; Ricard Vinyes, Montse Armengou and Ricard Belis, *Los niños perdidos del franquismo* (Barcelona: Plaza y Janés, 2002) pp. 59–71, 89–92; Antonio D. López Rodríguez, *Cruz, bandera y caudillo. El campo de concentración de Castuera* (Badajoz: CEDER-La Serena, 2007) pp. 226–63, 325–45.

6. Isaías Lafuente, *Esclavos por la patria. La explotación de los presos bajo el franquismo* (Madrid: Ediciones Temas de Hoy, 2002) pp. 57–63, 121–9, 135–70; Rafael Torres, *Los esclavos de Franco* (Madrid: Oberón, 2000) pp. 134–45; Javier Rodrigo, *Hasta la raíz. Violencia durante la guerra civil y la dictadura franquista* (Madrid: Alianza Editorial, 2008) pp. 138–57; Juan Miguel Baquero, '¿Qué empresas usaron a esclavos del franquismo?', *El Diario*, 26 April 2014 (https://www.eldiario.es/andalucia/empresas-usaron-esclavos-franquismo_0_251975222.html).

7. Gonzalo Acosta Bono, José Luis Gutiérrez Molina, Lola Martínez Macías and Ángel del Río Sánchez, *El canal de los presos (1940–1962). Trabajos forzados: de la represión política a la explotación económica* (Barcelona: Crítica, 2004) pp. xxxii–xxxvi, 173–88, 204–31.

8. Fernando Olmeda, *El Valle de los Caídos* (Barcelona: Ediciones Península, 2009) pp. 25, 43, 46–8, 54–78; Daniel Sueiro, *El Valle de los Caídos. Los secretos de la cripta franquista*, 2nd edn (Barcelona: Argos Vergara, 1983) pp. 8–24, 44–73, 118–43, 184–205.

9. Ramón Serrano Suñer, *Entre el silencio y la propaganda, la Historia como fue. Memorias* (Barcelona: Planeta, 1977) pp. 244–8.

10. Mónica Lanero Táboas, *Una milicia de la justicia. La política judicial del franquismo (1936–1945)* (Madrid: Centro de Estudios Constitucionales, 1996) pp. 318–19; Manuel Ballbé, *Orden público y militarismo en la España constitucional (1812–1983)* (Madrid: Alianza Editorial, 1983) pp. 402–9.

11. Lanero Táboas, *Una milicia de la justicia*, pp. 320–1; Pablo Gil, *La*

noche de los generales. Militares y represión en el régimen de Franco (Barcelona: Ediciones B, 2004) pp. 143–5; Peter Anderson, *The Francoist Military Trials: Terror and Complicity, 1939-1945* (New York: Routledge, 2010) pp. 53–9.

12. Manuel Álvaro Dueñas, '*Por ministerio de la ley y voluntad del Caudillo'. La Jurisdicción Especial de Responsabilidades Políticas (1939-1945)* (Madrid: Centro de Estudios Políticos y Constitucionales, 2006) pp. 68–80, 97–110; Manuel Ortiz Heras, *Violencia política en la II República y el primer franquismo. Albacete, 1936-1950* (Madrid: Siglo XXI de España, 1996) pp. 393–409; Julián Chaves Palacios, *La represión en la provincia de Cáceres durante la guerra civil (1936-1939)* (Cáceres: Universidad de Extremadura, 1995) pp. 87–91; Elena Franco Lanao, *Denuncias y represión en años de posguerra. El Tribunal de Responsabilidades Políticas en Huesca* (Huesca: Instituto de Estudios Altoaragoneses, 2005) pp. 43–52, 98–119; Santiago Vega Sombría, *De la esperanza a la persecución. La represión franquista en la provincia de Segovia* (Barcelona: Crítica, 2005) pp. 179–96; Glicerio Sánchez Recio, *Las responsabilidades políticas en la posguerra española. El partido judicial de Monóvar* (Alicante: Universidad de Alicante, 1984) pp. 6–40; Conxita Mir, Fabià Corretgé, Judit Farré and Joan Sagués, *Repressió econòmica i franquisme. L'actuació del Tribunal de Responsabilitats Polítiques a la provincia de Lleida* (Barcelona: Publicacions de l'Abadia de Montserrat, 1997) pp. 63–80; Mercè Barallat i Barés, *La repressió a la postguerra civil a Lleida (1938-*

1945) (Barcelona: Publicacions de l'Abadia de Montserrat, 1991) pp. 347–56; Óscar J. Rodríguez Barreira, *Migas con miedo. Prácticas de resistencia en el primer franquismo. Almería 1939-1952* (Almería: Universidad de Almería, 2008) pp. 81–101; Juan Carlos Berlinches Balbucid, *La rendición de la memoria. 200 casos de represión franquista en Guadalajara* (Guadalajara: Ediciones Bornova, 2004) pp. 97–128; Julius Ruiz, *Franco's Justice: Repression in Madrid after the Spanish Civil War* (Oxford: Clarendon Press, 2005) pp. 131–64.

13. Dionisio Ridruejo, *Escrito en España*, 2nd edn (Buenos Aires: Editorial Losada, 1964) pp. 98–104; Conxita Mir, 'El sino de los vencidos: la represión franquista en la Cataluña rural de posguerra', in Julián Casanova, ed., *Morir, matar, sobrevivir. La violencia en la dictadura de Franco* (Barcelona: Crítica, 2002) pp. 123–37; Ángela Cenarro, 'Matar, vigilar y delatar: la quiebra de la sociedad civil durante la guerra y la posguerra en España (1936-1948)', *Historia Social*, No. 44, 2002, pp. 65–86.

14. Borja de Riquer, *La dictadura de Franco* (Barcelona/Madrid: Crítica/Marcial Pons, 2010) pp. 247–89.

15. José Larraz, *Memorias* (Madrid: Real Academia de Ciencias Morales y Políticas, 2006) pp. 256–7.

16. *Ibid.*, pp. 181–6.

17. *Ibid.*, pp. 239–40, 249–55, 260.

18. *Ibid.*, pp. 166–74, 213–38, 283–308, 339–41, 350–1; Carlos Barciela, Inmaculada López, Joaquín Melgarejo and J. A. Miranda, *La España de Franco (1939-1975). Economía* (Madrid: Síntesis, 2001) pp. 46–52.

19. Francisco Franco Bahamonde, 'Fundamentos y directrices de un Plan de saneamiento de nuestra economía, armónico con nuestra reconstrucción nacional', *Historia 16*, No. 115, November 1985, pp. 44–9; Viñas et al., *Política comercial exterior*, I, pp. 268–81; Manuel Jesús González, *La economía política del franquismo (1940–1970). Dirigismo, mercado y planificación* (Madrid: Tecnos, 1979) pp. 46–7.

20. On Savarpoldi Hammaralt, see Ramón Garriga, *Nicolás Franco, el hermano brujo* (Barcelona: Planeta, 1980) pp. 128–30. On the gold, see *Mensaje del Caudillo a los españoles: discurso pronunciado por S.E. el Jefe del Estado la noche del 31 de diciembre de 1939* (Madrid, n.d.) p. 27; Ramón Garriga, *La España de Franco. Las relaciones con Hitler*, 2nd edn (Puebla, Mexico: Cajica, 1970) pp. 58, 126.

21. On the petrol scam, see *La Voz de Galicia*, 8 February; *La Vanguardia Española*, 21 January, 8 February 1940; Charles Foltz, Jr, *The Masquerade in Spain* (Boston: Houghton Mifflin, 1948) pp. 258–60; Juan Antonio Ansaldo, *¿Para qué ...? (de Alfonso XIII a Juan III)* (Buenos Aires: Editorial Vasca-Ekin, 1951) pp. 254–6; Larraz, *Memorias*, pp. 248–9; Ignacio Martínez de Pisón, *Filek. El estafador que engañó a Franco* (Barcelona: Seix Barral, 2018) pp. 141–99 (Felipe Polo at pp. 171–4).

22. Francisco Comín Comín, 'La corrupción permanente: el fraude fiscal en España', *Hispania Nova*, No. 16, 2018, pp. 481–521.

23. Klaus-Jörg Ruhl, *Franco, Falange y III Reich* (Madrid: Akal, 1986) pp. 49–50; José Maria Doussinague,

España tenía razón (Madrid: Espasa-Calpe, 1949) pp. 85–6; Viñas et al., *Política comercial exterior*, I, pp. 306–12.

24. Ángel Viñas, 'Hambre, corrupción y sobornos en el primer franquismo, 1939–1959', in Borja de Riquer, Joan Lluís Pérez Francesch, Gemma Rubí, Lluís Ferran Toledano and Oriol Luján, eds, *La corrupción política en la España contemporánea* (Madrid: Marcial Pons Historia, 2018) pp. 146–52.

25. Garriga, *Nicolás Franco*, pp. 167–84; Carlos Barciela, 'Franquismo y corrupción política', *Historia Social*, No. 30, 1998, pp. 83–96; 'El trágico final de la reforma agraria. La revolución "fascista" en el campo español', in Ángel Viñas, ed., *En el combate por la historia. La República, la guerra civil, el Franquismo* (Barcelona: Pasado y Presente, 2012) pp. 335–54; Ángel Viñas, 'Autarquía y política exterior en el primer franquismo 1939–1959', *Revista de Estudios Internacionales*, January–March 1980, pp. 61–92; Francisco Comín Comín, 'Presupuesto y corrupción en la España contemporánea (1808–2017): Lecciones de la historia', in Borja de Riquer et al., *La corrupción política*, pp. 93–100.

26. Barciela, 'Franquismo y corrupción', p. 91; Viñas, 'Hambre, corrupción y sobornos', pp. 153–60; Jaume Claret, *Ganar la Guerra, perder la paz. Memorias del general Latorre Roca* (Barcelona: Crítica, 2019) p. 288.

27. *Documentos inéditos para la historia del Generalísimo Franco* (Madrid: Fundación Nacional Francisco Franco, 1992), Vol. II-2, p. 370.

28. Ramón Garriga, *Los validos de Franco* (Barcelona: Planeta, 1981) pp. 163, 189; Jesús Aguirre, ed.,

Dionisio Ridruejo, de la Falange a la oposición (Madrid: Taurus Ediciones, 1976) pp. 91–4, 323–4; Ridruejo to Blas Pérez, 18 October 1942, reprinted in Dionisio Ridruejo, *Casi unas memorias* (Barcelona: Planeta, 1976) pp. 244–5; Ramón Garriga, *Franco-Serrano Suñer. Un drama político* (Barcelona: Planeta, 1986) p. 178.

29. David Eccles, ed., *By Safe Hand: Letters of Sybil and David Eccles 1939–1942* (London: Bodley Head, 1983) p. 206; *Documents on German Foreign Policy* (henceforth *DGFP*), Series D, Vol. XII (London: HMSO, 1962) pp. 36–7; Dirección General de Seguridad Informe, 16 January 1941, *Documentos inéditos*, II-2, pp. 19–22.

30. Carlos Martínez Campos to Varela, 28 August, Fidel Davila to Varela, 2 September 1940, reproduced in Federico Martínez Roda, *Varela. El general antifascista de Franco* (Madrid: La Esfera de los Libros, 2012) pp. 529–31.

31. José Martí Gómez, *La España del estraperlo (1936–1952)* (Barcelona: Planeta, 1995) pp. 127–45; Miguel Ángel del Arco Blanco, 'La corrupción en el franquismo: El fenómeno del "gran estraperlo"', *Hispania Nova*, No. 16, 2018, pp. 620–45; Laura de Andrés Creus, *El preu de la fam. L'estraperlo a la Catalunya de la postguerra* (Badalona: Ara Llibres, 2010) pp. 51–8, 63–6, 123–7; Rodríguez Barreira, *Migas con miedo*, pp. 167–281; Rafael Abella, *La vida cotidiana bajo el régimen de Franco* (Barcelona: Planeta, 1985) pp. 49–60; Rafael Abella, *Por el Imperio hacia Dios* (Barcelona: Planeta, 1978) pp. 101–32.

32. Barciela, 'Franquismo y corrupción', p. 91; Jaume Muñoz Jofre, *La*

España corrupta. Breve historia de la corrupción (de la Restauración a nuestros días, 1976–2016) (Granada: Comares, 2016) pp. 77–8.

33. Francisco Franco Bahamonde, *Palabras del Caudillo 19 abril 1937–7 diciembre 1942* (Madrid: Ediciones de la Vicesecretaría de Educación Popular, 1943) p. 102.

34. 'Normas para el paso de las fronteras españolas y modelo de solicitud de autorización para entrar en España', Equipo Nikor: http://www.derechos.org/nizkor/espana/doc/franco9.html; Bernd Rother, *Franco y el holocausto* (Madrid: Marcial Pons Historia, 2005) pp. 131–3.

35. Franco, *Palabras del Caudillo 19 abril 1937–7 diciembre 1942*, pp. 145, 213; *Mensaje del Caudillo 31 de diciembre de 1939*, p. 16.

36. José Antonio Ferrer Benimeli, *El contubernio judeo-masónico-comunista* (Madrid: Istmo, 1982) pp. 136–50, 191–3, 273–333; Javier Domínguez Arribas, *El enemigo judeo-masónico en la propaganda franquista (1936–1945)* (Madrid: Marcial Pons Historia, 2009) pp. 84–97.

37. Alfonso Lazo, *La Iglesia, la Falange y el fascismo (un estudio sobre la prensa española de postguerra)* (Seville: Universidad de Sevilla, 1995) pp. 179–220; Rother, *Franco y el holocausto*, pp. 127–9.

38. Jacobo Israel Garzón, 'España y los judíos (1939–1945). Una visión general', in Jacobo Israel Garzón and Alejandro Baer, *España y el Holocausto (1939–1945). Historia y testimonios* (Madrid: Ebraica Ediciones, 2007) pp. 18–23.

39. Pilar Vera, 'La huida silenciosa', *Diario de Cádiz*, 30 August 2009; Javier Dale, 'El éxodo de un judío

catalán', *La Vanguardia*, 26 March 2010; Jorge M. Reverte, 'La lista de Franco para el Holocausto', *El País*, 20 June 2010; Pedro Teotónio Pereira, *Memórias. Postos em que servi e algumas recordações pessoais*, 2 vols (Lisboa: Verbo, 1973) II, pp. 219–21.

40. Manuel Ros Agudo, *La guerra secreta de Franco* (Barcelona: Crítica, 2002) pp. 178–205.

41. On measures against Jews and freemasons during the Spanish Civil War, see Paul Preston, *El holocausto español. Odio y exterminio en la guerra civil y después* (Barcelona: Editorial Debate, 2011) pp. 633–4.

42. Marta Simó Sànchez, 'La memòria de l'Holocaust a l'Estat espanyol', unpublished doctoral thesis, Universitat Autònoma de Barcelona, 2018, pp. 118–48, 212–28.

43. United Nations, Security Council, Official Records, First Year: Second Series, Special Supplement, *Report of the Sub-Committee on the Spanish Question* (New York: Hunter College, 1946) pp. 17–21; Carlos Collado Seidel, *España, refugio nazi* (Madrid: Ediciones Temas de Hoy, 2005) pp. 25–53; Heleno Saña, *El franquismo sin mitos. Conversaciones con Serrano Suñer* (Barcelona: Grijalbo, 1982) pp. 305–8; Foltz, *The Masquerade*, pp. 283–5; Luis Suárez Fernández, *Francisco Franco y su tiempo*, 8 vols (Madrid: Fundación Nacional Francisco Franco, 1984) III, pp. 107–8.

44. *Franco ha dicho. Primer apéndice (contiene de 1º enero 1947 a 1º abril 1949)* (Madrid: Ediciones Voz, 1949) pp. 159–60; Antonio Marquina Barrio and Gloria Inés Ospina, *España y los judíos en el siglo XX* (Madrid: Espasa Calpe, 1987) p. 212.

45. *Foreign Relations of the United States* [henceforth *FRUS*] *1949* (Washington, DC: US Government Printing Office, 1975) IV, pp. 742–3; Raanan Rein, *In the Shadow of the Holocaust and the Inquisition: Israel's Relations with Francoist Spain* (London: Frank Cass, 1997) p. 35.

46. *España y los Judíos* (Madrid: Oficina de Información Diplomática, 1949) pp. 29, 43, 47; Isabelle Rohr, *The Spanish Right and the Jews, 1898–1945: Antisemitism and Opportunism* (Brighton: Sussex Academic Press, 2007) pp. 1–2; Rein, *In the Shadow*, pp. 36–47; Federico Ysart, *España y los judios en la segunda guerra mundial* (Barcelona: Dopesa, 1973); *Franco ha dicho. Primer apéndice*, pp. 159–60.

47. On Spain's strategic importance, see Denis Smyth, *Diplomacy and Strategy of Survival: British Policy and Franco's Spain, 1940–1941* (Cambridge: Cambridge University Press, 1986) pp. 1–4.

48. Mariano Sánchez Soler, *Villaverde. Fortuna y caída de la casa Franco* (Barcelona: Planeta, 1990) pp. 39–42; Javier Otero, 'El patrimonio oculto de Francisco Franco', *Tiempo*, 11 June 2010; Ángel Viñas, *La otra cara del Caudillo. Mitos y realidades en la biografía de Franco* (Barcelona: Crítica, 2015) pp. 295–6.

49. Carlos Babío Urkidi and Manuel Pérez Lorenzo, *Meirás. Un pazo, un caudillo, un espolio* (A Coruña: Fundación Galiza Sempre, 2017) pp. 57–85, 121–47, 162–83, 223–67; Sánchez Soler, *Villaverde*, pp. 45–8; Ramón Garriga, *La Señora de El Pardo* (Barcelona: Planeta, 1979) pp. 122–6.

50. *El País* and *La Voz de Galicia*, both 12 July 2019.

51. Javier Otero, 'El patrimonio oculto de Francisco Franco', *Tiempo*, 11 June 2010; María Luz de Prado Herrera, *La contribución popular a la financiación de la Guerra Civil. Salamanca, 1936-1939* (Salamanca: Ediciones Universidad de Salamanca, 2012) pp. 156-271, 367-77; Viñas, *La otra cara*, pp. 289, 292-3, 297-310, 316-30, 333-43; José Ángel Sánchez Asiaín, *La financiación de la guerra civil española. Una aproximación histórica* (Barcelona: Crítica, 2012) pp. 157-63, 712, 948-51.

52. Javier Otero, 'La familia Franco, inmune a la crisis', *Tiempo*, 15 November 2012.

53. Julio de Ramón-Laca, *Bajo la férula de Queipo. Como fue gobernada Andalucía* (Seville: Imprenta Comercial del Diario FE, 1939) pp. 36-7; Rúben Serém, *A Laboratory of Terror, Conspiracy, Coup d'état and Civil War in Seville, 1936-1939. History and Myth in Francoist Spain* (Brighton: Sussex Academic Press, 2017) pp. 149-89.

54. *La Unión*, 26 July 1936, 11 February, 27 May 1937; *ABC* (Seville), 10 August, 5 September, 16 November 1936.

55. *ABC* (Seville), 17 August, 18, 22 September, 9, 24, 25 December 1937; *La Unión*, 18, 22 September 1937; Ana Quevedo and Queipo de Llano, *Queipo de Llano. Gloria e infortunio de un general* (Barcelona: Planeta, 2001) pp. 496-8; Antonio Olmedo Delgado and General José Cuesta Monereo, *General Queipo de Llano (Aventura y audacia)* (Barcelona: AHR, 1958) pp. 335-9.

56. *DGFP*, Series D, vol. X (London: HMSO, 1957) pp. 514-15; *DGFP*, Series D, vol. XI (London: HMSO, 1961) pp. 153-5; Report of General Staff to Franco, October 1940, *Documentos inéditos*, II-1, pp. 371-4.

57. Gustau Nerín and Alfred Bosch, *El imperio que nunca existió. La aventura colonial discutida en Hendaya* (Barcelona: Plaza y Janés, 2001) pp. 19-35; Ros Agudo, *La guerra secreta*, pp. xxiii-xxvi, 35-51, 56-7, 66-71.

58. David Wingeate Pike, 'Franco and the Axis Stigma', *Journal of Contemporary History*, Vol. 17, No. 3, 1982, pp. 369-407. For the neutrality myth, see, *inter alia*, José María Sánchez Silva and José Luis Saenz de Heredia, *Franco ... ese hombre* (Madrid: Difusión Librera, 1975) p. 139; José Maria de Areilza, *Embajadores sobre España* (Madrid: Instituto de Estudios Políticos, 1947) pp. 4-5, 57-8; Doussinague, *España tenía razón, passim*; Brian Crozier, *Franco: A Biographical History* (London: Eyre & Spottiswoode, 1967) pp. 313-75.

59. David Wingeate Pike, *Franco and the Axis Stigma* (London: Palgrave Macmillan, 2008) pp. 11-15; E. O. Iredell, *Franco, valeroso caballero cristiano* (Buenos Aires: Editorial Américalee, 1945) pp. 166-82.

60. Víctor Alba, *Historia de la Segunda República Española* (Mexico City: Libro Mex, 1961) p. 287.

61. Ramon Serrano Suñer, *Entre la propaganda y la historia. La Historia como fue. Memorias* (Barcelona: Planeta, 1977) p. 358.

62. *Arriba*, 2, 3, 5, 10 May; *ABC*, 3, 11 May; *Informaciones*, 3, 7 May; *The Times*, 11 May 1945.

63. *DGFP*, Series D, Vol. IX (London: HMSO, 1956) pp. 396, 509-10, 620-1; Xavier Moreno Julià, *Hitler y Franco. Diplomacia en tiempos de guerra (1936-1945)* (Barcelona: Planeta, 2007) pp. 135-47.

64. Manuel Ros Agudo, *La gran tentación. Franco, el imperio colonial y los planes de intervención en la Segunda Guerra Mundial* (Barcelona: Styria de Ediciones, 2008) pp. 141-55; Jesús Albert Salueña, 'Protectorado español de Marruecos. Aspectos militares durante la II guerra mundial', *Ayeres en discusión Temas claves de Historia Contemporánea hoy. IX Congreso de la Asociación de Historia Contemporánea* (Murcia: ACH, 2008) pp. 111-15; Nerín and Bosch, *El imperio*, pp. 95-102.

65. *DGFP*, Series D, Vol. IX, pp. 449-53; Vol. XI, p. 445; Ros Agudo, *La guerra secreta*, pp. 72-85, 96-132, 205-17, 231-9, 248-51.

66. Mussolini to Franco, 9 June 1940, *I Documenti Diplomatici Italiani* [henceforth *DDI*] *9ª serie, vol. IV (9 aprile-10 giugno 1940)* (Rome: Libreria dello Stato, 1960) p. 60; Galeazzo Ciano, *L'Europa verso la catastrofe* (Milano: Mondadori, 1948) pp. 559-60.

67. *DGFP*, Series D, Vol. X (London: HMSO, 1957) p. 396; Sir Samuel Hoare, *Ambassador on Special Mission* (London: Collins, 1946) p. 44; Ramón Serrano Suñer, *Entre Hendaya y Gibraltar* (Madrid: Ediciones y Publicaciones Españolas, 1947) p. 65.

68. Memorandum by Stohrer, 8 August 1940, Note of the High Command, 10 August 1940, *DGFP*, Series D, Vol. X, pp. 442-5, 461-4.

69. *DGFP*, Series D, Vol. X, pp. 466-7, 499-500, 521.

70. *Ibid.*, pp. 514-15, 521, 561; Franco to Mussolini, 15 August 1940, *DDI 9ª serie, vol. V* (Rome: Libreria dello Stato, 1965) pp. 403-5; *DGFP*, Series D, Vol. X, pp. 484-6; Serrano Suñer, *Entre Hendaya y Gibraltar*, pp. 103-4.

71. *DGFP*, Series D, Vol. X, pp. 561-5, Vol. XI, pp. 37-40, 81-2; Walter Schellenberg, *The Schellenberg Memoirs: A Record of the Nazi Secret Service* (London: André Deutsch, 1956) pp. 135, 143.

72. *DGFP*, Series D, Vol. XI, pp. 83-102, 166-74; Serrano Suñer, *Entre Hendaya y Gibraltar*, pp. 165-83; Norman J. W. Goda, *Tomorrow the World: Hitler, Northwest Africa, and the Path toward America* (College Station, Tex.: A&M University Press, 1998) pp. 71-8; Gerhard L. Weinberg, *World in the Balance: Behind the Scenes of World War II* (Hanover, NH: University Press of New England, 1981) p. 122; Serrano Suñer, *Memorias*, pp. 335-7.

73. Franco to Serrano Suñer, 21 and 23 September 1940, reproduced in Serrano Suñer, *Memorias*, pp. 331-42; Serrano Suñer, *Entre Hendaya y Gibraltar*, p. 183.

74. Paul Preston, *The Politics of Revenge: Fascism and the Military in 20th Century Spain* (London: Unwin Hyman, 1990) pp. 91-3; Denis Smyth, 'The Moor and the Money-lender: Politics and Profits in Anglo-German Relations with Francoist Spain', in Marie-Luise Recker, ed., *Von der Konkurrenz zur Rivalität: Das Britische-Deutsche Verhältnis in den Länden der Europäischen Peripherie* (Stuttgart: Franz Steiner Verlag, 1986) pp. 171-4.

75. *DGFP*, Series D, Vol. XI, pp. 211-14; Galeazzo Ciano, *Diario 1939-1940* (Milano: Rizzoli, 1946) pp. 310-13; Colloquio Mussolini–Serrano Suñer, 1 October; Colloquio Mussolini–Hitler, 4 October 1940, *DDI, 9ª serie, vol. V*, pp. 639-40, 655-8; MacGregor Knox, *Mussolini Unleashed 1939-*

1941: Politics and Strategy in Fascist Italy's Last War (Cambridge: Cambridge University Press, 1982) pp. 189, 196.

76. Hugh Dalton, *The Second World War Diary of Hugh Dalton* (London: Jonathan Cape, 1986) 7 October 1940, p. 89; *FRUS 1940* (Washington, DC: US Government Printing Office, 1957) II, pp. 812-17.

77. *DDI, 9ª serie, vol. V*, pp. 720-2; *DGFP*, Series D, Vol. XI, pp. 331-4; Foltz, *The Masquerade*, p. 260.

78. Norman Rich, *Hitler's War Aims: Ideology, the Nazi State, and the Course of Expansion*, 2 vols (London: André Deutsch, 1973-4), I, pp. 169-70.

79. Franz Halder, *The Halder War Diary 1931-1942*, ed. Charles Burdick and Hans-Adolf Jacobsen (London: Greenhill, 1988) pp. 262, 273, 277-8.

80. José María Sánchez Silva and José Luis Saenz de Heredia, *Franco ... ese hombre* (Madrid: Difusión Librera, 1975) p. 139.

81. Serrano Suñer, *Memorias*, pp. 283-301; Paul Schmidt, *Hitler's Interpreter: The Secret History of German Diplomacy 1935-1945* (London: Heinemann, 1951) p. 196; *DGFP*, Series D, Vol. XI, pp. 371-9.

82. Ciano, *L'Europa verso la catastrofe*, pp. 603-4.

83. Heleno Saña, *El franquismo sin mitos. Conversaciones con Serrano Suñer* (Barcelona: Grijalbo, 1982) p. 193. See also the polemic between Serrano Suñer and Antonio Marquina in *El País*, 19, 21, 22, 26, 28, 29 November 1978.

84. *FRUS 1940*, II, p. 824.

85. Halder, *Diary*, 31 July 1940, pp. 244-6; Alan Bullock, *Hitler and Stalin: Parallel Lives* (London, 1991) pp. 754-5; Alan Clark, *Barbarossa:*

The Russian-German Conflict 1941-1945 (London, 1965) pp. 17-26. I am grateful to Professor Brian Bond for clarifying this point.

86. *DGFP*, Series D, Vol. XI, pp. 452, 478-9; Directive No. 18, 12 November 1940, *Hitler's War Directives 1939-1945*, ed. H. R. Trevor-Roper (London: Sidgwick & Jackson, 1964) pp. 39-42.

87. *DGFP*, Series D, Vol. XI, pp. 528-30, 574-6, 581-2, 787-8, 812, 816-17, 852-3, 990-4; *FRUS 1940*, II, pp. 829-38; Charles B. Burdick, *Germany's Military Strategy and Spain in World War II* (Syracuse: Syracuse University Press, 1968) pp. 77ff.; Heinz Höhne, *Canaris* (London: Secker & Warburg, 1979) pp. 440-1; André Brissaud, *Canaris* (London: Weidenfeld & Nicolson, 1973) pp. 224-6; Serrano Suñer, *Entre Hendaya y Gibraltar*, pp. 258-9.

88. *DGFP*, Series D, Vol. XI, pp. 1140-3, 1157-8, 1171-5.

89. *Ibid.*, Vol. XII, p. 30.

90. Stohrer to Wilhelmstrasse, 6 February 1941, *ibid.*, pp. 37-42, 51-3, 58, 78-9.

91. Ciano to Serrano Suñer, 22 January 1941, *DDI, 9ª serie, vol. VI (29 ottobre 1940-23 aprile 1941)* (Rome: Libreria dello Stato, 1986) p. 485; Serrano Suñer, *Entre Hendaya y Gibraltar*, pp. 262-3; Roberto Cantalupo, *Fu la Spagna. Ambasciata presso Franco. Febbraio-Aprile 1937* (Milan: Mondadori, 1948) pp. 288-9.

92. Hoare, *Ambassador*, pp. 95, 104.

93. Colloquio Mussolini-Franco, 12 February 1941, *DDI, 9ª serie, Vol. VI*, pp. 568-76; Serrano Suñer, *Entre Hendaya y Gibraltar*, pp. 261-4; Cantalupo, *Fu la Spagna*, pp. 291-3.

94. *DGFP*, Series D, Vol. XII, pp. 96–7, 131–2.
95. Burdick, *Germany's Military Strategy*, pp. 103ff.
96. *DGFP*, Series D, Vol. XII, pp. 194–5.
97. *FRUS 1941* (Washington, DC: US Government Printing Office, 1959) Vol. II, pp. 886–7.
98. Pereira to Salazar, 1 May 1941, *Correspondência de Pedro Teotónio Pereira para Oliveira Salazar, II (1940–1941)* (Lisbon: Presidência do Conselho de Ministros, 1989) pp. 286–7.
99. Denis Smyth, 'Hillgarth, Alan Hugh', in *Dictionary of National Biography 1971–1980* (Oxford: Oxford University Press, 1986) pp. 409–10; Josep Massot i Muntaner, *El cònsol Alan Hillgarth i les Illes Balears (1936–1939)* (Barcelona: Publicacions de l'Abadia de Montserrat, 1995) *passim*; Ángel Viñas, *Sobornos. De cómo Churchill y March compraron a los generales de Franco* (Barcelona: Crítica, 2016) p. 82.
100. Hillgarth Memorandum to Hoare, 2 June 1940, Templewood Papers, Cambridge University Library (henceforth TP), XIII/2/3; Hoare to Churchill, 12 June 1940, TP, XIII/16/1.
101. Denis Smyth, 'Les Chevaliers de Saint-George: la Grande-Bretagne et la corruption des généraux espagnols (1940–1942)', *Guerres mondiales et conflits contemporains*, No. 162, April 1991, pp. 29–54; Cabrera, *Juan March*, pp. 328–35; Viñas, *Sobornos*, pp. 75–8; Smyth, *Diplomacy*, pp. 225–6.
102. Many of the relevant documents can be found in two large files in TNA, Permanent Under-Secretary of State, Foreign Office, TNA, FO 1093-233 and FO 1093-234.
103. Viñas, *Sobornos*, pp. 83–4, 96–105, 109–13, 119–20, 157–9, 290–3; Richard Wigg, *Churchill and Spain: The Survival of the Franco Regime, 1940–45* (Brighton: Sussex Academic Press, 2008) pp. 45–6, 97, 113.
104. Viñas, *Sobornos*, pp. 454–65.
105. *Ibid.*, pp. 318–33.
106. Stohrer to Wilhelmstrasse, 22 April 1941, *DGFP*, Series D, Vol. XII, pp. 611–16.
107. Alfredo Kindelán, *La verdad de mis relaciones con Franco* (Barcelona: Planeta, 1981) pp. 117–18; Xavier Tusell and Genoveva García Queipo de Llano, *Franco y Mussolini. La política española durante la segunda guerra mundial* (Barcelona: Planeta, 1985) pp. 97–8; Viñas, *Sobornos*, pp. 236–40, 270.
108. Preston, *Franco*, pp. 427–35; Stanley G. Payne, *The Franco Regime 1936–1975* (Madison: University of Wisconsin Press, 1987) pp. 285–90.
109. Smyth, *Diplomacy*, pp. 226–7.
110. Pereira to Salazar, 11 May 1941, *Correspondência*, II, p. 310.
111. *DGFP*, Series D, Vol. XII, pp. 795–6; Pereira to Salazar, 18 June 1941, *Correspondência*, II, p. 366; Hoare, *Ambassador*, p. 112.
112. Pereira to Salazar, 18, 20, 22 May, 9 June 1941; *Correspondência*, II, pp. 314–16, 321–3, 327–8, 349–50.
113. Serrano Suñer, *Memorias*, pp. 200–1.
114. Hoare to Eden, 31 May 1941, TNA FO 954/27A/162.
115. *FRUS 1941*, II, pp. 891–903; *Arriba*, 31 May; *ABC*, 31 May, 6, 9 June 1941.
116. Hoare to Eden, 8 June 1941, TNA FO 954/27A/165.
117. *DGFP*, Series D, Vol. XII, pp. 1080–1.

118. Hoare, *Ambassador*, p. 140; José Luis Rodríguez Jiménez, *Los esclavos españoles de Hitler* (Barcelona: Planeta, 2002).

119. Denis Smyth, *Deathly Deception: The Real Story of Operation Mincemeat* (Oxford: Oxford University Press, 2010) pp. 150-1.

120. Hoare to Eden, 9 July 1941, TNA FO 954/27A/172.

121. 14 August 1941, *FRUS 1941*, II, pp. 911-13.

122. Wiehl, 6 September 1941, *DGFP*, Series D, Vol. XIII, pp. 459-60.

123. *FRUS 1941*, II, pp. 908-11; Serrano Suñer, *Memorias*, pp. 348-9.

124. *FRUS 1941*, II, pp. 913-25.

125. *Ibid.*, pp. 924-9.

126. *DDI, 9ª serie, vol. VIII (12 dicembre 1941-20 luglio 1942)* (Rome: Libreria dello Stato, 1988) pp. 322-3, 335-8; *Documents secrets du Ministère des Affaires Etrangères d'Allemagne: Espagne* (Paris: Éditions Paul Dupont, 1946) pp. 86-95; *FRUS 1942* (Washington, DC: US Government Printing Office, 1961) Vol. III, pp. 281-3; *The Times*, 13 February; *ABC*, 13 February 1942. Testimony of Serrano Suñer to the author.

127. Garriga, *La España de Franco*, pp. 345-6; Franco, *Palabras del Caudillo 19 abril 1937-7 diciembre 1942*, pp. 203-5.

128. *DDI, 9ª serie, vol. VIII*, pp. 113, 116-17, 123-4; *Arriba*, 13 January 1942.

129. Preston, *Franco*, pp. 464-9; Saña, *El franquismo*, pp. 271-6; Hoare, *Ambassador*, pp. 140, 164-71; Doussinague, *España tenía razón*, pp. 130-1, and Antonio Marquina Barrio, 'El atentado de Begoña', *Historia 16*, No. 76, August 1982, pp. 11-19; Martínez Roda, *Varela*, pp. 338-49. On the rumours about Serrano, Larraz, *Memorias*, p. 340;

Garriga, *Franco-Serrano Suñer*, p. 120.

130. *DDI, 9ª serie, vol. IX (21 luglio 1942-6 febbraio 1943)* (Rome: Libreria dello Stato, 1989) pp. 138-9; Serrano Suñer, *Entre Hendaya y Gibraltar*, pp. 211-18.

131. Denis Smyth, 'Screening "Torch": Allied Counter-Intelligence and the Spanish Threat to the Secrecy of the Allied Invasion of French North Africa in November 1942', *Intelligence and National Security*, Vol. 4, No. 2, April 1989, pp. 335-56, esp. pp. 344, 350-1.

132. Viñas, *Sobornos*, pp. 377-89.

133. Doussinague, *España tenía razón*, pp. 203-6.

134. Pedro Teotónio Pereira, *Correspondência de Pedro Teotónio Pereira para Oliveira Salazar, III (1942)* (Lisbon: Presidência do Conselho de Ministros, 1990) pp. 280-1; François Piétri, *Mes années d'Espagne 1940-1948* (Paris: Librairie Plon, 1954) p. 86; Ruhl, *Franco, Falange y III Reich*, pp. 49-50; Moltke to Wilhelmstrasse, 13, 24 January 1943, *Documents secrets*, pp. 127-34; Ramón Garriga, *La España de Franco. De la División Azul al pacto con los Estados Unidos (1943 a 1951)* (Puebla, Mexico: Cajica, 1971) p. 30.

135. Viñas, *Sobornos*, pp. 417-21.

136. Carlos Martínez de Campos, *Ayer 1931-1953* (Madrid: Instituto de Estudios Políticos, 1970) pp. 213-52; Gerald R. Kleinfeld and Lewis A. Tambs, *Hitler's Spanish Legion: The Blue Division in Russia* (Carbondale: Southern Illinois University Press, 1979) pp. 310-13.

137. Smyth, *Deathly Deception*, pp. 216-18; TNA, ADM 223/794, 'Mincemeat', Naval Intelligence, Division 12 ('Special Naval

Section') History of Naval
Intelligence and the Naval
Intelligence Department 1939–
1945, Vol. III, 'Naval Deception',
pp. 1–22; *Documentos inéditos*, IV,
pp. 223–5; Ruhl, *Franco, Falange y
III Reich*, p. 223.

138. Javier Tusell, *Franco, España y la II
guerra mundial. Entre el Eje y la
neutralidad* (Madrid: Temas de
Hoy, 1995) pp. 585–9; Eduardo
Martín de Pozuelo, *El Franquismo,
cómplice del Holocausto* (Barcelona:
La Vanguardia, 2012) pp. 39–40;
Rohr, *The Spanish Right and the
Jews*, pp. 123–56.

139. Rother, *Franco y el holocausto*,
pp. 128–9, 408–9; Marquina Barrio
and Inés Ospina, *España y los
judíos*, pp. 212–22; Diego Carcedo,
*Un español frente al Holocausto.
Así salvó Ángel Sanz Briz 5.000
judíos* (Madrid: Temas de Hoy,
2000) pp. 199–268; Rohr, *The
Spanish Right and the Jews*,
pp. 149–52; Juan Diego Quesada,
'Franco lo Supo. Excelencia, esto
ocurre en Auschwitz', *El País*, 21
March 2010.

140. *Arriba*, 18, 19, 20, 21 March, 2, 5,
12 May; *The Times*, 18 March; *ABC*,
2, 5, 7, 8, 9 May 1943; Doussinague,
España tenía razón, pp. 207–9.

141. *Bulletin of Spanish Studies*, Vol.
XXI, No. 82, April 1944, p. 85;
Hoare, *Ambassador*, pp. 239–40;
Preston, *The Politics of Revenge*,
pp. 100–4; José María Gil Robles,
*La monarquía por la que yo luché.
Páginas de un diario 1941–1954)*
(Madrid: Taurus, 1976) p. 55.

142. Abrahán Guillén, *25 años de
economía franquista* (Buenos Aires:
Periplo, 1963) p. 145; Payne, *The
Franco Regime*, pp. 285, 399, 425;
Gil Robles, *La monarquía*, pp. 74,
83, 86.

143. T. F. Burns, Memorandum for

Hoare, 11 April 1944, TP, XIII/6/28;
Viñas, *Sobornos*, pp. 444–6.

144. Ruhl, *Franco, Falange y III Reich*,
p. 68; Smyth, *Diplomacy*, p. 215;
Foltz, *The Masquerade*, pp. 126–9;
Gil Robles, *La monarquía*, pp. 28,
72, 77, 85.

145. Gil Robles, *La monarquía*, pp. 28,
33, 37–8, 53–9, 71, 74, 83.

146. Suárez Fernández, *Franco*, III,
p. 432; Claret, *Ganar la Guerra*,
pp. 277–8.

147. *Documentos inéditos*, IV,
pp. 679–80.

148. Collado Seidel, *España, refugio
nazi*, pp. 145–50, 223–5, 277–86.

149. Serrano Súñer, *Memorias*, p. 230;
Francisco Franco Salgado-Araujo,
*Mis conversaciones privadas con
Franco* (Barcelona: Planeta, 1976)
pp. 37, 178.

150. Claret, *Ganar la Guerra*, pp. 244–6,
267, 287–8.

151. Ridruejo, *Escrito en España*, p. 104;
Carlos Fernández Santander,
*Tensiones militares durante el
franquismo* (Barcelona: Plaza y
Janés, 1985) pp. 77–85.

152. Department of State, *The Spanish
Government and the Axis*
(Washington, DC: US Government
Printing Office, 1946) pp. 34–7;
Hoare, *Ambassador*, p. 258.

153. Rafael García Pérez, *Franquismo y
Tercer Reich. Las relaciones
económicas hispano-alemanas
durante la segunda guerra mundial*
(Madrid: Centro de Estudios
Constitucionales, 1994) pp. 453–73;
Garriga, *De la División Azul*,
pp. 338–42; Christian Leitz,
*Economic Relations between Nazi
Germany and Franco's Spain 1936–
1945* (Oxford: Oxford University
Press, 1996) pp. 190–2; Viñas et al.,
Política comercial exterior, I, p. 354,
362–3, 393–5, 410, 463–4; Viñas,
Sobornos, p. 446.

154. Burns, Memorandum, 11 April 1944, TP, XIII/6/28, p. 3.
155. Ramón J. Campo, *El oro de Canfranc* (Zaragoza: Biblioteca Aragonesa de Cultura, 2002) pp. 65-9, 79-85.
156. *FRUS 1943* (Washington, DC: US Government Printing Office, 1964) II, pp. 631-2, 722-38, 727-31; Doussinague, *España tenía razón*, pp. 88-9, 280-90; Hoare, *Ambassador*, pp. 249-56.
157. Warren F. Kimball, ed., *Churchill & Roosevelt: The Complete Correspondence*, 3 vols (Princeton, NJ: Princeton University Press, 1984) II, pp. 725-6, 728, 751; Sir Alexander Cadogan, *The Diaries of Sir Alexander Cadogan 1938-1945* (London: Cassell, 1971) pp. 602-3; *The Diaries of Edward R. Stettinius, Jr., 1943-1946* (New York: New Viewpoints, 1975) pp. 28-9; Hoare, *Ambassador*, pp. 257-62.
158. Kimball, ed., *Churchill & Roosevelt: Correspondence*, III, pp. 66-8, 99, 106-8, 114; Cadogan, *Diaries*, pp. 622-3; Hoare, *Ambassador*, pp. 262-8; Joan Maria Thomàs, *Roosevelt, Franco and the End of the Second World War* (London: Palgrave Macmillan, 2011) pp. 67-125.
159. Xavier Moreno Julià, *La División Azul. Sangre española en Rusia, 1941-1945* (Barcelona: Crítica, 2004) pp. 204-9, 295-305; Miguel Ezquerra, *Berlin, a vida o muerte* (Barcelona: Ediciones Acervo, 1975), pp. 15, 105-47; Fernando Vadillo, *La gran crónica de la División Azul. Los irreductibles* (Granada: García Hispán, 1993) pp. 225-65.
160. Hoare, *Ambassador*, pp. 283, 300-4.
161. Daniel Arasa, *La invasión de los maquis* (Barcelona: Belacqua de Ediciones, 2004) pp. 243-5,

299-306; Secundino Serrano, *Maquis. Historia de la guerrilla antifranquista* (Madrid: Ediciones Temas de Hoy, 2001) pp. 129-40; Tomas Cossias, *La lucha contra el 'maquis' en España* (Madrid: Editora Nacional, 1956) pp. 60-3; Fernando Martínez de Baños, *Hasta su total aniquilación. El Ejército contra el maquis en el Valle de Arán y en el Alto Aragón, 1944-1946* (Madrid: Almena Ediciones, 2002) pp. 137-8, 155-6.
162. Tusell, *Franco, España y la II guerra mundial*, p. 200.
163. *The Testament of Adolf Hitler: The Hitler-Bormann Documents* (London: Cassell, 1961) pp. 47-9.

Chapter 13: The Franco Regime: Corruption and Terror, 1945-1953

1. *Arriba*, 8 May; *ABC*, 8 May 1945.
2. Francisco Franco, *Textos de doctrina política. Palabras y escritos de 1945 a 1950* (Madrid: Publicaciones Españolas, 1951) pp. 612-13.
3. Bowker to Eden, 8, 14, 31 May 1945, TNA FO 371/49550, Z6008/2/41, Z6421/7/41 and Z7213/7/41; *ABC*, 26 April, 3, 11 May; *Arriba*, 3, 5, 10 May; *Informaciones*, 3, 7 May; *The Times*, 3, 11 May 1945.
4. Ramón Soriano, *La mano izquierda de Franco* (Barcelona: Planeta, 1981) p. 159; Borrell interview, María Mérida, *Testigos de Franco. Retablo íntimo de una dictadura* (Barcelona: Plaza y Janés, 1977) p. 225.
5. Rafael R. Tranche, 'La imagen de Franco "Caudillo" en la primera propaganda cinematográfica del Régimen', in Vicente Sánchez Biosca, ed., *Materiales para una iconografía de Francisco Franco*, 2 vols (Madrid: Archivos de la

Filmoteca, Nos 42–3, October 2002–February 2003) pp. 92–3.

6. Max Gallo, *Spain under Franco: A History* (London: Allen & Unwin, 1973), pp. 153–9.

7. *La Vanguardia Española*, 18 July; *The Times*, 18 July 1945; Franco, *Textos 1945–1950*, pp. 15–25.

8. Paul Preston, *Franco: A Biography* (London: HarperCollins, 1993) pp. 532–3.

9. Javier Tusell, *Franco y los católicos. La política interior española entre 1945 y 1957* (Madrid: Alianza Editorial, 1984) pp. 56–8.

10. *Ibid.*, pp. 61–77, 84–94, 118; Luis Suárez Fernández, *Francisco Franco y su tiempo*, 8 vols (Madrid: Fundación Nacional Francisco Franco, 1984) IV, p. 44; José María Gil Robles, *La monarquía por la que yo luché. Páginas de un diario 1941–1954)* (Madrid: Taurus, 1976) pp. 126–7; Ramón Garriga, *La España de Franco. De la División Azul al pacto con los Estados Unidos (1943 a 1951)* (Puebla, Mexico: Cajica, 1971) pp. 334–5; Florentino Portero, *Franco aislado. La cuestión española (1945–1950)* (Madrid: Aguilar, 1989) pp. 106–10.

11. Tusell, *Franco y los católicos*, pp. 58–9.

12. Suárez Fernández, *Franco*, I, p.. 19.

13. A. J. Lleonart y Anselem and Fernando María Castiella y Maiz, *España y ONU*, Vol. I: *1945–46* (Madrid: Consejo Superior de Investigaciones Científicas, 1978) pp. 30–3.

14. *The Times*, 18 June 1945.

15. Qasim Ahmad, *Britain, Franco Spain, and the Cold War, 1945–1950* (New York: Garland, 1992) pp. 33–40.

16. Lleonart and Castiella, *España y ONU*, I, pp. 42–4; *Foreign Relations of the United States* [henceforth

FRUS] *1945* (Washington, DC: US Government Printing Office, 1967) V, p. 683.

17. Speeches, 20 May, 20 June, 2, 17 July 1945, Franco, *Textos 1945–1950*, pp. 5–25.

18. Ángel Viñas, *Los pactos secretos de Franco con Estados Unidos. Bases, ayuda económica, recortes de soberanía* (Barcelona: Grijalbo, 1981) p. 27.

19. Laureano López Rodó, *La larga marcha hacia la monarquía* (Barcelona: Noguer, 1977) pp. 57–9; Tusell, *Franco y los católicos*, pp. 99–100.

20. Mallet to Bevin, 22 September, 6 October 1945, TNA FO 371/49590, Z10932/233/41, Z11432/233/41.

21. Portero, *Franco aislado*, pp. 133–4; Randolph Bernard Jones, 'The Spanish Question and the Cold War 1944–1953', unpublished PhD thesis, University of London, 1987, pp. 49–51.

22. See also speeches to the high command, 7 January 1946, to the general staff, 16 February 1946, Franco, *Textos 1945–1950*, pp. 539–49.

23. Garriga, *De la División Azul*, pp. 382–6; Heleno Saña, *El franquismo sin mitos. Conversaciones con Serrano Suñer* (Barcelona: Grijalbo, 1982) pp. 289–92, 301–3; Suárez Fernández, *Franco*, IV, pp. 52–3, 58–9; Tusell, *Franco y los católicos*, pp. 100–2.

24. *La Vanguardia Española*, 2 October; *Arriba*, 2 October 1945.

25. Tusell, *Franco y los católicos*, pp. 102–6; *ABC*, 12 October 1945.

26. *ABC*, 27 October; *Arriba*, 27 October 1945; Suárez Fernández, *Franco*, IV, p. 102; *FRUS 1946* (Washington, DC: US Government Printing Office, 1969) V, p. 1039.

27. Mallet to Bevin, 3 December 1945, TNA FO 371/49629, Z13504/1484/G41.

28. 'Informe Económico Octubre de 1946', Archivo Acción Republicana Democrática Española, Fundación Universitario Español, ARDE, Ind. 1-2. I am grateful to Ricardo Robledo for this information.

29. Garriga, De la División Azul, pp. 415-16.

30. Francisco Moreno Gómez, La resistencia armada contra Franco. Tragedia del maquis y la guerrilla (Barcelona: Crítica, 2001) pp. 471-9, 506-45, 549-51; Mercedes Yusta Rodrigo, Guerrilla y resistencia campesina. La resistencia armada contra el franquismo en Aragón (1939-1952) (Zaragoza: Prensas Universitarias de Zaragoza, 2003) pp. 169-73, 180-1; Secundino Serrano, Maquis. Historia de la guerrilla antifranquista (Madrid: Ediciones Temas de Hoy, 2001) pp. 231-9; Mundo Obrero, 11 September 1947, 5, 19 August, 30 September 1948.

31. Tusell, Franco y los católicos, p. 113.

32. Franco, Textos 1945-1950, pp. 334-5; Arriba, 5 January, 17, 19, 20 February; ABC, 5, 9 January, 22, 23 February; The Times, 11 February, 20 May 1946.

33. Mallet to Bevin, 15 February 1946, TNA FO 371/60373, Z2125/41/41; Gil Robles, La monarquía, pp. 161-9; López Rodó, La larga marcha, p. 62; Xavier Tusell, La oposición democrática al franquismo 1939-1962 (Barcelona: Planeta, 1977) pp. 114-16.

34. Torr memorandum, 20 February 1946, TNA FO 371/60373, Z1741/41/41; Alfredo Kindelán, La verdad de mis relaciones con Franco (Barcelona: Planeta, 1981) pp. 128-30, 254; Tusell, Franco y los

católicos, pp. 150-1; Suárez Fernández, Franco, IV, pp. 127-32, 153-7, 301.

35. Gregorio Morán, Miseria y grandeza del Partido Comunista de España 1939-1985 (Barcelona: Planeta, 1986) pp. 103, 107; David Wingeate Pike, Jours de gloire, jours de honte: le Parti Comuniste d'Espagne en France depuis son arrivée en 1939 jusqu'à son départ en 1950 (Paris: Société d'Édition d'Enseignement Supérieur, 1984) p. 59; Carlos Fernández Rodríguez, Madrid clandestino. La reestructuración del PCE (1939-1945) (Madrid: Fundación Domingo Malagón, 2002) pp. 370-6.

36. Hoyer Millar memorandum, 3 March 1946, TNA FO 371/60352, Z210/36/41.

37. The Times, 5 March 1946; Arthur P. Whitaker, Spain and the Defence of the West: Ally and Liability (New York: Harper & Brothers, 1961) pp. 25-7; Portero, Franco aislado, pp. 151-5.

38. Tusell, Franco y los católicos, p. 115.

39. Qasim Ahmad, Britain, Franco Spain, pp. 40-53.

40. Arriba, 8 March; ABC, 8 March 1946.

41. Arriba, 2 April 1946.

42. Arriba, 7 April 1946; Franco, Textos 1945-1950, pp. 551-2.

43. The Diaries of Edward R. Stettinius, Jr., 1943-1946 (New York: New Viewpoints, 1975) pp. 466-9; Lleonart and Castiella, España y ONU, I, pp. 81-3.

44. Franco, Textos 1945-1950, pp. 31-59; The Times, 15 May 1946.

45. United Nations, Security Council, Official Records, First Year: Second Series, Special Supplement, Report of the Sub-Committee on the Spanish Question (New York, June

1946); *FRUS 1946*, V, pp. 1072–4; Portero, *Franco aislado*, pp. 174–6.

46. Bonsal to Byrnes, *FRUS 1946*, V, pp. 1075–7; Lleonart and Castiella, *España y ONU*, I, pp. 104–20, 130–96.

47. Agustín del Río Cisneros, *Política internacional de España. El caso español en la ONU y en el mundo* (Madrid: Ediciones del Movimiento, 1946) *passim*.

48. Tusell, *Franco y los católicos*, p. 153.

49. *Ibid.*, p.116.

50. *Arriba*, 1, 2 October; *ABC*, 1, 2 October; *La Vanguardia Española*, 1, 2 October; *The Times*, 2 October 1946.

51. Lleonart and Castiella, *España y ONU*, I, pp. 215, 240–94; *Arriba*, 14 November 1946; *FRUS 1946*, V, pp. 1080–2.

52. *Arriba*, 30 November 1946; Tusell, *Franco y los católicos*, p. 154.

53. *Arriba*, 10 December; *La Vanguardia Española*, 10 December 1946.

54. *ABC*, 10, 11, 12, 13 December 1946; Lleonart and Castiella, *España y ONU*, I, pp. 310–89.

55. *The Times*, 17 December 1946; Garriga, *De la División Azul*, p. 469.

56. José María Pemán, *Mis encuentros con Franco* (Barcelona: Dopesa, 1976) pp. 118–19.

57. Jakim Boor (pseudonym of Francisco Franco Bahamonde), *Masonería* (Madrid: Gráficas Valera, 1952) p. 96.

58. *Arriba*, 14 December 1946; Boor, *Masonería*, pp. 8–9.

59. Francisco Franco Salgado-Araujo, *Mis conversaciones privadas con Franco* (Barcelona: Planeta, 1976) pp. 239, 366; Suárez Fernández, *Franco*, III, pp. 323–4, 394; Javier Domínguez Arribas, *El enemigo judeo-masónico en la propaganda*

franquista (1936–1945) (Madrid: Marcial Pons Historia, 2009) pp. 123–52.

60. López Rodó, *La larga marcha*, pp. 73, 529–32; Gil Robles, *La monarquía*, pp. 138, 173–4.

61. Gil Robles, *La monarquía*, p. 173.

62. Garriga, *De la División Azul*, pp. 472–4.

63. Portero, *Franco aislado*, p. 182.

64. Kenneth O. Morgan, *Labour in Power 1945–1951* (Oxford: Clarendon Press, 1984) pp. 251–3; Dean Acheson, *Present at the Creation: My Years in the State Department* (New York: Norton, 1969) pp. 294–301; Herbert Feis, *From Trust to Terror: The Onset of the Cold War 1945–1950* (London: Anthony Blond, 1970) pp. 191–8.

65. López Rodó, *La larga marcha*, pp. 75–89, 89–99; Gil Robles, *La monarquía*, pp. 206–14, 388–93; Tusell, *La oposición democrática*, pp. 161–9; Tusell, *Franco y los católicos*, pp. 161–2.

66. *FRUS 1947* (Washington, DC: US Government Printing Office, 1972) III, pp. 1066–80; Qasim Ahmad, *Britain, Franco Spain*, pp. 163–4; Bevin to Sargent, 25 April 1947, TNA FO 371/67868, Z4093/3/41.

67. *Mundo Obrero*, 8 May; *El Socialista*, 16 May 1947; José María Lorenzo Espinosa, *Rebelión en la Ría. Vizcaya 1947: obreros, empresarios y falangistas* (Bilbao: Universidad de Deusto, 1988) pp. 17–69.

68. Juan Carlos Jiménez de Aberasturi and Koldo San Sebastián, *La huelga general del 1º de mayo de 1947 (artículos y documentos)* (San Sebastián: Eusko Ikaskuntza, 1991) pp. 48–61.

69. *Le Monde*, 9 May 1947.

70. Ángel Viñas, *Guerra, dinero, dictadura. Ayuda fascista y autarquía en la España de Franco*

(Barcelona: Crítica, 1984) pp. 265–87; A. J. Lleonart y Anselem, *España y ONU*, Vol. II: *1947* (Madrid: Consejo Superior de Investigaciones Científicas, 1983) p. 117.

71. *Arriba*, 1 November 1946, 14 January; *ABC*, 14, 15, 16, 17 January 1947.

72. *Arriba*, 9, 10 June; *ABC*, 10 June; *The Times*, 9 June; *Observer*, 13 June 1947; Ramón Garriga, *La Señora de El Pardo* (Barcelona: Planeta, 1979) pp. 211–12.

73. José María de Areilza, *Memorias exteriores 1947–1964* (Barcelona: Planeta, 1984) p. 28.

74. Whitaker, *Spain*, p. 25; Areilza, *Memorias*, pp. 216–18.

75. *Ya*, 6 July; *Arriba*, 5, 6 July 1947.

76. Tusell, *Franco y los católicos*, pp. 163–5; Stanley G. Payne, *The Franco Regime 1936–1975* (Madison: Wisconsin University Press, 1987) p. 375; J. W. D. Trythall, *Franco* (London: Hart-Davis, 1970) pp. 203–6.

77. *FRUS 1947*, III, pp. 1084–7; FO to British Embassy (Washington), TNA FO 371/67869, Z7004/3/41.

78. *FRUS 1947*, III, pp. 1091–5; Walter Millis, ed., *The Forrestal Diaries* (New York: Viking Press, 1951) p. 328; Walter LaFeber, *America, Russia and the Cold War 1945–1975*, 3rd edn (New York: Wiley, 1976) pp. 66–7.

79. *FRUS 1947*, III, pp. 1096–7; Lleonart, *España y ONU*, II, pp. 230–313; Suárez Fernández, *Franco*, IV, pp. 212–14, 226; Franco, *Textos, 1945–1950*, pp. 111–14.

80. S. F. A. Coles, *Franco of Spain* (London: Neville Spearman, 1955) p. 63; Francisco Franco Salgado-Araujo, *Mi vida junto a Franco* (Barcelona: Planeta, 1977) p. 319.

81. *La Vanguardia Española*, 31 March; *The Times*, 1, 2 April 1948; Portero, *Franco aislado*, pp. 309–13; Suárez Fernández, *Franco*, IV, pp. 239–40.

82. Tusell, *La oposición democrática*, pp. 197–202; Suárez Fernández, *Franco*, IV, pp. 249–51

83. Gil Robles, *La monarquía*, pp. 265–73; Pedro Sainz Rodríguez, *Un reinado en la sombra* (Barcelona: Planeta, 1981) pp. 220–2; *FRUS 1948* (Washington, DC: US Government Printing Office, 1974) III, pp. 1050–1, 1059–63; *FRUS 1949* (Washington, DC: US Government Printing Office, 1975) IV, p. 755; Ramón de Alderete, ... *y estos borbones nos quieren gobernar* (Paris: Ruedo Ibérico, 1974) pp. 56–8; *The Times*, 28, 29 August 1948.

84. Gil Robles, *La monarquía*, pp. 272–5.

85. Tusell, *La oposición democrática*, pp. 203–5.

86. *ABC*, 10 November 1948; Gil Robles, *La monarquía*, pp. 276–81, 286.

87. Gil Robles, *La monarquía*, pp. 298–301.

88. María Jesús Cava Mesa, *Los diplomáticos de Franco. J. F. de Lequerica, temple y tenacidad (1890–1963)* (Bilbao: Universidad de Deusto, 1989) pp. 265–310; Theodore J. Lowi, 'Bases in Spain', in Harold Stein, ed., *American Civil–Military Decisions: A Book of Case Studies* (Birmingham, Ala.: University of Alabama Press, 1963) pp. 675–6; R. Richard Rubottom and J. Carter Murphy, *Spain and the United States since World War II* (New York: Praeger, 1984) pp. 10–11; Viñas, *Guerra, dictadura, dinero*, pp. 284–7; Whitaker, *Spain*, pp. 32–4.

89. Johnston to FO, 2 October 1948, TNA FO 371/73337, Z7957/84/41.
90. *Arriba*, 2 October; *ABC*, 2 October 1948; Suárez Fernández, *Franco*, IV, pp. 266–9.
91. *FRUS 1948*, III, pp. 1053–4; Suárez Fernández, *Franco*, IV, pp. 273–5.
92. *FRUS 1948*, III, p. 1063.
93. Moisés Llordén Miñambres, 'La política de vivienda del régimen franquista: nacimiento y despegue de los grandes constructores y promotores inmobiliarios en España, 1939–1960', in Glicerio Sánchez Recio and Julio Tascón Fernández, eds, *Los empresarios de Franco. Política y economía en España, 1936–1957* (Barcelona: Crítica, 2003) p. 149.
94. Bartolomé Barba Hernández, *Dos años al frente del Gobierno Civil de Barcelona y varios ensayos* (Madrid: Javier Morata, 1948) pp. 45–50; Rafael Abella, *Por el Imperio hacia Dios. Crónica de una posguerra (1939–1950)* (Barcelona: Planeta, 1978) pp. 101–32.
95. Portero, *Franco aislado*, pp. 316–17; *Daily Telegraph*, 1 February 1949; Franco, *Textos, 1945–1950*, pp. 277–81.
96. *FRUS 1949*, IV, pp. 729–30; Hankey to Bevin, 'Spain: Annual Report for 1949', 27 January 1950, TNA FO 371/89479, WS1011/1.
97. Whitaker, *Spain*, pp. 34–5; Gil Robles, *La monarquía*, pp. 291–2.
98. Whitaker, *Spain*, pp. 36–7.
99. *FRUS 1949*, IV, pp. 721–4, 730–5, 742–3; A. J. Lleonart y Anselem, *España y ONU*, Vol. III: *1948–1949: La 'cuestión española'* (Madrid: Consejo Superior de Investigaciones Científicas, 1985) pp. 54–8, 148–372.
100. Franco, *Textos, 1945–1950*, pp. 147–73.

101. Mercedes Cabrera, *Juan March (1880–1962)* (Madrid: Marcial Pons, 2011) pp. 347–92; Arturo Dixon, *Señor Monopolio. La asombrosa vida de Juan March* (Barcelona: Planeta, 1985) pp. 178–99; Ramón Garriga, *Los validos de Franco* (Barcelona: Planeta, 1981), pp. 198–202; Ramón Garriga, *Juan March y su tiempo* (Barcelona: Planeta, 1976) pp. 384, 388–94; Fabián Estapé, *Sin acuse de recibo* (Barcelona: Plaza y Janés, 2000) pp. 122–4, 202; Bernardo Díaz Nosty, *La irresistible ascensión de Juan March* (Madrid: Sedmay Ediciones, 1977) pp. 366–80; Pere Ferrer, *Juan March. El hombre más misterioso del mundo* (Barcelona: Ediciones B, 2008) pp. 415–27.
102. José Larraz, *Memorias* (Madrid: Real Academia de Ciencias Morales y Políticas, 2006) pp. 530–1.
103. Ramón Serrano Suñer, *Entre el silencio y la propaganda, la Historia como fue. Memorias* (Barcelona: Planeta, 1977) pp. 379–88.
104. Gil Robles, diary entries for 25, 26 September 1949, *La monarquía*, pp. 304–6.
105. *FRUS 1949*, IV, p. 761.
106. Benjamin Welles, *Spain: The Gentle Anarchy* (London: Pall Mall, 1965) pp. 286–7; Lowi, 'Bases', p. 692.
107. Cava Mesa, *Lequerica*, pp. 310–12; Lowi, 'Bases', pp. 677–80; Whitaker, *Spain*, pp. 23, 36–7; Viñas, *Los pactos*, pp. 43–4; Suárez Fernández, *Franco*, IV, pp. 366–7; Garriga, *De la División Azul*, pp. 548–9, 563–7.
108. *The Times*, 22, 24, 25, 28 October; *Arriba*, 22, 23, 25, 26, 27 October 1949; Gil Robles, *La monarquía*, pp. 308–12; Franco Salgado-Araujo, *Mi vida*, pp. 327–8.
109. Gil Robles, *La monarquía*, pp. 318–19.

110. Lowi, 'Bases', p. 683.

111. *FRUS 1950* (Washington, DC: US Government Printing Office, 1977) III, pp. 1549–55; Franks to FO, 19 January 1950, TNA FO 371/89496, WS10345/3, WS10345/4; Hoyer Millar to Bevin, 13 February 1950, FO 371/89496, WS10345/13.

112. Hankey to Shuckburgh, 25 January 1950, TNA FO 371/89496, WS10345/9; *Arriba*, 24, 25 January 1950.

113. Fernando Guirao, 'Spain and the "Green Pool": Challenge and Response, 1950 to 1955', in Richard T. Griffiths and Brian Girvin, eds, *The Green Pool and the Origins of the Common Agricultural Policy* (London: Lothian Press, 1995) pp. 261–87.

114. Indalecio Prieto, *Convulsiones de España. Pequeños detalles de grandes sucesos*, 3 vols (Mexico City: Oasis, 1967–9) I, pp. 307–8.

115. Mariano Sánchez Soler, *Villaverde. Fortuna y caída de la casa Franco* (Barcelona: Planeta, 1990) pp. 36–7, 52–3.

116. Madrid Embassy to FO, 16 April 1950, TNA FO 371/89487, WS1021/15.

117. *La Vanguardia Española*, 11, 12 April; *Arriba*, 11, 14 April; *ABC*, 11, 12 April 1950; Garriga, *La Señora*, pp. 222–4.

118. Garriga, *La Señora*, pp. 224–7, 243–4; Sánchez Soler, *Villaverde*, pp. 56–70, 76, 110–16; Jaume Claret, *Ganar la Guerra, perder la paz. Memorias del general Latorre Roca* (Barcelona: Crítica, 2019) p. 288.

119. Carlos Collado Seidel, *España, refugio nazi* (Madrid: Ediciones Temas de Hoy, 2005) pp. 184–5, 203–4.

120. Franco Salgado-Araujo, *Mis conversaciones*, pp. 9, 17–18, 189; Pilar Franco Bahamonde, *Nosotros*

los Franco (Barcelona: Planeta, 1980) pp. 144–6, 215–20; Mariano Sánchez Soler, *Ricos por la guerra civil de España* (Madrid: Raíces, 2007) pp. 66–7; Andrés Martínez-Bordiu Ortega, *Franco en familia. Cacerías en Jaén* (Barcelona: Planeta, 1994) pp. 26–8; Julián Lago, *Las contra-memorias de Franco* (Barcelona: Zeta, 1976) pp. 63–73.

121. Ángel Viñas, 'Hambre, corrupción y sobornos en el primer Franquismo (1939–1959)', in Borja de Riquer, Joan Lluís Pérez Francesch, Gemma Rubí, Lluís Ferran Toledano y Oriol Luján, eds, *La corrupción política en la España contemporánea* (Madrid: Marcial Pons Historia, 2018) pp. 165–7.

122. Sánchez Soler, *Villaverde*, pp. 39–51, 92–4, 122–4, 127, 131–9; Jaime Peñafiel, *El General y su tropa. Mis recuerdos de la familia Franco* (Madrid: Temas de Hoy, 1992) p. 149.

123. Javier Otero, 'El patrimonio oculto de Francisco Franco', *Tiempo*, 11 June 2010; Carlos Babío Urkidi and Manuel Pérez Lorenzo, *Meirás. Un pazo, un caudillo, un espolio* (A Coruña: Fundación Galiza Sempre, 2017) pp. 271–5.

124. Ramón Garriga, *Franco-Serrano Suñer. Un drama político* (Barcelona: Planeta, 1986) p. 179.

125. Franco Salgado-Araujo, *Mis conversaciones*, pp. 174, 195; Peñafiel, *El General y su tropa*, pp. 140–1; José Antonio Vaca de Osma, *Paisajes con Franco al fondo* (Barcelona: Plaza y Janés, 1987) p. 189; Pilar Jaraiz Franco, *Historia de una disidencia* (Barcelona: Planeta, 1981) p. 41.

126. Garriga, *La Señora*, pp. 225–7; Suárez Fernández, *Franco*, IV, pp. 271–3.

127. Franco Salgado-Araujo, *Mis conversaciones*, pp. 189, 195; Franco, *Nosotros*, p. 237.

128. Sánchez Soler, *Ricos*, pp. 108–11; Jaime Sánchez-Blanco, *La importancia de llamarse Franco. El negocio inmobiliario de doña Pilar* (Madrid: Edicusa, 1978) pp. 13–16, 21–49, 108–20, 139–58, 172–98, 243–84, 294–323, 337–41, 365–97.

129. On Hoffman, see Collado Seidel, *España, refugio nazi*, pp. 130, 312–15; Klaus-Jörg Ruhl, *Franco, Falange y III Reich* (Madrid: Akal, 1986) p. 208; José María Irujo, 'Un presunto nazi es el cónsul general de Alemania en Málaga desde 1974', *El País*, 1 April 1997; José Antonio Girón de Velasco, 'La casa de Girón legalmente edificada', *El País*, 31 October 1976; José Luis de Arrese, *Una etapa constituyente* (Barcelona: Planeta, 1982) pp. 59, 87, 92; Sánchez Soler, *Ricos*, pp. 143–8.

130. Mariano Sánchez Soler, *Los banqueros de Franco* (Madrid: Oberon, 2005) pp. 143–9; Víctor Mellado and Vicente Granados, eds, *Historia de la Costa del Sol* (Málaga: Prensa Malagueña, n.d.) pp. 115–16.

131. Sánchez Soler, *Ricos*, pp. 247–8; Rafael Porras, 'Franco y el "skyline" de Marbella', *El Mundo*, 8 December 2013.

132. *FRUS 1950*, III, pp. 1557–60; Suárez Fernández, *Franco*, IV, pp. 408–9.

133. Viñas, *Los pactos*, p. 59; Jakim Boor, *Masonería*, pp. 121–9, 137–41; Suárez Fernández, *Franco*, IV, pp. 431–3.

134. David Caute, *The Great Fear: The Anti-Communist Purge under Truman and Eisenhower* (London: Secker & Warburg, 1978) pp. 58–69, 566–7.

135. Memorandum of Chairman of the Joint Chiefs of Staff to the Secretary of Defense, 3 May, Truman to Acheson, 16 June 1950, *FRUS 1950*, III, pp. 1560–2.

136. Younger to Bevin, 3 August, TNA FO 371/89502, WS1031/39; W. I. Mallet to Bevin, 2 August, FO 371/89502, WS1051/39; W. I. Mallet to Hankey, 11 September 1950, FO 371/89503, WS1051/63.

137. Burrows (Washington) to Young, 4 September 1950, TNA FO 371/89503, WS1051/58.

138. A. J. Lleonart y Anselem, *España y ONU*, Vol. IV: *1950: La 'cuestión española'* (Madrid: Consejo Superior de Investigaciones Científicas, 1991) pp. 269–310; Qasim Ahmad, *Britain, Franco Spain*, pp. 197–8; *Arriba*, 5 November 1950.

139. *ABC*, 7 November 1950.

140. *FRUS 1950*, III, pp. 1573–4; Franks to FO, 18 November 1950, TNA FO 371/89507, WS1051/129.

141. Viñas, *Los pactos*, pp. 59–60; Garriga, *De la División Azul*, pp. 577–85.

142. Lequerica to Franco, 25 October 1950, Suárez Fernández, *Franco*, IV, pp. 440–1.

143. Suárez Fernández, *Franco*, IV, p. 413.

144. Francisco Franco, *Discursos y mensajes del Jefe del Estado 1951–1954* (Madrid: Publicaciones Españolas, 1955) pp. 33–7; Trythall, *Franco*, p. 211.

145. Randolph Bernard Jones, 'The Spanish Question and the Cold War 1944–1953', unpublished PhD thesis, University of London, 1987, pp. 195–211, 215–26.

146. Hankey to Young, 20 December 1950, TNA FO 371/89509, WS1051/170; Sebastian Balfour, *Dictatorship, Workers, and the City: Labour in Greater Barcelona since 1939* (Oxford: Clarendon Press, 1989) pp. 20–2.

147. Franco, *Discursos 1951–1954*, pp. 43–8.
148. *La Vanguardia Española*, 3 March 1951; Félix Fanés, *La vaga de tramvies del 1951* (Barcelona: Editorial Laia, 1977) pp. 28–33, 48–51.
149. *La Vanguardia Española*, 13, 14 March 1951; Fanés, *La vaga*, pp. 59–157; Gregorio López Raimundo, *Primera clandestinidad: segunda parte* (Barcelona: Editorial Antártida/Empúries, 1995) pp. 208–27; Balfour, *Dictatorship*, pp. 22–30; Michael Richards, 'Falange, Autarky and Crisis: The Barcelona General Strike of 1951', *European History Quarterly*, October 1999, pp. 543–85.
150. Garriga, *De la División Azul*, pp. 595–600.
151. Balfour to Morrison, 23 May 1951, TNA FO 371/96158, WS1016/56/51.
152. Franco, *Discursos 1951–1954*, pp. 50–1, 57; *Arriba*, 13, 15, 19 May 1951.
153. Stanton Griffis, *Lying in State* (New York: Doubleday, 1952) pp. 269–70, 287–9; Balfour to Young, 28 March 1951, TNA FO 371/96183, WS1071/36; Viñas, *Los pactos*, pp. 73–9.
154. López Rodó, *La larga marcha*, pp. 112–13, 550–4; Pemán, diary entry for 20 January 1951, quoted by Tusell, *Franco y los católicos*, p. 287.
155. Viñas, *Los pactos*, pp. 87–91; FO to Washington, 7 July, Francks to FO, 12 July 1951, TNA FO 371/96185, WS1071/69G and WS1071/71.
156. Welles, *Gentle Anarchy*, p. 287; Lowi, 'Bases', p. 692; Antonio Marquina Barrio, *España en la política de seguridad occidental 1939–1986* (Madrid: Ediciones Ejército, 1986) pp. 420–2; Viñas,

Los pactos, pp. 92–4; Boris N. Liedtke, *Embracing a Dictatorship: US Relations with Spain, 1945–53* (London: Macmillan, 1998) pp. 119–28.
157. *ABC*, 17 July; *The Times*, 19 July 1951; Viñas, *Los pactos*, pp. 95–102; Griffis, *Lying in State*, pp. 294–5; Marquina, *España*, pp. 422–4; Lowi, 'Bases', pp. 692–5; Cava Mesa, *Lequerica*, pp. 323–5.
158. Equipo Mundo, *Los 90 ministros de Franco* (Barcelona: Dopesa, 1970) pp. 203–46; Garriga, *De la División Azul*, pp. 624–9.
159. Ángel Viñas, Julio Viñuela, Fernando Eguidazu, Carlos Fernández Pulgar and Senen Florensa, *Política comercial exterior en España (1931–1975)*, 2 vols (Madrid: Banco Exterior de España, 1979) I, pp. 635–9, 671–2.
160. Balfour to Eden, 10 July 1952, Steel to Cheetham, 22 August, Murray to Cheetham, 28 August 1952, TNA FO 371/1020222, WS1102/21, WS1102/24G, WS1102/25; Viñas, *Los pactos*, pp. 120–1, 177; Franco Salgado-Araujo, *Mis conversaciones*, p. 56.
161. Balfour to Eden, 29 May 1952, TNA FO 371/102000, WS1015/2; Franco, *Discursos 1951–1954*, p. 173.
162. Lowi, 'Bases', pp. 696–7; Makins (Washington) to Eden, 18 February 1953, TNA FO 371/107687, WS1073/1; Viñas, *Los pactos*, pp. 165–9, 183–93, 252; Marquina, *España*, pp. 498–554.
163. Balfour to Cheetham, 29 April, 24 May, 31 July; Bellotti to FO, 26 June; Balfour to Young, 11 December 1953; Young memorandum, 8 December, Harrison to Minister of State, 17 December, Balfour memorandum, 17 December 1953, TNA FO 371/107682, WS1051/9,

WS1051/19WS1051/24, WS1051/38; FO 371/107686, WS10/2/6; FO 371/107690, WS1081/50; Franco, *Discursos 1951–1954*, pp. 360–4.

164. Balfour to Eden, 21 March 1953, FO 371/107731, WS1782/2; Tusell, *Franco y los católicos*, pp. 258–82; Guy Hermet, *Les Catholiques dans l'Espagne Franquiste*, 2 vols (Paris: Presses de la Fondation Nationale des Sciences Politiques, 1980–1) II, pp. 204–18; José Ángel Tello, *Ideología y política. La Iglesia católica española (1936–1959)* (Zaragoza: Libros Pórtico, 1984) pp. 111–16.

165. José Chao Rego, *La Iglesia en el franquismo* (Madrid: Ediciones Felmar, 1976) pp. 93–102; Norman B. Cooper, *Catholicism and the Franco Regime* (Beverly Hills Calif.: Sage, 1975) pp. 16–18; Rafael Gómez Pérez, *El franquismo y la Iglesia* (Madrid: Rialp, 1986) pp. 66–70; Feliciano Blázquez, *La traición de los clérigos en la España de Franco. Crónica de una intolerancia (1936–1975)* (Madrid: Editorial Trotta, 1991) pp. 103–5.

166. Lowi, 'Bases', pp. 696–7; Viñas, *Los pactos*, pp. 165–9, 183–93, 252; Liedtke, *Embracing a Dictatorship*, pp. 204–13; Arturo Jarque Iñiguez, *'Queremos esas bases'. El acercamiento de Estados Unidos a la España de Franco* (Alcalá de Henares: Universidad de Alcalá, 1998) pp. 351–63.

167. Hood minute, 5 November 1953, TNA FO 371/107686, WS1072/43; Viñas, *Los pactos*, pp. 195–202, 313–14; Ángel Viñas, *En las garras del águila. Los pactos con Estados Unidos, de Francisco Franco a Felipe González (1945–1995)* (Barcelona: Crítica, 2003) pp. 243–68.

168. José María de Areilza, *Diario de un ministro de la Monarquía* (Barcelona: Planeta, 1977) p. 45.

169. *ABC*, 27, 29, 30 September; *Arriba*, 27, 29, 30 September 1953.

170. Viñas, *Los pactos*, pp. 181–2, 203–50, 292; Lowi, 'Bases', pp. 697–8.

171. Viñas, *Los pactos*, pp. 261–75; Viñas et al., *Política comercial exterior*, I, pp. 497–501, 532–45.

172. Franco, *Discursos 1951–1954*, pp. 376–84; *La Vanguardia Española*, 1 October; *Arriba*, 1 October; *The Times*, 1 October 1953; Viñas, *Los pactos*, pp. 299–301.

173. *ABC*, 27, 30 September 1953; *Arriba*, 27, 29 September; Viñas, *Los pactos*, pp. 277–84.

174. *The Times*, 30 October 1953; Jean Créac'h, *Le cœur et l'épée: chroniques espagnoles* (Paris: Librairie Plon, 1958) pp. 319–20; Franco, *Discursos 1951–1954*, pp. 414–15.

Chapter 14: The Franco Regime: Corruption and Complacency, 1953–1969

1. Mariano Sánchez Soler, *Villaverde. Fortuna y caída de la casa Franco* (Barcelona: Planeta, 1990) pp. 63–8; Francisco Franco Salgado-Araujo, *Mis conversaciones privadas con Franco* (Barcelona: Planeta, 1976) pp. 9, 90–2, 111, 132.

2. Daniel Sueiro, *El Valle de los Caídos. Los secretos de la cripta franquista*, 2nd edn (Barcelona: Argos Vergara, 1983) pp. 123–43.

3. Gil Robles, diary entries for 13 May, 21, 22 June, 25 July, 7 September 1954; Don Juan to Franco, 16 July, Franco to Don Juan 17, 20 July 1954; José María Gil Robles, *La monarquía por la que yo luché. Páginas de un diario 1941–1954)*

(Madrid: Taurus, 1976) pp. 327–8, 411–18; Laureano López Rodó, *La larga marcha hacia la monarquía* (Barcelona: Noguer, 1977) pp. 115–17, 554–5.

4. Rafael Calvo Serer, *Franco frente al Rey. El proceso del régimen* (Paris: Autor/Ruedo Ibérico, 1972) pp. 29–30; Jean Créac'h, *Le cœur et l'épée: chroniques espagnoles* (Paris: Librairie Plon, 1958), pp. 317–18.

5. *ABC,* 20 October 1954; Créac'h, *Le cœur,* pp. 332–7; Luis Suárez Fernández, *Francisco Franco y su tiempo,* 8 vols (Madrid: Fundación Nacional Francisco Franco, 1984) V, p. 157; Franco Salgado-Araujo, *Mis conversaciones,* pp. 18, 23.

6. *Arriba,* 23 November 1954; Calvo Serer, *Franco frente al Rey,* pp. 29–30; Franco Salgado-Araujo, *Mis conversaciones,* p. 30; López Rodó, *La larga marcha,* p. 117; Créac'h, *Le cœur,* pp. 338–9; José María Toquero, *Franco y Don Juan. La oposición monárquica al franquismo* (Barcelona: Plaza y Janés, 1989) pp. 253–5.

7. Créac'h, *Le cœur,* pp. 339–40; Suárez Fernández, *Franco,* V, p. 159.

8. Franco to Don Juan, 2 December 1954, Pedro Sainz Rodríguez, *Un reinado en la sombra* (Barcelona: Planeta, 1981), pp. 383–4.

9. Mallet to Eden, 11 January 1955, TNA FO 371/117914, RS1942/4; Stirling to Macmillan, 19 April 1955, FO 371/117914, RS1942/15; Sainz Rodríguez, *Un reinado,* pp. 222–35; Créac'h, *Le cœur,* pp. 341–5; Franco Salgado-Araujo, *Mis conversaciones,* pp. 59–64; José María Pemán, *Mis encuentros con Franco* (Barcelona: Dopesa, 1976) p. 232; Xavier Tusell, *La oposición democrática al franquismo 1939–1962* (Barcelona: Planeta, 1977) pp. 235–6.

10. Francisco Franco, *Discursos y mensajes del Jefe del Estado 1951–1954* (Madrid: Publicaciones Españolas, 1955) pp. 551–3; *Arriba,* 23, 27 January; *ABC,* 1 March 1955; Mallet to Eden, 26 January 1955, TNA FO 371/117914, RS1942/6.

11. *Arriba,* 20 June 1955; Mallet to Macmillan, 5 July 1955, TNA FO 371/117914, RS1942/21.

12. *ABC,* 24 June 1955; Stirling to Macmillan, 26 July 1955; Balfour memorandum, 7 September 1955, TNA FO 371/117914, RS1942/25, RS1942/27; Créac'h, *Le cœur,* pp. 353–4.

13. Mary Vincent, *Spain 1833–2002: People and State* (Oxford: Oxford University Press, 2007) pp. 161–9; Antonio Cazorla Sánchez, *Las políticas de la victoria. La consolidación del Nuevo Estado franquista (1938–1953)* (Madrid: Marcial Pons, 2000) pp. 43–60, 98–110; Raymond Carr and Juan Pablo Fusi, *Spain: Dictatorship to Democracy* (London: Allen & Unwin, 1979) pp. 47–8.

14. Francisco Salva Miquel and Juan Vicente, *Francisco Franco (historia de un español)* (Barcelona: Ediciones Generales, 1959) pp. 293–7; Franco Salgado-Araujo, *Mis conversaciones,* pp. 84–5.

15. Franco Salgado-Araujo, *Mis conversaciones,* pp. 23, 32–3, 71–2; Carlos Rein Segura interview in Ángel Bayod, ed., *Franco visto por sus ministros* (Barcelona: Planeta, 1981) p. 78.

16. Franco Salgado-Araujo, *Mis conversaciones,* pp. 32–3, 36–7, 126; Ramón Garriga, *La Señora de El Pardo* (Barcelona: Planeta, 1979) pp. 249–53; Jaime Peñafiel, *El General y su tropa. Mis recuerdos de la familia Franco* (Madrid: Temas de Hoy, 1992) pp. 61–6.

17. *The Times*, 5 April 1956; Miguel Martín, *El colonialismo español en Marruecos (1860–1956)* (Paris: Ruedo Ibérico, 1973) pp. 227–39; Suárez Fernández, *Franco*, V, pp. 193–205; Ricardo de la Cierva, *Historia del franquismo*, Vol. II: *Aislamiento, transformación, agonía (1945–1975)* (Barcelona: Planeta, 1978) pp. 138, 146; Franco Salgado-Araujo, *Mis conversaciones*, pp. 170–3.

18. Chancery (Madrid) to Southern Department, 18 February 1955, TNA FO 371/117914, RS1942/10.

19. Calvo Serer, *Franco frente al Rey*, p. 14; Franco Salgado-Araujo, *Mis conversaciones*, pp. 146–7; Creac'h, *Le cœur*, p. 358.

20. Pedro Laín Entralgo, *Descargo de conciencia* (Barcelona: Barral Editores, 1976) pp. 414–18; Creac'h, *Le cœur*, pp. 359–60. The reports are printed in Roberto Mesa, ed., *Jaraneros y alborotadores. Documentos sobre los sucesos estudiantiles de febrero de 1956 en la Universidad Complutense de Madrid* (Madrid: Editorial de la Universidad Complutense, 1982) pp. 45–53, 58–64.

21. Washington Chancery to Madrid Chancery, 14 January 1956, TNA FO 371/124127, RS1015/4; Francisco Franco, *Discursos y mensajes del Jefe del Estado 1955–1959* (Madrid: Publicaciones Españolas, 1960) p. 136.

22. Mallet to Macmillan, 10 January, Mallet to Lloyd, 17 January 1956, TNA FO 371/124127, RS1015/2, RS1015/3, RS1015/6.

23. Mesa, ed., *Jaraneros*, pp. 109–12; Laín Entralgo, *Descargo*, pp. 418–23; Pablo Lizcano, *La generación del 56. La Universidad contra Franco* (Barcelona: Grijalbo, 1981) p. 142; Franco Salgado

Araujo, *Mis conversaciones*, pp. 163–4; Javier Tusell, *Franco y los católicos. La política interior española entre 1945 y 1957* (Madrid: Alianza Editorial, 1984) p. 382; Francisco Franco Salgado-Araujo, *Mi vida junto a Franco* (Barcelona: Planeta, 1977) p. 343; Creac'h, *Le cœur*, pp. 362–3.

24. Pilcher to Young, 12 October 1956, TNA FO 371/124128, RS1015/43; Stanley G. Payne, *Politics and the Military in Modern Spain* (Stanford, Calif.: Stanford University Press, 1967) p. 443.

25. *Arriba*, 9, 10 February; Mallet to Lloyd, 11 February 1956, TNA FO 371/124127, RS1015/12.

26. Testimony to the author of Rafael Calvo Serer, London 1976; Creac'h, *Le cœur*, pp. 364–5.

27. Creac'h, *Le cœur*, pp. 364–5; Tusell, *Franco y los católicos*, pp. 382–3; Franco Salgado-Araujo, *Mi vida*, p. 343; Franco Salgado-Araujo, *Mis conversaciones*, p. 159.

28. Tusell, *Franco y los Católicos*, pp. 383–4; Raimundo Fernández Cuesta, *Testimonio, recuerdos y reflexiones* (Madrid: Ediciones Dyrsa, 1985) pp. 241–5; José Luis de Arrese, *Una etapa constituyente* (Barcelona: Planeta, 1982) pp. 16–22; Equipo Mundo, *Los 90 Ministros de Franco* (Barcelona: Dopesa, 1970) pp. 249–53.

29. Mallet to Lloyd, 17, 18 February 1956, TNA FO 371/124127, RS1015/13, RS1015/14.

30. Madrid Chancery to Southern Department, 24 February 1956, TNA FO 371/124127, RS1015/18.

31. Pilar Franco Bahamonde, *Nosotros los Franco* (Barcelona: Planeta, 1980) pp. 147–8.

32. Madrid Chancery to Southern Department, 10 March 1956, TNA FO 371/124127, RS1015/21; Franco

Salgado-Araujo, *Mis conversaciones*, p. 166; Arrese, *Una etapa*, pp. 34–8; Suárez Fernández, *Franco*, V, pp. 264–5; *Arriba*, 6 March 1956.

33. Arrese, *Una etapa*, pp. 32–3.

34. Mallet to Lloyd, 29 May 1956, TNA FO 371/124128, RS1015/30; Llibert Ferri, Jordi Muixí and Eduardo Sanjuan, *Las huelgas contra Franco (1939–1956)* (Barcelona: Planeta, 1978) pp. 226–38; Faustino Miguélez, *La lucha de los mineros asturianos bajo el franquismo* (Barcelona: Editorial Laia, 1976) pp. 94–5.

35. Sainz Rodríguez, *Un reinado*, p. 163; Suárez Fernández, *Franco*, V, pp. 153, 266.

36. Arrese, *Una etapa*, pp. 42–5; Franco, *Discursos 1955–1959*, pp. 158–9, 163–5, 181–90; Madrid Chancery to Southern Department, 5 May 1954, TNA FO 371/124128, RS1015/23.

37. Arrese, *Una etapa*, pp. 44–8, 64, 66, 86–93.

38. Mallet to Young, 21 June 1956, TNA FO 371/124128, RS1015/34.

39. Laureano López Rodó, *Memorias* (Barcelona: Plaza y Janés, 1990) pp. 51–2; López Rodó, *La larga marcha*, pp. 124–30; Arrese, *Una etapa*, pp. 71, 80.

40. Arrese, *Una etapa*, p. 81; López Rodó, *Memorias*, pp. 58–9.

41. Payne, *Politics and the Military*, pp. 443; Arthur P. Whitaker, *Spain and the Defence of the West: Ally and Liability* (New York: Harper & Brothers, 1961) pp. 141–2.

42. Arrese, *Una etapa*, pp. 82–3.

43. *Ibid.*, pp. 98–104.

44. Franco, *Discursos 1955–1959*, pp. 214–15; Mallet to Lloyd, 20 July 1956, TNA FO 371/124128, RS1015/39A.

45. Suárez Fernández, *Franco*, V, p. 293.

46. Garriga, *La Señora*, p. 11.

47. Franco Salgado-Araujo, *Mis conversaciones*, pp. 174–9.

48. *The Times*, 1 October 1956; Franco, *Discursos 1955–1959*, pp. 233–8; Arrese, *Una etapa*, pp. 124–31; Madrid Chancery to Southern Department, 6 October 1956, TNA FO 371/124128, RS1015/42; López Rodó, *Memorias*, pp. 64–5; López Rodó, *La larga marcha*, pp. 132–3.

49. Arrese, *Una etapa*, pp. 132–5, 144–92; López Rodó, *Memorias*, pp. 65–77; López Rodó, *La larga marcha*, pp. 133–5; Créac'h, *Le cœur*, pp. 386–7.

50. Tusell, *Franco y los católicos*, pp. 409–25; Suárez Fernández, *Franco*, V, pp. 306–12.

51. Mallet to Lloyd, 15 January 1957, TNA FO 371/130325, RS1015/3; Arrese, *Una etapa*, pp. 234–42, 253–65; Suárez Fernández, *Franco*, V, pp. 314–15; Tusell, *Franco y los católicos*, pp. 426–8.

52. López Rodó, *Memorias*, pp. 66–9; López Rodó, *La larga marcha*, pp. 120–1.

53. Franco Salgado-Araujo, *Mis conversaciones*, p. 184; Calvo Serer, *Franco frente al Rey*, p. 36; Sainz Rodríguez, *Un reinado*, p. 164; López Rodó, *La larga marcha*, pp. 123–4; Suárez Fernández, *Franco*, V, pp. 319–20; Toquero, *Franco y Don Juan*, p. 266.

54. Madrid Chancery to Southern Department, TNA FO 371/130325, RS1015/5; Créac'h, *Le cœur*, pp. 387–8.

55. Luis Ramírez, *Nuestros primeros veinticinco años* (Paris: Ruedo Ibérico, 1964) pp. 111–12; Franco Salgado-Araujo, *Mis conversaciones*, p. 200; Jaume Fabre, Josep M. Huertas and Antoni Ribas, *Vint anys de resistència catalana*

(1939-1959) (Barcelona: Edicions de La Magrana, 1978) pp. 208-11.

56. Franco Salgado Araujo, *Mis conversaciones*, pp. 176, 195-8; Suárez Fernández, *Franco*, V, pp. 269, 319; López Rodó, *La larga marcha*, p. 124; Sainz Rodríguez, *Un reinado*, p. 166.

57. Calvo Serer, *Franco frente al Rey*, p. 37; La Cierva, *Franquismo*, II, p. 155.

58. Franco Salgado Araujo, diary entry for 6 April 1957, *Mis conversaciones*, pp. 198, 209; Sainz Rodríguez, *Un reinado*, p. 166; Ramírez, *Veinticinco años*, p. 117.

59. Jaume Claret, *Ganar la Guerra, perder la paz. Memorias del general Latorre Roca* (Barcelona: Crítica, 2019) p. 204.

60. Mallet to Lloyd, 16 January 1957, TNA FO 371/130349, RS1106/1; Créac'h, *Le cœur*, pp. 369-72.

61. Franco Salgado-Araujo, *Mis conversaciones*, p. 191; Ángel Viñas, Julio Viñuela, Fernando Eguidazu, Carlos Fernández Pulgar and Senen Florensa, *Política comercial exterior en España (1931-1975)*, 2 vols (Madrid: Banco Exterior de España, 1979) I, p. 665.

62. Garriga, *La Señora*, pp. 240-2; Arrese, *Una etapa*, pp. 87-8, 282; Mariano Sánchez Soler, *Ricos por la guerra civil de España* (Madrid: Raíces, 2007) pp. 132-4; Equipo Mundo, *Los 90 Ministros*, pp. 223-6; Borja de Riquer, *La dictadura de Franco* (Barcelona/ Madrid: Crítica/Marcial Pons, 2010) pp. 401-2; Ángel Viñas, 'Hambre, corrupción y sobornos en el primer Franquismo (1939-1959)', in Borja de Riquer, Joan Lluís Pérez Francesch, Gemma Rubí, Lluís Ferran Toledano y Oriol Luján, eds, *La corrupción política en la España*

contemporánea (Madrid: Marcial Pons Historia, 2018) p. 165.

63. López Rodó, *Memorias*, pp. 89-99; Suárez Fernández, *Franco*, V, pp. 320-1.

64. Mallet to Lloyd, 1 March 1957, TNA FO 371/130325, RS1015/9; López Rodó, *Memorias*, pp. 93-4; Benjamin Welles, *Spain: The Gentle Anarchy* (London: Pall Mall, 1965) p. 127; Arrese, *Una etapa*, p. 281.

65. Arrese, *Una etapa*, pp. 275-82; López Rodó, *Memorias*, pp. 92-3.

66. Mariano Navarro Rubio, *Mis memorias. Testimonio de una vida política truncada por el Caso MATESA* (Barcelona: Plaza y Janés, 1991) pp. 64-5; Jesús Ynfante, *La prodigiosa aventura del Opus Dei. Génesis y desarrollo de la Santa Mafia* (Paris: Ruedo Ibérico, 1970) pp. 163-207, 233-5; Daniel Artigues, *El Opus Dei en España 1928-1962. Su evolución ideológica y política de los orígenes al intento de dominio* (Paris: Ruedo Ibérico, 1971) pp. 181-95.

67. Ynfante, *Santa Mafia*, pp. 177-8; López Rodó, *Memorias*, pp. 66, 91; Navarro Rubio, *Mis memorias*, pp. 59-79; interview of Alberto Ullastres, *Diario 16*, in Justino Sinova, ed., *Historia del Franquismo*, 2 vols (Madrid: Información y Prensa, 1985) II, p. 471.

68. Navarro Rubio, *Mis memorias*, p. 240; López Rodó, *Memorias*, pp. 80-8, 96-108; Artigues, *Opus Dei*, pp. 185-7.

69. Manuel Jesús González, *La economía política del franquismo (1940-1970). Dirigismo, mercado y planificación* (Madrid: Tecnos, 1979) pp. 134-7; Franco Salgado-Araujo, *Mis conversaciones*, pp. 203, 228.

70. Toquero, *Franco y Don Juan*, p. 267.

71. López Rodó, *Memorias*, pp. 105–6; Ynfante, *Santa Mafia*, pp. 178–9.

72. Mariano Navarro Rubio, 'La batalla de la estabilización', *Anales de la Real Academia de Ciencias Morales y Políticas*, No. 53, 1976, pp. 175–8; Suárez Fernández, *Franco*, VI, p. 8; Navarro Rubio, *Mis memorias*, p. 78.

73. López Rodó, *La larga marcha*, pp. 145–8; Toquero, *Franco y Don Juan*, pp. 267–70.

74. Mallet to FO, 28 March 1958, TNA FO 371/136711, RS2183/1; Franco Salgado-Araujo, *Mis conversaciones*, p. 228.

75. López Rodó, *Memorias*, pp. 139–44; Franco Salgado-Araujo, *Mis conversaciones*, p. 236.

76. Navarro Rubio, 'La batalla de la estabilización', pp. 178–86.

77. Franco Salgado-Araujo, *Mis conversaciones*, pp. 248, 270.

78. Franco, *Discursos 1955–1959*, pp. 557–68. Cf. Chancery to Southern Department, 2 January 1959, TNA FO 371/144927, RS1015/1.

79. Report from Bank of London & South America, Madrid, 3 March 1959, TNA FO 371/144927, RS1015/9; Toquero, *Franco y Don Juan*, pp. 297–300; Suárez Fernández, *Franco*, VI, pp. 78–82.

80. Tusell, *La oposición democrática*, pp. 314–36, 340–57; Calvo Serer, *Franco frente al Rey*, pp. 55–8; Javier Tusell and José Calvo, *Giménez Fernández. Precursor de la democracia española* (Madrid: Mondadori, 1990) pp. 269–80; Sheelagh Ellwood, *Prietas las filas. Historia de Falange Española, 1933–1983* (Barcelona: Crítica, 1984) pp. 220–8.

81. Navarro Rubio, 'La batalla de la estabilización', pp. 188–96; Mallet to FO, 5, 11 February 1959, TNA FO 371/144927, RS1015/4, FO 371/144926, RS1013/1; Mallet to Selwyn Lloyd, 17 February 1959, FO 371/144950, RS1102/1.

82. Navarro Rubio, 'La batalla de la estabilización', pp. 196–9; Navarro Rubio, *Mis memorias*, pp. 124–6; Report from Bank of London & South America, Madrid, 3 March 1959, TNA FO 371/144927, RS1015/9; Calvo Serer, *Franco frente al Rey*, p. 79.

83. López Rodó, *Memorias*, p. 184; Navarro Rubio interview in Bayod, ed., *Franco*, p. 89; Calvo Serer, *Franco frente al Rey*, p. 79.

84. Navarro Rubio, 'La batalla de la estabilización', pp. 201–2.

85. Navarro Rubio, *Mis memorias*, pp. 140–1; Arrese interview, Navarro Rubio interview in Bayod, ed., *Franco*, pp. 59–61, 89; Ullastres interview in Sinova, ed., *Historia del franquismo*, II, p. 473.

86. Navarro Rubio, *Mis memorias*, pp. 141–8; Mariano Navarro Rubio, 'La batalla del desarrollo', *Anales de la Real Academia de Ciencias Morales y Políticas*, No. 54, 1977, pp. 198, 205–7; Franco Salgado-Araujo, *Mis conversaciones*, pp. 246–7; Calvo Serer, *Franco frente al Rey*, pp. 77–9.

87. Suárez Fernández, *Franco*, VI, p. 96; Franco Salgado-Araujo, *Mis conversaciones*, p. 259.

88. José Maravall, *El desarrollo económico y la clase obrera* (Barcelona: Ariel, 1970) pp. 91–2; Javier Domínguez, *Organizaciones obreras cristianas en la oposición al franquismo (1951–1975)* (Bilbao: Biblioteca Educación y Acción Social, 1985) pp. 47–66; *The Times*, 1 July 1959; Franco, *Discursos 1955–1959*, pp. 641–3.

89. Franco, *Discursos 1955–1959*, pp. 699–705; memorandum of

Eisenhower–Franco conversations, Suárez Fernández, *Franco*, VI, pp. 140–52; Welles, *Gentle Anarchy*, pp. 247–52; Franco, *Nosotros*, p. 115.

90. Joan Clavera, Joan M. Esteban, María Antonia Monés, Antoni Montserrat and Jacint Ros Hombravella, *Capitalismo español. De la autarquía a la estabilización*, 2 vols (Madrid: Edicusa, 1973) I, pp. 78–90; Juan Muñoz, Santiago Roldán and Angel Serrano, *La internacionalización del capital en España 1959-1977* (Madrid: Cuadernos para el Dialogo, 1978) pp. 17–43.

91. Franco Salgado-Araujo, *Mis conversaciones*, pp. 277, 280.

92. Franco to Don Juan, 12 March 1960, reprinted in Sainz Rodríguez, *Un reinado*, pp. 400–1 and 236–7; Franco Salgado-Araujo, *Mis conversaciones*, pp. 280–1, 304, 334; Toquero, *Franco y Don Juan*, pp. 280–3.

93. *The Times*, 31 March 1960; Toquero, *Franco y Don Juan*, pp. 280–4; Sainz Rodríguez, *Un reinado*, pp. 238–9; López Rodó, *Memorias*, pp. 214–15; Franco Salgado-Araujo, *Mis conversaciones*, p. 286; Don Juan to Franco, 11 April, Franco to Don Juan, 27 April 1960, reprinted in Sainz Rodriguez, *Un reinado*, pp. 402–3.

94. Sueiro, *Valle*, pp. 223–30; Franco Salgado-Araujo, *Mis conversaciones*, pp. 302–3.

95. López Rodó, *Memorias*, pp. 257–9.

96. Suárez Fernández, *Franco*, VI, pp. 202–3; Franco Salgado-Araujo, *Mis conversaciones*, pp. 307, 311–12, 324.

97. Suárez Fernández, *Franco*, VI, pp. 261–5; Marquina, *España*, pp. 746–9; Calvo Serer, *Franco frente al Rey*, pp. 58–66.

98. Francisco Franco, *Discursos y mensajes del Jefe del Estado 1960-1963* (Madrid: Publicaciones Españolas, 1964) pp. 207–53.

99. Franco, *Discursos 1960-1963*, pp. 291–306.

100. López Rodó, *La larga marcha*, pp. 189–90, 198–9.

101. Gregorio Morán, *Adolfo Suárez. Historia de una ambición* (Barcelona: Planeta, 1979) pp. 140–1.

102. Franco, *Discursos 1960-1963*, pp. 317–41.

103. Morán, *Adolfo Suárez*, p. 141.

104. López Rodó, *Memorias*, pp. 262–3; López Rodó, *La larga marcha*, p. 199.

105. *ABC*, 26, 27 December; *The Times*, 27 December 1961; Vicente Gil, *Cuarenta años junto a Franco* (Barcelona: Planeta, 1981) p. 131; Ramón Soriano, *La mano izquierda de Franco* (Barcelona: Planeta, 1981) pp. 14–20.

106. López Rodó, *La larga marcha*, pp. 195–6; Soriano, *La mano*, pp. 29–35.

107. José María de Areilza, *Crónica de libertad* (Barcelona: Planeta, 1985) pp. 36–7; López Rodó, *La larga marcha*, pp. 195–8; López Rodó, *Memorias*, pp. 301–2.

108. López Rodó, *Memorias*, pp. 306–11; Navarro Rubio, *Mis memorias*, pp. 227–30; López Rodó, *La larga marcha*, pp. 199–201.

109. López Rodó, *Memorias*, pp. 312–15, 538.

110. Franco Salgado-Araujo, *Mi vida*, p. 345; Soriano, *La mano*, pp. 87–93; Vicente Pozuelo, *Los últimos 476 días de Franco* (Barcelona: Planeta, 1980) pp. 35, 109, 178; Gil, *Cuarenta años*, pp. 84–5, 132; Carlos Fernández Santander, *El futbol durante la guerra civil y el franquismo*

(Madrid: Editorial San Martín, 1990) pp. 196–7.

111. Franco Salgado-Araujo, *Mis conversaciones*, p. 322; López Rodó, *Memorias*, pp. 315–17; José María de Areilza, *Memorias exteriores 1947–1964* (Barcelona: Planeta, 1984) pp. 169–70.

112. *Mundo Obrero*, 1 May; *The Times*, 12 May 1962; Gregorio Morán, *El cura y los mandarines. Historia no oficial del Bosque de los Letrados. Cultura y política en España 1962–1996* (Madrid: Akal, 2014) pp. 63–8; Ignacio Fernández de Castro and José Martínez, *España hoy* (Paris: Ruedo Ibérico, 1963) pp. 67–97, 103–28, 140–92; Parti Communiste Français, *Dos meses de huelgas* (Paris: Parti Communiste Français, 1962) pp. 41–95; Miguélez, *La lucha*, pp. 103–13.

113. Franco Salgado-Araujo, *Mis conversaciones*, pp. 337–41; *Arriba*, 27 May 1962; Franco, *Discursos 1960–1963*, pp. 389–97.

114. *ABC*, 9 June 1962; Morán, *El cura y los mandarines*, pp. 66–74; Franco Salgado-Araujo, *Mis conversaciones*, p. 343; Soriano, *La mano*, pp. 151–2; López Rodó, *Memorias*, pp. 335–6; Suárez Fernández, *Franco*, VI, pp. 357, 377.

115. Areilza, *Memorias exteriores*, pp. 170–82; Calvo Serer, *Franco frente al Rey*, pp. 112–13; Joaquín Satrústegui et al., eds, *Cuando la transición se hizo posible. El 'contubernio de Munich'* (Madrid: Editorial Tecnos, 1993) pp. 23–41; Morán, *El cura y los mandarines*, pp. 77–83; *Arriba*, 9, 10, 12 June; *ABC*, 9, 11, 12 June; *La Vanguardia Española*, 17 June; *The Times*, 18 June 1962; Franco, *Discursos 1960–1963*, pp. 399–404, 412, 423–4, 427.

116. Partido Comunista de España, *Declaración por la reconciliación nacional, por una solución democrática y pacífica del problema español* (Paris, 1956) pp. 3, 5, 29–31, 37–40; Paul Preston, *The Last Stalinist: The Life of Santiago Carrillo* (London: William Collins, 2014) pp. 217–32; Hilari Raguer, *Réquiem por la cristiandad. El Concilio Vaticano II y su impacto en España* (Barcelona: Ediciones Península, 2006) pp. 385–94.

117. Suárez Fernández, *Franco*, VI, pp. 394–5; Franco Salgado-Araujo, *Mis conversaciones*, pp. 343–4.

118. *ABC*, 11 July; *Le Monde*, 11 July 1962; López Rodó, *Memorias*, pp. 339–47; Franco Salgado-Araujo, *Mis conversaciones*, pp. 344–5; María Mérida, *Testigos de Franco. Retablo íntimo de una dictadura* (Barcelona: Plaza y Janés, 1977) pp. 68–70; Welles, *Gentle Anarchy*, pp. 88–99.

119. Manuel Fraga Iribarne, *Memoria breve de una vida pública* (Barcelona: Planeta, 1980) pp. 29–32.

120. Gabriel Tortella, *The Development of Modern Spain* (Cambridge, Mass.: Harvard University Press, 2000) pp. 327–37; Joseph Harrison, *The Spanish Economy in the Twentieth Century* (Beckenham: Croom Helm, 1985) pp. 144–57; Inbal Ofer, *Claiming the City and Contesting the State: Squatting, Community Formation and Democratization in Spain (1955–1986)* (New York: Routledge, 2017) ch. 2; Michael Richards, *After the Civil War: Making Memory and Re-Making Spain since 1936* (Cambridge: Cambridge University Press, 2013) pp. 156–78.

121. Maria Dolors Genovès, Josep M. Huertas, Salvador Tarragó, Manuel

Campo Vidal, Eugeni Giral and Rafael Pradas, 'La Barcelona de Porcioles', L'Avenç, No. 295, October 2004, pp. 28–40; Riquer, La dictadura de Franco, pp. 653–6.

122. Ernest Lluch, La vía valenciana (Valencia: Afers, 2003) p. 251; Jaume Muñoz Jofre, La España corrupta. Breve historia de la corrupción (de la Restauración a nuestros días) (Granada: Comares, 2016) p. 83.

123. Fraga, Memoria breve, p. 59; López Rodó, Memorias, pp. 359–60.

124. Fraga, Memoria breve, p. 52; Franco Salgado-Araujo, Mis conversaciones, pp. 382, 397; Gil, Cuarenta años, pp. 107–36.

125. Fraga, Memoria breve, pp. 33, 41–2.

126. Manuel Fernández Areal, La libertad de prensa en España 1938–1971 (Madrid: Edicusa, 1971) pp. 69–75; Javier Terrón Montero, La prensa de España durante el régimen de Franco (Madrid: Centro de Investigaciones Sociológicas, 1981) pp. 166–75; López Rodó, Memorias, pp. 364–5, 518–19.

127. Franco, typescript notes on freemasonry, 1963, Fundación Francisco Franco, Legajo 246, No. 4, in Manuscritos de Franco (Madrid: Fundación Nacional Francisco Franco, 1986) doc. 45; Franco Salgado-Araujo, Mis conversaciones, pp. 366–9; Pilar Jaraiz Franco, Historia de una disidencia (Barcelona: Planeta, 1981) p. 191.

128. Franco Salgado-Araujo, Mis conversaciones, p. 376.

129. Le Monde, 13, 18, 19 April 1962; Amandino Rodríguez Armada and José Antonio Novais, ¿Quién mató a Julián Grimau? (Madrid: Ediciones 99, 1976) pp. 17–103, 110–14.

130. Frances Lannon, Privilege, Persecution, and Prophecy: The Catholic Church in Spain 1875–1975 (Oxford: Oxford University Press, 1987) pp. 246–9; Franco Salgado-Araujo, Mis conversaciones, pp. 381–2.

131. ABC, 28 April 1962; López Rodó, Memorias, p. 379; Fraga, Memoria breve, pp. 69–70; Rodríguez Armada and Novais, Grimau, pp. 109–59.

132. Areilza, Memorias exteriores, pp. 164–5.

133. Octavio Alberola and Ariane Gransac, El anarquismo español y la acción revolucionaria 1961–1974 (Paris: Ruedo Ibérico, 1975) pp. 107–12; Edouard de Blaye, Franco and the Politics of Spain (Harmondsworth: Penguin, 1976) p. 221.

134. Suárez Fernández, Franco, VII, pp. 88–91; Calvo Serer, Franco frente al Rey, pp. 132–5; Fraga, Memoria breve, p. 77; Vincent, Spain, pp. 188–98.

135. Richards, After the Civil War, pp. 187–91, 198–201; Antonio Cazorla Sánchez, Franco. Biografía del mito (Madrid: Alianza Editorial, 2015) pp. 263–6; Morán, El cura y los mandarines, pp. 251–78.

136. Francisco Franco, Discursos y mensajes del Jefe del Estado 1964–1967 (Madrid: Publicaciones Españolas, 1968) pp. 19–40.

137. Fraga, Memoria breve, p. 107; López Rodó, Memorias, pp. 458–9.

138. Franco, Discursos 1964–1967, p. 43.

139. Miguélez, La lucha, pp. 121–6; López Rodó, Memorias, p. 456; Fraga, Memoria breve, pp. 108–10; Franco Salgado-Araujo, Mis conversaciones, p. 424.

140. Fraga, Memoria breve, pp. 112, 115; Franco Salgado-Araujo, Mis conversaciones, p. 426; Calvo Serer, Franco frente al Rey, p. 145.

141. Pere Ysàs, *Disidencia y subversión. La lucha del régimen franquista por la supervivencia, 1960–1975* (Barcelona: Crítica, 2004) pp. 17–46, 76–109.

142. Rafael Gómez Pérez, *El franquismo y la Iglesia* (Madrid: Rialp, 1986) pp. 104–6.

143. Franco, *Discursos 1964–1967*, pp. 51–92.

144. Fraga, *Memoria breve*, pp. 117–16; López Rodó, *Memorias*, pp. 475–8.

145. Ysàs, *Disidencia*, pp. 161–75; Feliciano Blázquez, *La traición de los clérigos en la España de Franco. Crónica de una intolerancia (1936–1975)* (Madrid: Editorial Trotta, 1991) pp. 158–64; Lannon, *Privilege*, pp. 250–1.

146. Franco Salgado-Araujo, *Mis conversaciones*, p. 407; Fraga, *Memoria breve*, pp. 89, 99, 103, 123–5.

147. López Rodó, *Memorias*, p. 498.

148. López Rodó, *La larga marcha*, pp. 226–7; Fraga, *Memoria breve*, p. 133; López Rodó, *Memorias*, p. 512; López Rodó, *La larga marcha*, pp. 227–8.

149. López Rodó, *Memorias*, pp. 519–20; López Rodó, *La larga marcha*, pp. 229–30; Fraga, *Memoria breve*, pp. 135–8.

150. López Rodó, *Memorias*, pp. 532–9; López Rodó, *La larga marcha*, pp. 235–6; Fraga, *Memoria breve*, p. 142.

151. Franco, typescript notes borrador de Ley de Prensa, 1964, Fundación Francisco Franco, Legajo 157, No. 1, in *Manuscritos de Franco*, doc. 46; Fraga, *Memoria breve*, pp. 144–5, 151, 158–9.

152. Joaquín Bardavío, *La rama trágica de los borbones* (Barcelona: Plaza y Janés, 1989) pp. 62–71, 111–18; Laureano López Rodó, *Memorias:*

años decisivos (Barcelona: Plaza y Janés, 1991) pp. 22, 33–4, 43.

153. López Rodó, *Memorias*, pp. 539–43, 564; Franco Salgado-Araujo, *Mis conversaciones*, pp. 455–6; Fraga, *Memoria breve*, pp. 159–60; Espinosa San Martín interview in Bayod, ed., *Franco*, pp. 150–1.

154. López Rodó, *Memorias: años decisivos*, pp. 18–20, 93; López Rodó, *La larga marcha*, pp. 238–43; Bardavío, *La rama trágica*, pp. 95–107; Franco Salgado-Araujo, *Mis conversaciones*, pp. 465, 506, 514.

155. Suárez Fernández, *Franco*, VII, pp. 328–9; López Rodó, *Memorias: años decisivos*, pp. 41–2.

156. Fraga, *Memoria breve*, p. 172.

157. Areilza, *Crónica*, pp. 19–21, 42–4; Toquero, *Franco y Don Juan*, pp. 343–8; Suárez Fernández, *Franco*, VII, pp. 171–2.

158. Franco Salgado-Araujo, *Mis conversaciones*, p. 469; Fraga, *Memoria breve*, pp. 64, 170–2.

159. Fraga, *Memoria breve*, pp. 174–5; López Rodó, *La larga marcha*, p. 248.

160. Calvo Serer, *Franco frente al Rey*, pp. 169–70; Fraga, *Memoria breve*, p. 183.

161. Franco, *Discursos 1964–1967*, pp. 219–51; Stanley G. Payne, *The Franco Regime 1936–1975* (Madison: Wisconsin University Press, 1987) p. 495.

162. Franco, *Discursos 1964–1967*, p. 259.

163. *Cuadernos de Ruedo Ibérico*, No. 10, December 1966–January 1967, pp. 27–63; Edouard de Blaye, *Franco and the Politics of Spain* (Harmondsworth: Pelican, 1976) pp. 236–8; Riquer, *La dictadura de Franco*, pp. 506–10.

164. Fraga, *Memoria breve*, p. 194; López Rodó, *La larga marcha*, pp. 263–5;

López Rodó, *Memorias: años decisivos*, p. 207; Calvo Serer, *Franco frente al Rey*, p. 171; Espinosa San Martín, in Bayod, ed., *Franco*, p. 154.

165. Franco Salgado-Araujo, *Mis conversaciones*, pp. 530, 533, 537; Fraga, *Memoria breve*, pp. 215–16, 243.

166. *Le Monde*, 14 March 1969; Franco Salgado-Araujo, *Mis conversaciones*, pp. 513–14, 540–1, 547.

167. Franco Salgado-Araujo, *Mis conversaciones*, pp. 538–9.

168. Francesc Amover, *Il carcere vaticano. Chiesa e fascismo in Spagna* (Milan: Gabriele Mazzotta Editore, 1975) pp. 28–47; Fernando Gutiérrez, *Curas represaliados en el franquismo* (Madrid: Akal, 1977) *passim*.

169. José Luis Rodríguez Jiménez, *Reaccionarios y golpistas. La extrema derecha en España: del tardofranquismo a la consolidación de la democracia (1967–1982)* (Madrid: Consejo Superior de Investigaciones Científicas, 1994) pp. 95–129; Xavier Casals i Meseguer, *Neonazis en España. De las audiciones wagnerianas a los skinheads (1966–1995)* (Barcelona: Grijalbo-Mondadori, 1995) pp. 57–65; Sophie Baby, *El mito de la transición pacífica. Violencia y política en España (1975–1982)* (Madrid: Ediciones Akal, 2018) pp. 104–9.

170. López Rodó, *Memorias: años decisivos*, pp. 308–18, 325.

171. Rafael Calvo Serer, *La solución presidencialista* (Barcelona: Plaza y Janés, 1979) p. 39.

172. López Rodó, *Memorias: años decisivos*, pp. 346–9, 355–7, 362–4.

173. *Ibid.*, pp. 366–7; Marquina, *España*, pp. 814–21.

174. Francisco Franco, *Discursos y mensajes del Jefe del Estado 1968–1970* (Madrid: Publicaciones Españolas, 1971) pp. 52–69.

175. López Rodó, *Memorias*, p. 542; Fraga, *Memoria breve*, pp. 234, 241; interview with López Rodó in Bayod, ed., *Franco*, p. 167; López Rodó, *Memorias: años decisivos*, pp. 358–9.

176. López Rodó, *La larga marcha*, pp. 279, 291–3, 301; López Rodó, *Memorias: años decisivos*, pp. 381–4; Fraga, *Memoria breve*, pp. 236–7; Suárez Fernández, *Franco*, VIII, pp. 66–72.

177. López Rodó, *Memorias: años decisivos*, p. 386.

178. López Rodó, *La larga marcha*, pp. 303–11; Espinosa San Martín interview in Bayod, ed., *Franco*, p. 160; Fraga, *Memoria breve*, pp. 245–6; Franco Salgado-Araujo, *Mis conversaciones*, pp. 544–5.

179. López Rodó, *Memorias: años decisivos*, pp. 423–6.

180. López Rodó, *La larga marcha*, pp. 320–5.

181. Joaquín Bardavío, *Los silencios del Rey* (Madrid: Strips Editores, 1979) p. 35; López Rodó, *La larga marcha*, pp. 325–36; López Rodó, *Memorias: años decisivos*, pp. 456–66.

182. Sainz Rodríguez, *Un reinado*, p. 276.

183. Franco, *Discursos 1968–1970*, pp. 85–97.

184. Bardavío, *Los silencios*, pp. 27, 49–52.

185. Carr and Fusi, *Spain*, pp. 179–88.

186. Navarro Rubio, *Mis memorias*, pp. 345–431; López Rodó, *Memorias: años decisivos*, pp. 494–521, 553–63.

187. Suárez Fernández, *Franco*, VIII, pp. 158–9.

188. *Arriba*, 24, 27 August 1969.

189. Franco Salgado-Araujo, *Mis conversaciones*, pp. 527, 530; Jaraiz Franco, *Historia*, p. 204; Franco, *Nosotros*, p. 158; López Rodó, *Memorias: años decisivos*, pp. 507–9, 682–90; Espinosa San Martín interview in Bayod, ed., *Franco*, pp. 161–3.

190. López Rodó, *La larga marcha*, pp. 654–9; Franco Salgado-Araujo, *Mis conversaciones*, p. 549; Fraga, *Memoria breve*, pp. 252–3; López Rodó, *Memorias: años decisivos*, pp. 499–505.

191. López Rodó, *La larga marcha*, pp. 390–5; Navarro Rubio, *Mis memorias*, p. 245; López Rodó, *Memorias: años decisivos*, pp. 520–3, 534–7; López Bravo interview, Bayod, ed., *Franco*, p. 120; *ABC*, 29 October 1969; Equipo Mundo, *Los 90 Ministros*, pp. 420–500; Rafael Calvo Serer, *La dictadura de los franquistas: El 'affaire' del MADRID y el futuro político* (Paris: Autor/Ruedo Ibérico, 1973) pp. 166, 168; Alfonso Armada, *Al servicio de la Corona* (Barcelona: Planeta, 1983) pp. 68, 72, 78, 93–4, 100–1, 119, 121, 135; José Ignacio San Martín, *Servicio especial. A las órdenes de Carrero Blanco* (Barcelona: Planeta, 1983) pp. 198, 253; López Rodó, *La larga marcha*, p. 200; Morán, *Suárez*, pp. 198–9, 204–5.

192. Franco, *Discursos 1968–1970*, pp. 107–21.

Chapter 15: The Twilight Years of a Corrupt Regime, 1969–1982

1. *ABC*, 22 July; *Ya*, 29 July; *Mundo Obrero*, 9 September 1970; *Horizonte español 1972*, 3 vols (Paris: Ruedo Ibérico, 1972) I, pp. 203–12.

2. Fernando Claudín, 'Dos concepciones de "la vía española al socialismo"', *Cuadernos de Ruedo Ibérico, Horizonte español 1966* (Paris: Ruedo Ibérico, 1966) pp. 59–100; Paul Preston, *The Last Stalinist: The Life of Santiago Carrillo* (London: William Collins, 2014) pp. 275–7.

3. Santiago Carrillo, *Libertad y socialismo* (Paris: Colección Ebro, 1971) pp. 56–66; *Nuestra Bandera*, No. 62, October–November 1969, pp. 22–5; Ignacio Gallego, *El partido de masas que necesitamos* (Paris: Editions Sociales, 1971) pp. 7–9.

4. *Le Monde*, 1, 5, 9, 12 September, 3, 5, 6 November; *Mundo Obrero*, 9, 30 September, 14 November 1970.

5. 'Ginés de Buitrago', 'Un poco de formalidad!', *ABC*, 2 April; *Mundo Obrero*, 29 April 1970.

6. Ramón Garriga, *La Señora de El Pardo* (Barcelona: Planeta, 1979) pp. 235, 289–92, 297–301; Joaquín Giménez Arnau, *Yo, Jimmy. Mi vida entre los Franco* (Barcelona: Planeta, 1981) p. 26; Laureano López Rodó, *La larga marcha hacia la monarquía* (Barcelona: Noguer, 1977), pp. 274–5, 286–9; Laureano López Rodó, *Memorias: años decisivos* (Barcelona: Plaza y Janés, 1991) p. 307; Manuel Fraga Iribarne, *Memoria breve de una vida pública* (Barcelona: Planeta, 1980) pp. 268, 272.

7. Laureano López Rodó, *El principio del fin. Memorias* (Barcelona: Plaza y Janés, 1992) pp. 84–5; Henry Kissinger, *The White House Years* (London: Weidenfeld & Nicolson/ Michael Joseph, 1979) pp. 930–2.

8. *ABC*, 22, 26 November; *Le Monde*, 5, 8 December 1970; Kepa Salaberri, *El proceso de Euskadi en Burgos. El sumarísimo 31.69* (Paris: Ruedo Ibérico, 1971) pp. 102–10, 165–7.

9. *Le Monde*, 2, 15, 16, 17, 18 December 1970; *Horizonte español 1972*, I, p. 235.

10. *Le Monde*, 18, 19, 21 December 1970; Vicente Gil, *Cuarenta años junto a Franco* (Barcelona: Planeta, 1981) pp. 98–103; Francisco Franco Salgado-Araujo, *Mis conversaciones privadas con Franco* (Barcelona: Planeta, 1976), p. 560; López Rodó, *El principio*, pp. 113–15; Salaberri, *Proceso*, pp. 263–72; *Horizonte español 1972*, I, pp. 266–71.

11. *Le Monde*, 29, 30, 31 December 1970; López Bravo and Garicano Goñi interviews in Ángel Bayod, ed., *Franco visto por sus ministros* (Barcelona: Planeta, 1981) pp. 124, 201–2, 239; López Rodó, *La larga marcha*, pp. 405–6; López Rodó, *El principio*, pp. 122–9, 579–82; Francisco Franco, *Discursos y mensajes del Jefe del Estado 1968–1970* (Madrid: Publicaciones Españolas, 1971) pp. 167–78; Salaberri, *Proceso*, pp. 293–318.

12. *Pensamiento político de Franco*, 2 vols (Madrid: Ediciones del Movimiento, 1975) II, pp. 718–19.

13. Vernon A. Walters, *Silent Missions* (New York: Doubleday, 1978) pp. 555–6.

14. López Rodó, *El principio*, p. 146; Joaquín Bardavío, *Los silencios del Rey* (Madrid: Strips Editores, 1979) pp. 53–4.

15. *Mundo Obrero*, 22 January; *Le Monde Diplomatique*, January 1971.

16. *Mundo Obrero*, 6, 19, February 1971; *Horizonte español 1972*, I, pp. 279, 288.

17. *Le Monde*, 31 January; *Mundo Obrero*, 3 April; *Madrid*, 24 November 1971; Luis Ramírez (pseudonym of Luciano Rincón), 'Morir en el bunker', *Horizonte Español 1972*, I, pp. 3–4.

18. *Le Monde*, 11 November 1971; *Horizonte español 1972*, I, p. 289; Rafael Calvo Serer, *Franco frente al rey* (Paris: Autor/Ruedo Ibérico, 1972) pp. 205–18.

19. *Arriba*, 2 October 1971; *Cuadernos de Ruedo Iberico*, Nos 33–5, October 1971–March 1972, pp. 3–19; *Horizonte español 1972*, I, pp. 326–35.

20. *Pensamiento político de Franco*, II, pp. 719–20; *ABC*, 2 October; *Mundo Obrero*, 15 October 1971; Rafael Calvo Serer, *La dictadura de los franquistas: El 'affaire' del MADRID y el futuro político* (Paris: Autor/Ruedo Ibérico, 1973) pp. 190–3; Fraga, *Memoria breve*, pp. 280–1.

21. *Pensamiento político de Franco*, I, pp. 3–17; Manuel Vázquez Montalbán, 'Los Creix', *El País*, 28 March 1985; David Ballester, *Vides truncades. Repressió, víctimes i impunitat a Catalunya (1964–1980)* (Valencia: Publicacions de la Universitat de València, 2018) pp. 43–60.

22. Norman Cooper, 'The Church. From Crusade to Christianity', in Paul Preston, ed., *Spain in Crisis: Evolution and Decline of the Franco Regime* (Hassocks: Harvester Press, 1976) pp. 72–4.

23. *Pensamiento político de Franco*, I, p. 270, II, pp. 720–1; *ABC*, 1 January; *Ya*, 6 January 1972; *Horizonte español 1972*, I, p. 336.

24. *Le Monde*, 12, 22 October, 2, 17, 24 November; *Mundo Obrero*, 15 July, 17 September, 2, 27 October, 12 November, 10 December 1971.

25. *Mundo Obrero*, 10 December 1971; *Horizonte español 1972*, I, pp. 315–16.

26. *Le Monde*, 1–2 February 1970; *Informaciones*, 6 November 1971, 17 April 1972, 26, 30 April 1973; *ABC*, 7 November 1971; *Mundo*

Obrero, 15 April 1972, 9 June 1973;
José Ignacio San Martín, *Servicio
especial. A las órdenes de Carrero
Blanco* (Barcelona: Planeta, 1983)
pp. 23–42; Ramírez, 'Morir en el
bunker', pp. 1–20; Paul Preston, *The
Politics of Revenge: Fascism and the
Military in 20th Century Spain*
(London: Allen & Unwin, 1990)
pp. 165–74; *Horizonte español 1972*,
I, pp. 311–14.

27. *Mundo Obrero*, 5 February, 10, 22
June 1972; *Horizonte español 1972*,
I, p. 370.

28. *Observer*, 19 March; *Mundo Obrero*,
14, 30 March, 15 April 1972.

29. Ángel Amigo, *Pertur: ETA 71–76*
(San Sebastián: Hordago
Publikapenak, 1978) pp. 44–8; José
María Garmendia, *Historia de ETA*,
2 vols (San Sebastián: L. Haranburu
Editor, 1980) II, pp. 164–73; Ortzi,
*Historia de Euskadi. El nacionalismo
vasco y ETA* (Paris: Ruedo Ibérico,
1975) pp. 397–401.

30. Ramón Garriga, *Nicolás Franco, el
hermano brujo* (Barcelona: Planeta,
1980) pp. 311–17; Gil, *Cuarenta
años*, pp. 87, 93; Mariano Sánchez
Soler, *Ricos por la guerra civil de
España* (Madrid: Editorial Raíces,
2007) pp. 89–102; Carlos Barciela,
'Franquismo y corrupción político',
Historia Social, No. 30, 1998,
pp. 83–96.

31. Gil, *Cuarenta años*, pp. 42–3, 60,
87–8, 91; López Rodó, *La larga
marcha*, pp. 323, 419, 435; López
Rodó, *El principio*, pp. 280–1;
Fraga, *Memoria breve*, pp. 285–92;
Rafael Calvo Serer, *La solución
presidencialista* (Barcelona: Plaza y
Janés, 1979) pp. 38–9.

32. Pilar Jaraiz Franco, *Historia de una
disidencia* (Barcelona: Planeta,
1981) pp. 156, 162–3, 174, 205.

33. Gil, *Cuarenta años*, pp. 50–1;
Torcuato Fernández-Miranda,

'Diario inédito', *ABC*, 20 December
1983, pp. 5–6; Carlos Fernández
Santander, *El Almirante Carrero*
(Barcelona: Plaza y Janés, 1985)
pp. 238–9; Javier Tusell, *Carrero. La
eminencia gris del régimen de
Franco* (Madrid: Ediciones Temas
de Hoy, 1993) pp. 399–400; Fraga,
Memoria breve, pp. 277, 288–9.

34. López Rodó, *El principio*, p. 325.

35. *Pensamiento político de Franco*, I,
pp. 27–34; López Rodó, *El principio*,
pp. 336–8.

36. López Rodó, *El principio*, p. 345.

37. *Mundo Obrero*, 3 March, 8 July
1972; 26 April 1973.

38. *Le Monde*, 15 August; *Le Socialiste*,
21 September 1972; PSOE,
Congresos del PSOE en el exilio, 2
vols (Madrid: Editorial Pablo
Iglesias, 1981) II, pp. 179–204.

39. Dionisio Ridruejo, *Casi unas
memorias* (Barcelona: Planeta,
1976) pp. 427–34; Rafael Calvo
Serer, *La solución presidencialista*
(Barcelona: Plaza y Janés, 1979)
pp. 48–53; Pilar Fernández-
Miranda Lozana and Alfonso
Fernández-Miranda Campoamor,
*Lo que el Rey me ha pedido.
Torcuato Fernández-Miranda y la
reforma política* (Barcelona: Plaza y
Janés, 1995) pp. 29–42; Miguel
Herrero, *El principio monárquico*
(Madrid: Cuadernos para el
Diálogo, 1972) *passim*; Jorge de
Esteban et al., *Desarrollo político y
constitución española* (Barcelona:
Ariel, 1973) *passim*.

40. *Mundo Obrero*, 28 April, 23 May
1973.

41. López Rodó, *La larga marcha*,
pp. 440–2.

42. *Le Monde*, 4, 5–6, 7 August 1973;
Javier Tusell and Genoveva García
Queipo de Llano, *Tiempo de
incertidumbre. Carlos Arias Navarro
entre el franquismo y la transición*

(1973–1976) (Barcelona: Crítica, 2003) pp. 39–48; Ismael Fuente, Javier García and Joaquín Prieto, *Golpe mortal. Asesinato de Carrero y agonía del franquismo* (Madrid: El País, 1983) p. 164; Carlos Arias interview in Bayod, ed., *Franco*, p. 308; Bardavío, *Los silencios*, pp. 61–2; López Rodó, *La larga marcha*, pp. 440–53.

43. Julen Agirre (pseudonym of Eva Forest), *Operación Ogro. Cómo y porqué ejecutamos a Carrero Blanco* (Hendaye/Paris: Ruedo Ibérico, 1974) p. 139; Joaquín Bardavío, *La crisis. Historia de quince días* (Madrid: Ediciones Sedmay, 1974) pp. 47–56; Fuente et al., *Golpe mortal*, p. 172.

44. José Utrera Molina, *Sin cambiar de bandera* (Barcelona: Planeta, 1989) pp. 70–4; Pilar Franco Bahamonde, *Nosotros los Franco* (Barcelona: Planeta, 1980) p. 150.

45. *Pueblo*, 22 December 1973; *El Socialista*, 2nd fortnight in January 1974, Marcel Niedergang, 'Le franquisme et ses ultras', *Le Monde*, 5–8 January 1974; Bardavío, *La crisis*, pp. 111–16; Fuente et al., *Golpe mortal*, pp. 184–7; Carlos Iniesta Cano, *Memorias y recuerdos* (Barcelona: Planeta, 1984) pp. 218–22; San Martín, *Servicio especial*, pp. 90–114.

46. Jaraiz Franco, *Historia*, p. 208; Ricardo de la Cierva, *Historia del franquismo*, Vol. II: *Aislamiento, transformación, agonía (1945–1975)* (Barcelona: Planeta, 1978) pp. 391–2.

47. Tusell and García Queipo de Llano, *Tiempo de incertidumbre*, pp. 53–69; Rafael Borrás Bertriu et al., *El día en que mataron a Carrero Blanco* (Barcelona: Planeta, 1974) pp. 252–6; *Mundo Obrero*, 5 January 1974; Gil, *Cuarenta años*,

pp. 139–63; Utrera, *Sin cambiar*, pp. 83–5; Bardavío, *Los silencios*, pp. 65–9; Fuente et al., *Golpe mortal*, pp. 172–3, 282–301; López Rodó, *La larga marcha*, pp. 459–61; Julio Rodríguez Martínez, *Impresiones de un ministro de Carrero Blanco* (Barcelona: Planeta, 1974) p. 96; Fraga, *Memoria breve*, pp. 309–10.

48. Borràs Betriu et al., *El dia en que mataron a Carrero Blanco*, pp. 252–6; *Le Monde*, 26 December; *Informaciones*, 21 December; *Daily Telegraph*, 31 December; *Guardian*, 31 December 1973, 4 January; *Financial Times*, 4 January; *Le Monde*, 4 January; *Mundo*, 5 January 1974; Fuente et al., *Golpe mortal*, pp. 50–1, 70.

49. *Pensamiento político de Franco*, I, pp. 35–8; Bardavío, *Los silencios*, p. 74.

50. *The Times*, 4 January; *Le Monde*, 4 January 1974.

51. Fuente et al., *Golpe mortal*, p. 283.

52. Utrera, *Sin cambiar*, pp. 85–92; La Cierva, *Franquismo*, II, p. 395.

53. *Mundo Obrero*, 28 November, 31 December; *Frente Libertario*, December 1973; *Financial Times*, 13 February; *Cambio 16*, 18 March; *Treball*, 12 March 1974; Wilebaldo Solano, 'Le développement des conflits sociaux', and Ramon Tamames, 'Expansion économique et démocratie', *Le Monde Diplomatique*, February 1974; Charles F. Gallagher, *Spain, Development and the Energy Crisis* (New York: AUFS, 1973) p. 3.

54. Licinio de la Fuente, '*Valió la pena*'. *Memorias* (Madrid: Editorial EDAF, 1998) pp. 207–11.

55. A. Saez Alba, *La otra cosa nostra. La Asociación Católica Nacional de Propagandistas y el caso de EL CORREO de Andalucía* (Paris:

Ruedo Ibérico, 1974) pp. CX–CXII, 293–323; Fernando Jaúregui and Manuel Soriano, *La otra historia de UCD* (Madrid: Emiliano Escolar Editor, 1980) pp. 41–2; *ABC*, 3 March 1974; Alfonso Osorio, *Trayectoria política de un ministro de la corona* (Barcelona: Planeta, 1980) pp. 26–7.

56. *The Times*, 13 February; *Le Monde*, 14 February 1974; Carlos Arias Navarro, *Discurso del Presidente del Gobierno a las Cortes Españolas, 12.II.1974* (Madrid: Ediciones del Movimiento, 1974); interview with Carro Martínez, Bayod, ed., *Franco*, pp. 348–9; De la Fuente, 'Valió la pena', pp. 211–12; Ferran Gallego, *El mito de la transición. La crisis del franquismo y los orígenes de la democracia (1973–1977)* (Barcelona: Crítica, 2008) pp. 40–54.

57. Utrera, *Sin cambiar*, pp. 98, 103; La Cierva, *Franquismo*, II, pp. 395–7.

58. José María de Areilza, *Diario de un ministro de la monarquía* (Barcelona: Planeta, 1977) p. 71; *Le Monde*, 26 February, 5, 9 March; *El Alcazar*, 7, 8 March; *Observer*, 10 March; *Guardian*, 11 March 1974; Ortzi, *Euskadi*, pp. 404–7; 'Il bastone e la garrota', *Panorama* (Rome), 14 March 1974.

59. Francesc Escribano, *Cuenta atrás. La historia de Salvador Puig Antich* (Barcelona: Ediciones Península, 2001) pp. 151–3; Gutmaro Gómez Bravo, *Puig Antich. La Transición Inacabada* (Madrid: Taurus, 2014) pp. 111–35.

60. *Arriba*, 28 April; *ABC*, 30 April; *Cambio 16*, 13 May 1974; Utrera, *Sin cambiar*, pp. 116–22; Gallego, *El mito*, pp. 64–6.

61. *Le Monde*, 15 May; *Financial Times*, 29 May 1974; Manuel Gutiérrez Mellado, *Un soldado para España*

(Barcelona: Argos Vergara, 1983) pp. 47–9; Paul Preston, *The Triumph of Democracy in Spain* (London: Methuen, 1986) pp. 60–2.

62. *ABC*, 29 May, 16 June; *Ya*, 16 June; *El Alcazar*, 16 June 1974.

63. Fraga, *Memoria breve*, p. 330.

64. Laureano López Rodó, *Claves de la transición. Memorias IV* (Barcelona: Plaza y Janés, 1993) pp. 57–8; Joaquín Bardavío, *La rama trágica de los Borbones* (Barcelona: Plaza y Janés, 1989) pp. 203–4.

65. José Oneto, *Arias entre dos crisis, 1973–1975* (Madrid: Cambio 16, 1975) p. 141; José Luis de Vilallonga, *El Rey. Conversaciones con D. Juan Carlos I de España* (Barcelona: Plaza y Janés, 1993) p. 215; Bardavío, *Los silencios*, pp. 95–101; Utrera, *Sin cambiar*, p. 147; Javier Figuero and Luis Herrero, *La muerte de Franco jamás contada* (Barcelona: Planeta, 1985) p. 130.

66. Gil, *Cuarenta años*, pp. 193–202, 209, 212; Vicente Pozuelo, *Los últimos 476 días de Franco* (Barcelona: Planeta, 1980) pp. 22–3; Jaime Peñafiel, *El General y su tropa. Mis recuerdos de la familia Franco* (Madrid: Temas de Hoy, 1992) pp. 155–6, 160.

67. *Le Monde*, 4–5 August; *Mundo Obrero*, 31 July 1974; Rafael Calvo Serer, *Mis enfrentamientos con el Poder* (Barcelona: Plaza y Janés, 1978) pp. 119–21; Carrillo's intervention at a private seminar held by the Fundación Ortega y Gasset in Toledo in May 1984.

68. Calvo Serer, *Mis enfrentamientos*, pp. 248–65.

69. *Le Monde*, 19 October; *Guardian*, 18 October 1974.

70. *Le Monde*, 4, 8, 18, 30, 31 October 1974; Oneto, *Arias entre dos crisis 1973–1975*, pp. 149–53; Carro

Martínez interview, Bayod, ed., *Franco*, pp. 354–6; Mariano Sánchez Soler, *Villaverde. Fortuna y caída de la casa Franco* (Barcelona: Planeta, 1990) p. 100; Utrera, *Sin cambiar*, pp. 173–5; La Cierva, *Franquismo*, II, p. 402; Gallego, *El mito*, pp. 103–7.

71. *Cambio 16*, 10 June 1974; Ramon Pi, *Joaquin Garrigues Walker* (Madrid: Cambio 16, 1977) p. 40.

72. *Ya*, 30, 31 October; *ABC*, 30 October; *Cambio 16*, 11–17, 18–24 November; *Le Monde*, 7 November 1974.

73. *Le Monde*, 20, 29, 30 November; *Guardian*, 28 November; *The Times*, 28 November; *Financial Times*, 28 November 1974; Fernando Álvarez de Miranda, *Del 'contubernio' al consenso* (Barcelona: Planeta, 1985) p. 83.

74. Bardavío, *Los silencios*, p. 102.

75. Pozuelo, *Los 476 últimos días*, pp. 126–9, 133–6, 141–7.

76. *Ibid.*, pp. 133, 177–8.

77. *Pensamiento político de Franco*, I, pp. 39–43.

78. Utrera, *Sin cambiar*, pp. 226–33.

79. Figuero and Herrero, *La muerte*, pp. 19–21.

80. De la Fuente, 'Valió la pena', pp. 223–8; interview with Licinio de la Fuente in Bayod, ed., *Franco*, pp. 240–2.

81. *Le Monde*, 5 March 1975; Utrera, *Sin cambiar*, pp. 248–59; Gregorio Morán, *Adolfo Suárez. Historia de una ambición* (Barcelona: Planeta, 1979) pp. 286–7; Carro Martínez interview, Bayod, ed., *Franco*, pp. 356–7.

82. Fraga, *Memoria breve*, pp. 346–9.

83. Utrera, *Sin cambiar*, pp. 266–73.

84. R. Richard Rubottom and J. Carter Murphy, *Spain and the United States since World War II* (New York: Praeger, 1984) pp. 113–14.

85. *Cambio 16*, 23–29 June 1975; Pozuelo, *Los 476 últimos días*, pp. 178–80; Gallego, *El mito*, pp. 133–9.

86. Osorio, *Trayectoria*, p. 183; Javier Figuero, *UCD. La 'empresa' que creo Adolfo Suárez* (Barcelona: Grijalbo, 1981) pp. 19–22; Morán, *Suárez*, pp. 74–5, 103–8, 121–7, 169–85; Jonathan Hopkin, *Party Formation and Democratic Transition in Spain: The Creation and Collapse of the Union of the Democratic Centre* (London: Macmillan, 1999) pp. 43–4.

87. Pedro J. Ramírez, *El año que murió Franco* (Barcelona: Plaza y Janés, 1985) pp. 51–2, 68–9; Morán, *Suárez*, pp. 295–6; Gallego, *El mito*, pp. 145–52.

88. *ABC*, 20 May 1975; Morán, *Suárez*, pp. 297–300.

89. Pozuelo, *Los 476 últimos días*, p. 157.

90. Franco, *Nosotros*, pp. 236–7.

91. Pozuelo, *Los 476 últimos días*, p. 187; Fraga, *Memoria breve*, p. 363.

92. *Arriba*, 16 July 1975.

93. Cooper, 'The Church', pp. 79–81.

94. *The Times*, 15 May 1975; Noticias del País Vasco, *Euskadi. El último estado de excepción* (Paris: Ruedo Ibérico, 1975) pp. 25–30, 45–77, 143–51; Javier Sánchez Erauskin, *Txiki-Otaegi. El viento y las raíces* (San Sebastián: Hordago Publikapenak, 1978) pp. 260–1, 283–93.

95. *Guardian*, 27 August; *Mundo Obrero*, 4th week of June, 3rd week of July 1975. Stock-market quotations derive from *Cambio 16* throughout the autumn of 1975.

96. Ramírez, *El año*, pp. 112, 118–21.

97. *Ya*, 30 September; *Sabado Grafico*, 24–30 September; *Guardian*, 26, 30 September, 3, 7 October; *Observer*,

5 October; *Sunday Times*, 5 October 1975; Pozuelo, *Los 476 últimos días*, pp. 208–10; Ramírez, *El año*, pp. 204–6.

98. *Cambio 16*, 23–29 June 1975; *Mundo Obrero*, 4th week of September 1975; Álvarez de Miranda, *Del 'contubernio'*, p. 88.

99. *Arriba*, 2 October; *Cambio 16*, 6 October 1975; Pozuelo, *Los 476 últimos días*, pp. 210–12.

100. Pio Moa Rodríguez, *De un tiempo y de un País* (Madrid: Ediciónes de la Torre, 1982) pp. 217–33.

101. Pozuelo, *Los últimos 476 días*, pp. 215–16; Rogelio Baón, *La cara humana de un Caudillo* (Madrid: Editorial San Martín, 1975) p. 227; José Luis Palma Gámiz, *El paciente de El Pardo* (Madrid: Rey Lear, 2004) pp. 19, 55, 59–60, 68–78; Jesús Palacios and Stanley G. Payne, *Franco, mi padre. Testimonio de Carmen Franco, la hija del Caudillo* (Madrid: La Esfera de los Libros, 2005) pp. 677–8.

102. Franco, *Nosotros*, pp. 167–8; Pozuelo, *Los 476 últimos días*, pp. 218–21; Figuero and Herrero, *La muerte*, p. 26.

103. Palma Gámiz, *El paciente*, pp. 118–23, 135–6; Palacios and Payne, *Franco, mi padre*, p. 679; Julio González Iglesias, *Los dientes de Franco* (Madrid: Editorial Fénix, 1996) pp. 366–9; *ABC*, 2, 7 November; *Ya*, 29, 30 October, 9, 14 18 November 1975; 'As Juan Carlos Sees It', *Newsweek*, 3 November 1975.

104. *Guardian*, 2, 31 October, 7, 12 November; *Sunday Times*, 26 October, 9 November; *ABC*, 7 November; *The Times*, 21 November 1975.

105. Manuel Hidalgo Huerta, *Cómo y por qué operé a Franco* (Madrid: Editorial Garsi, 1976) pp. 18–34;

Pozuelo, *Los 476 últimos días*, pp. 231–6; González Iglesias, *Los dientes*, p. 366; Palma Gámiz, *El paciente*, pp. 146–68; Juan Cobos Arévalo, *La vida privada de Franco. Confesiones del monaguillo del Palacio de El Pardo* (Cordoba: Editorial Almuzara, 2009) pp. 270–5.

106. Hidalgo Huerta, *Cómo y por qué*, pp. 35–55.

107. Gil, *Cuarenta años*, p. 212; Hidalgo Huerta, *Cómo y por qué*, pp. 55–8; Palma Gámiz, *El paciente*, pp. 176–81.

108. Peñafiel, *El General*, pp. 29–35; Ramírez, *El año*, p. 255; Palma Gámiz, *El paciente*, pp. 187–92.

109. Hidalgo Huerta, *Cómo y por qué*, pp. 59–69.

110. *Arriba*, 14, 18 November 1975; Figuero and Herrero, *La muerte*, pp. 35–6, 50–1.

111. *Arriba*, 20 November; *Ya*, 20 November 1975; Pozuelo, *Los 476 últimos días*, pp. 224–41; Baón, *La cara humana*, pp. 26–50; Figuero and Herrero, *La muerte*, pp. 102–12; Palacios and Payne, *Franco, mi padre*, pp. 684–5, 689–90; Hidalgo Huerta, *Cómo y por qué*, pp. 68–70; Luis Herrero, *El ocaso del régimen. Del asesinato de Carrero a la muerte de Franco* (Madrid: Ediciones Temas de Hoy, 1995) pp. 274–80; Pilar Cernuda, *30 días de noviembre. El mes que cambió la historia de España* (Barcelona: Planeta, 2000) pp. 133–40; Palma Gámiz, *El paciente*, pp. 205–12.

112. Juan Miguel Baquero, 'Franco acumuló una fortuna de 400 millones gracias a su entramado corrupto', *40 años de desmemoria* (Madrid: El Diario, 2015) at https://desmemoria.eldiario.es/fortuna-franco/.

113. Peñafiel, *El General*, pp. 132-6.
114. Giménez-Arnau, *Yo, Jimmy*, pp. 84, 164-5.
115. Inmaculada G. Mardones, 'Sin Franco no viven peor', *El País*, 20 November 1985; *Interviú*. No. 614, 17 February 1988; Giménez-Arnau, *Yo, Jimmy*, pp. 164ff.; Julia Navarro, *Señora Presidenta* (Barcelona: Plaza y Janés, 1999) p. 118.
116. *Guardian*, 21, 26, 28 November; *Daily Telegraph*, 21 November; *The Times*, 28 November; *Newsweek*, 1 December 1975; Figuero and Herrero, *La muerte*, pp. 135-7; Victoria Prego, *Así se hizo la Transición* (Barcelona: Plaza y Janés, 1995) pp. 332-6; Cernuda, *30 días*, pp. 165-9; Gallego, *El mito*, pp. 210-16.
117. Paul Preston, *Juan Carlos: Steering Spain from Dictatorship to Democracy* (London: Harper Perennial, 2005) pp. 318-28.
118. Federico Silva Muñoz, *Memorias políticas* (Barcelona: Planeta, 1993) pp. 228-9; Cernuda, *30 días*, pp. 12-13, 221.
119. *Cambio 16*, 17 November 1975; *Le Monde*, 29 January, 2 February 1974; Jose Luis Aranguren, *La cruz de la monarquía española actual* (Madrid: Taurus, 1974) *passim*.
120. *Mundo Obrero*, 25 November; *Servir al Pueblo*, No. 45, November; *Correo del Pueblo*, 18 November, 6 December; *Frente Libertario*, No. 57, December 1975.
121. Alfonso Armada, *Al servicio de la Corona* (Barcelona: Planeta, 1983); Carlos Fernández, *Los militares en la transición política* (Barcelona: Plaza y Janés, 1982) pp. 51-4.

Chapter 16: The Painful Creation of a Democracy, 1975-1982

1. Antonio Garrigues y Diaz-Cañabate, *Diálogos conmigo mismo* (Barcelona: Planeta, 1978) p. 163; José María de Areilza, *Diario de un ministro de la monarquía* (Barcelona: Planeta, 1977) pp. 13-16, 38; Manuel Fraga Iribarne, *En busca del tiempo servido* (Barcelona: Planeta, 1987) pp. 20-2.
2. Pilar Fernández-Miranda Lozana and Alfonso Fernández-Miranda Campoamor, *Lo que el Rey me ha pedido. Torcuato Fernández-Miranda y la reforma política* (Barcelona: Plaza y Janés, 1995) pp. 119-21; Gregorio Morán, *Adolfo Suárez. Historia de una ambición* (Barcelona: Planeta, 1979) pp. 15-20; *Guardian*, 12 December 1975; Joaquín Bardavío, *El dilema. Un pequeño caudillo o un gran Rey* (Madrid: Strips Editores, 1978) pp. 79-84; Paul Preston, *Juan Carlos: Steering Spain from Dictatorship to Democracy* (London: Harper Perennial, 2005) pp. 331-4; Ferran Gallego, *El mito de la transición. La crisis del franquismo y los orígenes de la democracia (1973-1977)* (Barcelona: Crítica, 2008) pp. 217-25.
3. Fernández-Miranda, *Lo que el Rey*, pp. 121, 147-51; Alfonso Osorio, *Trayectoria política de un ministro de la corona* (Barcelona: Planeta, 1980) pp. 54-62; *Arriba*, 29 January 1976; Areilza, *Diario*, pp. 73-6; Victoria Prego, *Así se hizo la Transición* (Barcelona: Plaza y Janés, 1995) pp. 391-4.
4. Areilza, *Diario*, p. 84; *Observer*, 1 February 1976; Bardavío, *El dilema*, p. 105; Osorio, *Trayectoria*, pp. 55, 65.
5. *Cambio 16*, 19-25 January; *Guardian*, 5, 7, 8, 9, 14, 15, 20 January; *Sunday Times*, 11, 18 January; *Mundo Obrero*, 20, 27

January 1976; Rodolfo Martín Villa, *Al servicio del Estado* (Barcelona: Planeta, 1984) pp. 16–17; Victor Diaz Cardiel et al., *Madrid en huelga. Enero 1976* (Madrid: Editorial Ayuso, 1976) pp. 91–150; Areilza, *Diario*, p. 51.

6. Preston, *Juan Carlos*, pp. 336–9.

7. *Mundo Obrero*, 4, 11 February; *Cambio 16*, 9–15 February; 1–7 March 1976.

8. Jose María Portell, *Euskadi. Amnistía arrancada* (Barcelona: Dopesa, 1977) pp. 37–42, 61–98; Mario Onaindía, *La lucha de clases en Euskadi (1939-1980)* (San Sebastián: Haranburu Editor, 1980) pp. 121–6; Gasteiz, *Vitoria, de la huelga a la matanza* (Paris: Ruedo Ibérico, 1976) pp. 117–32, 185–202; Martín Villa, *Al servicio*, pp. 26–8.

9. *Cambio 16*, 29 March–4 April, 19–25 April, 9–15 August, 23–29 August 1976, 12 February 1978; Ángel Amigo, *Pertur: ETA 71–76* (San Sebastián: Hordago Publikapenak, 1978) pp. 94–109, 124–8, 253–74; José María Garmendia, *Historia de ETA*, 2 vols (San Sebastián: L.Haranburu Editor, 1980) II, pp. 178–86; Natxo Arregi, *Memorias del KAS: 1975/78* (San Sebastián: Hordago Publikapenak, 1981) pp. 49–53; Sophie Baby, *El mito de la transición pacífica. Violencia y política en España (1975-1982)* (Madrid: Ediciones Akal, 2018) pp. 222–41.

10. *Mundo Obrero*, 27 January, 4, 11 February 1976; Fernando Claudín, *Santiago Carrillo. Crónica de un secretario general* (Barcelona: Planeta, 1983) pp. 231–4; Paul Preston, *The Last Stalinist: The Life of Santiago Carrillo* (London: William Collins, 2014) pp. 290–8; Areilza, *Diario*, p. 51.

11. *Mundo Obrero*, 9 April 1976; Osorio, *Trayectoria*, pp. 91–4; Areilza, *Diario*, p. 122.

12. Areilza, *Diario*, pp. 119–20, 122, 136–8, 146, 153; Emilio Attard, *Vida y muerte de UCD* (Barcelona: Planeta, 1983) p. 49; conversation of the author with Felipe González.

13. *Cambio 16*, 15–21 March 1976; Moran, *Suárez*, pp. 31–2; Osorio, *Trayectoria*, pp. 86–91; Martin Villa, *Al servicio*, pp. 28–9; Gasteiz, *Vitoria*, pp. 117–32; Preston, *Juan Carlos*, pp. 343–5.

14. Javier Figuero, *UCD. La 'empresa' que creo Adolfo Suárez* (Barcelona: Grijalbo, 1981) pp. 23–26; Areilza, *Diario*, p. 165; Antonio Izquierdo, *Yo, testigo de cargo* (Barcelona: Planeta, 1981) p. 41.

15. Minutes of Coordinación Democrática meeting, 9 April 1976, Oposición Española, *Documentos secretos* (Madrid: Sedmay Ediciones, 1976) pp. 108–12.

16. *Newsweek*, 26 April; *Guardian*, 3 July 1976; Areilza, *Diario*, pp. 105, 118, 124, 133–4, 146–8, 161–8, 178; José María de Areilza, *Cuadernos de la transicion* (Barcelona: Planeta, 1983) pp. 23–6; Preston, *Juan Carlos*, pp. 346–53; Javier Tusell and Genoveva García Queipo de Llano, *Tiempo de incertidumbre. Carlos Arias Navarro entre el franquismo y la transición (1973-1976)* (Barcelona: Crítica, 2003) pp. 321–6; Arias interview in Bayod, ed., *Franco*, p. 313; Gallego, *El mito*, pp. 383–410.

17. *El País*, 2, 4 July 1976; Osorio, *Trayectoria*, pp. 126–9; Morán, *Suárez*, pp. 55–61; Bardavío, *El dilema*, pp. 150–5; Izquierdo, *Yo, testigo*, p. 41; Preston, *Juan Carlos*, pp. 351–6; Gallego, *El mito*, pp. 411–20.

18. *Cambio 16*, 12–18, 19–25 July; *Mundo Obrero*, 14 July 1976; Adolfo Suárez's intervention at a private seminar held by the Fundación Ortega y Gasset in Toledo in May 1984 (henceforth FOG/Toledo).

19. *El País*, 6, 21 July; *Cambio 16*, 12–18 July 1976; Álvarez de Miranda, *Del 'contubernio'*, pp. 107–9; Areilza, *Cuadernos*, pp. 15–16, 39–40, 47–8, 56–8, 71–4; Osorio, *Trayectoria*, pp. 129–38; Bardavío, *El Dilema*, pp. 173–4.

20. Suárez, FOG/Toledo; *Cambio 16*, 9–15, 23–29 August; *Mundo Obrero*, 26 July–2 August, 1 September 1976; Joaquin Bardavío, *Sábado santo rojo* (Madrid: Ediciones Uve, 1980) pp. 42–4, 52; Morán, *Suárez*, p. 337; José J. A. Sagardoy and David León Blanco, *El poder sindical en España* (Barcelona: Planeta, 1982) p. 161.

21. Morán, *Suárez*, pp. 235–44, 331–2; Osorio, *Trayectoria*, pp. 141–2, 155, 162–4, 171–4; Figuero, *UCD*, pp. 48–51; *Cambio 16*, 26 July–1 August, 16–22 August 1976; remarks of Suárez, Gonzalez and Carrillo at FOG/Toledo.

22. *Cambio 16*, 13–20 September; *Mundo Obrero*, 8 September 1976.

23. Fernando Puell de la Villa, *Gutiérrez Mellado. Un militar del siglo XX (1912–1995)* (Madrid: Biblioteca Nueva, 1997) pp. 187–91; Manuel Gutiérrez Mellado, *Un Soldado para España* (Barcelona: Argos Vergara, 1983) pp. 40–1, 47; Areilza, *Diario*, pp. 76–7, 81, 152; Fernández, *Los militares*, p. 63; Preston, *Juan Carlos*, pp. 33–6.

24. *El Alcázar*, 23, 27 September; *Cambio 16*, 4–10, 11–17 October 1976; Osorio, *Trayectoria*, pp. 183–9; Fernández, *Los militares*, pp. 109–13; Colectivo Democracia, *Los Ejércitos ... más allá del golpe*

(Barcelona: Planeta, 1981) p. 63; Carlos Iniesta Cano, *Memorias y recuerdos* (Barcelona: Planeta, 1984) pp. 242–50; Bardavío, *El dilema*, pp. 184–92.

25. *El País*, 24 December; *El Alcázar*, 28 December 1976; *Cambio 16*, 3–9 January 1977; Martín Villa, *Al servicio*, p. 60.

26. *Mundo Obrero*, 15 September 1976; Osorio, *Trayectoria*, p. 206; Areilza, *Cuadernos*, pp. 47–8, 71, 78; Morán, *Suárez*, p. 334; Claudín, *Carrillo*, pp. 238–40; Eduardo Chamorro, *Felipe González. Un hombre a la espera* (Barcelona: Planeta, 1980) pp. 133–6; Gallego, *El mito*, pp. 482–98.

27. Suárez, FOG/Toledo; *El País*, 18, 19 November; *Cambio 16*, 22–28 November 1976; Emilio Attard, *La Constitución por dentro* (Barcelona: Argos Vergara, 1983) p. 76; Osorio, *Trayectoria*, pp. 230–46; Areilza, *Cuadernos*, p. 67; Morán, *Suárez*, pp. 312–16; Ignacio Sánchez-Cuenca, *Atado y bien atado. El suicidio institucional del franquismo y el surgimiento de la democracia* (Madrid: Alianza, 2014) pp. 205–82.

28. *Mundo Obrero*, 1–7, 15–21, 22 November; *Cambio 16*, 22–28 November, 5 December 1976; Osorio, *Trayectoria*, pp. 208–9; Martín Villa, *Al servicio*, pp. 54–7.

29. *El País*, 28 November; *Mundo Obrero*, 6–12 December 1976.

30. *Cambio 16*, 19 December 1976; Chamorro, *Felipe González*, pp. 136–43; PSOE, *XXVII Congreso* (Madrid: Avance, 1977) *passim*; Fernando Barciela, *La otra historia del PSOE* (Madrid: Emiliano Escolar, 1981) p. 19.

31. *El País*, 14, 15, 16, 17 December 1976; *Cambio 16*, 26 December, 27 December 1976–2 January 1977;

Osorio, *Trayectoria*, pp. 252–3; Felipe González, FOG/Toledo.

32. Osorio, *Trayectoria*, pp. 212–13; Manuel Durán, *Martín Villa* (San Sebastián: Hordago Publikapenak, 1979) *passim*; *Cambio 16*, 19–25 July, 2–8, 23–29 August, 11–17, 18–24 October 1976; Portell, *Amnistía*, pp. 170–4.

33. *Mundo Obrero*, 20–26 December 1976; Bardavío, *Sábado*, pp. 88–111; Osorio, *Trayectoria*, pp. 254–8; Claudín, *Carrillo*, pp. 2–9, 239–41; Preston, *The Last Stalinist*, pp. 302–5.

34. *El País*, 12 December 1976; *Cambio 16*, 31 January–6 February 1977; *Mundo Obrero*, 31 January–6 February 1977; Pio Moa Rodriguez, *De un tiempo y de un País* (Madrid: Ediciónes de la Torre, 1982) pp. 217–33; Durán, *Martín Villa*, p. 79; Bardavío, *Sábado*, pp. 142–7; Preston, *The Last Stalinist*, pp. 302–5.

35. Morán, *Suárez*, pp. 43–4, 324–8; Osorio, *Trayectoria*, pp. 97–108, 190–7, 291–9.

36. *Cambio 16*, 27 September–3 October, 18–24 October 1976; Areilza, *Cuadernos*, pp. 43–4, 50, 56; Osorio, *Trayectoria*, pp. 200–5; Pedro J. Ramírez, *Así se ganaron las elecciones* (Barcelona: Planeta, 1977) pp. 92–108; Christina Palomares, *The Quest for Survival after Franco: Moderate Francoism and the Slow Journey to the Polls, 1964–1977* (Brighton: Sussex Academic Press, 2004) pp. 165–80.

37. Jorge Verstrynge, *Memorias de un maldito* (Madrid: Grijalbo, 1999) pp. 211–13; Mariano Sánchez Soler, *Ricos por la guerra civil de España* (Madrid: Editorial Raíces, 2007) pp. 143–4; Fernando Jáuregui, *La derecha después de Fraga* (Madrid: El País, 1987) p. 181; Melchor

Miralles, *Dinero sucio. Diccionario de la corrupción en España* (Madrid: Temas de hoy, 1992) pp. 293–4.

38. Carlos Dávila and Luis Herrero, *De Fraga a Fraga. Crónica secreta de Alianza Popular* (Barcelona: Plaza y Janés, 1989) pp. 105–12.

39. Paul Preston, *The Triumph of Democracy in Spain* (London: Methuen, 1986) pp. 109–14.

40. Attard, *Vida y muerte*, pp. 34–53; Osorio, *Trayectoria*, pp. 190–7, 300–2; Álvarez de Miranda, *Del 'contubernio'*, pp. 112–20; Jáuregui and Soriano, *UCD*, pp. 43–8, 61–4; *El País*, 25 March; *Cambio 16*, 4–10 April 1977; Areilza, *Cuadernos*, pp. 92–4, 108–23; Ramírez, *Elecciones*, pp. 29–31; Figuero, *UCD*, pp. 57–61.

41. *Cambio 16*, 16–22 May; *El País*, 6, 7, 8 May 1977; *Diario 16*, 28 January 1978; Figuero, *UCD*, pp. 232–4; Attard, *Vida y muerte*, pp. 52–7; Ramírez, *Elecciones*, pp. 116–21, 139–49, 158–9; Álvarez de Miranda, *Del 'contubernio'*, pp. 127–9.

42. Preston, *Triumph*, pp. 108–14.

43. *Mundo Obrero*, 7–13, 21–27 March, 4–10, 11–17 April; *Cambio 16*, 18–24 April, 25 April–1 May, 2–8 May; *El País*, 15, 16 April; *ABC*, 14 April 1977; Suárez, FOG/Toledo; Morán, *Suárez*, pp. 320–1, 338; Claudín, *Carrillo*, pp. 245–8; Bardavío, *Sábado*, pp. 158–68, 196–200; Izquierdo, *Yo, testigo*, pp. 29, 63–4; Osorio, *Trayectoria*, pp. 288–91; Martín Villa, *Al servicio*, p. 69; Colectivo Democracia, *Los Ejércitos*, pp. 94–102; Pilar Urbano, *Con la venia. Yo indagué el 23 F* (Barcelona: Argos Vergara, 1982) p. 16; Preston, *The Last Stalinist*, pp. 306–12.

44. *Cambio 16*, 6–12 June 1977.
45. Ramírez, *Elecciones*, pp. 52, 127–32, 228–44, 304–6.
46. *Cambio 16*, 13–19 June 1977.
47. *Cambio 16*, 20–26 June, 27 June–3 July; *El País*, 15, 22, 29 May 1977; Ramírez, *Elecciones*, pp. 208–11, 248–9, 284–90.
48. Juan Luis Cebrián, *La España que bosteza* (Madrid: Taurus, 1981) pp. 22–5.
49. Juan J. Linz et al., *IV Informe FOESSA*, Vol. I: *Informe sociológico sobre el cambio político en España: 1975-1981* (Madrid: Euramérica, 1981) pp. 161–3.
50. Álvarez de Miranda, *Del 'contubernio'*, pp. 138–44; Jauregui and Soriano, *UCD*, pp. 48–9, 75–92; Figuero, *UCD*, pp. 82–4; Osorio, *Trayectoria*, pp. 331–6.
51. Durán, *Martín Villa*, pp. 113–25; *Cambio 16*, 19–25 September, 26 September–2 October, 3–9 October 1977; Álvarez de Miranda, *Del 'contubernio'*, pp. 157–9, 165; Martín Villa, *Al servicio*, pp. 150–8.
52. Unión Militar Democrática, *Los militares y la lucha por la democracia* (n.p., n.d. [but Madrid, 1976]) p. 47; José Luis Morales and Juan Celada, *La alternativa militar. El golpismo después de Franco* (Madrid: Editorial Revolución, 1981) pp. 67–85; Urbano, *Con la venia*, pp. 23–5; Fernández, *Los militares*, pp. 190–1.
53. *El País*, 20 September; *Cambio 16*, 3–9 October 1977; Fernández, *Los militares*, pp. 181–3; Amadeo Martínez Inglés, *La transición vigilada. Del Sábado Santo 'rojo' al 23-F* (Madrid: Ediciones Temas de Hoy, 1994) pp. 95–104.
54. Juan Pla, *La trama civil del golpe* (Barcelona: Planeta, 1982) p. 85; Urbano, *Con la venia*, p. 16; Alejandro Muñoz Alonso, *El*

terrorismo en España (Barcelona: Planeta, 1982) pp. 245–6; Colectivo Democracia, *Los Ejércitos*, p. 96.
55. *Cambio 16*, 24–30 October, 14–20 November 1977.
56. *Cambio 16*, 11–17 July, 10–16 October 1977; Suarez, FOG/Toledo; Osorio, *Trayectoria*, pp. 319–27; Martín Villa, *Al servicio*, pp. 174–8; Salvador Sánchez-Terán, *De Franco a la Generalitat* (Barcelona: Planeta, 1988) pp. 48–53, 282–320; Josep Tarradellas, *'Ja sóc aquí'. Recuerdo de un retorno* (Barcelona: Planeta, 1990) pp. 34–9, 110–58, 218–30; Preston, *Juan Carlos*, pp. 407–10.
57. *Cambio 16*, 17–23 October; *El País*, 4, 11 October 1977; Francisco Espinosa Maestre, 'Desclasifiquen las vergüenzas del franquismo', *Público*, 20 November 2015.
58. Miguel Castells Arteche, *El mejor defensor el pueblo* (San Sebastián: Ediciones Vascas, 1978) pp. 197–9; Txiki Benegas, *Euskadi. Sin la paz nada es posible* (Barcelona: Argos Vergara, 1984) pp. 80–2.
59. *Cambio 16*, 12–18 December, 26 December 1977–1 January 1978, 9–15 January 1978; Manuel Clavero Arévalo, *España, desde el centralismo a las autonomias* (Barcelona: Planeta, 1983) pp. 46–50.
60. Cf. Carrillo's speeches in the Cortes on 27 July, 14 September and 24 September 1977, reprinted in Santiago Carrillo, *Escritos sobre Eurocomunismo*, 2 vols (Madrid: Forma Ediciones, 1977) II, pp. 83–128; Victoria Prego, *Presidentes. Veinticinco años de historia narrada por los cuatro jefes de Gobierno de la democracia* (Barcelona: Plaza y Janés, 2000) pp. 70–3.
61. *Mundo Obrero*, 16 June, 16 August, 8–14 September, 2–19 December

1977; *Cambio 16*, 17–23, 24–30 October, 31 October–6 November, 7–13 November 1977; Santiago Carrillo, *Memorias* (Barcelona: Planeta, 1993) pp. 741–7; Claudin, *Carrillo*, pp. 275–9; Jesús Sánchez Rodríguez, *Teoría y práctica democrática en el PCE (1956–1982)* (Madrid: Fundación de Investigaciones Marxistas, 2004) pp. 286–9; Paul Heywood, 'Mirror Images: The PCE and the PSOE in the Transition to Democracy in Spain', *West European Politics*, Vol. 10, No. 10, April 1987, pp. 193–210.

62. *Informe Económico 1981* (Bilbao: Banco de Bilbao, 1982) pp. 154–61.

63. *Cambio 16*, 21–27 November 1977; Attard, *La Constitución*, pp. 77–90, 119–23, 223; Antonio Hernández Gil, *El cambio político español y la Constitución* (Barcelona: Planeta, 1984) pp. 283ff.

64. Attard, *La Constitución*, pp. 92–107; Martín Villa, *Al servicio*, p. 86; Álvarez de Miranda, *Del 'contubernio'*, pp. 179–95; *El Alcázar*, 6 July 1978.

65. *El País*, 13 January; *Cambio 16*, 23 July 1978; Preston, *Triumph*, pp. 138–41; Durán, *Martín Villa*, pp. 127–9.

66. *Cambio 16*, 5 February, 26 November 1978.

67. *Cambio 16*, 5, 12, 19 March, 29 April, 28 May, 4 June 1978; Attard, *Vida y muerte*, p. 67; Jauregui and Soriano, *UCD*, pp. 88, 115, 125.

68. *Cambio 16*, 23 July, 3, 10, 17 September 1978; Durán, *Martín Villa*, pp. 139–48, 167–94; Martín Villa, *Al servicio*, pp. 147–8; Benegas, *Euskadi*, pp. 102–3.

69. *Cambio 16*, 28 May, 9 July; *El País*, 29 June 1978; Luciano Rincón, *ETA (1974–1984)* (Barcelona: Plaza y Janés, 1985) pp. 163–6; Benegas, *Euskadi*, pp. 105–8; author's

interview with Rodolfo Martín Villa in Madrid in October 1984.

70. *Cambio 16*, 28 May, 4 June, 9, 30 July, 29 October, 12, 19 November; *El País*, 30 June, 29 July, 1 November 1978; Izquierdo, *Yo, testigo*, pp. 99–102; Rincón, *ETA*, pp. 21–2; Muñoz Alonso, *El terrorismo*, pp. 133–40; Benegas, *Euskadi*, pp. 88–9.

71. *El País*, 17, 19 November; *Cambio 16*, 3, 10 December; *El Alcázar*, 23 November 1978; Colectivo Democracia, *Los Ejércitos*, pp. 78–85; Morales and Celada, *La alternativa*, pp. 43–8; Martín Villa, *Al servicio*, pp. 134–5, 148–50; Urbano, *Con la venia*, p. 19; Izquierdo, *Yo, testigo*, pp. 49, 68–9; José Oneto, *La noche de Tejero* (Barcelona: Planeta, 1981) pp. 27–34; Antonio Izquierdo, *Claves para un día de febrero* (Barcelona: Planeta, 1982) pp. 28–9.

72. *El País*, 8, 9 December; *Cambio 16*, 17 December 1978; Ministerio del Interior, *Referendum Constitucional. Información sobre resultados provisionales de la votación* (Madrid: Ministerio del Interior, 1978).

73. Benegas, *Euskadi*, pp. 89–91.

74. Preston, *Triumph*, pp. 150–7; *Cambio 16*, 14 January, 11 February, 4, 11, 18 March; *El País*, 4 March 1979; Pedro J. Ramírez, *Así se ganaron las elecciones 1979* (Madrid: Prensa Española, 1979) pp. 179–263; Josep Meliá, *Asi cayó Adolfo Suárez* (Barcelona: Planeta, 1981) p. 29.

75. *El País*, 30, 31 March, 28, 29, 30 September, 2, 7 October; *Diario 16*, 1 October; *Mundo Obrero*, 2 October; *Cambio 16*, 15 April, 7 October 1979.

76. *El País*, 4, 5, 6 April; *Cambio 16*, 15 April 1979; Suarez, FOG/Toledo.

77. *Cambio 16*, 14, 28 May, 5, 12 October 1978; Ramírez, *Las elecciones 1979*, pp. 81, 103–16; Jaúregui and Soriano, *UCD*, pp. 101–4: Preston, *Triumph*, pp. 160–1.
78. *El País*, 12 May 1979; Armada, *Al servicio*, p. 215; Morales and Celada, *La alternativa*, pp. 51–3.
79. *Cambio 16*, 24 June, 1, 15, 22, 29 July, 5 August, 30 September, 7, 14 October, 4 November 1979; Attard, *Vida y muerte*, pp. 70–2; Jaúregui and Soriano, *UCD*, pp. 129–30.
80. *Cambio 16*, 13, 20 May, 21 October 1979; Miguel Castells Arteche, *Radiografía de un modelo represivo* (San Sebastián: Ediciones Vascas, 1982) pp. 33–8, 129–30.
81. *El Alcázar*, 21 September; *Cambio 16*, 7 October 1979.
82. Morales and Celada, *La alternativa*, pp. 74–7; Armada, *Al servicio*, pp. 216–17; Urbano, *Con la venia*, p. 21.
83. *El Alcázar*, 20 October 1979; *El País*, 27 January; *Diario 16*, 25 January; *Cambio 16*, 10 February 1980; Colectivo Democracia, *Los Ejércitos*, pp. 85–91; Morales and Celada, *La alternativa*, pp. 57–61; Urbano, *Con la venia*, pp. 21–3.
84. Martín Villa, *Al servicio*, p. 90.
85. *Cambio 16*, 16 December 1979, 27 January 1980.
86. *Cambio 16*, 3, 17, 24 February, 16, 30 March; *El País*, 18 February, 2, 3, 22 March 1980; Martín Villa, *Al servicio*, p. 90.
87. Preston, *Triumph*, pp. 172–4; *Cambio 16*, 2 March, 6, 13 April, 18, 25 May, 21 September 1980; Meliá, *Así cayó*, pp. 22, 39; Jaúregui and Soriano, *UCD*, pp. 31–6; José Oneto, *Los últimos días de un presidente* (Barcelona: Planeta,

1981) pp. 27, 35, 82; Martín Villa, *Al servicio*, p. 91.
88. *El País*, 3, 4, 21, 22, 23, 29, 30 May; *Cambio 16*, 16 March, 18 May, 1, 8, 29 June, 3 August 1980; Martín Villa, *Al servicio*, p. 94; Meliá, *Así cayó*, pp. 36–7; Oneto, *Los últimos días*, p. 50; Preston, *Triumph*, pp. 174–5.
89. *El País*, 8, 9, 30, 31 July; *Diario 16*, 8 July; *Cambio 16*, 13, 20, 27 July, 3, 10, 17 August 1980; Meliá, *Así cayó*, pp. 42–58; Oneto, *Los últimos días*, pp. 50–3; Jaúregui and Soriano, *UCD*, pp. 15–20, 34–7, 150–6; Jonathan Hopkin, *Party Formation and Democratic Transition in Spain: The Creation and Collapse of the Union of the Democratic Centre* (London: Macmillan, 1999) pp. 151–69.
90. *El País*, 22 June; *Cambio 16*, 13, 20 July, 17, 24 August, 7 September 1980; Rincón, *ETA*, p. 63.
91. *El País*, 10 September; *Cambio 16*, 21 September, 5, 12 October 1980; Meliá, *Así cayó*, pp. 51–9; Oneto, *Los últimos días*, pp. 67–8.
92. *Cambio 16*, 12, 19 October; *El País*, 2, 13 October 1980; Muñoz Alonso, *El terrorismo*, p. 227.
93. *El Alcázar*, 16, 21 September, 2 December 1980; conversation of the author with Felipe González in March 1981; *Cambio 16*, 9 March 1981; Armada, *Al servicio*, pp. 216, 223–7; Santiago Segura and Julio Merino, *Jaque al Rey. Las 'enigmas' y las 'incongruencias' del 23-F* (Barcelona: Planeta, 1983) pp. 53–4, 77–8; Morales and Celada, *La alternativa*, pp. 122–5; Santiago Segura and Julio Merino, *Visperas del 23-F* (Barcelona: Plaza y Janés, 1984) pp. 297–301; Urbano, *Con la venia*, pp. 33–5; Jesús Palacios, *23-F. El Rey y su secreto* (Madrid: Libros Libres, 2010) pp. 187–96.

94. *Cambio 16*, 5, 12, 19, 26 October, 3 November; *El País*, 24, 25, 26 October 1980.

95. *Cambio 16*, 10, 17, 24 November; *El País*, 11 November 1980; Benegas, *Euskadi*, pp. 110–11; Muñoz Alonso, *El terrorismo*, pp. 229–31.

96. *Cambio 16*, 17 November 1980; Urbano, *Con la venia*, pp. 24–5; Morales and Celada, *La alternativa*, pp. 89–91, 122–5; Jesús Palacios, *23-F: El golpe del CESID* (Barcelona: Planeta, 2001) pp. 25–30.

97. Fraga, *En busca*, pp. 223–4; Urbano, *Con la venia*, pp. 42–3.

98. Meliá, *Así cayó*, pp. 59–63; Oneto, *Los últimos días*, pp. 69–70; *Diario 16*, 12 January; *Cambio 16*, 26 January 1981.

99. Jaúregui and Soriano, *UCD*, pp. 195–9; Attard, *Vida y muerte*, pp. 180–1; Meliá, *Así cayó*, pp. 59–63; Oneto, *Los últimos días*, pp. 69–70; *Diario 16*, 12 January; *Cambio 16*, 26 January 1981.

100. Attard, *Vida y muerte*, p. 189; *Cambio 16*, 2 February 1981; Meliá, *Así cayó*, pp. 13–19, 68–74.

101. *El País*, 30 January; *El Alcázar*, 30 January; *Diario 16*, 30 January 1981; Oneto, *Los últimos días*, pp. 113, 119, 152; Meliá, *Así cayó*, pp. 74–5; Morales and Celada, *La alternativa*, pp. 125–6; Urbano, *Con la venia*, pp. 52–7.

102. *El Alcázar*, 24 January; *ABC*, 31 January 1981; Oneto, *Los últimos días*, pp. 74–5; Figuero, *UCD*, p. 4.

103. *Cambio 16*, 9 February 1981; Meliá, *Así cayó*, pp. 96–9, 118–19; Oneto, *Los últimos días*, pp. 124–6, 152–3, 159–63; Prego, *Presidentes*, pp. 113–21.

104. *Cambio 16*, 16 February 1981; Benegas, *Euskadi*, pp. 132–4; Urbano, *Con la venia*, pp. 73–5.

105. *Cambio 16*, 16, 23 February 1981; Rincón, *ETA*, pp. 123–4, 172–6.

106. *El Alcázar*, 8 February 1981.

107. *El Alcázar*, 17 December 1980, 22 January, 1 February; *Cambio 16*, 22 June 1981; Morales and Celada, *La alternativa*, pp. 127–30; Pla, *La trama civil*, pp. 59–69; Francisco Medina Ortega, *23F. La verdad* (Barcelona: Plaza y Janés, 2006) pp. 119–45; Urbano, *Con la venia*, pp. 47–8; Ricardo Pardo Zancada, *23-F. La pieza que falta. Testimonio de un protagonista* (Barcelona: Plaza y Janés, 1998) pp. 151–5; Javier Fernández López, *Diecisiete horas y media. El enigma del 23-F* (Madrid: Taurus, 2000) pp. 238–43; Pilar Cernuda, Fernando Jáuregui and Manuel Ángel Menéndez, *23-F. La conjura de los necios* (Madrid: Foca Ediciones, 2001) pp. 54–6; Palacios, *23-F. El golpe*, pp. 266–72.

108. *El País*, 7, 8, 22 February; *Diario 16*, 9 February; *Cambio 16*, 16 February 1981; Hopkin, *Party Formation*, pp. 179–92; Attard, *Vida y muerte*, pp. 193–207; Martín Villa, *Al servicio*, pp. 94–6.

109. *El País*, 3, 10, 13, 14 February; *Cambio 16*, 16, 23 February 1981; Izquierdo, *Claves*, pp. 99–103, 121–8, 135, 143; Morales and Celada, *La alternativa*, p. 132; Castells, *Radiografía*, pp. 31, 95, 159; Pla, *La trama civil*, pp. 46–50; Urbano, *Con la venia*, pp. 76–7.

110. *El País*, 24, 25, 26, 27, 28 February; *Cambio 16*, 2, 9 March 1981; Colectivo Democracia, *Los Ejércitos*, pp. 140ff.; Preston, *Juan Carlos*, pp. 467–72; Oneto, *La noche de Tejero*, passim; Urbano, *Con la venia*, pp. 143, 365–7; Armada, *Al servicio*, pp. 240–95; Segura and Merino, *Jaque*, pp. 75–188, 220–32; Morales and Celada, *La alternativa*, pp. 135–46.

111. Armada, *Al servicio*, pp. 231, 236; Segura and Merino, *Jaque*, pp. 56–8,

145–6; Martín Prieto, *Técnica de un golpe de Estado. El juicio del 23-F* (Barcelona: Grijalbo, 1982) pp. 88–94; José Oneto, *La verdad sobre el caso Tejero. El proceso del siglo* (Barcelona: Planeta, 1982) pp. 90, 116, 205–35.

112. Author's interviews with Sabino Fernández Campo and Alfonso Armada; Notes of General Quintana Lacaci, *El País*, 17 February 1991; Informe de Alberto Oliart al Congreso, *El País*, 18 March 1981; Fernando Reinlein, *Capitanes rebeldes. Los militares españoles durante la Transición: de la UMD al 23-F* (Madrid: La Esfera de los Libros, 2002) pp. 319–38; Cernuda, Jáuregui and Menéndez, *La conjura*, pp. 135–6, 142–8, 151–8, 200–2, 210, 216; Urbano, *Con la venia*, pp. 167–74; Fernández López, *Diecisiete horas y media*, pp. 133–5, 138–9, 147–57, 165–6; Palacios, *23-F. El Rey*, pp. 63–5, 212–19; Gabriel Cardona, *Las torres del honor. Un capitán del Ejército en la Transición y el golpe de Estado del 23-F* (Barcelona: Ediciones Destino, 2011) pp. 248–99; Andreu Farràs and Pere Cullell, *El 23-F a Catalunya* (Barcelona: Planeta, 1998) pp. 79–85; José Luis de Vilallonga, *Le Roi. Entretiens* (Paris: Fixot, 1993) pp. 169–70, 186, 195; Joaquín Prieto and José Luis Barbería, *El enigma del 'Elefante'. La conspiración del 23-F* (Madrid: El País-Aguilar, 1991) pp. 172–5, 300–1; Armada, *Al servicio*, pp. 240–3, 246–7; Javier Fernández López, *El Rey y otros militares. Los militares en el cambio de régimen político en España (1969-1982)* (Madrid: Editorial Trotta, 1998) pp. 167, 174–7; Manuel Soriano, *Sabino Fernández Campo. La sombra del Rey* (Madrid: Ediciones Temas de Hoy, 1995) pp. 351, 353–7; Diego Carcedo, *23-F. Los cabos sueltos* (Madrid: Ediciones Temas de Hoy, 2001) pp. 345–51, 356–9, 371–2, 375–6; Pardo Zancada, *23-F*, pp. 330–2, 340–65, 368–70; Eduardo Fuentes Gómez de Salazar, *El pacto del capó. El testimonio clave de un militar sobre el 23-F* (Madrid: Ediciones Temas de Hoy, 1994) pp. 105–36; Medina, *23-F. La verdad*, pp. 367–81.

113. Gregorio Morán, *Adolfo Suárez. Ambición y destino* (Barcelona: Debate, 2009) pp. 298–303; Oneto, *La verdad*, pp. 321–2; Cernuda, Jáuregui and Menéndez, *La conjura*, pp. 158–61.

114. Preston, *Juan Carlos*, pp. 473–85; Medina, *23-F. La verdad*, pp. 402–9. See also Javier Cercas, *Anatomía de un instante* (Barcelona: Mondadori, 2009).

115. Patricia Sverlo (pseudonym of Rebeca Quintans), *Un Rey golpe a golpe. Biografía no autorizada de Juan Carlos de Borbón* (Pamplona: Ardi Beltza, 2000) pp. 181–208; Rebeca Quintans, *Juan Carlos I. La biografía sin silencios* (Madrid: Akal, 2016) pp. 219–22; Amadeo Martínez Inglés, *23-F. El golpe que nunca existió* (Madrid: Foca Ediciones, 2001) pp. 99–119, 191–7; Palacios, *23-F. El golpe*, pp. 338–43; Juan Blanco, *23-F. Crónica fiel de un golpe anunciado* (Madrid: Fuerza Nueva Editorial, 1995) pp. 364–74; Palacios, *23-F. El Rey*, pp. 28–47, 196–229.

116. Ricardo Cid Cañaveral et al., *Todos al suelo: la conspiración y el golpe* (Madrid: Editorial Punto Crítico, 1981) pp. 205–7; Morales and Celada, *La alternativa*, pp. 146–8.

117. *Cambio 16*, 23 February, 9, 16 March, 8 June 1981.

118. Paul Preston and Denis Smyth, *Spain, the EEC and NATO* (London: Routledge & Kegan Paul, 1984) pp. 15-21, 53-4.

119. *El Alcázar*, 26, 27, 28 February; *Cambio 16*, 23 March, 20 April; *El País*, 6, 7, 20, 21, 22 March; *ABC*, 12 April 1981; Morales and Celada, *La alternativa*, pp. 166-8.

120. *El País*, 5, 6, 8, 9 May; *Cambio 16*, 11, 18 May 1981.

121. *El País*, 22, 24, 26 May; *Cambio 16*, 1, 8 June; *El Alcázar*, 27 May 1981.

122. *Cambio 16*, 29 June, 6 July 1981.

123. *Cambio 16*, 25 May, 29 June, 6 July 1981.

124. *Cambio 16*, 29 June, 6, 20 July, 17 August; *El Alcázar*, 27 May 1981.

125. *Cambio 16*, 3, 10, 17 August, 7, 14 September, 23 November; *El País*, 2 September, 4 November 1981; Martín Villa, *Al servicio*, p. 96; Attard, *Vida y muerte*, pp. 232-52; Hopkin, *Party Formation*, pp. 193-4.

126. *El País*, 21, 22 October; *Cambio 16*, 26 October, 2 November 1981; Attard, *Vida y muerte*, pp. 263-5.

127. *El País*, 20, 21, 22, 23 April; *Mundo Obrero*, 20, 23, 27 April 1978.

128. *Cambio 16*, 9, 16, 23, 30 November, 7 December; *El País*, 3, 14, 15, 23 November, 7, 8 December 1981; Attard, *Vida y muerte*, pp. 269-75; Martín Villa, *Al servicio*, pp. 100, 117.

129. *Cambio 16*, 3, 31 August, 7, 14, 21 December 1981.

130. *Cambio 16*, 18, 25 January, 1 February 1982.

131. For a day-by-day chronicle of the trial, see Martín Prieto, *Técnica*, pp. 13-310. For a full account of the defendants and witnesses, see Oneto, *La verdad*, pp. 3-259, 263-314. See also Francisco Mora, *Ni heroes ni bribones. Los personajes del 23-F* (Barcelona: Planeta, 1982)

pp. 19-199. An unashamedly pro-*golpista* version is given by Segura and Merino, *Jaque*.

132. *Cambio 16*, 29 March 1982; Pla, *La trama civil*, p. 28; Preston, *Triumph*, pp. 218-20.

133. *Cambio 16*, 17, 24, 31 May 1982; Martín Villa, *Al servicio*, p. 100.

134. *El País*, 4, 5 June; *Cambio 16*, 31 May, 7, 14 June 1982; Oneto, *La verdad*, pp. 379-406; Martín Prieto, *Técnica*, pp. 382-3; Segura and Merino, *Jaque*, pp. 214-40.

135. *El País*, 31 July; *Cambio 16*, 26 July, 2 August 1982; Prego, *Presidentes*, pp. 168-71.

136. Preston, *The Last Stalinist*, pp. 326-9.

137. *El País*, 1, 26, 27, 28 August; *Cambio 16*, 2, 9, 23, 30 August 1982.

138. *El País*, 14, 15 September; *Cambio 16*, 6, 13, 20 September 1982.

139. PSOE, *Por el cambio. Programa electoral* (Madrid: PSOE, 1982); *Cambio 16*, 27 September 1982.

140. *El País*, 3, 4, 5, 6, 7, 8, 14 October; *El Alcázar*, 6, 7 October; *Cambio 16*, 11, 18 October 1982; Cernuda, Jáuregui and Menéndez, *La conjura*, pp. 255-63.

141. *El País*, 29, 30 October; *Cambio 16*, 1 November 1982. The best account of the campaign and the results can be found in Alejandro Muñoz Alonso et al., *Las elecciones del cambio* (Barcelona: Editorial Argos Vergara, 1984).

Chapter 17: The Grandeur and Misery of a Newborn Democracy, 1982-2004

1. Paul Preston and Denis Smyth, *Spain, the EEC and NATO* (London: Routledge & Kegan Paul, 1984) pp. 75-80; Paul Preston, *Juan Carlos: Steering Spain from Dictatorship to Democracy* (London: Harper Perennial, 2005) pp. 495-500.

2. Javier Pradera, *Corrupción y política. Los costes de la democracia* (Barcelona: Galaxia Gutenberg, 2014) pp. 64–5.

3. 'Evolución del desempleo', *El País*, 20 November 2015; inflation figures from inflation.eu; Vicent Soler, 'Epíleg', in Ernest Lluch, *La vía valenciana* (Valencia: Afers, 2003) pp. 252–3.

4. *El País*, 5 February 1988; *ABC*, 19 April 1994; Pradera, *Corrupción y política*, pp. 66–7.

5. Charles T. Powell, *España en democracia, 1975–2000* (Barcelona: Plaza y Janés, 2001) pp. 417–24.

6. Paul Heywood, 'Analysing Political Corruption in Western Europe: Spain and the UK in Comparative Perspective', in Donatella Della Porta and Susan Rose-Ackerman, eds, *Corrupt Exchanges: Empirical Themes in the Politics and Political Economy of Corruption* (Baden-Baden: Nomos: 2002) pp. 49–52.

7. David Ruiz, *La España democrática (1975–2000). Política y sociedad* (Madrid: Síntesis, 2002) pp. 95–6.

8. Baltasar Garzón, *El fango. Cuarenta años de corrupción en España* (Barcelona: Debate, 2015) pp. 98–104; Paddy Woodworth, *Dirty War, Clean Hands. ETA, the GAL and Spanish Democracy* (Cork: Cork University Press, 2001) pp. 46–8, 66–83, 101–14, 220–1, 240–1, 268–76; Melchor Miralles and Ricardo Arques, *Amedo. El Estado contra ETA* (Barcelona: Plaza y Janés/Cambio 16, 1989) pp. 149–239, 322–64, 405–15; Paul Heywood, 'Corruption, Democracy and Governance in Contemporary Spain', in Sebastian Balfour, ed., *The Politics of Contemporary Spain* (London: Routledge, 2005) pp. 43–4.

9. *El País*, 8 June; *ABC* (Seville), 23 June 1996; Melchor Miralles, *Dinero sucio. Diccionario de la corrupción en España* (Madrid: Ediciones Temas de Hoy, 1992) p. 280.

10. *El País*, 11, 13 March 2011, 11 September 2013, 14 August 2014, 10 September 2015; *El Mundo*, 16 September 2016, 10 December 2018; Garzón, *El fango*, pp. 192–9.

11. *El País*, 25 July 1997; Carles Llorens, 'La gran estafa del postfranquisme', *Sàpiens*, No. 153, 2015, pp. 25–31; Garzón, *El fango*, pp. 307–8.

12. *El País*, 12 July 1986; Garzón, *El fango*, p. 586.

13. *El País*, 2 July 2006.

14. José Díaz Herrera and Isabel Durán Doussinague, *Los secretos del Poder. Del legado franquista al ocaso del felipismo: episodios inconfesables* (Madrid: Ediciones Temas de Hoy, 1994) pp. 380–98; Roger Cohen, 'Missing Millions – Kuwait's Bad Bet. A Special Report, Big Wallets and Little Supervision', *New York Times*, 28 September 1993; Garzón, *El fango*, pp. 309–10. On Grand Tibidabo, *El Mundo*, 27 June, 18 October 1999; *El País*, 28 June 2000, 15 March 2001, 15 January, 15 February, 14 June 2008.

15. *Interviú*, 21 August 1995; *Tiempo*, 30 July 1996; *El País*, 22 July 1995, 4 August 1996.

16. *El País*, 12 March, 3, 4 June 1996, 1, 3, 4, 5 April, 3, 5, 6 October 1997.

17. *El País*, 5, 16, 17, 18 May 1985.

18. *El País*, 7 January 1984, 7 January 1985; Narcís Serra, *The Military Transition: Democratic Reform of the Armed Forces* (Cambridge: Cambridge University Press, 2010) pp. 138–9, 178–80.

19. Numerous conversations of the author with Narcís Serra both

during his time as minister and after; Serra, *The Military Transition*, pp. 93–9, 103–34, 148–74, 181–5.

20. *El País*, 17 February 1991, 9 December 1997.

21. Sergio Gálvez Biesca, *La gran huelga general. El sindicalismo contra la 'modernización Socialista'* (Madrid: Siglo XXI de España, 2017) *passim*; Ruiz, *La España democrática*, pp. 89–93; Santos Juliá, *Un siglo de España. Política y sociedad* (Madrid: Marcial Pons, 1999) pp. 269–70.

22. Jorge Verstrynge, *Memorias de un maldito* (Madrid: Grijalbo, 1999) pp. 121, 164, 283.

23. Juliá, *Un siglo de España*, pp. 270–1; Pedro J. Ramirez, *La rosa y el capullo. Cara y cruz del felipismo* (Barcelona: Planeta, 1989) pp. 221–6.

24. Pradera, *Corrupción y política*, pp. 34–5, 75–83; Garzón, *El fango*, pp. 171–6; Juliá, *Un siglo de España*, pp. 264–5, 271–3; Miralles, *Dinero sucio*, pp. 304–11; Paul Heywood, 'Sleaze in Spain', *Parliamentary Affairs*, Vol. 48, No. 4, October 1995, pp. 726–8, 735–6.

25. *El Mundo*, 29 May 1991; Miralles, *Dinero sucio*, pp. 280–8; Garzón, *El fango*, pp. 92–7; Powell, *España en democracia*, pp. 510–12; Heywood, 'Sleaze in Spain', pp. 729–30; William Chislett, *Spain: What Everyone Needs to Know* (New York: Oxford University Press, 2013) p. 128.

26. *El País*, 14 January 1992, 28 June 2006; *El Mundo*, 22 September 1994; José Díaz Herrera and Isabel Durán, *El saqueo de España* (Madrid: Ediciones Temas de Hoy, 1996) pp. 241–80.

27. Garzón, *El fango*, pp. 116–20; Miralles, *Dinero sucio*, pp. 369–71; Powell, *España en democracia*,

pp. 510–11; José Díaz Herrera and Isabel Durán Doussinague, *Aznar. La vida desconocida de un presidente* (Barcelona: Planeta, 1999) pp. 460–73; Miguel Herrero de Miñón, *Memorias de estío* (Madrid: Ediciones Temas de Hoy, 1993) pp. 340–1; Heywood, 'Sleaze in Spain', pp. 730, 737; Ernesto Ekaizer, *Queríamos tanto a Luis* (Barcelona: Planeta, 2015) pp. 137–50.

28. *eldiario.es*, 5 May 2015.

29. Alfredo Grimaldos, *Zaplana. El brazo incorrupto del PP* (Madrid: FOCA, 2007) pp. 25–7, 289–97.

30. *El Mundo*, 25 May 2018; Grimaldos, *Zaplana*, pp. 139–62.

31. *El País*, 7 November 1998; Díaz Herrera and Durán, *Los secretos*, pp. 399–416.

32. Ruiz, *La España democrática*, pp. 103–8; Powell, *España en democracia*, pp. 442–63, 515–18.

33. Juliá, *Un siglo de España*, p. 274; *El País*, 14 May 1994.

34. *El País*, 5 May 1994; Díaz Herrera and Durán, *Los secretos*, pp. 338–47.

35. Garzón, *El fango*, pp. 316–24; Heywood, 'Sleaze in Spain', pp. 726–31; Ruiz, *La España democrática*, pp. 111–12.

36. *El País*, 29 May, 25 October 1983, 1 November 1986.

37. *El País*, 8 December 1993, 2, 5, 15 May 1994.

38. *El Mundo*, 3 May 1994; Garzón, *El fango*, pp. 106–16; Díaz Herrera and Durán, *Los secretos*, pp. 329–38.

39. *El País*, 7, 8 January; *El Mundo*, 10 January 1993; Manuel Soriano, *Sabino Fernández Campo. La sombra del Rey* (Madrid: Ediciones Temas de Hoy, 1995) pp. 491–502; Jesús Cacho, *El negocio de la libertad* (Madrid: Ediciones Foca, 1999) pp. 413–16, 430–4; Rebeca Quintans, *Juan Carlos I. La*

biografía sin silencios (Madrid: Akal, 2016) pp. 374–85.

40. *El País*, 10, 14, 17 November 1995, 4 November 1997; *Diario 16*, 10 November 1995; Cacho, *El negocio*, pp. 387–406, 434–8; Soriano, *Sabino Fernández Campo*, pp. 480–5; Díaz Herrera and Durán, *El saqueo*, pp. 19–87; Quintans, *Juan Carlos*, pp. 409–23.

41. Powell, *España en democracia*, pp. 519–21; Heywood, 'Sleaze in Spain', pp. 733–4, 737; Juliá, *Un siglo de España*, pp. 275–7.

42. Garzón, *El fango*, pp. 96–7.

43. *El País*, 20 April, 17, 29 June 1995; Woodworth, *Dirty War*, pp. 259, 265, 271–3, 304–10, 350–1; Ramirez, *La rosa y el capullo*, pp. 96–8.

44. Powell, *España en democracia*, pp. 522–46; Díaz Herrera and Durán, *Aznar*, pp. 525–6.

45. *El País*, 21 June 1997, 24 January, 28 February 2000; Juliá, *Un siglo de España*, pp. 280–2; Ruiz, *La España democrática*, pp. 125–8.

46. *El País*, 27 April 1996.

47. Powell, *España en democracia*, pp. 573–90; Ruiz, *La España democrática*, pp. 128–9.

48. Powell, *España en democracia*, pp. 596–8.

49. *El País*, 11 January, 21 February 1991; *El Mundo*, 31 August 1999; *El Plural*, 12 August 2014; Díaz Herrera and Durán, *Aznar*, pp. 526–7, 532.

50. *El Mundo*, 16 June 2000; *Informe del Consejo de la CNMV*, Madrid, 2 August 2000, https://www.elmundo.es/economia/cnmv/index.html.

51. *El Mundo*, 4 December 1997, 9 January 2002; *Wall Street Journal*, 18 July 2009; https://www.elmundo.es/especiales/2007/10/comunicacion/18elmundo/telefonica.html.

52. *El Mundo*, 2 March 1996; *El País*, 11, 18 March 1999.

53. *El País*, 15 September 1999.

54. *El Mundo*, 3 July; *El País*, 8 July 1997; Powell, *España en democracia*, pp. 599–601; Ruiz, *La España democrática*, p. 121.

55. Powell, *España en democracia*, pp. 616–25.

56. Heywood, 'Corruption, Democracy and Governance', p. 40; *El Mundo*, 23 April, 24 June 2015; *El Periódico*, 10 May; *El Diario*, 27 November 2016.

57. *El País*, 24 May 1997, 24 April, 31 August, 2, 8, 9 September 1999, 20 December 2000, 14 March, 28 July 2001; *El Mundo*, 23 April 2007.

58. *El País*, 12 June, 27 August 2001, 26 February, 20 November, 7 December, 2002, 4 December 2007, 28, 29 March 2008; *ABC*, 22 July 2001; *El Mundo*, 30 September 2001, 21 September 2002; *Cinco Días*, 27 March 2008.

59. *El País*, 9 January, 18 April, 6 May; *ABC*, 24 May 2002; Garzón, *El fango*, pp. 368–72.

60. *Interviú*, 9 September 2002; *El País*, 21 May; *El Mundo*, 6 February, 6 October 2009, 21 May 2013; *nuevatribuna.es*, 13 April 2010; Garzón, *El fango*, pp. 416–17.

61. Fernando Vallespín, 'La corrupción en la democracia española', introduction to Pradera, *Corrupción y política*, pp. viii–xii; *La Vanguardia*, 25 March 2018; Antonio Muñoz Molina, *Todo lo que era sólido* (Barcelona: Seix Barral, 2014) pp. 49–52, 55–6.

62. *El País*, 16 March 2011; Muñoz Molina, *Todo lo que era sólido*, pp. 99–102.

63. *El País*, 25 March 2011; 2, 3 June 2019; *El Mundo*, 30 April 2018; William Chislett, *Forty Years of Democratic Spain: Political*,

Economic, Foreign Policy and Social Change, 1978-2018 (Madrid: Elcano Royal Institute, 2018) p. 23.

64. Diego Docavo Pedraza, Cristina Gadea García and Juan García Rodríguez, *Fraude y corrupción en el sector inmobiliario* (Madrid: Universidad Autónoma, 2012) pp. 4-18, 25-30.

65. *El País*, 3 February, 31 April, 18 October, 17 November, 16 December 2007; *Información*, 17 May 2014; Linda Palfreeman, *Crisis in Catral: True Stories behind One of Spain's Worst Property Scandal Hotspots* (Milton Keynes: Native Spain, 2010) pp. 124-9; Muñoz Molina, *Todo lo que era sólido*, p. 157.

66. *Daily Mail*, 26 September 2012.

67. *ABC* (Seville), 8 December 2002, 18 October, 4 November, 12, 19 December 2006, 4 June 2018.

68. *El País*, 9 February 2007.

69. *El Mundo*, 28 December 2009; *El País*, 9 September, 1 December 2011; *Público*, 11 December 2017; Muñoz Molina, *Todo lo que era sólido*, pp. 157-9.

70. *El País*, 15 October 2009; *El Confidencial*, 25 March 2010; Garzón, *El fango*, pp. 202-14.

71. *El Mundo*, 6 July; *El País*, 29 October 2006, 8 July, 26 October 2010, 1 November 2011, 10 February, 8 June 2012, 3, 4 March 2014, 6 March 2019; Grimaldos, *Zaplana*, pp. 101-3.

72. *Levante*, 19 February 2012; *El Mundo*, 1, 12 July 2010; *El País*, 29 July, 26 September 2008, 11 July, 27 December 2010, 26 March 2011, 26 November 2013; Grimaldos, *Zaplana*, pp. 15, 92-4.

73. *La Vanguardia*, 18 November 2003.

74. *La Vanguardia*, 29, 30 January, 1 February 2004.

75. *El País*, 12 April 2013, 17 June, 29 August, 16 September, 1, 26 October, 2015; Garzón, *El fango*, pp. 35, 182-9.

76. *El Mundo*, 25 July 2014, 27 July 2018, *El País*, 25, 26 July, 26 September 2014; Garzón, *El fango*, pp. 293-7.

77. *El Mundo*, 3 December 2009; *El País*, 24 September, 27 October 2010, 7 February 2011, 18 December 2014, 16, 2 January, 18 March 2015, 13 March 2017, 18 April, 2 July, 30 September 2018; Garzón, *El fango*, pp. 254-7.

Chapter 18: The Triumph of Corruption and Incompetence, 2004-2018

1. Rubén Amón, 'El insoportable cinismo de Aznar', *El País*, 35 May 2018.

2. Ernesto Ekaizer, *Queríamos tanto a Luis* (Barcelona: Planeta, 2015) pp. 17-27; *El País*, 8 April 2010; Baltasar Garzón, *El fango. Cuarenta años de corrupción en España* (Barcelona: Debate, 2015) pp. 148-50.

3. *El Mundo*, 21 February 2012; Ekaizer, *Queríamos tanto a Luis*, pp. 40-51.

4. *El País*, 31 January, 3 February, 19 July; *El Mundo*, 8 January, 7, 14, 15 July 2013; Garzón, *El fango*, pp. 120-4; Ekaizer, *Queríamos tanto a Luis*, pp. 88-98, 136-41, 363-9.

5. *El País*, 19 October 2009, 30 August 2010, 3 October 2011; *El Mundo*, 12 April 2010; Sam Edwards, 'Spain's Watergate', *Guardian*, 1 March 2019; Garzón, *El fango*, pp. 120-38.

6. *El País*, 15 July, 28 December 2011.

7. *El Mundo*, 12 March; *El País*, 15 March 2009, 26 December 2011.

8. *Público*, 6 February 2011.

9. *El Mundo*, 24 May; *ABC*, 25 May 2018.

10. *El Mundo*, 9 December 2010.

11. *El Mundo*, 15 February 2018; *El País*, 8, 12 February, 2 May 2009.

12. *El País*, 27 January 2012.

13. *El País*, 14 October 2016; *El Mundo*, 18 November 2017.

14. *El País*, 27 July 2017.

15. *El Mundo*, 17 January, 22 February, 1, 8 April 2019.

16. *El Mundo*, 24 May, 13 June; *ABC*, 25 May 2018.

17. *El País*, 12 June 2018.

18. *El País*, 14 October 2005, 17 July 2006, 31 March 2011.

19. *El País*, 5 April; *El Mundo*, 5 April 2002; 'Los múltiples crímenes de Jesús Gil', *CTXT Revista Contexto*, No. 97, 28 December 2016, pp. 9–10.

20. *El País*, 1 April 1997.

21. Diego Docavo Pedraza, Cristina Gadea García and Juan García Rodríguez, *Fraude y corrupción en el sector inmobiliario* (Madrid: Universidad Autónoma, 2012) pp. 34–5; *ABC de Sevilla*, 15, 29 January 2002; *ABC*, 18 December 2006, 30 July 2012; *El País*, 12 December 2015, 30 March, 3 May 2016; *CTXT*, No. 97, 28 December 2016, pp. 9–10, 11–12.

22. *El Mundo*, 30 March; *El País*, 6 April 2006.

23. *El Mundo*, 1, 2, 7 April 2006.

24. *El Mundo*, 28 June 2006.

25. *El País*, 3 May 2007, 10 September 2012, 4, 15, 30 October 2013, 26 November 2015, 12 January 2016; *El Mundo*, 15 October 2014; *ABC*, 16 April 2013.

26. Blog de 'Audrey', 8 April 2006, http://www.zonalibre.org/blog/te/archives/092254.html.

27. *El Mundo*, 23 July 2007; *El País*, 26 September 2010.

28. Lorenzo Delgado Gómez-Escalonilla, 'El "error Aznar", o las consecuencias de secundar el unilateralismo de Estados Unidos',

Historia del Presente, No. 5, 2005, pp. 151–63; *El Mundo*, 16, 17 March 2003.

29. *El País*, 15 March 2017.

30. *El País*, 11 March, 3, 4 April 2006; Alberto Reig Tapia, *Anti Moa. La subversión neofranquista de la Historia de España* (Barcelona: Ediciones B, 2006) pp. 422–7; Giles Tremlett, *Ghosts of Spain. Travels through a Country's Hidden Past* (London: Faber & Faber, 2006) pp. 250–80.

31. Reig Tapia, *Anti Moa*, pp. 404–5; William Chislett, *Spain: What Everyone Needs to Know* (New York: Oxford University Press, 2013) pp. 158–60.

32. Reig Tapia, *Anti Moa*, pp. 434–6, 460–6; Alberto Reig Tapia, *Revisionismo y política. Pío Moa revisitado* (Madrid: Foca, 2008) p. 237.

33. Emilio Silva and Santiago Macías, *Las fosas de Franco. Los republicanos que el dictador dejó en las cunetas* (Madrid: Ediciones Temas de Hoy, 2003) pp. 60–119; Encarnación Barranquero Texeira and Lucía Prieto Borrego, *La derrota bajo tierra. Las fosas comunes del franquismo* (Granada: Comares, 2018) pp. 46–7.

34. Tremlett, *Ghosts of Spain*, pp. 3–32.

35. Alberto Reig Tapia, *La crítica de la crítica. Inconsecuentes, insustanciales, impotentes, prepotentes y equidistantes* (Madrid: Siglo XXI de España, 2017) pp. 169–70, 209–10, 259–60.

36. Banco de España, *Informe sobre la crisis financiera y bancaria en España, 2008–2014* (Madrid: Banco de España, 2017) pp. 78–87.

37. Javier Ayuso, 'Estrategia de construcción del enemigo español', *El País*, 2 December 2017; Alberto Reig Tapia, 'España y Cataluña. Un

inquietante malestar', in Álvaro
Soto Carmona, ed., *La democracia
herida. La tormenta perfecta*
(Madrid: Marcial Pons, 2019)
pp. 372–4.

38. J. H. Elliott, *Scots and Catalans:
Union and Disunion* (London: Yale
University Press, 2018) pp. 241–2;
Chislett, *Forty Years*, pp. 27–32;
Francesc de Carreras, 'Opinión
pública y secesionismo. El caso
catalán', *Cuadernos de Pensamiento
Político*, No. 44, 2014, pp. 23–38.

39. There are discrepancies between the
many opinion polls. Figures used
here are from the regular polls
carried out by the Centre d'Estudis
d'Opinió, Baròmetre d'Opinió
Política, June 2005–November
2006.

40. *El País*, 4 December 2005.

41. *El Mundo*, 19 June 2006; Elliott,
Scots and Catalans, pp. 238–9; Reig
Tapia, 'España y Cataluña',
pp. 375–8; Jaume Sobrequés i
Callicó, *La gran ignominia. Exiliats
y presos polítics a la Catalunya del
segle XXI* (Barcelona: Editorial
Base, 2018) pp. 11–13.

42. *El Mundo*, 24 October 2005; *El País*,
14 February 2006.

43. *El País*, 31 July, 1 August; *El Mundo*,
1 August 2006.

44. *El País*, 29 June, 10 July; *El Mundo*,
29 June, 10 July 2010.

45. Centre d'Estudis d'Opinió,
Baròmetre d'Opinió Política, 30 July
2010–25 January 2011.

46. *La Vanguardia*, 12 November; *El
País*, 29 September, 29 November
2010.

47. *El Mundo*, 3 August 2016; *El
Imparcial*, 25 June 2014; *El
Periódico*, 13 July 2017.

48. Ernesto Ekaizer, *El libro negro. La
crisis de Bankia y las Cajas*
(Barcelona: Espasa, 2018)
pp. 176–8.

49. *El País*, 12, 13 May 2010.

50. Banco de España, *Informe*,
pp. 89–98, 116–36; Ernesto Ekaizer,
*Indecentes. Crónica de un atraco
perfecto* (Barcelona: Espasa, 2012)
pp. 124–31; Iñigo de Barrón
Arniches, *El hundimiento de la
banca* (Madrid: Catarata, 2012)
pp. 145–63, 195–7, 255–66.

51. Ekaizer, *El libro negro*, pp. 220–7.

52. *El País*, 23 May, 6 June 2012;
Ekaizer, *El libro negro*, pp. 289–99,
309–18, 605–34; Barrón Arniches,
El hundimiento de la banca,
pp. 190–3, 199–253.

53. Barrón Arniches, *El hundimiento de
la banca*, pp. 264–78.

54. *El País*, 15, 16, 17, 18 May, 30 June
2011.

55. *El Mundo*, 9 May 2010; *El País*, 17
July 2012; Banco de España,
Informe, pp. 136–9; Ekaizer,
Indecentes, pp. 13–15, 183–9;
Ekaizer, *El libro negro*, pp. 148–61.

56. Centre d'Estudis d'Opinió,
Baròmetre d'Opinió Política, 29
June 2011–27 June 2012.

57. *El País*, 11, 20 September; *La
Vanguardia*, 11, 20 September 2012;
Ralph Minder, *The Struggle for
Catalonia: Rebel Politics in Spain*
(London: Hurst, 2017) pp. 2–7.

58. Centre d'Estudis d'Opinió,
Baròmetre d'Opinió Política, 27
June–8 November 2011.

59. *La Vanguardia*, 25 September 2012.

60. *Naciódigital*, 23 November 2012.

61. *El País*, 26 November, 18
December; *El Mundo*, 21 December
2012.

62. *El País*, 12 December 2013, 8 April,
19 July, 19 September, 13 October
2014; Sobrequés, *La gran
ignominia*, pp. 38–42.

63. *El País*, 10 November 2014; Elliott,
Scots and Catalans, p. 248.

64. *El País*, 19 November, 22 December
2014, 8 January, 25 February 2015.

65. *El País*, 14 January 2015.

66. *El País*, 31 March, 20 August 2015; Sobrequés, *La gran ignominia*, pp. 77–82.

67. *El País*, 21 February, 14, 15, 18 June 2015.

68. *El Mundo*, 16 November 2015; Sobrequés, *La gran ignominia*, p. 15.

69. *Público*, 21 June, 27 August; *El Periódico*, 11 July; *Ara*, 30 August 2016; *La Vanguardia*, 24 August 2017, 14 December 2018.

70. *El País*, 5, 10 November, 2 December; *El Mundo*, 10, 11 November 2015; Tobias Buck, *After the Fall: Crisis, Recovery and the Making of a New Spain* (London: Weidenfeld & Nicolson, 2019) pp. 49–52.

71. *La Vanguardia*, 28 September 2015, 11 January 2016; Sobrequés, *La gran ignominia*, pp. 84–95.

72. *La Vanguardia*, 24 July 2016.

73. *El País*, 10 January 2017.

74. *El Mundo*, 31 January; *La Vanguardia*, 5 February; *El País*, 6, 10 February, 13 March, 5 September 2017.

75. *El País*, 1 October, 12 December 2014, 23 February, 19 July 2017, 4, 26 October 2018.

76. *El País*, 2 February, 3 September, 30 December; *ABC*, 14 April, 25 November 2007.

77. Rebeca Quintans, *Juan Carlos I. La biografía sin silencios* (Madrid: Akal, 2016) pp. 591–3; Ana Romero, *Final de partida. La crónica de los hechos que llevaron a la abdicación de Juan Carlos I* (Madrid: La Esfera de los Libros, 2015) pp. 43–6.

78. *El País*, 14, 22 April; *El Mundo* 14 April 2012.

79. *El País*, 24 February 2012; *El Mundo*, 1, 2 December 2011, 7 May 2012; Quintans, *Juan Carlos*, pp. 595–7.

80. *Público*, 5 December; *El Mundo*, 29 November 2011.

81. *El País*, 24 February; *El Mundo*, 1 December 2011, 8 June 2012; Garzón, *El fango*, pp. 264–7.

82. *Público*, 5 December 2011; *El Mundo*, 18 November 2012.

83. *Público*, 5 December; *El Mundo*, 18, 24, 29 November, 4, 15 December 2011; *ABC*, 2 January, 26 February 2012; 'Urdangarín planeaba desviar cinco millones más a Belice', *El Mundo*, 9 December 2011.

84. *El Mundo*, 12 November; *ABC*, 18, 21 December 2011, 11 March 2012.

85. *ABC*, 23 April 2009, 2 December; *El País*, 12 November; *El Mundo*, 12 November 2011.

86. *El Mundo*, 8, 9, 13 December 2011, 25 February 2013; *El País*, 9 November, 10, 12, 13, 24 December 2011, 25 February 2013, 8 February 2014; *ABC*, 12, 13 November 2011, 11 March 2012; Romero, *Final de partida*, pp. 173–90; Garzón, *El fango*, pp. 267–79; Quintans, *Juan Carlos*, pp. 602–4, 610–13.

87. *El País*, 25 December; *El Mundo*, 26 December; *ABC*, 27 December 2011.

88. *Público*, 30 December; *ABC*, 29, 30 December 2011, 23 February, 3 April; *El País*, 22 April 2012, 12, 13 June 2018.

89. *ABC*, 14, 30 December 2011; *El Mundo*, 24 May 2012.

90. *ABC*, 11 March, 8 April; *El País*, 17 November 2007, 22 April 2012.

91. *ABC*, 14, 15, 16, 18 April 2012.

92. *ABC*, 3, 12 April; *El País*, 20, 22 April 2012.

93. *El País*, 18, 22 April; *ABC*, 16, 19 April 2012; Romero, *Final de partida*, pp. 51–9, 116.

94. *El Mundo*, interview with Peñafiel, 24 May; *ABC*, 18 May 2012; Romero, *Final de partida*, pp. 66–7, 93.

95. *ABC*, 14, 16, 17 April; *El País*, 16 April 2012.
96. *El País*, 18 April; *El Mundo*, 30 May 2012.
97. 'La bella princesa que triunfa en España', *El Mundo*, 20 March 2010; José Antonio Zarzalejos, 'Historia de cómo la Corona ha entrado en barrena', *elconfidencial.com*, 15 April 2012; Quintans, *Juan Carlos*, pp. 623–7. Romero, *Final de partida*, pp. 68–71 and photographs pp. 160ff.
98. *ABC*, 18 April; *El País*, 18, 22 April 2012.
99. Bob Colacello, 'King and Controversy', *Vanity Fair*, 10 September 2013.
100. *ABC*, 22 April; *El País*, 18, 22 April 2012; Romero, *Final de partida*, pp. 243–54; Quintans, *Juan Carlos*, pp. 672–4.
101. Santos Juliá, 'La erosión de la Monarquía', *El País*, 2 February 2014; Romero, *Final de partida*, pp. 307–33.
102. *El País*, 2 June; José Antonio Zarzalejos, 'El rey abdica para salvar a la Monarquía de la crisis institucional', *elconfidencial.com*, 2 June 2014.
103. *El País*, 9 April 2015; 3 February; *Público*, 8 February 2017.
104. *El Español*, 11, 15 July; *El País*, 11, 12, 23 July; *Daily Telegraph*, 16 July 2018.
105. *El País*, 22 December 2015, 24, 27 January; *El Mundo*, 22 January, 26 April, 3 May 2016.
106. *El País*, 28 June 2016.
107. Centre d'Estudis d'Opinió, Baròmetre d'Opinió Política, 22 July 2016; *El País*, 22 July 2016.
108. *Público*, 21 June, 27 August; *El Periódico*, 11 July; *Ara*, 30 August 2016: *La Vanguardia*, 24 August 2017, 14 December 2018.
109. *El Mundo*, 3 October; *Público*, 2 October; *El Periódico*, 5 October 2017; *El País*, 19 March 2019.
110. *La Vanguardia*, 2 November; *El País*, 25, 26, 27 October 2017; Xavier Vidal-Folch and Miquel Noguer, 'Los tres días que conmocionaron Cataluña', *El País*, 27 November 2017; Sobrequés, *La gran ignominia*, pp. 7–10; Elliott, *Scots and Catalans* pp. 251–7; Reig Tapia, 'España y Cataluña', pp. 378–80; Buck, *After the Fall*, pp. 52–8.
111. *El Mundo*, 15 May, 2 June; *El País*, 12, 21 May, 3 June, 6 September; *La Vanguardia* 14 May, 14 October 2018. For Torra's anti-Spanish views, see Quim Torra, 'La llengua i les bèsties', *MónTerrassa*, 19 December 2012.
112. *El País*, 3 June 2018.
113. *El País*, 29, 30 April 2019; Buck, *After the Fall*, pp. 137–8, 235–46.

Illustrations

A satirical cartoon published in the magazine *La Araña* in August 1885. 'Poor Spain. How beautiful she is. The more they strip her, the more beautiful she is.' Among the watching European leaders are Otto von Bismarck and King Umberto of Italy. Among those ripping the flag from her body are the architects of electoral corruption, Francisco Romero Robledo, Antonio Cánovas del Castillo and Práxedes Mateo Sagasta.

The USS *Maine*, blown up in Havana harbour, the excuse for the Spanish-American war of 1898. (The History Collection/Alamy)

A demonstration in Barcelona in protest against the repression that followed the *Semana Tragica* or Tragic Week. (The History Collection/Alamy)

Juan de la Cierva, the *cacique* from Murcia who fixed elections for Antonio Maura. (The History Collection/Alamy)

Alfonso XIII with the coalition government formed by Antonio Maura on 21 March 1918 in response to his threat to abdicate.

Severiano Martinez Anido, the brutal civil governor of Barcelona.

Miguel Primo de Rivera and Alfonso XIII, together with the generals of the recently formed Military Directory. (Hulton Royals Collection/Getty)

José Calvo Sotelo, Primo's Minister of Finance who would be assassinated in 1936 just before the outbreak of Civil War. (Universal History Archive/Getty)

A poster published in Valencia in 1831 to commemorate the Second Republic. (Heritage Image Partnership Ltd/Alamy Stock Photo)

Demonstration in the Madrid bull-ring during the Popular Front election campaign in February 1936 in support of the 30,000 Austrians imprisoned after the October 1934 uprising. (Shutterstock)

'The Last Pirate of the Mediterranean', the fabulously rich Juan March who helped finance Franco's war effort. (Dmitri Kessel/The LIFE Picture Collection/Getty)

Francisco Franco, as Generalísimo and his wife, Carmen Polo. (Hulton Archive/Getty)

Franco addresses crowd from the balcony of the Royal Palace of Madrid. (ullstein bild/Getty)

The heir to the Spanish throne, Don Juan de Borbón, in 1963 with his son Juan Carlos, the future King of Spain. (Express/Getty)

Prince Juan Carlos of Spain and Princess Sophia of Greece in Athens, married by the Greek Orthodox rite, May 1962. (AFP/Getty)

Spanish President Adolfo Suarez and King Juan Carlos, two of the architects of Spain's transition to democracy. (Gianni Ferrari/Getty)

The celebration in the Cortes of the 40th anniversary of the Spanish constitution in 2018. Four surviving prime ministers in the front row (from right to left: Felipe González, José María Aznar, José Luis Rodríguez Zapatero and Mariano Rajoy). (Zorstan/DYDPPA/ Shutterstock)

The protagonists of the Gürtel political corruption case. (AFP/Getty)

Index

as cadet in Military Academy, 48; on Alba, 162; and Morocco, 188–9, 190–1, 192, 193; Ben-Tieb incident/myth (1924), 190–1; supports execution of Jaca rebels, 222; on Primo de Rivera dictatorship, 225; and Azaña's reforms, 237; 'caudillo' title, 264; directs brutal repression in Asturias (1934), 274–5, 282, 297; made Chief of the General Staff (1935), 278, 297; advises Gil Robles against a coup, 281; and attempts to organize coup (February 1936), 286–7; and Comisión de Actas, 289; military commander of Canary Islands, 295, 298, 299–300; letter allegedly sent to Casares (June 1936), 296–7; decision to join 1936 conspiracy, 297–8, 299; air journey from Canaries to Morocco, 298, 299–300, 309; Nazi and fascist support during Civil War, 306–7, 309, 310, 313, 314, 317, 319, 320–1, 328–9; strategy during Civil War, 306, 319–20, 326, 327–8; becomes commander-in-chief (September 1936), 317; assumes full powers of head of state, 318; savage anti-Catalanism of, 327; and 'the covenant of blood,' 329; megalomaniac concept of his own place in history, 333, 335, 403; belief in alchemy, 338; and Filek's imaginary synthetic gasoline, 338, 350; anti-Semitism of, 341–3, 360–1, 378; shameless reinvention of the past by, 342, 343, 346, 347, 350, 369–70, 372, 374, 376; accumulation of huge personal fortune, 343–5, 353, 390, 466–7; estates and mansions of, 343–5, 389, 390, 403, 467; España y los Judíos (pamphlet, 1949), 343; gifts from Hitler, 345; Hendaye meeting with Hitler, 350, 351, 369; Bordighera meeting with Mussolini, 352; belief in own infallibility/lies, 370, 371; post-WW2 image as authoritarian Catholic, 371; articles in Arriba, 378; leisure pursuits, 381, 388, 403, 406–7, 415, 416, 417, 423, 426; grandchildren of, 389; failing acuity in 1950s/60s, 409, 419, 420–1, 425, 428, 429, 430, 431, 433; withdrawal from active

politics (from late 1950s), 415, 416, 417, 419–20, 423; hunting accident (1961), 422, 424; trial and execution of Grimau García (1963), 426–7; has Parkinson's disease, 429, 431, 432, 436, 443–4, 448, 457, 460; evidence of senility, 430, 431, 433; media coverage in old age, 431–2; drift into senility, 441, 442, 448–9, 459; day of 'national affirmation' (December 1970), 443; and death of Carrero, 451, 452; worsening health (1974–5), 457–8, 459–61, 462, 464–5; final illness, 464–6; last public appearance (1 October 1975), 464; implements Article 11 on death bed, 465; death of (20 November 1975), 466–7
Franco, Nicolás, 309, 318, 321, 339–40, 353, 359, 360, 362, 448, 459
Franco, Pilar, 339, 389, 391–2
Franco, Ramón, 217, 220, 221–2, 242
Franco dictatorship, xi, xiii, xiv, xv; repression as central pillar, 6, 334, 336, 341; use of violent crusade rhetoric, 270; Civil War victory institutionalizes, 329, 334; brutal policy towards the defeated, 330, 334, 336, 401; absolute power established (8 August 1939), 333–4; Organic Law of the State, 333–4, 421, 427–8, 429, 430–1, 432, 457–8, 465; ceremonial and choreography of, 334; malnutrition and starvation under, 334, 335, 339, 340, 351–2, 370, 382–3; pursuit and murder of prominent exiles, 334; sexual abuse of women prisoners, 334, 462; wild economic fantasies of, 337–8; autarkic policies, 337–9, 340, 373–4, 377, 385, 394, 398, 400, 405, 413–14; first peacetime government (1939), 337; use of state apparatus for private benefit, 339–40, 362–3, 388–93; myth of rescued Jews, 342–3, 360–1; as haven for Nazi and Vichy war criminals, 342, 369, 376, 381, 392; as 'Kleptocratic State,' 345–6; plans for attack on Gibraltar, 346; pro-Axis policy, 346, 347–9, 350, 355–7, 358–61, 364–5, 369, 376; smuggling of narcotics by, 347; monarchist-Falangist tensions, 349,